PETERSON'S COLLEGES FOR STUDENTS WITH LEARNING DISABILITIES OR ADD

7TH EDITION

THOMSON

PETERSON'S

Australia • Canada • Mexico • Singapore • Spain • United Kingdom • United States

ISSN 1525-3813
ISBN 0-7689-1268-7

Printed in the United States of America

10 9 8 7 6   07 06 05

Seventh Edition

CONTENTS

PREFACE

Welcome to *Colleges for Students with Learning Disabilities or ADD*.

Choosing a college that will provide the education and social life to suit his or her particular needs is a challenge for any student. For the student with LD or ADD, there are additional factors to take into account, but overall the process is more similar to that of other students than it is dissimilar. A successful search for a college depends on making the right match between your aspirations, an environment in which you feel comfortable, and the availability of support services. That being said, it is still no easy task to wade through the literature and Web pages that describe support services, and that is why this directory exists. While all the information about support services cannot be captured in a few pages, it is still very valuable to have basic information about support services in a single publication. The Association on Higher Education and Disability (AHEAD) feels that this guide is an important tool, and thus we were delighted when Peterson's asked us to assist them in revising it. In response to this request, AHEAD created a committee to review all aspects of the guide in order to provide the most accurate information possible. I would like to thank Scott Lissner, Ross Pollack, and Emily Silberberg for their work on this guide.

Let me tell you a few things about the process you are undertaking. Once you have narrowed your search using this book, Web sites, and other materials, there is no substitute for meeting with the people who run the programs that provide support services. These people rarely try to talk you into attending a school that is not right for you. They tell you what support they do and do not provide so you can make an informed decision. I talk to hundreds of prospective students and their parents every year, and they occasionally come armed with a list of questions that they think will allow them to get at the "truth" about the support services provided at my school. They quickly learn that I have nothing to hide. I readily

own up to what services are not provided. I tell them about the additional challenges of a large, competitive school. I tell them about other schools and what support they provide. Those of us who run support programs are every bit as invested as you are in finding you the right school. That is why we filled out the surveys used to create the profiles in this book, even though we don't like surveys. That is also why I and several of my colleagues consulted with Peterson's during the revision of this guide.

So far in this preface, I have been referring to the reader as "you," the prospective student. That is because I want to empower you to "own" this search, to ask the questions you want to ask, and to make decisions for yourself. That is not to say that your parents' opinions are not valuable; they are. However, we in this field often see something we call the "stereophonic effect" when a student and his or her parents come into our offices. One parent sits on either side of the student, and we look directly at the student and ask a question. Immediately, there are competing answers from the left and right side of the prospective student but nothing from the center channel. This worries us, as we have all seen students whose only visits to our offices are first the one they make as a prospective student and then the one they make after they are in deep academic trouble. While some schools do more to monitor a student's academic progress than others, all students benefit from a clear understanding of their cognitive strengths and weaknesses and the ability to know when they need help. This is not a concept unique to students with LD or ADD.

I believe you will find this guide to be helpful in your search. Good luck with your search, and maybe I will see you in Ann Arbor soon.

Sam Goodin is the Director of Services for Students for Disabilities at the University of Michigan. He is also a former President of the Association on Higher Education and Disability (AHEAD).

A NOTE FROM PETERSON'S EDITORS

Peterson's, in collaboration with AHEAD, is pleased to present this 7th edition of *Colleges for Students with Learning Disabilities or ADD*. With comprehensive profiles of programs at more than 1,100 colleges in the U.S. and Canada, this guide is designed to be the source of information for parents and students looking for LD programs and services.

Opportunities abound for students and this guide can help you find what you want in a number of ways:

You'll first want to read through the articles presented at the front of the guide. With authors specializing in the field of learning disabilities, as either directors of collegiate programs or as consultants in the private sector, they offer their guidance in the areas of *"Distinctions Between K—12 and Higher Education Requirements"* (Lydia S. Block), *"The College Experience"* (Emily Silberberg), *"Legal Considerations for Learning Disability Programs"* (Lydia S. Block), *"Documentation Required for College Eligibility"* (L. Scott Lissner), and *"Through the Eyes of an LD Director: Critical Steps for College Success"* (Ross Pollack).

The **College Listings Profiles,** divided into four categories: Four-Year Colleges with Structured/Proactive Programs, Four-Year Colleges with Self-Directed/ Decentralized Programs, Two-Year Colleges with Structured/ Proactive Programs, and Two-Year Colleges with Self-Directed/Decentralized Programs, have all the information you want to know about a college's LD program or unit, including details on orientation, summer programs, unique aids and services, subject-area tutoring, diagnostic testing, basic skills remediation, enrichment, student organization, fees, application, and written policies.

Finally, at the back of the guide, you'll find an **Alphabetical Index of Colleges** and a **Geographical Index of Colleges** for easy reference.

Peterson's publishes a full line of resources to help parents and students with any information you need to guide you through the college admissions process. Peterson's publications can be found at your local bookstore, library, and high school guidance office—or visit us on the Web at Petersons.com

Colleges will be pleased to know that Peterson's helped in this education search and selection process. Admissions staff member are more than happy to answer questions, address specific problems, and help in any way they can. The editors at Peterson's wish you great success in your college search!

DISTINCTIONS BETWEEN K–12 AND HIGHER EDUCATION REQUIREMENTS

The transition from high school to college is an experience that should be carefully planned for all students. Students with a learning disability (LD) who have received services during their K–12 school experiences have many factors to consider, and they must all be addressed thoughtfully.

There are many differences, some tangible and some more subtle, between the K–12 school experience and college, and it is important for students with learning disabilities to plan ahead so that they can make a good college choice. Self-understanding is very important as an LD student moves from the high school to the college setting. It is essential for them to understand what their disability is and how it impacts their learning in order to choose an institution where they can be successful.

During the K–12 experience, students generally have family and school personnel to guide them along the way. The college experience, even for those who stay near home, requires personal responsibility and independence on the part of the student. For the first time in their lives, students have to plan their own time and compete papers and projects without prompting and without automatic academic support. Most importantly, they have to learn how to be productive in the face of personal freedom that they have not experienced before.

The mission of colleges and universities is very different from that of K–12 institutions. Colleges are not required by law to seek out students with disabilities, and they are not required to do whatever it takes to help students succeed in a college setting. Colleges and universities are only required to provide "reasonable accommodations" to those students who identify themselves as learning disabled.

SELF-ADVOCACY

The Individuals with Disabilities Education Act (IDEA) protects the LD student during the K–12 school years. This means that it is the school's responsibility to seek out and identify students with disabilities and then serve them in the least restrictive environment possible. Under the IDEA, students and their families are guided through the education process. An Individual Education Plan (IEP) is developed and written for the student and carried out by the school each year. In addition, there is support in place. Students generally work with a guidance counselor to plan their courses each year. Students with learning disabilities can also usually rely on a resource teacher, a special education teacher, or a guidance counselor to tell their teachers what kind of academic support is needed. For example, if a student needs extended time on an exam, it will be arranged through these support services.

This is not the case at most colleges. The majority of colleges offer the services that are required by law and possibly some additional academic support. Most do not have trained learning disability specialists, and, if they do, they generally serve in a counseling role for many students. When LD students arrive at college, it is up to them to identify themselves to the Office for Disability Services and arrange for the help that they need. This is quite different from students knowing the help that they need will be there when they need it.

A new term that students are introduced to during the college admissions process is "disclosure." Students are expected from the very beginning to let others know about their learning disability if they want or need help. Students should understand and express the area(s) of their learning disability (e.g., written language), academic and personal strengths and weaknesses, the type of academic support they received in high school, what areas they think they will need help with in college, what accommodations they are requesting, and anything else that will help them both get admitted and have a good college experience.

THE ADMISSIONS PROCESS

In kindergarten through the twelfth grade, students with learning disabilities have others to advocate for them. When applying to colleges, students must fill out their own applications, write their own essays, and make their own case for why they are a good match for a particular institution. Though colleges cannot discriminate, they also are only required to accept students who are "otherwise qualified" for admittance to their institution. They are not required to overlook poor grades and test scores in order to admit a student; however, if there are compelling explanations for the low grades and test scores, this information may be taken into consideration during the admissions process.

Colleges usually have basic admissions requirements that students must meet to be admitted. They are as follows:

- 4 units of English;
- 3 units of mathematics (geometry, algebra I, algebra II);

1

- 3 units of science (including a laboratory science);
- 2 units of foreign language (sometimes 3);
- 3 units of social studies;
- 1 unit of practical arts;
- 2 units of health and physical education;
- a minimum grade point average;
- rank in high school class; and
- a minimum ACT Assessment or SAT score.

These are only basic requirements and they will differ from institution to institution. It is important to know that while colleges often consider extenuating circumstances, they are not *required* to consider them. If, for example, a student is identified with a learning disability in the middle of high school and has received poor grades up until then, a college will usually consider the improvement that may come after identification.

COURSE SUBSTITUTIONS

Colleges are in no way required to waive any course requirements. They are not required to substitute for any requirements. Very few colleges make a commitment to waive or substitute for a requirement before a student has been accepted by a school and has decided to enroll. Many factors are taken into consideration, and most schools have a policy and process in place that determines whether a waiver or substitution will be granted. This is rarely a decision that disability services personnel make independently. It usually involves faculty members and/or administrators.

One reason that this decision needs to be made carefully is that colleges do not want to—and are not required to—waive or substitute courses in a student's major academic area. There are exceptions. For example, if a student is majoring in chemistry and is doing well but has had a very difficult time learning a second language, a substitution may be granted. The college would consider if foreign language acquisition was affected by the student's learning disability and if there was enough evidence that the student would not be able to learn a language well enough to show proficiency. In a case like this, the college could ask the student to take substitute courses for the language. These course options could include culture classes, linguistics, or even computer classes.

Students who have a history of performing poorly in mathematics should know that substitutions for the mathematics requirement are rare and, again, must be tied to the functional limitations of a disability.

Students should never choose a college hoping that a specific requirement will be substituted or waived. A student can choose a major with minimal courses in a particular area, but students should look at a college curriculum with the idea that they will take all the required courses.

ACADEMIC SUPPORT

Colleges, by law, have the right to have their own eligibility standards or guidelines in place. Once accepted by a college, a student must submit his or her documentation to the Office for Disability Services in order to determine if he or she is eligible for services. The burden rests on the student to provide adequate documentation. Most disability services offices only review the documentation of admitted students, so students usually don't know before they are accepted if their documentation will be accepted. It is in the student's best interest to ask if a college will review documentation before admittance to allow for time to update or amend the documentation as necessary, as sometimes even if students have been served throughout elementary, middle, and high school, their documentation may be rejected by a specific college.

What academic support a student receives in college is directly related to the functional limitations and rationale described in his or her provided documentation. For example, if there is evidence that a student has a learning disability in the area of reading and is a slow reader because of it, the student may be eligible for a reader and extended time on exams. If the student has a learning disability in math and asks for extended time on English tests with essay questions, it may not be granted.

SUCCESS AND THE LD STUDENT

The adjustment to college life is difficult for most students. Students with learning disabilities who have been served throughout their schooling are used to having remedial services and guidance. In general, colleges do not offer remediation. College settings may have developmental courses, but the grades students receive in these courses often do not count toward graduation. Students who go on to college must be prepared for the rigors of the admissions process and then the course work, once they are admitted. In the K–12 arena, students and their families are used to the support given by the school and the structure that is provided. Parents are used to communicating with teachers, helping to shape their child's school experience. This type of communication changes at the college level, where students, not parents, are expected to communicate their own needs and work directly with the Office for Disability Services and faculty members to get the services they need.

The responsibility for success rests with the student. Students with learning disabilities should do their research carefully and be sure that the kind of support that they need is in place at the postsecondary institutions they are considering. It is critical that students evaluate the type of help they have received in high school and what type of academic support they will need in college. By carefully considering the factors that should be in place for a successful college experience ahead of time, students have a good chance of choosing a college where they can be successful.

Lydia S. Block, Ph.D., is an educational consultant in Columbus, Ohio. Dr. Block works with students with LD, ADD, head injuries, and other disabilities.

THE COLLEGE EXPERIENCE

As with any major life change, starting college is both exciting and frightening at the same time. One of the biggest challenges faced by all new students is negotiating the maze of requirements and services available to them. As a new arrival with learning disabilities, you may find additional bumps and turns in your road to a successful education. In addition to the normal maze of information that any new student receives, you also must be aware of the procedures required to ensure that your needed accommodations are provided.

After contacting the institution's Learning Disability Services Office, review the documentation guidelines for students with learning disabilities. Then allow plenty of time to prepare your documentation. You may need to request copies of evaluation results from your testing service provider or new and/or additional pieces of information. Preparing this documentation can take time, and delays can hold up receiving appropriate accommodations. Provide this information to the Learning Disability Services Office as early as possible. This allows plenty of time for the office to review the information and become familiar with your accommodation needs.

Next, try to visit the Learning Disability Services Office. This allows you the opportunity to become familiar with the office and its services, the campus, the accommodation procedures, and other university resources, as well as alleviating the stress associated with dealing with a new environment. Also take this opportunity to ask questions:

- What is the application process for students with learning disabilities?
- What are the services available to students with learning disabilities?
- What documentation is required?
- What will I need to do to receive these services once you have my documentation?
- Are there any additional fees for services?
- Are there other classes available for students with learning disabilities (e.g., skills)?
- Do you have any course substitution policies or a reduced course load option?
- Do you have tutors? Content tutors or skills tutors? Are they trained to work with students with learning disabilities?
- During orientation, are there placement tests given for which I will need accommodations?
- Is there a Learning Resource Center on campus?

The third step in preparation for college is to be aware of your individual needs when selecting classes and planning your course schedule. Organization is essential to staying focused. It is important to prioritize and think carefully about what academic and social opportunities you would like to explore and their time commitments. A reduced course load may be a viable option to help you acclimate to college life. The Learning Disability Services Office will help determine if this is an appropriate accommodation for you. When choosing a class schedule, avoid classes that accentuate your weaknesses. You will want to work with the Learning Disability Services Office for scheduling advice. Pick and choose classes and activities carefully. Use this opportunity to try new experiences. You may find something new that stimulates your interest. To stay focused, try the following:

- When planning your schedule, try to leave time between classes, as well as time for yourself.
- There are many activities available—budget your time wisely.
- Use your free time between classes to study.
- Keep a "To Do" list daily and cross things off when they are done.
- Assign priorities to your tasks.
- Learn to say no to friends, phone calls, and unexpected interruptions.
- Carry a calendar with classes, appointments, and homework due dates.

The fourth step in the preparation process is to become comfortable being your own self-advocate. In college, you are expected to participate in the processes associated with your education and you need to be able to define your individual learning style, strengths, and weaknesses. You must compensate for these strengths and weaknesses, with the help of the Learning Disability Services Office, while defining preferences and choices for learning. The Learning Disability Services Office can assist you in interpreting documentation and in defining strategies for approaching and communicating with faculty members. Meeting with faculty members frequently will serve to further enhance your education. Make sure you understand the information they give you by preparing in advance:

- Make an appointment (try to do it early in the semester).
- Be on time for the appointment.
- Introduce yourself.
- Tell the instructor the class in which you are enrolled.
- Show an interest in the class.
- Be calm and courteous (don't interrupt, and make sure to know the difference between passive, aggressive, and assertive responses).
- Bring with you accommodations information, informa-

tion on learning disabilities, and/or course materials you want to discuss.

- Be prepared to solve problems or look for alternative answers.
- Leave the instructor with a positive impression.

Being a student with a learning disability in college takes persistence, patience, perseverance, and desire, along with solid communication skills. Many students encounter problems in college as a result of ignorance about the services available to them and/or poor communication between themselves and their college. It is of paramount importance, therefore, to be informed about your learning disability and then actively seek out the services available at your chosen institution. This assuages problems and lessens the stress you may encounter.

The bottom line is to be proactive in the process. Knowing where to go and what services are available through the Learning Disability Services Office will ease the transition from high school to college. Even if you decide not avail yourself of the services, it is still important to be prepared with all of the required information. Remember though that these services are not retroactive. It is your education, and the choice to use or not use services should not be taken lightly. It cannot be stressed strongly enough that identifying yourself to the Learning Disability Services Office and providing them with the appropriate documentation enhances the institution's ability to provide timely services to meet your individual needs. You should know that the dedicated people who work in the field continually strive to improve the services of their institutions, to hone their individual skills in the field, and to educate the public overall—all to better serve your needs as a student with learning disabilities. Best of luck with this exciting time ahead of you!

Emily Silberberg

LEGAL CONSIDERATIONS FOR LEARNING DISABILITY PROGRAMS

Perhaps the largest legal issue facing students with learning disabilities (LD) or attention deficit disorder (ADD) and their families is the different laws that govern schools serving K–12 vs. schools in the postsecondary education arena. Until a student goes on to college or turns 21, he or she is protected by the Individuals with Disabilities Education Act (IDEA). Once a student enters college, the Rehabilitation Act of 1973, Section 504 (Section 504), and the Americans with Disabilities Act (ADA) take over.

LAWS GOVERNING K–12 EDUCATION

The ADA specifically requires that K–12 schools seek out students with disabilities and give them whatever help they need to be successful in the school setting. For this reason, students are tested at no charge by the school if a disability is suspected and have Individual Education Plans (IEPs) formulated by the school. They receive tutoring and other academic support during their school day as their IEP dictates. Transition services are also required by IDEA. The school is required to have a transition statement in the student's IEP by the time he or she is 14 and to have a plan in place when the student turns 16. It is important for parents to request that a transition plan be in place. It is this plan that helps ensure that the student has had the appropriate courses for college entrance and also helps the school and the family plan for the future.

High school students with learning disabilities or ADD are entitled to take college entrance exams (for instance, the ACT Assessment or SAT) with accommodations if they qualify. These accommodations can include a reader, a scribe, extended time, or additional breaks as needed. Until recently, the scores of students with disabilities were "flagged" by the testing agencies to show that the test had been taken with special accommodations. This is no longer the case. Students can now take these tests without being concerned that they will be discriminated against during the admissions process.

LAWS GOVERNING POSTSECONDARY EDUCATION

Colleges are not required to seek out students with learning disabilities and do not have to provide any diagnostic services. They also are only required to provide "reasonable accommodations." Students with learning disabilities and ADD may be entitled to reasonable academic support based on legislation that was enacted in 1973. The Rehabilitation Act of 1973, Section 504, was the first civil rights law that specifically addressed individuals with disabilities. It was also the first law that addressed students with disabilities in postsecondary settings. The law mandates that all colleges and universities in the United States that receive any federal financial assistance cannot discriminate in the recruitment, admission, or treatment of students with disabilities. This law allows students with documented disabilities to request modifications, academic support, or auxiliary aids that allow them to participate in and benefit from all of the activities and programs that colleges offer. The law states:

> *"No otherwise qualified handicapped individual in the United States shall, solely by reason of his handicap, be excluded from participation in, be denied the benefits of, or be subjected to discrimination under any program or activity receiving financial assistance."*

Under the provisions of Section 504, colleges and universities may not:

- Limit the number of students with disabilities they admit;
- Ask questions on application materials that require the student to disclose a disability;
- Ask students to take preadmissions tests without academic assistance for which they may be eligible;
- Exclude a student who is qualified from a particular major or course of study;
- Counsel students with disabilities out of a particular program due to the disability;
- Have rules or policies that discriminate against students with disabilities; or
- Limit eligibility to students with disabilities for scholarships, financial assistance, fellowships, internships, or assistantships.

Students should be able to disclose their disability when they apply to college without fear of discrimination. Some students who readily fit the admissions criteria for a par-

5

ticular school may choose not to disclose their disability. Even so, it is still important to communicate with the Office for Disability Services directly to determine if a college has appropriate services for the applicant. Once accepted, it is important to contact the Office for Disability Services immediately to determine eligibility for services and find out how they can be accessed.

Personnel Who Enforce These Laws

Each campus has an individual or individuals who have expertise in Section 504 and/or the ADA. On some campuses, particularly small ones, the Director of Disability Services may also be the ADA/504 Coordinator. On many campuses, the Director of Disability Services is also the 504 Coordinator and the ADA Coordinator is a separate position. This information should be posted on the college Web site. If it is not, students should call the college to find out how these positions are staffed.

Eligibility Guidelines

There is no guidance under IDEA, Section 504, or the ADA that requires colleges to accept documentation that does not meet their guidelines. Each college has the right to develop its own guidelines and adhere to them. It is for this reason that even schools within the same state may have different criteria for determining eligibility for learning disability services.

Where Records Are Kept

The Office for Disability Services should be the primary place on campus where all documentation, including medical records, is kept. Disability services offices are required to keep documentation of a disability in a separate file from the documentation of day-to-day interactions that a student has with the office.

Mandated Services

One of the major legal issues for colleges and universities in ensuring they have all services mandated for students with disabilities in place. There are not many services that are actually required by law. Mandated services are as follows:

- Extra time on exams;
- Permitting tests to be individually proctored, read orally, dictated, or typed;
- The use of notetakers;
- The provision of adaptive technology;
- The opportunity to register to vote; and
- The provision of materials in alternate media.

In college, academic support services are offered in the following ways:

Readers

- Readers can be asked to repeat information.
- Readers can only read what is on the written page; they cannot be asked to reword material.

Scribes

- Scribes can write down exactly what a student says; they cannot organize or reword the student's ideas.
- Scribes are responsible for spelling and punctuation.
- It is up to the student to review what is written and direct the scribe to make corrections.

Notetakers

- A notetaker can be a recruited volunteer from the class.
- A notetaker can be a hired student worker.
- Students are required to attend classes even when notes are taken for them.

Adaptive Technology

- Adaptive technology includes computer hardware and software that allows students to access materials. This technology may enlarge print, actually read material out loud, type for students as they speak, highlight material, and even (to some degree) organize written material.

Voter Registration

The Motor Voter Registration Act requires all public institutions to offer all students with disabilities the opportunity to register to vote.

Nonmandated Services

Many colleges also offer services beyond what the law states. Schools with learning centers in place and developmental courses often offer tutoring and study-skills workshops. It is important for students to ask about all of the services offered on a campus. Campuses that offer more than what is required by law often have campus climates that are conducive to learning for all students.

Confidentiality

Throughout students' K–12 school careers, the material that is generated regarding their disability has been kept confidential. The Family Educational Rights Privacy Act of 1974 (FERPA), also known as the Buckley Amendment, governs K–12 schools but has implications for college settings as well. In addition, the Americans with Disabilities Act also protects documentation and other materials from being shared without a student's explicit consent. These laws do not allow college faculty members to access disability-related information.

According to the Association on Higher Education and Disability (AHEAD), disability-related records provided by a physician, psychiatrist, psychologist, or other recognized professional are not subject to free access under FERPA. AHEAD also says, "It is only necessary to share with faculty the information that a student has a documented need for accommodation(s)." Students may request to review their own files; however, the contents of the file are the property of the Office for Disability Services. Nonetheless, the office cannot forward documentation to another institution or professional.

Grievance Procedures

Most colleges have a grievance procedure in place to handle concerns and complaints from students. Generally, if students feel that they have been denied a reasonable academic accommodation, they should first meet with the Disability Services Director. If the complaint cannot be resolved at that level, students should be informed of the process that is in place for filing a formal grievance and the specific time frame for filing. Complaints generally must be filed on a university-provided form and must include a written statement of the facts of the discriminatory incident in question. From that point on, the university then investigates the complaint.

RIGHTS FOR THE LD/ADD STUDENT

Students with LD/ADD are afforded the same protections under civil rights laws. They should not be discriminated against based on their disability. Most college campuses welcome students with disabilities and have policies and procedures in place that make requesting academic accommodations a smooth process. It is important to know what policies and procedures are in place at a college and who on campus has the responsibility for making sure that students with disabilities can access what they need to get the same education as their peers without disabilities.

Lydia S. Block, Ph.D., is an educational consultant in Columbus, Ohio. Dr. Block works with students with LD, ADD, head injuries, and other disabilities.

DOCUMENTATION REQUIRED FOR COLLEGE ELIGIBILITY

I was organizing my thoughts on documentation and considering what was most important to communicate. I thought through numerous presentations and conversations, and one family's story stuck in my mind as particularly representative. While each student is unique, I believe Tabatha's and her family's story is representative of the rigors surrounding documentation at the college level.

THE HIGH SCHOOL-TO-COLLEGE DISCONNECT

My first contact with the family came when the student's mother called me with a complaint. She said that her daughter had just been told by our Office for Disability Services that she no longer had a learning disability and would not be eligible for services as she moved into her first year of college.

Back in Elementary School

Tabatha (not her real name) was identified in third grade as having a specific learning disability impacting language, primarily reading and writing. Based on school performance, observations, and a full battery of psycho-educational tests, Tabatha was found to be eligible for special education services under the Individuals with Disabilities Education Act (IDEA). For three years, there were annual IEP meetings. Then, at the end of sixth grade, she was reevaluated.

Tabatha's learning behaviors were observed in class. Her school performance and progress, as represented by such indicators as homework, classroom tests, proficiency tests, and systemwide achievement tests, was reviewed. In addition, the teachers and special educators who had worked most closely with Tabatha provided input. Her performance had clearly improved, but it was still lagging in a few areas. Tabatha was eligible for continued special education services.

High School

Three years and IEPs later, Tabatha was completing ninth grade and her third evaluation. Happily, after six years of services and support, the review of classroom and standardized achievement tests showed she was now perform-

ing above grade level. Both Tabatha and her family were delighted to hear this. Satisfaction and pride changed to concern and panic as the team explained that Tabatha would no longer be eligible for special education services.

After some lengthy discussions with the high school, the family's concerns were addressed by developing a 504 Plan under Section 504 of the Rehabilitation Act. The plan identified accommodations (modifications to policies and procedures), including additional time to complete assignments, additional time to take tests, the opportunity to take tests in a different setting that minimized distractions, and access to a computer for essay tests and written work. With these modifications, Tabatha was successful in high school and was accepted by three of the four colleges to which she applied.

On to College

Once Tabatha selected a college, she and her parents registered for an August orientation session, paid her deposit, and began to plan for the fall. Tabatha contacted the Office for Disability Services, arranged an appointment during orientation, and had a copy of her "special education file" sent. The file included the paperwork from all three reviews, her seven IEPs, and her 504 Plan.

At the meeting, Tabatha was asked if she had any documentation she had not sent in. She was not positive but didn't think so; mostly, she wanted to know why the counselor was asking. The counselor said that the only diagnostic tests given were from third grade. "Tests that old don't tell us much about your current needs and limitations," the counselor added.

"Weren't all of the IEPs and the evaluations from sixth and ninth grade sent?" Tabatha asked.

The counselor explained that the neither of these evaluations contained any diagnostic tests (intelligence/aptitude, achievement, and cognitive process) used to diagnose a learning disability and determine its impact on adults. In addition, the ninth grade evaluation suggested that there were no longer any functional limitations since she was performing above grade level.

"I have always taken my tests with extra time!" Tabatha emphasized. The counselor said that they would provide accommodations through January to allow her to update her documentation.

Tabatha left the meeting upset. She talked to her mother, who then went to speak to the counselor. The counselor repeated the explanations that he had given to Tabatha. Tabatha's mother then pointed to the 504 Plan and said that she was told 504 applied to colleges. Didn't the college have to accept Tabatha's 504 Plan?

The counselor said that a plan developed by a high school or even one from another college does not automatically apply. Eligibility at the college level is based on documentation demonstrating that there is a current substantial limitation and identifying current impacts or limitations that are connected to the accommodations requested. The counselor added that every college has some latitude in establishing what documentation it wants. The counselor referred Tabatha and her mother to the office Web site, where the college's documentation guidelines were published.

WHAT DO YOU NEED?

Tabatha's story highlights several critical points about documentation at the college level. Typically, an IEP or 504 Plan will not be sufficient. Depending on the age, approach, and level of details included in your last eligibility evaluation, it may not be enough. So what is enough?

What Does the Government Say?

The U.S. Department of Education's Office for Civil Rights, which is the primary enforcement agency for college access under Section 504 and the Americans with Disabilities Act (ADA), has produced an excellent booklet focused on the transition to college, entitled "Students with Disabilities Preparing for Postsecondary Education: Know Your Rights and Responsibilities" (http://www.ed.gov/ocr/transition.html). The points made about documentation are:

"Schools may set reasonable standards for documentation. Some schools require more documentation than others. They may require you to provide documentation prepared by an appropriate professional, such as a medical doctor, psychologist, or other qualified diagnostician. The required documentation may include one or more of the following: a diagnosis of your current disability, the date of the diagnosis, how the diagnosis was reached, the credentials of the professional, how your disability affects a major life activity, and how the disability affects your academic performance. The documentation should provide enough information for you and your school to decide what is an appropriate academic adjustment.

"Although an Individual Education Plan (IEP) or Section 504 Plan, if you have one, may help identify services that have been effective for you, it generally is not sufficient documentation. This is because postsecondary education presents different demands than high school education, and what you need to meet these new demands may be different. Also, in some cases, the nature of a disability may change.

"If the documentation that you have does not meet the postsecondary school's requirements, a school official must tell you in a timely manner what additional documentation you need to provide. You may need a new evaluation in order to provide the required documentation."[1]

Six Elements of Comprehensive Documentation

Based on a review of decisions by the Office for Civil Rights, here are six core elements of documentation. You can use these elements to review existing documentation or to guide an evaluator in updating your documentation.

1. **A diagnostic statement identifying the condition(s).** Documentation should contain a clear statement identifying the disability. It is helpful if classification codes from the current editions of either the Diagnostic Statistical Manual (DSM) or the International Classifications of Disease (ICD) are included. The dates of the original diagnosis and any evaluations performed by referring professionals should be included, along with a date and description of the current evaluation being forwarded.

2. **Current functional impact of the condition(s).** The current functional impact on physical (including mobility dexterity, and endurance), perceptual, cognitive (including attention, distractibility, and communication), and behavioral abilities should be described as narrative. When formal or informal testing is used, the detailed results should be included. The combination of narrative and test results should provide a sense of severity, information on variability (over time, circumstance, or content), and potential environmental triggers.

3. **Treatments, medications, and assistive devices/services currently prescribed or in use.** This should include a description of treatments, medications, assistive devices, accommodations, and/or assistive services in current use and their estimated effectiveness in minimizing the impact of the condition(s). Also include any significant side effects that may impact physical, perceptual, behavioral, or cognitive performance.

4. **The expected progression or stability of the impacts described over time.** This description should provide an estimate of the change in the functional impacts of the condition(s) over time and/or recom-

[1] U.S. Department of Education, Office for Civil Rights, Students with Disabilities Preparing for Postsecondary Education: Know Your Rights and Responsibilities, Washington, D.C., 2002.

mendations concerning the predictable need for reevaluation of the condition(s). If the condition is variable (based on known cycles or environmental triggers), is the student under self-care for flare-ups or episodes?

5. **Recommended accommodations and services.** Recommendations should be logically connected to the impact of the condition. When connections are not obvious, they should be explained. Recommendations are not prescriptions and need to be evaluated by the college in the context of the student's academic program.

6. **Credentials of the evaluator.** If not clear from the letterhead or forms, the credentials of the evaluator should be included. If the evaluator's credentials are not those typically associated with diagnosis of the disability in question (for example, a general practitioner diagnosing attention deficit disorder), then a brief description of the evaluator's experience with this type of diagnosis should be included.

These six underlying elements for comprehensive documentation can be presented in a number of ways. You will recall that, according to the Office for Civil Rights, "Schools may set reasonable standards for documentation. Some schools require more documentation than others." So how do you know if your documentaion will be acceptable? If you know what colleges you are likely to attend, you should research their specific documentation requirements. Often, you can get these from the college's Web site. If you cannot find this information on the Web, you should contact the office and ask them to mail you a copy of their documentation guidelines. They will keep your request confidential.

The Highest Common Denominator

A psychoeducational battery consisting of standardized tests measuring aptitude, achievement, and cognitive processing is the most commonly accepted approach to identifying and quantifying the current functional impacts of a learning disability (the second of the six elements listed). Documentation containing such a battery is likely to meet the minimum standards for documentation at any institution and provides a foundation for anticipating accommodations in new settings and identifying compensatory strategies or tools you might use to minimize the impacts of your disability.

While the specific tests comprising a psychoeducational battery vary based on your educational history, there are five components that any complete battery should include:

1. **Adult referenced testing.** For tests relying on a norm or comparison group for interpretation, versions of the tests using an "adult" reference group may be considered necessary to show current impact (e.g., the Wechsler Adult Intelligence Scale vs. the Wechsler Intelligence Scale for Children). Typically, adult referenced tests begin to be administered around age 14.

2. **A measure of aptitude.** Commonly accepted aptitude measures include the Wechsler Adult Intelligence Scale,

Woodcock-Johnson Psychoeducational Battery's Tests of Cognitive Ability, Kaufman Adolescent and Adult Intelligence Test, or Stanford-Binet Intelligence Scale.

3. **A standardized measure of academic achievement.** Commonly accepted achievement batteries include the Stanford Test of Academic Skills, Woodcock-Johnson Psycho-educational Battery's Tests of Achievement, and the Wechsler Individual Achievement Tests. An evaluation of achievement can also be based on a collection of measures focused on specific areas of achievement, such as the Nelson-Denny Reading Skills Test, the Stanford Diagnostic Mathematics Test, the Test of Written Language, or the Woodcock Reading Mastery Tests.

4. **Measures of cognitive processes impacted.** Standardized tests that measure cognitive processes, such as memory, perception, auditory and visual processing, processing speed, or executive functioning, that are affected by the condition should be included. Commonly used instruments include the Detroit Tests of Learning Aptitude, subtests on the Wechsler Adult Intelligence Scale, and the Woodcock-Johnson Psychoeducational Battery's Tests of Cognitive Ability.

5. **Clinical observations.** This includes a narrative provided by the professional administering the tests that discusses test choice, testing conditions, and the individual's behaviors during testing.

Alternatives

There are a number of approaches to evaluating a learning disability that do not include a traditional psychoeducational evaluation. For example, a growing number of evaluators are moving away from using aptitude/achievement discrepancies in diagnosing adults and do not include achievement testing. Additionally, many public schools are moving toward observational evaluations instead of evaluations based on psychometric tests.

What is often missing from the documentation provided by these alternative evaluation approaches is a clear and descriptive narrative of what was observed by the evaluator. For example, in the documentation provided by Tabatha, the evaluator indicated where observations were made (e.g., in the classroom), what was looked at (classroom testing, proficiency tests, etc.), and that she was no longer eligible for special education services but would have these accommodations under a 504 Plan. There were no descriptions of what was observed in her testing behaviors or results that indicated that extended time was needed. There was no discussion of what about her writing by hand supported the use of a computer as an aid. A rationale connecting observations to accommodations and services can provide colleges with the kind of information from which they need to work.

In order to receive accommodations, your documentation must demonstrate that you have a disability as defined by the ADA and Section 504: "A mental or physical impairment that substantially limits one or more of the major live activitiesà" (28 CFR Part 36, Sec. 104). It is important to remember that there are many cases where a learning disability, attention deficit disorder, or other condition is present and causes some difficulties, but is not a substantial limitation. However, once the documentation has indicated that you have a disability, you are guaranteed equal treatment. For accommodations (extended testing time, books on tape, and other modifications or auxiliary aids), the documentation needs to identify current impacts of the disability that are rationally related to the requests you make.

L. Scott Lissner, M.A., is the University ADA Coordinator at The Ohio State University.

THROUGH THE EYES OF AN LD DIRECTOR: CRITICAL STEPS FOR COLLEGE SUCCESS

In one of many stories passed on throughout the ages, a local villager completed the arduous trek necessary to reach an esteemed Wise Man. The villager asked why one cannot cover the world in leather so one will never step on another thorn. The Wise Man replied, "There is no need to cover the world when one can achieve the same goal by covering the soles of one's feet with leather."

If students follow the advice dispensed by the many wise men and women located within collegiate support service offices, their transition to the postsecondary world will take shape without stepping on too many thorns.

K–12 THORNS

During the K–12 years, avoiding all academic thorns and simplifying all tasks to the lowest common denominator should be avoided when composing Individual Education Plans (IEP). Academic adjustments, auxiliary aids, and class selection must be based on clear and precise correlating strands stemming from comprehensive diagnostic evaluations. Having difficulty with particular course work in and of itself does not guarantee that antecedent variables stemming from a disability are in play. Cookie-cutter IEPs, in which the same set of accommodations is in place for all classes (a manifestation of the new generation of computerized, scantron-like IEPs), do not necessarily hold forth on the collegiate level. Collegiate support service personnel will not rubber-stamp high school IEPs.

Postgraduation summertime osmosis does not exist. Accommodations that maximized a student's potential in the high school world may disintegrate on the collegiate level. High school students who enjoyed 36 hours of teacher-driven class time and approximately 12 hours of at-home independent study each week must adapt to the mere 12 to 15 hours of collegiate professorial contact and budget 3 hours of study for each hour of class.

TRANSITIONING TO COLLEGE: SUMMER CLASSES

Families who expect the collegiate world to give carte blanche accommodations do have a litmus test. Summer classes offered throughout the country's two- and four-year postsecondary institutions are a wonderful venue to gauge a student's readiness for college. Enrolling in a summer class allows for a realistic shakedown of a student's skill base, alongside the possibility of parlaying the summer credits toward high school or postsecondary degrees. The compressed schedule of a summer class (typically, a sixteen-week class is completed in five to six weeks) ratchets up the workload to a level shadowing the time management and classroom skills necessary for a single class, surrounded by four additional courses within a standard fall/spring term. If the class is completed during the summer preceding the senior year, compensatory plans, based upon the summer class experience, can be developed and implemented throughout the student's final year in high school.

During the summer class, most students with learning disabilities discover the significant differences in the types of accommodations provided, the mode in which accommodations are carried out, and the new roles dictated to parents and students in the collegiate setting. If the student is planning to live on campus during college, it is important for parents to refrain from intervening during the summer school project, as parental structure will be nonexistent within the college dormitory setting. Students, not parents, are required to initiate contact with support service personnel in order to receive accommodations while concurrently creating lines of communication with faculty members.

STUDENT/FACULTY RELATIONSHIP

The student-faculty relationship is a cornerstone to a student's successful postsecondary transition. Faculty contact should be conducted within a faculty member's office during office hours, as impromptu discussions in the hall prior to or after class lack the confidentiality and time necessary for realistic advances with classroom material. Early in the semester (within the first week), students should hone in on information not detailed in the syllabus, which may pertain to specific accommodations they will be need. Academic accommodations will be based upon a range of variables, such as the types of exams to be administered. For example, if documentation supports the need for a word processor, this accommodation should be enlisted for an essay exam, but will have no relevance during a multiple-choice test. Throughout the semester, it is a good idea for students to discuss reading assignments prior to, not after, due dates with their professors. Most professors gladly review written assignments and return them with insightful feedback if they are handed in prior to the deadline (despite this extremely helpful point not usually being detailed on the syllabus).

COLLEGE COURSE SELECTION

Understanding a professor's teaching style and how it interacts with one's learning style makes the course selection process uniquely important, as inefficient class/professor selection in and of itself can lead to a catastrophic transition process. This is a variable given scant consideration throughout the K–12 learning continuum. While multimodality teaching, utilizing listening, speaking, reading, and writing, is the buzzword during K–12 education, students are likely to encounter a college professor utilizing a single-modality format (lecture), especially when classes are held in a theater-sized lecture hall. Thus, a visual learner should, whenever possible, seek out a whiteboard aficionado, while an auditory learner should seek the comfort of a strictly auditory lecture hall platform.

A second piece of a student's learning style revolves around course requirements. A strong writer would certainly prefer a course requiring three papers, while a strong reader would long for three multiple-choice exams. Students should not be swayed by student feedback surrounding the perceived difficulty level of a professor, as the tough professor may have been evaluated by an individual with an opposing learning style.

Securing preferred classes requires advance planning. Most schools offer multiple orientation dates during the late spring or early summer months. Creating first-semester schedules is a component of most of these orientations. Students who attend the earliest orientation have the pick of the litter for choosing professors, while students attending the last session may find it difficult to create an optimal set of classes. If final exams, proms, or graduation conflicts with early orientation dates, student should ask if it is possible to register early and attend a later orientation.

The selection of courses (although, as many undergraduates point out, one selects professors, not courses) is an active, not passive, process. Collaboration with support service personnel will help make the selection process a success.

SUPPORT SERVICE OFFICE

Attending a comprehensive, structured program does not transfer all responsibilities from the student to the school. The student is the conduit between classroom and dormitory life and support service personnel. Time is everything when it comes to problem solving within the support service office. Most support service personnel are quite competent when it comes to solving problems that may arise, *if* the problems are brought to the support service personnel within 48 hours (or two class periods) of the mishap. For example, a student's notetaker had the flu and the student received no notes for the two-week period prior to an exam. The student believed the professor would automatically locate a replacement, while the support service office continued to assume all was well, as the notetaker did not contact the office. The student took the exam, did poorly, and proceeded to complain to the support service office. If the student had contacted the professor or support service office in a timely manner, a substitute notetaker would have been located and/or the test postponed.

Students should plan to visit the support service office during orientation or, if logistics allow, over the summer months prior to the start of classes. If students create a bond with the staff under a stress-free environment, there is a greater likelihood that those seeking assistance to remedy a problem in the midst of a semester will visit the support service office in a timely manner.

_____

Ross Pollack, M.Ed., Ed.D., is Director of the Specialized Resource Center/ADA Coordinator at Manhattan College. He is one of four members of the New York State Department of Education's Standing Committee concerning the Task Force on Postsecondary Education and Disabilities.

HOW TO USE THIS GUIDE

In the following pages you'll find detailed information about learning disabilities (LD) and attention deficit disorder (ADD) programs and services at specific colleges. The profiles are organized into two primary divisions: four-year colleges, followed by two-year colleges. These two primary divisions are further subdivided into Colleges with Structured/Proactive Programs—programs offering more comprehensive services for students with LD or ADD, and Colleges with Self-Directed/Decentralized Programs—programs that may be less structured but do still provide a considerable number of special services to students with LD or ADD. The four sections of individual college profiles are presented in this order: Four-Year Colleges with Structured/Proactive Programs; Four-Year Colleges with Self-Directed/Decentralized Programs; Two-Year Colleges with Structured/Proactive Programs; Two-Year Colleges with Self-Directed/Decentralized Programs.

What Are the Differences between Colleges with Structured/Proactive Programs and Those with Self-Directed/Decentralized Programs?

Schools are classified as either Structured/Proactive or Self-Directed/Decentralized. Structured/Proactive Programs are more likely to have separate admissions processes and charge fees. These programs' services go well beyond those that are legally mandated and the student is provided with a more structured environment that includes low staff/student ratios. Self-Directed/Decentralized Programs usually have no separate admissions processes and eligibility for services must be established by the provision of disability documentation that meets institutional standards. Self-Directed/Decentralized Programs' services may be coordinated through the Disability Services Office and are based on need as specified by the student's documentation. Services may also be provided by other offices throughout the campus, and some services offered are not mandated by laws. Additionally, student progress is usually not monitored.

While all programs offer students with appropriate documentation academic adjustments and auxiliary aids, utilizing these support mechanisms will vary, falling within these two distinct categories. Structured/Proactive Programs are intrinsically school-centered decision making organizations, as compared to Self Directed/Decentralized Programs where support service decisions remain within the students' domain. Students with a tendency to cocoon themselves or wait until the eleventh hour to seek assistance when faced with academically induced stress will find a comfort zone associated with Structured/Proactive

Programs. Extra program fees, separate applications and a limit to the number of students accepted into the program allow Structured/Proactive Programs to maintain a student to staff ratio indicative of a structured format. Students in a Self-Directed/Decentralized Program line the continuum of support services from once a semester visits for academic adjustments to daily visits in order to receive a more comprehensive level of support.

COLLEGE PROFILE LISTINGS

Learning Disabilities Program or Unit Information

Each profile starts with the college name, address and contact information. You'll next find the program or unit name (when provided by the school) and the number of students served by the program or unit during the 2002–03 academic year, followed by the numbers of full-time and/or part-time staff members. The providers of services to the students (academic advisers, coaches, counselors, diagnostic specialists, graduate assistants/students, LD specialists, professional tutors, regular education teachers, remediation/learning, skill tutors, strategy tutors, special education tutors, teacher trainees, and/or trained peer tutors), as well as whether the service is provided as part of the LD program or unit and/or through a collaborative provider located on- or off-campus, completes this section.

Orientation

Schools offering orientation for new undergraduate students with LD have the program's required or optional status, the length of the program, and when the special orientation occurs listed here.

Summer Program

Schools offering summer programs to help students prepare for the demands of college have the program's required or optional status, the length of the program, and whether or not degree credit is earned listed here.

Unique Aids and Services

Unique aids and services, which include advocates, career counseling, digital textbooks, faculty training, parent workshops, personal coach, priority registration, support groups, and weekly meetings with faculty are enumerated.

Subject-area Tutoring

Subject-area tutoring, when available, is described as offered one-on-one, via small groups, and/or via class-size groups. Information is also provided on how the tutoring is provided (through the LD program or unit and/or collaboratively on- or off-campus) and how the tutoring is delivered (computer-based instruction, graduate, LD specialists, professional tutors, and trained peer tutors).

Diagnostic Testing

This section includes indications of diagnostic testing availability to undergraduate students through the LD program or unit and/or collaboratively on-or off-campus. The tests offered may include any of the following: auditory, handwriting, intelligence, learning strategies, learning styles, math, motor skills, neuropsychological, personality, reading, social skills, spelling, spoken language, study skills, written language, and visual processing.

Basic Skills Remediation

Basic skills remediation, when available, is described as offered one-on-one, via small groups, and/or via class-size groups. Information is also provided on how the basic skills remediation is provided (through the LD program or unit and/or collaboratively on- or off-campus) and how the basic skills remediation is delivered (computer-based instruction, graduate, LD specialists, professional tutors, regular education teachers, special education teachers, teacher trainees, and trained peer tutors). Basic skills remediation areas include auditory processing, computer skills, handwriting, learning strategies, math, motor skills, reading, social skills, spelling, spoken language, study skills, time management, visual processing, and written language.

Enrichment

Enrichment programs, when available, may be provided through the LD program or unit and/or collaboratively on- or off-campus. It will also be noted if the enrichment course/program is offered for credit. Enrichment programs include career planning, college survival skills, health and nutrition, learning strategies, math, medication management, oral communication skills, practical computer skills, reading, self-advocacy, stress management, study skills, test taking, time management, vocabulary development, and written composition skills.

Student Organization

The name of any student organizations for students with LD and the number of undergraduate student members are displayed here.

Fees

Listed here, if applicable, are costs (and reasons for variances) for non-mandated services, summer programs, orientation, and diagnostic testing.

Application

Information is given here pertaining to additional registration components, whether they are required or recommended for participation in the program or unit, and to whom the information should be sent upon application and upon acceptance. Deadlines for applying to the program or unit are also provided.

Written Policies

This section lists where students can find official policies regarding general/basic LD accommodations, substitutions and waivers of admissions requirements, substitutions and waivers of graduation requirements, course substitutions, reduced course loads, and grade forgiveness.

CRITERIA FOR INCLUSION IN THIS BOOK

The term "four-year college" is the commonly used designation for institutions that grant the baccalaureate degree. Four years is the expected amount of time required to earn this degree, although some bachelor's degree programs may be completed in three years, others require five years, and part-time programs may take considerably longer. Upper-level institutions offer only the junior and senior years and accept only students with two years of college-level credit. Therefore, "four-year college" is a conventional term that accurately describes most of the institutions included in this guide, but it should not be taken literally in all cases.

To be included in this guide, an institution must have full accreditation or be a candidate for accreditation (preaccreditation) status by an institutional or specialized accrediting body recognized by the U.S. Department of Education or the Council for Higher Education Accreditation (CHEA). Institutional accrediting bodies, which review each institution as a whole, include the six regional associations of schools and colleges (Middle States, New England, North Central, Northwest, Southern, and Western), each of which is responsible for a specified portion of the United States and its territories. Other institutional accrediting bodies are national in scope and accredit specific kinds of institutions (e.g., Bible colleges, independent colleges, and rabbinical and Talmudic schools). Program registration by the New York State Board of Regents is considered to be the equivalent of institutional accreditation, since the board requires that all programs offered by an institution meet its standards before recognition is granted. A Canadian institution must be chartered and authorized to grant degrees by the provincial government, affiliated with a chartered institution, or accredited by a recognized U.S. accrediting body This guide also includes institutions outside the United States that are accredited by these U.S. accrediting bodies. There are recognized specialized or professional accrediting bodies in more than forty different fields, each of which is authorized to accredit institutions for specific programs in its particular field. For specialized institutions that offer programs in one field only, we designate this to be the equivalent of institutional accreditation. A full explanation of the accrediting process and complete information on recognized, institutional (regional and national) and specialized accrediting bodies can be found online at www.chea.org or at www.ed.gov/offices/OPE/accreditation/index.html.

RESEARCH PROCEDURES

The data contained in the **College Profile Listings** were researched between spring and summer 2003 through Peterson's Learning Disabilities Online Survey. Questionnaires were sent to the more than 3,800 colleges that meet the criteria for inclusion in this guide. All data included in this edition have been submitted by officials (usually admission officers, institutional research personnel, or LD program coordinators) at the colleges themselves. All usable information received in time for publication has been included. The omission of any particular item from a profile listing signifies that either the item is not applicable to that institution or that data were not available. Because of the comprehensive editorial review that takes place in our offices and because all material comes directly from college officials, Peterson's has every reason to believe that the information presented in this guide is accurate at the time of printing. However, students should check with a specific college or university at the time of application to verify data, which may have changed since the publication of this volume.

Four-Year Colleges

WITH STRUCTURED/PROACTIVE PROGRAMS

Adelphi University
Learning Disabilities Program

South Avenue

Garden City, NY 11530

http://academics.adelphi.edu/ldprog/

Contact: Susan Spencer, Assistant Dean and Director. Phone: 516-877-4710. Fax: 516-877-4711. E-mail: ldprogram@adelphi.edu.

Learning Disabilities Program Approximately 140 registered undergraduate students were served during 2002-03. The program or unit includes 16 full-time staff members. Academic advisers, counselors, LD specialists, remediation/learning specialists, special education teachers, and strategy tutors are provided through the program or unit. Academic advisers are provided collaboratively through on-campus or off-campus services.

Orientation The program or unit offers a mandatory 5-week orientation for new students during summer prior to enrollment.

Summer Program To help prepare for the demands of college, there is a mandatory 5-week summer program prior to entering the school. Degree credit will be earned.

Unique Aids and Services Aids, services, or accommodations include parent workshops, priority registration, support groups, counseling.

Subject-area Tutoring Tutoring is offered in small groups for some subjects. Tutoring is provided collaboratively through on-campus or off-campus services via computer-based instruction, graduate assistants/students, and trained peer tutors.

Diagnostic Testing Testing is provided through the program or unit for learning strategies, learning styles, and reading. Testing for auditory processing, intelligence, and personality is provided collaboratively through on-campus or off-campus services.

Basic Skills Remediation Remediation is offered one-on-one for learning strategies, study skills, time management, and written language. Remediation is provided through the program or unit via LD specialists, special education teachers, and other.

Enrichment Enrichment programs are available through the program or unit for written composition skills.

Fees *LD Program or Service* fee is $4500. *Summer Program* fee is $1350. *Orientation* fee is $1350.

Application For admittance to the program or unit, students are required to apply to the program directly, provide a psychoeducational report (2 years old or less), provide documentation of high school services, and provide comprehensive diagnostic report. Upon application, materials documenting need for services should be sent only to the LD program or unit. Upon acceptance, documentation of need for services should be sent only to the LD program or unit. *Application deadline (institutional):* Continuous. *Application deadline (LD program):* 3/1 for fall. Rolling/continuous for spring.

Written Policies Written policies regarding general/basic LD accommodations and substitutions and waivers of admissions requirements are available on the program Web site. Written policies regarding course substitutions, general/basic LD accommodations, reduced course loads, and substitutions and waivers of admissions requirements are available through the program or unit directly.

American International College
Supportive Learning Services

1000 State Street

Springfield, MA 01109-3189

http://www.aic.edu/

Contact: Mrs. Anne M. Midura, Office Manager. Phone: 413-205-3426. Fax: 413-205-3908. E-mail: cbc2@aicstudent.com. Head of LD Program: Prof. Mary M. Saltus, Coordinator. Phone: 413-205-3426. Fax: 413-204-3908. E-mail: cbc2@aicstudent.com.

Supportive Learning Services Approximately 95 registered undergraduate students were served during 2002-03. The program or unit includes 12 full-time staff members. LD specialists and professional tutors are provided through the program or unit.

Orientation The program or unit offers a mandatory approximately 2-hour orientation for new students during the college orientation.

Subject-area Tutoring Tutoring is offered one-on-one and in small groups for all subjects. Tutoring is provided through the program or unit via LD specialists and professional tutors.

Enrichment Enrichment programs are available through the program or unit for learning strategies, study skills, test taking, time management, and written composition skills. Programs for career planning, college survival skills, and written composition skills are provided collaboratively through on-campus or off-campus services. Credit is offered for college survival skills.

Fees *LD Program or Service* fee is $350 to $2150 (fee varies according to level/tier of service). *Orientation* fee is $350 to $2150.

Application For admittance to the program or unit, students are required to provide a psychoeducational report (3 years old or less), provide documentation of high school services, and provide skill level testing. Upon application, materials documenting need for services should be sent only to the LD program or unit. *Application deadline (institutional):* Continuous. *Application deadline (LD program):* Rolling/continuous for fall and rolling/continuous for spring.

Written Policies Written policy regarding reduced course loads is outlined in the school's catalog/handbook. Written policy regarding general/basic LD accommodations is available through the program or unit directly.

American University
Academic Support Center

4400 Massachusetts Avenue, NW

Washington, DC 20016-8001

http://www.american.edu/asc

Contact: Ms. Melissa Scarfone, Coordinator of Learning Services Program. Phone: 202-885-3360. Fax: 202-885-1042. E-mail: asc@american.edu. Head of LD Program: Ms. Kathy Schwartz, Director of Academic Support Center. Phone: 202-885-3360. Fax: 202-885-1042. E-mail: asc@american.edu.

American University (continued)

Academic Support Center Approximately 300 registered undergraduate students were served during 2002-03. The program or unit includes 6 full-time and 7 part-time staff members. Graduate assistants/students, LD specialists, and trained peer tutors are provided through the program or unit. Academic advisers are provided collaboratively through on-campus or off-campus services.

Unique Aids and Services Aids, services, or accommodations include priority registration.

Subject-area Tutoring Tutoring is offered one-on-one for all subjects. Tutoring is provided collaboratively through on-campus or off-campus services via trained peer tutors.

Enrichment Enrichment programs are available through the program or unit for college survival skills, learning strategies, reading, self-advocacy, study skills, test taking, time management, and written composition skills. Programs for career planning, math, medication management, and stress management are provided collaboratively through on-campus or off-campus services.

Fees *LD Program or Service* fee is $1000 (fee varies according to level/tier of service).

Application For admittance to the program or unit, students are required to apply to the program directly and provide a psychoeducational report. Upon application, materials documenting need for services should be sent only to the LD program or unit. Upon acceptance, documentation of need for services should be sent only to the LD program or unit. *Application deadline (institutional):* 2/1. *Application deadline (LD program):* 2/1 for fall.

Written Policies Written policy regarding general/basic LD accommodations is available on the program Web site. Written policy regarding general/basic LD accommodations is outlined in the school's catalog/handbook. Written policies regarding general/basic LD accommodations and substitutions and waivers of admissions requirements are available through the program or unit directly.

Baker College of Jackson

2800 Springport Road

Jackson, MI 49202

http://www.baker.edu/

Contact: Mrs. Connie Hollmann, Student Adviser. Phone: 517-841-4505. Fax: 517-789-7331. E-mail: connie.hollmann@baker.edu.

The program or unit includes 1 full-time and 15 part-time staff members. Counselors, regular education teachers, and trained peer tutors are provided through the program or unit.

Unique Aids and Services Aids, services, or accommodations include advocates, career counseling, and personal coach.

Subject-area Tutoring Tutoring is offered one-on-one for some subjects. Tutoring is provided through the program or unit via computer-based instruction, trained peer tutors, and other.

Diagnostic Testing Testing is provided through the program or unit for math, reading, and written language.

Basic Skills Remediation Remediation is offered one-on-one for math, reading, and written language. Remediation is provided through the program or unit via computer-based instruction, regular education teachers, and trained peer tutors.

Enrichment Enrichment programs are available through the program or unit for career planning, college survival skills, math, oral communication skills, reading, and vocabulary development. Credit is offered for math and oral communication skills.

Application For admittance to the program or unit, students are required to provide documentation of high school services. It is recommended that students provide a psychoeducational report. Upon application, materials documenting need for services should be sent only to the LD program or unit. Upon acceptance, documentation of need for services should be sent only to the LD program or unit. *Application deadline (institutional):* 9/19. *Application deadline (LD program):* Rolling/continuous for fall and rolling/continuous for spring.

Written Policies Written policies regarding course substitutions, substitutions and waivers of admissions requirements, and substitutions and waivers of graduation requirements are outlined in the school's catalog/handbook.

Barry University
The Center for Advanced Learning Program (CAL)

11300 Northeast Second Avenue

Miami Shores, FL 33161-6695

http://www.barry.edu/

Contact: Ms. Vivian Castro, Director of Center for Advanced Learning Program. Phone: 305-899-3461. Fax: 305-899-3778. E-mail: vcastro@mail.barry.edu.

The Center for Advanced Learning Program (CAL) Approximately 45 registered undergraduate students were served during 2002-03. The program or unit includes 1 full-time and 15 part-time staff members. Academic advisers, counselors, LD specialists, and professional tutors are provided through the program or unit. Academic advisers and diagnostic specialists are provided collaboratively through on-campus or off-campus services.

Orientation The program or unit offers a mandatory half-day orientation for new students before classes begin.

Unique Aids and Services Aids, services, or accommodations include advocates, career counseling, and priority registration.

Subject-area Tutoring Tutoring is offered one-on-one and in small groups for most subjects. Tutoring is provided through the program or unit via professional tutors.

Diagnostic Testing Testing is provided through the program or unit for learning strategies, learning styles, and study skills.

Basic Skills Remediation Remediation is offered in class-size groups for computer skills, math, reading, study skills, time management, and written language. Remediation is provided through the program or unit.

Enrichment Enrichment programs are available through the program or unit for career planning, college survival skills, learning strategies, stress management, study skills, test taking, and time management. Programs for career planning, math, stress management, study skills, test taking, time management, vocabulary development, and written composition skills are provided collaboratively through on-campus or off-campus services. Credit is offered for college survival skills, learning strategies, study skills, test taking, and time management.

Fees *LD Program or Service* fee is $3900.

Application For admittance to the program or unit, students are required to apply to the program directly, provide a psychoeducational report (3 years old or less), provide documentation of high school services, and provide a letter of recommendation, personal statement, and have a personal interview. Upon application, materials documenting need for services should be sent only to the LD program or unit. Upon acceptance, documentation of need for services should be sent only to the LD program or unit. *Application deadline (institutional):* Continuous. *Application deadline (LD program):* Rolling/continuous for fall and rolling/continuous for spring.

Written Policies Written policies regarding course substitutions and general/basic LD accommodations are available on the program Web site. Written policies regarding course substitutions and general/basic LD accommodations are outlined in the school's catalog/handbook. Written policies regarding course substitutions and general/basic LD accommodations are available through the program or unit directly.

Beacon College

105 East Main Street

Leesburg, FL 34748

http://www.beaconcollege.edu/

Contact: Admissions Office. Phone: 352-787-7249. Fax: 352-787-0721. E-mail: admissions@beaconcollege.edu.

Approximately 76 registered undergraduate students were served during 2002-03. The program or unit includes 35 full-time staff members. Academic advisers, counselors, LD specialists, professional tutors, regular education teachers, remediation/learning specialists, skill tutors, special education teachers, and strategy tutors are provided through the program or unit. Academic advisers, counselors, LD specialists, professional tutors, regular education teachers, remediation/learning specialists, skill tutors, special education teachers, and strategy tutors are provided collaboratively through on-campus or off-campus services.

Summer Program To help prepare for the demands of college, there is an optional summer program prior to entering the school.

Unique Aids and Services Aids, services, or accommodations include advocates, career counseling, digital textbooks, faculty training, personal coach, support groups, and weekly meetings with faculty.

Subject-area Tutoring Tutoring is offered one-on-one, in small groups, and in class-size groups for all subjects. Tutoring is provided through the program or unit via computer-based instruction, LD specialists, and professional tutors. Tutoring is also provided collaboratively through on-campus or off-campus services via computer-based instruction, LD specialists, and professional tutors.

Basic Skills Remediation Remediation is offered one-on-one, in small groups, and in class-size groups for auditory processing, computer skills, handwriting, learning strategies, math, motor skills, reading, social skills, spelling, spoken language, study skills, time management, visual processing, and written language. Remediation is provided through the program or unit via computer-based instruction, LD specialists, professional tutors, regular education teachers, and special education teachers. Remediation is also provided

collaboratively through on-campus or off-campus services via computer-based instruction, LD specialists, professional tutors, regular education teachers, and special education teachers.

Enrichment Enrichment programs are available through the program or unit for career planning, college survival skills, health and nutrition, learning strategies, math, oral communication skills, practical computer skills, reading, self-advocacy, stress management, study skills, test taking, time management, vocabulary development, and written composition skills. Programs for career planning, college survival skills, health and nutrition, learning strategies, math, oral communication skills, practical computer skills, reading, self-advocacy, stress management, study skills, test taking, time management, vocabulary development, and written composition skills are provided collaboratively through on-campus or off-campus services. Credit is offered for career planning, health and nutrition, math, oral communication skills, practical computer skills, reading, vocabulary development, and written composition skills.

Student Organization There is a student organization consisting of 76 members.

Application For admittance to the program or unit, students are required to provide a psychoeducational report (3 years old or less) and provide WAIS. Upon application, materials documenting need for services should be sent only to admissions with institutional application materials. Upon acceptance, documentation of need for services should be sent only to admissions. *Application deadline (LD program):* Rolling/continuous for fall and rolling/continuous for spring.

Written Policies Written policies regarding course substitutions, general/basic LD accommodations, grade forgiveness, reduced course loads, substitutions and waivers of admissions requirements, and substitutions and waivers of graduation requirements are outlined in the school's catalog/handbook.

Bethany College
Special Advising Program

Main Street

Bethany, WV 26032

http://www.bethanywv.edu/

Contact: Phone: 304-829-7000. Fax: 304-829-7142.

Special Advising Program Approximately 22 registered undergraduate students were served during 2002-03. The program or unit includes 2 full-time staff members. Counselors, skill tutors, and strategy tutors are provided collaboratively through on-campus or off-campus services.

Orientation The program or unit offers a mandatory 5-day (Monday through Friday) orientation for new students during the week prior to the first week of school (end of August).

Unique Aids and Services Aids, services, or accommodations include weekly meetings with LD unit.

Subject-area Tutoring Tutoring is offered one-on-one and in small groups for most subjects. Tutoring is provided through the program or unit via trained peer tutors. Tutoring is also provided collaboratively through on-campus or off-campus services via trained peer tutors.

Bethany College (continued)

Basic Skills Remediation Remediation is available for learning strategies, math, reading, study skills, time management, and written language. Remediation is provided through the program or unit via regular education teachers. Remediation is also provided collaboratively through on-campus or off-campus services via regular education teachers.

Enrichment Enrichment programs are available through the program or unit for learning strategies, study skills, test taking, and time management. Credit is offered for learning strategies, study skills, test taking, and time management.

Fees *LD Program or Service* fee is $2500.

Application For admittance to the program or unit, students are required to provide a psychoeducational report (3 years old or less). It is recommended that students provide documentation of high school services. Upon acceptance, documentation of need for services should be sent to both admissions and the LD program or unit. *Application deadline (institutional):* 8/15. *Application deadline (LD program):* Rolling/continuous for fall and rolling/continuous for spring.

Written Policies Written policy regarding general/basic LD accommodations is outlined in the school's catalog/handbook. Written policy regarding general/basic LD accommodations is available through the program or unit directly.

Brenau University
Learning Center

One Centennial Circle
Gainesville, GA 30501-3697
http://www.brenau.edu/learningcenter

Contact: Dr. Vincent Jeffrey Yamilkoski, Professor of Education and Director of Learning Disabilities. Phone: 770-534-6134. Fax: 770-297-5883. E-mail: vyamilkoski@lib.brenau.edu.

Learning Center Approximately 40 registered undergraduate students were served during 2002-03. The program or unit includes 2 full-time staff members and 1 part-time staff member. Academic advisers, coaches, LD specialists, professional tutors, remediation/learning specialists, skill tutors, and strategy tutors are provided through the program or unit. Academic advisers and counselors are provided collaboratively through on-campus or off-campus services.

Orientation The program or unit offers a mandatory 1-hour orientation for new students during registration.

Summer Program To help prepare for the demands of college, there is an optional 8-week summer program prior to entering the school. Degree credit will be earned.

Unique Aids and Services Aids, services, or accommodations include advocates, career counseling, digital textbooks, faculty training, priority registration, and support groups.

Basic Skills Remediation Remediation is offered one-on-one for auditory processing, computer skills, learning strategies, math, reading, spoken language, study skills, time management, visual processing, and written language. Remediation is provided through the program or unit via LD specialists and professional tutors.

Enrichment Enrichment programs are available through the program or unit for career planning, college survival skills, learning strategies, math, medication management, oral communication skills, practical computer skills, reading, self-advocacy, stress management, study skills, test taking, time management, vocabulary development, and written composition skills. Programs for career planning, health and nutrition, math, medication management, practical computer skills, stress management, study skills, test taking, time management, and written composition skills are provided collaboratively through on-campus or off-campus services. Credit is offered for college survival skills, learning strategies, practical computer skills, and study skills.

Student Organization Brenau Organization for Learning Disabilities (BOLD) consists of 15 members.

Fees *LD Program or Service* fee is $900 to $5400 (fee varies according to level/tier of service). *Summer Program* fee is $450 to $1800.

Application For admittance to the program or unit, students are required to apply to the program directly and provide a psychoeducational report (3 years old or less). Upon application, materials documenting need for services should be sent only to admissions with institutional application materials. Upon acceptance, documentation of need for services should be sent only to the LD program or unit. *Application deadline (institutional):* Continuous. *Application deadline (LD program):* Rolling/continuous for fall and rolling/continuous for spring.

Written Policies Written policies regarding general/basic LD accommodations and reduced course loads are available on the program Web site. Written policies regarding general/basic LD accommodations and substitutions and waivers of admissions requirements are outlined in the school's catalog/handbook. Written policies regarding general/basic LD accommodations and reduced course loads are available through the program or unit directly.

Centenary College
Disability Services Office, Project ABLE

400 Jefferson Street
Hackettstown, NJ 07840-2100
http://www.centenarycollege.edu/

Contact: Mr. Jeffrey R. Zimdahl, Director of Disability Services. Phone: 908-852-1400 Ext. 2251. Fax: 908-979-4277. E-mail: jzimdahl@centenarycollege.edu.

Disability Services Office, Project ABLE Approximately 50 registered undergraduate students were served during 2002-03. The program or unit includes 2 full-time and 6 part-time staff members. LD specialists, professional tutors, remediation/learning specialists, and trained peer tutors are provided through the program or unit. Academic advisers, counselors, diagnostic specialists, LD specialists, professional tutors, remediation/learning specialists, and trained peer tutors are provided collaboratively through on-campus or off-campus services.

Orientation The program or unit offers an optional 1-hour orientation for new students during freshman orientation.

Summer Program To help prepare for the demands of college, there is an optional 6-week residential summer program prior to entering the school. Degree credit will be earned.

Unique Aids and Services Aids, services, or accommodations include advocates.

Subject-area Tutoring Tutoring is offered one-on-one for all subjects. Tutoring is provided through the program or unit via LD specialists, professional tutors, and trained peer tutors. Tutoring is also provided collaboratively through on-campus or off-campus services via LD specialists, professional tutors, and trained peer tutors.

Diagnostic Testing Testing for auditory processing, math, reading, spelling, and written language is provided collaboratively through on-campus or off-campus services.

Basic Skills Remediation Remediation is offered one-on-one and in small groups for math, reading, and written language. Remediation is provided through the program or unit via professional tutors. Remediation is also provided collaboratively through on-campus or off-campus services via professional tutors and other.

Enrichment Enrichment programs are available through the program or unit for college survival skills, learning strategies, math, self-advocacy, study skills, test taking, time management, and written composition skills. Programs for career planning, college survival skills, health and nutrition, learning strategies, math, medication management, self-advocacy, stress management, study skills, test taking, time management, and written composition skills are provided collaboratively through on-campus or off-campus services.

Fees *LD Program or Service* fee is $1850. *Summer Program* fee is $2350. *Diagnostic Testing* fee is $125.

Application For admittance to the program or unit, students are required to provide a psychoeducational report (3 years old or less) and provide documentation of high school services. Upon application, materials documenting need for services should be sent only to admissions with institutional application materials. Upon acceptance, documentation of need for services should be sent only to the LD program or unit. *Application deadline (institutional):* Continuous. *Application deadline (LD program):* Rolling/continuous for fall and rolling/continuous for spring.

Written Policies Written policies regarding general/basic LD accommodations and reduced course loads are available through the program or unit directly.

College of Mount St. Joseph
Project EXCEL

5701 Delhi Road
Cincinnati, OH 45233-1670
http://www.msj.edu/
Contact: Jane Pohlman, Director of Project EXCEL. Phone: 513-244-4623. Fax: 513-244-4222. E-mail: jane_pohlman@mail.msj.edu.

Project EXCEL Approximately 92 registered undergraduate students were served during 2002-03. The program or unit includes 7 full-time and 9 part-time staff members. Academic advisers, LD specialists, and professional tutors are provided through the program or unit. Academic advisers and counselors are provided collaboratively through on-campus or off-campus services.

Orientation The program or unit offers a mandatory semester-long orientation for new students during the fall semester of the freshman year (in the form of a course, EXC 103).

Subject-area Tutoring Tutoring is offered one-on-one and in small groups for most subjects. Tutoring is provided through the program or unit via computer-based instruction, LD specialists, and professional tutors.

Basic Skills Remediation Remediation is offered one-on-one and in small groups for computer skills, learning strategies, math, study skills, time management, and written language. Remediation is provided through the program or unit via computer-based instruction, LD specialists, and professional tutors.

Enrichment Enrichment programs are available through the program or unit for college survival skills, learning strategies, math, reading, self-advocacy, study skills, test taking, time management, and written composition skills. Programs for career planning, health and nutrition, math, practical computer skills, stress management, and written composition skills are provided collaboratively through on-campus or off-campus services. Credit is offered for career planning, learning strategies, math, practical computer skills, study skills, and written composition skills.

Fees *LD Program or Service* fee is $1530 to $3060 (fee varies according to level/tier of service).

Application For admittance to the program or unit, students are required to apply to the program directly and provide a psychoeducational report (3 years old or less). It is recommended that students provide documentation of high school services. Upon application, materials documenting need for services should be sent only to the LD program or unit. Upon acceptance, documentation of need for services should be sent only to the LD program or unit. *Application deadline (institutional):* 8/15. *Application deadline (LD program):* Rolling/continuous for fall and rolling/continuous for spring.

Written Policies Written policy regarding general/basic LD accommodations is available on the program Web site. Written policy regarding general/basic LD accommodations is available through the program or unit directly.

Concordia College
Concordia Connection

171 White Plains Road
Bronxville, NY 10708-1998
http://www.concordia.onlinecommunity.com/
attendingconcordia/ldstudents.htm
Contact: Dr. George Groth, Director of Concordia Connection. Phone: 914-337-9300 Ext. 2361. Fax: 914-395-4500. E-mail: ghg@concordia-ny.edu.

Concordia Connection Approximately 20 registered undergraduate students were served during 2002-03. The program or unit includes 1 full-time and 2 part-time staff members. LD specialists, skill tutors, special education teachers, and strategy tutors are provided through the program or unit.

Orientation The program or unit offers a mandatory 1-day orientation for new students before classes begin.

Unique Aids and Services Aids, services, or accommodations include career counseling and support groups.

Subject-area Tutoring Tutoring is offered one-on-one and in small groups for most subjects. Tutoring is provided through the program or unit via LD specialists, professional tutors, and trained peer tutors. Tutoring is also provided collaboratively through on-campus or off-campus services via trained peer tutors.

Diagnostic Testing Testing is provided through the program or unit for learning strategies, learning styles, math, personality, reading, social skills, spelling, study skills, and written language.

Concordia College (continued)

Basic Skills Remediation Remediation is offered one-on-one and in small groups for learning strategies, math, reading, study skills, time management, and written language. Remediation is provided through the program or unit via LD specialists, professional tutors, special education teachers, and trained peer tutors.

Enrichment Enrichment programs are available through the program or unit for college survival skills, math, reading, stress management, study skills, time management, and written composition skills.

Fees *LD Program or Service* fee is $2500 to $5000 (fee varies according to level/tier of service).

Application For admittance to the program or unit, students are required to provide a psychoeducational report and provide documentation of high school services. Upon application, materials documenting need for services should be sent only to admissions with institutional application materials. Upon acceptance, documentation of need for services should be sent only to admissions. *Application deadline (institutional):* 3/15. *Application deadline (LD program):* Rolling/continuous for fall and rolling/continuous for spring.

Written Policies Written policies regarding course substitutions, general/basic LD accommodations, reduced course loads, substitutions and waivers of admissions requirements, and substitutions and waivers of graduation requirements are available through the program or unit directly.

Curry College

1071 Blue Hill Avenue
Milton, MA 02186-9984
http://www.curry.edu/

Contact: Dr. Susan B. Pratt, Coordinator of Program for Advancement of Learning. Phone: 617-333-2250. Fax: 617-333-2018. E-mail: pal@curry.edu. Head of LD Program: Dr. Lisa Ijiri, Director of Program for Advancement of Learning. Phone: 617-333-2250. Fax: 617-333-2018. E-mail: pal@curry.edu.

Approximately 365 registered undergraduate students were served during 2002-03. The program or unit includes 17 full-time and 15 part-time staff members. Diagnostic specialists, LD specialists, remediation/learning specialists, and strategy tutors are provided through the program or unit. Academic advisers, counselors, professional tutors, regular education teachers, skill tutors, and trained peer tutors are provided collaboratively through on-campus or off-campus services.

Orientation The program or unit offers a mandatory 1-hour orientation for new students before classes begin and individually by special arrangement.

Summer Program To help prepare for the demands of college, there is an optional 3-week summer program prior to entering the school. Degree credit will be earned.

Unique Aids and Services Aids, services, or accommodations include advocates, career counseling, digital textbooks, personal coach, weekly meetings with faculty, assistive technology.

Subject-area Tutoring Tutoring is offered one-on-one and in small groups for most subjects. Tutoring is provided collaboratively through on-campus or off-campus services via computer-based instruction, professional tutors, and trained peer tutors.

Diagnostic Testing Testing is provided through the program or unit for auditory processing, intelligence, learning strategies, learning styles, math, reading, spelling, spoken language, study skills, visual processing, and written language.

Basic Skills Remediation Remediation is offered one-on-one for math and reading. Remediation is provided collaboratively through on-campus or off-campus services via computer-based instruction.

Enrichment Enrichment programs are available through the program or unit for learning strategies, reading, study skills, test taking, time management, and written composition skills. Programs for career planning, college survival skills, health and nutrition, learning strategies, math, oral communication skills, practical computer skills, reading, stress management, study skills, test taking, time management, and written composition skills are provided collaboratively through on-campus or off-campus services. Credit is offered for college survival skills, health and nutrition, learning strategies, math, oral communication skills, practical computer skills, reading, stress management, study skills, test taking, time management, and written composition skills.

Fees *LD Program or Service* fee is $1250 to $4500 (fee varies according to level/tier of service). *Summer Program* fee is $2200 to $2600. *Diagnostic Testing* fee is $450 to $1100.

Application For admittance to the program or unit, students are required to apply to the program directly and provide a psychoeducational report (3 years old or less). It is recommended that students provide documentation of high school services. Upon application, materials documenting need for services should be sent to both admissions and the LD program or unit. *Application deadline (institutional):* 4/1. *Application deadline (LD program):* 3/1 for fall. Rolling/continuous for spring.

Written Policies Written policies regarding general/basic LD accommodations and substitutions and waivers of admissions requirements are available on the program Web site. Written policies regarding general/basic LD accommodations and substitutions and waivers of admissions requirements are outlined in the school's catalog/handbook. Written policies regarding general/basic LD accommodations and substitutions and waivers of admissions requirements are available through the program or unit directly.

Davis & Elkins College
Supported Learning Program

100 Campus Drive
Elkins, WV 26241-3996
http://www.davisandelkins.edu

Contact: Mrs. Judith Sabol McCauley, Director of Supported Learning Program. Phone: 800-624-3157 Ext. 1229. Fax: 304-637-1413. E-mail: mccaulj@davisandelkins.edu.

Supported Learning Program Approximately 35 registered undergraduate students were served during 2002-03. The program or unit includes 2 full-time staff members. Diagnostic specialists and LD specialists are provided through the program or unit.

Orientation The program or unit offers a mandatory orientation for new students before registration and before classes begin.

Unique Aids and Services Aids, services, or accommodations include advocates, career counseling, faculty training, personal coach, weekly meetings with faculty, Kurzweil Readers, textbooks on tape, lab area, study groups, personal counseling, 3-way conferences .

Subject-area Tutoring Tutoring is offered one-on-one and in small groups for most subjects. Tutoring is provided through the program or unit via computer-based instruction, LD specialists, and trained peer tutors. Tutoring is also provided collaboratively through on-campus or off-campus services via trained peer tutors.

Diagnostic Testing Testing is provided through the program or unit for learning strategies, learning styles, reading, spelling, and study skills. Testing for math, personality, social skills, and written language is provided collaboratively through on-campus or off-campus services.

Basic Skills Remediation Remediation is offered one-on-one and in class-size groups for auditory processing, computer skills, learning strategies, math, reading, social skills, study skills, time management, visual processing, and written language. Remediation is provided through the program or unit via LD specialists. Remediation is also provided collaboratively through on-campus or off-campus services.

Enrichment Enrichment programs are available through the program or unit for college survival skills, learning strategies, medication management, self-advocacy, stress management, study skills, test taking, time management, vocabulary development, and written composition skills. Programs for career planning, college survival skills, health and nutrition, math, medication management, oral communication skills, practical computer skills, reading, stress management, study skills, test taking, time management, written composition skills, and other are provided collaboratively through on-campus or off-campus services. Credit is offered for college survival skills, health and nutrition, math, oral communication skills, practical computer skills, reading, written composition skills, and other.

Fees *LD Program or Service* fee is $2600.

Application For admittance to the program or unit, students are required to apply to the program directly, provide a psychoeducational report (3 years old or less), and provide a hand-written essay, letter of recommendation, and be interviewed. It is recommended that students provide documentation of high school services. Upon application, materials documenting need for services should be sent only to the LD program or unit. *Application deadline (institutional):* Continuous. *Application deadline (LD program):* 5/1 for spring.

Written Policies Written policies regarding course substitutions, substitutions and waivers of admissions requirements, and substitutions and waivers of graduation requirements are outlined in the school's catalog/handbook. Written policy regarding general/basic LD accommodations is available through the program or unit directly.

Edinboro University of Pennsylvania
Office for Students with Disabilities

Edinboro, PA 16444

http://www.edinboro.edu/

Contact: Ms. Kathleen K. Strosser, Assistant Director of Office for Students with Disabilities. Phone: 814-732-1399. Fax: 814-732-1120. E-mail: strosser@edinboro.edu.

Office for Students with Disabilities Approximately 235 registered undergraduate students were served during 2002-03. The program or unit includes 2 full-time and 2 part-time staff members.

Academic advisers, graduate assistants/students, LD specialists, and other are provided through the program or unit. Academic advisers and counselors are provided collaboratively through on-campus or off-campus services.

Unique Aids and Services Aids, services, or accommodations include priority registration.

Subject-area Tutoring Tutoring is offered in small groups for some subjects. Tutoring is provided collaboratively through on-campus or off-campus services via trained peer tutors.

Basic Skills Remediation Remediation is offered one-on-one for learning strategies, study skills, time management, and written language. Remediation is provided through the program or unit via graduate assistants/students, professional tutors, and trained peer tutors.

Enrichment Enrichment programs are available through the program or unit for self-advocacy, study skills, test taking, time management, and written composition skills. Programs for career planning, college survival skills, and health and nutrition are provided collaboratively through on-campus or off-campus services.

Fees *LD Program or Service* fee is $306 to $876 (fee varies according to level/tier of service).

Application For admittance to the program or unit, students are required to provide a psychoeducational report (3 years old or less). It is recommended that students provide documentation of high school services. Upon application, materials documenting need for services should be sent to both admissions and the LD program or unit. Upon acceptance, documentation of need for services should be sent only to the LD program or unit. *Application deadline (institutional):* Continuous. *Application deadline (LD program):* Rolling/continuous for fall and rolling/continuous for spring.

Written Policies Written policies regarding course substitutions and general/basic LD accommodations are available through the program or unit directly.

Fairleigh Dickinson University, College at Florham
The Regional Center for College Students with Learning Disabilities

285 Madison Avenue

Madison, NJ 07940-1099

http://www.fdu.edu/studentsvcs/rcsld.html

Contact: Mr. Vincent John Varrassi, Acting University Director. Phone: 201-692-2087. Fax: 201-692-2813. E-mail: varrassi@fdu.edu. Head of LD Program: Dr. Mary Lupiani Farrell, Project Director. Phone: 201-692-2087. Fax: 201-692-2813. E-mail: farrell@fdu.edu.

The Regional Center for College Students with Learning Disabilities Approximately 115 registered undergraduate students were served during 2002-03. The program or unit includes 7 full-time and 2 part-time staff members. LD specialists and professional tutors are provided through the program or unit. LD specialists and professional tutors are provided collaboratively through on-campus or off-campus services.

Fairleigh Dickinson University, College at Florham (continued)

Orientation The program or unit offers a mandatory 1-day orientation for new students before registration.

Unique Aids and Services Aids, services, or accommodations include career counseling, digital textbooks, and priority registration.

Subject-area Tutoring Tutoring is offered in small groups for most subjects. Tutoring is provided through the program or unit via LD specialists and professional tutors. Tutoring is also provided collaboratively through on-campus or off-campus services via LD specialists and professional tutors.

Diagnostic Testing Testing is provided through the program or unit for auditory processing, intelligence, learning strategies, math, motor skills, reading, spelling, spoken language, study skills, visual processing, and written language.

Basic Skills Remediation Remediation is offered in small groups for math, reading, and written language. Remediation is provided through the program or unit via LD specialists and special education teachers.

Enrichment Enrichment programs are available through the program or unit for career planning, college survival skills, learning strategies, practical computer skills, self-advocacy, study skills, test taking, time management, and written composition skills. Credit is offered for learning strategies, self-advocacy, and study skills.

Application For admittance to the program or unit, students are required to apply to the program directly, provide a psychoeducational report (2 years old or less), provide documentation of high school services, and provide other documentation. Upon application, materials documenting need for services should be sent only to the LD program or unit. Upon acceptance, documentation of need for services should be sent to both admissions and the LD program or unit. *Application deadline (institutional): 3/1. Application deadline (LD program):* Rolling/continuous for fall and rolling/continuous for spring.

Written Policies Written policies regarding course substitutions, general/basic LD accommodations, grade forgiveness, reduced course loads, substitutions and waivers of admissions requirements, and substitutions and waivers of graduation requirements are available through the program or unit directly.

were served during 2002-03. The program or unit includes 3 full-time and 4 part-time staff members. LD specialists and special education teachers are provided through the program or unit.

Orientation The program or unit offers a mandatory 1-day orientation for new students before registration.

Unique Aids and Services Aids, services, or accommodations include career counseling, digital textbooks, and priority registration.

Subject-area Tutoring Tutoring is offered in small groups for most subjects. Tutoring is provided through the program or unit via LD specialists and professional tutors. Tutoring is also provided collaboratively through on-campus or off-campus services via LD specialists and professional tutors.

Diagnostic Testing Testing is provided through the program or unit for auditory processing, intelligence, learning strategies, math, motor skills, reading, spelling, spoken language, study skills, visual processing, and written language.

Basic Skills Remediation Remediation is offered in small groups for math, reading, study skills, time management, and written language. Remediation is provided through the program or unit via LD specialists and professional tutors.

Enrichment Enrichment programs are available through the program or unit for career planning, college survival skills, learning strategies, practical computer skills, self-advocacy, study skills, test taking, time management, and written composition skills. Credit is offered for learning strategies and study skills.

Application For admittance to the program or unit, students are required to apply to the program directly, provide a psychoeducational report (2 years old or less), provide documentation of high school services, and provide other documentation. Upon application, materials documenting need for services should be sent only to the LD program or unit. Upon acceptance, documentation of need for services should be sent only to the LD program or unit. *Application deadline (institutional): 3/1. Application deadline (LD program):* Rolling/continuous for fall and rolling/continuous for spring.

Written Policies Written policies regarding course substitutions, general/basic LD accommodations, grade forgiveness, reduced course loads, substitutions and waivers of admissions requirements, and substitutions and waivers of graduation requirements are available through the program or unit directly.

Fairleigh Dickinson University, Metropolitan Campus
The Regional Center for College Students with Learning Disabilities

1000 River Road
Teaneck, NJ 07666-1914
http://www.fdu.edu/studentsvcs/rcsld.html

Contact: Mr. Vincent John Varrassi, Acting University Director. Phone: 201-692-2716. Fax: 201-692-2813. E-mail: varrassi@fdu.edu. Head of LD Program: Dr. Mary Lupiani Farrell, Project Director. Phone: 201-692-2716. Fax: 201-692-2716. E-mail: farrell@fdu.edu.

The Regional Center for College Students with Learning Disabilities Approximately 60 registered undergraduate students

Gannon University
Program for Students with Learning Disabilities (PSLD)

University Square
Erie, PA 16541-0001
http://www.gannon.edu/resource/psld/index.html

Contact: Sr. Joyce Lowrey SSJ, Director. Phone: 814-871-5326. Fax: 814-871-7499. E-mail: lowrey001@gannon.edu.

Program for Students with Learning Disabilities (PSLD) Approximately 65 registered undergraduate students were served during 2002-03. The program or unit includes 3 full-time and 3 part-time staff members. Academic advisers, coaches, counselors, diagnostic specialists, graduate assistants/students, LD specialists, professional tutors, regular education teachers, remediation/learning specialists, skill tutors, special education teachers, and strategy tutors are provided through the program or unit. Academic advisers and counselors are provided collaboratively through on-campus or off-campus services.

Unique Aids and Services Aids, services, or accommodations include advocates, career counseling, personal coach, and weekly meetings with faculty.

Subject-area Tutoring Tutoring is offered one-on-one. Tutoring is provided through the program or unit via LD specialists and professional tutors.

Basic Skills Remediation Remediation is offered one-on-one for computer skills, learning strategies, math, reading, study skills, time management, and written language. Remediation is provided through the program or unit via graduate assistants/students, LD specialists, professional tutors, regular education teachers, and special education teachers.

Enrichment Enrichment programs are available through the program or unit for college survival skills, learning strategies, math, oral communication skills, practical computer skills, reading, self-advocacy, stress management, study skills, test taking, time management, and written composition skills. Programs for career planning, college survival skills, health and nutrition, math, medication management, oral communication skills, practical computer skills, stress management, and study skills are provided collaboratively through on-campus or off-campus services. Credit is offered for college survival skills, learning strategies, self-advocacy, stress management, study skills, test taking, time management, and written composition skills.

Fees *LD Program or Service* fee is $600.

Application For admittance to the program or unit, students are required to apply to the program directly, provide a psychoeducational report (4 years old or less), and provide other documentation. It is recommended that students provide documentation of high school services. Upon application, materials documenting need for services should be sent only to admissions with institutional application materials. Upon acceptance, documentation of need for services should be sent only to the LD program or unit. *Application deadline (institutional):* Continuous. *Application deadline (LD program):* Rolling/continuous for fall and rolling/continuous for spring.

Written Policies Written policy regarding general/basic LD accommodations is available on the program Web site. Written policy regarding general/basic LD accommodations is outlined in the school's catalog/handbook. Written policy regarding general/basic LD accommodations is available through the program or unit directly.

George Mason University
Disability Resource Center

4400 University Drive
Fairfax, VA 22030
http://www.gmu.edu/
Contact: Ms. Deborah E. Wyne, Director. Phone: 703-993-2474. Fax: 703-993-2476. E-mail: dwyne@gmu.edu.

Disability Resource Center Approximately 792 registered undergraduate students were served during 2002-03. The program or unit includes 3 full-time staff members and 1 part-time staff member. Academic advisers and counselors are provided collaboratively through on-campus or off-campus services.

Summer Program To help prepare for the demands of college, there is an optional 1-day summer program prior to entering the school.

Unique Aids and Services Aids, services, or accommodations include career counseling, digital textbooks, faculty training, parent workshops, and priority registration.

Subject-area Tutoring Tutoring is offered for most subjects. Tutoring is provided through the program or unit via computer-based instruction, graduate assistants/students, LD specialists, professional tutors, trained peer tutors, and other.

Basic Skills Remediation Remediation is available for learning strategies, study skills, and time management. Remediation is provided through the program or unit via computer-based instruction, graduate assistants/students, and professional tutors.

Application For admittance to the program or unit, students are required to apply to the program directly and provide a psychoeducational report (3 years old or less). It is recommended that students provide documentation of high school services. Upon application, materials documenting need for services should be sent only to the LD program or unit. Upon acceptance, documentation of need for services should be sent only to the LD program or unit. *Application deadline (institutional):* 1/15. *Application deadline (LD program):* Rolling/continuous for fall and rolling/continuous for spring.

Written Policies Written policies regarding course substitutions, general/basic LD accommodations, reduced course loads, substitutions and waivers of admissions requirements, and substitutions and waivers of graduation requirements are available on the program Web site. Written policies regarding course substitutions, general/basic LD accommodations, substitutions and waivers of admissions requirements, and substitutions and waivers of graduation requirements are outlined in the school's catalog/handbook. Written policies regarding course substitutions, general/basic LD accommodations, reduced course loads, substitutions and waivers of admissions requirements, and substitutions and waivers of graduation requirements are available through the program or unit directly.

Graceland University

1 University Place
Lamoni, IA 50140
http://www.graceland.edu/
Contact: Susan Johnson Knotts, Director of Chance Program and Student Disability Services. Phone: 641-784-5421. Fax: 641-784-5446. E-mail: knotts@graceland.edu.

Approximately 90 registered undergraduate students were served during 2002-03. The program or unit includes 3 full-time staff members. Academic advisers and remediation/learning specialists are provided through the program or unit. Counselors, skill tutors, strategy tutors, and trained peer tutors are provided collaboratively through on-campus or off-campus services.

Unique Aids and Services Aids, services, or accommodations include advocates, career counseling, digital textbooks, and faculty training.

Subject-area Tutoring Tutoring is offered one-on-one and in small groups for most subjects. Tutoring is provided through the program or unit via LD specialists. Tutoring is also provided collaboratively through on-campus or off-campus services via computer-based instruction and trained peer tutors.

Graceland University (continued)

Basic Skills Remediation Remediation is offered one-on-one for auditory processing, learning strategies, math, reading, spelling, study skills, time management, and written language. Remediation is provided through the program or unit via LD specialists. Remediation is also provided collaboratively through on-campus or off-campus services via regular education teachers.

Enrichment Enrichment programs are available through the program or unit for career planning, college survival skills, learning strategies, practical computer skills, reading, self-advocacy, stress management, study skills, test taking, time management, vocabulary development, and written composition skills. Programs for career planning, college survival skills, health and nutrition, learning strategies, math, stress management, study skills, test taking, time management, vocabulary development, and written composition skills are provided collaboratively through on-campus or off-campus services. Credit is offered for career planning, college survival skills, health and nutrition, learning strategies, math, stress management, study skills, test taking, time management, vocabulary development, and written composition skills.

Fees *LD Program or Service* fee is $0 to $1300 (fee varies according to level/tier of service).

Application For admittance to the program or unit, students are required to apply to the program directly and provide a psychoeducational report (4 years old or less). It is recommended that students provide documentation of high school services. Upon application, materials documenting need for services should be sent only to admissions with institutional application materials. Upon acceptance, documentation of need for services should be sent only to admissions. *Application deadline (institutional):* Continuous. *Application deadline (LD program):* Rolling/continuous for fall and rolling/continuous for spring.

Written Policies Written policy regarding general/basic LD accommodations is outlined in the school's catalog/handbook. Written policies regarding course substitutions, grade forgiveness, reduced course loads, substitutions and waivers of admissions requirements, and substitutions and waivers of graduation requirements are available through the program or unit directly.

Hofstra University
Program for Academic Learning Skills (PALS)

100 Hofstra University
Hempstead, NY 11549
http://www.hofstra.edu/

Contact: PALS Information Line. Phone: 516-463-5761. Fax: 516-463-4049. E-mail: pals@hofstra.edu. Head of LD Program: Director. Phone: 516-463-5761. Fax: 516-463-4049. E-mail: pals@hofstra.edu.

Program for Academic Learning Skills (PALS) Approximately 200 registered undergraduate students were served during 2002-03. The program or unit includes 4 full-time staff members and 1 part-time staff member. Academic advisers, LD specialists, remediation/learning specialists, skill tutors, and strategy tutors are provided through the program or unit. Academic advisers, counselors, diagnostic specialists, graduate assistants/students, professional tutors, and trained peer tutors are provided collaboratively through on-campus or off-campus services.

Orientation The program or unit offers an optional orientation for new students after classes begin.

Unique Aids and Services Aids, services, or accommodations include digital textbooks, Kurzweil Reader voice activated computer.

Subject-area Tutoring Tutoring is offered one-on-one for all subjects. Tutoring is provided collaboratively through on-campus or off-campus services via trained peer tutors.

Diagnostic Testing Testing for auditory processing, intelligence, reading, spoken language, visual processing, and written language is provided collaboratively through on-campus or off-campus services.

Basic Skills Remediation Remediation is offered one-on-one for auditory processing, computer skills, learning strategies, reading, spelling, spoken language, study skills, time management, visual processing, written language, and test-taking strategies, self-advocacy, memory research. Remediation is provided through the program or unit via LD specialists.

Enrichment Enrichment programs are available through the program or unit for college survival skills, learning strategies, self-advocacy, study skills, test taking, time management, vocabulary development, and written composition skills. Programs for career planning, health and nutrition, math, oral communication skills, practical computer skills, reading, and stress management are provided collaboratively through on-campus or off-campus services.

Fees *LD Program or Service* fee is $6000. *Diagnostic Testing* fee is $375.

Application For admittance to the program or unit, students are required to provide a psychoeducational report (1 year old or less) and provide WAIS-III, achievement test results, full report, childhood history of ADD/ADHD. Upon application, materials documenting need for services should be sent only to admissions with institutional application materials. Upon acceptance, documentation of need for services should be sent to both admissions and the LD program or unit. *Application deadline (institutional):* Continuous. *Application deadline (LD program):* Rolling/continuous for fall and rolling/continuous for spring.

Written Policies Written policies regarding course substitutions, general/basic LD accommodations, and substitutions and waivers of graduation requirements are available on the program Web site. Written policies regarding course substitutions, general/basic LD accommodations, and substitutions and waivers of graduation requirements are outlined in the school's catalog/handbook. Written policy regarding general/basic LD accommodations is available through the program or unit directly.

Iona College

715 North Avenue
New Rochelle, NY 10801-1890
http://www.iona.edu/

Contact: Phone: 914-633-2000. Fax: 914-633-2096.

The program or unit includes 2 full-time and 10 part-time staff members. Counselors and LD specialists are provided through the program or unit.

Orientation The program or unit offers a mandatory orientation for new students during summer prior to enrollment.

Summer Program To help prepare for the demands of college, there is a mandatory 3-week summer program prior to entering the school.

Unique Aids and Services Aids, services, or accommodations include priority registration.

Basic Skills Remediation Remediation is offered one-on-one for auditory processing, learning strategies, study skills, time management, visual processing, and written language. Remediation is provided through the program or unit via LD specialists.

Fees *LD Program or Service* fee is $2600. *Summer Program* fee is $750.

Application For admittance to the program or unit, students are required to provide a psychoeducational report (2 years old or less), provide documentation of high school services, and provide WAIS report, standardized achievement test scores. Upon application, materials documenting need for services should be sent only to the LD program or unit. *Application deadline (institutional): 3/15. Application deadline (LD program):* Rolling/continuous for fall and rolling/continuous for spring.

Written Policies Written policy regarding general/basic LD accommodations is available on the program Web site. Written policy regarding general/basic LD accommodations is outlined in the school's catalog/handbook. Written policy regarding general/basic LD accommodations is available through the program or unit directly.

Jacksonville State University
Disability Support Services

700 Pelham Road North

Jacksonville, AL 36265-1602

http://dss.jsu.edu

Contact: Mr. Chris Lanier, Disability Specialist. Phone: 256-782-5095. Fax: 256-782-5025. E-mail: clanier@jsucc.jsu.edu. Head of LD Program: Mr. Daniel L. Miller, Director. Phone: 256-782-5095. Fax: 256-782-5025. E-mail: dss@jsucc.jsu.edu.

Disability Support Services Approximately 115 registered undergraduate students were served during 2002-03. The program or unit includes 1 full-time staff member. Academic advisers, coaches, LD specialists, professional tutors, remediation/learning specialists, skill tutors, and strategy tutors are provided through the program or unit. Academic advisers, counselors, graduate assistants/students, professional tutors, remediation/learning specialists, skill tutors, strategy tutors, and trained peer tutors are provided collaboratively through on-campus or off-campus services.

Summer Program To help prepare for the demands of college, there is an optional 5-week summer program prior to entering the school. Degree credit will be earned.

Unique Aids and Services Aids, services, or accommodations include career counseling, faculty training, personal coach, and priority registration.

Subject-area Tutoring Tutoring is offered one-on-one, in small groups, and in class-size groups. Tutoring is provided through the program or unit via computer-based instruction, graduate assistants/

students, LD specialists, and professional tutors. Tutoring is also provided collaboratively through on-campus or off-campus services via computer-based instruction, graduate assistants/students, LD specialists, and trained peer tutors.

Basic Skills Remediation Remediation is offered one-on-one, in small groups, and in class-size groups for learning strategies, math, reading, study skills, time management, and written language. Remediation is provided through the program or unit via computer-based instruction, graduate assistants/students, LD specialists, professional tutors, and special education teachers. Remediation is also provided collaboratively through on-campus or off-campus services via computer-based instruction, graduate assistants/students, LD specialists, and trained peer tutors.

Enrichment Enrichment programs are available through the program or unit for career planning, learning strategies, math, reading, self-advocacy, stress management, study skills, test taking, time management, vocabulary development, and written composition skills. Programs for career planning, college survival skills, health and nutrition, learning strategies, math, medication management, oral communication skills, reading, self-advocacy, stress management, study skills, test taking, time management, vocabulary development, and written composition skills are provided collaboratively through on-campus or off-campus services. Credit is offered for career planning, college survival skills, learning strategies, math, oral communication skills, reading, study skills, test taking, time management, vocabulary development, and written composition skills.

Student Organization Developing Scholars consists of 25 members.

Fees *Summer Program* fee is $750.

Application For admittance to the program or unit, students are required to apply to the program directly and provide a psychoeducational report (3 years old or less). It is recommended that students provide documentation of high school services. Upon acceptance, documentation of need for services should be sent only to the LD program or unit. *Application deadline (institutional):* Continuous. *Application deadline (LD program):* Rolling/continuous for fall.

Written Policies Written policy regarding general/basic LD accommodations is available on the program Web site. Written policies regarding general/basic LD accommodations and grade forgiveness are outlined in the school's catalog/handbook. Written policies regarding course substitutions and substitutions and waivers of graduation requirements are available through the program or unit directly.

King's College
FASP—First Year Academics Studies Program

133 North River Street

Wilkes-Barre, PA 18711-0801

http://www.kings.edu/frames/tb_frames/academics.html

Contact: Ms. Jacintha A. Burke, Director of Academics Skills Center. Phone: 570-208-5800. Fax: 570-825-9049. E-mail: jaburke@kings.edu.

FASP—First Year Academics Studies Program Approximately 75 registered undergraduate students were served during 2002-03. The program or unit includes 3 full-time and 2 part-time

King's College (continued)

staff members. Academic advisers and LD specialists are provided through the program or unit. Regular education teachers, trained peer tutors, and other are provided collaboratively through on-campus or off-campus services.

Orientation The program or unit offers a mandatory 1-day orientation for new students before registration, before classes begin, and during summer prior to enrollment.

Summer Program To help prepare for the demands of college, there is an optional 5-week summer program prior to entering the school. Degree credit will be earned.

Unique Aids and Services Aids, services, or accommodations include career counseling, faculty training, parent workshops, priority registration, and weekly meetings with faculty.

Subject-area Tutoring Tutoring is offered one-on-one and in small groups for most subjects. Tutoring is provided through the program or unit via LD specialists. Tutoring is also provided collaboratively through on-campus or off-campus services via trained peer tutors.

Diagnostic Testing Testing is provided through the program or unit for learning strategies, math, reading, spelling, study skills, and written language. Testing for intelligence, neuropsychological, personality, social skills, and visual processing is provided collaboratively through on-campus or off-campus services.

Enrichment Enrichment programs are available through the program or unit for college survival skills, learning strategies, medication management, self-advocacy, study skills, test taking, and time management. Programs for career planning, college survival skills, learning strategies, oral communication skills, practical computer skills, and written composition skills are provided collaboratively through on-campus or off-campus services. Credit is offered for career planning.

Fees *LD Program or Service* fee is $2400. *Summer Program* fee is $3000. *Diagnostic Testing* fee is applicable.

Application For admittance to the program or unit, students are required to apply to the program directly, provide a psychoeducational report (2 years old or less), and provide documentation of high school services. Upon application, materials documenting need for services should be sent to both admissions and the LD program or unit. Upon acceptance, documentation of need for services should be sent only to the LD program or unit. *Application deadline (institutional):* Continuous. *Application deadline (LD program):* Rolling/continuous for fall and rolling/continuous for spring.

Written Policies Written policy regarding general/basic LD accommodations is available on the program Web site. Written policy regarding general/basic LD accommodations is outlined in the school's catalog/handbook. Written policy regarding reduced course loads is available through the program or unit directly.

Limestone College
Program For Alternative Learning Styles

1115 College Drive
Gaffney, SC 29340-3799
http://www.limestone.edu

Contact: Ms. Karen W. Kearse, Program Director of PALS. Phone: 864-489-7151 Ext. 8223. Fax: 864-487-8706. E-mail: kkearsek@netscape.net.

Program For Alternative Learning Styles Approximately 18 registered undergraduate students were served during 2002-03. The program or unit includes 1 full-time and 1 part-time staff member. Academic advisers, graduate assistants/students, LD specialists, skill tutors, special education teachers, and strategy tutors are provided through the program or unit. Academic advisers, coaches, counselors, diagnostic specialists, graduate assistants/students, LD specialists, professional tutors, regular education teachers, remediation/learning specialists, skill tutors, special education teachers, strategy tutors, teacher trainees, and trained peer tutors are provided collaboratively through on-campus or off-campus services.

Orientation The program or unit offers a mandatory 1-day orientation for new students during registration and individually by special arrangement.

Unique Aids and Services Aids, services, or accommodations include advocates, career counseling, digital textbooks, faculty training, personal coach, and priority registration.

Subject-area Tutoring Tutoring is offered one-on-one and in small groups for all subjects. Tutoring is provided through the program or unit via graduate assistants/students, LD specialists, and trained peer tutors. Tutoring is also provided collaboratively through on-campus or off-campus services via computer-based instruction, graduate assistants/students, LD specialists, and trained peer tutors.

Diagnostic Testing Testing is provided through the program or unit for learning strategies, learning styles, personality, social skills, and study skills.

Basic Skills Remediation Remediation is offered in small groups and in class-size groups for auditory processing, computer skills, handwriting, learning strategies, math, motor skills, reading, social skills, spelling, spoken language, study skills, time management, visual processing, and written language. Remediation is provided through the program or unit via LD specialists, regular education teachers, and special education teachers. Remediation is also provided collaboratively through on-campus or off-campus services via LD specialists, regular education teachers, and special education teachers.

Enrichment Enrichment programs are available through the program or unit for college survival skills, learning strategies, self-advocacy, stress management, study skills, test taking, and time management. Programs for career planning, college survival skills, health and nutrition, learning strategies, oral communication skills, practical computer skills, reading, self-advocacy, stress management, study skills, test taking, time management, vocabulary development, and written composition skills are provided collaboratively through on-campus or off-campus services. Credit is offered for career planning, college survival skills, health and nutrition, learning strategies, oral communication skills, practical computer skills, reading, self-advocacy, stress management, study skills, test taking, time management, vocabulary development, and written composition skills.

Fees *LD Program or Service* fee is $1250 to $3000 (fee varies according to course level and level/tier of service).

Application For admittance to the program or unit, students are required to apply to the program directly, provide a psychoeducational report (3 years old or less), and provide documentation of high school services. Upon application, materials documenting need for services should be sent to both admissions and the LD program or unit. Upon acceptance, documentation of need for services should be sent to both admissions and the LD program or unit. *Application deadline (institutional):* Continuous. *Application deadline (LD program):* 7/3 for fall. 10/3 for spring.

Written Policies Written policy regarding general/basic LD accommodations is outlined in the school's catalog/handbook. Written policies regarding course substitutions, general/basic LD accommodations, grade forgiveness, reduced course loads, substitutions and waivers of admissions requirements, and substitutions and waivers of graduation requirements are available through the program or unit directly.

Written Policies Written policy regarding general/basic LD accommodations is available on the program Web site. Written policy regarding substitutions and waivers of admissions requirements is outlined in the school's catalog/handbook. Written policy regarding general/basic LD accommodations is available through the program or unit directly.

Long Island University, C.W. Post Campus

720 Northern Boulevard

Brookville, NY 11548-1300

http://www.cwpost.liunet.edu/cwis/cwp/post.html

Contact: Mrs. Mathilda Stucke, Director. Phone: 516-299-2937. Fax: 516-299-2126. E-mail: mstucke@liu.edu.

The program or unit includes 3 full-time and 17 part-time staff members. Counselors, diagnostic specialists, graduate assistants/students, LD specialists, professional tutors, skill tutors, and strategy tutors are provided through the program or unit. Academic advisers and coaches are provided collaboratively through on-campus or off-campus services.

Orientation The program or unit offers a mandatory 1-day orientation for new students before classes begin.

Unique Aids and Services Aids, services, or accommodations include career counseling.

Subject-area Tutoring Tutoring is offered one-on-one and in small groups for most subjects. Tutoring is provided through the program or unit via computer-based instruction, graduate assistants/students, LD specialists, and professional tutors.

Basic Skills Remediation Remediation is offered one-on-one and in small groups for computer skills, learning strategies, math, reading, social skills, spelling, study skills, time management, and written language. Remediation is provided through the program or unit via computer-based instruction, graduate assistants/students, and LD specialists.

Enrichment Enrichment programs are available through the program or unit for career planning, college survival skills, learning strategies, math, oral communication skills, practical computer skills, reading, self-advocacy, stress management, study skills, test taking, time management, vocabulary development, and written composition skills. Programs for career planning, college survival skills, health and nutrition, math, medication management, oral communication skills, practical computer skills, stress management, and written composition skills are provided collaboratively through on-campus or off-campus services. Credit is offered for oral communication skills and practical computer skills.

Fees *LD Program or Service* fee is $3200.

Application For admittance to the program or unit, students are required to apply to the program directly and provide a psychoeducational report (3 years old or less). It is recommended that students provide Woodcock-Johnson Test results. Upon acceptance, documentation of need for services should be sent only to the LD program or unit. *Application deadline (institutional):* Continuous. *Application deadline (LD program):* Rolling/continuous for fall and rolling/continuous for spring.

Loras College
Loras Learning Disabilities Program

1450 Alta Vista

Dubuque, IA 52004-0178

http://www.loras.edu/

Contact: Ms. Rochelle Fury, L.D. Secretary. Phone: 563-588-7134. Fax: 563-588-7147. E-mail: rfury@loras.edu. Head of LD Program: Ms. Dianne Gibson, Director of L.D. Program. Phone: 563-588-7223. Fax: 563-588-7147. E-mail: dgibson@loras.edu.

Loras Learning Disabilities Program Approximately 63 registered undergraduate students were served during 2002-03. The program or unit includes 4 full-time staff members. Academic advisers, graduate assistants/students, LD specialists, professional tutors, remediation/learning specialists, skill tutors, strategy tutors, and trained peer tutors are provided through the program or unit. Academic advisers, coaches, counselors, diagnostic specialists, graduate assistants/students, regular education teachers, and skill tutors are provided collaboratively through on-campus or off-campus services.

Unique Aids and Services Aids, services, or accommodations include digital textbooks, priority registration, credit class for first-year students.

Subject-area Tutoring Tutoring is offered one-on-one and in small groups for all subjects. Tutoring is provided through the program or unit via LD specialists and trained peer tutors. Tutoring is also provided collaboratively through on-campus or off-campus services via professional tutors and trained peer tutors.

Diagnostic Testing Testing for intelligence, math, personality, reading, spelling, and written language is provided collaboratively through on-campus or off-campus services.

Basic Skills Remediation Remediation is offered one-on-one and in class-size groups for computer skills, learning strategies, math, reading, study skills, time management, and written language. Remediation is provided through the program or unit via LD specialists and trained peer tutors. Remediation is also provided collaboratively through on-campus or off-campus services via computer-based instruction, professional tutors, and trained peer tutors.

Enrichment Enrichment programs are available through the program or unit for career planning, college survival skills, learning strategies, math, oral communication skills, reading, self-advocacy, stress management, study skills, test taking, time management, vocabulary development, and written composition skills. Programs for career planning, health and nutrition, math, oral communication skills, practical computer skills, and written composition skills are provided collaboratively through on-campus or off-campus services.

Fees *LD Program or Service* fee is $2850 to $3265 (fee varies according to level/tier of service).

Loras College (continued)

Application For admittance to the program or unit, students are required to provide a psychoeducational report (3 years old or less) and provide a personal essay. It is recommended that students provide documentation of high school services. Upon application, materials documenting need for services should be sent only to admissions with institutional application materials. *Application deadline (institutional):* Continuous. *Application deadline (LD program):* 11/1 for fall. Rolling/continuous for spring.

Written Policies Written policies regarding course substitutions, general/basic LD accommodations, substitutions and waivers of admissions requirements, and substitutions and waivers of graduation requirements are available through the program or unit directly.

Lynn University
Institute for Achievement and Learning, Comprehensive Support Program

3601 North Military Trail
Boca Raton, FL 33431-5598
http://www.lynn.edu/

Contact: Admissions. Phone: 561-237-7900. Fax: 561-237-7100. E-mail: admission@lynn.edu. Head of LD Program: Dr. Marsha Anne Glines, Executive Director of Institute for Achievement and Learning. Phone: 561-237-7881. Fax: 561-237-7100. E-mail: mglines@lynn.edu.

Institute for Achievement and Learning, Comprehensive Support Program Approximately 300 registered undergraduate students were served during 2002-03. The program or unit includes 10 full-time and 35 part-time staff members. Diagnostic specialists, LD specialists, professional tutors, remediation/learning specialists, skill tutors, and strategy tutors are provided through the program or unit.

Orientation The program or unit offers a mandatory 2-day orientation for new students before classes begin.

Unique Aids and Services Aids, services, or accommodations include advocates, career counseling, faculty training, priority registration, and support groups.

Subject-area Tutoring Tutoring is offered for all subjects. Tutoring is provided through the program or unit via professional tutors.

Diagnostic Testing Testing is provided through the program or unit for learning strategies, learning styles, personality, and study skills. Testing for math, personality, study skills, and written language is provided collaboratively through on-campus or off-campus services.

Basic Skills Remediation Remediation is offered one-on-one, in small groups, and in class-size groups for learning strategies. Remediation is provided through the program or unit via LD specialists.

Enrichment Enrichment programs are available through the program or unit for career planning, learning strategies, self-advocacy, study skills, test taking, and time management. Programs for career planning, college survival skills, health and nutrition, math, self-advocacy, stress management, study skills, time management, and written composition skills are provided collaboratively through on-campus or off-campus services.

Fees *LD Program or Service* fee is $7500 to $10,020 (fee varies according to level/tier of service).

Application For admittance to the program or unit, students are required to provide a psychoeducational report. It is recommended that students provide documentation of high school services. Upon application, materials documenting need for services should be sent to both admissions and the LD program or unit. *Application deadline (institutional):* Continuous. *Application deadline (LD program):* Rolling/continuous for fall and rolling/continuous for spring.

Written Policies Written policy regarding general/basic LD accommodations is available on the program Web site. Written policy regarding general/basic LD accommodations is available through the program or unit directly.

Marist College
Learning Disabilities Support Program

3399 North Road
Poughkeepsie, NY 12601-1387
http://www.marist.edu/

Contact: Ms. Gale Canale, Learning Disabilities Program Secretary. Phone: 845-575-3274. Fax: 845-575-3011. E-mail: gale.canale@marist.edu. Head of LD Program: Ms. Linda J. Cooper, Director Learning Disabilities Support Program. Phone: 845-575-3274. Fax: 845-575-3011. E-mail: linda.cooper@marist.edu.

Learning Disabilities Support Program Approximately 75 registered undergraduate students were served during 2002-03. The program or unit includes 3 full-time and 3 part-time staff members. LD specialists, special education teachers, and trained peer tutors are provided through the program or unit.

Unique Aids and Services Aids, services, or accommodations include career counseling and digital textbooks.

Subject-area Tutoring Tutoring is offered one-on-one and in small groups for most subjects. Tutoring is provided through the program or unit via LD specialists and trained peer tutors.

Basic Skills Remediation Remediation is offered one-on-one for learning strategies, study skills, time management, written language, and assistive technology. Remediation is provided through the program or unit via LD specialists and trained peer tutors.

Enrichment Enrichment programs are available through the program or unit for career planning, learning strategies, self-advocacy, stress management, study skills, test taking, time management, and written composition skills. Programs for math and written composition skills are provided collaboratively through on-campus or off-campus services.

Fees *LD Program or Service* fee is $3000.

Application For admittance to the program or unit, students are required to apply to the program directly, provide a psychoeducational report (3 years old or less), provide documentation of high school services, and provide achievement testing results in reading, writing and mathematics. Upon application, materials documenting need for services should be sent only to the LD program or unit. Upon acceptance, documentation of need for services should be sent only to the LD program or unit. *Application deadline (institutional):* 2/15. *Application deadline (LD program):* 2/15 for fall. 2/15 for spring.

Written Policies Written policy regarding general/basic LD accommodations is available on the program Web site. Written policy regarding general/basic LD accommodations is outlined in the school's catalog/handbook. Written policy regarding substitutions and waivers of admissions requirements is available through the program or unit directly.

Marshall University
Marshall University HELP Program

One John Marshall Drive
Huntington, WV 25755
http://www.marshall.edu/help
Contact: Phone: 304-696-3170. Fax: 304-696-3135.

Marshall University HELP Program The program or unit includes 11 full-time and 60 part-time staff members. Diagnostic specialists, graduate assistants/students, LD specialists, professional tutors, remediation/learning specialists, skill tutors, and strategy tutors are provided through the program or unit.
Orientation The program or unit offers a mandatory 1-day orientation for new students before registration, before classes begin, and during summer prior to enrollment.
Summer Program To help prepare for the demands of college, there is a mandatory 5-week summer program prior to entering the school. Degree credit will be earned.
Unique Aids and Services Aids, services, or accommodations include advocates, personal coach, priority registration, and support groups.
Subject-area Tutoring Tutoring is offered one-on-one for all subjects. Tutoring is provided through the program or unit via computer-based instruction, graduate assistants/students, LD specialists, and professional tutors.
Diagnostic Testing Testing is provided through the program or unit for auditory processing, handwriting, intelligence, learning strategies, learning styles, math, neuropsychological, reading, spelling, study skills, visual processing, written language, and other services.
Basic Skills Remediation Remediation is offered one-on-one for auditory processing, computer skills, handwriting, learning strategies, math, reading, spelling, study skills, time management, visual processing, and written language. Remediation is provided through the program or unit via computer-based instruction and LD specialists.
Enrichment Enrichment programs are available through the program or unit for career planning, college survival skills, learning strategies, math, practical computer skills, reading, self-advocacy, stress management, study skills, test taking, time management, vocabulary development, and written composition skills.
Student Organization HELPERS consists of 15 members.
Fees *LD Program or Service* fee is $275 to $475 (fee varies according to level/tier of service). *Summer Program* fee is $1200 to $2200. *Orientation* fee is $75. *Diagnostic Testing* fee is $500 to $1000.
Application For admittance to the program or unit, students are required to apply to the program directly, provide a psychoeducational report (3 years old or less), and provide 2 letters of recommendation and a 1 page essay. It is recommended that students provide documentation of high school services. Upon application, materials documenting need for services should be sent only to the LD program or unit. *Application deadline (institutional):* Continuous. *Application deadline (LD program):* 1/4 for fall.

Marymount Manhattan College

221 East 71st Street
New York, NY 10021-4597
http://marymount.mmm.edu/
Contact: Dr. Ann Jablon, Director of Program for Academic Access. Phone: 212-774-0724. E-mail: ajablon@mmm.edu. Head of LD Program: Dr. Ann Jablon, Director of Program for Academic Access. Phone: 212-774-0721. E-mail: ajablon@mmm.edu.

Approximately 50 registered undergraduate students were served during 2002-03. The program or unit includes 1 full-time and 2 part-time staff members. Diagnostic specialists and LD specialists are provided through the program or unit.
Orientation The program or unit offers a mandatory half-day orientation for new students during summer prior to enrollment.
Unique Aids and Services Aids, services, or accommodations include career counseling, priority registration, weekly meetings with faculty, one workshop per semester.
Subject-area Tutoring Tutoring is offered one-on-one for all subjects. Tutoring is provided collaboratively through on-campus or off-campus services via professional tutors and trained peer tutors.
Diagnostic Testing Testing for learning strategies, reading, spelling, spoken language, study skills, and written language is provided collaboratively through on-campus or off-campus services.
Basic Skills Remediation Remediation is offered in class-size groups for math, reading, study skills, time management, and written language. Remediation is provided collaboratively through on-campus or off-campus services via computer-based instruction and regular education teachers.
Enrichment Enrichment programs are available through the program or unit for college survival skills, learning strategies, medication management, reading, self-advocacy, stress management, study skills, test taking, time management, vocabulary development, and written composition skills. Programs for career planning, college survival skills, health and nutrition, learning strategies, math, oral communication skills, practical computer skills, and written composition skills are provided collaboratively through on-campus or off-campus services. Credit is offered for college survival skills, health and nutrition, learning strategies, math, oral communication skills, practical computer skills, and written composition skills.
Fees *LD Program or Service* fee is $3000.
Application For admittance to the program or unit, students are required to provide a psychoeducational report (2 years old or less). Upon application, materials documenting need for services should be sent only to the LD program or unit. *Application deadline (institutional):* Continuous. *Application deadline (LD program):* Rolling/continuous for fall and rolling/continuous for spring.
Written Policies Written policies regarding general/basic LD accommodations and reduced course loads are available on the program Web site. Written policy regarding general/basic LD accom-

Marymount Manhattan College (continued)

modations is outlined in the school's catalog/handbook. Written policies regarding general/basic LD accommodations and reduced course loads are available through the program or unit directly.

McDaniel College

2 College Hill

Westminster, MD 21157-4390

http://www.mcdaniel.edu/

Contact: Mr. Kevin Selby, Director Student Academic Support Services. Phone: 410-857-2479. Fax: 410-386-4617. E-mail: kselby@mcdaniel.edu.

Approximately 147 registered undergraduate students were served during 2002-03. The program or unit includes 2 full-time and 6 part-time staff members. Academic advisers, counselors, graduate assistants/students, LD specialists, professional tutors, skill tutors, strategy tutors, and trained peer tutors are provided through the program or unit. Academic advisers, counselors, diagnostic specialists, professional tutors, and trained peer tutors are provided collaboratively through on-campus or off-campus services.

Orientation The program or unit offers an optional 1-day orientation for new students during summer prior to enrollment.

Unique Aids and Services Aids, services, or accommodations include career counseling and priority registration.

Subject-area Tutoring Tutoring is offered one-on-one and in small groups for most subjects. Tutoring is provided through the program or unit via graduate assistants/students and LD specialists. Tutoring is also provided collaboratively through on-campus or off-campus services via professional tutors and trained peer tutors.

Diagnostic Testing Testing is provided through the program or unit for auditory processing, learning strategies, learning styles, personality, spoken language, study skills, and written language. Testing for math and written language is provided collaboratively through on-campus or off-campus services.

Basic Skills Remediation Remediation is offered one-on-one for learning strategies, math, social skills, study skills, and written language. Remediation is provided through the program or unit via computer-based instruction, graduate assistants/students, LD specialists, and professional tutors. Remediation is also provided collaboratively through on-campus or off-campus services via professional tutors.

Enrichment Enrichment programs are available through the program or unit for career planning, college survival skills, learning strategies, math, oral communication skills, self-advocacy, stress management, study skills, test taking, time management, vocabulary development, and written composition skills. Programs for career planning, college survival skills, health and nutrition, math, medication management, and written composition skills are provided collaboratively through on-campus or off-campus services.

Fees *LD Program or Service* fee is $0 to $1000 (fee varies according to level/tier of service).

Application For admittance to the program or unit, students are required to apply to the program directly and provide a psychoeducational report (3 years old or less). It is recommended that students provide documentation of high school services. Upon application, materials documenting need for services should be sent only to the

LD program or unit. Upon acceptance, documentation of need for services should be sent only to the LD program or unit. *Application deadline (institutional):* 2/1. *Application deadline (LD program):* Rolling/continuous for fall.

Written Policies Written policy regarding general/basic LD accommodations is available on the program Web site. Written policies regarding course substitutions, general/basic LD accommodations, and substitutions and waivers of graduation requirements are available through the program or unit directly.

Mercyhurst College
Learning Differences Program

501 East 38th Street

Erie, PA 16546

http://www.mercyhurst.edu/

Contact: Ms. Dianne D. Rogers, Director. Phone: 814-824-2450. Fax: 814-824-3063. E-mail: drogers@mercyhurst.edu.

Learning Differences Program Approximately 80 registered undergraduate students were served during 2002-03. The program or unit includes 1 full-time and 5 part-time staff members. Academic advisers, counselors, graduate assistants/students, and LD specialists are provided through the program or unit. Academic advisers, counselors, graduate assistants/students, remediation/learning specialists, skill tutors, and trained peer tutors are provided collaboratively through on-campus or off-campus services.

Orientation The program or unit offers a mandatory 1-day orientation for new students before registration, before classes begin, and individually by special arrangement.

Summer Program To help prepare for the demands of college, there is an optional 3-week summer program prior to entering the school. Degree credit will be earned.

Unique Aids and Services Aids, services, or accommodations include career counseling, priority registration, support groups, progress reports.

Subject-area Tutoring Tutoring is offered one-on-one, in small groups, and in class-size groups for all subjects. Tutoring is provided through the program or unit via graduate assistants/students, LD specialists, and trained peer tutors. Tutoring is also provided collaboratively through on-campus or off-campus services via graduate assistants/students, trained peer tutors, and other.

Basic Skills Remediation Remediation is offered in small groups and in class-size groups for computer skills, math, reading, and written language. Remediation is provided collaboratively through on-campus or off-campus services.

Enrichment Programs for career planning, college survival skills, health and nutrition, learning strategies, math, practical computer skills, reading, self-advocacy, stress management, study skills, test taking, time management, and written composition skills are provided collaboratively through on-campus or off-campus services.

Student Organization Learning Differences Program consists of 80 members.

Fees *LD Program or Service* fee is $1200. *Summer Program* fee is $1500 to $1700.

Application For admittance to the program or unit, students are required to provide a psychoeducational report (3 years old or less), provide documentation of high school services, and provide personal interview. Upon application, materials documenting need for services should be sent to both admissions and the LD program or unit. Upon acceptance, documentation of need for services should be sent only to the LD program or unit. *Application deadline (institutional):* Continuous. *Application deadline (LD program):* Rolling/continuous for fall and rolling/continuous for spring.

Written Policies Written policy regarding general/basic LD accommodations is available on the program Web site. Written policies regarding general/basic LD accommodations, grade forgiveness, and reduced course loads are outlined in the school's catalog/handbook. Written policies regarding course substitutions, general/basic LD accommodations, grade forgiveness, reduced course loads, substitutions and waivers of admissions requirements, and substitutions and waivers of graduation requirements are available through the program or unit directly.

Mitchell College
Learning Resource Center

437 Pequot Avenue
New London, CT 06320-4498
http://www.mitchell.edu/

Contact: Ms. Joanne Carnevale, Admissions Liaison. Phone: 860-701-5071. Fax: 860-701-5090. E-mail: carnevale_j@mitchell.edu. Head of LD Program: Dr. Peter F. Troiano, Associate Dean for Academic Support Services. Phone: 860-701-5141. Fax: 860-701-5090. E-mail: troiano_p@mitchell.edu.

Learning Resource Center Approximately 250 registered undergraduate students were served during 2002-03. The program or unit includes 28 full-time and 10 part-time staff members. Academic advisers, LD specialists, professional tutors, remediation/learning specialists, skill tutors, and strategy tutors are provided through the program or unit. Academic advisers, LD specialists, professional tutors, remediation/learning specialists, skill tutors, and strategy tutors are provided collaboratively through on-campus or off-campus services.

Orientation The program or unit offers an optional half-day orientation for new students immediately prior to new student orientation.

Summer Program To help prepare for the demands of college, there is an optional 4-week summer program prior to entering the school. Degree credit will be earned.

Unique Aids and Services Aids, services, or accommodations include advocates, career counseling, faculty training, parent workshops, and support groups.

Subject-area Tutoring Tutoring is offered one-on-one, in small groups, and in class-size groups for all subjects. Tutoring is provided through the program or unit via professional tutors.

Basic Skills Remediation Remediation is offered one-on-one, in small groups, and in class-size groups for auditory processing, computer skills, learning strategies, math, reading, study skills, time management, visual processing, and written language. Remediation is provided through the program or unit via LD specialists and professional tutors.

Enrichment Enrichment programs are available through the program or unit for learning strategies, math, reading, self-advocacy, stress management, study skills, test taking, time management,

vocabulary development, and written composition skills. Programs for career planning, college survival skills, health and nutrition, oral communication skills, practical computer skills, stress management, study skills, test taking, and time management are provided collaboratively through on-campus or off-campus services. Credit is offered for oral communication skills, practical computer skills, vocabulary development, and written composition skills.

Fees *LD Program or Service* fee is $3000 to $6000 (fee varies according to level/tier of service). *Summer Program* fee is $3500.

Application For admittance to the program or unit, students are required to apply to the program directly, provide a psychoeducational report (3 years old or less), and provide documentation of high school services. Upon application, materials documenting need for services should be sent only to admissions with institutional application materials. *Application deadline (institutional):* Continuous. *Application deadline (LD program):* Rolling/continuous for fall and rolling/continuous for spring.

Written Policies Written policies regarding course substitutions, general/basic LD accommodations, reduced course loads, substitutions and waivers of admissions requirements, and substitutions and waivers of graduation requirements are outlined in the school's catalog/handbook. Written policies regarding course substitutions, general/basic LD accommodations, reduced course loads, substitutions and waivers of admissions requirements, and substitutions and waivers of graduation requirements are available through the program or unit directly.

Morningside College
The Learning Disabilities Program

1501 Morningside Avenue
Sioux City, IA 51106-1751
http://www.morningside.edu/

Contact: Ms. Robbie Rohlena, Director of the Learning Disabilities Program. Phone: 712-274-5426. Fax: 712-274-5101. E-mail: rohlena@morningside.edu.

The Learning Disabilities Program Approximately 10 registered undergraduate students were served during 2002-03. The program or unit includes 1 full-time and 2 part-time staff members. Coaches, LD specialists, remediation/learning specialists, special education teachers, and strategy tutors are provided through the program or unit. Academic advisers, counselors, diagnostic specialists, graduate assistants/students, professional tutors, regular education teachers, skill tutors, teacher trainees, and trained peer tutors are provided collaboratively through on-campus or off-campus services.

Orientation The program or unit offers an optional 1-day orientation for new students before classes begin.

Unique Aids and Services Aids, services, or accommodations include advocates, career counseling, digital textbooks, faculty training, personal coach, and support groups.

Subject-area Tutoring Tutoring is offered one-on-one for all subjects. Tutoring is provided through the program or unit via LD specialists. Tutoring is also provided collaboratively through on-campus or off-campus services via graduate assistants/students, professional tutors, and trained peer tutors.

Morningside College (continued)

Diagnostic Testing Testing for auditory processing, intelligence, learning strategies, learning styles, math, neuropsychological, personality, reading, visual processing, and written language is provided collaboratively through on-campus or off-campus services.

Basic Skills Remediation Remediation is offered in small groups for learning strategies, math, reading, study skills, time management, and written language. Remediation is provided through the program or unit via LD specialists. Remediation is also provided collaboratively through on-campus or off-campus services via professional tutors, regular education teachers, and trained peer tutors.

Enrichment Enrichment programs are available through the program or unit for learning strategies, oral communication skills, reading, self-advocacy, study skills, test taking, time management, vocabulary development, and written composition skills. Programs for career planning, college survival skills, math, practical computer skills, and stress management are provided collaboratively through on-campus or off-campus services.

Student Organization Mentoring Program consists of 15 members.

Fees *LD Program or Service* fee is $800 to $1400 (fee varies according to level/tier of service).

Application For admittance to the program or unit, students are required to apply to the program directly, provide a psychoeducational report (5 years old or less), and provide documentation of high school services. Upon application, materials documenting need for services should be sent only to the LD program or unit. *Application deadline (institutional):* Continuous. *Application deadline (LD program):* Rolling/continuous for fall and rolling/continuous for spring.

Written Policies Written policy regarding general/basic LD accommodations is outlined in the school's catalog/handbook. Written policies regarding course substitutions and substitutions and waivers of graduation requirements are available through the program or unit directly.

Mount Ida College

777 Dedham Street
Newton Center, MA 02459-3310
http://www.mountida.edu/
Contact: Phone: 617-928-4500. Fax: 617-928-4507.

The program or unit includes 1 full-time and 8 part-time staff members. LD specialists are provided through the program or unit. LD specialists are provided collaboratively through on-campus or off-campus services.

Orientation The program or unit offers a mandatory 2-hour orientation for new students before classes begin and during orientation.

Unique Aids and Services Aids, services, or accommodations include personal coach.

Subject-area Tutoring Tutoring is offered one-on-one for some subjects. Tutoring is provided through the program or unit via LD specialists.

Enrichment Enrichment programs are available through the program or unit for college survival skills.

Fees *LD Program or Service* fee is $1500 to $2995 (fee varies according to level/tier of service). *Orientation* fee is $1500 to $2995.

Application For admittance to the program or unit, students are required to apply to the program directly, provide a psychoeducational report, provide documentation of high school services, and provide WAIS. Upon acceptance, documentation of need for services should be sent only to admissions. *Application deadline (institutional):* Continuous. *Application deadline (LD program):* Rolling/continuous for fall and rolling/continuous for spring.

Written Policies Written policies regarding general/basic LD accommodations and reduced course loads are available on the program Web site. Written policy regarding general/basic LD accommodations is outlined in the school's catalog/handbook. Written policies regarding general/basic LD accommodations and reduced course loads are available through the program or unit directly.

Muskingum College
PLUS Program

163 Stormont Street
New Concord, OH 43762
http://www.muskingum.edu/

Contact: Michelle Butler, Administrative Assistant. Phone: 740-826-8280. Fax: 740-826-8285. E-mail: butler@muskingum.edu. Head of LD Program: Dr. Eileen Henry, Director of Center for Advancement of Learning. Phone: 740-826-8284. Fax: 740-826-8285. E-mail: ehenry@muskingum.edu.

PLUS Program Approximately 160 registered undergraduate students were served during 2002-03. The program or unit includes 16 full-time and 4 part-time staff members. Professional tutors are provided through the program or unit.

Orientation The program or unit offers a mandatory orientation for new students prior to the first day of the fall semester.

Summer Program To help prepare for the demands of college, there is 2-week summer program prior to entering the school.

Unique Aids and Services Aids, services, or accommodations include priority registration.

Subject-area Tutoring Tutoring is offered one-on-one for all subjects. Tutoring is provided through the program or unit via professional tutors.

Enrichment Enrichment programs are available through the program or unit for career planning, learning strategies, study skills, test taking, and time management.

Student Organization ChatBack consists of 25 members.

Fees *LD Program or Service* fee is $2310 to $4620 (fee varies according to level/tier of service). *Summer Program* fee is $2000.

Application For admittance to the program or unit, students are required to provide a psychoeducational report (3 years old or less). It is recommended that students provide documentation of high school services. Upon application, materials documenting need for services should be sent only to the LD program or unit. *Application deadline (institutional):* 6/1. *Application deadline (LD program):* Rolling/continuous for fall and rolling/continuous for spring.

Written Policies Written policies regarding general/basic LD accommodations and reduced course loads are available through the program or unit directly.

New Jersey City University
Project Mentor: Regional Center for Students with Learning Disabilities

2039 Kennedy Boulevard

Jersey City, NJ 07305-1597

http://www.njcu.edu/PMentor_proj_ment_home.htm

Contact: Ms. Jennifer Aitken, Director and Project Mentor: Regional Center for Students with Learning Disabilities. Phone: 201-200-2091. Fax: 201-200-2575. E-mail: jaitken@njcu. Head of LD Program: Ms. Jennifer Aitken, Director and Project Mentor: Regional Center for Students with Learning Disabilities. Phone: 201-200-2091. Fax: 201-200-2575. E-mail: jaitken@njcu.edu.

Project Mentor: Regional Center for Students with Learning Disabilities Approximately 90 registered undergraduate students were served during 2002-03. The program or unit includes 1 full-time and 9 part-time staff members. Academic advisers, diagnostic specialists, graduate assistants/students, LD specialists, professional tutors, and strategy tutors are provided through the program or unit. Academic advisers are provided collaboratively through on-campus or off-campus services.

Orientation The program or unit offers an optional 1-semester orientation for new students during summer prior to enrollment and during the fall semester (1 degree credit).

Summer Program To help prepare for the demands of college, there is a mandatory 4-week summer program prior to entering the school.

Unique Aids and Services Aids, services, or accommodations include advocates, faculty training, parent workshops, priority registration, weekly meetings with mentors.

Subject-area Tutoring Tutoring is offered in small groups for some subjects. Tutoring is provided through the program or unit via graduate assistants/students and professional tutors.

Diagnostic Testing Testing is provided through the program or unit.

Basic Skills Remediation Remediation is offered in class-size groups for learning strategies, math, reading, spelling, study skills, time management, and written language. Remediation is provided through the program or unit via graduate assistants/students, professional tutors, and teacher trainees.

Enrichment Enrichment programs are available through the program or unit for career planning, college survival skills, learning strategies, math, practical computer skills, reading, self-advocacy, stress management, study skills, test taking, time management, and written composition skills. Programs for career planning, stress management, study skills, test taking, and time management are provided collaboratively through on-campus or off-campus services. Credit is offered for practical computer skills.

Fees *Summer Program* fee is $400. *Orientation* fee is $127.

Application For admittance to the program or unit, students are required to apply to the program directly, provide a psychoeducational report, provide documentation of high school services, and provide high school transcript, letters of recommendation. Upon application, materials documenting need for services should be sent only to the LD program or unit. Upon acceptance, documentation of need for services should be sent only to the LD program or unit. *Application deadline (institutional):* 4/1. *Application deadline (LD program):* 5/15 for fall. Rolling/continuous for spring.

Written Policies Written policy regarding general/basic LD accommodations is available on the program Web site. Written policy regarding general/basic LD accommodations is outlined in the school's catalog/handbook.

Nicholls State University
Louisiana Center for Dyslexia and Related Learning Disorders

906 East First Street

Thibodaux, LA 70310

http://www.nicholls.edu

Contact: Dr. Carol S. Ronka, Director. Phone: 985-448-4897. Fax: 985-448-4423. E-mail: dc-csr@nicholls.edu.

Louisiana Center for Dyslexia and Related Learning Disorders Approximately 90 registered undergraduate students were served during 2002-03. The program or unit includes 7 full-time staff members. Diagnostic specialists, graduate assistants/students, LD specialists, professional tutors, and remediation/learning specialists are provided through the program or unit. Academic advisers, coaches, and other are provided collaboratively through on-campus or off-campus services.

Orientation The program or unit offers a mandatory 2-hour orientation for new students before classes begin.

Unique Aids and Services Aids, services, or accommodations include priority registration and support groups.

Subject-area Tutoring Tutoring is offered one-on-one and in small groups for most subjects. Tutoring is provided through the program or unit via LD specialists.

Diagnostic Testing Testing is provided through the program or unit for auditory processing, intelligence, learning strategies, math, neuropsychological, reading, social skills, spelling, spoken language, study skills, visual processing, and written language.

Basic Skills Remediation Remediation is offered one-on-one and in small groups for math, reading, spelling, study skills, time management, and written language. Remediation is provided through the program or unit via LD specialists.

Enrichment Enrichment programs are available through the program or unit for career planning, college survival skills, math, oral communication skills, practical computer skills, reading, self-advocacy, study skills, test taking, time management, vocabulary development, and written composition skills.

Fees *LD Program or Service* fee is $750. *Diagnostic Testing* fee is $400.

Application For admittance to the program or unit, students are required to apply to the program directly and provide a psychoeducational report (3 years old or less). Upon application, materials documenting need for services should be sent only to the LD program or unit. Upon acceptance, documentation of need for services should be sent only to the LD program or unit. *Application deadline (institutional):* Continuous. *Application deadline (LD program):* 8/15 for fall. 1/5 for spring.

Written Policies Written policies regarding general/basic LD accommodations and substitutions and waivers of admissions requirements are outlined in the school's catalog/handbook.

Oak Hills Christian College
Assisted Learning Program

1600 Oak Hills Road, SW

Bemidji, MN 56601-8832

http://www.oakhills.edu/

Contact: Assisted Learning Program Director. Phone: 218-751-8670. Fax: 218-751-8825.

Assisted Learning Program Approximately 5 registered undergraduate students were served during 2002-03. The program or unit includes 1 part-time staff member. Academic advisers, counselors, diagnostic specialists, professional tutors, regular education teachers, remediation/learning specialists, skill tutors, and trained peer tutors are provided collaboratively through on-campus or off-campus services.

Unique Aids and Services Aids, services, or accommodations include personal coach and weekly meetings with faculty.

Subject-area Tutoring Tutoring is offered one-on-one and in small groups for some subjects. Tutoring is provided through the program or unit via trained peer tutors. Tutoring is also provided collaboratively through on-campus or off-campus services via trained peer tutors.

Diagnostic Testing Testing is provided through the program or unit for learning strategies and learning styles.

Fees *LD Program or Service* fee is $0 to $300 (fee varies according to level/tier of service).

Application For admittance to the program or unit, students are required to provide a psychoeducational report (5 years old or less). It is recommended that students provide documentation of high school services. Upon application, materials documenting need for services should be sent to both admissions and the LD program or unit. Upon acceptance, documentation of need for services should be sent only to the LD program or unit. *Application deadline (institutional):* Continuous. *Application deadline (LD program):* Rolling/continuous for fall and rolling/continuous for spring.

Written Policies Written policies regarding general/basic LD accommodations, substitutions and waivers of admissions requirements, and substitutions and waivers of graduation requirements are available on the program Web site. Written policies regarding general/basic LD accommodations, substitutions and waivers of admissions requirements, and substitutions and waivers of graduation requirements are outlined in the school's catalog/handbook.

Reinhardt College
Academic Support Office

7300 Reinhardt College Circle

Waleska, GA 30183-2981

http://www.reinhardt.edu/

Contact: Ms. Sylvia R. Robertson, Director of Academic Support Office. Phone: 770-720-5567. Fax: 770-720-5602. E-mail: srr@reinhardt.edu.

Academic Support Office Approximately 100 registered undergraduate students were served during 2002-03. The program or unit includes 4 full-time staff members. Academic advisers, LD special-ists, regular education teachers, remediation/learning specialists, special education teachers, strategy tutors, and other are provided through the program or unit. Counselors and diagnostic specialists are provided collaboratively through on-campus or off-campus services.

Orientation The program or unit offers a mandatory 1-day orientation for new students before classes begin.

Unique Aids and Services Aids, services, or accommodations include digital textbooks and priority registration.

Subject-area Tutoring Tutoring is offered in small groups for most subjects. Tutoring is provided through the program or unit via LD specialists and other.

Enrichment Enrichment programs are available through the program or unit for self-advocacy, test taking, time management, and written composition skills. Programs for career planning, college survival skills, health and nutrition, learning strategies, oral communication skills, stress management, and time management are provided collaboratively through on-campus or off-campus services. Credit is offered for college survival skills, health and nutrition, learning strategies, and oral communication skills.

Fees *LD Program or Service* fee is $861 to $7088 (fee varies according to level/tier of service).

Application For admittance to the program or unit, students are required to apply to the program directly, provide a psychoeducational report (3 years old or less), provide documentation of high school services, and provide 3 letters of reference. Upon application, materials documenting need for services should be sent only to admissions with institutional application materials. Upon acceptance, documentation of need for services should be sent only to admissions. *Application deadline (institutional):* Continuous. *Application deadline (LD program):* Rolling/continuous for fall and rolling/continuous for spring.

Written Policies Written policy regarding general/basic LD accommodations is outlined in the school's catalog/handbook.

Roosevelt University
Disabled Student Services, Learning and Support Services Program (LSSP)

430 South Michigan Avenue

Chicago, IL 60605-1394

http://www.roosevelt.edu/

Contact: Nancy Litke, Director of Learning and Support Services Program. Phone: 312-341-3810. Fax: 312-341-3735. E-mail: nlitke@roosevelt.edu.

Disabled Student Services, Learning and Support Services Program (LSSP) Approximately 20 registered undergraduate students were served during 2002-03. The program or unit includes 1 full-time and 3 part-time staff members. Academic advisers, coaches, LD specialists, professional tutors, remediation/learning specialists, skill tutors, and strategy tutors are provided through the program or unit. Academic advisers, counselors, graduate assistants/students, professional tutors, skill tutors, and strategy tutors are provided collaboratively through on-campus or off-campus services.

Orientation The program or unit offers an optional orientation for new students on a one-to-one, as needed basis.

Unique Aids and Services Aids, services, or accommodations include advocates, career counseling, support groups, and weekly meetings with faculty.

Subject-area Tutoring Tutoring is offered one-on-one and in small groups for most subjects. Tutoring is provided through the program or unit via computer-based instruction, graduate assistants/students, LD specialists, professional tutors, and trained peer tutors. Tutoring is also provided collaboratively through on-campus or off-campus services via computer-based instruction, graduate assistants/students, professional tutors, and trained peer tutors.

Basic Skills Remediation Remediation is offered one-on-one and in small groups for auditory processing, computer skills, learning strategies, math, reading, social skills, spelling, spoken language, study skills, time management, visual processing, and written language. Remediation is provided through the program or unit via computer-based instruction, LD specialists, and professional tutors. Remediation is also provided collaboratively through on-campus or off-campus services via computer-based instruction and professional tutors.

Enrichment Enrichment programs are available through the program or unit for career planning, college survival skills, learning strategies, math, oral communication skills, practical computer skills, reading, self-advocacy, stress management, study skills, test taking, time management, vocabulary development, and written composition skills. Programs for career planning, college survival skills, health and nutrition, learning strategies, math, oral communication skills, practical computer skills, reading, self-advocacy, stress management, study skills, test taking, time management, and written composition skills are provided collaboratively through on-campus or off-campus services.

Student Organization ADAPT consists of 15 members.

Fees *LD Program or Service* fee is $1000.

Application For admittance to the program or unit, students are required to apply to the program directly and provide a psychoeducational report. It is recommended that students provide documentation of high school services. Upon application, materials documenting need for services should be sent only to the LD program or unit. Upon acceptance, documentation of need for services should be sent only to the LD program or unit. *Application deadline (institutional):* 8/15. *Application deadline (LD program):* Rolling/continuous for fall and rolling/continuous for spring.

Written Policies Written policies regarding course substitutions, general/basic LD accommodations, reduced course loads, substitutions and waivers of admissions requirements, and substitutions and waivers of graduation requirements are available on the program Web site. Written policies regarding course substitutions, general/basic LD accommodations, reduced course loads, substitutions and waivers of admissions requirements, and substitutions and waivers of graduation requirements are available through the program or unit directly.

Sacred Heart University

5151 Park Avenue
Fairfield, CT 06825-1000
http://www.sacredheart.edu/
Contact: Mrs. Jill Elizabeth Angotta, Director of Special Services. Phone: 203-365-4730. Fax: 203-396-8049. E-mail: angottaj@sacredheart.edu.

Approximately 171 registered undergraduate students were served during 2002-03. The program or unit includes 5 full-time and 3 part-time staff members. LD specialists, professional tutors, remediation/learning specialists, skill tutors, strategy tutors, and trained peer tutors are provided through the program or unit. Academic advisers, coaches, counselors, and diagnostic specialists are provided collaboratively through on-campus or off-campus services.

Unique Aids and Services Aids, services, or accommodations include priority registration, books on tape, extended/separate environment testing, scribes.

Subject-area Tutoring Tutoring is offered one-on-one for most subjects. Tutoring is provided through the program or unit via LD specialists, professional tutors, and trained peer tutors.

Basic Skills Remediation Remediation is offered one-on-one and in class-size groups for learning strategies, math, reading, study skills, and time management. Remediation is provided through the program or unit via LD specialists, professional tutors, and trained peer tutors. Remediation is also provided collaboratively through on-campus or off-campus services via LD specialists, professional tutors, and trained peer tutors.

Enrichment Enrichment programs are available through the program or unit for learning strategies, math, oral communication skills, practical computer skills, reading, self-advocacy, study skills, test taking, time management, and written composition skills. Programs for career planning, college survival skills, health and nutrition, math, oral communication skills, practical computer skills, reading, study skills, test taking, time management, and written composition skills are provided collaboratively through on-campus or off-campus services.

Fees *LD Program or Service* fee is $1510 to $1950 (fee varies according to course level).

Application For admittance to the program or unit, students are required to provide a psychoeducational report (3 years old or less), provide documentation of high school services, and provide transitional plan and full evaluation. Upon application, materials documenting need for services should be sent only to the LD program or unit. Upon acceptance, documentation of need for services should be sent only to the LD program or unit. *Application deadline (institutional):* Continuous. *Application deadline (LD program):* Rolling/continuous for fall and rolling/continuous for spring.

Written Policies Written policy regarding general/basic LD accommodations is available on the program Web site. Written policies regarding course substitutions, general/basic LD accommodations, grade forgiveness, reduced course loads, substitutions and waivers of admissions requirements, and substitutions and waivers of graduation requirements are outlined in the school's catalog/handbook.

St. Gregory's University

1900 West MacArthur Drive
Shawnee, OK 74804-2499
http://www.sgc.edu/
Contact: Mrs. Susan Gay Faulk, Director of Partners in Learning. Phone: 405-878-5398. Fax: 405-878-5198. E-mail: sgfaulk@stgregorys.edu.

Approximately 24 registered undergraduate students were served during 2002-03. The program or unit includes 2 full-time and 50 part-time staff members. Academic advisers, counselors, graduate

St. Gregory's University (continued)

assistants/students, professional tutors, and trained peer tutors are provided through the program or unit. Academic advisers, counselors, graduate assistants/students, LD specialists, regular education teachers, remediation/learning specialists, and trained peer tutors are provided collaboratively through on-campus or off-campus services.

Unique Aids and Services Aids, services, or accommodations include advocates, career counseling, and faculty training.

Subject-area Tutoring Tutoring is offered one-on-one and in small groups for all subjects. Tutoring is provided through the program or unit via graduate assistants/students, professional tutors, and trained peer tutors. Tutoring is also provided collaboratively through on-campus or off-campus services via graduate assistants/students and trained peer tutors.

Basic Skills Remediation Remediation is offered in class-size groups for reading. Remediation is provided collaboratively through on-campus or off-campus services via regular education teachers.

Enrichment Programs for career planning, college survival skills, learning strategies, practical computer skills, reading, stress management, study skills, test taking, time management, and written composition skills are provided collaboratively through on-campus or off-campus services.

Fees *LD Program or Service* fee is $5600.

Application For admittance to the program or unit, students are required to apply to the program directly, provide a psychoeducational report (3 years old or less), and provide documentation of high school services. Upon acceptance, documentation of need for services should be sent only to the LD program or unit. *Application deadline (institutional):* Continuous. *Application deadline (LD program):* Rolling/continuous for fall and rolling/continuous for spring.

Written Policies Written policy regarding general/basic LD accommodations is outlined in the school's catalog/handbook. Written policies regarding course substitutions, grade forgiveness, reduced course loads, substitutions and waivers of admissions requirements, and substitutions and waivers of graduation requirements are available through the program or unit directly.

St. Thomas Aquinas College
The STAC Exchange

125 Route 340
Sparkill, NY 10976
http://www.stac.edu/

Contact: Dr. Richard F. Heath, Director of The STAC Exchange. Phone: 845-398-4230. Fax: 845-398-4229. E-mail: stacexch@stac.edu.

The STAC Exchange Approximately 78 registered undergraduate students were served during 2002-03. The program or unit includes 4 full-time and 7 part-time staff members. Academic advisers, LD specialists, professional tutors, strategy tutors, and other are provided through the program or unit. Academic advisers are provided collaboratively through on-campus or off-campus services.

Orientation The program or unit offers a mandatory 4-day, 3-night (residential) orientation for new students before classes begin and during summer prior to enrollment.

Unique Aids and Services Aids, services, or accommodations include priority registration.

Subject-area Tutoring Tutoring is offered one-on-one and in small groups for most subjects. Tutoring is provided through the program or unit via professional tutors and other. Tutoring is also provided collaboratively through on-campus or off-campus services via graduate assistants/students and trained peer tutors.

Basic Skills Remediation Remediation is offered one-on-one, in small groups, and in class-size groups for learning strategies, study skills, and time management. Remediation is provided through the program or unit via professional tutors and other. Remediation is also provided collaboratively through on-campus or off-campus services via graduate assistants/students and trained peer tutors.

Fees *LD Program or Service* fee is $3300. *Orientation* fee is $500 to $700.

Application For admittance to the program or unit, students are required to apply to the program directly and provide a psychoeducational report (3 years old or less). It is recommended that students provide documentation of high school services. Upon application, materials documenting need for services should be sent only to the LD program or unit. Upon acceptance, documentation of need for services should be sent only to the LD program or unit. *Application deadline (institutional):* Continuous. *Application deadline (LD program):* Rolling/continuous for fall.

Written Policies Written policies regarding course substitutions, general/basic LD accommodations, reduced course loads, substitutions and waivers of admissions requirements, and substitutions and waivers of graduation requirements are available through the program or unit directly.

Schreiner University

2100 Memorial Boulevard
Kerrville, TX 78028-5697

http://www.schreiner.edu/

Contact: Dr. Jude D. Gallik, Director. Phone: 830-792-7257. E-mail: jgallik@schreiner.edu.

Approximately 80 registered undergraduate students were served during 2002-03. The program or unit includes 4 full-time and 22 part-time staff members. LD specialists and professional tutors are provided through the program or unit.

Subject-area Tutoring Tutoring is offered one-on-one and in small groups for all subjects. Tutoring is provided through the program or unit via professional tutors.

Fees *LD Program or Service* fee is $5800.

Application For admittance to the program or unit, students are required to provide a psychoeducational report (1 year old or less) and provide WAIS III, achievement tests, and disability statement. It is recommended that students provide documentation of high school services. Upon application, materials documenting need for services should be sent only to the LD program or unit. *Application deadline (institutional):* 8/1. *Application deadline (LD program):* 4/15 for fall. 11/15 for spring.

Written Policies Written policies regarding course substitutions, general/basic LD accommodations, substitutions and waivers of admissions requirements, and substitutions and waivers of graduation requirements are outlined in the school's catalog/handbook.

Union College

3800 South 48th Street

Lincoln, NE 68506-4300

http://www.ucollege.edu/

Contact: Mrs. Jennifer Forbes, Director. Phone: 402-486-2506. Fax: 402-486-2895. E-mail: jeforbes@ucollege.edu.

Approximately 75 registered undergraduate students were served during 2002-03. The program or unit includes 3 full-time and 2 part-time staff members. Academic advisers, coaches, graduate assistants/students, LD specialists, professional tutors, remediation/learning specialists, skill tutors, special education teachers, and strategy tutors are provided through the program or unit. Counselors, diagnostic specialists, regular education teachers, and other are provided collaboratively through on-campus or off-campus services.

Orientation The program or unit offers a mandatory 3-hour orientation for new students after classes begin and individually by special arrangement.

Unique Aids and Services Aids, services, or accommodations include career counseling, faculty training, CD/taped textbooks.

Subject-area Tutoring Tutoring is offered one-on-one for most subjects. Tutoring is provided through the program or unit via LD specialists.

Diagnostic Testing Testing for auditory processing, intelligence, learning strategies, learning styles, math, neuropsychological, personality, reading, spelling, spoken language, study skills, and written language is provided collaboratively through on-campus or off-campus services.

Basic Skills Remediation Remediation is offered one-on-one and in class-size groups for computer skills, learning strategies, math, reading, social skills, spelling, study skills, time management, and written language. Remediation is provided through the program or unit via LD specialists.

Enrichment Enrichment programs are available through the program or unit for college survival skills, learning strategies, math, reading, self-advocacy, stress management, study skills, test taking, time management, and written composition skills. Programs for career planning, health and nutrition, math, oral communication skills, and practical computer skills are provided collaboratively through on-campus or off-campus services. Credit is offered for health and nutrition, math, oral communication skills, practical computer skills, and written composition skills.

Fees *LD Program or Service* fee is $0 to $495 (fee varies according to level/tier of service). *Diagnostic Testing* fee is $350.

Application For admittance to the program or unit, students are required to apply to the program directly, provide a psychoeducational report (5 years old or less), and provide documentation of high school services. Upon application, materials documenting need for services should be sent only to the LD program or unit. Upon acceptance, documentation of need for services should be sent only to the LD program or unit. *Application deadline (institutional):* Continuous. *Application deadline (LD program):* Rolling/continuous for fall and rolling/continuous for spring.

Written Policies Written policy regarding general/basic LD accommodations is available on the program Web site. Written policy regarding general/basic LD accommodations is available through the program or unit directly.

The University of Arizona

Tucson, AZ 85721

http://www.arizona.edu/

Contact: Shirley Ramsey, Assistant Director of Admissions. Phone: 520-621-8493. Fax: 520-621-9448. E-mail: ramsey@u.arizona.edu. Head of LD Program: Dr. Diane Perreira, Director. Phone: 520-621-1427. Fax: 520-621-9448. E-mail: perreird@u.arizona.edu.

Approximately 500 registered undergraduate students were served during 2002-03. The program or unit includes 22 full-time staff members and 1 part-time staff member. Coaches, counselors, graduate assistants/students, LD specialists, professional tutors, remediation/learning specialists, skill tutors, strategy tutors, trained peer tutors, and other are provided through the program or unit. Academic advisers and counselors are provided collaboratively through on-campus or off-campus services.

Orientation The program or unit offers a mandatory 1-day orientation for new students before registration and during summer prior to enrollment.

Unique Aids and Services Aids, services, or accommodations include advocates, parent workshops, priority registration, and support groups.

Subject-area Tutoring Tutoring is offered one-on-one, in small groups, and in class-size groups for most subjects. Tutoring is provided through the program or unit via computer-based instruction, graduate assistants/students, professional tutors, and trained peer tutors.

Enrichment Enrichment programs are available through the program or unit for career planning, college survival skills, health and nutrition, learning strategies, math, oral communication skills, reading, self-advocacy, stress management, study skills, test taking, time management, vocabulary development, and written composition skills. Programs for career planning, college survival skills, health and nutrition, learning strategies, math, medication management, oral communication skills, practical computer skills, stress management, study skills, test taking, time management, vocabulary development, and written composition skills are provided collaboratively through on-campus or off-campus services.

Fees *LD Program or Service* fee is $1600 to $3900 (fee varies according to level/tier of service). *Orientation* fee is $50 to $80.

Application For admittance to the program or unit, students are required to apply to the program directly, provide a psychoeducational report (3 years old or less), and provide a personal statement, questionnaire, and recommendations. Upon application, materials documenting need for services should be sent only to the LD program or unit. Upon acceptance, documentation of need for services should be sent only to the LD program or unit. *Application deadline (institutional):* 4/1. *Application deadline (LD program):* Rolling/continuous for fall and rolling/continuous for spring.

Written Policies Written policies regarding general/basic LD accommodations and substitutions and waivers of admissions requirements are available on the program Web site. Written policy regarding substitutions and waivers of admissions requirements is outlined in the school's catalog/handbook. Written policies regarding course substitutions, general/basic LD accommodations, reduced course loads, and substitutions and waivers of graduation requirements are available through the program or unit directly.

University of Denver
University Disability Services: Learning Effectiveness Program (LEP) and Disability Services Program (DSP)

University Park
2199 South University Park
Denver, CO 80208
http://www.du.edu/disability/

Contact: Mr. Dave Luker, Associate Director of Learning Effectiveness Program (LEP). Phone: 303-871-2372. Fax: 303-871-3939. E-mail: dluker@du.edu. Head of LD Program: Mr. Ted May, Director of University Disability Services. Phone: 303-871-2372. Fax: 303-871-3939. E-mail: tmay@du.edu.

University Disability Services: Learning Effectiveness Program (LEP) and Disability Services Program (DSP) Approximately 190 registered undergraduate students were served during 2002-03. The program or unit includes 11 full-time and 4 part-time staff members. Academic advisers, coaches, counselors, diagnostic specialists, graduate assistants/students, LD specialists, professional tutors, remediation/learning specialists, skill tutors, and strategy tutors are provided through the program or unit. Diagnostic specialists and graduate assistants/students are provided collaboratively through on-campus or off-campus services.

Orientation The program or unit offers an optional 1-day orientation for new students before registration, before classes begin, and individually by special arrangement.

Unique Aids and Services Aids, services, or accommodations include advocates, career counseling, faculty training, personal coach, priority registration, support groups, and weekly meetings with faculty.

Subject-area Tutoring Tutoring is offered one-on-one and in small groups for all subjects. Tutoring is provided through the program or unit via graduate assistants/students, LD specialists, and professional tutors. Tutoring is also provided collaboratively through on-campus or off-campus services via graduate assistants/students.

Diagnostic Testing Testing for auditory processing, intelligence, learning styles, math, neuropsychological, personality, reading, spelling, study skills, visual processing, and written language is provided collaboratively through on-campus or off-campus services.

Enrichment Enrichment programs are available through the program or unit for written composition skills. Programs for career planning, study skills, and time management are provided collaboratively through on-campus or off-campus services.

Student Organization Belay consists of 50 members.

Fees *LD Program or Service* fee is $2700. *Diagnostic Testing* fee is applicable.

Application For admittance to the program or unit, students are required to apply to the program directly and provide a psychoeducational report (3 years old or less). It is recommended that students provide documentation of high school services. Upon application, materials documenting need for services should be sent to both admissions and the LD program or unit. Upon acceptance, documentation of need for services should be sent only to the LD program or unit. *Application deadline (institutional):* 2/1. *Application deadline (LD program):* Rolling/continuous for fall and rolling/continuous for spring.

Written Policies Written policies regarding course substitutions, general/basic LD accommodations, and substitutions and waivers of graduation requirements are available on the program Web site. Written policies regarding course substitutions, general/basic LD accommodations, and substitutions and waivers of graduation requirements are available through the program or unit directly.

University of Indianapolis
Baccalaureate for University of Indianapolis Learning Disabled (BUILD)

1400 East Hanna Avenue
Indianapolis, IN 46227-3697
http://build.uindy.edu

Contact: Ms. Victoria Buzash, Associate Director. Phone: 317-788-3536. Fax: 317-788-3300. E-mail: vbuzash@uindy.edu. Head of LD Program: Ms. Deborah L. Spinney, Director. Phone: 317-788-3536. Fax: 317-788-3300. E-mail: dspinney@uindy.edu.

Baccalaureate for University of Indianapolis Learning Disabled (BUILD) Approximately 60 registered undergraduate students were served during 2002-03. The program or unit includes 2 full-time and 18 part-time staff members. Academic advisers, diagnostic specialists, graduate assistants/students, LD specialists, professional tutors, strategy tutors, and trained peer tutors are provided through the program or unit. Academic advisers, counselors, and special education teachers are provided collaboratively through on-campus or off-campus services.

Orientation The program or unit offers a mandatory 1-semester orientation for new students after classes begin.

Summer Program To help prepare for the demands of college, there is an optional 1-week summer program prior to entering the school.

Unique Aids and Services Aids, services, or accommodations include career counseling, digital textbooks, faculty training, and priority registration.

Subject-area Tutoring Tutoring is offered one-on-one and in small groups for some subjects. Tutoring is provided through the program or unit via graduate assistants/students, LD specialists, professional tutors, and trained peer tutors. Tutoring is also provided collaboratively through on-campus or off-campus services via computer-based instruction, graduate assistants/students, and trained peer tutors.

Diagnostic Testing Testing is provided through the program or unit for learning strategies, learning styles, and study skills. Testing for auditory processing, handwriting, intelligence, learning strategies, learning styles, math, motor skills, neuropsychological, personality, reading, social skills, spelling, spoken language, study skills, visual processing, written language, and other services is provided collaboratively through on-campus or off-campus services.

Basic Skills Remediation Remediation is offered in class-size groups for learning strategies, math, social skills, study skills, time management, and written language. Remediation is provided through the program or unit via graduate assistants/students, LD specialists, and regular education teachers.

Enrichment Enrichment programs are available through the program or unit for career planning, college survival skills, learning strategies, math, practical computer skills, reading, self-advocacy, stress management, study skills, test taking, time management, and written composition skills. Programs for career planning, college survival skills, health and nutrition, math, medication management, practical computer skills, reading, self-advocacy, stress management, and written composition skills are provided collaboratively through on-campus or off-campus services. Credit is offered for college survival skills, math, study skills, and written composition skills.

Fees *LD Program or Service* fee is $3900. *Summer Program* fee is $250. *Diagnostic Testing* fee is applicable.

Application For admittance to the program or unit, students are required to apply to the program directly and provide a psychoeducational report (3 years old or less). Upon application, materials documenting need for services should be sent only to the LD program or unit. *Application deadline (institutional):* Continuous. *Application deadline (LD program):* Rolling/continuous for fall and rolling/continuous for spring.

Written Policies Written policies regarding course substitutions, general/basic LD accommodations, grade forgiveness, and reduced course loads are available on the program Web site. Written policies regarding course substitutions, general/basic LD accommodations, grade forgiveness, and reduced course loads are outlined in the school's catalog/handbook. Written policies regarding course substitutions, general/basic LD accommodations, grade forgiveness, and reduced course loads are available through the program or unit directly.

The University of North Carolina at Chapel Hill
Learning Disabilities Services

Chapel Hill, NC 27599

http://www.unc.edu/depts/lds

Contact: Jane Byron, Director. Phone: 919-962-7227. Fax: 919-962-3674. E-mail: lds@unc.edu.

Learning Disabilities Services Approximately 260 registered undergraduate students were served during 2002-03. The program or unit includes 4 full-time and 2 part-time staff members. Academic advisers, coaches, LD specialists, special education teachers, strategy tutors, and other are provided through the program or unit. Academic advisers, coaches, counselors, diagnostic specialists, graduate assistants/students, professional tutors, remediation/learning specialists, and skill tutors are provided collaboratively through on-campus or off-campus services.

Unique Aids and Services Aids, services, or accommodations include personal coach, priority registration, individual meetings with LD specialists.

Subject-area Tutoring Tutoring is offered one-on-one and in small groups for all subjects. Tutoring is provided collaboratively through on-campus or off-campus services via graduate assistants/students, professional tutors, and trained peer tutors.

Basic Skills Remediation Remediation is available for learning strategies, math, reading, study skills, time management, and written language. Remediation is provided through the program or unit via LD specialists. Remediation is also provided collaboratively through on-campus or off-campus services via regular education teachers.

Enrichment Enrichment programs are available through the program or unit for college survival skills, learning strategies, medication management, self-advocacy, stress management, study skills, test taking, time management, written composition skills, and other. Programs for career planning, college survival skills, health and nutrition, math, oral communication skills, practical computer skills, reading, stress management, study skills, test taking, time management, vocabulary development, written composition skills, and other are provided collaboratively through on-campus or off-campus services.

Application For admittance to the program or unit, students are required to apply to the program directly, provide a psychoeducational report (3 years old or less), and provide evaluation of attention and co-morbid issues (for ADHD) . It is recommended that students provide documentation of high school services. Upon application, materials documenting need for services should be sent only to admissions with institutional application materials. Upon acceptance, documentation of need for services should be sent only to the LD program or unit. *Application deadline (institutional):* 1/15. *Application deadline (LD program):* Rolling/continuous for fall and rolling/continuous for spring.

Written Policies Written policy regarding general/basic LD accommodations is available through the program or unit directly.

University of North Texas

PO Box 311277

Denton, TX 76203

http://www.unt.edu/

Contact: Mr. James Renfro III, Interim Director of Office of Disability Accommodation. Phone: 940-565-4323. Fax: 940-565-4990. E-mail: jimmy@unt.edu.

Approximately 250 registered undergraduate students were served during 2002-03. The program or unit includes 4 full-time staff members. Counselors are provided through the program or unit. Skill tutors, strategy tutors, and trained peer tutors are provided collaboratively through on-campus or off-campus services.

Unique Aids and Services Aids, services, or accommodations include digital textbooks, faculty training, priority registration, testing accommodations, classroom note-takers.

Subject-area Tutoring Tutoring is offered one-on-one, in small groups, and in class-size groups for most subjects. Tutoring is provided collaboratively through on-campus or off-campus services via computer-based instruction, graduate assistants/students, and trained peer tutors.

Diagnostic Testing Testing for auditory processing, handwriting, intelligence, learning strategies, learning styles, math, motor skills, personality, reading, social skills, spelling, spoken language, study skills, and written language is provided collaboratively through on-campus or off-campus services.

Basic Skills Remediation Remediation is offered one-on-one, in small groups, and in class-size groups for learning strategies, math, study skills, and time management. Remediation is provided collaboratively through on-campus or off-campus services via computer-based instruction, graduate assistants/students, and trained peer tutors.

Enrichment Programs for college survival skills, learning strategies, math, reading, and study skills are provided collaboratively through on-campus or off-campus services.

University of North Texas (continued)

Fees *Diagnostic Testing* fee is $50 to $300.

Application For admittance to the program or unit, students are required to provide a psychoeducational report. It is recommended that students provide documentation of high school services. Upon application, materials documenting need for services should be sent only to the LD program or unit. Upon acceptance, documentation of need for services should be sent only to the LD program or unit. *Application deadline (institutional):* 6/15. *Application deadline (LD program):* Rolling/continuous for fall and rolling/continuous for spring.

Written Policies Written policies regarding course substitutions, general/basic LD accommodations, reduced course loads, substitutions and waivers of admissions requirements, and substitutions and waivers of graduation requirements are available on the program Web site. Written policy regarding general/basic LD accommodations is available through the program or unit directly.

The University of Tennessee at Chattanooga
College Access Program

615 McCallie Avenue
Chattanooga, TN 37403-2598
http://www.utc.edu/~utccap

Contact: Brenda Boyd, Learning Specialist. Phone: 423-425-5251. Fax: 423-425-4006. E-mail: brenda-boyd@utc.edu. Head of LD Program: Mrs. Debra Anderson, Director. Phone: 423-425-4006. Fax: 423-425-2288. E-mail: debra-anderson@utc.edu.

College Access Program Approximately 60 registered undergraduate students were served during 2002-03. The program or unit includes 3 full-time and 5 part-time staff members. LD specialists, professional tutors, and trained peer tutors are provided through the program or unit.

Orientation The program or unit offers an optional orientation for new students after classes begin and individually by special arrangement.

Unique Aids and Services Aids, services, or accommodations include career counseling, faculty training, study strategies classes.

Subject-area Tutoring Tutoring is offered one-on-one for all subjects. Tutoring is provided through the program or unit via computer-based instruction, LD specialists, professional tutors, and trained peer tutors. Tutoring is also provided collaboratively through on-campus or off-campus services via computer-based instruction, graduate assistants/students, and trained peer tutors.

Diagnostic Testing Testing is provided through the program or unit for learning strategies, learning styles, math, reading, spelling, study skills, and written language. Testing for learning strategies, learning styles, math, personality, and social skills is provided collaboratively through on-campus or off-campus services.

Enrichment Enrichment programs are available through the program or unit for college survival skills, learning strategies, math, practical computer skills, reading, self-advocacy, stress management, study skills, test taking, time management, and written com-

position skills. Programs for career planning, college survival skills, health and nutrition, math, and written composition skills are provided collaboratively through on-campus or off-campus services.

Fees *LD Program or Service* fee is $750.

Application For admittance to the program or unit, students are required to apply to the program directly and provide transcript, ACT/SAT scores, questionnaire, and recommendation. It is recommended that students provide documentation of high school services. Upon application, materials documenting need for services should be sent only to the LD program or unit. *Application deadline (institutional):* Continuous. *Application deadline (LD program):* Rolling/continuous for fall and rolling/continuous for spring.

Written Policies Written policy regarding general/basic LD accommodations is available on the program Web site. Written policy regarding general/basic LD accommodations is outlined in the school's catalog/handbook. Written policies regarding course substitutions, general/basic LD accommodations, and reduced course loads are available through the program or unit directly.

University of the Ozarks
Jones Learning Center

415 North College Avenue
Clarksville, AR 72830-2880
http://www.ozarks.edu/campusservices/jlc/index.html

Contact: Ms. Julia H. Frost, Director. Phone: 479-979-1403. Fax: 479-979-1429. E-mail: jlc@ozarks.edu.

Jones Learning Center Approximately 65 registered undergraduate students were served during 2002-03. The program or unit includes 19 full-time staff members and 1 part-time staff member. Academic advisers, diagnostic specialists, LD specialists, professional tutors, remediation/learning specialists, and trained peer tutors are provided through the program or unit. Academic advisers are provided collaboratively through on-campus or off-campus services.

Orientation The program or unit offers a mandatory 3-day orientation for new students before classes begin and during summer prior to enrollment.

Unique Aids and Services Aids, services, or accommodations include a program coordinator assigned to each student.

Subject-area Tutoring Tutoring is offered one-on-one and in small groups for all subjects. Tutoring is provided through the program or unit via LD specialists, professional tutors, and trained peer tutors.

Diagnostic Testing Testing is provided through the program or unit for auditory processing, intelligence, learning styles, math, reading, spelling, study skills, visual processing, and written language.

Basic Skills Remediation Remediation is offered one-on-one and in small groups for learning strategies, math, reading, study skills, time management, and written language. Remediation is provided through the program or unit via LD specialists and professional tutors.

Enrichment Enrichment programs are available through the program or unit for college survival skills, math, reading, self-advocacy, stress management, study skills, test taking, time management, and written composition skills. Programs for career planning and practical computer skills are provided collaboratively through on-campus or off-campus services. Credit is offered for career planning.

Student Organization Learning Center Ambassadors consists of 12 members.

Fees *Orientation* fee is $30 to $50. *Diagnostic Testing* fee is $450 to $750.

Application For admittance to the program or unit, students are required to apply to the program directly, provide a psychoeducational report (5 years old or less), and provide results of on-campus psychoeducational evaluation. It is recommended that students provide documentation of high school services. Upon application, materials documenting need for services should be sent only to the LD program or unit. *Application deadline (institutional):* Continuous. *Application deadline (LD program):* Rolling/continuous for fall and rolling/continuous for spring.

Written Policies Written policies regarding general/basic LD accommodations and substitutions and waivers of admissions requirements are available on the program Web site. Written policies regarding general/basic LD accommodations and substitutions and waivers of admissions requirements are outlined in the school's catalog/handbook. Written policies regarding course substitutions, reduced course loads, and substitutions and waivers of admissions requirements are available through the program or unit directly.

University of Wisconsin-Oshkosh

800 Algoma Boulevard

Oshkosh, WI 54901

http://www.uwosh.edu/

Contact: Dr. William R. Kitz, Director. Phone: 920-424-1033. Fax: 920-424-0858. E-mail: kitz@uwosh.edu.

Approximately 200 registered undergraduate students were served during 2002-03. The program or unit includes 3 full-time and 50 part-time staff members. Diagnostic specialists, graduate assistants/ students, LD specialists, remediation/learning specialists, skill tutors, special education teachers, strategy tutors, teacher trainees, and trained peer tutors are provided through the program or unit. Academic advisers, counselors, remediation/learning specialists, skill tutors, strategy tutors, teacher trainees, and trained peer tutors are provided collaboratively through on-campus or off-campus services.

Orientation The program or unit offers a mandatory 1-day orientation for new students before registration, before classes begin, and during summer prior to enrollment.

Summer Program To help prepare for the demands of college, there is a mandatory 6-week summer program prior to entering the school. Degree credit will be earned.

Unique Aids and Services Aids, services, or accommodations include advocates and digital textbooks.

Subject-area Tutoring Tutoring is offered one-on-one and in small groups for most subjects. Tutoring is provided through the program or unit via computer-based instruction, graduate assistants/ students, LD specialists, professional tutors, and trained peer tutors. Tutoring is also provided collaboratively through on-campus or off-campus services via computer-based instruction.

Diagnostic Testing Testing is provided through the program or unit for math, reading, spelling, spoken language, and written language.

Basic Skills Remediation Remediation is offered one-on-one, in small groups, and in class-size groups for computer skills, handwriting, learning strategies, math, reading, spelling, study skills, time management, and written language. Remediation is provided through the program or unit via computer-based instruction, graduate assistants/students, LD specialists, professional tutors, regular education teachers, special education teachers, teacher trainees, and trained peer tutors. Remediation is also provided collaboratively through on-campus or off-campus services via computer-based instruction.

Enrichment Enrichment programs are available through the program or unit for college survival skills, learning strategies, math, oral communication skills, practical computer skills, reading, self-advocacy, study skills, test taking, time management, vocabulary development, and written composition skills. Programs for career planning, college survival skills, health and nutrition, math, oral communication skills, practical computer skills, reading, stress management, study skills, test taking, time management, vocabulary development, and written composition skills are provided collaboratively through on-campus or off-campus services. Credit is offered for college survival skills, math, practical computer skills, reading, study skills, and written composition skills.

Student Organization No Limits consists of 30 members.

Application For admittance to the program or unit, students are required to apply to the program directly, provide a psychoeducational report (3 years old or less), and provide documentation of high school services. Upon application, materials documenting need for services should be sent only to the LD program or unit. Upon acceptance, documentation of need for services should be sent only to the LD program or unit. *Application deadline (institutional):* 8/1. *Application deadline (LD program):* Rolling/continuous for fall and rolling/continuous for spring.

Written Policies Written policies regarding course substitutions, general/basic LD accommodations, grade forgiveness, reduced course loads, substitutions and waivers of admissions requirements, and substitutions and waivers of graduation requirements are available through the program or unit directly.

Ursuline College
PSLD Program

2550 Lander Road

Pepper Pike, OH 44124-4398

http://www.ursuline.edu/

Contact: Ms. Annette Gromada, Learning Disabilities Specialist. Phone: 440-449-2046. E-mail: agromada@ursuline.edu.

PSLD Program Approximately 12 registered undergraduate students were served during 2002-03. The program or unit includes 2 full-time and 5 part-time staff members. Academic advisers, coaches, counselors, LD specialists, professional tutors, regular education teachers, and remediation/learning specialists are provided through the program or unit.

Orientation The program or unit offers a mandatory orientation for new students before classes begin, during registration, after classes begin, and individually by special arrangement.

Ursuline College (continued)

Unique Aids and Services Aids, services, or accommodations include career counseling, faculty training, parent workshops, personal coach, priority registration, support groups, weekly meetings with faculty, testing accommodations, computer programs, and separate computer lab.

Subject-area Tutoring Tutoring is offered one-on-one, in small groups, and in class-size groups for some subjects. Tutoring is provided through the program or unit via LD specialists and professional tutors. Tutoring is also provided collaboratively through on-campus or off-campus services via computer-based instruction, graduate assistants/students, and professional tutors.

Diagnostic Testing Testing is provided through the program or unit for learning strategies, learning styles, math, reading, study skills, and written language. Testing for auditory processing, intelligence, motor skills, neuropsychological, personality, social skills, and visual processing is provided collaboratively through on-campus or off-campus services.

Basic Skills Remediation Remediation is offered one-on-one, in small groups, and in class-size groups for learning strategies, math, reading, spoken language, study skills, time management, visual processing, and written language. Remediation is provided through the program or unit via LD specialists and professional tutors. Remediation is also provided collaboratively through on-campus or off-campus services via computer-based instruction, professional tutors, and regular education teachers.

Enrichment Enrichment programs are available through the program or unit for college survival skills, learning strategies, medication management, oral communication skills, self-advocacy, stress management, study skills, test taking, time management, and written composition skills. Programs for career planning, college survival skills, health and nutrition, learning strategies, math, reading, stress management, study skills, test taking, time management, vocabulary development, and written composition skills are provided collaboratively through on-campus or off-campus services.

Student Organization PSLD consists of 12 members.

Fees *LD Program or Service* fee is $1350. *Diagnostic Testing* fee is $0 to $500.

Application For admittance to the program or unit, students are required to apply to the program directly and provide a psychoeducational report (3 years old or less). It is recommended that students provide documentation of high school services. Upon application, materials documenting need for services should be sent only to the LD program or unit. *Application deadline (institutional):* Continuous. *Application deadline (LD program):* Rolling/continuous for fall and rolling/continuous for spring.

Written Policies Written policy regarding general/basic LD accommodations is outlined in the school's catalog/handbook. Written policy regarding general/basic LD accommodations is available through the program or unit directly.

Westminster College

501 Westminster Avenue
Fulton, MO 65251-1299
http://www.westminster-mo.edu/

Contact: Hank Ottinger, Director of Learning Disabilities Program. Phone: 573-592-5304. Fax: 573-592-5180. E-mail: ottingh@jaynet.wcmo.edu.

Approximately 48 registered undergraduate students were served during 2002-03. The program or unit includes 2 full-time staff members and 1 part-time staff member. Coaches, diagnostic specialists, LD specialists, professional tutors, remediation/learning specialists, skill tutors, strategy tutors, and trained peer tutors are provided through the program or unit. Academic advisers and counselors are provided collaboratively through on-campus or off-campus services.

Unique Aids and Services Aids, services, or accommodations include advocates, digital textbooks, and weekly meetings with faculty.

Subject-area Tutoring Tutoring is offered one-on-one and in small groups. Tutoring is provided through the program or unit via LD specialists and professional tutors. Tutoring is also provided collaboratively through on-campus or off-campus services via computer-based instruction.

Enrichment Enrichment programs are available through the program or unit for college survival skills, learning strategies, math, reading, study skills, test taking, time management, vocabulary development, and written composition skills. Programs for career planning, math, and stress management are provided collaboratively through on-campus or off-campus services. Credit is offered for career planning and college survival skills.

Fees *LD Program or Service* fee is $900 to $1800 (fee varies according to level/tier of service).

Application For admittance to the program or unit, students are required to apply to the program directly, provide a psychoeducational report (2 years old or less), and provide documentation of high school services. Upon application, materials documenting need for services should be sent only to admissions with institutional application materials. Upon acceptance, documentation of need for services should be sent only to admissions. *Application deadline (institutional):* Continuous. *Application deadline (LD program):* Rolling/continuous for fall and rolling/continuous for spring.

Written Policies Written policies regarding general/basic LD accommodations and reduced course loads are available on the program Web site. Written policies regarding general/basic LD accommodations and reduced course loads are available through the program or unit directly.

West Virginia Wesleyan College
Student Academic Support Services

59 College Avenue
Buckhannon, WV 26201
http://www.wvwc.edu/stu/sass

Contact: Ms. Shawn Mahoney Kuba, Director of Student Academic Support Services. Phone: 304-473-8563. Fax: 304-473-8497. E-mail: kuba_s@wvwc.edu.

Student Academic Support Services Approximately 95 registered undergraduate students were served during 2002-03. The program or unit includes 6 full-time and 7 part-time staff members. Academic advisers, counselors, diagnostic specialists, professional tutors, remediation/learning specialists, skill tutors, strategy tutors, and trained peer tutors are provided through the program or unit. Academic advisers and counselors are provided collaboratively through on-campus or off-campus services.

Orientation The program or unit offers a mandatory orientation for new students before registration and during the first day of first year orientation.

Unique Aids and Services Aids, services, or accommodations include faculty training, parent workshops, priority registration, weekly conferencing with LD adviser, assistive technology lab, LBP read program, test lab.

Subject-area Tutoring Tutoring is offered one-on-one and in small groups for most subjects. Tutoring is provided through the program or unit via computer-based instruction and trained peer tutors.

Basic Skills Remediation Remediation is offered one-on-one for auditory processing, learning strategies, reading, social skills, spelling, spoken language, study skills, time management, visual processing, written language, and Lindamood-Bell(tm) Learning Program. Remediation is provided through the program or unit via professional tutors, regular education teachers, and special education teachers.

Enrichment Enrichment programs are available through the program or unit for college survival skills, learning strategies, medication management, reading, self-advocacy, stress management, study skills, test taking, time management, vocabulary development, and written composition skills. Programs for career planning, college survival skills, health and nutrition, math, medication management, oral communication skills, practical computer skills, and stress management are provided collaboratively through on-campus or off-campus services. Credit is offered for career planning, college survival skills, health and nutrition, learning strategies, oral communication skills, practical computer skills, and study skills.

Fees *LD Program or Service* fee is $0 to $2400 (fee varies according to course level and level/tier of service).

Application For admittance to the program or unit, students are required to provide a psychoeducational report (2 years old or less). It is recommended that students provide documentation of high school services and provide recommendation of services and accommodations that will be helpful to student success. Upon acceptance, documentation of need for services should be sent only to the LD program or unit. *Application deadline (institutional):* 8/1. *Application deadline (LD program):* Rolling/continuous for fall and rolling/continuous for spring.

Written Policies Written policy regarding general/basic LD accommodations is available on the program Web site. Written policy regarding general/basic LD accommodations is available through the program or unit directly.

Four-Year Colleges

WITH SELF-DIRECTED/DECENTRALIZED PROGRAMS

Abilene Christian University

ACU Box 29100
Abilene, TX 79699-9100
http://www.acu.edu/

Contact: Dr. Gloria J. Bradshaw, Director of Alpha Academic Services. Phone: 325-674-2750. Fax: 325-674-6847. E-mail: bradshawg@acu.edu.

Approximately 105 registered undergraduate students were served during 2002-03. The program or unit includes 2 full-time staff members. Professional tutors and strategy tutors are provided through the program or unit. Academic advisers, counselors, diagnostic specialists, regular education teachers, skill tutors, and trained peer tutors are provided collaboratively through on-campus or off-campus services.

Orientation The program or unit offers a mandatory 2-hour orientation for new students after classes begin.

Subject-area Tutoring Tutoring is offered one-on-one and in small groups. Tutoring is provided through the program or unit via professional tutors and trained peer tutors. Tutoring is also provided collaboratively through on-campus or off-campus services via graduate assistants/students and trained peer tutors.

Diagnostic Testing Testing is provided through the program or unit for learning strategies and learning styles. Testing for intelligence, math, personality, reading, social skills, spelling, spoken language, visual processing, and written language is provided collaboratively through on-campus or off-campus services.

Basic Skills Remediation Remediation is offered in class-size groups for math, reading, study skills, time management, and written language. Remediation is provided collaboratively through on-campus or off-campus services via regular education teachers.

Enrichment Enrichment programs are available through the program or unit for learning strategies, stress management, study skills, test taking, time management, vocabulary development, and written composition skills. Programs for career planning, health and nutrition, stress management, study skills, test taking, time management, vocabulary development, and written composition skills are provided collaboratively through on-campus or off-campus services.

Fees *Diagnostic Testing* fee is $200.

Application For admittance to the program or unit, students are required to apply to the program directly and provide a psychoeducational report. It is recommended that students provide documentation of high school services. Upon application, materials documenting need for services should be sent only to admissions with institutional application materials. Upon acceptance, documentation of need for services should be sent only to the LD program or unit. *Application deadline (institutional):* 8/1. *Application deadline (LD program):* 8/1 for fall. 12/1 for spring.

Written Policies Written policy regarding general/basic LD accommodations is available through the program or unit directly.

Adrian College
Academic Services

110 South Madison Street
Adrian, MI 49221-2575

http://www.adrian.edu/

Contact: Mrs. Carol Tapp, Support Services Specialist. Phone: 517-265-5161 Ext. 4094. Fax: 517-264-3181. E-mail: ctapp@adrian.edu. Head of LD Program: Mrs. Jane McCloskey, Director of Academic Services. Phone: 517-265-5161 Ext. 4093. Fax: 517-264-3181. E-mail: jmccloskey@adrian.edu.

Academic Services Approximately 40 registered undergraduate students were served during 2002-03. The program or unit includes 4 full-time staff members and 1 part-time staff member. Academic advisers, LD specialists, remediation/learning specialists, skill tutors, strategy tutors, and trained peer tutors are provided through the program or unit. Academic advisers, coaches, counselors, and diagnostic specialists are provided collaboratively through on-campus or off-campus services.

Summer Program To help prepare for the demands of college, there is an optional 4-week summer program prior to entering the school. Degree credit will be earned.

Unique Aids and Services Aids, services, or accommodations include career counseling and faculty training.

Subject-area Tutoring Tutoring is offered one-on-one, in small groups, and in class-size groups for most subjects. Tutoring is provided through the program or unit via trained peer tutors.

Diagnostic Testing Testing is provided through the program or unit for learning styles, reading, and study skills. Testing for auditory processing, intelligence, math, and visual processing is provided collaboratively through on-campus or off-campus services.

Basic Skills Remediation Remediation is offered in class-size groups for learning strategies, math, reading, study skills, and time management. Remediation is provided through the program or unit via LD specialists and regular education teachers.

Enrichment Enrichment programs are available through the program or unit for college survival skills, learning strategies, reading, study skills, test taking, time management, and vocabulary development. Programs for career planning, math, and written composition skills are provided collaboratively through on-campus or off-campus services. Credit is offered for math, reading, and study skills.

Application For admittance to the program or unit, students are required to apply to the program directly and provide a psychoeducational report. It is recommended that students provide documentation of high school services. Upon application, materials documenting need for services should be sent only to admissions with institutional application materials. Upon acceptance, documentation of need for services should be sent only to the LD program or unit. *Application deadline (institutional):* 8/1. *Application deadline (LD program):* Rolling/continuous for fall and rolling/continuous for spring.

Written Policies Written policy regarding general/basic LD accommodations is available on the program Web site. Written policy regarding general/basic LD accommodations is available through the program or unit directly.

Alabama State University
Disabled Student Services, University Counseling Center

915 South Jackson Street
Montgomery, AL 36101-0271

Alabama State University (continued)
http://www.alasu.edu/
Contact: Mrs. Ashaki Nicole Means, Counselor and Coordinator of Groups. Phone: 334-229-4382 Ext. 4482. Fax: 334-229-6924. E-mail: ameans@asunet.alasu.edu. Head of LD Program: Mrs. Jessyca McCall Darrington, Director of Counseling Services. Phone: 334-229-4382 Ext. 4894. Fax: 334-229-6924. E-mail: jdarrington@asunet.alasu.edu.

Disabled Student Services, University Counseling Center
Approximately 60 registered undergraduate students were served during 2002-03. The program or unit includes 2 full-time staff members. Counselors and graduate assistants/students are provided through the program or unit. Academic advisers, diagnostic specialists, LD specialists, regular education teachers, skill tutors, and other are provided collaboratively through on-campus or off-campus services.
Unique Aids and Services Aids, services, or accommodations include career counseling, priority registration, and support groups.
Subject-area Tutoring Tutoring is offered one-on-one for most subjects. Tutoring is provided collaboratively through on-campus or off-campus services via computer-based instruction, graduate assistants/students, LD specialists, and other.
Basic Skills Remediation Remediation is offered in class-size groups for computer skills, math, reading, spelling, study skills, time management, and written language. Remediation is provided collaboratively through on-campus or off-campus services via regular education teachers.
Enrichment Enrichment programs are available through the program or unit for college survival skills, learning strategies, self-advocacy, stress management, study skills, test taking, and time management. Programs for career planning, college survival skills, health and nutrition, medication management, oral communication skills, practical computer skills, reading, time management, and written composition skills are provided collaboratively through on-campus or off-campus services. Credit is offered for health and nutrition, oral communication skills, practical computer skills, reading, study skills, and written composition skills.
Application For admittance to the program or unit, students are required to provide documentation of high school services. It is recommended that students provide a psychoeducational report (3 years old or less). Upon acceptance, documentation of need for services should be sent only to the LD program or unit. *Application deadline (institutional):* 7/30. *Application deadline (LD program):* Rolling/continuous for fall and rolling/continuous for spring.
Written Policies Written policy regarding general/basic LD accommodations is outlined in the school's catalog/handbook. Written policies regarding grade forgiveness and reduced course loads are available through the program or unit directly.

Alberta College of Art & Design
Services for Students with Disabilities

1407 14 Avenue NW
Calgary, AB T2N 4R3
Canada

http://www.acad.ab.ca/
Contact: Mr. Paul Roberge, Counsellor. Phone: 403-284-7666. Fax: 403-284-7636. E-mail: paul.roberge@acad.ca.

Services for Students with Disabilities Approximately 40 registered undergraduate students were served during 2002-03. The program or unit includes 1 full-time staff member. Academic advisers, coaches, counselors, and trained peer tutors are provided through the program or unit. Counselors, diagnostic specialists, LD specialists, professional tutors, remediation/learning specialists, skill tutors, and strategy tutors are provided collaboratively through on-campus or off-campus services.
Unique Aids and Services Aids, services, or accommodations include advocates, career counseling, and faculty training.
Subject-area Tutoring Tutoring is offered one-on-one for some subjects. Tutoring is provided through the program or unit via trained peer tutors. Tutoring is also provided collaboratively through on-campus or off-campus services via LD specialists and professional tutors.
Diagnostic Testing Testing for auditory processing, handwriting, intelligence, learning strategies, learning styles, math, motor skills, neuropsychological, reading, social skills, spelling, spoken language, study skills, visual processing, written language, and other services is provided collaboratively through on-campus or off-campus services.
Basic Skills Remediation Remediation is offered one-on-one for auditory processing, computer skills, handwriting, learning strategies, math, motor skills, reading, spelling, spoken language, study skills, time management, visual processing, and written language. Remediation is provided collaboratively through on-campus or off-campus services via LD specialists and professional tutors.
Enrichment Enrichment programs are available through the program or unit for reading, self-advocacy, stress management, time management, and written composition skills. Programs for career planning, college survival skills, health and nutrition, learning strategies, practical computer skills, reading, study skills, test taking, time management, and written composition skills are provided collaboratively through on-campus or off-campus services.
Fees *Diagnostic Testing* fee is $1500 to $2000.
Application For admittance to the program or unit, students are required to provide a psychoeducational report (2 years old or less). It is recommended that students provide documentation of high school services. Upon application, materials documenting need for services should be sent only to the LD program or unit. Upon acceptance, documentation of need for services should be sent only to the LD program or unit. *Application deadline (institutional):* 4/1. *Application deadline (LD program):* Rolling/continuous for fall and rolling/continuous for spring.

Albertson College of Idaho

2112 Cleveland Boulevard
Caldwell, ID 83605-4494
http://www.albertson.edu/
Contact: Phone: 208-459-5011. Fax: 208-454-2077.

The program or unit includes 1 full-time and 1 part-time staff member. Remediation/learning specialists are provided through the program or unit. Academic advisers, coaches, counselors, and remediation/learning specialists are provided collaboratively through on-campus or off-campus services.

Unique Aids and Services Aids, services, or accommodations include career counseling.

Subject-area Tutoring Tutoring is offered one-on-one and in small groups for some subjects. Tutoring is provided collaboratively through on-campus or off-campus services via graduate assistants/students.

Basic Skills Remediation Remediation is offered one-on-one for computer skills, learning strategies, math, reading, study skills, time management, and written language. Remediation is provided collaboratively through on-campus or off-campus services.

Application For admittance to the program or unit, students are required to provide a psychoeducational report (3 years old or less). It is recommended that students apply to the program directly and provide documentation of high school services. Upon application, materials documenting need for services should be sent only to the LD program or unit. Upon acceptance, documentation of need for services should be sent to both admissions and the LD program or unit. *Application deadline (institutional): 6/1. Application deadline (LD program):* Rolling/continuous for fall and rolling/continuous for spring.

Written Policies Written policies regarding general/basic LD accommodations and reduced course loads are available on the program Web site. Written policies regarding general/basic LD accommodations and reduced course loads are outlined in the school's catalog/handbook.

Albion College
Learning Support Center

611 East Porter Street
Albion, MI 49224-1831
http://www.albion/asc/lsc/disabilities.asp
Contact: Dr. Pamela Schwartz, Learning Support Specialist and Academic Assistant Director. Phone: 517-629-0825. Fax: 517-629-0509. E-mail: pschwartz@albion.edu.

Learning Support Center Approximately 75 registered undergraduate students were served during 2002-03. The program or unit includes 1 full-time and 3 part-time staff members. Coaches, LD specialists, remediation/learning specialists, and strategy tutors are provided through the program or unit. Academic advisers, counselors, diagnostic specialists, graduate assistants/students, skill tutors, and trained peer tutors are provided collaboratively through on-campus or off-campus services.

Orientation The program or unit offers a mandatory 1 to 2-hour orientation for new students individually by special arrangement.

Unique Aids and Services Aids, services, or accommodations include personal coach.

Subject-area Tutoring Tutoring is offered one-on-one and in small groups for all subjects. Tutoring is provided through the program or unit via LD specialists. Tutoring is also provided collaboratively through on-campus or off-campus services via trained peer tutors.

Diagnostic Testing Testing is provided through the program or unit for learning strategies, learning styles, math, and study skills.

Application For admittance to the program or unit, students are required to provide a psychoeducational report (5 years old or less). It is recommended that students provide documentation of high school services. Upon acceptance, documentation of need for services should be sent to both admissions and the LD program or unit. *Application deadline (institutional): 3/1. Application deadline (LD program):* Rolling/continuous for fall and rolling/continuous for spring.

Written Policies Written policies regarding general/basic LD accommodations and reduced course loads are available on the program Web site. Written policy regarding general/basic LD accommodations is available through the program or unit directly.

Albright College
Academic Support Services

13th and Bern Sreets, PO Box 15234
Reading, PA 19612-5234
http://www.albright.edu/
Contact: Dr. Tiffenia D. Archie, Assistant Academic Dean and Director of Academic Support. Phone: 610-921-7662. Fax: 610-921-7554. E-mail: tarchie@alb.edu.

Academic Support Services Approximately 22 registered undergraduate students were served during 2002-03. The program or unit includes 1 full-time staff member. Academic advisers and LD specialists are provided through the program or unit. Academic advisers and trained peer tutors are provided collaboratively through on-campus or off-campus services.

Unique Aids and Services Aids, services, or accommodations include advocates, career counseling, priority registration, support groups, extended time, notes.

Application For admittance to the program or unit, students are required to provide a psychoeducational report (3 years old or less). It is recommended that students provide documentation of high school services. Upon application, materials documenting need for services should be sent to both admissions and the LD program or unit. *Application deadline (institutional):* Continuous. *Application deadline (LD program):* Rolling/continuous for fall and rolling/continuous for spring.

Written Policies Written policy regarding general/basic LD accommodations is outlined in the school's catalog/handbook. Written policies regarding course substitutions, general/basic LD accommodations, reduced course loads, and substitutions and waivers of graduation requirements are available through the program or unit directly.

Alma College

614 West Superior Street
Alma, MI 48801-1599
http://www.alma.edu/
Contact: Ms. Janet Louise Tissue. Phone: 989-463-7225. Fax: 989-463-7353. E-mail: tissue@alma.edu.

Alma College (continued)

Approximately 75 registered undergraduate students were served during 2002-03.

Unique Aids and Services Aids, services, or accommodations include career counseling.

Subject-area Tutoring Tutoring is offered one-on-one and in small groups for most subjects. Tutoring is provided through the program or unit via trained peer tutors.

Diagnostic Testing Testing is provided through the program or unit for learning styles, math, personality, and study skills. Testing for auditory processing, handwriting, intelligence, learning strategies, motor skills, neuropsychological, reading, social skills, spelling, spoken language, visual processing, and written language is provided collaboratively through on-campus or off-campus services.

Basic Skills Remediation Remediation is available for learning strategies, math, reading, study skills, time management, and written language.

Enrichment Programs for career planning, college survival skills, learning strategies, math, medication management, reading, stress management, study skills, test taking, time management, and written composition skills are provided collaboratively through on-campus or off-campus services.

Application For admittance to the program or unit, students are required to provide a psychoeducational report (5 years old or less) and provide documentation of high school services. Upon acceptance, documentation of need for services should be sent only to the LD program or unit. *Application deadline (institutional):* Continuous. *Application deadline (LD program):* Rolling/continuous for fall and rolling/continuous for spring.

Written Policies Written policy regarding general/basic LD accommodations is available on the program Web site. Written policy regarding general/basic LD accommodations is outlined in the school's catalog/handbook.

Alverno College
Disability Services

3400 South 43rd Street, PO Box 343922

Milwaukee, WI 53234-3922

http://www.alverno.edu/

Contact: Colleen Barnett, Coordinator for Disability Services. Phone: 414-382-6026. Fax: 414-382-6354. E-mail: colleen.barnett@alverno.edu.

Disability Services Approximately 75 registered undergraduate students were served during 2002-03. The program or unit includes 1 full-time staff member. LD specialists are provided through the program or unit. Academic advisers, coaches, counselors, diagnostic specialists, professional tutors, regular education teachers, skill tutors, strategy tutors, and trained peer tutors are provided collaboratively through on-campus or off-campus services.

Unique Aids and Services Aids, services, or accommodations include career counseling and digital textbooks.

Subject-area Tutoring Tutoring is offered one-on-one and in small groups for some subjects. Tutoring is provided collaboratively through on-campus or off-campus services via professional tutors and trained peer tutors.

Diagnostic Testing Testing for auditory processing, intelligence, learning styles, math, neuropsychological, reading, spelling, spoken language, visual processing, and written language is provided collaboratively through on-campus or off-campus services.

Basic Skills Remediation Remediation is offered one-on-one for learning strategies, math, reading, study skills, time management, and written language. Remediation is provided collaboratively through on-campus or off-campus services via LD specialists, professional tutors, and trained peer tutors.

Enrichment Programs for career planning, college survival skills, learning strategies, math, oral communication skills, practical computer skills, reading, self-advocacy, stress management, study skills, test taking, time management, vocabulary development, and written composition skills are provided collaboratively through on-campus or off-campus services.

Application For admittance to the program or unit, students are required to provide a psychoeducational report (3 years old or less). It is recommended that students provide documentation of high school services. Upon application, materials documenting need for services should be sent only to the LD program or unit. Upon acceptance, documentation of need for services should be sent only to the LD program or unit. *Application deadline (institutional):* Continuous. *Application deadline (LD program):* Rolling/continuous for fall and rolling/continuous for spring.

Written Policies Written policies regarding course substitutions, general/basic LD accommodations, and substitutions and waivers of admissions requirements are available through the program or unit directly.

Amherst College

PO Box 5000

Amherst, MA 01002-5000

http://www.amherst.edu/

Contact: Frances Tuleja, Associate Dean of Students. Phone: 413-542-2529.

Approximately 11 registered undergraduate students were served during 2002-03. The program or unit includes 1 part-time staff member. Academic advisers, counselors, and trained peer tutors are provided collaboratively through on-campus or off-campus services.

Subject-area Tutoring Tutoring is offered one-on-one for some subjects. Tutoring is provided collaboratively through on-campus or off-campus services via trained peer tutors.

Application For admittance to the program or unit, students are required to provide documentation of high school services. Upon acceptance, documentation of need for services should be sent only to the LD program or unit. *Application deadline (institutional):* 12/31. *Application deadline (LD program):* Rolling/continuous for fall and rolling/continuous for spring.

Written Policies Written policy regarding general/basic LD accommodations is available through the program or unit directly.

Anderson University

1100 East Fifth Street

Anderson, IN 46012-3495

http://www.anderson.edu/

Contact: Rinda S. Vogelgesang, Director of Disabled Student Services. Phone: 765-641-4226. E-mail: rsvogelgesang@anderson.edu.

Approximately 50 registered undergraduate students were served during 2002-03. The program or unit includes 1 full-time and 2 part-time staff members. Academic advisers, coaches, counselors, LD specialists, regular education teachers, and remediation/learning specialists are provided through the program or unit. Academic advisers, counselors, regular education teachers, and trained peer tutors are provided collaboratively through on-campus or off-campus services.

Subject-area Tutoring Tutoring is offered one-on-one and in small groups for most subjects. Tutoring is provided through the program or unit via LD specialists and trained peer tutors. Tutoring is also provided collaboratively through on-campus or off-campus services via computer-based instruction.

Basic Skills Remediation Remediation is available for learning strategies, spelling, spoken language, study skills, time management, and written language. Remediation is provided through the program or unit via LD specialists and trained peer tutors.

Enrichment Enrichment programs are available through the program or unit for college survival skills, learning strategies, self-advocacy, study skills, test taking, time management, and written composition skills. Programs for career planning, health and nutrition, and math are provided collaboratively through on-campus or off-campus services. Credit is offered for career planning, college survival skills, health and nutrition, and study skills.

Application For admittance to the program or unit, students are required to provide a psychoeducational report (3 years old or less) and provide documentation of high school services. Upon application, materials documenting need for services should be sent only to the LD program or unit. *Application deadline (institutional):* 7/1. *Application deadline (LD program):* Rolling/continuous for fall and rolling/continuous for spring.

Written Policies Written policy regarding general/basic LD accommodations is available on the program Web site. Written policy regarding general/basic LD accommodations is outlined in the school's catalog/handbook.

Antioch University Los Angeles

13274 Fiji Way

Marina del Rey, CA 90292-7008

http://www.antiochla.edu/

Contact: Dr. Chloe T. Reid, Executive Dean. Phone: 310-578-1080 Ext. 244. E-mail: chloe_reid@antiochla.edu.

Approximately 15 registered undergraduate students were served during 2002-03. The program or unit includes 1 full-time staff member. Graduate assistants/students, professional tutors, regular education teachers, and remediation/learning specialists are provided collaboratively through on-campus or off-campus services.

Unique Aids and Services Aids, services, or accommodations include digital textbooks and priority registration.

Subject-area Tutoring Tutoring is offered one-on-one for some subjects. Tutoring is provided collaboratively through on-campus or off-campus services via graduate assistants/students and professional tutors.

Basic Skills Remediation Remediation is offered one-on-one for learning strategies, math, reading, spelling, and written language. Remediation is provided collaboratively through on-campus or off-campus services via computer-based instruction, graduate assistants/students, and professional tutors.

Application It is recommended that students provide a psychoeducational report (3 years old or less). Upon application, materials documenting need for services should be sent only to the LD program or unit. Upon acceptance, documentation of need for services should be sent only to the LD program or unit. *Application deadline (LD program):* Rolling/continuous for fall and rolling/continuous for spring.

Written Policies Written policies regarding course substitutions, general/basic LD accommodations, reduced course loads, substitutions and waivers of admissions requirements, and substitutions and waivers of graduation requirements are outlined in the school's catalog/handbook. Written policies regarding course substitutions, general/basic LD accommodations, reduced course loads, substitutions and waivers of admissions requirements, and substitutions and waivers of graduation requirements are available through the program or unit directly.

Antioch University Seattle
Disability Services

2326 Sixth Avenue

Seattle, WA 98121-1814

http://www.antiochsea.edu/

Contact: Ms. Capri St. Vil, Coordinator for Students with Disabilities. Phone: 206-268-4403. Fax: 206-441-3307. E-mail: cstvil@antiochsea.edu.

Disability Services Approximately 35 registered undergraduate students were served during 2002-03. The program or unit includes 1 part-time staff member. Academic advisers and regular education teachers are provided through the program or unit. Academic advisers, counselors, diagnostic specialists, graduate assistants/students, LD specialists, professional tutors, regular education teachers, remediation/learning specialists, skill tutors, strategy tutors, and trained peer tutors are provided collaboratively through on-campus or off-campus services.

Orientation The program or unit offers a mandatory orientation for new students before registration, during registration, and individually by special arrangement.

Unique Aids and Services Aids, services, or accommodations include weekly meetings with faculty, books on tape, note-takers, tutors, computer-assisted technology.

Subject-area Tutoring Tutoring is offered one-on-one for some subjects. Tutoring is provided collaboratively through on-campus or off-campus services via graduate assistants/students, professional tutors, and trained peer tutors.

Antioch University Seattle (continued)

Basic Skills Remediation Remediation is offered one-on-one for learning strategies, reading, spelling, spoken language, study skills, time management, and written language. Remediation is provided collaboratively through on-campus or off-campus services via graduate assistants/students, professional tutors, and trained peer tutors.

Enrichment Programs for career planning, health and nutrition, learning strategies, oral communication skills, practical computer skills, reading, self-advocacy, stress management, study skills, time management, vocabulary development, and written composition skills are provided collaboratively through on-campus or off-campus services. Credit is offered for career planning, health and nutrition, oral communication skills, practical computer skills, self-advocacy, and written composition skills.

Application For admittance to the program or unit, students are required to apply to the program directly and provide a psychoeducational report (7 years old or less). It is recommended that students provide documentation of high school services. Upon application, materials documenting need for services should be sent only to the LD program or unit. Upon acceptance, documentation of need for services should be sent only to the LD program or unit.

Written Policies Written policy regarding general/basic LD accommodations is available on the program Web site. Written policies regarding general/basic LD accommodations and substitutions and waivers of admissions requirements are outlined in the school's catalog/handbook. Written policies regarding general/basic LD accommodations and substitutions and waivers of admissions requirements are available through the program or unit directly.

Appalachian State University

Boone, NC 28608

http://www.appstate.edu/

Contact: Ms. Suzanne T. Wehner, Coordinator. Phone: 828-262-3053. Fax: 828-262-6834. E-mail: wehnerst@appstate.edu.

Approximately 424 registered undergraduate students were served during 2002-03. The program or unit includes 1 full-time staff member. Coaches, graduate assistants/students, and LD specialists are provided through the program or unit. Academic advisers, counselors, and professional tutors are provided collaboratively through on-campus or off-campus services.

Summer Program To help prepare for the demands of college, there is an optional 5-week summer program prior to entering the school. Degree credit will be earned.

Unique Aids and Services Aids, services, or accommodations include career counseling and priority registration.

Subject-area Tutoring Tutoring is offered one-on-one, in small groups, and in class-size groups for some subjects. Tutoring is provided through the program or unit via graduate assistants/students and LD specialists. Tutoring is also provided collaboratively through on-campus or off-campus services via computer-based instruction and trained peer tutors.

Diagnostic Testing Testing for auditory processing and spoken language is provided collaboratively through on-campus or off-campus services.

Enrichment Enrichment programs are available through the program or unit for learning strategies, self-advocacy, and time management. Programs for career planning, stress management, study skills, test taking, time management, and written composition skills are provided collaboratively through on-campus or off-campus services.

Fees *Summer Program* fee is $1306 to $2404. *Diagnostic Testing* fee is $100 to $500.

Application For admittance to the program or unit, students are required to apply to the program directly and provide a psychoeducational report (3 years old or less). It is recommended that students provide documentation of high school services. Upon application, materials documenting need for services should be sent only to admissions with institutional application materials. Upon acceptance, documentation of need for services should be sent only to the LD program or unit. *Application deadline (institutional):* Continuous. *Application deadline (LD program):* Rolling/continuous for fall and rolling/continuous for spring.

Written Policies Written policy regarding general/basic LD accommodations is available on the program Web site. Written policies regarding course substitutions, grade forgiveness, and reduced course loads are outlined in the school's catalog/handbook. Written policy regarding general/basic LD accommodations is available through the program or unit directly.

Argosy University-Sarasota

5250 17th Street

Sarasota, FL 34235-8246

http://www.sarasota.edu/

Contact: Phone: 941-379-0404. Fax: 941-379-9464.

Written Policies Written policy regarding general/basic LD accommodations is available through the program or unit directly.

Arkansas State University
Office of Disability Services

PO Box 10

Jonesboro, AR 72467

http://disability.astate.edu

Contact: Mrs. Kara Hubbard, Learning Disability Specialist. Phone: 870-972-3964. Fax: 870-910-8048. E-mail: kwright@mail.astate.edu. Head of LD Program: Dr. Jenifer Rice-Mason, Director of Disability Services. Phone: 870-972-3964. Fax: 870-910-8048. E-mail: jrmason@mail.astate.edu.

Office of Disability Services Approximately 150 registered undergraduate students were served during 2002-03. The program or unit includes 4 full-time and 2 part-time staff members. Counselors, graduate assistants/students, and LD specialists are provided through the program or unit. Academic advisers, counselors, diagnostic specialists, regular education teachers, and trained peer tutors are provided collaboratively through on-campus or off-campus services.

Unique Aids and Services Aids, services, or accommodations include advocates, career counseling, digital textbooks, and faculty training.

Subject-area Tutoring Tutoring is offered one-on-one and in small groups for some subjects. Tutoring is provided collaboratively through on-campus or off-campus services via graduate assistants/ students and trained peer tutors.

Basic Skills Remediation Remediation is offered one-on-one and in small groups for computer skills, learning strategies, social skills, study skills, and time management. Remediation is provided through the program or unit via graduate assistants/students and LD specialists. Remediation is also provided collaboratively through on-campus or off-campus services via graduate assistants/students, regular education teachers, and trained peer tutors.

Enrichment Enrichment programs are available through the program or unit for career planning, learning strategies, practical computer skills, self-advocacy, stress management, study skills, test taking, and time management. Programs for career planning, college survival skills, learning strategies, practical computer skills, self-advocacy, stress management, study skills, and test taking are provided collaboratively through on-campus or off-campus services. Credit is offered for practical computer skills.

Student Organization Delta Sigma Omicron consists of 20 members.

Application For admittance to the program or unit, students are required to apply to the program directly and provide a psychoeducational report (3 years old or less). It is recommended that students provide documentation of high school services. Upon application, materials documenting need for services should be sent only to the LD program or unit. Upon acceptance, documentation of need for services should be sent only to the LD program or unit. *Application deadline (institutional):* Continuous. *Application deadline (LD program):* Rolling/continuous for fall and rolling/continuous for spring.

Written Policies Written policies regarding course substitutions and general/basic LD accommodations are available through the program or unit directly.

Art Academy of Cincinnati

1125 Saint Gregory Street
Cincinnati, OH 45202-1799
http://www.artacademy.edu/
Contact: Phone: 513-721-5205. Fax: 513-562-8778.

The program or unit includes 1 part-time staff member. Counselors and trained peer tutors are provided collaboratively through on-campus or off-campus services.

Unique Aids and Services Aids, services, or accommodations include faculty training and personal coach.

Subject-area Tutoring Tutoring is offered one-on-one and in small groups for some subjects. Tutoring is provided collaboratively through on-campus or off-campus services via professional tutors and trained peer tutors.

Diagnostic Testing Testing for learning styles is provided collaboratively through on-campus or off-campus services.

Basic Skills Remediation Remediation is offered in class-size groups for computer skills, reading, study skills, and written language. Remediation is provided collaboratively through on-campus or off-campus services via regular education teachers.

Enrichment Programs for learning strategies, practical computer skills, reading, stress management, study skills, test taking, time management, and written composition skills are provided collaboratively through on-campus or off-campus services.

Application It is recommended that students provide a psychoeducational report (3 years old or less) and provide documentation of high school services. Upon application, materials documenting need for services should be sent only to admissions with institutional application materials. Upon acceptance, documentation of need for services should be sent only to the LD program or unit. *Application deadline (institutional):* 6/30. *Application deadline (LD program):* Rolling/continuous for fall and rolling/continuous for spring.

Written Policies Written policy regarding general/basic LD accommodations is available on the program Web site. Written policy regarding general/basic LD accommodations is outlined in the school's catalog/handbook.

The Art Institute of Atlanta
Disability Services

6600 Peachtree Dunwoody Road, 100 Embassy Row
Atlanta, GA 30328
http://www.aia.artinstitute.edu/
Contact: Phone: 770-394-8300. Fax: 770-394-0008. Head of LD Program: Mr. Shane D. Tratechaud, Disability Services Coordinator. Phone: 770-689-4912. Fax: 770-394-9798. E-mail: tratechs@aii.edu.

Disability Services Approximately 100 registered undergraduate students were served during 2002-03. The program or unit includes 1 full-time staff member. Academic advisers, counselors, regular education teachers, and trained peer tutors are provided collaboratively through on-campus or off-campus services.

Unique Aids and Services Aids, services, or accommodations include advocates, career counseling, faculty training, personal coach, and priority registration.

Subject-area Tutoring Tutoring is offered one-on-one for most subjects. Tutoring is provided collaboratively through on-campus or off-campus services via trained peer tutors.

Basic Skills Remediation Remediation is offered one-on-one for learning strategies, math, social skills, study skills, time management, and written language. Remediation is provided through the program or unit. Remediation is also provided collaboratively through on-campus or off-campus services via trained peer tutors.

Enrichment Enrichment programs are available through the program or unit for self-advocacy, stress management, study skills, test taking, and time management. Programs for career planning, college survival skills, health and nutrition, learning strategies, math, oral communication skills, practical computer skills, stress management, study skills, test taking, time management, and written composition skills are provided collaboratively through on-campus or off-campus services. Credit is offered for oral communication skills and practical computer skills.

Application For admittance to the program or unit, students are required to provide a psychoeducational report (3 years old or less) and provide an evaluation from a qualified health care provider. Upon application, materials documenting need for services should be sent only to the LD program or unit. Upon acceptance, docu-

The Art Institute of Atlanta (continued)

mentation of need for services should be sent only to the LD program or unit. *Application deadline (institutional): 9/29. Application deadline (LD program):* Rolling/continuous for fall and rolling/continuous for spring.

Written Policies Written policy regarding general/basic LD accommodations is available through the program or unit directly.

The Art Institute of Portland

1122 NW Davis Street
Portland, OR 97209
http://www.aipd.artinstitutes.edu/
Contact: Coordinator of Disability Services. Phone: 503-228-6528.

The program or unit includes 1 full-time staff member. Counselors are provided through the program or unit. Remediation/learning specialists and trained peer tutors are provided collaboratively through on-campus or off-campus services.

Unique Aids and Services Aids, services, or accommodations include digital textbooks and faculty training.

Subject-area Tutoring Tutoring is offered one-on-one for most subjects. Tutoring is provided through the program or unit via trained peer tutors. Tutoring is also provided collaboratively through on-campus or off-campus services via computer-based instruction and trained peer tutors.

Basic Skills Remediation Remediation is offered in small groups and in class-size groups for learning strategies, math, reading, spelling, study skills, time management, and written language. Remediation is provided through the program or unit via LD specialists. Remediation is also provided collaboratively through on-campus or off-campus services via regular education teachers.

Enrichment Enrichment programs are available through the program or unit for college survival skills, learning strategies, oral communication skills, reading, self-advocacy, stress management, study skills, test taking, and time management. Programs for career planning, college survival skills, and practical computer skills are provided collaboratively through on-campus or off-campus services. Credit is offered for college survival skills and practical computer skills.

Application For admittance to the program or unit, students are required to provide a psychoeducational report (3 years old or less). Upon application, materials documenting need for services should be sent to both admissions and the LD program or unit. Upon acceptance, documentation of need for services should be sent only to the LD program or unit. *Application deadline (institutional):* Continuous. *Application deadline (LD program):* Rolling/continuous for fall and rolling/continuous for spring.

Written Policies Written policy regarding general/basic LD accommodations is available through the program or unit directly.

Ashland University

401 College Avenue
Ashland, OH 44805-3702
http://www.ashland.edu/

Contact: Phone: 419-289-4142. Fax: 419-289-5999.

The program or unit includes 3 full-time staff members. LD specialists, remediation/learning specialists, and other are provided through the program or unit. LD specialists, remediation/learning specialists, and other are provided collaboratively through on-campus or off-campus services.

Orientation The program or unit offers a mandatory orientation for new students before classes begin, after classes begin, and individually by special arrangement.

Unique Aids and Services Aids, services, or accommodations include career counseling, priority registration, weekly meetings with faculty, taped textbooks.

Subject-area Tutoring Tutoring is offered one-on-one for most subjects. Tutoring is provided through the program or unit via trained peer tutors. Tutoring is also provided collaboratively through on-campus or off-campus services via trained peer tutors.

Basic Skills Remediation Remediation is offered one-on-one for auditory processing, learning strategies, social skills, spelling, spoken language, study skills, time management, visual processing, and written language. Remediation is provided through the program or unit via LD specialists. Remediation is also provided collaboratively through on-campus or off-campus services via LD specialists.

Enrichment Enrichment programs are available through the program or unit for career planning, college survival skills, learning strategies, oral communication skills, reading, self-advocacy, stress management, study skills, test taking, time management, and written composition skills. Programs for career planning, college survival skills, learning strategies, oral communication skills, self-advocacy, stress management, study skills, test taking, time management, and written composition skills are provided collaboratively through on-campus or off-campus services.

Application For admittance to the program or unit, students are required to provide a psychoeducational report (5 years old or less), provide documentation of high school services, and provide medical documentation. Upon acceptance, documentation of need for services should be sent only to the LD program or unit. *Application deadline (institutional):* Continuous. *Application deadline (LD program):* Rolling/continuous for fall and rolling/continuous for spring.

Written Policies Written policy regarding general/basic LD accommodations is available on the program Web site. Written policy regarding general/basic LD accommodations is outlined in the school's catalog/handbook. Written policies regarding course substitutions and general/basic LD accommodations are available through the program or unit directly.

Athens State University
Counseling and Career Services: Services to Students with Disabilities

300 North Beaty Street
Athens, AL 35611-1902
http://www.athens.edu/

Contact: Phone: 256-233-8100. Fax: 256-233-8164.

Counseling and Career Services: Services to Students with Disabilities Approximately 20 registered undergraduate students were served during 2002-03. The program or unit includes 1 full-time staff member. Counselors are provided collaboratively through on-campus or off-campus services.

Unique Aids and Services Aids, services, or accommodations include career counseling and priority registration.

Application For admittance to the program or unit, students are required to provide information from prior college. It is recommended that students provide documentation of high school services. Upon application, materials documenting need for services should be sent only to the LD program or unit. Upon acceptance, documentation of need for services should be sent only to the LD program or unit.

Written Policies Written policy regarding general/basic LD accommodations is available on the program Web site. Written policy regarding general/basic LD accommodations is outlined in the school's catalog/handbook.

Atlanta College of Art

1280 Peachtree Street, NE
Atlanta, GA 30309-3582
http://www.aca.edu/
Contact: Ms. Remi Stewart, Assistant Dean. Phone: 404-733-5090. Fax: 404-733-5201. E-mail: remi.stewart@woodruffcenter.org.

Approximately 20 registered undergraduate students were served during 2002-03. The program or unit includes 2 full-time staff members. Academic advisers are provided through the program or unit. Counselors and regular education teachers are provided collaboratively through on-campus or off-campus services.

Application For admittance to the program or unit, students are required to provide a psychoeducational report (3 years old or less). It is recommended that students provide documentation of high school services. Upon acceptance, documentation of need for services should be sent only to the LD program or unit. *Application deadline (institutional):* Continuous. *Application deadline (LD program):* Rolling/continuous for fall and rolling/continuous for spring.

Written Policies Written policy regarding general/basic LD accommodations is available on the program Web site. Written policy regarding general/basic LD accommodations is outlined in the school's catalog/handbook. Written policies regarding course substitutions and general/basic LD accommodations are available through the program or unit directly.

Auburn University

Auburn University, AL 36849
http://www.auburn.edu/disability
Contact: Dr. Kelly D. Haynes, Director. Phone: 334-844-2096. Fax: 334-844-2099. E-mail: haynemd@auburn.edu.

Approximately 209 registered undergraduate students were served during 2002-03. The program or unit includes 3 full-time staff members. Diagnostic specialists are provided through the program or unit. Trained peer tutors are provided collaboratively through on-campus or off-campus services.

Unique Aids and Services Aids, services, or accommodations include advocates, digital textbooks, and priority registration.

Subject-area Tutoring Tutoring is offered one-on-one and in small groups for some subjects. Tutoring is provided collaboratively through on-campus or off-campus services via trained peer tutors.

Student Organization Advocates for Disability Awareness consists of 20 members.

Application For admittance to the program or unit, students are required to apply to the program directly, provide a psychoeducational report (3 years old or less), and provide documentation as specified on Web site. It is recommended that students provide documentation of high school services. Upon application, materials documenting need for services should be sent only to the LD program or unit. Upon acceptance, documentation of need for services should be sent only to the LD program or unit. *Application deadline (institutional):* 8/1. *Application deadline (LD program):* Rolling/continuous for fall and rolling/continuous for spring.

Written Policies Written policy regarding general/basic LD accommodations is available on the program Web site. Written policy regarding general/basic LD accommodations is outlined in the school's catalog/handbook.

Auburn University Montgomery
Center for Special Services

PO Box 244023
Montgomery, AL 36124-4023
http://www.aum.edu/home/services/special/css.htm
Contact: Mrs. Tamara J. Massey-Garrett, Student Services Coordinator. Phone: 334-244-3631. Fax: 334-244-3907. E-mail: tmassey2@mail.aum.edu.

Center for Special Services Approximately 70 registered undergraduate students were served during 2002-03. The program or unit includes 4 full-time and 2 part-time staff members. Skill tutors, strategy tutors, and other are provided through the program or unit. Professional tutors, remediation/learning specialists, trained peer tutors, and other are provided collaboratively through on-campus or off-campus services.

Summer Program To help prepare for the demands of college, there is an optional 2-week summer program prior to entering the school.

Unique Aids and Services Aids, services, or accommodations include career counseling, digital textbooks, faculty training, priority registration, equipment, computer training, extended time on tests with a proctor to read and write.

Subject-area Tutoring Tutoring is offered one-on-one for some subjects. Tutoring is provided through the program or unit via computer-based instruction and other. Tutoring is also provided collaboratively through on-campus or off-campus services via professional tutors and trained peer tutors.

Auburn University Montgomery (continued)

Basic Skills Remediation Remediation is offered in class-size groups for math, reading, and written language. Remediation is provided collaboratively through on-campus or off-campus services via regular education teachers.

Enrichment Enrichment programs are available through the program or unit for oral communication skills and practical computer skills. Programs for career planning, college survival skills, learning strategies, self-advocacy, study skills, test taking, and time management are provided collaboratively through on-campus or off-campus services.

Application For admittance to the program or unit, students are required to provide a psychoeducational report (3 years old or less). Upon application, materials documenting need for services should be sent only to the LD program or unit. Upon acceptance, documentation of need for services should be sent only to the LD program or unit. *Application deadline (institutional):* Continuous. *Application deadline (LD program):* Rolling/continuous for fall and rolling/continuous for spring.

Written Policies Written policies regarding general/basic LD accommodations and grade forgiveness are available on the program Web site. Written policy regarding grade forgiveness is outlined in the school's catalog/handbook. Written policies regarding course substitutions, general/basic LD accommodations, and substitutions and waivers of graduation requirements are available through the program or unit directly.

Augsburg College
Center for Learning and Adaptive Student Services (CLASS)

2211 Riverside Avenue
Minneapolis, MN 55454-1351
http://www.augsburgcollege.edu/CLASS
Contact: Karena M. Jones, Disability Specialist. Phone: 612-330-1053. Fax: 612-330-1137. E-mail: class@augsburg.edu. Head of LD Program: James Hodgson PhD, Director of CLASS. Phone: 612-330-1053. Fax: 612-330-1137. E-mail: class@augsburg.edu.

Center for Learning and Adaptive Student Services (CLASS) Approximately 200 registered undergraduate students were served during 2002-03. The program or unit includes 6 full-time staff members. LD specialists, skill tutors, and strategy tutors are provided through the program or unit. Academic advisers, coaches, counselors, diagnostic specialists, graduate assistants/students, professional tutors, regular education teachers, remediation/learning specialists, special education teachers, teacher trainees, and trained peer tutors are provided collaboratively through on-campus or off-campus services.

Orientation The program or unit offers an optional orientation for new students during registration, after classes begin, and testing accommodations for the Augsburg placement tests.

Unique Aids and Services Aids, services, or accommodations include weekly meetings with disability specialist.

Basic Skills Remediation Remediation is offered one-on-one and in small groups for learning strategies, study skills, and time management. Remediation is provided through the program or unit via LD specialists.

Enrichment Enrichment programs are available through the program or unit for learning strategies, self-advocacy, study skills, test taking, and time management.

Application For admittance to the program or unit, students are required to apply to the program directly and provide a psychoeducational report (3 years old or less). It is recommended that students provide documentation of high school services. Upon acceptance, documentation of need for services should be sent only to the LD program or unit. *Application deadline (institutional):* 8/15. *Application deadline (LD program):* Rolling/continuous for fall and rolling/continuous for spring.

Written Policies Written policy regarding general/basic LD accommodations is available on the program Web site. Written policy regarding general/basic LD accommodations is outlined in the school's catalog/handbook. Written policies regarding course substitutions and general/basic LD accommodations are available through the program or unit directly.

Augustana College
Academic Development and Support Services Office

2001 South Summit Avenue
Sioux Falls, SD 57197
http://www.augie.edu/student_serv/disability.html
Contact: Susan J. Bies, Director of Academic Development and Support Services. Phone: 605-274-5516. Fax: 605-274-5229. E-mail: susan_bies@augie.edu.

Academic Development and Support Services Office Approximately 45 registered undergraduate students were served during 2002-03. The program or unit includes 1 part-time staff member. Academic advisers, coaches, counselors, regular education teachers, and trained peer tutors are provided collaboratively through on-campus or off-campus services.

Subject-area Tutoring Tutoring is offered one-on-one for some subjects. Tutoring is provided collaboratively through on-campus or off-campus services via computer-based instruction and trained peer tutors.

Enrichment Programs for career planning, college survival skills, health and nutrition, and learning strategies are provided collaboratively through on-campus or off-campus services. Credit is offered for career planning, college survival skills, and health and nutrition.

Application For admittance to the program or unit, students are required to provide a psychoeducational report (3 years old or less). Upon acceptance, documentation of need for services should be sent only to the LD program or unit. *Application deadline (institutional):* 8/1. *Application deadline (LD program):* Rolling/continuous for fall and rolling/continuous for spring.

Written Policies Written policy regarding general/basic LD accommodations is available on the program Web site. Written policy regarding general/basic LD accommodations is available through the program or unit directly.

Augusta State University

2500 Walton Way

Augusta, GA 30904-2200

http://www.aug.edu/

Contact: Ms. Angie S. Kitchens, Coordinator of Testing and Disability Services. Phone: 706-737-1471. Fax: 706-667-4350. E-mail: akitchens@aug.edu.

Approximately 50 registered undergraduate students were served during 2002-03. The program or unit includes 1 full-time and 1 part-time staff member. Academic advisers, counselors, regular education teachers, and remediation/learning specialists are provided collaboratively through on-campus or off-campus services.

Unique Aids and Services Aids, services, or accommodations include digital textbooks, faculty training, and priority registration.

Diagnostic Testing Testing for auditory processing, intelligence, learning strategies, math, motor skills, neuropsychological, personality, reading, social skills, spelling, spoken language, study skills, visual processing, and written language is provided collaboratively through on-campus or off-campus services.

Basic Skills Remediation Remediation is offered in class-size groups for math, reading, and written language. Remediation is provided collaboratively through on-campus or off-campus services via regular education teachers.

Enrichment Programs for career planning, college survival skills, learning strategies, math, stress management, study skills, test taking, and time management are provided collaboratively through on-campus or off-campus services.

Fees *Diagnostic Testing* fee is $400.

Application For admittance to the program or unit, students are required to apply to the program directly and provide a psychoeducational report (3 years old or less). It is recommended that students provide documentation of high school services. Upon application, materials documenting need for services should be sent only to the LD program or unit. Upon acceptance, documentation of need for services should be sent only to the LD program or unit. *Application deadline (institutional):* 7/21. *Application deadline (LD program):* Rolling/continuous for fall and rolling/continuous for spring.

Written Policies Written policies regarding course substitutions, general/basic LD accommodations, grade forgiveness, reduced course loads, substitutions and waivers of admissions requirements, and substitutions and waivers of graduation requirements are available on the program Web site. Written policies regarding course substitutions, general/basic LD accommodations, grade forgiveness, reduced course loads, substitutions and waivers of admissions requirements, and substitutions and waivers of graduation requirements are outlined in the school's catalog/handbook. Written policies regarding course substitutions, general/basic LD accommodations, and reduced course loads are available through the program or unit directly.

Aurora University
The Learning Center

347 South Gladstone Avenue

Aurora, IL 60506-4892

http://www.aurora.edu/learningcenter/

Contact: Mrs. Susan Lausier, Disabilities Services Coordinator. Phone: 630-844-5267. Fax: 630-844-5463. E-mail: slausier@aurora.edu. Head of LD Program: Mr. Eric

Schwarze, Director of the Learning Center. Phone: 630-844-5521. Fax: 630-844-5463. E-mail: eschwarz@aurora.edu.

The Learning Center Approximately 15 registered undergraduate students were served during 2002-03. The program or unit includes 3 full-time and 4 part-time staff members. Professional tutors, skill tutors, strategy tutors, and trained peer tutors are provided through the program or unit. Academic advisers and counselors are provided collaboratively through on-campus or off-campus services.

Unique Aids and Services Aids, services, or accommodations include advocates, readings on tape, testing accommodations, notetakers, typical classroom accommodations.

Subject-area Tutoring Tutoring is offered one-on-one and in small groups for all subjects. Tutoring is provided through the program or unit via computer-based instruction, professional tutors, and trained peer tutors.

Basic Skills Remediation Remediation is offered one-on-one for computer skills, learning strategies, math, reading, spelling, study skills, time management, and written language. Remediation is provided through the program or unit via computer-based instruction and professional tutors.

Enrichment Enrichment programs are available through the program or unit for college survival skills, learning strategies, practical computer skills, study skills, test taking, and time management. Programs for career planning and health and nutrition are provided collaboratively through on-campus or off-campus services.

Application For admittance to the program or unit, students are required to provide a psychoeducational report (3 years old or less). It is recommended that students provide documentation of high school services. Upon acceptance, documentation of need for services should be sent only to the LD program or unit. *Application deadline (institutional):* Continuous. *Application deadline (LD program):* Rolling/continuous for fall and rolling/continuous for spring.

Written Policies Written policy regarding general/basic LD accommodations is available on the program Web site. Written policy regarding general/basic LD accommodations is outlined in the school's catalog/handbook. Written policy regarding general/basic LD accommodations is available through the program or unit directly.

Austin College
Academic Skills Center

900 North Grand Avenue

Sherman, TX 75090-4400

http://artemis.austincollege.edu/asc/

Contact: Ms. Laura Marquez, Director of Academic Skills Center. Phone: 903-813-2454. Fax: 903-813-3188. E-mail: lmarquez@austincollege.edu. Head of LD Program: Ms. Laura Marquez, Director of Academic Skills Center. Phone: 903-813-2454903. Fax: 903-813-3188. E-mail: lmarquez@austincollege.edu.

Academic Skills Center Approximately 21 registered undergraduate students were served during 2002-03. The program or unit includes 1 full-time staff member. LD specialists are provided through

Austin College (continued)

the program or unit. Academic advisers, coaches, counselors, diagnostic specialists, professional tutors, and trained peer tutors are provided collaboratively through on-campus or off-campus services.
Unique Aids and Services Aids, services, or accommodations include career counseling, digital textbooks, and personal coach.
Subject-area Tutoring Tutoring is offered one-on-one and in small groups for most subjects. Tutoring is provided collaboratively through on-campus or off-campus services via trained peer tutors.
Enrichment Programs for career planning, health and nutrition, learning strategies, stress management, study skills, test taking, time management, and written composition skills are provided collaboratively through on-campus or off-campus services.
Application For admittance to the program or unit, students are required to provide a psychoeducational report (3 years old or less). Upon application, materials documenting need for services should be sent only to the LD program or unit. Upon acceptance, documentation of need for services should be sent only to the LD program or unit. *Application deadline (institutional):* 8/15.
Written Policies Written policy regarding general/basic LD accommodations is outlined in the school's catalog/handbook. Written policies regarding course substitutions, general/basic LD accommodations, reduced course loads, substitutions and waivers of admissions requirements, and substitutions and waivers of graduation requirements are available through the program or unit directly.

Averett University

420 West Main Street
Danville, VA 24541-3692
http://www.averett.edu/
Contact: Mrs. Julie T. Stockenberg, Assistant Dean for Student Retention. Phone: 434-791-5629. Fax: 434-791-5819. E-mail: julie.stockenberg@averett.edu.

Approximately 20 registered undergraduate students were served during 2002-03. The program or unit includes 1 full-time staff member. Academic advisers, coaches, counselors, diagnostic specialists, LD specialists, professional tutors, regular education teachers, remediation/learning specialists, skill tutors, special education teachers, strategy tutors, and trained peer tutors are provided collaboratively through on-campus or off-campus services.
Orientation The program or unit offers an optional orientation for new students individually by special arrangement.
Summer Program To help prepare for the demands of college, there is an optional 2-week summer program prior to entering the school.
Unique Aids and Services Aids, services, or accommodations include advocates, career counseling, faculty training, parent workshops, and personal coach.
Subject-area Tutoring Tutoring is offered one-on-one, in small groups, and in class-size groups for some subjects. Tutoring is provided collaboratively through on-campus or off-campus services via computer-based instruction, graduate assistants/students, LD specialists, professional tutors, and trained peer tutors.
Diagnostic Testing Testing for auditory processing, handwriting, intelligence, learning strategies, learning styles, math, motor skills, neuropsychological, personality, reading, social skills, spelling, spoken language, study skills, visual processing, and written language is provided collaboratively through on-campus or off-campus services.

Basic Skills Remediation Remediation is offered one-on-one, in small groups, and in class-size groups for handwriting, learning strategies, math, reading, social skills, spelling, spoken language, study skills, time management, visual processing, and written language. Remediation is provided collaboratively through on-campus or off-campus services via LD specialists, professional tutors, regular education teachers, and trained peer tutors.
Enrichment Programs for career planning, college survival skills, health and nutrition, learning strategies, math, medication management, oral communication skills, practical computer skills, reading, self-advocacy, stress management, study skills, test taking, time management, vocabulary development, and written composition skills are provided collaboratively through on-campus or off-campus services.
Fees *Diagnostic Testing* fee is applicable.
Application For admittance to the program or unit, students are required to provide a psychoeducational report. It is recommended that students provide documentation of high school services. Upon acceptance, documentation of need for services should be sent only to the LD program or unit. *Application deadline (institutional):* 9/1. *Application deadline (LD program):* Rolling/continuous for fall and rolling/continuous for spring.
Written Policies Written policy regarding general/basic LD accommodations is available through the program or unit directly.

Babson College
Disability Services

Wellesley, MA 02457-0310
http://www.babson.edu/classdeans
Contact: Ms. Erin M. Evans, Coordinator of Disability Services. Phone: 781-239-4508. Fax: 781-239-5567. E-mail: eevans@babson.edu.

Disability Services Approximately 70 registered undergraduate students were served during 2002-03. The program or unit includes 1 full-time staff member. Services are provided through the program or unit.
Basic Skills Remediation Remediation is offered one-on-one, in small groups, and in class-size groups for study skills and time management. Remediation is provided through the program or unit.
Enrichment Enrichment programs are available through the program or unit for self-advocacy, stress management, study skills, test taking, and time management. Programs for college survival skills, medication management, and written composition skills are provided collaboratively through on-campus or off-campus services.
Application For admittance to the program or unit, students are required to provide a psychoeducational report (3 years old or less). Upon acceptance, documentation of need for services should be sent only to the LD program or unit. *Application deadline (institutional):* 2/1. *Application deadline (LD program):* Rolling/continuous for fall and rolling/continuous for spring.
Written Policies Written policies regarding general/basic LD accommodations and reduced course loads are available on the program Web site. Written policy regarding general/basic LD accommodations is outlined in the school's catalog/handbook. Written policies regarding general/basic LD accommodations and reduced course loads are available through the program or unit directly.

Baker College of Auburn Hills
Counseling office

1500 University Drive
Auburn Hills, MI 48326-1586
http://www.baker.edu/
Contact: Phone: 248-340-0600.

Counseling office Approximately 45 registered undergraduate students were served during 2002-03. The program or unit includes 2 full-time staff members. Counselors, remediation/learning specialists, and trained peer tutors are provided through the program or unit.

Summer Program To help prepare for the demands of college, there is an optional 9-week summer program prior to entering the school. Degree credit will be earned.

Subject-area Tutoring Tutoring is offered one-on-one for most subjects. Tutoring is provided through the program or unit via computer-based instruction, LD specialists, and trained peer tutors.

Diagnostic Testing Testing is provided through the program or unit for learning styles and personality.

Basic Skills Remediation Remediation is offered in class-size groups for math, reading, and written language. Remediation is provided through the program or unit via computer-based instruction, regular education teachers, and trained peer tutors.

Enrichment Enrichment programs are available through the program or unit for career planning, learning strategies, stress management, study skills, test taking, and time management.

Application For admittance to the program or unit, students are required to apply to the program directly and provide a psychoeducational report (3 years old or less). It is recommended that students provide documentation of high school services and provide a letter from a doctor or counselor. Upon application, materials documenting need for services should be sent only to the LD program or unit. Upon acceptance, documentation of need for services should be sent only to the LD program or unit. *Application deadline (institutional):* Continuous. *Application deadline (LD program):* Rolling/continuous for fall and rolling/continuous for spring.

Written Policies Written policy regarding general/basic LD accommodations is available through the program or unit directly.

Baker College of Cadillac

9600 East 13th Street
Cadillac, MI 49601
http://www.baker.edu/
Contact: Phone: 231-876-3100. Fax: 231-775-8505.

The program or unit includes 2 full-time staff members. Academic advisers, skill tutors, and other are provided through the program or unit.

Unique Aids and Services Aids, services, or accommodations include note-takers.

Subject-area Tutoring Tutoring is offered one-on-one and in small groups for most subjects. Tutoring is provided through the program or unit via trained peer tutors.

Basic Skills Remediation Remediation is offered one-on-one for math, reading, and written language. Remediation is provided through the program or unit via computer-based instruction and trained peer tutors.

Application For admittance to the program or unit, students are required to provide a psychoeducational report (3 years old or less) and provide documentation of high school services. Upon acceptance, documentation of need for services should be sent only to admissions. *Application deadline (institutional):* Continuous.

Written Policies Written policy regarding general/basic LD accommodations is outlined in the school's catalog/handbook.

Ball State University
Disabled Student Development

2000 University Avenue
Muncie, IN 47306-1099
http://www.bsu.edu/dsd/
Contact: Mr. Richard Harris, Director. Phone: 765-285-5293. Fax: 765-285-5295. E-mail: dsd@bsu.edu.

Disabled Student Development Approximately 205 registered undergraduate students were served during 2002-03. Academic advisers, graduate assistants/students, regular education teachers, skill tutors, strategy tutors, and trained peer tutors are provided collaboratively through on-campus or off-campus services.

Orientation The program or unit offers an optional 2-hour orientation for new students after classes begin.

Unique Aids and Services Aids, services, or accommodations include digital textbooks and priority registration.

Subject-area Tutoring Tutoring is offered one-on-one, in small groups, and in class-size groups for most subjects. Tutoring is provided collaboratively through on-campus or off-campus services via computer-based instruction, graduate assistants/students, and trained peer tutors.

Basic Skills Remediation Remediation is offered one-on-one and in small groups for learning strategies, study skills, and time management. Remediation is provided collaboratively through on-campus or off-campus services via graduate assistants/students and trained peer tutors.

Enrichment Programs for career planning, learning strategies, study skills, and written composition skills are provided collaboratively through on-campus or off-campus services.

Application For admittance to the program or unit, students are required to provide a psychoeducational report (3 years old or less). Upon acceptance, documentation of need for services should be sent only to the LD program or unit. *Application deadline (institutional):* Continuous. *Application deadline (LD program):* Rolling/continuous for fall and rolling/continuous for spring.

Written Policies Written policy regarding general/basic LD accommodations is available on the program Web site. Written policy regarding general/basic LD accommodations is outlined in the school's catalog/handbook. Written policies regarding course substitutions, reduced course loads, and substitutions and waivers of graduation requirements are available through the program or unit directly.

The Baptist College of Florida

5400 College Drive
Graceville, FL 32440-1898
http://www.baptistcollege.edu/

Contact: Chris Bishop, Director of Admissions. Phone: 800-328-2660 Ext. 460. Fax: 850-263-7506.

Approximately 13 registered undergraduate students were served during 2002-03. The program or unit includes 1 full-time and 4 part-time staff members. Academic advisers are provided through the program or unit. Counselors, regular education teachers, and skill tutors are provided collaboratively through on-campus or off-campus services.

Unique Aids and Services Aids, services, or accommodations include career counseling.

Subject-area Tutoring Tutoring is offered one-on-one for all subjects. Tutoring is provided collaboratively through on-campus or off-campus services via trained peer tutors.

Basic Skills Remediation Remediation is offered one-on-one and in class-size groups for computer skills, math, reading, and written language. Remediation is provided collaboratively through on-campus or off-campus services via regular education teachers and trained peer tutors.

Application It is recommended that students provide documentation of high school services. Upon acceptance, documentation of need for services should be sent only to the LD program or unit. *Application deadline (institutional):* Continuous. *Application deadline (LD program):* Rolling/continuous for fall and rolling/continuous for spring.

Written Policies Written policy regarding general/basic LD accommodations is outlined in the school's catalog/handbook.

Baptist Missionary Association Theological Seminary

1530 East Pine Street
Jacksonville, TX 75766-5407
Contact: Phone: 903-586-2501.

Application *Application deadline (institutional):* 7/25.

Bard College

PO Box 5000
Annandale-on-Hudson, NY 12504
http://www.inside.bard.edu/academicservices

Contact: Dr. David Shein, Dean of Lower College Studies. Phone: 845-758-7454. Fax: 845-758-7646. E-mail: shein@bard.edu.

Approximately 100 registered undergraduate students were served during 2002-03. The program or unit includes 1 full-time staff member. Academic advisers, professional tutors, skill tutors, strategy tutors, and other are provided through the program or unit. Academic advisers, counselors, professional tutors, skill tutors, strategy tutors, trained peer tutors, and other are provided collaboratively through on-campus or off-campus services.

Orientation The program or unit offers an optional orientation for new students individually by special arrangement.

Unique Aids and Services Aids, services, or accommodations include faculty training, support groups, weekly meetings with faculty, test and classroom accommodations, academic advising and counseling.

Subject-area Tutoring Tutoring is offered one-on-one and in small groups for all subjects. Tutoring is provided through the program or unit via professional tutors and other. Tutoring is also provided collaboratively through on-campus or off-campus services via computer-based instruction, professional tutors, trained peer tutors, and other.

Basic Skills Remediation Remediation is offered one-on-one and in small groups for learning strategies, math, reading, study skills, time management, and written language. Remediation is provided through the program or unit via professional tutors and other. Remediation is also provided collaboratively through on-campus or off-campus services via computer-based instruction, professional tutors, trained peer tutors, and other.

Enrichment Enrichment programs are available through the program or unit for college survival skills, learning strategies, reading, self-advocacy, stress management, study skills, test taking, time management, written composition skills, and other. Programs for career planning, college survival skills, health and nutrition, learning strategies, math, practical computer skills, reading, stress management, study skills, test taking, time management, vocabulary development, written composition skills, and other are provided collaboratively through on-campus or off-campus services.

Student Organization LD Support Group.

Application For admittance to the program or unit, students are required to provide a psychoeducational report (5 years old or less) and provide disability registration form. It is recommended that students provide documentation of high school services. Upon application, materials documenting need for services should be sent only to admissions with institutional application materials. Upon acceptance, documentation of need for services should be sent only to the LD program or unit. *Application deadline (institutional):* 1/15. *Application deadline (LD program):* Rolling/continuous for fall and rolling/continuous for spring.

Written Policies Written policy regarding general/basic LD accommodations is available on the program Web site. Written policy regarding general/basic LD accommodations is outlined in the school's catalog/handbook.

Barton College
Academic Enrichment Center

PO Box 5000
Wilson, NC 27893-7000
http://www.barton.edu/

Contact: Ms. Leslie Stahlhut, Coordinator of Academic Enrichment Center. Phone: 252-399-6512. Fax: 252-399-6571. E-mail: lstahlhut@barton.edu.

Academic Enrichment Center Approximately 30 registered undergraduate students were served during 2002-03. The program or unit includes 1 full-time staff member. Skill tutors, strategy tutors, and trained peer tutors are provided through the program or unit. Academic advisers, regular education teachers, skill tutors, strategy tutors, and trained peer tutors are provided collaboratively through on-campus or off-campus services.

Subject-area Tutoring Tutoring is offered one-on-one and in small groups for some subjects.

Enrichment Programs for career planning, college survival skills, learning strategies, math, study skills, and test taking are provided collaboratively through on-campus or off-campus services.

Application For admittance to the program or unit, students are required to provide a neuropsychological evaluation. Upon acceptance, documentation of need for services should be sent only to the LD program or unit. *Application deadline (institutional):* Continuous. *Application deadline (LD program):* Rolling/continuous for fall and rolling/continuous for spring.

Written Policies Written policy regarding general/basic LD accommodations is available through the program or unit directly.

Bellarmine University
Disability Services

2001 Newburg Road

Louisville, KY 40205-0671

http://www.bellarmine.edu/studentaffairs/disabilityservices

Contact: Dr. J. Fred Ehrman, Assistant Dean of Students and Disability Services Coordinator. Phone: 502-452-8150. Fax: 502-452-8050. E-mail: fehrman@bellarmine.edu.

Disability Services Approximately 40 registered undergraduate students were served during 2002-03. The program or unit includes 1 full-time staff member. Academic advisers are provided through the program or unit. Academic advisers, counselors, diagnostic specialists, LD specialists, remediation/learning specialists, skill tutors, strategy tutors, and trained peer tutors are provided collaboratively through on-campus or off-campus services.

Subject-area Tutoring Tutoring is offered one-on-one and in small groups. Tutoring is provided collaboratively through on-campus or off-campus services via trained peer tutors.

Diagnostic Testing Testing for intelligence, learning strategies, learning styles, math, personality, reading, study skills, written language, and other services is provided collaboratively through on-campus or off-campus services.

Basic Skills Remediation Remediation is offered one-on-one and in small groups for computer skills, learning strategies, math, reading, spelling, study skills, and written language. Remediation is provided collaboratively through on-campus or off-campus services via trained peer tutors.

Enrichment Programs for college survival skills, health and nutrition, learning strategies, stress management, time management, and other are provided collaboratively through on-campus or off-campus services. Credit is offered for college survival skills, health and nutrition, learning strategies, stress management, time management, and other.

Application For admittance to the program or unit, students are required to provide a psychoeducational report (3 years old or less). It is recommended that students provide documentation of high school services. Upon application, materials documenting need for services should be sent only to the LD program or unit. Upon acceptance, documentation of need for services should be sent only to the LD program or unit. *Application deadline (institutional):* 2/1. *Application deadline (LD program):* Rolling/continuous for fall and rolling/continuous for spring.

Written Policies Written policy regarding general/basic LD accommodations is available on the program Web site. Written policy regarding general/basic LD accommodations is outlined in the school's catalog/handbook.

Beloit College
Learning Support Services Center

700 College Street

Beloit, WI 53511-5596

http://www.beloit.edu/~dss/

Contact: Ms. Diane M. Arnzen, Director. Phone: 608-363-2572. Fax: 608-363-7059. E-mail: arnzend@beloit.edu.

Learning Support Services Center Approximately 65 registered undergraduate students were served during 2002-03. The program or unit includes 2 full-time staff members. Diagnostic specialists, skill tutors, strategy tutors, and trained peer tutors are provided through the program or unit.

Unique Aids and Services Aids, services, or accommodations include faculty training.

Subject-area Tutoring Tutoring is offered one-on-one and in small groups for all subjects. Tutoring is provided through the program or unit via computer-based instruction and trained peer tutors.

Basic Skills Remediation Remediation is offered one-on-one and in small groups for auditory processing, learning strategies, reading, social skills, study skills, time management, and written language. Remediation is provided through the program or unit via computer-based instruction, trained peer tutors, and other.

Enrichment Enrichment programs are available through the program or unit for college survival skills, learning strategies, oral communication skills, stress management, study skills, test taking, and time management. Programs for career planning, college survival skills, health and nutrition, math, practical computer skills, reading, self-advocacy, stress management, and written composition skills are provided collaboratively through on-campus or off-campus services.

Application For admittance to the program or unit, students are required to provide a psychoeducational report. Upon application, materials documenting need for services should be sent only to the LD program or unit. Upon acceptance, documentation of need for services should be sent only to the LD program or unit. *Application deadline (institutional):* 2/1. *Application deadline (LD program):* Rolling/continuous for fall and rolling/continuous for spring.

Beloit College (continued)

Written Policies Written policy regarding general/basic LD accommodations is available on the program Web site. Written policy regarding general/basic LD accommodations is outlined in the school's catalog/handbook. Written policies regarding general/basic LD accommodations and reduced course loads are available through the program or unit directly.

Bemidji State University

1500 Birchmont Drive, NE
Bemidji, MN 56601-2699
http://www.bemidjistate.edu/

Contact: Kathi Hagen, Assistant Director, Disabilities.
Phone: 218-755-3883. E-mail: khagen@bemidjistate.edu.

The program or unit includes 1 full-time staff member. Regular education teachers are provided collaboratively through on-campus or off-campus services.

Unique Aids and Services Aids, services, or accommodations include career counseling and priority registration.

Subject-area Tutoring Tutoring is offered for some subjects.

Basic Skills Remediation Remediation is offered in class-size groups for study skills and time management. Remediation is provided collaboratively through on-campus or off-campus services.

Enrichment Programs for career planning, reading, study skills, and time management are provided collaboratively through on-campus or off-campus services. Credit is offered for career planning and study skills.

Application For admittance to the program or unit, students are required to apply to the program directly, provide a psychoeducational report (5 years old or less), and provide testing results and recommendations if applicable. Upon acceptance, documentation of need for services should be sent only to admissions. *Application deadline (institutional):* Continuous. *Application deadline (LD program):* Rolling/continuous for fall and rolling/continuous for spring.

Benedictine College

1020 North 2nd Street
Atchison, KS 66002-1499
http://www.benedictine.edu/

Contact: Ms. Camille Osborn, Director of General Studies Center. Phone: 913-367-5340 Ext. 2517. Fax: 913-367-5462.
E-mail: cosborn@benedictine.edu.

Approximately 30 registered undergraduate students were served during 2002-03. The program or unit includes 5 part-time staff members. Counselors and trained peer tutors are provided through the program or unit. Academic advisers, counselors, and trained peer tutors are provided collaboratively through on-campus or off-campus services.

Orientation The program or unit offers a mandatory orientation for new students before classes begin, during registration, after classes begin, and individually by special arrangement.

Unique Aids and Services Aids, services, or accommodations include advocates, digital textbooks, and weekly meetings with faculty.

Subject-area Tutoring Tutoring is offered one-on-one and in small groups for most subjects. Tutoring is provided through the program or unit via computer-based instruction and trained peer tutors.

Enrichment Enrichment programs are available through the program or unit for college survival skills and study skills. Programs for career planning, health and nutrition, learning strategies, stress management, and study skills are provided collaboratively through on-campus or off-campus services. Credit is offered for college survival skills.

Application For admittance to the program or unit, students are required to provide a psychoeducational report (3 years old or less). Upon application, materials documenting need for services should be sent only to admissions with institutional application materials. Upon acceptance, documentation of need for services should be sent only to admissions. *Application deadline (LD program):* Rolling/continuous for fall and rolling/continuous for spring.

Written Policies Written policy regarding general/basic LD accommodations is available through the program or unit directly.

Benedictine University

5700 College Road
Lisle, IL 60532-0900
http://www.ben.edu/

Contact: Ms. Tina Sonderby, Coordinator of Special Programs. Phone: 630-829-6512. Fax: 630-829-6663.
E-mail: tsonderby@ben.edu.

Approximately 9 registered undergraduate students were served during 2002-03. The program or unit includes 2 full-time staff members. LD specialists are provided through the program or unit. Academic advisers, professional tutors, and trained peer tutors are provided collaboratively through on-campus or off-campus services.

Subject-area Tutoring Tutoring is offered one-on-one for some subjects. Tutoring is provided through the program or unit via LD specialists, professional tutors, and trained peer tutors.

Basic Skills Remediation Remediation is offered one-on-one for learning strategies, math, reading, study skills, time management, and written language. Remediation is provided through the program or unit via LD specialists, professional tutors, and trained peer tutors.

Enrichment Enrichment programs are available through the program or unit for college survival skills, learning strategies, math, reading, stress management, study skills, test taking, time management, and written composition skills. Program for career planning is provided collaboratively through on-campus or off-campus services.

Application For admittance to the program or unit, students are required to provide a psychoeducational report (3 years old or less). Upon acceptance, documentation of need for services should be sent only to the LD program or unit. *Application deadline (institutional):* Continuous. *Application deadline (LD program):* Rolling/continuous for fall and rolling/continuous for spring.

Written Policies Written policy regarding general/basic LD accommodations is available through the program or unit directly.

Bennett College
Office of Students with Disabilities

900 East Washington Street

Greensboro, NC 27401-3239

http://www.bennett.edu/

Contact: Dr. Beth H. Holder, Coordinator for Students with Disabilities. Phone: 336-517-2178. E-mail: bholder@bennett.edu.

Office of Students with Disabilities Approximately 8 registered undergraduate students were served during 2002-03. The program or unit includes 1 full-time staff member. Academic advisers, LD specialists, and special education teachers are provided through the program or unit. Academic advisers, counselors, diagnostic specialists, professional tutors, regular education teachers, remediation/learning specialists, skill tutors, strategy tutors, and trained peer tutors are provided collaboratively through on-campus or off-campus services.

Orientation The program or unit offers an optional orientation for new students individually by special arrangement.

Unique Aids and Services Aids, services, or accommodations include advocates and faculty training.

Subject-area Tutoring Tutoring is offered one-on-one and in small groups for all subjects. Tutoring is provided collaboratively through on-campus or off-campus services via computer-based instruction and trained peer tutors.

Diagnostic Testing Testing for learning strategies, learning styles, math, personality, reading, social skills, spelling, study skills, and written language is provided collaboratively through on-campus or off-campus services.

Basic Skills Remediation Remediation is offered one-on-one and in class-size groups for auditory processing, computer skills, handwriting, learning strategies, math, motor skills, reading, social skills, spelling, spoken language, study skills, time management, visual processing, and written language. Remediation is provided collaboratively through on-campus or off-campus services via regular education teachers and trained peer tutors.

Enrichment Enrichment programs are available through the program or unit for self-advocacy. Programs for career planning, college survival skills, health and nutrition, learning strategies, math, oral communication skills, practical computer skills, reading, stress management, study skills, test taking, time management, and written composition skills are provided collaboratively through on-campus or off-campus services. Credit is offered for college survival skills, health and nutrition, math, oral communication skills, practical computer skills, reading, and written composition skills.

Application For admittance to the program or unit, students are required to apply to the program directly and provide a psychoeducational report (3 years old or less). It is recommended that students provide documentation of high school services. Upon application, materials documenting need for services should be sent only to the LD program or unit. Upon acceptance, documentation of need for services should be sent only to the LD program or unit. *Application deadline (institutional):* Continuous. *Application deadline (LD program):* Rolling/continuous for fall and rolling/continuous for spring.

Written Policies Written policies regarding course substitutions, general/basic LD accommodations, grade forgiveness, reduced course loads, substitutions and waivers of admissions requirements, and substitutions and waivers of graduation requirements are available through the program or unit directly.

Bentley College
Counseling and Student Development

175 Forest Street

Waltham, MA 02452-4705

http://ecampus.bentley.edu/dept/counsel/

Contact: Mr. Christopher Kennedy, Coordinator of Disability Services. Phone: 781-891-2274. Fax: 781-891-2474. E-mail: ckennedy@bentley.edu.

Counseling and Student Development Approximately 125 registered undergraduate students were served during 2002-03. The program or unit includes 1 full-time staff member. Academic advisers, coaches, LD specialists, skill tutors, and strategy tutors are provided through the program or unit. Academic advisers, counselors, diagnostic specialists, professional tutors, regular education teachers, remediation/learning specialists, special education teachers, teacher trainees, and trained peer tutors are provided collaboratively through on-campus or off-campus services.

Summer Program To help prepare for the demands of college, there is a mandatory 1-week summer program prior to entering the school.

Unique Aids and Services Aids, services, or accommodations include advocates, career counseling, digital textbooks, faculty training, parent workshops, personal coach, priority registration, support groups, and weekly meetings with faculty.

Subject-area Tutoring Tutoring is offered one-on-one for most subjects. Tutoring is provided through the program or unit via LD specialists. Tutoring is also provided collaboratively through on-campus or off-campus services via computer-based instruction, graduate assistants/students, professional tutors, and trained peer tutors.

Enrichment Enrichment programs are available through the program or unit for college survival skills, learning strategies, self-advocacy, stress management, study skills, test taking, and time management. Programs for career planning, college survival skills, health and nutrition, math, medication management, oral communication skills, practical computer skills, reading, stress management, study skills, test taking, time management, and written composition skills are provided collaboratively through on-campus or off-campus services.

Application For admittance to the program or unit, students are required to provide a psychoeducational report (5 years old or less). It is recommended that students provide documentation of high school services. Upon application, materials documenting need for services should be sent only to admissions with institutional application materials. Upon acceptance, documentation of need for services should be sent only to the LD program or unit. *Application deadline (institutional):* 2/1. *Application deadline (LD program):* Rolling/continuous for fall and rolling/continuous for spring.

Written Policies Written policies regarding course substitutions, general/basic LD accommodations, grade forgiveness, reduced course loads, and substitutions and waivers of graduation requirements are

Bentley College (continued)

available on the program Web site. Written policies regarding course substitutions, general/basic LD accommodations, grade forgiveness, reduced course loads, and substitutions and waivers of graduation requirements are outlined in the school's catalog/handbook.

Bethany College of the Assemblies of God
Educational Support Services

800 Bethany Drive
Scotts Valley, CA 95066-2820
http://www.bethany.edu/

Contact: Cynthia S.T. FitzGerald, Director of Educational Support Services. Phone: 831-438-3800 Ext. 2129. Fax: 831-439-9983. E-mail: cfitz@fc.bethany.edu.

Educational Support Services Approximately 45 registered undergraduate students were served during 2002-03. The program or unit includes 1 full-time and 6 part-time staff members. Academic advisers, counselors, LD specialists, remediation/learning specialists, skill tutors, strategy tutors, and trained peer tutors are provided through the program or unit. Academic advisers, skill tutors, strategy tutors, and trained peer tutors are provided collaboratively through on-campus or off-campus services.

Unique Aids and Services Aids, services, or accommodations include advocates, faculty training, peer tutors in the Student Individualized Learning Center, weekly meeting with educational therapist.

Subject-area Tutoring Tutoring is offered one-on-one and in small groups for all subjects. Tutoring is provided through the program or unit via LD specialists, professional tutors, and trained peer tutors. Tutoring is also provided collaboratively through on-campus or off-campus services via computer-based instruction, graduate assistants/students, and trained peer tutors.

Basic Skills Remediation Remediation is offered one-on-one and in class-size groups for computer skills, learning strategies, math, reading, study skills, time management, and written language. Remediation is provided through the program or unit via LD specialists, professional tutors, and trained peer tutors. Remediation is also provided collaboratively through on-campus or off-campus services via computer-based instruction, graduate assistants/students, regular education teachers, special education teachers, and trained peer tutors.

Enrichment Enrichment programs are available through the program or unit for college survival skills, learning strategies, reading, stress management, study skills, test taking, time management, vocabulary development, and written composition skills. Programs for math, oral communication skills, practical computer skills, reading, stress management, study skills, test taking, time management, and written composition skills are provided collaboratively through on-campus or off-campus services. Credit is offered for college survival skills, learning strategies, math, oral communication skills, stress management, study skills, test taking, time management, and written composition skills.

Application For admittance to the program or unit, students are required to provide a psychoeducational report (3 years old or less) and provide professional documentation of 504/ADA issues and

recommended accommodations. It is recommended that students provide documentation of high school services. Upon acceptance, documentation of need for services should be sent only to the LD program or unit. *Application deadline (institutional): 7/1. Application deadline (LD program):* Rolling/continuous for fall and rolling/continuous for spring.

Written Policies Written policies regarding course substitutions, general/basic LD accommodations, grade forgiveness, and substitutions and waivers of graduation requirements are available on the program Web site. Written policies regarding course substitutions, general/basic LD accommodations, grade forgiveness, and substitutions and waivers of graduation requirements are outlined in the school's catalog/handbook.

Bethel College
Disability Services

3900 Bethel Drive
St. Paul, MN 55112-6999
http://www.bethel.edu/Disability

Contact: Ms. Kathleen J. McGillivray, Director of Disability Services. Phone: 651-635-8759. Fax: 651-638-8880. E-mail: k-mcgillivray@bethel.edu.

Disability Services Approximately 25 registered undergraduate students were served during 2002-03. The program or unit includes 1 full-time and 2 part-time staff members. Academic advisers, coaches, diagnostic specialists, professional tutors, and special education teachers are provided through the program or unit. Academic advisers, coaches, diagnostic specialists, graduate assistants/students, LD specialists, remediation/learning specialists, and strategy tutors are provided collaboratively through on-campus or off-campus services.

Unique Aids and Services Aids, services, or accommodations include advocates, digital textbooks, faculty training, and weekly meetings with faculty.

Subject-area Tutoring Tutoring is offered one-on-one and in small groups for some subjects. Tutoring is provided collaboratively through on-campus or off-campus services via computer-based instruction, LD specialists, and other.

Enrichment Programs for career planning, college survival skills, learning strategies, study skills, test taking, time management, and written composition skills are provided collaboratively through on-campus or off-campus services. Credit is offered for college survival skills.

Application For admittance to the program or unit, students are required to provide a psychoeducational report. It is recommended that students provide documentation of high school services. Upon acceptance, documentation of need for services should be sent only to the LD program or unit. *Application deadline (institutional): 3/1. Application deadline (LD program):* Rolling/continuous for fall and rolling/continuous for spring.

Written Policies Written policy regarding general/basic LD accommodations is available on the program Web site. Written policy regarding general/basic LD accommodations is outlined in the school's catalog/handbook. Written policy regarding general/basic LD accommodations is available through the program or unit directly.

Bishop's University
Special Needs, Counselling Services

Lennoxville, QC J1M 1Z7

Canada

http://www.ubishops.ca/

Contact: Linda Nyiri, Special Needs Assistant. Phone: 819-822-9600 Ext. 2434. Fax: 819-822-9605. E-mail: lnyiri@ubishops.ca. Head of LD Program: Dr. Rosa Morelli, Director of Counseling Services. Phone: 819-822-9695. Fax: 819-822-9605. E-mail: rmorelli@ubishops.ca.

Special Needs, Counselling Services Approximately 56 registered undergraduate students were served during 2002-03. The program or unit includes 1 full-time and 1 part-time staff member. Counselors, diagnostic specialists, skill tutors, strategy tutors, trained peer tutors, and other are provided through the program or unit. Academic advisers are provided collaboratively through on-campus or off-campus services.

Orientation The program or unit offers an optional orientation for new students before classes begin, during registration, and individually by special arrangement.

Unique Aids and Services Aids, services, or accommodations include advocates, career counseling, and digital textbooks.

Subject-area Tutoring Tutoring is offered one-on-one for all subjects. Tutoring is provided through the program or unit via trained peer tutors.

Diagnostic Testing Testing is provided through the program or unit for intelligence, learning strategies, learning styles, math, reading, spelling, study skills, visual processing, and written language.

Basic Skills Remediation Remediation is available for learning strategies, reading, study skills, and time management.

Enrichment Enrichment programs are available through the program or unit for career planning, college survival skills, learning strategies, reading, stress management, study skills, test taking, and time management. Programs for college survival skills, health and nutrition, math, medication management, oral communication skills, practical computer skills, and written composition skills are provided collaboratively through on-campus or off-campus services.

Application For admittance to the program or unit, students are required to apply to the program directly, provide a psychoeducational report (5 years old or less), and provide documentation of high school services. It is recommended that students provide other documentation. Upon application, materials documenting need for services should be sent only to the LD program or unit. Upon acceptance, documentation of need for services should be sent only to the LD program or unit. *Application deadline (institutional):* 3/1. *Application deadline (LD program):* Rolling/continuous for fall and rolling/continuous for spring.

Written Policies Written policy regarding general/basic LD accommodations is outlined in the school's catalog/handbook.

Black Hills State University

1200 University Street

Spearfish, SD 57799

http://www.bhsu.edu/

Contact: Joan M. Wermers, Disability Services Adviser. Phone: 605-642-6099. Fax: 605-642-6497. E-mail: joanwermers@bhsu.edu.

Approximately 70 registered undergraduate students were served during 2002-03. The program or unit includes 1 full-time and 3 part-time staff members. Academic advisers, skill tutors, special education teachers, strategy tutors, and trained peer tutors are provided through the program or unit. Academic advisers, counselors, professional tutors, regular education teachers, remediation/learning specialists, skill tutors, strategy tutors, and trained peer tutors are provided collaboratively through on-campus or off-campus services.

Unique Aids and Services Aids, services, or accommodations include advocates, career counseling, support groups, academic accommodations based on disability documentation recommendations.

Subject-area Tutoring Tutoring is offered one-on-one, in small groups, and in class-size groups for some subjects. Tutoring is provided through the program or unit via computer-based instruction. Tutoring is also provided collaboratively through on-campus or off-campus services via professional tutors and trained peer tutors.

Diagnostic Testing Testing is provided through the program or unit for learning strategies, learning styles, and study skills. Testing for learning strategies, learning styles, math, study skills, and written language is provided collaboratively through on-campus or off-campus services.

Basic Skills Remediation Remediation is offered one-on-one, in small groups, and in class-size groups for computer skills, learning strategies, math, study skills, time management, and written language. Remediation is provided through the program or unit via computer-based instruction. Remediation is also provided collaboratively through on-campus or off-campus services via regular education teachers and trained peer tutors.

Enrichment Enrichment programs are available through the program or unit for self-advocacy. Programs for career planning, college survival skills, learning strategies, stress management, study skills, test taking, and time management are provided collaboratively through on-campus or off-campus services.

Student Organization Student Support Services Organization consists of 25 members.

Application For admittance to the program or unit, students are required to apply to the program directly, provide a psychoeducational report (3 years old or less), provide documentation of high school services, and provide a multidisciplinary evaluation team report. Upon application, materials documenting need for services should be sent only to the LD program or unit. Upon acceptance, documentation of need for services should be sent only to the LD program or unit. *Application deadline (institutional):* Continuous. *Application deadline (LD program):* Rolling/continuous for fall and rolling/continuous for spring.

Written Policies Written policy regarding general/basic LD accommodations is available on the program Web site. Written policy regarding general/basic LD accommodations is outlined in the school's catalog/handbook.

Bluffton College
Learning Resource Center, Disability Services

280 West College Avenue, Suite 1

Bluffton, OH 45817-1196

Bluffton College (continued)
http://www.bluffton.edu/

Contact: Diane Jones, Director of Learning Resources. Phone: 419-358-3019. Fax: 419-358-3323. E-mail: jonesd@bluffton.edu.

Learning Resource Center, Disability Services The program or unit includes 1 full-time staff member. Counselors and strategy tutors are provided through the program or unit. Academic advisers, diagnostic specialists, graduate assistants/students, LD specialists, skill tutors, teacher trainees, and trained peer tutors are provided collaboratively through on-campus or off-campus services.

Unique Aids and Services Aids, services, or accommodations include advocates, career counseling, and digital textbooks.

Subject-area Tutoring Tutoring is offered one-on-one and in small groups for all subjects. Tutoring is provided through the program or unit via other. Tutoring is also provided collaboratively through on-campus or off-campus services via other.

Basic Skills Remediation Remediation is offered one-on-one for learning strategies, study skills, and time management. Remediation is provided through the program or unit via teacher trainees and other.

Enrichment Enrichment programs are available through the program or unit for career planning, college survival skills, learning strategies, math, stress management, study skills, test taking, time management, and written composition skills. Programs for career planning, college survival skills, health and nutrition, learning strategies, stress management, study skills, test taking, time management, and written composition skills are provided collaboratively through on-campus or off-campus services.

Application For admittance to the program or unit, students are required to provide documentation of high school services. It is recommended that students apply to the program directly and provide a psychoeducational report. Upon application, materials documenting need for services should be sent to both admissions and the LD program or unit. Upon acceptance, documentation of need for services should be sent only to the LD program or unit. *Application deadline (institutional): 5/31. Application deadline (LD program):* Rolling/continuous for fall and rolling/continuous for spring.

Written Policies Written policy regarding substitutions and waivers of graduation requirements is outlined in the school's catalog/handbook. Written policy regarding general/basic LD accommodations is available through the program or unit directly.

Boston College

140 Commonwealth Avenue
Chestnut Hill, MA 02467-3800
http://www.bc.edu/

Contact: Dr. Kathleen Duggan, Assistant Director of Academic Development Center. Fax: 617-552-6075.

The program or unit includes 2 full-time staff members and 1 part-time staff member. Coaches, graduate assistants/students, LD specialists, strategy tutors, and trained peer tutors are provided through the program or unit. Academic advisers and counselors are provided collaboratively through on-campus or off-campus services.

Summer Program To help prepare for the demands of college, there is 6-week summer program prior to entering the school. Degree credit will be earned.

Unique Aids and Services Aids, services, or accommodations include personal coach and priority registration.

Subject-area Tutoring Tutoring is offered one-on-one for most subjects. Tutoring is provided through the program or unit via professional tutors and trained peer tutors. Tutoring is also provided collaboratively through on-campus or off-campus services via graduate assistants/students, professional tutors, and trained peer tutors.

Enrichment Programs for career planning, college survival skills, health and nutrition, learning strategies, math, medication management, reading, self-advocacy, stress management, study skills, test taking, time management, and written composition skills are provided collaboratively through on-campus or off-campus services.

Application For admittance to the program or unit, students are required to provide a psychoeducational report (4 years old or less). It is recommended that students provide documentation of high school services. Upon application, materials documenting need for services should be sent to both admissions and the LD program or unit. Upon acceptance, documentation of need for services should be sent only to the LD program or unit. *Application deadline (institutional): 1/2.*

Written Policies Written policy regarding general/basic LD accommodations is outlined in the school's catalog/handbook. Written policies regarding course substitutions and general/basic LD accommodations are available through the program or unit directly.

Boston University
Learning Disability Service

Boston, MA 02215
http://www.bu.edu/disability

Contact: Dr. Lorraine E. Wolf, Clinical Director. Phone: 617-353-3658. Fax: 617-353-9646. E-mail: lwolf@bu.edu.

Learning Disability Service Approximately 500 registered undergraduate students were served during 2002-03. The program or unit includes 2 full-time and 6 part-time staff members. Graduate assistants/students, remediation/learning specialists, strategy tutors, and other are provided through the program or unit.

Summer Program To help prepare for the demands of college, there is an optional 5-day summer program prior to entering the school.

Subject-area Tutoring Tutoring is offered one-on-one for most subjects. Tutoring is provided collaboratively through on-campus or off-campus services via graduate assistants/students and trained peer tutors.

Basic Skills Remediation Remediation is offered one-on-one and in small groups for learning strategies, study skills, time management, written language, and test-taking strategies.

Fees *LD Program or Service* fee is $1600. *Summer Program* fee is $2100.

Application For admittance to the program or unit, students are required to provide a psychoeducational report (3 years old or less) and provide full diagnostic report upon admission only. Upon application, materials documenting need for services should be sent only to the LD program or unit. Upon acceptance, documentation of need for services should be sent only to the LD program or unit. *Application deadline (institutional): 1/1.*

Written Policies Written policies regarding course substitutions, general/basic LD accommodations, substitutions and waivers of admissions requirements, and substitutions and waivers of graduation requirements are available on the program Web site. Written policies regarding course substitutions, general/basic LD accommodations, substitutions and waivers of admissions requirements, and substitutions and waivers of graduation requirements are outlined in the school's catalog/handbook. Written policies regarding course substitutions, general/basic LD accommodations, reduced course loads, substitutions and waivers of admissions requirements, and substitutions and waivers of graduation requirements are available through the program or unit directly.

Bradley University

1501 West Bradley Avenue
Peoria, IL 61625-0002
http://www.bradley.edu/
Contact: Phone: 309-676-7611.

The program or unit includes 3 full-time and 2 part-time staff members. Trained peer tutors are provided through the program or unit. Trained peer tutors are provided collaboratively through on-campus or off-campus services.

Unique Aids and Services Aids, services, or accommodations include advocates and faculty training.

Subject-area Tutoring Tutoring is offered one-on-one and in small groups for most subjects. Tutoring is provided through the program or unit via trained peer tutors. Tutoring is also provided collaboratively through on-campus or off-campus services via graduate assistants/students and trained peer tutors.

Diagnostic Testing Testing is provided through the program or unit for learning strategies, learning styles, reading, and study skills. Testing for learning styles, reading, and study skills is provided collaboratively through on-campus or off-campus services.

Basic Skills Remediation Remediation is offered one-on-one and in class-size groups for learning strategies, study skills, time management, and written language. Remediation is provided through the program or unit via trained peer tutors. Remediation is also provided collaboratively through on-campus or off-campus services via trained peer tutors.

Enrichment Enrichment programs are available through the program or unit for college survival skills, learning strategies, math, reading, stress management, study skills, test taking, and time management. Programs for career planning, college survival skills, learning strategies, practical computer skills, reading, stress management, study skills, test taking, time management, and written composition skills are provided collaboratively through on-campus or off-campus services.

Application For admittance to the program or unit, students are required to provide a psychoeducational report (3 years old or less). Upon acceptance, documentation of need for services should be sent only to the LD program or unit. *Application deadline (institutional):* Continuous. *Application deadline (LD program):* Rolling/continuous for fall and rolling/continuous for spring.

Written Policies Written policy regarding general/basic LD accommodations is available on the program Web site. Written policy regarding general/basic LD accommodations is outlined in the school's catalog/handbook. Written policy regarding general/basic LD accommodations is available through the program or unit directly.

Brandon University

270 18th Street
Brandon, MB R7A 6A9
Canada
http://www.brandonu.ca/
Contact: Darcy Bower, Registrar. Phone: 204-727-9635. Fax: 204-725-2143. E-mail: bower@brandonu.ca.

Unique Aids and Services Aids, services, or accommodations include career counseling and priority registration.

Subject-area Tutoring Tutoring is offered one-on-one and in small groups for all subjects. Tutoring is provided collaboratively through on-campus or off-campus services via trained peer tutors.

Basic Skills Remediation Remediation is offered one-on-one and in small groups for computer skills, learning strategies, math, spelling, study skills, time management, and written language. Remediation is provided collaboratively through on-campus or off-campus services.

Application For admittance to the program or unit, students are required to provide a psychoeducational report (3 years old or less). It is recommended that students provide documentation of high school services. Upon application, materials documenting need for services should be sent only to the LD program or unit. Upon acceptance, documentation of need for services should be sent to both admissions and the LD program or unit. *Application deadline (institutional):* Continuous. *Application deadline (LD program):* Rolling/continuous for fall and rolling/continuous for spring.

Written Policies Written policy regarding general/basic LD accommodations is available on the program Web site. Written policy regarding general/basic LD accommodations is outlined in the school's catalog/handbook. Written policy regarding general/basic LD accommodations is available through the program or unit directly.

Brevard College
Office for Students with Special Needs and Disabilities

400 North Broad Street
Brevard, NC 28712-3306
http://www.brevard.edu/
Contact: Ms. Susan Kuehn, Director of Office for Students with Special Needs and Disabilities. Phone: 828-884-8131. Fax: 828-884-3790. E-mail: skuehn@brevard.edu.

Office for Students with Special Needs and Disabilities Approximately 55 registered undergraduate students were served during 2002-03. The program or unit includes 1 full-time staff member. Academic advisers, counselors, professional tutors, remediation/learning specialists, and trained peer tutors are provided collaboratively through on-campus or off-campus services.

Summer Program To help prepare for the demands of college, there is an optional 5-week summer program prior to entering the school. Degree credit will be earned.

Subject-area Tutoring Tutoring is offered one-on-one and in small groups for most subjects. Tutoring is provided collaboratively through on-campus or off-campus services via professional tutors and trained peer tutors.

Brevard College (continued)

Diagnostic Testing Testing for learning styles, math, personality, reading, visual processing, and written language is provided collaboratively through on-campus or off-campus services.

Basic Skills Remediation Remediation is offered in class-size groups for math, reading, and written language. Remediation is provided collaboratively through on-campus or off-campus services via regular education teachers.

Enrichment Enrichment programs are available through the program or unit for self-advocacy. Programs for career planning, college survival skills, health and nutrition, learning strategies, math, medication management, oral communication skills, practical computer skills, reading, stress management, study skills, test taking, time management, vocabulary development, and written composition skills are provided collaboratively through on-campus or off-campus services. Credit is offered for college survival skills, health and nutrition, learning strategies, math, oral communication skills, practical computer skills, reading, stress management, study skills, test taking, time management, vocabulary development, and written composition skills.

Application For admittance to the program or unit, students are required to provide a psychoeducational report. It is recommended that students provide documentation of high school services. Upon application, materials documenting need for services should be sent only to the LD program or unit. Upon acceptance, documentation of need for services should be sent only to the LD program or unit. *Application deadline (institutional):* Continuous. *Application deadline (LD program):* Rolling/continuous for fall and rolling/continuous for spring.

Written Policies Written policies regarding course substitutions, general/basic LD accommodations, reduced course loads, substitutions and waivers of admissions requirements, and substitutions and waivers of graduation requirements are available on the program Web site. Written policies regarding grade forgiveness and substitutions and waivers of graduation requirements are outlined in the school's catalog/handbook. Written policies regarding course substitutions, general/basic LD accommodations, reduced course loads, substitutions and waivers of admissions requirements, and substitutions and waivers of graduation requirements are available through the program or unit directly.

Briar Cliff University

3303 Rebecca Street
Sioux City, IA 51104-0100
http://www.briarcliff.edu/

Contact: Sr. Jean Ann Beringer OSF, Director of Student Support Services. Phone: 712-279-5232. Fax: 712-279-5366. E-mail: beringer@briarcliff.edu.

The program or unit includes 1 part-time staff member. Counselors, skill tutors, and trained peer tutors are provided through the program or unit.

Application For admittance to the program or unit, students are required to apply to the program directly and provide a psychoeducational report (3 years old or less). It is recommended that students provide documentation of high school services. Upon application, materials documenting need for services should be sent only to the LD program or unit. Upon acceptance, documentation of need for

services should be sent only to the LD program or unit. *Application deadline (institutional):* Continuous. *Application deadline (LD program):* Rolling/continuous for fall and rolling/continuous for spring.

Written Policies Written policies regarding course substitutions, general/basic LD accommodations, reduced course loads, and substitutions and waivers of graduation requirements are available on the program Web site. Written policies regarding course substitutions, general/basic LD accommodations, reduced course loads, and substitutions and waivers of graduation requirements are available through the program or unit directly.

Brown University
Disability Support Services

Providence, RI 02912
http://www.brown.edu/Student_Services/
Office_of_Student_Life/dss/

Contact: Coordinator. Phone: 401-863-9588. E-mail: dss@brown.edu.

Disability Support Services Approximately 135 registered undergraduate students were served during 2002-03. The program or unit includes 1 full-time staff member. Academic advisers, coaches, counselors, diagnostic specialists, LD specialists, professional tutors, and skill tutors are provided collaboratively through on-campus or off-campus services.

Orientation The program or unit offers a mandatory 3 to 5-hour orientation for new students before classes begin and after classes begin.

Unique Aids and Services Aids, services, or accommodations include career counseling, personal coach, and support groups.

Subject-area Tutoring Tutoring is offered one-on-one and in small groups for some subjects. Tutoring is provided collaboratively through on-campus or off-campus services via graduate assistants/students, professional tutors, and trained peer tutors.

Diagnostic Testing Testing for auditory processing, handwriting, intelligence, learning strategies, learning styles, math, motor skills, neuropsychological, personality, reading, social skills, spelling, spoken language, study skills, visual processing, and written language is provided collaboratively through on-campus or off-campus services.

Basic Skills Remediation Remediation is offered one-on-one for learning strategies, reading, spelling, study skills, time management, and written language. Remediation is provided collaboratively through on-campus or off-campus services via professional tutors.

Enrichment Enrichment programs are available through the program or unit for self-advocacy. Programs for career planning, learning strategies, math, oral communication skills, practical computer skills, reading, self-advocacy, stress management, study skills, test taking, time management, and written composition skills are provided collaboratively through on-campus or off-campus services.

Student Organization Brown Disability Advocates consists of 45 members.

Fees *Diagnostic Testing* fee is $300 to $2000.

Application For admittance to the program or unit, students are required to provide a psychoeducational report (3 years old or less). Upon application, materials documenting need for services should be sent only to admissions with institutional application materials. Upon acceptance, documentation of need for services should be

sent only to the LD program or unit. *Application deadline (institutional): 1/1. Application deadline (LD program):* Rolling/continuous for fall and rolling/continuous for spring.
Written Policies Written policies regarding general/basic LD accommodations and reduced course loads are available on the program Web site. Written policy regarding general/basic LD accommodations is outlined in the school's catalog/handbook. Written policies regarding general/basic LD accommodations and reduced course loads are available through the program or unit directly.

Bryn Mawr College

101 North Merion Avenue
Bryn Mawr, PA 19010-2899
http://www.brynmawr.edu/
Contact: Stephanie Bell, Coordinator. Phone: 610-526-7351. Fax: 610-526-5451. E-mail: sbell@brynmawr.edu.

Approximately 30 registered undergraduate students were served during 2002-03. The program or unit includes 1 part-time staff member. LD specialists are provided through the program or unit. Academic advisers, counselors, diagnostic specialists, graduate assistants/students, regular education teachers, and trained peer tutors are provided collaboratively through on-campus or off-campus services.
Subject-area Tutoring Tutoring is offered one-on-one, in small groups, and in class-size groups for most subjects. Tutoring is provided collaboratively through on-campus or off-campus services via graduate assistants/students and trained peer tutors.
Diagnostic Testing Testing for auditory processing, intelligence, learning styles, math, motor skills, neuropsychological, personality, reading, spelling, spoken language, study skills, visual processing, and written language is provided collaboratively through on-campus or off-campus services.
Enrichment Enrichment programs are available through the program or unit for learning strategies, self-advocacy, study skills, test taking, and time management. Programs for career planning, health and nutrition, learning strategies, medication management, stress management, study skills, test taking, time management, and written composition skills are provided collaboratively through on-campus or off-campus services.
Fees *Diagnostic Testing* fee is $750 to $2400.
Application For admittance to the program or unit, students are required to provide a psychoeducational report. Upon acceptance, documentation of need for services should be sent only to the LD program or unit. *Application deadline (institutional): 1/15.*
Written Policies Written policies regarding general/basic LD accommodations and reduced course loads are outlined in the school's catalog/handbook. Written policies regarding course substitutions and general/basic LD accommodations are available through the program or unit directly.

Burlington College
Student Services

95 North Avenue
Burlington, VT 05401-2998

http://www.burlcol.edu/
Contact: Dr. Michael Watson, Dean of Students. Phone: 802-862-9616. E-mail: mwatson@burlcol.edu.

Student Services Approximately 10 registered undergraduate students were served during 2002-03. Academic advisers, diagnostic specialists, professional tutors, and regular education teachers are provided collaboratively through on-campus or off-campus services.
Unique Aids and Services Aids, services, or accommodations include advocates, career counseling, and personal coach.
Subject-area Tutoring Tutoring is offered one-on-one for some subjects. Tutoring is provided collaboratively through on-campus or off-campus services via professional tutors and trained peer tutors.
Diagnostic Testing Testing for auditory processing, handwriting, intelligence, learning strategies, learning styles, math, neuropsychological, reading, social skills, spelling, spoken language, study skills, visual processing, and written language is provided collaboratively through on-campus or off-campus services.
Basic Skills Remediation Remediation is offered one-on-one for computer skills, learning strategies, math, reading, social skills, study skills, and written language. Remediation is provided collaboratively through on-campus or off-campus services via professional tutors, regular education teachers, and trained peer tutors.
Enrichment Programs for career planning, college survival skills, learning strategies, math, oral communication skills, practical computer skills, reading, self-advocacy, stress management, study skills, test taking, time management, and written composition skills are provided collaboratively through on-campus or off-campus services. Credit is offered for oral communication skills, practical computer skills, and written composition skills.
Fees *Diagnostic Testing* fee is $0 to $1500.
Application For admittance to the program or unit, students are required to provide a psychoeducational report and provide documentation of high school services. *Application deadline (institutional): 8/1. Application deadline (LD program):* Rolling/continuous for fall and rolling/continuous for spring.
Written Policies Written policy regarding general/basic LD accommodations is available on the program Web site. Written policy regarding general/basic LD accommodations is outlined in the school's catalog/handbook.

Caldwell College

9 Ryerson Avenue
Caldwell, NJ 07006-6195
http://www.caldwell.edu/
Contact: Ms. Joan Serpico, Coordinator of Disability Services. Phone: 973-618-3645. Fax: 973-618-3488. E-mail: jserpico@caldwell.edu.

The program or unit includes 1 full-time staff member. LD specialists, remediation/learning specialists, skill tutors, and strategy tutors are provided through the program or unit. Academic advisers, coaches, counselors, LD specialists, professional tutors, regular education teachers, and trained peer tutors are provided collaboratively through on-campus or off-campus services.
Summer Program To help prepare for the demands of college, there is an optional 1-month summer program prior to entering the school. Degree credit will be earned.

Caldwell College (continued)

Unique Aids and Services Aids, services, or accommodations include career counseling and faculty training.

Subject-area Tutoring Tutoring is offered one-on-one and in small groups for all subjects. Tutoring is provided through the program or unit via LD specialists. Tutoring is also provided collaboratively through on-campus or off-campus services via computer-based instruction, graduate assistants/students, professional tutors, and trained peer tutors.

Basic Skills Remediation Remediation is offered in class-size groups for computer skills, learning strategies, math, reading, spelling, study skills, time management, and written language. Remediation is provided collaboratively through on-campus or off-campus services via regular education teachers.

Enrichment Enrichment programs are available through the program or unit for learning strategies, self-advocacy, study skills, test taking, and time management. Programs for career planning, college survival skills, health and nutrition, math, reading, study skills, test taking, and written composition skills are provided collaboratively through on-campus or off-campus services. Credit is offered for career planning, learning strategies, reading, and study skills.

Fees *Summer Program* fee is $1250.

Application For admittance to the program or unit, students are required to provide a psychoeducational report (3 years old or less). It is recommended that students provide documentation of high school services. Upon acceptance, documentation of need for services should be sent only to the LD program or unit. *Application deadline (institutional):* 3/15. *Application deadline (LD program):* Rolling/continuous for fall and rolling/continuous for spring.

Written Policies Written policies regarding course substitutions, general/basic LD accommodations, reduced course loads, substitutions and waivers of admissions requirements, and substitutions and waivers of graduation requirements are outlined in the school's catalog/handbook.

California Institute of the Arts
Office of Student Affairs

24700 McBean Parkway
Valencia, CA 91355-2340
http://www.calarts.edu/services/student_affairs/disabilities.html
Contact: Yvonne Guy, Dean of Student Affairs. Phone: 661-253-7891. Fax: 661-253-7872. E-mail: yguy@calarts.edu.

Office of Student Affairs Approximately 25 registered undergraduate students were served during 2002-03. The program or unit includes 2 full-time staff members. Counselors are provided through the program or unit. Academic advisers, diagnostic specialists, graduate assistants/students, LD specialists, and professional tutors are provided collaboratively through on-campus or off-campus services.

Unique Aids and Services Aids, services, or accommodations include career counseling and weekly meetings with faculty.

Subject-area Tutoring Tutoring is offered one-on-one. Tutoring is provided collaboratively through on-campus or off-campus services via graduate assistants/students, LD specialists, and professional tutors.

Basic Skills Remediation Remediation is offered one-on-one for computer skills, math, study skills, and time management. Remediation is provided collaboratively through on-campus or off-campus services via graduate assistants/students, LD specialists, and professional tutors.

Enrichment Programs for career planning, college survival skills, health and nutrition, learning strategies, math, practical computer skills, stress management, and time management are provided collaboratively through on-campus or off-campus services.

Application Upon application, materials documenting need for services should be sent only to admissions with institutional application materials. *Application deadline (institutional):* 1/5. *Application deadline (LD program):* Rolling/continuous for fall and rolling/continuous for spring.

Written Policies Written policies regarding course substitutions, general/basic LD accommodations, reduced course loads, substitutions and waivers of admissions requirements, and substitutions and waivers of graduation requirements are available on the program Web site. Written policies regarding course substitutions, general/basic LD accommodations, reduced course loads, substitutions and waivers of admissions requirements, and substitutions and waivers of graduation requirements are outlined in the school's catalog/handbook.

California Polytechnic State University, San Luis Obispo
Disability Resources Center

San Luis Obispo, CA 93407
http://drc.calpoly.edu/
Contact: Mr. William Bailey, Director. Phone: 805-756-1395. Fax: 805-756-5451. E-mail: wbailey@calpoly.edu.

Disability Resources Center Approximately 260 registered undergraduate students were served during 2002-03. The program or unit includes 4 full-time staff members. Academic advisers, diagnostic specialists, and LD specialists are provided through the program or unit.

Unique Aids and Services Aids, services, or accommodations include advocates, career counseling, faculty training, and priority registration.

Subject-area Tutoring Tutoring is offered one-on-one and in small groups for most subjects. Tutoring is provided through the program or unit via LD specialists.

Diagnostic Testing Testing for auditory processing, intelligence, learning strategies, learning styles, math, motor skills, neuropsychological, personality, reading, social skills, study skills, visual processing, and written language is provided collaboratively through on-campus or off-campus services.

Basic Skills Remediation Remediation is offered one-on-one and in small groups. Remediation is provided collaboratively through on-campus or off-campus services via LD specialists and trained peer tutors.

Enrichment Programs for career planning, college survival skills, health and nutrition, learning strategies, math, medication management, oral communication skills, practical computer skills, reading, stress management, study skills, test taking, time management, and written composition skills are provided collaboratively through on-campus or off-campus services.

Application For admittance to the program or unit, students are required to apply to the program directly and provide a psychoeducational report. Upon application, materials documenting need for services should be sent only to the LD program or unit. *Application deadline (institutional):* 11/30. *Application deadline (LD program):* Rolling/continuous for fall and rolling/continuous for spring.

Written Policies Written policy regarding general/basic LD accommodations is available on the program Web site. Written policies regarding course substitutions, grade forgiveness, reduced course loads, substitutions and waivers of admissions requirements, and substitutions and waivers of graduation requirements are available through the program or unit directly.

California State University, Bakersfield
Services for Students with Disabilities

9001 Stockdale Highway
Bakersfield, CA 93311-1099
http://www.csub.edu

Contact: Mrs. Jan Freshwater, Learning Disabilities Specialist. Phone: 661-664-3360. Fax: 661-664-2171. E-mail: jfreshwater@csub.edu. Head of LD Program: Mrs. Janice Clausen, Director. Phone: 661-664-3360. Fax: 661-664-2171. E-mail: jclausen@csub.edu.

Services for Students with Disabilities Approximately 250 registered undergraduate students were served during 2002-03. The program or unit includes 1 part-time staff member. Diagnostic specialists and LD specialists are provided through the program or unit. Academic advisers, counselors, diagnostic specialists, graduate assistants/students, professional tutors, regular education teachers, remediation/learning specialists, skill tutors, and strategy tutors are provided collaboratively through on-campus or off-campus services.

Unique Aids and Services Aids, services, or accommodations include career counseling and priority registration.

Subject-area Tutoring Tutoring is offered one-on-one for all subjects. Tutoring is provided collaboratively through on-campus or off-campus services via trained peer tutors.

Diagnostic Testing Testing is provided through the program or unit for auditory processing, intelligence, learning strategies, learning styles, math, reading, spelling, visual processing, and written language. Testing for study skills is provided collaboratively through on-campus or off-campus services.

Enrichment Enrichment programs are available through the program or unit for learning strategies and study skills. Programs for career planning, college survival skills, health and nutrition, learning strategies, math, reading, self-advocacy, stress management, study skills, test taking, time management, vocabulary development, and written composition skills are provided collaboratively through on-campus or off-campus services. Credit is offered for college survival skills, learning strategies, math, reading, self-advocacy, stress management, study skills, test taking, time management, vocabulary development, and written composition skills.

Application For admittance to the program or unit, students are required to apply to the program directly and provide a psychoeducational report. It is recommended that students provide documentation of high school services. Upon acceptance, documentation of

need for services should be sent only to the LD program or unit. *Application deadline (institutional):* 9/23. *Application deadline (LD program):* Rolling/continuous for fall and rolling/continuous for spring.

Written Policies Written policies regarding course substitutions, general/basic LD accommodations, and substitutions and waivers of admissions requirements are available through the program or unit directly.

California State University, Chico

400 West First Street
Chico, CA 95929-0722
http://www.csuchico.edu/

Contact: Mr. Van Alexander, Learning Disability Specialist. Phone: 530-898-5959. Fax: 530-898-4411. E-mail: valexander@csuchico.edu. Head of LD Program: Ms. Billie F. Jackson, Associate Director. Phone: 530-898-5959. Fax: 530-898-4411. E-mail: bfjackson@csuchico.edu.

Approximately 315 registered undergraduate students were served during 2002-03. The program or unit includes 2 full-time staff members. Diagnostic specialists, graduate assistants/students, and remediation/learning specialists are provided through the program or unit. Academic advisers, counselors, diagnostic specialists, graduate assistants/students, regular education teachers, remediation/learning specialists, skill tutors, special education teachers, strategy tutors, and trained peer tutors are provided collaboratively through on-campus or off-campus services.

Orientation The program or unit offers an optional 2-hour orientation for new students before classes begin and individually by special arrangement.

Unique Aids and Services Aids, services, or accommodations include digital textbooks and priority registration.

Subject-area Tutoring Tutoring is offered one-on-one and in small groups for most subjects. Tutoring is provided collaboratively through on-campus or off-campus services via graduate assistants/students and trained peer tutors.

Diagnostic Testing Testing is provided through the program or unit for auditory processing, intelligence, learning strategies, learning styles, math, motor skills, reading, spelling, spoken language, visual processing, and written language. Testing for auditory processing, intelligence, learning strategies, learning styles, personality, reading, spoken language, study skills, visual processing, and written language is provided collaboratively through on-campus or off-campus services.

Basic Skills Remediation Remediation is offered in class-size groups for learning strategies, math, study skills, time management, and written language. Remediation is provided collaboratively through on-campus or off-campus services via computer-based instruction, graduate assistants/students, teacher trainees, and trained peer tutors.

Enrichment Programs for career planning, college survival skills, health and nutrition, learning strategies, math, medication management, practical computer skills, study skills, time management, and written composition skills are provided collaboratively through on-campus or off-campus services.

California State University, Chico (continued)

Application For admittance to the program or unit, students are required to provide a psychoeducational report (5 years old or less) and provide reports of educational, medical, family histories and behavioral observations. Upon application, materials documenting need for services should be sent only to admissions with institutional application materials. Upon acceptance, documentation of need for services should be sent only to the LD program or unit. *Application deadline (institutional):* 11/30. *Application deadline (LD program):* Rolling/continuous for spring.

Written Policies Written policy regarding general/basic LD accommodations is available on the program Web site. Written policies regarding course substitutions, general/basic LD accommodations, grade forgiveness, reduced course loads, substitutions and waivers of admissions requirements, and substitutions and waivers of graduation requirements are outlined in the school's catalog/handbook. Written policy regarding general/basic LD accommodations is available through the program or unit directly.

Enrichment Programs for career planning, learning strategies, math, stress management, study skills, test taking, and time management are provided collaboratively through on-campus or off-campus services.

Application For admittance to the program or unit, students are required to apply to the program directly and provide a psychoeducational report (3 years old or less). It is recommended that students provide documentation of high school services. Upon application, materials documenting need for services should be sent only to the LD program or unit. Upon acceptance, documentation of need for services should be sent only to the LD program or unit. *Application deadline (institutional):* 11/30. *Application deadline (LD program):* Rolling/continuous for fall and rolling/continuous for spring.

Written Policies Written policies regarding course substitutions, general/basic LD accommodations, grade forgiveness, reduced course loads, substitutions and waivers of admissions requirements, and substitutions and waivers of graduation requirements are available through the program or unit directly.

California State University, Long Beach
Disabled Student Services, Stephen Benson Program

1250 Bellflower Boulevard

Long Beach, CA 90840

http://www.csulb.edu/

Contact: Phone: 562-985-4111.

Disabled Student Services, Stephen Benson Program
Approximately 550 registered undergraduate students were served during 2002-03. The program or unit includes 4 full-time and 8 part-time staff members. Academic advisers, counselors, diagnostic specialists, graduate assistants/students, LD specialists, skill tutors, and strategy tutors are provided through the program or unit. Academic advisers, coaches, professional tutors, remediation/learning specialists, skill tutors, and strategy tutors are provided collaboratively through on-campus or off-campus services.

Orientation The program or unit offers an optional orientation for new students before classes begin, during summer prior to enrollment, during registration, and individually by special arrangement.

Unique Aids and Services Aids, services, or accommodations include advocates, career counseling, faculty training, and priority registration.

Subject-area Tutoring Tutoring is offered one-on-one, in small groups, and in class-size groups for all subjects. Tutoring is provided collaboratively through on-campus or off-campus services via computer-based instruction, graduate assistants/students, professional tutors, and trained peer tutors.

Basic Skills Remediation Remediation is offered one-on-one and in small groups for auditory processing, computer skills, learning strategies, math, reading, spelling, study skills, time management, visual processing, and written language. Remediation is provided collaboratively through on-campus or off-campus services via computer-based instruction, graduate assistants/students, and professional tutors.

California State University, Sacramento
Services to Students with Disabilities

6000 J Street

Sacramento, CA 95819-6048

http://www.csus.edu/sswd/sswd.html

Contact: Dr. Davis Mertz, Learning Disabilities Specialist. Phone: 916-278-5279. Fax: 916-278-7825. E-mail: mertzdl@csus.edu. Head of LD Program: Patricia Sonntag, Director of Services to Students with Disabilities. Phone: 916-278-6955. Fax: 916-278-7825. E-mail: sonntagp@csus.edu.

Services to Students with Disabilities Approximately 400 registered undergraduate students were served during 2002-03. The program or unit includes 3 full-time staff members. Counselors, diagnostic specialists, LD specialists, remediation/learning specialists, strategy tutors, and other are provided through the program or unit. Academic advisers, coaches, graduate assistants/students, professional tutors, regular education teachers, skill tutors, and trained peer tutors are provided collaboratively through on-campus or off-campus services.

Unique Aids and Services Aids, services, or accommodations include digital textbooks and priority registration.

Subject-area Tutoring Tutoring is offered one-on-one, in small groups, and in class-size groups for most subjects. Tutoring is provided through the program or unit via LD specialists. Tutoring is also provided collaboratively through on-campus or off-campus services via computer-based instruction, graduate assistants/students, professional tutors, and trained peer tutors.

Diagnostic Testing Testing is provided through the program or unit for learning strategies, learning styles, and study skills. Testing for auditory processing, intelligence, math, personality, reading, social skills, spelling, spoken language, visual processing, and written language is provided collaboratively through on-campus or off-campus services.

Basic Skills Remediation Remediation is offered one-on-one, in small groups, and in class-size groups for computer skills, learning strategies, math, study skills, time management, and written language. Remediation is provided through the program or unit via LD specialists. Remediation is also provided collaboratively through on-campus or off-campus services via computer-based instruction, graduate assistants/students, professional tutors, regular education teachers, trained peer tutors, and other.

Enrichment Enrichment programs are available through the program or unit for college survival skills, learning strategies, math, practical computer skills, self-advocacy, stress management, study skills, test taking, and time management. Programs for career planning, health and nutrition, math, medication management, practical computer skills, stress management, vocabulary development, and written composition skills are provided collaboratively through on-campus or off-campus services. Credit is offered for college survival skills, learning strategies, math, practical computer skills, self-advocacy, stress management, study skills, test taking, and time management.

Student Organization Disabled Student Union consists of 20 members.

Application For admittance to the program or unit, students are required to apply to the program directly, provide a psychoeducational report (3 years old or less), provide documentation of high school services, and provide adult-normed assessment only. Upon application, materials documenting need for services should be sent only to the LD program or unit. Upon acceptance, documentation of need for services should be sent only to the LD program or unit. *Application deadline (institutional):* 5/1. *Application deadline (LD program):* Rolling/continuous for fall and rolling/continuous for spring.

Written Policies Written policy regarding general/basic LD accommodations is available on the program Web site. Written policies regarding course substitutions and general/basic LD accommodations are available through the program or unit directly.

California State University, San Bernardino
Services to Students with Disabilities

5500 University Parkway
San Bernardino, CA 92407-2397
http://enrollment.csusb.edu/~ssd

Contact: Dr. Doron A. Dula, Learning Disabilities Specialist. Phone: 909-880-5238. Fax: 909-880-7090. E-mail: ddula@csusb.edu.

Services to Students with Disabilities Approximately 60 registered undergraduate students were served during 2002-03. The program or unit includes 1 full-time staff member. Counselors, diagnostic specialists, and LD specialists are provided through the program or unit. Academic advisers and skill tutors are provided collaboratively through on-campus or off-campus services.

Unique Aids and Services Aids, services, or accommodations include priority registration.

Subject-area Tutoring Tutoring is offered one-on-one and in small groups for some subjects. Tutoring is provided collaboratively through on-campus or off-campus services via graduate assistants/ students.

Diagnostic Testing Testing is provided through the program or unit for auditory processing, handwriting, intelligence, math, reading, spelling, spoken language, visual processing, and written language.

Basic Skills Remediation Remediation is available for math, reading, spelling, and written language. Remediation is provided collaboratively through on-campus or off-campus services via professional tutors.

Enrichment Programs for career planning, college survival skills, math, practical computer skills, reading, study skills, test taking, time management, and written composition skills are provided collaboratively through on-campus or off-campus services.

Student Organization Uni Phi consists of 20 members.

Application For admittance to the program or unit, students are required to apply to the program directly, provide a psychoeducational report (3 years old or less), provide documentation of high school services, and provide concomitant medical/psychiatric for past and current treatment . Upon application, materials documenting need for services should be sent only to the LD program or unit. *Application deadline (institutional):* Continuous. *Application deadline (LD program):* Rolling/continuous for fall and rolling/continuous for spring.

Written Policies Written policies regarding course substitutions, general/basic LD accommodations, and substitutions and waivers of admissions requirements are available through the program or unit directly.

Calvin College
Student Academic Services (SAS)

3201 Burton Street, SE
Grand Rapids, MI 49546-4388
http://www.calvin.edu/academic/sas

Contact: June De Boer, Coordinator of Services to Students with Disabilities. Phone: 616-957-6113. Fax: 616-957-7066. E-mail: jed4@calvin.edu. Head of LD Program: Karen Broekstra, Coordinator of Services to Students with Disabilities. Phone: 616-957-6114. Fax: 616-957-7066. E-mail: kbroekst@calvin.edu.

Student Academic Services (SAS) Approximately 218 registered undergraduate students were served during 2002-03. The program or unit includes 2 full-time staff members and 1 part-time staff member. LD specialists are provided through the program or unit. Academic advisers, coaches, counselors, diagnostic specialists, skill tutors, strategy tutors, and trained peer tutors are provided collaboratively through on-campus or off-campus services.

Orientation The program or unit offers an optional 1-hour orientation for new students after classes begin and individually by special arrangement.

Unique Aids and Services Aids, services, or accommodations include advocates, personal coach, priority registration, books on tape/CD-ROM.

Subject-area Tutoring Tutoring is offered one-on-one, in small groups, and in class-size groups. Tutoring is provided collaboratively through on-campus or off-campus services via trained peer tutors.

Diagnostic Testing Testing is provided through the program or unit for intelligence, personality, and reading. Testing for auditory processing, handwriting, learning strategies, learning styles, math,

Calvin College (continued)

motor skills, neuropsychological, social skills, spelling, spoken language, study skills, visual processing, written language, and other services is provided collaboratively through on-campus or off-campus services.

Enrichment Programs for career planning, college survival skills, health and nutrition, learning strategies, math, medication management, oral communication skills, reading, self-advocacy, stress management, study skills, test taking, time management, and written composition skills are provided collaboratively through on-campus or off-campus services.

Fees *Diagnostic Testing* fee is applicable.

Application For admittance to the program or unit, students are required to provide a psychoeducational report (3 years old or less). It is recommended that students provide documentation of high school services. *Application deadline (institutional):* 8/15. *Application deadline (LD program):* Rolling/continuous for fall and rolling/continuous for spring.

Written Policies Written policy regarding grade forgiveness is outlined in the school's catalog/handbook. Written policy regarding general/basic LD accommodations is available through the program or unit directly.

Cambridge College

1000 Massachusetts Avenue
Cambridge, MA 02138-5304
http://www.cambridge.edu/

Contact: Deborah Davis McCarthy, Director of Student Services and Disability Support Coordinator. Phone: 800-877-4723 Ext. 200. Fax: 617-349-3558. E-mail: dmccarthy@cambridgecollege.edu.

Approximately 40 registered undergraduate students were served during 2002-03. The program or unit includes 1 full-time staff member. Academic advisers and counselors are provided through the program or unit. Professional tutors, regular education teachers, remediation/learning specialists, and skill tutors are provided collaboratively through on-campus or off-campus services.

Unique Aids and Services Aids, services, or accommodations include digital textbooks and faculty training.

Subject-area Tutoring Tutoring is offered one-on-one for some subjects. Tutoring is provided collaboratively through on-campus or off-campus services via professional tutors.

Basic Skills Remediation Remediation is available for computer skills, learning strategies, math, and written language. Remediation is provided collaboratively through on-campus or off-campus services via professional tutors and regular education teachers.

Enrichment Enrichment programs are available through the program or unit for college survival skills and self-advocacy. Programs for career planning, math, practical computer skills, study skills, test taking, and written composition skills are provided collaboratively through on-campus or off-campus services. Credit is offered for career planning, math, practical computer skills, and written composition skills.

Application For admittance to the program or unit, students are required to provide a psychoeducational report (5 years old or less) and provide medical documentation. Upon application, materials documenting need for services should be sent to both admissions and the LD program or unit. Upon acceptance, documentation of need for services should be sent only to the LD program or unit. *Application deadline (institutional):* Continuous. *Application deadline (LD program):* Rolling/continuous for fall and rolling/continuous for spring.

Written Policies Written policy regarding general/basic LD accommodations is available on the program Web site. Written policy regarding general/basic LD accommodations is outlined in the school's catalog/handbook. Written policies regarding general/basic LD accommodations, grade forgiveness, and reduced course loads are available through the program or unit directly.

Canisius College

2001 Main Street
Buffalo, NY 14208-1098
http://canisius.edu/dss/

Contact: Phone: 716-883-7000. Fax: 716-888-2377.

Approximately 70 registered undergraduate students were served during 2002-03. The program or unit includes 1 full-time and 1 part-time staff member. Professional tutors are provided through the program or unit. Academic advisers, counselors, and professional tutors are provided collaboratively through on-campus or off-campus services.

Subject-area Tutoring Tutoring is offered one-on-one for most subjects. Tutoring is provided through the program or unit via professional tutors. Tutoring is also provided collaboratively through on-campus or off-campus services via trained peer tutors.

Basic Skills Remediation Remediation is offered in small groups for math and reading.

Application For admittance to the program or unit, students are required to provide a psychoeducational report. It is recommended that students provide documentation of high school services. Upon application, materials documenting need for services should be sent only to the LD program or unit. Upon acceptance, documentation of need for services should be sent only to the LD program or unit. *Application deadline (institutional):* Continuous. *Application deadline (LD program):* Rolling/continuous for fall and rolling/continuous for spring.

Written Policies Written policies regarding general/basic LD accommodations and grade forgiveness are available on the program Web site. Written policies regarding general/basic LD accommodations and grade forgiveness are outlined in the school's catalog/handbook. Written policies regarding course substitutions, general/basic LD accommodations, reduced course loads, and substitutions and waivers of graduation requirements are available through the program or unit directly.

Capital University
Disability Services

2199 East Main Street
Columbus, OH 43209-2394
http://www.capital.edu/

Contact: Richard A. Schalinske, Coordinator of Disability Services. Phone: 614-236-6284. E-mail: rschalin@capital.edu.

Disability Services Approximately 40 registered undergraduate students were served during 2002-03. The program or unit includes 1 full-time staff member. Academic advisers, coaches, counselors, diagnostic specialists, graduate assistants/students, LD specialists, professional tutors, regular education teachers, remediation/learning specialists, skill tutors, special education teachers, strategy tutors, teacher trainees, and other are provided collaboratively through on-campus or off-campus services.

Unique Aids and Services Aids, services, or accommodations include advocates.

Subject-area Tutoring Tutoring is offered one-on-one for some subjects. Tutoring is provided collaboratively through on-campus or off-campus services via trained peer tutors.

Enrichment Programs for career planning, college survival skills, study skills, test taking, and time management are provided collaboratively through on-campus or off-campus services.

Application It is recommended that students apply to the program directly, provide a psychoeducational report (4 years old or less), and provide documentation of high school services. Upon application, materials documenting need for services should be sent only to the LD program or unit. *Application deadline (institutional):* 4/15.

Written Policies Written policy regarding general/basic LD accommodations is available through the program or unit directly.

Cardinal Stritch University
Academic Support Center

6801 North Yates Road
Milwaukee, WI 53217-3985
http://www.stritch.edu/

Contact: Marcia L. Laskey, Director Academic Support Center. Fax: 414-410-4239. E-mail: mllaskey@stritch.edu.

Academic Support Center The program or unit includes 3 full-time and 3 part-time staff members. LD specialists and professional tutors are provided through the program or unit.

Orientation The program or unit offers an optional orientation for new students individually by special arrangement.

Unique Aids and Services Aids, services, or accommodations include priority registration and weekly meetings with faculty.

Subject-area Tutoring Tutoring is offered one-on-one. Tutoring is provided through the program or unit via LD specialists and professional tutors.

Basic Skills Remediation Remediation is offered one-on-one and in class-size groups for learning strategies, math, reading, social skills, study skills, time management, visual processing, and written language. Remediation is provided through the program or unit via LD specialists and professional tutors.

Enrichment Enrichment programs are available through the program or unit for college survival skills, learning strategies, math, oral communication skills, reading, stress management, study skills, test taking, time management, and written composition skills.

Application For admittance to the program or unit, students are required to provide a psychoeducational report and provide documentation from a licensed professional with test results included.

Upon application, materials documenting need for services should be sent only to the LD program or unit. *Application deadline (institutional):* Continuous. *Application deadline (LD program):* Rolling/continuous for fall and rolling/continuous for spring.

Written Policies Written policy regarding general/basic LD accommodations is outlined in the school's catalog/handbook. Written policy regarding general/basic LD accommodations is available through the program or unit directly.

Carleton University
The Paul Menton Center

1125 Colonel By Drive
Ottawa, ON K1S 5B6
Canada
http://www.carleton.ca.pmc

Contact: Dr. Nancy McIntyre, Coordinator of Learning Disabilities. Phone: 613-520-6608. Fax: 613-520-3995. E-mail: nancy_mcintyre@carleton.ca.

The Paul Menton Center Approximately 250 registered undergraduate students were served during 2002-03. The program or unit includes 3 full-time staff members and 1 part-time staff member. Coaches, LD specialists, remediation/learning specialists, strategy tutors, trained peer tutors, and other are provided through the program or unit. Academic advisers, counselors, diagnostic specialists, graduate assistants/students, and professional tutors are provided collaboratively through on-campus or off-campus services.

Summer Program To help prepare for the demands of college, there is an optional 4-week summer program prior to entering the school.

Unique Aids and Services Aids, services, or accommodations include career counseling, digital textbooks, and faculty training.

Diagnostic Testing Testing for auditory processing, handwriting, intelligence, learning strategies, learning styles, math, motor skills, neuropsychological, personality, reading, social skills, spelling, spoken language, study skills, visual processing, written language, and other services is provided collaboratively through on-campus or off-campus services.

Enrichment Enrichment programs are available through the program or unit for college survival skills, learning strategies, practical computer skills, reading, self-advocacy, stress management, study skills, test taking, time management, vocabulary development, written composition skills, and other. Programs for career planning and medication management are provided collaboratively through on-campus or off-campus services.

Fees *Diagnostic Testing* fee is $1200 to $1500.

Application For admittance to the program or unit, students are required to provide a psychoeducational report (3 years old or less). It is recommended that students provide documentation of high school services. Upon application, materials documenting need for services should be sent only to the LD program or unit. *Application deadline (institutional):* 6/1. *Application deadline (LD program):* Rolling/continuous for fall and rolling/continuous for spring.

Written Policies Written policy regarding general/basic LD accommodations is available on the program Web site. Written policy regarding general/basic LD accommodations is available through the program or unit directly.

Carnegie Mellon University
Disability Resources

5000 Forbes Avenue
Pittsburgh, PA 15213-3891
http://hr.web.cmu.edu/eos.html

Contact: Mr. Larry Powell, Manager. Phone: 412-268-2013. Fax: 412-268-7472. E-mail: lpowell@andrew.cmu.edu.

Disability Resources Approximately 129 registered undergraduate students were served during 2002-03. The program or unit includes 2 full-time staff members. LD specialists are provided through the program or unit. Academic advisers, counselors, graduate assistants/students, LD specialists, and trained peer tutors are provided collaboratively through on-campus or off-campus services.
Unique Aids and Services Aids, services, or accommodations include digital textbooks.
Subject-area Tutoring Tutoring is offered one-on-one, in small groups, and in class-size groups for most subjects. Tutoring is provided collaboratively through on-campus or off-campus services via trained peer tutors.
Basic Skills Remediation Remediation is offered one-on-one for learning strategies, math, reading, study skills, time management, and written language. Remediation is provided collaboratively through on-campus or off-campus services via trained peer tutors.
Enrichment Programs for career planning, college survival skills, health and nutrition, learning strategies, math, medication management, stress management, study skills, test taking, time management, vocabulary development, and written composition skills are provided collaboratively through on-campus or off-campus services.
Application It is recommended that students provide a psychoeducational report and provide a neuropsychological report. Upon acceptance, documentation of need for services should be sent only to the LD program or unit. *Application deadline (institutional): 1/1. Application deadline (LD program):* Rolling/continuous for fall and rolling/continuous for spring.
Written Policies Written policy regarding general/basic LD accommodations is available on the program Web site. Written policies regarding course substitutions, grade forgiveness, reduced course loads, substitutions and waivers of admissions requirements, and substitutions and waivers of graduation requirements are outlined in the school's catalog/handbook. Written policy regarding general/basic LD accommodations is available through the program or unit directly.

Carroll College
Disabled Services

100 North East Avenue
Waukesha, WI 53186-5593
http://www.cc.edu/wyc

Contact: Ms. Andrea K. Broman, Disability Services Coordinator. Phone: 262-524-7335. Fax: 262-524-6892. E-mail: abroman@cc.edu.

Disabled Services Approximately 12 registered undergraduate students were served during 2002-03. The program or unit includes

1 part-time staff member. Coaches, counselors, LD specialists, regular education teachers, skill tutors, special education teachers, strategy tutors, teacher trainees, and trained peer tutors are provided through the program or unit. Academic advisers, counselors, diagnostic specialists, LD specialists, and remediation/learning specialists are provided collaboratively through on-campus or off-campus services.
Unique Aids and Services Aids, services, or accommodations include personal coach.
Subject-area Tutoring Tutoring is offered one-on-one and in small groups for most subjects. Tutoring is provided through the program or unit via trained peer tutors. Tutoring is also provided collaboratively through on-campus or off-campus services via professional tutors.
Diagnostic Testing Testing for auditory processing, handwriting, intelligence, learning strategies, learning styles, math, motor skills, neuropsychological, personality, reading, social skills, spelling, spoken language, study skills, visual processing, and written language is provided collaboratively through on-campus or off-campus services.
Basic Skills Remediation Remediation is offered one-on-one and in small groups for learning strategies, math, reading, social skills, study skills, and time management. Remediation is provided through the program or unit via trained peer tutors and other.
Enrichment Enrichment programs are available through the program or unit for learning strategies, self-advocacy, study skills, test taking, and time management. Programs for career planning, college survival skills, math, practical computer skills, self-advocacy, stress management, study skills, test taking, time management, and written composition skills are provided collaboratively through on-campus or off-campus services.
Fees *Diagnostic Testing* fee is applicable.
Application For admittance to the program or unit, students are required to apply to the program directly and provide a psychoeducational report (10 years old or less). It is recommended that students provide documentation of high school services. Upon application, materials documenting need for services should be sent only to the LD program or unit. Upon acceptance, documentation of need for services should be sent only to the LD program or unit. *Application deadline (institutional):* Continuous. *Application deadline (LD program):* Rolling/continuous for fall and rolling/continuous for spring.
Written Policies Written policies regarding general/basic LD accommodations and substitutions and waivers of graduation requirements are available on the program Web site. Written policies regarding course substitutions, general/basic LD accommodations, and reduced course loads are available through the program or unit directly.

Carroll College
Academic Resource Center

1601 North Benton Avenue
Helena, MT 59625-0002
http://www.carroll.edu/

Contact: Mrs. Joan M. Stottlemyer, Director of Academic Resource Center. Phone: 406-447-4504. Fax: 406-447-5476. E-mail: jstottle@carroll.edu.

Academic Resource Center The program or unit includes 1 part-time staff member. Academic advisers and other are provided collaboratively through on-campus or off-campus services.

Unique Aids and Services Aids, services, or accommodations include extended time on tests, note-taking.

Subject-area Tutoring Tutoring is offered one-on-one, in small groups, and in class-size groups for some subjects. Tutoring is provided through the program or unit via trained peer tutors and other. Tutoring is also provided collaboratively through on-campus or off-campus services via trained peer tutors and other.

Basic Skills Remediation Remediation is offered one-on-one for learning strategies, study skills, and time management. Remediation is provided through the program or unit. Remediation is also provided collaboratively through on-campus or off-campus services.

Application For admittance to the program or unit, students are required to apply to the program directly and provide a psychoeducational report (3 years old or less). It is recommended that students provide documentation of high school services. Upon acceptance, documentation of need for services should be sent only to the LD program or unit. *Application deadline (institutional):* 6/1. *Application deadline (LD program):* Rolling/continuous for fall and rolling/continuous for spring.

Written Policies Written policies regarding general/basic LD accommodations and reduced course loads are available on the program Web site. Written policies regarding general/basic LD accommodations and reduced course loads are outlined in the school's catalog/handbook.

Carson-Newman College

1646 Russell Avenue, PO Box 557

Jefferson City, TN 37760

http://www.cn.edu/

Contact: Laura Wadlington, Coordinator for Students with Disabilities. Phone: 865-471-3270. E-mail: lwadlington@cn.edu.

Approximately 28 registered undergraduate students were served during 2002-03. The program or unit includes 1 part-time staff member. Academic advisers, counselors, regular education teachers, remediation/learning specialists, and trained peer tutors are provided collaboratively through on-campus or off-campus services.

Subject-area Tutoring Tutoring is offered one-on-one, in small groups, and in class-size groups.

Basic Skills Remediation Remediation is offered in class-size groups for math, reading, study skills, and written language. Remediation is provided collaboratively through on-campus or off-campus services via regular education teachers and other.

Application For admittance to the program or unit, students are required to provide a psychoeducational report (3 years old or less) and provide a request for specific accommodations. It is recommended that students provide documentation of high school services. Upon acceptance, documentation of need for services should be sent only to the LD program or unit. *Application deadline (institutional):* 8/1. *Application deadline (LD program):* Rolling/continuous for fall.

Written Policies Written policy regarding general/basic LD accommodations is outlined in the school's catalog/handbook. Written policies regarding course substitutions and substitutions and waivers of graduation requirements are available through the program or unit directly.

Carthage College

2001 Alford Park Drive

Kenosha, WI 53140-1994

http://www.carthage.edu/

Contact: Diane Schowalter, Learning Specialist. Phone: 262-551-5802. E-mail: dschowalter1@carthage.edu.

The program or unit includes 1 part-time staff member. Academic advisers, coaches, diagnostic specialists, and other are provided collaboratively through on-campus or off-campus services.

Unique Aids and Services Aids, services, or accommodations include digital textbooks.

Subject-area Tutoring Tutoring is offered one-on-one for most subjects. Tutoring is provided collaboratively through on-campus or off-campus services via other.

Diagnostic Testing Testing is provided through the program or unit for auditory processing, intelligence, math, reading, spelling, visual processing, written language, and other services.

Application For admittance to the program or unit, students are required to provide a psychoeducational report (3 years old or less) and provide documentation of high school services. Upon application, materials documenting need for services should be sent only to the LD program or unit. Upon acceptance, documentation of need for services should be sent only to the LD program or unit. *Application deadline (institutional):* Continuous. *Application deadline (LD program):* Rolling/continuous for fall and rolling/continuous for spring.

Written Policies Written policy regarding general/basic LD accommodations is available on the program Web site. Written policy regarding general/basic LD accommodations is outlined in the school's catalog/handbook. Written policies regarding course substitutions and substitutions and waivers of admissions requirements are available through the program or unit directly.

Case Western Reserve University
Disability Services in Educational Support Services

10900 Euclid Avenue

Cleveland, OH 44106

http://www.cwru.edu/

Contact: Phone: 216-368-2000. Fax: 216-368-5111.

Disability Services in Educational Support Services Approximately 27 registered undergraduate students were served during 2002-03. The program or unit includes 1 full-time staff member.

Case Western Reserve University (continued)

Academic advisers, counselors, diagnostic specialists, regular education teachers, skill tutors, and trained peer tutors are provided collaboratively through on-campus or off-campus services.

Unique Aids and Services Aids, services, or accommodations include digital textbooks, faculty training, and priority registration.

Subject-area Tutoring Tutoring is offered one-on-one and in class-size groups. Tutoring is provided collaboratively through on-campus or off-campus services via computer-based instruction, graduate assistants/students, and trained peer tutors.

Diagnostic Testing Testing for auditory processing, intelligence, learning strategies, learning styles, neuropsychological, personality, reading, study skills, visual processing, and written language is provided collaboratively through on-campus or off-campus services.

Enrichment Programs for career planning, college survival skills, health and nutrition, learning strategies, practical computer skills, self-advocacy, stress management, study skills, test taking, time management, vocabulary development, and written composition skills are provided collaboratively through on-campus or off-campus services.

Application For admittance to the program or unit, students are required to provide a psychoeducational report (3 years old or less). Upon acceptance, documentation of need for services should be sent only to the LD program or unit. *Application deadline (institutional):* 2/1. *Application deadline (LD program):* Rolling/continuous for fall and rolling/continuous for spring.

Written Policies Written policy regarding general/basic LD accommodations is available on the program Web site. Written policy regarding general/basic LD accommodations is available through the program or unit directly.

The Catholic University of America
Disability Support Services

Cardinal Station
Washington, DC 20064
http://disabilityservices.cua.edu

Contact: Ms. Bonnie M. McClellan, Director of Disability Support Services. Phone: 202-319-5211. Fax: 202-319-5126. E-mail: cua-disabilityservices@cua.edu.

Disability Support Services Approximately 215 registered undergraduate students were served during 2002-03. The program or unit includes 2 full-time and 14 part-time staff members. Academic advisers, LD specialists, and remediation/learning specialists are provided through the program or unit. Academic advisers, counselors, graduate assistants/students, remediation/learning specialists, skill tutors, strategy tutors, trained peer tutors, and other are provided collaboratively through on-campus or off-campus services.

Orientation The program or unit offers an optional 1-hour parent and 1-hour student orientation for new students before classes begin, individually by special arrangement, and as a part of the 4-day freshman orientation.

Unique Aids and Services Aids, services, or accommodations include advocates, career counseling, digital textbooks, faculty training, priority registration, reading, writing, and organizational software, taped books.

Subject-area Tutoring Tutoring is offered one-on-one and in small groups for most subjects. Tutoring is provided collaboratively through on-campus or off-campus services via graduate assistants/students, professional tutors, trained peer tutors, and other.

Basic Skills Remediation Remediation is offered one-on-one, in small groups, and in class-size groups for learning strategies, reading, social skills, study skills, time management, written language, and anxiety/psychological support. Remediation is provided collaboratively through on-campus or off-campus services via graduate assistants/students and other.

Enrichment Enrichment programs are available through the program or unit for career planning, learning strategies, self-advocacy, and time management. Programs for career planning, college survival skills, health and nutrition, learning strategies, medication management, reading, self-advocacy, stress management, study skills, test taking, time management, written composition skills, and other are provided collaboratively through on-campus or off-campus services.

Application For admittance to the program or unit, students are required to provide a psychoeducational report and provide teacher recommendations in English, math, other. Upon application, materials documenting need for services should be sent only to admissions with institutional application materials. Upon acceptance, documentation of need for services should be sent only to the LD program or unit. *Application deadline (institutional):* 2/15. *Application deadline (LD program):* 2/15 for fall. 12/1 for spring.

Written Policies Written policies regarding course substitutions, general/basic LD accommodations, and substitutions and waivers of graduation requirements are available on the program Web site. Written policies regarding course substitutions, general/basic LD accommodations, and substitutions and waivers of graduation requirements are outlined in the school's catalog/handbook. Written policies regarding course substitutions, general/basic LD accommodations, reduced course loads, and substitutions and waivers of graduation requirements are available through the program or unit directly.

Cazenovia College

22 Sullivan Street
Cazenovia, NY 13035-1084
http://www.cazenovia.edu/

Contact: Ms. Cynthia-Anne Pratt, Director, Office of Special Services. Phone: 315-655-7308. Fax: 315-655-7398. E-mail: cpratt@cazenovia.edu.

Approximately 110 registered undergraduate students were served during 2002-03. The program or unit includes 1 full-time and 2 part-time staff members. Academic advisers, LD specialists, professional tutors, remediation/learning specialists, and skill tutors are provided through the program or unit. Academic advisers, professional tutors, remediation/learning specialists, and skill tutors are provided collaboratively through on-campus or off-campus services.

Unique Aids and Services Aids, services, or accommodations include advocates.

Subject-area Tutoring Tutoring is offered one-on-one and in small groups for most subjects. Tutoring is provided through the program or unit via LD specialists, professional tutors, and trained peer tutors. Tutoring is also provided collaboratively through on-campus or off-campus services via professional tutors and trained peer tutors.

Basic Skills Remediation Remediation is offered one-on-one and in small groups for learning strategies, math, reading, study skills, time management, and written language. Remediation is provided through the program or unit via LD specialists, professional tutors, and trained peer tutors. Remediation is also provided collaboratively through on-campus or off-campus services via professional tutors and trained peer tutors.

Enrichment Enrichment programs are available through the program or unit for learning strategies, reading, self-advocacy, stress management, study skills, test taking, time management, and written composition skills. Programs for career planning, college survival skills, learning strategies, math, medication management, reading, stress management, study skills, test taking, time management, and written composition skills are provided collaboratively through on-campus or off-campus services.

Application For admittance to the program or unit, students are required to provide a psychoeducational report (3 years old or less) and provide documentation of high school services. Upon application, materials documenting need for services should be sent only to the LD program or unit. Upon acceptance, documentation of need for services should be sent only to the LD program or unit. *Application deadline (institutional):* Continuous. *Application deadline (LD program):* Rolling/continuous for fall and rolling/continuous for spring.

Written Policies Written policies regarding general/basic LD accommodations and substitutions and waivers of admissions requirements are available on the program Web site. Written policies regarding general/basic LD accommodations and substitutions and waivers of admissions requirements are outlined in the school's catalog/handbook. Written policies regarding course substitutions and reduced course loads are available through the program or unit directly.

Cedar Crest College
Academic Services

100 College Drive
Allentown, PA 18104-6196

http://www.cedarcrest.edu/acadadvising

Contact: Christine M. Spindler, Director of Academic Services. Phone: 610-606-4628 Ext. 4628. Fax: 610-606-4673. E-mail: cmspindl@cedarcrest.edu.

Academic Services Approximately 65 registered undergraduate students were served during 2002-03. The program or unit includes 1 full-time and 1 part-time staff member. Academic advisers, professional tutors, skill tutors, strategy tutors, and trained peer tutors are provided through the program or unit. Academic advisers, coaches, counselors, diagnostic specialists, and regular education teachers are provided collaboratively through on-campus or off-campus services.

Unique Aids and Services Aids, services, or accommodations include career counseling and priority registration.

Subject-area Tutoring Tutoring is offered one-on-one and in small groups for most subjects. Tutoring is provided through the program or unit via professional tutors and trained peer tutors.

Basic Skills Remediation Remediation is offered one-on-one and in small groups for computer skills, learning strategies, math, reading, spelling, study skills, time management, and written language. Remediation is provided through the program or unit via computer-based instruction and professional tutors.

Application For admittance to the program or unit, students are required to apply to the program directly. It is recommended that students provide a psychoeducational report (5 years old or less) and provide documentation of high school services. Upon application, materials documenting need for services should be sent only to the LD program or unit. Upon acceptance, documentation of need for services should be sent only to the LD program or unit. *Application deadline (institutional):* Continuous. *Application deadline (LD program):* Rolling/continuous for fall and rolling/continuous for spring.

Written Policies Written policy regarding general/basic LD accommodations is available on the program Web site. Written policy regarding general/basic LD accommodations is outlined in the school's catalog/handbook. Written policy regarding general/basic LD accommodations is available through the program or unit directly.

Central Michigan University

Mount Pleasant, MI 48859

http://www.cmich.edu/

Contact: Mrs. Dorothy Kay McGrath Grossman, Assistant Director/Learning Disabilities. Phone: 989-774-3018. Fax: 989-774-1326. E-mail: mcgra1dk@cmich.edu.

Approximately 124 registered undergraduate students were served during 2002-03. The program or unit includes 1 full-time staff member. LD specialists are provided through the program or unit. LD specialists are provided collaboratively through on-campus or off-campus services.

Subject-area Tutoring Tutoring is offered in small groups for some subjects. Tutoring is provided collaboratively through on-campus or off-campus services via trained peer tutors.

Application For admittance to the program or unit, students are required to provide a psychoeducational report (3 years old or less) and provide documentation of high school services. Upon application, materials documenting need for services should be sent only to the LD program or unit. Upon acceptance, documentation of need for services should be sent only to the LD program or unit. *Application deadline (institutional):* Continuous. *Application deadline (LD program):* 8/1 for fall. 1/2 for spring.

Written Policies Written policies regarding substitutions and waivers of admissions requirements and substitutions and waivers of graduation requirements are outlined in the school's catalog/handbook. Written policy regarding general/basic LD accommodations is available through the program or unit directly.

Central Missouri State University
Office of Accessibility Services

PO Box 800
Warrensburg, MO 64093

Central Missouri State University (continued)
http://www.cmsu.edu/access

Contact: Dr. Barbara J. Mayfield, Director of ADA and 504 Coordinator. Phone: 660-543-4421. Fax: 660-543-4724. E-mail: mayfield@cmsu1.cmsu.edu.

Office of Accessibility Services Approximately 130 registered undergraduate students were served during 2002-03. The program or unit includes 2 full-time and 15 part-time staff members. Academic advisers, graduate assistants/students, LD specialists, remediation/ learning specialists, and strategy tutors are provided through the program or unit. Academic advisers, counselors, graduate assistants/ students, regular education teachers, skill tutors, strategy tutors, trained peer tutors, and other are provided collaboratively through on-campus or off-campus services.

Summer Program To help prepare for the demands of college, there is an optional summer program prior to entering the school. Degree credit will be earned.

Unique Aids and Services Aids, services, or accommodations include advocates, digital textbooks, faculty training, priority registration, and support groups.

Subject-area Tutoring Tutoring is offered in small groups for some subjects. Tutoring is provided collaboratively through on-campus or off-campus services via computer-based instruction, graduate assistants/students, and trained peer tutors.

Basic Skills Remediation Remediation is offered in small groups and in class-size groups for computer skills, learning strategies, math, reading, study skills, time management, and written language. Remediation is provided collaboratively through on-campus or off-campus services via computer-based instruction, graduate assistants/ students, professional tutors, and trained peer tutors.

Enrichment Enrichment programs are available through the program or unit for self-advocacy. Programs for career planning, college survival skills, learning strategies, math, oral communication skills, practical computer skills, reading, stress management, study skills, test taking, time management, vocabulary development, and written composition skills are provided collaboratively through on-campus or off-campus services. Credit is offered for college survival skills, learning strategies, math, oral communication skills, practical computer skills, reading, stress management, study skills, test taking, time management, vocabulary development, and written composition skills.

Student Organization United Students for Equal Access (USEA) consists of 12 members.

Fees *LD Program or Service* fee is $137. *Summer Program* fee is $137.

Application For admittance to the program or unit, students are required to apply to the program directly and provide a psychoeducational report. It is recommended that students provide documentation of high school services. Upon acceptance, documentation of need for services should be sent only to the LD program or unit. *Application deadline (institutional):* Continuous. *Application deadline (LD program):* Rolling/continuous for fall and rolling/continuous for spring.

Written Policies Written policy regarding general/basic LD accommodations is available on the program Web site. Written policy regarding general/basic LD accommodations is outlined in the school's catalog/handbook. Written policies regarding course substitutions, general/basic LD accommodations, grade forgiveness, reduced course loads, substitutions and waivers of admissions requirements, and substitutions and waivers of graduation requirements are available through the program or unit directly.

Central State University

1400 Brush Row Road
PO Box 1004
Wilberforce, OH 45384
http://www.centralstate.edu/

Contact: Ms. Vonya Le Thornton, Dean of Students and Director, Office of Disability Services. Phone: 937-376-6387. Fax: 937-376-6482. E-mail: vthornton@csu.ces.edu.

The program or unit includes 4 part-time staff members. Academic advisers, counselors, and trained peer tutors are provided collaboratively through on-campus or off-campus services.

Subject-area Tutoring Tutoring is offered one-on-one, in small groups, and in class-size groups for most subjects. Tutoring is provided collaboratively through on-campus or off-campus services via computer-based instruction, professional tutors, and trained peer tutors.

Enrichment Programs for career planning, college survival skills, health and nutrition, learning strategies, practical computer skills, stress management, study skills, test taking, time management, vocabulary development, and written composition skills are provided collaboratively through on-campus or off-campus services. Credit is offered for college survival skills, health and nutrition, learning strategies, practical computer skills, vocabulary development, and written composition skills.

Application For admittance to the program or unit, students are required to provide a psychoeducational report (3 years old or less) and provide documentation of high school services. Upon acceptance, documentation of need for services should be sent only to the LD program or unit. *Application deadline (institutional):* 6/15. *Application deadline (LD program):* Rolling/continuous for fall and rolling/ continuous for spring.

Written Policies Written policies regarding course substitutions, general/basic LD accommodations, substitutions and waivers of admissions requirements, and substitutions and waivers of graduation requirements are available through the program or unit directly.

Central Washington University
Disability Support Services

400 East 8th Avenue
Ellensburg, WA 98926-7463
http://www.cwu.edu/

Contact: Robert Campbell, Director of Disability Support Services. Phone: 509-963-2171. Fax: 509-963-3235. E-mail: campbelr@cwu.edu.

Disability Support Services Approximately 252 registered undergraduate students were served during 2002-03. The program or unit includes 4 full-time and 25 part-time staff members. Coaches are provided through the program or unit. Academic advisers, coaches, counselors, diagnostic specialists, professional tutors, and trained peer tutors are provided collaboratively through on-campus or off-campus services.

Subject-area Tutoring Tutoring is offered one-on-one, in small groups, and in class-size groups. Tutoring is provided collaboratively through on-campus or off-campus services via trained peer tutors.
Basic Skills Remediation Remediation is offered in class-size groups for learning strategies, math, reading, study skills, time management, and written language. Remediation is provided collaboratively through on-campus or off-campus services via computer-based instruction, graduate assistants/students, and trained peer tutors.
Application For admittance to the program or unit, students are required to provide a psychoeducational report (5 years old or less). *Application deadline (institutional):* Continuous. *Application deadline (LD program):* Rolling/continuous for fall and rolling/continuous for spring.
Written Policies Written policy regarding general/basic LD accommodations is available on the program Web site. Written policy regarding course substitutions is outlined in the school's catalog/handbook. Written policies regarding course substitutions, general/basic LD accommodations, and substitutions and waivers of graduation requirements are available through the program or unit directly.

Champlain College

PO Box 670
Burlington, VT 05402-0670
http://www.champlain.edu/
Contact: Coordinator of Support Services for Students with Disabilities. Phone: 802-860-2704. Fax: 802-860-2764.

Approximately 130 registered undergraduate students were served during 2002-03. The program or unit includes 1 part-time staff member. Academic advisers, counselors, regular education teachers, and trained peer tutors are provided collaboratively through on-campus or off-campus services.
Unique Aids and Services Aids, services, or accommodations include career counseling.
Subject-area Tutoring Tutoring is offered one-on-one and in small groups for all subjects. Tutoring is provided collaboratively through on-campus or off-campus services via trained peer tutors.
Enrichment Programs for career planning and college survival skills are provided collaboratively through on-campus or off-campus services. Credit is offered for college survival skills.
Application For admittance to the program or unit, students are required to provide a psychoeducational report (5 years old or less). It is recommended that students provide documentation of high school services. Upon acceptance, documentation of need for services should be sent only to the LD program or unit. *Application deadline (institutional):* Continuous. *Application deadline (LD program):* Rolling/continuous for fall and rolling/continuous for spring.

Charleston Southern University
Office of Disability Services

PO Box 118087
Charleston, SC 29423-8087

http://www.charlestonsouthern.edu/
Contact: Dr. Robert E. Ratliff, Assistant Dean for Counseling and Disability Services. Phone: 843-863-7212. Fax: 843-863-7197. E-mail: rratliff@csuniv.edu.

Office of Disability Services Approximately 40 registered undergraduate students were served during 2002-03. The program or unit includes 1 full-time staff member. Counselors and LD specialists are provided through the program or unit. Academic advisers, coaches, diagnostic specialists, professional tutors, and trained peer tutors are provided collaboratively through on-campus or off-campus services.
Orientation The program or unit offers an optional orientation for new students individually by special arrangement.
Unique Aids and Services Aids, services, or accommodations include faculty training, personal counseling by appointment.
Subject-area Tutoring Tutoring is offered one-on-one for most subjects. Tutoring is provided collaboratively through on-campus or off-campus services via trained peer tutors.
Basic Skills Remediation Remediation is offered one-on-one for learning strategies, social skills, study skills, and time management. Remediation is provided through the program or unit. Remediation is also provided collaboratively through on-campus or off-campus services via trained peer tutors.
Enrichment Programs for career planning, college survival skills, learning strategies, stress management, study skills, test taking, and time management are provided collaboratively through on-campus or off-campus services.
Application For admittance to the program or unit, students are required to apply to the program directly and provide a psychoeducational report (3 years old or less). It is recommended that students provide documentation of high school services. Upon application, materials documenting need for services should be sent only to admissions with institutional application materials. Upon acceptance, documentation of need for services should be sent only to the LD program or unit. *Application deadline (institutional):* Continuous. *Application deadline (LD program):* Rolling/continuous for fall and rolling/continuous for spring.
Written Policies Written policy regarding general/basic LD accommodations is available on the program Web site. Written policies regarding course substitutions, general/basic LD accommodations, and reduced course loads are available through the program or unit directly.

Chatham College

Woodland Road
Pittsburgh, PA 15232-2826
http://www.chatham.edu/
Contact: Mrs. Janet K. James, Director of Learning Center. Phone: 412-365-1611. Fax: 412-365-1660. E-mail: james@chatham.edu.

Approximately 26 registered undergraduate students were served during 2002-03. The program or unit includes 3 full-time and 2 part-time staff members. Academic advisers, coaches, counselors, diagnostic specialists, LD specialists, professional tutors, remediation/learning specialists, skill tutors, strategy tutors, and trained peer tutors are provided through the program or unit. Academic advisers,

Chatham College (continued)

coaches, counselors, graduate assistants/students, regular education teachers, special education teachers, and teacher trainees are provided collaboratively through on-campus or off-campus services.

Unique Aids and Services Aids, services, or accommodations include advocates, career counseling, digital textbooks, faculty training, parent workshops, and personal coach.

Subject-area Tutoring Tutoring is offered one-on-one and in small groups for all subjects. Tutoring is provided through the program or unit via computer-based instruction, graduate assistants/students, LD specialists, professional tutors, and trained peer tutors.

Diagnostic Testing Testing is provided through the program or unit for learning strategies, learning styles, math, reading, spelling, study skills, and written language. Testing for auditory processing, handwriting, intelligence, motor skills, neuropsychological, personality, social skills, spoken language, and visual processing is provided collaboratively through on-campus or off-campus services.

Basic Skills Remediation Remediation is offered one-on-one and in small groups for computer skills, learning strategies, math, reading, social skills, spelling, study skills, time management, and written language. Remediation is provided through the program or unit via computer-based instruction, graduate assistants/students, LD specialists, professional tutors, and trained peer tutors. Remediation is also provided collaboratively through on-campus or off-campus services via regular education teachers, special education teachers, and teacher trainees.

Enrichment Enrichment programs are available through the program or unit for college survival skills, learning strategies, math, practical computer skills, reading, stress management, study skills, test taking, time management, vocabulary development, and written composition skills. Programs for career planning, health and nutrition, math, medication management, oral communication skills, practical computer skills, self-advocacy, stress management, test taking, and time management are provided collaboratively through on-campus or off-campus services. Credit is offered for math, oral communication skills, and practical computer skills.

Application For admittance to the program or unit, students are required to provide a psychoeducational report (3 years old or less) and provide documentation of high school services. Upon acceptance, documentation of need for services should be sent to both admissions and the LD program or unit. *Application deadline (institutional):* Continuous. *Application deadline (LD program):* Rolling/continuous for fall and rolling/continuous for spring.

Written Policies Written policy regarding general/basic LD accommodations is outlined in the school's catalog/handbook. Written policies regarding course substitutions, general/basic LD accommodations, reduced course loads, and substitutions and waivers of graduation requirements are available through the program or unit directly.

The program or unit includes 1 part-time staff member. Academic advisers are provided collaboratively through on-campus or off-campus services.

Orientation The program or unit offers an optional orientation for new students individually by special arrangement.

Enrichment Programs for career planning, college survival skills, learning strategies, math, self-advocacy, stress management, study skills, test taking, time management, and written composition skills are provided collaboratively through on-campus or off-campus services.

Application For admittance to the program or unit, students are required to apply to the program directly and provide a psychoeducational report (3 years old or less). It is recommended that students provide documentation of high school services. Upon acceptance, documentation of need for services should be sent only to the LD program or unit. *Application deadline (institutional):* 3/1. *Application deadline (LD program):* Rolling/continuous for fall and rolling/continuous for spring.

Written Policies Written policies regarding course substitutions, general/basic LD accommodations, substitutions and waivers of admissions requirements, and substitutions and waivers of graduation requirements are available on the program Web site. Written policies regarding course substitutions, general/basic LD accommodations, substitutions and waivers of admissions requirements, and substitutions and waivers of graduation requirements are outlined in the school's catalog/handbook. Written policies regarding course substitutions, general/basic LD accommodations, substitutions and waivers of admissions requirements, and substitutions and waivers of graduation requirements are available through the program or unit directly.

City University

11900 NE First Street
Bellevue, WA 98005
http://www.cityu.edu/

Contact: Ms. Esther Hunt, Disability Resource/Project Coordinator. Phone: 800-426-5596 Ext. 5381. Fax: 425-709-5360. E-mail: ehunt@cityu.edu.

Application *Application deadline (institutional):* Continuous.

Christopher Newport University

1 University Place
Newport News, VA 23606-2998
http://www.cnu.edu/

Contact: Phone: 757-594-7000. Fax: 757-594-7333.

Claremont McKenna College

500 East 9th Street
Claremont, CA 91711
http://www.claremontmckenna.edu/directory/dean-students.htm

Contact: Mr. Jefferson Huang, Dean of Students. Phone: 909-621-8114. Fax: 909-621-8495. E-mail: jefferson.huang@claremontmckenna.edu.

Approximately 22 registered undergraduate students were served during 2002–03. The program or unit includes 7 full-time staff members. Academic advisers, coaches, counselors, diagnostic specialists, LD specialists, professional tutors, regular education teachers, skill tutors, strategy tutors, and other are provided collaboratively through on-campus or off-campus services.

Unique Aids and Services Aids, services, or accommodations include advocates, career counseling, personal coach, and weekly meetings with faculty.

Subject-area Tutoring Tutoring is offered one-on-one and in small groups for all subjects. Tutoring is provided collaboratively through on-campus or off-campus services via computer-based instruction, LD specialists, and trained peer tutors.

Diagnostic Testing Testing for auditory processing, handwriting, intelligence, learning strategies, learning styles, math, motor skills, neuropsychological, personality, reading, social skills, spelling, spoken language, study skills, visual processing, written language, and other services is provided collaboratively through on-campus or off-campus services.

Basic Skills Remediation Remediation is offered one-on-one and in small groups for auditory processing, computer skills, handwriting, learning strategies, math, motor skills, reading, social skills, spelling, spoken language, study skills, time management, visual processing, written language, and others. Remediation is provided collaboratively through on-campus or off-campus services via computer-based instruction, LD specialists, professional tutors, regular education teachers, and trained peer tutors.

Enrichment Programs for career planning, college survival skills, health and nutrition, learning strategies, math, medication management, oral communication skills, practical computer skills, reading, self-advocacy, stress management, study skills, test taking, time management, vocabulary development, written composition skills, and other are provided collaboratively through on-campus or off-campus services.

Application For admittance to the program or unit, students are required to provide a psychoeducational report (2 years old or less). It is recommended that students provide documentation of high school services. Upon application, materials documenting need for services should be sent only to admissions with institutional application materials. Upon acceptance, documentation of need for services should be sent to both admissions and the LD program or unit. *Application deadline (institutional): 1/2.*

Written Policies Written policy regarding general/basic LD accommodations is available on the program Web site. Written policy regarding general/basic LD accommodations is outlined in the school's catalog/handbook.

Clarke College
Learning Center

1550 Clarke Drive
Dubuque, IA 52001-3198
http://www.clarke.edu/

Contact: Ms. Myra Anne Benzer, Learning Center Director. Phone: 563-588-8107. E-mail: myra.benzer@clarke.edu.

Learning Center Approximately 30 registered undergraduate students were served during 2002-03. The program or unit includes 2 full-time staff members. Regular education teachers and remediation/learning specialists are provided through the program or unit. Aca-

demic advisers, coaches, counselors, diagnostic specialists, LD specialists, skill tutors, and trained peer tutors are provided collaboratively through on-campus or off-campus services.

Unique Aids and Services Aids, services, or accommodations include advocates, career counseling, faculty training, personal coach, and weekly meetings with faculty.

Subject-area Tutoring Tutoring is offered one-on-one and in small groups for some subjects. Tutoring is provided through the program or unit via computer-based instruction and LD specialists. Tutoring is also provided collaboratively through on-campus or off-campus services via computer-based instruction and trained peer tutors.

Diagnostic Testing Testing is provided through the program or unit for learning strategies, learning styles, and study skills. Testing for intelligence, math, reading, and written language is provided collaboratively through on-campus or off-campus services.

Basic Skills Remediation Remediation is offered one-on-one for computer skills, learning strategies, math, reading, spelling, study skills, time management, and written language. Remediation is provided through the program or unit via computer-based instruction and LD specialists. Remediation is also provided collaboratively through on-campus or off-campus services via computer-based instruction and trained peer tutors.

Enrichment Enrichment programs are available through the program or unit for college survival skills, learning strategies, oral communication skills, practical computer skills, reading, self-advocacy, stress management, study skills, test taking, time management, vocabulary development, and written composition skills. Programs for career planning, college survival skills, health and nutrition, math, medication management, reading, self-advocacy, stress management, time management, and written composition skills are provided collaboratively through on-campus or off-campus services.

Fees *Diagnostic Testing* fee is $0 to $350.

Application For admittance to the program or unit, students are required to provide a psychoeducational report. It is recommended that students provide documentation of high school services. Upon application, materials documenting need for services should be sent to both admissions and the LD program or unit. Upon acceptance, documentation of need for services should be sent only to the LD program or unit. *Application deadline (institutional):* Continuous. *Application deadline (LD program):* Rolling/continuous for fall and rolling/continuous for spring.

Written Policies Written policies regarding course substitutions, general/basic LD accommodations, reduced course loads, substitutions and waivers of admissions requirements, and substitutions and waivers of graduation requirements are available through the program or unit directly.

Clark University

950 Main Street
Worcester, MA 01610-1477
http://www.clarku.edu/

Contact: Sharon I. de Klerk, Coordinator of Disability Services. Phone: 508-793-7468. Fax: 508-421-3700. E-mail: sdeklerk@clarku.edu.

Clark University (continued)

Approximately 142 registered undergraduate students were served during 2002-03. The program or unit includes 1 full-time staff member. LD specialists are provided through the program or unit. Academic advisers and regular education teachers are provided collaboratively through on-campus or off-campus services.

Orientation The program or unit offers an optional 2-day orientation for new students before registration and before classes begin.

Unique Aids and Services Aids, services, or accommodations include career counseling.

Fees *Orientation* fee is $250.

Application For admittance to the program or unit, students are required to provide a psychoeducational report (3 years old or less). Upon acceptance, documentation of need for services should be sent only to the LD program or unit. *Application deadline (institutional):* 2/1. *Application deadline (LD program):* Rolling/continuous for fall and rolling/continuous for spring.

Written Policies Written policy regarding general/basic LD accommodations is available on the program Web site.

The Cleveland Institute of Art
Academic Services Office

11141 East Boulevard
Cleveland, OH 44106-1700
http://www.cia.edu/
Contact: Ms. Jill Milenski, Associate Director of Academic Services. Phone: 216-421-7462. Fax: 216-754-2557. E-mail: jmilenski@gate.cia.edu.

Academic Services Office Approximately 20 registered undergraduate students were served during 2002-03. The program or unit includes 1 part-time staff member. Academic advisers and trained peer tutors are provided through the program or unit.

Unique Aids and Services Aids, services, or accommodations include advocates.

Subject-area Tutoring Tutoring is offered one-on-one, in small groups, and in class-size groups for some subjects. Tutoring is provided through the program or unit via trained peer tutors. Tutoring is also provided collaboratively through on-campus or off-campus services via computer-based instruction.

Basic Skills Remediation Remediation is offered in class-size groups for learning strategies, study skills, and time management. Remediation is provided collaboratively through on-campus or off-campus services.

Enrichment Programs for career planning, learning strategies, study skills, test taking, time management, and written composition skills are provided collaboratively through on-campus or off-campus services.

Application It is recommended that students provide a psychoeducational report and provide documentation of high school services. Upon application, materials documenting need for services should be sent only to the LD program or unit. Upon acceptance, documentation of need for services should be sent only to the LD program or unit. *Application deadline (institutional):* Continuous. *Application deadline (LD program):* Rolling/continuous for fall and rolling/continuous for spring.

Written Policies Written policy regarding general/basic LD accommodations is outlined in the school's catalog/handbook.

Cleveland State University
Office of Disability Services

2121 Euclid Avenue
Cleveland, OH 44115
http://www.csuohio.edu/
Contact: Mr. Mike Zuccaro, Coordinator of Services for Persons with Disabilities. Phone: 216-687-2015. E-mail: m.zuccaro@csuohio.edu.

Office of Disability Services The program or unit includes 2 full-time and 3 part-time staff members. Counselors are provided through the program or unit. Counselors are provided collaboratively through on-campus or off-campus services.

Orientation The program or unit offers an optional 2-hour orientation for new students before registration, before classes begin, during summer prior to enrollment, during registration, after classes begin, and individually by special arrangement.

Summer Program To help prepare for the demands of college, there is an optional 12-week summer program prior to entering the school. Degree credit will be earned.

Unique Aids and Services Aids, services, or accommodations include advocates, career counseling, priority registration, and support groups.

Subject-area Tutoring Tutoring is offered one-on-one and in small groups for some subjects. Tutoring is provided collaboratively through on-campus or off-campus services via trained peer tutors.

Diagnostic Testing Testing is provided through the program or unit for math and written language. Testing for math and written language is provided collaboratively through on-campus or off-campus services.

Basic Skills Remediation Remediation is offered in class-size groups for math, reading, and written language. Remediation is provided collaboratively through on-campus or off-campus services via computer-based instruction and regular education teachers.

Enrichment Programs for career planning, college survival skills, math, practical computer skills, reading, self-advocacy, stress management, study skills, test taking, time management, and written composition skills are provided collaboratively through on-campus or off-campus services. Credit is offered for career planning, college survival skills, and reading.

Student Organization The Access Group consists of 50 members.

Application For admittance to the program or unit, students are required to provide a psychoeducational report (3 years old or less), provide documentation of high school services, and provide a transition to college statement. Upon acceptance, documentation of need for services should be sent only to the LD program or unit. *Application deadline (institutional):* Continuous. *Application deadline (LD program):* Rolling/continuous for fall and rolling/continuous for spring.

Written Policies Written policies regarding general/basic LD accommodations and grade forgiveness are available on the program Web site. Written policies regarding general/basic LD accommodations and grade forgiveness are outlined in the school's catalog/handbook. Written policies regarding course substitutions, general/basic LD accommodations, and grade forgiveness are available through the program or unit directly.

Coe College
Academic Achievement Program

1220 1st Avenue, NE
Cedar Rapids, IA 52402-5092
http://www.public.coe.edu/departments/AAP
Contact: Phone: 319-399-8000. Fax: 319-399-8816.

Academic Achievement Program Approximately 20 registered undergraduate students were served during 2002-03. The program or unit includes 3 full-time staff members and 1 part-time staff member. Academic advisers, counselors, remediation/learning specialists, skill tutors, and trained peer tutors are provided through the program or unit.
Orientation The program or unit offers an optional orientation for new students after classes begin and individually by special arrangement.
Subject-area Tutoring Tutoring is offered one-on-one and in small groups for most subjects. Tutoring is provided through the program or unit via LD specialists and trained peer tutors.
Basic Skills Remediation Remediation is offered one-on-one and in small groups for math, reading, study skills, and time management. Remediation is provided through the program or unit via computer-based instruction and LD specialists.
Enrichment Enrichment programs are available through the program or unit for career planning, college survival skills, learning strategies, math, reading, self-advocacy, study skills, test taking, and time management. Programs for career planning, health and nutrition, medication management, oral communication skills, practical computer skills, reading, stress management, and written composition skills are provided collaboratively through on-campus or off-campus services. Credit is offered for oral communication skills, reading, study skills, and written composition skills.
Application For admittance to the program or unit, students are required to provide a psychoeducational report (5 years old or less). It is recommended that students apply to the program directly and provide documentation of high school services. Upon application, materials documenting need for services should be sent only to the LD program or unit. Upon acceptance, documentation of need for services should be sent only to the LD program or unit. *Application deadline (institutional): 3/1. Application deadline (LD program):* Rolling/continuous for fall and rolling/continuous for spring.
Written Policies Written policies regarding general/basic LD accommodations and reduced course loads are available through the program or unit directly.

Cogswell Polytechnical College

1175 Bordeaux Drive
Sunnyvale, CA 94089-1299
http://www.cogswell.edu/
Contact: Ms. Garbriella Sechi, Academic Dean. Phone: 408-541-0100 Ext. 104. Fax: 408-747-0764. E-mail: dsechi@cogswell.edu.

Approximately 2 registered undergraduate students were served during 2002-03. The program or unit includes 3 full-time staff members. Academic advisers and regular education teachers are provided through the program or unit.
Unique Aids and Services Aids, services, or accommodations include advocates.
Subject-area Tutoring Tutoring is offered one-on-one for all subjects. Tutoring is provided through the program or unit via graduate assistants/students.
Basic Skills Remediation Remediation is offered one-on-one for learning strategies and math. Remediation is provided through the program or unit via graduate assistants/students and regular education teachers.
Application Upon application, materials documenting need for services should be sent only to admissions with institutional application materials. Upon acceptance, documentation of need for services should be sent only to the LD program or unit. *Application deadline (institutional): 6/1. Application deadline (LD program):* Rolling/continuous for fall and rolling/continuous for spring.
Written Policies Written policies regarding course substitutions, general/basic LD accommodations, grade forgiveness, reduced course loads, substitutions and waivers of admissions requirements, and substitutions and waivers of graduation requirements are outlined in the school's catalog/handbook.

Colby College

Mayflower Hill
Waterville, ME 04901-8840
http://www.colby.edu/dos/
Contact: Mr. Mark R. Serdjenian, Associate Dean of Students for Academics. Phone: 207-872-3106. Fax: 207-872-3076. E-mail: mrserdje@colby.edu.

Approximately 50 registered undergraduate students were served during 2002-03. The program or unit includes 1 part-time staff member. Academic advisers, counselors, skill tutors, and trained peer tutors are provided collaboratively through on-campus or off-campus services.
Subject-area Tutoring Tutoring is offered one-on-one for all subjects. Tutoring is provided collaboratively through on-campus or off-campus services via trained peer tutors.
Application For admittance to the program or unit, students are required to provide a psychoeducational report (5 years old or less). Upon application, materials documenting need for services should be sent only to admissions with institutional application materials. Upon acceptance, documentation of need for services should be sent only to the LD program or unit. *Application deadline (institutional): 1/1. Application deadline (LD program):* Rolling/continuous for fall and rolling/continuous for spring.
Written Policies Written policies regarding course substitutions, general/basic LD accommodations, reduced course loads, and substitutions and waivers of graduation requirements are available on the program Web site. Written policies regarding course substitutions, general/basic LD accommodations, reduced course loads, and substitutions and waivers of graduation requirements are outlined in the school's catalog/handbook. Written policies regarding course substitutions, general/basic LD accommodations, reduced course loads, and substitutions and waivers of graduation requirements are available through the program or unit directly.

Colgate University
Academic Program Support and Disability Services

13 Oak Drive
Hamilton, NY 13346-1386
http://offices.colgate.edu/disabilities
Contact: Ms. Lynn Waldman, Director of Academic Program Support and Disability Services. Phone: 315-228-7225. Fax: 315-228-7831. E-mail: lwaldman@mail.colgate.edu.

Academic Program Support and Disability Services Approximately 150 registered undergraduate students were served during 2002-03. The program or unit includes 1 full-time staff member. Remediation/learning specialists are provided through the program or unit. Academic advisers, coaches, counselors, diagnostic specialists, professional tutors, regular education teachers, and trained peer tutors are provided collaboratively through on-campus or off-campus services.
Unique Aids and Services Aids, services, or accommodations include services as determined on a case-by-case, course-by-course basis.
Subject-area Tutoring Tutoring is offered one-on-one, in small groups, and in class-size groups for most subjects. Tutoring is provided through the program or unit via LD specialists. Tutoring is also provided collaboratively through on-campus or off-campus services via computer-based instruction, graduate assistants/students, professional tutors, and trained peer tutors.
Enrichment Enrichment programs are available through the program or unit for career planning, college survival skills, learning strategies, math, medication management, oral communication skills, practical computer skills, reading, self-advocacy, stress management, study skills, test taking, time management, vocabulary development, written composition skills, and other. Programs for career planning, college survival skills, health and nutrition, learning strategies, math, medication management, oral communication skills, practical computer skills, stress management, study skills, test taking, time management, vocabulary development, written composition skills, and other are provided collaboratively through on-campus or off-campus services.
Application For admittance to the program or unit, students are required to provide a psychoeducational report. It is recommended that students provide documentation of high school services. Upon acceptance, documentation of need for services should be sent only to the LD program or unit. *Application deadline (institutional):* 1/15. *Application deadline (LD program):* Rolling/continuous for fall and rolling/continuous for spring.
Written Policies Written policy regarding general/basic LD accommodations is available on the program Web site. Written policy regarding general/basic LD accommodations is outlined in the school's catalog/handbook. Written policy regarding general/basic LD accommodations is available through the program or unit directly.

College Misericordia
Alternative Learners Project

301 Lake Street
Dallas, PA 18612-1098

http://www.misericordia.edu
Contact: Dr. Joseph Rogan, Program Director. Phone: 570-674-6347. Fax: 570-675-2441. E-mail: jrogan@misericordia.edu.

Alternative Learners Project Approximately 75 registered undergraduate students were served during 2002-03. The program or unit includes 4 full-time staff members. LD specialists and strategy tutors are provided through the program or unit. Academic advisers, counselors, LD specialists, professional tutors, remediation/learning specialists, and strategy tutors are provided collaboratively through on-campus or off-campus services.
Orientation The program or unit offers a mandatory 6-week orientation for new students after classes begin.
Unique Aids and Services Aids, services, or accommodations include advocates, career counseling, faculty training, parent workshops, and priority registration.
Subject-area Tutoring Tutoring is offered one-on-one and in small groups for all subjects. Tutoring is provided collaboratively through on-campus or off-campus services via computer-based instruction, professional tutors, and trained peer tutors.
Basic Skills Remediation Remediation is offered one-on-one and in small groups for learning strategies, math, reading, time management, and written language. Remediation is provided through the program or unit via LD specialists. Remediation is also provided collaboratively through on-campus or off-campus services via computer-based instruction, professional tutors, and trained peer tutors.
Enrichment Enrichment programs are available through the program or unit for college survival skills, learning strategies, and time management. Programs for career planning and medication management are provided collaboratively through on-campus or off-campus services.
Application For admittance to the program or unit, students are required to provide a psychoeducational report (2 years old or less) and provide documentation of high school services. Upon application, materials documenting need for services should be sent only to admissions with institutional application materials. Upon acceptance, documentation of need for services should be sent only to admissions. *Application deadline (institutional):* Continuous. *Application deadline (LD program):* 2/15 for fall. 2/15 for spring.
Written Policies Written policies regarding course substitutions, general/basic LD accommodations, grade forgiveness, reduced course loads, substitutions and waivers of admissions requirements, and substitutions and waivers of graduation requirements are available on the program Web site. Written policies regarding course substitutions, general/basic LD accommodations, grade forgiveness, reduced course loads, substitutions and waivers of admissions requirements, and substitutions and waivers of graduation requirements are outlined in the school's catalog/handbook. Written policies regarding course substitutions, general/basic LD accommodations, reduced course loads, substitutions and waivers of admissions requirements, and substitutions and waivers of graduation requirements are available through the program or unit directly.

College of Charleston
Center for Disability Services/SNAP

66 George Street
Charleston, SC 29424-0001

http://www.cofc.edu/~cds

Contact: Mrs. Bobbie Lindstrom, Director. Phone: 843-953-1431. Fax: 843-953-7731. E-mail: lindstromb@cofc.edu.

Center for Disability Services/SNAP Approximately 350 registered undergraduate students were served during 2002-03. The program or unit includes 2 full-time staff members and 1 part-time staff member. Academic advisers, coaches, and strategy tutors are provided through the program or unit. Academic advisers, counselors, diagnostic specialists, graduate assistants/students, professional tutors, remediation/learning specialists, skill tutors, strategy tutors, and trained peer tutors are provided collaboratively through on-campus or off-campus services.

Orientation The program or unit offers an optional half-day orientation for new students before classes begin and individually by special arrangement.

Unique Aids and Services Aids, services, or accommodations include career counseling, personal coach, and priority registration.

Subject-area Tutoring Tutoring is offered one-on-one and in small groups for most subjects. Tutoring is provided collaboratively through on-campus or off-campus services via graduate assistants/students, professional tutors, and trained peer tutors.

Diagnostic Testing Testing for auditory processing, intelligence, learning styles, math, personality, reading, spelling, study skills, visual processing, and written language is provided collaboratively through on-campus or off-campus services.

Enrichment Enrichment programs are available through the program or unit for self-advocacy and time management. Programs for career planning, learning strategies, stress management, study skills, test taking, time management, and written composition skills are provided collaboratively through on-campus or off-campus services.

Fees *Diagnostic Testing* fee is applicable.

Application For admittance to the program or unit, students are required to apply to the program directly and provide a psychoeducational report (3 years old or less). It is recommended that students provide documentation of high school services. Upon acceptance, documentation of need for services should be sent only to the LD program or unit. *Application deadline (institutional):* 4/1. *Application deadline (LD program):* Rolling/continuous for fall and rolling/continuous for spring.

Written Policies Written policies regarding course substitutions and general/basic LD accommodations are outlined in the school's catalog/handbook. Written policy regarding reduced course loads is available through the program or unit directly.

The College of New Jersey
The Office of Differing Abilities Services

PO Box 7718

Ewing, NJ 08628

http://www.tcnj.edu/%7Eodas

Contact: Ms. A. Terri Yamiolkowski, Coordinator. Phone: 609-771-2571. Fax: 609-771-5107. E-mail: yamiolko@tcnj.edu.

The Office of Differing Abilities Services Approximately 51 registered undergraduate students were served during 2002-03. The program or unit includes 1 full-time and 1 part-time staff member. Counselors and trained peer tutors are provided collaboratively through on-campus or off-campus services.

Unique Aids and Services Aids, services, or accommodations include advocates, career counseling, and digital textbooks.

Subject-area Tutoring Tutoring is offered one-on-one, in small groups, and in class-size groups for most subjects. Tutoring is provided collaboratively through on-campus or off-campus services via computer-based instruction and trained peer tutors.

Application For admittance to the program or unit, students are required to provide a psychoeducational report (3 years old or less). It is recommended that students provide documentation of high school services. Upon acceptance, documentation of need for services should be sent only to the LD program or unit. *Application deadline (institutional):* 2/15. *Application deadline (LD program):* Rolling/continuous for fall.

Written Policies Written policy regarding general/basic LD accommodations is available on the program Web site. Written policies regarding course substitutions, general/basic LD accommodations, grade forgiveness, and reduced course loads are available through the program or unit directly.

College of St. Catherine

2004 Randolph Avenue

St. Paul, MN 55105-1789

http://www.stkate.edu/

Contact: Phone: 651-690-6000. Fax: 651-690-6042.

The program or unit includes 2 part-time staff members. Coaches, counselors, diagnostic specialists, and LD specialists are provided through the program or unit. Academic advisers, graduate assistants/students, regular education teachers, and trained peer tutors are provided collaboratively through on-campus or off-campus services.

Orientation The program or unit offers an optional orientation for new students individually by special arrangement.

Unique Aids and Services Aids, services, or accommodations include career counseling, digital textbooks, faculty training, personal coach, and weekly meetings with faculty.

Subject-area Tutoring Tutoring is offered one-on-one and in small groups for most subjects. Tutoring is provided collaboratively through on-campus or off-campus services via trained peer tutors.

Diagnostic Testing Testing for auditory processing, intelligence, learning strategies, learning styles, math, personality, reading, spelling, visual processing, and written language is provided collaboratively through on-campus or off-campus services.

Basic Skills Remediation Remediation is offered one-on-one for learning strategies, study skills, and time management.

Enrichment Enrichment programs are available through the program or unit for self-advocacy, study skills, test taking, and time management. Programs for career planning, college survival skills, health and nutrition, learning strategies, math, medication management, stress management, study skills, test taking, time management, and written composition skills are provided collaboratively through on-campus or off-campus services. Credit is offered for career planning and learning strategies.

Fees *Diagnostic Testing* fee is $450.

Application For admittance to the program or unit, students are required to provide a psychoeducational report (3 years old or less). It is recommended that students provide documentation of high school services. Upon acceptance, documentation of need for ser-

College of St. Catherine (continued)

vices should be sent only to the LD program or unit. *Application deadline (institutional):* 8/15. *Application deadline (LD program):* Rolling/continuous for fall and rolling/continuous for spring.

Written Policies Written policies regarding general/basic LD accommodations and substitutions and waivers of graduation requirements are available on the program Web site. Written policies regarding grade forgiveness, reduced course loads, and substitutions and waivers of admissions requirements are outlined in the school's catalog/handbook. Written policies regarding course substitutions, general/basic LD accommodations, and substitutions and waivers of graduation requirements are available through the program or unit directly.

The College of Saint Rose
Learning Center: Disability Services

432 Western Avenue
Albany, NY 12203-1419
http://www.strose.edu/

Contact: Mrs. Kelly A. Hermann, Assistant Director for Special Services. Phone: 518-337-2335. Fax: 518-458-5330. E-mail: hermannk@strose.edu. Head of LD Program: Ms. Carol Schour, Director of The Learning Center. Phone: 518-458-5305. Fax: 518-458-5330. E-mail: schourc@strose.edu.

Learning Center: Disability Services Approximately 70 registered undergraduate students were served during 2002-03. The program or unit includes 3 full-time staff members. Graduate assistants/students and trained peer tutors are provided through the program or unit. Academic advisers and counselors are provided collaboratively through on-campus or off-campus services.

Subject-area Tutoring Tutoring is offered one-on-one, in small groups, and in class-size groups for most subjects. Tutoring is provided through the program or unit via computer-based instruction, graduate assistants/students, and trained peer tutors.

Basic Skills Remediation Remediation is offered one-on-one for learning strategies, study skills, and time management. Remediation is provided through the program or unit via graduate assistants/students and other.

Enrichment Enrichment programs are available through the program or unit for college survival skills, learning strategies, math, study skills, test taking, and time management. Program for career planning is provided collaboratively through on-campus or off-campus services.

Application For admittance to the program or unit, students are required to provide a psychoeducational report (3 years old or less). It is recommended that students provide documentation of high school services. Upon acceptance, documentation of need for services should be sent only to the LD program or unit. *Application deadline (institutional):* 5/1. *Application deadline (LD program):* Rolling/continuous for fall and rolling/continuous for spring.

Written Policies Written policies regarding general/basic LD accommodations and substitutions and waivers of admissions requirements are available through the program or unit directly.

College of Santa Fe
Disabilities Services, Center for Academic Excellence

1600 Saint Michael's Drive
Santa Fe, NM 87505-7634
http://www.csf.edu/cae

Contact: Ms. Donna Collins, Disabilities Services Coordinator. Phone: 505-473-6552. Fax: 505-473-6124. E-mail: dcollins@csf.edu.

Disabilities Services, Center for Academic Excellence Approximately 75 registered undergraduate students were served during 2002-03. The program or unit includes 1 full-time staff member. LD specialists are provided through the program or unit. Academic advisers, counselors, diagnostic specialists, professional tutors, regular education teachers, remediation/learning specialists, skill tutors, strategy tutors, and trained peer tutors are provided collaboratively through on-campus or off-campus services.

Unique Aids and Services Aids, services, or accommodations include digital textbooks, priority registration, and support groups.

Subject-area Tutoring Tutoring is offered one-on-one, in small groups, and in class-size groups for all subjects. Tutoring is provided through the program or unit via LD specialists. Tutoring is also provided collaboratively through on-campus or off-campus services via professional tutors and trained peer tutors.

Basic Skills Remediation Remediation is offered one-on-one, in small groups, and in class-size groups for computer skills, learning strategies, math, reading, study skills, time management, and written language. Remediation is provided through the program or unit via LD specialists. Remediation is also provided collaboratively through on-campus or off-campus services via professional tutors, regular education teachers, and trained peer tutors.

Student Organization Meeting of the Minds consists of 10 members.

Application For admittance to the program or unit, students are required to provide a psychoeducational report (3 years old or less). It is recommended that students provide documentation of high school services. Upon acceptance, documentation of need for services should be sent to both admissions and the LD program or unit. *Application deadline (institutional):* Continuous. *Application deadline (LD program):* Rolling/continuous for fall and rolling/continuous for spring.

Written Policies Written policy regarding general/basic LD accommodations is outlined in the school's catalog/handbook. Written policies regarding course substitutions and reduced course loads are available through the program or unit directly.

College of Staten Island of the City University of New York

2800 Victory Boulevard
Staten Island, NY 10314-6600
http://www.csi.cuny.edu/

Contact: Ms. Margaret Venditti, Director of Disability Services. Phone: 718-982-2510. Fax: 718-982-2117. E-mail: venditti@postbox.csi.cuny.edu.

The program or unit includes 2 full-time and 13 part-time staff members. Academic advisers, coaches, counselors, professional tutors, regular education teachers, and trained peer tutors are provided collaboratively through on-campus or off-campus services.

Orientation The program or unit offers an optional 2-hour orientation for new students before classes begin.

Unique Aids and Services Aids, services, or accommodations include advocates, career counseling, digital textbooks, faculty training, priority registration, and support groups.

Subject-area Tutoring Tutoring is offered one-on-one and in small groups for most subjects. Tutoring is provided through the program or unit via computer-based instruction, professional tutors, and trained peer tutors. Tutoring is also provided collaboratively through on-campus or off-campus services via computer-based instruction, professional tutors, and trained peer tutors.

Basic Skills Remediation Remediation is offered one-on-one and in small groups for learning strategies, math, reading, social skills, study skills, time management, and written language. Remediation is provided through the program or unit via professional tutors and trained peer tutors. Remediation is also provided collaboratively through on-campus or off-campus services via professional tutors and regular education teachers.

Enrichment Enrichment programs are available through the program or unit for college survival skills, learning strategies, math, oral communication skills, reading, self-advocacy, stress management, study skills, test taking, time management, and written composition skills. Programs for career planning, college survival skills, health and nutrition, learning strategies, math, practical computer skills, reading, stress management, study skills, test taking, time management, and written composition skills are provided collaboratively through on-campus or off-campus services. Credit is offered for career planning, college survival skills, health and nutrition, practical computer skills, study skills, test taking, time management, and written composition skills.

Student Organization Organization of Unique Individuals (OUI) consists of 25 members.

Application For admittance to the program or unit, students are required to provide a psychoeducational report (3 years old or less). It is recommended that students provide documentation of high school services. Upon application, materials documenting need for services should be sent only to the LD program or unit. Upon acceptance, documentation of need for services should be sent only to the LD program or unit. *Application deadline (institutional):* Continuous. *Application deadline (LD program):* Rolling/continuous for fall and rolling/continuous for spring.

Written Policies Written policy regarding general/basic LD accommodations is available on the program Web site. Written policy regarding general/basic LD accommodations is outlined in the school's catalog/handbook. Written policy regarding general/basic LD accommodations is available through the program or unit directly.

College of the Atlantic
Academic Services

105 Eden Street
Bar Harbor, ME 04609-1198
http://www.coa.edu/
Contact: Dr. Ken E. Hill, Associate Dean of Academic Services. Phone: 207-288-5015 Ext. 241. E-mail: khill@coa.edu.

Academic Services Approximately 16 registered undergraduate students were served during 2002-03. The program or unit includes 1 full-time and 5 part-time staff members. Counselors are provided through the program or unit. Academic advisers, counselors, diagnostic specialists, professional tutors, regular education teachers, skill tutors, and strategy tutors are provided collaboratively through on-campus or off-campus services.

Unique Aids and Services Aids, services, or accommodations include advocates, support groups, and weekly meetings with faculty.

Subject-area Tutoring Tutoring is offered one-on-one, in small groups, and in class-size groups for some subjects. Tutoring is provided collaboratively through on-campus or off-campus services via LD specialists, professional tutors, and trained peer tutors.

Basic Skills Remediation Remediation is offered one-on-one, in small groups, and in class-size groups for computer skills, learning strategies, math, social skills, study skills, time management, and written language. Remediation is provided collaboratively through on-campus or off-campus services via LD specialists, professional tutors, regular education teachers, and trained peer tutors.

Application It is recommended that students provide a psychoeducational report and provide documentation of high school services. Upon application, materials documenting need for services should be sent only to the LD program or unit. Upon acceptance, documentation of need for services should be sent only to the LD program or unit. *Application deadline (institutional):* 2/15. *Application deadline (LD program):* Rolling/continuous for fall and rolling/continuous for spring.

Written Policies Written policy regarding general/basic LD accommodations is outlined in the school's catalog/handbook.

College of the Holy Cross

1 College Street
Worcester, MA 01610-2395
http://www.holycross.edu/
Contact: Disability Services Office. Phone: 508-793-3693.

The program or unit includes 2 part-time staff members. Counselors are provided through the program or unit. Counselors are provided collaboratively through on-campus or off-campus services.

Unique Aids and Services Aids, services, or accommodations include career counseling.

Subject-area Tutoring Tutoring is offered one-on-one and in small groups for some subjects. Tutoring is provided collaboratively through on-campus or off-campus services via trained peer tutors.

Enrichment Programs for career planning, college survival skills, health and nutrition, learning strategies, math, stress management, study skills, and time management are provided collaboratively through on-campus or off-campus services.

Application For admittance to the program or unit, students are required to provide a psychoeducational report. It is recommended that students provide documentation of high school services. Upon acceptance, documentation of need for services should be sent only to the LD program or unit. *Application deadline (institutional):* 1/15. *Application deadline (LD program):* 1/15 for fall.

College of the Holy Cross (continued)

Written Policies Written policy regarding general/basic LD accommodations is available on the program Web site. Written policy regarding general/basic LD accommodations is outlined in the school's catalog/handbook. Written policy regarding general/basic LD accommodations is available through the program or unit directly.

College of the Ozarks

PO Box 17

Point Lookout, MO 65726

http://www.cofo.edu/

Contact: Sherry Jones, Assistant Registrar. Phone: 417-334-6411 Ext. 4223. Fax: 417-335-2618.

Approximately 3 registered undergraduate students were served during 2002-03. Academic advisers and skill tutors are provided collaboratively through on-campus or off-campus services.

Subject-area Tutoring Tutoring is offered one-on-one. Tutoring is provided collaboratively through on-campus or off-campus services via graduate assistants/students.

Enrichment Programs for career planning, learning strategies, math, oral communication skills, practical computer skills, stress management, and written composition skills are provided collaboratively through on-campus or off-campus services. Credit is offered for career planning, learning strategies, math, oral communication skills, practical computer skills, stress management, and written composition skills.

Application For admittance to the program or unit, students are required to provide a psychoeducational report and provide documentation of high school services. Upon acceptance, documentation of need for services should be sent only to admissions. *Application deadline (institutional): 2/15. Application deadline (LD program):* Rolling/continuous for fall and rolling/continuous for spring.

The College of William and Mary
Disability Services

PO Box 8795

Williamsburg, VA 23187-8795

http://www.wm.eduØSA÷ostud÷isserv.htm

Contact: Phone: 757-221-4000. Fax: 757-221-1242.

Disability Services Approximately 40 registered undergraduate students were served during 2002-03. The program or unit includes 1 full-time staff member. Academic advisers and regular education teachers are provided collaboratively through on-campus or off-campus services.

Diagnostic Testing Testing for study skills is provided collaboratively through on-campus or off-campus services.

Enrichment Programs for career planning, learning strategies, study skills, test taking, time management, and written composition skills are provided collaboratively through on-campus or off-campus services.

Application For admittance to the program or unit, students are required to provide a psychoeducational report (3 years old or less) and provide documentation as specified in "Documentation of Disability" (see Web site for details). Upon application, materials documenting need for services should be sent only to the LD program or unit. Upon acceptance, documentation of need for services should be sent only to the LD program or unit. *Application deadline (institutional): 1/7.*

Written Policies Written policies regarding course substitutions, general/basic LD accommodations, and reduced course loads are available on the program Web site. Written policies regarding general/basic LD accommodations and reduced course loads are outlined in the school's catalog/handbook. Written policy regarding course substitutions is available through the program or unit directly.

Colorado State University
Resources for Disabled Students

Fort Collins, CO 80523-0015

http://www.colostate.edu/Depts/RDS

Contact: Ms. Kathleen Ivy-Althoff, Counselor. Phone: 970-491-6385. Fax: 970-491-3457. E-mail: kivy@lamar.colostate.edu.

Resources for Disabled Students Approximately 400 registered undergraduate students were served during 2002-03. The program or unit includes 7 full-time staff members and 1 part-time staff member. Coaches and counselors are provided through the program or unit. Academic advisers, coaches, counselors, diagnostic specialists, skill tutors, strategy tutors, and trained peer tutors are provided collaboratively through on-campus or off-campus services.

Unique Aids and Services Aids, services, or accommodations include digital textbooks and priority registration.

Subject-area Tutoring Tutoring is offered one-on-one and in small groups. Tutoring is provided collaboratively through on-campus or off-campus services via computer-based instruction and trained peer tutors.

Diagnostic Testing Testing for auditory processing, intelligence, learning strategies, learning styles, math, neuropsychological, reading, spelling, study skills, visual processing, and written language is provided collaboratively through on-campus or off-campus services.

Enrichment Enrichment programs are available through the program or unit for self-advocacy. Programs for career planning, health and nutrition, learning strategies, practical computer skills, stress management, study skills, test taking, time management, and written composition skills are provided collaboratively through on-campus or off-campus services. Credit is offered for health and nutrition, practical computer skills, and written composition skills.

Application For admittance to the program or unit, students are required to provide professional assessment verifying diagnosis. It is recommended that students provide a psychoeducational report and provide documentation of high school services. Upon application, materials documenting need for services should be sent to both admissions and the LD program or unit. Upon acceptance, documentation of need for services should be sent only to the LD program or unit. *Application deadline (institutional): 7/1. Application deadline (LD program):* Rolling/continuous for fall and rolling/continuous for spring.

Written Policies Written policies regarding course substitutions, general/basic LD accommodations, reduced course loads, substitutions and waivers of admissions requirements, and substitutions and waivers of graduation requirements are available on the program Web site. Written policy regarding substitutions and waivers of graduation requirements is outlined in the school's catalog/handbook. Written policies regarding course substitutions, general/basic LD accommodations, reduced course loads, substitutions and waivers of admissions requirements, and substitutions and waivers of graduation requirements are available through the program or unit directly.

Columbia College Chicago
Services for Students with Disabilities (SSD)

600 South Michigan Avenue

Chicago, IL 60605-1996

http://www.colum.edu/student-life/conaway/SWD.html

Contact: Mrs. Suzan Snook, Coordinator of Services for Students with Disabilities. Phone: 312-344-8134. Fax: 312-344-8005. E-mail: ssnook@colum.edu.

Services for Students with Disabilities (SSD) Approximately 130 registered undergraduate students were served during 2002-03. The program or unit includes 2 part-time staff members. Counselors, graduate assistants/students, and LD specialists are provided collaboratively through on-campus or off-campus services.

Summer Program To help prepare for the demands of college, there is 4-week (sometimes required, sometimes recommended) summer program prior to entering the school.

Unique Aids and Services Aids, services, or accommodations include faculty training.

Subject-area Tutoring Tutoring is offered one-on-one for some subjects. Tutoring is provided collaboratively through on-campus or off-campus services via LD specialists, trained peer tutors, and other.

Basic Skills Remediation Remediation is offered one-on-one, in small groups, and in class-size groups for computer skills, learning strategies, math, reading, study skills, time management, and written language. Remediation is provided collaboratively through on-campus or off-campus services via LD specialists, professional tutors, trained peer tutors, and other.

Enrichment Enrichment programs are available through the program or unit for self-advocacy and time management. Programs for career planning, college survival skills, health and nutrition, learning strategies, math, practical computer skills, reading, stress management, study skills, test taking, time management, and written composition skills are provided collaboratively through on-campus or off-campus services. Credit is offered for college survival skills, health and nutrition, learning strategies, math, practical computer skills, and reading.

Application For admittance to the program or unit, students are required to apply to the program directly, provide a psychoeducational report (5 years old or less), and provide documentation of discrepancy between IQ & achievement, processing deficit in psychoeducational eval. It is recommended that students provide documentation of high school services. Upon acceptance, documentation of need

for services should be sent only to the LD program or unit. *Application deadline (institutional):* 7/15. *Application deadline (LD program):* Rolling/continuous for fall and rolling/continuous for spring.

Written Policies Written policies regarding general/basic LD accommodations and grade forgiveness are available on the program Web site. Written policies regarding general/basic LD accommodations and grade forgiveness are outlined in the school's catalog/handbook. Written policies regarding course substitutions, general/basic LD accommodations, reduced course loads, and substitutions and waivers of graduation requirements are available through the program or unit directly.

Columbus College of Art and Design
Disability Services

107 North Ninth Street

Columbus, OH 43215-1758

http://student.ccad.edu/s_adv_30.htm

Contact: Mr. Roderick C. Jungbauer, Director. Phone: 614-222-3292. Fax: 614-222-4040. E-mail: rjungbauer@ccad.edu.

Disability Services Approximately 93 registered undergraduate students were served during 2002-03. The program or unit includes 1 full-time staff member. Academic advisers and LD specialists are provided through the program or unit. Academic advisers, counselors, LD specialists, and remediation/learning specialists are provided collaboratively through on-campus or off-campus services.

Orientation The program or unit offers a mandatory 1-hour orientation for new students individually by special arrangement.

Unique Aids and Services Aids, services, or accommodations include priority registration, adjustment skills.

Enrichment Enrichment programs are available through the program or unit for learning strategies, self-advocacy, and study skills. Programs for career planning, college survival skills, health and nutrition, learning strategies, stress management, study skills, and time management are provided collaboratively through on-campus or off-campus services.

Application For admittance to the program or unit, students are required to provide a psychoeducational report (3 years old or less). Upon application, materials documenting need for services should be sent only to the LD program or unit. Upon acceptance, documentation of need for services should be sent only to the LD program or unit. *Application deadline (institutional):* Continuous. *Application deadline (LD program):* Rolling/continuous for fall and rolling/continuous for spring.

Written Policies Written policy regarding general/basic LD accommodations is available on the program Web site. Written policies regarding general/basic LD accommodations and grade forgiveness are outlined in the school's catalog/handbook. Written policies regarding course substitutions, general/basic LD accommodations, reduced course loads, substitutions and waivers of admissions requirements, and substitutions and waivers of graduation requirements are available through the program or unit directly.

Community Hospital of Roanoke Valley-College of Health Sciences
Counseling Services Department

PO Box 13186

Roanoke, VA 24031-3186

http://www.chs.edu

Contact: Ms. Barbara Awbrey, Counselor. Phone: 540-985-8513. Fax: 540-985-9773. E-mail: bawbrey@chs.edu.

Counseling Services Department Approximately 10 registered undergraduate students were served during 2002-03. The program or unit includes 1 full-time staff member. Counselors, graduate assistants/students, and remediation/learning specialists are provided through the program or unit. Academic advisers, counselors, diagnostic specialists, graduate assistants/students, regular education teachers, and skill tutors are provided collaboratively through on-campus or off-campus services.

Unique Aids and Services Aids, services, or accommodations include faculty training and weekly meetings with faculty.

Subject-area Tutoring Tutoring is offered one-on-one and in small groups for some subjects. Tutoring is provided collaboratively through on-campus or off-campus services via trained peer tutors.

Diagnostic Testing Testing is provided through the program or unit for learning strategies, learning styles, math, personality, reading, spelling, and study skills.

Basic Skills Remediation Remediation is offered one-on-one and in small groups for learning strategies, study skills, and time management. Remediation is provided through the program or unit.

Enrichment Enrichment programs are available through the program or unit for career planning, college survival skills, learning strategies, oral communication skills, self-advocacy, stress management, study skills, test taking, and time management. Programs for college survival skills, learning strategies, practical computer skills, stress management, study skills, test taking, time management, and written composition skills are provided collaboratively through on-campus or off-campus services. Credit is offered for college survival skills, learning strategies, practical computer skills, stress management, study skills, test taking, time management, and written composition skills.

Application For admittance to the program or unit, students are required to provide a psychoeducational report (4 years old or less). It is recommended that students provide documentation of high school services. Upon application, materials documenting need for services should be sent only to the LD program or unit. Upon acceptance, documentation of need for services should be sent only to the LD program or unit. *Application deadline (institutional):* 7/31. *Application deadline (LD program):* Rolling/continuous for fall and rolling/continuous for spring.

Written Policies Written policy regarding general/basic LD accommodations is available on the program Web site. Written policy regarding general/basic LD accommodations is outlined in the school's catalog/handbook. Written policies regarding course substitutions, general/basic LD accommodations, grade forgiveness, reduced course loads, substitutions and waivers of admissions requirements, and substitutions and waivers of graduation requirements are available through the program or unit directly.

Concord College
Office of Disability Services

Vermillion Street, PO Box 1000

Athens, WV 24712-1000

http://www.concord.edu/Pages/resources/Pages/ADA/ADA.html

Contact: Ms. Alice D. Dillon, Disability Services Coordinator. Phone: 304-384-5177. Fax: 304-384-7955. E-mail: ods@concord.edu.

Office of Disability Services Approximately 93 registered undergraduate students were served during 2002-03. The program or unit includes 1 full-time staff member. Academic advisers, remediation/learning specialists, skill tutors, and strategy tutors are provided through the program or unit. Academic advisers, counselors, remediation/learning specialists, skill tutors, and trained peer tutors are provided collaboratively through on-campus or off-campus services.

Orientation The program or unit offers an optional orientation for new students individually by special arrangement.

Unique Aids and Services Aids, services, or accommodations include advocates, career counseling, priority registration, recorded textbooks.

Subject-area Tutoring Tutoring is offered one-on-one and in small groups for most subjects. Tutoring is provided through the program or unit via other. Tutoring is also provided collaboratively through on-campus or off-campus services via computer-based instruction, trained peer tutors, and other.

Diagnostic Testing Testing is provided through the program or unit for learning strategies, learning styles, and study skills. Testing for learning strategies, learning styles, math, personality, study skills, written language, and other services is provided collaboratively through on-campus or off-campus services.

Basic Skills Remediation Remediation is offered one-on-one, in small groups, and in class-size groups for computer skills, learning strategies, math, reading, social skills, study skills, time management, and written language. Remediation is provided through the program or unit. Remediation is also provided collaboratively through on-campus or off-campus services via computer-based instruction, trained peer tutors, and other.

Enrichment Enrichment programs are available through the program or unit for college survival skills, learning strategies, medication management, self-advocacy, stress management, study skills, test taking, time management, and written composition skills. Programs for career planning, college survival skills, health and nutrition, learning strategies, math, oral communication skills, reading, self-advocacy, stress management, study skills, test taking, time management, vocabulary development, written composition skills, and other are provided collaboratively through on-campus or off-campus services. Credit is offered for college survival skills, health and nutrition, learning strategies, math, oral communication skills, reading, study skills, test taking, time management, vocabulary development, and written composition skills.

Application For admittance to the program or unit, students are required to provide a psychoeducational report (5 years old or less). It is recommended that students provide documentation of high school services. Upon acceptance, documentation of need for services should be sent only to the LD program or unit. *Application deadline (institutional):* Continuous. *Application deadline (LD program):* Rolling/continuous for fall and rolling/continuous for spring.

Written Policies Written policy regarding general/basic LD accommodations is available on the program Web site. Written policy regarding general/basic LD accommodations is outlined in the school's catalog/handbook. Written policy regarding general/basic LD accommodations is available through the program or unit directly.

Concordia University
Disability Services

275 Syndicate Street North
St. Paul, MN 55104-5494
http://www.csp.edu/studentsupportservices
Contact: Ms. Annette Carpenter, Disabilities Specialist. Phone: 651-641-8272. Fax: 651-659-0207. E-mail: carpenter@csp.edu.

Disability Services Approximately 20 registered undergraduate students were served during 2002-03. The program or unit includes 4 full-time staff members and 1 part-time staff member. Counselors, graduate assistants/students, LD specialists, remediation/learning specialists, trained peer tutors, and other are provided through the program or unit. Academic advisers are provided collaboratively through on-campus or off-campus services.

Orientation The program or unit offers an optional orientation for new students and students can meet with the LD specialist for additional information and registration assistance.

Unique Aids and Services Aids, services, or accommodations include career counseling, digital textbooks, faculty training, individual support.

Subject-area Tutoring Tutoring is offered one-on-one and in small groups for most subjects. Tutoring is provided through the program or unit via trained peer tutors. Tutoring is also provided collaboratively through on-campus or off-campus services via professional tutors and trained peer tutors.

Basic Skills Remediation Remediation is offered one-on-one, in small groups, and in class-size groups for computer skills, learning strategies, math, reading, social skills, spelling, study skills, time management, and written language. Remediation is provided through the program or unit via LD specialists, trained peer tutors, and other. Remediation is also provided collaboratively through on-campus or off-campus services via professional tutors.

Enrichment Enrichment programs are available through the program or unit for career planning, college survival skills, learning strategies, reading, self-advocacy, stress management, study skills, test taking, and time management. Programs for health and nutrition and practical computer skills are provided collaboratively through on-campus or off-campus services.

Application For admittance to the program or unit, students are required to provide a psychoeducational report (3 years old or less). It is recommended that students provide documentation of high school services. Upon acceptance, documentation of need for services should be sent only to the LD program or unit. *Application deadline (institutional):* 8/1. *Application deadline (LD program):* Rolling/continuous for fall and rolling/continuous for spring.

Written Policies Written policy regarding general/basic LD accommodations is available on the program Web site. Written policy regarding general/basic LD accommodations is available through the program or unit directly.

Cornerstone University
Cornerstone Learning Center (CLC)

1001 East Beltline Avenue, NE
Grand Rapids, MI 49525-5897
http://www.cornerstone.edu/
Contact: Dr. J. Stephen Neynaber, Director. Phone: 616-222-1596. Fax: 616-222-1595. E-mail: stephen_neynaber@cornerstone.edu.

Cornerstone Learning Center (CLC) Approximately 138 registered undergraduate students were served during 2002-03. The program or unit includes 3 full-time and 3 part-time staff members. Academic advisers, diagnostic specialists, graduate assistants/students, LD specialists, professional tutors, remediation/learning specialists, skill tutors, special education teachers, strategy tutors, and trained peer tutors are provided through the program or unit. Academic advisers, coaches, counselors, diagnostic specialists, regular education teachers, remediation/learning specialists, and trained peer tutors are provided collaboratively through on-campus or off-campus services.

Unique Aids and Services Aids, services, or accommodations include career counseling, digital textbooks, faculty training, parent workshops, personal coach, support groups, weekly meetings with faculty, a laptop computer with XP Office software that includes dictate software.

Subject-area Tutoring Tutoring is offered one-on-one, in small groups, and in class-size groups for all subjects. Tutoring is provided through the program or unit via computer-based instruction, graduate assistants/students, LD specialists, professional tutors, and trained peer tutors. Tutoring is also provided collaboratively through on-campus or off-campus services via computer-based instruction and trained peer tutors.

Diagnostic Testing Testing is provided through the program or unit for handwriting, learning strategies, learning styles, math, personality, reading, spelling, study skills, written language, and other services. Testing for learning strategies, learning styles, math, personality, spelling, study skills, and written language is provided collaboratively through on-campus or off-campus services.

Basic Skills Remediation Remediation is offered one-on-one, in small groups, and in class-size groups for computer skills, learning strategies, math, reading, spelling, study skills, time management, visual processing, written language, and English as a Second Language (ESL). Remediation is provided through the program or unit via computer-based instruction, graduate assistants/students, LD specialists, professional tutors, special education teachers, trained peer tutors, and other. Remediation is also provided collaboratively through on-campus or off-campus services via graduate assistants/students, regular education teachers, and trained peer tutors.

Enrichment Enrichment programs are available through the program or unit for career planning, college survival skills, learning strategies, reading, self-advocacy, stress management, study skills, test taking, time management, and written composition skills. Programs for career planning, health and nutrition, math, medication

Cornerstone University (continued)

management, practical computer skills, stress management, time management, and written composition skills are provided collaboratively through on-campus or off-campus services. Credit is offered for college survival skills, learning strategies, math, and written composition skills.

Application For admittance to the program or unit, students are required to apply to the program directly, provide documentation of high school services, and provide registration with the Health Center for students taking medications. It is recommended that students provide a psychoeducational report (2 years old or less). Upon application, materials documenting need for services should be sent only to the LD program or unit. Upon acceptance, documentation of need for services should be sent to both admissions and the LD program or unit. *Application deadline (institutional):* Continuous. *Application deadline (LD program):* Rolling/continuous for fall and rolling/continuous for spring.

Written Policies Written policies regarding course substitutions and general/basic LD accommodations are available on the program Web site. Written policies regarding course substitutions, general/basic LD accommodations, and reduced course loads are outlined in the school's catalog/handbook. Written policies regarding general/basic LD accommodations and reduced course loads are available through the program or unit directly.

Cornish College of the Arts
Student Affairs

1000 Lenora Street
Seattle, WA 98121
http://www.cornish.edu/
Contact: Mr. George Luis Sedano, Director of Student Affairs. Phone: 206-726-5111. Fax: 206-726-5097. E-mail: studentaffairs@cornish.edu.

Student Affairs Approximately 20 registered undergraduate students were served during 2002-03. The program or unit includes 2 full-time staff members.
Unique Aids and Services Aids, services, or accommodations include advocates and digital textbooks.
Enrichment Enrichment programs are available through the program or unit for career planning, college survival skills, health and nutrition, learning strategies, self-advocacy, stress management, study skills, test taking, and time management. Programs for career planning, college survival skills, learning strategies, oral communication skills, practical computer skills, stress management, study skills, test taking, time management, and written composition skills are provided collaboratively through on-campus or off-campus services. Credit is offered for oral communication skills, practical computer skills, and written composition skills.
Application For admittance to the program or unit, students are required to provide a psychoeducational report (3 years old or less). Upon acceptance, documentation of need for services should be sent only to the LD program or unit. *Application deadline (institutional):* 8/15. *Application deadline (LD program):* Rolling/continuous for fall and rolling/continuous for spring.
Written Policies Written policy regarding general/basic LD accommodations is available on the program Web site. Written policies regarding course substitutions, general/basic LD accommodations,

grade forgiveness, and substitutions and waivers of graduation requirements are outlined in the school's catalog/handbook. Written policies regarding course substitutions, general/basic LD accommodations, grade forgiveness, and substitutions and waivers of graduation requirements are available through the program or unit directly.

Creighton University
Office of Disability Accommodations

2500 California Plaza
Omaha, NE 68178-0001
http://www.creighton.edu/
Contact: Mr. Wade Pearson, Coordinator, Office of Disability Accommodations. Phone: 402-280-2749. Fax: 402-280-5579. E-mail: chess@creighton.edu.

Office of Disability Accommodations Approximately 100 registered undergraduate students were served during 2002-03. The program or unit includes 2 part-time staff members. Academic advisers, counselors, diagnostic specialists, graduate assistants/students, and trained peer tutors are provided collaboratively through on-campus or off-campus services.
Unique Aids and Services Aids, services, or accommodations include priority registration.
Subject-area Tutoring Tutoring is offered one-on-one for some subjects. Tutoring is provided collaboratively through on-campus or off-campus services via trained peer tutors.
Diagnostic Testing Testing for auditory processing, handwriting, intelligence, learning strategies, learning styles, math, motor skills, neuropsychological, personality, reading, social skills, spelling, spoken language, study skills, visual processing, and written language is provided collaboratively through on-campus or off-campus services.
Enrichment Programs for career planning, college survival skills, health and nutrition, learning strategies, oral communication skills, reading, self-advocacy, stress management, study skills, test taking, time management, and written composition skills are provided collaboratively through on-campus or off-campus services. Credit is offered for career planning, college survival skills, oral communication skills, and study skills.
Application For admittance to the program or unit, students are required to provide a psychoeducational report. Upon acceptance, documentation of need for services should be sent only to the LD program or unit. *Application deadline (institutional):* 8/1. *Application deadline (LD program):* Rolling/continuous for fall and rolling/continuous for spring.
Written Policies Written policy regarding general/basic LD accommodations is outlined in the school's catalog/handbook. Written policy regarding general/basic LD accommodations is available through the program or unit directly.

Crown College
SPACE for Success

6425 County Road 30
St. Bonifacius, MN 55375-9001
http://www.crown.edu/

Contact: Phone: 952-446-4100. Fax: 952-446-4149.

SPACE for Success Approximately 20 registered undergraduate students were served during 2002-03. The program or unit includes 1 full-time and 5 part-time staff members. Academic advisers, professional tutors, regular education teachers, and trained peer tutors are provided through the program or unit. Coaches, counselors, diagnostic specialists, graduate assistants/students, LD specialists, remediation/learning specialists, skill tutors, special education teachers, strategy tutors, teacher trainees, and other are provided collaboratively through on-campus or off-campus services.

Unique Aids and Services Aids, services, or accommodations include advocates.

Subject-area Tutoring Tutoring is offered one-on-one and in small groups for all subjects. Tutoring is provided through the program or unit via computer-based instruction, graduate assistants/students, LD specialists, and trained peer tutors. Tutoring is also provided collaboratively through on-campus or off-campus services via computer-based instruction, graduate assistants/students, professional tutors, and trained peer tutors.

Diagnostic Testing Testing is provided through the program or unit for learning strategies, learning styles, personality, reading, spelling, spoken language, study skills, and written language. Testing for auditory processing, handwriting, intelligence, learning strategies, math, motor skills, neuropsychological, social skills, spoken language, and visual processing is provided collaboratively through on-campus or off-campus services.

Basic Skills Remediation Remediation is offered one-on-one and in small groups for learning strategies, reading, spelling, spoken language, study skills, time management, and written language. Remediation is provided through the program or unit via computer-based instruction. Remediation is also provided collaboratively through on-campus or off-campus services via graduate assistants/students, LD specialists, professional tutors, regular education teachers, special education teachers, teacher trainees, trained peer tutors, and other.

Enrichment Enrichment programs are available through the program or unit for learning strategies, math, oral communication skills, practical computer skills, reading, study skills, test taking, time management, vocabulary development, and written composition skills. Programs for career planning, college survival skills, health and nutrition, learning strategies, math, oral communication skills, practical computer skills, reading, study skills, test taking, time management, vocabulary development, and written composition skills are provided collaboratively through on-campus or off-campus services. Credit is offered for written composition skills.

Fees *Diagnostic Testing* fee is applicable.

Application For admittance to the program or unit, students are required to provide documentation of high school services. It is recommended that students apply to the program directly and provide a psychoeducational report (3 years old or less). Upon application, materials documenting need for services should be sent only to admissions with institutional application materials. Upon acceptance, documentation of need for services should be sent only to the LD program or unit. *Application deadline (institutional):* Continuous. *Application deadline (LD program):* Rolling/continuous for fall.

Written Policies Written policy regarding general/basic LD accommodations is available on the program Web site. Written policies regarding general/basic LD accommodations, reduced course loads, and substitutions and waivers of admissions requirements are outlined in the school's catalog/handbook. Written policies regarding course substitutions and substitutions and waivers of admissions requirements are available through the program or unit directly.

The Culinary Institute of America
The Learning Strategies Center

1946 Campus Drive
Hyde Park, NY 12538-1499
http://www.ciachef.edu/
Contact: Mr. Jack Rittel, Disability Support Specialist. Phone: 845-451-1219. Fax: 845-451-1034. E-mail: j_rittel@culinary.edu. Head of LD Program: Ms. Jennifer R. Rosenberg, Director of the Learning Strategies Center. Phone: 845-451-1287. Fax: 845-451-1034. E-mail: j_rosenb@culinary.edu.

The Learning Strategies Center Approximately 190 registered undergraduate students were served during 2002-03. The program or unit includes 4 full-time staff members. LD specialists, remediation/learning specialists, and trained peer tutors are provided through the program or unit. Regular education teachers are provided collaboratively through on-campus or off-campus services.

Subject-area Tutoring Tutoring is offered one-on-one and in small groups for all subjects. Tutoring is provided through the program or unit via LD specialists and trained peer tutors.

Diagnostic Testing Testing for auditory processing, intelligence, learning strategies, math, motor skills, neuropsychological, reading, social skills, spelling, visual processing, and written language is provided collaboratively through on-campus or off-campus services.

Basic Skills Remediation Remediation is offered one-on-one and in class-size groups for learning strategies, math, study skills, time management, and written language. Remediation is provided through the program or unit via LD specialists and trained peer tutors. Remediation is also provided collaboratively through on-campus or off-campus services via regular education teachers.

Fees *Diagnostic Testing* fee is $350.

Application For admittance to the program or unit, students are required to provide a psychoeducational report (3 years old or less). Upon application, materials documenting need for services should be sent only to admissions with institutional application materials. Upon acceptance, documentation of need for services should be sent only to the LD program or unit. *Application deadline (institutional):* 1/15. *Application deadline (LD program):* Rolling/continuous for fall and rolling/continuous for spring.

Written Policies Written policy regarding general/basic LD accommodations is outlined in the school's catalog/handbook. Written policies regarding course substitutions, general/basic LD accommodations, and reduced course loads are available through the program or unit directly.

Cumberland College
Office of Academic Affairs

6178 College Station Drive
Williamsburg, KY 40769-1372

Cumberland College (continued)
http://www.cumberlandcollege.edu/

Contact: Mrs. Sue Weedman, Associate Dean. Phone: 606-539-4214. Fax: 606-539-4157. E-mail: sweedman@cumberlandcollege.edu.

Office of Academic Affairs Approximately 17 registered undergraduate students were served during 2002-03. Academic advisers, coaches, counselors, skill tutors, strategy tutors, and trained peer tutors are provided collaboratively through on-campus or off-campus services.

Unique Aids and Services Aids, services, or accommodations include career counseling and weekly meetings with faculty.

Subject-area Tutoring Tutoring is offered one-on-one, in small groups, and in class-size groups for all subjects. Tutoring is provided collaboratively through on-campus or off-campus services via computer-based instruction and trained peer tutors.

Enrichment Programs for career planning, college survival skills, health and nutrition, learning strategies, oral communication skills, practical computer skills, stress management, study skills, test taking, time management, and written composition skills are provided collaboratively through on-campus or off-campus services.

Application For admittance to the program or unit, students are required to apply to the program directly and provide a psychoeducational report (3 years old or less). Upon application, materials documenting need for services should be sent only to admissions with institutional application materials. Upon acceptance, documentation of need for services should be sent only to the LD program or unit. *Application deadline (institutional):* Continuous. *Application deadline (LD program):* Rolling/continuous for fall and rolling/continuous for spring.

Written Policies Written policy regarding general/basic LD accommodations is available through the program or unit directly.

Cumberland University

One Cumberland Square
Lebanon, TN 37087-3408
http://www.cumberland.edu/

Contact: Ms. Jeanne B. Lawson, Director of Student Disability Services Office. Phone: 615-444-2562 Ext. 1110. Fax: 615-444-2569. E-mail: jlawson@cumberland.edu.

Approximately 15 registered undergraduate students were served during 2002-03. The program or unit includes 1 part-time staff member. Academic advisers, coaches, counselors, professional tutors, regular education teachers, remediation/learning specialists, skill tutors, special education teachers, and strategy tutors are provided collaboratively through on-campus or off-campus services.

Orientation The program or unit offers before registration, before classes begin, during summer prior to enrollment, during registration, after classes begin, and individually by special arrangement.

Unique Aids and Services Aids, services, or accommodations include advocates, career counseling, and faculty training.

Subject-area Tutoring Tutoring is offered one-on-one, in small groups, and in class-size groups. Tutoring is provided through the program or unit via computer-based instruction and trained peer tutors. Tutoring is also provided collaboratively through on-campus or off-campus services via trained peer tutors.

Basic Skills Remediation Remediation is offered one-on-one, in small groups, and in class-size groups for computer skills, learning strategies, math, reading, study skills, and written language.

Enrichment Enrichment programs are available through the program or unit for math, reading, study skills, vocabulary development, and written composition skills. Credit is offered for math, reading, study skills, vocabulary development, and written composition skills.

Application For admittance to the program or unit, students are required to provide a psychoeducational report. Upon acceptance, documentation of need for services should be sent only to the LD program or unit. *Application deadline (institutional):* Continuous. *Application deadline (LD program):* Rolling/continuous for fall and rolling/continuous for spring.

Written Policies Written policy regarding general/basic LD accommodations is outlined in the school's catalog/handbook. Written policy regarding general/basic LD accommodations is available through the program or unit directly.

Daemen College
The Learning Center

4380 Main Street
Amherst, NY 14226-3592
http://www.daemen.edu/offices/learningcenter

Contact: Ms. Carol R. McPhillips, Coordinator. Phone: 716-839-8443. Fax: 716-839-8516. E-mail: cmcphill@daemen.edu. Head of LD Program: Dr. Kathleen Boone, Associate Dean and EE/AA Officer. Phone: 716-839-8301. E-mail: kboone@daemen.edu.

The Learning Center Approximately 30 registered undergraduate students were served during 2002-03. The program or unit includes 1 full-time staff member. Professional tutors, skill tutors, strategy tutors, and trained peer tutors are provided through the program or unit. Academic advisers are provided collaboratively through on-campus or off-campus services.

Subject-area Tutoring Tutoring is offered one-on-one, in small groups, and in class-size groups for most subjects. Tutoring is provided through the program or unit via professional tutors and trained peer tutors.

Basic Skills Remediation Remediation is offered one-on-one, in small groups, and in class-size groups for learning strategies, math, reading, study skills, time management, and written language. Remediation is provided through the program or unit via professional tutors and trained peer tutors. Remediation is also provided collaboratively through on-campus or off-campus services via regular education teachers.

Enrichment Programs for self-advocacy, study skills, test taking, and time management are provided collaboratively through on-campus or off-campus services.

Application For admittance to the program or unit, students are required to provide a psychoeducational report. It is recommended that students provide documentation of high school services. Upon application, materials documenting need for services should be sent only to the LD program or unit. Upon acceptance, documentation of need for services should be sent only to the LD program or unit. *Application deadline (institutional):* Continuous. *Application deadline (LD program):* Rolling/continuous for fall and rolling/continuous for spring.

Written Policies Written policies regarding general/basic LD accommodations, substitutions and waivers of admissions requirements, and substitutions and waivers of graduation requirements are available on the program Web site. Written policies regarding general/basic LD accommodations, substitutions and waivers of admissions requirements, and substitutions and waivers of graduation requirements are outlined in the school's catalog/handbook. Written policy regarding general/basic LD accommodations is available through the program or unit directly.

Dakota State University

820 North Washington
Madison, SD 57042-1799
http://www.dsu.edu/
Contact: Phone: 605-256-5111. Fax: 605-256-5316.

The program or unit includes 1 full-time staff member. Academic advisers, counselors, diagnostic specialists, regular education teachers, skill tutors, strategy tutors, and trained peer tutors are provided collaboratively through on-campus or off-campus services.
Unique Aids and Services Aids, services, or accommodations include digital textbooks, faculty training, priority registration, and weekly meetings with faculty.
Subject-area Tutoring Tutoring is offered one-on-one for most subjects. Tutoring is provided collaboratively through on-campus or off-campus services via trained peer tutors.
Diagnostic Testing Testing for auditory processing, handwriting, intelligence, learning strategies, learning styles, math, motor skills, neuropsychological, personality, reading, social skills, spelling, spoken language, study skills, visual processing, written language, and other services is provided collaboratively through on-campus or off-campus services.
Basic Skills Remediation Remediation is offered one-on-one and in class-size groups for auditory processing, learning strategies, math, reading, social skills, study skills, time management, visual processing, and written language. Remediation is provided collaboratively through on-campus or off-campus services via regular education teachers.
Enrichment Programs for career planning, college survival skills, health and nutrition, learning strategies, math, medication management, reading, stress management, study skills, test taking, time management, and written composition skills are provided collaboratively through on-campus or off-campus services.
Fees *Diagnostic Testing* fee is applicable.
Application For admittance to the program or unit, students are required to apply to the program directly, provide a psychoeducational report (3 years old or less), provide documentation of high school services, and provide results of a neuropsychological or psychoeducational evaluation by a qualified professional . Upon application, materials documenting need for services should be sent only to the LD program or unit. Upon acceptance, documentation of need for services should be sent only to the LD program or unit. *Application deadline (institutional):* Continuous. *Application deadline (LD program):* Rolling/continuous for fall and rolling/continuous for spring.
Written Policies Written policy regarding general/basic LD accommodations is available on the program Web site. Written policy regarding general/basic LD accommodations is outlined in the school's catalog/handbook. Written policy regarding general/basic LD accommodations is available through the program or unit directly.

Dalhousie University
Student Accessibility Services

Halifax, NS B3H 4R2
Canada
http://www.dal.ca/~services/ssd.html
Contact: Phone: 902-494-2211. Fax: 902-494-1630.

Student Accessibility Services Approximately 66 registered undergraduate students were served during 2002-03. The program or unit includes 1 full-time and 2 part-time staff members. Counselors are provided through the program or unit. Academic advisers, skill tutors, and strategy tutors are provided collaboratively through on-campus or off-campus services.
Unique Aids and Services Aids, services, or accommodations include regular meetings for students at high risk.
Diagnostic Testing Testing for learning strategies and study skills is provided collaboratively through on-campus or off-campus services.
Enrichment Enrichment programs are available through the program or unit for self-advocacy. Programs for career planning, college survival skills, learning strategies, oral communication skills, stress management, study skills, test taking, time management, and written composition skills are provided collaboratively through on-campus or off-campus services. Credit is offered for career planning, college survival skills, and written composition skills.
Application Upon application, materials documenting need for services should be sent only to the LD program or unit. Upon acceptance, documentation of need for services should be sent only to the LD program or unit. *Application deadline (institutional):* 6/1. *Application deadline (LD program):* Rolling/continuous for fall and rolling/continuous for spring.
Written Policies Written policies regarding general/basic LD accommodations and substitutions and waivers of admissions requirements are available on the program Web site. Written policy regarding substitutions and waivers of admissions requirements is outlined in the school's catalog/handbook. Written policy regarding general/basic LD accommodations is available through the program or unit directly.

Daniel Webster College
Office of Academic Resources

20 University Drive
Nashua, NH 03063-1300
http://www.dwc.edu/
Contact: Mrs. Melissa Plumb Kelleher, Director of Academic Resources. Phone: 603-577-6612. Fax: 603-577-6001.
E-mail: plumbkelleher@dwc.edu.

Office of Academic Resources Approximately 25 registered undergraduate students were served during 2002-03. The program or unit includes 1 full-time staff member. Academic advisers, counselors, and diagnostic specialists are provided collaboratively through on-campus or off-campus services.
Unique Aids and Services Aids, services, or accommodations include career counseling, weekly meetings with LD unit.

Daniel Webster College (continued)

Subject-area Tutoring Tutoring is offered one-on-one for most subjects. Tutoring is provided collaboratively through on-campus or off-campus services via trained peer tutors.

Diagnostic Testing Testing for auditory processing, intelligence, math, motor skills, neuropsychological, personality, reading, social skills, spelling, spoken language, visual processing, and written language is provided collaboratively through on-campus or off-campus services.

Basic Skills Remediation Remediation is offered one-on-one for computer skills, learning strategies, social skills, study skills, time management, and written language. Remediation is provided through the program or unit. Remediation is also provided collaboratively through on-campus or off-campus services via trained peer tutors.

Enrichment Enrichment programs are available through the program or unit for learning strategies, reading, self-advocacy, study skills, test taking, time management, vocabulary development, and written composition skills. Programs for career planning, college survival skills, math, practical computer skills, stress management, study skills, test taking, time management, vocabulary development, and written composition skills are provided collaboratively through on-campus or off-campus services. Credit is offered for college survival skills.

Fees *Diagnostic Testing* fee is applicable.

Application For admittance to the program or unit, students are required to provide a psychoeducational report (3 years old or less). It is recommended that students provide documentation of high school services. Upon application, materials documenting need for services should be sent only to the LD program or unit. Upon acceptance, documentation of need for services should be sent only to the LD program or unit. *Application deadline (institutional):* Continuous. *Application deadline (LD program):* Rolling/continuous for fall and rolling/continuous for spring.

Written Policies Written policies regarding course substitutions, general/basic LD accommodations, reduced course loads, substitutions and waivers of admissions requirements, and substitutions and waivers of graduation requirements are available through the program or unit directly.

Davidson College

Davidson, NC 28035

http://www.davidson.edu/

Contact: Phone: 704-894-2000. Fax: 704-894-2016.

Approximately 100 registered undergraduate students were served during 2002-03. The program or unit includes 1 full-time and 1 part-time staff member. Academic advisers, counselors, and LD specialists are provided collaboratively through on-campus or off-campus services.

Subject-area Tutoring Tutoring is offered one-on-one for all subjects. Tutoring is provided collaboratively through on-campus or off-campus services via LD specialists and trained peer tutors.

Enrichment Programs for career planning, college survival skills, health and nutrition, learning strategies, stress management, study skills, test taking, and time management are provided collaboratively through on-campus or off-campus services.

Student Organization Students for New Learning consists of 20 members.

Application For admittance to the program or unit, students are required to provide a psychoeducational report (3 years old or less). Upon acceptance, documentation of need for services should be sent only to the LD program or unit. *Application deadline (institutional):* 1/2. *Application deadline (LD program):* Rolling/continuous for fall and rolling/continuous for spring.

Written Policies Written policies regarding course substitutions, general/basic LD accommodations, reduced course loads, substitutions and waivers of admissions requirements, and substitutions and waivers of graduation requirements are outlined in the school's catalog/handbook. Written policy regarding general/basic LD accommodations is available through the program or unit directly.

Denison University
Office of Academic Support

Granville, OH 43023

http://www.denison.edu/acad-support/

Contact: Ms. Jennifer Grube Vestal, Associate Dean and Director of Academic Support. Phone: 740-587-6224. Fax: 740-587-5629. E-mail: vestal@denison.edu.

Office of Academic Support Approximately 140 registered undergraduate students were served during 2002-03. The program or unit includes 2 full-time staff members. Academic advisers, skill tutors, and trained peer tutors are provided through the program or unit. Trained peer tutors are provided collaboratively through on-campus or off-campus services.

Orientation The program or unit offers an optional 2-hour orientation for new students before classes begin.

Subject-area Tutoring Tutoring is offered one-on-one, in small groups, and in class-size groups for most subjects. Tutoring is provided through the program or unit via trained peer tutors. Tutoring is also provided collaboratively through on-campus or off-campus services via trained peer tutors.

Basic Skills Remediation Remediation is offered one-on-one and in small groups for learning strategies, study skills, time management, and written language. Remediation is provided through the program or unit. Remediation is also provided collaboratively through on-campus or off-campus services via trained peer tutors.

Enrichment Enrichment programs are available through the program or unit for college survival skills, learning strategies, stress management, study skills, test taking, and time management. Programs for career planning, health and nutrition, stress management, and written composition skills are provided collaboratively through on-campus or off-campus services.

Application For admittance to the program or unit, students are required to provide a psychoeducational report (3 years old or less). It is recommended that students provide documentation of high school services. Upon acceptance, documentation of need for services should be sent only to the LD program or unit. *Application deadline (institutional):* 2/1. *Application deadline (LD program):* Rolling/continuous for fall and rolling/continuous for spring.

Written Policies Written policy regarding general/basic LD accommodations is available on the program Web site. Written policy regarding general/basic LD accommodations is outlined in the

school's catalog/handbook. Written policies regarding course substitutions, general/basic LD accommodations, and reduced course loads are available through the program or unit directly.

DePaul University
Productive Learning Strategies (PLuS) Program

1 East Jackson Boulevard
Chicago, IL 60604-2287
http://condor.depaul.edu/~plus/
Contact: Mr. Stamatios Miras, Director of PLuS. Phone: 773-325-4239. Fax: 773-325-4673. E-mail: smiras@depaul.edu.

Productive Learning Strategies (PLuS) Program Approximately 136 registered undergraduate students were served during 2002-03. The program or unit includes 1 full-time and 5 part-time staff members. Coaches, diagnostic specialists, graduate assistants/students, LD specialists, remediation/learning specialists, skill tutors, and strategy tutors are provided through the program or unit. Academic advisers, counselors, graduate assistants/students, professional tutors, regular education teachers, special education teachers, teacher trainees, and trained peer tutors are provided collaboratively through on-campus or off-campus services.

Orientation The program or unit offers a mandatory 1 to 1.5-hour orientation for new students before classes begin, during summer prior to enrollment, individually by special arrangement, and during the university orientation dates.

Unique Aids and Services Aids, services, or accommodations include advocates, faculty training, personal coach, priority registration, organization/time management.

Subject-area Tutoring Tutoring is offered one-on-one for most subjects. Tutoring is provided through the program or unit via graduate assistants/students and LD specialists. Tutoring is also provided collaboratively through on-campus or off-campus services via trained peer tutors.

Diagnostic Testing Testing is provided through the program or unit for auditory processing, math, motor skills, reading, spelling, spoken language, study skills, visual processing, and written language. Testing for handwriting, intelligence, learning strategies, learning styles, neuropsychological, personality, and social skills is provided collaboratively through on-campus or off-campus services.

Basic Skills Remediation Remediation is offered one-on-one for learning strategies, math, reading, social skills, spelling, spoken language, study skills, time management, and written language. Remediation is provided through the program or unit via graduate assistants/students and LD specialists. Remediation is also provided collaboratively through on-campus or off-campus services via trained peer tutors.

Enrichment Enrichment programs are available through the program or unit for career planning, college survival skills, learning strategies, oral communication skills, reading, self-advocacy, study skills, test taking, time management, vocabulary development, and written composition skills. Programs for career planning, college survival skills, health and nutrition, math, practical computer skills, stress management, test taking, and written composition skills are provided collaboratively through on-campus or off-campus services.

Fees *LD Program or Service* fee is $750 to $1500 (fee varies according to degree level). *Diagnostic Testing* fee is $250 to $500.

Application For admittance to the program or unit, students are required to apply to the program directly and provide a psychoeducational report (3 years old or less). It is recommended that students provide documentation of high school services and provide an academic performance report from a specialist working with the student. Upon acceptance, documentation of need for services should be sent only to the LD program or unit. *Application deadline (institutional):* Continuous. *Application deadline (LD program):* Rolling/continuous for fall and rolling/continuous for spring.

Written Policies Written policies regarding course substitutions and general/basic LD accommodations are available on the program Web site.

DePauw University
Academic Services

313 South Locust Street
Greencastle, IN 46135-0037
http://www.depauw.edu/
Contact: Jacqueline D. Gardner, ADA Coordinator. Phone: 765-658-4027. Fax: 765-658-4021. E-mail: jgardner@depauw.edu.

Academic Services Approximately 5 registered undergraduate students were served during 2002-03. The program or unit includes 3 part-time staff members.

Subject-area Tutoring Tutoring is offered one-on-one, in small groups, and in class-size groups for most subjects. Tutoring is provided collaboratively through on-campus or off-campus services via trained peer tutors and other.

Enrichment Programs for career planning, college survival skills, health and nutrition, learning strategies, math, oral communication skills, practical computer skills, reading, stress management, study skills, test taking, time management, and written composition skills are provided collaboratively through on-campus or off-campus services.

Application For admittance to the program or unit, students are required to provide a psychoeducational report (3 years old or less). Upon acceptance, documentation of need for services should be sent only to the LD program or unit. *Application deadline (institutional):* 2/1. *Application deadline (LD program):* Rolling/continuous for fall.

Written Policies Written policy regarding general/basic LD accommodations is available on the program Web site. Written policy regarding general/basic LD accommodations is outlined in the school's catalog/handbook. Written policy regarding general/basic LD accommodations is available through the program or unit directly.

DeVry University

925 South Niagara Street
Denver, CO 80224
http://www.den.devry.edu/

DeVry University (continued)

Contact: Ms. Sheila Scott, Dean of Student Affairs. Phone: 303-280-7570. Fax: 303-280-7577. E-mail: sscott@den.devry.edu.

Approximately 5 registered undergraduate students were served during 2002-03. The program or unit includes 2 full-time staff members. Academic advisers and regular education teachers are provided collaboratively through on-campus or off-campus services.

Unique Aids and Services Aids, services, or accommodations include career counseling, digital textbooks, and faculty training.

Subject-area Tutoring Tutoring is offered one-on-one for all subjects. Tutoring is provided collaboratively through on-campus or off-campus services via professional tutors.

Enrichment Enrichment programs are available through the program or unit for college survival skills, health and nutrition, learning strategies, oral communication skills, stress management, study skills, and time management. Programs for career planning, college survival skills, math, oral communication skills, practical computer skills, reading, self-advocacy, test taking, and written composition skills are provided collaboratively through on-campus or off-campus services. Credit is offered for math, oral communication skills, practical computer skills, reading, and written composition skills.

Application Upon application, materials documenting need for services should be sent only to the LD program or unit. Upon acceptance, documentation of need for services should be sent only to the LD program or unit. *Application deadline (LD program):* Rolling/continuous for fall and rolling/continuous for spring.

Written Policies Written policy regarding general/basic LD accommodations is outlined in the school's catalog/handbook.

Dickinson College
Learning Support Services

PO Box 1773

Carlisle, PA 17013-2896

http://www.dickinson.edu/departments/disability/counseling.html

Contact: Mr. Keith E. Jervis, Coordinator of Learning Support Services. Phone: 717-245-1485 Ext. 1485. Fax: 717-245-1910. E-mail: jervis@dickinson.edu.

Learning Support Services Approximately 96 registered undergraduate students were served during 2002-03. The program or unit includes 1 full-time and 1 part-time staff member. Counselors and strategy tutors are provided through the program or unit. Trained peer tutors are provided collaboratively through on-campus or off-campus services.

Subject-area Tutoring Tutoring is offered one-on-one and in small groups for most subjects. Tutoring is provided through the program or unit via LD specialists. Tutoring is also provided collaboratively through on-campus or off-campus services via trained peer tutors.

Diagnostic Testing Testing is provided through the program or unit for learning strategies, learning styles, reading, study skills, and other services. Testing for auditory processing, handwriting, intelli-

gence, math, motor skills, neuropsychological, personality, reading, social skills, spelling, spoken language, study skills, visual processing, and written language is provided collaboratively through on-campus or off-campus services.

Basic Skills Remediation Remediation is available for learning strategies, reading, study skills, and time management. Remediation is provided through the program or unit via LD specialists.

Fees *Diagnostic Testing* fee is $250 to $800.

Application For admittance to the program or unit, students are required to provide a psychoeducational report (3 years old or less) and provide results of a psychoeducational battery assessing aptitude, achievement and information processing. It is recommended that students provide documentation of high school services. Upon application, materials documenting need for services should be sent only to the LD program or unit. Upon acceptance, documentation of need for services should be sent only to the LD program or unit. *Application deadline (institutional):* 2/1. *Application deadline (LD program):* Rolling/continuous for fall and rolling/continuous for spring.

Written Policies Written policies regarding course substitutions, general/basic LD accommodations, substitutions and waivers of admissions requirements, and substitutions and waivers of graduation requirements are outlined in the school's catalog/handbook.

Dickinson State University
Student Support Services

291 Campus Drive

Dickinson, ND 58601-4896

http://www.dsu.nodak.edu/

Contact: Ms. Lisa Cantlon, Director of Student Support Services. Phone: 701-483-2999. Fax: 701-483-2720. E-mail: lisa.cantlon@dsu.nodak.edu.

Student Support Services Approximately 35 registered undergraduate students were served during 2002-03. The program or unit includes 1 part-time staff member. Academic advisers, coaches, counselors, diagnostic specialists, and professional tutors are provided collaboratively through on-campus or off-campus services.

Subject-area Tutoring Tutoring is offered one-on-one and in small groups for most subjects. Tutoring is provided collaboratively through on-campus or off-campus services via computer-based instruction, professional tutors, and trained peer tutors.

Basic Skills Remediation Remediation is offered one-on-one, in small groups, and in class-size groups for learning strategies, math, social skills, study skills, time management, and written language. Remediation is provided collaboratively through on-campus or off-campus services via computer-based instruction, professional tutors, regular education teachers, and trained peer tutors.

Application For admittance to the program or unit, students are required to apply to the program directly and provide a psychoeducational report. It is recommended that students provide documentation of high school services. Upon acceptance, documentation of need for services should be sent only to the LD program or unit. *Application deadline (institutional):* Continuous. *Application deadline (LD program):* Rolling/continuous for fall and rolling/continuous for spring.

Written Policies Written policies regarding general/basic LD accommodations, reduced course loads, substitutions and waivers of admissions requirements, and substitutions and waivers of graduation requirements are outlined in the school's catalog/handbook.

Doane College
Academic Support Center

1014 Boswell Avenue

Crete, NE 68333-2430

http://www.doane.edu/crete_campus/Studentsupport/

Contact: Ms. Sherri A. Hanigan, Director. Phone: 402-826-8586. Fax: 402-826-8278. E-mail: shanigan@doane.edu.

Academic Support Center Approximately 12 registered undergraduate students were served during 2002-03. The program or unit includes 5 full-time staff members. Academic advisers, graduate assistants/students, regular education teachers, remediation/learning specialists, skill tutors, strategy tutors, and trained peer tutors are provided through the program or unit. Academic advisers, coaches, counselors, diagnostic specialists, LD specialists, and regular education teachers are provided collaboratively through on-campus or off-campus services.

Unique Aids and Services Aids, services, or accommodations include advocates, personal coach, weekly meetings with faculty, course accommodations based on functional limitations.

Subject-area Tutoring Tutoring is offered one-on-one and in small groups for most subjects. Tutoring is provided through the program or unit via computer-based instruction and trained peer tutors. Tutoring is also provided collaboratively through on-campus or off-campus services via trained peer tutors.

Diagnostic Testing Testing is provided through the program or unit for learning strategies, learning styles, math, reading, and written language. Testing for learning styles is provided collaboratively through on-campus or off-campus services.

Basic Skills Remediation Remediation is offered one-on-one and in class-size groups for learning strategies, math, reading, social skills, study skills, time management, and written language. Remediation is provided through the program or unit via computer-based instruction and regular education teachers.

Enrichment Program for other is provided collaboratively through on-campus or off-campus services.

Application For admittance to the program or unit, students are required to apply to the program directly and provide a psychoeducational report (3 years old or less). It is recommended that students provide documentation of high school services. Upon acceptance, documentation of need for services should be sent only to the LD program or unit. *Application deadline (institutional):* Continuous. *Application deadline (LD program):* Rolling/continuous for fall and rolling/continuous for spring.

Written Policies Written policy regarding general/basic LD accommodations is outlined in the school's catalog/handbook. Written policies regarding course substitutions, reduced course loads, and substitutions and waivers of graduation requirements are available through the program or unit directly.

Dominican University of California
Tutoring and Disability Services

50 Acacia Avenue

San Rafael, CA 94901-2298

http://www.dominican.edu/

Contact: Ms. Iris T. Crossley, Director of Tutoring and Disability Services. Phone: 415-257-0187. Fax: 415-257-1399. E-mail: crossley@dominican.edu.

Tutoring and Disability Services Approximately 40 registered undergraduate students were served during 2002-03. The program or unit includes 1 full-time staff member. Academic advisers, professional tutors, and skill tutors are provided through the program or unit.

Subject-area Tutoring Tutoring is offered one-on-one and in small groups for some subjects. Tutoring is provided collaboratively through on-campus or off-campus services via professional tutors.

Basic Skills Remediation Remediation is offered one-on-one and in small groups for study skills and time management. Remediation is provided collaboratively through on-campus or off-campus services.

Application For admittance to the program or unit, students are required to provide documentation of disability by a licensed professional. Upon acceptance, documentation of need for services should be sent only to the LD program or unit. *Application deadline (institutional):* Continuous. *Application deadline (LD program):* Rolling/continuous for fall and rolling/continuous for spring.

Written Policies Written policies regarding course substitutions, general/basic LD accommodations, substitutions and waivers of admissions requirements, and substitutions and waivers of graduation requirements are outlined in the school's catalog/handbook. Written policies regarding course substitutions, general/basic LD accommodations, substitutions and waivers of admissions requirements, and substitutions and waivers of graduation requirements are available through the program or unit directly.

Dordt College
Services for Students with Disabilities, Academic Skills Center

498 4th Avenue, NE

Sioux Center, IA 51250-1697

http://www.dordt.edu/academics/ask_center/services.shtml

Contact: Ms. Marliss Van Der Zwaag, Coordinator of Services for Students with Disabilities. Phone: 712-722-6490. Fax: 712-722-4498. E-mail: mvdzwaag@dordt.edu.

Services for Students with Disabilities, Academic Skills Center Approximately 35 registered undergraduate students were served during 2002-03. The program or unit includes 1 part-time staff member. Academic advisers, counselors, and remediation/

Dordt College (continued)

learning specialists are provided through the program or unit. Academic advisers, counselors, remediation/learning specialists, teacher trainees, and trained peer tutors are provided collaboratively through on-campus or off-campus services.

Orientation The program or unit offers a mandatory orientation for new students individually by special arrangement.

Unique Aids and Services Aids, services, or accommodations include advocates, career counseling, faculty training, priority registration, books on tape, testing accommodations, note-takers.

Subject-area Tutoring Tutoring is offered one-on-one and in class-size groups for most subjects. Tutoring is provided through the program or unit via computer-based instruction and trained peer tutors. Tutoring is also provided collaboratively through on-campus or off-campus services via trained peer tutors.

Basic Skills Remediation Remediation is offered one-on-one, in small groups, and in class-size groups for learning strategies, math, reading, study skills, time management, and written language. Remediation is provided through the program or unit via computer-based instruction, LD specialists, and trained peer tutors. Remediation is also provided collaboratively through on-campus or off-campus services via regular education teachers, teacher trainees, and trained peer tutors.

Enrichment Enrichment programs are available through the program or unit for college survival skills, learning strategies, self-advocacy, study skills, test taking, time management, and vocabulary development. Programs for career planning, college survival skills, learning strategies, math, reading, stress management, study skills, test taking, time management, vocabulary development, and written composition skills are provided collaboratively through on-campus or off-campus services. Credit is offered for math and written composition skills.

Application For admittance to the program or unit, students are required to provide a psychoeducational report. It is recommended that students provide documentation of high school services. Upon application, materials documenting need for services should be sent only to the LD program or unit. Upon acceptance, documentation of need for services should be sent only to the LD program or unit. *Application deadline (LD program):* Rolling/continuous for fall and rolling/continuous for spring.

Written Policies Written policy regarding general/basic LD accommodations is available on the program Web site. Written policies regarding course substitutions, general/basic LD accommodations, substitutions and waivers of admissions requirements, and substitutions and waivers of graduation requirements are outlined in the school's catalog/handbook. Written policies regarding course substitutions, general/basic LD accommodations, reduced course loads, and substitutions and waivers of graduation requirements are available through the program or unit directly.

Dowling College

Idle Hour Boulevard
Oakdale, NY 11769-1999
http://www.dowling.edu/

Contact: Prof. Katharine Ventimiglia, Reading/LD Specialist. Phone: 631-244-3335. E-mail: ventimik@dowling.edu. Head of LD Program: Ms. Eleanor Alster, Director of Hausmann Center. Phone: 631-244-3144. E-mail: alstere@dowling.edu.

Approximately 200 registered undergraduate students were served during 2002-03. The program or unit includes 2 full-time and 5 part-time staff members. Academic advisers, coaches, counselors, graduate assistants/students, LD specialists, professional tutors, regular education teachers, remediation/learning specialists, skill tutors, special education teachers, strategy tutors, teacher trainees, and trained peer tutors are provided collaboratively through on-campus or off-campus services.

Unique Aids and Services Aids, services, or accommodations include career counseling, digital textbooks, and priority registration.

Subject-area Tutoring Tutoring is offered one-on-one and in small groups for all subjects. Tutoring is provided through the program or unit via graduate assistants/students and LD specialists. Tutoring is also provided collaboratively through on-campus or off-campus services via computer-based instruction, professional tutors, and trained peer tutors.

Basic Skills Remediation Remediation is offered one-on-one, in small groups, and in class-size groups for computer skills, learning strategies, math, reading, study skills, time management, and written language. Remediation is provided through the program or unit via LD specialists. Remediation is also provided collaboratively through on-campus or off-campus services via computer-based instruction, graduate assistants/students, professional tutors, regular education teachers, and trained peer tutors.

Enrichment Enrichment programs are available through the program or unit for self-advocacy. Programs for career planning, college survival skills, health and nutrition, learning strategies, math, oral communication skills, practical computer skills, reading, stress management, study skills, test taking, time management, vocabulary development, and written composition skills are provided collaboratively through on-campus or off-campus services.

Application For admittance to the program or unit, students are required to provide a psychoeducational report (5 years old or less) and provide documentation of high school services. Upon application, materials documenting need for services should be sent only to admissions with institutional application materials. Upon acceptance, documentation of need for services should be sent to both admissions and the LD program or unit. *Application deadline (institutional):* Continuous. *Application deadline (LD program):* 9/10 for fall. 2/10 for spring.

Written Policies Written policy regarding general/basic LD accommodations is outlined in the school's catalog/handbook.

Drake University
Student Disability Services

2507 University Avenue
Des Moines, IA 50311-4516
http://www.drake.edu/

Contact: Chrystal Ann Stanley, Student Disability Services Coordinator. Phone: 515-271-1835. Fax: 515-271-1855. E-mail: chrystal.stanley@drake.edu.

Student Disability Services Approximately 97 registered undergraduate students were served during 2002-03. The program or unit includes 1 full-time staff member. Counselors, strategy tutors, and other are provided through the program or unit. Academic advisers, diagnostic specialists, regular education teachers, skill tutors, strategy tutors, and trained peer tutors are provided collaboratively through on-campus or off-campus services.

Unique Aids and Services Aids, services, or accommodations include advocates and faculty training.

Subject-area Tutoring Tutoring is offered one-on-one, in small groups, and in class-size groups for some subjects. Tutoring is provided collaboratively through on-campus or off-campus services via computer-based instruction and trained peer tutors.

Enrichment Enrichment programs are available through the program or unit for self-advocacy, stress management, study skills, test taking, and time management. Programs for career planning, health and nutrition, learning strategies, self-advocacy, stress management, study skills, test taking, time management, and written composition skills are provided collaboratively through on-campus or off-campus services.

Application For admittance to the program or unit, students are required to apply to the program directly and provide a psychoeducational report (3 years old or less). It is recommended that students provide documentation of high school services. Upon application, materials documenting need for services should be sent only to the LD program or unit. Upon acceptance, documentation of need for services should be sent only to the LD program or unit. *Application deadline (institutional):* Continuous. *Application deadline (LD program):* Rolling/continuous for fall and rolling/continuous for spring.

Written Policies Written policies regarding course substitutions, general/basic LD accommodations, and reduced course loads are outlined in the school's catalog/handbook. Written policies regarding course substitutions, general/basic LD accommodations, and reduced course loads are available through the program or unit directly.

Drexel University
Office of Disability Services

3141 Chestnut Street
Philadelphia, PA 19104-2875
http://www.drexel.edu/depts/affirmact/disability/default.html
Contact: Ms. Robin Stokes, Director. Phone: 215-895-1401. Fax: 215-895-1402. E-mail: robinstokes@drexel.edu. Head of LD Program: Dr. Cathy Schmidt, LD Coordinator. Phone: 215-895-1368. Fax: 215-895-1402. E-mail: catherine.a.schmidt@drexel.edu.

Office of Disability Services Approximately 86 registered undergraduate students were served during 2002-03. The program or unit includes 2 full-time staff members. Graduate assistants/students are provided through the program or unit. Academic advisers, counselors, professional tutors, and trained peer tutors are provided collaboratively through on-campus or off-campus services.

Orientation The program or unit offers an optional 2-hour orientation for new students before classes begin.

Summer Program To help prepare for the demands of college, there is an optional 2-day summer program prior to entering the school.

Unique Aids and Services Aids, services, or accommodations include faculty training.

Subject-area Tutoring Tutoring is offered in small groups for most subjects. Tutoring is provided collaboratively through on-campus or off-campus services via graduate assistants/students and trained peer tutors.

Enrichment Enrichment programs are available through the program or unit for college survival skills, learning strategies, self-advocacy, stress management, study skills, test taking, and time management. Programs for career planning, college survival skills, health and nutrition, learning strategies, math, study skills, test taking, time management, and written composition skills are provided collaboratively through on-campus or off-campus services.

Application For admittance to the program or unit, students are required to apply to the program directly and provide a psychoeducational report. It is recommended that students provide documentation of high school services. Upon acceptance, documentation of need for services should be sent only to the LD program or unit. *Application deadline (institutional):* 3/1. *Application deadline (LD program):* Rolling/continuous for fall.

Written Policies Written policy regarding general/basic LD accommodations is available on the program Web site. Written policy regarding general/basic LD accommodations is outlined in the school's catalog/handbook. Written policies regarding course substitutions, general/basic LD accommodations, and reduced course loads are available through the program or unit directly.

Drury University
Disabled Student Services

900 North Benton Avenue
Springfield, MO 65802-3791
http://www.drury.edu/
Contact: Ms. Barbara A. Nelms, Director of Student Development. Phone: 417-873-7419. Fax: 417-873-6833. E-mail: anelms@drury.edu.

Disabled Student Services Approximately 40 registered undergraduate students were served during 2002-03. The program or unit includes 5 full-time staff members. Counselors, graduate assistants/students, and skill tutors are provided through the program or unit. Academic advisers, diagnostic specialists, and skill tutors are provided collaboratively through on-campus or off-campus services.

Orientation The program or unit offers an optional 1-hour orientation for new students during registration.

Subject-area Tutoring Tutoring is offered one-on-one for most subjects. Tutoring is provided through the program or unit via graduate assistants/students and trained peer tutors.

Enrichment Enrichment programs are available through the program or unit for written composition skills. Programs for career planning, math, self-advocacy, and written composition skills are provided collaboratively through on-campus or off-campus services.

Student Organization Association for a Better Learning Environment (ABLE) consists of 6 members.

Application For admittance to the program or unit, students are required to provide a psychoeducational report (5 years old or less). It is recommended that students provide documentation of high school services. Upon acceptance, documentation of need for services should be sent to both admissions and the LD program or unit. *Application deadline (institutional):* 3/15. *Application deadline (LD program):* Rolling/continuous for fall.

Written Policies Written policy regarding general/basic LD accommodations is outlined in the school's catalog/handbook.

Duke University
Office of Services for Students with Disabilities

Durham, NC 27708-0586

http://www.duke.edu/web/skills

Contact: Dr. Emma Swain, Director. Phone: 919-684-5917. Fax: 919-684-8934. E-mail: eswain@duke.edu.

Office of Services for Students with Disabilities The program or unit includes 1 full-time staff member. Academic advisers, coaches, LD specialists, and trained peer tutors are provided collaboratively through on-campus or off-campus services.
Unique Aids and Services Aids, services, or accommodations include digital textbooks.
Subject-area Tutoring Tutoring is offered one-on-one for some subjects. Tutoring is provided collaboratively through on-campus or off-campus services via trained peer tutors.
Enrichment Programs for career planning, college survival skills, learning strategies, study skills, test taking, time management, and written composition skills are provided collaboratively through on-campus or off-campus services.
Application For admittance to the program or unit, students are required to provide a psychoeducational report (3 years old or less). It is recommended that students provide documentation of high school services. Upon application, materials documenting need for services should be sent only to the LD program or unit. Upon acceptance, documentation of need for services should be sent only to the LD program or unit. *Application deadline (institutional):* 1/2. *Application deadline (LD program):* 6/10 for fall. 11/10 for spring.
Written Policies Written policy regarding general/basic LD accommodations is available on the program Web site.

D'Youville College

320 Porter Avenue
Buffalo, NY 14201-1084

http://www.dyc.edu/

Contact: Ms. Isabelle R. Vecchio, Coordinator of Disability Services. Phone: 716-871-9263. Fax: 716-871-9263. E-mail: vecchioi@dyc.edu.

Approximately 58 registered undergraduate students were served during 2002-03. Counselors, graduate assistants/students, LD specialists, professional tutors, skill tutors, and trained peer tutors are provided collaboratively through on-campus or off-campus services.
Orientation The program or unit offers a mandatory orientation for new students individually by special arrangement.
Unique Aids and Services Aids, services, or accommodations include advocates, career counseling, priority registration, books on tape or CD .
Subject-area Tutoring Tutoring is offered one-on-one, in small groups, and in class-size groups for all subjects. Tutoring is provided collaboratively through on-campus or off-campus services via LD specialists, professional tutors, and trained peer tutors.

Diagnostic Testing Testing for math, reading, and written language is provided collaboratively through on-campus or off-campus services.
Basic Skills Remediation Remediation is offered one-on-one, in small groups, and in class-size groups for learning strategies, math, reading, study skills, time management, written language, and science. Remediation is provided collaboratively through on-campus or off-campus services via LD specialists, professional tutors, and trained peer tutors.
Enrichment Programs for career planning, college survival skills, learning strategies, math, reading, study skills, test taking, time management, vocabulary development, and written composition skills are provided collaboratively through on-campus or off-campus services. Credit is offered for math.
Student Organization The Phoenix Society consists of 7 members.
Application For admittance to the program or unit, students are required to provide a psychoeducational report (5 years old or less). It is recommended that students provide documentation of high school services. Upon application, materials documenting need for services should be sent only to the LD program or unit. Upon acceptance, documentation of need for services should be sent only to the LD program or unit. *Application deadline (institutional):* Continuous. *Application deadline (LD program):* Rolling/continuous for fall and rolling/continuous for spring.
Written Policies Written policy regarding general/basic LD accommodations is available on the program Web site. Written policies regarding course substitutions, general/basic LD accommodations, and reduced course loads are available through the program or unit directly.

Earlham College
Center for Academic Enrichment

801 National Road West
Richmond, IN 47374-4095

http://www.earlham.edu/~sas/support

Contact: Donna Keesling, Director of the Center for Academic Enrichment. Phone: 765-983-1341. Fax: 765-973-2120. E-mail: keesldo@earlham.edu.

Center for Academic Enrichment Approximately 67 registered undergraduate students were served during 2002-03. The program or unit includes 1 full-time and 1 part-time staff member. Academic advisers, coaches, counselors, diagnostic specialists, regular education teachers, and trained peer tutors are provided collaboratively through on-campus or off-campus services.
Unique Aids and Services Aids, services, or accommodations include digital textbooks.
Subject-area Tutoring Tutoring is offered one-on-one and in small groups for most subjects. Tutoring is provided collaboratively through on-campus or off-campus services via trained peer tutors and other.
Enrichment Program for career planning is provided collaboratively through on-campus or off-campus services.
Application For admittance to the program or unit, students are required to provide a psychoeducational report. Upon acceptance, documentation of need for services should be sent only to the LD program or unit. *Application deadline (institutional):* 2/15. *Application deadline (LD program):* Rolling/continuous for fall and rolling/continuous for spring.

Written Policies Written policy regarding general/basic LD accommodations is available on the program Web site. Written policy regarding general/basic LD accommodations is outlined in the school's catalog/handbook. Written policies regarding course substitutions and general/basic LD accommodations are available through the program or unit directly.

substitutions and waivers of graduation requirements are outlined in the school's catalog/handbook. Written policy regarding general/basic LD accommodations is available through the program or unit directly.

East Carolina University
Disability Support Services

East 5th Street
Greenville, NC 27858-4353
http://www.ecu.edu/studentlife/dss/

Contact: Ms. Liz Johnston, Director of Disability Support Services. Phone: 252-328-6799. Fax: 252-328-4883. E-mail: johnstone@mail.ecu.edu. Head of LD Program: Ms. Diane Majewski, Associate Director of Disability Support Services. Phone: 252-328-4884. Fax: 252-328-4883. E-mail: majewskid@mail.ecu.

Disability Support Services Approximately 500 registered undergraduate students were served during 2002-03. The program or unit includes 4 full-time staff members. Coaches, graduate assistants/students, and LD specialists are provided through the program or unit. Academic advisers, counselors, diagnostic specialists, professional tutors, regular education teachers, remediation/learning specialists, skill tutors, special education teachers, strategy tutors, teacher trainees, trained peer tutors, and other are provided collaboratively through on-campus or off-campus services.

Unique Aids and Services Aids, services, or accommodations include digital textbooks, faculty training, personal coach, and priority registration.

Subject-area Tutoring Tutoring is offered one-on-one, in small groups, and in class-size groups for most subjects. Tutoring is provided through the program or unit via computer-based instruction, graduate assistants/students, and LD specialists. Tutoring is also provided collaboratively through on-campus or off-campus services via computer-based instruction and graduate assistants/students.

Basic Skills Remediation Remediation is offered one-on-one for computer skills, learning strategies, math, reading, study skills, time management, and written language. Remediation is provided through the program or unit via graduate assistants/students and LD specialists.

Application For admittance to the program or unit, students are required to provide a psychoeducational report (3 years old or less) and provide other documentation (contact office for details). Upon application, materials documenting need for services should be sent only to the LD program or unit. Upon acceptance, documentation of need for services should be sent only to the LD program or unit. *Application deadline (institutional):* 3/15. *Application deadline (LD program):* Rolling/continuous for fall and rolling/continuous for spring.

Written Policies Written policies regarding general/basic LD accommodations, grade forgiveness, substitutions and waivers of admissions requirements, and substitutions and waivers of graduation requirements are available on the program Web site. Written policies regarding general/basic LD accommodations, grade forgiveness, substitutions and waivers of admissions requirements, and

East Central University
Student Support Services

1100 East 14th Street
Ada, OK 74820-6899
http://www.ecok.edu/

Contact: Mr. Dwain West, Director of Student Support Services. Phone: 580-310-5300. Fax: 580-580-5654. E-mail: dwest@mailclerk.ecok.edu.

Student Support Services Approximately 25 registered undergraduate students were served during 2002-03. The program or unit includes 5 full-time and 4 part-time staff members. Academic advisers, counselors, skill tutors, strategy tutors, and trained peer tutors are provided through the program or unit.

Orientation The program or unit offers an optional orientation for new students before registration, before classes begin, during summer prior to enrollment, during registration, after classes begin, and individually by special arrangement.

Unique Aids and Services Aids, services, or accommodations include advocates, career counseling, digital textbooks, priority registration, textbooks on tape.

Subject-area Tutoring Tutoring is offered one-on-one and in small groups for most subjects. Tutoring is provided through the program or unit via computer-based instruction, professional tutors, and trained peer tutors. Tutoring is also provided collaboratively through on-campus or off-campus services via computer-based instruction, professional tutors, and trained peer tutors.

Basic Skills Remediation Remediation is offered in class-size groups for math, reading, study skills, time management, written language, and science, English. Remediation is provided collaboratively through on-campus or off-campus services via computer-based instruction and regular education teachers.

Enrichment Enrichment programs are available through the program or unit for career planning, college survival skills, learning strategies, math, oral communication skills, self-advocacy, stress management, study skills, test taking, time management, vocabulary development, and written composition skills. Programs for career planning, learning strategies, math, practical computer skills, reading, and written composition skills are provided collaboratively through on-campus or off-campus services. Credit is offered for practical computer skills.

Application For admittance to the program or unit, students are required to apply to the program directly, provide a psychoeducational report (3 years old or less), and provide documentation from a qualified professional. Upon application, materials documenting need for services should be sent only to the LD program or unit. Upon acceptance, documentation of need for services should be sent only to the LD program or unit. *Application deadline (institutional):* 9/1. *Application deadline (LD program):* Rolling/continuous for fall and rolling/continuous for spring.

East Central University (continued)

Written Policies Written policies regarding course substitutions, grade forgiveness, reduced course loads, substitutions and waivers of admissions requirements, and substitutions and waivers of graduation requirements are outlined in the school's catalog/handbook. Written policy regarding general/basic LD accommodations is available through the program or unit directly.

Eastern Connecticut State University
Office of AccesAbility Services

83 Windham Street

Willimantic, CT 06226-2295

http://www.easternct.edu

Contact: Dr. Pamela J. Starr, Coordinator and Counselor OAS. Phone: 860-465-5573. Fax: 860-465-0136. E-mail: starrp@easternct.edu.

Office of AccesAbility Services Approximately 80 registered undergraduate students were served during 2002-03. The program or unit includes 1 full-time and 1 part-time staff member. Counselors and trained peer tutors are provided through the program or unit. Trained peer tutors are provided collaboratively through on-campus or off-campus services.

Orientation The program or unit offers individually by special arrangement.

Unique Aids and Services Aids, services, or accommodations include faculty training and priority registration.

Enrichment Enrichment programs are available through the program or unit for learning strategies, self-advocacy, study skills, test taking, time management, and other. Programs for career planning, college survival skills, health and nutrition, learning strategies, math, medication management, oral communication skills, practical computer skills, reading, stress management, study skills, test taking, time management, vocabulary development, written composition skills, and other are provided collaboratively through on-campus or off-campus services. Credit is offered for oral communication skills, practical computer skills, reading, vocabulary development, written composition skills, and other.

Application For admittance to the program or unit, students are required to apply to the program directly and provide a psychoeducational report. It is recommended that students provide documentation of high school services. Upon application, materials documenting need for services should be sent only to the LD program or unit. Upon acceptance, documentation of need for services should be sent only to the LD program or unit. *Application deadline (institutional):* 5/1. *Application deadline (LD program):* Rolling/continuous for fall and rolling/continuous for spring.

Written Policies Written policy regarding general/basic LD accommodations is available on the program Web site. Written policies regarding course substitutions, reduced course loads, and substitutions and waivers of graduation requirements are outlined in the school's catalog/handbook. Written policies regarding course substitutions, general/basic LD accommodations, and reduced course loads are available through the program or unit directly.

Eastern Illinois University

600 Lincoln Avenue

Charleston, IL 61920-3099

http://www.eiu.edu/

Contact: Ms. Kathryn L. Waggoner, Assistant Director. Phone: 217-581-6583. Fax: 217-581-7208. E-mail: cfkw@eiu.edu.

Approximately 60 registered undergraduate students were served during 2002-03. The program or unit includes 2 full-time staff members. Academic advisers, coaches, counselors, graduate assistants/students, regular education teachers, remediation/learning specialists, skill tutors, special education teachers, and strategy tutors are provided collaboratively through on-campus or off-campus services.

Summer Program To help prepare for the demands of college, there is 1-week summer program prior to entering the school.

Unique Aids and Services Aids, services, or accommodations include career counseling, faculty training, priority registration, notetakers, extended test time, permission to tape record classes, separate testing, interpreters.

Subject-area Tutoring Tutoring is offered one-on-one and in small groups for some subjects. Tutoring is provided collaboratively through on-campus or off-campus services via computer-based instruction and graduate assistants/students.

Basic Skills Remediation Remediation is offered in small groups for computer skills, learning strategies, math, reading, spoken language, study skills, time management, and written language. Remediation is provided collaboratively through on-campus or off-campus services via computer-based instruction.

Enrichment Enrichment programs are available through the program or unit for self-advocacy. Programs for career planning, college survival skills, health and nutrition, learning strategies, math, oral communication skills, practical computer skills, reading, self-advocacy, stress management, study skills, test taking, time management, and written composition skills are provided collaboratively through on-campus or off-campus services.

Fees *Summer Program* fee is $300.

Application For admittance to the program or unit, students are required to provide a psychoeducational report (3 years old or less), provide documentation of high school services, and provide results of adult normed and comprehensive testing . Upon application, materials documenting need for services should be sent only to the LD program or unit. Upon acceptance, documentation of need for services should be sent only to the LD program or unit. *Application deadline (institutional):* Continuous.

Written Policies Written policy regarding general/basic LD accommodations is available on the program Web site. Written policy regarding general/basic LD accommodations is available through the program or unit directly.

Eastern Mennonite University
Student Disability Support Services

1200 Park Road

Harrisonburg, VA 22802-2462

http://www.emu.edu/academicsupport/

Contact: Ms. Joyce Coryell Hedrick, Coordinator. Phone: 540-432-4233. Fax: 540-432-4631. E-mail: hedrickj@emu.edu.

Student Disability Support Services Approximately 80 registered undergraduate students were served during 2002-03. The program or unit includes 1 part-time staff member. Academic advisers, coaches, counselors, skill tutors, strategy tutors, and trained peer tutors are provided through the program or unit. Academic advisers, counselors, diagnostic specialists, regular education teachers, remediation/learning specialists, and trained peer tutors are provided collaboratively through on-campus or off-campus services.

Orientation The program or unit offers a mandatory orientation for new students individually by special arrangement.

Unique Aids and Services Aids, services, or accommodations include advocates, career counseling, digital textbooks, faculty training, personal coach, priority registration, support groups, mental health counseling.

Subject-area Tutoring Tutoring is offered one-on-one and in small groups for most subjects. Tutoring is provided through the program or unit via computer-based instruction and trained peer tutors. Tutoring is also provided collaboratively through on-campus or off-campus services via computer-based instruction and trained peer tutors.

Diagnostic Testing Testing is provided through the program or unit for learning strategies, learning styles, and reading. Testing for auditory processing, handwriting, intelligence, learning strategies, learning styles, math, motor skills, neuropsychological, personality, reading, social skills, spelling, spoken language, study skills, visual processing, written language, and other services is provided collaboratively through on-campus or off-campus services.

Basic Skills Remediation Remediation is offered one-on-one and in class-size groups for math, reading, study skills, time management, and written language. Remediation is provided through the program or unit via trained peer tutors and other. Remediation is also provided collaboratively through on-campus or off-campus services via computer-based instruction, regular education teachers, and trained peer tutors.

Enrichment Programs for career planning, college survival skills, health and nutrition, medication management, practical computer skills, reading, stress management, and written composition skills are provided collaboratively through on-campus or off-campus services. Credit is offered for reading and written composition skills.

Fees *Diagnostic Testing* fee is $0 to $500.

Application For admittance to the program or unit, students are required to apply to the program directly, provide a psychoeducational report (3 years old or less), and provide a psychoeducational report based on adult norms (3 years old or less). It is recommended that students provide documentation of high school services. Upon application, materials documenting need for services should be sent only to the LD program or unit. Upon acceptance, documentation of need for services should be sent only to the LD program or unit. *Application deadline (institutional):* 8/1. *Application deadline (LD program):* Rolling/continuous for fall and rolling/continuous for spring.

Written Policies Written policy regarding general/basic LD accommodations is outlined in the school's catalog/handbook. Written policies regarding course substitutions, general/basic LD accommo-

dations, reduced course loads, substitutions and waivers of admissions requirements, and substitutions and waivers of graduation requirements are available through the program or unit directly.

Eastern Michigan University
Access Services Office

Ypsilanti, MI 48197

http://www.emich.edu/public/students/disab.html

Contact: Mr. Donald J. Anderson, Director. Phone: 734-487-2470. Fax: 734-487-5784. E-mail: donald.anderson@emich.edu.

Access Services Office Approximately 267 registered undergraduate students were served during 2002-03. The program or unit includes 2 full-time staff members. Graduate assistants/students are provided through the program or unit. Academic advisers, coaches, counselors, diagnostic specialists, LD specialists, professional tutors, remediation/learning specialists, skill tutors, strategy tutors, trained peer tutors, and other are provided collaboratively through on-campus or off-campus services.

Unique Aids and Services Aids, services, or accommodations include digital textbooks and priority registration.

Subject-area Tutoring Tutoring is offered one-on-one and in small groups. Tutoring is provided collaboratively through on-campus or off-campus services via graduate assistants/students, professional tutors, and trained peer tutors.

Diagnostic Testing Testing for auditory processing, intelligence, learning strategies, learning styles, math, motor skills, neuropsychological, personality, reading, spelling, spoken language, study skills, visual processing, and written language is provided collaboratively through on-campus or off-campus services.

Basic Skills Remediation Remediation is offered one-on-one for auditory processing, learning strategies, math, reading, spelling, study skills, time management, and written language. Remediation is provided collaboratively through on-campus or off-campus services via graduate assistants/students, LD specialists, professional tutors, and trained peer tutors.

Enrichment Programs for career planning, college survival skills, health and nutrition, learning strategies, math, reading, stress management, study skills, test taking, time management, and written composition skills are provided collaboratively through on-campus or off-campus services.

Fees *Diagnostic Testing* fee is $50 to $1000.

Application For admittance to the program or unit, students are required to provide a psychoeducational report (5 years old or less). It is recommended that students provide documentation of high school services. Upon acceptance, documentation of need for services should be sent only to the LD program or unit. *Application deadline (institutional):* 6/30. *Application deadline (LD program):* Rolling/continuous for fall and rolling/continuous for spring.

Written Policies Written policy regarding general/basic LD accommodations is available on the program Web site. Written policy regarding general/basic LD accommodations is outlined in the school's catalog/handbook. Written policy regarding general/basic LD accommodations is available through the program or unit directly.

Eastern Michigan University (continued)

Eastern Nazarene College

23 East Elm Avenue

Quincy, MA 02170-2999

http://www.enc.edu/

Contact: Joyce Ann Klittich, Director of Academic Services. Phone: 617-745-3875. Fax: 617-745-3915. E-mail: klitticj@enc.edu.

Approximately 25 registered undergraduate students were served during 2002-03. The program or unit includes 1 full-time and 1 part-time staff member. Academic advisers, coaches, regular education teachers, trained peer tutors, and other are provided collaboratively through on-campus or off-campus services.

Unique Aids and Services Aids, services, or accommodations include career counseling and weekly meetings with faculty.

Subject-area Tutoring Tutoring is offered one-on-one and in small groups for most subjects. Tutoring is provided through the program or unit via trained peer tutors.

Basic Skills Remediation Remediation is offered one-on-one, in small groups, and in class-size groups for learning strategies, math, reading, study skills, time management, and written language. Remediation is provided through the program or unit via computer-based instruction, regular education teachers, and trained peer tutors.

Enrichment Enrichment programs are available through the program or unit for college survival skills, learning strategies, math, practical computer skills, reading, study skills, test taking, time management, vocabulary development, and written composition skills. Programs for career planning, health and nutrition, medication management, oral communication skills, self-advocacy, and stress management are provided collaboratively through on-campus or off-campus services. Credit is offered for career planning, college survival skills, health and nutrition, learning strategies, math, oral communication skills, reading, study skills, test taking, time management, vocabulary development, and written composition skills.

Application For admittance to the program or unit, students are required to provide a psychoeducational report (5 years old or less) and provide documentation of high school services. Upon application, materials documenting need for services should be sent to both admissions and the LD program or unit. Upon acceptance, documentation of need for services should be sent only to the LD program or unit. *Application deadline (institutional):* Continuous. *Application deadline (LD program):* Rolling/continuous for fall and rolling/continuous for spring.

Written Policies Written policy regarding general/basic LD accommodations is outlined in the school's catalog/handbook.

Eastern Washington University
Disability Support Services

526 5th Street

Cheney, WA 99004-2431

http://www.ewu.edu/StudentServ/dissup/

Contact: Ms. Karen Raver, Director of Disability Support Service and ADA Compliance. Phone: 509-359-2293. Fax: 509-359-4673. E-mail: kraver@mail.ewu.edu. Head of LD Program: Mr. Kevin Hills, Accommodation Specialist. Phone: 509-359-4706. Fax: 509-359-4673. E-mail: khills@mail.ewu.edu.

Disability Support Services Approximately 87 registered undergraduate students were served during 2002-03. The program or unit includes 3 full-time staff members. Academic advisers, coaches, counselors, diagnostic specialists, graduate assistants/students, regular education teachers, remediation/learning specialists, skill tutors, strategy tutors, and trained peer tutors are provided collaboratively through on-campus or off-campus services.

Unique Aids and Services Aids, services, or accommodations include career counseling, digital textbooks, faculty training, and priority registration.

Subject-area Tutoring Tutoring is offered one-on-one and in small groups for some subjects. Tutoring is provided collaboratively through on-campus or off-campus services via computer-based instruction, graduate assistants/students, professional tutors, and trained peer tutors.

Diagnostic Testing Testing for auditory processing, intelligence, learning strategies, learning styles, math, neuropsychological, personality, reading, social skills, spelling, study skills, and written language is provided collaboratively through on-campus or off-campus services.

Basic Skills Remediation Remediation is offered one-on-one and in small groups for auditory processing, learning strategies, math, reading, spelling, time management, visual processing, and written language. Remediation is provided collaboratively through on-campus or off-campus services via computer-based instruction, graduate assistants/students, and trained peer tutors.

Enrichment Enrichment programs are available through the program or unit for self-advocacy. Programs for career planning, college survival skills, health and nutrition, learning strategies, math, oral communication skills, practical computer skills, reading, self-advocacy, stress management, study skills, test taking, time management, vocabulary development, and written composition skills are provided collaboratively through on-campus or off-campus services. Credit is offered for college survival skills.

Application For admittance to the program or unit, students are required to provide a psychoeducational report. It is recommended that students provide documentation of high school services. Upon application, materials documenting need for services should be sent only to the LD program or unit. Upon acceptance, documentation of need for services should be sent only to the LD program or unit. *Application deadline (institutional):* Continuous. *Application deadline (LD program):* Rolling/continuous for fall and rolling/continuous for spring.

Written Policies Written policy regarding general/basic LD accommodations is available on the program Web site. Written policy regarding general/basic LD accommodations is available through the program or unit directly.

East Stroudsburg University of Pennsylvania

200 Prospect Street

East Stroudsburg, PA 18301-2999

http://www.esu.edu/

Contact: Ms. Adrian Wehmeyer, Assistive Technology Specialist and Outreach Coordinator. Phone: 570-422-3954. Fax: 570-422-3898. E-mail: awehmeyer@po-box.esu.edu. Head of LD Program: Dr. Edith Fisher Miller, Professor and Director of Disability Services. Phone: 570-422-3954. Fax: 570-422-3898. E-mail: emiller@po-box.esu.edu.

Approximately 175 registered undergraduate students were served during 2002-03. The program or unit includes 1 full-time and 2 part-time staff members. Academic advisers, graduate assistants/students, and LD specialists are provided through the program or unit. Academic advisers, counselors, professional tutors, regular education teachers, and trained peer tutors are provided collaboratively through on-campus or off-campus services.

Unique Aids and Services Aids, services, or accommodations include priority registration, taped textbooks, text-to-speech programs, reading pen, speech-to-text programs.

Subject-area Tutoring Tutoring is offered one-on-one and in small groups for most subjects. Tutoring is provided collaboratively through on-campus or off-campus services via professional tutors and trained peer tutors.

Enrichment Enrichment programs are available through the program or unit for career planning, college survival skills, learning strategies, oral communication skills, reading, self-advocacy, stress management, study skills, test taking, time management, and other.

Application For admittance to the program or unit, students are required to provide a psychoeducational report (3 years old or less). It is recommended that students provide documentation of high school services. Upon application, materials documenting need for services should be sent only to the LD program or unit. Upon acceptance, documentation of need for services should be sent only to the LD program or unit. *Application deadline (institutional):* 4/1. *Application deadline (LD program):* Rolling/continuous for fall and rolling/continuous for spring.

Written Policies Written policy regarding general/basic LD accommodations is available on the program Web site.

Elizabeth City State University
Center for Special Needs Students

1704 Weeksville Road

Elizabeth City, NC 27909-7806

http://www.ecsu.edu/

Contact: Mrs. Annie A. Hedgebeth, Coordinator of the Center for Special Needs Students. Phone: 252-335-3527. Fax: 252-335-3601. E-mail: aahedgebeth@mail.ecsu.edu.

Center for Special Needs Students Approximately 8 registered undergraduate students were served during 2002-03. The program or unit includes 1 full-time staff member. Academic advisers, coaches, counselors, diagnostic specialists, graduate assistants/students, professional tutors, regular education teachers, remediation/learning specialists, skill tutors, strategy tutors, and trained peer tutors are provided collaboratively through on-campus or off-campus services.

Unique Aids and Services Aids, services, or accommodations include digital textbooks, personal coach, and weekly meetings with faculty.

Subject-area Tutoring Tutoring is offered one-on-one, in small groups, and in class-size groups for most subjects. Tutoring is provided collaboratively through on-campus or off-campus services via computer-based instruction, graduate assistants/students, professional tutors, and trained peer tutors.

Basic Skills Remediation Remediation is offered one-on-one, in small groups, and in class-size groups for computer skills, learning strategies, math, reading, social skills, spelling, spoken language, study skills, time management, visual processing, and written language. Remediation is provided collaboratively through on-campus or off-campus services via computer-based instruction, graduate assistants/students, professional tutors, regular education teachers, and trained peer tutors.

Enrichment Programs for career planning, college survival skills, health and nutrition, learning strategies, math, medication management, oral communication skills, practical computer skills, reading, self-advocacy, stress management, study skills, test taking, time management, vocabulary development, and written composition skills are provided collaboratively through on-campus or off-campus services.

Application For admittance to the program or unit, students are required to apply to the program directly and provide a psychoeducational report (3 years old or less). It is recommended that students provide documentation of high school services. Upon application, materials documenting need for services should be sent to both admissions and the LD program or unit. Upon acceptance, documentation of need for services should be sent to both admissions and the LD program or unit. *Application deadline (institutional):* Continuous. *Application deadline (LD program):* Rolling/continuous for fall and rolling/continuous for spring.

Written Policies Written policy regarding general/basic LD accommodations is available on the program Web site. Written policy regarding general/basic LD accommodations is outlined in the school's catalog/handbook. Written policies regarding general/basic LD accommodations and reduced course loads are available through the program or unit directly.

Elmira College
Disability Services

One Park Place

Elmira, NY 14901

http://www.elmira.edu/

Contact: Ms. Carolyn Draht, Managing Director of Teacher Education Programs and Education Services. Phone: 607-735-1922. E-mail: cdraht@elmira.edu.

Disability Services Approximately 80 registered undergraduate students were served during 2002-03. The program or unit includes 1 full-time and 1 part-time staff member. Graduate assistants/students, skill tutors, strategy tutors, and trained peer tutors are provided through the program or unit. Academic advisers, coaches, counselors, graduate assistants/students, regular education teachers, and teacher trainees are provided collaboratively through on-campus or off-campus services.

Elmira College (continued)

Unique Aids and Services Aids, services, or accommodations include career counseling, digital textbooks, and priority registration.

Subject-area Tutoring Tutoring is offered one-on-one, in small groups, and in class-size groups for most subjects. Tutoring is provided collaboratively through on-campus or off-campus services via graduate assistants/students and trained peer tutors.

Application *Application deadline (institutional): 5/15.*

Written Policies Written policy regarding general/basic LD accommodations is outlined in the school's catalog/handbook. Written policy regarding general/basic LD accommodations is available through the program or unit directly.

Elon University
Disabilities Services

2700 Campus Box
Elon, NC 27244-2010
http://www.elon.edu/
Contact: Phone: 336-278-2000. Fax: 336-538-3986.

Disabilities Services Approximately 215 registered undergraduate students were served during 2002-03. The program or unit includes 1 full-time staff member. Academic advisers and LD specialists are provided through the program or unit. Academic advisers, coaches, counselors, and regular education teachers are provided collaboratively through on-campus or off-campus services.

Unique Aids and Services Aids, services, or accommodations include priority registration.

Subject-area Tutoring Tutoring is offered one-on-one and in small groups for most subjects. Tutoring is provided collaboratively through on-campus or off-campus services via trained peer tutors.

Basic Skills Remediation Remediation is offered in class-size groups for math, reading, and written language. Remediation is provided collaboratively through on-campus or off-campus services via regular education teachers.

Enrichment Programs for career planning, oral communication skills, practical computer skills, self-advocacy, and stress management are provided collaboratively through on-campus or off-campus services. Credit is offered for career planning.

Application For admittance to the program or unit, students are required to provide a psychoeducational report (4 years old or less). Upon acceptance, documentation of need for services should be sent only to the LD program or unit. *Application deadline (institutional):* Continuous. *Application deadline (LD program):* Rolling/continuous for fall and rolling/continuous for spring.

Written Policies Written policies regarding course substitutions, general/basic LD accommodations, and reduced course loads are available through the program or unit directly.

Emerson College

120 Boylston Street
Boston, MA 02116-4624
http://www.emerson.edu/

Contact: Anthony S. Bashir PhD, Disability Services Coordinator. Phone: 617-824-8415. Fax: 617-824-8941. E-mail: dso@emerson.edu.

Approximately 55 registered undergraduate students were served during 2002-03. The program or unit includes 2 full-time staff members. Academic advisers, counselors, graduate assistants/students, LD specialists, and trained peer tutors are provided collaboratively through on-campus or off-campus services.

Unique Aids and Services Aids, services, or accommodations include academic support services.

Subject-area Tutoring Tutoring is offered one-on-one and in small groups for some subjects. Tutoring is provided collaboratively through on-campus or off-campus services via graduate assistants/students and trained peer tutors.

Enrichment Programs for career planning, college survival skills, math, reading, self-advocacy, study skills, test taking, time management, and written composition skills are provided collaboratively through on-campus or off-campus services.

Application For admittance to the program or unit, students are required to provide a psychoeducational report and provide WAIS, Woodcock-Johnson (R), neuropsychological protocol. Upon acceptance, documentation of need for services should be sent only to the LD program or unit. *Application deadline (institutional): 2/1.*

Written Policies Written policies regarding course substitutions, general/basic LD accommodations, reduced course loads, and substitutions and waivers of graduation requirements are available through the program or unit directly.

Emory & Henry College

PO Box 947
Emory, VA 24327-0947
http://www.ehc.edu/

Contact: Ms. Karen Shuler Kilgore, Director of Academic Support Services. Phone: 276-944-6873. Fax: 276-944-6180. E-mail: kkilgore@ehc.edu.

Approximately 42 registered undergraduate students were served during 2002-03. The program or unit includes 1 full-time staff member. Academic advisers, coaches, counselors, and trained peer tutors are provided through the program or unit. Academic advisers, coaches, and counselors are provided collaboratively through on-campus or off-campus services.

Subject-area Tutoring Tutoring is offered one-on-one, in small groups, and in class-size groups for some subjects. Tutoring is provided through the program or unit via trained peer tutors.

Diagnostic Testing Testing is provided through the program or unit for study skills. Testing for auditory processing, intelligence, learning styles, math, motor skills, neuropsychological, personality, reading, social skills, spelling, study skills, visual processing, and written language is provided collaboratively through on-campus or off-campus services.

Fees *Diagnostic Testing* fee is $250.

Application For admittance to the program or unit, students are required to provide a psychoeducational report (3 years old or less). Upon acceptance, documentation of need for services should be sent only to the LD program or unit. *Application deadline (institutional):* Continuous. *Application deadline (LD program):* Rolling/continuous for fall and rolling/continuous for spring.

Written Policies Written policy regarding general/basic LD accommodations is outlined in the school's catalog/handbook.

Eugene Lang College, New School University
Student Disability Services

65 West 11th Street

New York, NY 10011-8601

http://www.lang.edu/

Contact: Mr. Tom McDonald, Director Student Disability Services. Phone: 212-229-5472. Fax: 212-229-8992. E-mail: sds@newschool.edu.

Student Disability Services Approximately 7 registered undergraduate students were served during 2002-03. The program or unit includes 1 full-time and 1 part-time staff member. Academic advisers, counselors, and other are provided collaboratively through on-campus or off-campus services.

Enrichment Programs for career planning, college survival skills, health and nutrition, learning strategies, self-advocacy, stress management, study skills, test taking, time management, and written composition skills are provided collaboratively through on-campus or off-campus services.

Application For admittance to the program or unit, students are required to apply to the program directly, provide a psychoeducational report (3 years old or less), and provide other documentation (contact office for guidelines). Upon acceptance, documentation of need for services should be sent only to the LD program or unit. *Application deadline (institutional):* 2/1. *Application deadline (LD program):* Rolling/continuous for fall.

Written Policies Written policy regarding general/basic LD accommodations is available on the program Web site. Written policy regarding general/basic LD accommodations is outlined in the school's catalog/handbook. Written policy regarding general/basic LD accommodations is available through the program or unit directly.

The Evergreen State College

2700 Evergreen Parkway, NW

Olympia, WA 98505

http://www.evergreen.edu/

Contact: Ms. Linda Pickering, Director of Access Services and ADA Compliance Officer. Phone: 360-867-6348. Fax: 360-867-5349. E-mail: pickeril@evergreen.edu.

Approximately 185 registered undergraduate students were served during 2002-03. The program or unit includes 1 full-time and 1 part-time staff member. Strategy tutors and other are provided through the program or unit. Academic advisers, counselors, professional tutors, remediation/learning specialists, and skill tutors are provided collaboratively through on-campus or off-campus services.

Unique Aids and Services Aids, services, or accommodations include career counseling, weekly meetings with faculty, books on tape, note-takers.

Subject-area Tutoring Tutoring is offered one-on-one and in small groups for most subjects. Tutoring is provided collaboratively through on-campus or off-campus services via computer-based instruction, professional tutors, and trained peer tutors.

Enrichment Enrichment programs are available through the program or unit for college survival skills, learning strategies, self-advocacy, stress management, study skills, and time management. Programs for career planning, college survival skills, learning strategies, practical computer skills, stress management, study skills, and written composition skills are provided collaboratively through on-campus or off-campus services. Credit is offered for career planning and college survival skills.

Application It is recommended that students provide a psychoeducational report (3 years old or less) and provide documentation of high school services. Upon acceptance, documentation of need for services should be sent only to the LD program or unit. *Application deadline (institutional):* 3/1. *Application deadline (LD program):* Rolling/continuous for fall and rolling/continuous for spring.

Written Policies Written policy regarding general/basic LD accommodations is available on the program Web site. Written policy regarding general/basic LD accommodations is available through the program or unit directly.

Farmingdale State University of New York

Route 110, 2350 Broadhollow Road

Farmingdale, NY 11735

http://www.farmingdale.edu/

Contact: Ms. Malka Edelman, Director. Phone: 631-420-2411. Fax: 631-420-2163. E-mail: malka.edelman@farmingdale.edu.

Approximately 195 registered undergraduate students were served during 2002-03. The program or unit includes 1 full-time and 2 part-time staff members. Counselors and LD specialists are provided through the program or unit. Academic advisers, counselors, LD specialists, professional tutors, and trained peer tutors are provided collaboratively through on-campus or off-campus services.

Orientation The program or unit offers an optional morning-long orientation for new students after classes begin.

Subject-area Tutoring Tutoring is offered one-on-one and in small groups for some subjects. Tutoring is provided through the program or unit via LD specialists. Tutoring is also provided collaboratively through on-campus or off-campus services via professional tutors and trained peer tutors.

Enrichment Programs for career planning, college survival skills, health and nutrition, learning strategies, math, self-advocacy, test taking, written composition skills, and other are provided collaboratively through on-campus or off-campus services.

Application For admittance to the program or unit, students are required to provide a psychoeducational report (3 years old or less) and provide documentation of high school services. Upon acceptance, documentation of need for services should be sent only to the LD program or unit. *Application deadline (institutional):* Continuous. *Application deadline (LD program):* Rolling/continuous for fall and rolling/continuous for spring.

Farmingdale State University of New York (continued)

Written Policies Written policy regarding general/basic LD accommodations is outlined in the school's catalog/handbook. Written policies regarding course substitutions, general/basic LD accommodations, reduced course loads, and substitutions and waivers of graduation requirements are available through the program or unit directly.

Fayetteville State University
Disabled Student Services

1200 Murchison Road
Fayetteville, NC 28301-4298

http://www.uncfsu.edu/studentaffairs/CFPD/cfpdservices.htm

Contact: Mr. Fred Sapp Jr., Director of the Center for Personal Development. Phone: 910-672-1222. Fax: 910-672-1389. E-mail: fsapp@uncfsu.edu.

Disabled Student Services Approximately 40 registered undergraduate students were served during 2002-03. The program or unit includes 2 full-time staff members. Counselors are provided through the program or unit. Academic advisers, diagnostic specialists, graduate assistants/students, LD specialists, professional tutors, regular education teachers, remediation/learning specialists, skill tutors, special education teachers, strategy tutors, and trained peer tutors are provided collaboratively through on-campus or off-campus services.

Unique Aids and Services Aids, services, or accommodations include career counseling and digital textbooks.

Subject-area Tutoring Tutoring is offered in small groups for all subjects. Tutoring is provided collaboratively through on-campus or off-campus services via graduate assistants/students, professional tutors, and trained peer tutors.

Diagnostic Testing Testing is provided through the program or unit for personality and study skills. Testing for auditory processing, intelligence, learning strategies, learning styles, math, motor skills, neuropsychological, reading, and visual processing is provided collaboratively through on-campus or off-campus services.

Basic Skills Remediation Remediation is offered in small groups for learning strategies, study skills, and time management. Remediation is provided collaboratively through on-campus or off-campus services via graduate assistants/students, professional tutors, and trained peer tutors.

Enrichment Programs for career planning, college survival skills, learning strategies, stress management, study skills, test taking, and time management are provided collaboratively through on-campus or off-campus services.

Application For admittance to the program or unit, students are required to apply to the program directly and provide a psychoeducational report (5 years old or less). Upon acceptance, documentation of need for services should be sent only to the LD program or unit. *Application deadline (institutional):* Continuous. *Application deadline (LD program):* Rolling/continuous for fall and rolling/continuous for spring.

Written Policies Written policy regarding general/basic LD accommodations is available on the program Web site. Written policy regarding course substitutions is outlined in the school's catalog/handbook.

Ferris State University
Disabilities Services Office

901 South State Street
Big Rapids, MI 49307

http://ferris.edu/colleges/university/disabilities.htm

Contact: Ms. Eunice C.W. Merwin, Educational Counselor for Students with Disabilities. Phone: 231-592-3772. Fax: 231-592-3686. E-mail: merwine@ferris.edu.

Disabilities Services Office Approximately 100 registered undergraduate students were served during 2002-03. The program or unit includes 1 full-time and 1 part-time staff member. Counselors are provided through the program or unit. Academic advisers, coaches, remediation/learning specialists, skill tutors, strategy tutors, and trained peer tutors are provided collaboratively through on-campus or off-campus services.

Orientation The program or unit offers an optional orientation for new students during registration.

Subject-area Tutoring Tutoring is offered one-on-one, in small groups, and in class-size groups for most subjects. Tutoring is provided collaboratively through on-campus or off-campus services via computer-based instruction, professional tutors, trained peer tutors, and other.

Diagnostic Testing Testing for learning strategies, learning styles, math, reading, spelling, and study skills is provided collaboratively through on-campus or off-campus services.

Basic Skills Remediation Remediation is offered one-on-one, in small groups, and in class-size groups for computer skills, learning strategies, math, reading, study skills, time management, and written language. Remediation is provided collaboratively through on-campus or off-campus services via computer-based instruction, professional tutors, regular education teachers, and trained peer tutors.

Enrichment Enrichment programs are available through the program or unit for self-advocacy, study skills, test taking, and time management. Programs for career planning, college survival skills, health and nutrition, learning strategies, math, practical computer skills, reading, stress management, study skills, test taking, time management, and written composition skills are provided collaboratively through on-campus or off-campus services. Credit is offered for career planning, college survival skills, health and nutrition, learning strategies, math, reading, stress management, study skills, test taking, time management, and written composition skills.

Application For admittance to the program or unit, students are required to apply to the program directly, provide a psychoeducational report, and provide test results from 9th grade and later. Upon application, materials documenting need for services should be sent only to the LD program or unit. Upon acceptance, documentation of need for services should be sent only to the LD program or unit. *Application deadline (institutional):* 8/4. *Application deadline (LD program):* Rolling/continuous for fall and rolling/continuous for spring.

Written Policies Written policies regarding course substitutions and general/basic LD accommodations are available on the program Web site. Written policies regarding course substitutions and general/basic LD accommodations are available through the program or unit directly.

Fitchburg State College
Office of Disability Services

160 Pearl Street

Fitchburg, MA 01420-2697

http://www.fsc.edu/disabilities

Contact: Director of Disability Services. Phone: 978-664-4020. Fax: 978-665-3021. E-mail: wpeterson@fsc.edu.

Office of Disability Services Approximately 100 registered undergraduate students were served during 2002-03. The program or unit includes 1 full-time and 4 part-time staff members. Counselors, diagnostic specialists, and graduate assistants/students are provided through the program or unit. Academic advisers, counselors, LD specialists, professional tutors, remediation/learning specialists, skill tutors, strategy tutors, trained peer tutors, and other are provided collaboratively through on-campus or off-campus services.

Orientation The program or unit offers an optional 1-day orientation for new students before classes begin, during summer prior to enrollment, and individually by special arrangement.

Unique Aids and Services Aids, services, or accommodations include career counseling, books on tape, assistive technology.

Subject-area Tutoring Tutoring is offered one-on-one for most subjects. Tutoring is provided through the program or unit via graduate assistants/students. Tutoring is also provided collaboratively through on-campus or off-campus services via graduate assistants/students, LD specialists, professional tutors, and trained peer tutors.

Diagnostic Testing Testing is provided through the program or unit for intelligence and other services. Testing for learning strategies and learning styles is provided collaboratively through on-campus or off-campus services.

Basic Skills Remediation Remediation is offered one-on-one, in small groups, and in class-size groups for computer skills, learning strategies, math, reading, study skills, and written language. Remediation is provided collaboratively through on-campus or off-campus services via LD specialists, professional tutors, and trained peer tutors.

Enrichment Enrichment programs are available through the program or unit for career planning, college survival skills, learning strategies, practical computer skills, self-advocacy, stress management, study skills, test taking, and time management. Programs for career planning, college survival skills, health and nutrition, learning strategies, math, oral communication skills, practical computer skills, reading, self-advocacy, stress management, study skills, test taking, time management, vocabulary development, and written composition skills are provided collaboratively through on-campus or off-campus services. Credit is offered for college survival skills, health and nutrition, oral communication skills, practical computer skills, reading, and written composition skills.

Application For admittance to the program or unit, students are required to apply to the program directly, provide a psychoeducational report (3 years old or less), and provide documentation of high school services. Upon application, materials documenting need for services should be sent only to admissions with institutional application materials. Upon acceptance, documentation of need for services should be sent only to the LD program or unit. *Application deadline (institutional):* 4/1. *Application deadline (LD program):* Rolling/continuous for fall and rolling/continuous for spring.

Written Policies Written policies regarding general/basic LD accommodations, reduced course loads, and substitutions and waivers of admissions requirements are available on the program Web site. Written policies regarding general/basic LD accommodations, reduced course loads, and substitutions and waivers of admissions requirements are outlined in the school's catalog/handbook. Written policies regarding course substitutions and general/basic LD accommodations are available through the program or unit directly.

Flagler College

74 King Street

PO Box 1027

St. Augustine, FL 32085-1027

http://www.flagler.edu/

Contact: Mary Jane Dillon, Director of External Programs and Special Projects. Phone: 904-819-6314. Fax: 904-824-6017. E-mail: dillonmj@flagler.edu.

The program or unit includes 1 full-time staff member. Services are provided through the program or unit.

Enrichment Programs for career planning, college survival skills, math, reading, and written composition skills are provided collaboratively through on-campus or off-campus services.

Application For admittance to the program or unit, students are required to provide a psychoeducational report (3 years old or less). It is recommended that students provide documentation of high school services. Upon acceptance, documentation of need for services should be sent only to the LD program or unit. *Application deadline (institutional):* 3/1. *Application deadline (LD program):* Rolling/continuous for fall and rolling/continuous for spring.

Written Policies Written policy regarding general/basic LD accommodations is outlined in the school's catalog/handbook.

Florida Agricultural and Mechanical University

Tallahassee, FL 32307-3200

http://www.famu.edu/

Contact: Dr. Sharon Mitchell Wooten, Director and Professor. Phone: 850-599-3168. Fax: 850-561-2513. E-mail: wootensm@aol.com.

The program or unit includes 7 full-time and 12 part-time staff members. Academic advisers, coaches, counselors, diagnostic specialists, graduate assistants/students, LD specialists, professional tutors, regular education teachers, remediation/learning specialists, skill tutors, special education teachers, strategy tutors, teacher trainees, trained peer tutors, and other are provided through the program or unit. Academic advisers, coaches, counselors, diagnostic specialists, graduate assistants/students, LD specialists, professional tutors, regular education teachers, remediation/learning specialists, teacher trainees, and trained peer tutors are provided collaboratively through on-campus or off-campus services.

Florida Agricultural and Mechanical University (continued)

Orientation The program or unit offers a mandatory 2-week orientation for new students before registration, before classes begin, and during summer prior to enrollment.

Summer Program To help prepare for the demands of college, there is a mandatory 2-week summer program prior to entering the school.

Unique Aids and Services Aids, services, or accommodations include advocates, career counseling, faculty training, parent workshops, support groups, and weekly meetings with faculty.

Subject-area Tutoring Tutoring is offered one-on-one, in small groups, and in class-size groups for all subjects. Tutoring is provided through the program or unit via computer-based instruction, graduate assistants/students, LD specialists, professional tutors, trained peer tutors, and other.

Diagnostic Testing Testing is provided through the program or unit for auditory processing, handwriting, learning strategies, learning styles, math, reading, social skills, spelling, study skills, visual processing, and written language. Testing for auditory processing, handwriting, intelligence, learning styles, math, motor skills, neuropsychological, personality, reading, social skills, spelling, spoken language, study skills, visual processing, and written language is provided collaboratively through on-campus or off-campus services.

Basic Skills Remediation Remediation is offered one-on-one, in small groups, and in class-size groups for computer skills, learning strategies, math, reading, social skills, spelling, spoken language, study skills, time management, and written language. Remediation is provided through the program or unit via computer-based instruction, graduate assistants/students, LD specialists, professional tutors, regular education teachers, special education teachers, teacher trainees, trained peer tutors, and other. Remediation is also provided collaboratively through on-campus or off-campus services via computer-based instruction, regular education teachers, and trained peer tutors.

Enrichment Enrichment programs are available through the program or unit for career planning, college survival skills, health and nutrition, learning strategies, math, oral communication skills, practical computer skills, reading, self-advocacy, stress management, study skills, test taking, time management, vocabulary development, written composition skills, and other. Programs for career planning, college survival skills, health and nutrition, math, oral communication skills, practical computer skills, reading, written composition skills, and other are provided collaboratively through on-campus or off-campus services. Credit is offered for college survival skills, health and nutrition, learning strategies, math, oral communication skills, reading, self-advocacy, stress management, study skills, test taking, time management, vocabulary development, and written composition skills.

Student Organization Excellence Through Caring consists of 25 members.

Fees *LD Program or Service* fee is $750 to $1500 (fee varies according to disability). *Summer Program* fee is $750 to $1500. *Diagnostic Testing* fee is $50 to $1000.

Application For admittance to the program or unit, students are required to apply to the program directly, provide a psychoeducational report, and provide teacher reports in English, math, and reading. Upon application, materials documenting need for services should be sent only to the LD program or unit. Upon acceptance, documentation of need for services should be sent only to the LD program or unit. *Application deadline (institutional):* 5/9. *Application deadline (LD program):* 4/30 for fall.

Written Policies Written policy regarding grade forgiveness is outlined in the school's catalog/handbook. Written policies regarding course substitutions, general/basic LD accommodations, reduced course loads, substitutions and waivers of admissions requirements, and substitutions and waivers of graduation requirements are available through the program or unit directly.

Florida Atlantic University

777 Glades Road, PO Box 3091
Boca Raton, FL 33431-0991
http://www.fau.edu/

Contact: Mrs. Nicole Rokos, Director. Phone: 561-297-3880. Fax: 561-297-2184. E-mail: nrokos@fau.edu.

Approximately 261 registered undergraduate students were served during 2002-03. The program or unit includes 8 full-time and 3 part-time staff members. Graduate assistants/students, LD specialists, skill tutors, strategy tutors, and other are provided through the program or unit. Academic advisers, counselors, diagnostic specialists, professional tutors, regular education teachers, remediation/learning specialists, skill tutors, strategy tutors, and trained peer tutors are provided collaboratively through on-campus or off-campus services.

Unique Aids and Services Aids, services, or accommodations include advocates and career counseling.

Subject-area Tutoring Tutoring is offered one-on-one and in small groups for some subjects. Tutoring is provided collaboratively through on-campus or off-campus services via computer-based instruction, graduate assistants/students, and trained peer tutors.

Basic Skills Remediation Remediation is offered one-on-one for learning strategies, study skills, time management, and standardized test preparation. Remediation is provided through the program or unit via LD specialists. Remediation is also provided collaboratively through on-campus or off-campus services via trained peer tutors.

Enrichment Enrichment programs are available through the program or unit for learning strategies, practical computer skills, self-advocacy, study skills, test taking, time management, and other. Programs for career planning, college survival skills, health and nutrition, learning strategies, math, oral communication skills, reading, stress management, study skills, test taking, time management, vocabulary development, written composition skills, and other are provided collaboratively through on-campus or off-campus services. Credit is offered for college survival skills, health and nutrition, learning strategies, oral communication skills, practical computer skills, and study skills.

Application For admittance to the program or unit, students are required to apply to the program directly and provide a psychoeducational report. It is recommended that students provide documentation of high school services and provide a letter from transferring institution of higher education regarding accommodations received. Upon acceptance, documentation of need for services should be sent only to the LD program or unit. *Application deadline (institutional):* 6/1. *Application deadline (LD program):* Rolling/continuous for fall and rolling/continuous for spring.

Written Policies Written policies regarding course substitutions, general/basic LD accommodations, substitutions and waivers of admissions requirements, and substitutions and waivers of graduation requirements are available on the program Web site. Written policies regarding general/basic LD accommodations and substitutions and waivers of admissions requirements are outlined in the school's catalog/handbook. Written policies regarding course substitutions, general/basic LD accommodations, substitutions and waivers of admissions requirements, and substitutions and waivers of graduation requirements are available through the program or unit directly.

Florida Gulf Coast University
The Office of Adaptive Services

10501 FGCU Boulevard South
Fort Myers, FL 33965-6565
http://www.fgcu.edu/adaptive
Contact: Ms. Cori Whiting, Coordinator of Adaptive Services. Phone: 239-590-7956 Ext. 7956. Fax: 239-590-7975. E-mail: cwhiting@fgcu.edu.

The Office of Adaptive Services Approximately 156 registered undergraduate students were served during 2002-03. The program or unit includes 1 full-time and 4 part-time staff members. Diagnostic specialists, graduate assistants/students, LD specialists, professional tutors, remediation/learning specialists, skill tutors, and strategy tutors are provided through the program or unit. Academic advisers, coaches, counselors, graduate assistants/students, regular education teachers, special education teachers, teacher trainees, and trained peer tutors are provided collaboratively through on-campus or off-campus services.
Unique Aids and Services Aids, services, or accommodations include faculty training, priority registration, and support groups.
Subject-area Tutoring Tutoring is offered one-on-one for all subjects. Tutoring is provided through the program or unit via graduate assistants/students, LD specialists, professional tutors, and trained peer tutors. Tutoring is also provided collaboratively through on-campus or off-campus services via computer-based instruction.
Diagnostic Testing Testing is provided through the program or unit for handwriting, learning strategies, learning styles, and study skills. Testing for auditory processing, intelligence, math, motor skills, neuropsychological, personality, reading, social skills, spelling, spoken language, visual processing, and written language is provided collaboratively through on-campus or off-campus services.
Basic Skills Remediation Remediation is offered one-on-one for computer skills, learning strategies, math, reading, spelling, study skills, time management, and written language. Remediation is provided through the program or unit via graduate assistants/students, LD specialists, and professional tutors. Remediation is also provided collaboratively through on-campus or off-campus services via computer-based instruction, regular education teachers, special education teachers, teacher trainees, and trained peer tutors.
Enrichment Enrichment programs are available through the program or unit for learning strategies, reading, self-advocacy, stress management, study skills, test taking, time management, vocabulary development, and written composition skills. Programs for career planning, college survival skills, health and nutrition, math, medication management, oral communication skills, and practical computer skills are provided collaboratively through on-campus or off-campus services.

Fees *Diagnostic Testing* fee is $300 to $3000.
Application For admittance to the program or unit, students are required to apply to the program directly and provide a psychoeducational report (3 years old or less). It is recommended that students provide documentation of high school services. Upon application, materials documenting need for services should be sent to both admissions and the LD program or unit. Upon acceptance, documentation of need for services should be sent only to the LD program or unit. *Application deadline (institutional):* 7/1. *Application deadline (LD program):* Rolling/continuous for fall and rolling/continuous for spring.
Written Policies Written policies regarding general/basic LD accommodations and substitutions and waivers of admissions requirements are available on the program Web site. Written policy regarding substitutions and waivers of admissions requirements is outlined in the school's catalog/handbook. Written policies regarding course substitutions, general/basic LD accommodations, grade forgiveness, reduced course loads, substitutions and waivers of admissions requirements, and substitutions and waivers of graduation requirements are available through the program or unit directly.

Florida Metropolitan University-North Orlando Campus
Campus Student Disability Services

5421 Diplomat Circle
Orlando, FL 32810-5674
Contact: Karen Oporto JD, Associate Dean. Phone: 407-628-5870 Ext. 104. Fax: 407-628-1344. E-mail: koporto@cci.edu. Head of LD Program: Dean George Karl Jr., Academic Dean. Phone: 407-628-5870 Ext. 147. Fax: 407-628-1344. E-mail: gkarl@cci.edu.

Campus Student Disability Services Approximately 1 registered undergraduate students were served during 2002-03. The program or unit includes 3 full-time staff members. Regular education teachers are provided through the program or unit. Regular education teachers are provided collaboratively through on-campus or off-campus services.
Unique Aids and Services Aids, services, or accommodations include advocates, career counseling, and weekly meetings with faculty.
Subject-area Tutoring Tutoring is offered one-on-one for most subjects. Tutoring is provided collaboratively through on-campus or off-campus services via professional tutors and trained peer tutors.
Enrichment Programs for career planning, college survival skills, math, oral communication skills, practical computer skills, and written composition skills are provided collaboratively through on-campus or off-campus services.
Application For admittance to the program or unit, students are required to apply to the program directly. Upon application, materials documenting need for services should be sent only to the LD program or unit. Upon acceptance, documentation of need for services should be sent only to the LD program or unit. *Application deadline (institutional):* Continuous. *Application deadline (LD program):* Rolling/continuous for fall and rolling/continuous for spring.

Florida Metropolitan University-North Orlando Campus (continued)

Written Policies Written policies regarding course substitutions, general/basic LD accommodations, grade forgiveness, reduced course loads, substitutions and waivers of admissions requirements, and substitutions and waivers of graduation requirements are available through the program or unit directly.

Florida State University

Tallahassee, FL 32306

http://www.fsu.edu/

Contact: Phone: 850-644-2525. Fax: 850-644-0197. Head of LD Program: Dr. Brenda Monk, Learning Specialist. Phone: 850-644-5928. Fax: 850-644-2188. E-mail: bmonk@admin.fsu.edu.

Approximately 40 registered undergraduate students were served during 2002-03. The program or unit includes 1 full-time and 8 part-time staff members. Academic advisers, coaches, counselors, diagnostic specialists, graduate assistants/students, LD specialists, professional tutors, remediation/learning specialists, and trained peer tutors are provided collaboratively through on-campus or off-campus services.

Subject-area Tutoring Tutoring is offered one-on-one, in small groups, and in class-size groups for most subjects. Tutoring is provided collaboratively through on-campus or off-campus services via computer-based instruction, graduate assistants/students, LD specialists, professional tutors, and trained peer tutors.

Diagnostic Testing Testing for auditory processing, intelligence, math, reading, social skills, visual processing, and written language is provided collaboratively through on-campus or off-campus services.

Basic Skills Remediation Remediation is offered in small groups for learning strategies, math, and reading. Remediation is provided collaboratively through on-campus or off-campus services via computer-based instruction, graduate assistants/students, LD specialists, professional tutors, and trained peer tutors.

Fees *Diagnostic Testing* fee is $500 to $1000.

Application For admittance to the program or unit, students are required to provide a psychoeducational report (3 years old or less). It is recommended that students provide documentation of high school services. Upon application, materials documenting need for services should be sent to both admissions and the LD program or unit. *Application deadline (institutional):* 3/1. *Application deadline (LD program):* Rolling/continuous for fall and rolling/continuous for spring.

Written Policies Written policies regarding course substitutions, general/basic LD accommodations, grade forgiveness, reduced course loads, substitutions and waivers of admissions requirements, and substitutions and waivers of graduation requirements are available on the program Web site.

Fontbonne University

6800 Wydown Boulevard

St. Louis, MO 63105-3098

http://www.fontbonne.edu/

Contact: Dr. Jane Daily Snyder, Director of Academic Resources. Phone: 314-719-3627. Fax: 314-719-3614. E-mail: jsnyder@fontbonne.edu.

The program or unit includes 3 full-time and 11 part-time staff members. Counselors, professional tutors, skill tutors, and trained peer tutors are provided collaboratively through on-campus or off-campus services.

Unique Aids and Services Aids, services, or accommodations include career counseling and faculty training.

Subject-area Tutoring Tutoring is offered one-on-one and in small groups for all subjects. Tutoring is provided collaboratively through on-campus or off-campus services via professional tutors and trained peer tutors.

Basic Skills Remediation Remediation is offered one-on-one, in small groups, and in class-size groups for learning strategies, math, reading, spoken language, study skills, time management, and written language. Remediation is provided collaboratively through on-campus or off-campus services via professional tutors and trained peer tutors.

Enrichment Programs for career planning, college survival skills, health and nutrition, learning strategies, math, oral communication skills, reading, stress management, study skills, test taking, time management, and written composition skills are provided collaboratively through on-campus or off-campus services. Credit is offered for health and nutrition and reading.

Application For admittance to the program or unit, students are required to apply to the program directly and provide a psychoeducational report (3 years old or less). Upon acceptance, documentation of need for services should be sent only to the LD program or unit. *Application deadline (institutional):* 8/1. *Application deadline (LD program):* Rolling/continuous for fall and rolling/continuous for spring.

Written Policies Written policy regarding general/basic LD accommodations is available through the program or unit directly.

Fordham University
Disability Services

441 East Fordham Road

New York, NY 10458

http://www.fordham.edu/dss

Contact: Ms. Jeanine Pirozzi-Blake, Director. Phone: 718-817-4362. Fax: 718-817-3735. E-mail: pirozzi@fordham.edu.

Disability Services Approximately 120 registered undergraduate students were served during 2002-03. The program or unit includes 1 full-time and 4 part-time staff members. Academic advisers, counselors, graduate assistants/students, skill tutors, strategy tutors, and other are provided through the program or unit. Academic advisers, counselors, regular education teachers, and trained peer tutors are provided collaboratively through on-campus or off-campus services.

Unique Aids and Services Aids, services, or accommodations include career counseling, digital textbooks, and priority registration.

Subject-area Tutoring Tutoring is offered one-on-one for most subjects. Tutoring is provided through the program or unit via graduate assistants/students. Tutoring is also provided collaboratively through on-campus or off-campus services via graduate assistants/ students and trained peer tutors.

Diagnostic Testing Testing for auditory processing, intelligence, learning strategies, learning styles, math, motor skills, neuropsychological, personality, reading, social skills, spelling, spoken language, study skills, visual processing, written language, and other services is provided collaboratively through on-campus or off-campus services.

Basic Skills Remediation Remediation is offered one-on-one for learning strategies, study skills, and time management. Remediation is provided through the program or unit via graduate assistants/students. Remediation is also provided collaboratively through on-campus or off-campus services via graduate assistants/students and trained peer tutors.

Enrichment Enrichment programs are available through the program or unit for learning strategies, study skills, test taking, time management, and other. Programs for career planning, college survival skills, health and nutrition, learning strategies, math, self-advocacy, stress management, study skills, test taking, time management, vocabulary development, written composition skills, and other are provided collaboratively through on-campus or off-campus services.

Fees *Diagnostic Testing* fee is $800.

Application For admittance to the program or unit, students are required to provide a psychoeducational report (3 years old or less) and provide documentation of high school services. Upon application, materials documenting need for services should be sent only to the LD program or unit. Upon acceptance, documentation of need for services should be sent only to the LD program or unit. *Application deadline (institutional): 2/1. Application deadline (LD program):* Rolling/continuous for fall and rolling/continuous for spring.

Written Policies Written policy regarding general/basic LD accommodations is available on the program Web site. Written policy regarding general/basic LD accommodations is available through the program or unit directly.

Fort Hays State University

600 Park Street
Hays, KS 67601-4099
http://www.fhsu.edu/

Contact: Ms. Carol Solko, Coordinator of Services for Students with Disabilities. Phone: 785-628-4276. Fax: 785-628-4113. E-mail: csolko@fhsu.edu.

Approximately 25 registered undergraduate students were served during 2002-03. The program or unit includes 1 full-time and 1 part-time staff member. Academic advisers, counselors, diagnostic specialists, graduate assistants/students, strategy tutors, and trained peer tutors are provided collaboratively through on-campus or off-campus services.

Unique Aids and Services Aids, services, or accommodations include advocates, career counseling, notes, test-taking accommodations.

Subject-area Tutoring Tutoring is offered one-on-one for most subjects. Tutoring is provided collaboratively through on-campus or off-campus services via computer-based instruction, graduate assistants/students, and trained peer tutors.

Diagnostic Testing Testing for auditory processing, intelligence, learning strategies, learning styles, math, neuropsychological, personality, reading, spoken language, study skills, and written language is provided collaboratively through on-campus or off-campus services.

Enrichment Programs for career planning, college survival skills, learning strategies, oral communication skills, stress management, study skills, test taking, time management, and vocabulary development are provided collaboratively through on-campus or off-campus services. Credit is offered for career planning, learning strategies, and oral communication skills.

Student Organization Creating Access for Today's Students (CATS) consists of 10 members.

Application For admittance to the program or unit, students are required to apply to the program directly, provide a psychoeducational report (3 years old or less), and provide documentation of high school services. Upon application, materials documenting need for services should be sent only to the LD program or unit. Upon acceptance, documentation of need for services should be sent only to the LD program or unit. *Application deadline (institutional):* Continuous. *Application deadline (LD program):* Rolling/continuous for fall and rolling/continuous for spring.

Written Policies Written policies regarding general/basic LD accommodations and reduced course loads are available through the program or unit directly.

Franciscan University of Steubenville

1235 University Boulevard
Steubenville, OH 43952-1763
http://www.franuniv.edu/

Contact: Mrs. Rose D. Kline, Director of Student Academic Support Services. Phone: 740-283-6245 Ext. 2112. Fax: 740-283-6401. E-mail: rkline@franciscan.edu.

Approximately 45 registered undergraduate students were served during 2002-03. The program or unit includes 2 full-time staff members. Academic advisers, counselors, graduate assistants/students, LD specialists, remediation/learning specialists, skill tutors, trained peer tutors, and other are provided through the program or unit. Academic advisers, counselors, regular education teachers, remediation/learning specialists, skill tutors, and trained peer tutors are provided collaboratively through on-campus or off-campus services.

Orientation The program or unit offers an optional 2-hour orientation for new students after classes begin and individually by special arrangement.

Unique Aids and Services Aids, services, or accommodations include advocates, digital textbooks, faculty training, and priority registration.

Subject-area Tutoring Tutoring is offered one-on-one and in small groups for most subjects. Tutoring is provided through the program or unit via LD specialists, professional tutors, and trained peer tutors. Tutoring is also provided collaboratively through on-campus or off-campus services via graduate assistants/students and trained peer tutors.

Basic Skills Remediation Remediation is offered one-on-one and in small groups for learning strategies, math, reading, study skills, time management, and written language. Remediation is provided through the program or unit via computer-based instruction, LD specialists, professional tutors, and trained peer tutors. Remediation is also provided collaboratively through on-campus or off-campus services via professional tutors and trained peer tutors.

Franciscan University of Steubenville (continued)

Enrichment Enrichment programs are available through the program or unit for college survival skills, learning strategies, reading, self-advocacy, stress management, study skills, test taking, time management, and written composition skills. Programs for career planning, college survival skills, learning strategies, stress management, study skills, test taking, time management, and written composition skills are provided collaboratively through on-campus or off-campus services.

Application For admittance to the program or unit, students are required to provide a psychoeducational report (3 years old or less). Upon application, materials documenting need for services should be sent only to the LD program or unit. Upon acceptance, documentation of need for services should be sent only to the LD program or unit. *Application deadline (institutional):* 5/1. *Application deadline (LD program):* Rolling/continuous for fall and rolling/continuous for spring.

Written Policies Written policy regarding general/basic LD accommodations is available on the program Web site. Written policies regarding general/basic LD accommodations and reduced course loads are outlined in the school's catalog/handbook. Written policies regarding general/basic LD accommodations and reduced course loads are available through the program or unit directly.

Franklin College

501 East Monroe
Franklin, IN 46131-2598
http://www.franklincollege.edu/
Contact: Ms. Jann Johnson, Assistant Dean for Academic Services. Phone: 317-738-8801. Fax: 317-738-8810. E-mail: jjohnson@franklincollege.edu.

Approximately 7 registered undergraduate students were served during 2002-03. The program or unit includes 1 part-time staff member. Academic advisers, coaches, counselors, regular education teachers, and trained peer tutors are provided collaboratively through on-campus or off-campus services.

Subject-area Tutoring Tutoring is offered one-on-one and in small groups for some subjects. Tutoring is provided collaboratively through on-campus or off-campus services via trained peer tutors.

Basic Skills Remediation Remediation is offered one-on-one, in small groups, and in class-size groups for learning strategies, math, reading, study skills, and time management. Remediation is provided collaboratively through on-campus or off-campus services via regular education teachers and trained peer tutors.

Enrichment Programs for career planning, college survival skills, learning strategies, math, study skills, test taking, time management, and written composition skills are provided collaboratively through on-campus or off-campus services. Credit is offered for career planning, college survival skills, learning strategies, math, and study skills.

Application For admittance to the program or unit, students are required to provide a psychoeducational report (5 years old or less). It is recommended that students provide documentation of high school services. Upon acceptance, documentation of need for services should be sent only to the LD program or unit. *Application deadline (institutional):* 5/1. *Application deadline (LD program):* Rolling/continuous for fall and rolling/continuous for spring.

Written Policies Written policy regarding general/basic LD accommodations is available through the program or unit directly.

Furman University
Disability Services

3300 Poinsett Highway
Greenville, SC 29613
http://www.furman.edu/
Contact: Susan Clark, Coordinator of Disability Services. Phone: 864-294-2322. Fax: 864-294-3044. E-mail: susan.clark@furman.edu.

Disability Services Approximately 75 registered undergraduate students were served during 2002-03. The program or unit includes 1 full-time and 1 part-time staff member. Services are provided through the program or unit. Diagnostic specialists are provided collaboratively through on-campus or off-campus services.

Unique Aids and Services Aids, services, or accommodations include digital textbooks and priority registration.

Subject-area Tutoring Tutoring is offered one-on-one for most subjects. Tutoring is provided through the program or unit via other.

Application For admittance to the program or unit, students are required to provide a psychoeducational report (3 years old or less). It is recommended that students provide documentation of high school services. Upon application, materials documenting need for services should be sent only to the LD program or unit. Upon acceptance, documentation of need for services should be sent only to the LD program or unit. *Application deadline (institutional):* 1/15. *Application deadline (LD program):* Rolling/continuous for fall and rolling/continuous for spring.

Written Policies Written policies regarding course substitutions, general/basic LD accommodations, and substitutions and waivers of graduation requirements are available on the program Web site. Written policies regarding course substitutions, general/basic LD accommodations, reduced course loads, and substitutions and waivers of graduation requirements are available through the program or unit directly.

Gallaudet University

800 Florida Avenue, NE
Washington, DC 20002-3625
http://www.gallaudet.edu/
Contact: Mr. Edgar Bernard Palmer, Director of Office for Students with Disabilities. Phone: 202-651-5652 Ext. 5807. Fax: 202-651-5887. E-mail: edgar.palmer@gallaudet.edu. Head of LD Program: Dr. Patricia M. Tesar, Coordinator of Office for Students with Disabilities. Phone: 202-651-5652 Ext. 3127. Fax: 202-651-5887. E-mail: patricia.tesar@gallaudet.edu.

Approximately 50 registered undergraduate students were served during 2002-03. The program or unit includes 7 full-time staff members. Academic advisers, coaches, counselors, diagnostic specialists, graduate assistants/students, LD specialists, professional tutors, regular education teachers, remediation/learning specialists, skill tutors, special education teachers, strategy tutors, teacher trainees, trained peer tutors, and other are provided through the program or unit.

Orientation The program or unit offers an optional 1-week orientation for new students before classes begin, during summer prior to enrollment, during registration, after classes begin, and individually by special arrangement.

Unique Aids and Services Aids, services, or accommodations include advocates, career counseling, faculty training, parent workshops, priority registration, support groups, and weekly meetings with faculty.

Subject-area Tutoring Tutoring is offered one-on-one for most subjects. Tutoring is provided collaboratively through on-campus or off-campus services via trained peer tutors.

Diagnostic Testing Testing for auditory processing, handwriting, intelligence, learning strategies, learning styles, math, motor skills, neuropsychological, personality, reading, social skills, spelling, spoken language, study skills, visual processing, written language, and other services is provided collaboratively through on-campus or off-campus services.

Basic Skills Remediation Remediation is offered one-on-one for computer skills, learning strategies, math, reading, social skills, study skills, time management, and written language. Remediation is provided through the program or unit via graduate assistants/students, LD specialists, and trained peer tutors. Remediation is also provided collaboratively through on-campus or off-campus services via special education teachers and trained peer tutors.

Enrichment Programs for career planning, college survival skills, math, reading, self-advocacy, stress management, study skills, test taking, time management, and written composition skills are provided collaboratively through on-campus or off-campus services.

Student Organization Organization for Unique Learners consists of 15 members.

Fees *Diagnostic Testing* fee is $550.

Application For admittance to the program or unit, students are required to apply to the program directly, provide a psychoeducational report, provide documentation of high school services, and provide psychoeducational adult testing results that meet Gallaudet University documentation standards. Upon application, materials documenting need for services should be sent to both admissions and the LD program or unit. Upon acceptance, documentation of need for services should be sent to both admissions and the LD program or unit. *Application deadline (institutional): 8/1. Application deadline (LD program):* Rolling/continuous for fall and rolling/continuous for spring.

Written Policies Written policies regarding general/basic LD accommodations and reduced course loads are available on the program Web site. Written policies regarding general/basic LD accommodations and reduced course loads are outlined in the school's catalog/handbook. Written policies regarding course substitutions, general/basic LD accommodations, reduced course loads, substitutions and waivers of admissions requirements, and substitutions and waivers of graduation requirements are available through the program or unit directly.

Gardner-Webb University
Noel Program for the Disabled

PO Box 997
Boiling Springs, NC 28017
http://www.gardner-webb.edu/

Contact: Ms. Cheryl Jenks Potter, Director of Noel Program for the Disabled. Phone: 704-406-4271. Fax: 704-406-3524. E-mail: cpotter@gardner-webb.edu.

Noel Program for the Disabled Approximately 101 registered undergraduate students were served during 2002-03. The program or unit includes 9 full-time staff members and 1 part-time staff member. LD specialists are provided through the program or unit. LD specialists are provided collaboratively through on-campus or off-campus services.

Orientation The program or unit offers an optional 2-hour orientation for new students before classes begin.

Unique Aids and Services Aids, services, or accommodations include career counseling, priority registration, weekly meetings with faculty, books on tape, readers, note-takers, books scanned on CD.

Subject-area Tutoring Tutoring is offered one-on-one, in small groups, and in class-size groups for all subjects. Tutoring is provided collaboratively through on-campus or off-campus services via graduate assistants/students.

Basic Skills Remediation Remediation is offered in class-size groups for math, reading, and written language. Remediation is provided collaboratively through on-campus or off-campus services via regular education teachers.

Enrichment Enrichment programs are available through the program or unit for career planning and study skills. Programs for career planning, college survival skills, math, reading, and written composition skills are provided collaboratively through on-campus or off-campus services.

Application For admittance to the program or unit, students are required to provide a psychoeducational report (3 years old or less). Upon application, materials documenting need for services should be sent only to the LD program or unit. Upon acceptance, documentation of need for services should be sent only to the LD program or unit. *Application deadline (institutional):* Continuous. *Application deadline (LD program):* Rolling/continuous for fall and rolling/continuous for spring.

Written Policies Written policy regarding general/basic LD accommodations is available on the program Web site. Written policy regarding general/basic LD accommodations is outlined in the school's catalog/handbook. Written policies regarding course substitutions, general/basic LD accommodations, reduced course loads, and substitutions and waivers of admissions requirements are available through the program or unit directly.

Geneva College

3200 College Avenue
Beaver Falls, PA 15010-3599
http://www.geneva.edu/

Geneva College (continued)

Contact: Mrs. Nancy I. Smith, Director of Student Support Services. Phone: 724-847-5566. Fax: 724-847-6991. E-mail: nismith@geneva.edu.

Approximately 70 registered undergraduate students were served during 2002–03. The program or unit includes 1 full-time and 1 part-time staff member. Trained peer tutors are provided through the program or unit. Academic advisers, regular education teachers, remediation/learning specialists, and trained peer tutors are provided collaboratively through on-campus or off-campus services.

Subject-area Tutoring Tutoring is offered one-on-one, in small groups, and in class-size groups for most subjects. Tutoring is provided through the program or unit via graduate assistants/students and trained peer tutors.

Diagnostic Testing Testing is provided through the program or unit for learning strategies and study skills. Testing for learning styles and math is provided collaboratively through on-campus or off-campus services.

Enrichment Programs for career planning, college survival skills, math, reading, and written composition skills are provided collaboratively through on-campus or off-campus services. Credit is offered for career planning, college survival skills, math, reading, and written composition skills.

Application For admittance to the program or unit, students are required to provide a psychoeducational report (3 years old or less). It is recommended that students provide documentation of high school services. Upon application, materials documenting need for services should be sent to both admissions and the LD program or unit. Upon acceptance, documentation of need for services should be sent only to the LD program or unit. *Application deadline (institutional):* Continuous. *Application deadline (LD program):* Rolling/continuous for fall and rolling/continuous for spring.

Written Policies Written policy regarding general/basic LD accommodations is outlined in the school's catalog/handbook. Written policy regarding general/basic LD accommodations is available through the program or unit directly.

Georgetown University
Learning and Disability Support Services

37th and O Streets, NW
Washington, DC 20057
http://www.georgetown.edu/
Contact: Phone: 202-687-5055. Fax: 202-687-6660.

Learning and Disability Support Services The program or unit includes 3 full-time staff members. LD specialists are provided through the program or unit. Academic advisers, counselors, regular education teachers, and other are provided collaboratively through on-campus or off-campus services.

Orientation The program or unit offers an optional 1-hour orientation for new students during freshman orientation.

Subject-area Tutoring Tutoring is offered for some subjects. Tutoring is provided collaboratively through on-campus or off-campus services via professional tutors and trained peer tutors.

Basic Skills Remediation Remediation is offered one-on-one and in small groups for study skills, time management, and written language. Remediation is provided collaboratively through on-campus or off-campus services via regular education teachers.

Enrichment Programs for learning strategies, study skills, test taking, time management, and written composition skills are provided collaboratively through on-campus or off-campus services.

Application For admittance to the program or unit, students are required to provide a psychoeducational report (3 years old or less). Upon acceptance, documentation of need for services should be sent only to the LD program or unit. *Application deadline (institutional):* 1/10.

Written Policies Written policy regarding general/basic LD accommodations is available on the program Web site. Written policy regarding general/basic LD accommodations is outlined in the school's catalog/handbook. Written policy regarding general/basic LD accommodations is available through the program or unit directly.

The George Washington University

2121 Eye Street, NW
Washington, DC 20052
http://www.gwu.edu/
Contact: Phone: 202-994-1000.

The program or unit includes 6 full-time and 4 part-time staff members. LD specialists and strategy tutors are provided through the program or unit. Academic advisers, counselors, graduate assistants/students, LD specialists, professional tutors, skill tutors, and trained peer tutors are provided collaboratively through on-campus or off-campus services.

Orientation The program or unit offers a mandatory orientation for new students after classes begin.

Unique Aids and Services Aids, services, or accommodations include advocates, career counseling, digital textbooks, faculty training, priority registration, support groups, and weekly meetings with faculty.

Subject-area Tutoring Tutoring is offered one-on-one for all subjects. Tutoring is provided collaboratively through on-campus or off-campus services via graduate assistants/students, professional tutors, and trained peer tutors.

Enrichment Enrichment programs are available through the program or unit for college survival skills, learning strategies, oral communication skills, reading, self-advocacy, stress management, study skills, test taking, time management, and written composition skills. Programs for career planning, college survival skills, health and nutrition, learning strategies, math, practical computer skills, stress management, study skills, test taking, time management, and written composition skills are provided collaboratively through on-campus or off-campus services.

Application For admittance to the program or unit, students are required to provide a psychoeducational report (3 years old or less). It is recommended that students provide documentation of high school services. Upon acceptance, documentation of need for services should be sent only to the LD program or unit. *Application deadline (institutional):* 1/15. *Application deadline (LD program):* Rolling/continuous for fall and rolling/continuous for spring.

Written Policies Written policy regarding general/basic LD accommodations is available on the program Web site. Written policy regarding reduced course loads is outlined in the school's catalog/handbook. Written policy regarding course substitutions is available through the program or unit directly.

Georgia Southwestern State University

800 Wheatley Street

Americus, GA 31709-4693

http://www.gsw.edu/

Contact: Disability Coordinator. Phone: 229-931-2294. Fax: 229-931-2832. Head of LD Program: Mr. John T. Spencer, Director. Phone: 229-931-2295. Fax: 229-931-2832. E-mail: jts@canes.gsw.edu.

Approximately 20 registered undergraduate students were served during 2002-03. The program or unit includes 1 full-time staff member. Academic advisers and skill tutors are provided through the program or unit. Coaches, counselors, and diagnostic specialists are provided collaboratively through on-campus or off-campus services.

Unique Aids and Services Aids, services, or accommodations include digital textbooks and faculty training.

Subject-area Tutoring Tutoring is offered one-on-one for most subjects. Tutoring is provided through the program or unit via trained peer tutors. Tutoring is also provided collaboratively through on-campus or off-campus services via trained peer tutors.

Application For admittance to the program or unit, students are required to apply to the program directly and provide a psychoeducational report. It is recommended that students provide documentation of high school services. Upon acceptance, documentation of need for services should be sent only to the LD program or unit. *Application deadline (institutional):* Continuous. *Application deadline (LD program):* Rolling/continuous for fall and rolling/continuous for spring.

Written Policies Written policy regarding grade forgiveness is outlined in the school's catalog/handbook. Written policies regarding course substitutions, general/basic LD accommodations, reduced course loads, and substitutions and waivers of graduation requirements are available through the program or unit directly.

Georgia State University

University Plaza

Atlanta, GA 30303-3083

http://www.gsu.edu/

Contact: Ms. Caroline E. Gergely, Director of Disability Services. Phone: 404-463-9044. Fax: 404-463-9049. E-mail: cgergely@gsu.edu.

The program or unit includes 3 full-time and 6 part-time staff members. LD specialists, skill tutors, and strategy tutors are provided through the program or unit. Academic advisers, counselors, diagnostic specialists, professional tutors, regular education teachers, remediation/learning specialists, skill tutors, and strategy tutors are provided collaboratively through on-campus or off-campus services.

Unique Aids and Services Aids, services, or accommodations include career counseling, faculty training, and priority registration.

Subject-area Tutoring Tutoring is offered one-on-one for some subjects. Tutoring is provided through the program or unit via LD specialists. Tutoring is also provided collaboratively through on-campus or off-campus services via graduate assistants/students and trained peer tutors.

Diagnostic Testing Testing for auditory processing, handwriting, intelligence, math, motor skills, neuropsychological, personality, reading, spelling, spoken language, visual processing, and written language is provided collaboratively through on-campus or off-campus services.

Enrichment Enrichment programs are available through the program or unit for college survival skills, learning strategies, self-advocacy, stress management, study skills, test taking, and time management. Programs for stress management and study skills are provided collaboratively through on-campus or off-campus services.

Fees *Diagnostic Testing* fee is $400.

Application For admittance to the program or unit, students are required to provide a psychoeducational report and provide LD evaluation results meeting Board of Regents guidelines and using adult norms. Upon acceptance, documentation of need for services should be sent only to the LD program or unit. *Application deadline (institutional):* 4/1. *Application deadline (LD program):* Rolling/continuous for fall and rolling/continuous for spring.

Written Policies Written policy regarding general/basic LD accommodations is available on the program Web site. Written policies regarding course substitutions and general/basic LD accommodations are available through the program or unit directly.

Glenville State College

200 High Street

Glenville, WV 26351-1200

http://www.glenville.edu/

Contact: Mr. Daniel A. Reed, Director. Phone: 304-462-7361. Fax: 304-462-7495. E-mail: reed@glenville.edu.

Approximately 21 registered undergraduate students were served during 2002-03. The program or unit includes 2 full-time staff members. Academic advisers, counselors, and trained peer tutors are provided through the program or unit.

Unique Aids and Services Aids, services, or accommodations include advocates and career counseling.

Subject-area Tutoring Tutoring is offered one-on-one and in small groups for all subjects. Tutoring is provided collaboratively through on-campus or off-campus services via trained peer tutors.

Application For admittance to the program or unit, students are required to apply to the program directly, provide a psychoeducational report (3 years old or less), provide documentation of high school services, and provide psychological report or medical report with original signatures. Upon application, materials documenting need for services should be sent only to the LD program or unit. Upon acceptance, documentation of need for services should be sent only to the LD program or unit. *Application deadline (institutional):* 8/1. *Application deadline (LD program):* Rolling/continuous for fall and rolling/continuous for spring.

Written Policies Written policy regarding general/basic LD accommodations is available on the program Web site. Written policy regarding general/basic LD accommodations is outlined in the school's catalog/handbook.

Gonzaga University
Disabilities Support Services

502 East Boone Avenue
Spokane, WA 99258
http://www.gonzaga.edu/campus+resources/offices+A-Z/
disabilities+support+services

Contact: Kathryne M. Shearer, Director of Disabilities
Support Services. Phone: 509-323-4134. Fax:
509-323-5523. E-mail: shearer@gonzaga.edu.

Disabilities Support Services Approximately 65 registered undergraduate students were served during 2002-03. The program or unit includes 3 full-time staff members. Graduate assistants/students are provided through the program or unit. Academic advisers, counselors, diagnostic specialists, skill tutors, and strategy tutors are provided collaboratively through on-campus or off-campus services.
Orientation The program or unit offers a mandatory 2-hour orientation for new students individually by special arrangement.
Unique Aids and Services Aids, services, or accommodations include advocates, career counseling, digital textbooks, faculty training, and priority registration.
Enrichment Enrichment programs are available through the program or unit for self-advocacy. Programs for career planning, college survival skills, health and nutrition, learning strategies, medication management, stress management, study skills, test taking, time management, and written composition skills are provided collaboratively through on-campus or off-campus services. Credit is offered for written composition skills.
Application For admittance to the program or unit, students are required to provide a psychoeducational report. It is recommended that students provide documentation of high school services. Upon application, materials documenting need for services should be sent only to the LD program or unit. Upon acceptance, documentation of need for services should be sent only to the LD program or unit. *Application deadline (institutional):* 2/1. *Application deadline (LD program):* Rolling/continuous for fall and rolling/continuous for spring.
Written Policies Written policy regarding general/basic LD accommodations is available on the program Web site. Written policy regarding general/basic LD accommodations is outlined in the school's catalog/handbook. Written policies regarding course substitutions, general/basic LD accommodations, reduced course loads, and substitutions and waivers of graduation requirements are available through the program or unit directly.

Gordon College
Academic Support Center

255 Grapevine Road
Wenham, MA 01984-1899
http://www.gordon.edu/

Contact: Chris Underation, Public Relations Specialist.
Phone: 978-927-2300 Ext. 4037. Fax: 978-867-4648. E-mail:
cunderation@hope.gordon.edu. Head of LD Program: Ann
Seavey, Director, Academic Support Center. Fax:
978-867-4648.

Academic Support Center Approximately 64 registered undergraduate students were served during 2002-03. The program or unit includes 2 full-time and 2 part-time staff members. Academic advisers, counselors, regular education teachers, skill tutors, strategy tutors, and trained peer tutors are provided through the program or unit.
Orientation The program or unit offers an optional approximately 1-hour orientation for new students individually by special arrangement.
Unique Aids and Services Aids, services, or accommodations include personal coach, regular meetings with tutors and/or staff.
Subject-area Tutoring Tutoring is offered one-on-one, in small groups, and in class-size groups for some subjects. Tutoring is provided through the program or unit via computer-based instruction, professional tutors, and trained peer tutors.
Basic Skills Remediation Remediation is offered one-on-one and in small groups for learning strategies, math, reading, study skills, time management, and others (check with ASC for offerings). Remediation is provided through the program or unit via LD specialists.
Enrichment Enrichment programs are available through the program or unit for learning strategies, study skills, test taking, and time management.
Application It is recommended that students provide documentation of high school services and provide disclosure of LD needs during the application process. Upon acceptance, documentation of need for services should be sent only to the LD program or unit. *Application deadline (institutional):* Continuous. *Application deadline (LD program):* Rolling/continuous for fall and rolling/continuous for spring.
Written Policies Written policies regarding general/basic LD accommodations and reduced course loads are available on the program Web site. Written policies regarding general/basic LD accommodations and reduced course loads are outlined in the school's catalog/handbook.

Governors State University
Disability Services

One University Parkway
University Park, IL 60466-0975
http://www.govst.edu/

Contact: Mrs. Robin Sweeney, Coordinator of Disability
Services. Phone: 708-235-3968. E-mail:
r-sweeney@govst.edu.

Disability Services Approximately 10 registered undergraduate students were served during 2002-03. The program or unit includes 1 full-time staff member. Academic advisers, counselors, graduate assistants/students, regular education teachers, trained peer tutors, and other are provided collaboratively through on-campus or off-campus services.
Unique Aids and Services Aids, services, or accommodations include career counseling, digital textbooks, and faculty training.
Subject-area Tutoring Tutoring is offered one-on-one, in small groups, and in class-size groups for some subjects. Tutoring is provided through the program or unit via graduate assistants/students, professional tutors, and other. Tutoring is also provided collaboratively through on-campus or off-campus services via graduate assistants/students, professional tutors, and other.

Diagnostic Testing Testing is provided through the program or unit for math and written language.

Application For admittance to the program or unit, students are required to provide a psychoeducational report. Upon application, materials documenting need for services should be sent only to the LD program or unit. Upon acceptance, documentation of need for services should be sent only to the LD program or unit. *Application deadline (LD program):* Rolling/continuous for fall and rolling/continuous for spring.

Written Policies Written policy regarding general/basic LD accommodations is available through the program or unit directly.

Grace College
Student Academic Achievement Center (SAAC)

200 Seminary Drive
Winona Lake, IN 46590-1294
http://www.grace.edu/
Contact: Mrs. Peggy S. Underwood, Director. Phone: 574-372-5100 Ext. 6422. E-mail: underwoodps@grace.edu.

Student Academic Achievement Center (SAAC) Approximately 21 registered undergraduate students were served during 2002-03. The program or unit includes 2 full-time staff members. Counselors, professional tutors, skill tutors, strategy tutors, and trained peer tutors are provided through the program or unit. Academic advisers, coaches, regular education teachers, and special education teachers are provided collaboratively through on-campus or off-campus services.

Unique Aids and Services Aids, services, or accommodations include career counseling and personal coach.

Subject-area Tutoring Tutoring is offered one-on-one and in small groups for most subjects. Tutoring is provided through the program or unit via trained peer tutors.

Diagnostic Testing Testing is provided through the program or unit.

Basic Skills Remediation Remediation is offered in class-size groups for computer skills, learning strategies, math, spelling, study skills, time management, and written language. Remediation is provided through the program or unit via trained peer tutors. Remediation is also provided collaboratively through on-campus or off-campus services via regular education teachers.

Application For admittance to the program or unit, students are required to provide a psychoeducational report (5 years old or less). It is recommended that students provide documentation of high school services. Upon acceptance, documentation of need for services should be sent only to the LD program or unit. *Application deadline (institutional):* 8/1. *Application deadline (LD program):* 5/1 for fall. 12/5 for spring.

Written Policies Written policy regarding grade forgiveness is outlined in the school's catalog/handbook. Written policy regarding general/basic LD accommodations is available through the program or unit directly.

Grace University

1311 South Ninth Street
Omaha, NE 68108
http://www.graceuniversity.edu/
Contact: Christi Jensen, Dean of Women. Phone: 402-449-2800 Ext. 2849. Fax: 402-341-9587. E-mail: cjensen@graceu.edu.

Approximately 5 registered undergraduate students were served during 2002-03. The program or unit includes 2 part-time staff members. Trained peer tutors and other are provided collaboratively through on-campus or off-campus services.

Orientation The program or unit offers an optional orientation for new students individually by special arrangement.

Unique Aids and Services Aids, services, or accommodations include large print or audio textbooks, faculty adviser.

Subject-area Tutoring Tutoring is offered one-on-one for most subjects. Tutoring is provided collaboratively through on-campus or off-campus services via graduate assistants/students, trained peer tutors, and other.

Basic Skills Remediation Remediation is offered one-on-one for study skills and time management. Remediation is provided collaboratively through on-campus or off-campus services via trained peer tutors and other.

Application For admittance to the program or unit, students are required to provide a psychoeducational report and provide medical or professional documentation. It is recommended that students provide documentation of high school services. Upon application, materials documenting need for services should be sent only to admissions with institutional application materials. Upon acceptance, documentation of need for services should be sent only to the LD program or unit. *Application deadline (institutional):* Continuous. *Application deadline (LD program):* Rolling/continuous for fall and rolling/continuous for spring.

Written Policies Written policy regarding general/basic LD accommodations is outlined in the school's catalog/handbook. Written policy regarding general/basic LD accommodations is available through the program or unit directly.

Grand Canyon University

3300 W Camelback Road, PO Box 11097
Phoenix, AZ 85017-1097
http://www.grand-canyon.edu/
Contact: Mrs. Gail Marie Weide, Student Disability Services Coordinator. Phone: 602-589-2047. Fax: 602-589-2759. E-mail: gweide@grand-canyon.edu.

Approximately 15 registered undergraduate students were served during 2002-03. The program or unit includes 1 part-time staff member. Regular education teachers and other are provided through the program or unit. Regular education teachers and other are provided collaboratively through on-campus or off-campus services.

Orientation The program or unit offers an optional orientation for new students individually by special arrangement.

Subject-area Tutoring Tutoring is offered one-on-one and in small groups for most subjects. Tutoring is provided collaboratively through on-campus or off-campus services via trained peer tutors.

Diagnostic Testing Testing for neuropsychological is provided collaboratively through on-campus or off-campus services.

Grand Canyon University (continued)

Enrichment Programs for career planning, college survival skills, health and nutrition, medication management, stress management, study skills, test taking, and time management are provided collaboratively through on-campus or off-campus services.

Fees *Diagnostic Testing* fee is $375.

Application For admittance to the program or unit, students are required to apply to the program directly and provide a psychoeducational report (10 years old or less). It is recommended that students provide documentation of high school services. Upon application, materials documenting need for services should be sent only to the LD program or unit. Upon acceptance, documentation of need for services should be sent only to the LD program or unit. *Application deadline (institutional):* Continuous. *Application deadline (LD program):* 8/1 for fall. 1/5 for spring.

Written Policies Written policies regarding general/basic LD accommodations, grade forgiveness, reduced course loads, substitutions and waivers of admissions requirements, and substitutions and waivers of graduation requirements are outlined in the school's catalog/handbook. Written policies regarding general/basic LD accommodations and substitutions and waivers of admissions requirements are available through the program or unit directly.

Grand View College

1200 Grandview Avenue

Des Moines, IA 50316-1599

http://www.gvc.edu/

Contact: Mrs. Carolyn M. Wassenaar, Director of Academic Success. Phone: 515-263-2971. Fax: 515-263-2971.

Approximately 10 registered undergraduate students were served during 2002-03. The program or unit includes 1 full-time staff member. Academic advisers, remediation/learning specialists, and trained peer tutors are provided collaboratively through on-campus or off-campus services.

Unique Aids and Services Aids, services, or accommodations include digital textbooks, Director of Academic Success advising and support.

Subject-area Tutoring Tutoring is offered one-on-one and in small groups for most subjects. Tutoring is provided collaboratively through on-campus or off-campus services via trained peer tutors.

Diagnostic Testing Testing for learning strategies, learning styles, math, reading, spelling, and study skills is provided collaboratively through on-campus or off-campus services.

Basic Skills Remediation Remediation is offered one-on-one, in small groups, and in class-size groups for learning strategies, math, reading, study skills, time management, and elements of English (grammar). Remediation is provided collaboratively through on-campus or off-campus services via LD specialists.

Enrichment Programs for career planning, college survival skills, health and nutrition, math, reading, self-advocacy, stress management, study skills, test taking, time management, vocabulary development, and written composition skills are provided collaboratively through on-campus or off-campus services. Credit is offered for college survival skills, health and nutrition, math, reading, and written composition skills.

Application For admittance to the program or unit, students are required to provide a psychoeducational report (3 years old or less). It is recommended that students provide documentation of high school services. Upon acceptance, documentation of need for services should be sent only to the LD program or unit. *Application deadline (institutional):* 8/15. *Application deadline (LD program):* Rolling/continuous for fall and rolling/continuous for spring.

Written Policies Written policy regarding general/basic LD accommodations is available on the program Web site. Written policies regarding general/basic LD accommodations and substitutions and waivers of admissions requirements are outlined in the school's catalog/handbook.

Green Mountain College
Calhoun Learning Center

One College Circle

Poultney, VT 05764-1199

http://www.greenmtn.edu/

Contact: Mrs. Nancy D. Ruby, Director of Academic Support Services. Phone: 802-287-8287 Ext. 8287. Fax: 802-287-8282. E-mail: rubyn@greenmtn.edu.

Calhoun Learning Center Approximately 85 registered undergraduate students were served during 2002-03. The program or unit includes 2 full-time and 2 part-time staff members. Remediation/learning specialists, strategy tutors, and trained peer tutors are provided through the program or unit.

Unique Aids and Services Aids, services, or accommodations include career counseling, faculty training, and support groups.

Subject-area Tutoring Tutoring is offered one-on-one and in small groups for most subjects. Tutoring is provided through the program or unit via LD specialists and trained peer tutors.

Diagnostic Testing Testing is provided through the program or unit for learning strategies, learning styles, math, and other services.

Basic Skills Remediation Remediation is offered one-on-one, in small groups, and in class-size groups for learning strategies, math, reading, social skills, spelling, study skills, time management, and written language. Remediation is provided through the program or unit via LD specialists and trained peer tutors.

Enrichment Enrichment programs are available through the program or unit for college survival skills, learning strategies, math, practical computer skills, reading, self-advocacy, stress management, study skills, test taking, time management, and written composition skills. Programs for career planning, health and nutrition, medication management, practical computer skills, stress management, and written composition skills are provided collaboratively through on-campus or off-campus services.

Student Organization Self Advocacy Group consists of 8 members.

Application For admittance to the program or unit, students are required to provide a psychoeducational report (3 years old or less). It is recommended that students apply to the program directly and provide documentation of high school services. Upon application, materials documenting need for services should be sent only to the LD program or unit. Upon acceptance, documentation of need for services should be sent only to the LD program or unit. *Application deadline (institutional):* Continuous. *Application deadline (LD program):* Rolling/continuous for fall and rolling/continuous for spring.

Written Policies Written policy regarding general/basic LD accommodations is available on the program Web site. Written policy regarding general/basic LD accommodations is outlined in the school's catalog/handbook.

Greensboro College

815 West Market Street

Greensboro, NC 27401-1875

http://www.gborocollege.edu/

Contact: Ms. Julie Yindra, Learning Disabilities Specialist. Phone: 336-272-7102 Ext. 591. Fax: 336-271-6634. E-mail: jyindra@gborocollege.edu.

Approximately 130 registered undergraduate students were served during 2002-03. The program or unit includes 2 full-time staff members and 1 part-time staff member. Academic advisers, counselors, diagnostic specialists, LD specialists, remediation/learning specialists, and strategy tutors are provided through the program or unit. Academic advisers, coaches, professional tutors, regular education teachers, skill tutors, and trained peer tutors are provided collaboratively through on-campus or off-campus services.

Orientation The program or unit offers an optional orientation for new students before classes begin, during summer prior to enrollment, during registration, and individually by special arrangement.

Unique Aids and Services Aids, services, or accommodations include advocates, career counseling, faculty training, and weekly meetings with faculty.

Subject-area Tutoring Tutoring is offered one-on-one for most subjects. Tutoring is provided through the program or unit via computer-based instruction and LD specialists. Tutoring is also provided collaboratively through on-campus or off-campus services via professional tutors and trained peer tutors.

Diagnostic Testing Testing is provided through the program or unit for learning strategies, learning styles, and study skills. Testing for auditory processing, handwriting, intelligence, math, motor skills, neuropsychological, personality, reading, spoken language, visual processing, and written language is provided collaboratively through on-campus or off-campus services.

Basic Skills Remediation Remediation is offered one-on-one for learning strategies, math, reading, study skills, time management, written language, and self-advocacy skills. Remediation is provided through the program or unit via computer-based instruction and LD specialists. Remediation is also provided collaboratively through on-campus or off-campus services via professional tutors.

Enrichment Enrichment programs are available through the program or unit for college survival skills, learning strategies, medication management, reading, self-advocacy, stress management, study skills, test taking, and time management. Programs for career planning, health and nutrition, math, and written composition skills are provided collaboratively through on-campus or off-campus services. Credit is offered for college survival skills.

Fees *Diagnostic Testing* fee is applicable.

Application For admittance to the program or unit, students are required to provide additional documentation based on the nature and scope of the disability. It is recommended that students provide a psychoeducational report (3 years old or less) and provide documentation of high school services. Upon application, materials documenting need for services should be sent only to the LD program or unit. Upon acceptance, documentation of need for services should be sent only to the LD program or unit. *Application deadline (institutional):* Continuous. *Application deadline (LD program):* Rolling/continuous for fall and rolling/continuous for spring.

Written Policies Written policy regarding general/basic LD accommodations is available on the program Web site. Written policies regarding course substitutions, general/basic LD accommodations, and substitutions and waivers of graduation requirements are outlined in the school's catalog/handbook. Written policies regarding course substitutions, general/basic LD accommodations, and substitutions and waivers of graduation requirements are available through the program or unit directly.

Grinnell College
Academic Advising Office

1121 Park Street

Grinnell, IA 50112-1690

http://www.grinnell.edu/offices/studentaffairs/acadadvising/disabilityservices/

Contact: Ms. Joyce M. Stern, Associate Dean and Director of Academic Advising. Phone: 641-269-3702. Fax: 641-269-3710. E-mail: sternjm@grinnell.edu.

Academic Advising Office Approximately 34 registered undergraduate students were served during 2002-03. The program or unit includes 1 part-time staff member. Academic advisers, counselors, professional tutors, skill tutors, and strategy tutors are provided collaboratively through on-campus or off-campus services.

Subject-area Tutoring Tutoring is offered one-on-one, in small groups, and in class-size groups for all subjects. Tutoring is provided collaboratively through on-campus or off-campus services via graduate assistants/students, professional tutors, and trained peer tutors.

Enrichment Programs for career planning, learning strategies, math, reading, study skills, test taking, and vocabulary development are provided collaboratively through on-campus or off-campus services.

Application For admittance to the program or unit, students are required to provide a psychoeducational report and provide other documentation (contact office for specific guidelines). It is recommended that students provide documentation of high school services. Upon application, materials documenting need for services should be sent only to the LD program or unit. Upon acceptance, documentation of need for services should be sent only to the LD program or unit. *Application deadline (institutional):* 1/20. *Application deadline (LD program):* Rolling/continuous for fall and rolling/continuous for spring.

Written Policies Written policy regarding general/basic LD accommodations is available on the program Web site. Written policy regarding general/basic LD accommodations is outlined in the school's catalog/handbook.

Guilford College

5800 West Friendly Avenue

Guilford College (continued)
Greensboro, NC 27410-4173
http://www.guilford.edu/
Contact: Dr. Sue Keith, Director of the Academic Skills Center. Phone: 336-316-2200. Fax: 336-316-2950. E-mail: skeith@guilford.edu. Head of LD Program: Kim Sellick, Alternative Learning Specialist. Phone: 336-316-2145. Fax: 336-316-2950. E-mail: ksellick@guilford.edu.

Approximately 265 registered undergraduate students were served during 2002-03. The program or unit includes 2 full-time and 3 part-time staff members. LD specialists, remediation/learning specialists, skill tutors, strategy tutors, and trained peer tutors are provided through the program or unit. Academic advisers, coaches, counselors, professional tutors, and regular education teachers are provided collaboratively through on-campus or off-campus services.
Orientation The program or unit offers an optional orientation for new students.
Unique Aids and Services Aids, services, or accommodations include career counseling, faculty training, personal coach, support groups, weekly meetings with faculty, Kurzweil Reader.
Subject-area Tutoring Tutoring is offered one-on-one, in small groups, and in class-size groups for most subjects. Tutoring is provided through the program or unit via LD specialists, professional tutors, and trained peer tutors. Tutoring is also provided collaboratively through on-campus or off-campus services via computer-based instruction.
Basic Skills Remediation Remediation is offered one-on-one, in small groups, and in class-size groups for learning strategies, reading, study skills, time management, and written language. Remediation is provided through the program or unit via LD specialists. Remediation is also provided collaboratively through on-campus or off-campus services via computer-based instruction, professional tutors, and trained peer tutors.
Enrichment Enrichment programs are available through the program or unit for college survival skills, learning strategies, reading, and study skills. Programs for career planning, practical computer skills, stress management, study skills, test taking, time management, vocabulary development, and written composition skills are provided collaboratively through on-campus or off-campus services. Credit is offered for college survival skills, learning strategies, reading, and study skills.
Student Organization LD Support Group.
Application For admittance to the program or unit, students are required to provide a psychoeducational report. Upon application, materials documenting need for services should be sent only to admissions with institutional application materials. *Application deadline (institutional):* 2/15.
Written Policies Written policy regarding general/basic LD accommodations is available on the program Web site. Written policy regarding general/basic LD accommodations is outlined in the school's catalog/handbook. Written policy regarding course substitutions is available through the program or unit directly.

Hamilton College

198 College Hill Road
Clinton, NY 13323-1296
http://www.hamilton.edu/

Contact: Ms. Nancy Rath Thompson, Senior Associate Dean of Students. Phone: 315-859-4022. Fax: 315-859-4077. E-mail: nthompso@hamilton.edu.

Approximately 40 registered undergraduate students were served during 2002-03. The program or unit includes 1 part-time staff member. Academic advisers, coaches, counselors, diagnostic specialists, skill tutors, and trained peer tutors are provided collaboratively through on-campus or off-campus services.
Subject-area Tutoring Tutoring is offered one-on-one and in small groups for some subjects. Tutoring is provided collaboratively through on-campus or off-campus services via trained peer tutors and other.
Application For admittance to the program or unit, students are required to provide a psychoeducational report (3 years old or less). Upon acceptance, documentation of need for services should be sent only to the LD program or unit. *Application deadline (institutional):* 1/15. *Application deadline (LD program):* Rolling/continuous for fall and rolling/continuous for spring.
Written Policies Written policy regarding general/basic LD accommodations is available on the program Web site. Written policy regarding general/basic LD accommodations is outlined in the school's catalog/handbook.

Hampden-Sydney College
Office of Academic Success

PO Box 667
Hampden-Sydney, VA 23943
http://www.hsc.edu/academics/success/
Contact: Mrs. Elizabeth Mccormack Ford, Associate Dean for Academic Support. Phone: 434-223-6286. Fax: 434-223-6347. E-mail: eford@hsc.edu.

Office of Academic Success Approximately 100 registered undergraduate students were served during 2002-03. The program or unit includes 1 full-time and 1 part-time staff member. Diagnostic specialists are provided through the program or unit. Academic advisers, counselors, and trained peer tutors are provided collaboratively through on-campus or off-campus services.
Subject-area Tutoring Tutoring is offered one-on-one and in small groups for most subjects. Tutoring is provided through the program or unit via professional tutors and trained peer tutors. Tutoring is also provided collaboratively through on-campus or off-campus services via trained peer tutors.
Enrichment Enrichment programs are available through the program or unit for college survival skills, learning strategies, stress management, study skills, test taking, and time management. Programs for career planning, college survival skills, health and nutrition, learning strategies, oral communication skills, and stress management are provided collaboratively through on-campus or off-campus services. Credit is offered for oral communication skills.
Application For admittance to the program or unit, students are required to provide a psychoeducational report (3 years old or less). It is recommended that students provide documentation of high school services. Upon acceptance, documentation of need for services should be sent only to the LD program or unit. *Application deadline (institutional):* 3/1. *Application deadline (LD program):* Rolling/continuous for fall and rolling/continuous for spring.

Written Policies Written policies regarding course substitutions, general/basic LD accommodations, reduced course loads, and substitutions and waivers of graduation requirements are available on the program Web site. Written policies regarding course substitutions, general/basic LD accommodations, reduced course loads, and substitutions and waivers of graduation requirements are outlined in the school's catalog/handbook. Written policies regarding course substitutions, general/basic LD accommodations, reduced course loads, and substitutions and waivers of graduation requirements are available through the program or unit directly.

Hampshire College
Center for Academic Support and Advising (CASA)

893 West Street
Amherst, MA 01002
http://www.hampshire.edu/cms/index.php?id=1667
Contact: Dr. Peter Cyril Stoll, Disability Service Coordinator. Phone: 413-559-5498. Fax: 413-559-6098. E-mail: pstoll@hampshire.edu.

Center for Academic Support and Advising (CASA) Approximately 80 registered undergraduate students were served during 2002-03. The program or unit includes 1 part-time staff member. LD specialists, skill tutors, and strategy tutors are provided through the program or unit. Academic advisers, counselors, LD specialists, skill tutors, strategy tutors, and trained peer tutors are provided collaboratively through on-campus or off-campus services.

Orientation The program or unit offers an optional orientation for new students before classes begin, during registration, after classes begin, and individually by special arrangement.

Unique Aids and Services Aids, services, or accommodations include advocates, career counseling, digital textbooks, personal coach, assistive technologies.

Subject-area Tutoring Tutoring is offered one-on-one and in small groups for some subjects. Tutoring is provided through the program or unit via LD specialists. Tutoring is also provided collaboratively through on-campus or off-campus services via LD specialists.

Basic Skills Remediation Remediation is offered one-on-one and in small groups for auditory processing, computer skills, learning strategies, motor skills, social skills, study skills, time management, visual processing, and written language. Remediation is provided through the program or unit via LD specialists. Remediation is also provided collaboratively through on-campus or off-campus services via computer-based instruction, regular education teachers, and trained peer tutors.

Enrichment Enrichment programs are available through the program or unit for college survival skills, learning strategies, oral communication skills, reading, self-advocacy, stress management, study skills, test taking, time management, and written composition skills. Programs for career planning, college survival skills, health and nutrition, learning strategies, math, medication management, oral communication skills, practical computer skills, reading, stress management, study skills, test taking, time management, vocabulary development, and written composition skills are provided collaboratively through on-campus or off-campus services. Credit is offered for health and nutrition.

Application For admittance to the program or unit, students are required to provide a psychoeducational report and provide Disability Service Request Form (available through admissions and student affairs). It is recommended that students provide documentation of high school services. Upon acceptance, documentation of need for services should be sent only to the LD program or unit. *Application deadline (institutional):* 2/1. *Application deadline (LD program):* Rolling/continuous for fall and rolling/continuous for spring.

Written Policies Written policy regarding general/basic LD accommodations is available on the program Web site. Written policies regarding general/basic LD accommodations and reduced course loads are available through the program or unit directly.

Hampton University
Office of Section 504 Compliance

Hampton, VA 23668
http://www.hamptonu.edu/
Contact: Ms. Janice Halimah Rashada, Section 504 Compliance Officer. Phone: 757-727-5493. Fax: 757-727-5998. E-mail: janice.rashada@hamptonu.edu.

Office of Section 504 Compliance Approximately 35 registered undergraduate students were served during 2002-03. The program or unit includes 2 full-time staff members. Counselors, regular education teachers, and trained peer tutors are provided collaboratively through on-campus or off-campus services.

Orientation The program or unit offers a mandatory approximately 30-minute orientation for new students individually by special arrangement.

Unique Aids and Services Aids, services, or accommodations include advocates, faculty training, and priority registration.

Subject-area Tutoring Tutoring is offered one-on-one for most subjects. Tutoring is provided collaboratively through on-campus or off-campus services via trained peer tutors.

Basic Skills Remediation Remediation is offered one-on-one, in small groups, and in class-size groups for learning strategies, math, reading, social skills, study skills, time management, and written language. Remediation is provided collaboratively through on-campus or off-campus services via regular education teachers and trained peer tutors.

Enrichment Programs for career planning, college survival skills, health and nutrition, learning strategies, medication management, self-advocacy, stress management, study skills, test taking, and time management are provided collaboratively through on-campus or off-campus services.

Application For admittance to the program or unit, students are required to provide a psychoeducational report (3 years old or less). Upon acceptance, documentation of need for services should be sent only to the LD program or unit. *Application deadline (institutional):* 3/1. *Application deadline (LD program):* Rolling/continuous for fall and rolling/continuous for spring.

Written Policies Written policy regarding general/basic LD accommodations is available on the program Web site. Written policy regarding general/basic LD accommodations is available through the program or unit directly.

Harding University
Student Support Services

900 East Center
Searcy, AR 72149-0001
http://www.harding.edu/

Contact: Mrs. Teresa McLeod, Disabilities Specialist and Counselor. Phone: 501-279-4019. Fax: 501-279-4217. E-mail: tmcleod@harding.edu.

Student Support Services Approximately 150 registered undergraduate students were served during 2002-03. The program or unit includes 6 full-time and 16 part-time staff members. Academic advisers, counselors, graduate assistants/students, LD specialists, skill tutors, and trained peer tutors are provided through the program or unit.

Unique Aids and Services Aids, services, or accommodations include career counseling, faculty training, personal coach, and priority registration.

Subject-area Tutoring Tutoring is offered one-on-one, in small groups, and in class-size groups for all subjects. Tutoring is provided through the program or unit via computer-based instruction, graduate assistants/students, and trained peer tutors. Tutoring is also provided collaboratively through on-campus or off-campus services via LD specialists.

Basic Skills Remediation Remediation is offered one-on-one, in small groups, and in class-size groups for learning strategies, math, reading, spelling, study skills, time management, and written language. Remediation is provided collaboratively through on-campus or off-campus services via computer-based instruction, graduate assistants/students, regular education teachers, and trained peer tutors.

Enrichment Programs for career planning, college survival skills, learning strategies, math, reading, study skills, test taking, time management, vocabulary development, and written composition skills are provided collaboratively through on-campus or off-campus services.

Application For admittance to the program or unit, students are required to apply to the program directly and provide a psychoeducational report (1 year old or less). It is recommended that students provide documentation of high school services. Upon acceptance, documentation of need for services should be sent to both admissions and the LD program or unit. *Application deadline (institutional):* 7/1. *Application deadline (LD program):* Rolling/continuous for fall and rolling/continuous for spring.

Written Policies Written policy regarding general/basic LD accommodations is available on the program Web site. Written policy regarding general/basic LD accommodations is outlined in the school's catalog/handbook.

Hastings College

800 North Turner Avenue
Hastings, NE 68901-7696
http://www.hastings.edu/

Contact: Dr. Kathleen M. Haverly, Learning Center Director. Phone: 402-461-7386 Ext. 7386. Fax: 402-461-7480. E-mail: khaverly@hastings.edu.

The program or unit includes 1 full-time and 1 part-time staff member. Academic advisers, counselors, graduate assistants/students, LD specialists, remediation/learning specialists, skill tutors, strategy tutors, and trained peer tutors are provided through the program or unit. Academic advisers, counselors, and regular education teachers are provided collaboratively through on-campus or off-campus services.

Orientation The program or unit offers a mandatory orientation for new students before registration, before classes begin, during summer prior to enrollment, during registration, after classes begin, and individually by special arrangement.

Unique Aids and Services Aids, services, or accommodations include advocates and career counseling.

Subject-area Tutoring Tutoring is offered one-on-one, in small groups, and in class-size groups for most subjects. Tutoring is provided through the program or unit via computer-based instruction, graduate assistants/students, LD specialists, and trained peer tutors. Tutoring is also provided collaboratively through on-campus or off-campus services via computer-based instruction, graduate assistants/students, and trained peer tutors.

Diagnostic Testing Testing is provided through the program or unit for learning strategies, learning styles, and study skills. Testing for learning styles and personality is provided collaboratively through on-campus or off-campus services.

Basic Skills Remediation Remediation is offered one-on-one, in small groups, and in class-size groups for computer skills, learning strategies, social skills, study skills, time management, and written language. Remediation is provided through the program or unit via graduate assistants/students, LD specialists, regular education teachers, and trained peer tutors. Remediation is also provided collaboratively through on-campus or off-campus services via graduate assistants/students, regular education teachers, and trained peer tutors.

Enrichment Programs for career planning, college survival skills, health and nutrition, learning strategies, oral communication skills, practical computer skills, stress management, study skills, test taking, time management, and written composition skills are provided collaboratively through on-campus or off-campus services. Credit is offered for college survival skills, health and nutrition, learning strategies, oral communication skills, practical computer skills, stress management, study skills, time management, and written composition skills.

Application For admittance to the program or unit, students are required to provide a psychoeducational report (3 years old or less). It is recommended that students provide documentation of high school services. Upon application, materials documenting need for services should be sent only to admissions with institutional application materials. Upon acceptance, documentation of need for services should be sent only to the LD program or unit. *Application deadline (institutional):* 8/1. *Application deadline (LD program):* Rolling/continuous for fall and rolling/continuous for spring.

Written Policies Written policies regarding general/basic LD accommodations, reduced course loads, substitutions and waivers of admissions requirements, and substitutions and waivers of graduation requirements are outlined in the school's catalog/handbook. Written policies regarding general/basic LD accommodations, reduced course loads, substitutions and waivers of admissions requirements, and substitutions and waivers of graduation requirements are available through the program or unit directly.

Haverford College
Office of Disabilities Services

370 Lancaster Avenue
Haverford, PA 19041-1392
http://www.haverford.edu/ods/ods
Contact: Dr. Richard E. Webb, Coordinator of Disabilities
Services. Phone: 610-896-1290. Fax: 610-896-2969.

Office of Disabilities Services Approximately 25 registered undergraduate students were served during 2002-03. The program or unit includes 1 part-time staff member. Academic advisers, coaches, counselors, and trained peer tutors are provided collaboratively through on-campus or off-campus services.

Subject-area Tutoring Tutoring is offered one-on-one for most subjects. Tutoring is provided collaboratively through on-campus or off-campus services via trained peer tutors.

Application For admittance to the program or unit, students are required to provide a psychoeducational report (3 years old or less). It is recommended that students provide documentation of high school services. Upon acceptance, documentation of need for services should be sent only to the LD program or unit. *Application deadline (institutional): 1/15. Application deadline (LD program):* Rolling/continuous for fall and rolling/continuous for spring.

Written Policies Written policies regarding course substitutions, general/basic LD accommodations, reduced course loads, and substitutions and waivers of graduation requirements are available on the program Web site. Written policies regarding course substitutions and substitutions and waivers of graduation requirements are available through the program or unit directly.

Basic Skills Remediation Remediation is offered one-on-one, in small groups, and in class-size groups for computer skills, learning strategies, math, reading, social skills, study skills, time management, and written language. Remediation is provided through the program or unit via professional tutors and trained peer tutors. Remediation is also provided collaboratively through on-campus or off-campus services via computer-based instruction, graduate assistants/students, and regular education teachers.

Enrichment Enrichment programs are available through the program or unit for career planning, college survival skills, learning strategies, math, self-advocacy, stress management, study skills, test taking, and time management. Programs for career planning, college survival skills, health and nutrition, math, oral communication skills, practical computer skills, reading, study skills, vocabulary development, and written composition skills are provided collaboratively through on-campus or off-campus services. Credit is offered for college survival skills, math, oral communication skills, practical computer skills, reading, and written composition skills.

Application For admittance to the program or unit, students are required to apply to the program directly and provide a psychoeducational report (4 years old or less). It is recommended that students provide documentation of high school services. Upon acceptance, documentation of need for services should be sent only to the LD program or unit. *Application deadline (institutional): 7/15. Application deadline (LD program):* Rolling/continuous for fall and rolling/continuous for spring.

Written Policies Written policy regarding general/basic LD accommodations is available on the program Web site. Written policy regarding general/basic LD accommodations is outlined in the school's catalog/handbook. Written policies regarding course substitutions, general/basic LD accommodations, and substitutions and waivers of graduation requirements are available through the program or unit directly.

Henderson State University
Disability Resource Center

1100 Henderson Street
Arkadelphia, AR 71999-0001
http://www.hsu.edu/dept/dis
Contact: Ms. Vickie Faust, Assistant Director. Phone: 870-230-5453. Fax: 870-230-5066. E-mail: faustv@hsu.edu.

Disability Resource Center Approximately 25 registered undergraduate students were served during 2002-03. The program or unit includes 4 full-time staff members. Academic advisers, counselors, LD specialists, skill tutors, strategy tutors, trained peer tutors, and other are provided through the program or unit. Academic advisers, counselors, diagnostic specialists, LD specialists, regular education teachers, and remediation/learning specialists are provided collaboratively through on-campus or off-campus services.

Unique Aids and Services Aids, services, or accommodations include career counseling, digital textbooks, priority registration, and support groups.

Subject-area Tutoring Tutoring is offered one-on-one and in small groups for some subjects. Tutoring is provided through the program or unit via professional tutors and trained peer tutors. Tutoring is also provided collaboratively through on-campus or off-campus services via computer-based instruction and graduate assistants/students.

Hendrix College
Academic Support; Counseling Services

1600 Washington Avenue
Conway, AR 72032-3080
http://www.hendrix.edu/counseling/disab.htm
Contact: Ms. Dionne Jackson, Coordinator of Academic Support. Phone: 501-450-1482. Fax: 501-450-3800. E-mail: jackson@hendrix.edu. Head of LD Program: Mary Anne Seibert PhD, Coordinator of Counseling Services. Phone: 501-450-1448. Fax: 501-450-1324. E-mail: seibert@hendrix.edu.

Academic Support; Counseling Services Approximately 15 registered undergraduate students were served during 2002-03. The program or unit includes 2 full-time staff members. Academic advisers, counselors, diagnostic specialists, LD specialists, professional tutors, remediation/learning specialists, skill tutors, strategy tutors, and trained peer tutors are provided collaboratively through on-campus or off-campus services.

Unique Aids and Services Aids, services, or accommodations include meetings with coordinator of academic support.

Subject-area Tutoring Tutoring is offered one-on-one for all subjects. Tutoring is provided collaboratively through on-campus or off-campus services via LD specialists, professional tutors, and trained peer tutors.

Hendrix College (continued)

Enrichment Programs for career planning, college survival skills, health and nutrition, learning strategies, medication management, oral communication skills, practical computer skills, reading, stress management, study skills, test taking, time management, written composition skills, and other are provided collaboratively through on-campus or off-campus services.

Application For admittance to the program or unit, students are required to provide a psychoeducational report (2 years old or less). It is recommended that students apply to the program directly. Upon application, materials documenting need for services should be sent only to admissions with institutional application materials. Upon acceptance, documentation of need for services should be sent only to the LD program or unit. *Application deadline (institutional):* Continuous. *Application deadline (LD program):* Rolling/continuous for fall and rolling/continuous for spring.

Written Policies Written policy regarding general/basic LD accommodations is available on the program Web site. Written policy regarding general/basic LD accommodations is outlined in the school's catalog/handbook. Written policy regarding general/basic LD accommodations is available through the program or unit directly.

High Point University
Academic Services Center

University Station, Montlieu Avenue
High Point, NC 27262-3598
http://www.highpoint.edu/academics/asc/
Contact: Ms. Kelly Norton, Director of the Academic Services Center. Phone: 336-841-9037. Fax: 336-841-5123. E-mail: knorton@highpoint.edu.

Academic Services Center Approximately 50 registered undergraduate students were served during 2002-03. The program or unit includes 1 full-time and 30 part-time staff members. Graduate assistants/students, LD specialists, remediation/learning specialists, teacher trainees, and trained peer tutors are provided through the program or unit. Academic advisers, counselors, graduate assistants/students, LD specialists, regular education teachers, remediation/learning specialists, teacher trainees, and trained peer tutors are provided collaboratively through on-campus or off-campus services.

Summer Program To help prepare for the demands of college, there is an optional 4-week summer program prior to entering the school. Degree credit will be earned.

Unique Aids and Services Aids, services, or accommodations include faculty training.

Subject-area Tutoring Tutoring is offered one-on-one and in small groups for most subjects. Tutoring is provided through the program or unit via computer-based instruction, graduate assistants/students, LD specialists, and trained peer tutors. Tutoring is also provided collaboratively through on-campus or off-campus services via graduate assistants/students, LD specialists, and trained peer tutors.

Basic Skills Remediation Remediation is offered one-on-one for computer skills, learning strategies, math, reading, spelling, study skills, and time management. Remediation is provided through the program or unit via graduate assistants/students and trained peer tutors. Remediation is also provided collaboratively through on-campus or off-campus services via graduate assistants/students and trained peer tutors.

Enrichment Enrichment programs are available through the program or unit for college survival skills, learning strategies, math, practical computer skills, stress management, study skills, test taking, time management, vocabulary development, and written composition skills. Programs for career planning, college survival skills, health and nutrition, learning strategies, math, reading, stress management, study skills, test taking, time management, vocabulary development, and written composition skills are provided collaboratively through on-campus or off-campus services. Credit is offered for college survival skills, health and nutrition, learning strategies, reading, stress management, study skills, test taking, and time management.

Fees *Summer Program* fee is $1600.

Application For admittance to the program or unit, students are required to provide a psychoeducational report (3 years old or less). It is recommended that students provide documentation of high school services. Upon application, materials documenting need for services should be sent only to the LD program or unit. Upon acceptance, documentation of need for services should be sent only to the LD program or unit. *Application deadline (institutional):* 8/15. *Application deadline (LD program):* Rolling/continuous for fall and rolling/continuous for spring.

Written Policies Written policies regarding course substitutions, general/basic LD accommodations, reduced course loads, and substitutions and waivers of graduation requirements are available on the program Web site. Written policies regarding course substitutions, general/basic LD accommodations, reduced course loads, and substitutions and waivers of graduation requirements are available through the program or unit directly.

Hiram College
Student Disability Services

Box 67
Hiram, OH 44234-0067
http://www.hiram.edu/
Contact: Dr. Lynn B. Taylor, Director of Counseling and Coordinator of Student Disability Services. Phone: 330-569-5952. Fax: 330-569-5398. E-mail: taylorlb@hiram.edu.

Student Disability Services Approximately 18 registered undergraduate students were served during 2002-03. The program or unit includes 1 full-time staff member. Counselors are provided through the program or unit. Academic advisers, coaches, regular education teachers, skill tutors, strategy tutors, and trained peer tutors are provided collaboratively through on-campus or off-campus services.

Subject-area Tutoring Tutoring is offered one-on-one, in small groups, and in class-size groups for all subjects. Tutoring is provided collaboratively through on-campus or off-campus services via trained peer tutors.

Enrichment Programs for career planning, college survival skills, health and nutrition, learning strategies, stress management, study skills, test taking, time management, and written composition skills are provided collaboratively through on-campus or off-campus services. Credit is offered for career planning.

Application For admittance to the program or unit, students are required to provide a psychoeducational report (3 years old or less) and provide documentation of high school services. Upon application, materials documenting need for services should be sent only to admissions with institutional application materials. Upon acceptance, documentation of need for services should be sent only to the LD program or unit. *Application deadline (institutional):* 2/1. *Application deadline (LD program):* Rolling/continuous for fall and rolling/continuous for spring.

Written Policies Written policy regarding general/basic LD accommodations is outlined in the school's catalog/handbook.

Holy Family University

Grant and Frankford Avenues

Philadelphia, PA 19114-2094

http://www.holyfamily.edu/

Contact: Disability Coordinator. Phone: 215-637-7700 Ext. 3232.

Approximately 35 registered undergraduate students were served during 2002-03. The program or unit includes 1 full-time and 1 part-time staff member. Counselors are provided through the program or unit. Academic advisers, professional tutors, and trained peer tutors are provided collaboratively through on-campus or off-campus services.

Unique Aids and Services Aids, services, or accommodations include career counseling.

Subject-area Tutoring Tutoring is offered for some subjects. Tutoring is provided collaboratively through on-campus or off-campus services via graduate assistants/students, professional tutors, and trained peer tutors.

Basic Skills Remediation Remediation is available for written language. Remediation is provided collaboratively through on-campus or off-campus services via graduate assistants/students, professional tutors, and trained peer tutors.

Enrichment Enrichment programs are available through the program or unit for career planning, college survival skills, self-advocacy, stress management, study skills, test taking, and time management. Programs for career planning, college survival skills, health and nutrition, learning strategies, math, stress management, study skills, test taking, time management, and written composition skills are provided collaboratively through on-campus or off-campus services.

Application For admittance to the program or unit, students are required to provide a psychoeducational report and provide documentation on case-by-case basis according to ADA and Section 504 guidelines. Upon application, materials documenting need for services should be sent only to the LD program or unit. Upon acceptance, documentation of need for services should be sent only to the LD program or unit. *Application deadline (institutional):* Continuous. *Application deadline (LD program):* Rolling/continuous for fall and rolling/continuous for spring.

Written Policies Written policy regarding general/basic LD accommodations is outlined in the school's catalog/handbook.

Holy Names College
Disability Support Services

3500 Mountain Boulevard

Oakland, CA 94619-1699

http://www.hnc.edu/site/college/disabled.html

Contact: Jennifer D. Bojanowski, Director of Disability Support Services. Phone: 510-436-1336. Fax: 510-436-1199. E-mail: dss@hnc.edu.

Disability Support Services Approximately 20 registered undergraduate students were served during 2002-03. The program or unit includes 1 part-time staff member. Academic advisers, coaches, counselors, diagnostic specialists, LD specialists, professional tutors, regular education teachers, remediation/learning specialists, and trained peer tutors are provided collaboratively through on-campus or off-campus services.

Orientation The program or unit offers a mandatory 1-hour (may vary based on needs) orientation for new students individually by special arrangement.

Summer Program To help prepare for the demands of college, there is an optional 6-week summer program prior to entering the school.

Subject-area Tutoring Tutoring is offered one-on-one and in small groups for some subjects. Tutoring is provided collaboratively through on-campus or off-campus services via computer-based instruction, LD specialists, professional tutors, and trained peer tutors.

Diagnostic Testing Testing is provided through the program or unit for math, reading, and written language. Testing for auditory processing, learning strategies, learning styles, study skills, and visual processing is provided collaboratively through on-campus or off-campus services.

Basic Skills Remediation Remediation is offered one-on-one, in small groups, and in class-size groups for learning strategies, math, social skills, study skills, time management, and written language. Remediation is provided through the program or unit. Remediation is also provided collaboratively through on-campus or off-campus services via LD specialists, professional tutors, regular education teachers, and trained peer tutors.

Enrichment Enrichment programs are available through the program or unit for self-advocacy and time management. Programs for career planning, college survival skills, learning strategies, math, study skills, and written composition skills are provided collaboratively through on-campus or off-campus services.

Student Organization Heumann Action Club consists of 5 members.

Application For admittance to the program or unit, students are required to provide a psychoeducational report (3 years old or less). Upon application, materials documenting need for services should be sent only to the LD program or unit. Upon acceptance, documentation of need for services should be sent only to the LD program or unit. *Application deadline (institutional):* 8/1. *Application deadline (LD program):* Rolling/continuous for fall and rolling/continuous for spring.

Written Policies Written policy regarding general/basic LD accommodations is available on the program Web site. Written policy regarding general/basic LD accommodations is outlined in the school's catalog/handbook. Written policy regarding general/basic LD accommodations is available through the program or unit directly.

Hood College

401 Rosemont Avenue

Hood College (continued)
Frederick, MD 21701-8575
http://www.hood.edu/
Contact: Julia Tackett, Learning Disabilities Coordinator. Phone: 301-696-3421. E-mail: tackett@hood.edu.

Orientation The program or unit offers an optional orientation for new students before classes begin, during registration, and individually by special arrangement.
Unique Aids and Services Aids, services, or accommodations include personal coach, support groups, and weekly meetings with faculty.
Subject-area Tutoring Tutoring is offered one-on-one for some subjects. Tutoring is provided through the program or unit via other. Tutoring is also provided collaboratively through on-campus or off-campus services via LD specialists, trained peer tutors, and other.
Basic Skills Remediation Remediation is offered in class-size groups for math, reading, study skills, and time management. Remediation is provided through the program or unit. Remediation is also provided collaboratively through on-campus or off-campus services via LD specialists, regular education teachers, trained peer tutors, and other.
Enrichment Enrichment programs are available through the program or unit for self-advocacy. Programs for math, reading, study skills, test taking, time management, and written composition skills are provided collaboratively through on-campus or off-campus services. Credit is offered for study skills and written composition skills.
Student Organization Students Managing Independent Learning Experiences (SMILE) Club consists of 10 members.
Application For admittance to the program or unit, students are required to provide a psychoeducational report (3 years old or less). It is recommended that students provide documentation of high school services. Upon acceptance, documentation of need for services should be sent only to the LD program or unit. *Application deadline (institutional):* 2/1. *Application deadline (LD program):* Rolling/continuous for fall and rolling/continuous for spring.
Written Policies Written policies regarding course substitutions, general/basic LD accommodations, reduced course loads, substitutions and waivers of admissions requirements, and substitutions and waivers of graduation requirements are available on the program Web site. Written policy regarding general/basic LD accommodations is outlined in the school's catalog/handbook. Written policies regarding course substitutions, general/basic LD accommodations, reduced course loads, substitutions and waivers of admissions requirements, and substitutions and waivers of graduation requirements are available through the program or unit directly.

Houston Baptist University
Enrichment Center

7502 Fondren Road
Houston, TX 77074-3298
http://www.hbu.edu/
Contact: Sebron Williams EdD, Director of Academic Testing. Phone: 281-649-3000 Ext. 3285. E-mail: swilliams@hbu.edu.

Enrichment Center Approximately 15 registered undergraduate students were served during 2002-03. Counselors are provided through the program or unit. Academic advisers and counselors are provided collaboratively through on-campus or off-campus services.
Unique Aids and Services Aids, services, or accommodations include career counseling.
Subject-area Tutoring Tutoring is offered one-on-one for some subjects. Tutoring is provided collaboratively through on-campus or off-campus services via professional tutors and trained peer tutors.
Diagnostic Testing Testing is provided through the program or unit for auditory processing, intelligence, learning strategies, learning styles, math, neuropsychological, personality, reading, study skills, visual processing, and written language. Testing for auditory processing, intelligence, learning strategies, learning styles, math, neuropsychological, personality, reading, study skills, visual processing, and written language is provided collaboratively through on-campus or off-campus services.
Basic Skills Remediation Remediation is offered one-on-one and in class-size groups for learning strategies, reading, social skills, study skills, time management, and written language. Remediation is provided through the program or unit via LD specialists and other. Remediation is also provided collaboratively through on-campus or off-campus services.
Enrichment Programs for career planning, college survival skills, learning strategies, math, medication management, oral communication skills, reading, self-advocacy, stress management, study skills, test taking, time management, vocabulary development, written composition skills, and other are provided collaboratively through on-campus or off-campus services.
Application Upon acceptance, documentation of need for services should be sent only to the LD program or unit. *Application deadline (institutional):* Continuous. *Application deadline (LD program):* Rolling/continuous for fall and rolling/continuous for spring.
Written Policies Written policy regarding general/basic LD accommodations is outlined in the school's catalog/handbook.

Humboldt State University

1 Harpst Street
Arcata, CA 95521-8299
http://www.humboldt.edu/
Contact: Mr. Ralph D. McFarland, Director. Phone: 707-826-4678. Fax: 707-826-5397. E-mail: rdm7001@humboldt.edu.

Approximately 200 registered undergraduate students were served during 2002-03. The program or unit includes 4 full-time staff members and 1 part-time staff member. LD specialists are provided through the program or unit.
Unique Aids and Services Aids, services, or accommodations include career counseling, digital textbooks, faculty training, priority registration, and support groups.
Subject-area Tutoring Tutoring is offered one-on-one and in small groups for some subjects. Tutoring is provided through the program or unit via LD specialists. Tutoring is also provided collaboratively through on-campus or off-campus services via computer-based instruction, graduate assistants/students, and trained peer tutors.

Diagnostic Testing Testing is provided through the program or unit for auditory processing, intelligence, learning styles, math, personality, reading, spelling, spoken language, study skills, and written language.

Basic Skills Remediation Remediation is offered in small groups for learning strategies, math, reading, study skills, and time management. Remediation is provided through the program or unit via LD specialists. Remediation is also provided collaboratively through on-campus or off-campus services via computer-based instruction and trained peer tutors.

Enrichment Enrichment programs are available through the program or unit for self-advocacy. Programs for career planning, college survival skills, health and nutrition, learning strategies, math, reading, stress management, study skills, test taking, time management, vocabulary development, written composition skills, and other are provided collaboratively through on-campus or off-campus services.

Application For admittance to the program or unit, students are required to provide a psychoeducational report and provide comprehensive diagnostic assessment. It is recommended that students provide documentation of high school services. Upon application, materials documenting need for services should be sent only to the LD program or unit. Upon acceptance, documentation of need for services should be sent only to the LD program or unit. *Application deadline (institutional):* Continuous. *Application deadline (LD program):* Rolling/continuous for fall and rolling/continuous for spring.

Written Policies Written policy regarding general/basic LD accommodations is available on the program Web site. Written policies regarding course substitutions, general/basic LD accommodations, substitutions and waivers of admissions requirements, and substitutions and waivers of graduation requirements are available through the program or unit directly.

Huntingdon College

1500 East Fairview Avenue
Montgomery, AL 36106-2148
http://www.huntingdon.edu/
Contact: Ms. Jennifer Salter, Director of Student Programs and Leadership Development. Phone: 334-833-4556. E-mail: jsalter@huntingdon.edu.

Approximately 10 registered undergraduate students were served during 2002-03. The program or unit includes 1 part-time staff member. Counselors are provided collaboratively through on-campus or off-campus services.

Diagnostic Testing Testing for auditory processing, handwriting, intelligence, learning strategies, learning styles, math, motor skills, neuropsychological, personality, reading, social skills, spelling, spoken language, study skills, visual processing, written language, and other services is provided collaboratively through on-campus or off-campus services.

Application For admittance to the program or unit, students are required to apply to the program directly, provide a psychoeducational report (3 years old or less), and provide documentation of high school services. Upon acceptance, documentation of need for services should be sent only to the LD program or unit. *Application deadline (institutional):* Continuous. *Application deadline (LD program):* Rolling/continuous for fall and rolling/continuous for spring.

Written Policies Written policy regarding general/basic LD accommodations is outlined in the school's catalog/handbook.

Huntington College

2303 College Avenue
Huntington, IN 46750-1299
http://www.huntington.edu/
Contact: Mrs. Kris Chafin, Director of Learning Assistance. Phone: 260-359-4290. Fax: 260-359-4077. E-mail: kchafin@huntington.edu.

Approximately 8 registered undergraduate students were served during 2002-03.

Unique Aids and Services Aids, services, or accommodations include personal coach.

Subject-area Tutoring Tutoring is offered one-on-one and in small groups for most subjects. Tutoring is provided through the program or unit via computer-based instruction and trained peer tutors.

Basic Skills Remediation Remediation is offered one-on-one for computer skills, learning strategies, math, spoken language, study skills, time management, and written language. Remediation is provided through the program or unit via computer-based instruction, trained peer tutors, and other.

Enrichment Enrichment programs are available through the program or unit for college survival skills, math, practical computer skills, self-advocacy, stress management, study skills, test taking, time management, and written composition skills. Programs for career planning, health and nutrition, and learning strategies are provided collaboratively through on-campus or off-campus services.

Application For admittance to the program or unit, students are required to provide a psychoeducational report (4 years old or less). It is recommended that students provide documentation of high school services. Upon application, materials documenting need for services should be sent only to the LD program or unit. Upon acceptance, documentation of need for services should be sent only to the LD program or unit. *Application deadline (institutional):* 8/1. *Application deadline (LD program):* Rolling/continuous for fall and rolling/continuous for spring.

Written Policies Written policies regarding course substitutions, general/basic LD accommodations, substitutions and waivers of admissions requirements, and substitutions and waivers of graduation requirements are available through the program or unit directly.

Husson College
Office of Student Affairs

One College Circle
Bangor, ME 04401-2999
http://www.husson.edu/
Contact: Mr. John Rubino, Dean of the College. Phone: 207-941-7107. Fax: 207-941-7190. E-mail: rubinoj@husson.edu.

Husson College (continued)

Office of Student Affairs Approximately 12 registered undergraduate students were served during 2002-03. Academic advisers, coaches, counselors, diagnostic specialists, graduate assistants/students, LD specialists, professional tutors, regular education teachers, remediation/learning specialists, skill tutors, and trained peer tutors are provided collaboratively through on-campus or off-campus services.

Subject-area Tutoring Tutoring is offered one-on-one and in small groups for some subjects. Tutoring is provided collaboratively through on-campus or off-campus services via professional tutors and trained peer tutors.

Basic Skills Remediation Remediation is offered one-on-one and in small groups for learning strategies, math, study skills, time management, and written language. Remediation is provided collaboratively through on-campus or off-campus services via regular education teachers and trained peer tutors.

Enrichment Programs for career planning, college survival skills, health and nutrition, learning strategies, math, medication management, reading, self-advocacy, stress management, study skills, test taking, time management, and written composition skills are provided collaboratively through on-campus or off-campus services.

Application For admittance to the program or unit, students are required to provide a psychoeducational report (3 years old or less) and provide documentation of high school services. Upon acceptance, documentation of need for services should be sent to both admissions and the LD program or unit. *Application deadline (institutional):* 9/1. *Application deadline (LD program):* Rolling/continuous for fall and rolling/continuous for spring.

Written Policies Written policy regarding general/basic LD accommodations is outlined in the school's catalog/handbook.

Idaho State University
ADA Disabilities and Resource Center

741 South 7th Avenue
Pocatello, ID 83209
http://www.isu.edu/ada4isu/
Contact: Dennis Toney, Director. Phone: 208-282-3599. Fax: 208-282-4617. E-mail: tonedenn@isu.edu.

ADA Disabilities and Resource Center Approximately 120 registered undergraduate students were served during 2002-03. Diagnostic specialists, graduate assistants/students, professional tutors, skill tutors, and strategy tutors are provided collaboratively through on-campus or off-campus services.

Subject-area Tutoring Tutoring is offered one-on-one, in small groups, and in class-size groups for some subjects. Tutoring is provided collaboratively through on-campus or off-campus services via computer-based instruction, graduate assistants/students, professional tutors, and trained peer tutors.

Diagnostic Testing Testing for auditory processing, handwriting, intelligence, learning strategies, learning styles, math, neuropsychological, personality, reading, spelling, spoken language, study skills, visual processing, and written language is provided collaboratively through on-campus or off-campus services.

Basic Skills Remediation Remediation is offered one-on-one, in small groups, and in class-size groups for computer skills, learning strategies, math, study skills, time management, and written language.

Remediation is provided collaboratively through on-campus or off-campus services via computer-based instruction, graduate assistants/students, professional tutors, and trained peer tutors.

Enrichment Programs for career planning, college survival skills, health and nutrition, learning strategies, math, oral communication skills, practical computer skills, reading, self-advocacy, study skills, test taking, time management, and written composition skills are provided collaboratively through on-campus or off-campus services. Credit is offered for college survival skills, health and nutrition, learning strategies, math, oral communication skills, practical computer skills, reading, study skills, test taking, time management, and written composition skills.

Fees *Diagnostic Testing* fee is $100.

Application For admittance to the program or unit, students are required to provide a psychoeducational report (3 years old or less). Upon acceptance, documentation of need for services should be sent only to the LD program or unit. *Application deadline (institutional):* 8/1. *Application deadline (LD program):* Rolling/continuous for fall and rolling/continuous for spring.

Written Policies Written policy regarding general/basic LD accommodations is available through the program or unit directly.

Illinois College
Templeton Counseling Center

1101 West College Avenue
Jacksonville, IL 62650-2299
http://www.ic.ed
Contact: Judy Norris, Director of Templeton Counseling Center. Phone: 217-245-3073. Fax: 217-245-3071. E-mail: jnorris@ic.edu.

Templeton Counseling Center Approximately 4 registered undergraduate students were served during 2002-03. The program or unit includes 1 part-time staff member. Counselors are provided through the program or unit. Academic advisers, counselors, diagnostic specialists, regular education teachers, and trained peer tutors are provided collaboratively through on-campus or off-campus services.

Unique Aids and Services Aids, services, or accommodations include career counseling.

Subject-area Tutoring Tutoring is offered one-on-one for all subjects. Tutoring is provided collaboratively through on-campus or off-campus services via trained peer tutors and other.

Diagnostic Testing Testing for auditory processing, intelligence, learning styles, math, personality, reading, spelling, spoken language, visual processing, written language, and other services is provided collaboratively through on-campus or off-campus services.

Enrichment Programs for career planning, college survival skills, health and nutrition, medication management, stress management, study skills, test taking, and time management are provided collaboratively through on-campus or off-campus services.

Fees *Diagnostic Testing* fee is applicable.

Application For admittance to the program or unit, students are required to provide a psychoeducational report. It is recommended that students provide documentation of high school services. *Application deadline (institutional):* 7/15. *Application deadline (LD program):* Rolling/continuous for fall and rolling/continuous for spring.

The Illinois Institute of Art
Student Services

350 North Orleans
Chicago, IL 60654
http://www.ilia.aii.edu/

Contact: Mr. Jamey DiVietro, Counselor. Phone: 312-475-6883. Fax: 312-475-6960. E-mail: divietrj@aii.edu.

Student Services Approximately 30 registered undergraduate students were served during 2002-03. The program or unit includes 1 full-time staff member. Counselors are provided through the program or unit. Academic advisers, graduate assistants/students, professional tutors, and regular education teachers are provided collaboratively through on-campus or off-campus services.
Unique Aids and Services Aids, services, or accommodations include career counseling and weekly meetings with faculty.
Subject-area Tutoring Tutoring is offered one-on-one, in small groups, and in class-size groups for most subjects. Tutoring is provided collaboratively through on-campus or off-campus services via computer-based instruction, graduate assistants/students, and professional tutors.
Basic Skills Remediation Remediation is offered in class-size groups for computer skills, learning strategies, math, reading, spelling, study skills, and time management. Remediation is provided collaboratively through on-campus or off-campus services via computer-based instruction, graduate assistants/students, professional tutors, and regular education teachers.
Enrichment Enrichment programs are available through the program or unit for college survival skills, stress management, study skills, test taking, and time management. Programs for career planning, learning strategies, math, oral communication skills, practical computer skills, reading, vocabulary development, and written composition skills are provided collaboratively through on-campus or off-campus services.
Application For admittance to the program or unit, students are required to provide documentation of high school services. It is recommended that students provide a psychoeducational report (2 years old or less). Upon application, materials documenting need for services should be sent only to the LD program or unit. Upon acceptance, documentation of need for services should be sent only to the LD program or unit. *Application deadline (institutional):* Continuous. *Application deadline (LD program):* Rolling/continuous for fall and rolling/continuous for spring.
Written Policies Written policy regarding general/basic LD accommodations is outlined in the school's catalog/handbook. Written policy regarding general/basic LD accommodations is available through the program or unit directly.

Illinois State University
Disability Concerns

Normal, IL 61790-2200
http://ilstu.edu/depts/disabilityconcerns

Contact: Ms. Sheryl J. Hogan, Coordinator of Learning Disability Services. Phone: 309-438-5853. Fax: 309-438-7713. E-mail: sjhogan@ilstu.edu. Head of LD

Program: Ms. Ann M. Caldwell, Director. Phone: 309-438-5853. Fax: 309-438-7713. E-mail: amcaldw@ilstu.edu.

Disability Concerns Approximately 175 registered undergraduate students were served during 2002-03. The program or unit includes 5 full-time staff members and 1 part-time staff member. Graduate assistants/students, LD specialists, and strategy tutors are provided through the program or unit. Academic advisers, counselors, diagnostic specialists, regular education teachers, skill tutors, strategy tutors, and trained peer tutors are provided collaboratively through on-campus or off-campus services.
Orientation The program or unit offers a mandatory orientation for new students individually by special arrangement.
Unique Aids and Services Aids, services, or accommodations include career counseling, digital textbooks, and faculty training.
Subject-area Tutoring Tutoring is offered one-on-one and in small groups for some subjects. Tutoring is provided collaboratively through on-campus or off-campus services via trained peer tutors.
Diagnostic Testing Testing for neuropsychological is provided collaboratively through on-campus or off-campus services.
Basic Skills Remediation Remediation is available for learning strategies, study skills, and time management. Remediation is provided through the program or unit via LD specialists.
Enrichment Enrichment programs are available through the program or unit for learning strategies, self-advocacy, study skills, test taking, and time management. Programs for career planning, college survival skills, health and nutrition, learning strategies, practical computer skills, stress management, study skills, test taking, and time management are provided collaboratively through on-campus or off-campus services.
Fees *Diagnostic Testing* fee is $400.
Application For admittance to the program or unit, students are required to apply to the program directly, provide a psychoeducational report, and provide documentation of high school services. Upon application, materials documenting need for services should be sent only to the LD program or unit. Upon acceptance, documentation of need for services should be sent only to the LD program or unit. *Application deadline (institutional):* 3/1. *Application deadline (LD program):* Rolling/continuous for fall and rolling/continuous for spring.
Written Policies Written policy regarding general/basic LD accommodations is available on the program Web site. Written policy regarding course substitutions is available through the program or unit directly.

Illinois Wesleyan University

PO Box 2900
Bloomington, IL 61702-2900
http://www.iwu.edu/

Contact: Dr. Roger Schanitter, Associate Provost. Phone: 309-556-3255. E-mail: rschnait@iwu.edu.

Approximately 15 registered undergraduate students were served during 2002-03. Academic advisers, coaches, counselors, and trained peer tutors are provided collaboratively through on-campus or off-campus services.
Unique Aids and Services Aids, services, or accommodations include extended examination time.

Illinois Wesleyan University (continued)

Subject-area Tutoring Tutoring is offered one-on-one and in small groups for some subjects. Tutoring is provided collaboratively through on-campus or off-campus services via trained peer tutors.
Application For admittance to the program or unit, students are required to provide a psychoeducational report. It is recommended that students provide documentation of high school services. Upon acceptance, documentation of need for services should be sent only to the LD program or unit. *Application deadline (institutional):* 3/1. *Application deadline (LD program):* Rolling/continuous for fall and rolling/continuous for spring.
Written Policies Written policy regarding general/basic LD accommodations is outlined in the school's catalog/handbook.

Immaculata University

1145 King Road
Immaculata, PA 19345
http://www.immaculata.edu/
Contact: Dr. Janet F. Kane, Dean of Women's College. Phone: 610-647-4400 Ext. 3019. Fax: 610-640-0836. E-mail: jkane@immaculta.edu.

Approximately 30 registered undergraduate students were served during 2002-03. Academic advisers, coaches, counselors, professional tutors, and regular education teachers are provided collaboratively through on-campus or off-campus services.
Subject-area Tutoring Tutoring is offered one-on-one for most subjects. Tutoring is provided collaboratively through on-campus or off-campus services via computer-based instruction, professional tutors, and trained peer tutors.
Enrichment Programs for career planning, college survival skills, health and nutrition, learning strategies, math, practical computer skills, stress management, study skills, time management, and written composition skills are provided collaboratively through on-campus or off-campus services.
Application For admittance to the program or unit, students are required to provide a psychoeducational report (5 years old or less) and provide documentation of high school services. Upon application, materials documenting need for services should be sent only to the LD program or unit. Upon acceptance, documentation of need for services should be sent only to the LD program or unit. *Application deadline (institutional):* 8/15. *Application deadline (LD program):* Rolling/continuous for fall and rolling/continuous for spring.
Written Policies Written policies regarding general/basic LD accommodations and reduced course loads are available through the program or unit directly.

Indiana University Bloomington
Disability Services for Students

Bloomington, IN 47405
http://www.indiana.edu/~iubdss

Contact: Jody K. Ferguson, Learning Disabilities Coordinator. Phone: 812-855-3508. Fax: 812-855-7650. E-mail: ferguson@indiana.edu. Head of LD Program: Martha P. Jacques, Director. Phone: 812-855-7578. Fax: 812-855-7650. E-mail: mjacques@indiana.edu.

Disability Services for Students Approximately 450 registered undergraduate students were served during 2002-03. The program or unit includes 2 full-time staff members and 1 part-time staff member.
Orientation The program or unit offers a mandatory 2-hour orientation for new students before classes begin.
Unique Aids and Services Aids, services, or accommodations include digital textbooks.
Student Organization Students for Improving Disability Awareness (SIDA).
Application For admittance to the program or unit, students are required to apply to the program directly, provide a psychoeducational report (2 years old or less), provide documentation of high school services, and provide an evaluation after age 16 with adult normed tests. Upon acceptance, documentation of need for services should be sent only to the LD program or unit. *Application deadline (institutional):* 2/1. *Application deadline (LD program):* Rolling/continuous for fall and rolling/continuous for spring.
Written Policies Written policies regarding course substitutions, general/basic LD accommodations, grade forgiveness, reduced course loads, substitutions and waivers of admissions requirements, and substitutions and waivers of graduation requirements are available on the program Web site. Written policies regarding course substitutions, general/basic LD accommodations, grade forgiveness, reduced course loads, substitutions and waivers of admissions requirements, and substitutions and waivers of graduation requirements are available through the program or unit directly.

Indiana University of Pennsylvania
Disability Support Services, Advising and Testing Center

Indiana, PA 15705-1087
http://www.iup.edu/advisingtesting/dss.html
Contact: Mr. Todd A. Van Wieren, Lead Disability Support Services Adviser. Phone: 724-357-4067. Fax: 724-357-2889. E-mail: toddvw@iup.edu. Head of LD Program: Dr. Catherine Dugan, Director of Disability Support Services. Phone: 724-357-4067. Fax: 724-357-2889. E-mail: cmdugan@iup.edu.

Disability Support Services, Advising and Testing Center Approximately 300 registered undergraduate students were served during 2002-03. The program or unit includes 3 full-time staff members. Academic advisers and graduate assistants/students are provided collaboratively through on-campus or off-campus services.
Orientation The program or unit offers an optional 1-hour orientation for new students the first week of classes.
Summer Program To help prepare for the demands of college, there is an optional 1-week summer program prior to entering the school.

Unique Aids and Services Aids, services, or accommodations include advocates, career counseling, priority registration, and weekly meetings with faculty.

Subject-area Tutoring Tutoring is offered in class-size groups for some subjects. Tutoring is provided collaboratively through on-campus or off-campus services via trained peer tutors.

Diagnostic Testing Testing for auditory processing, intelligence, learning styles, math, motor skills, personality, reading, spelling, spoken language, visual processing, and written language is provided collaboratively through on-campus or off-campus services.

Basic Skills Remediation Remediation is offered in class-size groups for learning strategies, math, reading, study skills, time management, and written language. Remediation is provided collaboratively through on-campus or off-campus services via regular education teachers.

Enrichment Programs for career planning, college survival skills, health and nutrition, learning strategies, math, oral communication skills, practical computer skills, and study skills are provided collaboratively through on-campus or off-campus services. Credit is offered for career planning, college survival skills, health and nutrition, learning strategies, math, oral communication skills, practical computer skills, and study skills.

Fees *Diagnostic Testing* fee is $75.

Application For admittance to the program or unit, students are required to provide a psychoeducational report (3 years old or less). It is recommended that students provide documentation of high school services. Upon application, materials documenting need for services should be sent only to the LD program or unit. Upon acceptance, documentation of need for services should be sent only to the LD program or unit. *Application deadline (institutional):* Continuous. *Application deadline (LD program):* Rolling/continuous for fall and rolling/continuous for spring.

Written Policies Written policy regarding general/basic LD accommodations is available on the program Web site. Written policy regarding general/basic LD accommodations is available through the program or unit directly.

Indiana University-Purdue University Indianapolis
Adaptive Educational Services

355 North Lansing
Indianapolis, IN 46202-2896
http://www.iupui.edu/it/aes_html/aes000.htm
Contact: Ms. Pamela A. King, Director. Phone: 317-274-3241. Fax: 317-278-2051. E-mail: pking@iupui.edu.

Adaptive Educational Services Approximately 400 registered undergraduate students were served during 2002-03. The program or unit includes 6 full-time staff members. Academic advisers, coaches, counselors, diagnostic specialists, graduate assistants/students, LD specialists, professional tutors, regular education teachers, remediation/learning specialists, skill tutors, special education teachers, strategy tutors, teacher trainees, and trained peer tutors are provided collaboratively through on-campus or off-campus services.

Unique Aids and Services Aids, services, or accommodations include career counseling and digital textbooks.

Application For admittance to the program or unit, students are required to apply to the program directly and provide a psychoeducational report (3 years old or less). It is recommended that students provide documentation of high school services. Upon application, materials documenting need for services should be sent only to the LD program or unit. Upon acceptance, documentation of need for services should be sent only to the LD program or unit. *Application deadline (institutional):* Continuous. *Application deadline (LD program):* Rolling/continuous for fall and rolling/continuous for spring.

Indiana University South Bend

1700 Mishawaka Avenue, PO Box 7111
South Bend, IN 46634-7111
http://www.indiana.edu/
Contact: Ms. Donna Lamborn, Learning Disabilities Specialist. Phone: 574-237-4832. Fax: 574-239-5018. E-mail: dlalmborn@iusb.edu.

Approximately 120 registered undergraduate students were served during 2002-03. The program or unit includes 1 full-time staff member. Academic advisers, LD specialists, regular education teachers, and trained peer tutors are provided through the program or unit. Diagnostic specialists are provided collaboratively through on-campus or off-campus services.

Orientation The program or unit offers a mandatory 1-hour orientation for new students individually by special arrangement.

Unique Aids and Services Aids, services, or accommodations include career counseling and faculty training.

Subject-area Tutoring Tutoring is offered one-on-one and in small groups for some subjects. Tutoring is provided through the program or unit via trained peer tutors. Tutoring is also provided collaboratively through on-campus or off-campus services via computer-based instruction.

Diagnostic Testing Testing is provided through the program or unit for learning strategies, learning styles, and study skills. Testing for auditory processing, handwriting, intelligence, math, motor skills, neuropsychological, personality, reading, spelling, spoken language, study skills, visual processing, and written language is provided collaboratively through on-campus or off-campus services.

Basic Skills Remediation Remediation is offered in small groups and in class-size groups for math, reading, and written language. Remediation is provided collaboratively through on-campus or off-campus services via computer-based instruction, regular education teachers, and trained peer tutors.

Enrichment Programs for career planning and written composition skills are provided collaboratively through on-campus or off-campus services.

Application For admittance to the program or unit, students are required to apply to the program directly, provide a psychoeducational report (3 years old or less), and provide a medical report if ADD. It is recommended that students provide documentation of high school services. Upon application, materials documenting need for services should be sent only to the LD program or unit. Upon acceptance, documentation of need for services should be sent only to the LD program or unit. *Application deadline (institutional):* 7/1. *Application deadline (LD program):* Rolling/continuous for fall and rolling/continuous for spring.

Indiana University South Bend (continued)

Written Policies Written policy regarding general/basic LD accommodations is available on the program Web site. Written policy regarding general/basic LD accommodations is available through the program or unit directly.

Indiana University Southeast
Office of Disability Services

4201 Grant Line Road
New Albany, IN 47150-6405
http://www.ius.edu/SSDis

Contact: Mr. Todd Alan Norris, Coordinator of Disability Services. Phone: 812-941-2243. Fax: 812-941-2542. E-mail: toanorri@ius.edu.

Office of Disability Services Approximately 200 registered undergraduate students were served during 2002-03. The program or unit includes 1 full-time and 1 part-time staff member. Academic advisers and counselors are provided through the program or unit. Academic advisers, coaches, diagnostic specialists, graduate assistants/students, professional tutors, regular education teachers, remediation/learning specialists, skill tutors, and trained peer tutors are provided collaboratively through on-campus or off-campus services.

Unique Aids and Services Aids, services, or accommodations include career counseling, priority registration, and support groups.

Subject-area Tutoring Tutoring is offered one-on-one, in small groups, and in class-size groups for most subjects. Tutoring is provided collaboratively through on-campus or off-campus services via computer-based instruction, graduate assistants/students, professional tutors, and trained peer tutors.

Basic Skills Remediation Remediation is offered one-on-one, in small groups, and in class-size groups for learning strategies, math, and study skills. Remediation is provided collaboratively through on-campus or off-campus services via professional tutors, regular education teachers, and special education teachers.

Enrichment Programs for career planning, college survival skills, learning strategies, math, study skills, and written composition skills are provided collaboratively through on-campus or off-campus services.

Application For admittance to the program or unit, students are required to provide a psychoeducational report (3 years old or less). Upon acceptance, documentation of need for services should be sent only to the LD program or unit. *Application deadline (institutional):* 7/15. *Application deadline (LD program):* Rolling/continuous for fall and rolling/continuous for spring.

Written Policies Written policy regarding general/basic LD accommodations is available on the program Web site. Written policies regarding course substitutions, general/basic LD accommodations, and substitutions and waivers of graduation requirements are available through the program or unit directly.

Indiana Wesleyan University
Center for Student Support Services

4201 South Washington Street
Marion, IN 46953-4974

http://www.indwes.edu/student_life/student_asst_services/

Contact: Jerry Harrell, Director of Center for Student Support Services. Phone: 765-677-2257. Fax: 765-677-2140. E-mail: jerry.harrell@indwes.edu.

Center for Student Support Services Approximately 100 registered undergraduate students were served during 2002-03. The program or unit includes 3 full-time staff members and 1 part-time staff member. Academic advisers, coaches, counselors, skill tutors, strategy tutors, trained peer tutors, and other are provided through the program or unit.

Unique Aids and Services Aids, services, or accommodations include advocates, career counseling, faculty training, personal coach, priority registration, academic advising, weekly meetings with counselors.

Subject-area Tutoring Tutoring is offered one-on-one and in small groups for most subjects. Tutoring is provided through the program or unit via trained peer tutors.

Basic Skills Remediation Remediation is offered one-on-one and in small groups for learning strategies, reading, social skills, study skills, time management, written language, and note-taking, learning styles. Remediation is provided through the program or unit via trained peer tutors and other.

Application For admittance to the program or unit, students are required to apply to the program directly and provide a psychoeducational report (3 years old or less). Upon application, materials documenting need for services should be sent only to the LD program or unit. Upon acceptance, documentation of need for services should be sent only to the LD program or unit. *Application deadline (institutional):* Continuous. *Application deadline (LD program):* Rolling/continuous for fall and rolling/continuous for spring.

Written Policies Written policies regarding course substitutions, general/basic LD accommodations, grade forgiveness, reduced course loads, substitutions and waivers of admissions requirements, and substitutions and waivers of graduation requirements are available through the program or unit directly.

Ithaca College
Academic Support Services for Students with Disabilities

100 Job Hall
Ithaca, NY 14850-7020
http://www.ithaca.edu/

Contact: Ms. Sandra Simkin, Administrative Assistant. Phone: 607-274-1005. Fax: 607-274-3957. E-mail: simkin@ithaca.edu. Head of LD Program: Ms. Leslie Schettino, Director of Academic Support Services. Phone: 607-274-1005. Fax: 607-274-3957. E-mail: lschettino@ithaca.edu.

Academic Support Services for Students with Disabilities Approximately 460 registered undergraduate students were served during 2002-03. The program or unit includes 3 full-time staff members. Counselors are provided through the program or unit. Academic advisers, counselors, diagnostic specialists, and trained peer tutors are provided collaboratively through on-campus or off-campus services.

Unique Aids and Services Aids, services, or accommodations include advocates, career counseling, faculty training, priority registration, and weekly meetings with faculty.

Enrichment Enrichment programs are available through the program or unit for self-advocacy, study skills, test taking, and time management. Programs for career planning, college survival skills, health and nutrition, math, medication management, oral communication skills, practical computer skills, stress management, and written composition skills are provided collaboratively through on-campus or off-campus services.

Application For admittance to the program or unit, students are required to provide a psychoeducational report (3 years old or less). It is recommended that students provide documentation of high school services. Upon acceptance, documentation of need for services should be sent only to the LD program or unit. *Application deadline (institutional):* 3/1. *Application deadline (LD program):* Rolling/continuous for fall and rolling/continuous for spring.

Written Policies Written policy regarding general/basic LD accommodations is available on the program Web site. Written policy regarding general/basic LD accommodations is outlined in the school's catalog/handbook. Written policies regarding course substitutions and general/basic LD accommodations are available through the program or unit directly.

Jacksonville University

2800 University Boulevard North

Jacksonville, FL 32211-3394

http://www.ju.edu/

Contact: Dr. John A. Balog, Vice President for Student Life. Phone: 904-256-7067 Ext. 7067. Fax: 904-256-7066 Ext. 7066. E-mail: jbalog@ju.edu.

Approximately 35 registered undergraduate students were served during 2002-03. The program or unit includes 2 full-time staff members. Services are provided through the program or unit. Services are provided collaboratively through on-campus or off-campus services.

Unique Aids and Services Aids, services, or accommodations include career counseling and faculty training.

Subject-area Tutoring Tutoring is offered one-on-one and in small groups for all subjects. Tutoring is provided collaboratively through on-campus or off-campus services via trained peer tutors and other.

Enrichment Programs for career planning, college survival skills, health and nutrition, math, reading, stress management, study skills, test taking, time management, and written composition skills are provided collaboratively through on-campus or off-campus services.

Application For admittance to the program or unit, students are required to provide a psychoeducational report (5 years old or less) and provide documentation of high school services. Upon application, materials documenting need for services should be sent only to the LD program or unit. Upon acceptance, documentation of need for services should be sent only to the LD program or unit. *Application deadline (institutional):* Continuous. *Application deadline (LD program):* Rolling/continuous for fall and rolling/continuous for spring.

Written Policies Written policies regarding general/basic LD accommodations, substitutions and waivers of admissions requirements, and substitutions and waivers of graduation requirements are

outlined in the school's catalog/handbook. Written policies regarding course substitutions, general/basic LD accommodations, reduced course loads, substitutions and waivers of admissions requirements, and substitutions and waivers of graduation requirements are available through the program or unit directly.

James Madison University

800 South Main Street

Harrisonburg, VA 22807

http://www.jmu.edu/

Contact: Louis J. Hedrick, Director. Phone: 540-568-6705. Fax: 540-568-7099. E-mail: disability-svcs@jmu.edu.

Approximately 250 registered undergraduate students were served during 2002-03. The program or unit includes 2 full-time and 2 part-time staff members. Graduate assistants/students and special education teachers are provided through the program or unit.

Unique Aids and Services Aids, services, or accommodations include career counseling, priority registration, other accommodations provided on an individual basis.

Subject-area Tutoring Tutoring is offered one-on-one, in small groups, and in class-size groups for some subjects. Tutoring is provided collaboratively through on-campus or off-campus services via graduate assistants/students, professional tutors, and trained peer tutors.

Diagnostic Testing Testing for auditory processing, intelligence, math, motor skills, neuropsychological, personality, reading, social skills, spelling, spoken language, study skills, visual processing, and written language is provided collaboratively through on-campus or off-campus services.

Enrichment Enrichment programs are available through the program or unit for college survival skills, learning strategies, reading, self-advocacy, test taking, and time management. Programs for career planning, college survival skills, health and nutrition, math, medication management, oral communication skills, practical computer skills, reading, stress management, study skills, test taking, time management, vocabulary development, and written composition skills are provided collaboratively through on-campus or off-campus services. Credit is offered for career planning.

Fees *Diagnostic Testing* fee is $100 to $200.

Application For admittance to the program or unit, students are required to provide a psychoeducational report (2 years old or less). It is recommended that students provide documentation of high school services. Upon acceptance, documentation of need for services should be sent only to the LD program or unit. *Application deadline (institutional):* 1/15. *Application deadline (LD program):* Rolling/continuous for fall and rolling/continuous for spring.

Written Policies Written policies regarding course substitutions, general/basic LD accommodations, substitutions and waivers of admissions requirements, and substitutions and waivers of graduation requirements are available on the program Web site. Written policies regarding course substitutions, general/basic LD accommodations, substitutions and waivers of admissions requirements, and substitutions and waivers of graduation requirements are outlined in the school's catalog/handbook. Written policies regarding course substitutions, substitutions and waivers of admissions requirements, and substitutions and waivers of graduation requirements are available through the program or unit directly.

Johnson & Wales University

8 Abbott Park Place
Providence, RI 02903-3703
http://www.jwu.edu/

Contact: Ms. Meryl Ann Berstein, Director of Center for Academic Support. Phone: 401-598-4689. Fax: 401-598-4657.

Approximately 600 registered undergraduate students were served during 2002-03. The program or unit includes 7 full-time and 46 part-time staff members. Counselors, graduate assistants/students, LD specialists, professional tutors, regular education teachers, remediation/learning specialists, skill tutors, strategy tutors, and trained peer tutors are provided through the program or unit. Counselors, graduate assistants/students, LD specialists, professional tutors, regular education teachers, remediation/learning specialists, skill tutors, strategy tutors, and trained peer tutors are provided collaboratively through on-campus or off-campus services.
Orientation The program or unit offers an optional 2-hour orientation for new students before classes begin.
Unique Aids and Services Aids, services, or accommodations include advocates, faculty training, and priority registration.
Subject-area Tutoring Tutoring is offered one-on-one, in small groups, and in class-size groups for all subjects. Tutoring is provided collaboratively through on-campus or off-campus services via computer-based instruction, graduate assistants/students, LD specialists, professional tutors, and trained peer tutors.
Basic Skills Remediation Remediation is offered one-on-one and in small groups for learning strategies, math, reading, spoken language, study skills, time management, and written language. Remediation is provided collaboratively through on-campus or off-campus services via LD specialists and professional tutors.
Application For admittance to the program or unit, students are required to provide psychoeducational report (3 years old or less) with testing. It is recommended that students provide documentation of high school services. Upon acceptance, documentation of need for services should be sent only to the LD program or unit. *Application deadline (institutional):* Continuous. *Application deadline (LD program):* Rolling/continuous for fall.
Written Policies Written policies regarding course substitutions and general/basic LD accommodations are outlined in the school's catalog/handbook. Written policies regarding course substitutions, general/basic LD accommodations, and reduced course loads are available through the program or unit directly.

Johnson & Wales University
Center for Academic Support

701 East Bay Street
Charleston, SC 29403
http://www.jwu.edu/

Contact: Ms. Meryl Ann Berstein, Director of Center for Academic Support. Phone: 401-598-4689. Fax: 401-598-4657. Head of LD Program: Ms. Susan R.

McConoughey, Director of Special Needs. Phone: 843-727-3031. Fax: 843-727-3094. E-mail: susan.mcconoughey@jwu.edu.

Center for Academic Support Approximately 130 registered undergraduate students were served during 2002-03. The program or unit includes 5 full-time and 46 part-time staff members. LD specialists, skill tutors, and special education teachers are provided collaboratively through on-campus or off-campus services.
Orientation The program or unit offers an optional 2-hour orientation for new students during registration.
Unique Aids and Services Aids, services, or accommodations include advocates, faculty training, and priority registration.
Subject-area Tutoring Tutoring is offered one-on-one and in small groups for most subjects. Tutoring is provided collaboratively through on-campus or off-campus services via graduate assistants/students, LD specialists, and trained peer tutors.
Basic Skills Remediation Remediation is offered one-on-one for computer skills, learning strategies, math, reading, spelling, study skills, and written language. Remediation is provided collaboratively through on-campus or off-campus services via LD specialists and special education teachers.
Enrichment Programs for learning strategies, math, reading, study skills, test taking, vocabulary development, and written composition skills are provided collaboratively through on-campus or off-campus services.
Application For admittance to the program or unit, students are required to provide a psychoeducational report (3 years old or less). It is recommended that students provide documentation of high school services. Upon application, materials documenting need for services should be sent to both admissions and the LD program or unit. Upon acceptance, documentation of need for services should be sent only to the LD program or unit. *Application deadline (institutional):* Continuous. *Application deadline (LD program):* Rolling/continuous for fall and rolling/continuous for spring.
Written Policies Written policy regarding general/basic LD accommodations is available on the program Web site. Written policy regarding general/basic LD accommodations is outlined in the school's catalog/handbook.

Johnson & Wales University

7150 Montview Boulevard
Denver, CO 80220
http://www.jwu.edu/

Contact: Ms. Joyce L. Scott, Director of Academic Achievement. Phone: 303-256-9451. Fax: 303-256-9476. E-mail: jscott@jwu.edu.

The program or unit includes 2 full-time staff members and 1 part-time staff member. Academic advisers, counselors, professional tutors, and trained peer tutors are provided through the program or unit. Regular education teachers are provided collaboratively through on-campus or off-campus services.
Unique Aids and Services Aids, services, or accommodations include career counseling, digital textbooks, faculty training, e-mail contact with faculty.

Subject-area Tutoring Tutoring is offered one-on-one and in small groups for all subjects. Tutoring is provided through the program or unit via computer-based instruction, professional tutors, and trained peer tutors. Tutoring is also provided collaboratively through on-campus or off-campus services via computer-based instruction.

Basic Skills Remediation Remediation is offered one-on-one for computer skills, learning strategies, math, reading, spelling, study skills, time management, and written language. Remediation is provided through the program or unit via computer-based instruction, professional tutors, and trained peer tutors. Remediation is also provided collaboratively through on-campus or off-campus services via regular education teachers and trained peer tutors.

Enrichment Enrichment programs are available through the program or unit for learning strategies, math, practical computer skills, reading, self-advocacy, stress management, study skills, test taking, time management, and written composition skills. Programs for career planning, health and nutrition, and practical computer skills are provided collaboratively through on-campus or off-campus services. Credit is offered for career planning, health and nutrition, and practical computer skills.

Application For admittance to the program or unit, students are required to provide a psychoeducational report. Upon acceptance, documentation of need for services should be sent only to the LD program or unit. *Application deadline (institutional):* Continuous. *Application deadline (LD program):* Rolling/continuous for fall and rolling/continuous for spring.

Written Policies Written policies regarding general/basic LD accommodations and reduced course loads are available through the program or unit directly.

Johnson & Wales University
Department of Student Success

1701 Northeast 127th Street
North Miami, FL 33181
http://www.jwu.edu/florida/stu_succ.htm
Contact: Dr. Martha Sacks, Director of Student Success. Phone: 305-892-7046. Fax: 305-892-5364. E-mail: martha.sacks@jwu.edu.

Department of Student Success Approximately 95 registered undergraduate students were served during 2002-03. The program or unit includes 3 full-time and 10 part-time staff members. Academic advisers, LD specialists, professional tutors, and trained peer tutors are provided through the program or unit.

Unique Aids and Services Aids, services, or accommodations include career counseling and priority registration.

Subject-area Tutoring Tutoring is offered one-on-one. Tutoring is provided through the program or unit via professional tutors and trained peer tutors.

Basic Skills Remediation Remediation is offered one-on-one for computer skills, learning strategies, math, reading, spelling, spoken language, study skills, time management, and written language. Remediation is provided through the program or unit via professional tutors and trained peer tutors.

Application For admittance to the program or unit, students are required to provide a psychoeducational report (3 years old or less). It is recommended that students provide documentation of high

school services. Upon application, materials documenting need for services should be sent only to the LD program or unit. Upon acceptance, documentation of need for services should be sent only to the LD program or unit. *Application deadline (institutional):* Continuous. *Application deadline (LD program):* Rolling/continuous for fall and rolling/continuous for spring.

Written Policies Written policy regarding general/basic LD accommodations is outlined in the school's catalog/handbook. Written policies regarding general/basic LD accommodations, grade forgiveness, reduced course loads, substitutions and waivers of admissions requirements, and substitutions and waivers of graduation requirements are available through the program or unit directly.

Johnson C. Smith University

100 Beatties Ford Road
Charlotte, NC 28216-5398
http://www.jcsu.edu/
Contact: Mr. James O. Cuthbertson Jr., Disability Services Coordinator. Phone: 704-378-1282. Fax: 704-330-1336. E-mail: jcuthbertson@jcsu.edu.

Approximately 15 registered undergraduate students were served during 2002-03. The program or unit includes 1 part-time staff member. Academic advisers, counselors, skill tutors, and strategy tutors are provided through the program or unit. Academic advisers, counselors, skill tutors, and strategy tutors are provided collaboratively through on-campus or off-campus services.

Unique Aids and Services Aids, services, or accommodations include advocates, career counseling, and faculty training.

Subject-area Tutoring Tutoring is offered one-on-one, in small groups, and in class-size groups.

Enrichment Programs for career planning, college survival skills, health and nutrition, learning strategies, math, oral communication skills, practical computer skills, reading, stress management, study skills, test taking, time management, vocabulary development, and written composition skills are provided collaboratively through on-campus or off-campus services.

Application For admittance to the program or unit, students are required to apply to the program directly, provide a psychoeducational report, and provide documentation of high school services. Upon acceptance, documentation of need for services should be sent only to the LD program or unit. *Application deadline (institutional):* 8/1. *Application deadline (LD program):* Rolling/continuous for fall and rolling/continuous for spring.

Written Policies Written policy regarding general/basic LD accommodations is available on the program Web site. Written policy regarding general/basic LD accommodations is outlined in the school's catalog/handbook. Written policies regarding course substitutions, general/basic LD accommodations, reduced course loads, substitutions and waivers of admissions requirements, and substitutions and waivers of graduation requirements are available through the program or unit directly.

Johnson State College
Academic Support Services

337 College Hill

Johnson, VT 05656-9405

http://www.johnsonstatecollege.edu/studentlife/
academicsupportsvs.html

Contact: Mr. Clyde Stats, Student Development Coordinator. Phone: 802-635-1263. Fax: 802-635-1454. E-mail: statsc@badger.jsc.vsc.edu. Head of LD Program: Ms. Dian Duranleau, Learning Specialist. Phone: 802-635-1264. Fax: 802-635-1454. E-mail: duranled@badger.jsc.vsc.edu.

Academic Support Services Approximately 120 registered undergraduate students were served during 2002-03. The program or unit includes 7 full-time staff members. Academic advisers, counselors, and LD specialists are provided through the program or unit. Professional tutors, skill tutors, and trained peer tutors are provided collaboratively through on-campus or off-campus services.

Summer Program To help prepare for the demands of college, there is a mandatory 1-week summer program prior to entering the school. Degree credit will be earned.

Unique Aids and Services Aids, services, or accommodations include career counseling, digital textbooks, priority registration, note-takers, extended time/alternate location on exams.

Subject-area Tutoring Tutoring is offered one-on-one and in small groups for most subjects. Tutoring is provided through the program or unit via graduate assistants/students, professional tutors, trained peer tutors, and other.

Diagnostic Testing Testing is provided through the program or unit for learning styles, math, reading, and written language.

Basic Skills Remediation Remediation is offered in class-size groups for math. Remediation is provided collaboratively through on-campus or off-campus services via regular education teachers.

Enrichment Enrichment programs are available through the program or unit for career planning, college survival skills, learning strategies, math, reading, self-advocacy, study skills, test taking, time management, vocabulary development, and written composition skills. Programs for career planning, stress management, vocabulary development, and written composition skills are provided collaboratively through on-campus or off-campus services.

Fees *Summer Program* fee is $650.

Application For admittance to the program or unit, students are required to provide a psychoeducational report (3 years old or less). It is recommended that students provide documentation of high school services. Upon acceptance, documentation of need for services should be sent only to the LD program or unit. *Application deadline (institutional):* Continuous. *Application deadline (LD program):* Rolling/continuous for fall and rolling/continuous for spring.

Written Policies Written policies regarding course substitutions, general/basic LD accommodations, and substitutions and waivers of graduation requirements are available on the program Web site. Written policies regarding course substitutions and substitutions and waivers of graduation requirements are outlined in the school's catalog/handbook. Written policies regarding general/basic LD accommodations and reduced course loads are available through the program or unit directly.

Kansas City Art Institute

4415 Warwick Boulevard

Kansas City, MO 64111-1874

http://www.kcai.edu/

Contact: Dr. Bambi N. Burgard, Assistant Dean for Academic Affairs/Student Achievement. Phone: 816-802-3376. Fax: 816-802-3480. E-mail: bburgard@kcai.edu.

Approximately 20 registered undergraduate students were served during 2002-03. The program or unit includes 1 full-time and 1 part-time staff member. Academic advisers, LD specialists, professional tutors, and trained peer tutors are provided through the program or unit.

Unique Aids and Services Aids, services, or accommodations include personal coach, weekly meetings with faculty, books on tape, oral testing, private test setting.

Subject-area Tutoring Tutoring is offered one-on-one for most subjects. Tutoring is provided through the program or unit via LD specialists, professional tutors, and trained peer tutors.

Basic Skills Remediation Remediation is offered one-on-one for learning strategies, reading, study skills, time management, and written language. Remediation is provided through the program or unit via LD specialists, professional tutors, and trained peer tutors.

Enrichment Enrichment programs are available through the program or unit for learning strategies, study skills, test taking, time management, and written composition skills. Programs for career planning, college survival skills, and stress management are provided collaboratively through on-campus or off-campus services.

Application For admittance to the program or unit, students are required to provide a psychoeducational report (3 years old or less) and provide documentation of high school services. Upon application, materials documenting need for services should be sent only to admissions with institutional application materials. Upon acceptance, documentation of need for services should be sent only to the LD program or unit. *Application deadline (institutional):* Continuous. *Application deadline (LD program):* Rolling/continuous for fall and rolling/continuous for spring.

Written Policies Written policy regarding grade forgiveness is outlined in the school's catalog/handbook. Written policy regarding general/basic LD accommodations is available through the program or unit directly.

Kansas State University

Manhattan, KS 66506

http://www.ksu.edu/

Contact: Ms. Andrea Blair, Learning Disabilities Specialist. Phone: 785-532-6441. Fax: 785-532-6457. E-mail: andreab@ksu.edu.

Approximately 400 registered undergraduate students were served during 2002-03. The program or unit includes 1 full-time staff member. Graduate assistants/students and LD specialists are provided through the program or unit.

Orientation The program or unit offers an optional 2-hour orientation for new students before classes begin.

Unique Aids and Services Aids, services, or accommodations include digital textbooks, faculty training, support groups, priority registration for students using taped texts.

Subject-area Tutoring Tutoring is offered one-on-one and in small groups for some subjects. Tutoring is provided through the program or unit via trained peer tutors.

Enrichment Enrichment programs are available through the program or unit for learning strategies. Credit is offered for learning strategies.

Application For admittance to the program or unit, students are required to apply to the program directly and provide a psychoeducational report. It is recommended that students provide documentation of high school services. Upon acceptance, documentation of need for services should be sent only to the LD program or unit. *Application deadline (institutional):* Continuous. *Application deadline (LD program):* Rolling/continuous for fall.

Written Policies Written policies regarding course substitutions and general/basic LD accommodations are available on the program Web site. Written policies regarding course substitutions and general/basic LD accommodations are outlined in the school's catalog/handbook. Written policies regarding course substitutions and general/basic LD accommodations are available through the program or unit directly.

Kennesaw State University
Disabled Student Support Services

1000 Chastain Road
Kennesaw, GA 30144-5591
http://www.kennesaw.edu/stu_dev/dsss
Contact: Ms. Carol J. Pope, Assistant Director for Disabled Student Support Services. Phone: 770-423-6443. Fax: 770-423-6667. E-mail: cpope@kennesaw.edu.

Disabled Student Support Services Approximately 75 registered undergraduate students were served during 2002-03. The program or unit includes 1 full-time and 1 part-time staff member. Academic advisers, coaches, counselors, LD specialists, remediation/learning specialists, skill tutors, and strategy tutors are provided through the program or unit. Academic advisers, counselors, and diagnostic specialists are provided collaboratively through on-campus or off-campus services.

Unique Aids and Services Aids, services, or accommodations include advocates, career counseling, digital textbooks, priority registration, and support groups.

Subject-area Tutoring Tutoring is offered in small groups for some subjects. Tutoring is provided through the program or unit via LD specialists. Tutoring is also provided collaboratively through on-campus or off-campus services via computer-based instruction, graduate assistants/students, and trained peer tutors.

Diagnostic Testing Testing is provided through the program or unit for learning strategies, learning styles, social skills, and study skills. Testing for auditory processing, handwriting, intelligence, math, motor skills, neuropsychological, personality, reading, spelling, spoken language, visual processing, and written language is provided collaboratively through on-campus or off-campus services.

Basic Skills Remediation Remediation is offered one-on-one and in small groups for computer skills, learning strategies, social skills, study skills, and time management. Remediation is provided through the program or unit via LD specialists.

Enrichment Enrichment programs are available through the program or unit for college survival skills, learning strategies, practical computer skills, self-advocacy, stress management, study skills, test taking, time management, and written composition skills. Programs for career planning, math, practical computer skills, stress management, and written composition skills are provided collaboratively through on-campus or off-campus services.

Student Organization Disabled Students Organization consists of 15 members.

Fees *Diagnostic Testing* fee is $400.

Application For admittance to the program or unit, students are required to apply to the program directly and provide a psychoeducational report (3 years old or less). It is recommended that students provide documentation of high school services. Upon acceptance, documentation of need for services should be sent only to the LD program or unit. *Application deadline (institutional):* 7/18. *Application deadline (LD program):* Rolling/continuous for fall and rolling/continuous for spring.

Written Policies Written policy regarding general/basic LD accommodations is available on the program Web site. Written policy regarding general/basic LD accommodations is available through the program or unit directly.

Kent State University
Student Disability Services

PO Box 5190
Kent, OH 44242-0001
http://www.kent.edu/
Contact: Anne L. Jannarone, Director. Phone: 330-672-3391. Fax: 330-672-3763. E-mail: ajannaro@kent.edu.

Student Disability Services Approximately 300 registered undergraduate students were served during 2002-03. The program or unit includes 5 full-time staff members and 1 part-time staff member. Counselors and graduate assistants/students are provided through the program or unit. Academic advisers, counselors, LD specialists, professional tutors, remediation/learning specialists, strategy tutors, teacher trainees, and trained peer tutors are provided collaboratively through on-campus or off-campus services.

Orientation The program or unit offers an optional 4-hour orientation for new students before classes begin.

Unique Aids and Services Aids, services, or accommodations include faculty training, priority registration, and support groups.

Subject-area Tutoring Tutoring is offered one-on-one and in small groups for some subjects. Tutoring is provided through the program or unit via graduate assistants/students and trained peer tutors.

Basic Skills Remediation Remediation is offered one-on-one and in small groups for learning strategies, study skills, and time management. Remediation is provided collaboratively through on-campus or off-campus services via graduate assistants/students, LD specialists, and trained peer tutors.

Enrichment Enrichment programs are available through the program or unit for learning strategies, study skills, and time management. Programs for career planning, health and nutrition, learning strategies, practical computer skills, reading, stress man-

Kent State University (continued)

agement, study skills, time management, and written composition skills are provided collaboratively through on-campus or off-campus services. Credit is offered for career planning, health and nutrition, and practical computer skills.

Student Organization Ability Unlimited consists of 30 members.

Application For admittance to the program or unit, students are required to provide a psychoeducational report (5 years old or less). It is recommended that students provide documentation of high school services. Upon acceptance, documentation of need for services should be sent only to the LD program or unit. *Application deadline (institutional):* 5/1. *Application deadline (LD program):* Rolling/continuous for fall and rolling/continuous for spring.

Written Policies Written policies regarding course substitutions, general/basic LD accommodations, and reduced course loads are available through the program or unit directly.

King College
The LINKing Center at King

1350 King College Road
Bristol, TN 37620-2699
http://www.king.edu/linking

Contact: Ms. Andrea Bloomer, Administrative Assistant. Phone: 423-652-4711. Fax: 423-652-6307. E-mail: aebloome@king.edu.

The LINKing Center at King Approximately 10 registered undergraduate students were served during 2002-03. The program or unit includes 3 part-time staff members. Counselors are provided through the program or unit. Academic advisers, coaches, counselors, LD specialists, and trained peer tutors are provided collaboratively through on-campus or off-campus services.

Unique Aids and Services Aids, services, or accommodations include career counseling and faculty training.

Subject-area Tutoring Tutoring is offered one-on-one, in small groups, and in class-size groups for most subjects. Tutoring is provided through the program or unit via trained peer tutors. Tutoring is also provided collaboratively through on-campus or off-campus services via trained peer tutors.

Basic Skills Remediation Remediation is offered one-on-one for learning strategies, math, reading, study skills, and time management. Remediation is provided through the program or unit via computer-based instruction and other.

Enrichment Enrichment programs are available through the program or unit for career planning, college survival skills, learning strategies, medication management, practical computer skills, self-advocacy, study skills, test taking, and time management. Programs for career planning, college survival skills, learning strategies, medication management, practical computer skills, vocabulary development, and written composition skills are provided collaboratively through on-campus or off-campus services. Credit is offered for college survival skills.

Application It is recommended that students provide a psychoeducational report and provide documentation of high school services. Upon application, materials documenting need for services should be sent to both admissions and the LD program or unit. Upon acceptance, documentation of need for services should be sent to both admissions and the LD program or unit. *Application deadline (institutional):* Continuous. *Application deadline (LD program):* Rolling/continuous for fall and rolling/continuous for spring.

Written Policies Written policies regarding general/basic LD accommodations, reduced course loads, and substitutions and waivers of admissions requirements are available through the program or unit directly.

The King's University College

9125 50th Street
Edmonton, AB T6B 2H3
Canada
http://www.kingsu.ca/

Contact: Ms. Ruth Wallace, Dean of Students. Phone: 780-465-3500. Fax: 780-465-3534. E-mail: ruth.wallace@kingsu.ca.

Approximately 8 registered undergraduate students were served during 2002-03. The program or unit includes 2 full-time staff members. Academic advisers and trained peer tutors are provided collaboratively through on-campus or off-campus services.

Orientation The program or unit offers an optional orientation for new students individually by special arrangement.

Unique Aids and Services Aids, services, or accommodations include career counseling, other accommodations as required.

Subject-area Tutoring Tutoring is offered one-on-one, in small groups, and in class-size groups for most subjects. Tutoring is provided collaboratively through on-campus or off-campus services via trained peer tutors.

Application For admittance to the program or unit, students are required to provide a psychoeducational report (3 years old or less). It is recommended that students provide documentation of high school services. Upon application, materials documenting need for services should be sent only to the LD program or unit. Upon acceptance, documentation of need for services should be sent only to the LD program or unit. *Application deadline (institutional):* Continuous. *Application deadline (LD program):* Rolling/continuous for fall.

Written Policies Written policy regarding general/basic LD accommodations is outlined in the school's catalog/handbook. Written policy regarding general/basic LD accommodations is available through the program or unit directly.

Kutztown University of Pennsylvania
Disabilities Services Office

15200 Kutztown Road
Kutztown, PA 19530-0730
http://www.kutztown.edu/

Contact: Mrs. Patricia J. Richter, Director of Disability Services for the Americans with Disabilities Act. Phone: 610-683-4108. Fax: 610-683-1520. E-mail: richter@kutztown.edu.

Disabilities Services Office Approximately 280 registered undergraduate students were served during 2002-03. Academic advisers, coaches, counselors, graduate assistants/students, LD specialists, skill tutors, strategy tutors, and trained peer tutors are provided collaboratively through on-campus or off-campus services.

Unique Aids and Services Aids, services, or accommodations include advocates, faculty training, priority registration, and support groups.

Subject-area Tutoring Tutoring is offered one-on-one and in small groups for most subjects. Tutoring is provided collaboratively through on-campus or off-campus services via computer-based instruction and trained peer tutors.

Enrichment Programs for career planning, college survival skills, health and nutrition, learning strategies, self-advocacy, stress management, study skills, test taking, time management, and written composition skills are provided collaboratively through on-campus or off-campus services.

Student Organization The Phoenix Group consists of 8 members.

Application For admittance to the program or unit, students are required to provide a psychoeducational report and provide updated documentation (4 years old or less). It is recommended that students provide documentation of high school services. Upon application, materials documenting need for services should be sent only to the LD program or unit. Upon acceptance, documentation of need for services should be sent only to the LD program or unit. *Application deadline (institutional):* 3/1. *Application deadline (LD program):* Rolling/continuous for fall and rolling/continuous for spring.

Written Policies Written policy regarding general/basic LD accommodations is available on the program Web site. Written policy regarding general/basic LD accommodations is outlined in the school's catalog/handbook. Written policies regarding course substitutions and general/basic LD accommodations are available through the program or unit directly.

Laboratory Institute of Merchandising

12 East 53rd Street
New York, NY 10022-5268
http://www.limcollege.edu/

Contact: Ellen Simpao PhD, Director of Counseling. Phone: 212-752-1530 Ext. 229. Fax: 212-752-5319. E-mail: esimpao@limcollege.edu.

Approximately 17 registered undergraduate students were served during 2002-03. The program or unit includes 2 full-time and 5 part-time staff members. Academic advisers and counselors are provided through the program or unit. Academic advisers, regular education teachers, and trained peer tutors are provided collaboratively through on-campus or off-campus services.

Unique Aids and Services Aids, services, or accommodations include career counseling, parent workshops, and weekly meetings with faculty.

Subject-area Tutoring Tutoring is offered one-on-one and in small groups for some subjects. Tutoring is provided collaboratively through on-campus or off-campus services via professional tutors, trained peer tutors, and other.

Basic Skills Remediation Remediation is offered one-on-one, in small groups, and in class-size groups for learning strategies, math, reading, spelling, study skills, time management, and written language. Remediation is provided collaboratively through on-campus or off-campus services via computer-based instruction, LD specialists, professional tutors, and trained peer tutors.

Enrichment Enrichment programs are available through the program or unit for career planning, college survival skills, health and nutrition, learning strategies, medication management, self-advocacy, stress management, study skills, test taking, time management, and other. Programs for career planning, college survival skills, health and nutrition, learning strategies, math, oral communication skills, practical computer skills, reading, self-advocacy, stress management, study skills, test taking, time management, vocabulary development, written composition skills, and other are provided collaboratively through on-campus or off-campus services. Credit is offered for college survival skills, math, oral communication skills, practical computer skills, and written composition skills.

Application For admittance to the program or unit, students are required to provide a psychoeducational report (3 years old or less). It is recommended that students provide documentation of high school services and provide neuropsychological reports. Upon acceptance, documentation of need for services should be sent only to the LD program or unit. *Application deadline (institutional):* Continuous. *Application deadline (LD program):* 12/31 for fall. 5/31 for spring.

Written Policies Written policy regarding general/basic LD accommodations is available on the program Web site. Written policy regarding general/basic LD accommodations is outlined in the school's catalog/handbook. Written policy regarding general/basic LD accommodations is available through the program or unit directly.

Lakehead University

955 Oliver Road
Thunder Bay, ON P7B 5E1
Canada
http://www.lakeheadu.ca/

Contact: Donna Patricia Grau, Coordinator Learning Assistance Centre. Phone: 807-343-8087. Fax: 807-346-7733. E-mail: donna.grau@lakeheadu.ca.

Approximately 100 registered undergraduate students were served during 2002-03. The program or unit includes 1 full-time and 2 part-time staff members. Academic advisers, graduate assistants/students, LD specialists, skill tutors, strategy tutors, and other are provided through the program or unit. Academic advisers, counselors, diagnostic specialists, graduate assistants/students, professional tutors, trained peer tutors, and other are provided collaboratively through on-campus or off-campus services.

Orientation The program or unit offers an optional orientation for new students individually by special arrangement.

Unique Aids and Services Aids, services, or accommodations include career counseling, personal coach, and support groups.

Lakehead University (continued)

Subject-area Tutoring Tutoring is offered one-on-one, in small groups, and in class-size groups for most subjects. Tutoring is provided through the program or unit via LD specialists. Tutoring is also provided collaboratively through on-campus or off-campus services via graduate assistants/students, professional tutors, and trained peer tutors.

Diagnostic Testing Testing for learning styles, math, motor skills, neuropsychological, personality, reading, social skills, spelling, spoken language, study skills, visual processing, and written language is provided collaboratively through on-campus or off-campus services.

Basic Skills Remediation Remediation is offered one-on-one and in small groups for computer skills, learning strategies, math, reading, spelling, study skills, time management, visual processing, and written language. Remediation is provided through the program or unit via computer-based instruction and LD specialists. Remediation is also provided collaboratively through on-campus or off-campus services via graduate assistants/students, professional tutors, and trained peer tutors.

Enrichment Enrichment programs are available through the program or unit for college survival skills, learning strategies, practical computer skills, reading, self-advocacy, study skills, test taking, time management, vocabulary development, and written composition skills. Programs for career planning, health and nutrition, math, oral communication skills, stress management, study skills, test taking, time management, and written composition skills are provided collaboratively through on-campus or off-campus services.

Fees *Diagnostic Testing* fee is $850.

Application For admittance to the program or unit, students are required to provide a psychoeducational report (4 years old or less), provide documentation of high school services, and provide documentation from other post-secondary institutions. Upon acceptance, documentation of need for services should be sent only to the LD program or unit. *Application deadline (institutional):* Continuous. *Application deadline (LD program):* Rolling/continuous for fall and rolling/continuous for spring.

Written Policies Written policy regarding general/basic LD accommodations is available on the program Web site. Written policy regarding general/basic LD accommodations is available through the program or unit directly.

Lakeland College
Hayssen Academic Resource Center

PO Box 359
Sheboygan, WI 53082-0359
http://www1.lakeland.edu/hayssen

Contact: Mr. Paul M. White, Director of Hayssen Academic Resource Center. Phone: 920-565-1412. Fax: 920-565-1231. E-mail: whitepm@lakeland.edu.

Hayssen Academic Resource Center Approximately 15 registered undergraduate students were served during 2002-03. The program or unit includes 1 full-time and 2 part-time staff members. Academic advisers, professional tutors, remediation/learning specialists, skill tutors, strategy tutors, and trained peer tutors are provided through the program or unit. Academic advisers, coaches, counselors, diagnostic specialists, regular education teachers, and remediation/learning specialists are provided collaboratively through on-campus or off-campus services.

Unique Aids and Services Aids, services, or accommodations include digital textbooks and faculty training.

Subject-area Tutoring Tutoring is offered one-on-one and in small groups for all subjects. Tutoring is provided through the program or unit via computer-based instruction, professional tutors, and trained peer tutors.

Diagnostic Testing Testing is provided through the program or unit for learning strategies, learning styles, math, reading, and study skills.

Basic Skills Remediation Remediation is offered one-on-one and in class-size groups for learning strategies, math, reading, spelling, study skills, time management, and written language. Remediation is provided through the program or unit via professional tutors and trained peer tutors. Remediation is also provided collaboratively through on-campus or off-campus services via computer-based instruction and regular education teachers.

Enrichment Enrichment programs are available through the program or unit for learning strategies, math, reading, stress management, study skills, test taking, time management, and written composition skills. Programs for career planning, college survival skills, health and nutrition, math, reading, and vocabulary development are provided collaboratively through on-campus or off-campus services.

Application For admittance to the program or unit, students are required to apply to the program directly and provide a psychoeducational report (3 years old or less). It is recommended that students provide documentation of high school services. Upon application, materials documenting need for services should be sent to both admissions and the LD program or unit. Upon acceptance, documentation of need for services should be sent only to the LD program or unit. *Application deadline (institutional):* 7/15. *Application deadline (LD program):* Rolling/continuous for fall and rolling/continuous for spring.

Written Policies Written policy regarding general/basic LD accommodations is outlined in the school's catalog/handbook. Written policies regarding course substitutions, general/basic LD accommodations, and reduced course loads are available through the program or unit directly.

Lake Superior State University
Disability Services, Resource Center for Students with Disabilities (RCSD)

650 W Easterday Avenue
Sault Sainte Marie, MI 49783-1626
http://www.lssu.edu/

Contact: Ms. Victoria Diane Fox, Coordinator of Disability Services. Phone: 906-632-6841 Ext. 2454. Fax: 906-635-7564. E-mail: vfox@lssu.edu. Head of LD Program: Mr. Dave Castner, Chair. Phone: 906-632-6841 Ext. 2453. Fax: 906-635-7564. E-mail: dcastner@.ssu.edu.

Disability Services, Resource Center for Students with Disabilities (RCSD) Approximately 128 registered undergraduate students were served during 2002-03. The program or unit includes 3 full-time staff members. Counselors are provided through the program or unit. Academic advisers, coaches, counselors, diagnostic specialists, LD specialists, regular education teachers, remediation/learning specialists, special education teachers, and trained peer tutors are provided collaboratively through on-campus or off-campus services.

Unique Aids and Services Aids, services, or accommodations include career counseling, digital textbooks, and faculty training.

Subject-area Tutoring Tutoring is offered one-on-one and in small groups for most subjects. Tutoring is provided collaboratively through on-campus or off-campus services via computer-based instruction, graduate assistants/students, and trained peer tutors.

Basic Skills Remediation Remediation is offered in class-size groups for math, reading, study skills, time management, and written language. Remediation is provided collaboratively through on-campus or off-campus services via regular education teachers, special education teachers, and trained peer tutors.

Enrichment Enrichment programs are available through the program or unit for self-advocacy. Programs for career planning, practical computer skills, reading, stress management, study skills, test taking, and time management are provided collaboratively through on-campus or off-campus services. Credit is offered for career planning.

Application For admittance to the program or unit, students are required to provide a psychoeducational report. It is recommended that students apply to the program directly, provide documentation of high school services, and provide recommendations for post-secondary accommodations from either IEP or psychoeducational report. Upon application, materials documenting need for services should be sent only to the LD program or unit. Upon acceptance, documentation of need for services should be sent only to the LD program or unit. *Application deadline (institutional):* 8/15. *Application deadline (LD program):* Rolling/continuous for fall and rolling/continuous for spring.

Written Policies Written policies regarding general/basic LD accommodations and reduced course loads are available through the program or unit directly.

Lamar University
Services for Students with Disabilities

4400 Martin Luther King Parkway
Beaumont, TX 77710

Contact: Mrs. Callie Faye Trahan, Coordinator of Services for Students with Disabilities. Phone: 409-880-8026. Fax: 409-880-2225. E-mail: trahancf@hal.lamar.edu.

Services for Students with Disabilities Approximately 225 registered undergraduate students were served during 2002-03. The program or unit includes 2 full-time and 2 part-time staff members. Academic advisers, counselors, regular education teachers, remediation/learning specialists, skill tutors, and strategy tutors are provided collaboratively through on-campus or off-campus services.

Orientation The program or unit offers an optional 1-day orientation for new students before classes begin, individually by special arrangement, and after registration.

Unique Aids and Services Aids, services, or accommodations include career counseling, digital textbooks, faculty training, and priority registration.

Subject-area Tutoring Tutoring is offered one-on-one and in small groups for some subjects. Tutoring is provided collaboratively through on-campus or off-campus services via computer-based instruction, graduate assistants/students, and other.

Basic Skills Remediation Remediation is offered in class-size groups for auditory processing, computer skills, handwriting, learning strategies, math, reading, study skills, time management, and written language. Remediation is provided collaboratively through on-campus or off-campus services via computer-based instruction, graduate assistants/students, regular education teachers, and other.

Enrichment Enrichment programs are available through the program or unit for college survival skills. Programs for career planning, health and nutrition, learning strategies, math, medication management, reading, stress management, study skills, test taking, time management, and written composition skills are provided collaboratively through on-campus or off-campus services. Credit is offered for health and nutrition, learning strategies, study skills, test taking, and time management.

Fees *Orientation* fee is $50.

Application For admittance to the program or unit, students are required to apply to the program directly and provide a psychoeducational report (3 years old or less). It is recommended that students provide documentation of high school services. Upon application, materials documenting need for services should be sent only to the LD program or unit. Upon acceptance, documentation of need for services should be sent only to the LD program or unit. *Application deadline (institutional):* 8/1. *Application deadline (LD program):* Rolling/continuous for fall and rolling/continuous for spring.

Written Policies Written policy regarding grade forgiveness is available on the program Web site. Written policies regarding course substitutions, general/basic LD accommodations, grade forgiveness, and substitutions and waivers of admissions requirements are outlined in the school's catalog/handbook. Written policies regarding course substitutions and substitutions and waivers of graduation requirements are available through the program or unit directly.

Langston University

PO Box 907
Langston, OK 73050-0907
http://www.lunet.edu/

Contact: Mr. Joseph L. Brown, ADA Compliance Officer. Phone: 405-466-3445. Fax: 405-466-3447. E-mail: jlbrown@lunet.edu.

Approximately 35 registered undergraduate students were served during 2002-03. The program or unit includes 1 full-time staff member. Academic advisers and counselors are provided through the program or unit. Academic advisers, counselors, professional tutors, skill tutors, strategy tutors, and trained peer tutors are provided collaboratively through on-campus or off-campus services.

Unique Aids and Services Aids, services, or accommodations include faculty training and weekly meetings with faculty.

Subject-area Tutoring Tutoring is offered one-on-one and in small groups for most subjects. Tutoring is provided collaboratively through on-campus or off-campus services via graduate assistants/students, professional tutors, and trained peer tutors.

Basic Skills Remediation Remediation is offered one-on-one, in small groups, and in class-size groups for math, reading, spelling, visual processing, and written language. Remediation is provided

Langston University (continued)

collaboratively through on-campus or off-campus services via computer-based instruction, graduate assistants/students, professional tutors, regular education teachers, and trained peer tutors.

Application For admittance to the program or unit, students are required to provide a psychoeducational report (2 years old or less) and provide documentation of high school services. Upon application, materials documenting need for services should be sent only to the LD program or unit. Upon acceptance, documentation of need for services should be sent only to the LD program or unit. *Application deadline (institutional):* Continuous. *Application deadline (LD program):* Rolling/continuous for fall and rolling/continuous for spring.

Written Policies Written policies regarding general/basic LD accommodations and substitutions and waivers of admissions requirements are outlined in the school's catalog/handbook. Written policies regarding general/basic LD accommodations and substitutions and waivers of admissions requirements are available through the program or unit directly.

La Roche College
Academic Enrichment Center

9000 Babcock Boulevard
Pittsburgh, PA 15237-5898
http://www.laroche.edu/

Contact: Mr. Lance Shaeffer, Assistant Dean of Academic Enrichment. Phone: 412-536-1295. Fax: 412-536-1118. E-mail: shaeffl1@laroche.edu.

Academic Enrichment Center Approximately 50 registered undergraduate students were served during 2002-03. The program or unit includes 3 full-time staff members and 1 part-time staff member. Counselors, LD specialists, professional tutors, skill tutors, strategy tutors, and trained peer tutors are provided through the program or unit. Academic advisers, coaches, counselors, diagnostic specialists, graduate assistants/students, LD specialists, professional tutors, regular education teachers, remediation/learning specialists, skill tutors, special education teachers, strategy tutors, teacher trainees, and trained peer tutors are provided collaboratively through on-campus or off-campus services.

Unique Aids and Services Aids, services, or accommodations include career counseling, weekly meetings with faculty, extended time for test-taking, note-taking.

Subject-area Tutoring Tutoring is offered one-on-one, in small groups, and in class-size groups for most subjects. Tutoring is provided through the program or unit via professional tutors and trained peer tutors. Tutoring is also provided collaboratively through on-campus or off-campus services via computer-based instruction, graduate assistants/students, professional tutors, and trained peer tutors.

Enrichment Programs for career planning, learning strategies, math, practical computer skills, stress management, study skills, test taking, and time management are provided collaboratively through on-campus or off-campus services.

Student Organization Project Achievement consists of 25 members.

Application It is recommended that students provide a psychoeducational report and provide documentation of high school services. Upon application, materials documenting need for services should be sent only to the LD program or unit. Upon acceptance, documentation of need for services should be sent only to the LD program or unit. *Application deadline (institutional):* 8/25. *Application deadline (LD program):* Rolling/continuous for fall and rolling/continuous for spring.

Written Policies Written policy regarding general/basic LD accommodations is available on the program Web site. Written policy regarding general/basic LD accommodations is outlined in the school's catalog/handbook. Written policy regarding general/basic LD accommodations is available through the program or unit directly.

Laurentian University
Special Needs Office

935 Ramsey Lake Road
Sudbury, ON P3E 2C6
Canada
http://www.laurentian.ca/specneeds/index.html

Contact: Mr. Raymond Morin, Study Skills Specialist and Assistive Technologist. Phone: 705-675-1151 Ext. 1086. Fax: 705-675-1151 Ext. 4807. E-mail: rjmorin@nickel.laurentian.ca.

Special Needs Office Approximately 125 registered undergraduate students were served during 2002-03. The program or unit includes 1 full-time and 1 part-time staff member. LD specialists and remediation/learning specialists are provided through the program or unit. Academic advisers, counselors, LD specialists, remediation/learning specialists, and trained peer tutors are provided collaboratively through on-campus or off-campus services.

Orientation The program or unit offers an optional 1-day orientation for new students before registration, before classes begin, during summer prior to enrollment, and individually by special arrangement.

Summer Program To help prepare for the demands of college, there is an optional 4-week summer program prior to entering the school.

Unique Aids and Services Aids, services, or accommodations include advocates and career counseling.

Subject-area Tutoring Tutoring is offered one-on-one for all subjects. Tutoring is provided through the program or unit via computer-based instruction and LD specialists. Tutoring is also provided collaboratively through on-campus or off-campus services via computer-based instruction, LD specialists, and trained peer tutors.

Basic Skills Remediation Remediation is offered one-on-one for computer skills, learning strategies, reading, study skills, time management, visual processing, and written language. Remediation is provided through the program or unit via computer-based instruction and LD specialists. Remediation is also provided collaboratively through on-campus or off-campus services via computer-based instruction, LD specialists, professional tutors, and trained peer tutors.

Enrichment Enrichment programs are available through the program or unit for learning strategies, reading, self-advocacy, study skills, time management, and written composition skills. Programs for career planning, college survival skills, learning strategies, math, reading, self-advocacy, stress management, study skills, test taking, time management, and written composition skills are provided collaboratively through on-campus or off-campus services.

Application For admittance to the program or unit, students are required to apply to the program directly and provide a psychoeducational report (3 years old or less). It is recommended that students provide documentation of high school services. Upon application, materials documenting need for services should be sent only to the LD program or unit. Upon acceptance, documentation of need for services should be sent only to the LD program or unit. *Application deadline (institutional):* 2/1. *Application deadline (LD program):* Rolling/continuous for fall and rolling/continuous for spring.

Lawrence University

PO Box 599
Appleton, WI 54912-0599
http://www.lawrence.edu
Contact: Mr. Geoff Gajewski, Assistant Dean of Student Academic Services. Phone: 920-832-6530. Fax: 920-832-6884. E-mail: geoffrey.c.gajewski@lawrence.edu.

Approximately 15 registered undergraduate students were served during 2002-03. The program or unit includes 2 part-time staff members. Academic advisers, graduate assistants/students, LD specialists, remediation/learning specialists, skill tutors, strategy tutors, and trained peer tutors are provided through the program or unit. Coaches, counselors, and diagnostic specialists are provided collaboratively through on-campus or off-campus services.

Unique Aids and Services Aids, services, or accommodations include career counseling, support groups, academic accommodations as needed.

Subject-area Tutoring Tutoring is offered one-on-one and in small groups for all subjects. Tutoring is provided through the program or unit via trained peer tutors.

Basic Skills Remediation Remediation is offered one-on-one and in small groups for computer skills, learning strategies, math, reading, spelling, spoken language, study skills, time management, and written language. Remediation is provided through the program or unit via trained peer tutors.

Enrichment Enrichment programs are available through the program or unit for college survival skills, learning strategies, math, oral communication skills, practical computer skills, reading, self-advocacy, stress management, study skills, test taking, time management, vocabulary development, and written composition skills. Programs for career planning, health and nutrition, and medication management are provided collaboratively through on-campus or off-campus services.

Student Organization ADAPT consists of 8 members.

Application For admittance to the program or unit, students are required to provide a psychoeducational report (3 years old or less). It is recommended that students provide documentation of high school services. Upon acceptance, documentation of need for services should be sent only to the LD program or unit. *Application deadline (institutional):* 1/15. *Application deadline (LD program):* Rolling/continuous for fall and rolling/continuous for spring.

Written Policies Written policy regarding general/basic LD accommodations is available on the program Web site. Written policy regarding general/basic LD accommodations is outlined in the school's catalog/handbook. Written policies regarding course substitutions, general/basic LD accommodations, reduced course loads, substitutions and waivers of admissions requirements, and substitutions and waivers of graduation requirements are available through the program or unit directly.

Lebanon Valley College
Office of Disability Services

101 North College Avenue
Annville, PA 17003-1400
http://www.lvc.edu/disability-services.html
Contact: Mrs. Anne H. Hohenwarter, Coordinator of Disability Services. Phone: 717-867-6158. Fax: 717-867-6910. E-mail: hohenwar@lvc.edu.

Office of Disability Services Approximately 63 registered undergraduate students were served during 2002-03. The program or unit includes 1 part-time staff member. Academic advisers, LD specialists, skill tutors, and strategy tutors are provided through the program or unit. Academic advisers, counselors, and trained peer tutors are provided collaboratively through on-campus or off-campus services.

Unique Aids and Services Aids, services, or accommodations include career counseling, faculty training, priority registration, extended time on exams in distraction-reduced room, books-on-tape, peer note-takers.

Subject-area Tutoring Tutoring is offered one-on-one for most subjects. Tutoring is provided collaboratively through on-campus or off-campus services via trained peer tutors.

Basic Skills Remediation Remediation is offered one-on-one for learning strategies, study skills, and time management. Remediation is provided through the program or unit via LD specialists.

Application For admittance to the program or unit, students are required to provide a psychoeducational report. It is recommended that students provide documentation of high school services. Upon acceptance, documentation of need for services should be sent only to the LD program or unit. *Application deadline (institutional):* Continuous. *Application deadline (LD program):* Rolling/continuous for fall and rolling/continuous for spring.

Written Policies Written policy regarding general/basic LD accommodations is available on the program Web site. Written policy regarding general/basic LD accommodations is outlined in the school's catalog/handbook. Written policies regarding course substitutions, general/basic LD accommodations, reduced course loads, and substitutions and waivers of graduation requirements are available through the program or unit directly.

Lee University
Academic Support Program

PO Box 3450
Cleveland, TN 37320-3450
http://www.leeuniversity.edu/

Lee University (continued)

Contact: Dr. Gayle Gallaher, Director. Phone: 423-614-8181. Fax: 423-614-8179. E-mail: ggallaher@leeuniversity.edu.

Academic Support Program Approximately 130 registered undergraduate students were served during 2002-03. The program or unit includes 1 full-time and 2 part-time staff members. Academic advisers, counselors, graduate assistants/students, and trained peer tutors are provided through the program or unit. Academic advisers, counselors, diagnostic specialists, graduate assistants/students, regular education teachers, and trained peer tutors are provided collaboratively through on-campus or off-campus services.

Subject-area Tutoring Tutoring is offered one-on-one and in small groups for all subjects. Tutoring is provided through the program or unit via graduate assistants/students and trained peer tutors. Tutoring is also provided collaboratively through on-campus or off-campus services via graduate assistants/students and trained peer tutors.

Basic Skills Remediation Remediation is offered in class-size groups for math, reading, spoken language, and written language. Remediation is provided through the program or unit via trained peer tutors. Remediation is also provided collaboratively through on-campus or off-campus services via regular education teachers and trained peer tutors.

Enrichment Programs for career planning, college survival skills, health and nutrition, practical computer skills, study skills, time management, and written composition skills are provided collaboratively through on-campus or off-campus services. Credit is offered for career planning, college survival skills, health and nutrition, practical computer skills, study skills, time management, and written composition skills.

Application For admittance to the program or unit, students are required to apply to the program directly. It is recommended that students provide a psychoeducational report and provide documentation of high school services. Upon application, materials documenting need for services should be sent to both admissions and the LD program or unit. Upon acceptance, documentation of need for services should be sent to both admissions and the LD program or unit. *Application deadline (institutional): 9/1. Application deadline (LD program):* Rolling/continuous for fall and rolling/continuous for spring.

Written Policies Written policy regarding general/basic LD accommodations is outlined in the school's catalog/handbook.

Lehigh University

27 Memorial Drive West
Bethlehem, PA 18015-3094
http://www.lehigh.edu/
Contact: Phone: 610-758-3000. Fax: 610-758-4361.

The program or unit includes 1 full-time and 1 part-time staff member. Coaches, graduate assistants/students, LD specialists, skill tutors, and strategy tutors are provided through the program or unit. Academic advisers, counselors, and trained peer tutors are provided collaboratively through on-campus or off-campus services.

Orientation The program or unit offers an optional 1-hour orientation for new students before classes begin, individually by special arrangement, and during new student orientation.

Unique Aids and Services Aids, services, or accommodations include faculty training, personal coach, and support groups.

Subject-area Tutoring Tutoring is offered one-on-one and in small groups for some subjects. Tutoring is provided through the program or unit via graduate assistants/students. Tutoring is also provided collaboratively through on-campus or off-campus services via trained peer tutors.

Basic Skills Remediation Remediation is offered one-on-one for learning strategies, study skills, and time management. Remediation is provided through the program or unit via graduate assistants/students and LD specialists.

Enrichment Enrichment programs are available through the program or unit for college survival skills, learning strategies, self-advocacy, study skills, test taking, time management, and written composition skills. Programs for career planning, college survival skills, health and nutrition, stress management, and written composition skills are provided collaboratively through on-campus or off-campus services.

Student Organization Peer Mentors consists of 20 members.

Application For admittance to the program or unit, students are required to provide a psychoeducational report (3 years old or less). It is recommended that students apply to the program directly and provide documentation of high school services. Upon acceptance, documentation of need for services should be sent only to the LD program or unit. *Application deadline (institutional): 1/1. Application deadline (LD program):* Rolling/continuous for fall and rolling/continuous for spring.

Written Policies Written policies regarding course substitutions and general/basic LD accommodations are available on the program Web site. Written policy regarding general/basic LD accommodations is outlined in the school's catalog/handbook. Written policies regarding course substitutions and general/basic LD accommodations are available through the program or unit directly.

Le Moyne College
Disability Support Services

1419 Salt Springs Road
Syracuse, NY 13214-1399
http://www.lemoyne.edu/academic_support_center/spneed.htm

Contact: Jennifer Reddy. Phone: 315-445-4118. Fax: 315-445-6014. E-mail: asc@lemoyne.edu. Head of LD Program: Bernardo DelSavio, Director of Disability Support Services. Phone: 315-445-4710. Fax: 315-445-6014. E-mail: delsavbf@lemoyne.edu.

Disability Support Services Approximately 107 registered undergraduate students were served during 2002-03. The program or unit includes 2 full-time staff members. Academic advisers, graduate assistants/students, LD specialists, and other are provided through the program or unit. Academic advisers, coaches, counselors, professional tutors, skill tutors, and trained peer tutors are provided collaboratively through on-campus or off-campus services.

Unique Aids and Services Aids, services, or accommodations include alternative formatting of exams and texts, assistance in finding note-takers, alternative testing.

Subject-area Tutoring Tutoring is offered one-on-one and in small groups for some subjects. Tutoring is provided through the program or unit via professional tutors and trained peer tutors. Tutoring is also provided collaboratively through on-campus or off-campus services via computer-based instruction, professional tutors, and trained peer tutors.

Basic Skills Remediation Remediation is offered one-on-one, in small groups, and in class-size groups for computer skills, learning strategies, math, reading, study skills, time management, and written language. Remediation is provided through the program or unit via trained peer tutors and other. Remediation is also provided collaboratively through on-campus or off-campus services via computer-based instruction, professional tutors, regular education teachers, trained peer tutors, and other.

Enrichment Enrichment programs are available through the program or unit for reading, self-advocacy, vocabulary development, and written composition skills. Programs for career planning, college survival skills, learning strategies, math, oral communication skills, practical computer skills, reading, stress management, study skills, test taking, time management, vocabulary development, and written composition skills are provided collaboratively through on-campus or off-campus services.

Application For admittance to the program or unit, students are required to provide a psychoeducational report (5 years old or less) and provide a meeting and review of documentation. It is recommended that students provide documentation of high school services. Upon acceptance, documentation of need for services should be sent only to the LD program or unit. *Application deadline (institutional):* 2/1. *Application deadline (LD program):* Rolling/continuous for fall and rolling/continuous for spring.

Written Policies Written policy regarding general/basic LD accommodations is available on the program Web site. Written policy regarding general/basic LD accommodations is outlined in the school's catalog/handbook. Written policies regarding course substitutions and general/basic LD accommodations are available through the program or unit directly.

LeMoyne-Owen College

807 Walker Avenue
Memphis, TN 38126-6595
http://www.lemoyne-owen.edu/
Contact: Ms. Jean B. Saulsberry, Director of Student Development. Phone: 901-942-6205. Fax: 901-775-7647. E-mail: jean_saulsberry@nile.loc.edu.

Approximately 7 registered undergraduate students were served during 2002-03. The program or unit includes 1 full-time staff member. Counselors and remediation/learning specialists are provided through the program or unit. Academic advisers, coaches, counselors, diagnostic specialists, regular education teachers, remediation/learning specialists, trained peer tutors, and other are provided collaboratively through on-campus or off-campus services.

Unique Aids and Services Aids, services, or accommodations include faculty training, priority registration, and support groups.

Subject-area Tutoring Tutoring is offered in small groups for most subjects. Tutoring is provided collaboratively through on-campus or off-campus services via professional tutors and trained peer tutors.

Diagnostic Testing Testing for auditory processing, learning strategies, learning styles, math, motor skills, neuropsychological, personality, reading, study skills, and visual processing is provided collaboratively through on-campus or off-campus services.

Basic Skills Remediation Remediation is offered one-on-one and in small groups for computer skills, learning strategies, math, reading, study skills, and time management. Remediation is provided collaboratively through on-campus or off-campus services via professional tutors, regular education teachers, and trained peer tutors.

Enrichment Programs for career planning, health and nutrition, learning strategies, math, study skills, time management, and written composition skills are provided collaboratively through on-campus or off-campus services.

Fees *Diagnostic Testing* fee is $20.

Application For admittance to the program or unit, students are required to apply to the program directly. Upon application, materials documenting need for services should be sent only to the LD program or unit. Upon acceptance, documentation of need for services should be sent only to the LD program or unit. *Application deadline (institutional):* 4/1. *Application deadline (LD program):* Rolling/continuous for fall and rolling/continuous for spring.

Written Policies Written policies regarding general/basic LD accommodations and substitutions and waivers of admissions requirements are outlined in the school's catalog/handbook. Written policies regarding course substitutions, general/basic LD accommodations, reduced course loads, substitutions and waivers of admissions requirements, and substitutions and waivers of graduation requirements are available through the program or unit directly.

Lenoir-Rhyne College
Disability Services Office

7th Avenue and 8th Street, NE
Hickory, NC 28603
http://www.lrc.edu/student/disabilities/disability_services.htm
Contact: Mr. Donavon Kirby, Disabilities Coordinator. Phone: 828-328-7296. Fax: 828-267-3441. E-mail: kirbydr@lrc.edu.

Disability Services Office Approximately 55 registered undergraduate students were served during 2002-03. The program or unit includes 1 full-time staff member. Academic advisers, coaches, counselors, and trained peer tutors are provided collaboratively through on-campus or off-campus services.

Subject-area Tutoring Tutoring is offered in small groups for some subjects. Tutoring is provided collaboratively through on-campus or off-campus services via trained peer tutors.

Application For admittance to the program or unit, students are required to provide a psychoeducational report (3 years old or less). Upon application, materials documenting need for services should be sent only to the LD program or unit. Upon acceptance, documentation of need for services should be sent only to the LD program or unit. *Application deadline (institutional):* Continuous. *Application deadline (LD program):* Rolling/continuous for fall and rolling/continuous for spring.

Written Policies Written policies regarding course substitutions, general/basic LD accommodations, and substitutions and waivers of admissions requirements are available on the program Web site. Written policies regarding course substitutions, general/basic LD

Lenoir-Rhyne College (continued)

accommodations, and substitutions and waivers of admissions requirements are outlined in the school's catalog/handbook. Written policies regarding course substitutions and general/basic LD accommodations are available through the program or unit directly.

LeTourneau University

PO Box 7001
Longview, TX 75607-7001
http://www.letu.edu/
Contact: Dr. William Howard Franklin, Dean of Student Services. Phone: 903-233-3130. Fax: 903-233-3129. E-mail: billfranklin@letu.edu.

The program or unit includes 1 full-time staff member. Counselors and regular education teachers are provided through the program or unit.

Subject-area Tutoring Tutoring is offered one-on-one, in small groups, and in class-size groups for most subjects. Tutoring is provided collaboratively through on-campus or off-campus services via graduate assistants/students and trained peer tutors.

Basic Skills Remediation Remediation is offered one-on-one and in small groups for learning strategies, math, reading, social skills, study skills, time management, and written language. Remediation is provided collaboratively through on-campus or off-campus services via graduate assistants/students and trained peer tutors.

Enrichment Programs for career planning, college survival skills, health and nutrition, learning strategies, math, reading, stress management, study skills, test taking, time management, and written composition skills are provided collaboratively through on-campus or off-campus services. Credit is offered for college survival skills and written composition skills.

Application For admittance to the program or unit, students are required to apply to the program directly and provide a psychoeducational report (1 year old or less). It is recommended that students provide documentation of high school services. Upon application, materials documenting need for services should be sent only to the LD program or unit. Upon acceptance, documentation of need for services should be sent only to the LD program or unit. *Application deadline (institutional):* 8/1. *Application deadline (LD program):* Rolling/continuous for fall and rolling/continuous for spring.

Written Policies Written policies regarding course substitutions, general/basic LD accommodations, and reduced course loads are available through the program or unit directly.

Lewis-Clark State College

500 Eighth Avenue
Lewiston, ID 83501-2698
http://www.lcsc.edu/
Contact: Ms. Debi Mundell, ADA Coordinator. Phone: 208-792-2378. Fax: 208-792-2453. E-mail: dmundell@lcsc.edu.

Approximately 200 registered undergraduate students were served during 2002-03. The program or unit includes 1 full-time staff member. Counselors, remediation/learning specialists, skill tutors, and trained peer tutors are provided collaboratively through on-campus or off-campus services.

Subject-area Tutoring Tutoring is offered one-on-one and in small groups for all subjects. Tutoring is provided collaboratively through on-campus or off-campus services via computer-based instruction and trained peer tutors.

Basic Skills Remediation Remediation is offered one-on-one and in small groups for learning strategies, math, reading, spelling, study skills, time management, and written language. Remediation is provided collaboratively through on-campus or off-campus services via computer-based instruction, special education teachers, and trained peer tutors.

Enrichment Programs for career planning, college survival skills, learning strategies, math, oral communication skills, practical computer skills, reading, self-advocacy, study skills, test taking, and time management are provided collaboratively through on-campus or off-campus services.

Application Upon application, materials documenting need for services should be sent only to the LD program or unit. Upon acceptance, documentation of need for services should be sent only to the LD program or unit. *Application deadline (institutional):* Continuous. *Application deadline (LD program):* Rolling/continuous for fall and rolling/continuous for spring.

Written Policies Written policy regarding general/basic LD accommodations is available on the program Web site. Written policy regarding general/basic LD accommodations is outlined in the school's catalog/handbook. Written policies regarding course substitutions, general/basic LD accommodations, substitutions and waivers of admissions requirements, and substitutions and waivers of graduation requirements are available through the program or unit directly.

Life Pacific College
Life Challenges

1100 Covina Boulevard
San Dimas, CA 91773-3298
http://www.lifepacific.edu/
Contact: Mrs. Susan Cape. E-mail: scape@lifepacific.edu.

Life Challenges Approximately 7 registered undergraduate students were served during 2002-03. Coaches are provided through the program or unit. Academic advisers, counselors, diagnostic specialists, graduate assistants/students, regular education teachers, and trained peer tutors are provided collaboratively through on-campus or off-campus services.

Diagnostic Testing Testing for auditory processing, learning strategies, learning styles, math, neuropsychological, reading, social skills, spelling, spoken language, study skills, visual processing, and written language is provided collaboratively through on-campus or off-campus services.

Enrichment Programs for career planning, college survival skills, learning strategies, math, oral communication skills, stress management, study skills, and time management are provided collaboratively through on-campus or off-campus services.

Fees *Diagnostic Testing* fee is $350.

Application For admittance to the program or unit, students are required to apply to the program directly. It is recommended that students provide a psychoeducational report (5 years old or less), provide documentation of high school services, and provide medical records. Upon application, materials documenting need for services should be sent only to the LD program or unit. Upon acceptance, documentation of need for services should be sent only to the LD program or unit. *Application deadline (institutional):* 7/1. *Application deadline (LD program):* Rolling/continuous for fall and rolling/continuous for spring.

Written Policies Written policy regarding general/basic LD accommodations is outlined in the school's catalog/handbook.

Long Island University, Brooklyn Campus

One University Plaza

Brooklyn, NY 11201-8423

http://www.liu.edu/

Contact: Mrs. Phyllis Brown-Richardson, Learning Disabilities Specialist. Phone: 718-488-1044. Fax: 718-834-6045. E-mail: phyllis.brown-richardson@liu.edu. Head of LD Program: Prof. Jeff Lambert, Director of Special Educational Services. Phone: 718-488-1044. Fax: 718-834-6045. E-mail: jlambert@liu.edu.

Approximately 50 registered undergraduate students were served during 2002-03. The program or unit includes 8 full-time and 12 part-time staff members. Academic advisers, counselors, graduate assistants/students, LD specialists, regular education teachers, skill tutors, strategy tutors, and trained peer tutors are provided collaboratively through on-campus or off-campus services.

Orientation The program or unit offers an optional orientation for new students before classes begin, after classes begin, and individually by special arrangement.

Unique Aids and Services Aids, services, or accommodations include advocates, career counseling, and faculty training.

Subject-area Tutoring Tutoring is offered one-on-one and in small groups. Tutoring is provided collaboratively through on-campus or off-campus services via computer-based instruction, graduate assistants/students, LD specialists, and trained peer tutors.

Basic Skills Remediation Remediation is offered one-on-one and in small groups. Remediation is provided collaboratively through on-campus or off-campus services via computer-based instruction, graduate assistants/students, LD specialists, regular education teachers, and trained peer tutors.

Enrichment Programs for career planning, college survival skills, learning strategies, math, oral communication skills, practical computer skills, self-advocacy, stress management, study skills, test taking, time management, vocabulary development, and written composition skills are provided collaboratively through on-campus or off-campus services.

Application It is recommended that students apply to the program directly, provide a psychoeducational report (3 years old or less), and provide documentation of high school services. Upon application, materials documenting need for services should be sent only to the LD program or unit. Upon acceptance, documentation of need

for services should be sent only to the LD program or unit. *Application deadline (institutional):* Continuous. *Application deadline (LD program):* Rolling/continuous for fall and rolling/continuous for spring.

Long Island University, Southampton College, Friends World Program

239 Montauk Highway

Southampton, NY 11968

http://www.southampton.liu.edu/fw/

Contact: Ms. Amy Urquhart, Associate Dean of Students. Phone: 631-287-8361. E-mail: amy.urquhart@liu.edu.

Approximately 5 registered undergraduate students were served during 2002-03. Academic advisers, graduate assistants/students, and trained peer tutors are provided collaboratively through on-campus or off-campus services.

Unique Aids and Services Aids, services, or accommodations include faculty training, support groups, and weekly meetings with faculty.

Subject-area Tutoring Tutoring is offered one-on-one and in small groups. Tutoring is provided collaboratively through on-campus or off-campus services via graduate assistants/students and other.

Basic Skills Remediation Remediation is offered one-on-one and in small groups for computer skills, learning strategies, study skills, and written language. Remediation is provided collaboratively through on-campus or off-campus services via graduate assistants/students, trained peer tutors, and other.

Enrichment Programs for learning strategies, oral communication skills, practical computer skills, self-advocacy, study skills, and written composition skills are provided collaboratively through on-campus or off-campus services.

Application It is recommended that students provide a psychoeducational report (3 years old or less) and provide documentation of high school services. Upon application, materials documenting need for services should be sent only to admissions with institutional application materials. Upon acceptance, documentation of need for services should be sent only to admissions. *Application deadline (institutional):* Continuous. *Application deadline (LD program):* Rolling/continuous for fall and rolling/continuous for spring.

Written Policies Written policy regarding general/basic LD accommodations is outlined in the school's catalog/handbook.

Longwood University
Disability Support Services

201 High Street

Farmville, VA 23909-1800

http://www.longwood.edu/

Contact: Susan E. Rood, Director of Disability Support Services. Phone: 434-395-2391. Fax: 434-395-2434. E-mail: srood@longwood.edu.

Longwood University (continued)

Disability Support Services Approximately 250 registered undergraduate students were served during 2002-03. The program or unit includes 1 full-time and 4 part-time staff members. Academic advisers, graduate assistants/students, skill tutors, and strategy tutors are provided through the program or unit. Coaches, counselors, regular education teachers, and skill tutors are provided collaboratively through on-campus or off-campus services.

Orientation The program or unit offers an optional orientation for new students during registration.

Subject-area Tutoring Tutoring is offered one-on-one and in small groups for most subjects. Tutoring is provided through the program or unit via trained peer tutors.

Diagnostic Testing Testing is provided through the program or unit for learning strategies, learning styles, personality, and study skills. Testing for auditory processing, intelligence, math, motor skills, neuropsychological, reading, spoken language, visual processing, and written language is provided collaboratively through on-campus or off-campus services.

Enrichment Enrichment programs are available through the program or unit for learning strategies, study skills, test taking, and time management. Programs for career planning, health and nutrition, medication management, and stress management are provided collaboratively through on-campus or off-campus services.

Student Organization Student Organization for Disability Awareness (SODA) consists of 15 members.

Application For admittance to the program or unit, students are required to provide a psychoeducational report (3 years old or less). It is recommended that students provide documentation of high school services. Upon application, materials documenting need for services should be sent to both admissions and the LD program or unit. Upon acceptance, documentation of need for services should be sent only to the LD program or unit. *Application deadline (institutional):* 3/1. *Application deadline (LD program):* Rolling/continuous for fall and rolling/continuous for spring.

Written Policies Written policies regarding course substitutions, general/basic LD accommodations, reduced course loads, and substitutions and waivers of graduation requirements are available on the program Web site. Written policies regarding course substitutions, general/basic LD accommodations, reduced course loads, and substitutions and waivers of graduation requirements are outlined in the school's catalog/handbook. Written policies regarding course substitutions, general/basic LD accommodations, reduced course loads, and substitutions and waivers of graduation requirements are available through the program or unit directly.

Louisiana State University and Agricultural and Mechanical College
Office of Disability Services

Baton Rouge, LA 70803

http://www.lsu.edu/disability

Contact: Ms. Wendy R. Devall, Assistant Director for Disability Services. Phone: 225-578-7100. Fax: 225-578-4560. E-mail: wdevall@lsu.edu.

Office of Disability Services Approximately 160 registered undergraduate students were served during 2002-03. The program or unit includes 1 full-time and 1 part-time staff member. Graduate assistants/students and LD specialists are provided through the program or unit. Academic advisers, counselors, and professional tutors are provided collaboratively through on-campus or off-campus services.

Unique Aids and Services Aids, services, or accommodations include priority registration, AlphaSmarts and other assistive technology.

Subject-area Tutoring Tutoring is offered in small groups for some subjects. Tutoring is provided collaboratively through on-campus or off-campus services via graduate assistants/students and trained peer tutors.

Diagnostic Testing Testing for auditory processing, intelligence, math, motor skills, neuropsychological, personality, reading, spelling, visual processing, and written language is provided collaboratively through on-campus or off-campus services.

Fees *Diagnostic Testing* fee is $250 to $300.

Application For admittance to the program or unit, students are required to apply to the program directly and provide a psychoeducational report (3 years old or less). Upon acceptance, documentation of need for services should be sent only to the LD program or unit. *Application deadline (institutional):* 4/15. *Application deadline (LD program):* Rolling/continuous for fall and rolling/continuous for spring.

Written Policies Written policy regarding general/basic LD accommodations is available on the program Web site. Written policy regarding general/basic LD accommodations is available through the program or unit directly.

Louisiana Tech University

PO Box 3168
Ruston, LA 71272

http://www.latech.edu/

Contact: William Carvel Fowler, Coordinator, Office of Disability Services. Phone: 318-257-4221. Fax: 318-257-2955. E-mail: wfowler@latech.edu.

Approximately 175 registered undergraduate students were served during 2002-03. The program or unit includes 2 full-time and 47 part-time staff members. Academic advisers, counselors, diagnostic specialists, graduate assistants/students, LD specialists, and other are provided through the program or unit. Academic advisers, counselors, graduate assistants/students, regular education teachers, and other are provided collaboratively through on-campus or off-campus services.

Unique Aids and Services Aids, services, or accommodations include career counseling, faculty training, parent workshops, and priority registration.

Subject-area Tutoring Tutoring is offered one-on-one and in small groups for most subjects. Tutoring is provided collaboratively through on-campus or off-campus services via computer-based instruction, graduate assistants/students, and other.

Diagnostic Testing Testing for auditory processing, intelligence, learning strategies, learning styles, motor skills, personality, reading, social skills, spelling, spoken language, study skills, visual processing, and written language is provided collaboratively through on-campus or off-campus services.

Enrichment Programs for career planning, college survival skills, learning strategies, oral communication skills, reading, self-advocacy, stress management, study skills, test taking, and time management are provided collaboratively through on-campus or off-campus services. Credit is offered for learning strategies, oral communication skills, reading, and time management.

Fees *Diagnostic Testing* fee is $50 to $150.

Application For admittance to the program or unit, students are required to apply to the program directly and provide a psychoeducational report (3 years old or less). Upon application, materials documenting need for services should be sent only to the LD program or unit. Upon acceptance, documentation of need for services should be sent only to the LD program or unit. *Application deadline (institutional):* 7/31. *Application deadline (LD program):* Rolling/continuous for fall and rolling/continuous for spring.

Written Policies Written policy regarding general/basic LD accommodations is available on the program Web site. Written policy regarding general/basic LD accommodations is available through the program or unit directly.

Lourdes College
Disability Services

6832 Convent Boulevard
Sylvania, OH 43560-2898
http://www.lourdes.edu/
Contact: Kim Grieve, Director of Disability Services. Phone: 419-824-3834. Fax: 419-824-3753. E-mail: kgrieve@lourdes.edu.

Disability Services Approximately 30 registered undergraduate students were served during 2002-03. The program or unit includes 2 part-time staff members. Professional tutors, trained peer tutors, and other are provided collaboratively through on-campus or off-campus services.

Orientation The program or unit offers an optional orientation for new students individually by special arrangement.

Unique Aids and Services Aids, services, or accommodations include advocates, digital textbooks, note-taking services.

Subject-area Tutoring Tutoring is offered one-on-one for most subjects. Tutoring is provided collaboratively through on-campus or off-campus services via trained peer tutors.

Enrichment Enrichment programs are available through the program or unit for self-advocacy, test taking, and other. Programs for career planning, college survival skills, learning strategies, oral communication skills, practical computer skills, stress management, study skills, time management, and written composition skills are provided collaboratively through on-campus or off-campus services.

Application For admittance to the program or unit, students are required to apply to the program directly and provide documentation of disability and service recommendations. It is recommended that students provide documentation of high school services. Upon application, materials documenting need for services should be sent only to the LD program or unit. Upon acceptance, documentation of need for services should be sent only to the LD program or unit. *Application deadline (institutional):* Continuous. *Application deadline (LD program):* Rolling/continuous for fall and rolling/continuous for spring.

Written Policies Written policies regarding general/basic LD accommodations and reduced course loads are available on the program Web site. Written policies regarding general/basic LD accommodations and reduced course loads are outlined in the school's catalog/handbook. Written policies regarding general/basic LD accommodations and reduced course loads are available through the program or unit directly.

Loyola Marymount University
Disability Support Services

One LMU Drive
Los Angeles, CA 90045-2659
http://www.lmu.edu/dss
Contact: Mr. James Stewart II, Coordinator. Phone: 310-338-4535. Fax: 310-338-7657. E-mail: jfstewart@lmu.edu.

Disability Support Services Approximately 160 registered undergraduate students were served during 2002-03. The program or unit includes 1 full-time staff member. Graduate assistants/students are provided through the program or unit. Counselors and diagnostic specialists are provided collaboratively through on-campus or off-campus services.

Unique Aids and Services Aids, services, or accommodations include advocates, faculty training, and priority registration.

Subject-area Tutoring Tutoring is offered one-on-one for most subjects. Tutoring is provided collaboratively through on-campus or off-campus services via computer-based instruction, graduate assistants/students, professional tutors, and trained peer tutors.

Enrichment Programs for career planning, college survival skills, health and nutrition, learning strategies, math, medication management, reading, stress management, study skills, test taking, time management, and written composition skills are provided collaboratively through on-campus or off-campus services.

Application For admittance to the program or unit, students are required to apply to the program directly and provide a psychoeducational report (3 years old or less). It is recommended that students provide documentation of high school services and provide letters from teachers, counselor, and previous standardized test scores/results. Upon application, materials documenting need for services should be sent only to the LD program or unit. Upon acceptance, documentation of need for services should be sent only to the LD program or unit. *Application deadline (institutional):* 2/1. *Application deadline (LD program):* Rolling/continuous for fall and rolling/continuous for spring.

Written Policies Written policy regarding general/basic LD accommodations is available on the program Web site. Written policy regarding general/basic LD accommodations is outlined in the school's catalog/handbook. Written policy regarding general/basic LD accommodations is available through the program or unit directly.

Loyola University Chicago
Services for Students with Disabilities

820 North Michigan Avenue
Chicago, IL 60611-2196

Loyola University Chicago (continued)
http://www.luc.edu/depts/lac/disabilities

Contact: Coordinator. Phone: 773-508-2471. Fax: 773-508-3123.

Services for Students with Disabilities Approximately 155 registered undergraduate students were served during 2002–03. The program or unit includes 1 full-time staff member. Academic advisers, coaches, counselors, graduate assistants/students, regular education teachers, remediation/learning specialists, and trained peer tutors are provided collaboratively through on-campus or off-campus services.

Subject-area Tutoring Tutoring is offered one-on-one and in small groups for most subjects. Tutoring is provided collaboratively through on-campus or off-campus services via graduate assistants/students and trained peer tutors.

Basic Skills Remediation Remediation is offered one-on-one, in small groups, and in class-size groups for learning strategies, study skills, and time management. Remediation is provided through the program or unit. Remediation is also provided collaboratively through on-campus or off-campus services via graduate assistants/students and other.

Enrichment Programs for career planning, college survival skills, health and nutrition, learning strategies, math, oral communication skills, practical computer skills, self-advocacy, stress management, study skills, test taking, time management, and written composition skills are provided collaboratively through on-campus or off-campus services. Credit is offered for career planning, college survival skills, health and nutrition, math, oral communication skills, practical computer skills, study skills, test taking, and time management.

Application For admittance to the program or unit, students are required to provide a psychoeducational report. It is recommended that students provide documentation of high school services. Upon application, materials documenting need for services should be sent only to the LD program or unit. Upon acceptance, documentation of need for services should be sent only to the LD program or unit. *Application deadline (institutional):* 4/1.

Written Policies Written policy regarding general/basic LD accommodations is available on the program Web site. Written policy regarding general/basic LD accommodations is outlined in the school's catalog/handbook. Written policy regarding general/basic LD accommodations is available through the program or unit directly.

MacMurray College

447 East College Avenue
Jacksonville, IL 62650
http://www.mac.edu/

Contact: Ms. Laura Covell, Director of Special Services. Phone: 217-479-7222. Fax: 217-291-0702. E-mail: lcovell@mac.edu.

Approximately 5 registered undergraduate students were served during 2002–03. The program or unit includes 2 full-time staff members. Academic advisers, coaches, LD specialists, remediation/learning specialists, skill tutors, and trained peer tutors are provided through the program or unit.

Unique Aids and Services Aids, services, or accommodations include advocates and career counseling.

Subject-area Tutoring Tutoring is offered one-on-one and in small groups. Tutoring is provided through the program or unit via computer-based instruction, graduate assistants/students, and trained peer tutors. Tutoring is also provided collaboratively through on-campus or off-campus services via computer-based instruction, graduate assistants/students, and trained peer tutors.

Basic Skills Remediation Remediation is offered one-on-one and in class-size groups for computer skills, learning strategies, math, reading, study skills, time management, and written language. Remediation is provided through the program or unit via computer-based instruction, regular education teachers, and trained peer tutors. Remediation is also provided collaboratively through on-campus or off-campus services via computer-based instruction, regular education teachers, and trained peer tutors.

Enrichment Programs for career planning, college survival skills, health and nutrition, learning strategies, math, oral communication skills, practical computer skills, reading, self-advocacy, stress management, study skills, test taking, time management, and written composition skills are provided collaboratively through on-campus or off-campus services.

Application It is recommended that students provide a psychoeducational report (3 years old or less) and provide documentation of high school services. Upon application, materials documenting need for services should be sent only to admissions with institutional application materials. Upon acceptance, documentation of need for services should be sent only to admissions. *Application deadline (institutional):* Continuous. *Application deadline (LD program):* Rolling/continuous for fall and rolling/continuous for spring.

Written Policies Written policies regarding general/basic LD accommodations and reduced course loads are available through the program or unit directly.

Magdalen College

511 Kearsarge Mountain Road
Warner, NH 03278
http://www.magdalen.edu/

Contact: Phone: 603-456-2656. Fax: 603-456-2660.

Academic advisers and counselors are provided collaboratively through on-campus or off-campus services.

Subject-area Tutoring Tutoring is offered one-on-one and in small groups for all subjects. Tutoring is provided collaboratively through on-campus or off-campus services via professional tutors.

Basic Skills Remediation Remediation is offered one-on-one and in small groups for math, reading, study skills, and written language. Remediation is provided collaboratively through on-campus or off-campus services via professional tutors and regular education teachers.

Application It is recommended that students apply to the program directly, provide a psychoeducational report, and provide documentation of high school services. Upon application, materials documenting need for services should be sent only to admissions with institutional application materials. *Application deadline (institutional):* 5/1. *Application deadline (LD program):* 5/1 for fall.

Maine College of Art
Disabled Student Services

97 Spring Street
Portland, ME 04101-3987
http://www.meca.edu/

Contact: Ms. Carmita Loretta McCoy, Dean of Students and Director of Student Affairs. Phone: 207-879-5742 Ext. 224. Fax: 207-772-5069. E-mail: cmccoy@meca.edu.

Disabled Student Services Approximately 50 registered undergraduate students were served during 2002-03. The program or unit includes 2 full-time staff members. Academic advisers, counselors, skill tutors, and trained peer tutors are provided through the program or unit. Diagnostic specialists and professional tutors are provided collaboratively through on-campus or off-campus services.
Unique Aids and Services Aids, services, or accommodations include ADA accommodations advising to faculty.
Subject-area Tutoring Tutoring is offered one-on-one for some subjects. Tutoring is provided through the program or unit via computer-based instruction and trained peer tutors. Tutoring is also provided collaboratively through on-campus or off-campus services via graduate assistants/students and professional tutors.
Enrichment Enrichment programs are available through the program or unit for self-advocacy. Programs for career planning, college survival skills, health and nutrition, learning strategies, math, stress management, study skills, time management, vocabulary development, and written composition skills are provided collaboratively through on-campus or off-campus services.
Application For admittance to the program or unit, students are required to provide a psychoeducational report (5 years old or less) and provide documentation of high school services. It is recommended that students apply to the program directly. Upon application, materials documenting need for services should be sent to both admissions and the LD program or unit. Upon acceptance, documentation of need for services should be sent only to the LD program or unit. *Application deadline (institutional):* Continuous. *Application deadline (LD program):* Rolling/continuous for fall and rolling/continuous for spring.
Written Policies Written policy regarding general/basic LD accommodations is available on the program Web site. Written policy regarding general/basic LD accommodations is outlined in the school's catalog/handbook. Written policies regarding general/basic LD accommodations and reduced course loads are available through the program or unit directly.

Malone College
Disability Support Services

515 25th Street, NW
Canton, OH 44709-3897
http://www.malone.edu/

Contact: Mrs. Patty Little, Director of Student Retention and Special Needs. Phone: 330-471-8359. Fax: 330-471-8149. E-mail: plittle@malone.edu.

Disability Support Services Approximately 40 registered undergraduate students were served during 2002-03. The program or unit includes 1 full-time staff member. Academic advisers, counselors, graduate assistants/students, regular education teachers, and trained peer tutors are provided collaboratively through on-campus or off-campus services.
Unique Aids and Services Aids, services, or accommodations include note-taking services, books on tape, tutors, distraction free/extended time testing.
Subject-area Tutoring Tutoring is offered one-on-one and in small groups for most subjects. Tutoring is provided collaboratively through on-campus or off-campus services via graduate assistants/students and trained peer tutors.
Application For admittance to the program or unit, students are required to apply to the program directly and provide a psychoeducational report (3 years old or less). It is recommended that students provide documentation of high school services. Upon application, materials documenting need for services should be sent only to the LD program or unit. Upon acceptance, documentation of need for services should be sent only to the LD program or unit. *Application deadline (institutional):* 7/1. *Application deadline (LD program):* Rolling/continuous for fall and rolling/continuous for spring.
Written Policies Written policy regarding general/basic LD accommodations is available on the program Web site. Written policy regarding general/basic LD accommodations is outlined in the school's catalog/handbook. Written policies regarding general/basic LD accommodations and reduced course loads are available through the program or unit directly.

Manchester College
Learning Support Services

604 College Avenue
North Manchester, IN 46962-1225
http://www.manchester.edu/

Contact: Phone: 260-982-5000. Fax: 260-982-5043.

Learning Support Services Approximately 40 registered undergraduate students were served during 2002-03. The program or unit includes 1 full-time staff member. LD specialists are provided through the program or unit. Academic advisers, counselors, and trained peer tutors are provided collaboratively through on-campus or off-campus services.
Unique Aids and Services Aids, services, or accommodations include weekly meetings with faculty.
Subject-area Tutoring Tutoring is offered one-on-one, in small groups, and in class-size groups. Tutoring is provided collaboratively through on-campus or off-campus services via trained peer tutors.
Application For admittance to the program or unit, students are required to provide a psychoeducational report (3 years old or less). It is recommended that students provide documentation of high school services and provide other documentation. Upon application, materials documenting need for services should be sent only to the LD program or unit. *Application deadline (institutional):* Continuous. *Application deadline (LD program):* Rolling/continuous for fall and rolling/continuous for spring.
Written Policies Written policy regarding general/basic LD accommodations is available through the program or unit directly.

Manhattan College
Specialized Resource Center

Manhattan College Parkway
Riverdale, NY 10471
http://www.manhattan.edu/sprscent

Contact: Dr. Ross Pollack, ADA Coordinator. Phone:
718-862-7101. Fax: 718-862-7808. E-mail:
ross.pollack@manhattan.edu.

Specialized Resource Center Approximately 125 registered
undergraduate students were served during 2002-03. The program
or unit includes 1 full-time and 1 part-time staff member. LD
specialists are provided through the program or unit. Academic
advisers, counselors, graduate assistants/students, professional tutors,
skill tutors, strategy tutors, and trained peer tutors are provided
collaboratively through on-campus or off-campus services.

Subject-area Tutoring Tutoring is offered one-on-one and in
small groups for most subjects. Tutoring is provided collaboratively
through on-campus or off-campus services via graduate assistants/
students, professional tutors, and trained peer tutors.

Enrichment Programs for career planning and college survival
skills are provided collaboratively through on-campus or off-
campus services.

Application For admittance to the program or unit, students are
required to provide a psychoeducational report. It is recommended
that students provide documentation of high school services. Upon
application, materials documenting need for services should be sent
only to the LD program or unit. Upon acceptance, documentation of
need for services should be sent only to the LD program or unit.
Application deadline (institutional): 3/1. *Application deadline (LD
program):* Rolling/continuous for fall and rolling/continuous for
spring.

Written Policies Written policies regarding course substitutions,
general/basic LD accommodations, reduced course loads, and substitutions and waivers of graduation requirements are available on
the program Web site.

Mannes College of Music, New School University
Student Disability Services

150 West 85th Street
New York, NY 10024-4402
http://www.newschool.edu

Contact: Phone: 212-580-0210. Fax: 212-580-1738.

Student Disability Services Approximately 1 registered undergraduate students were served during 2002-03. The program or unit
includes 1 full-time and 1 part-time staff member. Academic advisers, counselors, and other are provided collaboratively through
on-campus or off-campus services.

Enrichment Programs for career planning, college survival skills,
health and nutrition, learning strategies, self-advocacy, stress management, study skills, test taking, time management, and written
composition skills are provided collaboratively through on-campus
or off-campus services.

Application For admittance to the program or unit, students are
required to apply to the program directly and provide a psychoeducational report (3 years old or less). Upon acceptance, documentation of need for services should be sent only to the LD program or
unit. *Application deadline (institutional):* 12/1. *Application deadline (LD program):* Rolling/continuous for fall.

Written Policies Written policy regarding general/basic LD accommodations is available on the program Web site. Written policy
regarding general/basic LD accommodations is outlined in the
school's catalog/handbook. Written policy regarding general/basic
LD accommodations is available through the program or unit directly.

Marian College
Learning and Counseling Center— Academic Support Services Program

3200 Cold Spring Road
Indianapolis, IN 46222-1997
http://www.marian.edu/

Contact: Ms. Marjorie Batic, Director of Academic Support
Services. Phone: 317-955-6150. Fax: 317-955-6415. E-mail:
mbatic@marian.edu.

**Learning and Counseling Center—Academic Support Ser-
vices Program** Approximately 30 registered undergraduate students were served during 2002-03. The program or unit includes 1
full-time staff member. Graduate assistants/students, professional
tutors, and remediation/learning specialists are provided through the
program or unit. Academic advisers, coaches, counselors, LD specialists, regular education teachers, skill tutors, strategy tutors, and
trained peer tutors are provided collaboratively through on-campus
or off-campus services.

Unique Aids and Services Aids, services, or accommodations
include career counseling.

Subject-area Tutoring Tutoring is offered one-on-one and in
small groups for all subjects. Tutoring is provided through the
program or unit via computer-based instruction, LD specialists, and
professional tutors. Tutoring is also provided collaboratively through
on-campus or off-campus services via trained peer tutors.

Diagnostic Testing Testing is provided through the program or
unit for intelligence, learning strategies, learning styles, math, motor
skills, personality, reading, spelling, and study skills. Testing for
auditory processing, handwriting, intelligence, motor skills, neuropsychological, personality, social skills, spelling, spoken language,
visual processing, and written language is provided collaboratively
through on-campus or off-campus services.

Basic Skills Remediation Remediation is offered one-on-one, in
small groups, and in class-size groups for learning strategies, math,
reading, study skills, and organization, test-taking, note-taking. Remediation is provided through the program or unit via computer-based
instruction, LD specialists, and professional tutors. Remediation is
also provided collaboratively through on-campus or off-campus
services via regular education teachers and teacher trainees.

Enrichment Enrichment programs are available through the program or unit for college survival skills, learning strategies, math,
medication management, oral communication skills, reading, stress
management, study skills, test taking, time management, and written composition skills. Programs for career planning, health and

nutrition, and practical computer skills are provided collaboratively through on-campus or off-campus services. Credit is offered for college survival skills, health and nutrition, and practical computer skills.

Application For admittance to the program or unit, students are required to provide a psychoeducational report (3 years old or less). It is recommended that students provide documentation of high school services and provide a neuropsychological report. Upon acceptance, documentation of need for services should be sent only to the LD program or unit. *Application deadline (institutional):* 8/15.

Written Policies Written policy regarding general/basic LD accommodations is outlined in the school's catalog/handbook. Written policies regarding course substitutions, general/basic LD accommodations, reduced course loads, and substitutions and waivers of admissions requirements are available through the program or unit directly.

Marian College of Fond du Lac

45 South National Avenue

Fond du Lac, WI 54935-4699

http://www.mariancollege.edu/

Contact: Wendy Yurk, Coordinator of Disability Services. Phone: 920-923-7162. Fax: 920-923-8097. E-mail: wyurk@mariancollege.edu.

The program or unit includes 2 part-time staff members. Counselors are provided through the program or unit.

Unique Aids and Services Aids, services, or accommodations include advocates, career counseling, digital textbooks, faculty training, and support groups.

Subject-area Tutoring Tutoring is offered one-on-one for all subjects. Tutoring is provided collaboratively through on-campus or off-campus services via trained peer tutors.

Basic Skills Remediation Remediation is offered one-on-one and in small groups for computer skills, reading, social skills, spelling, study skills, time management, and written language. Remediation is provided collaboratively through on-campus or off-campus services via trained peer tutors and other.

Enrichment Programs for career planning, college survival skills, health and nutrition, learning strategies, medication management, practical computer skills, reading, self-advocacy, stress management, study skills, test taking, time management, vocabulary development, and written composition skills are provided collaboratively through on-campus or off-campus services.

Application For admittance to the program or unit, students are required to provide a psychoeducational report (5 years old or less). Upon application, materials documenting need for services should be sent only to the LD program or unit. Upon acceptance, documentation of need for services should be sent only to the LD program or unit. *Application deadline (institutional):* Continuous. *Application deadline (LD program):* Rolling/continuous for fall and rolling/continuous for spring.

Written Policies Written policy regarding general/basic LD accommodations is available through the program or unit directly.

Marietta College
Academic Resource Center

215 Fifth Street

Marietta, OH 45750-4000

http://mcnet.marietta.edu/~arc/students.html

Contact: Marilyn Pasquarelli, Disabilities Specialist. Phone: 740-376-4700. Fax: 740-376-4406. E-mail: pasquarm@marietta.edu. Head of LD Program: Debra R. Higgins, Director of the Academic Resource Center. Phone: 740-376-4700. Fax: 740-376-4406. E-mail: higginsd@marietta.edu.

Academic Resource Center Approximately 50 registered undergraduate students were served during 2002-03. The program or unit includes 2 full-time and 2 part-time staff members. LD specialists, skill tutors, strategy tutors, and trained peer tutors are provided through the program or unit. Academic advisers, coaches, counselors, regular education teachers, and other are provided collaboratively through on-campus or off-campus services.

Subject-area Tutoring Tutoring is offered one-on-one and in small groups for all subjects. Tutoring is provided through the program or unit via trained peer tutors.

Enrichment Enrichment programs are available through the program or unit for college survival skills, learning strategies, study skills, test taking, and time management. Programs for career planning, college survival skills, learning strategies, and written composition skills are provided collaboratively through on-campus or off-campus services.

Application For admittance to the program or unit, students are required to provide a psychoeducational report (3 years old or less) and provide test evaluations. It is recommended that students provide documentation of high school services. Upon acceptance, documentation of need for services should be sent to both admissions and the LD program or unit. *Application deadline (institutional):* 4/15. *Application deadline (LD program):* Rolling/continuous for fall and rolling/continuous for spring.

Written Policies Written policy regarding general/basic LD accommodations is outlined in the school's catalog/handbook.

Marlboro College
Academic Support Services

PO Box A, South Road

Marlboro, VT 05344

http://www.marlboro.edu/

Contact: Jeremy Lockwood Holch, Director of Academic Support Services. Phone: 802-258-9260 Ext. 260. E-mail: jholch@marlboro.edu.

Academic Support Services The program or unit includes 1 full-time staff member. Coaches, LD specialists, professional tutors, skill tutors, and strategy tutors are provided through the program or unit. Coaches, LD specialists, professional tutors, skill tutors, and strategy tutors are provided collaboratively through on-campus or off-campus services.

Marlboro College (continued)

Application For admittance to the program or unit, students are required to provide documentation of LD from a qualified health care provider. It is recommended that students provide a psycho-educational report (3 years old or less) and provide documentation of high school services. Upon application, materials documenting need for services should be sent only to admissions with institutional application materials. Upon acceptance, documentation of need for services should be sent only to the LD program or unit. *Application deadline (institutional): 3/1.*

Written Policies Written policy regarding general/basic LD accommodations is outlined in the school's catalog/handbook.

Martin Luther College

1995 Luther Court
New Ulm, MN 56073
http://www.mlc-wels.edu/

Contact: Dr. Alan M. Spurgin, Professor. Phone: 507-354-8221 Ext. 351. Fax: 507-354-8225. E-mail: spurgiam@mlc-wels.edu.

The program or unit includes 1 full-time staff member. Academic advisers, regular education teachers, special education teachers, and trained peer tutors are provided through the program or unit.

Subject-area Tutoring Tutoring is offered one-on-one and in small groups for most subjects. Tutoring is provided collaboratively through on-campus or off-campus services via trained peer tutors.

Diagnostic Testing Testing for learning styles and neuropsychological is provided collaboratively through on-campus or off-campus services.

Basic Skills Remediation Remediation is offered one-on-one for computer skills, math, spelling, study skills, and time management. Remediation is provided collaboratively through on-campus or off-campus services via regular education teachers and trained peer tutors.

Application It is recommended that students provide documentation of high school services. Upon application, materials documenting need for services should be sent only to admissions with institutional application materials. Upon acceptance, documentation of need for services should be sent only to admissions. *Application deadline (institutional): 4/15. Application deadline (LD program):* Rolling/continuous for spring.

Written Policies Written policy regarding general/basic LD accommodations is available through the program or unit directly.

Marymount University
Disability Support Services for Students

2807 North Glebe Road
Arlington, VA 22207-4299
http://www.marymount.edu/ssa/disabili/

Contact: Ms. Kelly L. DeSenti, Coordinator of Disability Support Services and Assistant Director of CCCS. Phone: 703-284-1605. Fax: 703-284-3841. E-mail: kelly.desenti@marymount.edu.

Disability Support Services for Students Approximately 65 registered undergraduate students were served during 2002-03. The program or unit includes 1 full-time staff member. Academic advisers, counselors, remediation/learning specialists, skill tutors, strategy tutors, and trained peer tutors are provided collaboratively through on-campus or off-campus services.

Unique Aids and Services Aids, services, or accommodations include weekly meetings with DSS coordinator .

Subject-area Tutoring Tutoring is offered one-on-one, in small groups, and in class-size groups for most subjects. Tutoring is provided collaboratively through on-campus or off-campus services via computer-based instruction, graduate assistants/students, trained peer tutors, and other.

Basic Skills Remediation Remediation is offered one-on-one, in small groups, and in class-size groups for learning strategies, math, reading, social skills, study skills, and time management. Remediation is provided collaboratively through on-campus or off-campus services via computer-based instruction, regular education teachers, and other.

Enrichment Programs for career planning, college survival skills, health and nutrition, learning strategies, math, practical computer skills, stress management, study skills, test taking, time management, and written composition skills are provided collaboratively through on-campus or off-campus services. Credit is offered for college survival skills, health and nutrition, practical computer skills, stress management, and written composition skills.

Application For admittance to the program or unit, students are required to provide a psychoeducational report (3 years old or less). Upon application, materials documenting need for services should be sent only to the LD program or unit. Upon acceptance, documentation of need for services should be sent only to the LD program or unit. *Application deadline (institutional):* Continuous. *Application deadline (LD program):* Rolling/continuous for fall and rolling/continuous for spring.

Written Policies Written policy regarding general/basic LD accommodations is outlined in the school's catalog/handbook. Written policies regarding course substitutions, general/basic LD accommodations, and substitutions and waivers of graduation requirements are available through the program or unit directly.

Marywood University

2300 Adams Avenue
Scranton, PA 18509-1598
http://www.marywood.edu/

Contact: Mr. Christopher Thomas Moy, Coordinator of Disability Services. Phone: 570-340-6045 Ext. 2549. Fax: 570-340-6028. E-mail: moy@es.marywood.edu.

Approximately 60 registered undergraduate students were served during 2002-03. The program or unit includes 1 full-time staff member. Academic advisers, counselors, and trained peer tutors are provided collaboratively through on-campus or off-campus services.

Orientation The program or unit offers before classes begin, during summer prior to enrollment, and individually by special arrangement.

Unique Aids and Services Aids, services, or accommodations include career counseling, digital textbooks, faculty training, and weekly meetings with faculty.

Subject-area Tutoring Tutoring is offered one-on-one for all subjects. Tutoring is provided through the program or unit via LD specialists. Tutoring is also provided collaboratively through on-campus or off-campus services via professional tutors and trained peer tutors.

Enrichment Enrichment programs are available through the program or unit for college survival skills, learning strategies, self-advocacy, stress management, study skills, and time management. Programs for career planning, college survival skills, practical computer skills, and written composition skills are provided collaboratively through on-campus or off-campus services.

Application For admittance to the program or unit, students are required to provide a psychoeducational report and provide documentation of high school services. Upon application, materials documenting need for services should be sent to both admissions and the LD program or unit. Upon acceptance, documentation of need for services should be sent only to the LD program or unit. *Application deadline (institutional):* Continuous. *Application deadline (LD program):* Rolling/continuous for fall and rolling/continuous for spring.

Written Policies Written policy regarding general/basic LD accommodations is available through the program or unit directly.

Massachusetts College of Liberal Arts
Learning Services Center

375 Church Street
North Adams, MA 01247-4100
http://www.mcla.mass.edu/Academics/Academic_Resources/
Learning_Services_Center/disabled.php
Contact: Ms. Claire Smith, Coordinator of Academic Support. Phone: 413-662-5318. Fax: 413-662-5319. E-mail: msmith1@mcla.mass.edu. Head of LD Program: Ms. Theresa Miller, Director of Learning Services. Phone: 413-662-5309. Fax: 413-662-5319. E-mail: tmiller@mcla.mass.edu.

Learning Services Center Approximately 80 registered undergraduate students were served during 2002-03. The program or unit includes 1 full-time staff member. Academic advisers, counselors, diagnostic specialists, LD specialists, and trained peer tutors are provided collaboratively through on-campus or off-campus services.

Summer Program To help prepare for the demands of college, there is an optional 4-week summer program prior to entering the school.

Unique Aids and Services Aids, services, or accommodations include priority registration.

Subject-area Tutoring Tutoring is offered in small groups for some subjects. Tutoring is provided collaboratively through on-campus or off-campus services via trained peer tutors.

Diagnostic Testing Testing for intelligence, math, reading, and written language is provided collaboratively through on-campus or off-campus services.

Basic Skills Remediation Remediation is offered in class-size groups for learning strategies and math. Remediation is provided collaboratively through on-campus or off-campus services via regular education teachers.

Application For admittance to the program or unit, students are required to provide a psychoeducational report (3 years old or less) and provide documentation of high school services. Upon application, materials documenting need for services should be sent only to admissions with institutional application materials. Upon acceptance, documentation of need for services should be sent only to the LD program or unit. *Application deadline (institutional):* Continuous. *Application deadline (LD program):* Rolling/continuous for fall and rolling/continuous for spring.

Written Policies Written policies regarding general/basic LD accommodations and substitutions and waivers of admissions requirements are available on the program Web site. Written policies regarding general/basic LD accommodations and substitutions and waivers of admissions requirements are available through the program or unit directly.

Mayville State University

330 3rd Street, NE
Mayville, ND 58257-1299
http://www.mayvillestate.edu/
Contact: Dr. Joyce Alton White, Director of Academic Support. Phone: 701-788-4674. Fax: 701-788-4731. E-mail: white@mail.masu.nodak.edu.

Approximately 30 registered undergraduate students were served during 2002-03. The program or unit includes 2 part-time staff members. Academic advisers, counselors, skill tutors, teacher trainees, and trained peer tutors are provided through the program or unit.

Orientation The program or unit offers an optional orientation for new students individually by special arrangement.

Unique Aids and Services Aids, services, or accommodations include career counseling, taped texts.

Subject-area Tutoring Tutoring is offered one-on-one and in small groups for most subjects. Tutoring is provided through the program or unit via computer-based instruction, trained peer tutors, and other.

Diagnostic Testing Testing is provided through the program or unit for learning strategies, learning styles, math, reading, study skills, and other services.

Basic Skills Remediation Remediation is offered in class-size groups for computer skills, learning strategies, math, reading, study skills, and time management. Remediation is provided through the program or unit via computer-based instruction, teacher trainees, and trained peer tutors. Remediation is also provided collaboratively through on-campus or off-campus services via computer-based instruction and regular education teachers.

Enrichment Enrichment programs are available through the program or unit for learning strategies, math, practical computer skills, reading, self-advocacy, stress management, study skills, test taking, and time management. Programs for career planning, college survival skills, health and nutrition, learning strategies, math, medication management, oral communication skills, practical computer skills, reading, study skills, and written composition skills are provided collaboratively through on-campus or off-campus services. Credit is offered for career planning, college survival skills, health and nutrition, learning strategies, math, oral communication skills, practical computer skills, reading, study skills, time management, and written composition skills.

Mayville State University (continued)

Application For admittance to the program or unit, students are required to provide a psychoeducational report (3 years old or less) and provide professional documentation of functional limitations. It is recommended that students provide documentation of high school services. Upon acceptance, documentation of need for services should be sent only to the LD program or unit. *Application deadline (institutional):* Continuous. *Application deadline (LD program):* Rolling/continuous for fall and rolling/continuous for spring.

Written Policies Written policy regarding general/basic LD accommodations is available on the program Web site. Written policy regarding general/basic LD accommodations is outlined in the school's catalog/handbook. Written policy regarding general/basic LD accommodations is available through the program or unit directly.

McKendree College
Students with Disabilities Support Services

701 College Road

Lebanon, IL 62254-1299

http://www.mckendree.edu/

Contact: Marjorie Snep, Coordinator of the Learning Center. Phone: 618-537-6850. E-mail: msnep@mckendree.edu.

Students with Disabilities Support Services Approximately 5 registered undergraduate students were served during 2002-03. The program or unit includes 1 full-time staff member. Counselors and remediation/learning specialists are provided collaboratively through on-campus or off-campus services.

Subject-area Tutoring Tutoring is offered one-on-one and in small groups for most subjects. Tutoring is provided collaboratively through on-campus or off-campus services via graduate assistants/students.

Basic Skills Remediation Remediation is offered one-on-one, in small groups, and in class-size groups for learning strategies, reading, study skills, time management, and written language. Remediation is provided collaboratively through on-campus or off-campus services via regular education teachers.

Enrichment Programs for career planning, college survival skills, health and nutrition, medication management, practical computer skills, reading, stress management, study skills, test taking, time management, vocabulary development, and written composition skills are provided collaboratively through on-campus or off-campus services. Credit is offered for college survival skills, reading, study skills, test taking, time management, vocabulary development, and written composition skills.

Application For admittance to the program or unit, students are required to provide a psychoeducational report and provide documentation of high school services. Upon acceptance, documentation of need for services should be sent only to the LD program or unit. *Application deadline (institutional):* Continuous. *Application deadline (LD program):* Rolling/continuous for fall and rolling/continuous for spring.

Written Policies Written policy regarding general/basic LD accommodations is outlined in the school's catalog/handbook.

McMaster University
Centre for Student Development, Assistive Technology, Learning and Academic Support (ATLAS) Program

1280 Main Street West

Hamilton, ON L8S 4M2

Canada

http://csd.mcmaster.ca/atlas/

Contact: Ms. Caroline Cayuga, Learning Disabilities Coordinator. Phone: 905-525-9140 Ext. 24354. Fax: 905-528-3749. E-mail: cayugac@mcmaster.ca.

Centre for Student Development, Assistive Technology, Learning and Academic Support (ATLAS) Program Approximately 125 registered undergraduate students were served during 2002-03. The program or unit includes 3 full-time staff members. Diagnostic specialists, LD specialists, remediation/learning specialists, trained peer tutors, and other are provided through the program or unit. Academic advisers and counselors are provided collaboratively through on-campus or off-campus services.

Summer Program To help prepare for the demands of college, there is summer program prior to entering the school.

Subject-area Tutoring Tutoring is offered one-on-one for some subjects. Tutoring is provided through the program or unit via trained peer tutors.

Diagnostic Testing Testing is provided through the program or unit for auditory processing, intelligence, learning strategies, learning styles, math, motor skills, reading, spelling, spoken language, study skills, visual processing, and written language. Testing for personality is provided collaboratively through on-campus or off-campus services.

Basic Skills Remediation Remediation is offered one-on-one for auditory processing, computer skills, learning strategies, reading, social skills, spelling, study skills, time management, visual processing, and written language. Remediation is provided through the program or unit via computer-based instruction, LD specialists, and trained peer tutors.

Enrichment Enrichment programs are available through the program or unit for learning strategies, math, oral communication skills, practical computer skills, reading, self-advocacy, study skills, test taking, time management, vocabulary development, and written composition skills. Programs for career planning, college survival skills, health and nutrition, medication management, and stress management are provided collaboratively through on-campus or off-campus services.

Application For admittance to the program or unit, students are required to provide a psychoeducational report. It is recommended that students provide documentation of high school services. Upon acceptance, documentation of need for services should be sent only to the LD program or unit. *Application deadline (institutional):* 7/15. *Application deadline (LD program):* 11/1 for fall. 6/1 for spring.

Written Policies Written policy regarding general/basic LD accommodations is available on the program Web site. Written policy regarding general/basic LD accommodations is outlined in the school's catalog/handbook.

McPherson College

1600 East Euclid, PO Box 1402
McPherson, KS 67460-1402
http://www.mcpherson.edu/

Contact: Kevin Hadduck, Director of Center for Academic Development. Phone: 620-241-0731. E-mail: hadduckk@mcpherson.edu.

The program or unit includes 2 part-time staff members. Counselors, remediation/learning specialists, skill tutors, and trained peer tutors are provided through the program or unit. Academic advisers and coaches are provided collaboratively through on-campus or off-campus services.

Unique Aids and Services Aids, services, or accommodations include advocates, career counseling, faculty training, and weekly meetings with faculty.

Subject-area Tutoring Tutoring is offered one-on-one and in small groups for all subjects. Tutoring is provided through the program or unit via graduate assistants/students and trained peer tutors.

Basic Skills Remediation Remediation is offered one-on-one and in small groups for computer skills, learning strategies, math, reading, study skills, and time management. Remediation is provided through the program or unit via regular education teachers and trained peer tutors.

Enrichment Enrichment programs are available through the program or unit for college survival skills, learning strategies, oral communication skills, reading, stress management, study skills, test taking, time management, and vocabulary development. Programs for career planning, math, practical computer skills, and written composition skills are provided collaboratively through on-campus or off-campus services. Credit is offered for learning strategies, math, reading, stress management, study skills, test taking, time management, and vocabulary development.

Application For admittance to the program or unit, students are required to provide a psychoeducational report (5 years old or less) and provide documentation of high school services. Upon application, materials documenting need for services should be sent to both admissions and the LD program or unit. Upon acceptance, documentation of need for services should be sent to both admissions and the LD program or unit. *Application deadline (institutional):* Continuous. *Application deadline (LD program):* Rolling/continuous for fall and rolling/continuous for spring.

Written Policies Written policies regarding course substitutions and general/basic LD accommodations are available through the program or unit directly.

Medaille College
Office of Disabilities Services

18 Agassiz Circle
Buffalo, NY 14214-2695
http://www.medaille.edu/

Contact: Ms. Debra McLoughlin, Director of Academic Advisement and Disabilities Services. Phone: 716-884-3411 Ext. 280. Fax: 716-884-0291. E-mail: dmcloughlin@medaille.edu.

Office of Disabilities Services Approximately 60 registered undergraduate students were served during 2002-03. The program or unit includes 2 full-time staff members. Academic advisers, counselors, professional tutors, regular education teachers, remediation/learning specialists, skill tutors, strategy tutors, trained peer tutors, and other are provided collaboratively through on-campus or off-campus services.

Orientation The program or unit offers a mandatory 1-hour orientation for new students individually by special arrangement.

Unique Aids and Services Aids, services, or accommodations include advocates, career counseling, digital textbooks, and faculty training.

Subject-area Tutoring Tutoring is offered one-on-one, in small groups, and in class-size groups for most subjects. Tutoring is provided collaboratively through on-campus or off-campus services via computer-based instruction, graduate assistants/students, professional tutors, and trained peer tutors.

Basic Skills Remediation Remediation is offered one-on-one, in small groups, and in class-size groups for computer skills, learning strategies, math, reading, spoken language, study skills, time management, and written language. Remediation is provided collaboratively through on-campus or off-campus services via computer-based instruction, professional tutors, regular education teachers, trained peer tutors, and other.

Application For admittance to the program or unit, students are required to provide a psychoeducational report. It is recommended that students provide documentation of high school services. Upon acceptance, documentation of need for services should be sent only to the LD program or unit. *Application deadline (institutional):* 8/1. *Application deadline (LD program):* Rolling/continuous for fall and rolling/continuous for spring.

Written Policies Written policies regarding course substitutions, general/basic LD accommodations, grade forgiveness, reduced course loads, substitutions and waivers of admissions requirements, and substitutions and waivers of graduation requirements are available through the program or unit directly.

Memorial University of Newfoundland
Glenn Roy Blundon Centre (Student Affairs and Services) for Students with Disabilities

Elizabeth Avenue
St. John's, NF A1C 5S7
Canada
http://www.mun.ca/student/disabilities/

Contact: Mrs. Ruth Marie North, Student Affairs Officer. Phone: 709-737-2156. Fax: 709-737-3096. E-mail: rnorth@mun.ca. Head of LD Program: Dr. George Hurley, Director of University Counselling Centre. Phone: 709-737-8874. Fax: 709-737-3011. E-mail: ghurley@mun.ca.

Glenn Roy Blundon Centre (Student Affairs and Services) for Students with Disabilities Approximately 65 registered undergraduate students were served during 2002-03. The program or unit includes 7 full-time staff members. Strategy tutors are provided

Memorial University of Newfoundland (continued)

through the program or unit. Academic advisers, coaches, counselors, diagnostic specialists, graduate assistants/students, LD specialists, professional tutors, remediation/learning specialists, skill tutors, and trained peer tutors are provided collaboratively through on-campus or off-campus services.

Orientation The program or unit offers an optional orientation for new students individually by special arrangement.

Unique Aids and Services Aids, services, or accommodations include advocates, career counseling, digital textbooks, faculty training, parent workshops, support groups, academic accommodations (e.g. for completing tests and exams).

Basic Skills Remediation Remediation is offered one-on-one, in small groups, and in class-size groups for learning strategies, math, reading, social skills, study skills, time management, and written language. Remediation is provided through the program or unit. Remediation is also provided collaboratively through on-campus or off-campus services via graduate assistants/students and trained peer tutors.

Enrichment Enrichment programs are available through the program or unit for learning strategies, study skills, test taking, and time management. Programs for career planning, college survival skills, health and nutrition, math, medication management, oral communication skills, practical computer skills, reading, self-advocacy, stress management, vocabulary development, and written composition skills are provided collaboratively through on-campus or off-campus services.

Student Organization Memorial University Disability Information and Support Centre.

Application For admittance to the program or unit, students are required to provide a psychoeducational report (2 years old or less). Upon application, materials documenting need for services should be sent only to the LD program or unit. Upon acceptance, documentation of need for services should be sent only to the LD program or unit. *Application deadline (institutional):* Continuous. *Application deadline (LD program):* Rolling/continuous for fall and rolling/continuous for spring.

Written Policies Written policy regarding general/basic LD accommodations is available through the program or unit directly.

Orientation The program or unit offers an optional orientation for new students individually by special arrangement.

Unique Aids and Services Aids, services, or accommodations include advocates, support groups, regular meetings with the Director of Academic Success Center.

Subject-area Tutoring Tutoring is offered one-on-one for most subjects. Tutoring is provided through the program or unit via computer-based instruction, graduate assistants/students, and LD specialists. Tutoring is also provided collaboratively through on-campus or off-campus services via other.

Basic Skills Remediation Remediation is offered in class-size groups for computer skills, learning strategies, social skills, study skills, time management, and written language. Remediation is provided through the program or unit via computer-based instruction, LD specialists, regular education teachers, and trained peer tutors. Remediation is also provided collaboratively through on-campus or off-campus services via LD specialists, professional tutors, special education teachers, and other.

Enrichment Enrichment programs are available through the program or unit for college survival skills, learning strategies, stress management, study skills, test taking, time management, vocabulary development, and written composition skills. Programs for career planning and self-advocacy are provided collaboratively through on-campus or off-campus services. Credit is offered for study skills.

Application For admittance to the program or unit, students are required to provide a psychoeducational report (3 years old or less), provide documentation of high school services, and provide documentation as specified on Web site. Upon acceptance, documentation of need for services should be sent only to the LD program or unit. *Application deadline (institutional):* Continuous. *Application deadline (LD program):* Rolling/continuous for fall and rolling/continuous for spring.

Written Policies Written policy regarding general/basic LD accommodations is available on the program Web site. Written policies regarding course substitutions and substitutions and waivers of admissions requirements are available through the program or unit directly.

Menlo College
Academic Success Center

1000 El Camino Real
Atherton, CA 94027-4301
http://www.menlo.edu/

Contact: Ms. Janet M. Miller, M.A., Director of the Academic Success Center. Phone: 650-543-3854. Fax: 650-543-4001. E-mail: jmiller@menlo.edu.

Academic Success Center Approximately 56 registered undergraduate students were served during 2002-03. The program or unit includes 1 full-time and 1 part-time staff member. Academic advisers, remediation/learning specialists, skill tutors, and strategy tutors are provided through the program or unit. Academic advisers, coaches, counselors, regular education teachers, strategy tutors, and trained peer tutors are provided collaboratively through on-campus or off-campus services.

Meredith College
Counseling Center/Disability Services

3800 Hillsborough Street
Raleigh, NC 27607-5298
http://www.meredith.edu/

Contact: Ms. LoriAnn S. Stretch, Assistant Counseling Director and Coordinator of Disability Services. Phone: 919-760-8427. Fax: 919-760-2383. E-mail: stretchl@meredith.edu.

Counseling Center/Disability Services Approximately 197 registered undergraduate students were served during 2002-03. The program or unit includes 3 full-time and 4 part-time staff members. Academic advisers, coaches, counselors, graduate assistants/students, and LD specialists are provided through the program or unit. Academic advisers, coaches, professional tutors, regular education teachers, remediation/learning specialists, skill tutors, special education teachers, strategy tutors, and trained peer tutors are provided collaboratively through on-campus or off-campus services.

Orientation The program or unit offers an optional 2-day orientation for new students before classes begin.

Unique Aids and Services Aids, services, or accommodations include advocates, career counseling, digital textbooks, faculty training, personal coach, priority registration, and weekly meetings with faculty.

Subject-area Tutoring Tutoring is offered one-on-one, in small groups, and in class-size groups for some subjects. Tutoring is provided collaboratively through on-campus or off-campus services via computer-based instruction, graduate assistants/students, and trained peer tutors.

Basic Skills Remediation Remediation is offered one-on-one, in small groups, and in class-size groups for computer skills, learning strategies, math, reading, social skills, study skills, time management, and written language. Remediation is provided through the program or unit via LD specialists. Remediation is also provided collaboratively through on-campus or off-campus services via computer-based instruction, graduate assistants/students, regular education teachers, teacher trainees, and trained peer tutors.

Enrichment Enrichment programs are available through the program or unit for college survival skills, learning strategies, medication management, self-advocacy, stress management, study skills, and time management. Programs for career planning, college survival skills, health and nutrition, learning strategies, math, oral communication skills, practical computer skills, reading, self-advocacy, stress management, study skills, test taking, time management, vocabulary development, and written composition skills are provided collaboratively through on-campus or off-campus services. Credit is offered for career planning, college survival skills, learning strategies, oral communication skills, practical computer skills, stress management, study skills, and written composition skills.

Student Organization Disability Support Organization consists of 20 members.

Fees *Orientation* fee is $50.

Application For admittance to the program or unit, students are required to apply to the program directly and provide a psychoeducational report (3 years old or less). It is recommended that students provide documentation of high school services. Upon application, materials documenting need for services should be sent only to the LD program or unit. Upon acceptance, documentation of need for services should be sent only to the LD program or unit. *Application deadline (institutional):* 2/15. *Application deadline (LD program):* Rolling/continuous for fall and rolling/continuous for spring.

Written Policies Written policies regarding course substitutions, general/basic LD accommodations, reduced course loads, substitutions and waivers of admissions requirements, and substitutions and waivers of graduation requirements are available on the program Web site. Written policies regarding course substitutions, general/basic LD accommodations, reduced course loads, substitutions and waivers of admissions requirements, and substitutions and waivers of graduation requirements are available through the program or unit directly.

Messiah College
Disability Services

One College Avenue
Grantham, PA 17027

http://www.messiah.edu/disability/disability.htm

Contact: Dr. Keith W. Drahn, Director of Disability Services and Associate Professor of Education. Phone: 717-796-5358. Fax: 717-796-5217. E-mail: kdrahn@messiah.edu.

Disability Services Approximately 20 registered undergraduate students were served during 2002-03. The program or unit includes 2 part-time staff members. Academic advisers, coaches, counselors, skill tutors, and trained peer tutors are provided collaboratively through on-campus or off-campus services.

Unique Aids and Services Aids, services, or accommodations include digital textbooks, priority registration, and weekly meetings with faculty.

Subject-area Tutoring Tutoring is offered one-on-one for most subjects. Tutoring is provided collaboratively through on-campus or off-campus services via trained peer tutors.

Diagnostic Testing Testing for auditory processing, intelligence, learning styles, math, neuropsychological, personality, reading, spelling, visual processing, written language, and other services is provided collaboratively through on-campus or off-campus services.

Basic Skills Remediation Remediation is offered one-on-one for study skills, time management, and written language. Remediation is provided through the program or unit.

Enrichment Enrichment programs are available through the program or unit for time management. Programs for career planning, college survival skills, health and nutrition, learning strategies, math, medication management, oral communication skills, practical computer skills, stress management, study skills, time management, and written composition skills are provided collaboratively through on-campus or off-campus services. Credit is offered for study skills.

Fees *Diagnostic Testing* fee is $400.

Application For admittance to the program or unit, students are required to provide a psychoeducational report. It is recommended that students provide documentation of high school services. Upon acceptance, documentation of need for services should be sent only to the LD program or unit. *Application deadline (institutional):* Continuous. *Application deadline (LD program):* Rolling/continuous for fall and rolling/continuous for spring.

Written Policies Written policy regarding general/basic LD accommodations is available on the program Web site. Written policies regarding course substitutions and reduced course loads are available through the program or unit directly.

Methodist College
Academic Development Center

5400 Ramsey Street
Fayetteville, NC 28311-1498

http://www.methodist.edu

Contact: Ms. Nicolette Starkie Campos, Assistant Dean for Academic Services. Phone: 910-630-7033. Fax: 910-630-7407. E-mail: ncampos@methodist.edu.

Academic Development Center Approximately 15 registered undergraduate students were served during 2002-03. The program or unit includes 2 full-time staff members. Academic advisers, professional tutors, skill tutors, and trained peer tutors are provided

Methodist College (continued)

through the program or unit. Academic advisers, coaches, counselors, regular education teachers, special education teachers, and teacher trainees are provided collaboratively through on-campus or off-campus services.

Unique Aids and Services Aids, services, or accommodations include advocates and priority registration.

Subject-area Tutoring Tutoring is offered one-on-one and in small groups for most subjects. Tutoring is provided through the program or unit via professional tutors and trained peer tutors.

Basic Skills Remediation Remediation is offered one-on-one and in small groups for auditory processing, computer skills, learning strategies, math, reading, spelling, study skills, time management, visual processing, and written language. Remediation is provided through the program or unit via professional tutors and trained peer tutors.

Enrichment Enrichment programs are available through the program or unit for college survival skills, learning strategies, reading, and study skills. Programs for career planning, college survival skills, health and nutrition, learning strategies, math, oral communication skills, practical computer skills, stress management, study skills, test taking, time management, and written composition skills are provided collaboratively through on-campus or off-campus services. Credit is offered for college survival skills, math, practical computer skills, study skills, and written composition skills.

Application For admittance to the program or unit, students are required to provide a psychoeducational report (3 years old or less). Upon application, materials documenting need for services should be sent only to the LD program or unit. Upon acceptance, documentation of need for services should be sent only to the LD program or unit. *Application deadline (institutional):* Continuous. *Application deadline (LD program):* Rolling/continuous for fall and rolling/continuous for spring.

Written Policies Written policy regarding general/basic LD accommodations is available through the program or unit directly.

Miami University
Bernard B. Rinella Jr. Learning Assistance Center

Oxford, OH 45056

http://www.muohio.edu/

Contact: Mr. Chuck Catania, Coordinator of Learning Disability Services. Phone: 513-529-8741. Fax: 513-529-8799. E-mail: catanica@muohio.edu.

Bernard B. Rinella Jr. Learning Assistance Center Approximately 400 registered undergraduate students were served during 2002-03. The program or unit includes 3 full-time and 2 part-time staff members. Graduate assistants/students, LD specialists, skill tutors, strategy tutors, and trained peer tutors are provided through the program or unit. Academic advisers, diagnostic specialists, and regular education teachers are provided collaboratively through on-campus or off-campus services.

Unique Aids and Services Aids, services, or accommodations include advocates, career counseling, personal coach, priority registration, and weekly meetings with faculty.

Subject-area Tutoring Tutoring is offered one-on-one, in small groups, and in class-size groups for all subjects. Tutoring is provided through the program or unit via graduate assistants/students and trained peer tutors.

Basic Skills Remediation Remediation is offered in small groups for learning strategies, study skills, and time management. Remediation is provided through the program or unit via graduate assistants/students, regular education teachers, and trained peer tutors.

Enrichment Enrichment programs are available through the program or unit for college survival skills, learning strategies, self-advocacy, study skills, test taking, and time management. Programs for career planning, health and nutrition, medication management, and stress management are provided collaboratively through on-campus or off-campus services.

Application For admittance to the program or unit, students are required to provide a psychoeducational report (3 years old or less) and provide documentation of high school services. Upon acceptance, documentation of need for services should be sent only to the LD program or unit. *Application deadline (institutional):* 1/31. *Application deadline (LD program):* Rolling/continuous for fall and rolling/continuous for spring.

Written Policies Written policy regarding general/basic LD accommodations is available on the program Web site. Written policies regarding course substitutions, general/basic LD accommodations, reduced course loads, substitutions and waivers of admissions requirements, and substitutions and waivers of graduation requirements are outlined in the school's catalog/handbook. Written policy regarding general/basic LD accommodations is available through the program or unit directly.

Michigan State University
Resource Center for Persons with Disabilities

East Lansing, MI 48824

http://www.rcpd.msu.edu

Contact: Elaine High, Learning Disabilities Specialist. Phone: 517-353-9642. Fax: 517-432-3191. E-mail: high@msu.edu. Head of LD Program: Mr. Michael J. Hudson, Director. Phone: 517-353-9642 Ext. 229. E-mail: mjh@msu.edu.

Resource Center for Persons with Disabilities Approximately 550 registered undergraduate students were served during 2002-03. The program or unit includes 2 full-time staff members. Coaches, diagnostic specialists, LD specialists, remediation/learning specialists, skill tutors, and strategy tutors are provided through the program or unit. Academic advisers, counselors, and trained peer tutors are provided collaboratively through on-campus or off-campus services.

Orientation The program or unit offers an optional 2.5-hour orientation for new students before classes begin.

Unique Aids and Services Aids, services, or accommodations include faculty training and priority registration.

Subject-area Tutoring Tutoring is offered one-on-one and in small groups for some subjects. Tutoring is provided collaboratively through on-campus or off-campus services via trained peer tutors.

Diagnostic Testing Testing is provided through the program or unit for learning strategies, learning styles, and study skills. Testing for intelligence, math, personality, reading, and spelling is provided collaboratively through on-campus or off-campus services.

Basic Skills Remediation Remediation is offered one-on-one, in small groups, and in class-size groups for learning strategies, reading, spelling, study skills, and time management. Remediation is provided through the program or unit via LD specialists. Remediation is also provided collaboratively through on-campus or off-campus services via LD specialists.

Enrichment Program for math is provided collaboratively through on-campus or off-campus services. Credit is offered for math.

Student Organization Council of Students with Disabilities consists of 14 members.

Fees *Diagnostic Testing* fee is $250.

Application For admittance to the program or unit, students are required to apply to the program directly and provide a psychoeducational report (3 years old or less). It is recommended that students provide documentation of high school services. Upon acceptance, documentation of need for services should be sent only to the LD program or unit. *Application deadline (LD program):* Rolling/continuous for fall and rolling/continuous for spring.

Written Policies Written policy regarding general/basic LD accommodations is available on the program Web site.

Michigan Technological University
Services for Students with Disabilities

1400 Townsend Drive
Houghton, MI 49931-1295

http://www.admin.mtu.edu/dos/disability.htm

Contact: Dr. Gloria B. Melton, Associate Dean of Student Affairs. Phone: 906-487-2212. Fax: 906-487-3060. E-mail: gbmelton@mtu.edu.

Services for Students with Disabilities Approximately 30 registered undergraduate students were served during 2002-03. The program or unit includes 1 part-time staff member. Academic advisers, coaches, counselors, diagnostic specialists, graduate assistants/students, LD specialists, professional tutors, regular education teachers, remediation/learning specialists, skill tutors, strategy tutors, and trained peer tutors are provided collaboratively through on-campus or off-campus services.

Unique Aids and Services Aids, services, or accommodations include advocates, career counseling, digital textbooks, personal coach, priority registration, and weekly meetings with faculty.

Subject-area Tutoring Tutoring is offered one-on-one and in small groups for most subjects. Tutoring is provided collaboratively through on-campus or off-campus services via graduate assistants/students, LD specialists, professional tutors, and trained peer tutors.

Enrichment Enrichment programs are available through the program or unit for self-advocacy, study skills, and time management. Programs for career planning, college survival skills, health and nutrition, learning strategies, math, medication management, oral communication skills, practical computer skills, reading, self-advocacy, stress management, study skills, test taking, time man-

agement, vocabulary development, and written composition skills are provided collaboratively through on-campus or off-campus services. Credit is offered for college survival skills, learning strategies, and math.

Application For admittance to the program or unit, students are required to provide a psychoeducational report (3 years old or less). It is recommended that students provide documentation of high school services. Upon acceptance, documentation of need for services should be sent only to the LD program or unit. *Application deadline (institutional):* Continuous. *Application deadline (LD program):* 8/30 for fall. 1/15 for spring.

Written Policies Written policy regarding general/basic LD accommodations is available on the program Web site. Written policy regarding general/basic LD accommodations is outlined in the school's catalog/handbook.

Middle Tennessee State University
Disabled Student Services

1301 East Main Street
Murfreesboro, TN 37132
http://www.mtsu.edu/

Contact: Amy Cagle, Assistant Director. Phone: 615-904-8246. Fax: 615-898-4893. E-mail: acagle@mtsu.edu.

Disabled Student Services Approximately 350 registered undergraduate students were served during 2002-03. The program or unit includes 4 full-time and 20 part-time staff members. Academic advisers, counselors, graduate assistants/students, LD specialists, and trained peer tutors are provided through the program or unit. Academic advisers, counselors, graduate assistants/students, LD specialists, and trained peer tutors are provided collaboratively through on-campus or off-campus services.

Summer Program To help prepare for the demands of college, there is a mandatory 2-day summer program prior to entering the school.

Unique Aids and Services Aids, services, or accommodations include digital textbooks, priority registration, weekly meetings with faculty, bi-weekly meetings with Assistant Director.

Subject-area Tutoring Tutoring is offered one-on-one and in small groups for most subjects. Tutoring is provided through the program or unit via computer-based instruction, graduate assistants/students, and professional tutors. Tutoring is also provided collaboratively through on-campus or off-campus services via graduate assistants/students and professional tutors.

Basic Skills Remediation Remediation is offered one-on-one and in small groups for computer skills, learning strategies, math, spelling, study skills, time management, and written language. Remediation is provided through the program or unit via graduate assistants/students and trained peer tutors. Remediation is also provided collaboratively through on-campus or off-campus services via graduate assistants/students and trained peer tutors.

Enrichment Enrichment programs are available through the program or unit for college survival skills, learning strategies, math, study skills, test taking, time management, and written composition skills. Programs for career planning, math, practical computer skills, and written composition skills are provided collaboratively through on-campus or off-campus services.

Middle Tennessee State University (continued)

Student Organization Sigma Delta Sigma consists of 25 members.

Fees *Summer Program* fee is $75.

Application For admittance to the program or unit, students are required to provide a psychoeducational report (5 years old or less). It is recommended that students provide documentation of high school services. Upon application, materials documenting need for services should be sent only to the LD program or unit. Upon acceptance, documentation of need for services should be sent only to the LD program or unit. *Application deadline (institutional):* Continuous. *Application deadline (LD program):* Rolling/continuous for fall and rolling/continuous for spring.

Written Policies Written policy regarding general/basic LD accommodations is available on the program Web site. Written policy regarding general/basic LD accommodations is available through the program or unit directly.

Midland Lutheran College
Academic Support Services

900 North Clarkson Street

Fremont, NE 68025-4200

http://www.mlc.edu/

Contact: Ms. Lisa Kramme, Director of Academic Support Services. Phone: 402-941-6257. Fax: 402-727-6223. E-mail: kramme@mlc.edu.

Academic Support Services Approximately 11 registered undergraduate students were served during 2002-03. The program or unit includes 2 full-time and 16 part-time staff members. Academic advisers, trained peer tutors, and other are provided collaboratively through on-campus or off-campus services.

Subject-area Tutoring Tutoring is offered one-on-one and in small groups for most subjects. Tutoring is provided collaboratively through on-campus or off-campus services via trained peer tutors and other.

Basic Skills Remediation Remediation is offered one-on-one and in class-size groups for learning strategies, study skills, and time management. Remediation is provided collaboratively through on-campus or off-campus services via regular education teachers, trained peer tutors, and other.

Enrichment Programs for career planning, college survival skills, health and nutrition, learning strategies, study skills, test taking, time management, and vocabulary development are provided collaboratively through on-campus or off-campus services. Credit is offered for college survival skills, learning strategies, study skills, test taking, time management, and vocabulary development.

Application For admittance to the program or unit, students are required to apply to the program directly and provide a psychoeducational report (4 years old or less). It is recommended that students provide documentation of high school services. Upon application, materials documenting need for services should be sent only to the LD program or unit. Upon acceptance, documentation of need for services should be sent only to the LD program or unit. *Application deadline (institutional):* Continuous. *Application deadline (LD program):* Rolling/continuous for fall and rolling/continuous for spring.

Written Policies Written policy regarding general/basic LD accommodations is outlined in the school's catalog/handbook.

Midwestern State University
Counseling and Disability Services

3410 Taft Boulevard

Wichita Falls, TX 76308

http://students.mwsu.edu/disability

Contact: Ms. Debra J. Higginbotham, Director. Phone: 940-397-4618. Fax: 940-397-4934. E-mail: debra.higginbotham@mwsu.edu.

Counseling and Disability Services Approximately 40 registered undergraduate students were served during 2002-03. The program or unit includes 1 full-time and 1 part-time staff member. Academic advisers and counselors are provided through the program or unit. Academic advisers, counselors, professional tutors, and regular education teachers are provided collaboratively through on-campus or off-campus services.

Orientation The program or unit offers a mandatory 1-hour orientation for new students individually by special arrangement.

Unique Aids and Services Aids, services, or accommodations include career counseling, digital textbooks, and priority registration.

Subject-area Tutoring Tutoring is offered one-on-one and in small groups for some subjects. Tutoring is provided through the program or unit via graduate assistants/students. Tutoring is also provided collaboratively through on-campus or off-campus services via graduate assistants/students and other.

Diagnostic Testing Testing is provided through the program or unit for intelligence, neuropsychological, reading, spelling, study skills, and written language. Testing for learning strategies, learning styles, personality, and study skills is provided collaboratively through on-campus or off-campus services.

Basic Skills Remediation Remediation is offered in class-size groups for math, reading, and written language. Remediation is provided collaboratively through on-campus or off-campus services via regular education teachers.

Enrichment Enrichment programs are available through the program or unit for career planning, learning strategies, self-advocacy, stress management, study skills, test taking, and time management. Programs for career planning, college survival skills, math, reading, self-advocacy, stress management, study skills, test taking, time management, and written composition skills are provided collaboratively through on-campus or off-campus services. Credit is offered for college survival skills, math, reading, and written composition skills.

Application For admittance to the program or unit, students are required to provide a psychoeducational report (3 years old or less) and provide diagnostic testing, scores, and recommendations. Upon application, materials documenting need for services should be sent only to the LD program or unit. Upon acceptance, documentation of need for services should be sent only to the LD program or unit. *Application deadline (institutional):* 8/7. *Application deadline (LD program):* Rolling/continuous for fall and rolling/continuous for spring.

Written Policies Written policy regarding general/basic LD accommodations is available on the program Web site. Written policy regarding general/basic LD accommodations is available through the program or unit directly.

Millersville University of Pennsylvania

PO Box 1002

Millersville, PA 17551-0302

http://www.millersville.edu/

Contact: Mrs. Sherlynn Bessick, Director of Office of Learning Services. Phone: 717-872-3178. Fax: 717-871-2129. E-mail: learning.services@millersville.edu.

Approximately 200 registered undergraduate students were served during 2002-03. The program or unit includes 2 full-time and 15 part-time staff members. Academic advisers, diagnostic specialists, graduate assistants/students, LD specialists, professional tutors, skill tutors, strategy tutors, teacher trainees, and trained peer tutors are provided through the program or unit. Academic advisers, counselors, diagnostic specialists, graduate assistants/students, LD specialists, professional tutors, skill tutors, special education teachers, strategy tutors, teacher trainees, and trained peer tutors are provided collaboratively through on-campus or off-campus services.

Unique Aids and Services Aids, services, or accommodations include career counseling, digital textbooks, faculty training, and priority registration.

Subject-area Tutoring Tutoring is offered one-on-one and in small groups for all subjects. Tutoring is provided through the program or unit via computer-based instruction, graduate assistants/students, LD specialists, professional tutors, and trained peer tutors. Tutoring is also provided collaboratively through on-campus or off-campus services via computer-based instruction, graduate assistants/students, professional tutors, and trained peer tutors.

Basic Skills Remediation Remediation is offered one-on-one and in small groups for computer skills, learning strategies, math, reading, study skills, time management, and written language. Remediation is provided through the program or unit via computer-based instruction, graduate assistants/students, LD specialists, professional tutors, teacher trainees, and trained peer tutors. Remediation is also provided collaboratively through on-campus or off-campus services via computer-based instruction, graduate assistants/students, professional tutors, teacher trainees, and trained peer tutors.

Enrichment Enrichment programs are available through the program or unit for career planning, college survival skills, learning strategies, math, practical computer skills, reading, study skills, test taking, time management, and written composition skills. Programs for career planning, college survival skills, health and nutrition, learning strategies, math, medication management, oral communication skills, practical computer skills, stress management, and written composition skills are provided collaboratively through on-campus or off-campus services. Credit is offered for health and nutrition.

Application For admittance to the program or unit, students are required to apply to the program directly and provide a psychoeducational report (3 years old or less). It is recommended that students provide documentation of high school services. Upon acceptance, documentation of need for services should be sent to both admissions and the LD program or unit. *Application deadline (institutional):* Continuous. *Application deadline (LD program):* Rolling/continuous for fall and rolling/continuous for spring.

Written Policies Written policy regarding general/basic LD accommodations is outlined in the school's catalog/handbook. Written policy regarding general/basic LD accommodations is available through the program or unit directly.

Millsaps College
ADA Services for Students

1701 North State Street

Jackson, MS 39210-0001

http://www.millsaps.edu/

Contact: Ms. Sherryly Wilburn, Director of ADA Services for Students. Phone: 601-974-1208. Fax: 601-974-1229. E-mail: wilbuse@millsaps.edu.

ADA Services for Students Approximately 48 registered undergraduate students were served during 2002-03. The program or unit includes 1 full-time staff member. Graduate assistants/students and regular education teachers are provided collaboratively through on-campus or off-campus services.

Unique Aids and Services Aids, services, or accommodations include personal advising to parents and students.

Subject-area Tutoring Tutoring is offered one-on-one. Tutoring is provided collaboratively through on-campus or off-campus services via trained peer tutors.

Application For admittance to the program or unit, students are required to provide a psychoeducational report and provide appropriate health provider information, and have a personal interview. Upon acceptance, documentation of need for services should be sent only to the LD program or unit. *Application deadline (institutional):* Continuous. *Application deadline (LD program):* Rolling/continuous for fall and rolling/continuous for spring.

Written Policies Written policy regarding general/basic LD accommodations is available through the program or unit directly.

Mills College

5000 MacArthur Boulevard

Oakland, CA 94613-1000

http://www.mills.edu/student_life/disabled.html

Contact: Ms. Kennedy F. Golden, Acting Disabled Students' Services Provider. Phone: 510-430-2264. Fax: 510-430-3235. E-mail: kennedyg@mills.edu.

The program or unit includes 1 part-time staff member. Academic advisers, coaches, counselors, diagnostic specialists, graduate assistants/students, and LD specialists are provided collaboratively through on-campus or off-campus services.

Orientation The program or unit offers an optional 1 to 2-day orientation for new students during summer prior to enrollment and individually by special arrangement.

Unique Aids and Services Aids, services, or accommodations include career counseling.

Mills College (continued)

Basic Skills Remediation Remediation is offered one-on-one for learning strategies, study skills, and time management. Remediation is provided collaboratively through on-campus or off-campus services via LD specialists.

Enrichment Programs for career planning, college survival skills, health and nutrition, learning strategies, self-advocacy, stress management, study skills, test taking, time management, and written composition skills are provided collaboratively through on-campus or off-campus services.

Application It is recommended that students apply to the program directly, provide a psychoeducational report (3 years old or less), and provide documentation of high school services. Upon application, materials documenting need for services should be sent only to the LD program or unit. Upon acceptance, documentation of need for services should be sent only to the LD program or unit. *Application deadline (institutional):* 3/1. *Application deadline (LD program):* Rolling/continuous for fall and rolling/continuous for spring.

Written Policies Written policy regarding general/basic LD accommodations is available through the program or unit directly.

Minneapolis College of Art and Design
Individualized Academic Success Program

2501 Stevens Avenue South

Minneapolis, MN 55404-4347

http://www.mcad.edu/

Contact: Ms. Margaret Anne McGee, Learning Center Director. Phone: 612-874-3633. Fax: 612-874-3702. E-mail: margaret_mcgee@mcad.edu.

Individualized Academic Success Program Approximately 15 registered undergraduate students were served during 2002-03. The program or unit includes 1 full-time and 1 part-time staff member. Graduate assistants/students, LD specialists, skill tutors, strategy tutors, and trained peer tutors are provided through the program or unit. Academic advisers and counselors are provided collaboratively through on-campus or off-campus services.

Unique Aids and Services Aids, services, or accommodations include career counseling and weekly meetings with faculty.

Subject-area Tutoring Tutoring is offered one-on-one for most subjects. Tutoring is provided through the program or unit via computer-based instruction, graduate assistants/students, LD specialists, and trained peer tutors.

Basic Skills Remediation Remediation is offered one-on-one for computer skills, learning strategies, reading, study skills, time management, and written language. Remediation is provided through the program or unit via graduate assistants/students and trained peer tutors.

Application It is recommended that students provide documentation of high school services and provide a diagnostic Letter from learning disability professional. Upon application, materials documenting need for services should be sent to both admissions and the LD program or unit. Upon acceptance, documentation of need for

services should be sent only to the LD program or unit. *Application deadline (institutional):* Continuous. *Application deadline (LD program):* Rolling/continuous for fall and rolling/continuous for spring.

Written Policies Written policy regarding general/basic LD accommodations is outlined in the school's catalog/handbook.

Minnesota State University, Mankato

228 Wiecking Center

Mankato, MN 56001

http://www.mnsu.edu/

Contact: Phone: 507-389-2463.

The program or unit includes 1 full-time and 5 part-time staff members. Graduate assistants/students are provided through the program or unit. Academic advisers, coaches, counselors, LD specialists, regular education teachers, skill tutors, strategy tutors, and trained peer tutors are provided collaboratively through on-campus or off-campus services.

Unique Aids and Services Aids, services, or accommodations include advocates, faculty training, and priority registration.

Subject-area Tutoring Tutoring is offered one-on-one and in small groups for some subjects. Tutoring is provided collaboratively through on-campus or off-campus services via graduate assistants/students and trained peer tutors.

Enrichment Enrichment programs are available through the program or unit for self-advocacy. Programs for career planning, college survival skills, health and nutrition, learning strategies, practical computer skills, stress management, study skills, test taking, and time management are provided collaboratively through on-campus or off-campus services.

Application For admittance to the program or unit, students are required to provide a psychoeducational report (3 years old or less). It is recommended that students provide documentation of high school services. Upon acceptance, documentation of need for services should be sent only to the LD program or unit. *Application deadline (institutional):* Continuous. *Application deadline (LD program):* Rolling/continuous for fall and rolling/continuous for spring.

Written Policies Written policies regarding course substitutions, general/basic LD accommodations, reduced course loads, and substitutions and waivers of graduation requirements are available on the program Web site. Written policies regarding course substitutions, general/basic LD accommodations, reduced course loads, and substitutions and waivers of graduation requirements are outlined in the school's catalog/handbook.

Minnesota State University, Moorhead

1104 7th Avenue South

Moorhead, MN 56563-0002

http://www.mnstate.edu/disability/

Contact: Mr. Greg Toutges, Coordinator of Disability Services. Phone: 218-236-2652. Fax: 218-287-5050. E-mail: toutges@mnstate.edu.

Approximately 90 registered undergraduate students were served during 2002–03. The program or unit includes 1 full-time and 5 part-time staff members. Academic advisers, coaches, counselors, diagnostic specialists, graduate assistants/students, LD specialists, professional tutors, regular education teachers, remediation/learning specialists, skill tutors, special education teachers, strategy tutors, teacher trainees, and trained peer tutors are provided collaboratively through on-campus or off-campus services.

Orientation The program or unit offers a mandatory 1-hour orientation for new students individually by special arrangement.

Unique Aids and Services Aids, services, or accommodations include career counseling, digital textbooks, priority registration, support groups, note-taking services, test accommodations, assistive technology, taped textbooks.

Subject-area Tutoring Tutoring is offered one-on-one and in class-size groups for some subjects. Tutoring is provided collaboratively through on-campus or off-campus services via graduate assistants/students and trained peer tutors.

Enrichment Enrichment programs are available through the program or unit for self-advocacy, test taking, time management, and other. Programs for career planning, college survival skills, health and nutrition, learning strategies, math, medication management, oral communication skills, practical computer skills, reading, stress management, study skills, vocabulary development, and written composition skills are provided collaboratively through on-campus or off-campus services. Credit is offered for career planning, college survival skills, math, oral communication skills, practical computer skills, reading, stress management, and study skills.

Student Organization Student Disability Association consists of 30 members.

Application For admittance to the program or unit, students are required to apply to the program directly and provide a psychoeducational report (3 years old or less). It is recommended that students provide documentation of high school services. Upon application, materials documenting need for services should be sent only to the LD program or unit. Upon acceptance, documentation of need for services should be sent only to the LD program or unit. *Application deadline (institutional):* 8/7. *Application deadline (LD program):* Rolling/continuous for fall and rolling/continuous for spring.

Written Policies Written policy regarding general/basic LD accommodations is available on the program Web site. Written policy regarding general/basic LD accommodations is available through the program or unit directly.

Minot State University
Student Development Center

500 University Avenue West

Minot, ND 58707-0002

http://www.misu.nodak.edu/

Contact: Ms. Evelyn Klimpel, Coordinator of Disability Services. Phone: 701-858-3371. Fax: 701-858-4341. E-mail: disability@minotstateu.edu.

Student Development Center Approximately 42 registered undergraduate students were served during 2002–03. The program or unit includes 2 full-time and 3 part-time staff members. Counselors, diagnostic specialists, graduate assistants/students, trained peer tutors, and other are provided through the program or unit. Academic advisers, coaches, counselors, diagnostic specialists, graduate assistants/students, LD specialists, professional tutors, regular education teachers, trained peer tutors, and other are provided collaboratively through on-campus or off-campus services.

Orientation The program or unit offers an optional 1-hour orientation for new students individually by special arrangement.

Unique Aids and Services Aids, services, or accommodations include digital textbooks, testing accommodations.

Subject-area Tutoring Tutoring is offered one-on-one, in small groups, and in class-size groups for all subjects. Tutoring is provided through the program or unit via graduate assistants/students and trained peer tutors. Tutoring is also provided collaboratively through on-campus or off-campus services via computer-based instruction, LD specialists, and professional tutors.

Diagnostic Testing Testing is provided through the program or unit for handwriting, learning strategies, learning styles, personality, reading, and study skills. Testing for auditory processing, intelligence, math, motor skills, neuropsychological, personality, reading, social skills, spelling, spoken language, study skills, visual processing, and written language is provided collaboratively through on-campus or off-campus services.

Enrichment Enrichment programs are available through the program or unit for college survival skills, learning strategies, self-advocacy, stress management, study skills, test taking, and time management. Programs for career planning, college survival skills, health and nutrition, learning strategies, math, medication management, oral communication skills, practical computer skills, reading, self-advocacy, stress management, study skills, test taking, time management, vocabulary development, and written composition skills are provided collaboratively through on-campus or off-campus services. Credit is offered for college survival skills, health and nutrition, learning strategies, stress management, study skills, test taking, and time management.

Application For admittance to the program or unit, students are required to apply to the program directly and provide a psychoeducational report (5 years old or less). It is recommended that students provide documentation of high school services. Upon application, materials documenting need for services should be sent only to the LD program or unit. Upon acceptance, documentation of need for services should be sent only to the LD program or unit. *Application deadline (institutional):* Continuous. *Application deadline (LD program):* Rolling/continuous for fall and rolling/continuous for spring.

Written Policies Written policies regarding general/basic LD accommodations, substitutions and waivers of admissions requirements, and substitutions and waivers of graduation requirements are outlined in the school's catalog/handbook. Written policy regarding general/basic LD accommodations is available through the program or unit directly.

Missouri Southern State College

3950 East Newman Road

Missouri Southern State College (continued)
Joplin, MO 64801-1595
http://www.mssc.edu/

Contact: Ms. Melissa A. Locher, Coordinator for Disability Service. Phone: 417-625-9373. Fax: 417-659-4456. E-mail: locher-m@mail.mssc.edu.

Approximately 50 registered undergraduate students were served during 2002-03. The program or unit includes 1 full-time and 35 part-time staff members. Academic advisers and LD specialists are provided through the program or unit. Academic advisers, counselors, diagnostic specialists, professional tutors, skill tutors, strategy tutors, and trained peer tutors are provided collaboratively through on-campus or off-campus services.

Unique Aids and Services Aids, services, or accommodations include priority registration.

Subject-area Tutoring Tutoring is offered one-on-one and in small groups for some subjects. Tutoring is provided collaboratively through on-campus or off-campus services via trained peer tutors.

Basic Skills Remediation Remediation is offered in class-size groups for math, study skills, and written language. Remediation is provided collaboratively through on-campus or off-campus services via regular education teachers.

Application For admittance to the program or unit, students are required to provide a psychoeducational report. It is recommended that students provide documentation of high school services. Upon application, materials documenting need for services should be sent only to the LD program or unit. Upon acceptance, documentation of need for services should be sent only to the LD program or unit. *Application deadline (institutional):* 8/3. *Application deadline (LD program):* Rolling/continuous for fall and rolling/continuous for spring.

Written Policies Written policies regarding general/basic LD accommodations, substitutions and waivers of admissions requirements, and substitutions and waivers of graduation requirements are outlined in the school's catalog/handbook. Written policies regarding course substitutions, general/basic LD accommodations, reduced course loads, substitutions and waivers of admissions requirements, and substitutions and waivers of graduation requirements are available through the program or unit directly.

Monmouth College
Office of Student Affairs

700 East Broadway
Monmouth, IL 61462-1998
http://www.monm.edu/

Contact: Jacquelyn Condon, Vice President for Student Life. Phone: 309-457-2113. Fax: 309-457-2363. E-mail: jackiec@monm.edu.

Office of Student Affairs Approximately 7 registered undergraduate students were served during 2002-03. Academic advisers, regular education teachers, trained peer tutors, and other are provided collaboratively through on-campus or off-campus services.

Subject-area Tutoring Tutoring is offered one-on-one and in small groups for most subjects. Tutoring is provided collaboratively through on-campus or off-campus services via graduate assistants/students and trained peer tutors.

Basic Skills Remediation Remediation is offered one-on-one for learning strategies, study skills, and time management. Remediation is provided collaboratively through on-campus or off-campus services via trained peer tutors.

Enrichment Programs for career planning, college survival skills, health and nutrition, learning strategies, stress management, study skills, test taking, and time management are provided collaboratively through on-campus or off-campus services.

Application For admittance to the program or unit, students are required to provide a psychoeducational report (5 years old or less) and provide documentation of high school services. Upon application, materials documenting need for services should be sent only to admissions with institutional application materials. Upon acceptance, documentation of need for services should be sent to both admissions and the LD program or unit. *Application deadline (institutional):* Continuous. *Application deadline (LD program):* Rolling/continuous for fall and rolling/continuous for spring.

Monmouth University

400 Cedar Avenue
West Long Branch, NJ 07764-1898
http://www.monmouth.edu/

Contact: Ms. Carolyne Chirichello, LD Specialist. E-mail: cchirich@monmouth.edu. Head of LD Program: Ms. Stacey Harris, Director of Disability Services. E-mail: sharris@monmouth.edu.

Approximately 175 registered undergraduate students were served during 2002-03. The program or unit includes 4 full-time staff members and 1 part-time staff member. LD specialists are provided through the program or unit. Counselors and other are provided collaboratively through on-campus or off-campus services.

Orientation The program or unit offers an optional orientation for new students during general orientation.

Unique Aids and Services Aids, services, or accommodations include faculty training and priority registration.

Basic Skills Remediation Remediation is offered one-on-one and in small groups for learning strategies, study skills, and time management. Remediation is provided collaboratively through on-campus or off-campus services via LD specialists.

Enrichment Enrichment programs are available through the program or unit for college survival skills, learning strategies, self-advocacy, study skills, and time management. Programs for career planning and college survival skills are provided collaboratively through on-campus or off-campus services.

Application For admittance to the program or unit, students are required to provide a psychoeducational report. It is recommended that students provide documentation of high school services. Upon acceptance, documentation of need for services should be sent only to the LD program or unit. *Application deadline (institutional):* 3/1. *Application deadline (LD program):* Rolling/continuous for fall and rolling/continuous for spring.

Written Policies Written policy regarding general/basic LD accommodations is available on the program Web site. Written policy regarding general/basic LD accommodations is outlined in the school's catalog/handbook. Written policy regarding general/basic LD accommodations is available through the program or unit directly.

Montana State University-Billings
Disability Support Services

1500 University Drive
Billings, MT 59101-0298
http://www.msubillings.edu

Contact: Ms. Trudy Ilene Carey, Interim Coordinator. Phone: 406-657-2283. Fax: 406-657-1658. E-mail: tcarey@msubillings.edu.

Disability Support Services Approximately 125 registered undergraduate students were served during 2002-03. The program or unit includes 1 full-time and 2 part-time staff members. Services are provided through the program or unit. Services are provided collaboratively through on-campus or off-campus services.
Unique Aids and Services Aids, services, or accommodations include digital textbooks, priority registration, alternative tests, notetakers, taping lectures.
Application For admittance to the program or unit, students are required to provide a psychoeducational report (5 years old or less). It is recommended that students provide documentation of high school services. Upon application, materials documenting need for services should be sent only to the LD program or unit. Upon acceptance, documentation of need for services should be sent only to the LD program or unit. *Application deadline (institutional):* 7/1. *Application deadline (LD program):* Rolling/continuous for fall and rolling/continuous for spring.
Written Policies Written policy regarding general/basic LD accommodations is available on the program Web site. Written policy regarding general/basic LD accommodations is outlined in the school's catalog/handbook.

Montana State University-Bozeman
Disability, Re-entry, and Veteran Services

Bozeman, MT 59717
http://www.montana.edu/www.res

Contact: Brenda K. York, Director. Phone: 406-994-2824. Fax: 406-994-3943. E-mail: byork@montana.edu.

Disability, Re-entry, and Veteran Services Approximately 124 registered undergraduate students were served during 2002-03. The program or unit includes 1 full-time staff member. Academic advisers, counselors, diagnostic specialists, and LD specialists are provided through the program or unit. Academic advisers, professional tutors, remediation/learning specialists, skill tutors, strategy tutors, and trained peer tutors are provided collaboratively through on-campus or off-campus services.
Unique Aids and Services Aids, services, or accommodations include digital textbooks, priority registration, extended time.
Subject-area Tutoring Tutoring is offered one-on-one for some subjects. Tutoring is provided collaboratively through on-campus or off-campus services via professional tutors and trained peer tutors.

Basic Skills Remediation Remediation is offered one-on-one, in small groups, and in class-size groups for computer skills, learning strategies, math, reading, study skills, time management, and written language. Remediation is provided collaboratively through on-campus or off-campus services via professional tutors and trained peer tutors.
Enrichment Programs for career planning, college survival skills, health and nutrition, learning strategies, math, practical computer skills, reading, stress management, study skills, test taking, time management, and written composition skills are provided collaboratively through on-campus or off-campus services.
Application For admittance to the program or unit, students are required to provide a psychoeducational report (3 years old or less). It is recommended that students provide documentation of high school services. Upon application, materials documenting need for services should be sent only to the LD program or unit. Upon acceptance, documentation of need for services should be sent only to the LD program or unit. *Application deadline (institutional):* Continuous. *Application deadline (LD program):* Rolling/continuous for fall and rolling/continuous for spring.
Written Policies Written policies regarding course substitutions, general/basic LD accommodations, and substitutions and waivers of graduation requirements are available on the program Web site. Written policies regarding course substitutions, general/basic LD accommodations, reduced course loads, and substitutions and waivers of graduation requirements are available through the program or unit directly.

Montana Tech of The University of Montana

1300 West Park Street
Butte, MT 59701-8997
http://www.mtech.edu/

Contact: Lee Barnett, Counselor and Career Coordinator. Phone: 406-496-3730. Fax: 406-496-3731. E-mail: lbarnett@mtech.edu. Head of LD Program: Paul Beatty, Dean of Students. Phone: 406-496-4198. Fax: 406-496-4757. E-mail: pbeatty@mtech.edu.

Approximately 10 registered undergraduate students were served during 2002-03. The program or unit includes 1 part-time staff member. Diagnostic specialists, LD specialists, and regular education teachers are provided collaboratively through on-campus or off-campus services.
Summer Program To help prepare for the demands of college, there is an optional 2-week summer program prior to entering the school.
Unique Aids and Services Aids, services, or accommodations include career counseling, weekly meetings with retention specialist, and mentor program.
Subject-area Tutoring Tutoring is offered one-on-one for most subjects. Tutoring is provided collaboratively through on-campus or off-campus services via trained peer tutors.
Basic Skills Remediation Remediation is available for math, study skills, time management, and written language. Remediation is provided collaboratively through on-campus or off-campus services via professional tutors, regular education teachers, and trained peer tutors.

Montana Tech of The University of Montana (continued)

Enrichment Programs for career planning, college survival skills, learning strategies, math, stress management, study skills, and time management are provided collaboratively through on-campus or off-campus services.

Application For admittance to the program or unit, students are required to provide a psychoeducational report and provide documentation from a certified professional specifying the disability and recommended accommodations. *Application deadline (institutional):* Continuous. *Application deadline (LD program):* Rolling/continuous for fall and rolling/continuous for spring.

Written Policies Written policy regarding general/basic LD accommodations is available on the program Web site. Written policy regarding general/basic LD accommodations is outlined in the school's catalog/handbook.

Montserrat College of Art

23 Essex Street, Box 26
Beverly, MA 01915
http://www.montserrat.edu/
Contact: Phone: 978-922-8222. Fax: 978-922-4268.

Strategy tutors are provided through the program or unit. Skill tutors and other are provided collaboratively through on-campus or off-campus services.

Unique Aids and Services Aids, services, or accommodations include weekly meetings with Vice President, Kurzweil software, books on tape.

Subject-area Tutoring Tutoring is offered one-on-one for some subjects. Tutoring is provided through the program or unit via other. Tutoring is also provided collaboratively through on-campus or off-campus services via computer-based instruction, professional tutors, and trained peer tutors.

Basic Skills Remediation Remediation is offered one-on-one for learning strategies, reading, spelling, study skills, time management, and written language. Remediation is provided through the program or unit. Remediation is also provided collaboratively through on-campus or off-campus services via computer-based instruction, professional tutors, and trained peer tutors.

Enrichment Enrichment programs are available through the program or unit for college survival skills, learning strategies, reading, self-advocacy, stress management, study skills, test taking, and time management. Programs for career planning, college survival skills, health and nutrition, stress management, study skills, test taking, time management, and written composition skills are provided collaboratively through on-campus or off-campus services. Credit is offered for college survival skills and written composition skills.

Application For admittance to the program or unit, students are required to provide a psychoeducational report (3 years old or less) and provide IEP, 504 Plan, or letter from psychiatrist/psychologist diagnosing special need. It is recommended that students apply to the program directly. Upon acceptance, documentation of need for services should be sent only to the LD program or unit. *Application deadline (institutional):* 8/1. *Application deadline (LD program):* Rolling/continuous for fall and rolling/continuous for spring.

Written Policies Written policy regarding general/basic LD accommodations is outlined in the school's catalog/handbook.

Moravian College
Office of Learning Services

1200 Main Street
Bethlehem, PA 18018-6650
http://www.moravian.edu/
Contact: Mrs. Laurie Morgan Roth, Director of Learning Services. Phone: 610-861-1510. Fax: 610-625-7935. E-mail: melmr01@moravian.edu.

Office of Learning Services Approximately 14 registered undergraduate students were served during 2002-03. The program or unit includes 1 full-time and 1 part-time staff member. Skill tutors, strategy tutors, and other are provided through the program or unit. Diagnostic specialists and other are provided collaboratively through on-campus or off-campus services.

Subject-area Tutoring Tutoring is offered one-on-one and in small groups for most subjects. Tutoring is provided through the program or unit via trained peer tutors. Tutoring is also provided collaboratively through on-campus or off-campus services via trained peer tutors.

Enrichment Enrichment programs are available through the program or unit for college survival skills, learning strategies, study skills, test taking, time management, and written composition skills. Programs for career planning, health and nutrition, math, medication management, stress management, and written composition skills are provided collaboratively through on-campus or off-campus services. Credit is offered for health and nutrition.

Application For admittance to the program or unit, students are required to provide a psychoeducational report (3 years old or less). It is recommended that students provide documentation of high school services. Upon acceptance, documentation of need for services should be sent only to the LD program or unit. *Application deadline (institutional):* 3/1. *Application deadline (LD program):* Rolling/continuous for fall and rolling/continuous for spring.

Written Policies Written policies regarding course substitutions and general/basic LD accommodations are available through the program or unit directly.

Mount Aloysius College

7373 Admiral Peary Highway
Cresson, PA 16630-1999
http://www.mtaloy.edu/
Contact: Dr. Dane Foust, Dean of Student Affairs. Phone: 814-886-6472. Fax: 814-886-6446. E-mail: dfoust@mtaloy.edu.

Approximately 25 registered undergraduate students were served during 2002-03. The program or unit includes 2 full-time staff members. Academic advisers, counselors, professional tutors, regular education teachers, remediation/learning specialists, and skill tutors are provided collaboratively through on-campus or off-campus services.

Unique Aids and Services Aids, services, or accommodations include advocates.

Subject-area Tutoring Tutoring is offered one-on-one and in small groups for most subjects. Tutoring is provided collaboratively through on-campus or off-campus services via professional tutors and trained peer tutors.

Basic Skills Remediation Remediation is offered one-on-one and in small groups for math, reading, spelling, spoken language, study skills, time management, and written language. Remediation is provided collaboratively through on-campus or off-campus services via professional tutors, regular education teachers, and trained peer tutors.

Enrichment Programs for career planning, college survival skills, health and nutrition, math, reading, stress management, study skills, test taking, and time management are provided collaboratively through on-campus or off-campus services. Credit is offered for career planning.

Application For admittance to the program or unit, students are required to apply to the program directly and provide a psychoeducational report (2 years old or less). It is recommended that students provide documentation of high school services. Upon application, materials documenting need for services should be sent only to the LD program or unit. Upon acceptance, documentation of need for services should be sent only to the LD program or unit. *Application deadline (institutional):* Continuous. *Application deadline (LD program):* Rolling/continuous for fall and rolling/continuous for spring.

Written Policies Written policy regarding general/basic LD accommodations is available through the program or unit directly.

Mount Holyoke College
Office of Learning Skills

50 College Street
South Hadley, MA 01075
http://www.mtholyoke.edu/offices/dcoll/ld

Contact: Dr. John Martin Body III, Associate Dean for Learning Skills. Phone: 413-538-2504. E-mail: jbody@mtholyoke.edu.

Office of Learning Skills Approximately 80 registered undergraduate students were served during 2002-03. The program or unit includes 1 full-time and 1 part-time staff member. Academic advisers, coaches, diagnostic specialists, graduate assistants/students, LD specialists, and strategy tutors are provided through the program or unit.

Unique Aids and Services Aids, services, or accommodations include assistive technology lab.

Subject-area Tutoring Tutoring is offered one-on-one, in small groups, and in class-size groups for most subjects. Tutoring is provided collaboratively through on-campus or off-campus services via graduate assistants/students and trained peer tutors.

Diagnostic Testing Testing is provided through the program or unit for intelligence, learning strategies, learning styles, math, reading, spelling, spoken language, study skills, visual processing, and written language.

Enrichment Enrichment programs are available through the program or unit for college survival skills, learning strategies, medication management, practical computer skills, self-advocacy, stress management, study skills, test taking, time management, written composition skills, and other.

Fees *Diagnostic Testing* fee is $25 to $650.

Application For admittance to the program or unit, students are required to provide a psychoeducational report (3 years old or less). It is recommended that students provide documentation of high school services. Upon acceptance, documentation of need for services should be sent only to the LD program or unit. *Application deadline (institutional):* 1/15. *Application deadline (LD program):* Rolling/continuous for fall and rolling/continuous for spring.

Written Policies Written policies regarding course substitutions, general/basic LD accommodations, reduced course loads, and substitutions and waivers of graduation requirements are available on the program Web site. Written policies regarding course substitutions, general/basic LD accommodations, reduced course loads, and substitutions and waivers of graduation requirements are outlined in the school's catalog/handbook.

Mount Mercy College
Academic Achievement Center

1330 Elmhurst Drive, NE
Cedar Rapids, IA 52402-4797
http://www.mtmercy.edu/

Contact: Mary Jean Stanton, Director Academic Achievement. Phone: 319-363-8213. Fax: 319-365-7977. E-mail: mstanton@mmc.mtmercy.edu.

Academic Achievement Center Approximately 25 registered undergraduate students were served during 2002-03. The program or unit includes 2 full-time staff members. Academic advisers, coaches, counselors, professional tutors, regular education teachers, and trained peer tutors are provided collaboratively through on-campus or off-campus services.

Orientation The program or unit offers a mandatory orientation for new students individually by special arrangement.

Subject-area Tutoring Tutoring is offered one-on-one and in small groups for some subjects. Tutoring is provided through the program or unit via professional tutors and trained peer tutors. Tutoring is also provided collaboratively through on-campus or off-campus services via trained peer tutors.

Diagnostic Testing Testing is provided through the program or unit for learning strategies, learning styles, math, reading, written language, and other services.

Basic Skills Remediation Remediation is offered in small groups and in class-size groups for learning strategies, math, reading, spoken language, study skills, time management, and written language. Remediation is provided through the program or unit via professional tutors, regular education teachers, and trained peer tutors. Remediation is also provided collaboratively through on-campus or off-campus services via trained peer tutors.

Enrichment Enrichment programs are available through the program or unit for learning strategies, math, oral communication skills, test taking, and written composition skills. Programs for career planning, college survival skills, practical computer skills, stress management, study skills, and time management are provided collaboratively through on-campus or off-campus services.

Student Organization Disability Awareness Group consists of 12 members.

Mount Mercy College (continued)

Application For admittance to the program or unit, students are required to provide a psychoeducational report (3 years old or less). It is recommended that students provide documentation of high school services. Upon application, materials documenting need for services should be sent only to the LD program or unit. Upon acceptance, documentation of need for services should be sent only to the LD program or unit. *Application deadline (institutional):* 8/30. *Application deadline (LD program):* Rolling/continuous for fall and rolling/continuous for spring.

Written Policies Written policy regarding general/basic LD accommodations is available on the program Web site. Written policy regarding general/basic LD accommodations is outlined in the school's catalog/handbook. Written policy regarding general/basic LD accommodations is available through the program or unit directly.

Mount Olive College

634 Henderson Street

Mount Olive, NC 28365

http://www.mountolivecollege.edu/

Contact: Phone: 919-658-2502. Fax: 919-658-8934.

Approximately 20 registered undergraduate students were served during 2002-03. The program or unit includes 1 full-time staff member.

Unique Aids and Services Aids, services, or accommodations include career counseling and faculty training.

Subject-area Tutoring Tutoring is offered one-on-one, in small groups, and in class-size groups for some subjects. Tutoring is provided through the program or unit via computer-based instruction, professional tutors, and trained peer tutors. Tutoring is also provided collaboratively through on-campus or off-campus services via computer-based instruction, professional tutors, and trained peer tutors.

Basic Skills Remediation Remediation is offered one-on-one, in small groups, and in class-size groups for computer skills, learning strategies, math, study skills, time management, and written language. Remediation is provided through the program or unit via trained peer tutors and other. Remediation is also provided collaboratively through on-campus or off-campus services via trained peer tutors.

Enrichment Enrichment programs are available through the program or unit for college survival skills, learning strategies, math, study skills, test taking, time management, and written composition skills. Programs for career planning, college survival skills, learning strategies, math, study skills, test taking, time management, and written composition skills are provided collaboratively through on-campus or off-campus services.

Application For admittance to the program or unit, students are required to provide a psychoeducational report. It is recommended that students provide documentation of high school services. Upon application, materials documenting need for services should be sent only to the LD program or unit. Upon acceptance, documentation of need for services should be sent only to the LD program or unit. *Application deadline (institutional):* Continuous. *Application deadline (LD program):* Rolling/continuous for fall and rolling/continuous for spring.

Written Policies Written policy regarding general/basic LD accommodations is outlined in the school's catalog/handbook. Written policy regarding general/basic LD accommodations is available through the program or unit directly.

Mount Saint Mary's College and Seminary
Learning Services

16300 Old Emmitsburg Road

Emmitsburg, MD 21727-7799

http://www.msmary.edu/

Contact: Mrs. Denise L. Marjarum, Director of Learning Services. Phone: 301-447-5006. Fax: 301-447-5918. E-mail: marjarum@msmary.edu.

Learning Services Approximately 75 registered undergraduate students were served during 2002-03. The program or unit includes 2 full-time and 3 part-time staff members. Academic advisers, graduate assistants/students, and LD specialists are provided through the program or unit. Academic advisers, regular education teachers, and trained peer tutors are provided collaboratively through on-campus or off-campus services.

Unique Aids and Services Aids, services, or accommodations include note-takers, scribes, interpreters, faculty interaction.

Subject-area Tutoring Tutoring is offered one-on-one for all subjects. Tutoring is provided through the program or unit via graduate assistants/students. Tutoring is also provided collaboratively through on-campus or off-campus services via trained peer tutors.

Diagnostic Testing Testing is provided through the program or unit for learning strategies, learning styles, and study skills.

Basic Skills Remediation Remediation is offered one-on-one for learning strategies, study skills, time management, and written language. Remediation is provided through the program or unit via graduate assistants/students, LD specialists, and trained peer tutors.

Enrichment Enrichment programs are available through the program or unit for college survival skills, learning strategies, self-advocacy, study skills, test taking, and time management. Programs for career planning, college survival skills, health and nutrition, medication management, practical computer skills, stress management, and written composition skills are provided collaboratively through on-campus or off-campus services.

Application For admittance to the program or unit, students are required to provide a psychoeducational report (3 years old or less). It is recommended that students provide documentation of high school services. Upon application, materials documenting need for services should be sent only to the LD program or unit. Upon acceptance, documentation of need for services should be sent only to the LD program or unit. *Application deadline (institutional):* Continuous. *Application deadline (LD program):* Rolling/continuous for fall and rolling/continuous for spring.

Written Policies Written policy regarding general/basic LD accommodations is outlined in the school's catalog/handbook. Written policy regarding general/basic LD accommodations is available through the program or unit directly.

Colleges for Students with Learning Disabilities or ADD

Mount Saint Vincent University

166 Bedford Highway
Halifax, NS B3M 2J6
Canada
http://www.msvu.ca/
Contact: Kim Beaton, Special Needs Coordinator. Phone: 902-457-6323. Fax: 902-445-2201. E-mail: kim.beaton@msvu.ca.

Approximately 70 registered undergraduate students were served during 2002-03. The program or unit includes 1 full-time and 2 part-time staff members. Counselors and graduate assistants/students are provided through the program or unit. Academic advisers, counselors, diagnostic specialists, and graduate assistants/students are provided collaboratively through on-campus or off-campus services.
Unique Aids and Services Aids, services, or accommodations include advocates, career counseling, digital textbooks, and support groups.
Subject-area Tutoring Tutoring is offered one-on-one and in small groups for some subjects. Tutoring is provided through the program or unit via graduate assistants/students. Tutoring is also provided collaboratively through on-campus or off-campus services via graduate assistants/students.
Basic Skills Remediation Remediation is offered one-on-one for learning strategies, social skills, study skills, time management, and written language. Remediation is provided through the program or unit via graduate assistants/students. Remediation is also provided collaboratively through on-campus or off-campus services via graduate assistants/students and other.
Enrichment Enrichment programs are available through the program or unit for career planning, college survival skills, learning strategies, oral communication skills, reading, self-advocacy, stress management, study skills, test taking, and time management. Programs for career planning, college survival skills, health and nutrition, learning strategies, math, reading, stress management, study skills, test taking, time management, and written composition skills are provided collaboratively through on-campus or off-campus services.
Application For admittance to the program or unit, students are required to provide a psychoeducational report (3 years old or less). Upon application, materials documenting need for services should be sent only to admissions with institutional application materials. Upon acceptance, documentation of need for services should be sent only to the LD program or unit. *Application deadline (institutional):* 3/14. *Application deadline (LD program):* Rolling/continuous for fall and rolling/continuous for spring.
Written Policies Written policy regarding general/basic LD accommodations is available on the program Web site. Written policy regarding general/basic LD accommodations is outlined in the school's catalog/handbook. Written policy regarding general/basic LD accommodations is available through the program or unit directly.

Mount Union College

1972 Clark Avenue

Alliance, OH 44601-3993
http://www.muc.edu/
Contact: Phone: 330-821-5320. Fax: 330-821-0425.

The program or unit includes 1 full-time staff member. Academic advisers are provided collaboratively through on-campus or off-campus services.
Orientation The program or unit offers an optional 1-hour orientation for new students during new student orientation.
Subject-area Tutoring Tutoring is offered in small groups for all subjects. Tutoring is provided through the program or unit via trained peer tutors. Tutoring is also provided collaboratively through on-campus or off-campus services via trained peer tutors.
Application For admittance to the program or unit, students are required to provide a psychoeducational report and provide documentation of high school services. Upon application, materials documenting need for services should be sent only to the LD program or unit. Upon acceptance, documentation of need for services should be sent only to the LD program or unit. *Application deadline (institutional):* Continuous. *Application deadline (LD program):* Rolling/continuous for fall and rolling/continuous for spring.
Written Policies Written policy regarding general/basic LD accommodations is available on the program Web site. Written policies regarding course substitutions and substitutions and waivers of graduation requirements are outlined in the school's catalog/handbook. Written policies regarding course substitutions, general/basic LD accommodations, and substitutions and waivers of graduation requirements are available through the program or unit directly.

Murray State University
Services for Students with Learning Disabilities

PO Box 9
Murray, KY 42071-0009
http://www.murraystate.edu/secsv/SSLD
Contact: Mrs. Cindy Clemson, Coordinator of Services for Students with Learning Disabilities. Phone: 270-762-2018. Fax: 270-762-4339. E-mail: cindy.clemson@murraystate.edu. Head of LD Program: Annazette Fields, Director of Equal Opportunity. Phone: 270-762-3155. Fax: 270-762-6887. E-mail: annazette.fields@murraystate.edu.

Services for Students with Learning Disabilities Approximately 300 registered undergraduate students were served during 2002-03. The program or unit includes 3 full-time and 45 part-time staff members. Academic advisers, coaches, graduate assistants/students, LD specialists, skill tutors, strategy tutors, and trained peer tutors are provided through the program or unit. Academic advisers, counselors, diagnostic specialists, and remediation/learning specialists are provided collaboratively through on-campus or off-campus services.
Orientation The program or unit offers a mandatory 1-semester orientation for new students twice a week during the first semester.
Unique Aids and Services Aids, services, or accommodations include advocates, career counseling, digital textbooks, faculty training, and priority registration.

Four-Year Colleges with Self-Directed/Decentralized Programs

Murray State University (continued)

Subject-area Tutoring Tutoring is offered one-on-one for most subjects. Tutoring is provided through the program or unit via graduate assistants/students and trained peer tutors.

Diagnostic Testing Testing is provided through the program or unit for learning strategies, learning styles, and study skills. Testing for auditory processing, handwriting, intelligence, math, neuropsychological, personality, reading, social skills, spelling, spoken language, and written language is provided collaboratively through on-campus or off-campus services.

Basic Skills Remediation Remediation is offered in class-size groups for learning strategies and study skills. Remediation is provided through the program or unit via LD specialists. Remediation is also provided collaboratively through on-campus or off-campus services via graduate assistants/students and regular education teachers.

Enrichment Enrichment programs are available through the program or unit for college survival skills, learning strategies, reading, self-advocacy, study skills, test taking, time management, and vocabulary development. Programs for practical computer skills and written composition skills are provided collaboratively through on-campus or off-campus services. Credit is offered for college survival skills, learning strategies, practical computer skills, reading, self-advocacy, study skills, test taking, time management, vocabulary development, and written composition skills.

Fees *LD Program or Service* fee is $300 to $750. *Diagnostic Testing* fee is $25 to $350.

Application For admittance to the program or unit, students are required to apply to the program directly, provide a psychoeducational report (3 years old or less), and provide documentation of high school services. Upon acceptance, documentation of need for services should be sent only to the LD program or unit. *Application deadline (institutional):* Continuous. *Application deadline (LD program):* 4/15 for fall. Rolling/continuous for spring.

Written Policies Written policies regarding course substitutions, general/basic LD accommodations, grade forgiveness, reduced course loads, substitutions and waivers of admissions requirements, and substitutions and waivers of graduation requirements are available through the program or unit directly.

Naropa University

2130 Arapahoe Avenue
Boulder, CO 80302-6697
http://www.naropa.edu/

Contact: Robert D. Cillo, Dean of Students. Phone: 303-546-3506. Fax: 303-245-4795. E-mail: bcillo@naropa.edu.

Approximately 5 registered undergraduate students were served during 2002-03. The program or unit includes 1 part-time staff member. LD specialists and other are provided through the program or unit.

Unique Aids and Services Aids, services, or accommodations include advocates.

Application For admittance to the program or unit, students are required to provide assessments from professionals in field. It is recommended that students apply to the program directly, provide a psychoeducational report (2 years old or less), and provide docu-

mentation of high school services. Upon application, materials documenting need for services should be sent only to the LD program or unit. Upon acceptance, documentation of need for services should be sent only to the LD program or unit. *Application deadline (institutional):* 1/15. *Application deadline (LD program):* Rolling/continuous for fall and rolling/continuous for spring.

Written Policies Written policy regarding general/basic LD accommodations is available on the program Web site. Written policy regarding general/basic LD accommodations is outlined in the school's catalog/handbook.

Neumann College

One Neumann Drive
Aston, PA 19014-1298
http://www.neumann.edu/

Contact: Mr. James P. Kain, Disabilities Services Coordinator. Phone: 610-361-5349. E-mail: jkain@neumann.edu.

The program or unit includes 1 part-time staff member. LD specialists are provided through the program or unit. Academic advisers, counselors, professional tutors, remediation/learning specialists, and skill tutors are provided collaboratively through on-campus or off-campus services.

Subject-area Tutoring Tutoring is offered one-on-one and in small groups for most subjects. Tutoring is provided collaboratively through on-campus or off-campus services via graduate assistants/students, LD specialists, professional tutors, and trained peer tutors.

Basic Skills Remediation Remediation is offered in class-size groups for math, reading, and written language. Remediation is provided through the program or unit via regular education teachers.

Enrichment Programs for career planning, college survival skills, learning strategies, math, stress management, study skills, test taking, time management, and written composition skills are provided collaboratively through on-campus or off-campus services.

Application For admittance to the program or unit, students are required to apply to the program directly and provide a psychoeducational report (5 years old or less). It is recommended that students provide documentation of high school services. Upon application, materials documenting need for services should be sent only to the LD program or unit. Upon acceptance, documentation of need for services should be sent only to the LD program or unit. *Application deadline (institutional):* 4/1. *Application deadline (LD program):* Rolling/continuous for fall and rolling/continuous for spring.

Written Policies Written policies regarding course substitutions, general/basic LD accommodations, reduced course loads, and substitutions and waivers of admissions requirements are available on the program Web site. Written policies regarding course substitutions, general/basic LD accommodations, reduced course loads, and substitutions and waivers of admissions requirements are outlined in the school's catalog/handbook. Written policies regarding course substitutions, general/basic LD accommodations, reduced course loads, and substitutions and waivers of admissions requirements are available through the program or unit directly.

184   *www.petersons.com*   *Colleges for Students with Learning Disabilities or ADD*

Newberry College
Disability Services

2100 College Street
Newberry, SC 29108-2197
http://www.newberry.edu/

Contact: Donna Taylor, Director of Disability Services.
Phone: 803-321-5187. E-mail: dtaylor@newberry.edu.

Disability Services Approximately 20 registered undergraduate students were served during 2002-03. The program or unit includes 1 part-time staff member. Academic advisers, coaches, counselors, regular education teachers, remediation/learning specialists, and trained peer tutors are provided collaboratively through on-campus or off-campus services.

Subject-area Tutoring Tutoring is offered one-on-one and in small groups. Tutoring is provided collaboratively through on-campus or off-campus services via trained peer tutors.

Basic Skills Remediation Remediation is offered one-on-one and in class-size groups for learning strategies, math, study skills, time management, and written language. Remediation is provided collaboratively through on-campus or off-campus services via regular education teachers and trained peer tutors.

Enrichment Programs for career planning, college survival skills, study skills, test taking, time management, and written composition skills are provided collaboratively through on-campus or off-campus services.

Application For admittance to the program or unit, students are required to provide a psychoeducational report (3 years old or less). It is recommended that students provide documentation of high school services. *Application deadline (institutional):* Continuous.

Written Policies Written policy regarding general/basic LD accommodations is outlined in the school's catalog/handbook. Written policies regarding course substitutions, general/basic LD accommodations, grade forgiveness, and reduced course loads are available through the program or unit directly.

New Mexico Highlands University

PO Box 9000
Las Vegas, NM 87701
http://www.nmhu.edu/
Contact: Phone: 505-454-3000. Fax: 505-454-3311.

The program or unit includes 1 full-time and 1 part-time staff member. Academic advisers and graduate assistants/students are provided through the program or unit. Professional tutors, skill tutors, and other are provided collaboratively through on-campus or off-campus services.

Unique Aids and Services Aids, services, or accommodations include digital textbooks and faculty training.

Subject-area Tutoring Tutoring is offered one-on-one and in small groups for some subjects. Tutoring is provided collaboratively through on-campus or off-campus services via computer-based instruction, graduate assistants/students, and trained peer tutors.

Diagnostic Testing Testing is provided through the program or unit for math, reading, and written language.

Basic Skills Remediation Remediation is offered in small groups and in class-size groups for reading. Remediation is provided collaboratively through on-campus or off-campus services via computer-based instruction and regular education teachers.

Enrichment Programs for career planning, reading, and written composition skills are provided collaboratively through on-campus or off-campus services.

Application For admittance to the program or unit, students are required to provide a psychoeducational report (5 years old or less) and provide documentation of disability form. It is recommended that students apply to the program directly. Upon application, materials documenting need for services should be sent only to the LD program or unit. Upon acceptance, documentation of need for services should be sent only to the LD program or unit. *Application deadline (institutional):* Continuous. *Application deadline (LD program):* Rolling/continuous for fall and rolling/continuous for spring.

Written Policies Written policy regarding general/basic LD accommodations is available on the program Web site. Written policy regarding general/basic LD accommodations is outlined in the school's catalog/handbook. Written policy regarding general/basic LD accommodations is available through the program or unit directly.

New Orleans Baptist Theological Seminary
Testing and Counseling Office

3939 Gentilly Boulevard
New Orleans, LA 70126-4858
http://www.nobts.edu/

Contact: Dr. Jeff Nave, Director of Testing and Counseling.
Phone: 504-816-8004. Fax: 504-816-8453. E-mail: jnave@nobts.edu.

Testing and Counseling Office Approximately 5 registered undergraduate students were served during 2002-03. The program or unit includes 1 full-time staff member. Counselors are provided through the program or unit. Academic advisers and regular education teachers are provided collaboratively through on-campus or off-campus services.

Enrichment Programs for career planning, health and nutrition, learning strategies, medication management, self-advocacy, stress management, study skills, test taking, and time management are provided collaboratively through on-campus or off-campus services.

Application It is recommended that students provide a psychoeducational report (5 years old or less) and provide documentation of high school services. Upon acceptance, documentation of need for services should be sent only to the LD program or unit. *Application deadline (institutional):* 8/9. *Application deadline (LD program):* Rolling/continuous for fall and rolling/continuous for spring.

New York School of Interior Design
Academic Advising Office

170 East 70th Street
New York, NY 10021-5110
http://www.nysid.edu
Contact: Mrs. Linda Sclafani, Academic Adviser. Phone: 212-472-1500 Ext. 303. Fax: 212-472-6577. E-mail: lindas@nysid.edu.

Academic Advising Office Approximately 3 registered undergraduate students were served during 2002-03. Academic advisers are provided through the program or unit.
Unique Aids and Services Aids, services, or accommodations include career counseling.
Subject-area Tutoring Tutoring is offered one-on-one for all subjects. Tutoring is provided through the program or unit via other.
Application For admittance to the program or unit, students are required to provide a psychoeducational report (1 year old or less). Upon application, materials documenting need for services should be sent only to admissions with institutional application materials. Upon acceptance, documentation of need for services should be sent only to admissions. *Application deadline (institutional):* Continuous. *Application deadline (LD program):* Rolling/continuous for fall and rolling/continuous for spring.

New York University
Henry and Lucy Moses Center for Students with Disabilities

70 Washington Square South
New York, NY 10012-1019
http://www.nyu.edu/osl/csd
Contact: Ms. Lakshmi Clark, Coordinator of Services for Students with Learning Disabilities and AD/HD. Phone: 212-998-4980. Fax: 212-995-4114. E-mail: lc83@nyu.edu.

Henry and Lucy Moses Center for Students with Disabilities Approximately 211 registered undergraduate students were served during 2002-03. The program or unit includes 1 full-time and 6 part-time staff members. LD specialists, remediation/learning specialists, and skill tutors are provided through the program or unit. Academic advisers, counselors, diagnostic specialists, graduate assistants/students, professional tutors, and trained peer tutors are provided collaboratively through on-campus or off-campus services.
Orientation The program or unit offers an optional 2 to 3-hour orientation for new students before classes begin and after classes begin.
Unique Aids and Services Aids, services, or accommodations include priority registration, workshops, assistive technology, accommodations based on documentation, referrals to NYU services.
Subject-area Tutoring Tutoring is offered one-on-one and in small groups for all subjects. Tutoring is provided collaboratively through on-campus or off-campus services via graduate assistants/students, professional tutors, and trained peer tutors.

Basic Skills Remediation Remediation is offered one-on-one for auditory processing, learning strategies, reading, study skills, time management, visual processing, and written language. Remediation is provided through the program or unit via graduate assistants/students and LD specialists. Remediation is also provided collaboratively through on-campus or off-campus services.
Enrichment Enrichment programs are available through the program or unit for learning strategies, reading, self-advocacy, study skills, test taking, time management, and written composition skills. Programs for career planning, college survival skills, health and nutrition, learning strategies, math, medication management, oral communication skills, practical computer skills, stress management, study skills, test taking, time management, and written composition skills are provided collaboratively through on-campus or off-campus services.
Application For admittance to the program or unit, students are required to apply to the program directly and provide a psychoeducational report (3 years old or less). It is recommended that students provide documentation of high school services. Upon application, materials documenting need for services should be sent only to admissions with institutional application materials. Upon acceptance, documentation of need for services should be sent only to the LD program or unit. *Application deadline (institutional):* 1/15. *Application deadline (LD program):* Rolling/continuous for fall and rolling/continuous for spring.
Written Policies Written policies regarding course substitutions, general/basic LD accommodations, and reduced course loads are available on the program Web site. Written policies regarding course substitutions, general/basic LD accommodations, and reduced course loads are available through the program or unit directly.

Niagara University
Office of Academic Support

Niagara Falls, NY 14109
http://www.niagara.edu/
Contact: Ms. Diane E. Stoelting, Coordinator of Specialized Support Services. Phone: 716-286-8076. Fax: 716-286-8063. E-mail: ds@niagara.edu.

Office of Academic Support Approximately 90 registered undergraduate students were served during 2002-03. The program or unit includes 1 full-time and 1 part-time staff member. Academic advisers, counselors, regular education teachers, remediation/learning specialists, skill tutors, trained peer tutors, and other are provided collaboratively through on-campus or off-campus services.
Unique Aids and Services Aids, services, or accommodations include digital textbooks, weekly meetings with the Coordinator of Specialized Support Services.
Subject-area Tutoring Tutoring is offered in small groups for some subjects. Tutoring is provided collaboratively through on-campus or off-campus services via trained peer tutors.
Basic Skills Remediation Remediation is offered in class-size groups for math, reading, study skills, and written language. Remediation is provided collaboratively through on-campus or off-campus services via regular education teachers.

Enrichment Programs for career planning, college survival skills, health and nutrition, learning strategies, math, reading, stress management, study skills, test taking, time management, vocabulary development, and written composition skills are provided collaboratively through on-campus or off-campus services.

Application For admittance to the program or unit, students are required to provide a psychoeducational report (3 years old or less). It is recommended that students provide documentation of high school services. Upon application, materials documenting need for services should be sent only to the LD program or unit. Upon acceptance, documentation of need for services should be sent only to the LD program or unit. *Application deadline (institutional):* 8/1. *Application deadline (LD program):* Rolling/continuous for fall and rolling/continuous for spring.

Written Policies Written policies regarding course substitutions, general/basic LD accommodations, and reduced course loads are available on the program Web site. Written policies regarding course substitutions, general/basic LD accommodations, and reduced course loads are available through the program or unit directly.

Nipissing University
Disability Services, Enhanced Services Program

100 College Drive, Box 5002
North Bay, ON P1B 8L7
Canada
http://www.nipissingu.ca/documents.cfm?smocid=1352

Contact: Mr. Mike Walker, Learning Strategist. Phone: 705-474-3450 Ext. 4333. Fax: 705-495-2850. E-mail: mikew@nipissingu.ca. Head of LD Program: Mr. Daniel Pletzer, Manager of Counseling and Disability Services. Phone: 705-474-3450 Ext. 4493. Fax: 705-495-2850. E-mail: danp@nipissingu.ca.

Disability Services, Enhanced Services Program Approximately 50 registered undergraduate students were served during 2002-03. The program or unit includes 2 full-time staff members. LD specialists, remediation/learning specialists, skill tutors, strategy tutors, and other are provided through the program or unit. Academic advisers, counselors, diagnostic specialists, professional tutors, skill tutors, and trained peer tutors are provided collaboratively through on-campus or off-campus services.

Orientation The program or unit offers an optional 3-day orientation for new students before classes begin and individually by special arrangement.

Unique Aids and Services Aids, services, or accommodations include career counseling, digital textbooks, support groups, test/examination and learning environment accommodations.

Subject-area Tutoring Tutoring is offered one-on-one for most subjects. Tutoring is provided collaboratively through on-campus or off-campus services via professional tutors and trained peer tutors.

Diagnostic Testing Testing is provided through the program or unit for learning strategies, learning styles, and study skills. Testing for auditory processing, intelligence, math, motor skills, neuropsychological, personality, reading, social skills, spelling, spoken language, visual processing, and written language is provided collaboratively through on-campus or off-campus services.

Basic Skills Remediation Remediation is offered one-on-one and in small groups for computer skills, learning strategies, social skills, study skills, time management, and written language. Remediation is provided through the program or unit via LD specialists. Remediation is also provided collaboratively through on-campus or off-campus services.

Enrichment Enrichment programs are available through the program or unit for college survival skills, learning strategies, oral communication skills, reading, self-advocacy, stress management, study skills, test taking, time management, and written composition skills. Programs for career planning, college survival skills, health and nutrition, learning strategies, math, oral communication skills, reading, self-advocacy, stress management, study skills, test taking, and written composition skills are provided collaboratively through on-campus or off-campus services. Credit is offered for career planning, college survival skills, health and nutrition, learning strategies, oral communication skills, reading, self-advocacy, stress management, study skills, test taking, time management, and written composition skills.

Fees *Diagnostic Testing* fee is $0 to $1500.

Application For admittance to the program or unit, students are required to provide a psychoeducational report (3 years old or less). It is recommended that students provide documentation of high school services and provide transition plan. Upon application, materials documenting need for services should be sent only to admissions with institutional application materials. Upon acceptance, documentation of need for services should be sent only to the LD program or unit. *Application deadline (institutional):* 6/1. *Application deadline (LD program):* Rolling/continuous for fall and rolling/continuous for spring.

Written Policies Written policies regarding general/basic LD accommodations and substitutions and waivers of admissions requirements are available on the program Web site. Written policy regarding substitutions and waivers of admissions requirements is outlined in the school's catalog/handbook. Written policies regarding general/basic LD accommodations and reduced course loads are available through the program or unit directly.

North Carolina Agricultural and Technical State University

1601 East Market Street
Greensboro, NC 27411
http://www.ncat.edu/

Contact: Ms. Peggy Oliphant, Director of Disability Support Services. Phone: 336-334-7765 Ext. 2901. Fax: 336-334-7333. E-mail: oliphant@ncat.edu.

Approximately 51 registered undergraduate students were served during 2002-03. The program or unit includes 1 full-time staff member. Academic advisers, counselors, diagnostic specialists, professional tutors, regular education teachers, special education teachers, trained peer tutors, and other are provided collaboratively through on-campus or off-campus services.

Unique Aids and Services Aids, services, or accommodations include advocates, faculty training, and support groups.

North Carolina Agricultural and Technical State University (continued)

Subject-area Tutoring Tutoring is offered one-on-one, in small groups, and in class-size groups for some subjects. Tutoring is provided collaboratively through on-campus or off-campus services via computer-based instruction, graduate assistants/students, and trained peer tutors.

Diagnostic Testing Testing for math, reading, and written language is provided collaboratively through on-campus or off-campus services.

Enrichment Enrichment programs are available through the program or unit for self-advocacy. Programs for career planning, college survival skills, health and nutrition, learning strategies, oral communication skills, practical computer skills, reading, stress management, study skills, test taking, time management, vocabulary development, written composition skills, and other are provided collaboratively through on-campus or off-campus services.

Application For admittance to the program or unit, students are required to provide a psychoeducational report (3 years old or less). It is recommended that students provide documentation of high school services. Upon application, materials documenting need for services should be sent only to the LD program or unit. Upon acceptance, documentation of need for services should be sent only to the LD program or unit. *Application deadline (institutional): 6/1. Application deadline (LD program):* Rolling/continuous for fall and rolling/continuous for spring.

Written Policies Written policy regarding general/basic LD accommodations is available on the program Web site. Written policy regarding general/basic LD accommodations is available through the program or unit directly.

North Carolina School of the Arts
Disabled Student Services

1533 South Main Street

PO Box 12189

Winston-Salem, NC 27127-2188

http://www.ncarts.edu/

Contact: Phone: 336-770-3399. Fax: 336-770-3370.

Disabled Student Services Approximately 40 registered undergraduate students were served during 2002-03. The program or unit includes 2 full-time staff members. LD specialists, remediation/ learning specialists, skill tutors, special education teachers, and strategy tutors are provided through the program or unit. Academic advisers, coaches, counselors, diagnostic specialists, professional tutors, regular education teachers, and teacher trainees are provided collaboratively through on-campus or off-campus services.

Subject-area Tutoring Tutoring is offered one-on-one for most subjects. Tutoring is provided through the program or unit via LD specialists.

Basic Skills Remediation Remediation is offered one-on-one for auditory processing, computer skills, learning strategies, reading, social skills, spelling, study skills, time management, visual processing, and written language. Remediation is provided through the program or unit via LD specialists.

Application For admittance to the program or unit, students are required to apply to the program directly, provide a psychoeducational report, and provide results of psychological conducted within the past 3 years. It is recommended that students provide documentation of high school services. Upon application, materials documenting need for services should be sent only to admissions with institutional application materials. Upon acceptance, documentation of need for services should be sent only to admissions. *Application deadline (institutional):* Continuous. *Application deadline (LD program):* Rolling/continuous for fall and rolling/continuous for spring.

Written Policies Written policies regarding general/basic LD accommodations and substitutions and waivers of admissions requirements are outlined in the school's catalog/handbook.

North Carolina Wesleyan College
Disability Support Services (DSS)

3400 North Wesleyan Boulevard

Rocky Mount, NC 27804-8677

http://www.ncwc.edu/

Contact: Wendy S. McFarland, Disabilities Coordinator and Pre-major Adviser. Phone: 252-985-5269. Fax: 252-985-5399. E-mail: wsmcfarland@ncwc.edu.

Disability Support Services (DSS) Approximately 35 registered undergraduate students were served during 2002-03. The program or unit includes 1 full-time staff member. Academic advisers are provided through the program or unit. Academic advisers, professional tutors, and trained peer tutors are provided collaboratively through on-campus or off-campus services.

Subject-area Tutoring Tutoring is offered one-on-one and in small groups for most subjects. Tutoring is provided collaboratively through on-campus or off-campus services via professional tutors and trained peer tutors.

Enrichment Programs for learning strategies, study skills, test taking, and time management are provided collaboratively through on-campus or off-campus services.

Application For admittance to the program or unit, students are required to apply to the program directly and provide a psychoeducational report (3 years old or less). It is recommended that students provide documentation of high school services. Upon application, materials documenting need for services should be sent to both admissions and the LD program or unit. Upon acceptance, documentation of need for services should be sent only to the LD program or unit. *Application deadline (institutional): 7/30. Application deadline (LD program):* Rolling/continuous for fall and rolling/continuous for spring.

Written Policies Written policies regarding course substitutions, general/basic LD accommodations, and substitutions and waivers of graduation requirements are available through the program or unit directly.

North Central College
Academic Support Services

30 North Brainard St, PO Box 3063
Naperville, IL 60566-7063
http://www.noctrl.edu/
Contact: Deanne M. Wiedeman, Director of LD Services.
Phone: 630-637-5264. E-mail: dmwiedem@noctrl.edu.

Academic Support Services Approximately 55 registered undergraduate students were served during 2002-03. The program or unit includes 2 full-time staff members. Academic advisers, counselors, LD specialists, skill tutors, and trained peer tutors are provided through the program or unit.
Orientation The program or unit offers an optional orientation for new students after classes begin.
Subject-area Tutoring Tutoring is offered for some subjects. Tutoring is provided through the program or unit via LD specialists and trained peer tutors.
Basic Skills Remediation Remediation is offered in small groups and in class-size groups for math, study skills, time management, and written language. Remediation is provided through the program or unit via LD specialists, regular education teachers, and other.
Enrichment Programs for career planning, college survival skills, learning strategies, math, study skills, time management, and written composition skills are provided collaboratively through on-campus or off-campus services.
Application It is recommended that students provide documentation of high school services. *Application deadline (institutional):* Continuous. *Application deadline (LD program):* Rolling/continuous for fall and rolling/continuous for spring.
Written Policies Written policies regarding general/basic LD accommodations, reduced course loads, and substitutions and waivers of admissions requirements are available through the program or unit directly.

North Dakota State University
Counseling and Disability Services

1301 North University Avenue
Fargo, ND 58105
http://www.ndsu.edu/counseling
Contact: Phone: 701-231-8011. Fax: 701-231-8802.

Counseling and Disability Services Approximately 50 registered undergraduate students were served during 2002-03. The program or unit includes 1 full-time and 1 part-time staff member. LD specialists are provided through the program or unit. Counselors are provided collaboratively through on-campus or off-campus services.
Unique Aids and Services Aids, services, or accommodations include priority registration, individual work with learning disability specialist.
Subject-area Tutoring Tutoring is offered one-on-one and in small groups for most subjects. Tutoring is provided through the program or unit via graduate assistants/students and trained peer tutors.

Basic Skills Remediation Remediation is offered in class-size groups for math and English. Remediation is provided through the program or unit via regular education teachers.
Application It is recommended that students provide a psychoeducational report (3 years old or less) and provide documentation of high school services. Upon application, materials documenting need for services should be sent only to the LD program or unit. Upon acceptance, documentation of need for services should be sent only to the LD program or unit. *Application deadline (institutional):* 8/15. *Application deadline (LD program):* Rolling/continuous for fall and rolling/continuous for spring.
Written Policies Written policies regarding course substitutions, general/basic LD accommodations, grade forgiveness, reduced course loads, substitutions and waivers of admissions requirements, and substitutions and waivers of graduation requirements are available on the program Web site.

Northeastern Illinois University
Accessibility Center: HELP Program

5500 North St Louis Avenue
Chicago, IL 60625-4699
http://www.neiu.edu/
Contact: Dr. Victoria Amey-Flippin, Director. Phone: 773-442-5495 Ext. 5496. Fax: 773-442-5499. E-mail: v-amey-flippin@neiu.edu.

Accessibility Center: HELP Program Approximately 156 registered undergraduate students were served during 2002-03. The program or unit includes 2 full-time staff members and 1 part-time staff member. Academic advisers, counselors, graduate assistants/students, and regular education teachers are provided collaboratively through on-campus or off-campus services.
Unique Aids and Services Aids, services, or accommodations include priority registration.
Subject-area Tutoring Tutoring is offered one-on-one and in small groups for most subjects. Tutoring is provided through the program or unit via graduate assistants/students, trained peer tutors, and other.
Basic Skills Remediation Remediation is offered in class-size groups for computer skills, math, reading, spelling, study skills, time management, and written language. Remediation is provided collaboratively through on-campus or off-campus services via regular education teachers.
Enrichment Programs for career planning, college survival skills, learning strategies, math, practical computer skills, reading, self-advocacy, stress management, study skills, test taking, time management, vocabulary development, written composition skills, and other are provided collaboratively through on-campus or off-campus services. Credit is offered for college survival skills, learning strategies, math, practical computer skills, reading, self-advocacy, stress management, study skills, test taking, time management, vocabulary development, written composition skills, and other.
Application For admittance to the program or unit, students are required to provide a psychoeducational report (3 years old or less) and provide documentation of high school services. Upon accep-

Northeastern Illinois University (continued)

tance, documentation of need for services should be sent only to the LD program or unit. *Application deadline (institutional): 7/1. Application deadline (LD program):* Rolling/continuous for fall and rolling/continuous for spring.

Written Policies Written policy regarding general/basic LD accommodations is available through the program or unit directly.

Northern Arizona University

South San Francisco Street

Flagstaff, AZ 86011

http://www.nau.edu/

Contact: Mr. Chad Loberger, Director. Phone: 928-523-8773. Fax: 928-523-8747. E-mail: chad.loberger@nau.edu.

Approximately 120 registered undergraduate students were served during 2002-03. The program or unit includes 6 full-time staff members. Academic advisers, counselors, skill tutors, strategy tutors, and trained peer tutors are provided collaboratively through on-campus or off-campus services.

Orientation The program or unit offers an optional 2-hour orientation for new students before classes begin.

Unique Aids and Services Aids, services, or accommodations include priority registration.

Subject-area Tutoring Tutoring is offered one-on-one for some subjects. Tutoring is provided collaboratively through on-campus or off-campus services via trained peer tutors.

Student Organization Advocates for Disability Issues on Campus consists of 5 members.

Application For admittance to the program or unit, students are required to provide a psychoeducational report (3 years old or less). Upon application, materials documenting need for services should be sent only to the LD program or unit. Upon acceptance, documentation of need for services should be sent only to the LD program or unit. *Application deadline (institutional):* Continuous. *Application deadline (LD program):* Rolling/continuous for fall and rolling/continuous for spring.

Written Policies Written policy regarding course substitutions is outlined in the school's catalog/handbook. Written policy regarding general/basic LD accommodations is available through the program or unit directly.

Northern Illinois University
Center for Access-Ability Resources (CAAR)

De Kalb, IL 60115-2854

http://www.niu.edu/uhs/caar

Contact: Mr. Garth Rubin, Coordinator. Phone: 815-753-1303. Fax: 815-753-9570. E-mail: grubin@niu.edu. Head of LD Program: Ms. Nancy J. Kasinski, Director. Phone: 815-753-9734. Fax: 815-753-9570. E-mail: nancyk@niu.edu.

Center for Access-Ability Resources (CAAR) Approximately 160 registered undergraduate students were served during 2002-03. The program or unit includes 1 full-time and 5 part-time staff members. Coaches, counselors, graduate assistants/students, and LD specialists are provided through the program or unit. Academic advisers, coaches, counselors, regular education teachers, and trained peer tutors are provided collaboratively through on-campus or off-campus services.

Orientation The program or unit offers a mandatory 1 to 3-hour orientation for new students before classes begin, individually by special arrangement, and during the year, upon notification of need.

Unique Aids and Services Aids, services, or accommodations include career counseling, faculty training, personal coach, priority registration, and support groups.

Subject-area Tutoring Tutoring is offered one-on-one and in small groups for some subjects. Tutoring is provided collaboratively through on-campus or off-campus services via computer-based instruction, graduate assistants/students, and trained peer tutors.

Diagnostic Testing Testing for auditory processing, handwriting, intelligence, learning styles, math, personality, reading, spelling, spoken language, study skills, visual processing, written language, and other services is provided collaboratively through on-campus or off-campus services.

Basic Skills Remediation Remediation is offered one-on-one and in small groups for auditory processing, learning strategies, math, spoken language, study skills, and time management. Remediation is provided through the program or unit via graduate assistants/students. Remediation is also provided collaboratively through on-campus or off-campus services via graduate assistants/students, regular education teachers, trained peer tutors, and other.

Enrichment Enrichment programs are available through the program or unit for career planning, college survival skills, learning strategies, self-advocacy, study skills, test taking, and time management. Programs for career planning, college survival skills, health and nutrition, learning strategies, oral communication skills, practical computer skills, stress management, study skills, test taking, time management, and written composition skills are provided collaboratively through on-campus or off-campus services. Credit is offered for career planning, college survival skills, health and nutrition, learning strategies, oral communication skills, and study skills.

Fees *Diagnostic Testing* fee is $0 to $400.

Application For admittance to the program or unit, students are required to provide a psychoeducational report (3 years old or less). It is recommended that students provide documentation of high school services. Upon application, materials documenting need for services should be sent only to the LD program or unit. Upon acceptance, documentation of need for services should be sent only to the LD program or unit. *Application deadline (institutional):* 8/1.

Written Policies Written policies regarding course substitutions, general/basic LD accommodations, reduced course loads, substitutions and waivers of admissions requirements, and substitutions and waivers of graduation requirements are available on the program Web site. Written policies regarding course substitutions, general/basic LD accommodations, reduced course loads, substitutions and waivers of admissions requirements, and substitutions and waivers of graduation requirements are available through the program or unit directly.

Northern Michigan University

1401 Presque Isle Avenue

Marquette, MI 49855-5301

http://www.nmu.edu/

Contact: Ms. Lynn Walden, Coordinator of Disability Services. Phone: 800-682-9797. Fax: 906-227-1714. E-mail: lwalden@nmu.edu.

Approximately 150 registered undergraduate students were served during 2002-03. The program or unit includes 1 full-time staff member. Graduate assistants/students are provided through the program or unit. Academic advisers, coaches, counselors, graduate assistants/students, trained peer tutors, and other are provided collaboratively through on-campus or off-campus services.

Summer Program To help prepare for the demands of college, there is an optional 6-week summer program prior to entering the school. Degree credit will be earned.

Unique Aids and Services Aids, services, or accommodations include taped texts, working with appropriate agencies and caseworkers.

Subject-area Tutoring Tutoring is offered one-on-one and in small groups. Tutoring is provided collaboratively through on-campus or off-campus services via computer-based instruction, graduate assistants/students, and trained peer tutors.

Basic Skills Remediation Remediation is available for learning strategies, math, reading, and study skills. Remediation is provided collaboratively through on-campus or off-campus services via computer-based instruction, graduate assistants/students, regular education teachers, and trained peer tutors.

Enrichment Programs for career planning, college survival skills, health and nutrition, learning strategies, math, oral communication skills, stress management, study skills, test taking, time management, and written composition skills are provided collaboratively through on-campus or off-campus services.

Student Organization Disabled Student Alliance.

Fees *Summer Program* fee is $325.

Application For admittance to the program or unit, students are required to apply to the program directly and provide a psychoeducational report (3 years old or less). It is recommended that students provide documentation of high school services. Upon application, materials documenting need for services should be sent to both admissions and the LD program or unit. *Application deadline (institutional):* Continuous. *Application deadline (LD program):* Rolling/continuous for fall and rolling/continuous for spring.

Written Policies Written policy regarding general/basic LD accommodations is available on the program Web site.

North Greenville College

PO Box 1892

Tigerville, SC 29688-1892

http://www.ngc.edu/

Contact: Mrs. Nancy A. Isgett, Learning Disabilities Liaison. Phone: 864-977-7129. Fax: 864-977-2089. E-mail: nisgett@ngc.edu.

Approximately 30 registered undergraduate students were served during 2002-03. The program or unit includes 1 full-time staff member. Academic advisers, counselors, regular education teachers, and remediation/learning specialists are provided collaboratively through on-campus or off-campus services.

Unique Aids and Services Aids, services, or accommodations include career counseling and priority registration.

Subject-area Tutoring Tutoring is offered one-on-one and in small groups for most subjects. Tutoring is provided collaboratively through on-campus or off-campus services via trained peer tutors.

Basic Skills Remediation Remediation is offered in class-size groups for computer skills, learning strategies, math, reading, study skills, and written language. Remediation is provided collaboratively through on-campus or off-campus services via regular education teachers.

Enrichment Programs for career planning, college survival skills, learning strategies, study skills, and written composition skills are provided collaboratively through on-campus or off-campus services.

Application For admittance to the program or unit, students are required to apply to the program directly and provide a psychoeducational report. It is recommended that students provide documentation of high school services. Upon application, materials documenting need for services should be sent to both admissions and the LD program or unit. Upon acceptance, documentation of need for services should be sent only to the LD program or unit. *Application deadline (institutional):* 8/18. *Application deadline (LD program):* Rolling/continuous for fall and rolling/continuous for spring.

Written Policies Written policy regarding general/basic LD accommodations is outlined in the school's catalog/handbook. Written policy regarding general/basic LD accommodations is available through the program or unit directly.

North Park University
Center for Academic Services

3225 West Foster Avenue

Chicago, IL 60625-4895

http://www.campus.northpark.edu/advising

Contact: Ms. Heather Walsh, Academic Services Counselor and Learning Specialist. Phone: 773-244-4990. Fax: 773-244-4954. E-mail: hwalsh@northpark.edu. Head of LD Program: Ms. Elizabeth Snezek, Director of Academic Services. Phone: 773-244-5664. Fax: 773-244-4954. E-mail: esnezek@northpark.edu.

Center for Academic Services Approximately 80 registered undergraduate students were served during 2002-03. The program or unit includes 5 full-time and 2 part-time staff members. Academic advisers, LD specialists, and remediation/learning specialists are provided through the program or unit. Counselors, skill tutors, and trained peer tutors are provided collaboratively through on-campus or off-campus services.

Unique Aids and Services Aids, services, or accommodations include career counseling, extended time for exams, note-takers, meetings with LD specialist, tape recorder in class.

Subject-area Tutoring Tutoring is offered one-on-one for all subjects. Tutoring is provided through the program or unit via LD specialists and trained peer tutors.

North Park University (continued)

Diagnostic Testing Testing is provided through the program or unit for learning strategies, learning styles, and study skills.

Basic Skills Remediation Remediation is offered one-on-one, in small groups, and in class-size groups for math, reading, study skills, written language, and memory and attention. Remediation is provided through the program or unit via LD specialists and trained peer tutors. Remediation is also provided collaboratively through on-campus or off-campus services via regular education teachers and special education teachers.

Enrichment Enrichment programs are available through the program or unit for career planning, college survival skills, learning strategies, study skills, test taking, time management, and other. Programs for career planning, reading, and written composition skills are provided collaboratively through on-campus or off-campus services. Credit is offered for career planning, college survival skills, learning strategies, reading, study skills, test taking, time management, written composition skills, and other.

Application For admittance to the program or unit, students are required to provide a psychoeducational report (3 years old or less). It is recommended that students apply to the program directly and provide documentation of high school services. Upon application, materials documenting need for services should be sent to both admissions and the LD program or unit. Upon acceptance, documentation of need for services should be sent only to the LD program or unit. *Application deadline (institutional):* Continuous. *Application deadline (LD program):* Rolling/continuous for fall and rolling/continuous for spring.

Written Policies Written policies regarding course substitutions and general/basic LD accommodations are available on the program Web site. Written policies regarding course substitutions and general/basic LD accommodations are outlined in the school's catalog/handbook. Written policy regarding reduced course loads is available through the program or unit directly.

Diagnostic Testing Testing for handwriting, learning strategies, learning styles, math, personality, reading, social skills, spoken language, and study skills is provided collaboratively through on-campus or off-campus services.

Basic Skills Remediation Remediation is offered one-on-one and in small groups for computer skills, learning strategies, math, reading, study skills, time management, and written language. Remediation is provided collaboratively through on-campus or off-campus services via computer-based instruction, graduate assistants/students, regular education teachers, teacher trainees, and trained peer tutors.

Enrichment Programs for career planning, college survival skills, health and nutrition, learning strategies, stress management, study skills, test taking, time management, and written composition skills are provided collaboratively through on-campus or off-campus services.

Fees *Diagnostic Testing* fee is applicable.

Application For admittance to the program or unit, students are required to provide a psychoeducational report (3 years old or less) and provide documentation of high school services. Upon application, materials documenting need for services should be sent to both admissions and the LD program or unit. *Application deadline (institutional):* Continuous. *Application deadline (LD program):* Rolling/continuous for fall and rolling/continuous for spring.

Written Policies Written policies regarding general/basic LD accommodations and reduced course loads are available on the program Web site. Written policies regarding general/basic LD accommodations and reduced course loads are outlined in the school's catalog/handbook. Written policy regarding general/basic LD accommodations is available through the program or unit directly.

Northwest Christian College
Student Life Department

828 East 11th Avenue

Eugene, OR 97401-3745

http://www.nwcc.edu/

Contact: Mr. Randy Worden, Dean of Students. Phone: 541-684-7248. Fax: 541-349-5260. E-mail: rworden@nwcc.edu.

Student Life Department Approximately 25 registered undergraduate students were served during 2002-03. The program or unit includes 1 part-time staff member. Academic advisers, counselors, diagnostic specialists, regular education teachers, skill tutors, strategy tutors, teacher trainees, and trained peer tutors are provided collaboratively through on-campus or off-campus services.

Unique Aids and Services Aids, services, or accommodations include advocates and career counseling.

Subject-area Tutoring Tutoring is offered one-on-one and in small groups for most subjects. Tutoring is provided collaboratively through on-campus or off-campus services via computer-based instruction, graduate assistants/students, and trained peer tutors.

Northwest Nazarene University

623 Holly Street

Nampa, ID 83686-5897

http://www.nnu.edu/

Contact: Mrs. Barbara Sosoka Howard, Adviser to Students with Learning Disabilities. Phone: 208-467-8669. E-mail: bshoward@nnu.edu.

Approximately 7 registered undergraduate students were served during 2002-03. The program or unit includes 1 part-time staff member. Academic advisers, coaches, counselors, graduate assistants/students, professional tutors, regular education teachers, remediation/learning specialists, skill tutors, and strategy tutors are provided through the program or unit.

Unique Aids and Services Aids, services, or accommodations include career counseling, personal coach, and weekly meetings with faculty.

Subject-area Tutoring Tutoring is offered one-on-one and in small groups for most subjects. Tutoring is provided collaboratively through on-campus or off-campus services via computer-based instruction, graduate assistants/students, LD specialists, and professional tutors.

Basic Skills Remediation Remediation is offered one-on-one and in small groups for computer skills, learning strategies, math, reading, spelling, study skills, time management, and written language. Remediation is provided collaboratively through on-campus or off-campus services via professional tutors and regular education teachers.

Enrichment Programs for career planning, college survival skills, health and nutrition, learning strategies, math, oral communication skills, practical computer skills, reading, study skills, test taking, time management, and written composition skills are provided collaboratively through on-campus or off-campus services. Credit is offered for career planning, college survival skills, health and nutrition, learning strategies, math, practical computer skills, reading, study skills, and written composition skills.

Application For admittance to the program or unit, students are required to provide documentation of high school services and provide test results. Upon acceptance, documentation of need for services should be sent only to the LD program or unit. *Application deadline (institutional):* 8/8. *Application deadline (LD program):* 8/1 for fall. 12/20 for spring.

Written Policies Written policy regarding general/basic LD accommodations is outlined in the school's catalog/handbook. Written policy regarding substitutions and waivers of graduation requirements is available through the program or unit directly.

Nova Scotia Agricultural College

PO Box 550

Truro, NS B2N 5E3

Canada

http://www.nsac.ns.ca/

Contact: Ms. Judy M. Smith, Dean of Student Services. Phone: 902-893-7915. Fax: 902-893-6545. E-mail: jsmith@nsac.ns.ca.

Approximately 6 registered undergraduate students were served during 2002-03. The program or unit includes 1 full-time staff member. LD specialists and trained peer tutors are provided through the program or unit. Academic advisers, diagnostic specialists, and LD specialists are provided collaboratively through on-campus or off-campus services.

Unique Aids and Services Aids, services, or accommodations include digital textbooks, disabilities resource facilitator.

Subject-area Tutoring Tutoring is offered one-on-one and in small groups for most subjects. Tutoring is provided through the program or unit via trained peer tutors.

Diagnostic Testing Testing is provided through the program or unit for math. Testing for auditory processing, learning strategies, learning styles, personality, reading, and visual processing is provided collaboratively through on-campus or off-campus services.

Basic Skills Remediation Remediation is offered one-on-one and in small groups for learning strategies, math, reading, study skills, and time management. Remediation is provided through the program or unit via computer-based instruction, LD specialists, and trained peer tutors.

Application For admittance to the program or unit, students are required to provide a psychoeducational report (6 years old or less) and provide documentation of high school services. It is recom-

mended that students apply to the program directly. Upon application, materials documenting need for services should be sent only to admissions with institutional application materials. Upon acceptance, documentation of need for services should be sent only to the LD program or unit. *Application deadline (institutional):* 8/1. *Application deadline (LD program):* Rolling/continuous for fall and rolling/continuous for spring.

Written Policies Written policies regarding general/basic LD accommodations and reduced course loads are available through the program or unit directly.

Nova Southeastern University
Farquhar College of Arts and Sciences, Academic Support Services

3301 College Avenue

Fort Lauderdale, FL 33314-7721

http://www.nova.edu/

Contact: Dr. Kenneth Gattis, Director of Academic Services. Phone: 954-262-8405. Fax: 954-262-3818. E-mail: gattis@nova.edu.

Farquhar College of Arts and Sciences, Academic Support Services Approximately 50 registered undergraduate students were served during 2002-03. The program or unit includes 1 full-time staff member. LD specialists are provided through the program or unit. Academic advisers and LD specialists are provided collaboratively through on-campus or off-campus services.

Unique Aids and Services Aids, services, or accommodations include digital textbooks and support groups.

Subject-area Tutoring Tutoring is offered one-on-one and in small groups for some subjects. Tutoring is provided collaboratively through on-campus or off-campus services via trained peer tutors and other.

Diagnostic Testing Testing is provided through the program or unit for learning strategies and study skills. Testing for auditory processing, handwriting, intelligence, learning styles, math, motor skills, neuropsychological, personality, reading, social skills, spelling, spoken language, visual processing, and written language is provided collaboratively through on-campus or off-campus services.

Basic Skills Remediation Remediation is offered in class-size groups for written language and others. Remediation is provided collaboratively through on-campus or off-campus services via regular education teachers.

Enrichment Programs for career planning, college survival skills, math, practical computer skills, reading, self-advocacy, study skills, test taking, time management, vocabulary development, and other are provided collaboratively through on-campus or off-campus services.

Application For admittance to the program or unit, students are required to provide a psychoeducational report. It is recommended that students provide documentation of high school services and provide other documentation. Upon acceptance, documentation of need for services should be sent only to the LD program or unit. *Application deadline (institutional):* Continuous. *Application deadline (LD program):* Rolling/continuous for fall and rolling/continuous for spring.

Nova Southeastern University (continued)

Written Policies Written policy regarding general/basic LD accommodations is available on the program Web site. Written policy regarding general/basic LD accommodations is outlined in the school's catalog/handbook. Written policies regarding course substitutions, general/basic LD accommodations, grade forgiveness, reduced course loads, and substitutions and waivers of graduation requirements are available through the program or unit directly.

Nyack College
Learning Disabilities Services

One South Boulevard
Nyack, NY 10960-3698
http://www.nyackcollege.edu/
Contact: Mrs. Elona Collins, Disabilities Services Coordinator. Phone: 845-358-1710 Ext. 570. Fax: 845-353-6334. E-mail: collinse@nyack.edu. Head of LD Program: Dr. Joyce Simons, Associate Dean and Director of Academic Development. Phone: 845-358-1710 Ext. 560. Fax: 845-353-6334. E-mail: simonsj@nyack.edu.

Learning Disabilities Services Approximately 20 registered undergraduate students were served during 2002-03. The program or unit includes 1 part-time staff member. Services are provided through the program or unit. Academic advisers, coaches, counselors, professional tutors, regular education teachers, and trained peer tutors are provided collaboratively through on-campus or off-campus services.
Orientation The program or unit offers an optional orientation for new students individually by special arrangement.
Unique Aids and Services Aids, services, or accommodations include advocates, digital textbooks, and priority registration.
Subject-area Tutoring Tutoring is offered one-on-one and in small groups for all subjects. Tutoring is provided collaboratively through on-campus or off-campus services via professional tutors and trained peer tutors.
Basic Skills Remediation Remediation is offered one-on-one and in small groups for learning strategies, study skills, time management, and written language. Remediation is provided collaboratively through on-campus or off-campus services via professional tutors, regular education teachers, and trained peer tutors.
Application For admittance to the program or unit, students are required to apply to the program directly, provide a psychoeducational report (3 years old or less), and provide documentation of high school services. Upon acceptance, documentation of need for services should be sent only to the LD program or unit. *Application deadline (institutional):* Continuous. *Application deadline (LD program):* Rolling/continuous for fall and rolling/continuous for spring.
Written Policies Written policy regarding general/basic LD accommodations is available through the program or unit directly.

Oakland University
Office of Disability Support Services

Rochester, MI 48309-4401
http://www.oakland.edu/

Contact: Linda Sisson, Director of Disability Support Services. Phone: 248-370-3266. Fax: 248-370-4989. E-mail: lgsisson@oakland.edu.

Office of Disability Support Services Approximately 210 registered undergraduate students were served during 2002-03. The program or unit includes 2 full-time and 2 part-time staff members. Academic advisers, diagnostic specialists, and trained peer tutors are provided collaboratively through on-campus or off-campus services.
Unique Aids and Services Aids, services, or accommodations include advocates, career counseling, digital textbooks, and priority registration.
Subject-area Tutoring Tutoring is offered one-on-one and in small groups for most subjects. Tutoring is provided collaboratively through on-campus or off-campus services via trained peer tutors.
Diagnostic Testing Testing for auditory processing, intelligence, math, reading, spelling, spoken language, visual processing, and written language is provided collaboratively through on-campus or off-campus services.
Basic Skills Remediation Remediation is offered one-on-one and in small groups for auditory processing, learning strategies, math, reading, spelling, study skills, time management, visual processing, and written language. Remediation is provided collaboratively through on-campus or off-campus services via graduate assistants/students and trained peer tutors.
Enrichment Programs for career planning, college survival skills, learning strategies, math, self-advocacy, stress management, study skills, test taking, time management, vocabulary development, and written composition skills are provided collaboratively through on-campus or off-campus services. Credit is offered for career planning, college survival skills, stress management, and written composition skills.
Student Organization Disability Awareness Group Integrating Students (DAGIS) consists of 5 members.
Fees *Diagnostic Testing* fee is $100.
Application For admittance to the program or unit, students are required to apply to the program directly, provide a psychoeducational report (3 years old or less), and provide all assessment scores, histories, and reports if submitting IEP as documentation. Upon acceptance, documentation of need for services should be sent only to the LD program or unit. *Application deadline (institutional):* Continuous.

Oberlin College
Student Academic Services, Services for Students with Disabilities

173 West Lorain Street
Oberlin, OH 44074
http://www.oberlin.edu/learning/SASmission.html
Contact: Mrs. Jane E. Boomer, Coordinator of Services for Students with Disabilities. Phone: 440-775-8467. Fax: 440-776-3010. E-mail: jane.boomer@oberlin.edu.

Student Academic Services, Services for Students with Disabilities Approximately 170 registered undergraduate students were served during 2002-03. The program or unit includes 2 full-time staff members. Academic advisers, coaches, LD specialists, and remediation/learning specialists are provided through the program or unit. Academic advisers, counselors, professional tutors, remediation/learning specialists, skill tutors, strategy tutors, and trained peer tutors are provided collaboratively through on-campus or off-campus services.

Orientation The program or unit offers an optional orientation for new students during registration.

Unique Aids and Services Aids, services, or accommodations include career counseling, digital textbooks, priority registration, support groups, and weekly meetings with faculty.

Subject-area Tutoring Tutoring is offered one-on-one for most subjects. Tutoring is provided collaboratively through on-campus or off-campus services via professional tutors and trained peer tutors.

Enrichment Enrichment programs are available through the program or unit for college survival skills, learning strategies, reading, self-advocacy, stress management, study skills, test taking, time management, vocabulary development, and written composition skills. Programs for college survival skills, learning strategies, math, oral communication skills, practical computer skills, reading, self-advocacy, study skills, test taking, time management, vocabulary development, and written composition skills are provided collaboratively through on-campus or off-campus services. Credit is offered for college survival skills, learning strategies, math, oral communication skills, practical computer skills, reading, self-advocacy, study skills, test taking, vocabulary development, and written composition skills.

Student Organization SOBIE consists of 15 members.

Application For admittance to the program or unit, students are required to provide a psychoeducational report. It is recommended that students provide documentation of high school services. Upon acceptance, documentation of need for services should be sent only to the LD program or unit. *Application deadline (institutional):* 1/15. *Application deadline (LD program):* Rolling/continuous for fall and rolling/continuous for spring.

Written Policies Written policy regarding general/basic LD accommodations is available on the program Web site. Written policy regarding general/basic LD accommodations is available through the program or unit directly.

Occidental College

1600 Campus Road
Los Angeles, CA 90041-3314
http://www.departments.oxy.edu/ctl/
services_for_disabilities.htm
Contact: Ms. Linda C. Whitney, Coordinator of Center for Teaching and Learning. Phone: 323-259-2849. E-mail: lwhitney@oxy.edu.

Approximately 60 registered undergraduate students were served during 2002-03. The program or unit includes 1 full-time and 1 part-time staff member. Academic advisers, coaches, LD specialists, and strategy tutors are provided through the program or unit.

Orientation The program or unit offers an optional 1-hour orientation for new students before classes begin.

Unique Aids and Services Aids, services, or accommodations include digital textbooks, personal coach, and priority registration.

Student Organization Learning Differences Association consists of 10 members.

Application For admittance to the program or unit, students are required to provide a psychoeducational report. Upon acceptance, documentation of need for services should be sent only to the LD program or unit. *Application deadline (institutional):* 1/15. *Application deadline (LD program):* Rolling/continuous for fall and rolling/continuous for spring.

Written Policies Written policy regarding general/basic LD accommodations is available on the program Web site. Written policies regarding general/basic LD accommodations and substitutions and waivers of admissions requirements are available through the program or unit directly.

The Ohio State University
Office for Disability Services

190 North Oval Mall
Columbus, OH 43210
http://www.ods.ohio-stste.edu
Contact: Ms. Lois J. Burke, Counselor. Phone: 614-292-3307. Fax: 614-292-4190. E-mail: burke.4@osu.edu. Head of LD Program: Ms. Patricia M. Carlton, Interim Director. Phone: 614-292-3307. Fax: 614-292-4190. E-mail: carlton.1@osu.edu.

Office for Disability Services Approximately 600 registered undergraduate students were served during 2002-03. The program or unit includes 8 full-time staff members. Counselors, LD specialists, and other are provided through the program or unit. Counselors, LD specialists, and other are provided collaboratively through on-campus or off-campus services.

Orientation The program or unit offers a mandatory 90-minute orientation for new students before classes begin, after classes begin, and individually by special arrangement.

Unique Aids and Services Aids, services, or accommodations include priority registration.

Diagnostic Testing Testing is provided through the program or unit for auditory processing, intelligence, math, reading, spelling, study skills, visual processing, and written language. Testing for auditory processing, intelligence, math, reading, spelling, spoken language, visual processing, and written language is provided collaboratively through on-campus or off-campus services.

Enrichment Programs for career planning, learning strategies, and study skills are provided collaboratively through on-campus or off-campus services. Credit is offered for learning strategies and study skills.

Fees *Diagnostic Testing* fee is $250.

Application For admittance to the program or unit, students are required to provide a psychoeducational report. It is recommended that students provide documentation of high school services. Upon application, materials documenting need for services should be sent only to the LD program or unit. Upon acceptance, documentation of need for services should be sent only to the LD program or unit. *Application deadline (institutional):* 2/15. *Application deadline (LD program):* Rolling/continuous for fall and rolling/continuous for spring.

Written Policies Written policy regarding general/basic LD accommodations is available on the program Web site. Written policies regarding course substitutions and general/basic LD accommodations are available through the program or unit directly.

The Ohio State University at Lima
Office for Disability Services

4240 Campus Drive
Lima, OH 45804-3576
http://www.ohio-state.edu/

Contact: Mrs. Karen M. Meyer, Coordinator for Disability Services. Phone: 419-995-8453. Fax: 419-995-8483. E-mail: meyer.193@osu.edu.

Office for Disability Services Approximately 25 registered undergraduate students were served during 2002-03. The program or unit includes 1 full-time and 1 part-time staff member. LD specialists are provided through the program or unit. Services are provided collaboratively through on-campus or off-campus services.

Unique Aids and Services Aids, services, or accommodations include priority registration and support groups.

Subject-area Tutoring Tutoring is offered one-on-one for most subjects. Tutoring is provided collaboratively through on-campus or off-campus services via trained peer tutors.

Application For admittance to the program or unit, students are required to apply to the program directly, provide a psychoeducational report (5 years old or less), and provide documentation of high school services. Upon application, materials documenting need for services should be sent only to the LD program or unit. Upon acceptance, documentation of need for services should be sent only to the LD program or unit. *Application deadline (institutional):* 7/1. *Application deadline (LD program):* Rolling/continuous for fall and rolling/continuous for spring.

Written Policies Written policy regarding general/basic LD accommodations is outlined in the school's catalog/handbook. Written policies regarding course substitutions, general/basic LD accommodations, grade forgiveness, reduced course loads, substitutions and waivers of admissions requirements, and substitutions and waivers of graduation requirements are available through the program or unit directly.

Ohio University
Office for Institutional Equity

Athens, OH 45701-2979
http://www.ohiou.edu/equity/disabilityservices/

Contact: Ms. Katherine M. Fahey, Assistant Director for Institutional Equity. Phone: 740-593-2620. Fax: 740-593-0790. E-mail: fahey@ohio.edu.

Office for Institutional Equity Approximately 325 registered undergraduate students were served during 2002-03. The program or unit includes 2 full-time staff members and 1 part-time staff member. Counselors are provided through the program or unit. Academic advisers, counselors, regular education teachers, skill tutors, and trained peer tutors are provided collaboratively through on-campus or off-campus services.

Unique Aids and Services Aids, services, or accommodations include advocates, digital textbooks, and priority registration.

Subject-area Tutoring Tutoring is offered one-on-one and in class-size groups for some subjects. Tutoring is provided collaboratively through on-campus or off-campus services via trained peer tutors.

Diagnostic Testing Testing for auditory processing, intelligence, neuropsychological, personality, reading, spoken language, written language, and other services is provided collaboratively through on-campus or off-campus services.

Enrichment Programs for career planning, health and nutrition, learning strategies, practical computer skills, reading, stress management, study skills, test taking, time management, and written composition skills are provided collaboratively through on-campus or off-campus services. Credit is offered for learning strategies, practical computer skills, and reading.

Fees *Diagnostic Testing* fee is $150 to $400.

Application For admittance to the program or unit, students are required to provide a psychoeducational report (3 years old or less). It is recommended that students provide documentation of high school services. Upon application, materials documenting need for services should be sent only to admissions with institutional application materials. Upon acceptance, documentation of need for services should be sent only to the LD program or unit. *Application deadline (institutional):* 2/1. *Application deadline (LD program):* Rolling/continuous for fall and rolling/continuous for spring.

Written Policies Written policy regarding general/basic LD accommodations is available on the program Web site. Written policy regarding general/basic LD accommodations is available through the program or unit directly.

Ohio Wesleyan University
Office of Academic Advising

61 South Sandusky Street
Delaware, OH 43015
http://web.owu.edu/

Contact: R. Blake Michael, Associate Dean for Academic Affairs. Phone: 740-368-3275. Fax: 740-368-3374. E-mail: acadvocp@owu.edu.

Office of Academic Advising Approximately 150 registered undergraduate students were served during 2002-03. The program or unit includes 1 part-time staff member. Academic advisers, skill tutors, and other are provided collaboratively through on-campus or off-campus services.

Basic Skills Remediation Remediation is offered one-on-one and in small groups for learning strategies, math, reading, study skills, time management, and written language. Remediation is provided collaboratively through on-campus or off-campus services via professional tutors and trained peer tutors.

Enrichment Programs for career planning, college survival skills, learning strategies, math, medication management, reading, study skills, time management, and written composition skills are provided collaboratively through on-campus or off-campus services. Credit is offered for college survival skills.

Application For admittance to the program or unit, students are required to provide a psychoeducational report (3 years old or less). It is recommended that students provide documentation of high school services. Upon acceptance, documentation of need for services should be sent only to the LD program or unit. *Application deadline (institutional):* 3/1.

Written Policies Written policies regarding course substitutions, general/basic LD accommodations, and reduced course loads are available through the program or unit directly.

Okanagan University College
Disability Services

3333 College Way
Kelowna, BC V1V 1V7
Canada
http://www.ouc.bc.ca/
Contact: Phone: 250-762-5445. Fax: 250-762-5470.

Disability Services Approximately 350 registered undergraduate students were served during 2002-03. The program or unit includes 5 full-time and 30 part-time staff members. Graduate assistants/students, professional tutors, remediation/learning specialists, skill tutors, strategy tutors, and trained peer tutors are provided through the program or unit. Academic advisers, coaches, counselors, diagnostic specialists, LD specialists, regular education teachers, special education teachers, and teacher trainees are provided collaboratively through on-campus or off-campus services.
Unique Aids and Services Aids, services, or accommodations include digital textbooks, faculty training, and priority registration.
Subject-area Tutoring Tutoring is offered one-on-one for most subjects. Tutoring is provided through the program or unit via computer-based instruction, graduate assistants/students, LD specialists, and trained peer tutors. Tutoring is also provided collaboratively through on-campus or off-campus services via professional tutors.
Diagnostic Testing Testing is provided through the program or unit for learning strategies, learning styles, and study skills. Testing for auditory processing, intelligence, math, neuropsychological, personality, reading, spelling, visual processing, and written language is provided collaboratively through on-campus or off-campus services.
Enrichment Enrichment programs are available through the program or unit for learning strategies, self-advocacy, study skills, test taking, time management, and written composition skills. Programs for career planning, college survival skills, health and nutrition, math, stress management, study skills, test taking, and time management are provided collaboratively through on-campus or off-campus services.
Fees *Diagnostic Testing* fee is $75.
Application For admittance to the program or unit, students are required to apply to the program directly and provide a psychoeducational report (5 years old or less). It is recommended that students provide documentation of high school services. Upon application, materials documenting need for services should be sent only to the LD program or unit. Upon acceptance, documentation of need for services should be sent to both admissions and the LD program or unit. *Application deadline (institutional):* Continuous. *Application deadline (LD program):* Rolling/continuous for fall and rolling/continuous for spring.
Written Policies Written policy regarding general/basic LD accommodations is outlined in the school's catalog/handbook. Written policies regarding general/basic LD accommodations and reduced course loads are available through the program or unit directly.

Oklahoma State University
Student Disability Services

Stillwater, OK 74078
http://www.okstate.edu/ucs/stdis/
Contact: Mr. Michael Shuttic, Coordinator of Student Disability Services and ADA Compliance. Phone: 405-744-7116. Fax: 405-744-8380. E-mail: shuttic@okstate.edu.

Student Disability Services Approximately 160 registered undergraduate students were served during 2002-03. The program or unit includes 4 full-time and 2 part-time staff members. Graduate assistants/students and strategy tutors are provided through the program or unit. Academic advisers, counselors, diagnostic specialists, remediation/learning specialists, skill tutors, strategy tutors, and trained peer tutors are provided collaboratively through on-campus or off-campus services.
Summer Program To help prepare for the demands of college, there is an optional 3 or 4-day summer program prior to entering the school.
Unique Aids and Services Aids, services, or accommodations include advocates, career counseling, digital textbooks, and faculty training.
Subject-area Tutoring Tutoring is offered one-on-one and in small groups for most subjects. Tutoring is provided collaboratively through on-campus or off-campus services via graduate assistants/students, professional tutors, and trained peer tutors.
Diagnostic Testing Testing is provided through the program or unit for learning strategies and learning styles. Testing for auditory processing, intelligence, learning strategies, learning styles, math, motor skills, neuropsychological, reading, spelling, spoken language, study skills, visual processing, and written language is provided collaboratively through on-campus or off-campus services.
Basic Skills Remediation Remediation is available for learning strategies, math, study skills, time management, and written language. Remediation is provided collaboratively through on-campus or off-campus services via graduate assistants/students, regular education teachers, and trained peer tutors.
Enrichment Programs for career planning, college survival skills, learning strategies, math, stress management, study skills, test taking, and time management are provided collaboratively through on-campus or off-campus services. Credit is offered for college survival skills, learning strategies, and math.
Fees *Diagnostic Testing* fee is $150 to $350.
Application For admittance to the program or unit, students are required to provide a psychoeducational report. It is recommended that students provide documentation of high school services. Upon application, materials documenting need for services should be sent only to the LD program or unit. Upon acceptance, documentation of need for services should be sent only to the LD program or unit. *Application deadline (institutional):* Continuous. *Application deadline (LD program):* Rolling/continuous for fall and rolling/continuous for spring.
Written Policies Written policies regarding course substitutions, general/basic LD accommodations, and substitutions and waivers of graduation requirements are available on the program Web site. Written policies regarding course substitutions and substitutions and waivers of graduation requirements are outlined in the school's

Oklahoma State University (continued)
catalog/handbook. Written policies regarding course substitutions, general/basic LD accommodations, and substitutions and waivers of graduation requirements are available through the program or unit directly.

Old Dominion University
Disability Services

5215 Hampton Boulevard
Norfolk, VA 23529
http://web.odu.edu/disabilityservices
Contact: Phone: 757-683-3000. Fax: 757-683-5357.

Disability Services Approximately 400 registered undergraduate students were served during 2002-03. The program or unit includes 3 full-time staff members and 1 part-time staff member. LD specialists are provided through the program or unit. Academic advisers, counselors, skill tutors, and strategy tutors are provided collaboratively through on-campus or off-campus services.
Unique Aids and Services Aids, services, or accommodations include priority registration.
Subject-area Tutoring Tutoring is offered one-on-one. Tutoring is provided collaboratively through on-campus or off-campus services via graduate assistants/students.
Basic Skills Remediation Remediation is offered in class-size groups for learning strategies, math, spelling, study skills, time management, and written language. Remediation is provided through the program or unit via LD specialists. Remediation is also provided collaboratively through on-campus or off-campus services via regular education teachers.
Enrichment Programs for learning strategies, math, stress management, study skills, test taking, time management, and written composition skills are provided collaboratively through on-campus or off-campus services.
Application For admittance to the program or unit, students are required to provide a psychoeducational report (3 years old or less). Upon acceptance, documentation of need for services should be sent only to admissions. *Application deadline (institutional):* 3/15. *Application deadline (LD program):* Rolling/continuous for fall and rolling/continuous for spring.
Written Policies Written policy regarding general/basic LD accommodations is available on the program Web site. Written policy regarding grade forgiveness is outlined in the school's catalog/handbook.

Olivet Nazarene University
Learning Development Center

One University Avenue
Bourbonnais, IL 60914-2271
http://www.olivet.edu/
Contact: Dr. Sue Ellen Rattin, Director Learning Development Center. Phone: 815-939-5150. Fax: 815-939-5169. E-mail: srattin@olivet.edu.

Learning Development Center Approximately 50 registered undergraduate students were served during 2002-03. The program or unit includes 2 full-time staff members. Academic advisers, coaches, counselors, diagnostic specialists, LD specialists, remediation/learning specialists, skill tutors, strategy tutors, and trained peer tutors are provided through the program or unit. Academic advisers, coaches, counselors, diagnostic specialists, skill tutors, strategy tutors, and trained peer tutors are provided collaboratively through on-campus or off-campus services.
Unique Aids and Services Aids, services, or accommodations include career counseling, personal coach, priority registration, support groups, and weekly meetings with faculty.
Subject-area Tutoring Tutoring is offered one-on-one and in small groups for most subjects. Tutoring is provided through the program or unit via computer-based instruction, LD specialists, and trained peer tutors. Tutoring is also provided collaboratively through on-campus or off-campus services via computer-based instruction, LD specialists, and trained peer tutors.
Diagnostic Testing Testing is provided through the program or unit for personality and reading.
Basic Skills Remediation Remediation is offered one-on-one, in small groups, and in class-size groups for computer skills, learning strategies, math, reading, study skills, time management, and written language. Remediation is provided through the program or unit via LD specialists. Remediation is also provided collaboratively through on-campus or off-campus services via LD specialists.
Enrichment Programs for career planning, college survival skills, health and nutrition, learning strategies, math, oral communication skills, practical computer skills, reading, self-advocacy, stress management, study skills, test taking, time management, and written composition skills are provided collaboratively through on-campus or off-campus services.
Application For admittance to the program or unit, students are required to provide a psychoeducational report (3 years old or less) and provide documentation of high school services. Upon acceptance, documentation of need for services should be sent to both admissions and the LD program or unit. *Application deadline (institutional):* Continuous. *Application deadline (LD program):* Rolling/continuous for fall and rolling/continuous for spring.
Written Policies Written policies regarding general/basic LD accommodations and reduced course loads are available through the program or unit directly.

Oregon Institute of Technology
Services for Students with Disabilities

3201 Campus Drive
Klamath Falls, OR 97601-8801
http://www.oit.edu/index.html?method=disb
Contact: Mr. Ron Douglas McCutcheon MSC, Director of Campus Access and Equal Opportunity. Phone: 541-885-1031. Fax: 541-885-1072. E-mail: mccutchr@oit.edu.

Services for Students with Disabilities Approximately 46 registered undergraduate students were served during 2002-03. The program or unit includes 1 full-time staff member. Skill tutors, strategy tutors, and other are provided through the program or unit. Academic advisers, counselors, diagnostic specialists, LD specialists, regular education teachers, remediation/learning specialists, skill tutors, trained peer tutors, and other are provided collaboratively through on-campus or off-campus services.

Unique Aids and Services Aids, services, or accommodations include digital textbooks, faculty training, priority registration, weekly meetings with faculty, note-taking, faculty notes, books on tape.

Subject-area Tutoring Tutoring is offered one-on-one and in small groups for some subjects. Tutoring is provided collaboratively through on-campus or off-campus services via computer-based instruction, trained peer tutors, and other.

Enrichment Enrichment programs are available through the program or unit for college survival skills, learning strategies, self-advocacy, study skills, test taking, and time management. Programs for career planning, college survival skills, health and nutrition, learning strategies, math, oral communication skills, practical computer skills, reading, self-advocacy, stress management, study skills, test taking, time management, vocabulary development, and written composition skills are provided collaboratively through on-campus or off-campus services.

Application For admittance to the program or unit, students are required to provide a psychoeducational report (3 years old or less). It is recommended that students provide documentation of high school services. Upon application, materials documenting need for services should be sent only to the LD program or unit. Upon acceptance, documentation of need for services should be sent only to the LD program or unit. *Application deadline (institutional): 6/1. Application deadline (LD program):* Rolling/continuous for fall and rolling/continuous for spring.

Written Policies Written policy regarding general/basic LD accommodations is available on the program Web site. Written policy regarding general/basic LD accommodations is available through the program or unit directly.

Oregon State University
Services for Students with Disabilities

Corvallis, OR 97331

http://oregonstate.edu/dept/ssd/

Contact: Dr. Tracy Bentley-Townlin, Director. Phone: 541-737-4098. Fax: 541-737-7354. E-mail: disability.services@oregonstate.edu.

Services for Students with Disabilities Approximately 250 registered undergraduate students were served during 2002-03. The program or unit includes 2 full-time staff members. Coaches are provided through the program or unit. Academic advisers, coaches, counselors, remediation/learning specialists, skill tutors, strategy tutors, and trained peer tutors are provided collaboratively through on-campus or off-campus services.

Orientation The program or unit offers an optional 1-hour orientation for new students individually by special arrangement and during a 10-hour class taught by students with disabilities currently using services.

Unique Aids and Services Aids, services, or accommodations include advocates and personal coach.

Subject-area Tutoring Tutoring is offered one-on-one and in small groups for some subjects. Tutoring is provided collaboratively through on-campus or off-campus services via computer-based instruction, graduate assistants/students, and trained peer tutors.

Basic Skills Remediation Remediation is offered one-on-one and in small groups for math, reading, study skills, time management, and written language. Remediation is provided collaboratively through on-campus or off-campus services.

Enrichment Programs for career planning, college survival skills, learning strategies, math, reading, self-advocacy, stress management, study skills, test taking, time management, vocabulary development, and written composition skills are provided collaboratively through on-campus or off-campus services. Credit is offered for career planning, learning strategies, math, and reading.

Application For admittance to the program or unit, students are required to apply to the program directly and provide a psychoeducational report (3 years old or less). It is recommended that students provide documentation of high school services. Upon acceptance, documentation of need for services should be sent only to the LD program or unit. *Application deadline (institutional): 3/1. Application deadline (LD program):* Rolling/continuous for fall and rolling/continuous for spring.

Written Policies Written policies regarding course substitutions, general/basic LD accommodations, reduced course loads, and substitutions and waivers of admissions requirements are available on the program Web site. Written policy regarding general/basic LD accommodations is outlined in the school's catalog/handbook. Written policies regarding course substitutions, general/basic LD accommodations, reduced course loads, and substitutions and waivers of admissions requirements are available through the program or unit directly.

Otterbein College
Academic Support Center

1 Otterbein College

Westerville, OH 43081

http://www.otterbein.edu/

Contact: Phone: 614-890-3000. Fax: 614-823-1200.

Academic Support Center The program or unit includes 3 full-time staff members. Remediation/learning specialists are provided collaboratively through on-campus or off-campus services.

Unique Aids and Services Aids, services, or accommodations include priority registration.

Subject-area Tutoring Tutoring is offered one-on-one for most subjects. Tutoring is provided collaboratively through on-campus or off-campus services via trained peer tutors.

Basic Skills Remediation Remediation is offered in class-size groups for learning strategies, math, reading, study skills, time management, and written language. Remediation is provided collaboratively through on-campus or off-campus services via regular education teachers.

Enrichment Programs for career planning, college survival skills, learning strategies, math, reading, study skills, test taking, time management, vocabulary development, and written composition skills are provided collaboratively through on-campus or off-campus services.

Otterbein College (continued)

Application For admittance to the program or unit, students are required to provide a psychoeducational report (3 years old or less) and provide documentation of high school services. Upon application, materials documenting need for services should be sent only to admissions with institutional application materials. Upon acceptance, documentation of need for services should be sent only to the LD program or unit. *Application deadline (institutional): 3/1. Application deadline (LD program):* Rolling/continuous for fall and rolling/continuous for spring.

Written Policies Written policies regarding course substitutions, general/basic LD accommodations, and substitutions and waivers of graduation requirements are available through the program or unit directly.

Our Lady of the Lake College
Counseling Services

7434 Perkins Road
Baton Rouge, LA 70808
http://www.ololcollege.edu/
Contact: Dr. Jacque R. Crehan, Dean of Student Services and Director of Counseling Services. Phone: 225-768-1713. Fax: 225-214-1945. E-mail: jcrehan@ololcollege.edu.

Counseling Services Approximately 45 registered undergraduate students were served during 2002-03. The program or unit includes 2 full-time and 7 part-time staff members. Counselors, diagnostic specialists, LD specialists, and skill tutors are provided through the program or unit. Skill tutors and trained peer tutors are provided collaboratively through on-campus or off-campus services.

Unique Aids and Services Aids, services, or accommodations include personal coach.

Subject-area Tutoring Tutoring is offered one-on-one for all subjects. Tutoring is provided through the program or unit via professional tutors and trained peer tutors. Tutoring is also provided collaboratively through on-campus or off-campus services via professional tutors and trained peer tutors.

Enrichment Enrichment programs are available through the program or unit for career planning, college survival skills, learning strategies, math, medication management, oral communication skills, reading, self-advocacy, stress management, study skills, test taking, time management, vocabulary development, and written composition skills. Programs for career planning, college survival skills, health and nutrition, learning strategies, math, oral communication skills, practical computer skills, reading, study skills, test taking, time management, vocabulary development, and written composition skills are provided collaboratively through on-campus or off-campus services. Credit is offered for practical computer skills.

Application For admittance to the program or unit, students are required to apply to the program directly and provide a psychoeducational report (3 years old or less). Upon application, materials documenting need for services should be sent only to the LD program or unit. Upon acceptance, documentation of need for services should be sent only to the LD program or unit. *Application deadline (institutional):* Continuous. *Application deadline (LD program):* Rolling/continuous for fall and rolling/continuous for spring.

Written Policies Written policy regarding general/basic LD accommodations is outlined in the school's catalog/handbook. Written policy regarding general/basic LD accommodations is available through the program or unit directly.

Pacific Union College
Learning disAbilities Services

One Angwin Avenue
Angwin, CA 94508-9707
http://www.puc.edu/studentlife/Career&Counseling Center
Contact: Rosemary Dibben, Director of Learning Resource Center. Phone: 707-965-6471. E-mail: rdibben@puc.edu.

Learning disAbilities Services Approximately 110 registered undergraduate students were served during 2002-03. The program or unit includes 1 full-time and 1 part-time staff member. Coaches and counselors are provided through the program or unit. Academic advisers, counselors, diagnostic specialists, regular education teachers, and trained peer tutors are provided collaboratively through on-campus or off-campus services.

Orientation The program or unit offers an optional 2-hour orientation for new students before registration and before classes begin.

Unique Aids and Services Aids, services, or accommodations include advocates, career counseling, priority registration, support groups, and weekly meetings with faculty.

Subject-area Tutoring Tutoring is offered one-on-one and in small groups for most subjects. Tutoring is provided collaboratively through on-campus or off-campus services via trained peer tutors.

Diagnostic Testing Testing for intelligence, math, neuropsychological, personality, reading, spelling, and written language is provided collaboratively through on-campus or off-campus services.

Basic Skills Remediation Remediation is offered in class-size groups for written language. Remediation is provided collaboratively through on-campus or off-campus services via regular education teachers.

Enrichment Programs for career planning, college survival skills, medication management, stress management, test taking, and time management are provided collaboratively through on-campus or off-campus services. Credit is offered for college survival skills.

Application For admittance to the program or unit, students are required to apply to the program directly and provide a psychoeducational report (3 years old or less). It is recommended that students provide documentation of high school services. Upon acceptance, documentation of need for services should be sent only to the LD program or unit. *Application deadline (institutional):* Continuous. *Application deadline (LD program):* Rolling/continuous for fall and rolling/continuous for spring.

Written Policies Written policies regarding course substitutions, general/basic LD accommodations, and substitutions and waivers of graduation requirements are available on the program Web site. Written policies regarding course substitutions, general/basic LD accommodations, and substitutions and waivers of graduation requirements are outlined in the school's catalog/handbook.

Parsons School of Design, New School University
Student Disability Services

66 Fifth Avenue
New York, NY 10011-8878
http://www.parsons.edu/
Contact: Mr. Tom McDonald, Director Student Disability Services. Phone: 212-229-5163. Fax: 212-229-8992. E-mail: sds@newschool.edu.

Student Disability Services Approximately 31 registered undergraduate students were served during 2002-03. The program or unit includes 1 full-time and 1 part-time staff member. Services are provided through the program or unit. Academic advisers, counselors, and other are provided collaboratively through on-campus or off-campus services.
Enrichment Enrichment programs are available through the program or unit for self-advocacy. Programs for career planning, college survival skills, health and nutrition, learning strategies, self-advocacy, stress management, study skills, test taking, time management, and written composition skills are provided collaboratively through on-campus or off-campus services.
Application For admittance to the program or unit, students are required to apply to the program directly, provide a psychoeducational report, and provide documentation (contact office for specific guidelines). Upon acceptance, documentation of need for services should be sent only to the LD program or unit. *Application deadline (institutional):* Continuous. *Application deadline (LD program):* Rolling/continuous for fall.
Written Policies Written policy regarding general/basic LD accommodations is available on the program Web site. Written policy regarding general/basic LD accommodations is outlined in the school's catalog/handbook. Written policy regarding general/basic LD accommodations is available through the program or unit directly.

Peace College

15 East Peace Street
Raleigh, NC 27604-1194
http://www.peace.edu/
Contact: Phone: 919-508-2000. Fax: 919-508-2328.

The program or unit includes 1 full-time and 8 part-time staff members. LD specialists, remediation/learning specialists, skill tutors, and strategy tutors are provided through the program or unit. Academic advisers, coaches, counselors, diagnostic specialists, graduate assistants/students, professional tutors, regular education teachers, special education teachers, and trained peer tutors are provided collaboratively through on-campus or off-campus services.
Unique Aids and Services Aids, services, or accommodations include career counseling.
Subject-area Tutoring Tutoring is offered one-on-one. Tutoring is provided through the program or unit via computer-based instruction, LD specialists, professional tutors, and trained peer tutors. Tutoring is also provided collaboratively through on-campus or off-campus services via computer-based instruction.

Basic Skills Remediation Remediation is offered one-on-one and in class-size groups for learning strategies, math, reading, spelling, study skills, time management, and written language. Remediation is provided through the program or unit via professional tutors and trained peer tutors. Remediation is also provided collaboratively through on-campus or off-campus services via regular education teachers.
Enrichment Enrichment programs are available through the program or unit for college survival skills, math, reading, self-advocacy, stress management, study skills, test taking, time management, and written composition skills. Programs for career planning, health and nutrition, learning strategies, math, oral communication skills, practical computer skills, and written composition skills are provided collaboratively through on-campus or off-campus services. Credit is offered for career planning, math, oral communication skills, practical computer skills, and written composition skills.
Application For admittance to the program or unit, students are required to apply to the program directly and provide a psychoeducational report. It is recommended that students provide documentation of high school services. Upon acceptance, documentation of need for services should be sent to both admissions and the LD program or unit. *Application deadline (institutional):* Continuous. *Application deadline (LD program):* Rolling/continuous for fall and rolling/continuous for spring.
Written Policies Written policy regarding general/basic LD accommodations is outlined in the school's catalog/handbook. Written policies regarding general/basic LD accommodations and substitutions and waivers of graduation requirements are available through the program or unit directly.

Pennsylvania College of Art & Design

204 North Prince Street, PO Box 59
Lancaster, PA 17608-0059
http://www.psad.org/
Contact: Pamela Richardson, Dean. Phone: 717-396-7833. Fax: 717-396-1339. E-mail: prichardson@psad.edu.

Application For admittance to the program or unit, students are required to provide a psychoeducational report. It is recommended that students provide documentation of high school services. Upon acceptance, documentation of need for services should be sent to both admissions and the LD program or unit. *Application deadline (institutional):* 5/1. *Application deadline (LD program):* Rolling/continuous for fall and rolling/continuous for spring.
Written Policies Written policy regarding general/basic LD accommodations is outlined in the school's catalog/handbook.

The Pennsylvania State University Abington College

1600 Woodland Road
Abington, PA 19001-3918
http://www.equity.psu.edu/ods

The Pennsylvania State University Abington College (continued)

Contact: Anne W. Prior, Disability Contact Liaison and Learning Center Director. Phone: 215-881-7537. Fax: 215-881-7317. E-mail: axp28@psu.edu.

Approximately 50 registered undergraduate students were served during 2002-03. The program or unit includes 1 part-time staff member.

Orientation The program or unit offers an optional 1-hour orientation for new students before classes begin and individually by special arrangement.

Unique Aids and Services Aids, services, or accommodations include priority registration, extended time for testing, note-takers.

Application For admittance to the program or unit, students are required to apply to the program directly and provide a psychoeducational report (3 years old or less). Upon acceptance, documentation of need for services should be sent only to the LD program or unit. *Application deadline (institutional):* Continuous. *Application deadline (LD program):* Rolling/continuous for fall and rolling/continuous for spring.

Written Policies Written policies regarding course substitutions, general/basic LD accommodations, and reduced course loads are available on the program Web site. Written policies regarding course substitutions, general/basic LD accommodations, and reduced course loads are outlined in the school's catalog/handbook.

The Pennsylvania State University Altoona College
Health and Wellness Center

3000 Ivyside Park
Altoona, PA 16601-3760
http://www.aa.psu.edu/healthwellness
Contact: Dr. Joy L. Himmel SAC, Director Health and Wellness Center. Phone: 814-949-5540. Fax: 814-949-5731. E-mail: jyh1@psu.edu.

Health and Wellness Center Approximately 150 registered undergraduate students were served during 2002-03. The program or unit includes 2 full-time staff members. LD specialists are provided through the program or unit. Academic advisers, counselors, LD specialists, professional tutors, remediation/learning specialists, skill tutors, and trained peer tutors are provided collaboratively through on-campus or off-campus services.

Orientation The program or unit offers an optional 2-hour orientation for new students before classes begin.

Unique Aids and Services Aids, services, or accommodations include career counseling, digital textbooks, faculty training, personal coach, priority registration, and support groups.

Subject-area Tutoring Tutoring is offered one-on-one and in small groups for most subjects. Tutoring is provided collaboratively through on-campus or off-campus services via computer-based instruction, professional tutors, and trained peer tutors.

Basic Skills Remediation Remediation is offered one-on-one and in small groups for learning strategies, math, reading, study skills, time management, and written language. Remediation is provided collaboratively through on-campus or off-campus services via computer-based instruction, professional tutors, and trained peer tutors.

Enrichment Enrichment programs are available through the program or unit for college survival skills, learning strategies, self-advocacy, study skills, and time management. Programs for career planning, college survival skills, health and nutrition, learning strategies, math, medication management, reading, stress management, study skills, time management, and written composition skills are provided collaboratively through on-campus or off-campus services. Credit is offered for college survival skills and math.

Student Organization EXCELL consists of 20 members.

Application For admittance to the program or unit, students are required to apply to the program directly, provide a psychoeducational report (3 years old or less), and provide documentation of high school services. Upon application, materials documenting need for services should be sent only to the LD program or unit. Upon acceptance, documentation of need for services should be sent only to the LD program or unit. *Application deadline (institutional):* Continuous. *Application deadline (LD program):* Rolling/continuous for fall and rolling/continuous for spring.

Written Policies Written policies regarding course substitutions and general/basic LD accommodations are available on the program Web site.

The Pennsylvania State University University Park Campus
The Office for Disability Services

201 Old Main
State College, PA 16802-1503
http://www.lions.psu.edu/ods/
Contact: Disability Specialist. Phone: 814-863-1807. Fax: 814-863-3217.

The Office for Disability Services Approximately 400 registered undergraduate students were served during 2002-03. The program or unit includes 9 full-time staff members. LD specialists are provided through the program or unit. Academic advisers, counselors, diagnostic specialists, graduate assistants/students, regular education teachers, and trained peer tutors are provided collaboratively through on-campus or off-campus services.

Unique Aids and Services Aids, services, or accommodations include digital textbooks, extended time testing, books on tape, readers, scribes.

Enrichment Enrichment programs are available through the program or unit for self-advocacy. Programs for career planning, college survival skills, health and nutrition, math, oral communication skills, practical computer skills, reading, stress management, study skills, test taking, time management, and written composition skills are provided collaboratively through on-campus or off-campus services. Credit is offered for career planning.

Application For admittance to the program or unit, students are required to apply to the program directly, provide a psychoeducational report, and provide documentation (refer to Penn State University LD guidelines). Upon acceptance, documentation of need for services should be sent to both admissions and the LD program or unit. *Application deadline (institutional):* Continuous. *Application deadline (LD program):* Rolling/continuous for fall and rolling/continuous for spring.

Written Policies Written policies regarding general/basic LD accommodations and substitutions and waivers of admissions requirements are available on the program Web site. Written policy regarding grade forgiveness is outlined in the school's catalog/handbook. Written policies regarding course substitutions and substitutions and waivers of graduation requirements are available through the program or unit directly.

Pfeiffer University

PO Box 960

Misenheimer, NC 28109-0960

http://www.pfeiffer.edu/

Contact: Mr. Jim E. Gulledge, Director of Academic Support Services. Phone: 704-463-1360 Ext. 2620. Fax: 704-463-1363. E-mail: gulledge@pfeiffer.edu.

Approximately 40 registered undergraduate students were served during 2002-03. The program or unit includes 3 full-time staff members and 1 part-time staff member. Remediation/learning specialists and trained peer tutors are provided through the program or unit. Professional tutors are provided collaboratively through on-campus or off-campus services.

Summer Program To help prepare for the demands of college, there is an optional 1 to 4-day summer program prior to entering the school.

Unique Aids and Services Aids, services, or accommodations include faculty training.

Subject-area Tutoring Tutoring is offered one-on-one and in small groups for most subjects. Tutoring is provided through the program or unit via trained peer tutors. Tutoring is also provided collaboratively through on-campus or off-campus services via professional tutors.

Basic Skills Remediation Remediation is offered in class-size groups for learning strategies, math, reading, study skills, and time management. Remediation is provided collaboratively through on-campus or off-campus services.

Enrichment Enrichment programs are available through the program or unit for learning strategies, self-advocacy, time management, vocabulary development, and written composition skills. Programs for career planning, college survival skills, health and nutrition, learning strategies, math, medication management, oral communication skills, practical computer skills, reading, stress management, study skills, test taking, time management, and written composition skills are provided collaboratively through on-campus or off-campus services. Credit is offered for college survival skills, learning strategies, math, oral communication skills, practical computer skills, reading, study skills, test taking, time management, and written composition skills.

Fees *Summer Program* fee is $15 to $150.

Application For admittance to the program or unit, students are required to provide a psychoeducational report (3 years old or less). It is recommended that students provide documentation of high school services. Upon acceptance, documentation of need for services should be sent only to the LD program or unit. *Application deadline (institutional):* Continuous. *Application deadline (LD program):* Rolling/continuous for fall and rolling/continuous for spring.

Written Policies Written policy regarding general/basic LD accommodations is available on the program Web site. Written policy regarding general/basic LD accommodations is outlined in the school's catalog/handbook.

Philadelphia Biblical University

200 Manor Avenue

Langhorne, PA 19047-2990

http://www.pbu.edu/

Contact: Mrs. Jean Minto. Phone: 215-702-4270. E-mail: jminto@pbu.edu.

Approximately 25 registered undergraduate students were served during 2002-03. The program or unit includes 1 part-time staff member. Regular education teachers and other are provided collaboratively through on-campus or off-campus services.

Subject-area Tutoring Tutoring is offered one-on-one for most subjects. Tutoring is provided through the program or unit via trained peer tutors and other.

Basic Skills Remediation Remediation is offered in class-size groups for learning strategies, reading, study skills, and written language. Remediation is provided collaboratively through on-campus or off-campus services via regular education teachers.

Application For admittance to the program or unit, students are required to provide report of the professional who diagnosed the disability. It is recommended that students provide documentation of high school services. Upon acceptance, documentation of need for services should be sent only to the LD program or unit. *Application deadline (institutional):* Continuous. *Application deadline (LD program):* Rolling/continuous for fall and rolling/continuous for spring.

Written Policies Written policy regarding general/basic LD accommodations is available on the program Web site. Written policy regarding general/basic LD accommodations is outlined in the school's catalog/handbook. Written policy regarding general/basic LD accommodations is available through the program or unit directly.

Philadelphia University
Disability Services Office

School House Lane and Henry Avenue

Philadelphia, PA 19144-5497

http://www.philau.edu/

Contact: Phone: 215-951-2700. Fax: 215-951-2907.

Disability Services Office Approximately 33 registered undergraduate students were served during 2002-03. The program or unit includes 4 part-time staff members. Academic advisers and graduate assistants/students are provided through the program or unit. Academic advisers, counselors, professional tutors, regular education teachers, remediation/learning specialists, skill tutors, strategy tutors, and trained peer tutors are provided collaboratively through on-campus or off-campus services.

Philadelphia University (continued)

Unique Aids and Services Aids, services, or accommodations include career counseling, digital textbooks, priority registration, extended time on exams, note-takers, tape recorded lectures.

Subject-area Tutoring Tutoring is offered one-on-one and in small groups for most subjects. Tutoring is provided collaboratively through on-campus or off-campus services via graduate assistants/students, professional tutors, and trained peer tutors.

Basic Skills Remediation Remediation is offered one-on-one for computer skills, learning strategies, math, reading, study skills, time management, written language, and science, foreign language, studio courses, ESL, test analysis. Remediation is provided collaboratively through on-campus or off-campus services via professional tutors, regular education teachers, and trained peer tutors.

Enrichment Enrichment programs are available through the program or unit for self-advocacy, stress management, study skills, test taking, and time management. Programs for career planning, college survival skills, health and nutrition, learning strategies, math, medication management, oral communication skills, practical computer skills, reading, self-advocacy, stress management, study skills, test taking, time management, and written composition skills are provided collaboratively through on-campus or off-campus services.

Application For admittance to the program or unit, students are required to apply to the program directly and provide psychoeducational report (3 years old or less) or psychoneurological report. It is recommended that students provide documentation of high school services. Upon application, materials documenting need for services should be sent only to the LD program or unit. Upon acceptance, documentation of need for services should be sent only to the LD program or unit. *Application deadline (institutional):* Continuous. *Application deadline (LD program):* Rolling/continuous for fall and rolling/continuous for spring.

Written Policies Written policy regarding general/basic LD accommodations is outlined in the school's catalog/handbook. Written policy regarding general/basic LD accommodations is available through the program or unit directly.

Piedmont College

PO Box 10

165 Central Avenue

Demorest, GA 30535-0010

http://www.piedmont.edu/

Contact: Debra K. Taylor, Director of Academic Support. Phone: 706-778-3000 Ext. 1359. Fax: 706-776-2811. E-mail: dtaylor@piedmont.edu.

Approximately 45 registered undergraduate students were served during 2002-03. The program or unit includes 1 full-time staff member. Academic advisers, coaches, counselors, graduate assistants/students, skill tutors, strategy tutors, and trained peer tutors are provided collaboratively through on-campus or off-campus services.

Unique Aids and Services Aids, services, or accommodations include priority registration, books on tape.

Subject-area Tutoring Tutoring is offered one-on-one and in small groups for some subjects. Tutoring is provided collaboratively through on-campus or off-campus services via graduate assistants/students and trained peer tutors.

Enrichment Programs for career planning, college survival skills, learning strategies, oral communication skills, practical computer skills, stress management, study skills, test taking, time management, and other are provided collaboratively through on-campus or off-campus services. Credit is offered for oral communication skills and practical computer skills.

Application For admittance to the program or unit, students are required to provide a psychoeducational report (3 years old or less). It is recommended that students provide documentation of high school services. Upon acceptance, documentation of need for services should be sent only to the LD program or unit. *Application deadline (institutional):* Continuous. *Application deadline (LD program):* Rolling/continuous for fall and rolling/continuous for spring.

Written Policies Written policy regarding general/basic LD accommodations is available on the program Web site. Written policy regarding general/basic LD accommodations is outlined in the school's catalog/handbook.

Pine Manor College

400 Heath Street

Chestnut Hill, MA 02467

http://www.pmc.edu/

Contact: Ms. Mary E. Walsh, Director of Brown Learning Resource Center. Phone: 617-731-7181. Fax: 617-731-7638. E-mail: walshmar@pmc.edu.

The program or unit includes 5 part-time staff members. LD specialists, professional tutors, skill tutors, and strategy tutors are provided through the program or unit.

Orientation The program or unit offers an optional 30-minute orientation for new students before registration, before classes begin, during summer prior to enrollment, individually by special arrangement, and during fall orientation.

Unique Aids and Services Aids, services, or accommodations include advocates, career counseling, faculty training, and priority registration.

Subject-area Tutoring Tutoring is offered one-on-one for most subjects. Tutoring is provided through the program or unit via LD specialists and professional tutors.

Basic Skills Remediation Remediation is offered one-on-one for computer skills, learning strategies, math, reading, spelling, study skills, time management, and written language. Remediation is provided through the program or unit via LD specialists and professional tutors.

Enrichment Enrichment programs are available through the program or unit for reading, self-advocacy, stress management, study skills, test taking, time management, vocabulary development, and written composition skills. Programs for career planning, college survival skills, health and nutrition, learning strategies, math, oral communication skills, practical computer skills, stress management, study skills, test taking, time management, and written composition skills are provided collaboratively through on-campus or off-campus services.

Application For admittance to the program or unit, students are required to provide a psychoeducational report. It is recommended that students provide documentation of high school services. Upon application, materials documenting need for services should be sent to both admissions and the LD program or unit. Upon acceptance, documentation of need for services should be sent only to the LD program or unit. *Application deadline (institutional):* Continuous. *Application deadline (LD program):* Rolling/continuous for fall and rolling/continuous for spring.

Written Policies Written policy regarding general/basic LD accommodations is available on the program Web site. Written policy regarding general/basic LD accommodations is outlined in the school's catalog/handbook. Written policies regarding course substitutions, general/basic LD accommodations, reduced course loads, and substitutions and waivers of graduation requirements are available through the program or unit directly.

Pittsburg State University

1701 South Broadway
Pittsburg, KS 66762
http://www.pittstate.edu/
Contact: Phone: 620-231-7000. Fax: 620-235-4080.

The program or unit includes 3 part-time staff members. Graduate assistants/students and LD specialists are provided through the program or unit.

Unique Aids and Services Aids, services, or accommodations include advocates.

Subject-area Tutoring Tutoring is offered one-on-one and in small groups for most subjects. Tutoring is provided through the program or unit via graduate assistants/students.

Enrichment Programs for career planning, college survival skills, and study skills are provided collaboratively through on-campus or off-campus services.

Application For admittance to the program or unit, students are required to provide a psychoeducational report and provide documentation of high school services. Upon acceptance, documentation of need for services should be sent only to the LD program or unit. *Application deadline (institutional):* Continuous.

Written Policies Written policy regarding general/basic LD accommodations is available on the program Web site.

Point Park College
Program for Academic Success

201 Wood Street
Pittsburgh, PA 15222-1984
http://www.ppc.edu/pas
Contact: Ms. Patricia A. Boykin, Director of Program for Academic Success. Phone: 412-392-4738. Fax: 412-392-3884. E-mail: pboykin@ppc.edu.

Program for Academic Success Approximately 5 registered undergraduate students were served during 2002-03. The program or unit includes 1 full-time staff member. Academic advisers, counselors, professional tutors, remediation/learning specialists, skill tutors, and trained peer tutors are provided collaboratively through on-campus or off-campus services.

Subject-area Tutoring Tutoring is offered one-on-one for some subjects. Tutoring is provided collaboratively through on-campus or off-campus services via professional tutors and trained peer tutors.
Diagnostic Testing Testing for math and written language is provided collaboratively through on-campus or off-campus services.
Basic Skills Remediation Remediation is offered one-on-one for learning strategies, math, study skills, time management, and written language. Remediation is provided collaboratively through on-campus or off-campus services via professional tutors and trained peer tutors.
Enrichment Enrichment programs are available through the program or unit for college survival skills, learning strategies, study skills, test taking, and time management. Programs for career planning, college survival skills, health and nutrition, learning strategies, math, stress management, study skills, test taking, time management, and written composition skills are provided collaboratively through on-campus or off-campus services. Credit is offered for career planning and college survival skills.
Application For admittance to the program or unit, students are required to apply to the program directly, provide a psychoeducational report (3 years old or less), and provide comprehensive testing, diagnostic statement and evidence, narrative report, accommodations rationale. It is recommended that students provide documentation of high school services. Upon acceptance, documentation of need for services should be sent only to the LD program or unit. *Application deadline (institutional):* Continuous. *Application deadline (LD program):* Rolling/continuous for fall and rolling/continuous for spring.
Written Policies Written policy regarding general/basic LD accommodations is available on the program Web site. Written policy regarding general/basic LD accommodations is outlined in the school's catalog/handbook. Written policy regarding general/basic LD accommodations is available through the program or unit directly.

Pratt Institute

200 Willoughby Avenue
Brooklyn, NY 11205-3899
http://www.pratt.edu/
Contact: Ms. Mai Linda McDonald, Coordinator of Disability Services Program. Phone: 718-636-3711. Fax: 718-636-3785. E-mail: mcdonald@pratt.edu.

Approximately 56 registered undergraduate students were served during 2002-03. The program or unit includes 1 full-time and 1 part-time staff member. Skill tutors, teacher trainees, and other are provided through the program or unit.
Unique Aids and Services Aids, services, or accommodations include advocates, career counseling, support groups, weekly meetings with faculty, time management assistance, tutoring in subjects such as art history and English.
Subject-area Tutoring Tutoring is offered one-on-one and in small groups for some subjects. Tutoring is provided through the program or unit via other. Tutoring is also provided collaboratively through on-campus or off-campus services via other.
Application For admittance to the program or unit, students are required to provide complete documentation as prescribed by AHEAD. It is recommended that students provide documentation of high school services. Upon acceptance, documentation of need for

Pratt Institute (continued)

services should be sent only to the LD program or unit. *Application deadline (institutional): 2/1. Application deadline (LD program):* Rolling/continuous for fall and rolling/continuous for spring.

Written Policies Written policy regarding general/basic LD accommodations is available on the program Web site. Written policy regarding general/basic LD accommodations is available through the program or unit directly.

Presbyterian College
Disabilities Services

503 South Broad Street

Clinton, SC 29325

http://www.presby.edu/

Contact: Ms. Cheryl R. Bryson, Administrative Assistant, Academic Affairs. Phone: 864-833-8234. Fax: 864-833-8481. E-mail: cbryson@presby.edu. Head of LD Program: Dr. J. David Gillespie, Vice President for Academic Affairs and ADA/504 Coordinator. Phone: 864-833-8233. Fax: 864-833-8481. E-mail: dgillesp@presby.edu.

Disabilities Services Approximately 65 registered undergraduate students were served during 2002-03. The program or unit includes 3 part-time staff members. LD specialists are provided through the program or unit. Academic advisers, coaches, counselors, professional tutors, regular education teachers, skill tutors, and other are provided collaboratively through on-campus or off-campus services.

Unique Aids and Services Aids, services, or accommodations include advocates, career counseling, faculty training, and parent workshops.

Subject-area Tutoring Tutoring is offered one-on-one, in small groups, and in class-size groups for most subjects. Tutoring is provided collaboratively through on-campus or off-campus services via graduate assistants/students, professional tutors, and other.

Basic Skills Remediation Remediation is available for computer skills, learning strategies, study skills, time management, and written language. Remediation is provided collaboratively through on-campus or off-campus services via graduate assistants/students, LD specialists, professional tutors, and other.

Enrichment Programs for career planning, college survival skills, learning strategies, oral communication skills, practical computer skills, stress management, study skills, time management, and written composition skills are provided collaboratively through on-campus or off-campus services. Credit is offered for career planning, college survival skills, oral communication skills, practical computer skills, study skills, and written composition skills.

Application For admittance to the program or unit, students are required to apply to the program directly and provide a psychoeducational report (3 years old or less). It is recommended that students provide documentation of high school services. Upon acceptance, documentation of need for services should be sent only to the LD program or unit. *Application deadline (institutional): 4/1. Application deadline (LD program):* Rolling/continuous for fall and rolling/continuous for spring.

Written Policies Written policy regarding general/basic LD accommodations is outlined in the school's catalog/handbook. Written policy regarding general/basic LD accommodations is available through the program or unit directly.

Prescott College

220 Grove Avenue

Prescott, AZ 86301-2990

http://www.prescott.edu/

Contact: Patricia Quinn-Kane, Learning Specialist. Phone: 928-778-2090 Ext. 1009. Fax: 928-776-5137. E-mail: pquinn-kane@prescott.edu.

The program or unit includes 1 part-time staff member. Academic advisers, LD specialists, regular education teachers, and trained peer tutors are provided collaboratively through on-campus or off-campus services.

Orientation The program or unit offers an optional 30-minute to 1-hour orientation for new students individually by special arrangement.

Unique Aids and Services Aids, services, or accommodations include career counseling and personal coach.

Subject-area Tutoring Tutoring is offered one-on-one for all subjects. Tutoring is provided collaboratively through on-campus or off-campus services via graduate assistants/students, LD specialists, and trained peer tutors.

Basic Skills Remediation Remediation is offered one-on-one for learning strategies, math, reading, social skills, study skills, written language, and self-advocacy skills. Remediation is provided through the program or unit via LD specialists and trained peer tutors.

Enrichment Enrichment programs are available through the program or unit for learning strategies, self-advocacy, stress management, study skills, time management, and written composition skills. Program for career planning is provided collaboratively through on-campus or off-campus services.

Application For admittance to the program or unit, students are required to provide a psychoeducational report. It is recommended that students provide documentation of high school services. Upon application, materials documenting need for services should be sent to both admissions and the LD program or unit. Upon acceptance, documentation of need for services should be sent only to the LD program or unit. *Application deadline (institutional): 2/1. Application deadline (LD program):* Rolling/continuous for fall and rolling/continuous for spring.

Written Policies Written policy regarding general/basic LD accommodations is available on the program Web site. Written policy regarding general/basic LD accommodations is outlined in the school's catalog/handbook.

Providence College
Office of Academic Services (OAS)

River Avenue and Eaton Street

Providence, RI 02918

http://www.providence.edu/academicservices

Contact: Ms. Rose A. Boyle, Disability Support Services Coordinator. Phone: 401-865-1121. Fax: 401-865-1219. E-mail: rboyle@providence.edu.

Office of Academic Services (OAS) Approximately 200 registered undergraduate students were served during 2002-03. The program or unit includes 1 full-time and 1 part-time staff member. Academic advisers are provided through the program or unit.

Unique Aids and Services Aids, services, or accommodations include digital textbooks and priority registration.

Subject-area Tutoring Tutoring is offered one-on-one and in small groups for most subjects. Tutoring is provided collaboratively through on-campus or off-campus services via trained peer tutors.

Application For admittance to the program or unit, students are required to provide a psychoeducational report (4 years old or less) and provide neuro/psychoeducational report. Upon acceptance, documentation of need for services should be sent only to the LD program or unit. *Application deadline (institutional): 1/15. Application deadline (LD program):* Rolling/continuous for fall and rolling/continuous for spring.

Purdue University North Central
Student Support Services

1401 South US Highway 421
Westville, IN 46391-9542
http://www.pnc.edu/sa/sss.html
Contact: Jodi James, Disability Services Coordinator. Phone: 219-785-5374. Fax: 219-785-5589. E-mail: jjames@pnc.edu.

Student Support Services Approximately 40 registered undergraduate students were served during 2002-03. The program or unit includes 1 full-time staff member. Counselors and trained peer tutors are provided through the program or unit. Academic advisers, professional tutors, and trained peer tutors are provided collaboratively through on-campus or off-campus services.

Unique Aids and Services Aids, services, or accommodations include career counseling, digital textbooks, and faculty training.

Subject-area Tutoring Tutoring is offered one-on-one and in small groups for most subjects. Tutoring is provided through the program or unit via trained peer tutors. Tutoring is also provided collaboratively through on-campus or off-campus services via trained peer tutors.

Basic Skills Remediation Remediation is offered in class-size groups for computer skills, learning strategies, math, reading, study skills, and time management. Remediation is provided through the program or unit via teacher trainees. Remediation is also provided collaboratively through on-campus or off-campus services via regular education teachers.

Enrichment Enrichment programs are available through the program or unit for career planning, learning strategies, math, reading, self-advocacy, stress management, study skills, test taking, and time management. Programs for career planning, college survival skills, health and nutrition, learning strategies, math, oral communication skills, practical computer skills, reading, stress management, study skills, test taking, vocabulary development, and written composition skills are provided collaboratively through on-campus or off-campus services. Credit is offered for health and nutrition, oral communication skills, practical computer skills, reading, vocabulary development, and written composition skills.

Application For admittance to the program or unit, students are required to provide a psychoeducational report (5 years old or less). It is recommended that students apply to the program directly and provide documentation of high school services. Upon application,

materials documenting need for services should be sent only to the LD program or unit. Upon acceptance, documentation of need for services should be sent only to the LD program or unit. *Application deadline (institutional): 8/6. Application deadline (LD program):* Rolling/continuous for fall and rolling/continuous for spring.

Written Policies Written policies regarding course substitutions, general/basic LD accommodations, reduced course loads, substitutions and waivers of admissions requirements, and substitutions and waivers of graduation requirements are available on the program Web site.

Queens University of Charlotte
Office of Academic Advising

1900 Selwyn Avenue
Charlotte, NC 28274-0002
http://www.queens.edu/
Contact: Mrs. Autumn Hyde Kennedy, Coordinator of Academic Advising. Phone: 704-337-2508. Fax: 704-337-2325. E-mail: kennedya@queens.edu.

Office of Academic Advising Approximately 30 registered undergraduate students were served during 2002-03. The program or unit includes 1 full-time staff member. Academic advisers, counselors, regular education teachers, and trained peer tutors are provided collaboratively through on-campus or off-campus services.

Unique Aids and Services Aids, services, or accommodations include career counseling, digital textbooks, and faculty training.

Subject-area Tutoring Tutoring is offered one-on-one for some subjects. Tutoring is provided collaboratively through on-campus or off-campus services via trained peer tutors.

Application For admittance to the program or unit, students are required to provide a psychoeducational report (3 years old or less). Upon acceptance, documentation of need for services should be sent only to the LD program or unit. *Application deadline (institutional):* Continuous. *Application deadline (LD program):* Rolling/continuous for fall and rolling/continuous for spring.

Randolph-Macon Woman's College
Learning Resources Center and Disability Services

2500 Rivermont Avenue
Lynchburg, VA 24503-1526
http://www.rmwc.edu/academics/resources_lrc.asp
Contact: Mrs. Tina T. Barnes, Director of Learning Resources Center and Disability Services. Phone: 434-947-8132. Fax: 434-947-8999. E-mail: tbarnes@rmwc.edu.

Learning Resources Center and Disability Services Approximately 20 registered undergraduate students were served during

Randolph-Macon Woman's College (continued)

2002-03. The program or unit includes 1 full-time and 1 part-time staff member. LD specialists are provided through the program or unit. Academic advisers, coaches, regular education teachers, skill tutors, strategy tutors, and trained peer tutors are provided collaboratively through on-campus or off-campus services.

Unique Aids and Services Aids, services, or accommodations include advocates, digital textbooks, personal coach, working with the student to determine appropriate outside agencies that can provide services.

Subject-area Tutoring Tutoring is offered one-on-one, in small groups, and in class-size groups for most subjects. Tutoring is provided collaboratively through on-campus or off-campus services via professional tutors and trained peer tutors.

Basic Skills Remediation Remediation is offered one-on-one, in small groups, and in class-size groups for computer skills, learning strategies, study skills, time management, and written language. Remediation is provided collaboratively through on-campus or off-campus services via trained peer tutors.

Enrichment Programs for career planning, learning strategies, practical computer skills, stress management, study skills, test taking, time management, and written composition skills are provided collaboratively through on-campus or off-campus services.

Application For admittance to the program or unit, students are required to apply to the program directly, provide a psychoeducational report (3 years old or less), and provide documentation appropriate to the disability by a credentialed individual. It is recommended that students provide documentation of high school services. Upon application, materials documenting need for services should be sent to both admissions and the LD program or unit. Upon acceptance, documentation of need for services should be sent only to the LD program or unit. *Application deadline (institutional): 3/1. Application deadline (LD program):* Rolling/continuous for fall and rolling/continuous for spring.

Written Policies Written policy regarding general/basic LD accommodations is available on the program Web site. Written policies regarding course substitutions, general/basic LD accommodations, substitutions and waivers of admissions requirements, and substitutions and waivers of graduation requirements are outlined in the school's catalog/handbook. Written policies regarding course substitutions, general/basic LD accommodations, and substitutions and waivers of graduation requirements are available through the program or unit directly.

Redeemer University College

Student Life Department—Services to Students with Disabilities

777 Garner Road East

Ancaster, ON L9K 1J4

Canada

http://www.redeemer.on.ca/

Contact: Phone: 905-648-2131. Fax: 905-648-2134.

Student Life Department—Services to Students with Disabilities Approximately 40 registered undergraduate students were

served during 2002-03. The program or unit includes 1 part-time staff member. Services are provided through the program or unit. Academic advisers, counselors, and diagnostic specialists are provided collaboratively through on-campus or off-campus services.

Unique Aids and Services Aids, services, or accommodations include career counseling, digital textbooks, and support groups.

Subject-area Tutoring Tutoring is offered one-on-one, in small groups, and in class-size groups for all subjects. Tutoring is provided through the program or unit via trained peer tutors and other.

Diagnostic Testing Testing is provided through the program or unit for learning strategies, learning styles, personality, and study skills. Testing for auditory processing, handwriting, intelligence, math, motor skills, neuropsychological, reading, spelling, visual processing, and written language is provided collaboratively through on-campus or off-campus services.

Basic Skills Remediation Remediation is offered one-on-one, in small groups, and in class-size groups for computer skills, learning strategies, math, reading, spelling, study skills, time management, and written language. Remediation is provided through the program or unit via trained peer tutors and other.

Fees *Diagnostic Testing* fee is $1200.

Application For admittance to the program or unit, students are required to provide a psychoeducational report (3 years old or less). It is recommended that students apply to the program directly and provide documentation of high school services. Upon application, materials documenting need for services should be sent only to the LD program or unit. Upon acceptance, documentation of need for services should be sent only to the LD program or unit. *Application deadline (institutional): 5/31. Application deadline (LD program):* Rolling/continuous for fall and rolling/continuous for spring.

Written Policies Written policies regarding course substitutions, general/basic LD accommodations, reduced course loads, and substitutions and waivers of admissions requirements are available through the program or unit directly.

Reformed Bible College

3333 East Beltline, NE

Grand Rapids, MI 49525-9749

http://www.reformed.edu/

Contact: Phone: 616-222-3000. Fax: 616-222-3045.

The program or unit includes 1 part-time staff member. Graduate assistants/students, LD specialists, and trained peer tutors are provided through the program or unit. Diagnostic specialists are provided collaboratively through on-campus or off-campus services.

Orientation The program or unit offers a mandatory orientation for new students individually by special arrangement.

Subject-area Tutoring Tutoring is offered in small groups and in class-size groups for some subjects. Tutoring is provided collaboratively through on-campus or off-campus services via graduate assistants/students and trained peer tutors.

Diagnostic Testing Testing for auditory processing, intelligence, reading, spelling, and visual processing is provided collaboratively through on-campus or off-campus services.

Basic Skills Remediation Remediation is offered one-on-one and in class-size groups for computer skills, learning strategies, reading, spelling, study skills, time management, and written language. Remediation is provided through the program or unit via special education teachers. Remediation is also provided collaboratively through on-campus or off-campus services via regular education teachers.

Enrichment Enrichment programs are available through the program or unit for learning strategies, reading, time management, and written composition skills. Programs for career planning, learning strategies, test taking, time management, and written composition skills are provided collaboratively through on-campus or off-campus services. Credit is offered for career planning, learning strategies, time management, and written composition skills.

Fees *Diagnostic Testing* fee is $100.

Application It is recommended that students apply to the program directly, provide a psychoeducational report (2 years old or less), and provide documentation of high school services. Upon application, materials documenting need for services should be sent only to admissions with institutional application materials. Upon acceptance, documentation of need for services should be sent only to the LD program or unit. *Application deadline (institutional):* Continuous. *Application deadline (LD program):* 7/15 for fall. 11/15 for spring.

Written Policies Written policy regarding reduced course loads is outlined in the school's catalog/handbook. Written policy regarding general/basic LD accommodations is available through the program or unit directly.

Regis College

235 Wellesley Street

Weston, MA 02493

http://www.regiscollege.edu/

Contact: Phone: 781-768-7000. Fax: 781-768-8339.

The program or unit includes 1 part-time staff member. Academic advisers, coaches, counselors, LD specialists, and regular education teachers are provided through the program or unit.

Orientation The program or unit offers an optional orientation for new students individually by special arrangement.

Unique Aids and Services Aids, services, or accommodations include ongoing meetings and counseling with LD Coordinator as needed .

Subject-area Tutoring Tutoring is offered one-on-one for most subjects. Tutoring is provided collaboratively through on-campus or off-campus services via LD specialists and trained peer tutors.

Application *Application deadline (institutional):* Continuous.

Written Policies Written policies regarding course substitutions, general/basic LD accommodations, substitutions and waivers of admissions requirements, and substitutions and waivers of graduation requirements are available on the program Web site. Written policies regarding course substitutions, general/basic LD accommodations, substitutions and waivers of admissions requirements, and substitutions and waivers of graduation requirements are outlined in the school's catalog/handbook. Written policies regarding course substitutions, general/basic LD accommodations, substitutions and waivers of admissions requirements, and substitutions and waivers of graduation requirements are available through the program or unit directly.

Rensselaer Polytechnic Institute
Disabled Student Services

110 8th Street

Troy, NY 12180-3590

http://www.rpi.edu/

Contact: Debra Hamilton, Assistant Dean of Students. Phone: 518-276-2746. Fax: 518-276-4839. E-mail: dss@rpi.edu.

Disabled Student Services Approximately 80 registered undergraduate students were served during 2002-03. The program or unit includes 2 part-time staff members. Counselors are provided through the program or unit. Counselors, LD specialists, remediation/learning specialists, and skill tutors are provided collaboratively through on-campus or off-campus services.

Orientation The program or unit offers an optional 1-hour orientation for new students individually by special arrangement and immediately following regular summer orientation.

Subject-area Tutoring Tutoring is offered one-on-one and in small groups for most subjects. Tutoring is provided collaboratively through on-campus or off-campus services via trained peer tutors.

Basic Skills Remediation Remediation is offered one-on-one and in small groups for learning strategies, reading, study skills, time management, and written language. Remediation is provided collaboratively through on-campus or off-campus services via LD specialists and trained peer tutors.

Application For admittance to the program or unit, students are required to provide a psychoeducational report. It is recommended that students provide documentation of high school services. Upon acceptance, documentation of need for services should be sent only to the LD program or unit. *Application deadline (institutional):* 1/1. *Application deadline (LD program):* Rolling/continuous for fall and rolling/continuous for spring.

Written Policies Written policy regarding general/basic LD accommodations is available on the program Web site. Written policies regarding general/basic LD accommodations and reduced course loads are available through the program or unit directly.

Rhodes College
Office of Student Disability Services

2000 North Parkway

Memphis, TN 38112-1690

http://www.rhodes.edu/disability

Contact: Ms. Melissa Butler, Coordinator of Disability and Career Services. Phone: 901-843-3994. Fax: 901-843-3040. E-mail: mbutler@rhodes.edu.

Office of Student Disability Services Approximately 27 registered undergraduate students were served during 2002-03. The program or unit includes 1 part-time staff member. Counselors are provided through the program or unit. Academic advisers, counselors, and trained peer tutors are provided collaboratively through on-campus or off-campus services.

Rhodes College (continued)

Unique Aids and Services Aids, services, or accommodations include career counseling, academic support services.

Subject-area Tutoring Tutoring is offered in small groups and in class-size groups for some subjects. Tutoring is provided collaboratively through on-campus or off-campus services via trained peer tutors and other.

Basic Skills Remediation Remediation is offered one-on-one and in small groups for study skills and time management. Remediation is provided collaboratively through on-campus or off-campus services.

Enrichment Programs for career planning, college survival skills, health and nutrition, learning strategies, math, medication management, self-advocacy, stress management, study skills, time management, and written composition skills are provided collaboratively through on-campus or off-campus services.

Application For admittance to the program or unit, students are required to apply to the program directly and provide a psychoeducational report (3 years old or less). It is recommended that students provide documentation of high school services. Upon application, materials documenting need for services should be sent only to the LD program or unit. Upon acceptance, documentation of need for services should be sent only to the LD program or unit. *Application deadline (institutional):* 2/1. *Application deadline (LD program):* Rolling/continuous for fall and rolling/continuous for spring.

Written Policies Written policies regarding general/basic LD accommodations and reduced course loads are available on the program Web site. Written policies regarding general/basic LD accommodations and reduced course loads are available through the program or unit directly.

The Richard Stockton College of New Jersey

PO Box 195, Jimmie Leeds Road
Pomona, NJ 08240-0195
http://www.stockton.edu/

Contact: Ms. Frances H. Bottone, Coordinator of Services for Students with Disabilities. Phone: 609-652-4988. Fax: 609-748-5550. E-mail: frances.bottone@stockton.edu.

The program or unit includes 1 full-time and 1 part-time staff member. Academic advisers, counselors, diagnostic specialists, LD specialists, and remediation/learning specialists are provided through the program or unit. Academic advisers, counselors, diagnostic specialists, professional tutors, skill tutors, and trained peer tutors are provided collaboratively through on-campus or off-campus services.

Unique Aids and Services Aids, services, or accommodations include advocates, digital textbooks, faculty training, priority registration, interpreters.

Subject-area Tutoring Tutoring is offered one-on-one for some subjects. Tutoring is provided through the program or unit via LD specialists. Tutoring is also provided collaboratively through on-campus or off-campus services via graduate assistants/students and trained peer tutors.

Basic Skills Remediation Remediation is offered one-on-one for math, study skills, time management, and written language. Remediation is provided through the program or unit via LD specialists. Remediation is also provided collaboratively through on-campus or off-campus services via trained peer tutors.

Enrichment Enrichment programs are available through the program or unit for learning strategies, stress management, study skills, test taking, time management, and written composition skills. Programs for career planning, college survival skills, health and nutrition, learning strategies, math, medication management, stress management, study skills, test taking, time management, and written composition skills are provided collaboratively through on-campus or off-campus services.

Application For admittance to the program or unit, students are required to provide a psychoeducational report (5 years old or less). It is recommended that students provide documentation of high school services. Upon application, materials documenting need for services should be sent only to the LD program or unit. Upon acceptance, documentation of need for services should be sent only to the LD program or unit. *Application deadline (institutional):* 5/1. *Application deadline (LD program):* Rolling/continuous for fall and rolling/continuous for spring.

Written Policies Written policy regarding general/basic LD accommodations is available on the program Web site. Written policy regarding general/basic LD accommodations is outlined in the school's catalog/handbook.

Rider University
Services for Students with Disabilities

2083 Lawrenceville Road
Lawrenceville, NJ 08648-3001
http://www.rider.edu/

Contact: Judy Wendell, Assistant Director of Services for Students with Disabilities. Phone: 609-896-5008. Fax: 609-895-5507. E-mail: jwendell@rider.edu.

Services for Students with Disabilities Approximately 100 registered undergraduate students were served during 2002-03. The program or unit includes 2 full-time staff members and 1 part-time staff member. Graduate assistants/students, LD specialists, professional tutors, remediation/learning specialists, and strategy tutors are provided through the program or unit. Counselors, diagnostic specialists, graduate assistants/students, professional tutors, remediation/learning specialists, strategy tutors, and trained peer tutors are provided collaboratively through on-campus or off-campus services.

Unique Aids and Services Aids, services, or accommodations include career counseling and support groups.

Subject-area Tutoring Tutoring is offered one-on-one, in small groups, and in class-size groups for most subjects. Tutoring is provided collaboratively through on-campus or off-campus services via graduate assistants/students and trained peer tutors.

Diagnostic Testing Testing for intelligence, math, reading, and written language is provided collaboratively through on-campus or off-campus services.

Basic Skills Remediation Remediation is offered in class-size groups for math and reading. Remediation is provided collaboratively through on-campus or off-campus services via regular education teachers.

Enrichment Enrichment programs are available through the program or unit for other.

Fees *Diagnostic Testing* fee is $125.

Application For admittance to the program or unit, students are required to provide a psychoeducational report (3 years old or less). It is recommended that students provide documentation of high school services. Upon application, materials documenting need for services should be sent to both admissions and the LD program or unit. Upon acceptance, documentation of need for services should be sent only to the LD program or unit. *Application deadline (institutional):* Continuous. *Application deadline (LD program):* Rolling/continuous for fall and rolling/continuous for spring.

Written Policies Written policies regarding general/basic LD accommodations, grade forgiveness, and reduced course loads are outlined in the school's catalog/handbook. Written policies regarding course substitutions and general/basic LD accommodations are available through the program or unit directly.

Ringling School of Art and Design
Academic Resource Center

2700 North Tamiami Trail
Sarasota, FL 34234-5895
http://www.arc.rsad.edu
Contact: Ms. Virginia B. DeMers, Director of Academic Resource Center. Phone: 941-359-7627 Ext. 7627. Fax: 941-359-6115. E-mail: vdemers@ringling.edu.

Academic Resource Center Approximately 40 registered undergraduate students were served during 2002-03. The program or unit includes 1 full-time and 1 part-time staff member. Professional tutors, remediation/learning specialists, and trained peer tutors are provided through the program or unit. Academic advisers, counselors, and regular education teachers are provided collaboratively through on-campus or off-campus services.

Subject-area Tutoring Tutoring is offered one-on-one and in small groups for some subjects. Tutoring is provided through the program or unit via LD specialists, professional tutors, and trained peer tutors.

Basic Skills Remediation Remediation is offered in class-size groups for learning strategies, spelling, study skills, time management, and written language. Remediation is provided through the program or unit via professional tutors and regular education teachers.

Enrichment Enrichment programs are available through the program or unit for reading, study skills, test taking, time management, and written composition skills. Programs for college survival skills, learning strategies, and written composition skills are provided collaboratively through on-campus or off-campus services.

Application For admittance to the program or unit, students are required to provide a psychoeducational report (3 years old or less). It is recommended that students provide documentation of high school services. Upon application, materials documenting need for services should be sent only to admissions with institutional application materials. Upon acceptance, documentation of need for services should be sent only to the LD program or unit. *Application deadline (institutional):* Continuous. *Application deadline (LD program):* Rolling/continuous for fall and rolling/continuous for spring.

Written Policies Written policy regarding general/basic LD accommodations is outlined in the school's catalog/handbook. Written policy regarding general/basic LD accommodations is available through the program or unit directly.

Roanoke College
Academic Services/Special Services

221 College Lane
Salem, VA 24153-3794
http://www.roanoke.edu/
Contact: Mr. Greg Wells, Coordinator of Special Services. Phone: 540-375-2248. Fax: 540-375-2092. E-mail: gwells@roanoke.edu.

Academic Services/Special Services Approximately 110 registered undergraduate students were served during 2002-03. The program or unit includes 1 part-time staff member. Regular education teachers, skill tutors, and strategy tutors are provided collaboratively through on-campus or off-campus services.

Subject-area Tutoring Tutoring is offered one-on-one and in small groups for most subjects. Tutoring is provided collaboratively through on-campus or off-campus services via trained peer tutors.

Application For admittance to the program or unit, students are required to provide a psychoeducational report (3 years old or less). It is recommended that students provide documentation of high school services. Upon application, materials documenting need for services should be sent only to the LD program or unit. Upon acceptance, documentation of need for services should be sent only to the LD program or unit. *Application deadline (institutional):* 3/1. *Application deadline (LD program):* Rolling/continuous for fall and rolling/continuous for spring.

Written Policies Written policy regarding general/basic LD accommodations is available through the program or unit directly.

Robert Morris University

6001 University Boulevard
Moon Township, PA 15108-1189
http://www.robert-morris.edu/
Contact: Ms. Cassandra Lee Oden, Director of Center for Student Success. Phone: 412-262-8349. Fax: 412-604-2589. E-mail: oden@rmu.edu.

Approximately 72 registered undergraduate students were served during 2002-03. The program or unit includes 4 full-time staff members. Academic advisers, coaches, counselors, graduate assistants/students, professional tutors, skill tutors, strategy tutors, and trained peer tutors are provided through the program or unit. Academic advisers, coaches, counselors, graduate assistants/students, professional tutors, skill tutors, strategy tutors, and trained peer tutors are provided collaboratively through on-campus or off-campus services.

Orientation The program or unit offers a mandatory orientation for new students individually by special arrangement.

Summer Program To help prepare for the demands of college, there is an optional summer program prior to entering the school.

Robert Morris University (continued)

Unique Aids and Services Aids, services, or accommodations include career counseling, digital textbooks, faculty training, and priority registration.

Subject-area Tutoring Tutoring is offered one-on-one and in small groups for most subjects. Tutoring is provided through the program or unit via computer-based instruction, graduate assistants/students, professional tutors, and trained peer tutors.

Basic Skills Remediation Remediation is offered in class-size groups for math, reading, and written language.

Enrichment Enrichment programs are available through the program or unit for self-advocacy. Programs for career planning, college survival skills, health and nutrition, learning strategies, math, medication management, oral communication skills, practical computer skills, reading, stress management, study skills, test taking, time management, vocabulary development, and written composition skills are provided collaboratively through on-campus or off-campus services.

Application For admittance to the program or unit, students are required to provide a psychoeducational report (3 years old or less). It is recommended that students apply to the program directly and provide documentation of high school services. Upon acceptance, documentation of need for services should be sent to both admissions and the LD program or unit. *Application deadline (institutional):* 7/1. *Application deadline (LD program):* Rolling/continuous for fall.

Written Policies Written policy regarding general/basic LD accommodations is available through the program or unit directly.

Roberts Wesleyan College
Learning Center

2301 Westside Drive
Rochester, NY 14624-1997
http://www.roberts.edu/
Contact: Prof. Bonnie C. Whitney, Learning Center Director. Phone: 585-594-6270. Fax: 585-594-6543. E-mail: whitney_bonnie@roberts.edu.

Learning Center Approximately 50 registered undergraduate students were served during 2002-03. The program or unit includes 2 full-time and 2 part-time staff members. LD specialists, regular education teachers, remediation/learning specialists, strategy tutors, and trained peer tutors are provided through the program or unit.

Unique Aids and Services Aids, services, or accommodations include faculty training.

Subject-area Tutoring Tutoring is offered one-on-one and in small groups for most subjects. Tutoring is provided through the program or unit via graduate assistants/students, LD specialists, and professional tutors. Tutoring is also provided collaboratively through on-campus or off-campus services via graduate assistants/students and trained peer tutors.

Basic Skills Remediation Remediation is offered one-on-one and in small groups for auditory processing, learning strategies, math, reading, spelling, study skills, time management, and written language. Remediation is provided through the program or unit via LD specialists, regular education teachers, and trained peer tutors. Remediation is also provided collaboratively through on-campus or off-campus services via graduate assistants/students and trained peer tutors.

Enrichment Enrichment programs are available through the program or unit for learning strategies, reading, stress management, study skills, test taking, time management, and written composition skills. Programs for career planning, medication management, and written composition skills are provided collaboratively through on-campus or off-campus services.

Application For admittance to the program or unit, students are required to provide a psychoeducational report (3 years old or less), provide documentation of high school services, and provide psychoeducational evaluation or medical information. Upon application, materials documenting need for services should be sent to both admissions and the LD program or unit. Upon acceptance, documentation of need for services should be sent only to the LD program or unit. *Application deadline (institutional):* 2/1. *Application deadline (LD program):* Rolling/continuous for fall and rolling/continuous for spring.

Written Policies Written policies regarding course substitutions, general/basic LD accommodations, and substitutions and waivers of graduation requirements are available on the program Web site. Written policies regarding course substitutions, general/basic LD accommodations, and substitutions and waivers of graduation requirements are outlined in the school's catalog/handbook.

Rochester Institute of Technology

One Lomb Memorial Drive
Rochester, NY 14623-5603
http://www.rit.edu/
Contact: Mrs. Lisa A. Fraser, Chairperson of Learning Support Services. Phone: 585-475-5296. Fax: 585-475-6682. E-mail: lafldc@rit.edu. Head of LD Program: Ms. Pamela A. Lloyd, Coordinator of Disability Services. Phone: 585-475-7804. Fax: 585-475-2215. E-mail: palldc@rit.edu.

Approximately 734 registered undergraduate students were served during 2002-03. The program or unit includes 9 full-time and 13 part-time staff members. Coaches, LD specialists, professional tutors, skill tutors, and strategy tutors are provided through the program or unit. Academic advisers, counselors, diagnostic specialists, graduate assistants/students, professional tutors, regular education teachers, skill tutors, and trained peer tutors are provided collaboratively through on-campus or off-campus services.

Orientation The program or unit offers a mandatory 2-hour orientation for new students before classes begin.

Unique Aids and Services Aids, services, or accommodations include career counseling, digital textbooks, faculty training, priority registration, textbooks on CD.

Subject-area Tutoring Tutoring is offered one-on-one and in small groups for all subjects. Tutoring is provided collaboratively through on-campus or off-campus services via graduate assistants/students, professional tutors, and trained peer tutors.

Diagnostic Testing Testing for handwriting, learning strategies, learning styles, math, personality, reading, social skills, spelling, spoken language, study skills, written language, and other services is provided collaboratively through on-campus or off-campus services.

Enrichment Enrichment programs are available through the program or unit for college survival skills, learning strategies, self-advocacy, stress management, study skills, test taking, and time management. Programs for career planning, college survival skills, health and nutrition, learning strategies, math, medication management, oral communication skills, practical computer skills, reading, stress management, test taking, time management, vocabulary development, and written composition skills are provided collaboratively through on-campus or off-campus services. Credit is offered for career planning.

Fees *LD Program or Service* fee is $440 to $950 (fee varies according to level/tier of service).

Application For admittance to the program or unit, students are required to apply to the program directly and provide a psychoeducational report (3 years old or less). It is recommended that students provide documentation of high school services. Upon acceptance, documentation of need for services should be sent only to the LD program or unit. *Application deadline (institutional):* 3/15. *Application deadline (LD program):* Rolling/continuous for fall and rolling/continuous for spring.

Written Policies Written policy regarding general/basic LD accommodations is available on the program Web site. Written policy regarding general/basic LD accommodations is outlined in the school's catalog/handbook. Written policies regarding general/basic LD accommodations and reduced course loads are available through the program or unit directly.

Rocky Mountain College

1511 Poly Drive
Billings, MT 59102-1796
http://www.rocky.edu/
Contact: Dr. Jane Van Dyk, Director. Phone: 406-657-1128. Fax: 406-259-9751. E-mail: vandykj@rocky.edu.

Approximately 30 registered undergraduate students were served during 2002-03. The program or unit includes 4 full-time staff members. Academic advisers, coaches, counselors, LD specialists, professional tutors, regular education teachers, remediation/learning specialists, skill tutors, strategy tutors, and trained peer tutors are provided through the program or unit.

Unique Aids and Services Aids, services, or accommodations include advocates, career counseling, personal coach, and weekly meetings with faculty.

Subject-area Tutoring Tutoring is offered one-on-one and in small groups for most subjects. Tutoring is provided through the program or unit via LD specialists, professional tutors, and trained peer tutors. Tutoring is also provided collaboratively through on-campus or off-campus services via trained peer tutors.

Basic Skills Remediation Remediation is offered one-on-one, in small groups, and in class-size groups for math, reading, study skills, and written language. Remediation is provided through the program or unit via regular education teachers.

Enrichment Enrichment programs are available through the program or unit for career planning, math, study skills, and written composition skills. Programs for career planning, college survival skills, and health and nutrition are provided collaboratively through on-campus or off-campus services. Credit is offered for college survival skills, health and nutrition, study skills, and written composition skills.

Application For admittance to the program or unit, students are required to apply to the program directly and provide a psychoeducational report (3 years old or less). It is recommended that students provide documentation of high school services. Upon application, materials documenting need for services should be sent only to the LD program or unit. Upon acceptance, documentation of need for services should be sent only to the LD program or unit. *Application deadline (institutional):* Continuous. *Application deadline (LD program):* Rolling/continuous for fall.

Written Policies Written policy regarding general/basic LD accommodations is available on the program Web site. Written policy regarding general/basic LD accommodations is outlined in the school's catalog/handbook. Written policy regarding general/basic LD accommodations is available through the program or unit directly.

Rocky Mountain College of Art & Design

1600 Pierce Street
Lakewood, CO 80214
http://www.rmcad.edu/
Contact: Ms. Kecia Leland, Dean of Students. Phone: 303-753-6046. Fax: 303-759-4970. E-mail: kleland@rmcad.edu.

Approximately 7 registered undergraduate students were served during 2002-03. The program or unit includes 1 full-time staff member. LD specialists are provided through the program or unit. Academic advisers, counselors, regular education teachers, and trained peer tutors are provided collaboratively through on-campus or off-campus services.

Unique Aids and Services Aids, services, or accommodations include faculty training and priority registration.

Subject-area Tutoring Tutoring is offered one-on-one and in small groups for all subjects. Tutoring is provided through the program or unit via trained peer tutors. Tutoring is also provided collaboratively through on-campus or off-campus services via trained peer tutors.

Enrichment Programs for career planning, college survival skills, learning strategies, stress management, study skills, test taking, and time management are provided collaboratively through on-campus or off-campus services.

Application For admittance to the program or unit, students are required to provide a psychoeducational report (3 years old or less) and provide letter from qualified MD or therapist. It is recommended that students provide documentation of high school services. Upon application, materials documenting need for services should be sent only to the LD program or unit. Upon acceptance, documentation of need for services should be sent only to the LD program or unit. *Application deadline (institutional):* Continuous. *Application deadline (LD program):* 9/1 for fall. 1/1 for spring.

Written Policies Written policy regarding general/basic LD accommodations is outlined in the school's catalog/handbook. Written policies regarding course substitutions, grade forgiveness, and reduced course loads are available through the program or unit directly.

Rogers State University

1701 West Will Rogers Boulevard

Rogers State University (continued)
Claremore, OK 74017-3252
http://www.rsu.edu/
Contact: Phone: 918-343-7777. Fax: 918-343-7898.

The program or unit includes 1 full-time staff member. Counselors and graduate assistants/students are provided through the program or unit. Counselors are provided collaboratively through on-campus or off-campus services.

Unique Aids and Services Aids, services, or accommodations include career counseling and digital textbooks.

Subject-area Tutoring Tutoring is offered one-on-one. Tutoring is provided collaboratively through on-campus or off-campus services via computer-based instruction and trained peer tutors.

Basic Skills Remediation Remediation is offered in class-size groups for handwriting, math, and reading. Remediation is provided collaboratively through on-campus or off-campus services via regular education teachers.

Enrichment Enrichment programs are available through the program or unit for career planning, college survival skills, health and nutrition, learning strategies, practical computer skills, self-advocacy, stress management, study skills, test taking, and time management. Programs for career planning, college survival skills, health and nutrition, learning strategies, math, oral communication skills, practical computer skills, reading, self-advocacy, stress management, study skills, test taking, time management, vocabulary development, and written composition skills are provided collaboratively through on-campus or off-campus services.

Application For admittance to the program or unit, students are required to apply to the program directly and provide a psychoeducational report (5 years old or less). It is recommended that students provide documentation of high school services. Upon application, materials documenting need for services should be sent only to the LD program or unit. Upon acceptance, documentation of need for services should be sent only to the LD program or unit. *Application deadline (institutional):* Continuous. *Application deadline (LD program):* Rolling/continuous for fall and rolling/continuous for spring.

Written Policies Written policy regarding general/basic LD accommodations is outlined in the school's catalog/handbook. Written policies regarding general/basic LD accommodations, substitutions and waivers of admissions requirements, and substitutions and waivers of graduation requirements are available through the program or unit directly.

Rollins College

1000 Holt Avenue
Winter Park, FL 32789-4499
http://www.rollins.edu/
Contact: Phone: 407-646-2000. Fax: 407-646-2600.

Academic advisers, graduate assistants/students, LD specialists, and trained peer tutors are provided collaboratively through on-campus or off-campus services.

Unique Aids and Services Aids, services, or accommodations include career counseling and weekly meetings with faculty.

Subject-area Tutoring Tutoring is offered one-on-one and in small groups for all subjects. Tutoring is provided collaboratively through on-campus or off-campus services via graduate assistants/students and trained peer tutors.

Enrichment Programs for career planning, college survival skills, health and nutrition, learning strategies, oral communication skills, practical computer skills, reading, stress management, study skills, test taking, time management, and written composition skills are provided collaboratively through on-campus or off-campus services. Credit is offered for career planning, college survival skills, health and nutrition, learning strategies, oral communication skills, practical computer skills, reading, and written composition skills.

Application For admittance to the program or unit, students are required to provide a psychoeducational report (3 years old or less). It is recommended that students provide documentation of high school services. Upon application, materials documenting need for services should be sent only to the LD program or unit. Upon acceptance, documentation of need for services should be sent only to the LD program or unit. *Application deadline (institutional):* 2/15.

Written Policies Written policies regarding course substitutions, general/basic LD accommodations, and reduced course loads are available on the program Web site.

Rowan University

201 Mullica Hill Road
Glassboro, NJ 08028-1701
http://www.rowan.edu/
Contact: Ms. Melissa J. Cox, Director of Academic Success Programs. Phone: 856-256-4260. Fax: 856-256-4438. E-mail: cox@rowan.edu.

Approximately 140 registered undergraduate students were served during 2002-03. The program or unit includes 3 full-time staff members. LD specialists, remediation/learning specialists, skill tutors, and trained peer tutors are provided through the program or unit.

Orientation The program or unit offers an optional 4-week (approximately 6 hours) orientation for new students after classes begin and during the first week of classes.

Unique Aids and Services Aids, services, or accommodations include career counseling, faculty training, parent workshops, priority registration, support groups, mentoring program.

Subject-area Tutoring Tutoring is offered one-on-one and in small groups for all subjects. Tutoring is provided through the program or unit via computer-based instruction, graduate assistants/students, LD specialists, and trained peer tutors. Tutoring is also provided collaboratively through on-campus or off-campus services via computer-based instruction and trained peer tutors.

Diagnostic Testing Testing is provided through the program or unit for learning strategies, learning styles, math, reading, study skills, and written language.

Basic Skills Remediation Remediation is offered in class-size groups for computer skills, learning strategies, reading, study skills, time management, and written language. Remediation is provided through the program or unit via computer-based instruction, graduate assistants/students, LD specialists, and trained peer tutors. Remediation is also provided collaboratively through on-campus or off-campus services via graduate assistants/students, regular education teachers, and trained peer tutors.

Enrichment Enrichment programs are available through the program or unit for career planning, college survival skills, learning strategies, self-advocacy, stress management, study skills, test taking, and time management. Programs for career planning, college survival skills, health and nutrition, learning strategies, math, practical computer skills, reading, stress management, study skills, test taking, time management, and written composition skills are provided collaboratively through on-campus or off-campus services. Credit is offered for math, practical computer skills, reading, and written composition skills.

Application For admittance to the program or unit, students are required to provide a psychoeducational report (2 years old or less) and provide documentation of disability, and LD testing results. Upon application, materials documenting need for services should be sent only to the LD program or unit. Upon acceptance, documentation of need for services should be sent only to the LD program or unit. *Application deadline (institutional): 3/15. Application deadline (LD program):* Rolling/continuous for fall and rolling/continuous for spring.

Written Policies Written policy regarding general/basic LD accommodations is available on the program Web site. Written policies regarding course substitutions, general/basic LD accommodations, and substitutions and waivers of graduation requirements are available through the program or unit directly.

Royal Roads University

2005 Sooke Road
Victoria, BC V9B 5Y2
Canada
http://www.royalroads.ca/
Contact: Mr. Kerry Wadsworth, Manager of Learner Services. Phone: 250-391-2505. Fax: 250-391-2522. E-mail: kerry.wadsworth@royalroads.ca. Head of LD Program: Ms. Ann Nightingale, Director of Learner Services and Registrar. Phone: 250-391-2552. Fax: 250-391-2522. E-mail: ann.nightingale@royalroads.ca.

Approximately 2 registered undergraduate students were served during 2002-03. Regular education teachers are provided collaboratively through on-campus or off-campus services.

Enrichment Programs for career planning, oral communication skills, practical computer skills, and study skills are provided collaboratively through on-campus or off-campus services.

Application For admittance to the program or unit, students are required to provide a psychoeducational report (5 years old or less). Upon application, materials documenting need for services should be sent only to admissions with institutional application materials. Upon acceptance, documentation of need for services should be sent only to admissions. *Application deadline (LD program):* Rolling/continuous for fall and rolling/continuous for spring.

Written Policies Written policy regarding general/basic LD accommodations is available on the program Web site.

The Sage Colleges
Disabilities Student Services

45 Ferry Street
Troy, NY 12180-4115

http://www.sage.edu
Contact: Ms. Katherine Norman, Coordinator of Disabilities Services. Phone: 518-244-2208. Fax: 518-244-4598. E-mail: normak@sage.edu.

Disabilities Student Services Approximately 33 registered undergraduate students were served during 2002-03. The program or unit includes 1 full-time staff member. Counselors are provided through the program or unit. Academic advisers, coaches, counselors, diagnostic specialists, graduate assistants/students, LD specialists, and trained peer tutors are provided collaboratively through on-campus or off-campus services.

Orientation The program or unit offers an optional orientation for new students individually by special arrangement.

Unique Aids and Services Aids, services, or accommodations include advocates, career counseling, faculty training, and weekly meetings with faculty.

Subject-area Tutoring Tutoring is offered one-on-one for most subjects. Tutoring is provided collaboratively through on-campus or off-campus services via computer-based instruction, graduate assistants/students, LD specialists, and trained peer tutors.

Basic Skills Remediation Remediation is offered one-on-one for computer skills, learning strategies, math, reading, study skills, and time management. Remediation is provided collaboratively through on-campus or off-campus services via computer-based instruction, LD specialists, and trained peer tutors.

Enrichment Programs for career planning, college survival skills, health and nutrition, learning strategies, math, medication management, oral communication skills, practical computer skills, reading, self-advocacy, stress management, study skills, test taking, time management, and written composition skills are provided collaboratively through on-campus or off-campus services.

Application For admittance to the program or unit, students are required to provide a psychoeducational report (3 years old or less). It is recommended that students provide documentation of high school services. Upon acceptance, documentation of need for services should be sent only to the LD program or unit. *Application deadline (LD program):* Rolling/continuous for fall and rolling/continuous for spring.

Written Policies Written policy regarding general/basic LD accommodations is outlined in the school's catalog/handbook. Written policies regarding course substitutions, general/basic LD accommodations, reduced course loads, and substitutions and waivers of graduation requirements are available through the program or unit directly.

Saginaw Valley State University
Disability Services

7400 Bay Road
University Center, MI 48710
http://www.svsu.edu/stuserv/disserv.html
Contact: Cynthia Woiderski, Director. Phone: 989-964-4168. Fax: 989-964-7258. E-mail: clbw@svsu.edu.

Saginaw Valley State University (continued)

Disability Services Approximately 150 registered undergraduate students were served during 2002-03. The program or unit includes 1 full-time staff member. Academic advisers, counselors, and trained peer tutors are provided collaboratively through on-campus or off-campus services.

Subject-area Tutoring Tutoring is offered one-on-one and in small groups for some subjects. Tutoring is provided collaboratively through on-campus or off-campus services via computer-based instruction and trained peer tutors.

Enrichment Program for career planning is provided collaboratively through on-campus or off-campus services.

Student Organization Ablers Club consists of 12 members.

Application For admittance to the program or unit, students are required to provide a psychoeducational report (3 years old or less). It is recommended that students provide documentation of high school services and provide transitional profile. Upon acceptance, documentation of need for services should be sent only to the LD program or unit. *Application deadline (institutional):* Continuous. *Application deadline (LD program):* Rolling/continuous for fall and rolling/continuous for spring.

Written Policies Written policy regarding general/basic LD accommodations is available on the program Web site.

St. Ambrose University
Services for Students with Disabilities

518 West Locust Street

Davenport, IA 52803-2898

http://www.sau.edu/

Contact: Mr. Ryan C. Saddler, Coordinator of Services for Students with Disabilities. Phone: 563-333-6275. Fax: 563-333-6243. E-mail: saddlerryanc@sau.edu.

Services for Students with Disabilities Approximately 100 registered undergraduate students were served during 2002-03. The program or unit includes 3 full-time staff members and 1 part-time staff member. LD specialists, professional tutors, remediation/learning specialists, skill tutors, and strategy tutors are provided through the program or unit. Academic advisers, coaches, counselors, diagnostic specialists, graduate assistants/students, regular education teachers, special education teachers, teacher trainees, trained peer tutors, and other are provided collaboratively through on-campus or off-campus services.

Summer Program To help prepare for the demands of college, there is an optional 4-week summer program prior to entering the school.

Unique Aids and Services Aids, services, or accommodations include advocates, career counseling, and faculty training.

Subject-area Tutoring Tutoring is offered one-on-one and in small groups for all subjects. Tutoring is provided through the program or unit via graduate assistants/students, LD specialists, and professional tutors. Tutoring is also provided collaboratively through on-campus or off-campus services via graduate assistants/students and trained peer tutors.

Basic Skills Remediation Remediation is offered one-on-one for auditory processing, learning strategies, math, reading, study skills, time management, visual processing, and written language.

Remediation is provided through the program or unit via graduate assistants/students, LD specialists, and professional tutors. Remediation is also provided collaboratively through on-campus or off-campus services via regular education teachers and trained peer tutors.

Enrichment Enrichment programs are available through the program or unit for learning strategies, self-advocacy, study skills, test taking, and time management. Programs for career planning, math, reading, stress management, study skills, test taking, time management, vocabulary development, and written composition skills are provided collaboratively through on-campus or off-campus services.

Fees *Summer Program* fee is $2625 to $2626.

Application For admittance to the program or unit, students are required to provide a psychoeducational report (3 years old or less). Upon acceptance, documentation of need for services should be sent to both admissions and the LD program or unit. *Application deadline (institutional):* Continuous. *Application deadline (LD program):* Rolling/continuous for fall and rolling/continuous for spring.

Written Policies Written policies regarding course substitutions, general/basic LD accommodations, reduced course loads, substitutions and waivers of admissions requirements, and substitutions and waivers of graduation requirements are available through the program or unit directly.

St. Andrews Presbyterian College
Disability Services

1700 Dogwood Mile

Laurinburg, NC 28352-5598

http://www.sapc.edu/access/index.html

Contact: Dorothy Wells, Director of Disability Services. Phone: 910-277-5331. Fax: 910-277-5746. E-mail: ods@sapc.edu.

Disability Services Approximately 27 registered undergraduate students were served during 2002-03. The program or unit includes 6 full-time and 12 part-time staff members. Counselors and other are provided through the program or unit. Academic advisers, counselors, regular education teachers, skill tutors, and trained peer tutors are provided collaboratively through on-campus or off-campus services.

Orientation The program or unit offers a mandatory 2-day orientation for new students before new student orientation.

Unique Aids and Services Aids, services, or accommodations include career counseling, digital textbooks, faculty training, parent workshops, adaptive technology.

Subject-area Tutoring Tutoring is offered one-on-one and in small groups for some subjects. Tutoring is provided collaboratively through on-campus or off-campus services via trained peer tutors.

Enrichment Enrichment programs are available through the program or unit for self-advocacy. Programs for career planning, math, practical computer skills, stress management, study skills, time management, and written composition skills are provided collaboratively through on-campus or off-campus services. Credit is offered for practical computer skills.

Application For admittance to the program or unit, students are required to apply to the program directly, provide a psychoeducational report (3 years old or less), and provide questionnaire completed by high school personnel. It is recommended that students provide documentation of high school services. Upon acceptance, documentation of need for services should be sent only to the LD program or unit. *Application deadline (institutional):* Continuous. *Application deadline (LD program):* Rolling/continuous for fall and rolling/continuous for spring.

Written Policies Written policy regarding general/basic LD accommodations is available on the program Web site. Written policies regarding course substitutions, general/basic LD accommodations, and reduced course loads are outlined in the school's catalog/handbook. Written policies regarding course substitutions, general/basic LD accommodations, and reduced course loads are available through the program or unit directly.

St. Bonaventure University
Disability Support Services

Route 417

St. Bonaventure, NY 14778-2284

http://www.sbu.edu/tlc/disability.html

Contact: Mrs. Nancy Ann Matthews, Coordinator of Disability Support Services. Phone: 716-375-2065. Fax: 716-375-2072. E-mail: nmatthew@sbu.edu.

Disability Support Services Approximately 113 registered undergraduate students were served during 2002-03. The program or unit includes 1 full-time and 1 part-time staff member. Graduate assistants/students and LD specialists are provided through the program or unit. Academic advisers, counselors, diagnostic specialists, and trained peer tutors are provided collaboratively through on-campus or off-campus services.

Unique Aids and Services Aids, services, or accommodations include advocates, career counseling, faculty training, personal coach, weekly meetings with faculty, peer mentors.

Subject-area Tutoring Tutoring is offered one-on-one and in small groups for most subjects. Tutoring is provided through the program or unit via LD specialists. Tutoring is also provided collaboratively through on-campus or off-campus services via graduate assistants/students, professional tutors, and trained peer tutors.

Enrichment Enrichment programs are available through the program or unit for learning strategies, self-advocacy, study skills, test taking, and time management. Programs for career planning, college survival skills, math, stress management, and written composition skills are provided collaboratively through on-campus or off-campus services. Credit is offered for college survival skills.

Application For admittance to the program or unit, students are required to provide a psychoeducational report (3 years old or less). It is recommended that students provide documentation of high school services. Upon application, materials documenting need for services should be sent only to the LD program or unit. Upon acceptance, documentation of need for services should be sent only to the LD program or unit. *Application deadline (institutional):* 4/15. *Application deadline (LD program):* Rolling/continuous for fall.

Written Policies Written policy regarding general/basic LD accommodations is outlined in the school's catalog/handbook. Written policies regarding course substitutions, general/basic LD accommodations, reduced course loads, and substitutions and waivers of graduation requirements are available through the program or unit directly.

St. Cloud State University
Student Disability Services

720 4th Avenue South

St. Cloud, MN 56301-4498

http://www.stcloudstate.edu/sds

Contact: Owen Zimpel, Director of Student Disability Services. Phone: 320-255-3117. Fax: 320-654-5100. E-mail: ojzimpel@stcloudstate.edu.

Student Disability Services Approximately 183 registered undergraduate students were served during 2002-03. The program or unit includes 8 full-time staff members. Services are provided through the program or unit. Counselors and graduate assistants/students are provided collaboratively through on-campus or off-campus services.

Orientation The program or unit offers an optional orientation for new students individually by special arrangement.

Unique Aids and Services Aids, services, or accommodations include priority registration and support groups.

Subject-area Tutoring Tutoring is offered one-on-one for some subjects. Tutoring is provided through the program or unit via other.

Enrichment Enrichment programs are available through the program or unit for self-advocacy, test taking, and time management. Programs for career planning, college survival skills, health and nutrition, reading, stress management, study skills, and written composition skills are provided collaboratively through on-campus or off-campus services.

Application For admittance to the program or unit, students are required to apply to the program directly and provide a psychoeducational report (3 years old or less). It is recommended that students provide documentation of high school services. Upon acceptance, documentation of need for services should be sent only to the LD program or unit. *Application deadline (LD program):* Rolling/continuous for fall and rolling/continuous for spring.

Written Policies Written policy regarding general/basic LD accommodations is available on the program Web site. Written policy regarding general/basic LD accommodations is available through the program or unit directly.

St. Edward's University
Student Disability Services (SDS)

3001 South Congress Avenue

Austin, TX 78704-6489

http://www.stedwards.edu/aps/sds.htm

St. Edward's University (continued)

Contact: Phone: 512-448-8400. Fax: 512-448-8492. Head of LD Program: Lorrain Perea, Student Disability Coordinator. Phone: 512-448-8660. E-mail: lorrainp@admin.stedwards.edu.

Student Disability Services (SDS) Approximately 200 registered undergraduate students were served during 2002-03. The program or unit includes 1 full-time and 2 part-time staff members. Academic advisers, counselors, and remediation/learning specialists are provided through the program or unit. Academic advisers, counselors, diagnostic specialists, LD specialists, regular education teachers, skill tutors, and strategy tutors are provided collaboratively through on-campus or off-campus services.

Orientation The program or unit offers a mandatory 1 to 2-hour orientation for new students individually by special arrangement.

Subject-area Tutoring Tutoring is offered one-on-one for most subjects. Tutoring is provided collaboratively through on-campus or off-campus services via computer-based instruction, graduate assistants/students, and trained peer tutors.

Basic Skills Remediation Remediation is offered one-on-one and in class-size groups for auditory processing, computer skills, learning strategies, math, reading, study skills, time management, and written language. Remediation is provided collaboratively through on-campus or off-campus services via professional tutors, regular education teachers, and trained peer tutors.

Enrichment Programs for career planning, college survival skills, health and nutrition, learning strategies, math, oral communication skills, practical computer skills, reading, self-advocacy, stress management, study skills, test taking, time management, and written composition skills are provided collaboratively through on-campus or off-campus services.

Application For admittance to the program or unit, students are required to provide a psychoeducational report (3 years old or less). Upon acceptance, documentation of need for services should be sent only to the LD program or unit. *Application deadline (institutional):* 7/1. *Application deadline (LD program):* Rolling/continuous for fall and rolling/continuous for spring.

Written Policies Written policy regarding general/basic LD accommodations is available on the program Web site. Written policies regarding course substitutions, general/basic LD accommodations, grade forgiveness, reduced course loads, substitutions and waivers of admissions requirements, and substitutions and waivers of graduation requirements are available through the program or unit directly.

St. Francis Xavier University
Program for Students with Disabilities

Box 5000

Antigonish, NS B2G 2W5

Canada

http://www.stfx.ca/campus/stu-serv/counselling/

Contact: Ms. Mary Ellen Clancy, Contact Person for Students with Disabilities. Phone: 902-867-2370. Fax: 902-867-2406. E-mail: mclancy@stfx.ca.

Program for Students with Disabilities Approximately 90 registered undergraduate students were served during 2002-03. The program or unit includes 1 full-time and 2 part-time staff members. Academic advisers, counselors, LD specialists, professional tutors, regular education teachers, strategy tutors, and trained peer tutors are provided through the program or unit. Academic advisers and trained peer tutors are provided collaboratively through on-campus or off-campus services.

Orientation The program or unit offers an optional 3-hour (varies as needed) orientation for new students before registration, before classes begin, during summer prior to enrollment, during registration, after classes begin, and individually by special arrangement.

Unique Aids and Services Aids, services, or accommodations include advocates, career counseling, digital textbooks, faculty training, parent workshops, and personal coach.

Subject-area Tutoring Tutoring is offered one-on-one and in small groups for most subjects. Tutoring is provided through the program or unit via LD specialists, professional tutors, and trained peer tutors. Tutoring is also provided collaboratively through on-campus or off-campus services via trained peer tutors.

Basic Skills Remediation Remediation is offered one-on-one and in small groups for computer skills, learning strategies, math, study skills, time management, and written language. Remediation is provided through the program or unit via computer-based instruction, LD specialists, professional tutors, regular education teachers, and trained peer tutors. Remediation is also provided collaboratively through on-campus or off-campus services via computer-based instruction and trained peer tutors.

Enrichment Enrichment programs are available through the program or unit for career planning, college survival skills, learning strategies, math, medication management, oral communication skills, practical computer skills, self-advocacy, stress management, study skills, test taking, time management, vocabulary development, and written composition skills. Programs for career planning, college survival skills, health and nutrition, learning strategies, math, medication management, practical computer skills, self-advocacy, stress management, study skills, test taking, time management, vocabulary development, and written composition skills are provided collaboratively through on-campus or off-campus services.

Application For admittance to the program or unit, students are required to provide a psychoeducational report. It is recommended that students provide documentation of high school services. Upon application, materials documenting need for services should be sent only to the LD program or unit. Upon acceptance, documentation of need for services should be sent only to the LD program or unit. *Application deadline (institutional):* Continuous. *Application deadline (LD program):* Rolling/continuous for fall and rolling/continuous for spring.

Written Policies Written policy regarding general/basic LD accommodations is available on the program Web site. Written policies regarding general/basic LD accommodations and reduced course loads are available through the program or unit directly.

St. John Fisher College

3690 East Avenue

Rochester, NY 14618-3597

http://www.sjfc.edu/

Contact: Christine L. Hogan, Counselor and Coordinator of Disability Services. Phone: 585-385-8034. Fax: 585-385-8117. E-mail: hogan@sjfc.edu.

Approximately 70 registered undergraduate students were served during 2002-03. The program or unit includes 1 part-time staff member. Academic advisers and trained peer tutors are provided collaboratively through on-campus or off-campus services.
Subject-area Tutoring Tutoring is offered one-on-one and in small groups for most subjects. Tutoring is provided collaboratively through on-campus or off-campus services via graduate assistants/students and other.
Enrichment Programs for career planning, college survival skills, health and nutrition, learning strategies, math, study skills, test taking, time management, and written composition skills are provided collaboratively through on-campus or off-campus services.
Application For admittance to the program or unit, students are required to provide a psychoeducational report and provide documentation of high school services. Upon acceptance, documentation of need for services should be sent only to the LD program or unit. *Application deadline (institutional):* Continuous.
Written Policies Written policies regarding general/basic LD accommodations and reduced course loads are available on the program Web site. Written policies regarding course substitutions, general/basic LD accommodations, reduced course loads, and substitutions and waivers of graduation requirements are available through the program or unit directly.

Saint John's University

PO Box 2000
Collegeville, MN 56321
http://www.csbsju.edu/
Contact: Susan R. Douma, Director of Academic Advising. Phone: 320-363-2248. Fax: 320-363-2714. E-mail: sdouma@csbsju.edu.

The program or unit includes 1 part-time staff member. Academic advisers and other are provided collaboratively through on-campus or off-campus services.
Application For admittance to the program or unit, students are required to provide a psychoeducational report (3 years old or less) and provide other documentation (varies depending on disability). It is recommended that students provide documentation of high school services. *Application deadline (institutional):* Continuous.
Written Policies Written policies regarding course substitutions, general/basic LD accommodations, and substitutions and waivers of admissions requirements are available through the program or unit directly.

St. Joseph's College, Suffolk Campus

155 West Roe Boulevard
Patchogue, NY 11772-2399
http://www.sjcny.edu/

Contact: Dr. Anna Bess Robinson, Director, Office of Counseling and Career Services. Phone: 631-447-3317. Fax: 631-654-1782. E-mail: abrobinson@sjcny.edu.

The program or unit includes 3 part-time staff members. Academic advisers, coaches, counselors, LD specialists, and remediation/learning specialists are provided collaboratively through on-campus or off-campus services.
Unique Aids and Services Aids, services, or accommodations include career counseling and faculty training.
Enrichment Programs for career planning, college survival skills, oral communication skills, and practical computer skills are provided collaboratively through on-campus or off-campus services. Credit is offered for career planning, college survival skills, oral communication skills, and practical computer skills.
Application *Application deadline (institutional):* Continuous.
Written Policies Written policies regarding general/basic LD accommodations, reduced course loads, substitutions and waivers of admissions requirements, and substitutions and waivers of graduation requirements are outlined in the school's catalog/handbook. Written policies regarding general/basic LD accommodations, substitutions and waivers of admissions requirements, and substitutions and waivers of graduation requirements are available through the program or unit directly.

St. Lawrence University

Canton, NY 13617-1455
http://www.stlawu.edu/
Contact: Mr. John Meagher, Director, Office of Accommodative Services. Phone: 315-229-5164. E-mail: jmeagher@stlawu.edu.

Approximately 112 registered undergraduate students were served during 2002-03. The program or unit includes 1 full-time and 1 part-time staff member. Academic advisers, counselors, diagnostic specialists, skill tutors, and trained peer tutors are provided through the program or unit. Academic advisers, coaches, counselors, teacher trainees, and trained peer tutors are provided collaboratively through on-campus or off-campus services.
Subject-area Tutoring Tutoring is offered one-on-one, in small groups, and in class-size groups for most subjects. Tutoring is provided collaboratively through on-campus or off-campus services via graduate assistants/students and trained peer tutors.
Enrichment Programs for career planning, learning strategies, stress management, study skills, test taking, time management, and written composition skills are provided collaboratively through on-campus or off-campus services.
Application For admittance to the program or unit, students are required to provide a psychoeducational report (3 years old or less) and provide documentation of high school services. Upon acceptance, documentation of need for services should be sent only to the LD program or unit. *Application deadline (institutional):* 2/15. *Application deadline (LD program):* Rolling/continuous for fall and rolling/continuous for spring.
Written Policies Written policy regarding general/basic LD accommodations is available on the program Web site. Written policy regarding general/basic LD accommodations is outlined in the school's catalog/handbook. Written policy regarding general/basic LD accommodations is available through the program or unit directly.

Saint Leo University
Office of Disability Services

PO Box 6665

Saint Leo, FL 33574-6665

http://www.saintleo.edu/

Contact: Dr. Karen A. Hahn, Director of Disability Services. Phone: 352-588-5464. Fax: 352-588-8605. E-mail: karen.hahn@saintleo.edu.

Office of Disability Services Approximately 50 registered undergraduate students were served during 2002-03. The program or unit includes 1 full-time staff member. LD specialists are provided through the program or unit. Academic advisers, coaches, counselors, professional tutors, and regular education teachers are provided collaboratively through on-campus or off-campus services.

Unique Aids and Services Aids, services, or accommodations include faculty training, personal coach, and priority registration.

Subject-area Tutoring Tutoring is offered one-on-one and in small groups for most subjects. Tutoring is provided collaboratively through on-campus or off-campus services via professional tutors and trained peer tutors.

Enrichment Enrichment programs are available through the program or unit for learning strategies, self-advocacy, stress management, study skills, test taking, and time management.

Application For admittance to the program or unit, students are required to provide a psychoeducational report (3 years old or less). Upon acceptance, documentation of need for services should be sent only to the LD program or unit. *Application deadline (institutional):* 8/15. *Application deadline (LD program):* Rolling/continuous for fall and rolling/continuous for spring.

Written Policies Written policies regarding course substitutions, general/basic LD accommodations, reduced course loads, substitutions and waivers of admissions requirements, and substitutions and waivers of graduation requirements are available on the program Web site. Written policies regarding course substitutions, general/basic LD accommodations, reduced course loads, substitutions and waivers of admissions requirements, and substitutions and waivers of graduation requirements are available through the program or unit directly.

Saint Luke's College
Learning Resource Center

4426 Wornall Road

Kansas City, MO 64111

http://www.saint-lukes.org/

Contact: Phone: 816-932-2233.

Learning Resource Center Approximately 3 registered undergraduate students were served during 2002-03. Academic advisers and regular education teachers are provided collaboratively through on-campus or off-campus services.

Unique Aids and Services Aids, services, or accommodations include faculty training.

Subject-area Tutoring Tutoring is offered one-on-one for most subjects. Tutoring is provided collaboratively through on-campus or off-campus services via computer-based instruction and other.

Basic Skills Remediation Remediation is offered one-on-one for computer skills, learning strategies, math, motor skills, study skills, time management, and visual processing. Remediation is provided collaboratively through on-campus or off-campus services via computer-based instruction, regular education teachers, and other.

Application It is recommended that students provide a psychoeducational report. Upon acceptance, documentation of need for services should be sent only to the LD program or unit. *Application deadline (LD program):* 12/1 for fall. 3/1 for spring.

Written Policies Written policy regarding general/basic LD accommodations is outlined in the school's catalog/handbook.

Saint Mary's University
Atlantic Centre of Support for Students with Disabilities

Halifax, NS B3H 3C3

Canada

http://www.stmarys.ca/administration/studentservices/atlcentr/atlantic.html

Contact: Ms. Madeleine Lelievre, Counsellor and Coordinator for Students with Learning Disabilities. Phone: 902-420-5837. Fax: 902-496-8122. E-mail: madeleine.lelievre@smu.ca.

Atlantic Centre of Support for Students with Disabilities Approximately 80 registered undergraduate students were served during 2002-03. The program or unit includes 1 full-time and 1 part-time staff member. Academic advisers, coaches, counselors, LD specialists, remediation/learning specialists, skill tutors, and strategy tutors are provided through the program or unit. Academic advisers and trained peer tutors are provided collaboratively through on-campus or off-campus services.

Orientation The program or unit offers an optional half-day orientation for new students before classes begin.

Unique Aids and Services Aids, services, or accommodations include advocates, digital textbooks, faculty training, personal coach, counseling, exam accommodation, assistive technology, volunteer note-takers, campus orientation.

Subject-area Tutoring Tutoring is offered one-on-one for most subjects. Tutoring is provided collaboratively through on-campus or off-campus services via graduate assistants/students and trained peer tutors.

Diagnostic Testing Testing is provided through the program or unit for learning strategies, learning styles, reading, spelling, study skills, and written language.

Basic Skills Remediation Remediation is offered one-on-one for computer skills, learning strategies, reading, study skills, time management, and written language. Remediation is provided through the program or unit via LD specialists.

Enrichment Enrichment programs are available through the program or unit for learning strategies, practical computer skills, self-advocacy, study skills, time management, and written composition skills. Programs for career planning, stress management, study skills, test taking, time management, and written composition skills are provided collaboratively through on-campus or off-campus services.

Application For admittance to the program or unit, students are required to apply to the program directly and provide a psychoeducational report (3 years old or less). It is recommended that students provide documentation of high school services. Upon acceptance, documentation of need for services should be sent only to the LD program or unit. *Application deadline (institutional): 7/1. Application deadline (LD program):* Rolling/continuous for fall and rolling/continuous for spring.

Written Policies Written policy regarding general/basic LD accommodations is available through the program or unit directly.

Saint Mary's University of Minnesota
Academic Skills Center Disability Services

700 Terrace Heights

Winona, MN 55987-1399

http://www.smumn.edu/

Contact: Ms. Bonnie M. Smith, Disability Services Coordinator. Phone: 507-457-1465. Fax: 507-457-1633. E-mail: bsmith@smumn.edu.

Academic Skills Center Disability Services Approximately 50 registered undergraduate students were served during 2002-03. The program or unit includes 2 full-time staff members and 1 part-time staff member. Academic advisers, LD specialists, skill tutors, strategy tutors, and trained peer tutors are provided through the program or unit. Academic advisers, counselors, regular education teachers, skill tutors, strategy tutors, and trained peer tutors are provided collaboratively through on-campus or off-campus services.

Unique Aids and Services Aids, services, or accommodations include advocates, digital textbooks, weekly meetings with faculty, testing accommodations, adaptive technology, note-takers.

Subject-area Tutoring Tutoring is offered one-on-one and in small groups for most subjects. Tutoring is provided through the program or unit via LD specialists and trained peer tutors. Tutoring is also provided collaboratively through on-campus or off-campus services via trained peer tutors.

Basic Skills Remediation Remediation is offered in class-size groups for learning strategies, reading, study skills, time management, and written language. Remediation is provided collaboratively through on-campus or off-campus services via regular education teachers.

Enrichment Programs for career planning and reading are provided collaboratively through on-campus or off-campus services. Credit is offered for career planning and reading.

Application For admittance to the program or unit, students are required to provide a psychoeducational report (3 years old or less). It is recommended that students provide documentation of high school services. Upon acceptance, documentation of need for services should be sent only to the LD program or unit. *Application deadline (institutional): 5/1. Application deadline (LD program):* Rolling/continuous for fall and rolling/continuous for spring.

Written Policies Written policy regarding general/basic LD accommodations is outlined in the school's catalog/handbook.

St. Mary's University of San Antonio

1 Camino Santa Maria

San Antonio, TX 78228-8507

http://www.stmarytx.edu

Contact: Ms. Karen A. Johnson, Dean of Students. Phone: 210-436-3714. Fax: 210-436-3300. E-mail: kjohnson@stmarytx.edu.

Approximately 30 registered undergraduate students were served during 2002-03. The program or unit includes 2 part-time staff members. Graduate assistants/students are provided through the program or unit. Counselors, graduate assistants/students, and trained peer tutors are provided collaboratively through on-campus or off-campus services.

Subject-area Tutoring Tutoring is offered one-on-one and in small groups. Tutoring is provided collaboratively through on-campus or off-campus services via graduate assistants/students and trained peer tutors.

Diagnostic Testing Testing for auditory processing, handwriting, intelligence, learning strategies, learning styles, math, neuropsychological, personality, reading, social skills, spelling, spoken language, study skills, visual processing, and written language is provided collaboratively through on-campus or off-campus services.

Enrichment Programs for career planning, college survival skills, health and nutrition, learning strategies, stress management, study skills, test taking, and time management are provided collaboratively through on-campus or off-campus services.

Application For admittance to the program or unit, students are required to apply to the program directly and provide a psychoeducational report (3 years old or less). Upon application, materials documenting need for services should be sent only to the LD program or unit. Upon acceptance, documentation of need for services should be sent only to the LD program or unit. *Application deadline (institutional):* Continuous. *Application deadline (LD program):* Rolling/continuous for fall and rolling/continuous for spring.

Written Policies Written policy regarding general/basic LD accommodations is available on the program Web site. Written policies regarding course substitutions and general/basic LD accommodations are available through the program or unit directly.

Saint Michael's College
Program for Students with Special Needs

One Winooski Park

Colchester, VT 05439

http://www.smcvt.edu/

Contact: Ms. Antonia Messuri, Liaison for Students with Special Needs. Phone: 802-654-2818. Fax: 802-654-2697. E-mail: amessuri@smcvt.edu.

Program for Students with Special Needs Approximately 150 registered undergraduate students were served during 2002-03.

Saint Michael's College (continued)

The program or unit includes 1 full-time staff member. Academic advisers, counselors, diagnostic specialists, LD specialists, and trained peer tutors are provided collaboratively through on-campus or off-campus services.

Orientation The program or unit offers an optional 1-hour orientation for new students during summer prior to enrollment, during registration, after classes begin, and individually by special arrangement.

Unique Aids and Services Aids, services, or accommodations include career counseling, faculty training, and support groups.

Subject-area Tutoring Tutoring is offered one-on-one and in small groups for most subjects. Tutoring is provided collaboratively through on-campus or off-campus services via trained peer tutors.

Diagnostic Testing Testing for auditory processing, handwriting, intelligence, learning strategies, learning styles, math, motor skills, neuropsychological, personality, reading, social skills, spelling, spoken language, study skills, visual processing, and written language is provided collaboratively through on-campus or off-campus services.

Enrichment Programs for career planning, college survival skills, health and nutrition, learning strategies, math, medication management, practical computer skills, self-advocacy, stress management, study skills, test taking, and time management are provided collaboratively through on-campus or off-campus services.

Fees *Diagnostic Testing* fee is $800.

Application For admittance to the program or unit, students are required to provide a psychoeducational report (3 years old or less). It is recommended that students provide documentation of high school services. Upon application, materials documenting need for services should be sent only to admissions with institutional application materials. Upon acceptance, documentation of need for services should be sent to both admissions and the LD program or unit. *Application deadline (institutional):* 2/1. *Application deadline (LD program):* Rolling/continuous for fall and rolling/continuous for spring.

Written Policies Written policy regarding general/basic LD accommodations is available on the program Web site. Written policies regarding general/basic LD accommodations and substitutions and waivers of admissions requirements are outlined in the school's catalog/handbook. Written policies regarding general/basic LD accommodations, reduced course loads, and substitutions and waivers of admissions requirements are available through the program or unit directly.

St. Norbert College
Academic Support Services

100 Grant Street
De Pere, WI 54115-2099
http://www.snc.edu/

Contact: Ms. Karen Goode-Bartholomew, Director of Academic Support Services. Phone: 920-403-1326. Fax: 920-403-4021. E-mail: karen.goode-bartholomew@snc.edu.

Academic Support Services Approximately 120 registered undergraduate students were served during 2002-03. The program or unit includes 2 full-time staff members. Coaches, remediation/learning specialists, skill tutors, strategy tutors, and trained peer tutors are provided through the program or unit. Academic advisers, counselors, diagnostic specialists, and graduate assistants/students are provided collaboratively through on-campus or off-campus services.

Unique Aids and Services Aids, services, or accommodations include career counseling, personal coach, and priority registration.

Subject-area Tutoring Tutoring is offered one-on-one and in small groups for most subjects. Tutoring is provided through the program or unit via trained peer tutors.

Diagnostic Testing Testing is provided through the program or unit for learning styles, reading, and study skills.

Enrichment Enrichment programs are available through the program or unit for learning strategies, reading, stress management, study skills, test taking, time management, and vocabulary development. Programs for career planning, college survival skills, health and nutrition, learning strategies, math, medication management, reading, study skills, test taking, time management, and vocabulary development are provided collaboratively through on-campus or off-campus services. Credit is offered for college survival skills, math, reading, study skills, test taking, time management, and vocabulary development.

Application For admittance to the program or unit, students are required to provide a psychoeducational report (3 years old or less). Upon application, materials documenting need for services should be sent only to the LD program or unit. Upon acceptance, documentation of need for services should be sent only to the LD program or unit. *Application deadline (institutional):* Continuous. *Application deadline (LD program):* Rolling/continuous for fall and rolling/continuous for spring.

Written Policies Written policies regarding course substitutions, reduced course loads, and substitutions and waivers of graduation requirements are outlined in the school's catalog/handbook. Written policies regarding course substitutions, general/basic LD accommodations, reduced course loads, and substitutions and waivers of graduation requirements are available through the program or unit directly.

St. Olaf College
Student Disability Services

1520 St Olaf Avenue
Northfield, MN 55057-1098
http://www.stolaf.edu/

Contact: Mrs. Kathy Ann Quade, Coordinator of Student Disability Services. Phone: 507-646-3288. Fax: 507-646-3750. E-mail: quadek@stolaf.edu.

Student Disability Services Approximately 20 registered undergraduate students were served during 2002-03. The program or unit includes 1 full-time staff member. Coaches and counselors are provided through the program or unit. Academic advisers, counselors, skill tutors, strategy tutors, and trained peer tutors are provided collaboratively through on-campus or off-campus services.

Unique Aids and Services Aids, services, or accommodations include advocates, career counseling, personal coach, weekly meetings with disability provider.

Subject-area Tutoring Tutoring is offered one-on-one and in small groups for all subjects. Tutoring is provided collaboratively through on-campus or off-campus services via trained peer tutors.

Enrichment Programs for career planning, college survival skills, learning strategies, math, stress management, study skills, test taking, time management, and written composition skills are provided collaboratively through on-campus or off-campus services.

Application For admittance to the program or unit, students are required to provide a psychoeducational report (3 years old or less). It is recommended that students provide documentation of high school services. Upon acceptance, documentation of need for services should be sent only to the LD program or unit. *Application deadline (institutional):* Continuous.

Written Policies Written policies regarding reduced course loads and substitutions and waivers of graduation requirements are available on the program Web site. Written policy regarding substitutions and waivers of graduation requirements is outlined in the school's catalog/handbook. Written policies regarding general/basic LD accommodations and reduced course loads are available through the program or unit directly.

St. Thomas University
Department of Student Affairs

51 Dineen Drive
Fredericton, NB E3B 5G3
Canada
http://www.stu.ca
Contact: Mr. Kelly Arthur Lamrock, Director of Student Affairs. Phone: 506-452-0616. Fax: 506-460-0319. E-mail: lamrock@stu.ca.

Department of Student Affairs Approximately 50 registered undergraduate students were served during 2002-03. The program or unit includes 4 full-time staff members. Academic advisers are provided through the program or unit. Academic advisers, coaches, counselors, and trained peer tutors are provided collaboratively through on-campus or off-campus services.

Orientation The program or unit offers an optional 1-day orientation for new students individually by special arrangement.

Unique Aids and Services Aids, services, or accommodations include advocates, career counseling, faculty training, scribes, recorders.

Subject-area Tutoring Tutoring is offered one-on-one for all subjects. Tutoring is provided through the program or unit via trained peer tutors. Tutoring is also provided collaboratively through on-campus or off-campus services via professional tutors.

Enrichment Programs for career planning, college survival skills, learning strategies, reading, stress management, study skills, test taking, time management, and written composition skills are provided collaboratively through on-campus or off-campus services.

Application Upon application, materials documenting need for services should be sent only to admissions with institutional application materials. Upon acceptance, documentation of need for services should be sent only to the LD program or unit. *Application deadline (institutional):* 7/31. *Application deadline (LD program):* Rolling/continuous for fall and rolling/continuous for spring.

Written Policies Written policies regarding general/basic LD accommodations and substitutions and waivers of admissions requirements are available on the program Web site. Written policies regarding general/basic LD accommodations and substitutions and waivers of admissions requirements are outlined in the school's catalog/handbook.

Saint Vincent College
Academic Affairs

300 Fraser Purchase Road
Latrobe, PA 15650-2690
http://www.stvincent.edu/
Contact: Ms. Jennifer A. Brown, Academic Counselor. Phone: 724-805-2371. Fax: 724-532-5082. E-mail: jennifer.brown@email.stvincent.edu.

Academic Affairs Approximately 9 registered undergraduate students were served during 2002-03. The program or unit includes 1 part-time staff member. Academic advisers and counselors are provided through the program or unit. Coaches, diagnostic specialists, LD specialists, professional tutors, regular education teachers, remediation/learning specialists, and trained peer tutors are provided collaboratively through on-campus or off-campus services.

Unique Aids and Services Aids, services, or accommodations include career counseling, priority registration, and support groups.

Subject-area Tutoring Tutoring is offered one-on-one and in small groups. Tutoring is provided collaboratively through on-campus or off-campus services via trained peer tutors.

Enrichment Programs for career planning, college survival skills, health and nutrition, learning strategies, oral communication skills, self-advocacy, stress management, study skills, test taking, time management, and written composition skills are provided collaboratively through on-campus or off-campus services. Credit is offered for study skills.

Application For admittance to the program or unit, students are required to provide a psychoeducational report (3 years old or less). It is recommended that students provide documentation of high school services. Upon application, materials documenting need for services should be sent only to the LD program or unit. Upon acceptance, documentation of need for services should be sent only to the LD program or unit. *Application deadline (institutional):* 5/1. *Application deadline (LD program):* Rolling/continuous for fall and rolling/continuous for spring.

Written Policies Written policy regarding general/basic LD accommodations is available through the program or unit directly.

Salem International University

223 West Main Street, PO Box 500
Salem, WV 26426-0500
http://www.salemiu.edu/
Contact: Ms. Deborah S. Woods, Disability Services Coordinator. Phone: 304-782-5608. Fax: 304-782-5588. E-mail: woods@salemiu.edu.

Approximately 5 registered undergraduate students were served during 2002-03. The program or unit includes 1 full-time staff member. Academic advisers are provided through the program or unit.

Unique Aids and Services Aids, services, or accommodations include extended test time, quiet test area, test read.

Salem International University (continued)

Subject-area Tutoring Tutoring is offered in small groups for some subjects. Tutoring is provided collaboratively through on-campus or off-campus services via trained peer tutors.

Basic Skills Remediation Remediation is offered one-on-one and in class-size groups for math, social skills, study skills, time management, and English. Remediation is provided through the program or unit. Remediation is also provided collaboratively through on-campus or off-campus services via regular education teachers.

Application For admittance to the program or unit, students are required to apply to the program directly and provide adult level psychoeducational report (3 years old or less). Upon application, materials documenting need for services should be sent only to the LD program or unit. Upon acceptance, documentation of need for services should be sent only to the LD program or unit. *Application deadline (institutional):* Continuous. *Application deadline (LD program):* Rolling/continuous for fall and rolling/continuous for spring.

Written Policies Written policies regarding general/basic LD accommodations and substitutions and waivers of admissions requirements are available through the program or unit directly.

Sam Houston State University
Counseling Center, Counseling Services and Services for Students with Disabilities

Huntsville, TX 77341
http://www.shsu.edu/counsel
Contact: Phone: 936-294-1111.

Counseling Center, Counseling Services and Services for Students with Disabilities Approximately 200 registered undergraduate students were served during 2002-03. The program or unit includes 1 full-time staff member. Counselors are provided through the program or unit. Academic advisers are provided collaboratively through on-campus or off-campus services.

Subject-area Tutoring Tutoring is offered one-on-one, in small groups, and in class-size groups for some subjects. Tutoring is provided collaboratively through on-campus or off-campus services via computer-based instruction, graduate assistants/students, and trained peer tutors.

Enrichment Programs for career planning, college survival skills, health and nutrition, learning strategies, math, medication management, stress management, study skills, test taking, time management, and written composition skills are provided collaboratively through on-campus or off-campus services.

Student Organization Challenged Students consists of 5 members.

Application For admittance to the program or unit, students are required to provide a psychoeducational report. It is recommended that students provide documentation of high school services. Upon acceptance, documentation of need for services should be sent only to the LD program or unit. *Application deadline (institutional):* Continuous.

Written Policies Written policy regarding general/basic LD accommodations is available on the program Web site. Written policy regarding general/basic LD accommodations is outlined in the school's catalog/handbook.

San Diego State University

5500 Campanile Drive
San Diego, CA 92182
http://www.sdsu.edu/
Contact: Margo Behr, Coordinator of Learning Disabilities Program. Phone: 619-594-6473. Fax: 619-594-4315. E-mail: mbehr@mail.sdsu.edu.

Approximately 250 registered undergraduate students were served during 2002-03. The program or unit includes 3 full-time staff members. Counselors, diagnostic specialists, graduate assistants/students, LD specialists, professional tutors, and remediation/learning specialists are provided through the program or unit. Academic advisers, coaches, counselors, diagnostic specialists, and regular education teachers are provided collaboratively through on-campus or off-campus services.

Orientation The program or unit offers a mandatory 1-hour orientation for new students before using accommodations authorized by DSS program.

Unique Aids and Services Aids, services, or accommodations include advocates, career counseling, and priority registration.

Subject-area Tutoring Tutoring is offered one-on-one and in small groups for some subjects. Tutoring is provided through the program or unit via graduate assistants/students, professional tutors, and trained peer tutors. Tutoring is also provided collaboratively through on-campus or off-campus services via graduate assistants/students and trained peer tutors.

Diagnostic Testing Testing is provided through the program or unit for auditory processing, intelligence, math, neuropsychological, spelling, spoken language, visual processing, and written language. Testing for auditory processing and reading is provided collaboratively through on-campus or off-campus services.

Basic Skills Remediation Remediation is offered in class-size groups for learning strategies, math, study skills, time management, and written language. Remediation is provided through the program or unit via regular education teachers and trained peer tutors. Remediation is also provided collaboratively through on-campus or off-campus services via regular education teachers and trained peer tutors.

Enrichment Enrichment programs are available through the program or unit for college survival skills, learning strategies, self-advocacy, study skills, test taking, time management, and written composition skills. Programs for career planning, college survival skills, health and nutrition, math, medication management, practical computer skills, reading, stress management, and written composition skills are provided collaboratively through on-campus or off-campus services. Credit is offered for college survival skills, math, study skills, test taking, time management, and written composition skills.

Application For admittance to the program or unit, students are required to apply to the program directly. It is recommended that students provide a psychoeducational report, provide documentation of high school services, and provide documentation from community college (for transfer students). Upon application, materials documenting need for services should be sent only to the LD program or unit. Upon acceptance, documentation of need for services should be sent only to the LD program or unit. *Application deadline (institutional):* 11/30. *Application deadline (LD program):* 12/1 for fall. 5/1 for spring.

Written Policies Written policies regarding general/basic LD accommodations and substitutions and waivers of graduation requirements are available on the program Web site. Written policies regarding course substitutions, substitutions and waivers of admissions requirements, and substitutions and waivers of graduation requirements are outlined in the school's catalog/handbook. Written policies regarding general/basic LD accommodations and substitutions and waivers of admissions requirements are available through the program or unit directly.

San Francisco State University
Disability Programs and Resource Center

1600 Holloway Avenue
San Francisco, CA 94132-1722
http://www.sfsu.edu/~dprc/

Contact: Zi Hengstler, Learning Specialist. Phone: 415-338-7878. Fax: 415-338-1041. E-mail: zibelle@sfsu.edu.

Disability Programs and Resource Center Approximately 300 registered undergraduate students were served during 2002-03. The program or unit includes 2 part-time staff members. Academic advisers and LD specialists are provided through the program or unit. Academic advisers, professional tutors, and skill tutors are provided collaboratively through on-campus or off-campus services.
Unique Aids and Services Aids, services, or accommodations include priority registration.
Subject-area Tutoring Tutoring is offered in small groups for most subjects. Tutoring is provided collaboratively through on-campus or off-campus services via trained peer tutors.
Enrichment Enrichment programs are available through the program or unit for self-advocacy. Programs for career planning and study skills are provided collaboratively through on-campus or off-campus services.
Application For admittance to the program or unit, students are required to apply to the program directly and provide a psychoeducational report (3 years old or less). It is recommended that students provide documentation of high school services. Upon acceptance, documentation of need for services should be sent only to the LD program or unit. *Application deadline (institutional):* Continuous. *Application deadline (LD program):* Rolling/continuous for fall and rolling/continuous for spring.
Written Policies Written policies regarding course substitutions, general/basic LD accommodations, reduced course loads, substitutions and waivers of admissions requirements, and substitutions and waivers of graduation requirements are available through the program or unit directly.

Santa Clara University
Disabilities Resources

500 El Camino Real
Santa Clara, CA 95053
http://www.scu.edu/advising/

Contact: Ann Ravenscroft, Coordinator of Disabilities Resources. Phone: 408-554-4111. Fax: 408-554-5136. E-mail: eravenscroft@scu.edu.

Disabilities Resources Approximately 77 registered undergraduate students were served during 2002-03. The program or unit includes 1 full-time and 2 part-time staff members. Academic advisers, graduate assistants/students, and LD specialists are provided through the program or unit. Academic advisers, counselors, regular education teachers, skill tutors, strategy tutors, and trained peer tutors are provided collaboratively through on-campus or off-campus services.
Orientation The program or unit offers a mandatory 2-hour orientation for new students before classes begin and individually by special arrangement.
Unique Aids and Services Aids, services, or accommodations include career counseling and priority registration.
Subject-area Tutoring Tutoring is offered one-on-one and in small groups for most subjects. Tutoring is provided collaboratively through on-campus or off-campus services via computer-based instruction, graduate assistants/students, and trained peer tutors.
Application For admittance to the program or unit, students are required to apply to the program directly, provide a psychoeducational report (3 years old or less), and provide documentation from an appropriate professional. It is recommended that students provide documentation of high school services. Upon acceptance, documentation of need for services should be sent only to the LD program or unit. *Application deadline (institutional):* 1/15. *Application deadline (LD program):* Rolling/continuous for fall and rolling/continuous for spring.
Written Policies Written policies regarding course substitutions and general/basic LD accommodations are available on the program Web site. Written policy regarding general/basic LD accommodations is available through the program or unit directly.

Savannah College of Art and Design
Disability Services

342 Bull Street, PO Box 3146
Savannah, GA 31402-3146
http://www.scad.edu/

Contact: Ms. Lita Clary, Coordinator for Disability Resource Services. Phone: 912-525-4665. Fax: 912-525-4955. E-mail: lclary@scad.edu.

Disability Services The program or unit includes 2 full-time staff members. Counselors are provided through the program or unit. Academic advisers are provided collaboratively through on-campus or off-campus services.
Subject-area Tutoring Tutoring is offered one-on-one and in small groups for some subjects. Tutoring is provided collaboratively through on-campus or off-campus services via trained peer tutors and other.
Basic Skills Remediation Remediation is offered one-on-one and in small groups for study skills, time management, and others. Remediation is provided collaboratively through on-campus or off-campus services via trained peer tutors.

Savannah College of Art and Design (continued)

Application Upon acceptance, documentation of need for services should be sent to both admissions and the LD program or unit. *Application deadline (institutional):* Continuous. *Application deadline (LD program):* Rolling/continuous for fall and rolling/continuous for spring.

Written Policies Written policy regarding general/basic LD accommodations is available through the program or unit directly.

School of the Art Institute of Chicago
The Learning Center

37 South Wabash
Chicago, IL 60603-3103
http://www.artic.edu/saic/

Contact: Learning Center. Phone: 312-345-9478. Fax: 312-345-9490.

The Learning Center Approximately 100 registered undergraduate students were served during 2002-03. The program or unit includes 2 full-time staff members. LD specialists and remediation/learning specialists are provided through the program or unit. Academic advisers and counselors are provided collaboratively through on-campus or off-campus services.

Unique Aids and Services Aids, services, or accommodations include advocates, career counseling, priority registration, and weekly meetings with faculty.

Subject-area Tutoring Tutoring is offered one-on-one for most subjects. Tutoring is provided through the program or unit via LD specialists.

Basic Skills Remediation Remediation is offered one-on-one and in class-size groups for learning strategies, reading, study skills, time management, and written language. Remediation is provided through the program or unit via LD specialists. Remediation is also provided collaboratively through on-campus or off-campus services via regular education teachers.

Application For admittance to the program or unit, students are required to provide a psychoeducational report (3 years old or less). Upon application, materials documenting need for services should be sent only to the LD program or unit. Upon acceptance, documentation of need for services should be sent only to the LD program or unit. *Application deadline (institutional):* 8/15. *Application deadline (LD program):* Rolling/continuous for fall and rolling/continuous for spring.

Written Policies Written policy regarding general/basic LD accommodations is outlined in the school's catalog/handbook. Written policy regarding reduced course loads is available through the program or unit directly.

Seattle Pacific University
Disability Support Services

3307 Third Avenue West
Seattle, WA 98119-1997

http://www.spu.edu/students/campus/disabled/html

Contact: Mrs. Sara Wetzel, Program Coordinator for Learning Services. Phone: 206-281-2475. Fax: 206-286-7348. E-mail: sjrobbie@spu.edu.

Disability Support Services Approximately 20 registered undergraduate students were served during 2002-03. The program or unit includes 1 full-time staff member. Remediation/learning specialists are provided collaboratively through on-campus or off-campus services.

Unique Aids and Services Aids, services, or accommodations include books on tape, extra time for exams, note-takers.

Subject-area Tutoring Tutoring is offered one-on-one and in small groups for most subjects. Tutoring is provided collaboratively through on-campus or off-campus services via graduate assistants/students and trained peer tutors.

Basic Skills Remediation Remediation is offered one-on-one and in class-size groups for learning strategies, math, reading, spelling, study skills, time management, and written language. Remediation is provided collaboratively through on-campus or off-campus services via graduate assistants/students and regular education teachers.

Enrichment Enrichment programs are available through the program or unit for reading, self-advocacy, study skills, test taking, and time management. Programs for career planning, college survival skills, health and nutrition, learning strategies, math, medication management, reading, stress management, study skills, test taking, time management, and written composition skills are provided collaboratively through on-campus or off-campus services. Credit is offered for career planning, college survival skills, learning strategies, math, reading, stress management, study skills, test taking, and time management.

Application For admittance to the program or unit, students are required to provide a psychoeducational report. Upon acceptance, documentation of need for services should be sent only to the LD program or unit. *Application deadline (institutional):* 6/1. *Application deadline (LD program):* Rolling/continuous for fall and rolling/continuous for spring.

Written Policies Written policies regarding course substitutions, general/basic LD accommodations, reduced course loads, and substitutions and waivers of graduation requirements are available through the program or unit directly.

Seattle University
Disabilities Services

900 Broadway
Seattle, WA 98122
http://www.seattleu.edu/student/lc

Contact: Mr. Richard Okamoto, Disabilities Specialist. Phone: 206-296-5744. Fax: 206-296-5747. E-mail: okamotr@seattleu.edu. Head of LD Program: Ms. Carol Schneider, Learning Center Director. Phone: 206-296-5741. Fax: 206-296-5747. E-mail: carolsch@seattleu.edu.

Disabilities Services Approximately 90 registered undergraduate students were served during 2002-03. The program or unit includes 2 full-time staff members. Academic advisers, counselors, strategy tutors, and trained peer tutors are provided collaboratively through on-campus or off-campus services.

Subject-area Tutoring Tutoring is offered one-on-one and in small groups for some subjects. Tutoring is provided through the program or unit via trained peer tutors. Tutoring is also provided collaboratively through on-campus or off-campus services via trained peer tutors.

Basic Skills Remediation Remediation is offered one-on-one for learning strategies, study skills, and time management. Remediation is provided collaboratively through on-campus or off-campus services via professional tutors.

Enrichment Programs for career planning, learning strategies, study skills, test taking, and time management are provided collaboratively through on-campus or off-campus services.

Application For admittance to the program or unit, students are required to provide a psychoeducational report. Upon acceptance, documentation of need for services should be sent only to the LD program or unit. *Application deadline (institutional):* 7/1. *Application deadline (LD program):* Rolling/continuous for fall and rolling/continuous for spring.

Written Policies Written policies regarding course substitutions, general/basic LD accommodations, and reduced course loads are available on the program Web site. Written policies regarding course substitutions, general/basic LD accommodations, and reduced course loads are available through the program or unit directly.

Seton Hall University
Disability Support Services

400 South Orange Avenue
South Orange, NJ 07079-2697
http://www.shu.edu/

Contact: Ms. Linda R. Walter, Director. Phone: 973-313-6003. Fax: 973-761-9185. E-mail: walterli@shu.edu.

Disability Support Services Approximately 350 registered undergraduate students were served during 2002-03. The program or unit includes 1 full-time and 1 part-time staff member. Graduate assistants/students, LD specialists, professional tutors, remediation/learning specialists, skill tutors, and strategy tutors are provided through the program or unit. Academic advisers and counselors are provided collaboratively through on-campus or off-campus services.

Summer Program To help prepare for the demands of college, there is an optional summer program prior to entering the school.

Unique Aids and Services Aids, services, or accommodations include career counseling, digital textbooks, faculty training, parent workshops, priority registration, and support groups.

Subject-area Tutoring Tutoring is offered one-on-one and in small groups for most subjects. Tutoring is provided through the program or unit via computer-based instruction, graduate assistants/students, and LD specialists. Tutoring is also provided collaboratively through on-campus or off-campus services via computer-based instruction and trained peer tutors.

Diagnostic Testing Testing for math, reading, and written language is provided collaboratively through on-campus or off-campus services.

Basic Skills Remediation Remediation is offered in small groups and in class-size groups for computer skills, learning strategies, math, social skills, study skills, time management, and written

language. Remediation is provided through the program or unit via special education teachers. Remediation is also provided collaboratively through on-campus or off-campus services via computer-based instruction and regular education teachers.

Enrichment Enrichment programs are available through the program or unit for college survival skills, learning strategies, medication management, oral communication skills, practical computer skills, self-advocacy, stress management, study skills, test taking, time management, and written composition skills. Programs for career planning, college survival skills, health and nutrition, math, medication management, oral communication skills, practical computer skills, reading, stress management, study skills, test taking, time management, and written composition skills are provided collaboratively through on-campus or off-campus services.

Application For admittance to the program or unit, students are required to provide a psychoeducational report (3 years old or less), provide documentation of high school services, and provide a complete evaluation using AHEAD guidelines. Upon application, materials documenting need for services should be sent only to the LD program or unit. Upon acceptance, documentation of need for services should be sent only to the LD program or unit. *Application deadline (institutional):* 3/1.

Written Policies Written policies regarding course substitutions, general/basic LD accommodations, reduced course loads, substitutions and waivers of admissions requirements, and substitutions and waivers of graduation requirements are available on the program Web site. Written policies regarding course substitutions, general/basic LD accommodations, reduced course loads, substitutions and waivers of admissions requirements, and substitutions and waivers of graduation requirements are available through the program or unit directly.

Seton Hill University
Office of Disability Services

Seton Hill Drive
Greensburg, PA 15601
http://www.setonhill.edu/

Contact: Ms. Teresa Ann Bassi, Director of Counseling and Coordinator of Disability Services. Phone: 724-838-4295. Fax: 724-830-4733. E-mail: bassi@setonhill.edu.

Office of Disability Services Approximately 40 registered undergraduate students were served during 2002-03. The program or unit includes 1 part-time staff member. Academic advisers and counselors are provided through the program or unit. Academic advisers, coaches, counselors, regular education teachers, skill tutors, strategy tutors, and trained peer tutors are provided collaboratively through on-campus or off-campus services.

Orientation The program or unit offers an optional 3-day orientation for new students before classes begin and after classes begin.

Summer Program To help prepare for the demands of college, there is an optional 3-day summer program prior to entering the school.

Unique Aids and Services Aids, services, or accommodations include career counseling, digital textbooks, faculty training, personal coach, and support groups.

Seton Hill University (continued)

Subject-area Tutoring Tutoring is offered one-on-one and in small groups for most subjects. Tutoring is provided collaboratively through on-campus or off-campus services via computer-based instruction and trained peer tutors.

Basic Skills Remediation Remediation is offered one-on-one, in small groups, and in class-size groups for handwriting, learning strategies, math, social skills, spelling, study skills, time management, and written language. Remediation is provided collaboratively through on-campus or off-campus services via computer-based instruction, regular education teachers, and teacher trainees.

Enrichment Enrichment programs are available through the program or unit for medication management, self-advocacy, stress management, test taking, and time management. Programs for career planning, college survival skills, learning strategies, math, medication management, oral communication skills, practical computer skills, study skills, test taking, time management, vocabulary development, and written composition skills are provided collaboratively through on-campus or off-campus services. Credit is offered for study skills and time management.

Student Organization There is a student organization consisting of 15 members.

Application For admittance to the program or unit, students are required to provide a diagnostic report with recommendation. It is recommended that students provide a psychoeducational report (3 years old or less) and provide documentation of high school services. Upon application, materials documenting need for services should be sent only to the LD program or unit. Upon acceptance, documentation of need for services should be sent only to the LD program or unit. *Application deadline (institutional): 8/15. Application deadline (LD program):* Rolling/continuous for fall and rolling/continuous for spring.

Written Policies Written policy regarding general/basic LD accommodations is outlined in the school's catalog/handbook. Written policies regarding course substitutions, general/basic LD accommodations, reduced course loads, and substitutions and waivers of admissions requirements are available through the program or unit directly.

Shawnee State University
Office of Disability Services

940 Second Street
Portsmouth, OH 45662-4344
http://www.shawnee.edu/student/ssc/disability.html
Contact: J. Scott Douthat, Coordinator of Disability Services. Phone: 740-351-3276. Fax: 740-351-3107. E-mail: sdouthat@shawnee.edu.

Office of Disability Services Approximately 90 registered undergraduate students were served during 2002-03. The program or unit includes 5 full-time staff members and 1 part-time staff member. Academic advisers, counselors, LD specialists, professional tutors, remediation/learning specialists, skill tutors, special education teachers, strategy tutors, trained peer tutors, and other are provided through the program or unit. Coaches, counselors, diagnostic specialists, regular education teachers, remediation/learning specialists, skill tutors, strategy tutors, teacher trainees, trained peer tutors, and other are provided collaboratively through on-campus or off-campus services.

Unique Aids and Services Aids, services, or accommodations include advocates, career counseling, digital textbooks, faculty training, priority registration, support groups, adaptive equipment and computer technologies.

Subject-area Tutoring Tutoring is offered one-on-one and in small groups for most subjects. Tutoring is provided through the program or unit via computer-based instruction, LD specialists, professional tutors, trained peer tutors, and other. Tutoring is also provided collaboratively through on-campus or off-campus services via computer-based instruction, professional tutors, trained peer tutors, and other.

Diagnostic Testing Testing is provided through the program or unit for learning strategies, learning styles, math, reading, spelling, study skills, and written language. Testing for auditory processing, handwriting, intelligence, motor skills, neuropsychological, personality, social skills, spoken language, and visual processing is provided collaboratively through on-campus or off-campus services.

Basic Skills Remediation Remediation is offered one-on-one and in small groups for computer skills, learning strategies, math, reading, social skills, spelling, study skills, time management, visual processing, and written language. Remediation is provided through the program or unit via computer-based instruction, LD specialists, professional tutors, trained peer tutors, and other. Remediation is also provided collaboratively through on-campus or off-campus services via computer-based instruction, professional tutors, regular education teachers, teacher trainees, trained peer tutors, and other.

Enrichment Enrichment programs are available through the program or unit for career planning, college survival skills, learning strategies, math, practical computer skills, reading, self-advocacy, stress management, study skills, test taking, time management, written composition skills, and other. Programs for career planning, college survival skills, health and nutrition, learning strategies, math, medication management, oral communication skills, practical computer skills, reading, self-advocacy, stress management, study skills, test taking, time management, vocabulary development, written composition skills, and other are provided collaboratively through on-campus or off-campus services. Credit is offered for career planning, college survival skills, health and nutrition, learning strategies, math, oral communication skills, practical computer skills, reading, stress management, study skills, test taking, time management, vocabulary development, written composition skills, and other.

Fees *Diagnostic Testing* fee is applicable.

Application For admittance to the program or unit, students are required to provide a diagnosis from a licensed professional (e.g. MD or clinical psychologist). It is recommended that students provide a psychoeducational report (5 years old or less) and provide documentation of high school services. Upon acceptance, documentation of need for services should be sent only to the LD program or unit. *Application deadline (institutional):* Continuous. *Application deadline (LD program):* Rolling/continuous for fall and rolling/continuous for spring.

Written Policies Written policy regarding general/basic LD accommodations is outlined in the school's catalog/handbook. Written policy regarding general/basic LD accommodations is available through the program or unit directly.

Shenandoah University

1460 University Drive

Winchester, VA 22601-5195

http://www.su.edu/

Contact: Judith Landes, Director of Academic Support Services. Phone: 540-665-4928. Fax: 540-665-5470. E-mail: jlandes@su.edu.

Academic advisers, coaches, counselors, regular education teachers, and trained peer tutors are provided collaboratively through on-campus or off-campus services.

Unique Aids and Services Aids, services, or accommodations include career counseling and priority registration.

Subject-area Tutoring Tutoring is offered one-on-one and in small groups for most subjects. Tutoring is provided collaboratively through on-campus or off-campus services via trained peer tutors.

Enrichment Programs for career planning, college survival skills, math, stress management, study skills, test taking, time management, and written composition skills are provided collaboratively through on-campus or off-campus services. Credit is offered for college survival skills, math, and study skills.

Application For admittance to the program or unit, students are required to provide a psychoeducational report. It is recommended that students provide documentation of high school services. Upon acceptance, documentation of need for services should be sent only to the LD program or unit. *Application deadline (institutional):* Continuous. *Application deadline (LD program):* Rolling/continuous for fall and rolling/continuous for spring.

Written Policies Written policies regarding course substitutions, general/basic LD accommodations, reduced course loads, substitutions and waivers of admissions requirements, and substitutions and waivers of graduation requirements are available on the program Web site. Written policy regarding general/basic LD accommodations is outlined in the school's catalog/handbook. Written policies regarding course substitutions, general/basic LD accommodations, reduced course loads, substitutions and waivers of admissions requirements, and substitutions and waivers of graduation requirements are available through the program or unit directly.

Shippensburg University of Pennsylvania

1871 Old Main Drive

Shippensburg, PA 17257-2299

http://www.ship.edu/

Contact: Paula Madey, Assistant Director of Social Equity and Coordinator of Disabled Student Services. Phone: 717-477-1161. Fax: 717-477-4001. E-mail: pdmade@wharf.ship.edu.

Approximately 288 registered undergraduate students were served during 2002-03. The program or unit includes 3 full-time staff members. LD specialists are provided through the program or unit. Academic advisers, coaches, counselors, graduate assistants/students, LD specialists, professional tutors, remediation/learning specialists, skill tutors, strategy tutors, and trained peer tutors are provided collaboratively through on-campus or off-campus services.

Orientation The program or unit offers a mandatory approximately 30-minute orientation for new students before registration, before classes begin, during summer prior to enrollment, during registration, after classes begin, and individually by special arrangement.

Unique Aids and Services Aids, services, or accommodations include career counseling and priority registration.

Subject-area Tutoring Tutoring is offered one-on-one and in small groups. Tutoring is provided collaboratively through on-campus or off-campus services via graduate assistants/students, LD specialists, professional tutors, trained peer tutors, and other.

Basic Skills Remediation Remediation is offered one-on-one and in small groups for learning strategies, math, reading, social skills, spelling, study skills, time management, visual processing, and written language. Remediation is provided collaboratively through on-campus or off-campus services via graduate assistants/students, LD specialists, professional tutors, trained peer tutors, and other.

Enrichment Programs for career planning, college survival skills, health and nutrition, learning strategies, math, reading, stress management, study skills, test taking, time management, and written composition skills are provided collaboratively through on-campus or off-campus services.

Application For admittance to the program or unit, students are required to apply to the program directly. It is recommended that students provide a psychoeducational report and provide documentation of high school services. Upon acceptance, documentation of need for services should be sent only to the LD program or unit. *Application deadline (institutional):* Continuous. *Application deadline (LD program):* Rolling/continuous for fall and rolling/continuous for spring.

Written Policies Written policies regarding general/basic LD accommodations and substitutions and waivers of admissions requirements are available on the program Web site. Written policies regarding general/basic LD accommodations, substitutions and waivers of admissions requirements, and substitutions and waivers of graduation requirements are outlined in the school's catalog/handbook. Written policies regarding general/basic LD accommodations, substitutions and waivers of admissions requirements, and substitutions and waivers of graduation requirements are available through the program or unit directly.

Siena College
Office of Tutoring and Services for Students with Disabilities

515 Loudon Road

Loudonville, NY 12211-1462

http://www.siena.edu/advising

Contact: Ms. Renee Zullo, Director. Phone: 518-783-4239. Fax: 518-786-5013. E-mail: zullo@siena.edu.

Office of Tutoring and Services for Students with Disabilities Approximately 59 registered undergraduate students were served during 2002-03. The program or unit includes 1 full-time staff member. Graduate assistants/students, LD specialists, and trained peer tutors are provided through the program or unit. Academic advisers and counselors are provided collaboratively through on-campus or off-campus services.

Unique Aids and Services Aids, services, or accommodations include priority registration.

Subject-area Tutoring Tutoring is offered in small groups for some subjects. Tutoring is provided through the program or unit via graduate assistants/students and trained peer tutors.

Siena College (continued)

Enrichment Enrichment programs are available through the program or unit for stress management, study skills, and test taking.

Application For admittance to the program or unit, students are required to provide a psychoeducational report (3 years old or less). It is recommended that students provide documentation of high school services. Upon acceptance, documentation of need for services should be sent only to the LD program or unit. *Application deadline (institutional): 3/1. Application deadline (LD program):* Rolling/continuous for fall and rolling/continuous for spring.

Written Policies Written policy regarding general/basic LD accommodations is available on the program Web site. Written policy regarding general/basic LD accommodations is available through the program or unit directly.

Silver Lake College

2406 South Alverno Road
Manitowoc, WI 54220-9319

http://www.sl.edu/

Contact: Ms. Carol Schevers, Director of Learning Resource Center. Phone: 920-686-6115. Fax: 920-684-7082. E-mail: cschevers@silver.sl.edu.

Approximately 1 registered undergraduate students were served during 2002-03. The program or unit includes 1 full-time staff member. Remediation/learning specialists, skill tutors, and strategy tutors are provided through the program or unit. Academic advisers, diagnostic specialists, and regular education teachers are provided collaboratively through on-campus or off-campus services.

Diagnostic Testing Testing for auditory processing, intelligence, math, reading, visual processing, and written language is provided collaboratively through on-campus or off-campus services.

Basic Skills Remediation Remediation is offered one-on-one and in small groups for learning strategies, reading, study skills, time management, and written language. Remediation is provided collaboratively through on-campus or off-campus services via regular education teachers.

Application *Application deadline (institutional): 8/31.*

Written Policies Written policy regarding general/basic LD accommodations is outlined in the school's catalog/handbook. Written policy regarding general/basic LD accommodations is available through the program or unit directly.

Simmons College
Academic Support Center

300 The Fenway
Boston, MA 02115

http://www.simmons.edu/

Contact: Ms. Margaret U. Suby Sr., Learning Disabilities Specialist. Phone: 617-521-2473. Fax: 617-521-3079. E-mail: suby@simmons.edu.

Academic Support Center Approximately 120 registered undergraduate students were served during 2002-03. The program or unit includes 1 part-time staff member. Diagnostic specialists, remediation/learning specialists, strategy tutors, and trained peer tutors are provided through the program or unit. Diagnostic specialists, LD specialists, remediation/learning specialists, strategy tutors, trained peer tutors, and other are provided collaboratively through on-campus or off-campus services.

Unique Aids and Services Aids, services, or accommodations include advocates, personal coach, support groups, weekly meetings with faculty, extended time for tests, private room for tests and papers, use of a computer to take tests.

Subject-area Tutoring Tutoring is offered one-on-one and in small groups for most subjects. Tutoring is provided through the program or unit via computer-based instruction, graduate assistants/students, LD specialists, professional tutors, and trained peer tutors.

Diagnostic Testing Testing is provided through the program or unit for intelligence, learning strategies, learning styles, math, reading, spelling, study skills, visual processing, and written language. Testing for auditory processing, intelligence, math, neuropsychological, personality, reading, social skills, spelling, spoken language, visual processing, written language, and other services is provided collaboratively through on-campus or off-campus services.

Basic Skills Remediation Remediation is offered one-on-one for learning strategies, reading, study skills, time management, and written language. Remediation is provided through the program or unit via computer-based instruction, LD specialists, professional tutors, and trained peer tutors.

Enrichment Enrichment programs are available through the program or unit for college survival skills, learning strategies, reading, self-advocacy, stress management, study skills, test taking, time management, and written composition skills. Programs for career planning, health and nutrition, math, practical computer skills, self-advocacy, stress management, and written composition skills are provided collaboratively through on-campus or off-campus services.

Fees *Diagnostic Testing* fee is $500 to $850.

Application For admittance to the program or unit, students are required to provide a psychoeducational report (3 years old or less) and provide letters from doctors or therapists treating student, especially for an emotionally-based disability. Upon application, materials documenting need for services should be sent only to the LD program or unit. Upon acceptance, documentation of need for services should be sent only to the LD program or unit. *Application deadline (institutional): 2/2. Application deadline (LD program):* Rolling/continuous for fall and rolling/continuous for spring.

Written Policies Written policies regarding course substitutions, general/basic LD accommodations, substitutions and waivers of admissions requirements, and substitutions and waivers of graduation requirements are outlined in the school's catalog/handbook. Written policy regarding general/basic LD accommodations is available through the program or unit directly.

Simon Fraser University
Centre for Students with Disabilities (CSD)

8888 University Drive
Burnaby, BC V5A 1S6
Canada

http://www.sfu.ca/ccs/csd/

Contact: Mr. Ron Snitz, Learning Specialist. Phone: 604-291-5381. Fax: 604-291-4384. E-mail: rsnitz@sfu.ca.

Centre for Students with Disabilities (CSD) Approximately 50 registered undergraduate students were served during 2002-03. The program or unit includes 4 full-time staff members. Diagnostic specialists, LD specialists, remediation/learning specialists, special education teachers, and trained peer tutors are provided through the program or unit. Academic advisers, coaches, counselors, graduate assistants/students, professional tutors, regular education teachers, skill tutors, strategy tutors, and teacher trainees are provided collaboratively through on-campus or off-campus services.

Unique Aids and Services Aids, services, or accommodations include career counseling, digital textbooks, and priority registration.

Subject-area Tutoring Tutoring is offered one-on-one for most subjects. Tutoring is provided through the program or unit via graduate assistants/students, LD specialists, professional tutors, and trained peer tutors.

Enrichment Programs for career planning, college survival skills, health and nutrition, learning strategies, math, medication management, practical computer skills, reading, self-advocacy, stress management, study skills, test taking, time management, and written composition skills are provided collaboratively through on-campus or off-campus services.

Application For admittance to the program or unit, students are required to apply to the program directly and provide a psychoeducational report. Upon application, materials documenting need for services should be sent only to the LD program or unit. Upon acceptance, documentation of need for services should be sent only to the LD program or unit. *Application deadline (institutional):* 4/30. *Application deadline (LD program):* Rolling/continuous for fall and rolling/continuous for spring.

Written Policies Written policies regarding course substitutions, general/basic LD accommodations, grade forgiveness, reduced course loads, substitutions and waivers of admissions requirements, and substitutions and waivers of graduation requirements are available on the program Web site.

Simpson College
Hawley Academic Resource Center

701 North C Street

Indianola, IA 50125-1297

http://www.simpson.edu/

Contact: Mr. Todd Little, Director of Hawley Academic Resource Center. Phone: 515-961-1524. E-mail: little@simpson.edu.

Hawley Academic Resource Center Approximately 15 registered undergraduate students were served during 2002-03. The program or unit includes 2 full-time staff members. Skill tutors, strategy tutors, and trained peer tutors are provided through the program or unit. Academic advisers, coaches, counselors, regular education teachers, skill tutors, strategy tutors, and trained peer tutors are provided collaboratively through on-campus or off-campus services.

Unique Aids and Services Aids, services, or accommodations include career counseling.

Subject-area Tutoring Tutoring is offered one-on-one and in small groups for most subjects. Tutoring is provided through the program or unit via graduate assistants/students and trained peer tutors. Tutoring is also provided collaboratively through on-campus or off-campus services via graduate assistants/students and trained peer tutors.

Basic Skills Remediation Remediation is offered one-on-one and in small groups for learning strategies, reading, study skills, and time management. Remediation is provided through the program or unit via LD specialists and professional tutors.

Enrichment Programs for career planning, college survival skills, learning strategies, reading, stress management, study skills, test taking, time management, and written composition skills are provided collaboratively through on-campus or off-campus services.

Application For admittance to the program or unit, students are required to provide documentation of high school services. Upon application, materials documenting need for services should be sent only to the LD program or unit. Upon acceptance, documentation of need for services should be sent only to the LD program or unit. *Application deadline (institutional):* 8/15. *Application deadline (LD program):* Rolling/continuous for fall and rolling/continuous for spring.

Written Policies Written policies regarding course substitutions, general/basic LD accommodations, reduced course loads, substitutions and waivers of admissions requirements, and substitutions and waivers of graduation requirements are outlined in the school's catalog/handbook.

Slippery Rock University of Pennsylvania

Slippery Rock, PA 16057

http://www.sru.edu/

Contact: Ms. Linda M. Smith, Director of Office for Students with Disabilities. Phone: 724-738-2203. Fax: 724-738-4399. E-mail: linda.smith@sru.edu.

Approximately 150 registered undergraduate students were served during 2002-03. The program or unit includes 1 full-time staff member.

Unique Aids and Services Aids, services, or accommodations include priority registration.

Subject-area Tutoring Tutoring is offered one-on-one for some subjects. Tutoring is provided collaboratively through on-campus or off-campus services via trained peer tutors.

Basic Skills Remediation Remediation is offered one-on-one for learning strategies, math, study skills, and time management. Remediation is provided collaboratively through on-campus or off-campus services via trained peer tutors.

Enrichment Programs for learning strategies, math, study skills, test taking, and time management are provided collaboratively through on-campus or off-campus services.

Application For admittance to the program or unit, students are required to provide a psychoeducational report (3 years old or less). It is recommended that students apply to the program directly and provide documentation of high school services. Upon acceptance, documentation of need for services should be sent only to the LD program or unit. *Application deadline (LD program):* Rolling/continuous for fall.

Slippery Rock University of Pennsylvania (continued)
Written Policies Written policy regarding general/basic LD accommodations is available on the program Web site.

Sonoma State University
Disabled Student Services

1801 East Cotati Avenue
Rohnert Park, CA 94928-3609
http://www.sonoma.edu/

Contact: Ms. Aurelia Melgar, Support Services Coordinator. Phone: 707-664-2677. Fax: 707-664-3330. E-mail: aurelia.melgar@sonoma.edu. Head of LD Program: Ms. Linda R. Lipps, Managing Director. Phone: 707-664-2677. Fax: 707-664-3330.

Disabled Student Services Approximately 180 registered undergraduate students were served during 2002-03. The program or unit includes 5 full-time staff members. Academic advisers, remediation/learning specialists, skill tutors, and trained peer tutors are provided through the program or unit.
Unique Aids and Services Aids, services, or accommodations include advocates and priority registration.
Subject-area Tutoring Tutoring is offered one-on-one, in small groups, and in class-size groups for some subjects. Tutoring is provided through the program or unit via graduate assistants/students, LD specialists, and trained peer tutors. Tutoring is also provided collaboratively through on-campus or off-campus services via graduate assistants/students, professional tutors, and trained peer tutors.
Basic Skills Remediation Remediation is offered one-on-one, in small groups, and in class-size groups for learning strategies, math, reading, study skills, time management, and written language. Remediation is provided through the program or unit via graduate assistants/students, LD specialists, and trained peer tutors. Remediation is also provided collaboratively through on-campus or off-campus services via graduate assistants/students, LD specialists, and professional tutors.
Enrichment Enrichment programs are available through the program or unit for learning strategies, math, oral communication skills, reading, stress management, study skills, test taking, time management, and written composition skills. Programs for career planning, college survival skills, health and nutrition, learning strategies, math, self-advocacy, stress management, study skills, test taking, and time management are provided collaboratively through on-campus or off-campus services. Credit is offered for career planning, college survival skills, learning strategies, math, stress management, study skills, test taking, and time management.
Student Organization Disabled Students and Friends Club consists of 12 members.
Application For admittance to the program or unit, students are required to apply to the program directly and provide a psychoeducational report (3 years old or less). It is recommended that students provide documentation of high school services. Upon application, materials documenting need for services should be sent only to the LD program or unit. Upon acceptance, documentation of need for services should be sent only to the LD program or unit. *Application deadline (institutional):* 12/31. *Application deadline (LD program):* Rolling/continuous for fall and rolling/continuous for spring.

Written Policies Written policy regarding general/basic LD accommodations is available on the program Web site.

South Dakota State University

PO Box 2201
Brookings, SD 57007
http://www.sdstate.edu/

Contact: Nancy L. Schade, Coordinator of Disability Services. Phone: 605-688-4504. Fax: 605-688-4032. E-mail: nancy_schade@sdstate.edu.

The program or unit includes 1 full-time and 1 part-time staff member. Counselors, graduate assistants/students, regular education teachers, skill tutors, and other are provided collaboratively through on-campus or off-campus services.
Orientation The program or unit offers an optional 1-day orientation for new students before registration.
Unique Aids and Services Aids, services, or accommodations include advocates, digital textbooks, faculty training, priority registration.
Subject-area Tutoring Tutoring is offered for some subjects. Tutoring is provided through the program or unit via graduate assistants/students. Tutoring is also provided collaboratively through on-campus or off-campus services via graduate assistants/students and other.
Enrichment Programs for career planning, college survival skills, health and nutrition, medication management, self-advocacy, stress management, study skills, test taking, time management, written composition skills, and other are provided collaboratively through on-campus or off-campus services.
Student Organization Students Taking Responsibility in Diversifying Education (STRIDE) consists of 12 members.
Application For admittance to the program or unit, students are required to apply to the program directly, provide a psychoeducational report (3 years old or less), and provide documentation of high school services. Upon application, materials documenting need for services should be sent only to the LD program or unit. Upon acceptance, documentation of need for services should be sent only to the LD program or unit. *Application deadline (institutional):* Continuous. *Application deadline (LD program):* Rolling/continuous for fall and rolling/continuous for spring.
Written Policies Written policies regarding course substitutions, grade forgiveness, and reduced course loads are outlined in the school's catalog/handbook. Written policies regarding course substitutions, general/basic LD accommodations, grade forgiveness, reduced course loads, and substitutions and waivers of admissions requirements are available through the program or unit directly.

Southeastern Bible College

3001 Highway 280 East
Birmingham, AL 35243-4181
http://www.sebc.edu/

Contact: Miss Stacy Ann Monk, Equity Coordinator. Phone: 205-970-9208. Fax: 205-970-9207. E-mail: smonk@sebc.edu.

Approximately 3 registered undergraduate students were served during 2002-03. The program or unit includes 1 full-time staff member. Academic advisers and regular education teachers are provided collaboratively through on-campus or off-campus services.
Unique Aids and Services Aids, services, or accommodations include advocates and faculty training.
Subject-area Tutoring Tutoring is offered one-on-one and in class-size groups for most subjects. Tutoring is provided through the program or unit via LD specialists. Tutoring is also provided collaboratively through on-campus or off-campus services via computer-based instruction.
Basic Skills Remediation Remediation is offered one-on-one and in class-size groups for learning strategies, math, reading, study skills, time management, and written language. Remediation is provided through the program or unit via LD specialists. Remediation is also provided collaboratively through on-campus or off-campus services via computer-based instruction and regular education teachers.
Application For admittance to the program or unit, students are required to apply to the program directly and provide a psychoeducational report (3 years old or less). It is recommended that students provide documentation of high school services. Upon application, materials documenting need for services should be sent only to the LD program or unit. Upon acceptance, documentation of need for services should be sent only to the LD program or unit. *Application deadline (institutional):* Continuous. *Application deadline (LD program):* 8/1 for fall. 12/1 for spring.
Written Policies Written policy regarding general/basic LD accommodations is outlined in the school's catalog/handbook. Written policies regarding course substitutions, general/basic LD accommodations, and reduced course loads are available through the program or unit directly.

Southeastern Louisiana University
Office of Disability Services

Hammond, LA 70402

http://www.selu.edu/

Contact: Ms. Sharon Eaton, Director, Office of Disability Services. Phone: 985-549-2247. Fax: 985-549-3482. E-mail: seaton@selu.edu.

Office of Disability Services The program or unit includes 2 full-time staff members. Academic advisers, coaches, counselors, graduate assistants/students, skill tutors, strategy tutors, and trained peer tutors are provided collaboratively through on-campus or off-campus services.
Unique Aids and Services Aids, services, or accommodations include priority registration.
Subject-area Tutoring Tutoring is offered one-on-one for most subjects. Tutoring is provided collaboratively through on-campus or off-campus services via trained peer tutors.

Basic Skills Remediation Remediation is offered in small groups for learning strategies, social skills, study skills, time management, and written language. Remediation is provided collaboratively through on-campus or off-campus services via computer-based instruction, graduate assistants/students, regular education teachers, trained peer tutors, and other.
Application For admittance to the program or unit, students are required to provide a psychoeducational report (3 years old or less). Upon acceptance, documentation of need for services should be sent only to the LD program or unit. *Application deadline (institutional):* 7/15. *Application deadline (LD program):* Rolling/continuous for fall and rolling/continuous for spring.
Written Policies Written policy regarding general/basic LD accommodations is available on the program Web site. Written policies regarding course substitutions and general/basic LD accommodations are available through the program or unit directly.

Southeastern Oklahoma State University

Fifth and University

Durant, OK 74701-0609

http://www.sosu.edu/

Contact: Phone: 580-745-2000. Fax: 580-745-7490.

The program or unit includes 3 part-time staff members. Academic advisers, counselors, LD specialists, and remediation/learning specialists are provided collaboratively through on-campus or off-campus services.
Unique Aids and Services Aids, services, or accommodations include career counseling, tutoring, frequent contact.
Subject-area Tutoring Tutoring is offered in small groups for all subjects. Tutoring is provided collaboratively through on-campus or off-campus services via trained peer tutors.
Basic Skills Remediation Remediation is offered in class-size groups for math, reading, written language, and science. Remediation is provided collaboratively through on-campus or off-campus services via graduate assistants/students.
Enrichment Programs for career planning, learning strategies, stress management, study skills, test taking, and time management are provided collaboratively through on-campus or off-campus services.
Application For admittance to the program or unit, students are required to provide a psychoeducational report and provide appropriate testing/evaluation documentation. Upon acceptance, documentation of need for services should be sent only to the LD program or unit. *Application deadline (institutional):* Continuous. *Application deadline (LD program):* Rolling/continuous for fall and rolling/continuous for spring.
Written Policies Written policies regarding course substitutions, general/basic LD accommodations, substitutions and waivers of admissions requirements, and substitutions and waivers of graduation requirements are available through the program or unit directly.

Southern Adventist University
Center for Learning Success

PO Box 370

Collegedale, TN 37315-0370

http://cls.southern.edu

Contact: Dr. Hollis James, Disabilities Services Coordinator. Phone: 423-238-2577. Fax: 423-238-2575. E-mail: cls@southern.edu.

Center for Learning Success Approximately 60 registered undergraduate students were served during 2002-03. The program or unit includes 3 full-time and 10 part-time staff members. Academic advisers, graduate assistants/students, LD specialists, skill tutors, strategy tutors, teacher trainees, and trained peer tutors are provided through the program or unit. Academic advisers, counselors, diagnostic specialists, and regular education teachers are provided collaboratively through on-campus or off-campus services.

Unique Aids and Services Aids, services, or accommodations include advocates, career counseling, faculty training, priority registration, Brain Gym.

Subject-area Tutoring Tutoring is offered one-on-one and in small groups for most subjects. Tutoring is provided through the program or unit via computer-based instruction, graduate assistants/students, and trained peer tutors.

Basic Skills Remediation Remediation is offered one-on-one and in small groups for computer skills, handwriting, learning strategies, math, reading, social skills, spelling, spoken language, study skills, time management, and written language. Remediation is provided through the program or unit via computer-based instruction, graduate assistants/students, regular education teachers, special education teachers, teacher trainees, and trained peer tutors.

Enrichment Enrichment programs are available through the program or unit for college survival skills, learning strategies, oral communication skills, reading, self-advocacy, study skills, test taking, time management, vocabulary development, written composition skills, and other. Programs for career planning, college survival skills, health and nutrition, medication management, and stress management are provided collaboratively through on-campus or off-campus services.

Application For admittance to the program or unit, students are required to provide a psychoeducational report (3 years old or less) and provide psychoeducational testing and DSM-IV diagnosis (must be done on adult-normed instruments). It is recommended that students provide documentation of high school services. Upon application, materials documenting need for services should be sent only to the LD program or unit. Upon acceptance, documentation of need for services should be sent only to the LD program or unit. *Application deadline (institutional):* Continuous. *Application deadline (LD program):* Rolling/continuous for fall.

Written Policies Written policies regarding course substitutions and general/basic LD accommodations are outlined in the school's catalog/handbook. Written policy regarding general/basic LD accommodations is available through the program or unit directly.

Southern Illinois University Carbondale

Carbondale, IL 62901

http://www.siu.edu/siuc/

Contact: Mr. Roger Pugh, Learning Skills Specialist. Phone: 618-453-2369 Ext. 10. Fax: 618-453-3711. E-mail: rpugh@siu.edu. Head of LD Program: Mrs. Sally Dedecker, Coordinator. Phone: 618-453-6131 Ext. 41. Fax: 618-453-3711. E-mail: lukidawg@siu.edu.

Approximately 150 registered undergraduate students were served during 2002-03. The program or unit includes 6 full-time staff members. Diagnostic specialists, graduate assistants/students, LD specialists, professional tutors, remediation/learning specialists, skill tutors, special education teachers, strategy tutors, teacher trainees, and trained peer tutors are provided through the program or unit. Academic advisers, coaches, counselors, diagnostic specialists, and regular education teachers are provided collaboratively through on-campus or off-campus services.

Orientation The program or unit offers an optional 4-day orientation for new students before classes begin.

Summer Program To help prepare for the demands of college, there is an optional 4-day summer program prior to entering the school.

Unique Aids and Services Aids, services, or accommodations include advocates, career counseling, faculty training, and support groups.

Subject-area Tutoring Tutoring is offered one-on-one and in small groups for all subjects. Tutoring is provided through the program or unit via computer-based instruction, graduate assistants/students, LD specialists, professional tutors, and trained peer tutors.

Diagnostic Testing Testing is provided through the program or unit for auditory processing, handwriting, intelligence, learning strategies, learning styles, math, motor skills, reading, spelling, spoken language, visual processing, written language, and other services. Testing for auditory processing, neuropsychological, personality, spelling, visual processing, and written language is provided collaboratively through on-campus or off-campus services.

Basic Skills Remediation Remediation is offered one-on-one for computer skills, learning strategies, math, reading, spelling, spoken language, study skills, time management, written language, and organization and test-taking strategies. Remediation is provided through the program or unit via computer-based instruction, graduate assistants/students, LD specialists, professional tutors, special education teachers, teacher trainees, and trained peer tutors.

Enrichment Enrichment programs are available through the program or unit for career planning, college survival skills, learning strategies, math, practical computer skills, reading, self-advocacy, study skills, test taking, time management, vocabulary development, and written composition skills. Programs for health and nutrition, stress management, study skills, test taking, and time management are provided collaboratively through on-campus or off-campus services.

Fees *LD Program or Service* fee is $2200 to $4400 (fee varies according to level/tier of service). *Diagnostic Testing* fee is $1000.

Application For admittance to the program or unit, students are required to apply to the program directly, provide a psychoeducational report, and provide documentation of high school services. Upon application, materials documenting need for services should be sent only to the LD program or unit. Upon acceptance, documentation of need for services should be sent only to the LD program or unit. *Application deadline (institutional):* Continuous. *Application deadline (LD program):* Rolling/continuous for fall and rolling/continuous for spring.

Written Policies Written policy regarding general/basic LD accommodations is available on the program Web site. Written policy regarding general/basic LD accommodations is outlined in the school's catalog/handbook. Written policies regarding course substitutions, general/basic LD accommodations, and substitutions and waivers of admissions requirements are available through the program or unit directly.

Southern Illinois University Edwardsville
Disability Support Services

Edwardsville, IL 62026-0001

http://www.siue.edu/DSS

Contact: Jim Boyle, Learning Disabilities Specialist. Phone: 618-650-3726 Ext. 2568. Fax: 618-650-5691. E-mail: jboyle@siue.edu.

Disability Support Services Approximately 60 registered undergraduate students were served during 2002-03. The program or unit includes 2 full-time staff members. Academic advisers, diagnostic specialists, and LD specialists are provided through the program or unit. Coaches, counselors, graduate assistants/students, professional tutors, regular education teachers, remediation/learning specialists, skill tutors, and trained peer tutors are provided collaboratively through on-campus or off-campus services.

Orientation The program or unit offers a mandatory 5-hour orientation for new students before classes begin.

Unique Aids and Services Aids, services, or accommodations include faculty training, priority registration, and support groups.

Subject-area Tutoring Tutoring is offered one-on-one and in small groups for most subjects. Tutoring is provided through the program or unit via LD specialists and professional tutors. Tutoring is also provided collaboratively through on-campus or off-campus services via computer-based instruction, graduate assistants/students, and trained peer tutors.

Diagnostic Testing Testing is provided through the program or unit for auditory processing, intelligence, learning styles, math, motor skills, neuropsychological, reading, social skills, spelling, spoken language, study skills, visual processing, and written language.

Basic Skills Remediation Remediation is offered in class-size groups for computer skills, learning strategies, math, reading, spelling, study skills, time management, and written language. Remediation is provided through the program or unit via LD specialists and professional tutors. Remediation is also provided collaboratively through on-campus or off-campus services via computer-based instruction, graduate assistants/students, regular education teachers, and trained peer tutors.

Enrichment Programs for career planning, college survival skills, health and nutrition, learning strategies, math, oral communication skills, practical computer skills, reading, self-advocacy, stress management, study skills, test taking, time management, vocabulary development, and written composition skills are provided collaboratively through on-campus or off-campus services. Credit is offered for career planning, college survival skills, health and nutrition, math, oral communication skills, practical computer skills, reading, study skills, vocabulary development, and written composition skills.

Student Organization New Horizons consists of 15 members.

Application For admittance to the program or unit, students are required to provide a psychoeducational report (3 years old or less) and provide documentation of high school services. Upon acceptance, documentation of need for services should be sent only to the LD program or unit. *Application deadline (institutional):* 5/31. *Application deadline (LD program):* Rolling/continuous for fall and rolling/continuous for spring.

Written Policies Written policy regarding general/basic LD accommodations is available on the program Web site. Written policies regarding general/basic LD accommodations and substitutions and waivers of admissions requirements are available through the program or unit directly.

Southern Methodist University
Services for Students with Disabilities

6425 Boaz

Dallas, TX 75275

http://www.smu.edu/studentlife/OSSD_Facts.html

Contact: Ms. Rebecca Marin, Coordinator. Phone: 214-768-4557. Fax: 214-768-1255. E-mail: rmarin@smu.edu.

Services for Students with Disabilities Approximately 200 registered undergraduate students were served during 2002-03. The program or unit includes 1 full-time and 1 part-time staff member. Academic advisers, counselors, diagnostic specialists, and LD specialists are provided collaboratively through on-campus or off-campus services.

Unique Aids and Services Aids, services, or accommodations include priority registration and support groups.

Subject-area Tutoring Tutoring is offered one-on-one and in small groups for some subjects. Tutoring is provided collaboratively through on-campus or off-campus services via graduate assistants/students and trained peer tutors.

Diagnostic Testing Testing for intelligence, math, motor skills, personality, reading, spelling, spoken language, and written language is provided collaboratively through on-campus or off-campus services.

Enrichment Programs for college survival skills, learning strategies, reading, self-advocacy, stress management, study skills, test taking, time management, and vocabulary development are provided collaboratively through on-campus or off-campus services. Credit is offered for college survival skills, learning strategies, reading, self-advocacy, stress management, study skills, test taking, time management, and vocabulary development.

Fees *Diagnostic Testing* fee is $400.

Application For admittance to the program or unit, students are required to provide a psychoeducational report (3 years old or less). Upon application, materials documenting need for services should be sent only to the LD program or unit. Upon acceptance, docu-

Southern Methodist University (continued)

mentation of need for services should be sent only to the LD program or unit. *Application deadline (institutional): 1/15. Application deadline (LD program):* Rolling/continuous for fall and rolling/continuous for spring.

Written Policies Written policies regarding course substitutions, general/basic LD accommodations, grade forgiveness, substitutions and waivers of admissions requirements, and substitutions and waivers of graduation requirements are available on the program Web site. Written policies regarding grade forgiveness and substitutions and waivers of admissions requirements are outlined in the school's catalog/handbook. Written policies regarding course substitutions, general/basic LD accommodations, substitutions and waivers of admissions requirements, and substitutions and waivers of graduation requirements are available through the program or unit directly.

Southern Nazarene University

Academic Center for Excellence, Disability Support

6729 Northwest 39th Expressway

Bethany, OK 73008

http://www.snu.edu/

Contact: Mrs. Jeanette Hanson, Disability Support. Phone: 405-789-6400 Ext. 6272. E-mail: jhanson@snu.edu. Head of LD Program: Mrs. Loral McDonald Henck, Director of Academic Center for Excellence. Phone: 405-789-6400 Ext. 6694. E-mail: lhenck@snu.edu.

Academic Center for Excellence, Disability Support Approximately 32 registered undergraduate students were served during 2002-03. The program or unit includes 1 full-time and 1 part-time staff member. LD specialists, remediation/learning specialists, and trained peer tutors are provided through the program or unit. Academic advisers, counselors, diagnostic specialists, skill tutors, strategy tutors, and trained peer tutors are provided collaboratively through on-campus or off-campus services.

Unique Aids and Services Aids, services, or accommodations include advocates, career counseling, digital textbooks, faculty training, and personal coach.

Subject-area Tutoring Tutoring is offered one-on-one for most subjects. Tutoring is provided collaboratively through on-campus or off-campus services via computer-based instruction and trained peer tutors.

Diagnostic Testing Testing is provided through the program or unit for auditory processing, intelligence, neuropsychological, personality, and social skills.

Basic Skills Remediation Remediation is offered one-on-one for learning strategies, math, reading, study skills, time management, and written language. Remediation is provided collaboratively through on-campus or off-campus services via computer-based instruction and trained peer tutors.

Enrichment Enrichment programs are available through the program or unit for learning strategies, reading, self-advocacy, stress management, study skills, test taking, time management, vocabulary development, and written composition skills. Programs for career planning, college survival skills, health and nutrition, math,

medication management, practical computer skills, self-advocacy, time management, and written composition skills are provided collaboratively through on-campus or off-campus services. Credit is offered for college survival skills.

Application For admittance to the program or unit, students are required to provide a psychoeducational report (3 years old or less) and provide documentation of high school services. It is recommended that students apply to the program directly and provide other documentation. Upon application, materials documenting need for services should be sent only to the LD program or unit. Upon acceptance, documentation of need for services should be sent only to the LD program or unit. *Application deadline (institutional): 8/15. Application deadline (LD program):* Rolling/continuous for fall and rolling/continuous for spring.

Written Policies Written policies regarding course substitutions, substitutions and waivers of admissions requirements, and substitutions and waivers of graduation requirements are outlined in the school's catalog/handbook. Written policies regarding general/basic LD accommodations and substitutions and waivers of graduation requirements are available through the program or unit directly.

Southern Polytechnic State University

1100 South Marietta Parkway

Marietta, GA 30060-2896

http://www.spsu.edu/

Contact: Mrs. Freida Williams Castleberry, Disability Services and Testing Adviser. Phone: 770-528-7244. Fax: 770-528-7913. E-mail: fcastleb@spsu.edu.

Approximately 40 registered undergraduate students were served during 2002-03. The program or unit includes 1 full-time staff member. Academic advisers and other are provided through the program or unit. Academic advisers and other are provided collaboratively through on-campus or off-campus services.

Unique Aids and Services Aids, services, or accommodations include career counseling, digital textbooks, priority registration, and support groups.

Subject-area Tutoring Tutoring is offered one-on-one for some subjects. Tutoring is provided collaboratively through on-campus or off-campus services via graduate assistants/students and trained peer tutors.

Diagnostic Testing Testing for auditory processing, handwriting, intelligence, learning strategies, learning styles, math, motor skills, neuropsychological, personality, reading, social skills, spelling, spoken language, study skills, visual processing, and written language is provided collaboratively through on-campus or off-campus services.

Fees *Diagnostic Testing* fee is $400.

Application For admittance to the program or unit, students are required to provide a psychoeducational report (3 years old or less). Upon acceptance, documentation of need for services should be sent only to the LD program or unit. *Application deadline (institutional): 8/1. Application deadline (LD program):* Rolling/continuous for fall and rolling/continuous for spring.

Written Policies Written policies regarding course substitutions, general/basic LD accommodations, grade forgiveness, reduced course loads, substitutions and waivers of admissions requirements, and substitutions and waivers of graduation requirements are available on the program Web site.

Southern Utah University

351 West Center

Cedar City, UT 84720-2498

http://www.suu.edu/

Contact: Mrs. Carmen Rosa Alldredge, Coordinator of Services for Students with Disabilities. Phone: 435-865-8022. Fax: 435-865-8235. E-mail: alldredge@suu.edu.

Approximately 43 registered undergraduate students were served during 2002-03. The program or unit includes 1 full-time staff member. Academic advisers, coaches, counselors, diagnostic specialists, regular education teachers, skill tutors, and trained peer tutors are provided collaboratively through on-campus or off-campus services.

Unique Aids and Services Aids, services, or accommodations include advocates, career counseling, faculty training, priority registration, and support groups.

Subject-area Tutoring Tutoring is offered in small groups for most subjects. Tutoring is provided collaboratively through on-campus or off-campus services via computer-based instruction, graduate assistants/students, and trained peer tutors.

Diagnostic Testing Testing for intelligence, learning strategies, learning styles, math, motor skills, personality, reading, social skills, spelling, spoken language, study skills, and written language is provided collaboratively through on-campus or off-campus services.

Basic Skills Remediation Remediation is offered in small groups for learning strategies, math, reading, spelling, study skills, time management, and written language. Remediation is provided collaboratively through on-campus or off-campus services via graduate assistants/students and trained peer tutors.

Enrichment Programs for career planning, college survival skills, health and nutrition, learning strategies, math, medication management, oral communication skills, practical computer skills, reading, self-advocacy, stress management, study skills, test taking, time management, vocabulary development, and written composition skills are provided collaboratively through on-campus or off-campus services. Credit is offered for career planning, college survival skills, health and nutrition, learning strategies, math, stress management, study skills, test taking, time management, and written composition skills.

Student Organization Elite Achiever's Club consists of 12 members.

Fees *Diagnostic Testing* fee is $100.

Application For admittance to the program or unit, students are required to provide a psychoeducational report (3 years old or less). It is recommended that students provide documentation of high school services. Upon application, materials documenting need for services should be sent only to admissions with institutional application materials. Upon acceptance, documentation of need for services should be sent only to admissions. *Application deadline (institutional):* 7/1. *Application deadline (LD program):* 7/1 for fall. 12/1 for spring.

Written Policies Written policy regarding general/basic LD accommodations is available on the program Web site. Written policy regarding general/basic LD accommodations is outlined in the school's catalog/handbook. Written policy regarding general/basic LD accommodations is available through the program or unit directly.

Southern Vermont College
Disabilities Support Program

982 Mansion Drive

Bennington, VT 05201-6002

http://www.svc.edu/

Contact: Mr. Todd Gerson, Coordinator. Phone: 802-447-6360. Fax: 802-447-4695. E-mail: tgerson@svc.edu.

Disabilities Support Program Approximately 72 registered undergraduate students were served during 2002-03. The program or unit includes 2 full-time staff members. LD specialists, professional tutors, remediation/learning specialists, skill tutors, and strategy tutors are provided through the program or unit. Academic advisers, coaches, counselors, diagnostic specialists, regular education teachers, and trained peer tutors are provided collaboratively through on-campus or off-campus services.

Orientation The program or unit offers an optional orientation for new students before registration, before classes begin, during registration, and individually by special arrangement.

Subject-area Tutoring Tutoring is offered one-on-one and in small groups for all subjects. Tutoring is provided through the program or unit via computer-based instruction and LD specialists. Tutoring is also provided collaboratively through on-campus or off-campus services via computer-based instruction and trained peer tutors.

Diagnostic Testing Testing is provided through the program or unit for learning styles, reading, visual processing, and written language. Testing for auditory processing, intelligence, math, neuropsychological, and personality is provided collaboratively through on-campus or off-campus services.

Basic Skills Remediation Remediation is available for computer skills, learning strategies, math, reading, spelling, study skills, time management, visual processing, and written language. Remediation is provided through the program or unit via LD specialists and professional tutors. Remediation is also provided collaboratively through on-campus or off-campus services via computer-based instruction, regular education teachers, and trained peer tutors.

Enrichment Enrichment programs are available through the program or unit for career planning, college survival skills, learning strategies, stress management, study skills, test taking, time management, vocabulary development, and written composition skills. Programs for math, stress management, study skills, and test taking are provided collaboratively through on-campus or off-campus services.

Fees *Diagnostic Testing* fee is applicable.

Application For admittance to the program or unit, students are required to provide a psychoeducational report (3 years old or less) and provide documentation of high school services. Upon application, materials documenting need for services should be sent only to the LD program or unit. Upon acceptance, documentation of need for services should be sent only to the LD program or unit. *Application deadline (institutional):* Continuous. *Application deadline (LD program):* Rolling/continuous for fall and rolling/continuous for spring.

Written Policies Written policy regarding general/basic LD accommodations is available on the program Web site. Written policy regarding general/basic LD accommodations is outlined in the

Southern Vermont College (continued)

school's catalog/handbook. Written policies regarding course substitutions, general/basic LD accommodations, and reduced course loads are available through the program or unit directly.

South University
Student Services

5355 Vaughn Road
Montgomery, AL 36116-1120
http://www.southuniversity.edu/

Contact: Ms. Patricia K. Byrnside, Dean of Student Affairs. Phone: 334-395-8800. Fax: 334-396-8859. E-mail: pbyrnside@southuniversity.edu.

Student Services Approximately 5 registered undergraduate students were served during 2002-03. Counselors and regular education teachers are provided through the program or unit.
Subject-area Tutoring Tutoring is offered one-on-one, in small groups, and in class-size groups for most subjects. Tutoring is provided through the program or unit via trained peer tutors and other.
Application For admittance to the program or unit, students are required to apply to the program directly and provide a psychoeducational report (5 years old or less). It is recommended that students provide documentation of high school services. Upon application, materials documenting need for services should be sent only to the LD program or unit. Upon acceptance, documentation of need for services should be sent only to the LD program or unit. *Application deadline (LD program):* Rolling/continuous for fall and rolling/continuous for spring.
Written Policies Written policy regarding general/basic LD accommodations is outlined in the school's catalog/handbook. Written policies regarding general/basic LD accommodations and reduced course loads are available through the program or unit directly.

Southwestern University

1001 East University Avenue
Georgetown, TX 78626
http://www.southwestern.edu/

Contact: Ms. Deb McCarthy, Academic Services Coordinator. Phone: 512-863-1286. E-mail: mccarthd@southwestern.edu.

The program or unit includes 4 full-time and 3 part-time staff members. Academic advisers and trained peer tutors are provided through the program or unit. Counselors and diagnostic specialists are provided collaboratively through on-campus or off-campus services.
Unique Aids and Services Aids, services, or accommodations include advocates, digital textbooks, faculty training, priority registration, extended testing time.
Subject-area Tutoring Tutoring is offered one-on-one for some subjects. Tutoring is provided through the program or unit via trained peer tutors and other.

Basic Skills Remediation Remediation is offered one-on-one for learning strategies, reading, social skills, study skills, time management, written language, and other areas as needed. Remediation is provided through the program or unit via trained peer tutors and other.
Application For admittance to the program or unit, students are required to provide a psychoeducational report (3 years old or less). Upon application, materials documenting need for services should be sent only to admissions with institutional application materials. Upon acceptance, documentation of need for services should be sent only to the LD program or unit. *Application deadline (institutional):* 2/15. *Application deadline (LD program):* Rolling/continuous for fall and rolling/continuous for spring.
Written Policies Written policy regarding course substitutions is available on the program Web site. Written policies regarding course substitutions and general/basic LD accommodations are outlined in the school's catalog/handbook. Written policies regarding course substitutions, general/basic LD accommodations, and reduced course loads are available through the program or unit directly.

Texas State University-San Marcos
Office of Disability Services

601 University Drive
San Marcos, TX 78666
http://www.ods.swt.edu

Contact: Ms. Tina Schultz, Director. Phone: 512-245-3451. Fax: 512-245-3452. E-mail: tina@swt.edu.

Office of Disability Services Approximately 260 registered undergraduate students were served during 2002-03. The program or unit includes 1 full-time staff member. Diagnostic specialists and LD specialists are provided through the program or unit. Academic advisers, coaches, counselors, and graduate assistants/students are provided collaboratively through on-campus or off-campus services.
Unique Aids and Services Aids, services, or accommodations include priority registration.
Subject-area Tutoring Tutoring is offered one-on-one for some subjects. Tutoring is provided collaboratively through on-campus or off-campus services via computer-based instruction and trained peer tutors.
Enrichment Programs for career planning, college survival skills, and math are provided collaboratively through on-campus or off-campus services.
Application For admittance to the program or unit, students are required to provide a psychoeducational report (5 years old or less). It is recommended that students provide documentation of high school services. Upon application, materials documenting need for services should be sent only to the LD program or unit. Upon acceptance, documentation of need for services should be sent only to the LD program or unit. *Application deadline (institutional):* 7/1. *Application deadline (LD program):* Rolling/continuous for fall and rolling/continuous for spring.
Written Policies Written policies regarding course substitutions, general/basic LD accommodations, reduced course loads, substitutions and waivers of admissions requirements, and substitutions and waivers of graduation requirements are available on the program

Web site. Written policies regarding general/basic LD accommodations and substitutions and waivers of admissions requirements are outlined in the school's catalog/handbook. Written policies regarding course substitutions, general/basic LD accommodations, reduced course loads, substitutions and waivers of admissions requirements, and substitutions and waivers of graduation requirements are available through the program or unit directly.

Springfield College
Office of Student Support Services

263 Alden Street

Springfield, MA 01109-3797

http://www.spfldcol.edu/student life/student support

Contact: Ms. Deb Dickens, Director of Student Support Services. Phone: 413-748-3768. Fax: 413-748-3937. E-mail: ddickens@spfldcol.edu.

Office of Student Support Services Approximately 125 registered undergraduate students were served during 2002-03. The program or unit includes 1 full-time and 1 part-time staff member. Academic advisers, coaches, and LD specialists are provided through the program or unit. Academic advisers and trained peer tutors are provided collaboratively through on-campus or off-campus services.

Unique Aids and Services Aids, services, or accommodations include advocates, digital textbooks, and personal coach.

Subject-area Tutoring Tutoring is offered one-on-one and in small groups for most subjects. Tutoring is provided through the program or unit via LD specialists. Tutoring is also provided collaboratively through on-campus or off-campus services via graduate assistants/students and trained peer tutors.

Basic Skills Remediation Remediation is offered one-on-one for computer skills, learning strategies, study skills, and time management. Remediation is provided through the program or unit via LD specialists.

Enrichment Enrichment programs are available through the program or unit for learning strategies, practical computer skills, self-advocacy, study skills, test taking, and time management. Programs for study skills, test taking, and time management are provided collaboratively through on-campus or off-campus services.

Application For admittance to the program or unit, students are required to provide a psychoeducational report (3 years old or less). It is recommended that students provide documentation of high school services. Upon acceptance, documentation of need for services should be sent only to the LD program or unit. *Application deadline (institutional): 4/1. Application deadline (LD program):* Rolling/continuous for fall and rolling/continuous for spring.

Written Policies Written policy regarding general/basic LD accommodations is available on the program Web site. Written policies regarding course substitutions, general/basic LD accommodations, reduced course loads, substitutions and waivers of admissions requirements, and substitutions and waivers of graduation requirements are outlined in the school's catalog/handbook. Written policy regarding general/basic LD accommodations is available through the program or unit directly.

Stanford University
Schwab Learning Center

Stanford, CA 94305-9991

http://www.stanford.edu/

Contact: Sue Willows-Raznikov, M.A., Learning Strategies Coordinator. Phone: 650-725-3163. Fax: 650-725-5301. E-mail: willows@stanford.edu. Head of LD Program: Joan M. Bisagno PhD, Assistant Dean of Students and Director. Phone: 650-723-1039. Fax: 650-725-5301. E-mail: joan.bisagno@stanford.edu.

Schwab Learning Center The program or unit includes 1 full-time and 11 part-time staff members. Coaches, diagnostic specialists, graduate assistants/students, LD specialists, professional tutors, skill tutors, strategy tutors, and trained peer tutors are provided through the program or unit. Academic advisers and counselors are provided collaboratively through on-campus or off-campus services.

Orientation The program or unit offers an optional 2-hour orientation for new students before classes begin, during summer prior to enrollment, after classes begin, individually by special arrangement, and throughout the academic year.

Unique Aids and Services Aids, services, or accommodations include career counseling, digital textbooks, and support groups.

Subject-area Tutoring Tutoring is offered one-on-one, in small groups, and in class-size groups for all subjects. Tutoring is provided through the program or unit via computer-based instruction, graduate assistants/students, LD specialists, professional tutors, and trained peer tutors. Tutoring is also provided collaboratively through on-campus or off-campus services via computer-based instruction, graduate assistants/students, LD specialists, professional tutors, and trained peer tutors.

Diagnostic Testing Testing is provided through the program or unit for auditory processing, handwriting, intelligence, learning strategies, learning styles, math, motor skills, neuropsychological, reading, spelling, spoken language, study skills, visual processing, and written language. Testing for auditory processing, handwriting, intelligence, learning strategies, learning styles, math, motor skills, neuropsychological, personality, reading, social skills, spelling, spoken language, study skills, visual processing, and written language is provided collaboratively through on-campus or off-campus services.

Basic Skills Remediation Remediation is offered one-on-one for auditory processing, computer skills, handwriting, math, motor skills, reading, spelling, spoken language, study skills, time management, visual processing, and written language. Remediation is provided through the program or unit via computer-based instruction, graduate assistants/students, LD specialists, and professional tutors. Remediation is also provided collaboratively through on-campus or off-campus services via computer-based instruction, graduate assistants/students, LD specialists, and professional tutors.

Enrichment Enrichment programs are available through the program or unit for career planning, college survival skills, learning strategies, oral communication skills, practical computer skills, self-advocacy, stress management, study skills, test taking, time management, vocabulary development, and written composition skills. Programs for career planning, college survival skills, health and nutrition, learning strategies, math, medication management, oral communication skills, practical computer skills, stress management, study skills, test taking, time management, and written composition

Stanford University (continued)

skills are provided collaboratively through on-campus or off-campus services. Credit is offered for learning strategies, oral communication skills, practical computer skills, and time management. **Application** For admittance to the program or unit, students are required to provide screening evaluation completed by LD staff. It is recommended that students provide a psychoeducational report (3 years old or less). Upon application, materials documenting need for services should be sent only to the LD program or unit. Upon acceptance, documentation of need for services should be sent only to the LD program or unit. *Application deadline (institutional):* 12/15. *Application deadline (LD program):* Rolling/continuous for fall and rolling/continuous for spring.

Written Policies Written policies regarding course substitutions, general/basic LD accommodations, and reduced course loads are available on the program Web site. Written policies regarding course substitutions, general/basic LD accommodations, and reduced course loads are available through the program or unit directly.

State University of New York at Albany

1400 Washington Avenue

Albany, NY 12222-0001

http://www.albany.edu/

Contact: Mrs. Carolyn B. Malloch, Learning Disability Specialist. Phone: 518-442-5566. Fax: 518-442-5589. E-mail: cmalloch@uamail.albany.edu.

Approximately 185 registered undergraduate students were served during 2002-03. The program or unit includes 1 full-time staff member. Coaches, LD specialists, skill tutors, and strategy tutors are provided through the program or unit. Academic advisers and counselors are provided collaboratively through on-campus or off-campus services.

Unique Aids and Services Aids, services, or accommodations include personal coach and priority registration.

Subject-area Tutoring Tutoring is offered one-on-one, in small groups, and in class-size groups for most subjects. Tutoring is provided collaboratively through on-campus or off-campus services via graduate assistants/students and trained peer tutors.

Enrichment Enrichment programs are available through the program or unit for college survival skills, learning strategies, self-advocacy, study skills, and time management.

Application For admittance to the program or unit, students are required to provide a psychoeducational report (3 years old or less) and provide supporting testing documentation if course substitution or exemption is requested. It is recommended that students provide documentation of high school services. Upon application, materials documenting need for services should be sent only to the LD program or unit. Upon acceptance, documentation of need for services should be sent only to the LD program or unit. *Application deadline (institutional):* 3/1. *Application deadline (LD program):* Rolling/continuous for fall and rolling/continuous for spring.

Written Policies Written policy regarding general/basic LD accommodations is available on the program Web site. Written policies regarding course substitutions, general/basic LD accommodations, and substitutions and waivers of graduation requirements are outlined in the school's catalog/handbook.

State University of New York College at Cortland

PO Box 2000

Cortland, NY 13045

http://www.cortland.edu/

Contact: Ute G. Gomez, Assistant Coordinator Student Disability Services. Phone: 607-753-2066. Fax: 607-753-5495. E-mail: gomezu@cortland.edu.

Approximately 500 registered undergraduate students were served during 2002-03. The program or unit includes 2 full-time staff members and 1 part-time staff member. Counselors are provided through the program or unit. Academic advisers, counselors, graduate assistants/students, professional tutors, skill tutors, and other are provided collaboratively through on-campus or off-campus services.

Orientation The program or unit offers an optional orientation for new students before classes begin and individually by special arrangement.

Unique Aids and Services Aids, services, or accommodations include career counseling, books on tape, Kurzweil Reader, test-taking center.

Subject-area Tutoring Tutoring is offered one-on-one, in small groups, and in class-size groups for most subjects. Tutoring is provided through the program or unit via computer-based instruction and other. Tutoring is also provided collaboratively through on-campus or off-campus services via computer-based instruction, graduate assistants/students, professional tutors, and trained peer tutors.

Diagnostic Testing Testing for learning strategies, learning styles, study skills, and other services is provided collaboratively through on-campus or off-campus services.

Enrichment Programs for career planning, health and nutrition, learning strategies, medication management, practical computer skills, stress management, study skills, test taking, time management, and written composition skills are provided collaboratively through on-campus or off-campus services.

Application For admittance to the program or unit, students are required to apply to the program directly and provide a psychoeducational report (3 years old or less). It is recommended that students provide documentation of high school services. Upon acceptance, documentation of need for services should be sent only to the LD program or unit. *Application deadline (LD program):* Rolling/continuous for fall and rolling/continuous for spring.

Written Policies Written policies regarding course substitutions, general/basic LD accommodations, substitutions and waivers of admissions requirements, and substitutions and waivers of graduation requirements are available on the program Web site. Written policy regarding general/basic LD accommodations is outlined in the school's catalog/handbook. Written policies regarding course substitutions, general/basic LD accommodations, reduced course loads, substitutions and waivers of admissions requirements, and substitutions and waivers of graduation requirements are available through the program or unit directly.

State University of New York College at Fredonia
Disability Support Services for Students

Fredonia, NY 14063-1136

http://www.fredonia.edu/tlc/dsshandbook.html

Contact: Ms. Carolyn L. Boone, Coordinator of Disability Support Services for Students. Phone: 716-673-3270. Fax: 716-673-3801. E-mail: boone@fredonia.edu.

Disability Support Services for Students Approximately 66 registered undergraduate students were served during 2002-03. The program or unit includes 1 full-time staff member. Trained peer tutors and other are provided collaboratively through on-campus or off-campus services.

Subject-area Tutoring Tutoring is offered one-on-one and in small groups for most subjects. Tutoring is provided through the program or unit via trained peer tutors.

Enrichment Enrichment programs are available through the program or unit for self-advocacy. Programs for oral communication skills and stress management are provided collaboratively through on-campus or off-campus services.

Application For admittance to the program or unit, students are required to provide a psychoeducational report. It is recommended that students provide documentation of high school services. Upon acceptance, documentation of need for services should be sent only to the LD program or unit. *Application deadline (institutional):* Continuous. *Application deadline (LD program):* Rolling/continuous for fall and rolling/continuous for spring.

Written Policies Written policy regarding general/basic LD accommodations is available on the program Web site. Written policy regarding general/basic LD accommodations is outlined in the school's catalog/handbook. Written policy regarding general/basic LD accommodations is available through the program or unit directly.

State University of New York College at Geneseo

1 College Circle

Geneseo, NY 14454-1401

http://www.geneseo.edu/

Contact: Ms. Tabitha Buggie-Hunt, Director, Office of Disability Services. Phone: 585-245-5112. Fax: 585-245-5032. E-mail: tbuggieh@geneseo.edu.

Approximately 100 registered undergraduate students were served during 2002-03. The program or unit includes 1 full-time staff member.

Subject-area Tutoring Tutoring is offered one-on-one and in small groups for most subjects. Tutoring is provided collaboratively through on-campus or off-campus services via trained peer tutors and other.

Application For admittance to the program or unit, students are required to provide a psychoeducational report (5 years old or less). Upon acceptance, documentation of need for services should be

sent only to the LD program or unit. *Application deadline (institutional):* 1/15. *Application deadline (LD program):* Rolling/continuous for fall and rolling/continuous for spring.

Written Policies Written policies regarding general/basic LD accommodations and substitutions and waivers of admissions requirements are available on the program Web site. Written policies regarding general/basic LD accommodations and substitutions and waivers of admissions requirements are available through the program or unit directly.

State University of New York College at Old Westbury

PO Box 210

Old Westbury, NY 11568-0210

http://www.oldwestbury.edu/

Contact: Phone: 516-876-3000. Fax: 516-876-3307.

The program or unit includes 2 full-time staff members and 1 part-time staff member. Academic advisers, coaches, counselors, graduate assistants/students, LD specialists, regular education teachers, skill tutors, strategy tutors, trained peer tutors, and other are provided through the program or unit. Academic advisers are provided collaboratively through on-campus or off-campus services.

Unique Aids and Services Aids, services, or accommodations include career counseling, faculty training, priority registration, and support groups.

Subject-area Tutoring Tutoring is offered one-on-one and in small groups for most subjects. Tutoring is provided through the program or unit via computer-based instruction, graduate assistants/students, LD specialists, trained peer tutors, and other.

Basic Skills Remediation Remediation is offered one-on-one and in small groups for computer skills, learning strategies, math, motor skills, reading, social skills, spelling, spoken language, study skills, time management, visual processing, and written language. Remediation is provided through the program or unit via computer-based instruction, graduate assistants/students, LD specialists, regular education teachers, teacher trainees, trained peer tutors, and other. Remediation is also provided collaboratively through on-campus or off-campus services via graduate assistants/students and other.

Enrichment Enrichment programs are available through the program or unit for career planning, college survival skills, learning strategies, oral communication skills, practical computer skills, self-advocacy, stress management, study skills, test taking, time management, written composition skills, and other. Programs for career planning, college survival skills, learning strategies, self-advocacy, stress management, study skills, test taking, time management, and written composition skills are provided collaboratively through on-campus or off-campus services. Credit is offered for career planning and college survival skills.

Student Organization Access for All consists of 20 members.

Application For admittance to the program or unit, students are required to provide a psychoeducational report. It is recommended that students provide documentation of high school services and provide reports from any other professionals seen. Upon accep-

State University of New York College at Old Westbury (continued)

tance, documentation of need for services should be sent only to the LD program or unit. *Application deadline (institutional):* Continuous. *Application deadline (LD program):* Rolling/continuous for fall and rolling/continuous for spring.

Written Policies Written policies regarding course substitutions and substitutions and waivers of graduation requirements are outlined in the school's catalog/handbook. Written policy regarding general/basic LD accommodations is available through the program or unit directly.

State University of New York College at Oneonta
Student Disability Services (SDS)

Ravine Parkway
Oneonta, NY 13820-4015
http://www.oneonta.edu/

Contact: Mr. Craig Levins, Coordinator. Phone: 607-436-2137. Fax: 607-436-3167. E-mail: sds@oneonta.edu.

Student Disability Services (SDS) Approximately 225 registered undergraduate students were served during 2002-03. The program or unit includes 2 full-time staff members and 1 part-time staff member. Academic advisers, diagnostic specialists, graduate assistants/students, and trained peer tutors are provided through the program or unit. Academic advisers, coaches, counselors, regular education teachers, remediation/learning specialists, skill tutors, strategy tutors, and trained peer tutors are provided collaboratively through on-campus or off-campus services.

Subject-area Tutoring Tutoring is offered one-on-one for most subjects. Tutoring is provided through the program or unit via trained peer tutors. Tutoring is also provided collaboratively through on-campus or off-campus services via graduate assistants/students, professional tutors, and trained peer tutors.

Basic Skills Remediation Remediation is offered in class-size groups for computer skills, learning strategies, math, study skills, time management, and written language. Remediation is provided collaboratively through on-campus or off-campus services via professional tutors and regular education teachers.

Enrichment Enrichment programs are available through the program or unit for self-advocacy. Programs for career planning, college survival skills, health and nutrition, learning strategies, math, stress management, study skills, test taking, time management, and written composition skills are provided collaboratively through on-campus or off-campus services.

Student Organization Peer Mentor Program consists of 11 members.

Application For admittance to the program or unit, students are required to provide a psychoeducational report (3 years old or less). It is recommended that students provide documentation of high school services. Upon application, materials documenting need for services should be sent only to the LD program or unit. Upon acceptance, documentation of need for services should be sent only to the LD program or unit. *Application deadline (institutional):* Continuous. *Application deadline (LD program):* Rolling/continuous for fall and rolling/continuous for spring.

Written Policies Written policy regarding general/basic LD accommodations is available on the program Web site.

State University of New York College at Potsdam

44 Pierrepont Avenue
Potsdam, NY 13676
http://www.potsdam.edu/

Contact: Ms. Sharon House, Director of Accommodative Services. Phone: 315-267-3267. Fax: 315-267-3267. E-mail: housese@potsdam.edu.

The program or unit includes 1 full-time staff member. Academic advisers, counselors, and trained peer tutors are provided collaboratively through on-campus or off-campus services.

Unique Aids and Services Aids, services, or accommodations include career counseling, faculty training, and priority registration.

Subject-area Tutoring Tutoring is offered one-on-one and in small groups for most subjects. Tutoring is provided collaboratively through on-campus or off-campus services via trained peer tutors.

Enrichment Programs for career planning, college survival skills, learning strategies, math, stress management, study skills, test taking, and time management are provided collaboratively through on-campus or off-campus services.

Application For admittance to the program or unit, students are required to provide a psychoeducational report. It is recommended that students provide documentation of high school services. Upon acceptance, documentation of need for services should be sent only to the LD program or unit. *Application deadline (institutional):* Continuous.

Written Policies Written policy regarding general/basic LD accommodations is available on the program Web site. Written policy regarding general/basic LD accommodations is outlined in the school's catalog/handbook. Written policy regarding general/basic LD accommodations is available through the program or unit directly.

State University of New York College of Environmental Science and Forestry
Office of Student Life

1 Forestry Drive
Syracuse, NY 13210-2779
http://www.esf.edu/

Contact: Mr. Thomas O. Slocum, Director of Career and Counseling Services. Phone: 315-470-6660. Fax: 315-470-4728. E-mail: toslocum@esf.edu.

Office of Student Life Approximately 33 registered undergraduate students were served during 2002-03. The program or unit includes 4 full-time staff members. Coaches, diagnostic specialists, LD specialists, professional tutors, remediation/learning specialists, skill tutors, special education teachers, strategy tutors, teacher trainees, and trained peer tutors are provided through the program or unit. Academic advisers, counselors, graduate assistants/students, and regular education teachers are provided collaboratively through on-campus or off-campus services.

Unique Aids and Services Aids, services, or accommodations include advocates and career counseling.

Subject-area Tutoring Tutoring is offered one-on-one and in small groups for some subjects. Tutoring is provided through the program or unit via LD specialists. Tutoring is also provided collaboratively through on-campus or off-campus services via graduate assistants/students and trained peer tutors.

Application For admittance to the program or unit, students are required to provide a psychoeducational report (3 years old or less). It is recommended that students provide documentation of high school services. Upon acceptance, documentation of need for services should be sent only to the LD program or unit. *Application deadline (institutional):* Continuous. *Application deadline (LD program):* Rolling/continuous for fall and rolling/continuous for spring.

Written Policies Written policy regarding general/basic LD accommodations is outlined in the school's catalog/handbook. Written policy regarding reduced course loads is available through the program or unit directly.

State University of West Georgia
Student Disability Services

1600 Maple Street
Carrollton, GA 30118
http://www.westga.edu/~dserve
Contact: Dr. Ann Phillips, Coordinator. Phone: 770-836-6428. Fax: 770-838-2562. E-mail: aphillip@westga.edu.

Student Disability Services Approximately 500 registered undergraduate students were served during 2002-03. The program or unit includes 2 part-time staff members. Academic advisers, counselors, diagnostic specialists, skill tutors, and strategy tutors are provided through the program or unit. Academic advisers, counselors, diagnostic specialists, and remediation/learning specialists are provided collaboratively through on-campus or off-campus services.

Unique Aids and Services Aids, services, or accommodations include career counseling, priority registration, individualized special accommodations report .

Subject-area Tutoring Tutoring is offered one-on-one for some subjects. Tutoring is provided through the program or unit via graduate assistants/students. Tutoring is also provided collaboratively through on-campus or off-campus services via other.

Diagnostic Testing Testing is provided through the program or unit for personality. Testing for auditory processing, intelligence, reading, spelling, and written language is provided collaboratively through on-campus or off-campus services.

Basic Skills Remediation Remediation is offered in class-size groups for math, reading, and written language. Remediation is provided collaboratively through on-campus or off-campus services via regular education teachers.

Enrichment Enrichment programs are available through the program or unit for self-advocacy. Programs for career planning, health and nutrition, math, medication management, oral communication skills, practical computer skills, reading, study skills, test taking, time management, and written composition skills are provided collaboratively through on-campus or off-campus services. Credit is offered for health and nutrition, math, oral communication skills, practical computer skills, reading, and written composition skills.

Fees *Diagnostic Testing* fee is $400.

Application For admittance to the program or unit, students are required to apply to the program directly and provide a psychoeducational report (3 years old or less). Upon application, materials documenting need for services should be sent only to the LD program or unit. Upon acceptance, documentation of need for services should be sent only to the LD program or unit. *Application deadline (institutional):* 7/31. *Application deadline (LD program):* Rolling/continuous for fall and rolling/continuous for spring.

Written Policies Written policy regarding general/basic LD accommodations is available on the program Web site. Written policy regarding general/basic LD accommodations is outlined in the school's catalog/handbook. Written policies regarding course substitutions and general/basic LD accommodations are available through the program or unit directly.

Stephen F. Austin State University
Disability Services

1936 North Street
Nacogdoches, TX 75962
http://www.sfasu.edu/disabilityservices/index.htm
Contact: Mr. Chuck Lopez, Director of Disability Services. Phone: 936-468-3004. Fax: 936-468-1368. E-mail: clopez@sfasu.edu.

Disability Services Approximately 65 registered undergraduate students were served during 2002-03. Counselors, graduate assistants/students, skill tutors, and strategy tutors are provided through the program or unit. Academic advisers, counselors, diagnostic specialists, graduate assistants/students, regular education teachers, remediation/learning specialists, skill tutors, strategy tutors, and trained peer tutors are provided collaboratively through on-campus or off-campus services.

Unique Aids and Services Aids, services, or accommodations include career counseling, digital textbooks, faculty training, and personal coach.

Subject-area Tutoring Tutoring is offered one-on-one, in small groups, and in class-size groups for all subjects. Tutoring is provided collaboratively through on-campus or off-campus services via graduate assistants/students and trained peer tutors.

Diagnostic Testing Testing is provided through the program or unit for learning strategies, learning styles, and study skills. Testing for auditory processing, handwriting, intelligence, learning strategies, learning styles, math, motor skills, neuropsychological, personality, reading, spelling, spoken language, visual processing, and written language is provided collaboratively through on-campus or off-campus services.

Stephen F. Austin State University (continued)

Basic Skills Remediation Remediation is offered in class-size groups for auditory processing, math, reading, study skills, time management, and written language. Remediation is provided collaboratively through on-campus or off-campus services via graduate assistants/students, professional tutors, regular education teachers, trained peer tutors, and other.

Enrichment Enrichment programs are available through the program or unit for career planning, college survival skills, learning strategies, self-advocacy, stress management, study skills, test taking, and time management. Programs for career planning, college survival skills, health and nutrition, math, medication management, oral communication skills, practical computer skills, reading, self-advocacy, stress management, study skills, test taking, time management, vocabulary development, and written composition skills are provided collaboratively through on-campus or off-campus services. Credit is offered for college survival skills, learning strategies, math, oral communication skills, practical computer skills, reading, study skills, test taking, time management, vocabulary development, and written composition skills.

Fees *Diagnostic Testing* fee is $150 to $200.

Application For admittance to the program or unit, students are required to provide a psychoeducational report (3 years old or less). It is recommended that students provide documentation of high school services. Upon application, materials documenting need for services should be sent only to the LD program or unit. Upon acceptance, documentation of need for services should be sent only to the LD program or unit. *Application deadline (institutional):* Continuous. *Application deadline (LD program):* Rolling/continuous for fall and rolling/continuous for spring.

Written Policies Written policies regarding course substitutions, general/basic LD accommodations, and substitutions and waivers of graduation requirements are available on the program Web site. Written policy regarding general/basic LD accommodations is outlined in the school's catalog/handbook. Written policies regarding course substitutions, general/basic LD accommodations, and substitutions and waivers of graduation requirements are available through the program or unit directly.

Sterling College

PO Box 98
Sterling, KS 67579-0098
http://www.sterling.edu/

Contact: Ms. Jan Schierling, Director of Academic Support. Phone: 620-278-4202. Fax: 620-278-4370. E-mail: jschiering@stering.edu.

Approximately 12 registered undergraduate students were served during 2002-03. The program or unit includes 1 full-time staff member. Academic advisers, coaches, regular education teachers, and trained peer tutors are provided collaboratively through on-campus or off-campus services.

Subject-area Tutoring Tutoring is provided through the program or unit via computer-based instruction and trained peer tutors.

Diagnostic Testing Testing is provided through the program or unit for learning styles, math, personality, and reading.

Basic Skills Remediation Remediation is offered one-on-one for math, reading, study skills, time management, and written language. Remediation is provided through the program or unit via computer-based instruction and trained peer tutors. Remediation is also provided collaboratively through on-campus or off-campus services via regular education teachers.

Enrichment Enrichment programs are available through the program or unit for college survival skills, study skills, test taking, and time management. Program for math is provided collaboratively through on-campus or off-campus services. Credit is offered for college survival skills and math.

Application It is recommended that students provide a psychoeducational report (5 years old or less) and provide documentation of high school services. Upon application, materials documenting need for services should be sent to both admissions and the LD program or unit. Upon acceptance, documentation of need for services should be sent only to the LD program or unit. *Application deadline (institutional):* Continuous. *Application deadline (LD program):* Rolling/continuous for fall and rolling/continuous for spring.

Written Policies Written policies regarding substitutions and waivers of admissions requirements and substitutions and waivers of graduation requirements are outlined in the school's catalog/handbook. Written policy regarding general/basic LD accommodations is available through the program or unit directly.

Stonehill College
Academic Resource Center

320 Washington Street
Easton, MA 02357-5510
http://www.stonehill.edu/

Contact: Ms. Autumn Grant-Kimball, Director of the Academic Resource Center. Phone: 508-565-1033. Fax: 508-565-1492. E-mail: akimball@stonehill.edu.

Academic Resource Center Approximately 45 registered undergraduate students were served during 2002-03. The program or unit includes 1 full-time and 1 part-time staff member. LD specialists are provided through the program or unit. Academic advisers, counselors, diagnostic specialists, LD specialists, skill tutors, strategy tutors, and trained peer tutors are provided collaboratively through on-campus or off-campus services.

Subject-area Tutoring Tutoring is offered one-on-one and in small groups for most subjects. Tutoring is provided collaboratively through on-campus or off-campus services via trained peer tutors.

Diagnostic Testing Testing for learning styles, neuropsychological, and study skills is provided collaboratively through on-campus or off-campus services.

Basic Skills Remediation Remediation is offered in class-size groups for learning strategies, study skills, and time management. Remediation is provided collaboratively through on-campus or off-campus services via regular education teachers.

Enrichment Programs for college survival skills, learning strategies, stress management, study skills, test taking, time management, and written composition skills are provided collaboratively through on-campus or off-campus services. Credit is offered for college survival skills.

Application For admittance to the program or unit, students are required to provide a psychoeducational report (3 years old or less). It is recommended that students provide documentation of high school services. Upon acceptance, documentation of need for services should be sent only to the LD program or unit. *Application deadline (institutional): 1/15. Application deadline (LD program):* Rolling/continuous for fall and rolling/continuous for spring.

Written Policies Written policy regarding reduced course loads is available on the program Web site. Written policies regarding course substitutions, general/basic LD accommodations, and substitutions and waivers of admissions requirements are available through the program or unit directly.

Stony Brook University, State University of New York
Disability Support Services

Nicolls Road

Stony Brook, NY 11794

http://studentaffairs.stonybrook.edu/disabilityservices/

Contact: Donna Molloy, Assistant Director and Learning Disabilities Specialist. Phone: 631-632-6748. Fax: 631-632-6747. E-mail: dmolloy@notes.cc.sunysb.edu. Head of LD Program: Joanna Harris, Director Disability Support Services. Phone: 631-632-6748. E-mail: jjharris@notes.cc.sunysb.edu.

Disability Support Services Approximately 170 registered undergraduate students were served during 2002-03. The program or unit includes 6 full-time staff members and 1 part-time staff member. Counselors, graduate assistants/students, and LD specialists are provided through the program or unit. Academic advisers, coaches, and regular education teachers are provided collaboratively through on-campus or off-campus services.

Orientation The program or unit offers an optional 2-day orientation for new students before classes begin and during summer prior to enrollment.

Enrichment Programs for career planning, college survival skills, learning strategies, medication management, oral communication skills, practical computer skills, stress management, and written composition skills are provided collaboratively through on-campus or off-campus services. Credit is offered for oral communication skills.

Application For admittance to the program or unit, students are required to provide a psychoeducational report (3 years old or less). It is recommended that students provide documentation of high school services. Upon application, materials documenting need for services should be sent only to admissions with institutional application materials. Upon acceptance, documentation of need for services should be sent only to the LD program or unit. *Application deadline (LD program):* Rolling/continuous for fall and rolling/continuous for spring.

Written Policies Written policy regarding general/basic LD accommodations is available on the program Web site. Written policies regarding general/basic LD accommodations and reduced course loads are available through the program or unit directly.

Suffolk University
Ballotti Learning Center

8 Ashburton Place

Boston, MA 02108-2770

http://www.suffolk.edu

Contact: Ms. Joyce M. Atkinson, Learning Disabilities Specialist. Phone: 617-573-8235. Fax: 617-742-6761. E-mail: jatkinso@suffolk.edu. Head of LD Program: Mr. Christopher M. Giordano, Assistant Dean of Students. Phone: 617-573-8239. Fax: 617-742-2582. E-mail: cgiordan@suffolk.edu.

Ballotti Learning Center Approximately 80 registered undergraduate students were served during 2002-03. The program or unit includes 2 full-time and 2 part-time staff members. Coaches, graduate assistants/students, LD specialists, and trained peer tutors are provided through the program or unit. Academic advisers and counselors are provided collaboratively through on-campus or off-campus services.

Orientation The program or unit offers an optional orientation for new students individually by special arrangement and during family orientation.

Unique Aids and Services Aids, services, or accommodations include digital textbooks, faculty training, parent workshops, personal coach, priority registration, support groups, meetings with Assistant Dean of students.

Subject-area Tutoring Tutoring is offered one-on-one and in small groups for most subjects. Tutoring is provided through the program or unit via graduate assistants/students and trained peer tutors. Tutoring is also provided collaboratively through on-campus or off-campus services via computer-based instruction.

Basic Skills Remediation Remediation is offered one-on-one for computer skills, learning strategies, math, study skills, time management, and written language. Remediation is provided through the program or unit via computer-based instruction and graduate assistants/students. Remediation is also provided collaboratively through on-campus or off-campus services via trained peer tutors.

Enrichment Enrichment programs are available through the program or unit for learning strategies, self-advocacy, study skills, test taking, time management, and written composition skills. Programs for career planning, college survival skills, math, medication management, oral communication skills, practical computer skills, reading, stress management, and written composition skills are provided collaboratively through on-campus or off-campus services. Credit is offered for math, oral communication skills, and reading.

Student Organization ACCESS consists of 10 members.

Application For admittance to the program or unit, students are required to provide a psychoeducational report (3 years old or less). It is recommended that students apply to the program directly and provide documentation of high school services. Upon acceptance, documentation of need for services should be sent only to the LD program or unit. *Application deadline (institutional): 3/15. Application deadline (LD program):* Rolling/continuous for fall and rolling/continuous for spring.

Written Policies Written policy regarding general/basic LD accommodations is available on the program Web site. Written policy regarding general/basic LD accommodations is outlined in the

Suffolk University (continued)

school's catalog/handbook. Written policies regarding course substitutions, general/basic LD accommodations, and reduced course loads are available through the program or unit directly.

Sul Ross State University
Disabilities Services

East Highway 90
Alpine, TX 79832
http://www.sulross.edu/

Contact: Ms. Joyce Christine Sesters, Disabilities Services Coordinator. Phone: 432-837-8178. Fax: 432-837-8724. E-mail: jsesters@sulross.edu.

Disabilities Services Approximately 100 registered undergraduate students were served during 2002-03. The program or unit includes 2 full-time staff members. Counselors are provided through the program or unit.

Unique Aids and Services Aids, services, or accommodations include career counseling, digital textbooks, and faculty training.

Subject-area Tutoring Tutoring is offered one-on-one and in small groups for all subjects. Tutoring is provided collaboratively through on-campus or off-campus services via computer-based instruction, trained peer tutors, and other.

Basic Skills Remediation Remediation is offered in small groups for handwriting, learning strategies, math, reading, study skills, time management, and written language. Remediation is provided collaboratively through on-campus or off-campus services via computer-based instruction, regular education teachers, and trained peer tutors.

Enrichment Programs for career planning, college survival skills, learning strategies, math, reading, stress management, study skills, test taking, time management, and written composition skills are provided collaboratively through on-campus or off-campus services.

Application For admittance to the program or unit, students are required to apply to the program directly and provide a psychoeducational report (5 years old or less). It is recommended that students provide documentation of high school services. Upon application, materials documenting need for services should be sent to both admissions and the LD program or unit. Upon acceptance, documentation of need for services should be sent to both admissions and the LD program or unit. *Application deadline (institutional):* Continuous. *Application deadline (LD program):* Rolling/continuous for fall and rolling/continuous for spring.

Written Policies Written policy regarding general/basic LD accommodations is outlined in the school's catalog/handbook. Written policies regarding course substitutions, general/basic LD accommodations, grade forgiveness, reduced course loads, substitutions and waivers of admissions requirements, and substitutions and waivers of graduation requirements are available through the program or unit directly.

Sweet Briar College

Sweet Briar, VA 24595

http://www.sbc.edu/

Contact: Dr. Jonathan Green, Associate Dean of Academic Affairs. Phone: 434-381-6205. Fax: 434-381-6489. E-mail: jgreen@sbc.edu.

Approximately 84 registered undergraduate students were served during 2002-03. Academic advisers, coaches, counselors, diagnostic specialists, LD specialists, skill tutors, and strategy tutors are provided collaboratively through on-campus or off-campus services.

Unique Aids and Services Aids, services, or accommodations include career counseling and digital textbooks.

Subject-area Tutoring Tutoring is offered one-on-one for all subjects. Tutoring is provided collaboratively through on-campus or off-campus services via computer-based instruction, professional tutors, and trained peer tutors.

Diagnostic Testing Testing for auditory processing, intelligence, learning strategies, learning styles, math, motor skills, neuropsychological, reading, spoken language, study skills, visual processing, and written language is provided collaboratively through on-campus or off-campus services.

Basic Skills Remediation Remediation is offered one-on-one for learning strategies, math, reading, spelling, time management, and written language. Remediation is provided collaboratively through on-campus or off-campus services via computer-based instruction and trained peer tutors.

Enrichment Programs for career planning, college survival skills, health and nutrition, learning strategies, math, reading, stress management, study skills, test taking, time management, and written composition skills are provided collaboratively through on-campus or off-campus services.

Fees *Diagnostic Testing* fee is applicable.

Application For admittance to the program or unit, students are required to provide a psychoeducational report (5 years old or less). Upon application, materials documenting need for services should be sent only to admissions with institutional application materials. Upon acceptance, documentation of need for services should be sent only to the LD program or unit. *Application deadline (institutional):* 2/1. *Application deadline (LD program):* Rolling/continuous for fall and rolling/continuous for spring.

Written Policies Written policies regarding course substitutions, general/basic LD accommodations, grade forgiveness, substitutions and waivers of admissions requirements, and substitutions and waivers of graduation requirements are outlined in the school's catalog/handbook.

Syracuse University
Office of Disability Services

Syracuse, NY 13244-0003

http://sumweb.syr.edu/ssr/dserv/

Contact: Ms. Patricia C. Jones, Administrative Assistant. Phone: 315-443-4498. Fax: 315-443-1312. E-mail: pcjones@syr.edu. Head of LD Program: Mr. Stephen H. Simon, Director of Disability Services. Phone: 315-443-4498. Fax: 315-443-1312. E-mail: shsimon@syr.edu.

Office of Disability Services Approximately 547 registered undergraduate students were served during 2002-03. The program or unit includes 6 full-time staff members and 1 part-time staff member.

Counselors and LD specialists are provided through the program or unit. Academic advisers, coaches, counselors, diagnostic specialists, graduate assistants/students, LD specialists, skill tutors, strategy tutors, and trained peer tutors are provided collaboratively through on-campus or off-campus services.

Subject-area Tutoring Tutoring is offered one-on-one, in small groups, and in class-size groups for some subjects. Tutoring is provided collaboratively through on-campus or off-campus services via graduate assistants/students, LD specialists, and trained peer tutors.

Diagnostic Testing Testing is provided through the program or unit for learning styles and study skills. Testing for auditory processing, handwriting, intelligence, learning strategies, learning styles, math, motor skills, neuropsychological, personality, reading, spelling, spoken language, study skills, visual processing, and written language is provided collaboratively through on-campus or off-campus services.

Enrichment Enrichment programs are available through the program or unit for college survival skills, self-advocacy, stress management, study skills, test taking, and time management. Programs for career planning, college survival skills, health and nutrition, learning strategies, math, medication management, oral communication skills, practical computer skills, reading, stress management, study skills, test taking, time management, vocabulary development, and written composition skills are provided collaboratively through on-campus or off-campus services. Credit is offered for health and nutrition, learning strategies, math, oral communication skills, practical computer skills, study skills, test taking, and time management.

Fees *Diagnostic Testing* fee is applicable.

Application For admittance to the program or unit, students are required to provide a psychoeducational report (3 years old or less). It is recommended that students apply to the program directly. Upon application, materials documenting need for services should be sent only to the LD program or unit. Upon acceptance, documentation of need for services should be sent only to admissions. *Application deadline (institutional): 1/1. Application deadline (LD program):* Rolling/continuous for fall and rolling/continuous for spring.

Written Policies Written policy regarding general/basic LD accommodations is available on the program Web site. Written policy regarding general/basic LD accommodations is available through the program or unit directly.

Taylor University

236 West Reade Avenue
Upland, IN 46989-1001
http://www.tayloru.edu/
Contact: Dr. R. Edwin Welch, Coordinator of Academic Support Services. Phone: 765-998-5523. E-mail: edwelch@tayloru.edu.

The program or unit includes 1 full-time staff member. Services are provided through the program or unit. Regular education teachers and trained peer tutors are provided collaboratively through on-campus or off-campus services.

Unique Aids and Services Aids, services, or accommodations include accommodations on a case-by-case basis.

Subject-area Tutoring Tutoring is offered one-on-one and in small groups for most subjects. Tutoring is provided collaboratively through on-campus or off-campus services via trained peer tutors.

Basic Skills Remediation Remediation is offered in small groups for learning strategies, math, reading, study skills, time management, and written language. Remediation is provided collaboratively through on-campus or off-campus services via regular education teachers.

Application For admittance to the program or unit, students are required to apply to the program directly and provide a psychoeducational report (3 years old or less). It is recommended that students provide documentation of high school services. Upon acceptance, documentation of need for services should be sent only to the LD program or unit. *Application deadline (institutional): 2/15. Application deadline (LD program):* Rolling/continuous for fall and rolling/continuous for spring.

Written Policies Written policies regarding course substitutions, general/basic LD accommodations, and substitutions and waivers of graduation requirements are available on the program Web site. Written policies regarding course substitutions, general/basic LD accommodations, and substitutions and waivers of graduation requirements are available through the program or unit directly.

Temple University
Disability Resources and Service

1801 North Broad Street
Philadelphia, PA 19122-6096
http://www.temple.edu/disability
Contact: Ms. Wendy E. Kohler, Learning Disability Coordinator. Phone: 215-204-1280. Fax: 215-204-6794. E-mail: wendy.kohler@temple.edu.

Disability Resources and Service Approximately 600 registered undergraduate students were served during 2002-03. The program or unit includes 1 full-time and 1 part-time staff member. LD specialists are provided through the program or unit. Academic advisers, coaches, counselors, regular education teachers, skill tutors, and strategy tutors are provided collaboratively through on-campus or off-campus services.

Unique Aids and Services Aids, services, or accommodations include career counseling and digital textbooks.

Diagnostic Testing Testing for auditory processing, intelligence, learning strategies, learning styles, math, personality, reading, spelling, spoken language, visual processing, and written language is provided collaboratively through on-campus or off-campus services.

Enrichment Programs for career planning, college survival skills, health and nutrition, learning strategies, math, medication management, stress management, study skills, test taking, time management, and written composition skills are provided collaboratively through on-campus or off-campus services.

Fees *Diagnostic Testing* fee is applicable.

Application For admittance to the program or unit, students are required to provide a psychoeducational report (5 years old or less). It is recommended that students provide documentation of high school services and provide a current evaluation. Upon acceptance, documentation of need for services should be sent only to the LD program or unit. *Application deadline (institutional): 4/1. Application deadline (LD program):* Rolling/continuous for fall and rolling/continuous for spring.

Temple University (continued)

Written Policies Written policy regarding general/basic LD accommodations is available on the program Web site. Written policies regarding course substitutions, general/basic LD accommodations, and substitutions and waivers of graduation requirements are available through the program or unit directly.

Tennessee State University

3500 John A Merritt Boulevard

Nashville, TN 37209-1561

http://www.tnstate.edu/

Contact: Mrs. Patricia M. Scudder, Coordinator. Phone: 615-963-7872. Fax: 615-963-2176. E-mail: pscudder@tnstate.edu.

Approximately 75 registered undergraduate students were served during 2002-03. The program or unit includes 1 full-time staff member. LD specialists and remediation/learning specialists are provided collaboratively through on-campus or off-campus services.
Unique Aids and Services Aids, services, or accommodations include digital textbooks.
Subject-area Tutoring Tutoring is offered one-on-one and in small groups for most subjects. Tutoring is provided collaboratively through on-campus or off-campus services via computer-based instruction, graduate assistants/students, and trained peer tutors.
Enrichment Programs for career planning, college survival skills, study skills, and written composition skills are provided collaboratively through on-campus or off-campus services.
Application For admittance to the program or unit, students are required to apply to the program directly and provide a psychoeducational report. Upon acceptance, documentation of need for services should be sent only to the LD program or unit. *Application deadline (institutional):* 8/1. *Application deadline (LD program):* Rolling/continuous for fall and rolling/continuous for spring.
Written Policies Written policies regarding course substitutions, general/basic LD accommodations, reduced course loads, substitutions and waivers of admissions requirements, and substitutions and waivers of graduation requirements are outlined in the school's catalog/handbook. Written policy regarding general/basic LD accommodations is available through the program or unit directly.

Texas A&M University

College Station, TX 77843

http://www.tamu.edu/

Contact: Dr. Anne Reber, Assistant Director of Student Life. Phone: 979-845-1637. Fax: 979-458-1214. E-mail: anne@studentlife.tamu.edu.

Approximately 275 registered undergraduate students were served during 2002-03. The program or unit includes 4 full-time staff members and 1 part-time staff member. LD specialists, skill tutors, and strategy tutors are provided through the program or unit. Academic advisers, counselors, diagnostic specialists, graduate assistants/students, professional tutors, remediation/learning specialists, skill tutors, and strategy tutors are provided collaboratively through on-campus or off-campus services.
Unique Aids and Services Aids, services, or accommodations include advocates, digital textbooks, and priority registration.
Diagnostic Testing Testing for auditory processing, intelligence, math, neuropsychological, personality, reading, spelling, spoken language, study skills, visual processing, and written language is provided collaboratively through on-campus or off-campus services.
Basic Skills Remediation Remediation is offered in class-size groups for learning strategies, math, reading, study skills, time management, and written language. Remediation is provided collaboratively through on-campus or off-campus services via computer-based instruction, graduate assistants/students, and regular education teachers.
Enrichment Enrichment programs are available through the program or unit for learning strategies and self-advocacy. Programs for career planning, college survival skills, learning strategies, math, reading, stress management, study skills, test taking, time management, and written composition skills are provided collaboratively through on-campus or off-campus services. Credit is offered for career planning, college survival skills, math, reading, and written composition skills.
Student Organization Networks consists of 15 members.
Fees *Diagnostic Testing* fee is $350 to $1000.
Application For admittance to the program or unit, students are required to provide a psychoeducational report (3 years old or less). It is recommended that students provide documentation of high school services. Upon application, materials documenting need for services should be sent only to the LD program or unit. Upon acceptance, documentation of need for services should be sent only to the LD program or unit. *Application deadline (institutional):* 2/1. *Application deadline (LD program):* Rolling/continuous for fall and rolling/continuous for spring.
Written Policies Written policies regarding course substitutions, general/basic LD accommodations, grade forgiveness, reduced course loads, and substitutions and waivers of graduation requirements are available through the program or unit directly.

Texas Tech University
Access TECH Disability Support Program

Lubbock, TX 79409

http://www.studentaffairs.ttu.edu/accesstech

Contact: Mr. Frank V. Silvas, Director. Phone: 806-742-2405. Fax: 806-742-4837. E-mail: frank.silvas@ttu.edu.

Access TECH Disability Support Program Approximately 300 registered undergraduate students were served during 2002-03. The program or unit includes 11 full-time staff members. LD specialists are provided through the program or unit. Counselors and skill tutors are provided collaboratively through on-campus or off-campus services.
Orientation The program or unit offers an optional 30-minute orientation for new students during registration.

Unique Aids and Services Aids, services, or accommodations include advocates, career counseling, faculty training, priority registration, and support groups.

Subject-area Tutoring Tutoring is offered one-on-one and in small groups for some subjects. Tutoring is provided collaboratively through on-campus or off-campus services via computer-based instruction, graduate assistants/students, and other.

Diagnostic Testing Testing is provided through the program or unit for auditory processing. Testing for handwriting, intelligence, math, motor skills, neuropsychological, personality, reading, spelling, spoken language, study skills, visual processing, written language, and other services is provided collaboratively through on-campus or off-campus services.

Basic Skills Remediation Remediation is offered one-on-one and in small groups for math, reading, study skills, time management, and written language. Remediation is provided collaboratively through on-campus or off-campus services via computer-based instruction, graduate assistants/students, professional tutors, and other.

Enrichment Enrichment programs are available through the program or unit for college survival skills, self-advocacy, study skills, and time management. Programs for career planning, college survival skills, health and nutrition, learning strategies, math, medication management, oral communication skills, practical computer skills, reading, stress management, study skills, test taking, time management, vocabulary development, written composition skills, and other are provided collaboratively through on-campus or off-campus services.

Fees *Diagnostic Testing* fee is $550 to $4000.

Application For admittance to the program or unit, students are required to apply to the program directly, provide a psychoeducational report (3 years old or less), and provide documentation of high school services. Upon application, materials documenting need for services should be sent only to the LD program or unit. Upon acceptance, documentation of need for services should be sent only to the LD program or unit. *Application deadline (institutional):* Continuous. *Application deadline (LD program):* Rolling/continuous for fall and rolling/continuous for spring.

Written Policies Written policies regarding course substitutions, general/basic LD accommodations, grade forgiveness, reduced course loads, substitutions and waivers of admissions requirements, and substitutions and waivers of graduation requirements are outlined in the school's catalog/handbook.

Thiel College
Office of Special Needs (OSS)

75 College Avenue
Greenville, PA 16125-2181
http://www.thiel.edu/

Contact: Ms. Susan Cowan, Coordinator of Office of Special Needs. Phone: 724-589-2063. Fax: 724-589-2850. E-mail: scowan@thiel.edu.

Office of Special Needs (OSS) Approximately 40 registered undergraduate students were served during 2002-03. The program or unit includes 1 full-time staff member. Academic advisers, counselors, professional tutors, remediation/learning specialists, and trained peer tutors are provided collaboratively through on-campus or off-campus services.

Subject-area Tutoring Tutoring is offered one-on-one. Tutoring is provided collaboratively through on-campus or off-campus services via trained peer tutors.

Basic Skills Remediation Remediation is offered in class-size groups for learning strategies, math, reading, study skills, time management, and written language. Remediation is provided collaboratively through on-campus or off-campus services via professional tutors, regular education teachers, trained peer tutors, and other.

Enrichment Programs for career planning, college survival skills, learning strategies, math, oral communication skills, reading, stress management, study skills, test taking, time management, and written composition skills are provided collaboratively through on-campus or off-campus services. Credit is offered for math, stress management, study skills, test taking, time management, and written composition skills.

Application For admittance to the program or unit, students are required to provide documentation from professional DSM-IV diagnosis. It is recommended that students provide documentation of high school services. Upon application, materials documenting need for services should be sent only to the LD program or unit. Upon acceptance, documentation of need for services should be sent only to the LD program or unit. *Application deadline (institutional):* 8/15. *Application deadline (LD program):* Rolling/continuous for fall and rolling/continuous for spring.

Written Policies Written policy regarding general/basic LD accommodations is outlined in the school's catalog/handbook. Written policy regarding general/basic LD accommodations is available through the program or unit directly.

Thomas Edison State College
Office of Students with Disabilities

101 West State Street
Trenton, NJ 08608-1176
http://www.tesc.edu/

Contact: Ms. Janice Toliver, ADA Coordinator. Phone: 609-984-1141 Ext. 3415. Fax: 609-777-2956. E-mail: jtoliver@tesc.edu.

Office of Students with Disabilities Approximately 20 registered undergraduate students were served during 2002-03. The program or unit includes 1 full-time staff member. Academic advisers and LD specialists are provided through the program or unit. Academic advisers and LD specialists are provided collaboratively through on-campus or off-campus services.

Unique Aids and Services Aids, services, or accommodations include books on tape via Recording for the Blind.

Application For admittance to the program or unit, students are required to provide LD evaluation. It is recommended that students provide a psychoeducational report (5 years old or less) and provide documentation of high school services. Upon application, materials documenting need for services should be sent only to the LD program or unit. Upon acceptance, documentation of need for services should be sent only to the LD program or unit. *Application deadline (LD program):* Rolling/continuous for fall and rolling/continuous for spring.

Thomas Edison State College (continued)

Written Policies Written policy regarding general/basic LD accommodations is outlined in the school's catalog/handbook. Written policies regarding course substitutions, substitutions and waivers of admissions requirements, and substitutions and waivers of graduation requirements are available through the program or unit directly.

Thomas More College

333 Thomas More Parkway
Crestview Hills, KY 41017-3495
http://www.thomasmore.edu/
Contact: Mrs. Barbara S. Davis, Director of Student Services and Advising. Phone: 859-344-3521. Fax: 859-344-3607. E-mail: barb.davis@thomasmore.edu.

Approximately 35 registered undergraduate students were served during 2002-03. The program or unit includes 2 part-time staff members. Counselors, diagnostic specialists, LD specialists, professional tutors, remediation/learning specialists, skill tutors, strategy tutors, trained peer tutors, and other are provided through the program or unit. Academic advisers, coaches, regular education teachers, special education teachers, teacher trainees, and other are provided collaboratively through on-campus or off-campus services.
Unique Aids and Services Aids, services, or accommodations include advocates, career counseling, and support groups.
Subject-area Tutoring Tutoring is offered one-on-one and in small groups for most subjects. Tutoring is provided through the program or unit via professional tutors and trained peer tutors.
Basic Skills Remediation Remediation is offered in class-size groups for learning strategies, math, reading, spelling, study skills, time management, and written language. Remediation is provided through the program or unit via LD specialists and trained peer tutors.
Enrichment Enrichment programs are available through the program or unit for learning strategies, math, medication management, oral communication skills, reading, self-advocacy, stress management, study skills, test taking, time management, vocabulary development, and written composition skills. Programs for career planning, health and nutrition, learning strategies, math, medication management, oral communication skills, practical computer skills, reading, self-advocacy, stress management, study skills, test taking, time management, vocabulary development, and written composition skills are provided collaboratively through on-campus or off-campus services.
Application For admittance to the program or unit, students are required to provide a psychoeducational report (3 years old or less). It is recommended that students provide documentation of high school services. Upon application, materials documenting need for services should be sent only to the LD program or unit. *Application deadline (institutional):* 8/15. *Application deadline (LD program):* Rolling/continuous for fall.
Written Policies Written policy regarding general/basic LD accommodations is available on the program Web site. Written policy regarding general/basic LD accommodations is outlined in the school's catalog/handbook. Written policies regarding course substitutions, general/basic LD accommodations, reduced course loads, substitutions and waivers of admissions requirements, and substitutions and waivers of graduation requirements are available through the program or unit directly.

Toccoa Falls College

Alt Hwy 17
Toccoa Falls, GA 30598
http://www.toccoafalls.edu/
Contact: Sabrina Armour, Director of Learning Support Services. Phone: 706-886-7299 Ext. 5465. Fax: 706-282-6012. E-mail: sarmour@tfc.edu.

Approximately 25 registered undergraduate students were served during 2002-03. The program or unit includes 1 full-time and 20 part-time staff members. Academic advisers, coaches, counselors, diagnostic specialists, graduate assistants/students, LD specialists, trained peer tutors, and other are provided through the program or unit. Academic advisers, counselors, diagnostic specialists, graduate assistants/students, trained peer tutors, and other are provided collaboratively through on-campus or off-campus services.
Unique Aids and Services Aids, services, or accommodations include personal coach, support groups, meetings with faculty, advisers, and others on case-by-case basis.
Subject-area Tutoring Tutoring is offered one-on-one for all subjects. Tutoring is provided through the program or unit via graduate assistants/students and trained peer tutors. Tutoring is also provided collaboratively through on-campus or off-campus services via graduate assistants/students and trained peer tutors.
Basic Skills Remediation Remediation is offered one-on-one and in small groups for computer skills, handwriting, learning strategies, math, reading, spelling, spoken language, study skills, time management, and most campus taught courses. Remediation is provided through the program or unit via computer-based instruction, LD specialists, and trained peer tutors. Remediation is also provided collaboratively through on-campus or off-campus services via computer-based instruction, LD specialists, and trained peer tutors.
Enrichment Enrichment programs are available through the program or unit for career planning, college survival skills, learning strategies, practical computer skills, reading, stress management, study skills, test taking, time management, and written composition skills. Programs for career planning, health and nutrition, learning strategies, and written composition skills are provided collaboratively through on-campus or off-campus services.
Application For admittance to the program or unit, students are required to provide a psychoeducational report (4 years old or less). It is recommended that students apply to the program directly and provide documentation of high school services. Upon application, materials documenting need for services should be sent only to the LD program or unit. *Application deadline (institutional):* Continuous. *Application deadline (LD program):* Rolling/continuous for fall and rolling/continuous for spring.
Written Policies Written policy regarding general/basic LD accommodations is available on the program Web site. Written policy regarding general/basic LD accommodations is outlined in the school's catalog/handbook.

Transylvania University

300 North Broadway
Lexington, KY 40508-1797
http://www.transy.edu/

Contact: Ms. Marian Molle', ADA Coordinator. Phone: 859-233-8215. Fax: 859-233-8797. E-mail: mmolle@transy.edu.

Approximately 4 registered undergraduate students were served during 2002-03. The program or unit includes 1 part-time staff member. Academic advisers, counselors, diagnostic specialists, and regular education teachers are provided collaboratively through on-campus or off-campus services.

Subject-area Tutoring Tutoring is offered one-on-one and in small groups for some subjects. Tutoring is provided collaboratively through on-campus or off-campus services via trained peer tutors.

Enrichment Programs for career planning, college survival skills, health and nutrition, learning strategies, stress management, study skills, time management, and written composition skills are provided collaboratively through on-campus or off-campus services.

Application For admittance to the program or unit, students are required to apply to the program directly and provide a psychoeducational report. It is recommended that students provide documentation of high school services. Upon application, materials documenting need for services should be sent only to the LD program or unit. *Application deadline (institutional):* 2/1. *Application deadline (LD program):* Rolling/continuous for fall and rolling/continuous for spring.

Written Policies Written policy regarding general/basic LD accommodations is outlined in the school's catalog/handbook.

Trent University
Learning Integration Program

1600 West Bank Drive
Peterborough, ON K9J 7B8
Canada
http://www.Trentu.ca/specialneeds
Contact: Ms. Eunice Lund-Lucas, Coordinator Special Needs. Phone: 705-748-1281. Fax: 705-748-1509. E-mail: elundlucas@Trentu.ca.

Learning Integration Program Approximately 85 registered undergraduate students were served during 2002-03. The program or unit includes 3 full-time and 3 part-time staff members. Coaches, diagnostic specialists, LD specialists, professional tutors, and remediation/learning specialists are provided through the program or unit. Academic advisers, counselors, graduate assistants/students, regular education teachers, skill tutors, and strategy tutors are provided collaboratively through on-campus or off-campus services.

Unique Aids and Services Aids, services, or accommodations include advocates, career counseling, faculty training, and personal coach.

Subject-area Tutoring Tutoring is offered one-on-one for most subjects. Tutoring is provided through the program or unit via professional tutors. Tutoring is also provided collaboratively through on-campus or off-campus services via trained peer tutors.

Diagnostic Testing Testing is provided through the program or unit for auditory processing, handwriting, intelligence, learning strategies, learning styles, math, motor skills, neuropsychological, personality, reading, social skills, spelling, spoken language, study skills, visual processing, and written language. Testing for learning styles, reading, spelling, and study skills is provided collaboratively through on-campus or off-campus services.

Basic Skills Remediation Remediation is offered one-on-one for learning strategies, math, reading, social skills, study skills, time management, written language, and motivational issues. Remediation is provided through the program or unit via LD specialists and professional tutors.

Enrichment Enrichment programs are available through the program or unit for health and nutrition, self-advocacy, and time management. Programs for career planning, learning strategies, reading, stress management, study skills, test taking, and written composition skills are provided collaboratively through on-campus or off-campus services.

Fees *Diagnostic Testing* fee is $1300.

Application For admittance to the program or unit, students are required to provide documentation of high school services. It is recommended that students provide a psychoeducational report. Upon application, materials documenting need for services should be sent to both admissions and the LD program or unit. Upon acceptance, documentation of need for services should be sent only to the LD program or unit. *Application deadline (institutional):* 6/1. *Application deadline (LD program):* Rolling/continuous for fall.

Written Policies Written policy regarding general/basic LD accommodations is available on the program Web site. Written policy regarding general/basic LD accommodations is outlined in the school's catalog/handbook.

Trinity Baptist College
Program to Assist Learning Disabled Students

800 Hammond Boulevard
Jacksonville, FL 32221
http://www.tbc.edu/
Contact: Dr. Lois Schaefer, Associate Professor. Phone: 904-596-2506. Fax: 904-596-2531. E-mail: lschaefer@tbc.edu.

Program to Assist Learning Disabled Students Approximately 20 registered undergraduate students were served during 2002-03. The program or unit includes 1 full-time staff member. Diagnostic specialists and LD specialists are provided through the program or unit. Academic advisers, counselors, professional tutors, and regular education teachers are provided collaboratively through on-campus or off-campus services.

Orientation The program or unit offers a mandatory approximately 30-minute orientation for new students after classes begin and individually by special arrangement.

Unique Aids and Services Aids, services, or accommodations include advocates, faculty training, meetings with faculty adviser/special education counselor.

Subject-area Tutoring Tutoring is offered one-on-one. Tutoring is provided through the program or unit via LD specialists. Tutoring is also provided collaboratively through on-campus or off-campus services via computer-based instruction and trained peer tutors.

Diagnostic Testing Testing is provided through the program or unit for auditory processing, handwriting, intelligence, learning strategies, learning styles, reading, and visual processing. Testing for reading and spelling is provided collaboratively through on-campus or off-campus services.

Trinity Baptist College (continued)

Basic Skills Remediation Remediation is offered in class-size groups for handwriting, learning strategies, math, reading, spelling, study skills, time management, visual processing, and written language. Remediation is provided collaboratively through on-campus or off-campus services via regular education teachers and trained peer tutors.

Enrichment Enrichment programs are available through the program or unit for reading, self-advocacy, study skills, test taking, and time management. Programs for career planning, college survival skills, learning strategies, math, self-advocacy, time management, vocabulary development, and written composition skills are provided collaboratively through on-campus or off-campus services.

Application For admittance to the program or unit, students are required to provide a psychoeducational report, provide documentation of high school services, and provide in person conference with LD unit personnel. It is recommended that students apply to the program directly. Upon application, materials documenting need for services should be sent only to admissions with institutional application materials. *Application deadline (institutional):* Continuous. *Application deadline (LD program):* Rolling/continuous for fall and rolling/continuous for spring.

Written Policies Written policies regarding general/basic LD accommodations, grade forgiveness, and reduced course loads are outlined in the school's catalog/handbook.

Trinity Christian College
Office Of Academic Support and Services (TASS)

6601 West College Drive

Palos Heights, IL 60463-0929

http://www.trnty.edu/

Contact: Phone: 708-597-3000. Fax: 708-239-3995.

Office Of Academic Support and Services (TASS) Approximately 46 registered undergraduate students were served during 2002-03. The program or unit includes 1 full-time and 1 part-time staff member. Coaches, counselors, remediation/learning specialists, strategy tutors, and trained peer tutors are provided through the program or unit. Coaches, counselors, diagnostic specialists, remediation/learning specialists, strategy tutors, and trained peer tutors are provided collaboratively through on-campus or off-campus services.

Orientation The program or unit offers an optional orientation for new students individually by special arrangement.

Summer Program To help prepare for the demands of college, there is an optional 1-week summer program prior to entering the school. Degree credit will be earned.

Unique Aids and Services Aids, services, or accommodations include career counseling, digital textbooks, and support groups.

Subject-area Tutoring Tutoring is offered one-on-one, in small groups, and in class-size groups for most subjects. Tutoring is provided through the program or unit via computer-based instruction, trained peer tutors, and other.

Diagnostic Testing Testing is provided through the program or unit for learning strategies, learning styles, personality, reading, study skills, and other services. Testing for auditory processing, handwriting, intelligence, math, motor skills, neuropsychological, social skills, spelling, and spoken language is provided collaboratively through on-campus or off-campus services.

Basic Skills Remediation Remediation is offered one-on-one for learning strategies, spoken language, study skills, time management, and written language. Remediation is provided through the program or unit via regular education teachers and trained peer tutors. Remediation is also provided collaboratively through on-campus or off-campus services via regular education teachers and trained peer tutors.

Enrichment Enrichment programs are available through the program or unit for career planning, college survival skills, health and nutrition, learning strategies, self-advocacy, stress management, study skills, test taking, time management, written composition skills, and other.

Application For admittance to the program or unit, students are required to provide a psychoeducational report (3 years old or less) and provide documentation of high school services. It is recommended that students provide results of updated testing at a local facility (application provided). Upon application, materials documenting need for services should be sent only to the LD program or unit. Upon acceptance, documentation of need for services should be sent only to the LD program or unit. *Application deadline (institutional):* Continuous. *Application deadline (LD program):* Rolling/continuous for fall and rolling/continuous for spring.

Written Policies Written policy regarding general/basic LD accommodations is outlined in the school's catalog/handbook. Written policy regarding general/basic LD accommodations is available through the program or unit directly.

Trinity College of Nursing and Health Sciences Schools

555 6th Street, Suite 300

Moline, IL 61265-1216

http://www.trinitycollegeqc.edu/

Contact: Ms. Alethea Kaiser, Director of Learner Services. Phone: 309-779-7720. Fax: 309-779-7748. E-mail: kaisera@trinityqc.com.

Approximately 3 registered undergraduate students were served during 2002-03. The program or unit includes 1 full-time staff member. Academic advisers are provided collaboratively through on-campus or off-campus services.

Unique Aids and Services Aids, services, or accommodations include faculty training, personal coach, and weekly meetings with faculty.

Subject-area Tutoring Tutoring is offered one-on-one and in small groups for most subjects. Tutoring is provided collaboratively through on-campus or off-campus services via trained peer tutors.

Diagnostic Testing Testing for auditory processing, handwriting, intelligence, learning styles, neuropsychological, personality, reading, study skills, and visual processing is provided collaboratively through on-campus or off-campus services.

Enrichment Programs for career planning, learning strategies, study skills, and test taking are provided collaboratively through on-campus or off-campus services.

Application It is recommended that students provide a psychoeducational report (3 years old or less) and provide documentation of high school services. Upon acceptance, documentation of need for services should be sent only to the LD program or unit. *Application deadline (institutional): 6/1. Application deadline (LD program):* Rolling/continuous for fall and rolling/continuous for spring.

Written Policies Written policy regarding general/basic LD accommodations is outlined in the school's catalog/handbook.

Trinity University
Disability Services for Students

715 Stadium Drive
San Antonio, TX 78212-7200
http://www.trinity.edu/dss

Contact: Coordinator of Disability Services. Phone: 210-999-7411. Fax: 210-999-7848. E-mail: dss@trinity.edu.

Disability Services for Students Approximately 15 registered undergraduate students were served during 2002-03. The program or unit includes 1 part-time staff member. Academic advisers and counselors are provided collaboratively through on-campus or off-campus services.

Subject-area Tutoring Tutoring is offered one-on-one for most subjects. Tutoring is provided collaboratively through on-campus or off-campus services via other.

Enrichment Enrichment programs are available through the program or unit for college survival skills and self-advocacy. Programs for career planning, practical computer skills, stress management, study skills, test taking, and time management are provided collaboratively through on-campus or off-campus services. Credit is offered for practical computer skills.

Application For admittance to the program or unit, students are required to apply to the program directly and provide a psychoeducational report (3 years old or less). Upon acceptance, documentation of need for services should be sent only to the LD program or unit. *Application deadline (institutional): 2/1. Application deadline (LD program):* Rolling/continuous for fall and rolling/continuous for spring.

Written Policies Written policies regarding course substitutions, general/basic LD accommodations, reduced course loads, and substitutions and waivers of graduation requirements are available on the program Web site. Written policies regarding course substitutions, general/basic LD accommodations, reduced course loads, and substitutions and waivers of graduation requirements are available through the program or unit directly.

Troy State University
Adaptive Needs Program

University Avenue
Troy, AL 36082
http://www.troyst.edu/

Contact: Deborah G. Sellers, Adaptive Needs Program Director. Phone: 334-670-3220. Fax: 334-670-3810. E-mail: dsellers@troyst.edu.

Adaptive Needs Program Approximately 55 registered undergraduate students were served during 2002-03. The program or unit includes 1 full-time staff member. Academic advisers, graduate assistants/students, and skill tutors are provided through the program or unit.

Orientation The program or unit offers an optional 1 to 2-hour orientation for new students individually by special arrangement.

Unique Aids and Services Aids, services, or accommodations include career counseling, faculty training, priority registration, textbooks on tape, academic advising.

Subject-area Tutoring Tutoring is offered one-on-one and in small groups. Tutoring is provided collaboratively through on-campus or off-campus services via computer-based instruction and trained peer tutors.

Basic Skills Remediation Remediation is offered in class-size groups for math, study skills, time management, and written language. Remediation is provided collaboratively through on-campus or off-campus services via regular education teachers and trained peer tutors.

Enrichment Enrichment programs are available through the program or unit for self-advocacy. Program for career planning is provided collaboratively through on-campus or off-campus services. Credit is offered for career planning.

Student Organization Students Concerned About Disability Awareness (SCADA) consists of 25 members.

Application For admittance to the program or unit, students are required to provide a psychoeducational report (3 years old or less) and provide documentation of high school services. Upon application, materials documenting need for services should be sent only to the LD program or unit. Upon acceptance, documentation of need for services should be sent only to the LD program or unit. *Application deadline (institutional): Continuous. Application deadline (LD program):* Rolling/continuous for fall and rolling/continuous for spring.

Written Policies Written policy regarding general/basic LD accommodations is available through the program or unit directly.

Troy State University Montgomery
Disability Services Office

PO Drawer 4419
Montgomery, AL 36103-4419
http://www.tsum.edu/

Contact: Mrs. Jane Currey Rudick, Coordinator. Phone: 334-241-5486 Ext. 486. Fax: 334-241-5455. E-mail: jrudick@tsum.edu.

Disability Services Office Approximately 200 registered undergraduate students were served during 2002-03. The program or unit includes 1 full-time and 1 part-time staff member. Academic advisers, counselors, diagnostic specialists, professional tutors, regular education teachers, remediation/learning specialists, skill tutors, and strategy tutors are provided collaboratively through on-campus or off-campus services.

Troy State University Montgomery (continued)

Orientation The program or unit offers an optional orientation for new students individually by special arrangement.

Unique Aids and Services Aids, services, or accommodations include career counseling, digital textbooks, priority registration, and support groups.

Subject-area Tutoring Tutoring is offered one-on-one for some subjects. Tutoring is provided collaboratively through on-campus or off-campus services via computer-based instruction, graduate assistants/students, and professional tutors.

Diagnostic Testing Testing for auditory processing, handwriting, intelligence, learning strategies, learning styles, math, motor skills, neuropsychological, personality, reading, social skills, spelling, spoken language, study skills, visual processing, and written language is provided collaboratively through on-campus or off-campus services.

Basic Skills Remediation Remediation is offered one-on-one and in class-size groups for learning strategies, math, reading, study skills, time management, and written language. Remediation is provided collaboratively through on-campus or off-campus services via computer-based instruction, graduate assistants/students, professional tutors, and regular education teachers.

Enrichment Programs for career planning, college survival skills, learning strategies, math, oral communication skills, practical computer skills, reading, study skills, test taking, time management, vocabulary development, and written composition skills are provided collaboratively through on-campus or off-campus services. Credit is offered for college survival skills, learning strategies, math, oral communication skills, practical computer skills, reading, study skills, test taking, time management, vocabulary development, and written composition skills.

Application For admittance to the program or unit, students are required to apply to the program directly and provide a psychoeducational report (3 years old or less). Upon application, materials documenting need for services should be sent only to the LD program or unit. Upon acceptance, documentation of need for services should be sent only to the LD program or unit. *Application deadline (institutional):* Continuous. *Application deadline (LD program):* Rolling/continuous for fall and rolling/continuous for spring.

Written Policies Written policies regarding course substitutions, general/basic LD accommodations, grade forgiveness, substitutions and waivers of admissions requirements, and substitutions and waivers of graduation requirements are available through the program or unit directly.

Truman State University

100 East Normal Street
Kirksville, MO 63501-4221
http://www.truman.edu/

Contact: Mrs. Vicky L. Wehner RN, Coordinator. Phone: 660-785-4478. Fax: 660-785-4011. E-mail: vwehner@truman.edu.

Approximately 75 registered undergraduate students were served during 2002-03. The program or unit includes 10 part-time staff members. Academic advisers, graduate assistants/students, LD specialists, professional tutors, remediation/learning specialists, skill tutors, strategy tutors, and trained peer tutors are provided through

the program or unit. Academic advisers, coaches, counselors, diagnostic specialists, graduate assistants/students, LD specialists, professional tutors, regular education teachers, remediation/learning specialists, skill tutors, and trained peer tutors are provided collaboratively through on-campus or off-campus services.

Unique Aids and Services Aids, services, or accommodations include advocates, career counseling, digital textbooks, faculty training, personal coach, and priority registration.

Subject-area Tutoring Tutoring is offered one-on-one, in small groups, and in class-size groups for most subjects. Tutoring is provided through the program or unit via graduate assistants/students. Tutoring is also provided collaboratively through on-campus or off-campus services via graduate assistants/students and trained peer tutors.

Basic Skills Remediation Remediation is offered one-on-one for learning strategies, math, study skills, and time management. Remediation is provided through the program or unit via computer-based instruction, graduate assistants/students, and trained peer tutors. Remediation is also provided collaboratively through on-campus or off-campus services via regular education teachers and trained peer tutors.

Enrichment Enrichment programs are available through the program or unit for college survival skills, learning strategies, self-advocacy, study skills, test taking, and time management. Programs for career planning, college survival skills, health and nutrition, math, medication management, oral communication skills, self-advocacy, stress management, study skills, and written composition skills are provided collaboratively through on-campus or off-campus services. Credit is offered for oral communication skills.

Application For admittance to the program or unit, students are required to provide a psychoeducational report (3 years old or less) and provide medical documentation for chronic, psychiatric, or temporary physical disability. It is recommended that students provide documentation of high school services. Upon application, materials documenting need for services should be sent only to the LD program or unit. Upon acceptance, documentation of need for services should be sent only to the LD program or unit. *Application deadline (institutional):* 3/1. *Application deadline (LD program):* Rolling/continuous for fall and rolling/continuous for spring.

Written Policies Written policies regarding general/basic LD accommodations and reduced course loads are available through the program or unit directly.

Tulane University
Office of Disability Services

6823 St Charles Avenue
New Orleans, LA 70118-5669
http://www.tulane.edu/

Contact: David Tylicki, Accommodations Coordinator. Phone: 504-862-8433. Fax: 504-862-8435. E-mail: dtylicki@tulane.edu. Head of LD Program: Manager of Disability Services. Phone: 504-862-8433. Fax: 504-862-8435.

Office of Disability Services Approximately 202 registered undergraduate students were served during 2002-03. The program or unit includes 3 full-time staff members. LD specialists, skill tutors, and strategy tutors are provided through the program or unit. Academic advisers, coaches, counselors, diagnostic specialists, graduate assistants/students, regular education teachers, and trained peer tutors are provided collaboratively through on-campus or off-campus services.

Orientation The program or unit offers a mandatory 30-minute to 1-hour orientation for new students before classes begin, during registration, after classes begin, and individually by special arrangement.

Unique Aids and Services Aids, services, or accommodations include career counseling, digital textbooks, personal coach, support groups, note-takers, books-on-tape, testing accommodations, extended time, distraction-reduced environment.

Subject-area Tutoring Tutoring is offered one-on-one, in small groups, and in class-size groups for some subjects. Tutoring is provided collaboratively through on-campus or off-campus services via graduate assistants/students and trained peer tutors.

Diagnostic Testing Testing for learning styles, personality, reading, visual processing, and other services is provided collaboratively through on-campus or off-campus services.

Basic Skills Remediation Remediation is offered one-on-one, in small groups, and in class-size groups for learning strategies, study skills, time management, and stress management, test-taking strategies. Remediation is provided through the program or unit via LD specialists.

Enrichment Enrichment programs are available through the program or unit for college survival skills, learning strategies, stress management, study skills, test taking, and time management. Programs for career planning, health and nutrition, oral communication skills, practical computer skills, self-advocacy, stress management, time management, and written composition skills are provided collaboratively through on-campus or off-campus services.

Fees *Diagnostic Testing* fee is $0 to $75.

Application *Application deadline (institutional):* 1/15. *Application deadline (LD program):* Rolling/continuous for fall and rolling/continuous for spring.

Written Policies Written policies regarding course substitutions, general/basic LD accommodations, and substitutions and waivers of graduation requirements are available on the program Web site. Written policies regarding course substitutions, general/basic LD accommodations, and substitutions and waivers of graduation requirements are available through the program or unit directly.

Tusculum College
Disabilities Office

60 Shiloh Road

Greeneville, TN 37743-9997

http://www.tusculum.edu/learning/

Contact: Ms. Lori N. McCallister, Director. Phone: 423-636-7300 Ext. 5651. E-mail: lmccalli@tusculum.edu.

Disabilities Office Approximately 16 registered undergraduate students were served during 2002-03. The program or unit includes 1 full-time staff member. Academic advisers, coaches, counselors, graduate assistants/students, skill tutors, strategy tutors, and trained peer tutors are provided collaboratively through on-campus or off-campus services.

Summer Program To help prepare for the demands of college, there is an optional 2-week summer program prior to entering the school. Degree credit will be earned.

Unique Aids and Services Aids, services, or accommodations include career counseling, digital textbooks, faculty training, and personal coach.

Subject-area Tutoring Tutoring is offered one-on-one, in small groups, and in class-size groups for most subjects. Tutoring is provided collaboratively through on-campus or off-campus services via professional tutors and trained peer tutors.

Basic Skills Remediation Remediation is offered one-on-one, in small groups, and in class-size groups for computer skills, learning strategies, math, reading, study skills, time management, and written language. Remediation is provided collaboratively through on-campus or off-campus services via professional tutors and trained peer tutors.

Enrichment Programs for career planning, college survival skills, learning strategies, math, oral communication skills, practical computer skills, reading, stress management, study skills, test taking, time management, and written composition skills are provided collaboratively through on-campus or off-campus services. Credit is offered for oral communication skills, practical computer skills, and written composition skills.

Application For admittance to the program or unit, students are required to provide a psychoeducational report (3 years old or less). It is recommended that students provide documentation of high school services. Upon application, materials documenting need for services should be sent only to the LD program or unit. Upon acceptance, documentation of need for services should be sent only to the LD program or unit. *Application deadline (institutional):* Continuous. *Application deadline (LD program):* Rolling/continuous for fall and rolling/continuous for spring.

Written Policies Written policy regarding general/basic LD accommodations is available on the program Web site. Written policy regarding general/basic LD accommodations is outlined in the school's catalog/handbook. Written policy regarding general/basic LD accommodations is available through the program or unit directly.

Union Institute & University
Academic Support Network

440 East McMillan Street

Cincinnati, OH 45206-1925

http://www.tui.edu/universityoffices/ASN

Contact: Ms. Anne E. Connor, Director of Academic Support Network. Phone: 802-828-8801. Fax: 802-828-8565. E-mail: anne.connor@tui.edu.

Academic Support Network Approximately 35 registered undergraduate students were served during 2002-03. The program or unit includes 1 full-time and 2 part-time staff members. Coaches, professional tutors, regular education teachers, remediation/learning specialists, skill tutors, and strategy tutors are provided through the program or unit.

Orientation The program or unit offers an optional variable length (as needed) orientation for new students individually by special arrangement and after general orientation.

Unique Aids and Services Aids, services, or accommodations include advocates, faculty training, and personal coach.

Union Institute & University (continued)

Diagnostic Testing Testing is provided through the program or unit for learning strategies, learning styles, and reading.

Basic Skills Remediation Remediation is offered one-on-one, in small groups, and in class-size groups for computer skills, learning strategies, reading, social skills, spoken language, study skills, time management, and written language. Remediation is provided through the program or unit via computer-based instruction, professional tutors, and regular education teachers.

Application For admittance to the program or unit, students are required to apply to the program directly and provide a psychoeducational report (3 years old or less). Upon acceptance, documentation of need for services should be sent only to the LD program or unit. *Application deadline (institutional):* 10/1. *Application deadline (LD program):* Rolling/continuous for fall and rolling/continuous for spring.

Written Policies Written policy regarding general/basic LD accommodations is available on the program Web site. Written policy regarding general/basic LD accommodations is outlined in the school's catalog/handbook. Written policy regarding general/basic LD accommodations is available through the program or unit directly.

Union University
Support Service(s)

1050 Union University Drive

Jackson, TN 38305-3697

http://www.uu.edu/

Contact: Dr. Paul Deschenes, Director of Counseling Services. Fax: 731-661-5017. E-mail: pdeschen@uu.edu.

Support Service(s) Approximately 19 registered undergraduate students were served during 2002-03. Academic advisers, counselors, and other are provided collaboratively through on-campus or off-campus services.

Unique Aids and Services Aids, services, or accommodations include advocates and faculty training.

Subject-area Tutoring Tutoring is offered one-on-one. Tutoring is provided collaboratively through on-campus or off-campus services via trained peer tutors.

Diagnostic Testing Testing for intelligence, personality, and other services is provided collaboratively through on-campus or off-campus services.

Enrichment Programs for career planning, learning strategies, stress management, study skills, test taking, and time management are provided collaboratively through on-campus or off-campus services.

Fees *Diagnostic Testing* fee is $200.

Application For admittance to the program or unit, students are required to provide a psychoeducational report (3 years old or less) and provide documentation of high school services. *Application deadline (institutional):* Continuous. *Application deadline (LD program):* Rolling/continuous for fall and rolling/continuous for spring.

Written Policies Written policy regarding general/basic LD accommodations is available through the program or unit directly.

Unity College
Learning Resource Center

90 Quaker Hill Road

Unity, ME 04988

http://www.unity.edu/lrc/lrc.htm

Contact: Ms. Ann Dailey, Learning Disabilities Specialist. Phone: 207-948-3131 Ext. 285. Fax: 207-948-6277. E-mail: adailey@unity.edu.

Learning Resource Center Approximately 25 registered undergraduate students were served during 2002-03. The program or unit includes 2 full-time staff members. Academic advisers, LD specialists, remediation/learning specialists, strategy tutors, and trained peer tutors are provided through the program or unit. Academic advisers, counselors, regular education teachers, skill tutors, and trained peer tutors are provided collaboratively through on-campus or off-campus services.

Orientation The program or unit offers an optional orientation for new students individually by special arrangement.

Unique Aids and Services Aids, services, or accommodations include advocates and career counseling.

Subject-area Tutoring Tutoring is offered one-on-one and in small groups for most subjects. Tutoring is provided through the program or unit via LD specialists and trained peer tutors. Tutoring is also provided collaboratively through on-campus or off-campus services via trained peer tutors.

Basic Skills Remediation Remediation is offered one-on-one for computer skills, learning strategies, math, study skills, time management, and written language. Remediation is provided through the program or unit via LD specialists and trained peer tutors. Remediation is also provided collaboratively through on-campus or off-campus services via trained peer tutors.

Enrichment Enrichment programs are available through the program or unit for college survival skills, learning strategies, math, practical computer skills, self-advocacy, stress management, study skills, test taking, time management, and written composition skills. Programs for career planning, college survival skills, health and nutrition, learning strategies, math, practical computer skills, reading, stress management, study skills, time management, and written composition skills are provided collaboratively through on-campus or off-campus services.

Application For admittance to the program or unit, students are required to provide a psychoeducational report (3 years old or less) and provide documentation of high school services. Upon application, materials documenting need for services should be sent only to admissions with institutional application materials. Upon acceptance, documentation of need for services should be sent only to the LD program or unit. *Application deadline (institutional):* Continuous. *Application deadline (LD program):* Rolling/continuous for fall and rolling/continuous for spring.

Written Policies Written policy regarding general/basic LD accommodations is outlined in the school's catalog/handbook.

University at Buffalo, The State University of New York

Capen Hall
Buffalo, NY 14260
http://www.buffalo.edu/

Contact: Mr. Randy Borst, Director of Disability Services. Phone: 716-645-2608. Fax: 716-645-3116. E-mail: stu-disability@buffalo.edu.

Approximately 135 registered undergraduate students were served during 2002-03. The program or unit includes 4 full-time staff members. Graduate assistants/students are provided through the program or unit. Academic advisers, counselors, graduate assistants/students, remediation/learning specialists, skill tutors, strategy tutors, and trained peer tutors are provided collaboratively through on-campus or off-campus services.

Unique Aids and Services Aids, services, or accommodations include career counseling and digital textbooks.

Subject-area Tutoring Tutoring is offered for all subjects. Tutoring is provided collaboratively through on-campus or off-campus services via trained peer tutors.

Basic Skills Remediation Remediation is offered one-on-one, in small groups, and in class-size groups for learning strategies, math, social skills, study skills, time management, and written language. Remediation is provided collaboratively through on-campus or off-campus services via graduate assistants/students, regular education teachers, and trained peer tutors.

Enrichment Enrichment programs are available through the program or unit for self-advocacy and time management. Programs for career planning, college survival skills, health and nutrition, learning strategies, math, medication management, oral communication skills, practical computer skills, reading, self-advocacy, stress management, study skills, test taking, time management, and written composition skills are provided collaboratively through on-campus or off-campus services. Credit is offered for career planning, college survival skills, health and nutrition, learning strategies, math, oral communication skills, and study skills.

Application For admittance to the program or unit, students are required to apply to the program directly and provide a psychoeducational report (3 years old or less). It is recommended that students provide documentation of high school services. Upon application, materials documenting need for services should be sent only to the LD program or unit. Upon acceptance, documentation of need for services should be sent only to the LD program or unit. *Application deadline (institutional):* Continuous. *Application deadline (LD program):* Rolling/continuous for fall and rolling/continuous for spring.

Written Policies Written policies regarding course substitutions and general/basic LD accommodations are available through the program or unit directly.

University College of the Cariboo

PO Box 3010, Station Terminal
Kamloops, BC V2C 5N3
Canada
http://www.cariboo.bc.ca/

Contact: Ms. Davina Neve, Disability Services Adviser. Phone: 250-828-5369. Fax: 250-371-5772. E-mail: dneve@cariboo.bc.ca.

The program or unit includes 8 full-time staff members and 1 part-time staff member. Academic advisers, counselors, diagnostic specialists, and professional tutors are provided through the program or unit. Academic advisers, counselors, diagnostic specialists, and professional tutors are provided collaboratively through on-campus or off-campus services.

Orientation The program or unit offers an optional orientation for new students individually by special arrangement.

Summer Program To help prepare for the demands of college, there is an optional 6-week summer program prior to entering the school. Degree credit will be earned.

Unique Aids and Services Aids, services, or accommodations include career counseling, digital textbooks, faculty training, and priority registration.

Subject-area Tutoring Tutoring is offered one-on-one for most subjects. Tutoring is provided through the program or unit via LD specialists and professional tutors. Tutoring is also provided collaboratively through on-campus or off-campus services via LD specialists and professional tutors.

Basic Skills Remediation Remediation is offered one-on-one for auditory processing, computer skills, handwriting, learning strategies, math, motor skills, reading, social skills, spelling, spoken language, study skills, time management, visual processing, and written language. Remediation is provided through the program or unit via LD specialists, professional tutors, and special education teachers. Remediation is also provided collaboratively through on-campus or off-campus services via LD specialists, professional tutors, and special education teachers.

Enrichment Enrichment programs are available through the program or unit for career planning, college survival skills, learning strategies, stress management, study skills, test taking, and time management. Programs for career planning, college survival skills, learning strategies, stress management, study skills, test taking, and time management are provided collaboratively through on-campus or off-campus services. Credit is offered for career planning.

Application For admittance to the program or unit, students are required to apply to the program directly and provide a psychoeducational report (5 years old or less). It is recommended that students provide documentation of high school services. Upon application, materials documenting need for services should be sent to both admissions and the LD program or unit. Upon acceptance, documentation of need for services should be sent only to the LD program or unit. *Application deadline (institutional):* 3/1. *Application deadline (LD program):* Rolling/continuous for fall and rolling/continuous for spring.

Written Policies Written policy regarding general/basic LD accommodations is available on the program Web site. Written policy regarding general/basic LD accommodations is outlined in the school's catalog/handbook. Written policy regarding general/basic LD accommodations is available through the program or unit directly.

The University of Alabama in Huntsville

301 Sparkman Drive
Huntsville, AL 35899
http://www.uah.edu/

Contact: Ms. Rosemary Robinson, Associate Director of Student Affairs Programs. Phone: 256-824-6203. Fax: 256-824-6672. E-mail: robinsr@email.uah.edu.

Approximately 160 registered undergraduate students were served during 2002-03. The program or unit includes 1 full-time and 3 part-time staff members. Academic advisers, counselors, graduate assistants/students, regular education teachers, teacher trainees, and trained peer tutors are provided collaboratively through on-campus or off-campus services.

Unique Aids and Services Aids, services, or accommodations include advocates, career counseling, faculty training, and priority registration.

Subject-area Tutoring Tutoring is offered one-on-one and in small groups for most subjects. Tutoring is provided collaboratively through on-campus or off-campus services via computer-based instruction, graduate assistants/students, and trained peer tutors.

Enrichment Enrichment programs are available through the program or unit for college survival skills, self-advocacy, study skills, test taking, and time management. Programs for career planning, college survival skills, health and nutrition, learning strategies, math, stress management, study skills, test taking, time management, and written composition skills are provided collaboratively through on-campus or off-campus services.

Application For admittance to the program or unit, students are required to provide a psychoeducational report (5 years old or less). It is recommended that students provide documentation of high school services. Upon application, materials documenting need for services should be sent only to the LD program or unit. Upon acceptance, documentation of need for services should be sent only to the LD program or unit. *Application deadline (institutional):* 8/15. *Application deadline (LD program):* Rolling/continuous for fall and rolling/continuous for spring.

Written Policies Written policy regarding general/basic LD accommodations is available on the program Web site. Written policy regarding general/basic LD accommodations is outlined in the school's catalog/handbook. Written policies regarding course substitutions, general/basic LD accommodations, reduced course loads, substitutions and waivers of admissions requirements, and substitutions and waivers of graduation requirements are available through the program or unit directly.

University of Alaska Anchorage
Disability Support Services

3211 Providence Drive
Anchorage, AK 99508-8060
http://www.uaa.alaska.edu/

Contact: Ms. Kaela Parks, Accommodations Coordinator. Phone: 907-786-4535. Fax: 907-786-4531. E-mail: ankmk4@uaa.alaska.edu.

Disability Support Services Approximately 80 registered undergraduate students were served during 2002-03.

Unique Aids and Services Aids, services, or accommodations include digital textbooks and priority registration.

Subject-area Tutoring Tutoring is offered one-on-one for most subjects. Tutoring is provided collaboratively through on-campus or off-campus services via computer-based instruction, graduate assistants/students, and trained peer tutors.

Basic Skills Remediation Remediation is offered one-on-one and in class-size groups for computer skills, learning strategies, math, reading, spoken language, study skills, time management, and written language. Remediation is provided collaboratively through on-campus or off-campus services via computer-based instruction, graduate assistants/students, regular education teachers, and trained peer tutors.

Enrichment Programs for career planning, college survival skills, learning strategies, math, stress management, study skills, test taking, time management, and written composition skills are provided collaboratively through on-campus or off-campus services. Credit is offered for college survival skills, learning strategies, math, stress management, study skills, test taking, time management, and written composition skills.

Application For admittance to the program or unit, students are required to provide a psychoeducational report (3 years old or less) and provide an interview to discuss accommodation options. It is recommended that students provide documentation of high school services. Upon application, materials documenting need for services should be sent only to the LD program or unit. Upon acceptance, documentation of need for services should be sent only to the LD program or unit. *Application deadline (institutional):* 8/1. *Application deadline (LD program):* Rolling/continuous for fall and rolling/continuous for spring.

Written Policies Written policies regarding course substitutions, general/basic LD accommodations, grade forgiveness, reduced course loads, substitutions and waivers of admissions requirements, and substitutions and waivers of graduation requirements are available on the program Web site. Written policy regarding general/basic LD accommodations is outlined in the school's catalog/handbook. Written policies regarding course substitutions, general/basic LD accommodations, grade forgiveness, reduced course loads, substitutions and waivers of admissions requirements, and substitutions and waivers of graduation requirements are available through the program or unit directly.

University of Arkansas
Center for Students with Disabilities

Fayetteville, AR 72701-1201
http://www.uark.edu/

Contact: Dr. Linda Watts, Associate Director. Phone: 479-575-3104. Fax: 479-575-7445. E-mail: lwatts@uark.edu.

Center for Students with Disabilities Approximately 300 registered undergraduate students were served during 2002-03. The program or unit includes 5 full-time and 15 part-time staff members.

Academic advisers, coaches, counselors, diagnostic specialists, graduate assistants/students, LD specialists, professional tutors, regular education teachers, remediation/learning specialists, skill tutors, special education teachers, strategy tutors, teacher trainees, trained peer tutors, and other are provided collaboratively through on-campus or off-campus services.

Unique Aids and Services Aids, services, or accommodations include career counseling, digital textbooks, and priority registration.

Subject-area Tutoring Tutoring is offered one-on-one, in small groups, and in class-size groups. Tutoring is provided collaboratively through on-campus or off-campus services via computer-based instruction, graduate assistants/students, LD specialists, professional tutors, and trained peer tutors.

Diagnostic Testing Testing for auditory processing, handwriting, intelligence, learning strategies, learning styles, math, motor skills, neuropsychological, personality, reading, social skills, spelling, spoken language, study skills, visual processing, and written language is provided collaboratively through on-campus or off-campus services.

Basic Skills Remediation Remediation is offered one-on-one, in small groups, and in class-size groups for computer skills, handwriting, learning strategies, math, reading, social skills, spelling, spoken language, study skills, time management, and written language. Remediation is provided collaboratively through on-campus or off-campus services via computer-based instruction, graduate assistants/students, LD specialists, professional tutors, regular education teachers, and special education teachers.

Enrichment Programs for career planning, college survival skills, health and nutrition, learning strategies, math, medication management, oral communication skills, practical computer skills, reading, self-advocacy, stress management, study skills, test taking, time management, vocabulary development, and written composition skills are provided collaboratively through on-campus or off-campus services. Credit is offered for college survival skills.

Application For admittance to the program or unit, students are required to apply to the program directly and provide a psychoeducational report. It is recommended that students provide documentation of high school services. Upon application, materials documenting need for services should be sent only to the LD program or unit. *Application deadline (institutional):* 8/15. *Application deadline (LD program):* Rolling/continuous for fall and rolling/continuous for spring.

Written Policies Written policies regarding course substitutions, general/basic LD accommodations, substitutions and waivers of admissions requirements, and substitutions and waivers of graduation requirements are available on the program Web site. Written policies regarding course substitutions, grade forgiveness, substitutions and waivers of admissions requirements, and substitutions and waivers of graduation requirements are outlined in the school's catalog/handbook. Written policy regarding general/basic LD accommodations is available through the program or unit directly.

University of Arkansas at Fort Smith

PO Box 3649
Fort Smith, AR 72913-3649
http://www.uafortsmith.edu/

Contact: Mr. Roger A. Young, ADA Student Services Coordinator. Phone: 479-788-7577 Ext. 7577. Fax: 479-788-7587 Ext. 7587. E-mail: ryoung@uafortsmith.edu.

The program or unit includes 2 full-time staff members. Academic advisers, coaches, counselors, professional tutors, regular education teachers, remediation/learning specialists, skill tutors, and trained peer tutors are provided through the program or unit.

Orientation The program or unit offers a mandatory 1-hour orientation for new students individually by special arrangement.

Unique Aids and Services Aids, services, or accommodations include career counseling and priority registration.

Subject-area Tutoring Tutoring is offered one-on-one and in small groups for all subjects. Tutoring is provided collaboratively through on-campus or off-campus services via computer-based instruction, graduate assistants/students, professional tutors, and trained peer tutors.

Basic Skills Remediation Remediation is offered one-on-one, in small groups, and in class-size groups for learning strategies, math, reading, spelling, study skills, time management, and written language. Remediation is provided collaboratively through on-campus or off-campus services via computer-based instruction, graduate assistants/students, professional tutors, regular education teachers, and trained peer tutors.

Enrichment Programs for career planning, college survival skills, health and nutrition, math, oral communication skills, practical computer skills, reading, stress management, study skills, test taking, time management, and written composition skills are provided collaboratively through on-campus or off-campus services.

Student Organization Students with Disabilities consists of 14 members.

Application For admittance to the program or unit, students are required to apply to the program directly and provide a psychoeducational report. It is recommended that students provide documentation of high school services. Upon acceptance, documentation of need for services should be sent only to the LD program or unit. *Application deadline (institutional):* Continuous. *Application deadline (LD program):* Rolling/continuous for fall and rolling/continuous for spring.

Written Policies Written policies regarding course substitutions, general/basic LD accommodations, grade forgiveness, reduced course loads, substitutions and waivers of admissions requirements, and substitutions and waivers of graduation requirements are outlined in the school's catalog/handbook.

University of Baltimore

1420 North Charles Street
Baltimore, MD 21201-5779
http://www.ubalt.edu/

Contact: Ms. Jacquelyn Noelle Truelove-DeSimone, Director. Phone: 410-837-4775. Fax: 410-837-4932. E-mail: jtruelove@ubmail.ubalt.edu.

The program or unit includes 1 full-time staff member. Academic advisers and other are provided collaboratively through on-campus or off-campus services.

Unique Aids and Services Aids, services, or accommodations include priority registration, weekly meetings with the DSS Director.

University of Baltimore (continued)

Subject-area Tutoring Tutoring is offered one-on-one for most subjects. Tutoring is provided collaboratively through on-campus or off-campus services via professional tutors and trained peer tutors.

Application For admittance to the program or unit, students are required to provide a psychoeducational report (5 years old or less). Upon application, materials documenting need for services should be sent only to the LD program or unit. Upon acceptance, documentation of need for services should be sent only to the LD program or unit. *Application deadline (LD program):* Rolling/continuous for fall and rolling/continuous for spring.

Written Policies Written policy regarding general/basic LD accommodations is available on the program Web site. Written policy regarding general/basic LD accommodations is available through the program or unit directly.

University of Calgary
Disability Resource Center

2500 University Drive, NW
Calgary, AB T2N 1N4
Canada
http://www.ucalgary.ca/drc
Contact: Phone: 403-220-5110. Fax: 403-289-1253.

Disability Resource Center Approximately 320 registered undergraduate students were served during 2002-03. The program or unit includes 1 full-time and 1 part-time staff member. Diagnostic specialists and LD specialists are provided through the program or unit. Coaches, counselors, graduate assistants/students, professional tutors, strategy tutors, and trained peer tutors are provided collaboratively through on-campus or off-campus services.

Orientation The program or unit offers an optional 1-week orientation for new students before classes begin.

Summer Program To help prepare for the demands of college, there is an optional 1-week summer program prior to entering the school.

Unique Aids and Services Aids, services, or accommodations include career counseling, digital textbooks, faculty training, and personal coach.

Basic Skills Remediation Remediation is offered one-on-one for auditory processing, computer skills, learning strategies, reading, spelling, spoken language, study skills, time management, visual processing, and written language. Remediation is provided through the program or unit via computer-based instruction, graduate assistants/students, and LD specialists. Remediation is also provided collaboratively through on-campus or off-campus services via professional tutors and trained peer tutors.

Enrichment Enrichment programs are available through the program or unit for career planning, learning strategies, medication management, oral communication skills, reading, self-advocacy, stress management, study skills, time management, vocabulary development, and written composition skills. Programs for college survival skills, health and nutrition, practical computer skills, and test taking are provided collaboratively through on-campus or off-campus services.

Fees *LD Program or Service* fee is $460 Canadian dollars. *Summer Program* fee is $460 Canadian dollars. *Orientation* fee is $460 Canadian dollars.

Application For admittance to the program or unit, students are required to provide a psychoeducational report (5 years old or less). Upon application, materials documenting need for services should be sent only to the LD program or unit. Upon acceptance, documentation of need for services should be sent only to the LD program or unit. *Application deadline (institutional): 6/1. Application deadline (LD program):* Rolling/continuous for fall and rolling/continuous for spring.

Written Policies Written policy regarding general/basic LD accommodations is available on the program Web site. Written policy regarding general/basic LD accommodations is available through the program or unit directly.

University of California, Berkeley

Berkeley, CA 94720-1500
http://dsp.berkeley.edu and http://dsptrio.berkeley.edu
Contact: Dr. Connie Chiba, Disability Services Coordinator. Phone: 510-642-0518. E-mail: cchiba@uclink.berkeley.edu.

Approximately 200 registered undergraduate students were served during 2002-03. The program or unit includes 2 full-time and 2 part-time staff members. LD specialists are provided through the program or unit.

Orientation The program or unit offers an optional 2 to 3-hour orientation for new students before classes begin.

Unique Aids and Services Aids, services, or accommodations include priority registration and support groups.

Enrichment Enrichment programs are available through the program or unit for career planning, college survival skills, learning strategies, reading, self-advocacy, study skills, test taking, and time management.

Student Organization Disabled Students' Union (For students with various types of disabilities).

Application For admittance to the program or unit, students are required to provide a psychoeducational report. Upon application, materials documenting need for services should be sent only to the LD program or unit. *Application deadline (institutional):* 11/30. *Application deadline (LD program):* 11/30 for fall.

Written Policies Written policies regarding general/basic LD accommodations and reduced course loads are available on the program Web site. Written policies regarding course substitutions and substitutions and waivers of graduation requirements are available through the program or unit directly.

University of California, Davis
Student Disability Center

One Shields Avenue
Davis, CA 95616
http://sdc.ucdavis.edu
Contact: LD Specialist. Phone: 530-752-3184. Fax: 530-752-0161. E-mail: sdc@ucdavis.edu. Head of LD

Program: Coordinator of Student Disability Center. Phone: 530-752-3184. Fax: 530-752-0161. E-mail: sdc@ucdavis.edu.

Student Disability Center Approximately 150 registered undergraduate students were served during 2002-03. The program or unit includes 2 full-time staff members. LD specialists are provided through the program or unit. Academic advisers, counselors, diagnostic specialists, graduate assistants/students, professional tutors, skill tutors, strategy tutors, and trained peer tutors are provided collaboratively through on-campus or off-campus services.
Unique Aids and Services Aids, services, or accommodations include career counseling, digital textbooks, faculty training, and support groups.
Subject-area Tutoring Tutoring is offered in small groups and in class-size groups for some subjects. Tutoring is provided collaboratively through on-campus or off-campus services via computer-based instruction, graduate assistants/students, professional tutors, and trained peer tutors.
Enrichment Enrichment programs are available through the program or unit for learning strategies, self-advocacy, and study skills. Programs for career planning, college survival skills, health and nutrition, learning strategies, math, oral communication skills, practical computer skills, stress management, study skills, test taking, time management, and written composition skills are provided collaboratively through on-campus or off-campus services.
Student Organization Disabled Student Union consists of 10 members.
Application For admittance to the program or unit, students are required to provide a psychoeducational report (3 years old or less). Upon acceptance, documentation of need for services should be sent only to the LD program or unit. *Application deadline (institutional):* 11/30. *Application deadline (LD program):* Rolling/continuous for fall and rolling/continuous for spring.
Written Policies Written policy regarding general/basic LD accommodations is available on the program Web site. Written policy regarding general/basic LD accommodations is outlined in the school's catalog/handbook. Written policy regarding general/basic LD accommodations is available through the program or unit directly.

University of California, Los Angeles

405 Hilgard Avenue
Los Angeles, CA 90095
http://www.ucla.edu/

Contact: Dr. Julie Morris, Coordinator of Learning Disabilities Program. Phone: 310-794-5732. Fax: 310-825-9656. E-mail: jmorris@saonet.ucla.edu.

Approximately 300 registered undergraduate students were served during 2002-03. The program or unit includes 2 full-time staff members and 1 part-time staff member. Counselors, diagnostic specialists, and LD specialists are provided through the program or unit. Academic advisers, counselors, diagnostic specialists, skill tutors, strategy tutors, and trained peer tutors are provided collaboratively through on-campus or off-campus services.

Orientation The program or unit offers an optional orientation for new students before classes begin and during orientation just prior to the start of classes.
Unique Aids and Services Aids, services, or accommodations include support groups.
Subject-area Tutoring Tutoring is offered one-on-one and in small groups for some subjects. Tutoring is provided collaboratively through on-campus or off-campus services via trained peer tutors.
Enrichment Enrichment programs are available through the program or unit for learning strategies, reading, test taking, time management, and written composition skills.
Student Organization Disabled Student Union.
Application For admittance to the program or unit, students are required to provide a psychoeducational report (3 years old or less). It is recommended that students provide adult versions of tests for LD documentation. Upon acceptance, documentation of need for services should be sent only to the LD program or unit. *Application deadline (institutional):* 11/30. *Application deadline (LD program):* Rolling/continuous for fall and rolling/continuous for spring.
Written Policies Written policy regarding general/basic LD accommodations is available on the program Web site. Written policies regarding course substitutions, general/basic LD accommodations, and reduced course loads are available through the program or unit directly.

University of California, San Diego
Office for Students with Disabilities

9500 Gilman Drive
La Jolla, CA 92093
http://www.ucsd.edu/

Contact: Phone: 858-534-2230. Head of LD Program: Ms. Roberta Gimblett, Director of Office for Students with Disabilities. Phone: 858-534-4382. Fax: 858-534-4650. E-mail: rgimblett@ucsd.edu.

Office for Students with Disabilities Approximately 160 registered undergraduate students were served during 2002-03. Academic advisers, coaches, counselors, diagnostic specialists, and LD specialists are provided collaboratively through on-campus or off-campus services.
Orientation The program or unit offers a mandatory 1-hour orientation for new students before classes begin and individually by special arrangement.
Unique Aids and Services Aids, services, or accommodations include advocates, digital textbooks, support groups, separate test location, extended time, note-takers.
Subject-area Tutoring Tutoring is offered one-on-one and in small groups for some subjects. Tutoring is provided collaboratively through on-campus or off-campus services via computer-based instruction, graduate assistants/students, professional tutors, and trained peer tutors.
Basic Skills Remediation Remediation is offered one-on-one and in small groups for learning strategies, math, reading, spelling, study skills, time management, and written language. Remediation is provided collaboratively through on-campus or off-campus services via computer-based instruction, graduate assistants/students, professional tutors, and trained peer tutors.

University of California, San Diego (continued)

Enrichment Programs for career planning, college survival skills, health and nutrition, learning strategies, math, medication management, oral communication skills, practical computer skills, reading, stress management, study skills, test taking, time management, vocabulary development, and written composition skills are provided collaboratively through on-campus or off-campus services.

Student Organization OSD Peer Mentor Support Group and Disabled Student Organization consists of 20 members.

Application For admittance to the program or unit, students are required to apply to the program directly, provide a psychoeducational report (3 years old or less), and provide history, scores, and co-morbidity. It is recommended that students provide documentation of high school services. Upon acceptance, documentation of need for services should be sent only to admissions. *Application deadline (institutional):* 11/30. *Application deadline (LD program):* Rolling/continuous for fall and rolling/continuous for spring.

Written Policies Written policies regarding course substitutions, general/basic LD accommodations, and reduced course loads are available on the program Web site. Written policies regarding course substitutions, general/basic LD accommodations, and reduced course loads are outlined in the school's catalog/handbook. Written policy regarding general/basic LD accommodations is available through the program or unit directly.

University of California, Santa Barbara
Disabled Students Program

Santa Barbara, CA 93106
http://www.sa.ucsb.edu/dsp
Contact: Disabled Students Program. Phone: 805-893-2668. Fax: 805-893-7127.

Disabled Students Program Approximately 200 registered undergraduate students were served during 2002-03. The program or unit includes 7 full-time staff members. LD specialists are provided through the program or unit. Academic advisers, coaches, counselors, diagnostic specialists, graduate assistants/students, professional tutors, regular education teachers, skill tutors, strategy tutors, and teacher trainees are provided collaboratively through on-campus or off-campus services.

Orientation The program or unit offers a mandatory orientation for new students before classes begin and individually by special arrangement.

Unique Aids and Services Aids, services, or accommodations include advocates, priority registration, special test-taking arrangements, note-takers.

Subject-area Tutoring Tutoring is offered in small groups for some subjects. Tutoring is provided collaboratively through on-campus or off-campus services via computer-based instruction, graduate assistants/students, and professional tutors.

Application For admittance to the program or unit, students are required to apply to the program directly and provide documentation as specified on Web site. It is recommended that students provide a psychoeducational report (3 years old or less). Upon acceptance, documentation of need for services should be sent only to the LD program or unit. *Application deadline (institutional):* 11/30. *Application deadline (LD program):* 6/15 for fall. 1/15 for spring.

Written Policies Written policy regarding general/basic LD accommodations is available on the program Web site.

University of Central Oklahoma
Disability Support Services

100 North University Drive
Edmond, OK 73034-5209
http://www.ucok.edu/disability_support/
Contact: Phone: 405-974-2000. Fax: 405-974-4964.

Disability Support Services Approximately 230 registered undergraduate students were served during 2002-03. The program or unit includes 2 full-time and 3 part-time staff members. Academic advisers, coaches, and counselors are provided through the program or unit. Academic advisers, coaches, counselors, skill tutors, and strategy tutors are provided collaboratively through on-campus or off-campus services.

Orientation The program or unit offers an optional orientation for new students during registration and individually by special arrangement.

Unique Aids and Services Aids, services, or accommodations include support groups.

Enrichment Enrichment programs are available through the program or unit for career planning, college survival skills, learning strategies, oral communication skills, stress management, study skills, and time management. Programs for career planning, college survival skills, learning strategies, math, oral communication skills, stress management, study skills, and time management are provided collaboratively through on-campus or off-campus services.

Student Organization Students with Disabilities Organization consists of 30 members.

Application For admittance to the program or unit, students are required to provide a psychoeducational report and provide other documentation. It is recommended that students provide documentation of high school services. Upon acceptance, documentation of need for services should be sent only to the LD program or unit. *Application deadline (institutional):* Continuous. *Application deadline (LD program):* Rolling/continuous for fall.

Written Policies Written policies regarding course substitutions, general/basic LD accommodations, substitutions and waivers of admissions requirements, and substitutions and waivers of graduation requirements are available through the program or unit directly.

University of Colorado at Boulder
Academic Access and Resources

Boulder, CO 80309
http://www.colorado.edu/disabilityservices
Contact: Jayne MacArthur, Coordinator of Academic Access and Resources Program. Phone: 303-492-8671. Fax: 303-492-5601. E-mail: dsinfo@spot.colorado.edu.

Academic Access and Resources Approximately 250 registered undergraduate students were served during 2002-03. The program or unit includes 3 full-time and 10 part-time staff members. Academic advisers, diagnostic specialists, LD specialists, and strategy tutors are provided through the program or unit. Academic advisers, counselors, diagnostic specialists, professional tutors, regular education teachers, remediation/learning specialists, strategy tutors, and trained peer tutors are provided collaboratively through on-campus or off-campus services.

Orientation The program or unit offers an optional 1.5-hour orientation for new students before classes begin.

Unique Aids and Services Aids, services, or accommodations include advocates, career counseling, digital textbooks, faculty training, support groups, individualized meetings with students.

Subject-area Tutoring Tutoring is offered one-on-one and in small groups for most subjects. Tutoring is provided collaboratively through on-campus or off-campus services via graduate assistants/students, professional tutors, and trained peer tutors.

Diagnostic Testing Testing is provided through the program or unit for auditory processing, handwriting, intelligence, math, neuropsychological, reading, spelling, spoken language, visual processing, and written language. Testing for auditory processing, intelligence, learning styles, math, neuropsychological, personality, reading, spelling, spoken language, visual processing, and written language is provided collaboratively through on-campus or off-campus services.

Enrichment Enrichment programs are available through the program or unit for career planning, learning strategies, self-advocacy, study skills, test taking, time management, and written composition skills. Programs for career planning, college survival skills, learning strategies, oral communication skills, practical computer skills, stress management, study skills, test taking, time management, and written composition skills are provided collaboratively through on-campus or off-campus services.

Fees *Diagnostic Testing* fee is $300.

Application For admittance to the program or unit, students are required to provide a psychoeducational report (3 years old or less). Upon application, materials documenting need for services should be sent only to the LD program or unit. Upon acceptance, documentation of need for services should be sent only to the LD program or unit. *Application deadline (institutional):* 1/15. *Application deadline (LD program):* Rolling/continuous for fall and rolling/continuous for spring.

Written Policies Written policies regarding general/basic LD accommodations and substitutions and waivers of graduation requirements are available on the program Web site. Written policy regarding general/basic LD accommodations is outlined in the school's catalog/handbook. Written policies regarding general/basic LD accommodations, substitutions and waivers of admissions requirements, and substitutions and waivers of graduation requirements are available through the program or unit directly.

University of Colorado at Colorado Springs

1420 Austin Bluffs Parkway
PO Box 7150
Colorado Springs, CO 80918
http://www.uccs.edu/

Contact: Ms. Kaye J. Simonton, Coordinator of Disability Services. Phone: 719-262-3653. Fax: 719-262-3195. E-mail: ksimonto@uccs.edu.

The program or unit includes 1 full-time staff member. Academic advisers are provided through the program or unit. Academic advisers, counselors, and graduate assistants/students are provided collaboratively through on-campus or off-campus services.

Unique Aids and Services Aids, services, or accommodations include career counseling and digital textbooks.

Subject-area Tutoring Tutoring is offered one-on-one and in small groups for most subjects. Tutoring is provided collaboratively through on-campus or off-campus services via graduate assistants/students.

Enrichment Programs for career planning, college survival skills, health and nutrition, math, stress management, study skills, test taking, and time management are provided collaboratively through on-campus or off-campus services.

Application For admittance to the program or unit, students are required to provide a psychoeducational report (3 years old or less). It is recommended that students provide documentation of high school services. Upon application, materials documenting need for services should be sent only to the LD program or unit. Upon acceptance, documentation of need for services should be sent only to the LD program or unit. *Application deadline (institutional):* 7/1. *Application deadline (LD program):* Rolling/continuous for fall and rolling/continuous for spring.

Written Policies Written policy regarding general/basic LD accommodations is available through the program or unit directly.

University of Connecticut
University Program for College Students with Learning Disabilities (UPLD)

Storrs, CT 06269

http://www.uconn.edu/

Contact: Dr. Joseph W. Madaus, Director, University Program for College Students with Learning Disabilities. Phone: 860-486-0178. Fax: 860-486-5799.

University Program for College Students with Learning Disabilities (UPLD) Approximately 170 registered undergraduate students were served during 2002-03. The program or unit includes 1 full-time and 4 part-time staff members. Graduate assistants/students and LD specialists are provided through the program or unit. Academic advisers, coaches, counselors, and trained peer tutors are provided collaboratively through on-campus or off-campus services.

Unique Aids and Services Aids, services, or accommodations include reasonable accommodations and aids determined on a case-by-case basis.

Application For admittance to the program or unit, students are required to provide a psychoeducational report (3 years old or less). It is recommended that students provide documentation of high school services. Upon acceptance, documentation of need for services should be sent only to the LD program or unit. *Application deadline (institutional):* 3/1.

University of Connecticut (continued)

Written Policies Written policies regarding course substitutions and general/basic LD accommodations are available on the program Web site. Written policies regarding course substitutions and general/basic LD accommodations are outlined in the school's catalog/handbook. Written policies regarding course substitutions, general/basic LD accommodations, and reduced course loads are available through the program or unit directly.

University of Dayton
LEAD: Disability Services

300 College Park
Dayton, OH 45469-1300
http://academic.udayton.edu/osd/

Contact: Ms. Brenda D. Cooper, Program Coordinator of LEAD: Disability Services. Phone: 937-229-2066. Fax: 937-229-3270. E-mail: brenda.cooper@notes.udayton.edu. Head of LD Program: Lisa B. Rhine PhD, Director of LEAD Services. Phone: 937-229-2066. Fax: 937-229-3270. E-mail: lisa.rhine@notes.udayton.edu.

LEAD: Disability Services Approximately 360 registered undergraduate students were served during 2002-03. The program or unit includes 3 full-time staff members and 1 part-time staff member. Counselors, LD specialists, remediation/learning specialists, and special education teachers are provided through the program or unit. Academic advisers, coaches, counselors, diagnostic specialists, regular education teachers, skill tutors, special education teachers, and trained peer tutors are provided collaboratively through on-campus or off-campus services.

Unique Aids and Services Aids, services, or accommodations include digital textbooks, faculty training, and priority registration.

Subject-area Tutoring Tutoring is offered one-on-one, in small groups, and in class-size groups for all subjects. Tutoring is provided collaboratively through on-campus or off-campus services via computer-based instruction and trained peer tutors.

Basic Skills Remediation Remediation is offered one-on-one and in small groups for math, study skills, time management, and written language. Remediation is provided collaboratively through on-campus or off-campus services via trained peer tutors.

Enrichment Enrichment programs are available through the program or unit for self-advocacy, stress management, study skills, test taking, and time management. Programs for career planning, health and nutrition, learning strategies, math, practical computer skills, self-advocacy, stress management, study skills, test taking, time management, and written composition skills are provided collaboratively through on-campus or off-campus services.

Application For admittance to the program or unit, students are required to provide a psychoeducational report (5 years old or less). It is recommended that students provide documentation of high school services and provide diagnostic report/summary. Upon application, materials documenting need for services should be sent to both admissions and the LD program or unit. Upon acceptance, documentation of need for services should be sent only to the LD program or unit.

Written Policies Written policy regarding general/basic LD accommodations is available on the program Web site. Written policy regarding general/basic LD accommodations is outlined in the school's catalog/handbook. Written policy regarding general/basic LD accommodations is available through the program or unit directly.

University of Delaware
LD/ADHD Services, Academic Services Center

Newark, DE 19716
http://www.udel.edu/ASC

Contact: Ms. Ruth A. Smith, Staff Assistant. Phone: 302-831-2805. Fax: 302-831-4128. E-mail: rasmith@udel.edu. Head of LD Program: Ms. Lysbet J. Murray, Associate Director of Academic Services Center. Phone: 302-831-2805. Fax: 302-831-4128. E-mail: lysbet@udel.edu.

LD/ADHD Services, Academic Services Center Approximately 250 registered undergraduate students were served during 2002-03. The program or unit includes 2 full-time staff members. LD specialists are provided through the program or unit. Academic advisers, graduate assistants/students, skill tutors, and trained peer tutors are provided collaboratively through on-campus or off-campus services.

Summer Program To help prepare for the demands of college, there is summer program prior to entering the school.

Subject-area Tutoring Tutoring is offered one-on-one and in small groups for some subjects. Tutoring is provided collaboratively through on-campus or off-campus services via trained peer tutors.

Application For admittance to the program or unit, students are required to apply to the program directly, provide a psychoeducational report (3 years old or less), and provide evidence of current impact on academic performance. It is recommended that students provide documentation of high school services. Upon application, materials documenting need for services should be sent only to the LD program or unit. Upon acceptance, documentation of need for services should be sent only to the LD program or unit. *Application deadline (institutional):* 2/15. *Application deadline (LD program):* Rolling/continuous for fall and rolling/continuous for spring.

Written Policies Written policy regarding general/basic LD accommodations is available on the program Web site. Written policy regarding course substitutions is outlined in the school's catalog/handbook. Written policy regarding general/basic LD accommodations is available through the program or unit directly.

University of Detroit Mercy
UAS/Disability Support Services

4001 W McNichols Rd, PO Box 19900
Detroit, MI 48219-0900
http://www.udmercy.edu/

Contact: Emilie A. Gallegos, Director of UAS/Disability Support Services. Phone: 313-578-0310. Fax: 313-578-0342. E-mail: gallegem@udmercy.edu.

UAS/Disability Support Services Approximately 75 registered undergraduate students were served during 2002-03. The program or unit includes 2 full-time staff members. Professional tutors, remediation/learning specialists, skill tutors, strategy tutors, and trained peer tutors are provided through the program or unit. Academic advisers, diagnostic specialists, and LD specialists are provided collaboratively through on-campus or off-campus services.

Unique Aids and Services Aids, services, or accommodations include advocates and faculty training.

Subject-area Tutoring Tutoring is offered one-on-one and in small groups for most subjects. Tutoring is provided through the program or unit via computer-based instruction, graduate assistants/students, professional tutors, and trained peer tutors.

Diagnostic Testing Testing is provided through the program or unit for learning strategies, learning styles, math, personality, reading, spelling, and study skills. Testing for intelligence, motor skills, personality, reading, and social skills is provided collaboratively through on-campus or off-campus services.

Basic Skills Remediation Remediation is offered one-on-one and in small groups for computer skills, learning strategies, math, reading, study skills, time management, and written language. Remediation is provided through the program or unit via computer-based instruction, graduate assistants/students, professional tutors, teacher trainees, and trained peer tutors.

Enrichment Enrichment programs are available through the program or unit for college survival skills, learning strategies, math, reading, stress management, study skills, test taking, time management, vocabulary development, and written composition skills. Programs for career planning, health and nutrition, math, and written composition skills are provided collaboratively through on-campus or off-campus services. Credit is offered for career planning, college survival skills, health and nutrition, learning strategies, reading, and vocabulary development.

Fees *Diagnostic Testing* fee is $0 to $300.

Application For admittance to the program or unit, students are required to provide a psychoeducational report (3 years old or less). It is recommended that students provide documentation of high school services. Upon application, materials documenting need for services should be sent only to the LD program or unit. Upon acceptance, documentation of need for services should be sent only to the LD program or unit. *Application deadline (institutional):* 7/1. *Application deadline (LD program):* Rolling/continuous for fall and rolling/continuous for spring.

Written Policies Written policies regarding course substitutions, general/basic LD accommodations, and substitutions and waivers of graduation requirements are available on the program Web site. Written policy regarding general/basic LD accommodations is outlined in the school's catalog/handbook. Written policies regarding course substitutions, general/basic LD accommodations, reduced course loads, and substitutions and waivers of graduation requirements are available through the program or unit directly.

University of Florida

Gainesville, FL 32611
http://www.ufl.edu/

Contact: Ms. Carole S. Burrowbridge, Learning Disabilities Specialist. Phone: 352-392-1261 Ext. 228. Fax: 352-392-1430. E-mail: burrowbr@ufl.edu.

The program or unit includes 2 full-time staff members and 1 part-time staff member. Graduate assistants/students and LD specialists are provided through the program or unit. Academic advisers, counselors, diagnostic specialists, remediation/learning specialists, skill tutors, strategy tutors, teacher trainees, and trained peer tutors are provided collaboratively through on-campus or off-campus services.

Unique Aids and Services Aids, services, or accommodations include digital textbooks, faculty training, parent workshops, personal coach, priority registration, and support groups.

Subject-area Tutoring Tutoring is offered one-on-one for some subjects. Tutoring is provided through the program or unit via LD specialists. Tutoring is also provided collaboratively through on-campus or off-campus services via graduate assistants/students and trained peer tutors.

Diagnostic Testing Testing is provided through the program or unit for learning strategies, learning styles, and study skills. Testing for auditory processing, handwriting, intelligence, learning strategies, learning styles, math, motor skills, neuropsychological, personality, reading, social skills, spelling, spoken language, study skills, visual processing, and written language is provided collaboratively through on-campus or off-campus services.

Basic Skills Remediation Remediation is offered one-on-one for auditory processing, reading, spoken language, and written language. Remediation is provided collaboratively through on-campus or off-campus services via graduate assistants/students and teacher trainees.

Enrichment Enrichment programs are available through the program or unit for college survival skills, health and nutrition, learning strategies, medication management, self-advocacy, stress management, study skills, test taking, time management, and written composition skills. Programs for career planning, college survival skills, health and nutrition, medication management, oral communication skills, practical computer skills, self-advocacy, stress management, study skills, test taking, time management, vocabulary development, and written composition skills are provided collaboratively through on-campus or off-campus services. Credit is offered for health and nutrition and stress management.

Student Organization Union of Students with Disabilities consists of 50 members.

Fees *Diagnostic Testing* fee is $0 to $800.

Application For admittance to the program or unit, students are required to provide a psychoeducational report. It is recommended that students provide documentation of high school services. Upon application, materials documenting need for services should be sent only to admissions with institutional application materials. Upon acceptance, documentation of need for services should be sent only to the LD program or unit. *Application deadline (institutional):* 1/13. *Application deadline (LD program):* Rolling/continuous for fall and rolling/continuous for spring.

Written Policies Written policies regarding course substitutions, general/basic LD accommodations, reduced course loads, substitutions and waivers of admissions requirements, and substitutions and waivers of graduation requirements are available on the program Web site. Written policies regarding course substitutions, general/

University of Florida (continued)

basic LD accommodations, reduced course loads, substitutions and waivers of admissions requirements, and substitutions and waivers of graduation requirements are available through the program or unit directly.

University of Georgia

Athens, GA 30602

http://www.uga.edu/

Contact: Noel Gregg PhD, Director. Phone: 706-542-4589. Fax: 706-583-0001. E-mail: ngregg@coe.uga.edu.

The program or unit includes 16 full-time and 4 part-time staff members. Diagnostic specialists, graduate assistants/students, LD specialists, and strategy tutors are provided through the program or unit. Academic advisers, counselors, professional tutors, skill tutors, and strategy tutors are provided collaboratively through on-campus or off-campus services.

Orientation The program or unit offers a mandatory orientation for new students before registration, before classes begin, and during summer prior to enrollment.

Unique Aids and Services Aids, services, or accommodations include digital textbooks, faculty training, priority registration, support groups, and weekly meetings with faculty.

Subject-area Tutoring Tutoring is offered in small groups for some subjects. Tutoring is provided collaboratively through on-campus or off-campus services via computer-based instruction, graduate assistants/students, and trained peer tutors.

Diagnostic Testing Testing is provided through the program or unit for auditory processing, intelligence, math, motor skills, neuropsychological, personality, reading, social skills, spelling, spoken language, study skills, visual processing, written language, and other services. Testing for auditory processing, intelligence, learning strategies, learning styles, math, motor skills, neuropsychological, personality, reading, social skills, spelling, spoken language, study skills, visual processing, written language, and other services is provided collaboratively through on-campus or off-campus services.

Basic Skills Remediation Remediation is offered in small groups for computer skills, learning strategies, math, reading, study skills, time management, and written language. Remediation is provided collaboratively through on-campus or off-campus services via computer-based instruction, graduate assistants/students, and professional tutors.

Enrichment Enrichment programs are available through the program or unit for learning strategies, self-advocacy, study skills, test taking, and time management. Programs for career planning, college survival skills, health and nutrition, learning strategies, math, medication management, practical computer skills, reading, stress management, study skills, test taking, time management, and written composition skills are provided collaboratively through on-campus or off-campus services. Credit is offered for career planning, college survival skills, learning strategies, and practical computer skills.

Student Organization Student Advisory Board consists of 8 members.

Fees *Diagnostic Testing* fee is $400 to $500.

Application For admittance to the program or unit, students are required to provide a psychoeducational report (3 years old or less) and provide documentation meeting the Georgia Regents Center

criteria. Upon application, materials documenting need for services should be sent only to the LD program or unit. Upon acceptance, documentation of need for services should be sent only to the LD program or unit. *Application deadline (institutional):* 2/1. *Application deadline (LD program):* Rolling/continuous for fall and rolling/continuous for spring.

Written Policies Written policies regarding course substitutions, general/basic LD accommodations, reduced course loads, substitutions and waivers of admissions requirements, and substitutions and waivers of graduation requirements are available on the program Web site. Written policy regarding general/basic LD accommodations is outlined in the school's catalog/handbook. Written policies regarding course substitutions, general/basic LD accommodations, reduced course loads, and substitutions and waivers of admissions requirements, and substitutions and waivers of graduation requirements are available through the program or unit directly.

University of Great Falls

1301 Twentieth Street South

Great Falls, MT 59405

http://www.ugf.edu/

Contact: Sue Romsa, Director of Student Support Services. Phone: 406-791-5212. Fax: 406-791-5220. E-mail: sromsa@ugf.edu.

Approximately 60 registered undergraduate students were served during 2002-03. The program or unit includes 5 full-time and 10 part-time staff members. Counselors, diagnostic specialists, LD specialists, professional tutors, remediation/learning specialists, skill tutors, strategy tutors, and trained peer tutors are provided through the program or unit. Academic advisers, graduate assistants/students, regular education teachers, special education teachers, teacher trainees, and other are provided collaboratively through on-campus or off-campus services.

Orientation The program or unit offers an optional orientation for new students during registration and individually by special arrangement.

Summer Program To help prepare for the demands of college, there is an optional 15-week (drop-in service) summer program prior to entering the school.

Unique Aids and Services Aids, services, or accommodations include advocates, career counseling, faculty training, priority registration, support groups, and weekly meetings with faculty.

Subject-area Tutoring Tutoring is offered one-on-one, in small groups, and in class-size groups for all subjects. Tutoring is provided through the program or unit via LD specialists, professional tutors, and trained peer tutors. Tutoring is also provided collaboratively through on-campus or off-campus services via computer-based instruction and graduate assistants/students.

Diagnostic Testing Testing is provided through the program or unit for learning strategies, learning styles, reading, social skills, spelling, spoken language, and study skills. Testing for auditory processing, handwriting, intelligence, math, motor skills, neuropsychological, personality, visual processing, and written language is provided collaboratively through on-campus or off-campus services.

Basic Skills Remediation Remediation is offered one-on-one, in small groups, and in class-size groups for computer skills, learning strategies, math, reading, social skills, spelling, spoken language, study skills, time management, visual processing, and written language. Remediation is provided through the program or unit via LD specialists, professional tutors, and trained peer tutors. Remediation is also provided collaboratively through on-campus or off-campus services via computer-based instruction, graduate assistants/students, regular education teachers, special education teachers, and teacher trainees.

Enrichment Enrichment programs are available through the program or unit for career planning, college survival skills, health and nutrition, learning strategies, math, oral communication skills, practical computer skills, reading, self-advocacy, stress management, study skills, test taking, time management, vocabulary development, and written composition skills. Programs for career planning, college survival skills, health and nutrition, learning strategies, math, medication management, oral communication skills, practical computer skills, reading, self-advocacy, stress management, study skills, test taking, time management, vocabulary development, and written composition skills are provided collaboratively through on-campus or off-campus services. Credit is offered for practical computer skills and written composition skills.

Application For admittance to the program or unit, students are required to apply to the program directly, provide a psychoeducational report, and provide documentation of high school services. Upon application, materials documenting need for services should be sent to both admissions and the LD program or unit. Upon acceptance, documentation of need for services should be sent to both admissions and the LD program or unit. *Application deadline (institutional):* 8/1. *Application deadline (LD program):* Rolling/continuous for fall and rolling/continuous for spring.

Written Policies Written policies regarding course substitutions, general/basic LD accommodations, grade forgiveness, reduced course loads, and substitutions and waivers of graduation requirements are outlined in the school's catalog/handbook. Written policy regarding general/basic LD accommodations is available through the program or unit directly.

University of Hartford
Learning Plus, L+

200 Bloomfield Avenue
West Hartford, CT 06117-1599
http://uhaweb.edu/ldsupport
Contact: Ms. E. Lynne Golden, Director of Learning Plus. Phone: 860-768-4312. Fax: 860-768-4183. E-mail: golden@hartford.edu.

Learning Plus, L+ Approximately 175 registered undergraduate students were served during 2002-03. The program or unit includes 1 full-time and 6 part-time staff members. LD specialists and strategy tutors are provided through the program or unit. Counselors and professional tutors are provided collaboratively through on-campus or off-campus services.

Orientation The program or unit offers an optional orientation for new students before classes begin.

Unique Aids and Services Aids, services, or accommodations include digital textbooks.

Enrichment Enrichment programs are available through the program or unit for college survival skills, learning strategies, math, reading, self-advocacy, stress management, study skills, test taking,

time management, and written composition skills. Programs for career planning, reading, stress management, and written composition skills are provided collaboratively through on-campus or off-campus services.

Application For admittance to the program or unit, students are required to provide a psychoeducational report (3 years old or less) and provide aptitude test (e.g. WAIS III), achievement test (e.g. WIAT or WJR), and information processing. Upon acceptance, documentation of need for services should be sent only to the LD program or unit. *Application deadline (institutional):* Continuous. *Application deadline (LD program):* Rolling/continuous for fall and rolling/continuous for spring.

Written Policies Written policy regarding general/basic LD accommodations is available on the program Web site. Written policies regarding general/basic LD accommodations, substitutions and waivers of admissions requirements, and substitutions and waivers of graduation requirements are outlined in the school's catalog/handbook. Written policies regarding course substitutions, general/basic LD accommodations, reduced course loads, substitutions and waivers of admissions requirements, and substitutions and waivers of graduation requirements are available through the program or unit directly.

University of Hawaii at Hilo

200 West Kawili Street
Hilo, HI 96720-4091
http://www.uhh.hawaii.edu/
Contact: Susan Shirachi Gonsalves, Director. Phone: 808-933-0816. Fax: 808-974-7691. E-mail: shirachi@hawaii.edu.

The program or unit includes 3 part-time staff members. Academic advisers, counselors, regular education teachers, skill tutors, special education teachers, and trained peer tutors are provided collaboratively through on-campus or off-campus services.

Unique Aids and Services Aids, services, or accommodations include advocates, faculty training, priority registration, and support groups.

Subject-area Tutoring Tutoring is offered one-on-one, in small groups, and in class-size groups for some subjects. Tutoring is provided collaboratively through on-campus or off-campus services via computer-based instruction, graduate assistants/students, professional tutors, and trained peer tutors.

Basic Skills Remediation Remediation is offered in class-size groups for math, reading, and written language. Remediation is provided collaboratively through on-campus or off-campus services via regular education teachers and trained peer tutors.

Enrichment Programs for career planning, college survival skills, health and nutrition, learning strategies, math, oral communication skills, practical computer skills, self-advocacy, stress management, study skills, test taking, time management, vocabulary development, and written composition skills are provided collaboratively through on-campus or off-campus services. Credit is offered for college survival skills, health and nutrition, learning strategies, math, oral communication skills, practical computer skills, and written composition skills.

Application For admittance to the program or unit, students are required to apply to the program directly and provide documentation of learning disability from a doctor, psychologist, etc.. It is

University of Hawaii at Hilo (continued)

recommended that students provide a psychoeducational report and provide documentation of high school services. Upon application, materials documenting need for services should be sent only to the LD program or unit. Upon acceptance, documentation of need for services should be sent only to the LD program or unit. *Application deadline (institutional): 7/1. Application deadline (LD program):* Rolling/continuous for fall and rolling/continuous for spring.

Written Policies Written policy regarding general/basic LD accommodations is available on the program Web site. Written policies regarding general/basic LD accommodations and substitutions and waivers of admissions requirements are available through the program or unit directly.

University of Hawaii at Manoa
KOKUA Program

2444 Dole Street
Honolulu, HI 96822
http://www.uhm.hawaii.edu/
Contact: Phone: 808-956-8111.

KOKUA Program Approximately 250 registered undergraduate students were served during 2002-03. Academic advisers, counselors, and regular education teachers are provided through the program or unit. Academic advisers, counselors, and regular education teachers are provided collaboratively through on-campus or off-campus services.

Orientation The program or unit offers an optional orientation for new students individually by special arrangement.

Unique Aids and Services Aids, services, or accommodations include advocates and priority registration.

Application For admittance to the program or unit, students are required to provide a psychoeducational report. It is recommended that students provide documentation of high school services. Upon application, materials documenting need for services should be sent only to the LD program or unit. Upon acceptance, documentation of need for services should be sent only to the LD program or unit. *Application deadline (institutional): 6/1. Application deadline (LD program):* Rolling/continuous for fall and rolling/continuous for spring.

University of Houston
Justin Dart Jr., Center for Students with DisABILITIES

4800 Calhoun Road
Houston, TX 77204
http://www.uh.edu/csd
Contact: Scott Crain, Counselor. Phone: 713-743-5400. Fax: 713-743-5396. E-mail: wscrain@mail.uh.edu. Head of

LD Program: Cheryl Amoruso, Director. Phone: 713-743-5400. Fax: 713-743-5396. E-mail: camoruso@mail.uh.edu.

Justin Dart Jr., Center for Students with DisABILITIES Approximately 375 registered undergraduate students were served during 2002-03. The program or unit includes 6 full-time and 5 part-time staff members. Coaches, counselors, LD specialists, and strategy tutors are provided through the program or unit. Academic advisers, coaches, counselors, diagnostic specialists, graduate assistants/students, LD specialists, professional tutors, regular education teachers, remediation/learning specialists, skill tutors, special education teachers, strategy tutors, teacher trainees, and trained peer tutors are provided collaboratively through on-campus or off-campus services.

Orientation The program or unit offers a mandatory orientation for new students individually by special arrangement and during the "Cougar Preview" .

Unique Aids and Services Aids, services, or accommodations include career counseling, digital textbooks, personal coach, priority registration, and support groups.

Subject-area Tutoring Tutoring is offered one-on-one, in small groups, and in class-size groups for most subjects. Tutoring is provided collaboratively through on-campus or off-campus services via computer-based instruction, graduate assistants/students, professional tutors, and trained peer tutors.

Diagnostic Testing Testing for auditory processing, intelligence, learning strategies, learning styles, math, motor skills, personality, reading, social skills, spelling, spoken language, study skills, visual processing, and written language is provided collaboratively through on-campus or off-campus services.

Basic Skills Remediation Remediation is offered in small groups and in class-size groups for computer skills, learning strategies, math, reading, social skills, spelling, study skills, time management, and written language. Remediation is provided collaboratively through on-campus or off-campus services via graduate assistants/students, professional tutors, teacher trainees, and trained peer tutors.

Enrichment Enrichment programs are available through the program or unit for college survival skills, learning strategies, self-advocacy, study skills, test taking, and time management. Programs for career planning, college survival skills, health and nutrition, learning strategies, math, medication management, oral communication skills, practical computer skills, reading, self-advocacy, stress management, study skills, test taking, time management, vocabulary development, and written composition skills are provided collaboratively through on-campus or off-campus services.

Student Organization DisABLED Student Association consists of 400 members.

Fees *Diagnostic Testing* fee is $200.

Application For admittance to the program or unit, students are required to provide a psychoeducational report (3 years old or less). It is recommended that students provide documentation of high school services and provide documentation of previous higher education accommodations. Upon application, materials documenting need for services should be sent only to the LD program or unit. Upon acceptance, documentation of need for services should be sent only to the LD program or unit. *Application deadline (institutional): 5/1. Application deadline (LD program):* Rolling/continuous for fall and rolling/continuous for spring.

Written Policies Written policies regarding course substitutions, general/basic LD accommodations, reduced course loads, substitutions and waivers of admissions requirements, and substitutions and waivers of graduation requirements are available on the program Web site. Written policies regarding course substitutions, general/basic LD accommodations, substitutions and waivers of admissions requirements, and substitutions and waivers of graduation requirements are outlined in the school's catalog/handbook. Written policies regarding course substitutions, general/basic LD accommodations, and reduced course loads are available through the program or unit directly.

University of Houston-Downtown
Disabled Student Services

One Main Street
Houston, TX 77002-1001
http://www.uhd.edu/
Contact: Duraese Hall, Coordinator of DSS. Phone: 713-226-5227. Fax: 713-226-5293. E-mail: halld@uhd.edu.

Disabled Student Services Approximately 26 registered undergraduate students were served during 2002-03. The program or unit includes 2 full-time staff members and 1 part-time staff member. Academic advisers and counselors are provided through the program or unit. Academic advisers, counselors, diagnostic specialists, graduate assistants/students, LD specialists, professional tutors, regular education teachers, remediation/learning specialists, skill tutors, special education teachers, strategy tutors, teacher trainees, and trained peer tutors are provided collaboratively through on-campus or off-campus services.
Orientation The program or unit offers a mandatory 1-hour orientation for new students individually by special arrangement.
Unique Aids and Services Aids, services, or accommodations include career counseling, faculty training, priority registration, and support groups.
Subject-area Tutoring Tutoring is offered one-on-one. Tutoring is provided collaboratively through on-campus or off-campus services via computer-based instruction and trained peer tutors.
Basic Skills Remediation Remediation is offered in class-size groups for math, reading, spelling, study skills, time management, and written language. Remediation is provided collaboratively through on-campus or off-campus services via computer-based instruction and regular education teachers.
Enrichment Programs for career planning, college survival skills, learning strategies, practical computer skills, stress management, study skills, test taking, and time management are provided collaboratively through on-campus or off-campus services. Credit is offered for college survival skills, learning strategies, practical computer skills, stress management, study skills, test taking, and time management.
Student Organization Student Handicapped Organization at Work (SHOW) consists of 10 members.
Application For admittance to the program or unit, students are required to provide a psychoeducational report (4 years old or less). Upon acceptance, documentation of need for services should be sent only to the LD program or unit. *Application deadline (institutional):* 8/1. *Application deadline (LD program):* Rolling/continuous for fall and rolling/continuous for spring.

Written Policies Written policy regarding general/basic LD accommodations is available through the program or unit directly.

University of Illinois at Urbana-Champaign
Division of Rehabilitation Education Services (DRES)

601 East John Street
Champaign, IL 61820
http://www.rehab.uiuc.edu
Contact: Ms. Karen L. Wold, Learning Disabilities Specialist. Phone: 217-333-8705. Fax: 217-333-0248. E-mail: kwold2@uiuc.edu.

Division of Rehabilitation Education Services (DRES) Approximately 175 registered undergraduate students were served during 2002-03. The program or unit includes 2 full-time and 2 part-time staff members. Diagnostic specialists, graduate assistants/students, LD specialists, remediation/learning specialists, skill tutors, strategy tutors, and other are provided through the program or unit. Academic advisers, coaches, and counselors are provided collaboratively through on-campus or off-campus services.
Unique Aids and Services Aids, services, or accommodations include advocates, career counseling, digital textbooks, faculty training, personal coach, priority registration, and support groups.
Basic Skills Remediation Remediation is offered one-on-one for computer skills, learning strategies, reading, social skills, spelling, study skills, time management, and written language. Remediation is provided through the program or unit via LD specialists.
Enrichment Enrichment programs are available through the program or unit for career planning, college survival skills, learning strategies, oral communication skills, practical computer skills, reading, self-advocacy, stress management, study skills, test taking, time management, vocabulary development, and written composition skills. Programs for career planning, college survival skills, health and nutrition, learning strategies, math, medication management, practical computer skills, stress management, study skills, test taking, time management, and written composition skills are provided collaboratively through on-campus or off-campus services.
Student Organization Delta Sigma Omicron consists of 30 members.
Application For admittance to the program or unit, students are required to apply to the program directly and provide a psychoeducational report (3 years old or less). Upon application, materials documenting need for services should be sent only to the LD program or unit. Upon acceptance, documentation of need for services should be sent only to the LD program or unit. *Application deadline (institutional):* 1/1. *Application deadline (LD program):* Rolling/continuous for fall and rolling/continuous for spring.
Written Policies Written policies regarding course substitutions, general/basic LD accommodations, reduced course loads, substitutions and waivers of admissions requirements, and substitutions and waivers of graduation requirements are available on the program Web site. Written policy regarding course substitutions is outlined in the school's catalog/handbook. Written policies regarding course

University of Illinois at Urbana-Champaign (continued)

substitutions, general/basic LD accommodations, reduced course loads, substitutions and waivers of admissions requirements, and substitutions and waivers of graduation requirements are available through the program or unit directly.

University of Kansas
Services for Students with Disabilities

Lawrence, KS 66045

http://www.ku.edu/~ssdis

Contact: Mr. Andrew Shoemaker, Learning Disabilities Specialist. Phone: 785-864-2620. Fax: 785-864-2817. E-mail: shoe@ku.edu.

Services for Students with Disabilities Approximately 267 registered undergraduate students were served during 2002-03. The program or unit includes 1 full-time and 1 part-time staff member. LD specialists are provided through the program or unit. Academic advisers, coaches, counselors, diagnostic specialists, graduate assistants/students, LD specialists, regular education teachers, remediation/learning specialists, skill tutors, strategy tutors, and trained peer tutors are provided collaboratively through on-campus or off-campus services.

Unique Aids and Services Aids, services, or accommodations include digital textbooks.

Subject-area Tutoring Tutoring is offered one-on-one and in small groups for some subjects. Tutoring is provided collaboratively through on-campus or off-campus services via graduate assistants/students, LD specialists, professional tutors, and trained peer tutors.

Diagnostic Testing Testing for auditory processing, handwriting, intelligence, learning strategies, learning styles, math, motor skills, neuropsychological, personality, reading, social skills, spelling, spoken language, study skills, visual processing, and written language is provided collaboratively through on-campus or off-campus services.

Basic Skills Remediation Remediation is offered one-on-one, in small groups, and in class-size groups for learning strategies, study skills, and time management. Remediation is provided collaboratively through on-campus or off-campus services via graduate assistants/students and regular education teachers.

Enrichment Programs for career planning, college survival skills, health and nutrition, learning strategies, math, oral communication skills, practical computer skills, reading, self-advocacy, stress management, study skills, test taking, time management, and written composition skills are provided collaboratively through on-campus or off-campus services. Credit is offered for career planning, college survival skills, and math.

Fees *Diagnostic Testing* fee is $225 to $1500.

Application For admittance to the program or unit, students are required to provide a psychoeducational report (3 years old or less). It is recommended that students provide documentation of high school services. Upon acceptance, documentation of need for services should be sent only to the LD program or unit. *Application deadline (institutional):* 4/1. *Application deadline (LD program):* Rolling/continuous for fall and rolling/continuous for spring.

Written Policies Written policy regarding general/basic LD accommodations is available on the program Web site. Written policies regarding course substitutions, general/basic LD accommodations, and substitutions and waivers of graduation requirements are available through the program or unit directly.

University of Kentucky
Disability Resource Center

Lexington, KY 40506-0032

http://www.uky.edu/StudentAffairs/DisabilityResourceCenter/

Contact: Leisa Pickering, Cognitive Disability Specialist. Phone: 859-257-2754. Fax: 859-257-1980. E-mail: lmpick@uky.edu. Head of LD Program: Jake Karnes, Assistant Dean of Students. Phone: 859-257-2754. Fax: 859-257-1980. E-mail: msfogg0@pop.uky.edu.

Disability Resource Center Approximately 450 registered undergraduate students were served during 2002-03. The program or unit includes 1 full-time staff member. Coaches, LD specialists, and strategy tutors are provided through the program or unit. Academic advisers, counselors, and strategy tutors are provided collaboratively through on-campus or off-campus services.

Unique Aids and Services Aids, services, or accommodations include advocates, career counseling, digital textbooks, personal coach, priority registration, support groups, faculty consultations as needed.

Diagnostic Testing Testing for auditory processing, intelligence, math, motor skills, neuropsychological, personality, reading, social skills, spelling, spoken language, visual processing, and written language is provided collaboratively through on-campus or off-campus services.

Basic Skills Remediation Remediation is offered in class-size groups for computer skills, learning strategies, math, spoken language, study skills, time management, and written language. Remediation is provided collaboratively through on-campus or off-campus services via regular education teachers and other.

Enrichment Programs for career planning, college survival skills, health and nutrition, learning strategies, math, medication management, oral communication skills, practical computer skills, stress management, study skills, test taking, time management, and written composition skills are provided collaboratively through on-campus or off-campus services. Credit is offered for health and nutrition, math, oral communication skills, practical computer skills, and written composition skills.

Fees *Diagnostic Testing* fee is $275 to $700.

Application For admittance to the program or unit, students are required to apply to the program directly and provide a psychoeducational report (3 years old or less). Upon acceptance, documentation of need for services should be sent only to the LD program or unit. *Application deadline (institutional):* 2/15. *Application deadline (LD program):* Rolling/continuous for fall and rolling/continuous for spring.

Written Policies Written policy regarding general/basic LD accommodations is available on the program Web site. Written policy regarding general/basic LD accommodations is outlined in the school's catalog/handbook. Written policy regarding general/basic LD accommodations is available through the program or unit directly.

University of King's College

6350 Coburg Road

Halifax, NS B3H 2A1

Canada

http://www.ukings.ns.ca/
Contact: Elizabeth Yeo, Registrar. Phone: 902-422-1271 Ext. 122. Fax: 902-423-3357. E-mail: elizabeth.yeo@ukings.ns.ca.

Academic advisers, counselors, and diagnostic specialists are provided collaboratively through on-campus or off-campus services.
Application For admittance to the program or unit, students are required to provide a psychoeducational report. Upon application, materials documenting need for services should be sent only to admissions with institutional application materials. Upon acceptance, documentation of need for services should be sent only to admissions. *Application deadline (institutional):* 3/1.
Written Policies Written policies regarding general/basic LD accommodations and substitutions and waivers of admissions requirements are outlined in the school's catalog/handbook.

University of Louisiana at Lafayette
Services for Students with Disabilities

Lafayette, LA 70504
http://disability.louisiana.edu
Contact: Ms. Page T. Salley, Coordinator of Services for Students with Disabilities. Phone: 337-482-5252. Fax: 337-482-1340. E-mail: salley@louisiana.edu.

Services for Students with Disabilities Approximately 200 registered undergraduate students were served during 2002-03. The program or unit includes 2 full-time staff members. Academic advisers, counselors, graduate assistants/students, remediation/learning specialists, skill tutors, and trained peer tutors are provided collaboratively through on-campus or off-campus services.
Unique Aids and Services Aids, services, or accommodations include advocates, career counseling, and priority registration.
Subject-area Tutoring Tutoring is offered one-on-one and in small groups for most subjects. Tutoring is provided collaboratively through on-campus or off-campus services via computer-based instruction, graduate assistants/students, and trained peer tutors.
Diagnostic Testing Testing for intelligence, math, reading, spelling, and written language is provided collaboratively through on-campus or off-campus services.
Basic Skills Remediation Remediation is offered one-on-one for learning strategies, spoken language, study skills, time management, and written language. Remediation is provided collaboratively through on-campus or off-campus services via computer-based instruction, graduate assistants/students, and other.
Enrichment Enrichment programs are available through the program or unit for learning strategies, self-advocacy, stress management, study skills, test taking, and time management. Programs for career planning, college survival skills, health and nutrition, math, oral communication skills, and practical computer skills are provided collaboratively through on-campus or off-campus services. Credit is offered for career planning, college survival skills, health and nutrition, math, oral communication skills, and practical computer skills.
Student Organization Beacon Club consists of 5 members.

Application For admittance to the program or unit, students are required to apply to the program directly, provide a psychoeducational report, and provide college testing. It is recommended that students provide documentation of high school services. Upon acceptance, documentation of need for services should be sent only to the LD program or unit. *Application deadline (institutional):* Continuous. *Application deadline (LD program):* Rolling/continuous for fall and rolling/continuous for spring.
Written Policies Written policy regarding general/basic LD accommodations is outlined in the school's catalog/handbook.

University of Maine
Disability Support Services

Orono, ME 04469
http://www.umaine.edu/
Contact: Ann Smith, Coordinator of Disability Services. Phone: 207-581-2319. Fax: 207-581-4252. E-mail: ann.smith@umit.maine.edu.

Disability Support Services Approximately 100 registered undergraduate students were served during 2002-03. The program or unit includes 2 full-time staff members and 1 part-time staff member. Counselors are provided through the program or unit. Counselors are provided collaboratively through on-campus or off-campus services.
Unique Aids and Services Aids, services, or accommodations include digital textbooks.
Subject-area Tutoring Tutoring is offered in small groups for some subjects. Tutoring is provided collaboratively through on-campus or off-campus services via trained peer tutors.
Enrichment Enrichment programs are available through the program or unit for learning strategies, study skills, time management, and other.
Application For admittance to the program or unit, students are required to provide a psychoeducational report (3 years old or less). It is recommended that students provide documentation of high school services. Upon application, materials documenting need for services should be sent only to admissions with institutional application materials. Upon acceptance, documentation of need for services should be sent only to the LD program or unit. *Application deadline (institutional):* Continuous.
Written Policies Written policies regarding course substitutions, general/basic LD accommodations, and reduced course loads are available on the program Web site. Written policies regarding general/basic LD accommodations and grade forgiveness are outlined in the school's catalog/handbook. Written policies regarding general/basic LD accommodations and reduced course loads are available through the program or unit directly.

The University of Maine at Augusta
Learning Support Services

46 University Drive
Augusta, ME 04330-9410

The University of Maine at Augusta (continued)
http://www.uma.maine.edu

Contact: Mr. Donald T. Osier, Director of Learning Support Services. Phone: 207-621-3066. Fax: 207-621-3491. E-mail: donald.osier@maine.edu.

Learning Support Services Approximately 25 registered undergraduate students were served during 2002-03. The program or unit includes 3 full-time and 3 part-time staff members. Academic advisers, counselors, professional tutors, remediation/learning specialists, and trained peer tutors are provided collaboratively through on-campus or off-campus services.

Unique Aids and Services Aids, services, or accommodations include digital textbooks, note-takers, extended time for tests.

Subject-area Tutoring Tutoring is offered one-on-one and in small groups for some subjects. Tutoring is provided collaboratively through on-campus or off-campus services via professional tutors and trained peer tutors.

Basic Skills Remediation Remediation is offered in class-size groups for math, reading, and written language. Remediation is provided collaboratively through on-campus or off-campus services via regular education teachers.

Application For admittance to the program or unit, students are required to provide a psychoeducational report (3 years old or less). It is recommended that students provide documentation of high school services. Upon application, materials documenting need for services should be sent only to the LD program or unit. Upon acceptance, documentation of need for services should be sent only to the LD program or unit. *Application deadline (institutional):* Continuous. *Application deadline (LD program):* Rolling/continuous for fall and rolling/continuous for spring.

Written Policies Written policies regarding general/basic LD accommodations and substitutions and waivers of graduation requirements are available on the program Web site. Written policies regarding general/basic LD accommodations and substitutions and waivers of graduation requirements are outlined in the school's catalog/handbook.

University of Maine at Fort Kent
Academic and Counseling Services

23 University Drive

Fort Kent, ME 04743-1292

http://www.umfk.maine.edu/acserv

Contact: Phone: 207-834-7500. Fax: 207-834-7609.

Academic and Counseling Services Approximately 20 registered undergraduate students were served during 2002-03. The program or unit includes 2 full-time and 2 part-time staff members. Academic advisers, counselors, professional tutors, remediation/learning specialists, skill tutors, and trained peer tutors are provided through the program or unit. Academic advisers, counselors, professional tutors, regular education teachers, remediation/learning specialists, and skill tutors are provided collaboratively through on-campus or off-campus services.

Summer Program To help prepare for the demands of college, there is an optional 3-week summer program prior to entering the school. Degree credit will be earned.

Subject-area Tutoring Tutoring is offered for all subjects. Tutoring is provided through the program or unit via professional tutors and trained peer tutors. Tutoring is also provided collaboratively through on-campus or off-campus services via professional tutors and trained peer tutors.

Basic Skills Remediation Remediation is offered one-on-one for computer skills, learning strategies, math, reading, study skills, time management, and written language. Remediation is provided through the program or unit via professional tutors and regular education teachers.

Fees *Summer Program* fee is $300.

Application For admittance to the program or unit, students are required to provide a psychoeducational report (3 years old or less). Upon acceptance, documentation of need for services should be sent only to the LD program or unit. *Application deadline (institutional):* Continuous. *Application deadline (LD program):* Rolling/continuous for fall and rolling/continuous for spring.

Written Policies Written policy regarding general/basic LD accommodations is available on the program Web site. Written policy regarding general/basic LD accommodations is outlined in the school's catalog/handbook.

University of Maine at Machias

9 O'Brien Avenue

Machias, ME 04654-1321

http://www.umm.maine.edu/

Contact: Ms. Jean Schild, Student Resources Coordinator. Phone: 207-255-1228. Fax: 207-255-4864. E-mail: schild@maine.edu.

Approximately 63 registered undergraduate students were served during 2002-03.

Unique Aids and Services Aids, services, or accommodations include digital textbooks, personal coach, one-on-one services as needed.

Enrichment Enrichment programs are available through the program or unit for college survival skills, learning strategies, self-advocacy, study skills, test taking, and time management. Programs for career planning, college survival skills, health and nutrition, math, practical computer skills, stress management, vocabulary development, and written composition skills are provided collaboratively through on-campus or off-campus services. Credit is offered for college survival skills, vocabulary development, and written composition skills.

Application For admittance to the program or unit, students are required to provide a psychoeducational report (3 years old or less). *Application deadline (institutional):* Continuous. *Application deadline (LD program):* Rolling/continuous for fall and rolling/continuous for spring.

Written Policies Written policy regarding general/basic LD accommodations is available on the program Web site. Written policy regarding general/basic LD accommodations is outlined in the school's catalog/handbook.

University of Manitoba
Disability Services

Winnipeg, MB R3T 2N2
Canada

http://www.umanitoba.ca/

Contact: Ms. Janalee Morris-Wales, Coordinator. Phone: 204-474-6213. E-mail: morriswa@ms.umanitoba.ca.

Disability Services Approximately 125 registered undergraduate students were served during 2002-03. The program or unit includes 1 part-time staff member. LD specialists are provided through the program or unit. Academic advisers, counselors, diagnostic specialists, LD specialists, and skill tutors are provided collaboratively through on-campus or off-campus services.

Unique Aids and Services Aids, services, or accommodations include advocates, career counseling, digital textbooks, faculty training, priority registration, and support groups.

Diagnostic Testing Testing for auditory processing, intelligence, math, motor skills, neuropsychological, reading, spelling, visual processing, written language, and other services is provided collaboratively through on-campus or off-campus services.

Basic Skills Remediation Remediation is offered one-on-one, in small groups, and in class-size groups for learning strategies, math, reading, spelling, study skills, time management, and written language. Remediation is provided collaboratively through on-campus or off-campus services via LD specialists, professional tutors, and trained peer tutors.

Enrichment Enrichment programs are available through the program or unit for college survival skills, learning strategies, reading, self-advocacy, study skills, test taking, time management, and written composition skills. Programs for career planning, college survival skills, learning strategies, math, practical computer skills, reading, study skills, test taking, time management, and written composition skills are provided collaboratively through on-campus or off-campus services. Credit is offered for college survival skills, learning strategies, practical computer skills, reading, study skills, time management, and written composition skills.

Application For admittance to the program or unit, students are required to apply to the program directly and provide a psychoeducational report. It is recommended that students provide documentation of high school services. Upon application, materials documenting need for services should be sent only to the LD program or unit. Upon acceptance, documentation of need for services should be sent only to the LD program or unit. *Application deadline (institutional):* 7/1. *Application deadline (LD program):* Rolling/continuous for fall and rolling/continuous for spring.

Written Policies Written policy regarding general/basic LD accommodations is available on the program Web site. Written policies regarding general/basic LD accommodations, grade forgiveness, and reduced course loads are available through the program or unit directly.

University of Mary

7500 University Drive
Bismarck, ND 58504-9652

http://www.umary.edu/

Contact: Ms. Mary Jo Wocken, Director of Learning Skills Services. Phone: 701-355-8264.

Approximately 18 registered undergraduate students were served during 2002-03. The program or unit includes 1 part-time staff member. Academic advisers, LD specialists, and professional tutors are provided through the program or unit.

Application For admittance to the program or unit, students are required to apply to the program directly and provide documentation of high school services. It is recommended that students provide a psychoeducational report. Upon application, materials documenting need for services should be sent only to the LD program or unit. Upon acceptance, documentation of need for services should be sent only to the LD program or unit. *Application deadline (institutional):* Continuous. *Application deadline (LD program):* 9/15 for fall. 1/15 for spring.

University of Mary Hardin-Baylor
Counseling and Testing Center and the Meadows Center for Academic Excellence

900 College Street
Belton, TX 76513

http://www.umhb.edu/

Contact: Nate Williams, Director of Counseling and Testing. Phone: 254-295-4696. Fax: 254-295-4196. E-mail: nwilliams@umhb.edu.

Counseling and Testing Center and the Meadows Center for Academic Excellence Approximately 75 registered undergraduate students were served during 2002-03. The program or unit includes 3 full-time and 3 part-time staff members. Academic advisers, counselors, diagnostic specialists, regular education teachers, remediation/learning specialists, skill tutors, strategy tutors, trained peer tutors, and other are provided collaboratively through on-campus or off-campus services.

Unique Aids and Services Aids, services, or accommodations include advocates, career counseling, faculty training, and personal coach.

Subject-area Tutoring Tutoring is offered one-on-one and in small groups for most subjects. Tutoring is provided collaboratively through on-campus or off-campus services via computer-based instruction, graduate assistants/students, LD specialists, trained peer tutors, and other.

Diagnostic Testing Testing for handwriting, intelligence, learning strategies, learning styles, math, neuropsychological, personality, reading, social skills, spelling, study skills, written language, and other services is provided collaboratively through on-campus or off-campus services.

Basic Skills Remediation Remediation is offered one-on-one, in small groups, and in class-size groups for learning strategies, math, reading, social skills, spelling, study skills, time management, and written language. Remediation is provided collaboratively through on-campus or off-campus services via computer-based instruction, graduate assistants/students, LD specialists, regular education teachers, and trained peer tutors.

University of Mary Hardin-Baylor (continued)

Enrichment Programs for career planning, college survival skills, health and nutrition, learning strategies, medication management, self-advocacy, stress management, study skills, test taking, and time management are provided collaboratively through on-campus or off-campus services.

Application For admittance to the program or unit, students are required to provide a psychoeducational report (3 years old or less) and provide a diagnostic report from a professional qualified to make the respective diagnosis. It is recommended that students apply to the program directly. Upon acceptance, documentation of need for services should be sent only to the LD program or unit. *Application deadline (institutional):* Continuous. *Application deadline (LD program):* Rolling/continuous for fall and rolling/continuous for spring.

Written Policies Written policy regarding general/basic LD accommodations is outlined in the school's catalog/handbook. Written policy regarding general/basic LD accommodations is available through the program or unit directly.

University of Maryland, College Park

College Park, MD 20742

http://www.maryland.edu/

Contact: Ms. Susan C. McMenamin, Coordinator. Phone: 301-314-7682. Fax: 301-405-0813. E-mail: smcmenam@wam.umd.edu. Head of LD Program: Dr. Alan Marcus, Director. Phone: 301-314-7682. Fax: 301-405-0813. E-mail: almarcus@wam.umd.edu.

Approximately 850 registered undergraduate students were served during 2002-03. The program or unit includes 2 full-time and 3 part-time staff members. Graduate assistants/students and LD specialists are provided through the program or unit. Academic advisers and counselors are provided collaboratively through on-campus or off-campus services.

Unique Aids and Services Aids, services, or accommodations include priority registration.

Subject-area Tutoring Tutoring is offered one-on-one, in small groups, and in class-size groups for some subjects. Tutoring is provided collaboratively through on-campus or off-campus services via computer-based instruction and graduate assistants/students.

Basic Skills Remediation Remediation is offered in small groups for math. Remediation is provided collaboratively through on-campus or off-campus services via computer-based instruction and other.

Enrichment Enrichment programs are available through the program or unit for self-advocacy and time management. Programs for career planning, learning strategies, math, stress management, study skills, test taking, time management, and written composition skills are provided collaboratively through on-campus or off-campus services. Credit is offered for career planning and learning strategies.

Application For admittance to the program or unit, students are required to apply to the program directly and provide a psychoeducational report (3 years old or less). Upon application, materials documenting need for services should be sent only to admissions with institutional application materials. Upon acceptance, documen-

tation of need for services should be sent only to the LD program or unit. *Application deadline (institutional):* 1/20. *Application deadline (LD program):* Rolling/continuous for fall and rolling/continuous for spring.

Written Policies Written policies regarding course substitutions, general/basic LD accommodations, grade forgiveness, reduced course loads, substitutions and waivers of admissions requirements, and substitutions and waivers of graduation requirements are available on the program Web site. Written policies regarding course substitutions, general/basic LD accommodations, grade forgiveness, reduced course loads, substitutions and waivers of admissions requirements, and substitutions and waivers of graduation requirements are outlined in the school's catalog/handbook. Written policies regarding course substitutions, general/basic LD accommodations, grade forgiveness, reduced course loads, substitutions and waivers of admissions requirements, and substitutions and waivers of graduation requirements are available through the program or unit directly.

University of Massachusetts Amherst

Learning Disabilities Support Services (LDSS)

Amherst, MA 01003

http://www.umass.edu/ldss

Contact: Learning Disabilities Support Services. Phone: 413-545-4602. Fax: 413-577-0691. E-mail: ldssinfo@acad.umass.edu.

Learning Disabilities Support Services (LDSS) Approximately 400 registered undergraduate students were served during 2002-03. The program or unit includes 3 full-time and 9 part-time staff members. Graduate assistants/students, LD specialists, professional tutors, remediation/learning specialists, skill tutors, special education teachers, and strategy tutors are provided through the program or unit. Academic advisers, counselors, diagnostic specialists, graduate assistants/students, and trained peer tutors are provided collaboratively through on-campus or off-campus services.

Unique Aids and Services Aids, services, or accommodations include weekly meetings with faculty.

Subject-area Tutoring Tutoring is offered one-on-one for some subjects. Tutoring is provided through the program or unit via graduate assistants/students. Tutoring is also provided collaboratively through on-campus or off-campus services via graduate assistants/students and trained peer tutors.

Diagnostic Testing Testing for auditory processing, intelligence, math, neuropsychological, personality, visual processing, written language, and other services is provided collaboratively through on-campus or off-campus services.

Fees *Diagnostic Testing* fee is applicable.

Application For admittance to the program or unit, students are required to provide a psychoeducational report and provide diagnosis of a learning disability . It is recommended that students provide documentation of high school services. Upon acceptance, documentation of need for services should be sent only to the LD program or unit. *Application deadline (institutional):* 1/15. *Application deadline (LD program):* Rolling/continuous for fall and rolling/continuous for spring.

Written Policies Written policies regarding course substitutions, general/basic LD accommodations, substitutions and waivers of admissions requirements, and substitutions and waivers of graduation requirements are available on the program Web site.

University of Massachusetts Boston
Ross Center for Disability Services

100 Morrissey Boulevard
Boston, MA 02125-3393
http://www.rosscenter.umb.edu

Contact: Dr. Renee L. Goldberg, Assistant Director. Phone: 617-287-7400. Fax: 617-287-7466. E-mail: renee.goldberg@umb.edu. Head of LD Program: Sheila Petruccelli, Director. Phone: 617-287-7400. Fax: 617-287-7466. E-mail: sheila.petrucelli@umb.edu.

Ross Center for Disability Services Approximately 90 registered undergraduate students were served during 2002-03. The program or unit includes 1 full-time and 1 part-time staff member. Academic advisers, counselors, graduate assistants/students, LD specialists, skill tutors, and strategy tutors are provided through the program or unit. Academic advisers, counselors, graduate assistants/students, professional tutors, remediation/learning specialists, skill tutors, strategy tutors, and trained peer tutors are provided collaboratively through on-campus or off-campus services.

Unique Aids and Services Aids, services, or accommodations include digital textbooks, priority registration, note-takers, testing accommodations.

Subject-area Tutoring Tutoring is offered one-on-one and in small groups for some subjects. Tutoring is provided collaboratively through on-campus or off-campus services via computer-based instruction, graduate assistants/students, LD specialists, professional tutors, and trained peer tutors.

Enrichment Enrichment programs are available through the program or unit for college survival skills, learning strategies, self-advocacy, study skills, test taking, time management, and written composition skills. Programs for career planning, college survival skills, health and nutrition, learning strategies, math, oral communication skills, practical computer skills, reading, self-advocacy, stress management, study skills, test taking, time management, and written composition skills are provided collaboratively through on-campus or off-campus services.

Student Organization Center for Students with Disabilities consists of 25 members.

Application For admittance to the program or unit, students are required to provide a psychoeducational report (3 years old or less). Upon application, materials documenting need for services should be sent only to admissions with institutional application materials. Upon acceptance, documentation of need for services should be sent only to the LD program or unit. *Application deadline (institutional):* Continuous.

Written Policies Written policy regarding general/basic LD accommodations is available on the program Web site. Written policy regarding substitutions and waivers of admissions requirements is outlined in the school's catalog/handbook. Written policy regarding general/basic LD accommodations is available through the program or unit directly.

University of Massachusetts Dartmouth

285 Old Westport Road
North Dartmouth, MA 02747-2300
http://www.umassd.edu/

Contact: Ms. Carole Johnson, Director of Disabled Student Services. Phone: 508-999-8711. E-mail: cjohnson@umassd.edu.

Approximately 300 registered undergraduate students were served during 2002-03. The program or unit includes 1 full-time and 9 part-time staff members. Academic advisers, counselors, graduate assistants/students, skill tutors, strategy tutors, and trained peer tutors are provided through the program or unit. Academic advisers, counselors, diagnostic specialists, LD specialists, professional tutors, regular education teachers, and trained peer tutors are provided collaboratively through on-campus or off-campus services.

Unique Aids and Services Aids, services, or accommodations include advocates, faculty training, and priority registration.

Subject-area Tutoring Tutoring is offered one-on-one for most subjects. Tutoring is provided through the program or unit via computer-based instruction, graduate assistants/students, and trained peer tutors. Tutoring is also provided collaboratively through on-campus or off-campus services via graduate assistants/students and trained peer tutors.

Diagnostic Testing Testing for auditory processing, handwriting, intelligence, learning strategies, learning styles, math, motor skills, neuropsychological, personality, reading, social skills, spelling, spoken language, study skills, visual processing, written language, and other services is provided collaboratively through on-campus or off-campus services.

Basic Skills Remediation Remediation is offered one-on-one and in small groups for auditory processing, computer skills, handwriting, learning strategies, math, motor skills, reading, social skills, spelling, spoken language, study skills, time management, visual processing, written language, and others. Remediation is provided through the program or unit via computer-based instruction, graduate assistants/students, and trained peer tutors. Remediation is also provided collaboratively through on-campus or off-campus services via computer-based instruction, graduate assistants/students, LD specialists, professional tutors, regular education teachers, and trained peer tutors.

Enrichment Enrichment programs are available through the program or unit for college survival skills, learning strategies, self-advocacy, stress management, study skills, test taking, and time management.

Student Organization Disabled Student Coalition consists of 10 members.

Fees *Diagnostic Testing* fee is $500.

Application For admittance to the program or unit, students are required to provide documentation of high school services. It is recommended that students provide a psychoeducational report (3 years old or less). Upon application, materials documenting need for services should be sent only to the LD program or unit. Upon acceptance, documentation of need for services should be sent only to the LD program or unit. *Application deadline (institutional):* Continuous. *Application deadline (LD program):* Rolling/continuous for fall and rolling/continuous for spring.

University of Massachusetts Dartmouth (continued)
Written Policies Written policies regarding course substitutions, general/basic LD accommodations, substitutions and waivers of admissions requirements, and substitutions and waivers of graduation requirements are outlined in the school's catalog/handbook. Written policies regarding course substitutions, general/basic LD accommodations, reduced course loads, substitutions and waivers of admissions requirements, and substitutions and waivers of graduation requirements are available through the program or unit directly.

The University of Memphis
Student Disability Services, Learning Disabilities-AD/HD Program

Memphis, TN 38152

http://www.people.memphis.edu/~sds/

Contact: Ms. Susan C. Te Paske, Director. Phone: 901-678-2880. Fax: 901-678-3070. E-mail: stepaske@memphis.edu.

Student Disability Services, Learning Disabilities-AD/HD Program Approximately 450 registered undergraduate students were served during 2002–03. The program or unit includes 3 full-time and 2 part-time staff members. Academic advisers, coaches, counselors, graduate assistants/students, LD specialists, professional tutors, remediation/learning specialists, skill tutors, strategy tutors, and trained peer tutors are provided through the program or unit. Academic advisers, counselors, diagnostic specialists, professional tutors, regular education teachers, skill tutors, strategy tutors, and trained peer tutors are provided collaboratively through on-campus or off-campus services.
Orientation The program or unit offers a mandatory 3-hour orientation for new students before classes begin and individually by special arrangement.
Unique Aids and Services Aids, services, or accommodations include advocates, career counseling, faculty training, parent workshops, personal coach, and priority registration.
Subject-area Tutoring Tutoring is offered one-on-one and in small groups for some subjects. Tutoring is provided through the program or unit via computer-based instruction, graduate assistants/students, and LD specialists. Tutoring is also provided collaboratively through on-campus or off-campus services via computer-based instruction, LD specialists, and trained peer tutors.
Diagnostic Testing Testing for auditory processing, intelligence, math, motor skills, personality, reading, social skills, spelling, spoken language, visual processing, and written language is provided collaboratively through on-campus or off-campus services.
Basic Skills Remediation Remediation is offered one-on-one and in small groups for computer skills, learning strategies, math, motor skills, reading, social skills, spoken language, study skills, time management, written language, and organizational strategies. Remediation is provided through the program or unit via computer-based instruction and LD specialists. Remediation is also provided collaboratively through on-campus or off-campus services via computer-based instruction, regular education teachers, and trained peer tutors.
Enrichment Enrichment programs are available through the program or unit for career planning, college survival skills, learning strategies, math, medication management, oral communication skills,

practical computer skills, reading, self-advocacy, stress management, study skills, test taking, time management, vocabulary development, and written composition skills. Programs for career planning, college survival skills, health and nutrition, learning strategies, math, oral communication skills, practical computer skills, reading, stress management, study skills, test taking, time management, and written composition skills are provided collaboratively through on-campus or off-campus services. Credit is offered for college survival skills.
Fees *Diagnostic Testing* fee is $150.
Application For admittance to the program or unit, students are required to apply to the program directly and provide a psychoeducational report (3 years old or less). It is recommended that students provide documentation of high school services. Upon application, materials documenting need for services should be sent only to the LD program or unit. Upon acceptance, documentation of need for services should be sent only to the LD program or unit. *Application deadline (institutional):* 8/1. *Application deadline (LD program):* Rolling/continuous for fall and rolling/continuous for spring.
Written Policies Written policies regarding course substitutions, general/basic LD accommodations, reduced course loads, and substitutions and waivers of graduation requirements are available on the program Web site. Written policies regarding course substitutions, general/basic LD accommodations, reduced course loads, and substitutions and waivers of graduation requirements are available through the program or unit directly.

University of Miami
Office of Disability Services

University of Miami Branch
Coral Gables, FL 33124
http://www.miami.edu/
Contact: Phone: 305-284-2211. Fax: 305-284-2507.

Subject-area Tutoring Tutoring is offered for some subjects.
Application For admittance to the program or unit, students are required to provide a psychoeducational report (3 years old or less) and provide complete, comprehensive, current psychoeducational test report. Upon acceptance, documentation of need for services should be sent only to the LD program or unit. *Application deadline (institutional):* 2/1. *Application deadline (LD program):* Rolling/continuous for fall.
Written Policies Written policy regarding general/basic LD accommodations is available through the program or unit directly.

University of Michigan

Ann Arbor, MI 48109
http://www.umich.edu/
Contact: Dr. Stuart Segal, Coordinator. Phone: 734-763-3000. Fax: 734-936-3947. E-mail: sssegal@umich.edu.

Approximately 450 registered undergraduate students were served during 2002–03. The program or unit includes 2 full-time staff members. Graduate assistants/students and LD specialists are provided through the program or unit. Academic advisers, counselors, diagnostic specialists, and remediation/learning specialists are provided collaboratively through on-campus or off-campus services.

Orientation The program or unit offers before classes begin.

Unique Aids and Services Aids, services, or accommodations include advocates and priority registration.

Subject-area Tutoring Tutoring is offered one-on-one for some subjects. Tutoring is provided collaboratively through on-campus or off-campus services via graduate assistants/students and trained peer tutors.

Diagnostic Testing Testing is provided through the program or unit for reading and study skills. Testing for auditory processing, handwriting, intelligence, learning strategies, learning styles, math, motor skills, neuropsychological, spelling, and written language is provided collaboratively through on-campus or off-campus services.

Basic Skills Remediation Remediation is offered one-on-one for math and written language. Remediation is provided collaboratively through on-campus or off-campus services via graduate assistants/students, LD specialists, professional tutors, and trained peer tutors.

Enrichment Programs for career planning, college survival skills, study skills, time management, and written composition skills are provided collaboratively through on-campus or off-campus services.

Application For admittance to the program or unit, students are required to provide a psychoeducational report. Upon application, materials documenting need for services should be sent only to the LD program or unit. Upon acceptance, documentation of need for services should be sent only to the LD program or unit. *Application deadline (institutional):* 2/1. *Application deadline (LD program):* Rolling/continuous for fall and rolling/continuous for spring.

Written Policies Written policy regarding general/basic LD accommodations is available on the program Web site.

University of Minnesota, Duluth

10 University Drive
Duluth, MN 55812-2496
http://www.d.umn.edu/

Contact: Judith W. Bromen, Coordinator. Phone: 218-726-7965. Fax: 218-726-6244. E-mail: jbromen@d.umn.edu.

Approximately 95 registered undergraduate students were served during 2002-03. The program or unit includes 2 full-time staff members. Academic advisers, diagnostic specialists, and LD specialists are provided through the program or unit. Academic advisers, counselors, skill tutors, and strategy tutors are provided collaboratively through on-campus or off-campus services.

Unique Aids and Services Aids, services, or accommodations include priority registration.

Subject-area Tutoring Tutoring is offered one-on-one, in small groups, and in class-size groups for some subjects. Tutoring is provided collaboratively through on-campus or off-campus services via trained peer tutors.

Diagnostic Testing Testing is provided through the program or unit for intelligence, math, reading, spelling, and spoken language. Testing for auditory processing, intelligence, and spoken language is provided collaboratively through on-campus or off-campus services.

Basic Skills Remediation Remediation is offered in class-size groups for math, study skills, and written language. Remediation is provided collaboratively through on-campus or off-campus services via regular education teachers.

Enrichment Enrichment programs are available through the program or unit for learning strategies, self-advocacy, and time management. Programs for career planning, college survival skills, health and nutrition, math, medication management, practical computer skills, stress management, study skills, and written composition skills are provided collaboratively through on-campus or off-campus services. Credit is offered for health and nutrition, math, study skills, and written composition skills.

Student Organization Access for All consists of 8 members.

Fees *Diagnostic Testing* fee is $0 to $50.

Application For admittance to the program or unit, students are required to provide a psychoeducational report (3 years old or less). It is recommended that students provide documentation of high school services. Upon application, materials documenting need for services should be sent only to the LD program or unit. Upon acceptance, documentation of need for services should be sent only to the LD program or unit. *Application deadline (institutional):* 2/1. *Application deadline (LD program):* Rolling/continuous for fall and rolling/continuous for spring.

Written Policies Written policy regarding general/basic LD accommodations is available on the program Web site. Written policy regarding general/basic LD accommodations is outlined in the school's catalog/handbook. Written policy regarding general/basic LD accommodations is available through the program or unit directly.

University of Minnesota, Morris

600 East 4th Street
Morris, MN 56267-2134
http://www.mrs.umn.edu/

Contact: Phone: 320-589-2211. Fax: 320-589-6399.

The program or unit includes 2 full-time staff members and 1 part-time staff member. Counselors, strategy tutors, and trained peer tutors are provided through the program or unit. Counselors, strategy tutors, and trained peer tutors are provided collaboratively through on-campus or off-campus services.

Unique Aids and Services Aids, services, or accommodations include digital textbooks, personal coach, priority registration, test accommodations.

Subject-area Tutoring Tutoring is offered one-on-one and in small groups for most subjects. Tutoring is provided collaboratively through on-campus or off-campus services via trained peer tutors and other.

Basic Skills Remediation Remediation is offered one-on-one, in small groups, and in class-size groups for auditory processing, learning strategies, math, reading, study skills, time management, and written language. Remediation is provided collaboratively through on-campus or off-campus services.

Enrichment Enrichment programs are available through the program or unit for learning strategies, self-advocacy, and stress management. Programs for career planning, college survival skills, learning strategies, math, reading, self-advocacy, stress manage-

University of Minnesota, Morris (continued)

ment, study skills, test taking, time management, and written composition skills are provided collaboratively through on-campus or off-campus services. Credit is offered for college survival skills.

Application For admittance to the program or unit, students are required to provide a psychoeducational report (3 years old or less). It is recommended that students provide documentation of high school services. Upon application, materials documenting need for services should be sent only to admissions with institutional application materials. Upon acceptance, documentation of need for services should be sent only to the LD program or unit. *Application deadline (institutional): 3/15. Application deadline (LD program):* Rolling/continuous for fall and rolling/continuous for spring.

Written Policies Written policies regarding course substitutions, general/basic LD accommodations, grade forgiveness, reduced course loads, substitutions and waivers of admissions requirements, and substitutions and waivers of graduation requirements are available through the program or unit directly.

University of Mississippi
Office of Student Disability Services

Oxford, MS 38677

http://www.olemiss.edu/depts/sds

Contact: Ms. Stacey Reycraft, Assistant Director and Disability Specialist. Phone: 662-915-7128. Fax: 662-915-5972. E-mail: sds@olemiss.edu.

Office of Student Disability Services Approximately 300 registered undergraduate students were served during 2002-03. The program or unit includes 5 full-time staff members.

Unique Aids and Services Aids, services, or accommodations include priority registration.

Application For admittance to the program or unit, students are required to apply to the program directly and provide a psychoeducational report (3 years old or less). Upon acceptance, documentation of need for services should be sent only to the LD program or unit. *Application deadline (institutional): 7/20. Application deadline (LD program):* Rolling/continuous for fall and rolling/continuous for spring.

Written Policies Written policy regarding general/basic LD accommodations is available on the program Web site. Written policy regarding general/basic LD accommodations is outlined in the school's catalog/handbook.

University of Missouri-Columbia
Office of Disability Services

Columbia, MO 65211

http://web.missouri.edu/~accesscm/

Contact: Mr. Eric Vinson, Learning Disabilities Specialist. Phone: 573-882-4696. Fax: 573-884-9272. E-mail: disabilityservices@missouri.edu. Head of LD Program: Dr.

Sarah Colby Weaver, Director. Phone: 573-882-4696. Fax: 573-884-9272. E-mail: disabilityservices@missouri.edu.

Office of Disability Services Approximately 606 registered undergraduate students were served during 2002-03. The program or unit includes 8 full-time staff members and 1 part-time staff member. Graduate assistants/students, LD specialists, remediation/learning specialists, skill tutors, and strategy tutors are provided through the program or unit. Academic advisers, coaches, counselors, diagnostic specialists, professional tutors, regular education teachers, teacher trainees, and trained peer tutors are provided collaboratively through on-campus or off-campus services.

Unique Aids and Services Aids, services, or accommodations include career counseling, digital textbooks, faculty training, personal coach, priority registration, weekly meetings with faculty, extra testing time, private testing room, classroom note-takers, test-readers, and test-scribes.

Subject-area Tutoring Tutoring is offered one-on-one, in small groups, and in class-size groups for most subjects. Tutoring is provided collaboratively through on-campus or off-campus services via graduate assistants/students, professional tutors, and trained peer tutors.

Diagnostic Testing Testing is provided through the program or unit for learning strategies, learning styles, and study skills. Testing for auditory processing, handwriting, intelligence, math, motor skills, neuropsychological, personality, reading, social skills, spelling, spoken language, visual processing, and written language is provided collaboratively through on-campus or off-campus services.

Basic Skills Remediation Remediation is offered one-on-one for learning strategies, study skills, and time management. Remediation is provided through the program or unit via LD specialists.

Enrichment Programs for career planning, college survival skills, health and nutrition, learning strategies, math, oral communication skills, practical computer skills, reading, self-advocacy, stress management, study skills, test taking, time management, and written composition skills are provided collaboratively through on-campus or off-campus services. Credit is offered for career planning, college survival skills, health and nutrition, learning strategies, math, oral communication skills, practical computer skills, reading, self-advocacy, stress management, study skills, test taking, time management, and written composition skills.

Fees *Diagnostic Testing* fee is $700.

Application For admittance to the program or unit, students are required to provide a psychoeducational report (5 years old or less). It is recommended that students provide documentation of high school services. Upon application, materials documenting need for services should be sent only to the LD program or unit. Upon acceptance, documentation of need for services should be sent only to the LD program or unit. *Application deadline (institutional):* Continuous. *Application deadline (LD program):* Rolling/continuous for fall and rolling/continuous for spring.

Written Policies Written policy regarding general/basic LD accommodations is available on the program Web site. Written policies regarding substitutions and waivers of admissions requirements and substitutions and waivers of graduation requirements are outlined in the school's catalog/handbook. Written policy regarding general/basic LD accommodations is available through the program or unit directly.

University of Missouri-Kansas City
Office of Services for Students with Disabilities

5100 Rockhill Road

Kansas City, MO 64110-2499

http://www.umkc.edu/disability

Contact: Mr. R. Scott Laurent, Coordinator. Phone: 816-235-5696. Fax: 816-235-6363. E-mail: disability@umkc.edu.

Office of Services for Students with Disabilities Approximately 85 registered undergraduate students were served during 2002-03. The program or unit includes 1 full-time and 6 part-time staff members. Academic advisers, counselors, diagnostic specialists, skill tutors, strategy tutors, and trained peer tutors are provided collaboratively through on-campus or off-campus services.

Unique Aids and Services Aids, services, or accommodations include career counseling, digital textbooks, faculty training, and priority registration.

Subject-area Tutoring Tutoring is offered in small groups for some subjects. Tutoring is provided collaboratively through on-campus or off-campus services via graduate assistants/students and trained peer tutors.

Diagnostic Testing Testing for auditory processing, handwriting, intelligence, learning strategies, learning styles, math, motor skills, neuropsychological, personality, reading, social skills, spelling, spoken language, study skills, visual processing, written language, and other services is provided collaboratively through on-campus or off-campus services.

Basic Skills Remediation Remediation is offered one-on-one and in class-size groups for learning strategies, math, study skills, time management, and written language. Remediation is provided through the program or unit. Remediation is also provided collaboratively through on-campus or off-campus services via graduate assistants/students and trained peer tutors.

Enrichment Enrichment programs are available through the program or unit for self-advocacy, test taking, and time management. Programs for career planning, college survival skills, health and nutrition, learning strategies, math, oral communication skills, practical computer skills, stress management, study skills, test taking, and written composition skills are provided collaboratively through on-campus or off-campus services. Credit is offered for college survival skills, oral communication skills, and practical computer skills.

Student Organization There is a student organization consisting of 20 members.

Fees *Diagnostic Testing* fee is applicable.

Application For admittance to the program or unit, students are required to provide a psychoeducational report (3 years old or less). It is recommended that students provide documentation of high school services. Upon acceptance, documentation of need for services should be sent only to the LD program or unit. *Application deadline (institutional):* Continuous. *Application deadline (LD program):* Rolling/continuous for fall and rolling/continuous for spring.

Written Policies Written policy regarding general/basic LD accommodations is available on the program Web site. Written policies regarding general/basic LD accommodations and reduced course loads are available through the program or unit directly.

University of Missouri-Rolla
Disability Support Services

1870 Miner Circle

Rolla, MO 65409-0910

http://campus.umr.edu/dss/

Contact: Ms. Connie Arthur, Student Disabilities Services Adviser. Phone: 573-341-4222. Fax: 573-341-6179. E-mail: dss@umr.edu.

Disability Support Services Approximately 44 registered undergraduate students were served during 2002-03. The program or unit includes 1 full-time staff member. Academic advisers, coaches, counselors, professional tutors, skill tutors, strategy tutors, and trained peer tutors are provided collaboratively through on-campus or off-campus services.

Orientation The program or unit offers a mandatory 5-day orientation for new students before classes begin.

Unique Aids and Services Aids, services, or accommodations include digital textbooks, priority registration, and support groups.

Subject-area Tutoring Tutoring is offered in small groups for some subjects. Tutoring is provided collaboratively through on-campus or off-campus services via computer-based instruction, graduate assistants/students, and trained peer tutors.

Diagnostic Testing Testing is provided through the program or unit for learning strategies, learning styles, study skills, and visual processing. Testing for personality and written language is provided collaboratively through on-campus or off-campus services.

Enrichment Enrichment programs are available through the program or unit for learning strategies, medication management, self-advocacy, stress management, study skills, test taking, and time management. Programs for career planning, college survival skills, oral communication skills, practical computer skills, reading, and written composition skills are provided collaboratively through on-campus or off-campus services.

Fees *Orientation* fee is $135.

Application For admittance to the program or unit, students are required to provide a psychoeducational report (3 years old or less). It is recommended that students apply to the program directly and provide documentation of high school services. Upon application, materials documenting need for services should be sent only to the LD program or unit. Upon acceptance, documentation of need for services should be sent only to the LD program or unit. *Application deadline (institutional):* 7/1. *Application deadline (LD program):* Rolling/continuous for fall and rolling/continuous for spring.

Written Policies Written policy regarding general/basic LD accommodations is available on the program Web site. Written policy regarding general/basic LD accommodations is outlined in the school's catalog/handbook.

University of Missouri-St. Louis
Disability Access Services

8001 Natural Bridge Road

St. Louis, MO 63121-4499

http://www.umsl.edu/services/disabled/

Contact: Mrs. Marilyn Ditto-Pernell, Director of Disability Access Services. Phone: 314-516-6554. Fax: 314-516-6561. E-mail: mditto@umsl.edu.

Disability Access Services Approximately 125 registered undergraduate students were served during 2002-03. The program or unit includes 1 full-time staff member. Academic advisers, counselors, and other are provided collaboratively through on-campus or off-campus services.

Unique Aids and Services Aids, services, or accommodations include career counseling, digital textbooks, and priority registration.

Enrichment Programs for career planning, stress management, study skills, test taking, time management, and other are provided collaboratively through on-campus or off-campus services.

Student Organization Students with disAbilities Association consists of 75 members.

Application For admittance to the program or unit, students are required to apply to the program directly, provide a psychoeducational report (5 years old or less), and provide a specific DSM-IV diagnosis, assessment test scores, summary and recommendations. Upon application, materials documenting need for services should be sent only to the LD program or unit. Upon acceptance, documentation of need for services should be sent only to the LD program or unit. *Application deadline (institutional):* Continuous. *Application deadline (LD program):* 7/7 for fall. 12/1 for spring.

Written Policies Written policy regarding general/basic LD accommodations is available on the program Web site. Written policy regarding general/basic LD accommodations is outlined in the school's catalog/handbook. Written policy regarding general/basic LD accommodations is available through the program or unit directly.

University of Mobile

PO Box 13220

Mobile, AL 36663-0220

http://www.umobile.edu/

Contact: Mrs. Barbara N. Smith, ADA Coordinator. Phone: 251-442-2276 Ext. 251. Fax: 251-442-2513. E-mail: barbaras@mail.umobile.edu.

Approximately 15 registered undergraduate students were served during 2002-03. The program or unit includes 1 part-time staff member. Academic advisers and trained peer tutors are provided collaboratively through on-campus or off-campus services.

Subject-area Tutoring Tutoring is offered one-on-one for some subjects. Tutoring is provided collaboratively through on-campus or off-campus services via computer-based instruction and trained peer tutors.

Basic Skills Remediation Remediation is offered one-on-one for learning strategies, math, study skills, time management, and written language. Remediation is provided collaboratively through on-campus or off-campus services via trained peer tutors.

Application For admittance to the program or unit, students are required to apply to the program directly and provide a psychoeducational report. Upon acceptance, documentation of need for services should be sent to both admissions and the LD program or unit. *Application deadline (institutional):* Continuous. *Application deadline (LD program):* Rolling/continuous for fall and rolling/continuous for spring.

Written Policies Written policy regarding general/basic LD accommodations is available on the program Web site. Written policy regarding general/basic LD accommodations is outlined in the school's catalog/handbook.

The University of Montana-Missoula
Disability Services for Students

Missoula, MT 59812-0002

http://www.umt.edu/dss

Contact: Phone: 406-243-0211. Fax: 406-243-5711. Head of LD Program: Mr. James Marks, Director. Phone: 406-243-2243. Fax: 406-243-5330.

Disability Services for Students Approximately 260 registered undergraduate students were served during 2002-03. The program or unit includes 9 full-time and 3 part-time staff members. Academic advisers, coaches, counselors, diagnostic specialists, graduate assistants/students, LD specialists, professional tutors, regular education teachers, and trained peer tutors are provided collaboratively through on-campus or off-campus services.

Orientation The program or unit offers an optional 2-hour orientation for new students during summer prior to enrollment.

Unique Aids and Services Aids, services, or accommodations include advocates, career counseling, digital textbooks, priority registration, and support groups.

Subject-area Tutoring Tutoring is offered one-on-one for most subjects. Tutoring is provided collaboratively through on-campus or off-campus services via graduate assistants/students and trained peer tutors.

Enrichment Programs for career planning, college survival skills, health and nutrition, learning strategies, math, medication management, oral communication skills, practical computer skills, self-advocacy, stress management, study skills, test taking, time management, and written composition skills are provided collaboratively through on-campus or off-campus services. Credit is offered for college survival skills, health and nutrition, learning strategies, math, oral communication skills, practical computer skills, and study skills.

Student Organization Alliance for Disability and Students at University of Montana (ADSUM).

Application For admittance to the program or unit, students are required to apply to the program directly and provide a psychoeducational report (5 years old or less). It is recommended that students provide documentation of high school services. Upon application, materials documenting need for services should be sent only to the LD program or unit. Upon acceptance, documentation of need for services should be sent only to the LD program or unit. *Application deadline (institutional):* 7/1. *Application deadline (LD program):* Rolling/continuous for fall and rolling/continuous for spring.

Written Policies Written policies regarding course substitutions, general/basic LD accommodations, substitutions and waivers of admissions requirements, and substitutions and waivers of graduation requirements are available on the program Web site. Written policy regarding substitutions and waivers of admissions requirements is outlined in the school's catalog/handbook. Written policies regarding course substitutions, general/basic LD accommodations, and substitutions and waivers of graduation requirements are available through the program or unit directly.

The University of Montana-Western
Student Life Office

710 South Atlantic
Dillon, MT 59725-3598
http://www.umwestern.edu/StuLife
Contact: Dr. Eric W. Murray, Dean of Students. Phone: 406-683-7565. Fax: 406-683-7570. E-mail: e_murray@umwestern.edu.

Student Life Office Approximately 20 registered undergraduate students were served during 2002-03. The program or unit includes 4 part-time staff members. Graduate assistants/students and LD specialists are provided through the program or unit.

Unique Aids and Services Aids, services, or accommodations include books-on-tape, note-taking, private testing.

Subject-area Tutoring Tutoring is offered one-on-one and in small groups for most subjects. Tutoring is provided collaboratively through on-campus or off-campus services via graduate assistants/students.

Application It is recommended that students provide a psychoeducational report (3 years old or less) and provide documentation of high school services. Upon application, materials documenting need for services should be sent only to the LD program or unit. Upon acceptance, documentation of need for services should be sent only to the LD program or unit. *Application deadline (institutional):* 7/1. *Application deadline (LD program):* Rolling/continuous for fall and rolling/continuous for spring.

Written Policies Written policy regarding general/basic LD accommodations is available on the program Web site. Written policies regarding course substitutions, reduced course loads, and substitutions and waivers of graduation requirements are outlined in the school's catalog/handbook. Written policy regarding general/basic LD accommodations is available through the program or unit directly.

University of Montevallo
Services for Students with Disabilities

Station 6001
Montevallo, AL 35115
http://www.montevallo.edu/sswd

Contact: Ms. Deborah S. McCune, Coordinator of Services for Students with Disabilities. Phone: 205-665-6250. Fax: 205-665-6255. E-mail: mccuned@montevallo.edu.

Services for Students with Disabilities Approximately 75 registered undergraduate students were served during 2002-03. The program or unit includes 1 full-time and 1 part-time staff member. Academic advisers and counselors are provided through the program or unit. Academic advisers, counselors, skill tutors, strategy tutors, and trained peer tutors are provided collaboratively through on-campus or off-campus services.

Unique Aids and Services Aids, services, or accommodations include career counseling, faculty training, and priority registration.

Subject-area Tutoring Tutoring is offered one-on-one and in small groups for most subjects. Tutoring is provided collaboratively through on-campus or off-campus services via graduate assistants/students and trained peer tutors.

Diagnostic Testing Testing for learning strategies, learning styles, personality, spoken language, and study skills is provided collaboratively through on-campus or off-campus services.

Basic Skills Remediation Remediation is offered one-on-one and in small groups for auditory processing, learning strategies, math, spoken language, study skills, and time management. Remediation is provided collaboratively through on-campus or off-campus services via graduate assistants/students, trained peer tutors, and other.

Enrichment Programs for career planning, health and nutrition, learning strategies, stress management, study skills, test taking, time management, and written composition skills are provided collaboratively through on-campus or off-campus services.

Application For admittance to the program or unit, students are required to apply to the program directly and provide a psychoeducational report. It is recommended that students provide documentation of high school services. Upon application, materials documenting need for services should be sent only to the LD program or unit. Upon acceptance, documentation of need for services should be sent only to the LD program or unit. *Application deadline (institutional):* 8/1. *Application deadline (LD program):* Rolling/continuous for fall and rolling/continuous for spring.

Written Policies Written policy regarding general/basic LD accommodations is available on the program Web site. Written policy regarding grade forgiveness is outlined in the school's catalog/handbook. Written policies regarding course substitutions and general/basic LD accommodations are available through the program or unit directly.

University of Nebraska at Omaha
Services for Students with disABILITIES

6001 Dodge Street
Omaha, NE 68182
http://www.unomaha.edu/%7ewwwud/ssd.html
Contact: Kate Benecke. Phone: 402-554-2872. E-mail: mbenecke@mail.unomaha.edu.

Services for Students with disABILITIES Approximately 45 registered undergraduate students were served during 2002-03. The program or unit includes 3 full-time staff members and 1 part-time

University of Nebraska at Omaha (continued)

staff member. Academic advisers, coaches, counselors, diagnostic specialists, graduate assistants/students, LD specialists, professional tutors, regular education teachers, remediation/learning specialists, skill tutors, special education teachers, strategy tutors, teacher trainees, and trained peer tutors are provided collaboratively through on-campus or off-campus services.

Unique Aids and Services Aids, services, or accommodations include advocates and priority registration.

Subject-area Tutoring Tutoring is offered one-on-one, in small groups, and in class-size groups for most subjects. Tutoring is provided collaboratively through on-campus or off-campus services via computer-based instruction, graduate assistants/students, LD specialists, professional tutors, and trained peer tutors.

Enrichment Enrichment programs are available through the program or unit for self-advocacy. Programs for career planning, college survival skills, health and nutrition, learning strategies, math, reading, stress management, study skills, test taking, time management, and written composition skills are provided collaboratively through on-campus or off-campus services.

Student Organization Network for disABLED Students.

Application For admittance to the program or unit, students are required to provide a psychoeducational report (3 years old or less). It is recommended that students provide documentation of high school services. Upon application, materials documenting need for services should be sent only to the LD program or unit. Upon acceptance, documentation of need for services should be sent only to the LD program or unit. *Application deadline (institutional):* 8/1. *Application deadline (LD program):* Rolling/continuous for fall and rolling/continuous for spring.

University of Nebraska-Lincoln

14th and R Streets
Lincoln, NE 68588
http://www.unl.edu/
Contact: Mrs. Veva Cheney, Director of Services for Students with Disabilities. Phone: 402-472-3787. Fax: 402-472-0080. E-mail: vcheney@unl.edu.

The program or unit includes 2 full-time staff members and 1 part-time staff member. Academic advisers, coaches, counselors, diagnostic specialists, and skill tutors are provided collaboratively through on-campus or off-campus services.

Unique Aids and Services Aids, services, or accommodations include digital textbooks and priority registration.

Diagnostic Testing Testing for auditory processing, intelligence, math, reading, spelling, visual processing, and written language is provided collaboratively through on-campus or off-campus services.

Fees *Diagnostic Testing* fee is applicable.

Application For admittance to the program or unit, students are required to provide a psychoeducational report (3 years old or less). It is recommended that students provide documentation of high school services. Upon application, materials documenting need for services should be sent only to the LD program or unit. Upon acceptance, documentation of need for services should be sent only to the LD program or unit. *Application deadline (institutional):* 6/30. *Application deadline (LD program):* Rolling/continuous for fall and rolling/continuous for spring.

Written Policies Written policies regarding general/basic LD accommodations and substitutions and waivers of admissions requirements are available on the program Web site. Written policies regarding course substitutions, general/basic LD accommodations, grade forgiveness, reduced course loads, substitutions and waivers of admissions requirements, and substitutions and waivers of graduation requirements are available through the program or unit directly.

University of Nevada, Las Vegas
Learning Enhancement Services

4505 Maryland Parkway
Las Vegas, NV 89154-9900
http://www.unlv.edu/studentlife/les/
Contact: Mr. Phillip A. Pownall, Coordinator of Disability Services. Phone: 702-895-0866. Fax: 702-895-0651. E-mail: ppownall@ccmail.nevada.edu. Head of LD Program: Ms. Anita H. Stockbauer, Director of Learning Enhancement Services. Phone: 702-895-0866. Fax: 702-895-0651. E-mail: anitas@ccmail.nevada.edu.

Learning Enhancement Services Approximately 333 registered undergraduate students were served during 2002-03. The program or unit includes 5 full-time staff members and 1 part-time staff member. Counselors are provided through the program or unit.

Unique Aids and Services Aids, services, or accommodations include advocates, career counseling, digital textbooks, faculty training, and priority registration.

Enrichment Programs for career planning, college survival skills, learning strategies, study skills, test taking, and time management are provided collaboratively through on-campus or off-campus services.

Application For admittance to the program or unit, students are required to provide a psychoeducational report (3 years old or less). Upon application, materials documenting need for services should be sent only to the LD program or unit. Upon acceptance, documentation of need for services should be sent only to the LD program or unit. *Application deadline (institutional):* 5/1. *Application deadline (LD program):* Rolling/continuous for fall and rolling/continuous for spring.

Written Policies Written policy regarding general/basic LD accommodations is available through the program or unit directly.

University of New Brunswick Fredericton
Centre of Excellence for Students with Disabilities

PO Box 4400
Fredericton, NB E3B 5A3
Canada
http://www.unb.ca/

Contact: Phone: 506-453-4666. Fax: 506-453-5016.

Centre of Excellence for Students with Disabilities The program or unit includes 2 full-time and 15 part-time staff members. Academic advisers, coaches, counselors, diagnostic specialists, graduate assistants/students, LD specialists, regular education teachers, and skill tutors are provided through the program or unit.

Unique Aids and Services Aids, services, or accommodations include digital textbooks and personal coach.

Subject-area Tutoring Tutoring is offered one-on-one for all subjects. Tutoring is provided through the program or unit via graduate assistants/students, LD specialists, professional tutors, and trained peer tutors. Tutoring is also provided collaboratively through on-campus or off-campus services via computer-based instruction, graduate assistants/students, professional tutors, and trained peer tutors.

Diagnostic Testing Testing is provided through the program or unit for auditory processing, handwriting, learning strategies, learning styles, math, motor skills, neuropsychological, reading, spelling, study skills, visual processing, and written language. Testing for handwriting and math is provided collaboratively through on-campus or off-campus services.

Basic Skills Remediation Remediation is offered one-on-one for computer skills, learning strategies, math, reading, social skills, spelling, spoken language, study skills, time management, and written language. Remediation is provided through the program or unit via graduate assistants/students, LD specialists, professional tutors, regular education teachers, special education teachers, teacher trainees, and trained peer tutors.

Enrichment Enrichment programs are available through the program or unit for study skills, test taking, and time management.

Application For admittance to the program or unit, students are required to provide a psychoeducational report (10 years old or less). It is recommended that students provide documentation of high school services. Upon acceptance, documentation of need for services should be sent only to the LD program or unit. *Application deadline (institutional):* Continuous.

Written Policies Written policy regarding general/basic LD accommodations is available on the program Web site. Written policy regarding general/basic LD accommodations is outlined in the school's catalog/handbook. Written policy regarding general/basic LD accommodations is available through the program or unit directly.

University of New Brunswick Saint John
Student Life and Support Services

PO Box 5050

Saint John, NB E2L 4L5

Canada

http://www.unbsj.ca/stu_serv

Contact: Mr. Ken Craft, Student Development Coordinator. Phone: 506-648-5962. Fax: 506-648-5681. E-mail: kcraft@unbsj.ca.

Student Life and Support Services Approximately 15 registered undergraduate students were served during 2002-03. The pro-

gram or unit includes 1 full-time staff member. Academic advisers, counselors, skill tutors, and trained peer tutors are provided collaboratively through on-campus or off-campus services.

Unique Aids and Services Aids, services, or accommodations include advocates and career counseling.

Basic Skills Remediation Remediation is offered one-on-one for learning strategies, reading, study skills, time management, and written language. Remediation is provided through the program or unit.

Enrichment Enrichment programs are available through the program or unit for college survival skills, learning strategies, reading, study skills, test taking, and time management. Programs for career planning, college survival skills, learning strategies, math, oral communication skills, reading, self-advocacy, stress management, study skills, test taking, time management, and written composition skills are provided collaboratively through on-campus or off-campus services.

Application For admittance to the program or unit, students are required to provide a psychoeducational report. It is recommended that students provide documentation of high school services. Upon acceptance, documentation of need for services should be sent only to the LD program or unit. *Application deadline (institutional):* Continuous. *Application deadline (LD program):* Rolling/continuous for fall and rolling/continuous for spring.

Written Policies Written policy regarding general/basic LD accommodations is available on the program Web site. Written policy regarding general/basic LD accommodations is outlined in the school's catalog/handbook. Written policy regarding general/basic LD accommodations is available through the program or unit directly.

University of New England
Disability Services

Hills Beach Road

Biddeford, ME 04005-9526

http://www.une.edu/studentlife/dsd/index.html

Contact: Susan M. Church, Coordinator Disability Services. Phone: 207-283-0170 Ext. 2815. Fax: 207-294-5931. E-mail: schurch@une.edu.

Disability Services Approximately 65 registered undergraduate students were served during 2002-03. The program or unit includes 2 full-time staff members. Academic advisers, counselors, professional tutors, remediation/learning specialists, skill tutors, strategy tutors, and trained peer tutors are provided collaboratively through on-campus or off-campus services.

Unique Aids and Services Aids, services, or accommodations include digital textbooks and priority registration.

Subject-area Tutoring Tutoring is offered in small groups for most subjects. Tutoring is provided collaboratively through on-campus or off-campus services via professional tutors and trained peer tutors.

Enrichment Enrichment programs are available through the program or unit for self-advocacy. Programs for career planning, college survival skills, learning strategies, math, reading, stress management, study skills, test taking, time management, and written composition skills are provided collaboratively through on-campus or off-campus services.

University of New England (continued)

Application For admittance to the program or unit, students are required to provide a psychoeducational report (3 years old or less). It is recommended that students provide documentation of high school services. Upon application, materials documenting need for services should be sent only to the LD program or unit. Upon acceptance, documentation of need for services should be sent only to the LD program or unit. *Application deadline (institutional):* Continuous. *Application deadline (LD program):* Rolling/continuous for fall and rolling/continuous for spring.

Written Policies Written policies regarding course substitutions, general/basic LD accommodations, and reduced course loads are available on the program Web site. Written policies regarding course substitutions, general/basic LD accommodations, and reduced course loads are available through the program or unit directly.

University of New Hampshire
Access Office, Support Services for Students with Disabilities

Durham, NH 03824

http://unhinfo.unh.edu/access/index.html

Contact: Mr. Christopher J.V. Paris, Academic Assistant. Phone: 603-862-2607. Fax: 603-862-4043. E-mail: christopher.paris@unh.edu. Head of LD Program: Ms. Maxine J. Little, Director. Phone: 603-862-2648. Fax: 603-862-4043. E-mail: maxine.little@unh.edu.

Access Office, Support Services for Students with Disabilities Approximately 185 registered undergraduate students were served during 2002-03. The program or unit includes 2 full-time and 2 part-time staff members. Academic advisers, counselors, LD specialists, and strategy tutors are provided through the program or unit. Academic advisers, counselors, diagnostic specialists, professional tutors, regular education teachers, skill tutors, strategy tutors, and trained peer tutors are provided collaboratively through on-campus or off-campus services.

Unique Aids and Services Aids, services, or accommodations include advocates, priority registration, texts on tape.

Enrichment Enrichment programs are available through the program or unit for self-advocacy. Programs for career planning, college survival skills, health and nutrition, learning strategies, math, oral communication skills, practical computer skills, self-advocacy, stress management, study skills, test taking, time management, and written composition skills are provided collaboratively through on-campus or off-campus services.

Application For admittance to the program or unit, students are required to apply to the program directly and provide a psychoeducational report (3 years old or less). It is recommended that students provide documentation of high school services and provide other pertinent data on information processing. Upon application, materials documenting need for services should be sent only to the LD program or unit. Upon acceptance, documentation of need for services should be sent only to the LD program or unit. *Application deadline (institutional):* 2/1. *Application deadline (LD program):* Rolling/continuous for fall and rolling/continuous for spring.

Written Policies Written policy regarding general/basic LD accommodations is available on the program Web site. Written policy regarding general/basic LD accommodations is outlined in the school's catalog/handbook. Written policies regarding course substitutions, general/basic LD accommodations, and reduced course loads are available through the program or unit directly.

University of New Hampshire at Manchester

400 Commercial Street

Manchester, NH 03101-1113

http://www.unh.edu/unhm/

Contact: Phone: 603-641-4321. Fax: 603-641-4125.

The program or unit includes 3 part-time staff members. Academic advisers, professional tutors, regular education teachers, skill tutors, strategy tutors, and trained peer tutors are provided collaboratively through on-campus or off-campus services.

Unique Aids and Services Aids, services, or accommodations include career counseling, faculty training, and priority registration.

Subject-area Tutoring Tutoring is offered one-on-one and in small groups for some subjects. Tutoring is provided through the program or unit via graduate assistants/students, LD specialists, professional tutors, and trained peer tutors.

Basic Skills Remediation Remediation is offered one-on-one and in small groups for learning strategies, math, reading, study skills, and time management. Remediation is provided through the program or unit via graduate assistants/students, LD specialists, and trained peer tutors.

Application *Application deadline (institutional):* 6/15.

Written Policies Written policies regarding course substitutions, general/basic LD accommodations, substitutions and waivers of admissions requirements, and substitutions and waivers of graduation requirements are available on the program Web site. Written policies regarding course substitutions, general/basic LD accommodations, substitutions and waivers of admissions requirements, and substitutions and waivers of graduation requirements are outlined in the school's catalog/handbook. Written policies regarding general/basic LD accommodations and reduced course loads are available through the program or unit directly.

University of New Haven
Disability Services and Resources

300 Orange Avenue

West Haven, CT 06516-1916

http://www.newhaven.edu/campuslife/disabilities.html

Contact: Ms. Linda Copney-Okeke, Director of Disability Services and Resources. Phone: 203-932-7332. Fax: 203-931-6082. E-mail: lcopney-okeke@newhaven.edu.

Disability Services and Resources Approximately 200 registered undergraduate students were served during 2002-03. The program or unit includes 1 full-time staff member. Academic advisers, counselors, graduate assistants/students, LD specialists, and skill tutors are provided through the program or unit. Academic advisers, counselors, diagnostic specialists, professional tutors, skill tutors, and strategy tutors are provided collaboratively through on-campus or off-campus services.

Unique Aids and Services Aids, services, or accommodations include career counseling and faculty training.

Subject-area Tutoring Tutoring is offered one-on-one and in small groups for most subjects. Tutoring is provided through the program or unit via computer-based instruction and graduate assistants/students. Tutoring is also provided collaboratively through on-campus or off-campus services via graduate assistants/students and professional tutors.

Diagnostic Testing Testing is provided through the program or unit for learning strategies and learning styles. Testing for intelligence, math, personality, reading, spelling, study skills, written language, and other services is provided collaboratively through on-campus or off-campus services.

Basic Skills Remediation Remediation is offered one-on-one, in small groups, and in class-size groups for computer skills, learning strategies, math, reading, social skills, study skills, and time management. Remediation is provided collaboratively through on-campus or off-campus services via regular education teachers and other.

Enrichment Enrichment programs are available through the program or unit for math, study skills, test taking, time management, and written composition skills. Programs for career planning, health and nutrition, learning strategies, math, oral communication skills, practical computer skills, reading, stress management, study skills, test taking, time management, and written composition skills are provided collaboratively through on-campus or off-campus services. Credit is offered for math, oral communication skills, practical computer skills, reading, and written composition skills.

Application For admittance to the program or unit, students are required to provide a psychoeducational report. It is recommended that students provide documentation of high school services. Upon acceptance, documentation of need for services should be sent only to the LD program or unit. *Application deadline (institutional):* Continuous. *Application deadline (LD program):* Rolling/continuous for fall and rolling/continuous for spring.

Written Policies Written policies regarding course substitutions, general/basic LD accommodations, and reduced course loads are available through the program or unit directly.

University of New Orleans
Office of Disability Services

Lake Front
New Orleans, LA 70148
http://www.uno.edu/~stlf/ODS%20Manual/ods_manual_frames.htm
Contact: Mrs. Amy A. King, Assistant Director. Phone: 504-280-7284. E-mail: aaking@uno.edu.

Office of Disability Services Approximately 100 registered undergraduate students were served during 2002-03. The program or unit includes 3 full-time and 2 part-time staff members.

Unique Aids and Services Aids, services, or accommodations include digital textbooks.

Subject-area Tutoring Tutoring is offered one-on-one and in small groups for some subjects. Tutoring is provided collaboratively through on-campus or off-campus services via trained peer tutors.

Enrichment Programs for career planning, college survival skills, oral communication skills, practical computer skills, stress management, study skills, time management, and written composition skills are provided collaboratively through on-campus or off-campus services. Credit is offered for oral communication skills, study skills, and written composition skills.

Application For admittance to the program or unit, students are required to provide a psychoeducational report (3 years old or less) and provide documentation from MD or psychologist/psychiatrist (for Attention Deficit Disorder). Upon application, materials documenting need for services should be sent only to the LD program or unit. Upon acceptance, documentation of need for services should be sent only to the LD program or unit. *Application deadline (institutional):* Continuous. *Application deadline (LD program):* Rolling/continuous for fall and rolling/continuous for spring.

Written Policies Written policies regarding course substitutions and general/basic LD accommodations are available on the program Web site. Written policy regarding grade forgiveness is outlined in the school's catalog/handbook. Written policies regarding course substitutions and general/basic LD accommodations are available through the program or unit directly.

University of North Alabama
Developmental Services

One Harrison Plaza
Florence, AL 35632-0001
http://www2.una.edu/devservices
Contact: Mrs. Jennifer S. Adams, Associate Director of Student Life for Developmental Services. Phone: 256-765-4907. Fax: 256-765-6016. E-mail: jsadams@una.edu.

Developmental Services Approximately 100 registered undergraduate students were served during 2002-03. The program or unit includes 2 full-time staff members. Academic advisers, coaches, counselors, graduate assistants/students, remediation/learning specialists, skill tutors, strategy tutors, trained peer tutors, and other are provided through the program or unit. Academic advisers, coaches, counselors, diagnostic specialists, graduate assistants/students, LD specialists, professional tutors, regular education teachers, remediation/learning specialists, skill tutors, special education teachers, strategy tutors, trained peer tutors, and other are provided collaboratively through on-campus or off-campus services.

Summer Program To help prepare for the demands of college, there is 2-day summer program prior to entering the school.

Unique Aids and Services Aids, services, or accommodations include advocates, personal coach, and priority registration.

Subject-area Tutoring Tutoring is offered one-on-one and in small groups for most subjects. Tutoring is provided through the program or unit via computer-based instruction, graduate assistants/students, trained peer tutors, and other. Tutoring is also provided collaboratively through on-campus or off-campus services via computer-based instruction, graduate assistants/students, trained peer tutors, and other.

University of North Alabama (continued)

Basic Skills Remediation Remediation is offered one-on-one, in small groups, and in class-size groups for computer skills, learning strategies, math, reading, spelling, study skills, time management, and memory/concentration. Remediation is provided through the program or unit via computer-based instruction, graduate assistants/ students, LD specialists, and trained peer tutors. Remediation is also provided collaboratively through on-campus or off-campus services via computer-based instruction, graduate assistants/students, LD specialists, and trained peer tutors.

Enrichment Enrichment programs are available through the program or unit for college survival skills, learning strategies, practical computer skills, reading, self-advocacy, stress management, study skills, test taking, time management, and written composition skills. Programs for career planning, college survival skills, health and nutrition, learning strategies, math, medication management, oral communication skills, practical computer skills, reading, stress management, study skills, test taking, time management, and written composition skills are provided collaboratively through on-campus or off-campus services.

Fees *Summer Program* fee is $60.

Application For admittance to the program or unit, students are required to apply to the program directly. It is recommended that students provide a psychoeducational report (5 years old or less) and provide documentation of high school services. Upon application, materials documenting need for services should be sent only to the LD program or unit. Upon acceptance, documentation of need for services should be sent only to the LD program or unit. *Application deadline (institutional):* Continuous. *Application deadline (LD program):* Rolling/continuous for fall and rolling/continuous for spring.

Written Policies Written policies regarding general/basic LD accommodations and grade forgiveness are available on the program Web site. Written policies regarding general/basic LD accommodations, grade forgiveness, substitutions and waivers of admissions requirements, and substitutions and waivers of graduation requirements are outlined in the school's catalog/handbook. Written policies regarding course substitutions, general/basic LD accommodations, grade forgiveness, and reduced course loads are available through the program or unit directly.

The University of North Carolina at Asheville

One University Heights

Asheville, NC 28804-3299

http://www.unca.edu/

Contact: Dr. Heidi Kelley, Director of Liberal Arts Learning and Disability Services. Phone: 828-251-6980. Fax: 828-251-6023. E-mail: hkelley@unca.edu.

The program or unit includes 1 part-time staff member. Academic advisers, coaches, counselors, regular education teachers, and trained peer tutors are provided collaboratively through on-campus or off-campus services.

Unique Aids and Services Aids, services, or accommodations include faculty training, priority registration, support groups, and weekly meetings with faculty.

Subject-area Tutoring Tutoring is offered one-on-one for all subjects. Tutoring is provided collaboratively through on-campus or off-campus services via trained peer tutors.

Student Organization Equal Access consists of 10 members.

Application For admittance to the program or unit, students are required to provide a psychoeducational report (3 years old or less), provide documentation of high school services, and provide specific diagnosis. Upon application, materials documenting need for services should be sent only to the LD program or unit. Upon acceptance, documentation of need for services should be sent only to the LD program or unit. *Application deadline (institutional):* 3/15. *Application deadline (LD program):* Rolling/continuous for fall and rolling/ continuous for spring.

Written Policies Written policy regarding general/basic LD accommodations is available on the program Web site. Written policy regarding general/basic LD accommodations is outlined in the school's catalog/handbook.

The University of North Carolina at Greensboro
Disability Services

1000 Spring Garden Street

Greensboro, NC 27412-5001

http://www.uncg.edu/ods

Contact: Patricia L. Bailey, Director. Phone: 336-334-5440. Fax: 336-334-4412. E-mail: plbailey@uncg.edu.

Disability Services Approximately 200 registered undergraduate students were served during 2002-03. The program or unit includes 5 full-time and 2 part-time staff members. Counselors and LD specialists are provided through the program or unit. Skill tutors and trained peer tutors are provided collaboratively through on-campus or off-campus services.

Unique Aids and Services Aids, services, or accommodations include advocates, career counseling, faculty training, and priority registration.

Subject-area Tutoring Tutoring is offered one-on-one and in small groups for most subjects. Tutoring is provided through the program or unit via graduate assistants/students and LD specialists. Tutoring is also provided collaboratively through on-campus or off-campus services via graduate assistants/students and trained peer tutors.

Diagnostic Testing Testing is provided through the program or unit for learning styles. Testing for auditory processing, intelligence, math, personality, reading, spelling, spoken language, study skills, visual processing, and written language is provided collaboratively through on-campus or off-campus services.

Enrichment Enrichment programs are available through the program or unit for career planning, learning strategies, math, self-advocacy, stress management, study skills, test taking, time management, vocabulary development, and written composition skills. Programs for career planning, college survival skills, math, oral communication skills, reading, stress management, study skills, test taking, time management, and written composition skills are provided collaboratively through on-campus or off-campus services. Credit is offered for career planning, college survival skills, and oral communication skills.

Fees *Diagnostic Testing* fee is $50 to $600.

Application For admittance to the program or unit, students are required to apply to the program directly and provide a psychoeducational report (3 years old or less). It is recommended that students provide documentation of high school services. Upon application, materials documenting need for services should be sent only to the LD program or unit. Upon acceptance, documentation of need for services should be sent only to the LD program or unit. *Application deadline (institutional):* 8/1. *Application deadline (LD program):* Rolling/continuous for fall and rolling/continuous for spring.

Written Policies Written policies regarding course substitutions, general/basic LD accommodations, reduced course loads, and substitutions and waivers of graduation requirements are available on the program Web site. Written policies regarding course substitutions, reduced course loads, and substitutions and waivers of graduation requirements are outlined in the school's catalog/handbook. Written policies regarding general/basic LD accommodations, reduced course loads, and substitutions and waivers of graduation requirements are available through the program or unit directly.

The University of North Carolina at Wilmington
Disability Services, SEA Lab

601 South College Road
Wilmington, NC 28403-3297
http://www.uncwil.edu/stuaff/SDS/disability.html

Contact: Mr. Christopher Stone, Learning Specialist, Disability Services. Phone: 910-962-7846. Fax: 910-962-7124. E-mail: stonec@uncw.edu.

Disability Services, SEA Lab Approximately 135 registered undergraduate students were served during 2002-03. The program or unit includes 3 full-time staff members. LD specialists, skill tutors, and strategy tutors are provided through the program or unit. Regular education teachers and trained peer tutors are provided collaboratively through on-campus or off-campus services.

Unique Aids and Services Aids, services, or accommodations include priority registration.

Subject-area Tutoring Tutoring is offered one-on-one, in small groups, and in class-size groups for most subjects. Tutoring is provided collaboratively through on-campus or off-campus services via trained peer tutors.

Enrichment Enrichment programs are available through the program or unit for learning strategies, self-advocacy, stress management, study skills, test taking, and time management. Programs for career planning, health and nutrition, learning strategies, stress management, study skills, test taking, time management, and written composition skills are provided collaboratively through on-campus or off-campus services.

Application For admittance to the program or unit, students are required to provide a psychoeducational report (3 years old or less). It is recommended that students provide documentation of high school services. Upon acceptance, documentation of need for services should be sent only to the LD program or unit. *Application deadline (institutional):* 2/1. *Application deadline (LD program):* Rolling/continuous for fall and rolling/continuous for spring.

Written Policies Written policy regarding general/basic LD accommodations is available on the program Web site. Written policies regarding course substitutions, general/basic LD accommodations, and substitutions and waivers of admissions requirements are available through the program or unit directly.

University of North Dakota
Disability Support Services

Grand Forks, ND 58202
http://www.und.edu/dept/dss

Contact: Debrah Glennen, Director. Phone: 701-777-3425. Fax: 701-777-4170. E-mail: deb_glennen@mail.und.nodak.edu.

Disability Support Services Approximately 125 registered undergraduate students were served during 2002-03. The program or unit includes 5 full-time and 2 part-time staff members. LD specialists are provided through the program or unit. Academic advisers, counselors, diagnostic specialists, professional tutors, and remediation/learning specialists are provided collaboratively through on-campus or off-campus services.

Orientation The program or unit offers an optional orientation for new students after classes begin and individually by special arrangement.

Unique Aids and Services Aids, services, or accommodations include digital textbooks and priority registration.

Subject-area Tutoring Tutoring is offered in small groups for some subjects. Tutoring is provided collaboratively through on-campus or off-campus services via computer-based instruction, graduate assistants/students, and trained peer tutors.

Diagnostic Testing Testing for auditory processing, intelligence, learning strategies, learning styles, math, motor skills, neuropsychological, personality, reading, spelling, spoken language, study skills, visual processing, and written language is provided collaboratively through on-campus or off-campus services.

Basic Skills Remediation Remediation is offered in small groups and in class-size groups for learning strategies, math, spelling, study skills, time management, visual processing, and written language. Remediation is provided collaboratively through on-campus or off-campus services via LD specialists and professional tutors.

Enrichment Enrichment programs are available through the program or unit for learning strategies, self-advocacy, study skills, test taking, and time management. Programs for career planning, college survival skills, health and nutrition, math, medication management, practical computer skills, reading, stress management, study skills, test taking, time management, vocabulary development, and written composition skills are provided collaboratively through on-campus or off-campus services. Credit is offered for career planning, college survival skills, study skills, and vocabulary development.

Fees *Diagnostic Testing* fee is $350 to $1000.

Application For admittance to the program or unit, students are required to provide a psychoeducational report. It is recommended that students provide documentation of high school services. Upon acceptance, documentation of need for services should be sent only to the LD program or unit. *Application deadline (institutional):* 7/1. *Application deadline (LD program):* Rolling/continuous for fall and rolling/continuous for spring.

University of North Dakota (continued)

Written Policies Written policy regarding general/basic LD accommodations is outlined in the school's catalog/handbook. Written policies regarding course substitutions, grade forgiveness, reduced course loads, and substitutions and waivers of graduation requirements are available through the program or unit directly.

University of Northern Colorado
Disability Access Center

Greeley, CO 80639

http://www.unco.edu/dac

Contact: Ms. Nancy L. Kauffman, Director. Phone: 970-351-2289. Fax: 970-351-4166. E-mail: nancy.kauffman@unco.edu.

Disability Access Center Approximately 132 registered undergraduate students were served during 2002-03. The program or unit includes 2 full-time and 2 part-time staff members. Coaches, graduate assistants/students, and strategy tutors are provided through the program or unit. Academic advisers, counselors, diagnostic specialists, regular education teachers, skill tutors, strategy tutors, and trained peer tutors are provided collaboratively through on-campus or off-campus services.

Orientation The program or unit offers a mandatory orientation for new students individually by special arrangement.

Unique Aids and Services Aids, services, or accommodations include advocates, digital textbooks, and support groups.

Subject-area Tutoring Tutoring is offered one-on-one, in small groups, and in class-size groups for some subjects. Tutoring is provided through the program or unit via graduate assistants/students. Tutoring is also provided collaboratively through on-campus or off-campus services via trained peer tutors.

Enrichment Enrichment programs are available through the program or unit for learning strategies, self-advocacy, stress management, study skills, test taking, and time management. Programs for career planning, college survival skills, math, stress management, study skills, test taking, time management, and written composition skills are provided collaboratively through on-campus or off-campus services.

Student Organization People Redefining Disabilities through Disability Education consists of 5 members.

Application For admittance to the program or unit, students are required to apply to the program directly, provide a psychoeducational report, and provide documentation of high school services. Upon application, materials documenting need for services should be sent only to the LD program or unit. Upon acceptance, documentation of need for services should be sent only to the LD program or unit. *Application deadline (institutional):* Continuous. *Application deadline (LD program):* Rolling/continuous for fall and rolling/continuous for spring.

Written Policies Written policy regarding general/basic LD accommodations is available on the program Web site. Written policy regarding grade forgiveness is outlined in the school's catalog/handbook. Written policy regarding general/basic LD accommodations is available through the program or unit directly.

University of North Florida
Disability Resource Center

4567 St. Johns Bluff Road South
Jacksonville, FL 32224-2645

http://www.unf.edu/

Contact: Dr. Robert E. Lee, Director. Phone: 904-620-2769. Fax: 904-620-3874. E-mail: rlee@unf.edu.

Disability Resource Center Approximately 100 registered undergraduate students were served during 2002-03. The program or unit includes 3 full-time staff members. Academic advisers, counselors, regular education teachers, remediation/learning specialists, skill tutors, strategy tutors, and trained peer tutors are provided collaboratively through on-campus or off-campus services.

Unique Aids and Services Aids, services, or accommodations include career counseling and priority registration.

Subject-area Tutoring Tutoring is offered one-on-one and in small groups for some subjects. Tutoring is provided collaboratively through on-campus or off-campus services via trained peer tutors.

Enrichment Programs for career planning, college survival skills, learning strategies, math, stress management, study skills, test taking, time management, vocabulary development, and written composition skills are provided collaboratively through on-campus or off-campus services.

Application For admittance to the program or unit, students are required to provide a psychoeducational report (3 years old or less). It is recommended that students provide documentation of high school services. Upon application, materials documenting need for services should be sent only to the LD program or unit. Upon acceptance, documentation of need for services should be sent only to the LD program or unit. *Application deadline (institutional):* 7/2. *Application deadline (LD program):* Rolling/continuous for fall and rolling/continuous for spring.

Written Policies Written policies regarding general/basic LD accommodations, substitutions and waivers of admissions requirements, and substitutions and waivers of graduation requirements are available on the program Web site. Written policies regarding course substitutions, general/basic LD accommodations, substitutions and waivers of admissions requirements, and substitutions and waivers of graduation requirements are available through the program or unit directly.

University of Notre Dame

Notre Dame, IN 46556

http://www.nd.edu/

Contact: Mr. Scott Howland, Program Coordinator. Phone: 574-631-7141. Fax: 574-631-7939. E-mail: showland@nd.edu.

The program or unit includes 1 full-time staff member. Academic advisers, counselors, diagnostic specialists, and trained peer tutors are provided collaboratively through on-campus or off-campus services.

Unique Aids and Services Aids, services, or accommodations include priority registration.

Subject-area Tutoring Tutoring is offered one-on-one and in small groups for some subjects. Tutoring is provided collaboratively through on-campus or off-campus services via trained peer tutors.

Enrichment Programs for career planning, health and nutrition, test taking, time management, and written composition skills are provided collaboratively through on-campus or off-campus services.

Application For admittance to the program or unit, students are required to provide a psychoeducational report (3 years old or less). Upon acceptance, documentation of need for services should be sent only to the LD program or unit. *Application deadline (institutional):* 1/9. *Application deadline (LD program):* Rolling/continuous for fall.

Written Policies Written policy regarding general/basic LD accommodations is outlined in the school's catalog/handbook. Written policies regarding course substitutions, general/basic LD accommodations, and reduced course loads are available through the program or unit directly.

University of Oregon
Disability Services

Eugene, OR 97403

http://ds.uoregon.edu

Contact: Mr. Steve Pickett, Director of Disability Services and Associate Director of Academic Advising. Phone: 541-346-1155. Fax: 541-346-6013. E-mail: spickett@uoregon.edu.

Disability Services Approximately 350 registered undergraduate students were served during 2002-03. The program or unit includes 4 full-time and 3 part-time staff members. Academic advisers, coaches, counselors, diagnostic specialists, graduate assistants/students, LD specialists, professional tutors, regular education teachers, remediation/learning specialists, skill tutors, and strategy tutors are provided collaboratively through on-campus or off-campus services.

Orientation The program or unit offers a mandatory variable length (based on needs) orientation for new students before registration, before classes begin, during summer prior to enrollment, during registration, after classes begin, and individually by special arrangement.

Unique Aids and Services Aids, services, or accommodations include faculty training, priority registration, regularly scheduled appointments with a DS adviser.

Subject-area Tutoring Tutoring is offered one-on-one and in small groups for most subjects. Tutoring is provided collaboratively through on-campus or off-campus services via computer-based instruction, graduate assistants/students, LD specialists, professional tutors, and trained peer tutors.

Diagnostic Testing Testing for auditory processing, handwriting, intelligence, learning strategies, learning styles, math, motor skills, neuropsychological, personality, reading, social skills, spelling, spoken language, study skills, visual processing, written language, and other services is provided collaboratively through on-campus or off-campus services.

Basic Skills Remediation Remediation is offered one-on-one and in small groups for auditory processing, computer skills, learning strategies, math, reading, spelling, spoken language, study skills, time management, visual processing, and written language. Reme-

diation is provided collaboratively through on-campus or off-campus services via computer-based instruction, graduate assistants/students, LD specialists, professional tutors, regular education teachers, and trained peer tutors.

Enrichment Programs for career planning, college survival skills, health and nutrition, learning strategies, math, medication management, oral communication skills, practical computer skills, reading, self-advocacy, stress management, study skills, test taking, time management, vocabulary development, and written composition skills are provided collaboratively through on-campus or off-campus services.

Fees *Diagnostic Testing* fee is $300.

Application For admittance to the program or unit, students are required to provide a psychoeducational report (3 years old or less) and provide assessment appropriate to the disabling condition. It is recommended that students apply to the program directly and provide documentation of high school services. Upon application, materials documenting need for services should be sent only to admissions with institutional application materials. Upon acceptance, documentation of need for services should be sent only to the LD program or unit. *Application deadline (institutional):* 1/15. *Application deadline (LD program):* Rolling/continuous for fall and rolling/continuous for spring.

Written Policies Written policies regarding general/basic LD accommodations and substitutions and waivers of admissions requirements are available on the program Web site. Written policies regarding course substitutions, general/basic LD accommodations, grade forgiveness, reduced course loads, substitutions and waivers of admissions requirements, and substitutions and waivers of graduation requirements are outlined in the school's catalog/handbook. Written policy regarding general/basic LD accommodations is available through the program or unit directly.

University of Pennsylvania
Student Disabilities Services

3451 Walnut Street

Philadelphia, PA 19104

http://dolphin.upenn.edu/~lrcenter/sds

Contact: Dr. Jerome F. Knast, Director of Student Disabilities Services. Phone: 215-573-9235. Fax: 215-746-6326. E-mail: sdsmail@pobox.upenn.edu.

Student Disabilities Services Approximately 200 registered undergraduate students were served during 2002-03. The program or unit includes 4 full-time staff members and 1 part-time staff member. Diagnostic specialists, LD specialists, strategy tutors, and other are provided through the program or unit. Academic advisers, counselors, remediation/learning specialists, skill tutors, trained peer tutors, and other are provided collaboratively through on-campus or off-campus services.

Orientation The program or unit offers an optional 2-hour orientation for new students before classes begin and individually by special arrangement.

Summer Program To help prepare for the demands of college, there is an optional 4-week summer program prior to entering the school. Degree credit will be earned.

University of Pennsylvania (continued)

Unique Aids and Services Aids, services, or accommodations include career counseling, faculty training, support groups, assistive technology, auxiliary aids and services.

Subject-area Tutoring Tutoring is offered one-on-one and in small groups for some subjects. Tutoring is provided collaboratively through on-campus or off-campus services via graduate assistants/students and trained peer tutors.

Enrichment Enrichment programs are available through the program or unit for college survival skills, learning strategies, oral communication skills, reading, self-advocacy, study skills, test taking, time management, vocabulary development, written composition skills, and other. Programs for career planning, college survival skills, health and nutrition, learning strategies, math, medication management, oral communication skills, practical computer skills, reading, self-advocacy, stress management, study skills, test taking, time management, vocabulary development, written composition skills, and other are provided collaboratively through on-campus or off-campus services.

Student Organization Student Disabilities Services Student Advisory Board consists of 20 members.

Application For admittance to the program or unit, students are required to provide a psychoeducational report (3 years old or less). It is recommended that students provide documentation of high school services and provide related histories and medical documentation. Upon acceptance, documentation of need for services should be sent only to the LD program or unit. *Application deadline (institutional):* 1/1. *Application deadline (LD program):* Rolling/continuous for fall and rolling/continuous for spring.

Written Policies Written policy regarding general/basic LD accommodations is available on the program Web site. Written policy regarding general/basic LD accommodations is outlined in the school's catalog/handbook. Written policy regarding general/basic LD accommodations is available through the program or unit directly.

University of Phoenix-Nevada Campus
ADA Office

333 North Rancho Drive
Suite 300
Las Vegas, NV 89106-3797
http://www.phoenix.edu/

Contact: Ms. Sophie Marie Ainsworth, Administration Specialist. Phone: 702-638-7279 Ext. 1168. Fax: 702-638-8064. E-mail: sophie.ainsworth@phoenix.edu.

ADA Office Approximately 12 registered undergraduate students were served during 2002-03. The program or unit includes 2 full-time staff members. LD specialists are provided through the program or unit.

Orientation The program or unit offers an optional orientation for new students individually by special arrangement.

Unique Aids and Services Aids, services, or accommodations include advocates, digital textbooks, faculty training, additional support provided by ADA officer upon request.

Enrichment Programs for health and nutrition, learning strategies, math, oral communication skills, practical computer skills, study skills, vocabulary development, written composition skills, and other are provided collaboratively through on-campus or off-campus services. Credit is offered for health and nutrition, learning strategies, math, oral communication skills, practical computer skills, study skills, vocabulary development, written composition skills, and other.

Application For admittance to the program or unit, students are required to apply to the program directly, provide a psychoeducational report, and provide medical documentation. Upon application, materials documenting need for services should be sent only to the LD program or unit. Upon acceptance, documentation of need for services should be sent only to the LD program or unit. *Application deadline (institutional):* Continuous. *Application deadline (LD program):* Rolling/continuous for fall and rolling/continuous for spring.

Written Policies Written policies regarding general/basic LD accommodations, reduced course loads, and substitutions and waivers of admissions requirements are available through the program or unit directly.

University of Pittsburgh
Disability Resources and Services

4200 Fifth Avenue
Pittsburgh, PA 15260
http://www.drs.pitt.edu

Contact: Noreen J. Mazzocca, Disability Specialist. Phone: 412-648-7890. Fax: 412-624-3346. E-mail: njm974@pitt.edu. Head of LD Program: Lynnett Van Slyke, Director. Phone: 412-648-7890. Fax: 412-624-3346. E-mail: vanslyke@pitt.edu.

Disability Resources and Services Approximately 380 registered undergraduate students were served during 2002-03. The program or unit includes 6 full-time staff members. LD specialists, remediation/learning specialists, skill tutors, and strategy tutors are provided through the program or unit. Academic advisers, coaches, counselors, diagnostic specialists, graduate assistants/students, professional tutors, regular education teachers, special education teachers, teacher trainees, and trained peer tutors are provided collaboratively through on-campus or off-campus services.

Subject-area Tutoring Tutoring is offered one-on-one and in small groups for most subjects. Tutoring is provided collaboratively through on-campus or off-campus services via graduate assistants/students, professional tutors, and trained peer tutors.

Diagnostic Testing Testing for auditory processing, handwriting, intelligence, learning strategies, learning styles, math, motor skills, neuropsychological, personality, reading, social skills, spelling, spoken language, study skills, visual processing, and written language is provided collaboratively through on-campus or off-campus services.

Enrichment Enrichment programs are available through the program or unit for learning strategies, self-advocacy, study skills, test taking, and time management. Programs for career planning, college survival skills, health and nutrition, math, medication management, oral communication skills, reading, stress management, study skills, test taking, time management, vocabulary development, and written composition skills are provided collaboratively through on-campus or off-campus services.

Fees *Diagnostic Testing* fee is applicable.

Application For admittance to the program or unit, students are required to apply to the program directly and provide a psychoeducational report (5 years old or less). Upon application, materials documenting need for services should be sent only to the LD program or unit. Upon acceptance, documentation of need for services should be sent only to the LD program or unit. *Application deadline (institutional):* Continuous. *Application deadline (LD program):* Rolling/continuous for fall and rolling/continuous for spring.

Written Policies Written policies regarding course substitutions, general/basic LD accommodations, substitutions and waivers of admissions requirements, and substitutions and waivers of graduation requirements are available on the program Web site. Written policy regarding general/basic LD accommodations is outlined in the school's catalog/handbook. Written policies regarding course substitutions, general/basic LD accommodations, substitutions and waivers of admissions requirements, and substitutions and waivers of graduation requirements are available through the program or unit directly.

University of Pittsburgh at Johnstown
Disability Services/Learning Resource Center

450 Schoolhouse Road

Johnstown, PA 15904-2990

http://info.pitt.edu/~upjweb/

Contact: Coordinator of Disability Services. Phone: 814-269-7001. Fax: 814-269-7177.

Disability Services/Learning Resource Center Approximately 50 registered undergraduate students were served during 2002-03. Academic advisers, counselors, diagnostic specialists, LD specialists, professional tutors, regular education teachers, skill tutors, strategy tutors, and trained peer tutors are provided through the program or unit. Academic advisers, counselors, diagnostic specialists, LD specialists, professional tutors, regular education teachers, skill tutors, strategy tutors, and trained peer tutors are provided collaboratively through on-campus or off-campus services.

Unique Aids and Services Aids, services, or accommodations include career counseling, digital textbooks, priority registration, and weekly meetings with faculty.

Subject-area Tutoring Tutoring is offered one-on-one and in small groups for most subjects. Tutoring is provided through the program or unit via LD specialists and trained peer tutors. Tutoring is also provided collaboratively through on-campus or off-campus services via professional tutors and trained peer tutors.

Diagnostic Testing Testing is provided through the program or unit for math. Testing for auditory processing, intelligence, learning strategies, learning styles, math, motor skills, neuropsychological, personality, reading, social skills, spelling, and visual processing is provided collaboratively through on-campus or off-campus services.

Basic Skills Remediation Remediation is offered one-on-one and in small groups for learning strategies, math, study skills, and time management. Remediation is provided through the program or unit via trained peer tutors. Remediation is also provided collaboratively through on-campus or off-campus services via professional tutors and trained peer tutors.

Enrichment Programs for career planning, college survival skills, learning strategies, stress management, study skills, time management, and written composition skills are provided collaboratively through on-campus or off-campus services. Credit is offered for college survival skills.

Fees *Diagnostic Testing* fee is applicable.

Application For admittance to the program or unit, students are required to apply to the program directly and provide a psychoeducational report (3 years old or less). It is recommended that students provide documentation of high school services. Upon application, materials documenting need for services should be sent only to the LD program or unit. Upon acceptance, documentation of need for services should be sent only to the LD program or unit. *Application deadline (institutional):* Continuous. *Application deadline (LD program):* Rolling/continuous for fall and rolling/continuous for spring.

Written Policies Written policy regarding general/basic LD accommodations is available on the program Web site. Written policy regarding general/basic LD accommodations is outlined in the school's catalog/handbook. Written policy regarding general/basic LD accommodations is available through the program or unit directly.

University of Portland
Office for Students with Disabilities

5000 North Willamette Boulevard

Portland, OR 97203-5798

http://www.up.edu/
up_sub.asp?ctnt=145&mnu=50&chl=200&lvl=2

Contact: Ms. Melanie Gangle, Coordinator of Office for Students with Disabilities. Phone: 503-943-7134. Fax: 503-943-7199. E-mail: gangle@up.edu.

Office for Students with Disabilities Approximately 28 registered undergraduate students were served during 2002-03. The program or unit includes 1 full-time staff member. Academic advisers, coaches, counselors, graduate assistants/students, regular education teachers, strategy tutors, trained peer tutors, and other are provided collaboratively through on-campus or off-campus services.

Unique Aids and Services Aids, services, or accommodations include accommodations and services provided on a case-by-case basis.

Subject-area Tutoring Tutoring is offered one-on-one, in small groups, and in class-size groups for some subjects. Tutoring is provided collaboratively through on-campus or off-campus services via computer-based instruction, graduate assistants/students, and trained peer tutors.

Enrichment Programs for career planning, college survival skills, health and nutrition, learning strategies, math, medication management, practical computer skills, reading, stress management, study skills, test taking, time management, and written composition skills are provided collaboratively through on-campus or off-campus services.

University of Portland (continued)

Application For admittance to the program or unit, students are required to provide a psychoeducational report and provide completed accommodation request form. Upon acceptance, documentation of need for services should be sent only to the LD program or unit. *Application deadline (institutional):* 6/1.

Written Policies Written policy regarding general/basic LD accommodations is available on the program Web site. Written policy regarding general/basic LD accommodations is outlined in the school's catalog/handbook. Written policy regarding general/basic LD accommodations is available through the program or unit directly.

University of Redlands

1200 E. Colton Avenue
PO Box 3080
Redlands, CA 92373-0999
http://www.redlands.edu/
Contact: Judy Bowman, Director of Academic Support and Disabled Student Services. Phone: 909-335-4079. Fax: 909-335-5297. E-mail: judy_bowman@redlands.edu.

Approximately 150 registered undergraduate students were served during 2002-03. The program or unit includes 1 full-time staff member. Academic advisers and counselors are provided through the program or unit. Academic advisers, counselors, diagnostic specialists, and skill tutors are provided collaboratively through on-campus or off-campus services.

Unique Aids and Services Aids, services, or accommodations include career counseling, digital textbooks, faculty training, and personal coach.

Subject-area Tutoring Tutoring is offered one-on-one for most subjects. Tutoring is provided collaboratively through on-campus or off-campus services via trained peer tutors.

Enrichment Enrichment programs are available through the program or unit for self-advocacy. Programs for career planning, college survival skills, health and nutrition, learning strategies, practical computer skills, stress management, study skills, test taking, time management, vocabulary development, and written composition skills are provided collaboratively through on-campus or off-campus services. Credit is offered for career planning, college survival skills, learning strategies, practical computer skills, study skills, test taking, time management, vocabulary development, and written composition skills.

Application Upon application, materials documenting need for services should be sent only to admissions with institutional application materials. Upon acceptance, documentation of need for services should be sent only to the LD program or unit. *Application deadline (institutional):* 12/15. *Application deadline (LD program):* Rolling/continuous for fall and rolling/continuous for spring.

Written Policies Written policies regarding course substitutions, general/basic LD accommodations, and reduced course loads are available on the program Web site. Written policies regarding course substitutions, general/basic LD accommodations, and reduced course loads are available through the program or unit directly.

University of Rhode Island

Kingston, RI 02881

http://www.uri.edu

Contact: Ms. Bette Nee, Coordinator of Disability Services for Students. Phone: 401-874-2098. Fax: 401-874-5574. E-mail: bnee@uri.edu. Head of LD Program: Ms. Pamela A. Rohland, Director of Disability Services for Students. Phone: 401-874-2098. Fax: 401-874-2098. E-mail: rohland@uri.edu.

Approximately 400 registered undergraduate students were served during 2002-03. The program or unit includes 2 full-time and 2 part-time staff members. Graduate assistants/students, LD specialists, remediation/learning specialists, skill tutors, special education teachers, and strategy tutors are provided through the program or unit. Academic advisers, coaches, counselors, diagnostic specialists, graduate assistants/students, regular education teachers, skill tutors, strategy tutors, teacher trainees, trained peer tutors, and other are provided collaboratively through on-campus or off-campus services.

Orientation The program or unit offers an optional 30-minute orientation for new students before registration, during summer prior to enrollment, and during the university first-year student orientation.

Unique Aids and Services Aids, services, or accommodations include advocates, career counseling, digital textbooks, faculty training, priority registration, support groups, and weekly meetings with faculty.

Subject-area Tutoring Tutoring is offered one-on-one and in small groups for some subjects. Tutoring is provided through the program or unit via LD specialists. Tutoring is also provided collaboratively through on-campus or off-campus services via computer-based instruction, graduate assistants/students, professional tutors, and trained peer tutors.

Basic Skills Remediation Remediation is offered one-on-one and in small groups for learning strategies, math, study skills, time management, and written language. Remediation is provided through the program or unit via special education teachers. Remediation is also provided collaboratively through on-campus or off-campus services via LD specialists, professional tutors, and trained peer tutors.

Enrichment Enrichment programs are available through the program or unit for college survival skills, self-advocacy, study skills, test taking, and time management. Programs for career planning, college survival skills, health and nutrition, learning strategies, math, medication management, oral communication skills, reading, self-advocacy, study skills, test taking, time management, and written composition skills are provided collaboratively through on-campus or off-campus services. Credit is offered for college survival skills, learning strategies, and written composition skills.

Application For admittance to the program or unit, students are required to apply to the program directly and provide a psychoeducational report (3 years old or less). Upon application, materials documenting need for services should be sent only to admissions with institutional application materials. Upon acceptance, documentation of need for services should be sent only to the LD program or unit. *Application deadline (institutional):* 3/1. *Application deadline (LD program):* Rolling/continuous for fall and rolling/continuous for spring.

Written Policies Written policies regarding course substitutions, general/basic LD accommodations, reduced course loads, substitutions and waivers of admissions requirements, and substitutions and waivers of graduation requirements are available on the program

Web site. Written policies regarding course substitutions, general/basic LD accommodations, reduced course loads, and substitutions and waivers of graduation requirements are available through the program or unit directly.

University of Rio Grande
Department of Accessibility

218 North College Avenue
Rio Grande, OH 45674
http://www.rio.edu/
Contact: Ms. Marshall E. Kimmel, Counselor. Phone: 740-245-7339. Fax: 740-245-7446. E-mail: mkimmel@rio.edu.

Department of Accessibility Approximately 57 registered undergraduate students were served during 2002-03. The program or unit includes 1 full-time and 1 part-time staff member. Academic advisers, counselors, diagnostic specialists, and LD specialists are provided through the program or unit. Coaches, regular education teachers, remediation/learning specialists, skill tutors, strategy tutors, and trained peer tutors are provided collaboratively through on-campus or off-campus services.
Orientation The program or unit offers an optional 1-hour orientation for new students before classes begin, during summer prior to enrollment, and individually by special arrangement.
Unique Aids and Services Aids, services, or accommodations include career counseling and support groups.
Subject-area Tutoring Tutoring is offered one-on-one and in small groups for all subjects. Tutoring is provided collaboratively through on-campus or off-campus services via trained peer tutors.
Basic Skills Remediation Remediation is offered in class-size groups for learning strategies, math, reading, study skills, and time management. Remediation is provided collaboratively through on-campus or off-campus services via computer-based instruction and regular education teachers.
Enrichment Enrichment programs are available through the program or unit for college survival skills, stress management, and other. Programs for career planning, health and nutrition, learning strategies, math, medication management, oral communication skills, practical computer skills, reading, self-advocacy, study skills, test taking, time management, vocabulary development, and written composition skills are provided collaboratively through on-campus or off-campus services. Credit is offered for health and nutrition, math, and written composition skills.
Application For admittance to the program or unit, students are required to provide a psychoeducational report (3 years old or less). It is recommended that students provide documentation of high school services. Upon application, materials documenting need for services should be sent only to the LD program or unit. Upon acceptance, documentation of need for services should be sent only to the LD program or unit. *Application deadline (institutional):* Continuous. *Application deadline (LD program):* Rolling/continuous for fall and rolling/continuous for spring.
Written Policies Written policy regarding general/basic LD accommodations is outlined in the school's catalog/handbook. Written policies regarding course substitutions, general/basic LD accommodations, reduced course loads, and substitutions and waivers of admissions requirements are available through the program or unit directly.

University of Rochester
Learning Assistance Services

Wilson Boulevard
Rochester, NY 14627-0250
http://www.rochester.edu/College/las
Contact: Gina Tonogbanua, Disability Support Coordinator. Phone: 585-275-9044. Fax: 585-273-1116. Head of LD Program: Vicki Roth, Assistant Dean for Learning Assistance. Phone: 585-275-9049. Fax: 585-273-1116. E-mail: vrth@mail.rochester.edu.

Learning Assistance Services Approximately 144 registered undergraduate students were served during 2002-03. The program or unit includes 2 full-time and 2 part-time staff members. Graduate assistants/students, LD specialists, skill tutors, strategy tutors, and trained peer tutors are provided through the program or unit. Academic advisers and counselors are provided collaboratively through on-campus or off-campus services.
Orientation The program or unit offers an optional 1-hour orientation for new students individually by special arrangement.
Unique Aids and Services Aids, services, or accommodations include career counseling and priority registration.
Subject-area Tutoring Tutoring is offered one-on-one and in small groups for most subjects. Tutoring is provided through the program or unit via graduate assistants/students and trained peer tutors. Tutoring is also provided collaboratively through on-campus or off-campus services via computer-based instruction and trained peer tutors.
Diagnostic Testing Testing is provided through the program or unit for reading and study skills.
Enrichment Enrichment programs are available through the program or unit for college survival skills, learning strategies, reading, self-advocacy, stress management, study skills, test taking, and time management. Programs for career planning, health and nutrition, medication management, stress management, and written composition skills are provided collaboratively through on-campus or off-campus services.
Application For admittance to the program or unit, students are required to provide a psychoeducational report (3 years old or less). Upon acceptance, documentation of need for services should be sent only to the LD program or unit. *Application deadline (institutional):* 1/15. *Application deadline (LD program):* Rolling/continuous for fall and rolling/continuous for spring.
Written Policies Written policy regarding general/basic LD accommodations is available on the program Web site. Written policies regarding reduced course loads and substitutions and waivers of admissions requirements are outlined in the school's catalog/handbook. Written policies regarding general/basic LD accommodations and reduced course loads are available through the program or unit directly.

University of Saint Francis
Student Learning Center

2701 Spring Street
Fort Wayne, IN 46808-3994

University of Saint Francis (continued)
http://www.sf.edu/
Contact: Ms. Michelle Lavonne Kruyer, Director of Student Learning Center. Phone: 260-434-7677. Fax: 260-434-7444. E-mail: mkruyer@sf.edu.

Student Learning Center Approximately 35 registered undergraduate students were served during 2002-03. The program or unit includes 1 full-time staff member. LD specialists and trained peer tutors are provided through the program or unit. Skill tutors are provided collaboratively through on-campus or off-campus services.

Orientation The program or unit offers a mandatory 2-hour orientation for new students individually by special arrangement.

Subject-area Tutoring Tutoring is offered one-on-one and in small groups for some subjects. Tutoring is provided through the program or unit via computer-based instruction, LD specialists, and trained peer tutors. Tutoring is also provided collaboratively through on-campus or off-campus services via computer-based instruction and trained peer tutors.

Basic Skills Remediation Remediation is offered in class-size groups for math, reading, and written language. Remediation is provided collaboratively through on-campus or off-campus services via regular education teachers.

Application For admittance to the program or unit, students are required to provide a psychoeducational report and provide documentation of high school services. Upon acceptance, documentation of need for services should be sent only to the LD program or unit. *Application deadline (institutional):* Continuous. *Application deadline (LD program):* Rolling/continuous for fall and rolling/continuous for spring.

Written Policies Written policies regarding course substitutions, general/basic LD accommodations, reduced course loads, substitutions and waivers of admissions requirements, and substitutions and waivers of graduation requirements are available through the program or unit directly.

University of St. Thomas
Enhancement Program—Disability Services

2115 Summit Avenue
St. Paul, MN 55105-1096
http://www.stthomas.edu/enhancementprog
Contact: Ms. Kimberly Schumann, Director. Phone: 651-962-6315. Fax: 651-962-6710. E-mail: kjschumann@stthomas.edu.

Enhancement Program—Disability Services Approximately 125 registered undergraduate students were served during 2002-03. The program or unit includes 1 full-time and 1 part-time staff member. Academic advisers, counselors, graduate assistants/students, and LD specialists are provided through the program or unit. Academic advisers, counselors, diagnostic specialists, graduate assistants/students, remediation/learning specialists, skill tutors, strategy tutors, and trained peer tutors are provided collaboratively through on-campus or off-campus services.

Unique Aids and Services Aids, services, or accommodations include advocates, digital textbooks, faculty training, note-takers, extended exam time, reader, adaptive technology.

Subject-area Tutoring Tutoring is offered one-on-one, in small groups, and in class-size groups for most subjects. Tutoring is provided through the program or unit via graduate assistants/students and trained peer tutors. Tutoring is also provided collaboratively through on-campus or off-campus services via graduate assistants/students and trained peer tutors.

Diagnostic Testing Testing is provided through the program or unit for learning strategies, study skills, and written language. Testing for auditory processing, intelligence, learning strategies, learning styles, math, motor skills, neuropsychological, personality, reading, spelling, spoken language, study skills, visual processing, and written language is provided collaboratively through on-campus or off-campus services.

Basic Skills Remediation Remediation is offered one-on-one and in small groups for learning strategies, math, reading, spelling, study skills, time management, and written language. Remediation is provided through the program or unit via graduate assistants/students and trained peer tutors. Remediation is also provided collaboratively through on-campus or off-campus services via graduate assistants/students, trained peer tutors, and other.

Enrichment Enrichment programs are available through the program or unit for self-advocacy, stress management, study skills, test taking, time management, and written composition skills. Programs for career planning, health and nutrition, learning strategies, math, medication management, practical computer skills, reading, stress management, study skills, test taking, time management, and written composition skills are provided collaboratively through on-campus or off-campus services.

Fees *Diagnostic Testing* fee is $400.

Application For admittance to the program or unit, students are required to provide a psychoeducational report (3 years old or less). Upon acceptance, documentation of need for services should be sent only to the LD program or unit. *Application deadline (institutional):* Continuous. *Application deadline (LD program):* Rolling/continuous for fall and rolling/continuous for spring.

Written Policies Written policies regarding course substitutions, general/basic LD accommodations, reduced course loads, and substitutions and waivers of graduation requirements are available through the program or unit directly.

University of San Francisco

2130 Fulton Street
San Francisco, CA 94117-1080
http://www.usfca.edu/
Contact: Tom Merrell, Director of Student Disability Services. Phone: 415-422-6876. Fax: 415-422-5906. E-mail: merrellt@usfca.edu.

Approximately 150 registered undergraduate students were served during 2002-03. The program or unit includes 2 full-time and 3 part-time staff members. Coaches, LD specialists, remediation/learning specialists, skill tutors, and strategy tutors are provided through the program or unit. Academic advisers, professional tutors, regular education teachers, and trained peer tutors are provided collaboratively through on-campus or off-campus services.

Unique Aids and Services Aids, services, or accommodations include digital textbooks, faculty training, personal coach, priority registration, and support groups.

Subject-area Tutoring Tutoring is offered one-on-one, in small groups, and in class-size groups for most subjects. Tutoring is provided through the program or unit via LD specialists and professional tutors. Tutoring is also provided collaboratively through on-campus or off-campus services via computer-based instruction, graduate assistants/students, and trained peer tutors.

Basic Skills Remediation Remediation is offered one-on-one for learning strategies, reading, social skills, study skills, time management, and written language. Remediation is provided through the program or unit via LD specialists. Remediation is also provided collaboratively through on-campus or off-campus services via professional tutors.

Enrichment Enrichment programs are available through the program or unit for career planning, college survival skills, learning strategies, oral communication skills, practical computer skills, reading, self-advocacy, stress management, study skills, test taking, time management, and written composition skills. Programs for career planning, college survival skills, learning strategies, math, practical computer skills, reading, stress management, study skills, test taking, time management, and written composition skills are provided collaboratively through on-campus or off-campus services. Credit is offered for career planning, college survival skills, learning strategies, math, practical computer skills, reading, stress management, study skills, test taking, time management, and written composition skills.

Application For admittance to the program or unit, students are required to provide a psychoeducational report (3 years old or less) and provide an intake interview. Upon application, materials documenting need for services should be sent only to admissions with institutional application materials. Upon acceptance, documentation of need for services should be sent only to the LD program or unit. *Application deadline (institutional):* 2/1. *Application deadline (LD program):* Rolling/continuous for fall and rolling/continuous for spring.

Written Policies Written policy regarding general/basic LD accommodations is available on the program Web site. Written policy regarding general/basic LD accommodations is outlined in the school's catalog/handbook. Written policies regarding course substitutions, general/basic LD accommodations, reduced course loads, and substitutions and waivers of graduation requirements are available through the program or unit directly.

University of Science and Arts of Oklahoma
Student Services

1727 West Alabama

Chickasha, OK 73018

http://www.usao.edu/

Contact: Ms. Lesli Courtney, Counselor. Phone: 405-574-1326. Fax: 405-574-1220. E-mail: lcourtney@usao.edu.

Student Services Approximately 25 registered undergraduate students were served during 2002-03. The program or unit includes 2 full-time staff members. Academic advisers, counselors, and LD specialists are provided through the program or unit. Academic advisers, coaches, graduate assistants/students, professional tutors,

regular education teachers, remediation/learning specialists, skill tutors, strategy tutors, and trained peer tutors are provided collaboratively through on-campus or off-campus services.

Subject-area Tutoring Tutoring is offered one-on-one and in small groups for most subjects. Tutoring is provided collaboratively through on-campus or off-campus services via computer-based instruction, graduate assistants/students, and trained peer tutors.

Basic Skills Remediation Remediation is offered in class-size groups for computer skills, learning strategies, math, study skills, time management, written language, and science. Remediation is provided collaboratively through on-campus or off-campus services via computer-based instruction, LD specialists, regular education teachers, and trained peer tutors.

Enrichment Programs for career planning, learning strategies, math, stress management, study skills, test taking, time management, and written composition skills are provided collaboratively through on-campus or off-campus services.

Application For admittance to the program or unit, students are required to provide a psychoeducational report (2 years old or less) and provide documentation of high school services. Upon acceptance, documentation of need for services should be sent only to the LD program or unit. *Application deadline (institutional):* 9/3. *Application deadline (LD program):* 8/15 for fall. 12/15 for spring.

Written Policies Written policy regarding general/basic LD accommodations is outlined in the school's catalog/handbook.

University of South Carolina
Office of Student Disability Services

Columbia, SC 29208

http://www.sa.sc.edu/dss/

Contact: Mrs. Deborah Clement Haynes, Director of Student Disability Services. Phone: 803-777-6142. Fax: 803-777-6741. E-mail: debbieh@gwm.sc.edu.

Office of Student Disability Services Approximately 275 registered undergraduate students were served during 2002-03. The program or unit includes 2 full-time and 5 part-time staff members. Academic advisers and graduate assistants/students are provided through the program or unit.

Unique Aids and Services Aids, services, or accommodations include priority registration.

Enrichment Programs for career planning, college survival skills, study skills, test taking, and time management are provided collaboratively through on-campus or off-campus services.

Application For admittance to the program or unit, students are required to provide a psychoeducational report (3 years old or less). Upon acceptance, documentation of need for services should be sent only to the LD program or unit. *Application deadline (institutional):* 5/15. *Application deadline (LD program):* Rolling/continuous for fall and rolling/continuous for spring.

Written Policies Written policies regarding course substitutions, general/basic LD accommodations, reduced course loads, substitutions and waivers of admissions requirements, and substitutions and waivers of graduation requirements are available on the program Web site.

University of South Carolina Aiken
Office of Disability Services

471 University Parkway
Aiken, SC 29801-6309
http://www.usca.edu/ds/

Contact: Dr. Kay B. Benitez, Director of Assistive Technology Center and Disability Services. Phone: 803-641-3609. Fax: 803-641-3677. E-mail: kayb@usca.edu.

Office of Disability Services Approximately 250 registered undergraduate students were served during 2002-03. The program or unit includes 1 full-time and 8 part-time staff members. Counselors, graduate assistants/students, LD specialists, remediation/learning specialists, skill tutors, special education teachers, strategy tutors, teacher trainees, and trained peer tutors are provided through the program or unit. Academic advisers, coaches, counselors, diagnostic specialists, graduate assistants/students, LD specialists, regular education teachers, special education teachers, and teacher trainees are provided collaboratively through on-campus or off-campus services.

Orientation The program or unit offers an optional orientation for new students individually by special arrangement.

Unique Aids and Services Aids, services, or accommodations include advocates, career counseling, digital textbooks, faculty training, priority registration, support groups, assistive technology .

Subject-area Tutoring Tutoring is offered one-on-one for most subjects. Tutoring is provided through the program or unit via computer-based instruction, graduate assistants/students, LD specialists, and trained peer tutors. Tutoring is also provided collaboratively through on-campus or off-campus services via computer-based instruction and graduate assistants/students.

Enrichment Enrichment programs are available through the program or unit for career planning, college survival skills, health and nutrition, learning strategies, math, practical computer skills, reading, self-advocacy, vocabulary development, and written composition skills. Programs for career planning, college survival skills, health and nutrition, learning strategies, math, oral communication skills, practical computer skills, self-advocacy, stress management, study skills, test taking, time management, vocabulary development, and written composition skills are provided collaboratively through on-campus or off-campus services. Credit is offered for career planning, college survival skills, health and nutrition, math, oral communication skills, practical computer skills, reading, and written composition skills.

Application For admittance to the program or unit, students are required to apply to the program directly, provide a psychoeducational report (3 years old or less), and provide documentation by a licensed professional. It is recommended that students provide documentation of high school services. Upon application, materials documenting need for services should be sent only to the LD program or unit. Upon acceptance, documentation of need for services should be sent only to the LD program or unit. *Application deadline (institutional):* 8/1. *Application deadline (LD program):* Rolling/continuous for fall and rolling/continuous for spring.

Written Policies Written policies regarding course substitutions, general/basic LD accommodations, reduced course loads, and substitutions and waivers of graduation requirements are available on the program Web site. Written policies regarding course substitutions, general/basic LD accommodations, reduced course loads, and

substitutions and waivers of graduation requirements are outlined in the school's catalog/handbook. Written policies regarding course substitutions, general/basic LD accommodations, reduced course loads, and substitutions and waivers of graduation requirements are available through the program or unit directly.

University of South Carolina Spartanburg
Office of Disability Services

800 University Way
Spartanburg, SC 29303-4999
http://www.uscs.edu/student_life/development/ods

Contact: Mr. Jim Gorske, Assistant Director of Student Development. Phone: 864-503-5199. Fax: 864-503-5100. E-mail: jgorske@gw.uscs.edu.

Office of Disability Services Approximately 60 registered undergraduate students were served during 2002-03. The program or unit includes 1 full-time staff member. Academic advisers, counselors, regular education teachers, and trained peer tutors are provided collaboratively through on-campus or off-campus services.

Unique Aids and Services Aids, services, or accommodations include digital textbooks, priority registration, note-taking services, alternative test administration .

Subject-area Tutoring Tutoring is offered one-on-one and in small groups for most subjects. Tutoring is provided collaboratively through on-campus or off-campus services via trained peer tutors.

Enrichment Programs for career planning, college survival skills, stress management, study skills, test taking, and time management are provided collaboratively through on-campus or off-campus services.

Student Organization Special Education Club consists of 10 members.

Application For admittance to the program or unit, students are required to apply to the program directly and provide a psychoeducational report. It is recommended that students provide documentation of high school services. Upon application, materials documenting need for services should be sent only to the LD program or unit. Upon acceptance, documentation of need for services should be sent only to the LD program or unit. *Application deadline (LD program):* Rolling/continuous for fall and rolling/continuous for spring.

Written Policies Written policy regarding general/basic LD accommodations is available on the program Web site. Written policies regarding course substitutions, grade forgiveness, reduced course loads, substitutions and waivers of admissions requirements, and substitutions and waivers of graduation requirements are outlined in the school's catalog/handbook. Written policy regarding general/basic LD accommodations is available through the program or unit directly.

The University of South Dakota
Disability Services

414 East Clark Street

Vermillion, SD 57069-2390

http://www.usd.edu/disabrs

Contact: Ms. Elaine Pearson, Director. Phone: 605-677-6389. Fax: 605-677-3172. E-mail: epearson@usd.edu.

Disability Services Approximately 400 registered undergraduate students were served during 2002-03. The program or unit includes 2 full-time and 8 part-time staff members. Graduate assistants/students, LD specialists, remediation/learning specialists, skill tutors, and strategy tutors are provided through the program or unit. Academic advisers, coaches, counselors, diagnostic specialists, professional tutors, regular education teachers, special education teachers, teacher trainees, and trained peer tutors are provided collaboratively through on-campus or off-campus services.
Orientation The program or unit offers an optional orientation for new students individually by special arrangement.
Unique Aids and Services Aids, services, or accommodations include digital textbooks, faculty training, priority registration, and support groups.
Subject-area Tutoring Tutoring is offered in small groups. Tutoring is provided through the program or unit via graduate assistants/students and trained peer tutors. Tutoring is also provided collaboratively through on-campus or off-campus services via computer-based instruction, LD specialists, and trained peer tutors.
Diagnostic Testing Testing for auditory processing, intelligence, learning strategies, learning styles, math, motor skills, neuropsychological, personality, reading, social skills, spelling, spoken language, study skills, visual processing, and written language is provided collaboratively through on-campus or off-campus services.
Basic Skills Remediation Remediation is offered one-on-one for auditory processing, computer skills, learning strategies, math, reading, spelling, spoken language, visual processing, and written language. Remediation is provided through the program or unit via LD specialists.
Enrichment Enrichment programs are available through the program or unit for learning strategies, self-advocacy, stress management, study skills, test taking, and written composition skills. Programs for career planning, learning strategies, math, oral communication skills, practical computer skills, reading, self-advocacy, stress management, study skills, test taking, and written composition skills are provided collaboratively through on-campus or off-campus services.
Application For admittance to the program or unit, students are required to apply to the program directly, provide a psychoeducational report (5 years old or less), and provide documentation of high school services. Upon application, materials documenting need for services should be sent only to the LD program or unit. Upon acceptance, documentation of need for services should be sent only to the LD program or unit. *Application deadline (institutional):* Continuous. *Application deadline (LD program):* Rolling/continuous for fall.

Written Policies Written policy regarding general/basic LD accommodations is available on the program Web site. Written policy regarding substitutions and waivers of admissions requirements is outlined in the school's catalog/handbook. Written policy regarding general/basic LD accommodations is available through the program or unit directly.

University of Southern Indiana
Counseling Center

8600 University Boulevard

Evansville, IN 47712-3590

http://www.usi.edu/

Contact: Mrs. Leslie M. Smith, Assistant Director of Counseling. Phone: 812-464-1867. Fax: 812-461-5288. E-mail: lmsmith@usi.edu.

Counseling Center Approximately 120 registered undergraduate students were served during 2002-03. The program or unit includes 3 part-time staff members. Academic advisers, counselors, diagnostic specialists, regular education teachers, remediation/learning specialists, skill tutors, strategy tutors, and trained peer tutors are provided collaboratively through on-campus or off-campus services.
Unique Aids and Services Aids, services, or accommodations include advocates and career counseling.
Subject-area Tutoring Tutoring is offered one-on-one and in small groups for some subjects. Tutoring is provided collaboratively through on-campus or off-campus services via trained peer tutors.
Basic Skills Remediation Remediation is offered in class-size groups for learning strategies, math, reading, spelling, study skills, time management, and written language. Remediation is provided collaboratively through on-campus or off-campus services.
Enrichment Programs for career planning, college survival skills, health and nutrition, learning strategies, math, reading, study skills, test taking, time management, and written composition skills are provided collaboratively through on-campus or off-campus services. Credit is offered for career planning, college survival skills, health and nutrition, math, and study skills.
Application For admittance to the program or unit, students are required to apply to the program directly and provide a psychoeducational report. It is recommended that students provide documentation of high school services. Upon acceptance, documentation of need for services should be sent only to the LD program or unit. *Application deadline (institutional):* 8/15. *Application deadline (LD program):* Rolling/continuous for fall and rolling/continuous for spring.
Written Policies Written policy regarding general/basic LD accommodations is available on the program Web site. Written policy regarding general/basic LD accommodations is available through the program or unit directly.

The University of Tennessee
Office of Disability Services

Knoxville, TN 37996

http://ods.utk.edu

The University of Tennessee (continued)

Contact: LD Coordinator. Phone: 865-974-3873. Fax: 865-974-9552. E-mail: ods@tennessee.edu.

Office of Disability Services Approximately 600 registered undergraduate students were served during 2002-03. The program or unit includes 3 full-time staff members. Counselors, diagnostic specialists, and LD specialists are provided through the program or unit. Academic advisers, coaches, graduate assistants/students, professional tutors, regular education teachers, remediation/learning specialists, skill tutors, special education teachers, strategy tutors, teacher trainees, trained peer tutors, and other are provided collaboratively through on-campus or off-campus services.

Unique Aids and Services Aids, services, or accommodations include career counseling.

Enrichment Enrichment programs are available through the program or unit for career planning, learning strategies, practical computer skills, study skills, test taking, and time management.

Application For admittance to the program or unit, students are required to provide a psychoeducational report (3 years old or less). It is recommended that students provide documentation of high school services. Upon acceptance, documentation of need for services should be sent only to the LD program or unit. *Application deadline (institutional):* 2/1. *Application deadline (LD program):* Rolling/continuous for fall and rolling/continuous for spring.

Written Policies Written policy regarding general/basic LD accommodations is available on the program Web site. Written policies regarding course substitutions, general/basic LD accommodations, and substitutions and waivers of admissions requirements are available through the program or unit directly.

The University of Tennessee at Martin
PACE-Program Access for College Enhancement

University Street
Martin, TN 38238-1000
http://www.utm.edu/
Contact: Ms. Mia Barber, PACE Coordinator. Phone: 731-587-7195. E-mail: mbarber@utm.edu.

PACE-Program Access for College Enhancement Approximately 50 registered undergraduate students were served during 2002-03. The program or unit includes 2 full-time staff members. Academic advisers, counselors, graduate assistants/students, skill tutors, and strategy tutors are provided through the program or unit. Academic advisers, counselors, teacher trainees, and trained peer tutors are provided collaboratively through on-campus or off-campus services.

Orientation The program or unit offers a mandatory 2-hour orientation for new students after classes begin and individually by special arrangement.

Unique Aids and Services Aids, services, or accommodations include faculty training.

Subject-area Tutoring Tutoring is offered one-on-one for some subjects. Tutoring is provided through the program or unit via trained peer tutors. Tutoring is also provided collaboratively through on-campus or off-campus services via computer-based instruction and trained peer tutors.

Application For admittance to the program or unit, students are required to apply to the program directly and provide a psychoeducational report (3 years old or less). It is recommended that students provide documentation of high school services. Upon application, materials documenting need for services should be sent only to the LD program or unit. Upon acceptance, documentation of need for services should be sent to both admissions and the LD program or unit. *Application deadline (institutional):* Continuous. *Application deadline (LD program):* Rolling/continuous for fall and rolling/continuous for spring.

Written Policies Written policy regarding general/basic LD accommodations is available on the program Web site. Written policy regarding general/basic LD accommodations is outlined in the school's catalog/handbook.

The University of Texas at Arlington
Office for Students with Disabilities (OSD)

701 South Nedderman Drive
Arlington, TX 76019
http://www.uta.edu/disability
Contact: Phone: 817-272-2222. Fax: 817-272-5656.

Office for Students with Disabilities (OSD) Approximately 160 registered undergraduate students were served during 2002-03. The program or unit includes 1 full-time staff member. Services are provided through the program or unit. Counselors and professional tutors are provided collaboratively through on-campus or off-campus services.

Subject-area Tutoring Tutoring is offered one-on-one, in small groups, and in class-size groups for some subjects. Tutoring is provided collaboratively through on-campus or off-campus services via trained peer tutors.

Application For admittance to the program or unit, students are required to apply to the program directly and provide a psychoeducational report. Upon application, materials documenting need for services should be sent only to the LD program or unit. Upon acceptance, documentation of need for services should be sent only to the LD program or unit. *Application deadline (institutional):* Continuous. *Application deadline (LD program):* Rolling/continuous for fall and rolling/continuous for spring.

Written Policies Written policy regarding general/basic LD accommodations is available on the program Web site. Written policies regarding course substitutions, general/basic LD accommodations, and reduced course loads are available through the program or unit directly.

The University of Texas at Austin

Austin, TX 78712-1111
http://www.utexas.edu/

Contact: Student Affairs Administrator. Phone: 512-471-6259. Fax: 512-475-7730. E-mail: ssd@uts.cc.utexas.edu.

The program or unit includes 2 full-time staff members and 1 part-time staff member. Diagnostic specialists, graduate assistants/students, and LD specialists are provided through the program or unit. Academic advisers, coaches, counselors, diagnostic specialists, graduate assistants/students, remediation/learning specialists, skill tutors, strategy tutors, and trained peer tutors are provided collaboratively through on-campus or off-campus services.

Unique Aids and Services Aids, services, or accommodations include digital textbooks, faculty training, priority registration, and support groups.

Subject-area Tutoring Tutoring is offered one-on-one, in small groups, and in class-size groups for some subjects. Tutoring is provided collaboratively through on-campus or off-campus services via computer-based instruction, graduate assistants/students, professional tutors, and trained peer tutors.

Basic Skills Remediation Remediation is offered one-on-one, in small groups, and in class-size groups for learning strategies, math, reading, study skills, time management, and written language. Remediation is provided collaboratively through on-campus or off-campus services via computer-based instruction, graduate assistants/students, professional tutors, and trained peer tutors.

Enrichment Enrichment programs are available through the program or unit for self-advocacy. Programs for career planning, college survival skills, health and nutrition, learning strategies, math, medication management, reading, stress management, study skills, test taking, time management, and written composition skills are provided collaboratively through on-campus or off-campus services.

Student Organization SOAR consists of 10 members.

Application For admittance to the program or unit, students are required to apply to the program directly and provide a psychoeducational report (3 years old or less). It is recommended that students provide documentation of high school services. Upon application, materials documenting need for services should be sent only to the LD program or unit. *Application deadline (institutional): 2/1. Application deadline (LD program):* Rolling/continuous for fall and rolling/continuous for spring.

Written Policies Written policies regarding general/basic LD accommodations and reduced course loads are available through the program or unit directly.

The University of Texas at Brownsville

80 Fort Brown
Brownsville, TX 78520-4991
http://www.utb.edu/
Contact: Mr. Stephen D. Wilder, Counselor/Coordinator. Phone: 956-983-7374. Fax: 956-983-7861. E-mail: wilder@utb.edu.

Academic advisers, coaches, counselors, professional tutors, regular education teachers, remediation/learning specialists, skill tutors, and trained peer tutors are provided collaboratively through on-campus or off-campus services.

Subject-area Tutoring Tutoring is offered one-on-one, in small groups, and in class-size groups for some subjects. Tutoring is provided collaboratively through on-campus or off-campus services via computer-based instruction, professional tutors, and trained peer tutors.

Basic Skills Remediation Remediation is offered one-on-one, in small groups, and in class-size groups for math, reading, and written language. Remediation is provided collaboratively through on-campus or off-campus services via computer-based instruction, professional tutors, regular education teachers, and trained peer tutors.

Enrichment Programs for career planning and study skills are provided collaboratively through on-campus or off-campus services.

Application For admittance to the program or unit, students are required to provide a psychoeducational report (3 years old or less) and provide comprehensive individual assessment. It is recommended that students provide documentation of high school services. Upon application, materials documenting need for services should be sent only to the LD program or unit. Upon acceptance, documentation of need for services should be sent only to the LD program or unit. *Application deadline (LD program):* Rolling/continuous for fall and rolling/continuous for spring.

Written Policies Written policy regarding course substitutions is outlined in the school's catalog/handbook. Written policy regarding general/basic LD accommodations is available through the program or unit directly.

The University of Texas at El Paso
Disabled Student Services

500 West University Avenue
El Paso, TX 79968-0001
http://www.utep.edu/dsso
Contact: Phone: 915-747-5000. Fax: 915-747-5122.

Disabled Student Services Approximately 60 registered undergraduate students were served during 2002-03. The program or unit includes 4 full-time and 4 part-time staff members. Diagnostic specialists are provided through the program or unit. Academic advisers and counselors are provided collaboratively through on-campus or off-campus services.

Unique Aids and Services Aids, services, or accommodations include digital textbooks and priority registration.

Subject-area Tutoring Tutoring is offered in small groups for some subjects. Tutoring is provided collaboratively through on-campus or off-campus services via computer-based instruction and trained peer tutors.

Diagnostic Testing Testing is provided through the program or unit for auditory processing, intelligence, math, motor skills, reading, spelling, spoken language, visual processing, and written language. Testing for auditory processing, intelligence, math, motor skills, reading, spelling, spoken language, visual processing, and written language is provided collaboratively through on-campus or off-campus services.

Basic Skills Remediation Remediation is offered in class-size groups for learning strategies, math, reading, study skills, and time management. Remediation is provided collaboratively through on-campus or off-campus services via computer-based instruction, regular education teachers, and trained peer tutors.

The University of Texas at El Paso (continued)

Enrichment Programs for career planning, health and nutrition, math, reading, stress management, study skills, test taking, and time management are provided collaboratively through on-campus or off-campus services.

Application For admittance to the program or unit, students are required to provide a psychoeducational report (5 years old or less). Upon application, materials documenting need for services should be sent only to the LD program or unit. Upon acceptance, documentation of need for services should be sent only to the LD program or unit. *Application deadline (institutional): 7/31. Application deadline (LD program):* Rolling/continuous for fall and rolling/continuous for spring.

Written Policies Written policy regarding general/basic LD accommodations is available on the program Web site. Written policy regarding general/basic LD accommodations is available through the program or unit directly.

The University of Texas at San Antonio

6900 North Loop 1604 West
San Antonio, TX 78249-0617
http://www.utsa.edu/
Contact: Lorraine Harrison, Director of Disability Services. Phone: 210-458-4157. Fax: 210-458-4980. E-mail: lharrison@utsa.edu.

Approximately 110 registered undergraduate students were served during 2002-03. The program or unit includes 2 full-time staff members. Services are provided through the program or unit.

Subject-area Tutoring Tutoring is offered in small groups for some subjects. Tutoring is provided collaboratively through on-campus or off-campus services via computer-based instruction and trained peer tutors.

Diagnostic Testing Testing for auditory processing, intelligence, math, personality, reading, spelling, spoken language, visual processing, and written language is provided collaboratively through on-campus or off-campus services.

Basic Skills Remediation Remediation is offered in small groups and in class-size groups for learning strategies, math, reading, study skills, time management, and written language. Remediation is provided collaboratively through on-campus or off-campus services via regular education teachers and trained peer tutors.

Enrichment Enrichment programs are available through the program or unit for self-advocacy. Programs for career planning, college survival skills, health and nutrition, learning strategies, math, practical computer skills, reading, stress management, study skills, test taking, time management, and written composition skills are provided collaboratively through on-campus or off-campus services. Credit is offered for college survival skills.

Fees *Diagnostic Testing* fee is $50.

Application For admittance to the program or unit, students are required to provide a psychoeducational report (3 years old or less). Upon application, materials documenting need for services should be sent only to the LD program or unit. Upon acceptance, documentation of need for services should be sent only to the LD program or unit. *Application deadline (institutional): 7/1. Application deadline (LD program):* Rolling/continuous for fall and rolling/continuous for spring.

Written Policies Written policy regarding general/basic LD accommodations is available on the program Web site. Written policy regarding general/basic LD accommodations is available through the program or unit directly.

The University of the Arts
Learning Skills Support Program

320 South Broad Street
Philadelphia, PA 19102-4944
http://www.uarts.edu/
Contact: Ms. Neila Douglas, Learning Skills Specialist. Phone: 215-717-6616. Fax: 215-717-6611. E-mail: ndouglas@uarts.edu.

Learning Skills Support Program Approximately 32 registered undergraduate students were served during 2002-03. The program or unit includes 2 part-time staff members. LD specialists are provided through the program or unit. Counselors, professional tutors, and trained peer tutors are provided collaboratively through on-campus or off-campus services.

Subject-area Tutoring Tutoring is offered for most subjects. Tutoring is provided through the program or unit via LD specialists. Tutoring is also provided collaboratively through on-campus or off-campus services via professional tutors and trained peer tutors.

Diagnostic Testing Testing is provided through the program or unit for learning styles.

Application For admittance to the program or unit, students are required to provide psychoeducational evaluation or IEP/504. Upon application, materials documenting need for services should be sent to both admissions and the LD program or unit. Upon acceptance, documentation of need for services should be sent to both admissions and the LD program or unit. *Application deadline (institutional):* Continuous. *Application deadline (LD program):* Rolling/continuous for fall and rolling/continuous for spring.

Written Policies Written policies regarding general/basic LD accommodations and reduced course loads are available through the program or unit directly.

University of the Pacific
Office of Services for Students with Disabilities (SSD)

3601 Pacific Avenue
Stockton, CA 95211-0197
http://www.uop.edu/education/ssd
Contact: Lisa Cooper, Coordinator. Phone: 209-946-2458. Fax: 209-946-2278. E-mail: ssd@uop.edu.

Office of Services for Students with Disabilities (SSD) Approximately 100 registered undergraduate students were served during 2002-03. The program or unit includes 1 full-time and 10 part-time staff members. Remediation/learning specialists, skill tutors, trained peer tutors, and other are provided through the program or unit. Academic advisers, counselors, diagnostic specialists, remediation/learning specialists, skill tutors, trained peer tutors, and other are provided collaboratively through on-campus or off-campus services.

Orientation The program or unit offers an optional orientation for new students individually by special arrangement and during the summer orientation programs.

Unique Aids and Services Aids, services, or accommodations include advocates, faculty training, priority registration, assistive technology.

Subject-area Tutoring Tutoring is offered one-on-one and in small groups for most subjects. Tutoring is provided through the program or unit via computer-based instruction, graduate assistants/students, trained peer tutors, and other. Tutoring is also provided collaboratively through on-campus or off-campus services via graduate assistants/students, trained peer tutors, and other.

Diagnostic Testing Testing is provided through the program or unit for math, reading, written language, and other services. Testing for math, reading, written language, and other services is provided collaboratively through on-campus or off-campus services.

Basic Skills Remediation Remediation is offered in class-size groups for math, reading, and written language. Remediation is provided through the program or unit via regular education teachers and trained peer tutors. Remediation is also provided collaboratively through on-campus or off-campus services via regular education teachers and trained peer tutors.

Enrichment Enrichment programs are available through the program or unit for math, reading, self-advocacy, written composition skills, and other. Programs for career planning, health and nutrition, learning strategies, math, medication management, oral communication skills, practical computer skills, reading, stress management, study skills, test taking, time management, and written composition skills are provided collaboratively through on-campus or off-campus services. Credit is offered for career planning, math, reading, and written composition skills.

Application For admittance to the program or unit, students are required to apply to the program directly and provide a psychoeducational report. It is recommended that students provide documentation of high school services. Upon acceptance, documentation of need for services should be sent only to the LD program or unit. *Application deadline (institutional):* 1/15. *Application deadline (LD program):* Rolling/continuous for fall and rolling/continuous for spring.

Written Policies Written policy regarding general/basic LD accommodations is available on the program Web site. Written policy regarding general/basic LD accommodations is outlined in the school's catalog/handbook. Written policy regarding general/basic LD accommodations is available through the program or unit directly.

University of the South
University Counseling Service

735 University Avenue
Sewanee, TN 37383-1000
http://www.sewanee.edu/

Contact: University Counseling Service. Phone: 931-598-1325. Fax: 931-598-1261. E-mail: prambo@sewanee.edu.

University Counseling Service Approximately 35 registered undergraduate students were served during 2002-03. The program or unit includes 2 full-time staff members and 1 part-time staff member. Counselors, professional tutors, and trained peer tutors are provided through the program or unit. Academic advisers, coaches, diagnostic specialists, LD specialists, regular education teachers, remediation/learning specialists, skill tutors, strategy tutors, and teacher trainees are provided collaboratively through on-campus or off-campus services.

Summer Program To help prepare for the demands of college, there is an optional 6-week summer program prior to entering the school. Degree credit will be earned.

Unique Aids and Services Aids, services, or accommodations include career counseling, personal coach, and weekly meetings with faculty.

Subject-area Tutoring Tutoring is offered one-on-one and in small groups for most subjects. Tutoring is provided collaboratively through on-campus or off-campus services via computer-based instruction, LD specialists, professional tutors, and trained peer tutors.

Enrichment Enrichment programs are available through the program or unit for career planning, college survival skills, learning strategies, medication management, stress management, study skills, test taking, and time management. Programs for health and nutrition, math, oral communication skills, practical computer skills, reading, self-advocacy, vocabulary development, and written composition skills are provided collaboratively through on-campus or off-campus services.

Application For admittance to the program or unit, students are required to provide a psychoeducational report (3 years old or less) and provide a neuropsychological report. It is recommended that students provide documentation of high school services. *Application deadline (institutional):* 2/1. *Application deadline (LD program):* Rolling/continuous for fall and rolling/continuous for spring.

Written Policies Written policy regarding general/basic LD accommodations is outlined in the school's catalog/handbook. Written policy regarding general/basic LD accommodations is available through the program or unit directly.

University of Toledo
Office of Accessibility

2801 West Bancroft
Toledo, OH 43606-3398
http://www.utoledo.edu

Contact: Dr. Mary Ann G. Stibbe, Learning Disabilities Specialist. Phone: 419-530-4981. E-mail: mstibbe@utnet.utoledo.edu.

Office of Accessibility Approximately 120 registered undergraduate students were served during 2002-03. The program or unit includes 1 full-time staff member. Academic advisers are provided through the program or unit. Academic advisers, coaches, and LD specialists are provided collaboratively through on-campus or off-campus services.

Unique Aids and Services Aids, services, or accommodations include career counseling, digital textbooks, faculty training, and priority registration.

University of Toledo (continued)

Subject-area Tutoring Tutoring is offered for most subjects. Tutoring is provided collaboratively through on-campus or off-campus services via trained peer tutors and other.

Basic Skills Remediation Remediation is offered in class-size groups for auditory processing, learning strategies, math, spoken language, study skills, time management, and written language. Remediation is provided collaboratively through on-campus or off-campus services via regular education teachers.

Enrichment Programs for career planning, college survival skills, learning strategies, math, oral communication skills, stress management, study skills, test taking, time management, and written composition skills are provided collaboratively through on-campus or off-campus services.

Application For admittance to the program or unit, students are required to provide a psychoeducational report (1 year old or less). It is recommended that students provide documentation of high school services. Upon acceptance, documentation of need for services should be sent only to the LD program or unit. *Application deadline (institutional):* Continuous. *Application deadline (LD program):* Rolling/continuous for fall and rolling/continuous for spring.

Written Policies Written policies regarding course substitutions, general/basic LD accommodations, substitutions and waivers of admissions requirements, and substitutions and waivers of graduation requirements are available on the program Web site. Written policies regarding course substitutions, general/basic LD accommodations, substitutions and waivers of admissions requirements, and substitutions and waivers of graduation requirements are available through the program or unit directly.

University of Toronto
Accessibility Services, Programs and Services for Students with a Disability

Toronto, ON M5S 1A1

Canada

http://disability.sa.utoronto.ca

Contact: Dr. Pearl Levey, Learning Disability Specialist. Phone: 416-978-1724. Fax: 416-978-8246. E-mail: pearl.levey@utoronto.ca.

Accessibility Services, Programs and Services for Students with a Disability Approximately 500 registered undergraduate students were served during 2002-03. The program or unit includes 1 full-time and 5 part-time staff members. Counselors, diagnostic specialists, LD specialists, remediation/learning specialists, and strategy tutors are provided through the program or unit. Academic advisers, coaches, counselors, diagnostic specialists, professional tutors, remediation/learning specialists, and skill tutors are provided collaboratively through on-campus or off-campus services.

Orientation The program or unit offers an optional half-day orientation for new students before registration, before classes begin, during summer prior to enrollment, and individually by special arrangement.

Summer Program To help prepare for the demands of college, there is an optional summer program prior to entering the school.

Unique Aids and Services Aids, services, or accommodations include advocates, career counseling, digital textbooks, personal coach, support groups, adaptive technology .

Subject-area Tutoring Tutoring is offered one-on-one for most subjects. Tutoring is provided through the program or unit via LD specialists. Tutoring is also provided collaboratively through on-campus or off-campus services via graduate assistants/students and professional tutors.

Diagnostic Testing Testing is provided through the program or unit for auditory processing, intelligence, learning strategies, learning styles, math, motor skills, reading, social skills, spelling, spoken language, study skills, visual processing, and written language. Testing for handwriting, motor skills, neuropsychological, personality, spoken language, study skills, visual processing, and written language is provided collaboratively through on-campus or off-campus services.

Basic Skills Remediation Remediation is offered one-on-one and in small groups for auditory processing, computer skills, learning strategies, math, reading, social skills, spelling, spoken language, study skills, time management, visual processing, written language, and second-language learning. Remediation is provided through the program or unit via computer-based instruction and LD specialists. Remediation is also provided collaboratively through on-campus or off-campus services via professional tutors and other.

Enrichment Enrichment programs are available through the program or unit for college survival skills, learning strategies, oral communication skills, practical computer skills, reading, self-advocacy, stress management, study skills, test taking, time management, vocabulary development, and written composition skills. Programs for career planning, college survival skills, health and nutrition, learning strategies, math, medication management, oral communication skills, practical computer skills, reading, self-advocacy, stress management, study skills, test taking, time management, vocabulary development, and written composition skills are provided collaboratively through on-campus or off-campus services.

Fees *Diagnostic Testing* fee is $900.

Application For admittance to the program or unit, students are required to apply to the program directly and provide a psychoeducational report (3 years old or less). It is recommended that students provide documentation of high school services. Upon application, materials documenting need for services should be sent only to the LD program or unit. Upon acceptance, documentation of need for services should be sent only to the LD program or unit. *Application deadline (institutional):* 3/1. *Application deadline (LD program):* Rolling/continuous for fall and rolling/continuous for spring.

Written Policies Written policies regarding general/basic LD accommodations and reduced course loads are available on the program Web site. Written policies regarding general/basic LD accommodations and reduced course loads are available through the program or unit directly.

University of Tulsa
Center for Student Academic Support

600 South College Avenue

Tulsa, OK 74104-3189

http://www.utulsa.edu/

Contact: Dr. Jane Randall Corso, Director of Center for Student Academic Support. Phone: 918-631-2334. Fax: 918-631-3459. E-mail: jane-corso@utulsa.edu.

Center for Student Academic Support Approximately 125 registered undergraduate students were served during 2002-03. The program or unit includes 3 full-time and 10 part-time staff members. Academic advisers, counselors, graduate assistants/students, and trained peer tutors are provided through the program or unit. Diagnostic specialists and LD specialists are provided collaboratively through on-campus or off-campus services.

Orientation The program or unit offers an optional orientation for new students during registration, after classes begin, and individually by special arrangement.

Unique Aids and Services Aids, services, or accommodations include career counseling, priority registration, and support groups.

Subject-area Tutoring Tutoring is offered one-on-one for most subjects. Tutoring is provided through the program or unit via graduate assistants/students and trained peer tutors.

Basic Skills Remediation Remediation is offered one-on-one, in small groups, and in class-size groups for learning strategies, reading, study skills, and time management. Remediation is provided through the program or unit via graduate assistants/students, trained peer tutors, and other.

Enrichment Enrichment programs are available through the program or unit for college survival skills, learning strategies, oral communication skills, stress management, study skills, test taking, and time management. Programs for career planning, health and nutrition, math, medication management, practical computer skills, reading, vocabulary development, and written composition skills are provided collaboratively through on-campus or off-campus services.

Application For admittance to the program or unit, students are required to apply to the program directly, provide a psychoeducational report, and provide documentation of high school services. Upon application, materials documenting need for services should be sent only to the LD program or unit. Upon acceptance, documentation of need for services should be sent only to the LD program or unit. *Application deadline (institutional):* Continuous. *Application deadline (LD program):* Rolling/continuous for fall and rolling/continuous for spring.

Written Policies Written policy regarding general/basic LD accommodations is available on the program Web site. Written policy regarding general/basic LD accommodations is outlined in the school's catalog/handbook. Written policies regarding course substitutions, general/basic LD accommodations, reduced course loads, substitutions and waivers of admissions requirements, and substitutions and waivers of graduation requirements are available through the program or unit directly.

University of Utah

201 South University Street

Salt Lake City, UT 84112-1107

http://www.utah.edu/

Contact: Mrs. Christine Anderson, Disabilities Adviser. Phone: 801-585-1815. Fax: 801-581-5487. E-mail: canderson@sa.utah.edu.

Approximately 260 registered undergraduate students were served during 2002-03. The program or unit includes 7 full-time and 20 part-time staff members. Counselors are provided collaboratively through on-campus or off-campus services.

Orientation The program or unit offers an optional 1 to 2-hour orientation for new students before classes begin and individually by special arrangement.

Unique Aids and Services Aids, services, or accommodations include advocates, faculty training, priority registration, support groups, books on tape.

Subject-area Tutoring Tutoring is offered one-on-one and in small groups for most subjects. Tutoring is provided collaboratively through on-campus or off-campus services via graduate assistants/students, professional tutors, and trained peer tutors.

Diagnostic Testing Testing for auditory processing, intelligence, learning strategies, learning styles, math, motor skills, neuropsychological, reading, social skills, spelling, study skills, visual processing, and written language is provided collaboratively through on-campus or off-campus services.

Basic Skills Remediation Remediation is offered one-on-one for computer skills, learning strategies, math, study skills, and time management. Remediation is provided collaboratively through on-campus or off-campus services via professional tutors and trained peer tutors.

Enrichment Enrichment programs are available through the program or unit for practical computer skills. Programs for career planning, college survival skills, health and nutrition, learning strategies, math, practical computer skills, stress management, study skills, and time management are provided collaboratively through on-campus or off-campus services. Credit is offered for career planning, college survival skills, health and nutrition, learning strategies, math, stress management, study skills, and time management.

Student Organization Students Together Able Not Disabled (STAND) consists of 20 members.

Fees *Diagnostic Testing* fee is $115.

Application For admittance to the program or unit, students are required to provide a psychoeducational report (3 years old or less). It is recommended that students provide documentation of high school services. Upon application, materials documenting need for services should be sent only to the LD program or unit. Upon acceptance, documentation of need for services should be sent only to the LD program or unit. *Application deadline (institutional):* 5/1. *Application deadline (LD program):* Rolling/continuous for fall and rolling/continuous for spring.

Written Policies Written policy regarding general/basic LD accommodations is available on the program Web site. Written policies regarding course substitutions, general/basic LD accommodations, substitutions and waivers of admissions requirements, and substitutions and waivers of graduation requirements are available through the program or unit directly.

University of Vermont

Burlington, VT 05405

http://www.uvm.edu/

Contact: Margaret Ottinger, Assistant Director of Academic Support Programs/ACCESS. Phone: 802-656-7753. Fax: 802-656-7753. E-mail: margaret.ottinger@uvm.edu.

University of Vermont (continued)

Approximately 500 registered undergraduate students were served during 2002-03. The program or unit includes 7 full-time and 2 part-time staff members. LD specialists, remediation/learning specialists, skill tutors, and strategy tutors are provided through the program or unit. Academic advisers, coaches, counselors, diagnostic specialists, graduate assistants/students, professional tutors, remediation/learning specialists, skill tutors, strategy tutors, and trained peer tutors are provided collaboratively through on-campus or off-campus services.

Orientation The program or unit offers an optional 1 to 2-hour orientation for new students before registration, before classes begin, during summer prior to enrollment, during registration, after classes begin, and individually by special arrangement.

Unique Aids and Services Aids, services, or accommodations include career counseling, digital textbooks, faculty training, parent workshops, priority registration, regular meetings with specialist or study skills tutor.

Subject-area Tutoring Tutoring is offered one-on-one and in small groups for most subjects. Tutoring is provided collaboratively through on-campus or off-campus services via graduate assistants/students, professional tutors, and trained peer tutors.

Diagnostic Testing Testing for auditory processing, handwriting, intelligence, learning strategies, learning styles, math, motor skills, neuropsychological, personality, reading, social skills, spelling, spoken language, study skills, visual processing, and written language is provided collaboratively through on-campus or off-campus services.

Basic Skills Remediation Remediation is offered one-on-one, in small groups, and in class-size groups for learning strategies, math, reading, spelling, study skills, time management, and written language. Remediation is provided through the program or unit via LD specialists. Remediation is also provided collaboratively through on-campus or off-campus services via graduate assistants/students, LD specialists, professional tutors, trained peer tutors, and other.

Enrichment Enrichment programs are available through the program or unit for college survival skills, learning strategies, self-advocacy, stress management, study skills, test taking, and time management. Programs for career planning, college survival skills, health and nutrition, learning strategies, math, medication management, oral communication skills, practical computer skills, reading, self-advocacy, stress management, study skills, test taking, time management, vocabulary development, and written composition skills are provided collaboratively through on-campus or off-campus services. Credit is offered for college survival skills, learning strategies, self-advocacy, stress management, study skills, test taking, and time management.

Fees *Diagnostic Testing* fee is applicable.

Application For admittance to the program or unit, students are required to provide a psychoeducational report (3 years old or less). It is recommended that students provide documentation of high school services and provide a letter from student and/or educational support services professional addressing impact of the LD. Upon application, materials documenting need for services should be sent only to the LD program or unit. Upon acceptance, documentation of need for services should be sent only to the LD program or unit. *Application deadline (institutional):* 1/15. *Application deadline (LD program):* Rolling/continuous for fall and rolling/continuous for spring.

Written Policies Written policies regarding course substitutions, general/basic LD accommodations, reduced course loads, substitutions and waivers of admissions requirements, and substitutions and waivers of graduation requirements are available on the program Web site. Written policies regarding course substitutions, general/basic LD accommodations, reduced course loads, and substitutions and waivers of graduation requirements are outlined in the school's catalog/handbook. Written policies regarding course substitutions, general/basic LD accommodations, reduced course loads, substitutions and waivers of admissions requirements, and substitutions and waivers of graduation requirements are available through the program or unit directly.

The University of Virginia's College at Wise

1 College Avenue
Wise, VA 24293
http://www.uvawise.edu/

Contact: Ms. Narda N. Porter, ADA Coordinator. Phone: 276-328-0177. Fax: 276-376-1076. E-mail: nnb3h@uvawise.edu.

Approximately 45 registered undergraduate students were served during 2002-03. The program or unit includes 1 full-time and 1 part-time staff member. Counselors, graduate assistants/students, skill tutors, strategy tutors, trained peer tutors, and other are provided through the program or unit. Counselors, graduate assistants/students, skill tutors, strategy tutors, trained peer tutors, and other are provided collaboratively through on-campus or off-campus services.

Unique Aids and Services Aids, services, or accommodations include priority registration.

Subject-area Tutoring Tutoring is offered one-on-one and in small groups for most subjects. Tutoring is provided through the program or unit via computer-based instruction, trained peer tutors, and other.

Basic Skills Remediation Remediation is offered one-on-one, in small groups, and in class-size groups for computer skills, learning strategies, math, reading, spelling, spoken language, study skills, time management, visual processing, and written language. Remediation is provided through the program or unit via trained peer tutors. Remediation is also provided collaboratively through on-campus or off-campus services via regular education teachers.

Enrichment Enrichment programs are available through the program or unit for career planning, college survival skills, learning strategies, math, oral communication skills, self-advocacy, stress management, study skills, test taking, time management, vocabulary development, and written composition skills. Programs for career planning, college survival skills, health and nutrition, learning strategies, math, oral communication skills, practical computer skills, reading, vocabulary development, and written composition skills are provided collaboratively through on-campus or off-campus services. Credit is offered for health and nutrition, math, oral communication skills, practical computer skills, reading, vocabulary development, and written composition skills.

Application For admittance to the program or unit, students are required to provide a psychoeducational report. It is recommended that students apply to the program directly and provide documentation of high school services. Upon application, materials documenting need for services should be sent only to the LD program or unit. Upon acceptance, documentation of need for services should be sent only to the LD program or unit. *Application deadline (institutional):* 8/1. *Application deadline (LD program):* Rolling/continuous for fall and rolling/continuous for spring.

Written Policies Written policy regarding general/basic LD accommodations is available on the program Web site. Written policies regarding course substitutions, general/basic LD accommodations, and reduced course loads are available through the program or unit directly.

University of Waterloo
Office for Persons with Disabilities

200 University Avenue West

Waterloo, ON N2L 3G1

Canada

http://www.studentservices.uwaterloo.ca/disabilities

Contact: Mrs. Alice Schmidt, Learning Specialist. Phone: 519-888-4567 Ext. 5660. Fax: 519-746-2401. E-mail: arschmid@uwaterloo.ca. Head of LD Program: Ms. Rose Padacz, Director. Phone: 519-888-4567 Ext. 5231. Fax: 519-746-2401. E-mail: rmpadacz@uwaterloo.ca.

Office for Persons with Disabilities Approximately 200 registered undergraduate students were served during 2002-03. The program or unit includes 3 full-time staff members and 1 part-time staff member. Coaches, counselors, diagnostic specialists, LD specialists, professional tutors, remediation/learning specialists, strategy tutors, and trained peer tutors are provided through the program or unit. Academic advisers, counselors, diagnostic specialists, graduate assistants/students, professional tutors, skill tutors, and teacher trainees are provided collaboratively through on-campus or off-campus services.

Unique Aids and Services Aids, services, or accommodations include career counseling, digital textbooks, applications of technology, academic accommodations, transportation and housing.

Subject-area Tutoring Tutoring is offered one-on-one for all subjects. Tutoring is provided through the program or unit via LD specialists. Tutoring is also provided collaboratively through on-campus or off-campus services via graduate assistants/students, professional tutors, and trained peer tutors.

Diagnostic Testing Testing is provided through the program or unit for auditory processing, learning strategies, learning styles, reading, study skills, and other services. Testing for auditory processing, handwriting, intelligence, learning strategies, learning styles, math, motor skills, neuropsychological, personality, reading, social skills, spelling, spoken language, study skills, visual processing, written language, and other services is provided collaboratively through on-campus or off-campus services.

Basic Skills Remediation Remediation is offered one-on-one for auditory processing, computer skills, learning strategies, math, motor skills, reading, social skills, spelling, spoken language, study skills, time management, visual processing, and written language. Remediation is provided collaboratively through on-campus or off-campus services via computer-based instruction, graduate assistants/students, LD specialists, professional tutors, and trained peer tutors.

Enrichment Enrichment programs are available through the program or unit for career planning, college survival skills, learning strategies, oral communication skills, reading, self-advocacy, stress management, study skills, test taking, time management, vocabu-lary development, and written composition skills. Programs for career planning, college survival skills, health and nutrition, learning strategies, math, medication management, oral communication skills, practical computer skills, stress management, study skills, test taking, time management, and written composition skills are provided collaboratively through on-campus or off-campus services. Credit is offered for career planning and college survival skills.

Fees *Diagnostic Testing* fee is $1500 to $2400.

Application It is recommended that students apply to the program directly, provide a psychoeducational report, provide documentation of high school services, and provide a letter from a physician or other professional letter of reference. Upon application, materials documenting need for services should be sent to both admissions and the LD program or unit. Upon acceptance, documentation of need for services should be sent only to the LD program or unit. *Application deadline (LD program):* Rolling/continuous for fall and rolling/continuous for spring.

University of West Florida
Disabled Student Services

11000 University Parkway

Pensacola, FL 32514-5750

http://www.uwf.edu/DSS

Contact: Ms. Barbara Fitzpatrick, Director of Disabled Student Services. Phone: 850-474-2387. Fax: 850-857-6188. E-mail: bfitzpat@uwf.edu. Head of LD Program: Dr. Doglas Pearson, Associate Vice President of Student Affairs. Phone: 850-474-2384. Fax: 850-857-6188. E-mail: dpearson@uwf.edu.

Disabled Student Services Approximately 139 registered undergraduate students were served during 2002-03. The program or unit includes 2 full-time and 4 part-time staff members. Academic advisers, coaches, counselors, graduate assistants/students, and professional tutors are provided through the program or unit. Academic advisers, coaches, counselors, graduate assistants/students, and professional tutors are provided collaboratively through on-campus or off-campus services.

Summer Program To help prepare for the demands of college, there is an optional summer program prior to entering the school. Degree credit will be earned.

Unique Aids and Services Aids, services, or accommodations include career counseling, priority registration, support groups, reasonable accommodations as requested.

Subject-area Tutoring Tutoring is offered one-on-one and in small groups. Tutoring is provided collaboratively through on-campus or off-campus services via graduate assistants/students, professional tutors, and other.

Basic Skills Remediation Remediation is offered one-on-one and in small groups for learning strategies, math, reading, spelling, study skills, time management, visual processing, and written language. Remediation is provided collaboratively through on-campus or off-campus services via graduate assistants/students, professional tutors, teacher trainees, and trained peer tutors.

Student Organization Students with Alternative Needs (SWANS) consists of 12 members.

University of West Florida (continued)

Application For admittance to the program or unit, students are required to provide registration with Disabled Student Services. Upon application, materials documenting need for services should be sent only to the LD program or unit. *Application deadline (institutional):* 6/30. *Application deadline (LD program):* Rolling/continuous for fall and rolling/continuous for spring.

Written Policies Written policy regarding general/basic LD accommodations is available on the program Web site. Written policies regarding course substitutions, general/basic LD accommodations, grade forgiveness, substitutions and waivers of admissions requirements, and substitutions and waivers of graduation requirements are outlined in the school's catalog/handbook.

University of Windsor

401 Sunset Avenue

Windsor, ON N9B 3P4

Canada

http://www.uwindsor.ca/

Contact: Ms. Margaret E. Crawford, Special Needs Coordinator. Phone: 519-253-3000 Ext. 3298. Fax: 519-973-7095. E-mail: crawfm@uwindsor.ca. Head of LD Program: Ms. Michelle Petherick, Learning Strategist. Phone: 519-253-3000 Ext. 3935. Fax: 519-973-7095. E-mail: mpeth@uwindsor.ca.

Approximately 76 registered undergraduate students were served during 2002-03. The program or unit includes 2 full-time staff members. Academic advisers, coaches, counselors, diagnostic specialists, graduate assistants/students, LD specialists, remediation/learning specialists, and strategy tutors are provided through the program or unit. Academic advisers, diagnostic specialists, and LD specialists are provided collaboratively through on-campus or off-campus services.

Orientation The program or unit offers an optional 2 to 4-hour orientation for new students after classes begin and individually by special arrangement.

Summer Program To help prepare for the demands of college, there is an optional 3-week (subject to change) summer program prior to entering the school.

Unique Aids and Services Aids, services, or accommodations include advocates, career counseling, digital textbooks, faculty training, and support groups.

Subject-area Tutoring Tutoring is offered in small groups for some subjects. Tutoring is provided through the program or unit via LD specialists and trained peer tutors.

Diagnostic Testing Testing is provided through the program or unit for auditory processing, intelligence, learning strategies, learning styles, math, neuropsychological, personality, reading, social skills, spelling, study skills, visual processing, and written language.

Basic Skills Remediation Remediation is offered in small groups for computer skills, learning strategies, reading, study skills, and time management. Remediation is provided through the program or unit via computer-based instruction.

Enrichment Enrichment programs are available through the program or unit for learning strategies, practical computer skills, reading, self-advocacy, and written composition skills. Programs for

career planning, college survival skills, health and nutrition, math, medication management, stress management, study skills, test taking, and time management are provided collaboratively through on-campus or off-campus services.

Fees *Summer Program* fee is $25 to $100. *Diagnostic Testing* fee is $700 to $701.

Application For admittance to the program or unit, students are required to provide a psychoeducational report (3 years old or less). It is recommended that students apply to the program directly, provide documentation of high school services, and provide IPRC reports. Upon application, materials documenting need for services should be sent to both admissions and the LD program or unit. Upon acceptance, documentation of need for services should be sent only to the LD program or unit. *Application deadline (institutional):* Continuous. *Application deadline (LD program):* Rolling/continuous for fall and rolling/continuous for spring.

Written Policies Written policies regarding general/basic LD accommodations and reduced course loads are available through the program or unit directly.

The University of Winnipeg
Disability Services

515 Portage Avenue

Winnipeg, MB R3B 2E9

Canada

http://www.uwinnipeg.ca/web/current/services/disability.shtml

Contact: Mr. Jess Roebuck, Coordinator of the Disability Resource Centre. Phone: 204-786-9771. Fax: 204-786-8656. E-mail: j.roebuck@uwinnipeg.ca. Head of LD Program: Mr. Colin Russell, Director of Academic Advising and Special Needs Services. Phone: 204-786-9776. Fax: 204-786-8656. E-mail: c.russell@uwinnipeg.ca.

Disability Services Approximately 108 registered undergraduate students were served during 2002-03. The program or unit includes 2 full-time staff members and 1 part-time staff member. Academic advisers are provided through the program or unit. Academic advisers, counselors, diagnostic specialists, professional tutors, remediation/learning specialists, and strategy tutors are provided collaboratively through on-campus or off-campus services.

Orientation The program or unit offers an optional orientation for new students before registration, before classes begin, and individually by special arrangement.

Summer Program To help prepare for the demands of college, there is an optional 1-day summer program prior to entering the school.

Unique Aids and Services Aids, services, or accommodations include advocates, faculty training, and priority registration.

Subject-area Tutoring Tutoring is offered for some subjects. Tutoring is provided collaboratively through on-campus or off-campus services via professional tutors and trained peer tutors.

Basic Skills Remediation Remediation is offered one-on-one and in small groups for study skills and time management. Remediation is provided collaboratively through on-campus or off-campus services.

Enrichment Programs for career planning, learning strategies, practical computer skills, stress management, study skills, test taking, time management, and written composition skills are provided collaboratively through on-campus or off-campus services.

Student Organization Adaptive Services Students Directorate in the Students Association consists of 197 members.

Application For admittance to the program or unit, students are required to apply to the program directly and provide a psychoeducational report (3 years old or less). It is recommended that students provide documentation of high school services. Upon application, materials documenting need for services should be sent only to the LD program or unit. Upon acceptance, documentation of need for services should be sent only to the LD program or unit. *Application deadline (institutional): 8/9. Application deadline (LD program):* Rolling/continuous for fall and rolling/continuous for spring.

University of Wisconsin-Eau Claire
Services for Students with Disabilities

PO Box 4004

Eau Claire, WI 54702-4004

http://www.uwec.edu/ssd

Contact: Elizabeth Ann Hicks, Director of Services for Students with Disabilities. Phone: 715-836-4542. Fax: 715-836-3712. E-mail: hicksea@uwec.edu.

Services for Students with Disabilities Approximately 100 registered undergraduate students were served during 2002-03. The program or unit includes 2 part-time staff members. Counselors and LD specialists are provided through the program or unit. Academic advisers, counselors, diagnostic specialists, remediation/learning specialists, skill tutors, strategy tutors, and trained peer tutors are provided collaboratively through on-campus or off-campus services.

Unique Aids and Services Aids, services, or accommodations include career counseling, digital textbooks, and priority registration.

Subject-area Tutoring Tutoring is offered one-on-one and in small groups for most subjects. Tutoring is provided collaboratively through on-campus or off-campus services via computer-based instruction and trained peer tutors.

Diagnostic Testing Testing for learning strategies, learning styles, math, personality, reading, study skills, and written language is provided collaboratively through on-campus or off-campus services.

Basic Skills Remediation Remediation is offered one-on-one and in small groups for learning strategies, math, reading, study skills, time management, and written language. Remediation is provided collaboratively through on-campus or off-campus services via computer-based instruction and trained peer tutors.

Enrichment Programs for career planning, college survival skills, health and nutrition, learning strategies, medication management, self-advocacy, stress management, study skills, test taking, time management, and written composition skills are provided collaboratively through on-campus or off-campus services. Credit is offered for learning strategies and study skills.

Application For admittance to the program or unit, students are required to apply to the program directly and provide a psychoeducational report (3 years old or less). It is recommended that students provide documentation of high school services. Upon application, materials documenting need for services should be sent only to the LD program or unit. Upon acceptance, documentation of need for

services should be sent only to the LD program or unit. *Application deadline (institutional):* Continuous. *Application deadline (LD program):* Rolling/continuous for fall and rolling/continuous for spring.

Written Policies Written policies regarding course substitutions, general/basic LD accommodations, grade forgiveness, reduced course loads, substitutions and waivers of admissions requirements, and substitutions and waivers of graduation requirements are available on the program Web site. Written policies regarding course substitutions, general/basic LD accommodations, grade forgiveness, reduced course loads, substitutions and waivers of admissions requirements, and substitutions and waivers of graduation requirements are outlined in the school's catalog/handbook. Written policies regarding course substitutions, general/basic LD accommodations, reduced course loads, substitutions and waivers of admissions requirements, and substitutions and waivers of graduation requirements are available through the program or unit directly.

University of Wisconsin-Green Bay
Disability Services Office

2420 Nicolet Drive

Green Bay, WI 54311-7001

http://www.uwgb.edu/esms/ds.htm

Contact: Mrs. Lynn Niemi, Coordinator of Disability Services. Phone: 920-465-2841. Fax: 920-465-2954. E-mail: niemil@uwgb.edu.

Disability Services Office Approximately 50 registered undergraduate students were served during 2002-03. The program or unit includes 1 part-time staff member. Academic advisers are provided collaboratively through on-campus or off-campus services.

Unique Aids and Services Aids, services, or accommodations include determining and implementing accommodations.

Subject-area Tutoring Tutoring is offered one-on-one and in small groups for some subjects. Tutoring is provided collaboratively through on-campus or off-campus services via trained peer tutors.

Basic Skills Remediation Remediation is offered in class-size groups for math, reading, study skills, and written language. Remediation is provided collaboratively through on-campus or off-campus services via regular education teachers.

Enrichment Program for career planning is provided collaboratively through on-campus or off-campus services.

Application For admittance to the program or unit, students are required to provide a psychoeducational report. It is recommended that students provide documentation of high school services. Upon application, materials documenting need for services should be sent only to the LD program or unit. Upon acceptance, documentation of need for services should be sent only to the LD program or unit. *Application deadline (institutional): 2/1. Application deadline (LD program):* Rolling/continuous for fall and rolling/continuous for spring.

Written Policies Written policy regarding general/basic LD accommodations is available on the program Web site. Written policies regarding course substitutions, general/basic LD accommodations, and substitutions and waivers of graduation requirements are available through the program or unit directly.

University of Wisconsin-La Crosse

1725 State Street

La Crosse, WI 54601-3742

http://www.uwlax.edu/

Contact: Ms. June A. Reinert, Director of Disability Resource Services. Phone: 608-785-6900. Fax: 608-785-6910. E-mail: reinert.june@uwlax.edu.

The program or unit includes 1 full-time and 2 part-time staff members. Academic advisers, counselors, LD specialists, and remediation/learning specialists are provided collaboratively through on-campus or off-campus services.

Orientation The program or unit offers a mandatory 2-hour orientation for new students before classes begin and during registration.

Unique Aids and Services Aids, services, or accommodations include digital textbooks, faculty training, priority registration, and support groups.

Subject-area Tutoring Tutoring is offered in small groups for most subjects. Tutoring is provided collaboratively through on-campus or off-campus services via computer-based instruction.

Student Organization Students Advocating Potential Ability consists of 19 members.

Application For admittance to the program or unit, students are required to apply to the program directly and provide a psychoeducational report (3 years old or less). It is recommended that students provide documentation of high school services. Upon acceptance, documentation of need for services should be sent only to the LD program or unit. *Application deadline (institutional):* Continuous. *Application deadline (LD program):* Rolling/continuous for spring.

Written Policies Written policies regarding course substitutions, general/basic LD accommodations, reduced course loads, and substitutions and waivers of graduation requirements are available on the program Web site.

University of Wisconsin-Madison

McBurney Disability Resource Center

500 Lincoln Drive

Madison, WI 53706-1380

http://www.mcburney.wisc.edu/

Contact: McBurney Disability Resource Center Transition Services. Phone: 608-263-2741. Fax: 608-263-2741. E-mail: mcburney@uwmadmail.services.wisc.edu. Head of LD Program: Cathy Trueba, LD Services Coordinator. Phone: 608-263-5177. Fax: 608-265-2998. E-mail: cmtrueba@wisc.edu.

McBurney Disability Resource Center Approximately 450 registered undergraduate students were served during 2002-03. The program or unit includes 1 full-time and 1 part-time staff member. Academic advisers, counselors, graduate assistants/students, and LD specialists are provided through the program or unit. Counse-

lors, diagnostic specialists, graduate assistants/students, professional tutors, remediation/learning specialists, skill tutors, and strategy tutors are provided collaboratively through on-campus or off-campus services.

Orientation The program or unit offers a mandatory 1-4 hour orientation for new students before classes begin.

Subject-area Tutoring Tutoring is offered in small groups for some subjects. Tutoring is provided collaboratively through on-campus or off-campus services via graduate assistants/students, trained peer tutors, and other.

Diagnostic Testing Testing for auditory processing, handwriting, intelligence, math, reading, spelling, spoken language, visual processing, written language, and other services is provided collaboratively through on-campus or off-campus services.

Enrichment Enrichment programs are available through the program or unit for self-advocacy and study skills. Programs for career planning, learning strategies, math, medication management, stress management, study skills, and written composition skills are provided collaboratively through on-campus or off-campus services. Credit is offered for learning strategies and study skills.

Fees *Diagnostic Testing* fee is $150.

Application For admittance to the program or unit, students are required to apply to the program directly. It is recommended that students provide documentation of high school services. Upon application, materials documenting need for services should be sent to both admissions and the LD program or unit. Upon acceptance, documentation of need for services should be sent only to the LD program or unit. *Application deadline (institutional):* 2/1. *Application deadline (LD program):* Rolling/continuous for fall and rolling/continuous for spring.

Written Policies Written policies regarding course substitutions, general/basic LD accommodations, and substitutions and waivers of graduation requirements are available on the program Web site. Written policy regarding course substitutions is outlined in the school's catalog/handbook. Written policy regarding substitutions and waivers of graduation requirements is available through the program or unit directly.

University of Wisconsin-Milwaukee

Learning Disabilities Program, Student Accessibility Center

PO Box 413

Milwaukee, WI 53201-0413

http://www.uwm.edu/Dept/DSAD/SAC

Contact: Laurie B. Petersen, Learning Disabilities Program Manager. Phone: 414-229-6239. Fax: 414-229-2237. E-mail: lauriep@uwm.edu.

Learning Disabilities Program, Student Accessibility Center Approximately 200 registered undergraduate students were served during 2002-03. The program or unit includes 2 full-time staff members. Coaches and LD specialists are provided through the program or unit. Counselors, diagnostic specialists, remediation/learning specialists, skill tutors, and trained peer tutors are provided collaboratively through on-campus or off-campus services.

Orientation The program or unit offers an optional orientation for new students individually by special arrangement.

Unique Aids and Services Aids, services, or accommodations include advocates, digital textbooks, faculty training, test accommodations, note-taking services, progress reports, assistive technology lab.

Subject-area Tutoring Tutoring is offered one-on-one and in small groups for most subjects. Tutoring is provided collaboratively through on-campus or off-campus services via computer-based instruction, graduate assistants/students, and trained peer tutors.

Diagnostic Testing Testing for intelligence, learning strategies, learning styles, math, neuropsychological, personality, reading, social skills, spelling, spoken language, study skills, visual processing, and written language is provided collaboratively through on-campus or off-campus services.

Basic Skills Remediation Remediation is offered in class-size groups for computer skills, learning strategies, math, reading, spoken language, study skills, time management, and written language. Remediation is provided collaboratively through on-campus or off-campus services via graduate assistants/students, regular education teachers, and trained peer tutors.

Enrichment Enrichment programs are available through the program or unit for self-advocacy, stress management, study skills, test taking, and time management. Programs for career planning, college survival skills, health and nutrition, learning strategies, math, oral communication skills, practical computer skills, reading, study skills, test taking, time management, and written composition skills are provided collaboratively through on-campus or off-campus services. Credit is offered for career planning, college survival skills, health and nutrition, learning strategies, reading, study skills, test taking, and time management.

Fees *Diagnostic Testing* fee is $225 to $350.

Application For admittance to the program or unit, students are required to apply to the program directly, provide a psychoeducational report, provide documentation of high school services, and provide psychoeducational evaluation (for ADHD). Upon application, materials documenting need for services should be sent only to the LD program or unit. Upon acceptance, documentation of need for services should be sent only to the LD program or unit. *Application deadline (institutional):* 8/1. *Application deadline (LD program):* Rolling/continuous for fall and rolling/continuous for spring.

Written Policies Written policy regarding general/basic LD accommodations is available on the program Web site. Written policy regarding general/basic LD accommodations is available through the program or unit directly.

University of Wisconsin-Platteville

1 University Plaza
Platteville, WI 53818-3099
http://www.uwplatt.edu/

Contact: Ms. Rebecca L. Peters, Coordinator of Services for Students with Disabilities. Phone: 608-342-1818. Fax: 608-342-1918. E-mail: petersre@uwplatt.edu.

Approximately 100 registered undergraduate students were served during 2002-03. The program or unit includes 2 part-time staff members. LD specialists are provided through the program or unit.

Academic advisers, counselors, diagnostic specialists, remediation/learning specialists, skill tutors, and trained peer tutors are provided collaboratively through on-campus or off-campus services.

Unique Aids and Services Aids, services, or accommodations include digital textbooks and support groups.

Subject-area Tutoring Tutoring is offered one-on-one and in small groups for most subjects. Tutoring is provided collaboratively through on-campus or off-campus services via trained peer tutors.

Diagnostic Testing Testing for reading is provided collaboratively through on-campus or off-campus services.

Basic Skills Remediation Remediation is offered one-on-one and in small groups for computer skills, learning strategies, reading, study skills, and time management. Remediation is provided collaboratively through on-campus or off-campus services via computer-based instruction, regular education teachers, and trained peer tutors.

Enrichment Programs for career planning, college survival skills, health and nutrition, learning strategies, reading, stress management, study skills, test taking, time management, and written composition skills are provided collaboratively through on-campus or off-campus services. Credit is offered for career planning and college survival skills.

Student Organization Students Planning for Success consists of 15 members.

Application For admittance to the program or unit, students are required to provide a psychoeducational report (3 years old or less) and provide documentation of high school services. Upon application, materials documenting need for services should be sent only to admissions with institutional application materials. Upon acceptance, documentation of need for services should be sent only to the LD program or unit. *Application deadline (institutional):* Continuous. *Application deadline (LD program):* Rolling/continuous for fall and rolling/continuous for spring.

Written Policies Written policy regarding general/basic LD accommodations is available on the program Web site. Written policies regarding course substitutions, general/basic LD accommodations, reduced course loads, substitutions and waivers of admissions requirements, and substitutions and waivers of graduation requirements are available through the program or unit directly.

University of Wisconsin-Stout

Menomonie, WI 54751
http://www.uwstout.edu/

Contact: Ms. Debra Joan Shefchik, Director of Disability Services. Phone: 715-232-2995. Fax: 715-232-2996. E-mail: shefchikd@uwstout.edu.

The program or unit includes 1 full-time and 3 part-time staff members. Academic advisers, LD specialists, and other are provided through the program or unit.

Orientation The program or unit offers a mandatory 2-hour orientation for new students before classes begin, after classes begin, and individually by special arrangement.

Unique Aids and Services Aids, services, or accommodations include advocates, career counseling, digital textbooks, personal coach, priority registration, support groups, test accommodations, peer note-takers.

University of Wisconsin-Stout (continued)

Subject-area Tutoring Tutoring is offered one-on-one and in small groups for some subjects. Tutoring is provided collaboratively through on-campus or off-campus services via trained peer tutors.

Diagnostic Testing Testing for auditory processing, intelligence, learning styles, math, motor skills, neuropsychological, personality, reading, spelling, visual processing, and written language is provided collaboratively through on-campus or off-campus services.

Basic Skills Remediation Remediation is offered in class-size groups for math and written language. Remediation is provided collaboratively through on-campus or off-campus services via regular education teachers.

Enrichment Enrichment programs are available through the program or unit for career planning, college survival skills, learning strategies, reading, self-advocacy, stress management, study skills, test taking, time management, and written composition skills. Programs for career planning, math, and written composition skills are provided collaboratively through on-campus or off-campus services.

Fees *Diagnostic Testing* fee is $75.

Application For admittance to the program or unit, students are required to provide a psychoeducational report (3 years old or less) and provide documentation of high school services. Upon acceptance, documentation of need for services should be sent only to the LD program or unit. *Application deadline (institutional):* Continuous. *Application deadline (LD program):* Rolling/continuous for fall and rolling/continuous for spring.

Written Policies Written policy regarding general/basic LD accommodations is available on the program Web site. Written policies regarding course substitutions, general/basic LD accommodations, and substitutions and waivers of graduation requirements are outlined in the school's catalog/handbook. Written policies regarding course substitutions, general/basic LD accommodations, and substitutions and waivers of graduation requirements are available through the program or unit directly.

University of Wisconsin-Whitewater

800 West Main Street
Whitewater, WI 53190-1790
http://www.uww.edu/

Contact: Nancy Amacher, Director. Phone: 262-472-4788. E-mail: amachern@uww.edu.

Approximately 147 registered undergraduate students were served during 2002-03. The program or unit includes 3 full-time and 40 part-time staff members. Academic advisers, graduate assistants/students, LD specialists, skill tutors, strategy tutors, and trained peer tutors are provided through the program or unit. Counselors are provided collaboratively through on-campus or off-campus services.

Orientation The program or unit offers an optional 30-minute orientation for new students during summer prior to enrollment, during registration, and individually by special arrangement.

Summer Program To help prepare for the demands of college, there is an optional 4-week summer program prior to entering the school.

Unique Aids and Services Aids, services, or accommodations include career counseling, digital textbooks, and priority registration.

Subject-area Tutoring Tutoring is offered one-on-one and in small groups for all subjects. Tutoring is provided through the program or unit via LD specialists and trained peer tutors.

Basic Skills Remediation Remediation is offered one-on-one, in small groups, and in class-size groups for computer skills, learning strategies, math, reading, study skills, time management, and written language. Remediation is provided through the program or unit via LD specialists and trained peer tutors. Remediation is also provided collaboratively through on-campus or off-campus services via regular education teachers.

Enrichment Enrichment programs are available through the program or unit for career planning, college survival skills, learning strategies, math, practical computer skills, self-advocacy, stress management, study skills, test taking, time management, and written composition skills. Programs for career planning, college survival skills, health and nutrition, and written composition skills are provided collaboratively through on-campus or off-campus services. Credit is offered for career planning, college survival skills, health and nutrition, and written composition skills.

Fees *LD Program or Service* fee is $700 to $950 (fee varies according to course level). *Summer Program* fee is $1700 to $2900.

Application For admittance to the program or unit, students are required to apply to the program directly, provide a psychoeducational report (3 years old or less), and provide 2 letters of recommendation. It is recommended that students provide documentation of high school services. Upon application, materials documenting need for services should be sent only to the LD program or unit. *Application deadline (institutional):* Continuous. *Application deadline (LD program):* Rolling/continuous for fall and rolling/continuous for spring.

University of Wyoming
Disability Support Services

Laramie, WY 82071
http://www.uwyo.edu click on A-Z directory, then select Disability Support Services

Contact: Ms. Chris Primus, Director of University Disability Support Services. Phone: 307-766-6189. Fax: 307-766-4010. E-mail: cfprimus@uwyo.edu.

Disability Support Services Approximately 75 registered undergraduate students were served during 2002-03. The program or unit includes 4 full-time and 25 part-time staff members. Counselors are provided through the program or unit. Academic advisers, counselors, diagnostic specialists, skill tutors, strategy tutors, and trained peer tutors are provided collaboratively through on-campus or off-campus services.

Orientation The program or unit offers an optional half-day orientation for new students before classes begin and individually by special arrangement.

Unique Aids and Services Aids, services, or accommodations include advocates and priority registration.

Subject-area Tutoring Tutoring is offered one-on-one and in small groups for most subjects. Tutoring is provided collaboratively through on-campus or off-campus services via computer-based instruction, graduate assistants/students, and trained peer tutors.

Diagnostic Testing Testing for auditory processing, intelligence, learning styles, math, neuropsychological, personality, reading, spelling, visual processing, and written language is provided collaboratively through on-campus or off-campus services.

Basic Skills Remediation Remediation is offered one-on-one and in small groups for learning strategies, math, reading, study skills, time management, and written language. Remediation is provided collaboratively through on-campus or off-campus services via computer-based instruction, graduate assistants/students, and trained peer tutors.

Enrichment Programs for career planning, college survival skills, health and nutrition, learning strategies, math, practical computer skills, reading, stress management, study skills, test taking, time management, and written composition skills are provided collaboratively through on-campus or off-campus services.

Student Organization WyoACCESS consists of 15 members.

Fees *Diagnostic Testing* fee is applicable.

Application For admittance to the program or unit, students are required to apply to the program directly and provide a psychoeducational report. It is recommended that students provide documentation of high school services. Upon application, materials documenting need for services should be sent only to the LD program or unit. Upon acceptance, documentation of need for services should be sent only to the LD program or unit. *Application deadline (institutional):* 8/10. *Application deadline (LD program):* Rolling/continuous for fall and rolling/continuous for spring.

Written Policies Written policies regarding course substitutions, general/basic LD accommodations, and substitutions and waivers of graduation requirements are available on the program Web site. Written policies regarding course substitutions, substitutions and waivers of admissions requirements, and substitutions and waivers of graduation requirements are outlined in the school's catalog/handbook. Written policies regarding course substitutions, general/basic LD accommodations, and substitutions and waivers of graduation requirements are available through the program or unit directly.

Utica College
Academic Support Services Center

1600 Burrstone Road
Utica, NY 13502-4892
http://www.utica.edu/

Contact: Mrs. Kateri Teresa Henkel, Coordinator of Learning Services. Phone: 315-792-3032. Fax: 315-792-3292. E-mail: khenkel@utica.edu. Head of LD Program: Mr. Stephen Pattarini, Director of Student Development. Phone: 315-792-3032. Fax: 315-792-3292. E-mail: spattarini@utica.edu.

Academic Support Services Center Approximately 100 registered undergraduate students were served during 2002-03. The program or unit includes 1 full-time staff member. Academic advisers and LD specialists are provided through the program or unit. Academic advisers, counselors, diagnostic specialists, professional tutors, regular education teachers, skill tutors, strategy tutors, and trained peer tutors are provided collaboratively through on-campus or off-campus services.

Unique Aids and Services Aids, services, or accommodations include advocates, career counseling, and priority registration.

Subject-area Tutoring Tutoring is offered one-on-one and in small groups for most subjects. Tutoring is provided through the program or unit via professional tutors. Tutoring is also provided collaboratively through on-campus or off-campus services via professional tutors and trained peer tutors.

Basic Skills Remediation Remediation is offered one-on-one and in small groups for computer skills, learning strategies, study skills, and time management. Remediation is provided through the program or unit via LD specialists. Remediation is also provided collaboratively through on-campus or off-campus services.

Enrichment Enrichment programs are available through the program or unit for self-advocacy, study skills, test taking, and time management. Programs for career planning, college survival skills, learning strategies, math, oral communication skills, practical computer skills, study skills, test taking, time management, and written composition skills are provided collaboratively through on-campus or off-campus services. Credit is offered for college survival skills, oral communication skills, and practical computer skills.

Application For admittance to the program or unit, students are required to provide a psychoeducational report (3 years old or less). It is recommended that students provide documentation of high school services. Upon application, materials documenting need for services should be sent to both admissions and the LD program or unit. Upon acceptance, documentation of need for services should be sent only to the LD program or unit. *Application deadline (institutional):* Continuous. *Application deadline (LD program):* Rolling/continuous for fall and rolling/continuous for spring.

Written Policies Written policies regarding course substitutions, general/basic LD accommodations, and substitutions and waivers of graduation requirements are available through the program or unit directly.

Valley City State University
Student Academic Services, DSS

101 College Street, SW
Valley City, ND 58072
http://www.vcsu.edu/

Contact: Ms. Jan Drake, Director of Student Academic Services. Phone: 701-845-0981. Fax: 701-845-7299. E-mail: jan_drake@mail.vcsu.nodak.edu.

Student Academic Services, DSS Approximately 24 registered undergraduate students were served during 2002-03. The program or unit includes 1 full-time and 1 part-time staff member. Academic advisers, counselors, graduate assistants/students, regular education teachers, and trained peer tutors are provided through the program or unit. Diagnostic specialists and regular education teachers are provided collaboratively through on-campus or off-campus services.

Unique Aids and Services Aids, services, or accommodations include digital textbooks and priority registration.

Subject-area Tutoring Tutoring is offered one-on-one, in small groups, and in class-size groups for all subjects. Tutoring is provided through the program or unit via computer-based instruction and trained peer tutors. Tutoring is also provided collaboratively through on-campus or off-campus services via computer-based instruction and trained peer tutors.

Valley City State University (continued)

Enrichment Programs for career planning, college survival skills, learning strategies, math, stress management, time management, and written composition skills are provided collaboratively through on-campus or off-campus services. Credit is offered for career planning, college survival skills, learning strategies, math, stress management, time management, and written composition skills.

Application For admittance to the program or unit, students are required to provide a psychoeducational report (5 years old or less) and provide documentation of high school services. Upon acceptance, documentation of need for services should be sent only to the LD program or unit. *Application deadline (institutional):* Continuous. *Application deadline (LD program):* Rolling/continuous for fall and rolling/continuous for spring.

Written Policies Written policy regarding general/basic LD accommodations is available through the program or unit directly.

Valparaiso University
Disability Support Services (DSS) Office

651 South College Avenue

Valparaiso, IN 46383-6493

http://www.valpo.edu/

Contact: Dr. Christina H. Grabarek, Director of Disability Support Services. Phone: 219-464-5318. Fax: 219-464-5511. E-mail: christina.grabarek@valpo.edu.

Disability Support Services (DSS) Office Approximately 40 registered undergraduate students were served during 2002-03. The program or unit includes 1 full-time staff member. LD specialists are provided through the program or unit. Academic advisers, counselors, professional tutors, regular education teachers, remediation/learning specialists, skill tutors, strategy tutors, and trained peer tutors are provided collaboratively through on-campus or off-campus services.

Unique Aids and Services Aids, services, or accommodations include priority registration.

Subject-area Tutoring Tutoring is offered one-on-one, in small groups, and in class-size groups for most subjects. Tutoring is provided collaboratively through on-campus or off-campus services via professional tutors and trained peer tutors.

Basic Skills Remediation Remediation is offered in class-size groups for learning strategies and study skills. Remediation is provided collaboratively through on-campus or off-campus services via regular education teachers.

Enrichment Programs for career planning, learning strategies, medication management, stress management, study skills, and written composition skills are provided collaboratively through on-campus or off-campus services.

Application For admittance to the program or unit, students are required to provide a psychoeducational report (3 years old or less), provide documentation of high school services, and provide a letter requesting accommodations. Upon acceptance, documentation of need for services should be sent only to the LD program or unit. *Application deadline (institutional):* 8/15. *Application deadline (LD program):* Rolling/continuous for fall and rolling/continuous for spring.

Written Policies Written policy regarding general/basic LD accommodations is available on the program Web site. Written policy regarding general/basic LD accommodations is outlined in the school's catalog/handbook. Written policy regarding general/basic LD accommodations is available through the program or unit directly.

Vanguard University of Southern California
Learning Assistance

55 Fair Drive

Costa Mesa, CA 92626-9601

http://www.vanguard.edu/

Contact: Mrs. Barbi Ann Rouse, Director of Learning Skills. Phone: 714-556-3610 Ext. 227. Fax: 714-662-5222. E-mail: brouse@vanguard.edu.

Learning Assistance Approximately 29 registered undergraduate students were served during 2002-03. The program or unit includes 1 full-time and 2 part-time staff members. Academic advisers, regular education teachers, skill tutors, strategy tutors, and other are provided through the program or unit. Academic advisers, counselors, regular education teachers, and trained peer tutors are provided collaboratively through on-campus or off-campus services.

Unique Aids and Services Aids, services, or accommodations include career counseling, regular appointments with Director of Learning Skills.

Subject-area Tutoring Tutoring is offered for most subjects. Tutoring is provided collaboratively through on-campus or off-campus services via graduate assistants/students and trained peer tutors.

Basic Skills Remediation Remediation is offered in small groups for learning strategies, reading, study skills, time management, and editing. Remediation is provided collaboratively through on-campus or off-campus services via regular education teachers and trained peer tutors.

Enrichment Enrichment programs are available through the program or unit for college survival skills, learning strategies, stress management, study skills, test taking, time management, and written composition skills. Programs for career planning, learning strategies, practical computer skills, reading, study skills, test taking, and time management are provided collaboratively through on-campus or off-campus services. Credit is offered for college survival skills, learning strategies, practical computer skills, reading, study skills, test taking, and time management.

Application For admittance to the program or unit, students are required to apply to the program directly, provide a psychoeducational report (3 years old or less), provide documentation of high school services, and provide medical doctor verification in some cases. Upon application, materials documenting need for services should be sent only to admissions with institutional application materials. Upon acceptance, documentation of need for services should be sent to both admissions and the LD program or unit. *Application deadline (institutional):* 3/2. *Application deadline (LD program):* Rolling/continuous for fall and rolling/continuous for spring.

Written Policies Written policies regarding general/basic LD accommodations and substitutions and waivers of admissions requirements are available through the program or unit directly.

Vermont College
Academic Support Network (ASN)

36 College Street
Montpelier, VT 05602
http://www.tui.edu/universityoffices/ASN.asp
Contact: Anne Connor, Director of Academic Support Network. Phone: 802-828-8801. Fax: 802-828-8565. E-mail: anne.connor@tui.edu.

Academic Support Network (ASN) Approximately 15 registered undergraduate students were served during 2002-03. The program or unit includes 1 full-time and 1 part-time staff member. Coaches, diagnostic specialists, professional tutors, regular education teachers, remediation/learning specialists, skill tutors, and strategy tutors are provided through the program or unit. Coaches, diagnostic specialists, professional tutors, regular education teachers, remediation/learning specialists, skill tutors, and strategy tutors are provided collaboratively through on-campus or off-campus services.
Orientation The program or unit offers an optional orientation for new students before classes begin.
Unique Aids and Services Aids, services, or accommodations include faculty training, personal coach, regular meetings with faculty.
Subject-area Tutoring Tutoring is offered one-on-one. Tutoring is provided through the program or unit via professional tutors. Tutoring is also provided collaboratively through on-campus or off-campus services via professional tutors.
Diagnostic Testing Testing is provided through the program or unit for learning strategies and reading.
Basic Skills Remediation Remediation is offered one-on-one for learning strategies and written language. Remediation is provided through the program or unit via professional tutors and regular education teachers. Remediation is also provided collaboratively through on-campus or off-campus services via professional tutors and regular education teachers.
Enrichment Enrichment programs are available through the program or unit for college survival skills, learning strategies, reading, self-advocacy, stress management, study skills, test taking, time management, and written composition skills. Programs for college survival skills, learning strategies, reading, self-advocacy, stress management, study skills, test taking, time management, and written composition skills are provided collaboratively through on-campus or off-campus services.
Application For admittance to the program or unit, students are required to provide a psychoeducational report (3 years old or less). Upon application, materials documenting need for services should be sent only to the LD program or unit. *Application deadline (LD program):* Rolling/continuous for fall and rolling/continuous for spring.
Written Policies Written policy regarding general/basic LD accommodations is available on the program Web site. Written policy regarding general/basic LD accommodations is outlined in the school's catalog/handbook. Written policy regarding general/basic LD accommodations is available through the program or unit directly.

Vermont Technical College

PO Box 500

Randolph Center, VT 05061-0500
http://www.vtc.edu
Contact: Robin C. Goodall, Learning Specialist. Phone: 802-728-1278. Fax: 802-728-1714. E-mail: rgoodall@vtc.edu.

Approximately 75 registered undergraduate students were served during 2002-03. The program or unit includes 1 full-time staff member. Counselors, LD specialists, skill tutors, and strategy tutors are provided through the program or unit. Academic advisers, counselors, LD specialists, professional tutors, skill tutors, strategy tutors, and trained peer tutors are provided collaboratively through on-campus or off-campus services.
Summer Program To help prepare for the demands of college, there is an optional 1-day summer program prior to entering the school.
Unique Aids and Services Aids, services, or accommodations include career counseling, digital textbooks, personal coach, and weekly meetings with faculty.
Subject-area Tutoring Tutoring is offered one-on-one and in small groups for all subjects. Tutoring is provided through the program or unit via computer-based instruction and LD specialists. Tutoring is also provided collaboratively through on-campus or off-campus services via computer-based instruction, professional tutors, and trained peer tutors.
Basic Skills Remediation Remediation is offered one-on-one for computer skills, learning strategies, math, study skills, time management, and written language. Remediation is provided collaboratively through on-campus or off-campus services via computer-based instruction, professional tutors, and trained peer tutors.
Enrichment Programs for learning strategies and self-advocacy are provided collaboratively through on-campus or off-campus services.
Application For admittance to the program or unit, students are required to provide a psychoeducational report (3 years old or less). Upon application, materials documenting need for services should be sent only to admissions with institutional application materials. Upon acceptance, documentation of need for services should be sent to both admissions and the LD program or unit. *Application deadline (institutional):* Continuous. *Application deadline (LD program):* Rolling/continuous for fall and rolling/continuous for spring.
Written Policies Written policy regarding general/basic LD accommodations is available on the program Web site. Written policies regarding general/basic LD accommodations and reduced course loads are outlined in the school's catalog/handbook. Written policies regarding general/basic LD accommodations and reduced course loads are available through the program or unit directly.

Villanova University
Learning Support Services

800 Lancaster Avenue
Villanova, PA 19085-1699
http://learningsupportservices.villanova.edu
Contact: Ms. Nancy Mott, Director of Learning Support Services. Phone: 610-591-5636. Fax: 610-519-8015. E-mail: nancy.mott@villanova.edu.

Villanova University (continued)

Learning Support Services Approximately 175 registered undergraduate students were served during 2002-03. The program or unit includes 1 full-time and 1 part-time staff member. Coaches, graduate assistants/students, LD specialists, remediation/learning specialists, skill tutors, strategy tutors, and trained peer tutors are provided through the program or unit. Academic advisers, counselors, graduate assistants/students, regular education teachers, skill tutors, strategy tutors, and trained peer tutors are provided collaboratively through on-campus or off-campus services.

Unique Aids and Services Aids, services, or accommodations include career counseling, digital textbooks, personal coach, support groups, and weekly meetings with faculty.

Subject-area Tutoring Tutoring is offered one-on-one, in small groups, and in class-size groups for most subjects. Tutoring is provided through the program or unit via computer-based instruction, graduate assistants/students, and LD specialists. Tutoring is also provided collaboratively through on-campus or off-campus services via computer-based instruction, graduate assistants/students, and trained peer tutors.

Diagnostic Testing Testing is provided through the program or unit for learning strategies, learning styles, and study skills. Testing for learning strategies, learning styles, and study skills is provided collaboratively through on-campus or off-campus services.

Enrichment Enrichment programs are available through the program or unit for college survival skills, learning strategies, self-advocacy, stress management, study skills, test taking, and time management. Programs for career planning, health and nutrition, learning strategies, math, stress management, study skills, test taking, time management, and written composition skills are provided collaboratively through on-campus or off-campus services. Credit is offered for college survival skills, learning strategies, self-advocacy, stress management, study skills, test taking, and time management.

Application For admittance to the program or unit, students are required to provide a psychoeducational report. It is recommended that students provide documentation of high school services. Upon acceptance, documentation of need for services should be sent only to the LD program or unit. *Application deadline (institutional):* 1/7. *Application deadline (LD program):* Rolling/continuous for fall and rolling/continuous for spring.

Written Policies Written policies regarding general/basic LD accommodations, reduced course loads, and substitutions and waivers of graduation requirements are available on the program Web site. Written policies regarding general/basic LD accommodations and substitutions and waivers of graduation requirements are outlined in the school's catalog/handbook. Written policies regarding general/basic LD accommodations, reduced course loads, and substitutions and waivers of graduation requirements are available through the program or unit directly.

Virginia Commonwealth University

901 West Franklin Street
Richmond, VA 23284-9005
http://www.vcu.edu/

Contact: Ms. Joyce Belinda Knight, Coordinator. Phone: 804-828-2253. Fax: 804-828-1944. E-mail: jbknight@vcu.edu.

Approximately 300 registered undergraduate students were served during 2002-03. The program or unit includes 1 full-time staff member. Graduate assistants/students, LD specialists, and trained peer tutors are provided through the program or unit. Graduate assistants/students, LD specialists, and trained peer tutors are provided collaboratively through on-campus or off-campus services.

Orientation The program or unit offers an optional 1-day orientation for new students before classes begin.

Unique Aids and Services Aids, services, or accommodations include advocates, career counseling, digital textbooks, faculty training, parent workshops, personal coach, priority registration, and support groups.

Subject-area Tutoring Tutoring is offered one-on-one for some subjects. Tutoring is provided collaboratively through on-campus or off-campus services via trained peer tutors.

Enrichment Programs for career planning, college survival skills, health and nutrition, learning strategies, study skills, test taking, time management, and written composition skills are provided collaboratively through on-campus or off-campus services.

Application For admittance to the program or unit, students are required to provide a psychoeducational report (3 years old or less). Upon application, materials documenting need for services should be sent only to the LD program or unit. Upon acceptance, documentation of need for services should be sent only to admissions. *Application deadline (institutional):* 2/1. *Application deadline (LD program):* Rolling/continuous for fall.

Written Policies Written policy regarding general/basic LD accommodations is available on the program Web site. Written policy regarding general/basic LD accommodations is available through the program or unit directly.

Virginia Intermont College
Student Support Services

1013 Moore Street
Bristol, VA 24201-4298
http://www.vic.edu/

Contact: Ms. Barbara L. Holbrook, School Psychologist and Learning Disabilities Specialist. Phone: 276-466-7906. Fax: 276-645-6493. E-mail: barbaraholbrook@vic.edu.

Student Support Services Approximately 25 registered undergraduate students were served during 2002-03. The program or unit includes 3 full-time staff members. Counselors, diagnostic specialists, and LD specialists are provided through the program or unit.

Unique Aids and Services Aids, services, or accommodations include advocates, faculty training, support groups, academic advising.

Subject-area Tutoring Tutoring is offered one-on-one and in small groups for most subjects. Tutoring is provided through the program or unit via trained peer tutors.

Diagnostic Testing Testing is provided through the program or unit for auditory processing, intelligence, learning strategies, learning styles, math, motor skills, reading, spelling, spoken language, study skills, visual processing, and written language.

Basic Skills Remediation Remediation is offered in small groups for learning strategies, reading, study skills, and time management. Remediation is provided through the program or unit via LD specialists and trained peer tutors. Remediation is also provided collaboratively through on-campus or off-campus services via regular education teachers.

Enrichment Enrichment programs are available through the program or unit for college survival skills, learning strategies, stress management, study skills, test taking, and time management. Program for career planning is provided collaboratively through on-campus or off-campus services. Credit is offered for study skills, test taking, and time management.

Application For admittance to the program or unit, students are required to provide a psychoeducational report (5 years old or less). It is recommended that students provide documentation of high school services. Upon acceptance, documentation of need for services should be sent only to the LD program or unit. *Application deadline (institutional):* Continuous. *Application deadline (LD program):* Rolling/continuous for fall and rolling/continuous for spring.

Written Policies Written policy regarding general/basic LD accommodations is available on the program Web site. Written policy regarding general/basic LD accommodations is outlined in the school's catalog/handbook. Written policies regarding course substitutions, general/basic LD accommodations, reduced course loads, and substitutions and waivers of graduation requirements are available through the program or unit directly.

Virginia Polytechnic Institute and State University
Services for Students with Disabilities

Blacksburg, VA 24061

http://www.ssd.vt.edu

Contact: Dr. Susan P. Angle, Director of Services for Students with Disabilities. Phone: 540-231-3788. Fax: 540-231-3232. E-mail: spangle@vt.edu.

Services for Students with Disabilities Approximately 205 registered undergraduate students were served during 2002-03. The program or unit includes 3 full-time staff members and 1 part-time staff member. Diagnostic specialists, graduate assistants/students, LD specialists, and strategy tutors are provided through the program or unit. Academic advisers, counselors, diagnostic specialists, graduate assistants/students, LD specialists, professional tutors, regular education teachers, skill tutors, strategy tutors, and trained peer tutors are provided collaboratively through on-campus or off-campus services.

Orientation The program or unit offers an optional 3-hour orientation for new students before classes begin.

Unique Aids and Services Aids, services, or accommodations include faculty training and priority registration.

Subject-area Tutoring Tutoring is offered one-on-one, in small groups, and in class-size groups for some subjects. Tutoring is provided collaboratively through on-campus or off-campus services via computer-based instruction, graduate assistants/students, professional tutors, and trained peer tutors.

Enrichment Programs for career planning, college survival skills, health and nutrition, learning strategies, math, medication management, oral communication skills, practical computer skills, stress management, study skills, test taking, time management, and written composition skills are provided collaboratively through on-campus or off-campus services. Credit is offered for career planning, math, oral communication skills, practical computer skills, and written composition skills.

Student Organization Students with Disabilities Student Advisory Board consists of 15 members.

Application For admittance to the program or unit, students are required to provide a psychoeducational report. It is recommended that students provide documentation of high school services. Upon application, materials documenting need for services should be sent only to the LD program or unit. Upon acceptance, documentation of need for services should be sent only to the LD program or unit. *Application deadline (institutional):* 1/15. *Application deadline (LD program):* Rolling/continuous for fall and rolling/continuous for spring.

Written Policies Written policies regarding course substitutions and general/basic LD accommodations are available on the program Web site. Written policy regarding general/basic LD accommodations is outlined in the school's catalog/handbook. Written policies regarding course substitutions and general/basic LD accommodations are available through the program or unit directly.

Wake Forest University

Reynolda Station

Winston-Salem, NC 27109

http://www.wfu.edu/

Contact: Van D. Westervelt PhD, Director of Learning Assistance Center. Phone: 336-758-5929. Fax: 336-758-1991.

The program or unit includes 3 full-time and 3 part-time staff members. Graduate assistants/students, strategy tutors, and trained peer tutors are provided through the program or unit.

Subject-area Tutoring Tutoring is offered one-on-one and in small groups for some subjects. Tutoring is provided through the program or unit via graduate assistants/students and trained peer tutors.

Application For admittance to the program or unit, students are required to provide a psychoeducational report (3 years old or less). It is recommended that students provide documentation of high school services. Upon acceptance, documentation of need for services should be sent only to the LD program or unit. *Application deadline (institutional):* 1/15. *Application deadline (LD program):* Rolling/continuous for fall and rolling/continuous for spring.

Written Policies Written policy regarding general/basic LD accommodations is available on the program Web site. Written policy regarding reduced course loads is available through the program or unit directly.

Washburn University
Student Services/Services for Students with Disabilities Office (SSWDO)

1700 SW College Avenue

Topeka, KS 66621

http://www.washburn.edu./services/studentaffairs/stuservices

Contact: Phone: 785-231-1010. Fax: 785-231-1089.

Application For admittance to the program or unit, students are required to provide a psychoeducational report. Upon acceptance, documentation of need for services should be sent only to the LD program or unit. *Application deadline (institutional):* Continuous.

Written Policies Written policy regarding general/basic LD accommodations is available on the program Web site. Written policies regarding general/basic LD accommodations and substitutions and waivers of graduation requirements are available through the program or unit directly.

Washington & Jefferson College
Center for Excellence in Teaching and Learning

60 South Lincoln Street

Washington, PA 15301-4801

http://www.washjeff.edu/CETL

Contact: Dr. James M. Sloat, Director of Center for Excellence in Teaching and Learning. Phone: 724-250-3533. Fax: 724-250-3463. E-mail: cetl@washjeff.edu.

Center for Excellence in Teaching and Learning Approximately 15 registered undergraduate students were served during 2002-03. The program or unit includes 1 full-time staff member. Academic advisers, skill tutors, and trained peer tutors are provided through the program or unit. Academic advisers are provided collaboratively through on-campus or off-campus services.

Orientation The program or unit offers an optional orientation for new students individually by special arrangement.

Unique Aids and Services Aids, services, or accommodations include weekly meetings with faculty.

Subject-area Tutoring Tutoring is offered one-on-one and in small groups for some subjects. Tutoring is provided through the program or unit via trained peer tutors. Tutoring is also provided collaboratively through on-campus or off-campus services via trained peer tutors.

Basic Skills Remediation Remediation is offered one-on-one for learning strategies, math, spoken language, study skills, time management, and written language. Remediation is provided through the program or unit via trained peer tutors and other.

Enrichment Enrichment programs are available through the program or unit for learning strategies, math, oral communication skills, reading, self-advocacy, stress management, study skills, test taking, time management, and written composition skills. Program for career planning is provided collaboratively through on-campus or off-campus services.

Application For admittance to the program or unit, students are required to apply to the program directly and provide a psychoeducational report (3 years old or less). It is recommended that students provide documentation of high school services. Upon acceptance, documentation of need for services should be sent to both admissions and the LD program or unit. *Application deadline (institutional):* 3/1. *Application deadline (LD program):* Rolling/continuous for fall and rolling/continuous for spring.

Written Policies Written policies regarding course substitutions, general/basic LD accommodations, and substitutions and waivers of graduation requirements are available through the program or unit directly.

Washington and Lee University

Lexington, VA 24450-0303

http://counsel.wlu.edu/policy/ugrpol1.htm

Contact: Dr. Jeanine Stewart, Associate Dean of the College. Phone: 540-458-8746. Fax: 540-458-8945. E-mail: stewartj@wlu.edu.

Approximately 37 registered undergraduate students were served during 2002-03. Academic advisers, counselors, and other are provided collaboratively through on-campus or off-campus services.

Subject-area Tutoring Tutoring is offered one-on-one for most subjects. Tutoring is provided collaboratively through on-campus or off-campus services via trained peer tutors and other.

Enrichment Programs for career planning, college survival skills, health and nutrition, learning strategies, medication management, practical computer skills, stress management, study skills, time management, and written composition skills are provided collaboratively through on-campus or off-campus services.

Application For admittance to the program or unit, students are required to apply to the program directly, provide a psychoeducational report (2 years old or less), and provide a meeting with Associate Dean. It is recommended that students provide documentation of high school services. Upon application, materials documenting need for services should be sent only to the LD program or unit. Upon acceptance, documentation of need for services should be sent only to the LD program or unit. *Application deadline (institutional):* 1/15. *Application deadline (LD program):* Rolling/continuous for fall and rolling/continuous for spring.

Written Policies Written policy regarding general/basic LD accommodations is available on the program Web site.

Washington State University

Pullman, WA 99164

http://www.wsu.edu/

Contact: Dr. Susan V. Schaeffer, Director. Phone: 509-335-3417. Fax: 509-335-8511. E-mail: schaeff@wsu.edu.

The program or unit includes 4 full-time staff members and 1 part-time staff member. LD specialists and remediation/learning specialists are provided through the program or unit. Academic advisers, counselors, diagnostic specialists, regular education teachers, and trained peer tutors are provided collaboratively through on-campus or off-campus services.

Unique Aids and Services Aids, services, or accommodations include priority registration.

Subject-area Tutoring Tutoring is offered one-on-one for most subjects. Tutoring is provided collaboratively through on-campus or off-campus services via trained peer tutors.

Student Organization Disability Resource Center consists of 6 members.

Application For admittance to the program or unit, students are required to apply to the program directly and provide a psychoeducational report. It is recommended that students provide documentation of high school services. Upon acceptance, documentation of need for services should be sent only to the LD program or unit. *Application deadline (LD program):* Rolling/continuous for fall and rolling/continuous for spring.

Written Policies Written policy regarding general/basic LD accommodations is available on the program Web site. Written policies regarding course substitutions and general/basic LD accommodations are available through the program or unit directly.

Waynesburg College

51 West College Street
Waynesburg, PA 15370-1222
http://www.waynesburg.edu/
Contact: Thomas Helmick Thomas Helmick, Director of Human Resources and Disability Services. Phone: 724-852-3210. Fax: 724-852-3269. E-mail: thelmick@waynesburg.com.

Approximately 20 registered undergraduate students were served during 2002-03. The program or unit includes 1 full-time staff member. Academic advisers, professional tutors, and regular education teachers are provided collaboratively through on-campus or off-campus services.

Subject-area Tutoring Tutoring is offered one-on-one and in small groups for some subjects. Tutoring is provided collaboratively through on-campus or off-campus services via professional tutors.

Application It is recommended that students provide a psychoeducational report (1 year old or less) and provide documentation of high school services. Upon application, materials documenting need for services should be sent only to admissions with institutional application materials. Upon acceptance, documentation of need for services should be sent only to the LD program or unit. *Application deadline (institutional):* Continuous. *Application deadline (LD program):* Rolling/continuous for fall and rolling/continuous for spring.

Written Policies Written policies regarding course substitutions, general/basic LD accommodations, grade forgiveness, reduced course loads, substitutions and waivers of admissions requirements, and substitutions and waivers of graduation requirements are outlined in the school's catalog/handbook.

Wayne State College

1111 Main Street

Wayne, NE 68787
http://www.wsc.edu/
Contact: Dr. Jeff B. Carstens, Assistant Dean for Student Life. Phone: 402-375-7213. Fax: 402-375-7079. E-mail: jecarst1@wsc.edu.

Approximately 25 registered undergraduate students were served during 2002-03. The program or unit includes 1 part-time staff member. Counselors and graduate assistants/students are provided through the program or unit. Academic advisers, counselors, diagnostic specialists, LD specialists, regular education teachers, and trained peer tutors are provided collaboratively through on-campus or off-campus services.

Unique Aids and Services Aids, services, or accommodations include advocates and priority registration.

Subject-area Tutoring Tutoring is offered one-on-one, in small groups, and in class-size groups for most subjects. Tutoring is provided collaboratively through on-campus or off-campus services via graduate assistants/students and trained peer tutors.

Diagnostic Testing Testing for auditory processing, intelligence, math, neuropsychological, personality, reading, spelling, spoken language, and written language is provided collaboratively through on-campus or off-campus services.

Enrichment Enrichment programs are available through the program or unit for self-advocacy. Programs for career planning, college survival skills, health and nutrition, learning strategies, stress management, study skills, test taking, time management, vocabulary development, and written composition skills are provided collaboratively through on-campus or off-campus services. Credit is offered for college survival skills, health and nutrition, and stress management.

Student Organization Able Capable and Equal (ACE) consists of 15 members.

Application For admittance to the program or unit, students are required to provide a psychoeducational report (3 years old or less). It is recommended that students provide documentation of high school services. Upon application, materials documenting need for services should be sent only to the LD program or unit. Upon acceptance, documentation of need for services should be sent only to the LD program or unit. *Application deadline (institutional):* Continuous. *Application deadline (LD program):* Rolling/continuous for fall and rolling/continuous for spring.

Written Policies Written policy regarding general/basic LD accommodations is available on the program Web site. Written policy regarding general/basic LD accommodations is outlined in the school's catalog/handbook.

Wayne State University
Educational Accessibility Services, Academic Success Center

656 West Kirby Street
Detroit, MI 48202
http://www.eas.wayne.edu
Contact: Ms. Deborah E. Wright, University Counselor. Phone: 313-577-1851. Fax: 313-577-4898. E-mail: deborah.wright@wayne.edu. Head of LD Program: Dr.

Wayne State University (continued)
Susan L. Neste, Director of Academic Success Center.
Phone: 313-577-3165. E-mail: sneste@wayne.edu.

Educational Accessibility Services, Academic Success Center Approximately 70 registered undergraduate students were served during 2002-03. The program or unit includes 10 full-time and 20 part-time staff members. Counselors, diagnostic specialists, graduate assistants/students, professional tutors, remediation/learning specialists, skill tutors, and strategy tutors are provided through the program or unit. Academic advisers, coaches, LD specialists, regular education teachers, special education teachers, teacher trainees, trained peer tutors, and other are provided collaboratively through on-campus or off-campus services.

Unique Aids and Services Aids, services, or accommodations include advocates, priority registration, books on tape, alternative testing.

Subject-area Tutoring Tutoring is offered one-on-one and in small groups for most subjects. Tutoring is provided through the program or unit via computer-based instruction, graduate assistants/students, LD specialists, professional tutors, and trained peer tutors.

Diagnostic Testing Testing is provided through the program or unit for learning strategies, learning styles, reading, spoken language, study skills, and written language. Testing for auditory processing, handwriting, intelligence, math, motor skills, neuropsychological, personality, social skills, spelling, and visual processing is provided collaboratively through on-campus or off-campus services.

Basic Skills Remediation Remediation is offered one-on-one and in small groups for auditory processing, computer skills, learning strategies, math, reading, spelling, study skills, time management, visual processing, and written language. Remediation is provided through the program or unit via computer-based instruction, graduate assistants/students, LD specialists, professional tutors, regular education teachers, special education teachers, teacher trainees, and trained peer tutors.

Enrichment Enrichment programs are available through the program or unit for career planning, college survival skills, health and nutrition, learning strategies, math, oral communication skills, practical computer skills, reading, self-advocacy, stress management, study skills, test taking, time management, vocabulary development, and written composition skills. Program for stress management is provided collaboratively through on-campus or off-campus services.

Student Organization Abled Student Organization consists of 100 members.

Application For admittance to the program or unit, students are required to apply to the program directly, provide a psychoeducational report (3 years old or less), and provide a medical report. It is recommended that students provide documentation of high school services. Upon application, materials documenting need for services should be sent only to the LD program or unit. Upon acceptance, documentation of need for services should be sent only to the LD program or unit. *Application deadline (institutional):* 8/1. *Application deadline (LD program):* Rolling/continuous for fall and rolling/continuous for spring.

Written Policies Written policies regarding course substitutions, general/basic LD accommodations, grade forgiveness, reduced course loads, substitutions and waivers of admissions requirements, and substitutions and waivers of graduation requirements are available through the program or unit directly.

Webster University
Services for Students with Disabilities

470 East Lockwood Avenue
St. Louis, MO 63119-3194
http://www.webster.edu/acadaffairs/asp/arc.htm
Contact: Phone: 314-968-6900. Fax: 314-968-7115.

Services for Students with Disabilities Approximately 130 registered undergraduate students were served during 2002-03. The program or unit includes 2 full-time and 2 part-time staff members. Coaches, LD specialists, skill tutors, strategy tutors, and trained peer tutors are provided through the program or unit. Academic advisers, coaches, counselors, diagnostic specialists, graduate assistants/students, and professional tutors are provided collaboratively through on-campus or off-campus services.

Unique Aids and Services Aids, services, or accommodations include career counseling, digital textbooks, faculty training, and weekly meetings with faculty.

Subject-area Tutoring Tutoring is offered one-on-one and in small groups for all subjects. Tutoring is provided through the program or unit via computer-based instruction, graduate assistants/students, LD specialists, trained peer tutors, and other.

Diagnostic Testing Testing is provided through the program or unit for learning strategies, learning styles, math, reading, spelling, study skills, and written language. Testing for auditory processing, handwriting, intelligence, motor skills, neuropsychological, social skills, spoken language, and visual processing is provided collaboratively through on-campus or off-campus services.

Basic Skills Remediation Remediation is offered one-on-one and in class-size groups for computer skills, learning strategies, math, study skills, time management, and written language. Remediation is provided through the program or unit via LD specialists and trained peer tutors.

Enrichment Enrichment programs are available through the program or unit for learning strategies, self-advocacy, study skills, test taking, time management, vocabulary development, and written composition skills. Programs for career planning, college survival skills, health and nutrition, learning strategies, math, medication management, oral communication skills, stress management, test taking, time management, vocabulary development, and written composition skills are provided collaboratively through on-campus or off-campus services.

Fees *Diagnostic Testing* fee is applicable.

Application For admittance to the program or unit, students are required to apply to the program directly and provide a psychoeducational report. It is recommended that students provide documentation of high school services. Upon acceptance, documentation of need for services should be sent only to the LD program or unit. *Application deadline (institutional):* 7/1. *Application deadline (LD program):* Rolling/continuous for fall and rolling/continuous for spring.

Written Policies Written policy regarding general/basic LD accommodations is available on the program Web site. Written policy regarding general/basic LD accommodations is outlined in the school's catalog/handbook. Written policies regarding course substitutions, general/basic LD accommodations, reduced course loads, substitutions and waivers of admissions requirements, and substitutions and waivers of graduation requirements are available through the program or unit directly.

Wells College

170 Main Street
Aurora, NY 13026
http://www.wells.edu/

Contact: Diane Kay Koester, Associate Dean for Academic and Learning Resources. Phone: 315-364-3241. Fax: 315-364-3383. E-mail: dkoester@wells.edu.

Approximately 10 registered undergraduate students were served during 2002-03. The program or unit includes 1 part-time staff member. Academic advisers, coaches, counselors, regular education teachers, and trained peer tutors are provided collaboratively through on-campus or off-campus services.

Subject-area Tutoring Tutoring is offered one-on-one and in small groups for some subjects. Tutoring is provided collaboratively through on-campus or off-campus services via trained peer tutors.

Enrichment Programs for career planning, learning strategies, math, study skills, test taking, and time management are provided collaboratively through on-campus or off-campus services.

Application For admittance to the program or unit, students are required to provide a psychoeducational report and provide documentation of high school services. It is recommended that students apply to the program directly. Upon acceptance, documentation of need for services should be sent to both admissions and the LD program or unit. *Application deadline (institutional): 3/1. Application deadline (LD program):* Rolling/continuous for fall and rolling/continuous for spring.

Written Policies Written policy regarding general/basic LD accommodations is outlined in the school's catalog/handbook.

Wesleyan University

Middletown, CT 06459-0260
http://www.wesleyan.edu/

Contact: Ms. Vancenia Rutherford, Associate Dean of the College. Phone: 860-685-2765. Fax: 860-685-3940. E-mail: vrutherford@wesleyan.edu.

The program or unit includes 1 part-time staff member. Academic advisers, counselors, regular education teachers, and trained peer tutors are provided collaboratively through on-campus or off-campus services.

Orientation The program or unit offers a mandatory orientation for new students individually by special arrangement.

Unique Aids and Services Aids, services, or accommodations include faculty consultation as needed.

Subject-area Tutoring Tutoring is offered one-on-one, in small groups, and in class-size groups for most subjects. Tutoring is provided collaboratively through on-campus or off-campus services via graduate assistants/students, trained peer tutors, and other.

Enrichment Programs for career planning, college survival skills, health and nutrition, math, self-advocacy, stress management, study skills, time management, and written composition skills are provided collaboratively through on-campus or off-campus services.

Application For admittance to the program or unit, students are required to provide a psychoeducational report (3 years old or less). It is recommended that students apply to the program directly and

provide documentation of high school services. Upon acceptance, documentation of need for services should be sent only to the LD program or unit. *Application deadline (institutional): 1/1. Application deadline (LD program):* Rolling/continuous for fall and rolling/continuous for spring.

Written Policies Written policy regarding general/basic LD accommodations is outlined in the school's catalog/handbook. Written policy regarding general/basic LD accommodations is available through the program or unit directly.

West Chester University of Pennsylvania
Office of Services for Students with Disabilities (OSSD)

University Avenue and High Street
West Chester, PA 19383
http://www.wcupa.edu/

Contact: Phone: 610-436-1000.

Office of Services for Students with Disabilities (OSSD)
Approximately 350 registered undergraduate students were served during 2002-03. The program or unit includes 3 full-time and 10 part-time staff members. Coaches, diagnostic specialists, graduate assistants/students, LD specialists, professional tutors, remediation/learning specialists, skill tutors, and strategy tutors are provided through the program or unit. Academic advisers, counselors, and regular education teachers are provided collaboratively through on-campus or off-campus services.

Orientation The program or unit offers an optional orientation for new students before classes begin and during summer prior to enrollment.

Unique Aids and Services Aids, services, or accommodations include digital textbooks, faculty training, personal coach, priority registration, support groups, and weekly meetings with faculty.

Subject-area Tutoring Tutoring is offered one-on-one and in small groups for some subjects. Tutoring is provided through the program or unit via graduate assistants/students, LD specialists, and professional tutors. Tutoring is also provided collaboratively through on-campus or off-campus services via trained peer tutors.

Basic Skills Remediation Remediation is offered in class-size groups. Remediation is provided collaboratively through on-campus or off-campus services via regular education teachers.

Enrichment Enrichment programs are available through the program or unit for learning strategies, math, self-advocacy, study skills, test taking, and time management. Programs for college survival skills, health and nutrition, stress management, and written composition skills are provided collaboratively through on-campus or off-campus services.

Student Organization Association for Disability Awareness consists of 7 members.

Application For admittance to the program or unit, students are required to provide a psychoeducational report. It is recommended that students apply to the program directly and provide documentation of high school services. Upon acceptance, documentation of need for services should be sent only to the LD program or unit. *Application deadline (institutional): Continuous. Application deadline (LD program):* Rolling/continuous for fall and rolling/continuous for spring.

West Chester University of Pennsylvania (continued)

Written Policies Written policy regarding general/basic LD accommodations is available on the program Web site. Written policy regarding general/basic LD accommodations is outlined in the school's catalog/handbook. Written policy regarding substitutions and waivers of admissions requirements is available through the program or unit directly.

Western Carolina University
Student Support Services

Cullowhee, NC 28723

http://www.wcu.edu/

Contact: Ms. Carol M. Mellen, Director of Student Support Services. Phone: 828-227-7127. Fax: 828-227-7078. E-mail: mellen@email.wcu.edu.

Student Support Services Approximately 90 registered undergraduate students were served during 2002-03. The program or unit includes 5 full-time staff members and 1 part-time staff member. Academic advisers, coaches, counselors, graduate assistants/students, professional tutors, regular education teachers, skill tutors, and trained peer tutors are provided through the program or unit. Academic advisers, coaches, counselors, graduate assistants/students, professional tutors, regular education teachers, skill tutors, and trained peer tutors are provided collaboratively through on-campus or off-campus services.

Unique Aids and Services Aids, services, or accommodations include career counseling, faculty training, and priority registration.

Subject-area Tutoring Tutoring is offered one-on-one and in small groups for most subjects. Tutoring is provided through the program or unit via graduate assistants/students, professional tutors, and trained peer tutors. Tutoring is also provided collaboratively through on-campus or off-campus services via graduate assistants/students, professional tutors, and trained peer tutors.

Enrichment Enrichment programs are available through the program or unit for career planning, learning strategies, self-advocacy, stress management, study skills, test taking, time management, and written composition skills. Programs for career planning, college survival skills, health and nutrition, math, oral communication skills, practical computer skills, reading, stress management, study skills, test taking, time management, vocabulary development, and written composition skills are provided collaboratively through on-campus or off-campus services. Credit is offered for college survival skills, health and nutrition, math, oral communication skills, practical computer skills, reading, study skills, test taking, time management, vocabulary development, and written composition skills.

Application For admittance to the program or unit, students are required to provide a psychoeducational report. It is recommended that students provide documentation of high school services. Upon acceptance, documentation of need for services should be sent only to the LD program or unit. *Application deadline (institutional):* 8/1. *Application deadline (LD program):* Rolling/continuous for fall and rolling/continuous for spring.

Written Policies Written policy regarding general/basic LD accommodations is outlined in the school's catalog/handbook.

Western Illinois University
Disability Support Services

1 University Circle

Macomb, IL 61455-1390

http://www.student.services.wiu.edu/dss/

Contact: Ms. Gretchen Steil Weiss, Learning Specialist. Phone: 309-298-2512. Fax: 309-298-2361. E-mail: ge-steilweiss@wiu.edu.

Disability Support Services Approximately 120 registered undergraduate students were served during 2002-03. The program or unit includes 2 full-time staff members. Graduate assistants/students, LD specialists, remediation/learning specialists, skill tutors, strategy tutors, and trained peer tutors are provided through the program or unit. Academic advisers, coaches, counselors, diagnostic specialists, regular education teachers, special education teachers, teacher trainees, and trained peer tutors are provided collaboratively through on-campus or off-campus services.

Orientation The program or unit offers an optional 1-hour orientation for new students before classes begin, after classes begin, and individually by special arrangement.

Unique Aids and Services Aids, services, or accommodations include faculty training, personal coach, priority registration, alternative textbook formats.

Subject-area Tutoring Tutoring is offered one-on-one for some subjects. Tutoring is provided through the program or unit via graduate assistants/students. Tutoring is also provided collaboratively through on-campus or off-campus services via trained peer tutors.

Basic Skills Remediation Remediation is offered in class-size groups for math and written language. Remediation is provided collaboratively through on-campus or off-campus services via regular education teachers.

Enrichment Enrichment programs are available through the program or unit for college survival skills, learning strategies, self-advocacy, study skills, test taking, and time management. Programs for career planning, health and nutrition, learning strategies, math, oral communication skills, practical computer skills, stress management, study skills, test taking, and time management are provided collaboratively through on-campus or off-campus services. Credit is offered for college survival skills, math, oral communication skills, and practical computer skills.

Student Organization Promoting the Rights of Individuals with Disabilities Everywhere consists of 10 members.

Application For admittance to the program or unit, students are required to apply to the program directly and provide a psychoeducational report (3 years old or less). It is recommended that students provide documentation of high school services and provide individualized transitional plan. Upon application, materials documenting need for services should be sent only to the LD program or unit. Upon acceptance, documentation of need for services should be sent only to the LD program or unit. *Application deadline (institutional):* 8/1. *Application deadline (LD program):* Rolling/continuous for fall and rolling/continuous for spring.

Written Policies Written policies regarding course substitutions, general/basic LD accommodations, and substitutions and waivers of graduation requirements are available on the program Web site. Written policy regarding grade forgiveness is outlined in the school's catalog/handbook. Written policies regarding course substitutions, general/basic LD accommodations, and substitutions and waivers of graduation requirements are available through the program or unit directly.

Western Kentucky University
Student Disability Services

1 Big Red Way
Bowling Green, KY 42101-3576
http://www.wku.edu/Dept/Support/Legal/EOO/sds.htm
Contact: Mr. Matt Davis, Coordinator of Student Disability Services. Phone: 270-745-5004. Fax: 270-745-6289. E-mail: matt.davis@wku.edu.

Student Disability Services Approximately 120 registered undergraduate students were served during 2002-03. The program or unit includes 2 full-time staff members. Regular education teachers are provided through the program or unit. Academic advisers, coaches, counselors, diagnostic specialists, graduate assistants/students, LD specialists, professional tutors, remediation/learning specialists, skill tutors, special education teachers, strategy tutors, teacher trainees, and trained peer tutors are provided collaboratively through on-campus or off-campus services.
Summer Program To help prepare for the demands of college, there is an optional 5-day summer program prior to entering the school.
Unique Aids and Services Aids, services, or accommodations include career counseling and priority registration.
Subject-area Tutoring Tutoring is offered one-on-one and in small groups for most subjects. Tutoring is provided collaboratively through on-campus or off-campus services via computer-based instruction, graduate assistants/students, and trained peer tutors.
Diagnostic Testing Testing for auditory processing, intelligence, math, neuropsychological, reading, spelling, visual processing, and written language is provided collaboratively through on-campus or off-campus services.
Enrichment Programs for career planning, college survival skills, health and nutrition, learning strategies, math, medication management, oral communication skills, practical computer skills, reading, self-advocacy, stress management, study skills, test taking, time management, vocabulary development, and written composition skills are provided collaboratively through on-campus or off-campus services. Credit is offered for college survival skills, health and nutrition, math, oral communication skills, practical computer skills, reading, and study skills.
Fees *Summer Program* fee is $100.
Application For admittance to the program or unit, students are required to provide a psychoeducational report (3 years old or less). It is recommended that students provide documentation of high school services. Upon application, materials documenting need for services should be sent only to the LD program or unit. Upon acceptance, documentation of need for services should be sent only to the LD program or unit. *Application deadline (institutional):* 8/1. *Application deadline (LD program):* Rolling/continuous for fall and rolling/continuous for spring.

Written Policies Written policies regarding course substitutions, general/basic LD accommodations, grade forgiveness, reduced course loads, substitutions and waivers of admissions requirements, and substitutions and waivers of graduation requirements are available on the program Web site. Written policies regarding course substitutions, grade forgiveness, reduced course loads, substitutions and waivers of admissions requirements, and substitutions and waivers of graduation requirements are outlined in the school's catalog/handbook. Written policy regarding general/basic LD accommodations is available through the program or unit directly.

Western New England College
Student Disability Services

1215 Wilbraham Road
Springfield, MA 01119-2654
http://www.wnec.edu/html/VA.html#student
Contact: Dr. Bonni Alpert, Director of Student Disability Services. Phone: 413-782-1257. Fax: 413-782-1746. E-mail: balpert@wnec.edu.

Student Disability Services Approximately 100 registered undergraduate students were served during 2002-03. The program or unit includes 2 full-time staff members and 1 part-time staff member. Coaches, graduate assistants/students, LD specialists, professional tutors, regular education teachers, remediation/learning specialists, skill tutors, and strategy tutors are provided through the program or unit. Academic advisers, counselors, diagnostic specialists, graduate assistants/students, professional tutors, regular education teachers, remediation/learning specialists, skill tutors, and trained peer tutors are provided collaboratively through on-campus or off-campus services.
Orientation The program or unit offers an optional orientation for new students during registration and individually by special arrangement.
Summer Program To help prepare for the demands of college, there is an optional summer program prior to entering the school.
Unique Aids and Services Aids, services, or accommodations include advocates, career counseling, digital textbooks, faculty training, personal coach, priority registration, tutoring, accommodations.
Subject-area Tutoring Tutoring is offered one-on-one. Tutoring is provided through the program or unit via graduate assistants/students, LD specialists, professional tutors, and trained peer tutors. Tutoring is also provided collaboratively through on-campus or off-campus services via graduate assistants/students, professional tutors, and trained peer tutors.
Basic Skills Remediation Remediation is offered in class-size groups for math, reading, and written language. Remediation is provided collaboratively through on-campus or off-campus services via graduate assistants/students and regular education teachers.
Enrichment Enrichment programs are available through the program or unit for learning strategies, self-advocacy, stress management, study skills, test taking, and time management. Programs for career planning, college survival skills, health and nutrition, learning strategies, math, oral communication skills, practical computer skills, reading, stress management, study skills, time management, and written composition skills are provided collaboratively through

Western New England College (continued)

on-campus or off-campus services. Credit is offered for college survival skills, health and nutrition, learning strategies, math, oral communication skills, practical computer skills, reading, time management, and written composition skills.

Application For admittance to the program or unit, students are required to apply to the program directly and provide a psychoeducational report. It is recommended that students provide documentation of high school services. Upon acceptance, documentation of need for services should be sent only to the LD program or unit. *Application deadline (institutional):* Continuous. *Application deadline (LD program):* Rolling/continuous for fall and rolling/continuous for spring.

Written Policies Written policy regarding general/basic LD accommodations is outlined in the school's catalog/handbook. Written policy regarding general/basic LD accommodations is available through the program or unit directly.

Western Oregon University
Office of Disability Services

345 North Monmouth Avenue

Monmouth, OR 97361-1394

http://www.wou.edu/student/disability/

Contact: Ms. Annette Leonard, Director. Phone: 503-838-8250. Fax: 503-838-8721. E-mail: ods@wou.edu.

Office of Disability Services Approximately 75 registered undergraduate students were served during 2002-03. The program or unit includes 2 full-time staff members. Counselors are provided through the program or unit. Academic advisers, counselors, skill tutors, strategy tutors, and trained peer tutors are provided collaboratively through on-campus or off-campus services.

Unique Aids and Services Aids, services, or accommodations include priority registration, support groups, limited academic coaching.

Subject-area Tutoring Tutoring is offered one-on-one for most subjects. Tutoring is provided collaboratively through on-campus or off-campus services via graduate assistants/students, trained peer tutors, and other.

Diagnostic Testing Testing for auditory processing, intelligence, learning strategies, learning styles, math, neuropsychological, reading, spelling, study skills, visual processing, written language, and other services is provided collaboratively through on-campus or off-campus services.

Fees *Diagnostic Testing* fee is applicable.

Application For admittance to the program or unit, students are required to apply to the program directly and provide a psychoeducational report (3 years old or less). It is recommended that students provide documentation of high school services. Upon acceptance, documentation of need for services should be sent only to the LD program or unit. *Application deadline (institutional):* Continuous. *Application deadline (LD program):* Rolling/continuous for fall and rolling/continuous for spring.

Written Policies Written policy regarding general/basic LD accommodations is available on the program Web site. Written policy regarding general/basic LD accommodations is available through the program or unit directly.

Western State College of Colorado
Disability Services, Learning Assistance Center

600 North Adams Street

Gunnison, CO 81231

http://www.western.edu

Contact: Ms. Jan Edwards, Director of Learning Assistance Center. Phone: 970-943-7056. Fax: 970-943-3409. E-mail: jedwards@western.edu.

Disability Services, Learning Assistance Center Approximately 100 registered undergraduate students were served during 2002-03. The program or unit includes 1 full-time and 1 part-time staff member. Academic advisers, counselors, remediation/learning specialists, and other are provided through the program or unit. Academic advisers, counselors, regular education teachers, trained peer tutors, and other are provided collaboratively through on-campus or off-campus services.

Orientation The program or unit offers an optional 2-hour orientation for new students after classes begin and individually by special arrangement.

Unique Aids and Services Aids, services, or accommodations include priority registration.

Subject-area Tutoring Tutoring is offered one-on-one and in small groups for some subjects. Tutoring is provided collaboratively through on-campus or off-campus services via trained peer tutors.

Basic Skills Remediation Remediation is offered one-on-one and in small groups for learning strategies, study skills, and time management. Remediation is provided through the program or unit. Remediation is also provided collaboratively through on-campus or off-campus services.

Enrichment Enrichment programs are available through the program or unit for college survival skills, learning strategies, self-advocacy, stress management, study skills, test taking, and time management. Programs for career planning, college survival skills, learning strategies, stress management, study skills, test taking, and time management are provided collaboratively through on-campus or off-campus services.

Student Organization Community of Abled Students consists of 20 members.

Application For admittance to the program or unit, students are required to provide a psychoeducational report (3 years old or less). It is recommended that students provide documentation of high school services and provide a completed Request for Disability Support Services form. Upon acceptance, documentation of need for services should be sent only to the LD program or unit. *Application deadline (institutional):* Continuous. *Application deadline (LD program):* Rolling/continuous for fall and rolling/continuous for spring.

Written Policies Written policies regarding course substitutions and general/basic LD accommodations are available on the program Web site. Written policies regarding course substitutions and general/basic LD accommodations are available through the program or unit directly.

Western Washington University
Disability Resources for Students

516 High Street

Bellingham, WA 98225-5996

http://www.ac.wwu.edu/~osl/drs/drsindex.html

Contact: David Brunnemer, Associate Director, Office of Student Life. Phone: 360-650-3844. Fax: 360-650-3715. E-mail: david.brunnemer@wwu.edu.

Disability Resources for Students Approximately 224 registered undergraduate students were served during 2002-03. The program or unit includes 1 full-time and 3 part-time staff members. Academic advisers, counselors, graduate assistants/students, LD specialists, regular education teachers, and strategy tutors are provided collaboratively through on-campus or off-campus services.

Unique Aids and Services Aids, services, or accommodations include career counseling, faculty training, and priority registration.

Subject-area Tutoring Tutoring is offered one-on-one and in small groups. Tutoring is provided collaboratively through on-campus or off-campus services via graduate assistants/students and trained peer tutors.

Enrichment Programs for career planning, health and nutrition, learning strategies, math, medication management, reading, self-advocacy, stress management, study skills, test taking, time management, and written composition skills are provided collaboratively through on-campus or off-campus services.

Application For admittance to the program or unit, students are required to provide a psychoeducational report. It is recommended that students provide documentation of high school services. Upon application, materials documenting need for services should be sent only to the LD program or unit. *Application deadline (institutional):* 3/1. *Application deadline (LD program):* Rolling/continuous for fall.

Written Policies Written policy regarding general/basic LD accommodations is available on the program Web site. Written policies regarding course substitutions, general/basic LD accommodations, reduced course loads, and substitutions and waivers of graduation requirements are available through the program or unit directly.

West Liberty State College

PO Box 295

West Liberty, WV 26074

http://www.wlsc.edu/

Contact: Phone: 304-336-5000. Fax: 304-336-8285.

The program or unit includes 1 full-time and 1 part-time staff member. Graduate assistants/students and other are provided through the program or unit. Academic advisers, coaches, counselors, regular education teachers, and special education teachers are provided collaboratively through on-campus or off-campus services.

Subject-area Tutoring Tutoring is offered one-on-one for most subjects. Tutoring is provided collaboratively through on-campus or off-campus services via trained peer tutors.

Diagnostic Testing Testing for auditory processing, intelligence, learning styles, math, motor skills, neuropsychological, personality, reading, spelling, spoken language, visual processing, written language, and other services is provided collaboratively through on-campus or off-campus services.

Enrichment Programs for career planning, college survival skills, health and nutrition, learning strategies, self-advocacy, stress management, study skills, test taking, and time management are provided collaboratively through on-campus or off-campus services.

Application For admittance to the program or unit, students are required to provide a psychoeducational report and provide psychological report only if psychoeducational report is not available. It is recommended that students provide documentation of high school services. Upon application, materials documenting need for services should be sent to both admissions and the LD program or unit. Upon acceptance, documentation of need for services should be sent only to the LD program or unit. *Application deadline (LD program):* 8/31 for fall. 1/31 for spring.

Written Policies Written policies regarding general/basic LD accommodations and substitutions and waivers of admissions requirements are available through the program or unit directly.

Westminster College
Disabilities Services for Students

319 South Market Street

New Wilmington, PA 16172-0001

http://www.westminster.edu/

Contact: Dr. Linda P. Domanski, Assistant Professor of Education. Phone: 724-946-7182. Fax: 724-946-6180. E-mail: domanslp@westminster.edu. Head of LD Program: Dr. Neal A. Edman, Dean of Student Affairs. Phone: 724-946-7110. Fax: 724-946-7171. E-mail: nedman@westminster.edu.

Disabilities Services for Students Approximately 35 registered undergraduate students were served during 2002-03. The program or unit includes 2 part-time staff members. LD specialists and special education teachers are provided through the program or unit. Academic advisers, counselors, graduate assistants/students, LD specialists, regular education teachers, skill tutors, special education teachers, and trained peer tutors are provided collaboratively through on-campus or off-campus services.

Unique Aids and Services Aids, services, or accommodations include weekly meetings with faculty.

Subject-area Tutoring Tutoring is offered one-on-one for most subjects. Tutoring is provided through the program or unit via LD specialists. Tutoring is also provided collaboratively through on-campus or off-campus services via graduate assistants/students and LD specialists.

Basic Skills Remediation Remediation is offered in class-size groups for reading and study skills. Remediation is provided collaboratively through on-campus or off-campus services via regular education teachers.

Enrichment Programs for career planning, health and nutrition, oral communication skills, study skills, test taking, and time management are provided collaboratively through on-campus or off-campus services.

Westminster College (continued)

Application For admittance to the program or unit, students are required to provide a psychoeducational report (3 years old or less), provide documentation of high school services, and provide documentation from Office of Vocational Rehabilitation. Upon acceptance, documentation of need for services should be sent only to the LD program or unit. *Application deadline (institutional):* 5/1. *Application deadline (LD program):* Rolling/continuous for fall and rolling/continuous for spring.

Written Policies Written policy regarding general/basic LD accommodations is outlined in the school's catalog/handbook. Written policy regarding general/basic LD accommodations is available through the program or unit directly.

Westminster College

1840 South 1300 East

Salt Lake City, UT 84105-3697

http://www.wcslc.edu/

Contact: Ms. Ginny DeWitt, Associate Director of START Center and Coordinator of SSD Program. Phone: 801-832-2280. Fax: 801-832-3101. E-mail: gdewitt@westminstercollege.edu.

The program or unit includes 1 full-time staff member. Diagnostic specialists are provided through the program or unit. Academic advisers, counselors, diagnostic specialists, and regular education teachers are provided collaboratively through on-campus or off-campus services.

Unique Aids and Services Aids, services, or accommodations include priority registration.

Subject-area Tutoring Tutoring is offered one-on-one for most subjects. Tutoring is provided collaboratively through on-campus or off-campus services via trained peer tutors.

Basic Skills Remediation Remediation is offered one-on-one for computer skills, learning strategies, math, study skills, time management, and written language. Remediation is provided through the program or unit. Remediation is also provided collaboratively through on-campus or off-campus services via trained peer tutors and other.

Enrichment Programs for career planning, college survival skills, learning strategies, practical computer skills, self-advocacy, stress management, study skills, test taking, time management, and written composition skills are provided collaboratively through on-campus or off-campus services. Credit is offered for college survival skills and practical computer skills.

Application For admittance to the program or unit, students are required to provide a psychoeducational report. It is recommended that students provide documentation of high school services. Upon acceptance, documentation of need for services should be sent only to the LD program or unit. *Application deadline (institutional):* Continuous. *Application deadline (LD program):* Rolling/continuous for fall and rolling/continuous for spring.

Written Policies Written policy regarding general/basic LD accommodations is available on the program Web site. Written policies regarding general/basic LD accommodations and reduced course loads are available through the program or unit directly.

West Texas A&M University
Student Disability Services

2501 4th Avenue

Canyon, TX 79016-0001

http://www.wtamu.edu/

Contact: James Eric Lathrop, Coordinator of Student Disability Services. Phone: 806-651-2335. Fax: 806-651-2362. E-mail: elathrop@mail.wtamu.edu.

Student Disability Services Approximately 105 registered undergraduate students were served during 2002-03. The program or unit includes 3 full-time staff members and 1 part-time staff member. Academic advisers, counselors, and strategy tutors are provided through the program or unit. Academic advisers, counselors, professional tutors, regular education teachers, remediation/learning specialists, skill tutors, special education teachers, teacher trainees, and trained peer tutors are provided collaboratively through on-campus or off-campus services.

Unique Aids and Services Aids, services, or accommodations include advocates and career counseling.

Subject-area Tutoring Tutoring is offered one-on-one for most subjects. Tutoring is provided collaboratively through on-campus or off-campus services via professional tutors and trained peer tutors.

Diagnostic Testing Testing is provided through the program or unit for learning strategies and learning styles. Testing for auditory processing, intelligence, learning strategies, learning styles, math, motor skills, neuropsychological, reading, spelling, spoken language, visual processing, and written language is provided collaboratively through on-campus or off-campus services.

Basic Skills Remediation Remediation is offered in class-size groups for auditory processing, math, reading, spoken language, and written language. Remediation is provided collaboratively through on-campus or off-campus services via professional tutors, regular education teachers, and trained peer tutors.

Application For admittance to the program or unit, students are required to provide a psychoeducational report (3 years old or less). It is recommended that students provide documentation of high school services. Upon application, materials documenting need for services should be sent only to admissions with institutional application materials. Upon acceptance, documentation of need for services should be sent only to the LD program or unit. *Application deadline (institutional):* Continuous. *Application deadline (LD program):* 5/31 for fall. 12/31 for spring.

Written Policies Written policies regarding course substitutions, general/basic LD accommodations, grade forgiveness, reduced course loads, substitutions and waivers of admissions requirements, and substitutions and waivers of graduation requirements are outlined in the school's catalog/handbook. Written policy regarding substitutions and waivers of admissions requirements is available through the program or unit directly.

West Virginia University

University Avenue

Morgantown, WV 26506

http://www.wvu.edu/

Contact: Ms. Rebecca Frances Berger, Disability Services Counselor and Interpreting Coordinator. Phone: 304-293-6700. Fax: 304-293-3861. E-mail: rebecca.berger@mail.wvu.edu. Head of LD Program: Dr. Richard Strasburger, Disability Services Counselor. Phone: 304-293-6700. Fax: 304-293-3861. E-mail: richard.strasburger@mail.wvu.edu.

Approximately 800 registered undergraduate students were served during 2002-03. The program or unit includes 3 full-time staff members. LD specialists are provided through the program or unit. Academic advisers, coaches, counselors, diagnostic specialists, regular education teachers, and skill tutors are provided collaboratively through on-campus or off-campus services.

Unique Aids and Services Aids, services, or accommodations include career counseling, priority registration, weekly meetings with faculty, classroom accommodations.

Diagnostic Testing Testing for auditory processing, intelligence, math, motor skills, neuropsychological, personality, spelling, visual processing, written language, and other services is provided collaboratively through on-campus or off-campus services.

Fees *Diagnostic Testing* fee is $150.

Application For admittance to the program or unit, students are required to apply to the program directly and provide a psychoeducational report (5 years old or less). It is recommended that students provide documentation of high school services. Upon application, materials documenting need for services should be sent only to the LD program or unit. Upon acceptance, documentation of need for services should be sent only to the LD program or unit. *Application deadline (institutional): 8/1. Application deadline (LD program):* Rolling/continuous for fall and rolling/continuous for spring.

Written Policies Written policy regarding general/basic LD accommodations is available on the program Web site. Written policies regarding course substitutions, general/basic LD accommodations, reduced course loads, substitutions and waivers of admissions requirements, and substitutions and waivers of graduation requirements are available through the program or unit directly.

Wheaton College

501 East College Avenue
Wheaton, IL 60187-5593
http://www.wheaton.edu/
Contact: Phone: 630-752-5000. Fax: 630-752-5285.

Approximately 19 registered undergraduate students were served during 2002-03. The program or unit includes 1 part-time staff member. Academic advisers, coaches, counselors, diagnostic specialists, and trained peer tutors are provided collaboratively through on-campus or off-campus services.

Unique Aids and Services Aids, services, or accommodations include support groups.

Subject-area Tutoring Tutoring is offered one-on-one for some subjects. Tutoring is provided collaboratively through on-campus or off-campus services via trained peer tutors and other.

Diagnostic Testing Testing for auditory processing, intelligence, learning strategies, learning styles, neuropsychological, personality, reading, social skills, study skills, visual processing, and written language is provided collaboratively through on-campus or off-campus services.

Enrichment Programs for career planning, health and nutrition, learning strategies, medication management, stress management, study skills, time management, and written composition skills are provided collaboratively through on-campus or off-campus services.

Application For admittance to the program or unit, students are required to apply to the program directly and provide a psychoeducational report (3 years old or less). It is recommended that students provide documentation of high school services. Upon acceptance, documentation of need for services should be sent only to the LD program or unit. *Application deadline (institutional): 1/15. Application deadline (LD program):* Rolling/continuous for fall and rolling/continuous for spring.

Written Policies Written policy regarding general/basic LD accommodations is available on the program Web site. Written policy regarding general/basic LD accommodations is outlined in the school's catalog/handbook. Written policy regarding course substitutions is available through the program or unit directly.

Wheelock College
Disability Services

200 The Riverway
Boston, MA 02215
http://www.wheelock.edu/dis/dishome.htm
Contact: Samantha G. Daley, Coordinator of Disability Services. Phone: 617-879-2304. Fax: 617-734-7103. E-mail: sdaley@wheelock.edu.

Disability Services Approximately 79 registered undergraduate students were served during 2002-03. The program or unit includes 1 full-time staff member. LD specialists, skill tutors, and strategy tutors are provided through the program or unit. Academic advisers, coaches, counselors, regular education teachers, remediation/learning specialists, skill tutors, strategy tutors, and trained peer tutors are provided collaboratively through on-campus or off-campus services.

Unique Aids and Services Aids, services, or accommodations include career counseling, digital textbooks, faculty training, and priority registration.

Subject-area Tutoring Tutoring is offered one-on-one, in small groups, and in class-size groups for all subjects. Tutoring is provided through the program or unit via LD specialists and professional tutors. Tutoring is also provided collaboratively through on-campus or off-campus services via professional tutors and trained peer tutors.

Basic Skills Remediation Remediation is offered one-on-one and in small groups for learning strategies, math, reading, spelling, study skills, time management, and written language. Remediation is provided through the program or unit via LD specialists and professional tutors. Remediation is also provided collaboratively through on-campus or off-campus services via professional tutors and trained peer tutors.

Enrichment Enrichment programs are available through the program or unit for college survival skills, learning strategies, math, reading, self-advocacy, study skills, test taking, time management, vocabulary development, and written composition skills. Programs for career planning, health and nutrition, learning strategies, math, medication management, oral communication skills, reading, stress management, study skills, test taking, time management, vocabu-

Wheelock College (continued)

lary development, and written composition skills are provided collaboratively through on-campus or off-campus services. Credit is offered for math, oral communication skills, stress management, and written composition skills.

Application For admittance to the program or unit, students are required to provide a psychoeducational report (5 years old or less). Upon acceptance, documentation of need for services should be sent only to the LD program or unit. *Application deadline (institutional): 3/1. Application deadline (LD program):* Rolling/continuous for fall and rolling/continuous for spring.

Written Policies Written policy regarding general/basic LD accommodations is available on the program Web site. Written policy regarding general/basic LD accommodations is outlined in the school's catalog/handbook. Written policy regarding general/basic LD accommodations is available through the program or unit directly.

Whitman College
Academic Resources

345 Boyer Avenue

Walla Walla, WA 99362-2083

http://www.whitman.edu/academic_resources/

Contact: Ms. Clare Carson, Director of Academic Resources. Phone: 509-527-5213. Fax: 509-526-4770. E-mail: carsonc@whitman.edu.

Academic Resources Approximately 90 registered undergraduate students were served during 2002-03.

Unique Aids and Services Aids, services, or accommodations include support groups, note-takers, peer tutors, assistive technology.

Subject-area Tutoring Tutoring is offered one-on-one. Tutoring is provided through the program or unit via trained peer tutors.

Basic Skills Remediation Remediation is offered one-on-one for learning strategies, math, reading, spelling, study skills, time management, and written language. Remediation is provided through the program or unit via professional tutors.

Application For admittance to the program or unit, students are required to provide a psychoeducational report (3 years old or less). Upon acceptance, documentation of need for services should be sent only to the LD program or unit. *Application deadline (institutional): 1/1. Application deadline (LD program):* Rolling/continuous for fall and rolling/continuous for spring.

Written Policies Written policy regarding general/basic LD accommodations is available on the program Web site. Written policy regarding general/basic LD accommodations is available through the program or unit directly.

Whittier College

13406 E Philadelphia Street

Whittier, CA 90608-0634

http://www.whittier.edu/

Contact: Ms. Joan Smith, Director. Phone: 562-907-4840. Fax: 562-907-4980. E-mail: jsmith@whittier.edu.

Approximately 60 registered undergraduate students were served during 2002-03. The program or unit includes 1 part-time staff member. Academic advisers, skill tutors, and trained peer tutors are provided collaboratively through on-campus or off-campus services.

Unique Aids and Services Aids, services, or accommodations include digital textbooks.

Subject-area Tutoring Tutoring is offered in small groups for all subjects. Tutoring is provided collaboratively through on-campus or off-campus services via trained peer tutors.

Basic Skills Remediation Remediation is offered one-on-one and in class-size groups for learning strategies, study skills, and time management. Remediation is provided collaboratively through on-campus or off-campus services via computer-based instruction and regular education teachers.

Enrichment Programs for career planning, college survival skills, health and nutrition, learning strategies, study skills, test taking, time management, and written composition skills are provided collaboratively through on-campus or off-campus services. Credit is offered for career planning, college survival skills, health and nutrition, and learning strategies.

Application For admittance to the program or unit, students are required to provide complete diagnostic documentation from a licensed professional. It is recommended that students provide documentation of high school services. Upon acceptance, documentation of need for services should be sent only to the LD program or unit. *Application deadline (institutional):* Continuous.

Written Policies Written policies regarding course substitutions, general/basic LD accommodations, reduced course loads, substitutions and waivers of admissions requirements, and substitutions and waivers of graduation requirements are available on the program Web site. Written policies regarding course substitutions, general/basic LD accommodations, reduced course loads, substitutions and waivers of admissions requirements, and substitutions and waivers of graduation requirements are outlined in the school's catalog/handbook. Written policies regarding course substitutions, general/basic LD accommodations, reduced course loads, substitutions and waivers of admissions requirements, and substitutions and waivers of graduation requirements are available through the program or unit directly.

Wichita State University
Office of Disability Services

1845 North Fairmount

Wichita, KS 67260

http://webs.wichita.edu/disserv/graphics.html

Contact: Mr. Grady L. Landrum, Director. Phone: 316-978-6970. Fax: 316-978-3114. E-mail: grady.landrum@wichita.edu.

Office of Disability Services Approximately 60 registered undergraduate students were served during 2002-03. The program or unit includes 2 full-time staff members. Academic advisers are provided collaboratively through on-campus or off-campus services.

Summer Program To help prepare for the demands of college, there is summer program prior to entering the school.

Unique Aids and Services Aids, services, or accommodations include career counseling and digital textbooks.

Diagnostic Testing Testing for auditory processing, intelligence, learning strategies, learning styles, visual processing, and written language is provided collaboratively through on-campus or off-campus services.

Enrichment Programs for career planning, college survival skills, learning strategies, practical computer skills, self-advocacy, stress management, study skills, test taking, and time management are provided collaboratively through on-campus or off-campus services. Credit is offered for college survival skills and practical computer skills.

Fees *Diagnostic Testing* fee is $250.

Application For admittance to the program or unit, students are required to provide a psychoeducational report (5 years old or less). It is recommended that students provide documentation of high school services. Upon acceptance, documentation of need for services should be sent only to the LD program or unit. *Application deadline (LD program):* 7/30 for fall. 1/15 for spring.

Written Policies Written policy regarding general/basic LD accommodations is outlined in the school's catalog/handbook. Written policy regarding general/basic LD accommodations is available through the program or unit directly.

Widener University
Enable

One University Place

Chester, PA 19013-5792

http://www.widener.edu/sss/sssenable.html

Contact: Mrs. Susan Cortese, Secretary, Academic Support Services. Phone: 610-499-1266. Fax: 610-499-1192. E-mail: susan.m.cortese@widener.edu. Head of LD Program: Dr. Rebecca Corsey McKeogh, Director of Enable. Phone: 610-499-4179. Fax: 610-499-1192.

Enable Approximately 220 registered undergraduate students were served during 2002-03. The program or unit includes 1 full-time and 7 part-time staff members. Coaches, counselors, graduate assistants/students, and LD specialists are provided through the program or unit. Counselors, professional tutors, skill tutors, strategy tutors, and trained peer tutors are provided collaboratively through on-campus or off-campus services.

Unique Aids and Services Aids, services, or accommodations include advocates and personal coach.

Subject-area Tutoring Tutoring is offered one-on-one and in small groups for most subjects. Tutoring is provided collaboratively through on-campus or off-campus services via graduate assistants/students, professional tutors, and trained peer tutors.

Basic Skills Remediation Remediation is offered one-on-one and in small groups for learning strategies, math, reading, study skills, time management, and written language. Remediation is provided collaboratively through on-campus or off-campus services via graduate assistants/students, professional tutors, and regular education teachers.

Application For admittance to the program or unit, students are required to provide a psychoeducational report (3 years old or less) and provide Request for Accommodation form (if accommodations are needed; not needed for academic coaching). Upon acceptance,

documentation of need for services should be sent only to the LD program or unit. *Application deadline (institutional):* Continuous. *Application deadline (LD program):* Rolling/continuous for fall and rolling/continuous for spring.

Written Policies Written policies regarding course substitutions, general/basic LD accommodations, and reduced course loads are available on the program Web site. Written policy regarding general/basic LD accommodations is outlined in the school's catalog/handbook. Written policies regarding course substitutions, general/basic LD accommodations, and reduced course loads are available through the program or unit directly.

Wilkes University

170 South Franklin St, PO Box 111

Wilkes-Barre, PA 18766-0002

http://www.wilkes.edu/

Contact: Mr. Thomas James Thomas, Director of University Learning Center. Phone: 570-408-4150. Fax: 570-408-4907. E-mail: thomast@wilkes.edu.

Approximately 30 registered undergraduate students were served during 2002-03. The program or unit includes 1 full-time and 4 part-time staff members. Academic advisers, professional tutors, remediation/learning specialists, and skill tutors are provided through the program or unit.

Unique Aids and Services Aids, services, or accommodations include advocates, career counseling, personal coach, and priority registration.

Subject-area Tutoring Tutoring is offered one-on-one and in small groups for most subjects. Tutoring is provided through the program or unit via LD specialists and professional tutors. Tutoring is also provided collaboratively through on-campus or off-campus services via computer-based instruction, professional tutors, and trained peer tutors.

Diagnostic Testing Testing is provided through the program or unit for learning strategies, learning styles, and study skills. Testing for intelligence, learning styles, math, neuropsychological, personality, reading, social skills, visual processing, and written language is provided collaboratively through on-campus or off-campus services.

Basic Skills Remediation Remediation is offered one-on-one, in small groups, and in class-size groups for learning strategies, math, study skills, time management, and written language. Remediation is provided through the program or unit via LD specialists and professional tutors. Remediation is also provided collaboratively through on-campus or off-campus services via computer-based instruction, professional tutors, regular education teachers, and trained peer tutors.

Enrichment Enrichment programs are available through the program or unit for career planning, college survival skills, learning strategies, self-advocacy, study skills, test taking, and time management. Programs for health and nutrition, math, medication management, oral communication skills, practical computer skills, reading, stress management, vocabulary development, and written composition skills are provided collaboratively through on-campus or off-campus services. Credit is offered for learning strategies, math, oral communication skills, practical computer skills, and written composition skills.

Wilkes University (continued)

Application For admittance to the program or unit, students are required to provide a psychoeducational report (2 years old or less). It is recommended that students provide documentation of high school services. Upon application, materials documenting need for services should be sent only to the LD program or unit. Upon acceptance, documentation of need for services should be sent only to the LD program or unit. *Application deadline (institutional):* Continuous. *Application deadline (LD program):* Rolling/continuous for fall and rolling/continuous for spring.

Written Policies Written policy regarding general/basic LD accommodations is available on the program Web site. Written policy regarding general/basic LD accommodations is outlined in the school's catalog/handbook. Written policies regarding course substitutions, reduced course loads, and substitutions and waivers of graduation requirements are available through the program or unit directly.

Willamette University

900 State Street

Salem, OR 97301-3931

http://www.willamette.edu/

Contact: Phone: 503-370-6300. Fax: 503-375-5363.

The program or unit includes 1 full-time and 2 part-time staff members. Coaches, counselors, LD specialists, and remediation/learning specialists are provided through the program or unit.

Unique Aids and Services Aids, services, or accommodations include career counseling and personal coach.

Subject-area Tutoring Tutoring is offered one-on-one, in small groups, and in class-size groups for most subjects. Tutoring is provided collaboratively through on-campus or off-campus services via computer-based instruction and trained peer tutors.

Basic Skills Remediation Remediation is offered one-on-one for learning strategies, reading, study skills, time management, and written language. Remediation is provided through the program or unit via LD specialists.

Enrichment Enrichment programs are available through the program or unit for college survival skills, learning strategies, self-advocacy, stress management, study skills, test taking, time management, and written composition skills. Programs for career planning, health and nutrition, practical computer skills, reading, stress management, and written composition skills are provided collaboratively through on-campus or off-campus services.

Application *Application deadline (institutional):* 2/1. *Application deadline (LD program):* Rolling/continuous for fall and rolling/continuous for spring.

Written Policies Written policies regarding course substitutions, general/basic LD accommodations, substitutions and waivers of admissions requirements, and substitutions and waivers of graduation requirements are available on the program Web site. Written policies regarding course substitutions, substitutions and waivers of admissions requirements, and substitutions and waivers of graduation requirements are outlined in the school's catalog/handbook.

William Penn University
Office of Services for Students with Disabilities (OSSD)

201 Trueblood Avenue

Oskaloosa, IA 52577-1799

http://www.wmpenn.edu/

Contact: Dr. D. A. Wilcox, Dean, College of Arts, Sciences and Professional Studies. Phone: 641-673-1010. E-mail: wilcoxd@wmpenn.edu.

Office of Services for Students with Disabilities (OSSD)

Approximately 20 registered undergraduate students were served during 2002-03. The program or unit includes 1 part-time staff member. Academic advisers, counselors, remediation/learning specialists, skill tutors, and trained peer tutors are provided collaboratively through on-campus or off-campus services.

Subject-area Tutoring Tutoring is offered one-on-one and in small groups for most subjects. Tutoring is provided collaboratively through on-campus or off-campus services via computer-based instruction, professional tutors, and trained peer tutors.

Basic Skills Remediation Remediation is offered one-on-one and in small groups for computer skills, learning strategies, math, reading, study skills, time management, and written language. Remediation is provided collaboratively through on-campus or off-campus services via computer-based instruction, professional tutors, and trained peer tutors.

Application For admittance to the program or unit, students are required to provide a psychoeducational report (5 years old or less). It is recommended that students provide documentation of high school services. Upon acceptance, documentation of need for services should be sent only to the LD program or unit. *Application deadline (LD program):* Rolling/continuous for fall.

Written Policies Written policy regarding general/basic LD accommodations is available on the program Web site. Written policy regarding general/basic LD accommodations is outlined in the school's catalog/handbook. Written policy regarding general/basic LD accommodations is available through the program or unit directly.

Williams College
Disabilities and Accommodations/Dean's Office

PO Box 687

988 Main Street

Williamstown, MA 01267

http://www.williams.edu/dean/disable.htm

Contact: Amy Pettengill Fahnestock Amy Pettengill Fahnestock, Assistant Dean. Phone: 413-597-4264. Fax: 413-597-3507. E-mail: apetteng@williams.edu. Head of LD Program: Dr. Charles R. Toomajian, Associate Dean and Registrar. Phone: 413-597-4286. Fax: 413-597-4010. E-mail: charles.r.toomajian@williams.edu.

Disabilities and Accommodations/Dean's Office Approximately 55 registered undergraduate students were served during

2002-03. The program or unit includes 1 full-time and 1 part-time staff member. Academic advisers, counselors, skill tutors, and trained peer tutors are provided through the program or unit. Academic advisers, counselors, diagnostic specialists, LD specialists, skill tutors, and trained peer tutors are provided collaboratively through on-campus or off-campus services.

Unique Aids and Services Aids, services, or accommodations include advocates, weekly meetings with faculty, regular meetings with Coordinator of Disability Services.

Subject-area Tutoring Tutoring is offered one-on-one and in small groups for all subjects. Tutoring is provided through the program or unit via trained peer tutors. Tutoring is also provided collaboratively through on-campus or off-campus services via trained peer tutors.

Enrichment Programs for career planning, math, stress management, study skills, test taking, time management, and written composition skills are provided collaboratively through on-campus or off-campus services.

Application For admittance to the program or unit, students are required to provide a psychoeducational report (3 years old or less). Upon acceptance, documentation of need for services should be sent only to the LD program or unit. *Application deadline (institutional):* 1/1. *Application deadline (LD program):* Rolling/continuous for fall and rolling/continuous for spring.

Written Policies Written policies regarding general/basic LD accommodations and reduced course loads are available on the program Web site. Written policies regarding general/basic LD accommodations and reduced course loads are outlined in the school's catalog/handbook. Written policies regarding general/basic LD accommodations and reduced course loads are available through the program or unit directly.

William Woods University
Office of Disability Services

One University Avenue
Fulton, MO 65251-1098
http://www.williamwoods.edu/

Contact: Ms. Carrie L. McCray, Coordinator. Phone: 573-592-1194. Fax: 573-592-1180. E-mail: cmccray@williamwoods.edu.

Office of Disability Services Approximately 35 registered undergraduate students were served during 2002-03. The program or unit includes 1 full-time staff member. Academic advisers and trained peer tutors are provided collaboratively through on-campus or off-campus services.

Unique Aids and Services Aids, services, or accommodations include faculty training and personal coach.

Subject-area Tutoring Tutoring is offered one-on-one and in small groups for most subjects. Tutoring is provided collaboratively through on-campus or off-campus services via trained peer tutors.

Application For admittance to the program or unit, students are required to provide a psychoeducational report (4 years old or less). It is recommended that students provide documentation of high school services. Upon application, materials documenting need for services should be sent only to the LD program or unit. Upon

acceptance, documentation of need for services should be sent only to the LD program or unit. *Application deadline (institutional):* Continuous. *Application deadline (LD program):* Rolling/continuous for fall and rolling/continuous for spring.

Written Policies Written policies regarding course substitutions, general/basic LD accommodations, grade forgiveness, reduced course loads, substitutions and waivers of admissions requirements, and substitutions and waivers of graduation requirements are available through the program or unit directly.

Wilmington College
Student Affairs

320 DuPont Highway
New Castle, DE 19720-6491
http://www.wilmcoll.edu/

Contact: Ms. Linda M. Doran, Assistant Director of Athletics and Student Affairs Associate. Phone: 302-328-9401 Ext. 225. Fax: 302-328-7376. E-mail: ldora@wilmcoll.edu. Head of LD Program: Dr. LaVerne T. Harmon, Vice President of Student Affairs. Phone: 302-328-9401 Ext. 101. Fax: 302-328-7376. E-mail: lharm@wilmcoll.edu.

Student Affairs Approximately 28 registered undergraduate students were served during 2002-03. The program or unit includes 1 full-time staff member. Services are provided through the program or unit.

Orientation The program or unit offers an optional orientation for new students individually by special arrangement.

Subject-area Tutoring Tutoring is offered one-on-one for some subjects. Tutoring is provided collaboratively through on-campus or off-campus services via other.

Enrichment Programs for career planning, stress management, study skills, test taking, and time management are provided collaboratively through on-campus or off-campus services.

Application For admittance to the program or unit, students are required to provide a psychoeducational report (4 years old or less). It is recommended that students provide documentation of high school services. Upon application, materials documenting need for services should be sent only to the LD program or unit. Upon acceptance, documentation of need for services should be sent to both admissions and the LD program or unit. *Application deadline (institutional):* Continuous. *Application deadline (LD program):* Rolling/continuous for fall and rolling/continuous for spring.

Written Policies Written policy regarding general/basic LD accommodations is available through the program or unit directly.

Winona State University
Disability Resource Center

PO Box 5838
Winona, MN 55987-5838
http://www.winona.edu/disabilityservices/

Winona State University (continued)

Contact: Ms. Nancy Dumke, Disability Services Coordinator. Phone: 507-457-2391. Fax: 507-457-2427. E-mail: ndumke@winona.edu.

Disability Resource Center Approximately 30 registered undergraduate students were served during 2002-03. The program or unit includes 1 full-time and 2 part-time staff members. Academic advisers and graduate assistants/students are provided through the program or unit. Academic advisers, counselors, professional tutors, skill tutors, strategy tutors, and trained peer tutors are provided collaboratively through on-campus or off-campus services.

Unique Aids and Services Aids, services, or accommodations include priority registration, taped textbooks.

Subject-area Tutoring Tutoring is offered one-on-one and in small groups for most subjects. Tutoring is provided collaboratively through on-campus or off-campus services via professional tutors and trained peer tutors.

Application For admittance to the program or unit, students are required to apply to the program directly, provide a psychoeducational report (3 years old or less), and provide specific diagnosis, significant functional limitations, recommended accommodations. It is recommended that students provide documentation of high school services. Upon acceptance, documentation of need for services should be sent only to the LD program or unit. *Application deadline (institutional):* Continuous. *Application deadline (LD program):* Rolling/continuous for fall and rolling/continuous for spring.

Written Policies Written policy regarding general/basic LD accommodations is available on the program Web site. Written policy regarding course substitutions is outlined in the school's catalog/handbook. Written policies regarding general/basic LD accommodations and substitutions and waivers of admissions requirements are available through the program or unit directly.

Worcester State College

486 Chandler Street

Worcester, MA 01602-2597

http://www.worcester.edu/

Contact: Dennis L. Lindblom, Coordinator. Phone: 508-929-8733. Fax: 508-929-8147. E-mail: dlindblom@worcester.edu.

The program or unit includes 1 part-time staff member. LD specialists are provided through the program or unit.

Unique Aids and Services Aids, services, or accommodations include career counseling, priority registration, and support groups.

Basic Skills Remediation Remediation is offered one-on-one for learning strategies, reading, social skills, study skills, time management, and written language. Remediation is provided through the program or unit via LD specialists.

Enrichment Enrichment programs are available through the program or unit for college survival skills, practical computer skills, reading, self-advocacy, study skills, test taking, time management, and written composition skills.

Application For admittance to the program or unit, students are required to apply to the program directly and provide a psychoeducational report. It is recommended that students provide documentation of high school services. Upon application, materials documenting need for services should be sent only to admissions with

institutional application materials. Upon acceptance, documentation of need for services should be sent only to the LD program or unit. *Application deadline (institutional): 6/1. Application deadline (LD program):* Rolling/continuous for fall and rolling/continuous for spring.

Written Policies Written policies regarding general/basic LD accommodations and substitutions and waivers of admissions requirements are available on the program Web site. Written policies regarding general/basic LD accommodations and substitutions and waivers of admissions requirements are outlined in the school's catalog/handbook. Written policies regarding general/basic LD accommodations and reduced course loads are available through the program or unit directly.

Wright State University
Office of Disability Services

3640 Colonel Glenn Highway

Dayton, OH 45435

http://www.wright.edu

Contact: Cassandra Mitchell, Academic Support Services Specialist. Phone: 937-775-5680. Fax: 937-775-5795. E-mail: cassandra.mitchell@wright.edu. Head of LD Program: Mr. Jeffrey Vernooy, Director. Phone: 937-775-5680. Fax: 937-775-5795. E-mail: disability_services@wright.edu.

Office of Disability Services Approximately 225 registered undergraduate students were served during 2002-03. The program or unit includes 6 full-time and 2 part-time staff members. LD specialists are provided through the program or unit. Academic advisers, counselors, diagnostic specialists, skill tutors, trained peer tutors, and other are provided collaboratively through on-campus or off-campus services.

Unique Aids and Services Aids, services, or accommodations include career counseling, digital textbooks, and faculty training.

Subject-area Tutoring Tutoring is offered one-on-one for all subjects. Tutoring is provided through the program or unit via trained peer tutors. Tutoring is also provided collaboratively through on-campus or off-campus services via trained peer tutors.

Diagnostic Testing Testing is provided through the program or unit for intelligence, math, personality, reading, spelling, written language, and other services. Testing for intelligence, math, neuropsychological, personality, reading, spelling, written language, and other services is provided collaboratively through on-campus or off-campus services.

Basic Skills Remediation Remediation is offered in class-size groups for math, reading, and written language. Remediation is provided through the program or unit via LD specialists. Remediation is also provided collaboratively through on-campus or off-campus services via regular education teachers and trained peer tutors.

Enrichment Enrichment programs are available through the program or unit for career planning, practical computer skills, and time management. Programs for career planning, college survival skills, practical computer skills, study skills, and time management are provided collaboratively through on-campus or off-campus services. Credit is offered for career planning, college survival skills, practical computer skills, study skills, and time management.

Fees *LD Program or Service* fee is $6 to $500 (fee varies according to level/tier of service).

Application For admittance to the program or unit, students are required to apply to the program directly and provide a psychoeducational report (3 years old or less). It is recommended that students provide documentation of high school services. Upon application, materials documenting need for services should be sent to both admissions and the LD program or unit. Upon acceptance, documentation of need for services should be sent only to the LD program or unit. *Application deadline (institutional):* Continuous. *Application deadline (LD program):* Rolling/continuous for fall and rolling/continuous for spring.

Written Policies Written policies regarding course substitutions, general/basic LD accommodations, grade forgiveness, reduced course loads, substitutions and waivers of admissions requirements, and substitutions and waivers of graduation requirements are available on the program Web site. Written policies regarding course substitutions, grade forgiveness, reduced course loads, substitutions and waivers of admissions requirements, and substitutions and waivers of graduation requirements are outlined in the school's catalog/handbook. Written policy regarding general/basic LD accommodations is available through the program or unit directly.

Xavier University

3800 Victory Parkway
Cincinnati, OH 45207
http://www.xu.edu/

Contact: Ms. Sarah M. Kelly, Associate Vice President for Student Development. Phone: 513-745-3280. Fax: 513-745-3877. E-mail: kelly@xavier.edu.

Approximately 150 registered undergraduate students were served during 2002-03. The program or unit includes 2 full-time and 35 part-time staff members. Graduate assistants/students, LD specialists, skill tutors, strategy tutors, and trained peer tutors are provided through the program or unit. Academic advisers, counselors, diagnostic specialists, professional tutors, and regular education teachers are provided collaboratively through on-campus or off-campus services.

Unique Aids and Services Aids, services, or accommodations include career counseling and digital textbooks.

Subject-area Tutoring Tutoring is offered one-on-one and in small groups for most subjects. Tutoring is provided through the program or unit via trained peer tutors. Tutoring is also provided collaboratively through on-campus or off-campus services via trained peer tutors.

Diagnostic Testing Testing is provided through the program or unit for learning strategies, learning styles, and study skills. Testing for auditory processing, intelligence, learning strategies, learning styles, personality, social skills, study skills, visual processing, and written language is provided collaboratively through on-campus or off-campus services.

Basic Skills Remediation Remediation is offered one-on-one for learning strategies, math, reading, study skills, and time management. Remediation is provided through the program or unit via trained peer tutors. Remediation is also provided collaboratively through on-campus or off-campus services via trained peer tutors.

Enrichment Enrichment programs are available through the program or unit for learning strategies, study skills, test taking, and time management. Programs for career planning, college survival skills, learning strategies, stress management, study skills, and time management are provided collaboratively through on-campus or off-campus services. Credit is offered for college survival skills.

Application For admittance to the program or unit, students are required to provide a psychoeducational report (3 years old or less). It is recommended that students provide documentation of high school services. Upon acceptance, documentation of need for services should be sent only to the LD program or unit. *Application deadline (institutional):* 2/1.

Written Policies Written policies regarding course substitutions, general/basic LD accommodations, and substitutions and waivers of graduation requirements are available on the program Web site. Written policy regarding general/basic LD accommodations is outlined in the school's catalog/handbook. Written policies regarding course substitutions and substitutions and waivers of graduation requirements are available through the program or unit directly.

Yale University

New Haven, CT 06520
http://www.yale.edu/

Contact: Judy York, Director of Resource Office on Disabilities. Phone: 203-432-2324. Fax: 203-432-7884. E-mail: judith.york@yale.edu.

The program or unit includes 2 full-time staff members. Academic advisers, diagnostic specialists, graduate assistants/students, and trained peer tutors are provided collaboratively through on-campus or off-campus services.

Unique Aids and Services Aids, services, or accommodations include extended time on tests, note-takers.

Enrichment Programs for career planning, health and nutrition, and written composition skills are provided collaboratively through on-campus or off-campus services.

Application For admittance to the program or unit, students are required to apply to the program directly and provide a psychoeducational report (5 years old or less). Upon acceptance, documentation of need for services should be sent only to the LD program or unit. *Application deadline (institutional):* 12/31. *Application deadline (LD program):* Rolling/continuous for fall and rolling/continuous for spring.

Written Policies Written policy regarding substitutions and waivers of graduation requirements is outlined in the school's catalog/handbook. Written policy regarding general/basic LD accommodations is available through the program or unit directly.

Youngstown State University
Disability Services

One University Plaza
Youngstown, OH 44555-0001
http://www.ysu.edu/services/disabilityservices

Youngstown State University (continued)

Contact: Jain Savage, Coordinator. Phone: 330-941-1372. Fax: 330-941-7470. E-mail: jasavage@ysu.edu.

Disability Services The program or unit includes 1 full-time and 1 part-time staff member. Graduate assistants/students are provided through the program or unit. Academic advisers, trained peer tutors, and other are provided collaboratively through on-campus or off-campus services.

Unique Aids and Services Aids, services, or accommodations include digital textbooks and priority registration.

Subject-area Tutoring Tutoring is offered one-on-one and in small groups for most subjects. Tutoring is provided through the program or unit via graduate assistants/students. Tutoring is also provided collaboratively through on-campus or off-campus services via computer-based instruction, LD specialists, trained peer tutors, and other.

Basic Skills Remediation Remediation is available for learning strategies, math, reading, study skills, time management, and written language. Remediation is provided collaboratively through on-campus or off-campus services via computer-based instruction, graduate assistants/students, and trained peer tutors.

Enrichment Programs for career planning, college survival skills, learning strategies, math, reading, study skills, test taking, time management, and written composition skills are provided collaboratively through on-campus or off-campus services.

Application For admittance to the program or unit, students are required to apply to the program directly, provide a psychoeducational report (3 years old or less), and provide documentation of high school services. It is recommended that students provide multi-factored evaluation or educational specialist. Upon application, materials documenting need for services should be sent only to the LD program or unit. Upon acceptance, documentation of need for services should be sent only to the LD program or unit. *Application deadline (institutional):* 8/15. *Application deadline (LD program):* Rolling/continuous for fall and rolling/continuous for spring.

Written Policies Written policy regarding general/basic LD accommodations is available on the program Web site. Written policy regarding grade forgiveness is outlined in the school's catalog/handbook. Written policy regarding general/basic LD accommodations is available through the program or unit directly.

Two-Year Colleges

WITH STRUCTURED/PROACTIVE PROGRAMS

Andrew College
Support Services for Students with Learning Disabilities and AD/HD

413 College Street

Cuthbert, GA 39840-1313

http://www.andrewcollege.edu/

Contact: Sherri K. Taylor, Director of The Focus Program. Phone: 229-732-5908. Fax: 229-732-5905. E-mail: focus@andrewcollege.edu.

Support Services for Students with Learning Disabilities and AD/HD Approximately 20 registered undergraduate students were served during 2002-03. The program or unit includes 1 full-time and 6 part-time staff members. Academic advisers, coaches, counselors, LD specialists, professional tutors, regular education teachers, remediation/learning specialists, skill tutors, special education teachers, and strategy tutors are provided through the program or unit. Academic advisers and trained peer tutors are provided collaboratively through on-campus or off-campus services.

Orientation The program or unit offers a mandatory 1-night orientation for new students after classes begin.

Unique Aids and Services Aids, services, or accommodations include advocates, career counseling, faculty training, personal coach, priority registration, and support groups.

Subject-area Tutoring Tutoring is offered one-on-one and in small groups for most subjects. Tutoring is provided through the program or unit via computer-based instruction, LD specialists, and professional tutors. Tutoring is also provided collaboratively through on-campus or off-campus services via computer-based instruction, graduate assistants/students, and trained peer tutors.

Basic Skills Remediation Remediation is offered in class-size groups for learning strategies, math, reading, social skills, study skills, time management, and written language. Remediation is provided through the program or unit via LD specialists, professional tutors, regular education teachers, and special education teachers. Remediation is also provided collaboratively through on-campus or off-campus services via computer-based instruction and other.

Enrichment Enrichment programs are available through the program or unit for career planning, college survival skills, learning strategies, math, medication management, oral communication skills, practical computer skills, reading, self-advocacy, stress management, study skills, test taking, time management, vocabulary development, and written composition skills. Programs for career planning, college survival skills, math, oral communication skills, practical computer skills, stress management, study skills, test taking, time management, vocabulary development, and written composition skills are provided collaboratively through on-campus or off-campus services. Credit is offered for college survival skills, math, and reading.

Fees *LD Program or Service* fee is $5000.

Application For admittance to the program or unit, students are required to apply to the program directly, provide a psychoeducational report (3 years old or less), and provide other documentation. It is recommended that students provide documentation of high school services. Upon application, materials documenting need for services should be sent only to the LD program or unit. Upon acceptance, documentation of need for services should be sent only to the LD program or unit. *Application deadline (institutional): 8/15. Application deadline (LD program):* Rolling/continuous for fall and rolling/continuous for spring.

Written Policies Written policy regarding general/basic LD accommodations is available on the program Web site. Written policies regarding course substitutions, general/basic LD accommodations, and reduced course loads are available through the program or unit directly.

Bishop State Community College

351 North Broad Street

Mobile, AL 36603-5898

http://www.bscc.cc.al.us/

Contact: Mr. Arvin Trotter, ADA Coordinator. Phone: 251-690-6874. Fax: 251-690-6814. E-mail: atrotter@bscc.edu.

The program or unit includes 1 full-time and 28 part-time staff members. Academic advisers, counselors, professional tutors, regular education teachers, remediation/learning specialists, skill tutors, special education teachers, strategy tutors, and trained peer tutors are provided collaboratively through on-campus or off-campus services.

Unique Aids and Services Aids, services, or accommodations include advocates, career counseling, digital textbooks, personal coach, priority registration, support groups, and weekly meetings with faculty.

Subject-area Tutoring Tutoring is offered one-on-one and in small groups. Tutoring is provided collaboratively through on-campus or off-campus services via computer-based instruction, professional tutors, and trained peer tutors.

Basic Skills Remediation Remediation is offered one-on-one and in small groups for auditory processing, computer skills, handwriting, learning strategies, math, reading, social skills, spelling, spoken language, study skills, time management, visual processing, and written language. Remediation is provided collaboratively through on-campus or off-campus services via computer-based instruction, professional tutors, regular education teachers, teacher trainees, and trained peer tutors.

Enrichment Programs for career planning, health and nutrition, learning strategies, math, medication management, oral communication skills, practical computer skills, reading, study skills, test taking, time management, vocabulary development, and written composition skills are provided collaboratively through on-campus or off-campus services. Credit is offered for health and nutrition, math, oral communication skills, practical computer skills, reading, vocabulary development, and written composition skills.

Student Organization Students with Different Abilities (SDA) consists of 53 members.

Application It is recommended that students apply to the program directly, provide a psychoeducational report, and provide documentation of high school services. Upon application, materials documenting need for services should be sent only to the LD program or unit. Upon acceptance, documentation of need for services should

335

Bishop State Community College (continued)

be sent only to the LD program or unit. *Application deadline (institutional):* Continuous. *Application deadline (LD program):* Rolling/continuous for fall and rolling/continuous for spring.

Written Policies Written policy regarding general/basic LD accommodations is available through the program or unit directly.

Community College of Allegheny County
Supportive Services

800 Allegheny Avenue

Pittsburgh, PA 15233-1894

http://www.ccac.edu/default.aspx?id=137533

Contact: Ms. Marilyn Gleser, LD Coordinator. Phone: 412-237-4613. Fax: 412-237-2721. E-mail: mgleser@ccac.edu.

Supportive Services Approximately 220 registered undergraduate students were served during 2002-03. The program or unit includes 2 full-time and 4 part-time staff members. Academic advisers, counselors, LD specialists, remediation/learning specialists, strategy tutors, and trained peer tutors are provided through the program or unit. Professional tutors, regular education teachers, remediation/learning specialists, skill tutors, strategy tutors, and trained peer tutors are provided collaboratively through on-campus or off-campus services.

Orientation The program or unit offers an optional 3-hour orientation for new students before classes begin.

Summer Program To help prepare for the demands of college, there is an optional 4-week summer program prior to entering the school. Degree credit will be earned.

Unique Aids and Services Aids, services, or accommodations include career counseling, digital textbooks, faculty training, priority registration, and weekly meetings with faculty.

Subject-area Tutoring Tutoring is offered one-on-one and in small groups for most subjects. Tutoring is provided through the program or unit via trained peer tutors. Tutoring is also provided collaboratively through on-campus or off-campus services via professional tutors and trained peer tutors.

Basic Skills Remediation Remediation is offered in class-size groups for learning strategies, math, reading, study skills, time management, and written language. Remediation is provided collaboratively through on-campus or off-campus services via LD specialists, regular education teachers, and special education teachers.

Enrichment Enrichment programs are available through the program or unit for career planning, college survival skills, learning strategies, math, reading, self-advocacy, study skills, test taking, time management, vocabulary development, and written composition skills. Programs for career planning, learning strategies, math, reading, study skills, vocabulary development, and written composition skills are provided collaboratively through on-campus or off-campus services. Credit is offered for career planning, college survival skills, learning strategies, math, reading, self-advocacy, study skills, vocabulary development, and written composition skills.

Student Organization Using Personal Potential Student Club consists of 15 members.

Application For admittance to the program or unit, students are required to apply to the program directly and provide a psychoeducational report. It is recommended that students provide documentation of high school services. Upon application, materials documenting need for services should be sent only to the LD program or unit. *Application deadline (institutional):* Continuous. *Application deadline (LD program):* Rolling/continuous for fall and rolling/continuous for spring.

Written Policies Written policy regarding general/basic LD accommodations is available on the program Web site. Written policy regarding general/basic LD accommodations is outlined in the school's catalog/handbook. Written policies regarding course substitutions and substitutions and waivers of graduation requirements are available through the program or unit directly.

Dean College
Arch Program

99 Main Street

Franklin, MA 02038-1994

http://www.dean.edu/

Contact: Larry Walter Thode, Assistant Director of Admissions. Phone: 508-541-1510. Fax: 508-541-8726. E-mail: lthode@dean.edu. Head of LD Program: Paul Hastings, Director of Arch Program and Disabilities Support Services. Phone: 508-541-1764. Fax: 508-541-8726. E-mail: phastings@dean.edu.

Arch Program Approximately 45 registered undergraduate students were served during 2002-03. The program or unit includes 5 full-time and 15 part-time staff members. Academic advisers, counselors, diagnostic specialists, LD specialists, professional tutors, remediation/learning specialists, skill tutors, special education teachers, strategy tutors, and trained peer tutors are provided through the program or unit.

Unique Aids and Services Aids, services, or accommodations include faculty training, personal coach, priority registration, and support groups.

Subject-area Tutoring Tutoring is offered in small groups for all subjects. Tutoring is provided collaboratively through on-campus or off-campus services via professional tutors.

Basic Skills Remediation Remediation is offered in class-size groups for computer skills, learning strategies, math, reading, study skills, time management, and written language. Remediation is provided collaboratively through on-campus or off-campus services via regular education teachers and special education teachers.

Enrichment Programs for career planning, college survival skills, learning strategies, reading, self-advocacy, study skills, test taking, time management, and written composition skills are provided collaboratively through on-campus or off-campus services.

Fees *LD Program or Service* fee is $2500.

Application For admittance to the program or unit, students are required to provide a psychoeducational report (3 years old or less) and provide documentation of high school services. Upon application, materials documenting need for services should be sent only to the LD program or unit. *Application deadline (institutional):* Continuous. *Application deadline (LD program):* Rolling/continuous for fall.

Written Policies Written policies regarding course substitutions, general/basic LD accommodations, reduced course loads, and substitutions and waivers of admissions requirements are outlined in the school's catalog/handbook.

Dorothea Hopfer School of Nursing at The Mount Vernon Hospital

53 Valentine Street

Mount Vernon, NY 10550

Contact: Phone: 914-664-8000 Ext. 3221. Fax: 914-665-7047.

Academic advisers and professional tutors are provided collaboratively through on-campus or off-campus services.

Unique Aids and Services Aids, services, or accommodations include advocates and career counseling.

Subject-area Tutoring Tutoring is offered one-on-one for all subjects. Tutoring is provided collaboratively through on-campus or off-campus services via computer-based instruction and professional tutors.

Basic Skills Remediation Remediation is offered one-on-one for learning strategies, study skills, and time management. Remediation is provided collaboratively through on-campus or off-campus services via computer-based instruction and regular education teachers.

Enrichment Programs for math, study skills, test taking, and time management are provided collaboratively through on-campus or off-campus services.

Application Upon application, materials documenting need for services should be sent only to admissions with institutional application materials. Upon acceptance, documentation of need for services should be sent only to admissions. *Application deadline (LD program):* Rolling/continuous for fall and rolling/continuous for spring.

Written Policies Written policies regarding course substitutions, general/basic LD accommodations, grade forgiveness, reduced course loads, substitutions and waivers of admissions requirements, and substitutions and waivers of graduation requirements are outlined in the school's catalog/handbook.

Fresno City College
Disabled Students Programs and Services

1101 East University Avenue

Fresno, CA 93741-0002

http://www.sccd.com

Contact: Ms. Linda Lee Kane, Learning Disability Specialist. Phone: 559-442-8237. Fax: 559-485-7304. E-mail: linda.kane@sccd.com. Head of LD Program: Dr. Janice Emerzian, Director. Phone: 559-442-8237. Fax: 559-485-7304. E-mail: emerzian@sccd.org.

Disabled Students Programs and Services Approximately 350 registered undergraduate students were served during 2002-03. Academic advisers, counselors, diagnostic specialists, graduate assistants/students, LD specialists, professional tutors, and regular education teachers are provided collaboratively through on-campus or off-campus services.

Orientation The program or unit offers an optional 1-hour orientation for new students before registration, before classes begin, during summer prior to enrollment, during registration, after classes begin, and individually by special arrangement.

Summer Program To help prepare for the demands of college, there is an optional 6-week summer program prior to entering the school.

Unique Aids and Services Aids, services, or accommodations include career counseling, digital textbooks, priority registration, and support groups.

Subject-area Tutoring Tutoring is offered one-on-one for most subjects. Tutoring is provided collaboratively through on-campus or off-campus services via computer-based instruction and trained peer tutors.

Diagnostic Testing Testing is provided through the program or unit for auditory processing, intelligence, learning strategies, learning styles, math, reading, spelling, spoken language, study skills, visual processing, and written language.

Basic Skills Remediation Remediation is offered in class-size groups for auditory processing, computer skills, learning strategies, math, reading, social skills, spelling, study skills, time management, visual processing, and written language. Remediation is provided collaboratively through on-campus or off-campus services via computer-based instruction, regular education teachers, and special education teachers.

Enrichment Programs for career planning, college survival skills, learning strategies, math, oral communication skills, practical computer skills, reading, self-advocacy, stress management, study skills, test taking, time management, vocabulary development, and written composition skills are provided collaboratively through on-campus or off-campus services.

Fees *Summer Program* fee is $33.

Application For admittance to the program or unit, students are required to apply to the program directly and provide a psychoeducational report. It is recommended that students provide documentation of high school services. Upon application, materials documenting need for services should be sent only to the LD program or unit. Upon acceptance, documentation of need for services should be sent only to the LD program or unit. *Application deadline (institutional):* Continuous. *Application deadline (LD program):* Rolling/continuous for fall and rolling/continuous for spring.

Written Policies Written policies regarding general/basic LD accommodations, substitutions and waivers of admissions requirements, and substitutions and waivers of graduation requirements are available on the program Web site. Written policies regarding general/basic LD accommodations, substitutions and waivers of admissions requirements, and substitutions and waivers of graduation requirements are outlined in the school's catalog/handbook. Written policies regarding course substitutions, general/basic LD accommodations, grade forgiveness, reduced course loads, substitutions and waivers of admissions requirements, and substitutions and waivers of graduation requirements are available through the program or unit directly.

Holyoke Community College
Office for Students with Disabilities and Deaf Services

303 Homestead Avenue

Holyoke, MA 01040-1099

http://www.hcc.mass.edu/

Contact: Ms. Maureen L. Conroy, Director of Office for Students with Disabilities and Deaf Services. Phone: 413-552-2417. Fax: 413-534-8975. E-mail: mconroy@hcc.mass.edu. Head of LD Program: Ms. Maureen L. Conroy, Director of Office for Students with Disabilities and Deaf Services. Phone: 413-552-2582. Fax: 413-534-8975. E-mail: mconroy@hcc.mass.edu.

Office for Students with Disabilities and Deaf Services Approximately 450 registered undergraduate students were served during 2002-03. The program or unit includes 4 full-time and 3 part-time staff members. Academic advisers and LD specialists are provided through the program or unit. Academic advisers, coaches, counselors, diagnostic specialists, graduate assistants/students, professional tutors, regular education teachers, and skill tutors are provided collaboratively through on-campus or off-campus services.

Orientation The program or unit offers an optional approximately 1-hour orientation for new students before classes begin.

Unique Aids and Services Aids, services, or accommodations include advocates, career counseling, faculty training, and support groups.

Subject-area Tutoring Tutoring is offered one-on-one for most subjects. Tutoring is provided collaboratively through on-campus or off-campus services via trained peer tutors and other.

Basic Skills Remediation Remediation is offered one-on-one for computer skills, learning strategies, math, reading, social skills, spoken language, study skills, time management, and written language. Remediation is provided collaboratively through on-campus or off-campus services via trained peer tutors.

Enrichment Programs for career planning, college survival skills, health and nutrition, learning strategies, math, oral communication skills, practical computer skills, reading, self-advocacy, stress management, study skills, test taking, time management, and written composition skills are provided collaboratively through on-campus or off-campus services. Credit is offered for health and nutrition, learning strategies, math, oral communication skills, practical computer skills, and reading.

Application For admittance to the program or unit, students are required to provide a psychoeducational report (2 years old or less). It is recommended that students apply to the program directly and provide documentation of high school services. Upon application, materials documenting need for services should be sent only to the LD program or unit. Upon acceptance, documentation of need for services should be sent only to the LD program or unit. *Application deadline (institutional):* Continuous. *Application deadline (LD program):* Rolling/continuous for fall and rolling/continuous for spring.

Written Policies Written policy regarding general/basic LD accommodations is available on the program Web site. Written policy regarding general/basic LD accommodations is outlined in the school's catalog/handbook. Written policies regarding course sub-

stitutions, general/basic LD accommodations, reduced course loads, and substitutions and waivers of admissions requirements are available through the program or unit directly.

Iowa Lakes Community College
SAVE (Student Alternative Vocational Education)

19 South 7th Street

Estherville, IA 51334-2295

http://www.iowalakes.edu

Contact: Phone: 712-362-2604.

SAVE (Student Alternative Vocational Education) Approximately 50 registered undergraduate students were served during 2002-03. The program or unit includes 4 full-time and 2 part-time staff members. Special education teachers are provided through the program or unit.

Fees *LD Program or Service* fee varies according to academic program.

Application For admittance to the program or unit, students are required to provide documentation of high school services. It is recommended that students apply to the program directly and provide a psychoeducational report (3 years old or less). Upon application, materials documenting need for services should be sent only to the LD program or unit. Upon acceptance, documentation of need for services should be sent only to the LD program or unit. *Application deadline (institutional):* Continuous.

Landmark College

River Road South

Putney, VT 05346

http://www.landmark.edu

Contact: John Capriotti, Associate Dean of Admissions. Phone: 802-387-6718. Fax: 802-387-6868. E-mail: jcapriotti@landmark.edu.

Approximately 365 registered undergraduate students were served during 2002-03. Academic advisers, coaches, counselors, diagnostic specialists, LD specialists, regular education teachers, and remediation/learning specialists are provided collaboratively through on-campus or off-campus services.

Orientation The program or unit offers before classes begin.

Summer Program To help prepare for the demands of college, there is an optional 6-week summer program prior to entering the school.

Basic Skills Remediation Remediation is offered one-on-one, in small groups, and in class-size groups for computer skills, learning strategies, math, reading, spelling, spoken language, study skills, time management, and written language. Remediation is provided collaboratively through on-campus or off-campus services via LD specialists and regular education teachers.

Enrichment Programs for career planning, learning strategies, medication management, oral communication skills, practical computer skills, reading, self-advocacy, stress management, study skills, time management, vocabulary development, and written composition skills are provided collaboratively through on-campus or off-campus services.

Student Organization Student Governance Association consists of 20 members.

Fees *Summer Program* fee is $7875.

Application For admittance to the program or unit, students are required to provide a psychoeducational report (3 years old or less) and provide transcripts. It is recommended that students provide documentation of high school services. Upon application, materials documenting need for services should be sent only to admissions with institutional application materials. Upon acceptance, documentation of need for services should be sent only to admissions. *Application deadline (institutional):* 5/15. *Application deadline (LD program):* Rolling/continuous for fall and rolling/continuous for spring.

Written Policies Written policy regarding general/basic LD accommodations is available on the program Web site. Written policy regarding general/basic LD accommodations is outlined in the school's catalog/handbook.

Lewis and Clark Community College
Student Development and Counseling

5800 Godfrey Road
Godfrey, IL 62035-2466
http://www.lc.edu/

Contact: Ms. Kathy Haberer, Special Learning Needs Counselor. Phone: 618-468-4126. Fax: 618-468-7257. E-mail: khaberer@lc.edu.

Student Development and Counseling Approximately 125 registered undergraduate students were served during 2002-03. The program or unit includes 4 full-time and 25 part-time staff members. Academic advisers, counselors, diagnostic specialists, LD specialists, professional tutors, regular education teachers, remediation/learning specialists, skill tutors, special education teachers, and strategy tutors are provided through the program or unit. Coaches, regular education teachers, and remediation/learning specialists are provided collaboratively through on-campus or off-campus services.

Orientation The program or unit offers an optional 1-hour orientation for new students before registration, before classes begin, and individually by special arrangement.

Unique Aids and Services Aids, services, or accommodations include career counseling, digital textbooks, faculty training, parent workshops, personal coach, priority registration, support groups, weekly meetings with faculty, assistive technology .

Subject-area Tutoring Tutoring is offered one-on-one and in small groups for most subjects. Tutoring is provided through the program or unit via computer-based instruction, LD specialists, professional tutors, and trained peer tutors. Tutoring is also provided collaboratively through on-campus or off-campus services via computer-based instruction, professional tutors, and trained peer tutors.

Diagnostic Testing Testing is provided through the program or unit for auditory processing, learning strategies, learning styles, math, motor skills, reading, social skills, spelling, spoken language, study skills, visual processing, and written language. Testing for intelligence, neuropsychological, personality, and reading is provided collaboratively through on-campus or off-campus services.

Basic Skills Remediation Remediation is offered one-on-one, in small groups, and in class-size groups for auditory processing, computer skills, learning strategies, math, reading, social skills, spelling, spoken language, study skills, time management, visual processing, and written language. Remediation is provided through the program or unit via computer-based instruction, LD specialists, professional tutors, regular education teachers, special education teachers, and trained peer tutors. Remediation is also provided collaboratively through on-campus or off-campus services via computer-based instruction, professional tutors, regular education teachers, special education teachers, and trained peer tutors.

Enrichment Enrichment programs are available through the program or unit for career planning, college survival skills, health and nutrition, learning strategies, math, oral communication skills, practical computer skills, reading, self-advocacy, stress management, study skills, test taking, time management, vocabulary development, written composition skills, and other. Programs for career planning, college survival skills, health and nutrition, learning strategies, math, oral communication skills, practical computer skills, reading, self-advocacy, stress management, study skills, test taking, time management, vocabulary development, written composition skills, and other are provided collaboratively through on-campus or off-campus services. Credit is offered for career planning, college survival skills, health and nutrition, learning strategies, math, oral communication skills, practical computer skills, reading, self-advocacy, study skills, test taking, time management, vocabulary development, written composition skills, and other.

Student Organization People First consists of 30 members.

Fees *LD Program or Service* fee is $0 to $900 (fee varies according to academic program, disability, course level, and level/tier of service).

Application For admittance to the program or unit, students are required to apply to the program directly. It is recommended that students provide a psychoeducational report (5 years old or less) and provide documentation of high school services. Upon application, materials documenting need for services should be sent only to the LD program or unit. Upon acceptance, documentation of need for services should be sent only to the LD program or unit. *Application deadline (institutional):* Continuous. *Application deadline (LD program):* Rolling/continuous for fall and rolling/continuous for spring.

Written Policies Written policy regarding general/basic LD accommodations is available on the program Web site. Written policy regarding general/basic LD accommodations is outlined in the school's catalog/handbook.

Longview Community College
ABLE (Academic Bridges to Learning Effectiveness)

500 Southwest Longview Road
Lee's Summit, MO 64081-2105

Longview Community College (continued)
http://www.kcmetro./programs/able.html

Contact: Ms. Mary Ellen Jenison, ABLE Program Director. Phone: 816-672-2366. Fax: 816-672-2025. E-mail: maryellen.jenison@kcmetro.edu.

ABLE (Academic Bridges to Learning Effectiveness) Approximately 90 registered undergraduate students were served during 2002-03. The program or unit includes 2 full-time and 15 part-time staff members. Academic advisers, counselors, graduate assistants/students, LD specialists, remediation/learning specialists, and special education teachers are provided through the program or unit.

Orientation The program or unit offers a mandatory 2½-hour orientation for new students before classes begin.

Unique Aids and Services Aids, services, or accommodations include advocates, career counseling, support groups, weekly meetings with faculty, parent support groups, books on tape.

Subject-area Tutoring Tutoring is offered in small groups for most subjects. Tutoring is provided through the program or unit via graduate assistants/students, LD specialists, and trained peer tutors. Tutoring is also provided collaboratively through on-campus or off-campus services via graduate assistants/students, LD specialists, and trained peer tutors.

Basic Skills Remediation Remediation is offered in small groups for auditory processing, learning strategies, math, reading, social skills, spelling, spoken language, study skills, time management, visual processing, and written language. Remediation is provided through the program or unit via graduate assistants/students, LD specialists, regular education teachers, special education teachers, and trained peer tutors. Remediation is also provided collaboratively through on-campus or off-campus services via graduate assistants/students, LD specialists, regular education teachers, special education teachers, and trained peer tutors.

Enrichment Programs for career planning, college survival skills, learning strategies, math, oral communication skills, reading, self-advocacy, stress management, study skills, test taking, time management, vocabulary development, and written composition skills are provided collaboratively through on-campus or off-campus services. Credit is offered for career planning, college survival skills, learning strategies, math, oral communication skills, reading, self-advocacy, stress management, study skills, test taking, time management, vocabulary development, and written composition skills.

Fees *LD Program or Service* fee is $35.

Application For admittance to the program or unit, students are required to apply to the program directly and provide a psychoeducational report. It is recommended that students provide documentation of high school services and provide neuropsychological report. Upon application, materials documenting need for services should be sent only to the LD program or unit. *Application deadline (institutional):* Continuous. *Application deadline (LD program):* 7/15 for fall. 12/21 for spring.

Written Policies Written policies regarding course substitutions, general/basic LD accommodations, substitutions and waivers of admissions requirements, and substitutions and waivers of graduation requirements are outlined in the school's catalog/handbook. Written policy regarding reduced course loads is available through the program or unit directly.

Louisburg College

501 North Main Street
Louisburg, NC 27549-2399
http://www.louisburg.edu/

Contact: Regina Lynn Burger, Director of Learning Services. Phone: 919-497-3276. Fax: 919-496-6733. E-mail: rburger@louisburg.edu.

The program or unit includes 5 full-time staff members and 1 part-time staff member. Academic advisers, coaches, counselors, LD specialists, professional tutors, regular education teachers, remediation/learning specialists, skill tutors, and strategy tutors are provided through the program or unit. Regular education teachers and remediation/learning specialists are provided collaboratively through on-campus or off-campus services.

Orientation The program or unit offers a mandatory 1-day orientation for new students before registration, before classes begin, and during summer prior to enrollment.

Summer Program To help prepare for the demands of college, there is an optional 4-week summer program prior to entering the school. Degree credit will be earned.

Unique Aids and Services Aids, services, or accommodations include career counseling, personal coach, priority registration, and weekly meetings with faculty.

Subject-area Tutoring Tutoring is offered one-on-one for some subjects. Tutoring is provided through the program or unit via LD specialists and professional tutors.

Diagnostic Testing Testing is provided through the program or unit for learning strategies, learning styles, and study skills.

Basic Skills Remediation Remediation is offered in class-size groups for math, reading, and written language. Remediation is provided collaboratively through on-campus or off-campus services via regular education teachers.

Enrichment Enrichment programs are available through the program or unit for career planning, college survival skills, learning strategies, math, reading, self-advocacy, stress management, study skills, test taking, time management, vocabulary development, and written composition skills. Credit is offered for college survival skills.

Fees *LD Program or Service* fee is $4400. *Summer Program* fee is $375.

Application For admittance to the program or unit, students are required to apply to the program directly and provide a psychoeducational report (3 years old or less). It is recommended that students provide documentation of high school services. Upon application, materials documenting need for services should be sent only to the LD program or unit. *Application deadline (institutional):* Continuous. *Application deadline (LD program):* Rolling/continuous for fall and rolling/continuous for spring.

Written Policies Written policy regarding general/basic LD accommodations is outlined in the school's catalog/handbook. Written policy regarding general/basic LD accommodations is available through the program or unit directly.

Rockford Business College

730 North Church Street

Rockford, IL 61103
http://www.rbcsuccess.com/
Contact: Phone: 815-965-8616. Fax: 815-965-0360.

Counselors are provided collaboratively through on-campus or off-campus services.
Application *Application deadline (institutional):* 9/4.
Written Policies Written policy regarding general/basic LD accommodations is outlined in the school's catalog/handbook.

St. Philip's College

1801 Martin Luther King Drive
San Antonio, TX 78203-2098
http://www.accd.edu/spc/
Contact: Mrs. Joannis K. Flatley, Director of Educational Support Services. Phone: 210-531-3502. Fax: 210-531-3513. E-mail: jflatley@accd.edu.

Approximately 450 registered undergraduate students were served during 2002-03. The program or unit includes 3 full-time and 15 part-time staff members. Academic advisers, counselors, diagnostic specialists, LD specialists, professional tutors, skill tutors, and trained peer tutors are provided through the program or unit. Academic advisers, counselors, regular education teachers, and remediation/learning specialists are provided collaboratively through on-campus or off-campus services.
Unique Aids and Services Aids, services, or accommodations include faculty training, extended test time, readers, testing in a non-distracting environment.
Subject-area Tutoring Tutoring is offered one-on-one and in small groups for all subjects. Tutoring is provided through the program or unit via professional tutors and trained peer tutors.
Basic Skills Remediation Remediation is offered in class-size groups for math, reading, and English.
Enrichment Enrichment programs are available through the program or unit for career planning, college survival skills, learning strategies, math, reading, self-advocacy, stress management, study skills, test taking, time management, and written composition skills. Programs for career planning, math, reading, study skills, and written composition skills are provided collaboratively through on-campus or off-campus services. Credit is offered for math, reading, study skills, and written composition skills.
Application *Application deadline (institutional):* Continuous. *Application deadline (LD program):* Rolling/continuous for fall and rolling/continuous for spring.
Written Policies Written policy regarding general/basic LD accommodations is available on the program Web site. Written policy regarding general/basic LD accommodations is outlined in the school's catalog/handbook. Written policy regarding general/basic LD accommodations is available through the program or unit directly.

Spencerian College-Lexington
Education Department

2355 Harrodsburg Road
Lexington, KY 40504

http://www.spencerian.edu/
Contact: Karen S. Whalen, Director of Education. Phone: 859-223-9608 Ext. 8012. Fax: 859-224-7744. E-mail: kwhalen@spencerian.edu.

Education Department Approximately 5 registered undergraduate students were served during 2002-03. The program or unit includes 10 full-time and 5 part-time staff members. Academic advisers, coaches, counselors, graduate assistants/students, regular education teachers, skill tutors, trained peer tutors, and other are provided through the program or unit.
Orientation The program or unit offers an optional orientation for new students individually by special arrangement.
Unique Aids and Services Aids, services, or accommodations include advocates, career counseling, faculty training, and personal coach.
Subject-area Tutoring Tutoring is offered one-on-one, in small groups, and in class-size groups for all subjects. Tutoring is provided through the program or unit via computer-based instruction, graduate assistants/students, professional tutors, and trained peer tutors. Tutoring is also provided collaboratively through on-campus or off-campus services via computer-based instruction, graduate assistants/students, professional tutors, and trained peer tutors.
Diagnostic Testing Testing is provided through the program or unit for math, personality, reading, and written language.
Basic Skills Remediation Remediation is offered one-on-one for computer skills, learning strategies, math, study skills, and time management. Remediation is provided through the program or unit via professional tutors and regular education teachers. Remediation is also provided collaboratively through on-campus or off-campus services via professional tutors and regular education teachers.
Enrichment Enrichment programs are available through the program or unit for career planning, practical computer skills, stress management, study skills, test taking, and time management. Programs for career planning, learning strategies, practical computer skills, stress management, study skills, test taking, and time management are provided collaboratively through on-campus or off-campus services. Credit is offered for practical computer skills.
Application It is recommended that students provide a psychoeducational report (2 years old or less) and provide documentation of high school services. Upon application, materials documenting need for services should be sent only to admissions with institutional application materials. Upon acceptance, documentation of need for services should be sent to both admissions and the LD program or unit. *Application deadline (institutional):* Continuous. *Application deadline (LD program):* Rolling/continuous for fall and rolling/continuous for spring.
Written Policies Written policy regarding general/basic LD accommodations is outlined in the school's catalog/handbook.

Terra State Community College

2830 Napoleon Road
Fremont, OH 43420-9670
http://www.terra.edu/
Contact: Ms. Cheryl Lynn Chesney, Coordinator. Phone: 800-334-3886 Ext. 208. Fax: 419-334-2300. E-mail: cchesney@terra.edu.

Terra State Community College (continued)

The program or unit includes 1 full-time and 15 part-time staff members. Academic advisers and counselors are provided through the program or unit. Counselors are provided collaboratively through on-campus or off-campus services.

Orientation The program or unit offers a mandatory 1-hour orientation for new students individually by special arrangement.

Unique Aids and Services Aids, services, or accommodations include career counseling and faculty training.

Subject-area Tutoring Tutoring is offered one-on-one for all subjects. Tutoring is provided through the program or unit via graduate assistants/students, professional tutors, and trained peer tutors.

Basic Skills Remediation Remediation is offered in class-size groups for math, reading, spelling, study skills, time management, and written language. Remediation is provided collaboratively through on-campus or off-campus services via computer-based instruction and regular education teachers.

Enrichment Enrichment programs are available through the program or unit for learning strategies, math, reading, self-advocacy, stress management, study skills, test taking, time management, vocabulary development, and written composition skills. Programs for math, reading, study skills, test taking, time management, vocabulary development, and written composition skills are provided collaboratively through on-campus or off-campus services.

Student Organization Special Populations Advisory Board consists of 7 members.

Application For admittance to the program or unit, students are required to apply to the program directly, provide a psychoeducational report (3 years old or less), provide documentation of high school services, and provide a medical diagnosis from a physician. Upon application, materials documenting need for services should be sent only to the LD program or unit. Upon acceptance, documentation of need for services should be sent only to the LD program or unit. *Application deadline (institutional):* Continuous. *Application deadline (LD program):* 8/25 for fall. 3/30 for spring.

Written Policies Written policy regarding general/basic LD accommodations is available on the program Web site. Written policies regarding course substitutions, general/basic LD accommodations, grade forgiveness, substitutions and waivers of admissions requirements, and substitutions and waivers of graduation requirements are outlined in the school's catalog/handbook. Written policy regarding general/basic LD accommodations is available through the program or unit directly.

William Rainey Harper College
Access and Disability Services—Program for Achieving Student Success (PASS)

1200 West Algonquin Road

Palatine, IL 60067-7398

http://www.harpercollege.edu

Contact: Mrs. Pascuala Herrera, Coordinator of LD Services. Phone: 847-925-6266. Fax: 847-925-6267. E-mail: pherrera@harpercollege.edu.

Access and Disability Services—Program for Achieving Student Success (PASS) Approximately 60 registered undergraduate students were served during 2002-03. The program or unit includes 1 full-time and 8 part-time staff members. Diagnostic specialists, LD specialists, professional tutors, remediation/learning specialists, skill tutors, and strategy tutors are provided through the program or unit. Academic advisers, coaches, counselors, and regular education teachers are provided collaboratively through on-campus or off-campus services.

Orientation The program or unit offers an optional 2-day orientation for new students before classes begin.

Unique Aids and Services Aids, services, or accommodations include faculty training, parent workshops, priority registration, early warning progress monitoring.

Subject-area Tutoring Tutoring is offered one-on-one for most subjects. Tutoring is provided through the program or unit via computer-based instruction, LD specialists, and professional tutors. Tutoring is also provided collaboratively through on-campus or off-campus services via trained peer tutors.

Diagnostic Testing Testing is provided through the program or unit for auditory processing, handwriting, intelligence, learning styles, math, reading, spelling, study skills, visual processing, and written language. Testing for learning styles, math, reading, spelling, study skills, and written language is provided collaboratively through on-campus or off-campus services.

Basic Skills Remediation Remediation is offered one-on-one and in class-size groups for computer skills, learning strategies, math, reading, spelling, study skills, time management, and written language. Remediation is provided through the program or unit via computer-based instruction, LD specialists, and professional tutors. Remediation is also provided collaboratively through on-campus or off-campus services via regular education teachers and trained peer tutors.

Enrichment Enrichment programs are available through the program or unit for career planning, college survival skills, learning strategies, math, practical computer skills, reading, self-advocacy, stress management, study skills, test taking, time management, and written composition skills. Programs for career planning, college survival skills, health and nutrition, learning strategies, math, practical computer skills, reading, stress management, study skills, test taking, time management, and written composition skills are provided collaboratively through on-campus or off-campus services. Credit is offered for career planning, college survival skills, health and nutrition, learning strategies, math, practical computer skills, reading, study skills, test taking, and time management.

Student Organization ADS Success Club consists of 12 members.

Fees *LD Program or Service* fee is $450 to $600 (fee varies according to level/tier of service). *Orientation* fee is $70. *Diagnostic Testing* fee is $300.

Application For admittance to the program or unit, students are required to provide documentation of high school services. It is recommended that students apply to the program directly and provide a psychoeducational report (3 years old or less). Upon application, materials documenting need for services should be sent only to the LD program or unit. Upon acceptance, documentation of need for services should be sent only to the LD program or unit. *Application deadline (institutional):* Continuous. *Application deadline (LD program):* Rolling/continuous for fall and rolling/continuous for spring.

Written Policies Written policy regarding general/basic LD accommodations is available on the program Web site. Written policies regarding course substitutions, general/basic LD accommodations, grade forgiveness, reduced course loads, and substitutions and waivers of admissions requirements are available through the program or unit directly.

Two-Year Colleges

WITH SELF-DIRECTED/DECENTRALIZED PROGRAMS

Abraham Baldwin Agricultural College
Learning Disabilities Services

2802 Moore Highway
Tifton, GA 31793
http://www.abac.edu/

Contact: Ms. Rita Wade, Service Provider. Phone: 229-386-3489. Fax: 229-386-3579. E-mail: rwade@abac.edu.

Learning Disabilities Services Approximately 46 registered undergraduate students were served during 2002-03. The program or unit includes 2 full-time staff members. Academic advisers and other are provided through the program or unit. Counselors and diagnostic specialists are provided collaboratively through on-campus or off-campus services.

Orientation The program or unit offers an optional 30-minute orientation for new students during new student orientation.

Unique Aids and Services Aids, services, or accommodations include priority registration.

Subject-area Tutoring Tutoring is offered one-on-one and in small groups for all subjects. Tutoring is provided through the program or unit via professional tutors. Tutoring is also provided collaboratively through on-campus or off-campus services via other.

Diagnostic Testing Testing for auditory processing, intelligence, motor skills, spoken language, visual processing, and written language is provided collaboratively through on-campus or off-campus services.

Enrichment Enrichment programs are available through the program or unit for other.

Application For admittance to the program or unit, students are required to provide a psychoeducational report (3 years old or less). It is recommended that students provide documentation of high school services. Upon application, materials documenting need for services should be sent to both admissions and the LD program or unit. Upon acceptance, documentation of need for services should be sent to both admissions and the LD program or unit. *Application deadline (institutional):* 9/24. *Application deadline (LD program):* Rolling/continuous for fall and rolling/continuous for spring.

Written Policies Written policies regarding course substitutions, substitutions and waivers of admissions requirements, and substitutions and waivers of graduation requirements are available on the program Web site. Written policy regarding general/basic LD accommodations is outlined in the school's catalog/handbook. Written policy regarding general/basic LD accommodations is available through the program or unit directly.

Adirondack Community College

640 Bay Road
Queensbury, NY 12804
http://www.sunyacc.edu/

Contact: Mr. Jamin Totino, Director of Accessibility Services. Phone: 518-743-2282. Fax: 518-743-2241. E-mail: totinoj@acc.sunyacc.edu.

Approximately 165 registered undergraduate students were served during 2002-03. The program or unit includes 2 full-time staff members. Academic advisers, counselors, LD specialists, remediation/learning specialists, and strategy tutors are provided through the program or unit. Academic advisers, counselors, and professional tutors are provided collaboratively through on-campus or off-campus services.

Unique Aids and Services Aids, services, or accommodations include advocates, career counseling, and priority registration.

Subject-area Tutoring Tutoring is offered one-on-one and in small groups for some subjects. Tutoring is provided collaboratively through on-campus or off-campus services via professional tutors and trained peer tutors.

Diagnostic Testing Testing is provided through the program or unit for learning strategies, learning styles, reading, study skills, and written language. Testing for learning strategies, math, reading, spelling, and written language is provided collaboratively through on-campus or off-campus services.

Basic Skills Remediation Remediation is offered one-on-one for learning strategies, math, reading, spelling, study skills, time management, and written language. Remediation is provided through the program or unit via computer-based instruction and LD specialists.

Enrichment Enrichment programs are available through the program or unit for learning strategies, self-advocacy, study skills, test taking, time management, and written composition skills. Programs for career planning, college survival skills, health and nutrition, learning strategies, math, oral communication skills, practical computer skills, reading, stress management, study skills, test taking, time management, and written composition skills are provided collaboratively through on-campus or off-campus services. Credit is offered for college survival skills and health and nutrition.

Application For admittance to the program or unit, students are required to apply to the program directly, provide a psychoeducational report (3 years old or less), and provide documentation from a qualified clinician verifying disability status. It is recommended that students provide documentation of high school services. Upon acceptance, documentation of need for services should be sent only to the LD program or unit. *Application deadline (institutional):* 8/15. *Application deadline (LD program):* Rolling/continuous for fall and rolling/continuous for spring.

Written Policies Written policies regarding course substitutions, general/basic LD accommodations, reduced course loads, and substitutions and waivers of graduation requirements are available on the program Web site. Written policies regarding course substitutions, general/basic LD accommodations, reduced course loads, and substitutions and waivers of graduation requirements are available through the program or unit directly.

Aims Community College

Box 69
Greeley, CO 80632-0069
http://www.aims.edu/

Contact: Ms. Janet Krause, Director of Supplemental Services. Phone: 970-330-8008 Ext. 6388. Fax: 970-339-6474. E-mail: jkrause@aims.edu.

347

Aims Community College (continued)

The program or unit includes 35 part-time staff members. Academic advisers, counselors, professional tutors, regular education teachers, remediation/learning specialists, skill tutors, and trained peer tutors are provided collaboratively through on-campus or off-campus services.

Subject-area Tutoring Tutoring is offered one-on-one and in small groups for most subjects. Tutoring is provided collaboratively through on-campus or off-campus services via computer-based instruction, professional tutors, and trained peer tutors.

Basic Skills Remediation Remediation is offered in class-size groups for math, reading, spelling, study skills, and written language. Remediation is provided collaboratively through on-campus or off-campus services via computer-based instruction and regular education teachers.

Enrichment Programs for career planning, math, reading, study skills, vocabulary development, and written composition skills are provided collaboratively through on-campus or off-campus services. Credit is offered for career planning, math, reading, study skills, vocabulary development, and written composition skills.

Application For admittance to the program or unit, students are required to provide appropriate tests by appropriate person with recommendations. It is recommended that students provide documentation of high school services. Upon acceptance, documentation of need for services should be sent only to the LD program or unit. *Application deadline (institutional):* Continuous. *Application deadline (LD program):* Rolling/continuous for fall.

Alabama Southern Community College
Disability Services

PO Box 2000
Monroeville, AL 36461
http://www.ascc.edu/
Contact: Ms. Bridgett Loree Shewmake MT, ADA Coordinator. Phone: 334-636-9642 Ext. 620. Fax: 334-636-1380. E-mail: bshewmake@ascc.edu. Head of LD Program: Ms. Ann Clanton, Dean of Students. Phone: 334-636-9642 Ext. 639. Fax: 334-636-1380.

Disability Services Approximately 5 registered undergraduate students were served during 2002-03. The program or unit includes 4 part-time staff members. Services are provided collaboratively through on-campus or off-campus services.

Unique Aids and Services Aids, services, or accommodations include career counseling, faculty training, and priority registration.

Subject-area Tutoring Tutoring is offered one-on-one for all subjects. Tutoring is provided collaboratively through on-campus or off-campus services via computer-based instruction, graduate assistants/students, and trained peer tutors.

Diagnostic Testing Testing for learning strategies, learning styles, math, and reading is provided collaboratively through on-campus or off-campus services.

Basic Skills Remediation Remediation is offered in class-size groups for computer skills, learning strategies, math, reading, study skills, time management, and written language. Remediation is provided collaboratively through on-campus or off-campus services via computer-based instruction and regular education teachers.

Enrichment Programs for career planning, college survival skills, health and nutrition, learning strategies, math, practical computer skills, reading, stress management, study skills, test taking, time management, and written composition skills are provided collaboratively through on-campus or off-campus services. Credit is offered for career planning, college survival skills, health and nutrition, learning strategies, math, practical computer skills, reading, stress management, study skills, test taking, time management, and written composition skills.

Application It is recommended that students apply to the program directly, provide a psychoeducational report (2 years old or less), and provide documentation of high school services. Upon application, materials documenting need for services should be sent only to the LD program or unit. Upon acceptance, documentation of need for services should be sent only to the LD program or unit. *Application deadline (institutional):* 9/10. *Application deadline (LD program):* Rolling/continuous for fall and rolling/continuous for spring.

Written Policies Written policy regarding general/basic LD accommodations is outlined in the school's catalog/handbook. Written policy regarding general/basic LD accommodations is available through the program or unit directly.

Albuquerque Technical Vocational Institute
Special Services

525 Buena Vista, SE
Albuquerque, NM 87106-4096
http://www.tvi.cc.nm.us/
Contact: Phone: 505-224-3000. Fax: 505-224-4740.

Special Services Approximately 250 registered undergraduate students were served during 2002-03. The program or unit includes 9 full-time staff members. Counselors and diagnostic specialists are provided through the program or unit.

Subject-area Tutoring Tutoring is offered in small groups for some subjects. Tutoring is provided collaboratively through on-campus or off-campus services via professional tutors.

Application For admittance to the program or unit, students are required to apply to the program directly and provide a psychoeducational report (3 years old or less). It is recommended that students provide documentation of high school services. Upon application, materials documenting need for services should be sent only to the LD program or unit. Upon acceptance, documentation of need for services should be sent only to the LD program or unit. *Application deadline (institutional):* Continuous. *Application deadline (LD program):* Rolling/continuous for fall and rolling/continuous for spring.

Alexandria Technical College
Support Services Department

1601 Jefferson Street
Alexandria, MN 56308-3707

http://www.alextech.org/CollegeServices.htm

Contact: Ms. Mary J. Ackerman, Support Services Coordinator. Phone: 320-762-4673. Fax: 320-762-4501. E-mail: marya@alx.tec.mn.us.

Support Services Department Approximately 290 registered undergraduate students were served during 2002-03. The program or unit includes 3 part-time staff members. Diagnostic specialists, professional tutors, remediation/learning specialists, skill tutors, and strategy tutors are provided through the program or unit. Academic advisers, counselors, graduate assistants/students, regular education teachers, and trained peer tutors are provided collaboratively through on-campus or off-campus services.

Unique Aids and Services Aids, services, or accommodations include career counseling and parent workshops.

Subject-area Tutoring Tutoring is offered one-on-one and in small groups for most subjects. Tutoring is provided through the program or unit via graduate assistants/students, professional tutors, and trained peer tutors.

Diagnostic Testing Testing is provided through the program or unit for learning styles. Testing for math, reading, and written language is provided collaboratively through on-campus or off-campus services.

Basic Skills Remediation Remediation is offered in class-size groups for math and written language. Remediation is provided collaboratively through on-campus or off-campus services via computer-based instruction and regular education teachers.

Enrichment Enrichment programs are available through the program or unit for learning strategies, math, oral communication skills, practical computer skills, self-advocacy, stress management, study skills, test taking, time management, vocabulary development, and written composition skills. Program for career planning is provided collaboratively through on-campus or off-campus services.

Application For admittance to the program or unit, students are required to provide a psychoeducational report (3 years old or less), provide documentation of high school services, and provide assessment summary report. Upon application, materials documenting need for services should be sent only to the LD program or unit. Upon acceptance, documentation of need for services should be sent only to the LD program or unit. *Application deadline (institutional):* Continuous. *Application deadline (LD program):* Rolling/continuous for fall and rolling/continuous for spring.

Written Policies Written policy regarding general/basic LD accommodations is outlined in the school's catalog/handbook. Written policy regarding general/basic LD accommodations is available through the program or unit directly.

Allan Hancock College

800 South College Drive

Santa Maria, CA 93454-6399

http://www.hancockcollege.edu/

Contact: Mark Malangko, Director. Phone: 805-922-6966 Ext. 3274. Fax: 805-922-3556. E-mail: mmalangko@hancock.cc.ca.us.

The program or unit includes 17 full-time staff members. Academic advisers, counselors, diagnostic specialists, LD specialists, professional tutors, remediation/learning specialists, skill tutors, and strat-

egy tutors are provided through the program or unit. Counselors, professional tutors, and regular education teachers are provided collaboratively through on-campus or off-campus services.

Orientation The program or unit offers an optional 1-day orientation for new students before registration and before classes begin.

Unique Aids and Services Aids, services, or accommodations include digital textbooks and priority registration.

Subject-area Tutoring Tutoring is offered one-on-one and in small groups for most subjects. Tutoring is provided through the program or unit via computer-based instruction and LD specialists. Tutoring is also provided collaboratively through on-campus or off-campus services via computer-based instruction, graduate assistants/students, professional tutors, and trained peer tutors.

Diagnostic Testing Testing is provided through the program or unit for auditory processing, intelligence, learning styles, math, neuropsychological, reading, spelling, spoken language, study skills, visual processing, and written language.

Basic Skills Remediation Remediation is offered one-on-one for computer skills, learning strategies, math, reading, spelling, study skills, time management, and written language. Remediation is provided through the program or unit via computer-based instruction and LD specialists. Remediation is also provided collaboratively through on-campus or off-campus services via computer-based instruction, graduate assistants/students, professional tutors, regular education teachers, and trained peer tutors.

Enrichment Enrichment programs are available through the program or unit for learning strategies, math, self-advocacy, test taking, time management, vocabulary development, and written composition skills. Programs for career planning, college survival skills, health and nutrition, math, practical computer skills, reading, stress management, study skills, test taking, time management, and written composition skills are provided collaboratively through on-campus or off-campus services. Credit is offered for college survival skills, health and nutrition, math, practical computer skills, reading, self-advocacy, study skills, and written composition skills.

Application For admittance to the program or unit, students are required to apply to the program directly and provide a psychoeducational report (3 years old or less). It is recommended that students provide documentation of high school services. Upon application, materials documenting need for services should be sent only to the LD program or unit. *Application deadline (institutional):* Continuous. *Application deadline (LD program):* Rolling/continuous for fall and rolling/continuous for spring.

Written Policies Written policy regarding general/basic LD accommodations is available on the program Web site. Written policies regarding course substitutions, general/basic LD accommodations, substitutions and waivers of admissions requirements, and substitutions and waivers of graduation requirements are outlined in the school's catalog/handbook. Written policies regarding course substitutions, general/basic LD accommodations, substitutions and waivers of admissions requirements, and substitutions and waivers of graduation requirements are available through the program or unit directly.

Allen County Community College

1801 North Cottonwood Street

Iola, KS 66749-1607

Allen County Community College (continued)
http://www.allencc.net/

Contact: Dan Kinney, Dean of Student Affairs. Phone: 620-365-5116 Ext. 213. Fax: 620-365-7406. E-mail: dkinney@allencc.edu.

Academic advisers, coaches, counselors, regular education teachers, remediation/learning specialists, and trained peer tutors are provided collaboratively through on-campus or off-campus services.

Unique Aids and Services Aids, services, or accommodations include career counseling and faculty training.

Subject-area Tutoring Tutoring is offered one-on-one. Tutoring is provided collaboratively through on-campus or off-campus services via computer-based instruction and trained peer tutors.

Diagnostic Testing Testing for math, reading, and written language is provided collaboratively through on-campus or off-campus services.

Basic Skills Remediation Remediation is offered one-on-one, in small groups, and in class-size groups for math, reading, study skills, time management, and written language. Remediation is provided collaboratively through on-campus or off-campus services via computer-based instruction, regular education teachers, and trained peer tutors.

Enrichment Programs for career planning, learning strategies, math, reading, stress management, study skills, test taking, time management, vocabulary development, and written composition skills are provided collaboratively through on-campus or off-campus services. Credit is offered for learning strategies, math, reading, stress management, study skills, test taking, time management, vocabulary development, and written composition skills.

Application For admittance to the program or unit, students are required to provide documentation of high school services. Upon acceptance, documentation of need for services should be sent only to the LD program or unit. *Application deadline (institutional):* 8/24. *Application deadline (LD program):* Rolling/continuous for fall and rolling/continuous for spring.

Written Policies Written policy regarding general/basic LD accommodations is available on the program Web site. Written policies regarding general/basic LD accommodations and substitutions and waivers of admissions requirements are outlined in the school's catalog/handbook.

Allentown Business School
Student Services Department

2809 East Saucon Valley Road
Center Valley, PA 18034
http://www.chooseabs.com/

Contact: Student Services Coordinator. Phone: 800-227-9109. Fax: 610-791-7810.

Student Services Department Approximately 150 registered undergraduate students were served during 2002-03. The program or unit includes 3 full-time staff members. Academic advisers, counselors, and LD specialists are provided through the program or unit. Academic advisers, counselors, LD specialists, professional tutors, regular education teachers, skill tutors, strategy tutors, trained peer tutors, and other are provided collaboratively through on-campus or off-campus services.

Orientation The program or unit offers an optional 11-week orientation for new students after classes begin and individually by special arrangement.

Unique Aids and Services Aids, services, or accommodations include career counseling, digital textbooks, priority registration, and support groups.

Subject-area Tutoring Tutoring is offered one-on-one, in small groups, and in class-size groups for all subjects. Tutoring is provided through the program or unit via computer-based instruction. Tutoring is also provided collaboratively through on-campus or off-campus services via professional tutors, trained peer tutors, and other.

Basic Skills Remediation Remediation is offered one-on-one and in small groups for computer skills, learning strategies, math, reading, social skills, spoken language, study skills, and time management. Remediation is provided through the program or unit via computer-based instruction and other.

Enrichment Enrichment programs are available through the program or unit for self-advocacy. Programs for college survival skills, learning strategies, math, practical computer skills, stress management, study skills, test taking, time management, and written composition skills are provided collaboratively through on-campus or off-campus services.

Application It is recommended that students apply to the program directly, provide a psychoeducational report (5 years old or less), and provide documentation of high school services. Upon application, materials documenting need for services should be sent to both admissions and the LD program or unit. Upon acceptance, documentation of need for services should be sent only to the LD program or unit. *Application deadline (institutional):* Continuous. *Application deadline (LD program):* Rolling/continuous for fall and rolling/continuous for spring.

Written Policies Written policies regarding course substitutions, general/basic LD accommodations, grade forgiveness, reduced course loads, and substitutions and waivers of graduation requirements are available through the program or unit directly.

Alvin Community College
Office of Support Services for Students with Disabilities

3110 Mustang Road
Alvin, TX 77511-4898
http://www.alvincollege.edu/

Contact: Ms. Eileen Cross, ADA Counselor. Phone: 281-756-3531. Fax: 281-756-3843. E-mail: ecross@alvin.cc.tx.us.

Office of Support Services for Students with Disabilities Approximately 70 registered undergraduate students were served during 2002-03. The program or unit includes 1 full-time and 1 part-time staff member. LD specialists are provided through the program or unit.

Diagnostic Testing Testing is provided through the program or unit for learning strategies and learning styles.

Basic Skills Remediation Remediation is offered one-on-one and in small groups for math, reading, and written language. Remediation is provided collaboratively through on-campus or off-campus services via computer-based instruction, professional tutors, and trained peer tutors.

Enrichment Programs for career planning, college survival skills, learning strategies, math, stress management, study skills, test taking, and time management are provided collaboratively through on-campus or off-campus services.

Student Organization Student Organization for Disability Awareness (SODA).

Application For admittance to the program or unit, students are required to apply to the program directly, provide a psychoeducational report (5 years old or less), and provide documentation of high school services. Upon application, materials documenting need for services should be sent to both admissions and the LD program or unit. Upon acceptance, documentation of need for services should be sent only to the LD program or unit. *Application deadline (institutional):* Continuous. *Application deadline (LD program):* Rolling/continuous for fall and rolling/continuous for spring.

Written Policies Written policy regarding general/basic LD accommodations is available on the program Web site. Written policy regarding general/basic LD accommodations is available through the program or unit directly.

Amarillo College
Accessibility Services

PO Box 447

Amarillo, TX 79178-0001

http://www.actx.edu/

Contact: Ms. Brenda Jeanne Wilkes, Coordinator of Accessibility Services. Phone: 806-371-5436. Fax: 806-371-5997. E-mail: wilkes-bj@actx.edu.

Accessibility Services Approximately 185 registered undergraduate students were served during 2002-03. The program or unit includes 2 full-time and 4 part-time staff members. Academic advisers, diagnostic specialists, and remediation/learning specialists are provided collaboratively through on-campus or off-campus services.

Orientation The program or unit offers an optional 2-hour orientation for new students before registration, before classes begin, during summer prior to enrollment, during registration, after classes begin, and individually by special arrangement.

Unique Aids and Services Aids, services, or accommodations include career counseling, priority registration, and support groups.

Subject-area Tutoring Tutoring is offered one-on-one and in small groups for some subjects. Tutoring is provided through the program or unit via LD specialists. Tutoring is also provided collaboratively through on-campus or off-campus services via computer-based instruction and trained peer tutors.

Diagnostic Testing Testing for intelligence, learning strategies, math, neuropsychological, personality, reading, spelling, and written language is provided collaboratively through on-campus or off-campus services.

Basic Skills Remediation Remediation is offered one-on-one, in small groups, and in class-size groups for learning strategies, math, reading, and study skills. Remediation is provided through the program or unit via LD specialists. Remediation is also provided collaboratively through on-campus or off-campus services via computer-based instruction, regular education teachers, and trained peer tutors.

Enrichment Enrichment programs are available through the program or unit for career planning, learning strategies, math, reading, stress management, study skills, test taking, and written composition skills. Programs for career planning, college survival skills, learning strategies, math, practical computer skills, reading, stress management, study skills, test taking, and written composition skills are provided collaboratively through on-campus or off-campus services. Credit is offered for career planning, college survival skills, math, practical computer skills, reading, study skills, and written composition skills.

Student Organization ACcessibility Aware consists of 25 members.

Fees *Diagnostic Testing* fee is applicable.

Application For admittance to the program or unit, students are required to apply to the program directly and provide a psychoeducational report (5 years old or less). It is recommended that students provide documentation of high school services. Upon application, materials documenting need for services should be sent only to the LD program or unit. Upon acceptance, documentation of need for services should be sent only to the LD program or unit. *Application deadline (LD program):* Rolling/continuous for fall and rolling/continuous for spring.

Written Policies Written policies regarding general/basic LD accommodations, substitutions and waivers of admissions requirements, and substitutions and waivers of graduation requirements are outlined in the school's catalog/handbook. Written policy regarding general/basic LD accommodations is available through the program or unit directly.

Anoka-Ramsey Community College, Cambridge Campus
Disability/Access Services

300 Polk Street South

Cambridge, MN 55008-5706

http://www.an.cc.mn.us/

Contact: Maria Struthers-Barlage, Academic Adviser. Phone: 763-689-7000. Fax: 763-689-7050. E-mail: maria.struthers-barlage@anokaramsey.edu.

Disability/Access Services Approximately 10 registered undergraduate students were served during 2002-03. Academic advisers, counselors, and professional tutors are provided collaboratively through on-campus or off-campus services.

Unique Aids and Services Aids, services, or accommodations include career counseling and priority registration.

Subject-area Tutoring Tutoring is offered one-on-one, in small groups, and in class-size groups for most subjects. Tutoring is provided collaboratively through on-campus or off-campus services via trained peer tutors.

Basic Skills Remediation Remediation is offered in class-size groups for computer skills, learning strategies, math, reading, and written language. Remediation is provided collaboratively through on-campus or off-campus services via regular education teachers and trained peer tutors.

Anoka-Ramsey Community College, Cambridge Campus (continued)

Enrichment Programs for career planning, health and nutrition, math, oral communication skills, practical computer skills, reading, stress management, and written composition skills are provided collaboratively through on-campus or off-campus services. Credit is offered for career planning, health and nutrition, math, oral communication skills, practical computer skills, reading, stress management, and written composition skills.

Application It is recommended that students apply to the program directly, provide a psychoeducational report, and provide documentation of high school services. Upon application, materials documenting need for services should be sent only to the LD program or unit. *Application deadline (institutional):* Continuous.

Written Policies Written policy regarding general/basic LD accommodations is available on the program Web site. Written policies regarding general/basic LD accommodations and substitutions and waivers of graduation requirements are outlined in the school's catalog/handbook. Written policies regarding general/basic LD accommodations and substitutions and waivers of graduation requirements are available through the program or unit directly.

Antelope Valley College
Disabled Student Services

3041 West Avenue K
Lancaster, CA 93536-5426
http://www.avc.edu/

Contact: Mr. David Greenleaf, Learning Disability Specialist. Phone: 661-722-6300 Ext. 6162. E-mail: dgreenleaf@avc.edu.

Disabled Student Services Approximately 250 registered undergraduate students were served during 2002-03. The program or unit includes 2 full-time staff members. LD specialists are provided through the program or unit.

Unique Aids and Services Aids, services, or accommodations include career counseling, digital textbooks, faculty training, and priority registration.

Diagnostic Testing Testing is provided through the program or unit for auditory processing, intelligence, math, reading, spelling, visual processing, and written language.

Application For admittance to the program or unit, students are required to apply to the program directly and provide documentation of high school services. Upon application, materials documenting need for services should be sent only to the LD program or unit. Upon acceptance, documentation of need for services should be sent only to the LD program or unit. *Application deadline (institutional):* Continuous. *Application deadline (LD program):* Rolling/continuous for fall and rolling/continuous for spring.

Written Policies Written policies regarding course substitutions, general/basic LD accommodations, substitutions and waivers of admissions requirements, and substitutions and waivers of graduation requirements are available through the program or unit directly.

Arapahoe Community College
Center for Academic Resources

5900 South Santa Fe Drive, PO Box 9002
Littleton, CO 80160-9002
http://www.arapahoe.edu/

Contact: Ms. Linda J. Heesch, Director of Center for Academic Resources. Phone: 303-797-5806. Fax: 303-797-5810. E-mail: linda.heesch@arapahoe.edu.

Center for Academic Resources Approximately 83 registered undergraduate students were served during 2002-03. The program or unit includes 2 full-time staff members. Diagnostic specialists and professional tutors are provided through the program or unit. Diagnostic specialists are provided collaboratively through on-campus or off-campus services.

Unique Aids and Services Aids, services, or accommodations include digital textbooks.

Subject-area Tutoring Tutoring is offered one-on-one and in small groups for most subjects. Tutoring is provided collaboratively through on-campus or off-campus services via professional tutors and trained peer tutors.

Basic Skills Remediation Remediation is offered in class-size groups for math, reading, spelling, study skills, and written language. Remediation is provided collaboratively through on-campus or off-campus services via regular education teachers.

Enrichment Enrichment programs are available through the program or unit for self-advocacy. Programs for career planning, learning strategies, math, oral communication skills, reading, self-advocacy, study skills, test taking, time management, and written composition skills are provided collaboratively through on-campus or off-campus services. Credit is offered for career planning, learning strategies, math, oral communication skills, reading, self-advocacy, study skills, and written composition skills.

Application For admittance to the program or unit, students are required to provide a psychoeducational report (3 years old or less), provide documentation of high school services, and provide appropriate documentation. Upon acceptance, documentation of need for services should be sent only to the LD program or unit. *Application deadline (institutional):* Continuous. *Application deadline (LD program):* Rolling/continuous for fall and rolling/continuous for spring.

Written Policies Written policy regarding general/basic LD accommodations is available on the program Web site. Written policies regarding course substitutions, general/basic LD accommodations, reduced course loads, and substitutions and waivers of graduation requirements are available through the program or unit directly.

Argosy University-Twin Cities

1515 Central Parkway
Eagen, MN 55121
http://www.argosyu.edu/

Contact: Dr. Jack O'Regan, Special Services Coordinator. Phone: 952-252-7575. E-mail: joregan@argosyu.edu.

Approximately 12 registered undergraduate students were served during 2002-03. The program or unit includes 1 part-time staff member. Academic advisers, counselors, graduate assistants/students, and professional tutors are provided collaboratively through on-campus or off-campus services.

Unique Aids and Services Aids, services, or accommodations include career counseling.

Subject-area Tutoring Tutoring is offered one-on-one. Tutoring is provided collaboratively through on-campus or off-campus services via graduate assistants/students, professional tutors, and trained peer tutors.

Diagnostic Testing Testing for intelligence, learning strategies, learning styles, math, neuropsychological, personality, reading, social skills, spelling, study skills, and written language is provided collaboratively through on-campus or off-campus services.

Basic Skills Remediation Remediation is offered one-on-one for math, reading, study skills, and time management. Remediation is provided collaboratively through on-campus or off-campus services via graduate assistants/students, regular education teachers, and trained peer tutors.

Application For admittance to the program or unit, students are required to apply to the program directly and provide a psychoeducational report (3 years old or less). Upon application, materials documenting need for services should be sent only to admissions with institutional application materials. Upon acceptance, documentation of need for services should be sent only to the LD program or unit. *Application deadline (institutional):* Continuous. *Application deadline (LD program):* Rolling/continuous for fall and rolling/continuous for spring.

Written Policies Written policy regarding general/basic LD accommodations is available on the program Web site. Written policies regarding course substitutions, general/basic LD accommodations, and substitutions and waivers of admissions requirements are outlined in the school's catalog/handbook.

Arizona Western College

PO Box 929

Yuma, AZ 85366-0929

http://www.azwestern.edu/

Contact: Phone: 928-317-6000. Fax: 928-344-7730.

The program or unit includes 1 full-time staff member. Academic advisers, coaches, counselors, diagnostic specialists, LD specialists, regular education teachers, and trained peer tutors are provided collaboratively through on-campus or off-campus services.

Unique Aids and Services Aids, services, or accommodations include advocates, career counseling, and digital textbooks.

Subject-area Tutoring Tutoring is offered in small groups for most subjects. Tutoring is provided collaboratively through on-campus or off-campus services via computer-based instruction and trained peer tutors.

Basic Skills Remediation Remediation is offered in small groups for computer skills, learning strategies, study skills, and time management. Remediation is provided collaboratively through on-campus or off-campus services via computer-based instruction and other.

Application For admittance to the program or unit, students are required to provide a psychoeducational report (5 years old or less). It is recommended that students provide documentation of high school services. Upon application, materials documenting need for services should be sent only to the LD program or unit. Upon acceptance, documentation of need for services should be sent only to the LD program or unit. *Application deadline (institutional):* Continuous. *Application deadline (LD program):* 5/1 for fall. 11/1 for spring.

Written Policies Written policies regarding course substitutions, general/basic LD accommodations, substitutions and waivers of admissions requirements, and substitutions and waivers of graduation requirements are available on the program Web site. Written policies regarding course substitutions, general/basic LD accommodations, substitutions and waivers of admissions requirements, and substitutions and waivers of graduation requirements are outlined in the school's catalog/handbook. Written policy regarding general/basic LD accommodations is available through the program or unit directly.

Arkansas State University-Beebe

PO Box 1000

Beebe, AR 72012-1000

http://www.asub.edu

Contact: Mrs. Kristi Tucker, Counselor and Coordinator of Disability Services. Phone: 501-882-8263. Fax: 501-882-8301. E-mail: kntucker@asub.edu. Head of LD Program: Dr. Mark Taylor, Director of Guidance Services. Phone: 501-882-8279. Fax: 501-882-8279. E-mail: mltaylor@asub.edu.

Approximately 50 registered undergraduate students were served during 2002-03. The program or unit includes 2 full-time staff members. Counselors, LD specialists, professional tutors, and other are provided through the program or unit.

Unique Aids and Services Aids, services, or accommodations include career counseling, digital textbooks, and faculty training.

Subject-area Tutoring Tutoring is offered one-on-one, in small groups, and in class-size groups for all subjects. Tutoring is provided collaboratively through on-campus or off-campus services via computer-based instruction, graduate assistants/students, professional tutors, and trained peer tutors.

Basic Skills Remediation Remediation is offered in class-size groups for math, reading, and written language. Remediation is provided collaboratively through on-campus or off-campus services.

Enrichment Enrichment programs are available through the program or unit for self-advocacy and stress management. Programs for career planning, college survival skills, math, oral communication skills, practical computer skills, reading, study skills, test taking, time management, vocabulary development, and written composition skills are provided collaboratively through on-campus or off-campus services. Credit is offered for career planning, college survival skills, math, oral communication skills, practical computer skills, reading, study skills, test taking, time management, vocabulary development, and written composition skills.

Arkansas State University-Beebe (continued)

Application For admittance to the program or unit, students are required to apply to the program directly and provide a psychoeducational report (5 years old or less). It is recommended that students provide documentation of high school services. Upon application, materials documenting need for services should be sent only to the LD program or unit. Upon acceptance, documentation of need for services should be sent only to the LD program or unit. *Application deadline (institutional):* Continuous. *Application deadline (LD program):* Rolling/continuous for fall and rolling/continuous for spring.

Written Policies Written policy regarding general/basic LD accommodations is outlined in the school's catalog/handbook.

The Art Institute of California-Los Angeles

2900 31st Street

Santa Monica, CA 90405-3035

http://www.aicala.artinstitutes.edu/

Contact: Ms. Mary A. Coleman, Director of Counseling Services. Phone: 310-314-6000 Ext. 5049. E-mail: colemanm@aii.edu.

Approximately 25 registered undergraduate students were served during 2002-03. The program or unit includes 1 full-time staff member. Counselors and LD specialists are provided through the program or unit.

Unique Aids and Services Aids, services, or accommodations include personal coach.

Application For admittance to the program or unit, students are required to provide a psychoeducational report (5 years old or less) and provide diagnosis by a psychologist or other qualified person. Upon application, materials documenting need for services should be sent only to the LD program or unit. *Application deadline (LD program):* Rolling/continuous for fall and rolling/continuous for spring.

Written Policies Written policy regarding substitutions and waivers of admissions requirements is available on the program Web site. Written policies regarding general/basic LD accommodations and substitutions and waivers of admissions requirements are outlined in the school's catalog/handbook. Written policy regarding general/basic LD accommodations is available through the program or unit directly.

The Art Institute of New York City

75 Varick Street, 16th Floor

New York, NY 10013

http://www.nyrs.artinstitutes.edu/

Contact: Ms. Jennifer Fallon, Counselor. Phone: 212-226-5500 Ext. 6700. E-mail: fallonj@aii.edu.

The program or unit includes 1 full-time staff member. Counselors are provided through the program or unit. Academic advisers and regular education teachers are provided collaboratively through on-campus or off-campus services.

Unique Aids and Services Aids, services, or accommodations include career counseling.

Subject-area Tutoring Tutoring is offered one-on-one, in small groups, and in class-size groups.

Basic Skills Remediation Remediation is offered one-on-one, in small groups, and in class-size groups for math, reading, study skills, and time management. Remediation is provided collaboratively through on-campus or off-campus services via regular education teachers, trained peer tutors, and other.

Enrichment Enrichment programs are available through the program or unit for health and nutrition, math, oral communication skills, practical computer skills, stress management, study skills, and time management. Programs for career planning, college survival skills, learning strategies, study skills, test taking, and time management are provided collaboratively through on-campus or off-campus services. Credit is offered for health and nutrition, math, oral communication skills, and practical computer skills.

Application For admittance to the program or unit, students are required to apply to the program directly, provide a psychoeducational report, and provide documentation completed by an appropriate professional relevant to the disability. Upon application, materials documenting need for services should be sent only to the LD program or unit. Upon acceptance, documentation of need for services should be sent only to the LD program or unit. *Application deadline (LD program):* Rolling/continuous for fall and rolling/continuous for spring.

Written Policies Written policies regarding general/basic LD accommodations and substitutions and waivers of graduation requirements are outlined in the school's catalog/handbook. Written policies regarding general/basic LD accommodations, substitutions and waivers of admissions requirements, and substitutions and waivers of graduation requirements are available through the program or unit directly.

The Art Institute of Philadelphia
The Academic Achievement Center

1622 Chestnut Street

Philadelphia, PA 19103-5198

http://www.aiph.artinstitutes.edu/

Contact: Mrs. Anita J. Rudman, Director of Academic Achievement. Phone: 800-275-2474 Ext. 6344. Fax: 215-405-6399. E-mail: rudmana@aii.edu.

The Academic Achievement Center Approximately 85 registered undergraduate students were served during 2002-03. The program or unit includes 1 full-time staff member. Academic advisers are provided through the program or unit. Academic advisers, counselors, regular education teachers, and trained peer tutors are provided collaboratively through on-campus or off-campus services.

Subject-area Tutoring Tutoring is offered one-on-one for all subjects. Tutoring is provided collaboratively through on-campus or off-campus services via trained peer tutors.

Diagnostic Testing Testing is provided through the program or unit for math, reading, and written language. Testing for math, reading, and written language is provided collaboratively through on-campus or off-campus services.

Basic Skills Remediation Remediation is offered in class-size groups for math, reading, and written language. Remediation is provided collaboratively through on-campus or off-campus services via regular education teachers.

Enrichment Enrichment programs are available through the program or unit for self-advocacy. Programs for career planning, college survival skills, health and nutrition, learning strategies, stress management, study skills, test taking, and time management are provided collaboratively through on-campus or off-campus services.

Application For admittance to the program or unit, students are required to provide a psychoeducational report (3 years old or less), provide documentation of high school services, and provide a medical evaluation, if appropriate. Upon application, materials documenting need for services should be sent to both admissions and the LD program or unit. *Application deadline (institutional):* Continuous. *Application deadline (LD program):* Rolling/continuous for fall and rolling/continuous for spring.

Written Policies Written policy regarding general/basic LD accommodations is outlined in the school's catalog/handbook.

The Art Institute of Pittsburgh
Disability Services

420 Boulevard of the Allies

Pittsburgh, PA 15219

http://www.aip.aii.edu/

Contact: Jenna Templeton, Director of Student Life. Phone: 412-291-6291. Fax: 412-263-3805. E-mail: templetj@aii.edu.

Disability Services Approximately 100 registered undergraduate students were served during 2002-03. The program or unit includes 1 full-time staff member. Academic advisers, counselors, remediation/learning specialists, and trained peer tutors are provided collaboratively through on-campus or off-campus services.

Unique Aids and Services Aids, services, or accommodations include faculty training.

Subject-area Tutoring Tutoring is offered one-on-one and in small groups for most subjects. Tutoring is provided collaboratively through on-campus or off-campus services via graduate assistants/students and trained peer tutors.

Basic Skills Remediation Remediation is offered in class-size groups for math and written language. Remediation is provided collaboratively through on-campus or off-campus services via computer-based instruction and regular education teachers.

Application For admittance to the program or unit, students are required to provide a psychoeducational report. It is recommended that students provide documentation of high school services. Upon application, materials documenting need for services should be sent only to the LD program or unit. Upon acceptance, documentation of need for services should be sent only to the LD program or unit. *Application deadline (institutional):* Continuous. *Application deadline (LD program):* Rolling/continuous for fall and rolling/continuous for spring.

Written Policies Written policies regarding course substitutions, general/basic LD accommodations, substitutions and waivers of admissions requirements, and substitutions and waivers of graduation requirements are outlined in the school's catalog/handbook.

The Art Institute of Seattle
Special Needs/Disabilities Office

2323 Elliott Avenue

Seattle, WA 98121-1642

http://www.ais.edu/

Contact: Ms. Karen Ehnat, Director of Special Needs/Disabilities. Phone: 206-239-2308. Fax: 206-441-3475. E-mail: ehnatk@aii.edu.

Special Needs/Disabilities Office Counselors, regular education teachers, skill tutors, strategy tutors, and trained peer tutors are provided collaboratively through on-campus or off-campus services.

Subject-area Tutoring Tutoring is offered one-on-one and in small groups for most subjects. Tutoring is provided collaboratively through on-campus or off-campus services via trained peer tutors and other.

Application For admittance to the program or unit, students are required to provide a psychoeducational report and provide results of current testing at the adult level. It is recommended that students provide documentation of high school services. Upon acceptance, documentation of need for services should be sent only to the LD program or unit. *Application deadline (institutional):* Continuous. *Application deadline (LD program):* Rolling/continuous for fall and rolling/continuous for spring.

Written Policies Written policy regarding general/basic LD accommodations is available on the program Web site. Written policy regarding general/basic LD accommodations is outlined in the school's catalog/handbook. Written policy regarding general/basic LD accommodations is available through the program or unit directly.

The Art Institutes International Minnesota

15 South 9th Street

Minneapolis, MN 55402-3137

http://www.aim.artinstitutes.edu/

Contact: Ms. Lara Derksen, Director of Student Life. Phone: 612-332-3361 Ext. 165. Fax: 612-332-3934. E-mail: derksenl@aii.edu.

Approximately 5 registered undergraduate students were served during 2002-03. Counselors, remediation/learning specialists, and trained peer tutors are provided through the program or unit. Academic advisers, coaches, counselors, regular education teachers, remediation/learning specialists, skill tutors, and trained peer tutors are provided collaboratively through on-campus or off-campus services.

Unique Aids and Services Aids, services, or accommodations include digital textbooks and personal coach.

The Art Institutes International Minnesota (continued)

Subject-area Tutoring Tutoring is offered one-on-one and in small groups. Tutoring is provided collaboratively through on-campus or off-campus services via computer-based instruction and trained peer tutors.

Basic Skills Remediation Remediation is offered in small groups and in class-size groups for computer skills, math, reading, spelling, and written language. Remediation is provided collaboratively through on-campus or off-campus services via regular education teachers.

Application Upon application, materials documenting need for services should be sent only to the LD program or unit. Upon acceptance, documentation of need for services should be sent only to the LD program or unit. *Application deadline (institutional):* Continuous. *Application deadline (LD program):* Rolling/continuous for fall and rolling/continuous for spring.

Written Policies Written policy regarding general/basic LD accommodations is outlined in the school's catalog/handbook.

Asheville-Buncombe Technical Community College
Disability Services Office

340 Victoria Road
Asheville, NC 28801-4897
http://www.abtech.edu/Student_Services/counseling/disability/default.asp

Contact: Annie Clingenpeel, Disability Services Coordinator and Counselor. Phone: 828-254-1921 Ext. 141. Fax: 828-281-9704. E-mail: aclingenpeel@abtech.edu.

Disability Services Office Approximately 119 registered undergraduate students were served during 2002-03. The program or unit includes 1 full-time staff member. Counselors are provided through the program or unit. Academic advisers, remediation/learning specialists, skill tutors, and trained peer tutors are provided collaboratively through on-campus or off-campus services.

Orientation The program or unit offers an optional 1-hour orientation for new students individually by special arrangement.

Unique Aids and Services Aids, services, or accommodations include career counseling, faculty training, priority registration, meetings with faculty.

Subject-area Tutoring Tutoring is offered in class-size groups for some subjects. Tutoring is provided collaboratively through on-campus or off-campus services via computer-based instruction, trained peer tutors, and other.

Basic Skills Remediation Remediation is offered in class-size groups for math, reading, and written language. Remediation is provided collaboratively through on-campus or off-campus services via computer-based instruction, professional tutors, regular education teachers, special education teachers, and teacher trainees.

Enrichment Enrichment programs are available through the program or unit for learning strategies, self-advocacy, stress management, study skills, test taking, time management, and other. Programs for career planning, college survival skills, health and nutrition, learning strategies, math, oral communication skills, practical computer skills, reading, stress management, study skills, time manage-

ment, vocabulary development, and written composition skills are provided collaboratively through on-campus or off-campus services. Credit is offered for college survival skills, health and nutrition, learning strategies, math, oral communication skills, practical computer skills, reading, stress management, study skills, time management, and written composition skills.

Application For admittance to the program or unit, students are required to provide a psychoeducational report (5 years old or less). It is recommended that students apply to the program directly and provide documentation of high school services. Upon application, materials documenting need for services should be sent only to the LD program or unit. Upon acceptance, documentation of need for services should be sent only to the LD program or unit. *Application deadline (institutional):* Continuous. *Application deadline (LD program):* Rolling/continuous for fall and rolling/continuous for spring.

Written Policies Written policy regarding general/basic LD accommodations is available on the program Web site. Written policies regarding course substitutions, general/basic LD accommodations, reduced course loads, and substitutions and waivers of graduation requirements are available through the program or unit directly.

Ashland Community and Technical College
Disability Services

1400 College Drive
Ashland, KY 41101-3683
http://www.ashland.kctcs.edu/

Contact: Ms. Nancy Coldiron Preston, Disability Services Coordinator. Phone: 606-326-2051. Fax: 606-326-2192. E-mail: nancy.preston@kctcs.edu.

Disability Services Approximately 50 registered undergraduate students were served during 2002-03. The program or unit includes 5 part-time staff members. Academic advisers, counselors, and regular education teachers are provided through the program or unit. Academic advisers, counselors, professional tutors, regular education teachers, skill tutors, and trained peer tutors are provided collaboratively through on-campus or off-campus services.

Orientation The program or unit offers individually by special arrangement.

Unique Aids and Services Aids, services, or accommodations include advocates, career counseling, digital textbooks, faculty training, priority registration, and support groups.

Subject-area Tutoring Tutoring is offered one-on-one and in small groups for most subjects. Tutoring is provided through the program or unit via computer-based instruction. Tutoring is also provided collaboratively through on-campus or off-campus services via computer-based instruction and trained peer tutors.

Basic Skills Remediation Remediation is offered in small groups and in class-size groups for auditory processing, computer skills, learning strategies, math, reading, spelling, study skills, time management, and written language. Remediation is provided through the program or unit via computer-based instruction. Remediation is also provided collaboratively through on-campus or off-campus services via computer-based instruction, regular education teachers, special education teachers, and trained peer tutors.

Enrichment Enrichment programs are available through the program or unit for career planning. Programs for career planning, college survival skills, learning strategies, math, reading, study skills, test taking, time management, vocabulary development, and written composition skills are provided collaboratively through on-campus or off-campus services.

Application For admittance to the program or unit, students are required to apply to the program directly and provide a psychoeducational report (3 years old or less). It is recommended that students provide documentation of high school services. Upon application, materials documenting need for services should be sent only to the LD program or unit. Upon acceptance, documentation of need for services should be sent only to the LD program or unit. *Application deadline (institutional):* 8/20. *Application deadline (LD program):* Rolling/continuous for fall and rolling/continuous for spring.

Written Policies Written policies regarding course substitutions, general/basic LD accommodations, substitutions and waivers of admissions requirements, and substitutions and waivers of graduation requirements are available on the program Web site. Written policies regarding course substitutions, general/basic LD accommodations, substitutions and waivers of admissions requirements, and substitutions and waivers of graduation requirements are outlined in the school's catalog/handbook. Written policies regarding course substitutions, general/basic LD accommodations, substitutions and waivers of admissions requirements, and substitutions and waivers of graduation requirements are available through the program or unit directly.

Asnuntuck Community College
Student Services

170 Elm Street
Enfield, CT 06082-3800
http://www.acc.commnet.edu
Contact: P. Maki McHenry, Counselor and Accommodations Coordinator. Phone: 860-253-3021. Fax: 860-253-3029. E-mail: mmchenry@acc.commnet.edu.

Student Services Approximately 75 registered undergraduate students were served during 2002-03.
Unique Aids and Services Aids, services, or accommodations include advocates, career counseling, faculty training, personal coach, priority registration, support groups.
Subject-area Tutoring Tutoring is offered one-on-one, in small groups, and in class-size groups for some subjects. Tutoring is provided collaboratively through on-campus or off-campus services via computer-based instruction, professional tutors, and other.
Basic Skills Remediation Remediation is offered one-on-one, in small groups, and in class-size groups for computer skills, learning strategies, math, reading, social skills, spelling, study skills, time management, and written language. Remediation is provided collaboratively through on-campus or off-campus services via computer-based instruction, professional tutors, regular education teachers, and other.
Enrichment Programs for career planning, college survival skills, health and nutrition, learning strategies, math, oral communication skills, practical computer skills, reading, self-advocacy, stress man-

agement, study skills, test taking, time management, vocabulary development, and written composition skills are provided collaboratively through on-campus or off-campus services. Credit is offered for college survival skills, health and nutrition, learning strategies, reading, study skills, test taking, time management, vocabulary development, and written composition skills.

Application For admittance to the program or unit, students are required to provide a psychoeducational report. It is recommended that students provide documentation of high school services. Upon application, materials documenting need for services should be sent only to the LD program or unit. Upon acceptance, documentation of need for services should be sent only to the LD program or unit. *Application deadline (institutional):* Continuous. *Application deadline (LD program):* Rolling/continuous for fall and rolling/continuous for spring.

Written Policies Written policy regarding general/basic LD accommodations is available on the program Web site. Written policies regarding course substitutions, general/basic LD accommodations, grade forgiveness, reduced course loads, substitutions and waivers of admissions requirements, and substitutions and waivers of graduation requirements are outlined in the school's catalog/handbook. Written policies regarding course substitutions, general/basic LD accommodations, grade forgiveness, reduced course loads, substitutions and waivers of admissions requirements, and substitutions and waivers of graduation requirements are available through the program or unit directly.

Athens Technical College
Office of Student Support Services

800 US Highway 29 North
Athens, GA 30601-1500
http://www.athenstech.org
Contact: Jim Synan, Disabilities Counselor. Phone: 706-355-5006. Fax: 706-369-5756. E-mail: jsynan@athenstech.org.

Office of Student Support Services Approximately 100 registered undergraduate students were served during 2002-03. The program or unit includes 2 full-time staff members. Academic advisers, counselors, and trained peer tutors are provided through the program or unit. Academic advisers and trained peer tutors are provided collaboratively through on-campus or off-campus services.
Unique Aids and Services Aids, services, or accommodations include career counseling and digital textbooks.
Subject-area Tutoring Tutoring is offered one-on-one, in small groups, and in class-size groups for some subjects. Tutoring is provided collaboratively through on-campus or off-campus services via computer-based instruction, graduate assistants/students, professional tutors, and trained peer tutors.
Basic Skills Remediation Remediation is offered one-on-one and in small groups for math, reading, spelling, and written language. Remediation is provided collaboratively through on-campus or off-campus services via computer-based instruction and regular education teachers.
Enrichment Enrichment programs are available through the program or unit for career planning and college survival skills.

Athens Technical College (continued)

Application For admittance to the program or unit, students are required to provide a psychoeducational report (3 years old or less). It is recommended that students provide documentation of high school services. Upon application, materials documenting need for services should be sent only to the LD program or unit. Upon acceptance, documentation of need for services should be sent only to the LD program or unit. *Application deadline (institutional):* Continuous. *Application deadline (LD program):* Rolling/continuous for fall and rolling/continuous for spring.

Written Policies Written policy regarding general/basic LD accommodations is available on the program Web site. Written policies regarding course substitutions and general/basic LD accommodations are outlined in the school's catalog/handbook. Written policies regarding general/basic LD accommodations and reduced course loads are available through the program or unit directly.

Austin Community College
Office for Students with Disabilities

5930 Middle Fiskville Road
Austin, TX 78752-4390
http://www2.austincc.edu/osd/index.html
Contact: Ms. Judy Lynn Hay, Supervisor. Phone: 512-223-3143. Fax: 512-223-3408. E-mail: jhaymull@austincc.edu.

Office for Students with Disabilities The program or unit includes 6 full-time and 12 part-time staff members. Academic advisers, coaches, counselors, LD specialists, regular education teachers, remediation/learning specialists, and skill tutors are provided collaboratively through on-campus or off-campus services.

Orientation The program or unit offers a mandatory 1½-hour orientation for new students before classes begin and individually by special arrangement.

Unique Aids and Services Aids, services, or accommodations include advocates, career counseling, faculty training, and priority registration.

Subject-area Tutoring Tutoring is offered in small groups for most subjects. Tutoring is provided collaboratively through on-campus or off-campus services via computer-based instruction and trained peer tutors.

Basic Skills Remediation Remediation is offered in class-size groups for learning strategies, math, reading, and written language. Remediation is provided collaboratively through on-campus or off-campus services via computer-based instruction and regular education teachers.

Enrichment Programs for career planning, college survival skills, learning strategies, and written composition skills are provided collaboratively through on-campus or off-campus services.

Application For admittance to the program or unit, students are required to apply to the program directly and provide a psychoeducational report (3 years old or less). Upon application, materials documenting need for services should be sent only to the LD program or unit. Upon acceptance, documentation of need for services should be sent only to the LD program or unit. *Application deadline (institutional):* Continuous. *Application deadline (LD program):* Rolling/continuous for fall and rolling/continuous for spring.

Written Policies Written policies regarding course substitutions, general/basic LD accommodations, grade forgiveness, reduced course loads, substitutions and waivers of admissions requirements, and substitutions and waivers of graduation requirements are available on the program Web site. Written policies regarding course substitutions, general/basic LD accommodations, grade forgiveness, reduced course loads, substitutions and waivers of admissions requirements, and substitutions and waivers of graduation requirements are outlined in the school's catalog/handbook. Written policies regarding course substitutions, general/basic LD accommodations, grade forgiveness, reduced course loads, substitutions and waivers of admissions requirements, and substitutions and waivers of graduation requirements are available through the program or unit directly.

Bay de Noc Community College

2001 North Lincoln Road
Escanaba, MI 49829-2511
http://www.baydenoc.cc.mi.us/
Contact: Marlene Paavilainen, Director of Special Populations. Phone: 906-786-5802 Ext. 1128. Fax: 906-789-6912. E-mail: paavilam@baydenoc.cc.mi.us.

Enrichment Programs for career planning, college survival skills, learning strategies, math, oral communication skills, practical computer skills, reading, stress management, study skills, test taking, time management, vocabulary development, and written composition skills are provided collaboratively through on-campus or off-campus services.

Application *Application deadline (institutional):* 8/15.

Beaufort County Community College

PO Box 1069
Washington, NC 27889-1069
http://www.beaufort.cc.nc.us/
Contact: Ms. Lisa Bunting, Special Population Coordinator. Phone: 252-940-6351. E-mail: lisab@email.beaufort.cc.nc.us.

The program or unit includes 1 part-time staff member. Academic advisers, coaches, counselors, diagnostic specialists, graduate assistants/students, LD specialists, professional tutors, regular education teachers, remediation/learning specialists, skill tutors, special education teachers, teacher trainees, trained peer tutors, and other are provided collaboratively through on-campus or off-campus services.

Orientation The program or unit offers an optional orientation for new students individually by special arrangement.

Unique Aids and Services Aids, services, or accommodations include advocates and career counseling.

Subject-area Tutoring Tutoring is offered one-on-one and in small groups. Tutoring is provided collaboratively through on-campus or off-campus services via computer-based instruction, graduate assistants/students, LD specialists, trained peer tutors, and other.

Basic Skills Remediation Remediation is offered in class-size groups for computer skills, learning strategies, math, reading, study skills, time management, and written language. Remediation is provided collaboratively through on-campus or off-campus services via computer-based instruction, graduate assistants/students, LD specialists, professional tutors, regular education teachers, special education teachers, teacher trainees, trained peer tutors, and other.

Enrichment Programs for career planning, college survival skills, health and nutrition, learning strategies, math, oral communication skills, practical computer skills, reading, self-advocacy, stress management, study skills, test taking, time management, vocabulary development, written composition skills, and other are provided collaboratively through on-campus or off-campus services. Credit is offered for college survival skills, health and nutrition, math, practical computer skills, reading, study skills, test taking, time management, and written composition skills.

Application For admittance to the program or unit, students are required to apply to the program directly and provide a psychoeducational report. It is recommended that students provide documentation of high school services. Upon application, materials documenting need for services should be sent only to the LD program or unit. Upon acceptance, documentation of need for services should be sent only to the LD program or unit. *Application deadline (institutional):* Continuous.

Written Policies Written policy regarding general/basic LD accommodations is outlined in the school's catalog/handbook. Written policy regarding general/basic LD accommodations is available through the program or unit directly.

Bergen Community College

400 Paramus Road

Paramus, NJ 07652-1595

http://www.bergen.edu/

Contact: Ms. Nancy Carr, Director. Phone: 201-612-5270. Fax: 201-493-1839. E-mail: ncarr@bergen.edu.

Approximately 800 registered undergraduate students were served during 2002-03. The program or unit includes 11 full-time staff members. Academic advisers, counselors, and LD specialists are provided through the program or unit. Diagnostic specialists, professional tutors, and regular education teachers are provided collaboratively through on-campus or off-campus services.

Orientation The program or unit offers an optional 2-day orientation for new students during summer prior to enrollment and individually by special arrangement.

Summer Program To help prepare for the demands of college, there is an optional 2-day summer program prior to entering the school.

Unique Aids and Services Aids, services, or accommodations include career counseling, faculty training, parent workshops, and priority registration.

Subject-area Tutoring Tutoring is offered one-on-one for most subjects. Tutoring is provided collaboratively through on-campus or off-campus services via computer-based instruction, graduate assistants/students, professional tutors, and trained peer tutors.

Diagnostic Testing Testing is provided through the program or unit for auditory processing. Testing for auditory processing is provided collaboratively through on-campus or off-campus services.

Basic Skills Remediation Remediation is offered one-on-one for math, reading, spoken language, and written language. Remediation is provided collaboratively through on-campus or off-campus services via computer-based instruction, professional tutors, and trained peer tutors.

Fees *Diagnostic Testing* fee is applicable.

Application For admittance to the program or unit, students are required to apply to the program directly, provide a psychoeducational report (3 years old or less), and provide documentation of high school services. Upon application, materials documenting need for services should be sent only to the LD program or unit. *Application deadline (institutional):* 7/31. *Application deadline (LD program):* Rolling/continuous for fall and rolling/continuous for spring.

Written Policies Written policies regarding course substitutions, general/basic LD accommodations, substitutions and waivers of admissions requirements, and substitutions and waivers of graduation requirements are available through the program or unit directly.

Berkshire Community College
Disabled Student Services

1350 West Street

Pittsfield, MA 01201-5786

http://www.berkshirecc.edu

Contact: Phone: 413-499-4660. Fax: 606-224-7744.

Disabled Student Services Approximately 60 registered undergraduate students were served during 2002-03. The program or unit includes 1 full-time staff member. LD specialists are provided through the program or unit. Academic advisers, counselors, regular education teachers, skill tutors, strategy tutors, and trained peer tutors are provided collaboratively through on-campus or off-campus services.

Unique Aids and Services Aids, services, or accommodations include advocates, career counseling, and faculty training.

Subject-area Tutoring Tutoring is offered one-on-one and in small groups. Tutoring is provided collaboratively through on-campus or off-campus services via computer-based instruction, graduate assistants/students, and trained peer tutors.

Basic Skills Remediation Remediation is offered in small groups and in class-size groups for math, reading, study skills, time management, and written language. Remediation is provided collaboratively through on-campus or off-campus services via regular education teachers.

Enrichment Enrichment programs are available through the program or unit for college survival skills, learning strategies, self-advocacy, stress management, study skills, test taking, and time management. Programs for career planning, college survival skills, health and nutrition, learning strategies, math, oral communication skills, practical computer skills, reading, stress management, study skills, test taking, time management, vocabulary development, and written composition skills are provided collaboratively through on-campus or off-campus services.

Berkshire Community College (continued)

Application For admittance to the program or unit, students are required to apply to the program directly and provide a psychoeducational report. It is recommended that students provide documentation of high school services. Upon application, materials documenting need for services should be sent only to the LD program or unit. Upon acceptance, documentation of need for services should be sent only to the LD program or unit. *Application deadline (institutional):* Continuous. *Application deadline (LD program):* Rolling/continuous for fall and rolling/continuous for spring.

Written Policies Written policies regarding course substitutions, general/basic LD accommodations, substitutions and waivers of admissions requirements, and substitutions and waivers of graduation requirements are available on the program Web site. Written policy regarding general/basic LD accommodations is outlined in the school's catalog/handbook. Written policies regarding course substitutions, general/basic LD accommodations, substitutions and waivers of admissions requirements, and substitutions and waivers of graduation requirements are available through the program or unit directly.

Bessemer State Technical College
Special Needs Services

PO Box 308

Bessemer, AL 35021-0308

http://www.bessemertech.com/

Contact: Ms. Renay Herndon, Retention and Assessment Coordinator. Phone: 205-426-7335 Ext. 335. Fax: 205-426-7306. E-mail: rherndon@bstc.cc.al.us. Head of LD Program: Dr. Cynthia Anthony, Dean of Student Development Services. Phone: 205-426-7319 Ext. 319. Fax: 205-426-7306. E-mail: canthony@bstc.cc.al.us.

Special Needs Services Approximately 105 registered undergraduate students were served during 2002-03. The program or unit includes 5 full-time staff members. Counselors and LD specialists are provided through the program or unit. Academic advisers, counselors, diagnostic specialists, LD specialists, professional tutors, regular education teachers, remediation/learning specialists, and trained peer tutors are provided collaboratively through on-campus or off-campus services.

Orientation The program or unit offers an optional orientation for new students individually by special arrangement.

Unique Aids and Services Aids, services, or accommodations include career counseling, faculty training, priority registration, and weekly meetings with faculty.

Subject-area Tutoring Tutoring is offered one-on-one for all subjects. Tutoring is provided through the program or unit via other. Tutoring is also provided collaboratively through on-campus or off-campus services via computer-based instruction and trained peer tutors.

Basic Skills Remediation Remediation is offered one-on-one and in small groups for computer skills, learning strategies, math, reading, social skills, study skills, time management, and written

language. Remediation is provided through the program or unit via LD specialists. Remediation is also provided collaboratively through on-campus or off-campus services via computer-based instruction and trained peer tutors.

Enrichment Enrichment programs are available through the program or unit for career planning, self-advocacy, and stress management. Programs for college survival skills, learning strategies, math, oral communication skills, practical computer skills, reading, study skills, test taking, time management, vocabulary development, and written composition skills are provided collaboratively through on-campus or off-campus services. Credit is offered for career planning, college survival skills, learning strategies, math, oral communication skills, practical computer skills, reading, self-advocacy, stress management, study skills, test taking, time management, vocabulary development, and written composition skills.

Application For admittance to the program or unit, students are required to provide a psychoeducational report (3 years old or less). Upon application, materials documenting need for services should be sent only to the LD program or unit. *Application deadline (institutional):* 8/4. *Application deadline (LD program):* Rolling/continuous for fall and rolling/continuous for spring.

Written Policies Written policies regarding course substitutions, general/basic LD accommodations, and grade forgiveness are outlined in the school's catalog/handbook. Written policy regarding general/basic LD accommodations is available through the program or unit directly.

Bismarck State College
Disability Support Services

PO Box 5587

Bismarck, ND 58506-5587

http://www.bismarckstate.edu/student/disability

Contact: Ms. Marlene Seaworth, Disability Support Services Coordinator. Phone: 701-224-5554. Fax: 701-224-5550. E-mail: marlene.seaworth@bsc.nodak.edu.

Disability Support Services Approximately 50 registered undergraduate students were served during 2002-03. The program or unit includes 1 full-time staff member. Academic advisers, counselors, graduate assistants/students, regular education teachers, and trained peer tutors are provided collaboratively through on-campus or off-campus services.

Subject-area Tutoring Tutoring is offered in small groups for some subjects. Tutoring is provided collaboratively through on-campus or off-campus services via trained peer tutors.

Enrichment Programs for learning strategies, study skills, test taking, and time management are provided collaboratively through on-campus or off-campus services.

Application For admittance to the program or unit, students are required to apply to the program directly and provide a psychoeducational report (3 years old or less). It is recommended that students provide documentation of high school services. Upon application, materials documenting need for services should be sent only to the LD program or unit. Upon acceptance, documentation of need for services should be sent only to the LD program or unit. *Application deadline (institutional):* Continuous. *Application deadline (LD program):* Rolling/continuous for fall and rolling/continuous for spring.

Written Policies Written policy regarding general/basic LD accommodations is available on the program Web site. Written policy regarding general/basic LD accommodations is outlined in the school's catalog/handbook. Written policy regarding general/basic LD accommodations is available through the program or unit directly.

Blackhawk Technical College

PO Box 5009
Janesville, WI 53547-5009
http://www.blackhawk.edu/
Contact: Ms. Christine A. Flottum, Instructor and Program Manager. Phone: 608-757-7796. Fax: 608-743-4409. E-mail: cflottum@blackhawk.edu.

Approximately 57 registered undergraduate students were served during 2002-03. The program or unit includes 4 full-time and 3 part-time staff members. LD specialists, professional tutors, remediation/learning specialists, skill tutors, special education teachers, strategy tutors, and trained peer tutors are provided through the program or unit. Academic advisers, counselors, and regular education teachers are provided collaboratively through on-campus or off-campus services.
Orientation The program or unit offers an optional orientation for new students during summer prior to enrollment and individually by special arrangement.
Summer Program To help prepare for the demands of college, there is an optional 1-week summer program prior to entering the school.
Unique Aids and Services Aids, services, or accommodations include career counseling, parent workshops, and priority registration.
Subject-area Tutoring Tutoring is offered one-on-one and in small groups for most subjects. Tutoring is provided through the program or unit via computer-based instruction, LD specialists, professional tutors, and trained peer tutors. Tutoring is also provided collaboratively through on-campus or off-campus services via computer-based instruction.
Diagnostic Testing Testing is provided through the program or unit for learning strategies, learning styles, math, reading, spelling, study skills, and written language.
Basic Skills Remediation Remediation is offered in small groups and in class-size groups for computer skills, learning strategies, math, reading, spelling, study skills, time management, and written language. Remediation is provided collaboratively through on-campus or off-campus services via computer-based instruction, professional tutors, regular education teachers, and trained peer tutors.
Enrichment Enrichment programs are available through the program or unit for college survival skills, learning strategies, self-advocacy, study skills, test taking, time management, and written composition skills. Programs for career planning, college survival skills, learning strategies, math, practical computer skills, reading, study skills, test taking, time management, vocabulary development, and written composition skills are provided collaboratively through on-campus or off-campus services.
Application For admittance to the program or unit, students are required to provide a psychoeducational report and provide documentation of high school services. Upon application, materials documenting need for services should be sent only to the LD program or

unit. Upon acceptance, documentation of need for services should be sent only to the LD program or unit. *Application deadline (institutional):* Continuous. *Application deadline (LD program):* Rolling/continuous for fall and rolling/continuous for spring.
Written Policies Written policy regarding general/basic LD accommodations is outlined in the school's catalog/handbook.

Blinn College

902 College Avenue
Brenham, TX 77833-4049
http://www.blinn.edu/
Contact: Ms. Patricia E. Moran, Director of Disability Services. Phone: 979-830-4157. Fax: 979-830-4410. E-mail: pmoran@blinn.edu.

Approximately 550 registered undergraduate students were served during 2002-03. The program or unit includes 4 full-time and 4 part-time staff members. Academic advisers and counselors are provided through the program or unit. Regular education teachers, remediation/learning specialists, and skill tutors are provided collaboratively through on-campus or off-campus services.
Unique Aids and Services Aids, services, or accommodations include one-on-one counseling on disability related issues.
Subject-area Tutoring Tutoring is offered in small groups for most subjects. Tutoring is provided collaboratively through on-campus or off-campus services via computer-based instruction, trained peer tutors, and other.
Basic Skills Remediation Remediation is offered in class-size groups for learning strategies, math, reading, study skills, and written language. Remediation is provided collaboratively through on-campus or off-campus services via computer-based instruction and regular education teachers.
Enrichment Programs for career planning, learning strategies, math, practical computer skills, reading, stress management, study skills, test taking, time management, and written composition skills are provided collaboratively through on-campus or off-campus services. Credit is offered for learning strategies, math, practical computer skills, reading, study skills, and written composition skills.
Application For admittance to the program or unit, students are required to provide a psychoeducational report (5 years old or less). It is recommended that students provide documentation of high school services. Upon application, materials documenting need for services should be sent only to the LD program or unit. Upon acceptance, documentation of need for services should be sent only to the LD program or unit. *Application deadline (institutional):* Continuous. *Application deadline (LD program):* Rolling/continuous for fall and rolling/continuous for spring.
Written Policies Written policies regarding course substitutions, general/basic LD accommodations, substitutions and waivers of admissions requirements, and substitutions and waivers of graduation requirements are available through the program or unit directly.

Blue Mountain Community College
Services for Students with Disabilities

2411 Northwest Carden Avenue
PO Box 100

Blue Mountain Community College (continued)
Pendleton, OR 97801-1000

http://www.bmcc.cc.or.us/bmcc_web/service/disability/
Disable.shtml

Contact: Amy Spiegel, Coordinator of Services for Students with Disabilities. Phone: 541-278-5807. Fax: 541-278-5888. E-mail: aspiegel@bluecc.edu.

Services for Students with Disabilities Approximately 73 registered undergraduate students were served during 2002-03. The program or unit includes 1 part-time staff member. Academic advisers, coaches, counselors, diagnostic specialists, professional tutors, regular education teachers, remediation/learning specialists, and trained peer tutors are provided collaboratively through on-campus or off-campus services.

Orientation The program or unit offers an optional orientation for new students before registration, before classes begin, during summer prior to enrollment, during registration, after classes begin, and individually by special arrangement.

Unique Aids and Services Aids, services, or accommodations include advocates, career counseling, digital textbooks, faculty training, personal coach, support groups, and weekly meetings with faculty.

Subject-area Tutoring Tutoring is offered one-on-one and in small groups for most subjects. Tutoring is provided collaboratively through on-campus or off-campus services via computer-based instruction, professional tutors, and trained peer tutors.

Diagnostic Testing Testing for auditory processing, handwriting, intelligence, learning strategies, learning styles, math, motor skills, neuropsychological, personality, reading, social skills, spelling, spoken language, study skills, visual processing, and written language is provided collaboratively through on-campus or off-campus services.

Basic Skills Remediation Remediation is offered one-on-one, in small groups, and in class-size groups for auditory processing, computer skills, handwriting, learning strategies, math, reading, social skills, spelling, spoken language, study skills, time management, visual processing, and written language. Remediation is provided collaboratively through on-campus or off-campus services via computer-based instruction, professional tutors, and trained peer tutors.

Enrichment Programs for career planning, college survival skills, health and nutrition, learning strategies, math, oral communication skills, practical computer skills, reading, self-advocacy, stress management, study skills, test taking, time management, vocabulary development, and written composition skills are provided collaboratively through on-campus or off-campus services. Credit is offered for career planning, college survival skills, health and nutrition, math, oral communication skills, practical computer skills, reading, stress management, study skills, test taking, time management, vocabulary development, and written composition skills.

Fees *Diagnostic Testing* fee is $40.

Application For admittance to the program or unit, students are required to provide a psychoeducational report (3 years old or less). Upon application, materials documenting need for services should be sent only to the LD program or unit. Upon acceptance, documentation of need for services should be sent only to the LD program or unit. *Application deadline (institutional):* Continuous. *Application deadline (LD program):* Rolling/continuous for fall and rolling/continuous for spring.

Written Policies Written policies regarding general/basic LD accommodations, grade forgiveness, reduced course loads, and substitutions and waivers of admissions requirements are available on the program Web site. Written policies regarding general/basic LD accommodations, grade forgiveness, reduced course loads, and substitutions and waivers of admissions requirements are outlined in the school's catalog/handbook. Written policies regarding course substitutions and substitutions and waivers of graduation requirements are available through the program or unit directly.

Blue Ridge Community College

PO Box 80
Weyers Cave, VA 24486-0080

http://www.brcc.edu/

Contact: Ms. Carlita McCombs, Student Services Coordinator. Phone: 540-234-9261 Ext. 2289. Fax: 540-453-2437. E-mail: mccombsc@brcc.edu.

The program or unit includes 1 full-time staff member. Academic advisers are provided through the program or unit.

Subject-area Tutoring Tutoring is offered one-on-one for most subjects. Tutoring is provided collaboratively through on-campus or off-campus services via trained peer tutors.

Basic Skills Remediation Remediation is offered in class-size groups for math, reading, study skills, time management, and written language. Remediation is provided collaboratively through on-campus or off-campus services via regular education teachers.

Enrichment Programs for career planning, college survival skills, health and nutrition, learning strategies, math, oral communication skills, practical computer skills, reading, stress management, study skills, test taking, time management, and written composition skills are provided collaboratively through on-campus or off-campus services. Credit is offered for career planning, college survival skills, health and nutrition, learning strategies, oral communication skills, stress management, study skills, test taking, and time management.

Application For admittance to the program or unit, students are required to provide a psychoeducational report. Upon application, materials documenting need for services should be sent only to the LD program or unit. Upon acceptance, documentation of need for services should be sent only to the LD program or unit. *Application deadline (institutional):* Continuous. *Application deadline (LD program):* Rolling/continuous for fall and rolling/continuous for spring.

Written Policies Written policy regarding general/basic LD accommodations is outlined in the school's catalog/handbook. Written policy regarding general/basic LD accommodations is available through the program or unit directly.

Blue Ridge Community College

College Drive
Flat Rock, NC 28731-9624

http://www.blueridge.edu/

Contact: Judy Stoneham, Director for Disability Services. Phone: 828-694-1813. E-mail: judys@blueridge.com.

The program or unit includes 2 full-time staff members. Regular education teachers and other are provided collaboratively through on-campus or off-campus services.

Subject-area Tutoring Tutoring is offered one-on-one and in small groups for some subjects. Tutoring is provided collaboratively through on-campus or off-campus services via computer-based instruction and other.

Basic Skills Remediation Remediation is available for math, reading, study skills, and written language. Remediation is provided collaboratively through on-campus or off-campus services via computer-based instruction and regular education teachers.

Application For admittance to the program or unit, students are required to provide a psychoeducational report (3 years old or less). It is recommended that students provide documentation of high school services. Upon acceptance, documentation of need for services should be sent to both admissions and the LD program or unit. *Application deadline (institutional):* Continuous. *Application deadline (LD program):* Rolling/continuous for fall and rolling/continuous for spring.

Written Policies Written policy regarding general/basic LD accommodations is available on the program Web site. Written policies regarding course substitutions, general/basic LD accommodations, reduced course loads, substitutions and waivers of admissions requirements, and substitutions and waivers of graduation requirements are outlined in the school's catalog/handbook. Written policy regarding general/basic LD accommodations is available through the program or unit directly.

Brevard Community College
Office for Students with Disabilities

1519 Clearlake Road

Cocoa, FL 32922-6597

http://www.brevardcc.edu/osd

Contact: Dr. Lyndi Kolack Fertel, Director of Office for Students with Disabilities. Phone: 321-632-1111 Ext. 63607. Fax: 321-634-3709. E-mail: fertell@brevardcc.edu.

Office for Students with Disabilities Approximately 300 registered undergraduate students were served during 2002-03. The program or unit includes 9 part-time staff members. LD specialists, professional tutors, and remediation/learning specialists are provided through the program or unit.

Unique Aids and Services Aids, services, or accommodations include advocates, priority registration, and support groups.

Subject-area Tutoring Tutoring is offered one-on-one for some subjects. Tutoring is provided through the program or unit via LD specialists and professional tutors. Tutoring is also provided collaboratively through on-campus or off-campus services via computer-based instruction, graduate assistants/students, professional tutors, and trained peer tutors.

Diagnostic Testing Testing is provided through the program or unit for auditory processing, learning strategies, learning styles, math, motor skills, reading, spelling, study skills, visual processing, and written language.

Basic Skills Remediation Remediation is offered in small groups for computer skills, learning strategies, math, reading, spelling, study skills, time management, and written language. Remediation is provided through the program or unit via LD specialists and professional tutors. Remediation is also provided collaboratively through on-campus or off-campus services via computer-based instruction, regular education teachers, and trained peer tutors.

Enrichment Enrichment programs are available through the program or unit for math and practical computer skills. Programs for career planning, college survival skills, learning strategies, math, oral communication skills, practical computer skills, reading, study skills, test taking, time management, and written composition skills are provided collaboratively through on-campus or off-campus services. Credit is offered for college survival skills, learning strategies, math, oral communication skills, reading, study skills, test taking, time management, and written composition skills.

Student Organization Students Overcoming Life's Obstacles (SOLO) Club consists of 15 members.

Application For admittance to the program or unit, students are required to provide a psychoeducational report (3 years old or less). It is recommended that students provide documentation of high school services. Upon application, materials documenting need for services should be sent only to the LD program or unit. *Application deadline (institutional):* Continuous. *Application deadline (LD program):* Rolling/continuous for fall and rolling/continuous for spring.

Written Policies Written policies regarding course substitutions, general/basic LD accommodations, grade forgiveness, substitutions and waivers of admissions requirements, and substitutions and waivers of graduation requirements are available on the program Web site. Written policy regarding general/basic LD accommodations is outlined in the school's catalog/handbook. Written policies regarding course substitutions, general/basic LD accommodations, grade forgiveness, reduced course loads, substitutions and waivers of admissions requirements, and substitutions and waivers of graduation requirements are available through the program or unit directly.

Bristol Community College
Office of Disability Services

777 Elsbree Street

Fall River, MA 02720-7395

http://www.BristolCommunityCollege.edu

Contact: Ms. Jan Baptist, Director. Phone: 508-678-2811 Ext. 2319. Fax: 508-675-2294. E-mail: jbaptist@bristol.mass.edu.

Office of Disability Services Approximately 423 registered undergraduate students were served during 2002-03. The program or unit includes 3 full-time and 7 part-time staff members. LD specialists, remediation/learning specialists, skill tutors, strategy tutors, trained peer tutors, and other are provided through the program or unit.

Summer Program To help prepare for the demands of college, there is an optional 1-week summer program prior to entering the school.

Unique Aids and Services Aids, services, or accommodations include advocates, career counseling, faculty training, parent workshops, personal coach, progress reports from faculty.

Bristol Community College (continued)

Subject-area Tutoring Tutoring is offered one-on-one and in small groups for most subjects. Tutoring is provided through the program or unit via LD specialists and trained peer tutors.

Basic Skills Remediation Remediation is offered one-on-one, in small groups, and in class-size groups for math, reading, study skills, and written language. Remediation is provided through the program or unit via LD specialists and trained peer tutors. Remediation is also provided collaboratively through on-campus or off-campus services via regular education teachers.

Enrichment Programs for career planning, college survival skills, health and nutrition, oral communication skills, reading, stress management, study skills, test taking, and time management are provided collaboratively through on-campus or off-campus services.

Application For admittance to the program or unit, students are required to apply to the program directly and provide a psychoeducational report (3 years old or less). It is recommended that students provide documentation of high school services. Upon acceptance, documentation of need for services should be sent only to the LD program or unit. *Application deadline (LD program):* Rolling/continuous for fall and rolling/continuous for spring.

Written Policies Written policy regarding general/basic LD accommodations is available on the program Web site. Written policy regarding general/basic LD accommodations is outlined in the school's catalog/handbook. Written policies regarding course substitutions, reduced course loads, substitutions and waivers of admissions requirements, and substitutions and waivers of graduation requirements are available through the program or unit directly.

Broward Community College
The Office of Disability Services

225 East Las Olas Boulevard
Fort Lauderdale, FL 33301-2298
http://www.broward.edu/
Contact: Mrs. Beverly A. Cranmer, Coordinator of Disability Services. Phone: 954-201-7655. Fax: 954-201-7492. E-mail: bcranmer@broward.edu.

The Office of Disability Services Approximately 130 registered undergraduate students were served during 2002-03. The program or unit includes 3 full-time and 2 part-time staff members. LD specialists are provided through the program or unit. Academic advisers, counselors, regular education teachers, remediation/learning specialists, and trained peer tutors are provided collaboratively through on-campus or off-campus services.

Unique Aids and Services Aids, services, or accommodations include digital textbooks, faculty training, support groups, isolated testing, extended time on projects and testing, use of a tape recorder, adaptive software.

Subject-area Tutoring Tutoring is offered in small groups and in class-size groups for some subjects. Tutoring is provided collaboratively through on-campus or off-campus services via computer-based instruction, graduate assistants/students, and trained peer tutors.

Basic Skills Remediation Remediation is offered in class-size groups for math, reading, study skills, and written language. Remediation is provided collaboratively through on-campus or off-campus services via computer-based instruction and regular education teachers.

Enrichment Enrichment programs are available through the program or unit for learning strategies, self-advocacy, study skills, test taking, and time management. Programs for career planning, college survival skills, health and nutrition, learning strategies, stress management, study skills, test taking, time management, and written composition skills are provided collaboratively through on-campus or off-campus services. Credit is offered for college survival skills and health and nutrition.

Application For admittance to the program or unit, students are required to apply to the program directly and provide a psychoeducational report (3 years old or less). It is recommended that students provide documentation of high school services. Upon application, materials documenting need for services should be sent only to the LD program or unit. Upon acceptance, documentation of need for services should be sent only to the LD program or unit. *Application deadline (LD program):* Rolling/continuous for fall and rolling/continuous for spring.

Written Policies Written policies regarding course substitutions, general/basic LD accommodations, and substitutions and waivers of graduation requirements are available on the program Web site. Written policies regarding course substitutions, general/basic LD accommodations, and substitutions and waivers of graduation requirements are outlined in the school's catalog/handbook. Written policies regarding course substitutions, general/basic LD accommodations, and substitutions and waivers of graduation requirements are available through the program or unit directly.

Brunswick Community College
Student Development

PO Box 30
Supply, NC 28462-0030
http://www.brunswick.cc.nc.us/
Contact: Matlynn Yeoman, Vice President for Student Development. Phone: 910-755-7321. Fax: 910-754-9609. E-mail: yeomanm@brunswick.cc.nc.us.

Student Development Approximately 20 registered undergraduate students were served during 2002-03. Academic advisers, counselors, professional tutors, remediation/learning specialists, and other are provided collaboratively through on-campus or off-campus services.

Unique Aids and Services Aids, services, or accommodations include advocates, career counseling, and priority registration.

Subject-area Tutoring Tutoring is offered one-on-one for some subjects. Tutoring is provided through the program or unit via other. Tutoring is also provided collaboratively through on-campus or off-campus services via professional tutors.

Diagnostic Testing Testing is provided through the program or unit for math, reading, and written language. Testing for learning styles is provided collaboratively through on-campus or off-campus services.

Basic Skills Remediation Remediation is offered in class-size groups for math, reading, and written language. Remediation is provided collaboratively through on-campus or off-campus services via regular education teachers.

Application For admittance to the program or unit, students are required to apply to the program directly, provide a psychoeducational report (3 years old or less), and provide documentation of high school services. Upon application, materials documenting need for services should be sent only to the LD program or unit. Upon acceptance, documentation of need for services should be sent only to the LD program or unit. *Application deadline (institutional):* Continuous. *Application deadline (LD program):* Rolling/continuous for fall and rolling/continuous for spring.

Written Policies Written policies regarding course substitutions, general/basic LD accommodations, grade forgiveness, substitutions and waivers of admissions requirements, and substitutions and waivers of graduation requirements are available on the program Web site. Written policies regarding course substitutions, general/basic LD accommodations, grade forgiveness, substitutions and waivers of admissions requirements, and substitutions and waivers of graduation requirements are outlined in the school's catalog/handbook.

Bryant and Stratton College

953 James Street
Syracuse, NY 13203-2502
http://www.bryantstratton.edu/
Contact: Ms. Beatrice M. Owens, Student Advisor. Phone: 315-472-6603 Ext. 244. E-mail: bowens@bryantstratton.edu.

Approximately 20 registered undergraduate students were served during 2002-03. The program or unit includes 5 part-time staff members. Academic advisers are provided through the program or unit. Counselors, LD specialists, regular education teachers, remediation/learning specialists, and trained peer tutors are provided collaboratively through on-campus or off-campus services.

Orientation The program or unit offers an optional half-day orientation for new students individually by special arrangement.

Unique Aids and Services Aids, services, or accommodations include advocates, career counseling, and support groups.

Subject-area Tutoring Tutoring is offered for some subjects. Tutoring is provided collaboratively through on-campus or off-campus services via trained peer tutors and other.

Basic Skills Remediation Remediation is offered one-on-one and in small groups for math, study skills, and time management. Remediation is provided collaboratively through on-campus or off-campus services via regular education teachers and trained peer tutors.

Enrichment Programs for learning strategies, practical computer skills, stress management, study skills, test taking, time management, and written composition skills are provided collaboratively through on-campus or off-campus services.

Application For admittance to the program or unit, students are required to provide documentation of high school services. It is recommended that students provide a psychoeducational report. Upon application, materials documenting need for services should be sent to both admissions and the LD program or unit. Upon acceptance, documentation of need for services should be sent to both admissions and the LD program or unit. *Application deadline (institutional):* Continuous. *Application deadline (LD program):* Rolling/continuous for fall and rolling/continuous for spring.

Written Policies Written policy regarding general/basic LD accommodations is outlined in the school's catalog/handbook. Written policy regarding course substitutions is available through the program or unit directly.

Bucks County Community College

275 Swamp Road
Newtown, PA 18940-1525
http://www.bucks.edu/
Contact: Ms. Marge Zipin, Learning Disabilities Specialist. Phone: 215-968-8465. Fax: 215-968-8464. E-mail: zipinm@bucks.edu.

Approximately 85 registered undergraduate students were served during 2002-03. The program or unit includes 1 full-time staff member. Academic advisers, LD specialists, and strategy tutors are provided through the program or unit. Counselors, diagnostic specialists, remediation/learning specialists, skill tutors, and trained peer tutors are provided collaboratively through on-campus or off-campus services.

Orientation The program or unit offers an optional 3-day orientation for new students before classes begin, during summer prior to enrollment, and during registration.

Unique Aids and Services Aids, services, or accommodations include career counseling, faculty training, and priority registration.

Subject-area Tutoring Tutoring is offered one-on-one for some subjects. Tutoring is provided through the program or unit via computer-based instruction and LD specialists. Tutoring is also provided collaboratively through on-campus or off-campus services via computer-based instruction and trained peer tutors.

Basic Skills Remediation Remediation is offered one-on-one for computer skills, learning strategies, math, reading, social skills, spelling, study skills, time management, and written language. Remediation is provided through the program or unit via computer-based instruction and LD specialists. Remediation is also provided collaboratively through on-campus or off-campus services via computer-based instruction and trained peer tutors.

Application For admittance to the program or unit, students are required to provide a psychoeducational report. It is recommended that students provide documentation of high school services. Upon application, materials documenting need for services should be sent only to the LD program or unit. *Application deadline (institutional):* 5/1. *Application deadline (LD program):* Rolling/continuous for fall and rolling/continuous for spring.

Written Policies Written policy regarding general/basic LD accommodations is available on the program Web site. Written policies regarding course substitutions, general/basic LD accommodations, and reduced course loads are available through the program or unit directly.

Bunker Hill Community College

250 New Rutherford Avenue
Boston, MA 02129-2925
http://www.bhcc.mass.edu/
Contact: Ms. Andrea F. Lausier, Coordinator of Disability Support Services. Phone: 617-228-3415. E-mail: alausier@bhcc.mass.edu.

Bunker Hill Community College (continued)

The program or unit includes 1 full-time and 1 part-time staff member. Academic advisers, coaches, counselors, graduate assistants/students, professional tutors, regular education teachers, skill tutors, special education teachers, strategy tutors, teacher trainees, and trained peer tutors are provided through the program or unit. Diagnostic specialists, LD specialists, and remediation/learning specialists are provided collaboratively through on-campus or off-campus services.

Orientation The program or unit offers an optional orientation for new students individually by special arrangement.

Summer Program To help prepare for the demands of college, there is an optional summer program prior to entering the school.

Unique Aids and Services Aids, services, or accommodations include faculty training, priority registration, and support groups.

Subject-area Tutoring Tutoring is offered one-on-one and in small groups for some subjects. Tutoring is provided through the program or unit via graduate assistants/students and trained peer tutors.

Basic Skills Remediation Remediation is offered one-on-one and in small groups for learning strategies, math, social skills, study skills, time management, and written language. Remediation is provided through the program or unit via computer-based instruction, graduate assistants/students, LD specialists, and trained peer tutors.

Enrichment Enrichment programs are available through the program or unit for college survival skills, learning strategies, math, reading, and self-advocacy. Programs for career planning, study skills, test taking, time management, and written composition skills are provided collaboratively through on-campus or off-campus services.

Application For admittance to the program or unit, students are required to provide a psychoeducational report. It is recommended that students provide documentation of high school services. Upon application, materials documenting need for services should be sent only to the LD program or unit. Upon acceptance, documentation of need for services should be sent only to the LD program or unit. *Application deadline (institutional):* Continuous. *Application deadline (LD program):* Rolling/continuous for fall and rolling/continuous for spring.

Written Policies Written policy regarding general/basic LD accommodations is available on the program Web site. Written policy regarding general/basic LD accommodations is outlined in the school's catalog/handbook. Written policies regarding general/basic LD accommodations and reduced course loads are available through the program or unit directly.

Burlington County College
Special Populations Program

Route 530
Pemberton, NJ 08068-1599
http://www.bcc.edu/

Contact: William Murphy, Learning Disabilities Specialist. Phone: 609-894-9311 Ext. 7789. Fax: 609-894-0764. E-mail: wmurphy@bcc.edu. Head of LD Program: Barbara Ericson, Coordinator of Special Populations. Phone: 609-894-9311 Ext. 7208. Fax: 609-894-0764. E-mail: ericson@bcc.edu.

Special Populations Program Approximately 172 registered undergraduate students were served during 2002-03. The program or unit includes 1 full-time and 1 part-time staff member. Academic advisers, counselors, diagnostic specialists, LD specialists, strategy tutors, and trained peer tutors are provided through the program or unit. Academic advisers, counselors, professional tutors, regular education teachers, remediation/learning specialists, skill tutors, and trained peer tutors are provided collaboratively through on-campus or off-campus services.

Orientation The program or unit offers an optional 1-day orientation for new students before classes begin.

Unique Aids and Services Aids, services, or accommodations include career counseling, priority registration, other aids and services dependent upon appropriate documentation submitted.

Subject-area Tutoring Tutoring is offered one-on-one for most subjects. Tutoring is provided through the program or unit via LD specialists. Tutoring is also provided collaboratively through on-campus or off-campus services via computer-based instruction, professional tutors, and trained peer tutors.

Basic Skills Remediation Remediation is offered one-on-one for computer skills, learning strategies, math, reading, study skills, and written language. Remediation is provided through the program or unit via LD specialists and trained peer tutors. Remediation is also provided collaboratively through on-campus or off-campus services via computer-based instruction, professional tutors, regular education teachers, and trained peer tutors.

Enrichment Enrichment programs are available through the program or unit for learning strategies and self-advocacy. Programs for career planning, college survival skills, and study skills are provided collaboratively through on-campus or off-campus services. Credit is offered for college survival skills and study skills.

Application For admittance to the program or unit, students are required to provide a psychoeducational report (3 years old or less) and provide documentation of high school services. Upon acceptance, documentation of need for services should be sent only to the LD program or unit. *Application deadline (institutional):* Continuous. *Application deadline (LD program):* Rolling/continuous for fall and rolling/continuous for spring.

Butte College

3536 Butte Campus Drive
Oroville, CA 95965-8399
http://www.butte.edu/

Contact: Phone: 530-895-2511. Fax: 530-895-2345. Head of LD Program: Mr. Richard Dunn, Coordinator of Disabled Student Programs and Services. Phone: 530-895-2455. Fax: 530-895-2235. E-mail: dsps@butte.edu.

Approximately 140 registered undergraduate students were served during 2002-03. The program or unit includes 4 full-time staff members and 1 part-time staff member. Diagnostic specialists, LD specialists, skill tutors, strategy tutors, trained peer tutors, and other are provided through the program or unit. Academic advisers, coaches, counselors, professional tutors, regular education teachers, remediation/learning specialists, skill tutors, trained peer tutors, and other are provided collaboratively through on-campus or off-campus services.

Unique Aids and Services Aids, services, or accommodations include advocates, career counseling, digital textbooks, faculty training, personal coach, priority registration, extended time for exams, adapted computer stations, cognitive skills development classes.

Subject-area Tutoring Tutoring is offered one-on-one and in small groups for most subjects. Tutoring is provided collaboratively through on-campus or off-campus services via computer-based instruction, LD specialists, professional tutors, and trained peer tutors.

Diagnostic Testing Testing is provided through the program or unit for auditory processing, intelligence, learning strategies, learning styles, math, reading, spelling, spoken language, study skills, visual processing, written language, and other services.

Basic Skills Remediation Remediation is offered one-on-one, in small groups, and in class-size groups for computer skills, learning strategies, math, motor skills, reading, spelling, study skills, time management, and written language. Remediation is provided collaboratively through on-campus or off-campus services via computer-based instruction, professional tutors, regular education teachers, trained peer tutors, and other.

Enrichment Enrichment programs are available through the program or unit for learning strategies, practical computer skills, and self-advocacy. Programs for career planning, college survival skills, health and nutrition, learning strategies, math, medication management, practical computer skills, reading, stress management, study skills, test taking, time management, vocabulary development, written composition skills, and other are provided collaboratively through on-campus or off-campus services. Credit is offered for career planning, college survival skills, health and nutrition, learning strategies, math, practical computer skills, reading, stress management, study skills, vocabulary development, written composition skills, and other.

Application For admittance to the program or unit, students are required to apply to the program directly, provide a psychoeducational report (3 years old or less), and provide documentation of high school services. Upon application, materials documenting need for services should be sent only to the LD program or unit. Upon acceptance, documentation of need for services should be sent only to the LD program or unit. *Application deadline (institutional):* Continuous. *Application deadline (LD program):* Rolling/continuous for fall and rolling/continuous for spring.

Written Policies Written policy regarding general/basic LD accommodations is available on the program Web site. Written policy regarding general/basic LD accommodations is outlined in the school's catalog/handbook. Written policies regarding course substitutions, general/basic LD accommodations, reduced course loads, and substitutions and waivers of graduation requirements are available through the program or unit directly.

Cabrillo College
Learning Skills Program

6500 Soquel Drive
Aptos, CA 95003-3194
http://www.cabrillo.edu/

Contact: Ms. Deborah Shulman, Director of Learning Skills Program. Phone: 831-479-6220. Fax: 831-479-6393. E-mail: deshulma@cabrillo.edu.

Learning Skills Program Approximately 560 registered undergraduate students were served during 2002-03. The program or unit includes 2 full-time and 7 part-time staff members. Academic advisers, diagnostic specialists, LD specialists, remediation/learning specialists, skill tutors, special education teachers, and strategy tutors are provided through the program or unit. Academic advisers, counselors, diagnostic specialists, professional tutors, remediation/learning specialists, skill tutors, special education teachers, strategy tutors, and trained peer tutors are provided collaboratively through on-campus or off-campus services.

Orientation The program or unit offers a mandatory 1 to 2-hour orientation for new students individually by special arrangement and at various times throughout the fall and spring semesters.

Summer Program To help prepare for the demands of college, there is an optional 4-week summer program prior to entering the school.

Unique Aids and Services Aids, services, or accommodations include priority registration, testing accommodations, note-takers.

Subject-area Tutoring Tutoring is offered in small groups for most subjects. Tutoring is provided through the program or unit via computer-based instruction, LD specialists, and professional tutors. Tutoring is also provided collaboratively through on-campus or off-campus services via computer-based instruction, professional tutors, and trained peer tutors.

Diagnostic Testing Testing is provided through the program or unit for auditory processing, intelligence, learning strategies, math, neuropsychological, reading, spelling, study skills, visual processing, and written language. Testing for motor skills, personality, and social skills is provided collaboratively through on-campus or off-campus services.

Basic Skills Remediation Remediation is offered in small groups and in class-size groups for computer skills, learning strategies, math, reading, spelling, study skills, time management, and written language. Remediation is provided through the program or unit via LD specialists and special education teachers. Remediation is also provided collaboratively through on-campus or off-campus services via computer-based instruction, professional tutors, and regular education teachers.

Enrichment Enrichment programs are available through the program or unit for college survival skills, learning strategies, self-advocacy, stress management, study skills, test taking, and time management. Programs for career planning, college survival skills, math, practical computer skills, reading, stress management, study skills, test taking, time management, vocabulary development, and written composition skills are provided collaboratively through on-campus or off-campus services.

Fees *LD Program or Service* fee is $40 to $205 (fee varies according to level/tier of service). *Summer Program* fee is $40 to $205. *Orientation* fee is $40 to $205. *Diagnostic Testing* fee is $40.

Application For admittance to the program or unit, students are required to apply to the program directly. It is recommended that students provide a psychoeducational report (3 years old or less) and provide documentation of high school services. Upon application, materials documenting need for services should be sent only to the LD program or unit. Upon acceptance, documentation of need for services should be sent only to the LD program or unit. *Application deadline (institutional):* Continuous. *Application deadline (LD program):* Rolling/continuous for fall and rolling/continuous for spring.

Cabrillo College (continued)

Written Policies Written policies regarding course substitutions, general/basic LD accommodations, substitutions and waivers of admissions requirements, and substitutions and waivers of graduation requirements are available on the program Web site. Written policies regarding course substitutions, general/basic LD accommodations, substitutions and waivers of admissions requirements, and substitutions and waivers of graduation requirements are outlined in the school's catalog/handbook. Written policies regarding course substitutions, general/basic LD accommodations, substitutions and waivers of admissions requirements, and substitutions and waivers of graduation requirements are available through the program or unit directly.

Camden County College
Program for the Academically Challenged Student (PACS)

PO Box 200
Blackwood, NJ 08012-0200
http://camdencc.edu

Contact: Joanne Kinzy, Director. Phone: 856-227-7200 Ext. 4430. Fax: 856-374-4913. E-mail: jkinzy@camdencc.edu.

Program for the Academically Challenged Student (PACS) The program or unit includes 2 full-time and 2 part-time staff members. LD specialists, professional tutors, and other are provided through the program or unit.

Orientation The program or unit offers an optional half-day orientation for new students during summer prior to enrollment.

Summer Program To help prepare for the demands of college, there is an optional 6-week summer program prior to entering the school. Degree credit will be earned.

Unique Aids and Services Aids, services, or accommodations include career counseling, priority registration, extended time on tests and assistive technology.

Subject-area Tutoring Tutoring is offered one-on-one and in small groups for most subjects. Tutoring is provided collaboratively through on-campus or off-campus services via computer-based instruction, professional tutors, and trained peer tutors.

Basic Skills Remediation Remediation is offered in class-size groups for learning strategies, math, reading, study skills, time management, and written language. Remediation is provided through the program or unit via regular education teachers. Remediation is also provided collaboratively through on-campus or off-campus services via regular education teachers.

Application For admittance to the program or unit, students are required to provide a psychoeducational report and provide documentation of high school services. Upon application, materials documenting need for services should be sent only to the LD program or unit. *Application deadline (institutional):* Continuous. *Application deadline (LD program):* Rolling/continuous for fall and rolling/continuous for spring.

Written Policies Written policies regarding general/basic LD accommodations and grade forgiveness are available on the program Web site. Written policies regarding general/basic LD accommodations and grade forgiveness are outlined in the school's catalog/handbook. Written policy regarding course substitutions is available through the program or unit directly.

Carteret Community College

3505 Arendell Street
Morehead City, NC 28557-2989
http://www.carteret.edu/

Contact: Mr. Mark Johnson, Counselor. Phone: 252-222-6148. Fax: 252-222-6265. E-mail: maj@carteret.edu.

The program or unit includes 3 part-time staff members. Counselors are provided through the program or unit. Academic advisers, counselors, diagnostic specialists, remediation/learning specialists, and skill tutors are provided collaboratively through on-campus or off-campus services.

Subject-area Tutoring Tutoring is offered in small groups for most subjects. Tutoring is provided collaboratively through on-campus or off-campus services via computer-based instruction, professional tutors, and trained peer tutors.

Basic Skills Remediation Remediation is offered in class-size groups for math, reading, study skills, and written language. Remediation is provided collaboratively through on-campus or off-campus services via regular education teachers and special education teachers.

Application For admittance to the program or unit, students are required to apply to the program directly and provide a psychoeducational report (3 years old or less). Upon acceptance, documentation of need for services should be sent only to the LD program or unit. *Application deadline (institutional):* Continuous. *Application deadline (LD program):* Rolling/continuous for fall and rolling/continuous for spring.

Written Policies Written policy regarding general/basic LD accommodations is available on the program Web site. Written policy regarding general/basic LD accommodations is outlined in the school's catalog/handbook.

Central Carolina Community College
Special Populations Office

1105 Kelly Drive
Sanford, NC 27330-9000
http://www.cccc.edu/student_services.mgi

Contact: Mr. David C. Oates, Special Populations Director. Phone: 919-718-7273. Fax: 919-718-7379. E-mail: doates@cccc.edu.

Special Populations Office Approximately 20 registered undergraduate students were served during 2002-03.

Subject-area Tutoring Tutoring is offered one-on-one for most subjects. Tutoring is provided collaboratively through on-campus or off-campus services via trained peer tutors.

Application For admittance to the program or unit, students are required to apply to the program directly, provide a psychoeducational report (3 years old or less), and provide documentation of high school services. Upon acceptance, documentation of need for services should be sent to both admissions and the LD program or unit. *Application deadline (institutional):* Continuous. *Application deadline (LD program):* Rolling/continuous for fall and rolling/continuous for spring.

Written Policies Written policies regarding course substitutions, general/basic LD accommodations, reduced course loads, and substitutions and waivers of graduation requirements are available through the program or unit directly.

Central Lakes College

501 West College Drive
Brainerd, MN 56401-3904
http://www.clcmn.edu/
Contact: Judy Richer, Disability Coordinator. Phone: 218-855-8128. Fax: 218-894-5149. E-mail: jricher@clcmn.edu.

Approximately 258 registered undergraduate students were served during 2002-03. The program or unit includes 2 full-time staff members. LD specialists, professional tutors, skill tutors, and trained peer tutors are provided through the program or unit. Academic advisers, counselors, and regular education teachers are provided collaboratively through on-campus or off-campus services.

Orientation The program or unit offers a mandatory 1-hour orientation for new students individually by special arrangement.

Unique Aids and Services Aids, services, or accommodations include career counseling, digital textbooks, faculty training, and priority registration.

Subject-area Tutoring Tutoring is offered one-on-one and in small groups for most subjects. Tutoring is provided through the program or unit via computer-based instruction, professional tutors, and trained peer tutors. Tutoring is also provided collaboratively through on-campus or off-campus services via computer-based instruction.

Enrichment Enrichment programs are available through the program or unit for college survival skills, math, practical computer skills, study skills, test taking, and written composition skills. Programs for career planning, college survival skills, health and nutrition, math, practical computer skills, stress management, and time management are provided collaboratively through on-campus or off-campus services. Credit is offered for career planning and college survival skills.

Application For admittance to the program or unit, students are required to apply to the program directly. It is recommended that students provide a psychoeducational report (3 years old or less) and provide documentation of high school services. Upon acceptance, documentation of need for services should be sent only to the LD program or unit. *Application deadline (institutional):* Continuous. *Application deadline (LD program):* Rolling/continuous for fall and rolling/continuous for spring.

Written Policies Written policy regarding general/basic LD accommodations is available on the program Web site. Written policy regarding general/basic LD accommodations is outlined in the school's catalog/handbook. Written policies regarding course substitutions, general/basic LD accommodations, substitutions and waivers of admissions requirements, and substitutions and waivers of graduation requirements are available through the program or unit directly.

Central Ohio Technical College

1179 University Drive
Newark, OH 43055-1767
http://www.cotc.tec.oh.us/
Contact: Phone: 740-366-1351. Fax: 740-366-5047.

The program or unit includes 4 full-time staff members. Diagnostic specialists, LD specialists, remediation/learning specialists, and trained peer tutors are provided through the program or unit. Academic advisers, counselors, graduate assistants/students, and regular education teachers are provided collaboratively through on-campus or off-campus services.

Summer Program To help prepare for the demands of college, there is an optional 3-day summer program prior to entering the school.

Unique Aids and Services Aids, services, or accommodations include career counseling.

Subject-area Tutoring Tutoring is offered one-on-one for some subjects. Tutoring is provided through the program or unit via trained peer tutors.

Diagnostic Testing Testing is provided through the program or unit for intelligence, learning styles, math, reading, and written language.

Enrichment Enrichment programs are available through the program or unit for career planning, college survival skills, learning strategies, practical computer skills, reading, stress management, study skills, and test taking. Credit is offered for college survival skills, practical computer skills, and reading.

Application For admittance to the program or unit, students are required to provide a psychoeducational report (3 years old or less). It is recommended that students provide documentation of high school services. Upon acceptance, documentation of need for services should be sent only to the LD program or unit. *Application deadline (institutional):* Continuous. *Application deadline (LD program):* Rolling/continuous for fall and rolling/continuous for spring.

Written Policies Written policies regarding course substitutions, grade forgiveness, reduced course loads, substitutions and waivers of admissions requirements, and substitutions and waivers of graduation requirements are outlined in the school's catalog/handbook. Written policy regarding general/basic LD accommodations is available through the program or unit directly.

Central Piedmont Community College

PO Box 35009
Charlotte, NC 28235-5009
http://www.cpcc.cc.nc.us/
Contact: Mrs. Pat G. Adams, Counselor. Phone: 704-330-6556. Fax: 704-330-6230. E-mail: patricia.adams@cpcc.edu.

Approximately 160 registered undergraduate students were served during 2002-03. The program or unit includes 2 full-time and 5

Central Piedmont Community College (continued)

part-time staff members. Academic advisers, counselors, LD specialists, professional tutors, and skill tutors are provided through the program or unit. Academic advisers, counselors, diagnostic specialists, professional tutors, regular education teachers, skill tutors, and trained peer tutors are provided collaboratively through on-campus or off-campus services.

Orientation The program or unit offers an optional orientation for new students individually by special arrangement.

Unique Aids and Services Aids, services, or accommodations include advocates, career counseling, faculty training, and support groups.

Subject-area Tutoring Tutoring is offered one-on-one and in small groups for most subjects. Tutoring is provided collaboratively through on-campus or off-campus services via computer-based instruction, professional tutors, and trained peer tutors.

Basic Skills Remediation Remediation is offered in class-size groups for learning strategies, math, reading, study skills, and time management. Remediation is provided collaboratively through on-campus or off-campus services via regular education teachers.

Student Organization Student Organization for Learning Differences Awareness (SOLDA) consists of 10 members.

Application For admittance to the program or unit, students are required to provide a psychoeducational report (3 years old or less) and provide psychological evaluation results. It is recommended that students provide documentation of high school services. Upon application, materials documenting need for services should be sent only to the LD program or unit. Upon acceptance, documentation of need for services should be sent only to the LD program or unit. *Application deadline (institutional):* Continuous. *Application deadline (LD program):* Rolling/continuous for fall and rolling/continuous for spring.

Written Policies Written policy regarding general/basic LD accommodations is available on the program Web site. Written policy regarding general/basic LD accommodations is outlined in the school's catalog/handbook. Written policy regarding general/basic LD accommodations is available through the program or unit directly.

Central Texas College
Learning Disabilities

PO Box 1800
Killeen, TX 76540-1800
http://www.ctcd.cc.tx.us/

Contact: Mrs. Geneva A. Weedon, Learning Disabilities Counselor and Coordinator. Phone: 254-526-1863. Fax: 254-690-1323. E-mail: lrndisab@ctcd.edu.cc.tx.us.

Learning Disabilities Approximately 120 registered undergraduate students were served during 2002-03. The program or unit includes 2 full-time staff members. Counselors, LD specialists, remediation/learning specialists, skill tutors, and trained peer tutors are provided through the program or unit. Academic advisers, counselors, diagnostic specialists, graduate assistants/students, professional tutors, regular education teachers, remediation/learning specialists, skill tutors, and trained peer tutors are provided collaboratively through on-campus or off-campus services.

Orientation The program or unit offers an optional orientation for new students individually by special arrangement.

Unique Aids and Services Aids, services, or accommodations include career counseling and priority registration.

Subject-area Tutoring Tutoring is offered one-on-one and in small groups for most subjects. Tutoring is provided collaboratively through on-campus or off-campus services via computer-based instruction, graduate assistants/students, LD specialists, and trained peer tutors.

Basic Skills Remediation Remediation is offered one-on-one and in small groups for learning strategies, math, reading, study skills, time management, and written language. Remediation is provided collaboratively through on-campus or off-campus services via computer-based instruction, graduate assistants/students, LD specialists, and trained peer tutors.

Enrichment Enrichment programs are available through the program or unit for career planning, college survival skills, and learning strategies. Programs for career planning, college survival skills, learning strategies, math, reading, self-advocacy, stress management, study skills, test taking, time management, vocabulary development, and written composition skills are provided collaboratively through on-campus or off-campus services. Credit is offered for reading, vocabulary development, and written composition skills.

Application For admittance to the program or unit, students are required to provide a psychoeducational report (5 years old or less) and provide medical reports for ADHD. It is recommended that students provide documentation of high school services. Upon acceptance, documentation of need for services should be sent only to the LD program or unit. *Application deadline (institutional):* Continuous. *Application deadline (LD program):* Rolling/continuous for fall and rolling/continuous for spring.

Written Policies Written policy regarding general/basic LD accommodations is outlined in the school's catalog/handbook. Written policy regarding general/basic LD accommodations is available through the program or unit directly.

Central Wyoming College
Disabilities Assistance Office

2660 Peck Avenue
Riverton, WY 82501-2273
http://www.cwc.edu/

Contact: Dr. Mohammed Waheed, Dean, Student Services. Phone: 307-855-2186. Fax: 307-855-2155. E-mail: mwaheed@cwc.edu.

Disabilities Assistance Office Approximately 35 registered undergraduate students were served during 2002-03. The program or unit includes 1 part-time staff member. Academic advisers, counselors, diagnostic specialists, regular education teachers, and trained peer tutors are provided collaboratively through on-campus or off-campus services.

Orientation The program or unit offers an optional orientation for new students individually by special arrangement.

Unique Aids and Services Aids, services, or accommodations include career counseling, individual academic accommodations.

Subject-area Tutoring Tutoring is offered one-on-one for most subjects. Tutoring is provided collaboratively through on-campus or off-campus services via computer-based instruction and trained peer tutors.

Diagnostic Testing Testing for intelligence, learning strategies, learning styles, math, reading, spelling, spoken language, visual processing, and written language is provided collaboratively through on-campus or off-campus services.

Basic Skills Remediation Remediation is offered one-on-one for learning strategies, math, reading, spelling, study skills, and written language. Remediation is provided collaboratively through on-campus or off-campus services via professional tutors.

Enrichment Enrichment programs are available through the program or unit for career planning, learning strategies, math, reading, and written composition skills. Programs for career planning, college survival skills, learning strategies, math, reading, stress management, study skills, and written composition skills are provided collaboratively through on-campus or off-campus services. Credit is offered for study skills.

Application For admittance to the program or unit, students are required to apply to the program directly, provide a psychoeducational report (5 years old or less), provide documentation of high school services, and provide new evaluation if no records are obtainable. Upon application, materials documenting need for services should be sent only to the LD program or unit. Upon acceptance, documentation of need for services should be sent only to the LD program or unit. *Application deadline (institutional):* Continuous. *Application deadline (LD program):* Rolling/continuous for fall and rolling/continuous for spring.

Written Policies Written policy regarding general/basic LD accommodations is outlined in the school's catalog/handbook. Written policy regarding general/basic LD accommodations is available through the program or unit directly.

Cerro Coso Community College

3000 College Heights Boulevard
Ridgecrest, CA 93555-9571
http://www.cerrocoso.edu/
Contact: Phone: 760-384-6100. Fax: 760-375-4776.

The program or unit includes 1 full-time and 6 part-time staff members. LD specialists, remediation/learning specialists, and strategy tutors are provided through the program or unit. Counselors are provided collaboratively through on-campus or off-campus services.

Orientation The program or unit offers a mandatory 1½ to 2-hour orientation for new students after classes begin and individually by special arrangement.

Unique Aids and Services Aids, services, or accommodations include advocates, career counseling, digital textbooks, priority registration, and support groups.

Subject-area Tutoring Tutoring is offered one-on-one and in small groups for most subjects. Tutoring is provided through the program or unit via computer-based instruction, LD specialists, and professional tutors. Tutoring is also provided collaboratively through on-campus or off-campus services via computer-based instruction and trained peer tutors.

Diagnostic Testing Testing is provided through the program or unit for auditory processing, handwriting, intelligence, learning strategies, learning styles, reading, spelling, spoken language, visual processing, and written language.

Basic Skills Remediation Remediation is offered one-on-one, in small groups, and in class-size groups for auditory processing, computer skills, learning strategies, math, motor skills, reading, social skills, spelling, study skills, time management, visual processing, and written language. Remediation is provided through the program or unit via computer-based instruction and LD specialists. Remediation is also provided collaboratively through on-campus or off-campus services via computer-based instruction.

Enrichment Programs for career planning, college survival skills, learning strategies, math, practical computer skills, reading, self-advocacy, stress management, study skills, test taking, time management, vocabulary development, and written composition skills are provided collaboratively through on-campus or off-campus services.

Student Organization Special Services Club consists of 60 members.

Application For admittance to the program or unit, students are required to apply to the program directly and provide a psychoeducational report (3 years old or less). It is recommended that students provide documentation of high school services and provide other documentation. Upon application, materials documenting need for services should be sent only to the LD program or unit. *Application deadline (institutional):* Continuous. *Application deadline (LD program):* Rolling/continuous for fall and rolling/continuous for spring.

Written Policies Written policy regarding general/basic LD accommodations is available on the program Web site. Written policies regarding course substitutions, general/basic LD accommodations, and substitutions and waivers of admissions requirements are outlined in the school's catalog/handbook. Written policies regarding course substitutions, general/basic LD accommodations, reduced course loads, substitutions and waivers of admissions requirements, and substitutions and waivers of graduation requirements are available through the program or unit directly.

Chaffey College

5885 Haven Avenue
Rancho Cucamonga, CA 91737-3002
http://www.chaffey.edu/
Contact: Phone: 909-987-1737. Fax: 909-941-2783.

The program or unit includes 2 full-time and 25 part-time staff members. Counselors, diagnostic specialists, LD specialists, remediation/learning specialists, and trained peer tutors are provided through the program or unit. Academic advisers, coaches, regular education teachers, skill tutors, and trained peer tutors are provided collaboratively through on-campus or off-campus services.

Orientation The program or unit offers an optional 1-day orientation for new students individually by special arrangement.

Unique Aids and Services Aids, services, or accommodations include priority registration and support groups.

Subject-area Tutoring Tutoring is offered one-on-one and in small groups for all subjects. Tutoring is provided collaboratively through on-campus or off-campus services via computer-based instruction and trained peer tutors.

Diagnostic Testing Testing is provided through the program or unit for auditory processing, intelligence, math, reading, spelling, visual processing, and written language.

Chaffey College (continued)

Basic Skills Remediation Remediation is offered in class-size groups for learning strategies, math, reading, spelling, spoken language, study skills, time management, and written language. Remediation is provided collaboratively through on-campus or off-campus services via computer-based instruction, regular education teachers, and trained peer tutors.

Application For admittance to the program or unit, students are required to apply to the program directly. It is recommended that students provide a psychoeducational report and provide documentation of high school services. *Application deadline (institutional):* Continuous. *Application deadline (LD program):* Rolling/continuous for fall and rolling/continuous for spring.

Written Policies Written policy regarding general/basic LD accommodations is available on the program Web site. Written policies regarding course substitutions, general/basic LD accommodations, reduced course loads, substitutions and waivers of admissions requirements, and substitutions and waivers of graduation requirements are available through the program or unit directly.

Chaparral College

4585 East Speedway, No 204
Tucson, AZ 85712
http://www.chap-col.edu/
Contact: Ms. Carol Ann Jenkins, ESI/GED Instructor.
Phone: 520-327-6866. Fax: 520-325-0108.

Approximately 20 registered undergraduate students were served during 2002-03.
Subject-area Tutoring Tutoring is offered one-on-one and in small groups for some subjects. Tutoring is provided collaboratively through on-campus or off-campus services via professional tutors and other.
Application *Application deadline (institutional):* Continuous.
Written Policies Written policy regarding substitutions and waivers of admissions requirements is outlined in the school's catalog/handbook.

Chattahoochee Technical College
Disability Services

980 South Cobb Drive
Marietta, GA 30060
http://www.chat-tec.com/
Contact: Ms. Mary Frances Bernard, Disability Services Counselor. Phone: 770-528-4529. Fax: 770-528-4578.
E-mail: mfbernard@chat-tec.com.

Disability Services The program or unit includes 1 full-time staff member. Counselors are provided through the program or unit.
Unique Aids and Services Aids, services, or accommodations include advocates, career counseling, digital textbooks, faculty training, priority registration, assistive technology.

Subject-area Tutoring Tutoring is offered one-on-one for some subjects. Tutoring is provided collaboratively through on-campus or off-campus services via computer-based instruction and other.
Basic Skills Remediation Remediation is offered one-on-one for math, reading, spelling, study skills, and written language. Remediation is provided collaboratively through on-campus or off-campus services via computer-based instruction and regular education teachers.
Enrichment Programs for career planning, practical computer skills, and study skills are provided collaboratively through on-campus or off-campus services. Credit is offered for practical computer skills and study skills.
Application For admittance to the program or unit, students are required to apply to the program directly and provide a psychoeducational report. It is recommended that students provide documentation of high school services. Upon application, materials documenting need for services should be sent only to the LD program or unit. Upon acceptance, documentation of need for services should be sent only to the LD program or unit. *Application deadline (institutional):* Continuous. *Application deadline (LD program):* Rolling/continuous for fall and rolling/continuous for spring.
Written Policies Written policy regarding general/basic LD accommodations is outlined in the school's catalog/handbook. Written policy regarding general/basic LD accommodations is available through the program or unit directly.

Chattanooga State Technical Community College

4501 Amnicola Highway
Chattanooga, TN 37406-1097
http://www.chattanoogastate.edu/Student_Services/disability/dimain.asp
Contact: Ms. Shelly Boatner, Learning Disabilities Specialist. Phone: 423-697-2436. Fax: 423-697-2693. E-mail: shelly.boatner@chattanoogastate.edu.

Approximately 175 registered undergraduate students were served during 2002-03. The program or unit includes 3 full-time and 2 part-time staff members. Academic advisers and LD specialists are provided through the program or unit. Academic advisers, counselors, professional tutors, regular education teachers, remediation/learning specialists, skill tutors, strategy tutors, and trained peer tutors are provided collaboratively through on-campus or off-campus services.
Unique Aids and Services Aids, services, or accommodations include career counseling and support groups.
Subject-area Tutoring Tutoring is offered one-on-one and in small groups for some subjects. Tutoring is provided collaboratively through on-campus or off-campus services via computer-based instruction, professional tutors, and trained peer tutors.
Basic Skills Remediation Remediation is offered in class-size groups for learning strategies, math, reading, study skills, time management, and written language. Remediation is provided collaboratively through on-campus or off-campus services via computer-based instruction, professional tutors, regular education teachers, and trained peer tutors.

Enrichment Enrichment programs are available through the program or unit for study skills, test taking, and time management. Programs for career planning, learning strategies, math, reading, stress management, study skills, test taking, and time management are provided collaboratively through on-campus or off-campus services.

Student Organization Student Awareness Association consists of 15 members.

Application For admittance to the program or unit, students are required to provide a psychoeducational report (5 years old or less). Upon application, materials documenting need for services should be sent only to the LD program or unit. Upon acceptance, documentation of need for services should be sent only to the LD program or unit. *Application deadline (institutional):* Continuous. *Application deadline (LD program):* Rolling/continuous for fall and rolling/continuous for spring.

Written Policies Written policies regarding course substitutions and general/basic LD accommodations are available on the program Web site. Written policies regarding course substitutions and general/basic LD accommodations are outlined in the school's catalog/handbook. Written policies regarding course substitutions and general/basic LD accommodations are available through the program or unit directly.

Cisco Junior College
Counselor/Special Populations

Box 3, Route 3
Cisco, TX 76437-9321
http://www.cisco.cc.tx.us/
Contact: Mrs. Linda R. Grant, Counselor. Phone: 325-673-4567 Ext. 224. E-mail: lgrant@cisco.cc.tx.us.

Counselor/Special Populations Approximately 40 registered undergraduate students were served during 2002-03. The program or unit includes 2 part-time staff members. Academic advisers, coaches, counselors, regular education teachers, remediation/learning specialists, and other are provided collaboratively through on-campus or off-campus services.

Unique Aids and Services Aids, services, or accommodations include career counseling, digital textbooks, faculty training, and priority registration.

Subject-area Tutoring Tutoring is offered one-on-one and in small groups for most subjects. Tutoring is provided collaboratively through on-campus or off-campus services via computer-based instruction, trained peer tutors, and other.

Basic Skills Remediation Remediation is offered in class-size groups for math, reading, and written language. Remediation is provided collaboratively through on-campus or off-campus services via computer-based instruction and regular education teachers.

Enrichment Programs for career planning, college survival skills, learning strategies, math, reading, and written composition skills are provided collaboratively through on-campus or off-campus services.

Application For admittance to the program or unit, students are required to provide a psychoeducational report (5 years old or less) and provide documentation of high school services. Upon application, materials documenting need for services should be sent only to the LD program or unit. Upon acceptance, documentation of need

for services should be sent only to the LD program or unit. *Application deadline (institutional):* Continuous. *Application deadline (LD program):* Rolling/continuous for fall and rolling/continuous for spring.

Written Policies Written policy regarding general/basic LD accommodations is available on the program Web site. Written policy regarding general/basic LD accommodations is outlined in the school's catalog/handbook. Written policy regarding general/basic LD accommodations is available through the program or unit directly.

City Colleges of Chicago, Richard J. Daley College
Special Needs

7500 South Pulaski Road
Chicago, IL 60652-1242
http://daley.ccc.edu/
Contact: Karen Barnett-Lee, Special Needs Coordinator. Phone: 773-838-7578. Fax: 773-838-7524. E-mail: kbarnett@ccc.edu.

Special Needs Approximately 50 registered undergraduate students were served during 2002-03. The program or unit includes 1 full-time and 1 part-time staff member. Academic advisers, counselors, and graduate assistants/students are provided through the program or unit. Academic advisers, counselors, graduate assistants/students, professional tutors, regular education teachers, skill tutors, and strategy tutors are provided collaboratively through on-campus or off-campus services.

Orientation The program or unit offers an optional orientation for new students before classes begin, during registration, after classes begin, and individually by special arrangement.

Unique Aids and Services Aids, services, or accommodations include advocates and career counseling.

Subject-area Tutoring Tutoring is offered one-on-one. Tutoring is provided through the program or unit via computer-based instruction. Tutoring is also provided collaboratively through on-campus or off-campus services via computer-based instruction and professional tutors.

Basic Skills Remediation Remediation is offered one-on-one and in small groups for computer skills, learning strategies, math, reading, study skills, and written language. Remediation is provided collaboratively through on-campus or off-campus services via professional tutors and regular education teachers.

Enrichment Enrichment programs are available through the program or unit for oral communication skills, self-advocacy, study skills, test taking, and time management. Programs for career planning, college survival skills, learning strategies, math, practical computer skills, reading, study skills, test taking, time management, and written composition skills are provided collaboratively through on-campus or off-campus services.

Application For admittance to the program or unit, students are required to provide a psychoeducational report and provide documentation of high school services. Upon application, materials documenting need for services should be sent only to the LD program or unit. Upon acceptance, documentation of need for services should be sent only to the LD program or unit. *Application deadline (institutional):* Continuous.

City Colleges of Chicago, Richard J. Daley College (continued)
Written Policies Written policies regarding course substitutions, general/basic LD accommodations, grade forgiveness, reduced course loads, substitutions and waivers of admissions requirements, and substitutions and waivers of graduation requirements are available through the program or unit directly.

Cleveland State Community College
Disability Support Services

PO Box 3570
Cleveland, TN 37320-3570
http://www.clevelandstatecc.edu50
Contact: Ms. Amy L. Derrick, Coordinator of Disability Support Services. Phone: 423-478-6217. Fax: 423-614-8724. E-mail: aderrick@clscc.cc.tn.us.

Disability Support Services Approximately 60 registered undergraduate students were served during 2002-03. The program or unit includes 1 full-time staff member. Academic advisers, coaches, regular education teachers, and trained peer tutors are provided through the program or unit. Academic advisers, coaches, counselors, regular education teachers, and trained peer tutors are provided collaboratively through on-campus or off-campus services.
Orientation The program or unit offers a mandatory 1-hour orientation for new students individually by special arrangement.
Unique Aids and Services Aids, services, or accommodations include advocates and career counseling.
Subject-area Tutoring Tutoring is offered in small groups for most subjects. Tutoring is provided through the program or unit via graduate assistants/students. Tutoring is also provided collaboratively through on-campus or off-campus services via graduate assistants/students.
Enrichment Programs for career planning, college survival skills, health and nutrition, learning strategies, stress management, study skills, test taking, and time management are provided collaboratively through on-campus or off-campus services.
Application For admittance to the program or unit, students are required to apply to the program directly and provide a psychoeducational report (3 years old or less). It is recommended that students provide documentation of high school services. Upon application, materials documenting need for services should be sent only to the LD program or unit. Upon acceptance, documentation of need for services should be sent only to the LD program or unit. *Application deadline (institutional):* Continuous. *Application deadline (LD program):* Rolling/continuous for fall and rolling/continuous for spring.
Written Policies Written policy regarding general/basic LD accommodations is available on the program Web site. Written policy regarding general/basic LD accommodations is outlined in the school's catalog/handbook. Written policy regarding general/basic LD accommodations is available through the program or unit directly.

Clinton Community College

1000 Lincoln Boulevard

Clinton, IA 52732-6299
http://www.eicc.edu/ccc/
Contact: Phone: 563-244-7001. Fax: 563-244-7107.

The program or unit includes 1 full-time staff member. Academic advisers, professional tutors, regular education teachers, and other are provided collaboratively through on-campus or off-campus services.
Subject-area Tutoring Tutoring is offered in small groups for most subjects. Tutoring is provided collaboratively through on-campus or off-campus services via trained peer tutors.
Basic Skills Remediation Remediation is offered in class-size groups for computer skills, learning strategies, math, reading, study skills, and time management. Remediation is provided collaboratively through on-campus or off-campus services via regular education teachers and trained peer tutors.
Enrichment Programs for career planning, college survival skills, learning strategies, practical computer skills, stress management, study skills, test taking, and time management are provided collaboratively through on-campus or off-campus services.
Application For admittance to the program or unit, students are required to provide a psychoeducational report. It is recommended that students provide documentation of high school services. Upon application, materials documenting need for services should be sent only to the LD program or unit. *Application deadline (institutional):* Continuous. *Application deadline (LD program):* Rolling/continuous for fall and rolling/continuous for spring.
Written Policies Written policies regarding course substitutions, general/basic LD accommodations, and reduced course loads are available through the program or unit directly.

Clinton Community College

136 Clinton Point Drive
Plattsburgh, NY 12901-9573
http://clintoncc.suny.edu/
Contact: Phone: 518-562-4200. Fax: 518-562-8621.

The program or unit includes 1 full-time and 2 part-time staff members. Academic advisers, counselors, diagnostic specialists, LD specialists, professional tutors, regular education teachers, and remediation/learning specialists are provided collaboratively through on-campus or off-campus services.
Orientation The program or unit offers an optional orientation for new students before registration and when they apply for services.
Unique Aids and Services Aids, services, or accommodations include faculty training and priority registration.
Subject-area Tutoring Tutoring is offered in small groups for some subjects. Tutoring is provided collaboratively through on-campus or off-campus services via professional tutors.
Basic Skills Remediation Remediation is offered in class-size groups for computer skills, math, reading, study skills, and written language. Remediation is provided collaboratively through on-campus or off-campus services via professional tutors.
Application For admittance to the program or unit, students are required to provide a psychoeducational report (3 years old or less). *Application deadline (institutional):* 9/3.

Written Policies Written policy regarding general/basic LD accommodations is available on the program Web site. Written policy regarding general/basic LD accommodations is outlined in the school's catalog/handbook. Written policy regarding general/basic LD accommodations is available through the program or unit directly.

Cloud County Community College

2221 Campus Drive, PO Box 1002
Concordia, KS 66901-1002
http://www.cloud.edu/

Contact: Leslie L. Hemphill, Director of Advisement and Counseling. Phone: 785-243-1435 Ext. 317. Fax: 785-243-1839. E-mail: lhemphill@cloud.edu. Head of LD Program: Sue Regan, Director of Learning Skills Center. Phone: 785-243-1435 Ext. 230. Fax: 785-243-1043. E-mail: sregan@cloud.edu.

The program or unit includes 3 full-time staff members and 1 part-time staff member. Academic advisers, coaches, counselors, LD specialists, professional tutors, remediation/learning specialists, skill tutors, strategy tutors, and trained peer tutors are provided collaboratively through on-campus or off-campus services.
Unique Aids and Services Aids, services, or accommodations include career counseling.
Subject-area Tutoring Tutoring is offered one-on-one and in small groups for most subjects. Tutoring is provided collaboratively through on-campus or off-campus services via computer-based instruction, LD specialists, professional tutors, and trained peer tutors.
Diagnostic Testing Testing for intelligence, learning strategies, learning styles, math, reading, spelling, and study skills is provided collaboratively through on-campus or off-campus services.
Basic Skills Remediation Remediation is offered in small groups and in class-size groups for computer skills, learning strategies, math, reading, spelling, study skills, time management, and written language. Remediation is provided collaboratively through on-campus or off-campus services via computer-based instruction, LD specialists, professional tutors, and trained peer tutors.
Enrichment Programs for career planning, college survival skills, health and nutrition, learning strategies, math, practical computer skills, reading, stress management, study skills, test taking, time management, vocabulary development, and written composition skills are provided collaboratively through on-campus or off-campus services. Credit is offered for career planning, college survival skills, health and nutrition, math, practical computer skills, and reading.
Fees *Diagnostic Testing* fee is $0 to $500.
Application For admittance to the program or unit, students are required to provide a psychoeducational report (3 years old or less). It is recommended that students apply to the program directly and provide documentation of high school services. Upon acceptance, documentation of need for services should be sent only to the LD program or unit. *Application deadline (institutional):* 9/11. *Application deadline (LD program):* Rolling/continuous for fall and rolling/continuous for spring.

Written Policies Written policy regarding general/basic LD accommodations is outlined in the school's catalog/handbook. Written policies regarding course substitutions, general/basic LD accommodations, grade forgiveness, reduced course loads, and substitutions and waivers of graduation requirements are available through the program or unit directly.

Clovis Community College

417 Schepps Boulevard
Clovis, NM 88101-8381
http://www.clovis.edu/

Contact: Susan Cage, Special Services Coordinator. Phone: 505-769-4098. Fax: 505-769-4190. E-mail: susan.cage@clovis.edu.

Approximately 100 registered undergraduate students were served during 2002-03. The program or unit includes 2 full-time staff members. Academic advisers and counselors are provided through the program or unit. Coaches, diagnostic specialists, graduate assistants/students, LD specialists, professional tutors, regular education teachers, remediation/learning specialists, skill tutors, special education teachers, strategy tutors, teacher trainees, trained peer tutors, and other are provided collaboratively through on-campus or off-campus services.
Subject-area Tutoring Tutoring is offered one-on-one for all subjects. Tutoring is provided collaboratively through on-campus or off-campus services via computer-based instruction and trained peer tutors.
Application For admittance to the program or unit, students are required to apply to the program directly and provide a psychoeducational report (5 years old or less). It is recommended that students provide documentation of high school services. Upon application, materials documenting need for services should be sent only to the LD program or unit. Upon acceptance, documentation of need for services should be sent to both admissions and the LD program or unit. *Application deadline (LD program):* Rolling/continuous for fall and rolling/continuous for spring.
Written Policies Written policy regarding general/basic LD accommodations is available through the program or unit directly.

Coastal Georgia Community College

3700 Altama Avenue
Brunswick, GA 31520-3644
http://www.cgcc.peachnet.edu

Contact: Mr. Sherrel L. Bees, Disability Services Coordinator. Phone: 912-264-7220. Fax: 912-261-3900. E-mail: sbees@cgcc.edu.

The program or unit includes 1 full-time staff member. Academic advisers, counselors, regular education teachers, skill tutors, and trained peer tutors are provided collaboratively through on-campus or off-campus services.

Coastal Georgia Community College (continued)

Unique Aids and Services Aids, services, or accommodations include faculty training and priority registration.

Subject-area Tutoring Tutoring is offered one-on-one and in small groups for all subjects. Tutoring is provided collaboratively through on-campus or off-campus services via computer-based instruction and trained peer tutors.

Diagnostic Testing Testing for auditory processing, intelligence, learning strategies, math, neuropsychological, personality, reading, visual processing, and written language is provided collaboratively through on-campus or off-campus services.

Basic Skills Remediation Remediation is offered in class-size groups for math, reading, and written language. Remediation is provided collaboratively through on-campus or off-campus services via computer-based instruction, regular education teachers, and trained peer tutors.

Enrichment Programs for career planning, college survival skills, learning strategies, math, practical computer skills, reading, study skills, test taking, time management, and written composition skills are provided collaboratively through on-campus or off-campus services. Credit is offered for college survival skills.

Fees *Diagnostic Testing* fee is $400.

Application For admittance to the program or unit, students are required to apply to the program directly and provide a psychoeducational report (3 years old or less). It is recommended that students provide documentation of high school services. Upon application, materials documenting need for services should be sent only to the LD program or unit. Upon acceptance, documentation of need for services should be sent only to the LD program or unit. *Application deadline (institutional):* 8/19. *Application deadline (LD program):* Rolling/continuous for fall and rolling/continuous for spring.

Written Policies Written policies regarding course substitutions, general/basic LD accommodations, substitutions and waivers of admissions requirements, and substitutions and waivers of graduation requirements are available on the program Web site. Written policies regarding general/basic LD accommodations, substitutions and waivers of admissions requirements, and substitutions and waivers of graduation requirements are outlined in the school's catalog/handbook. Written policies regarding course substitutions, general/basic LD accommodations, substitutions and waivers of admissions requirements, and substitutions and waivers of graduation requirements are available through the program or unit directly.

Cochran School of Nursing

967 North Broadway
Yonkers, NY 10701
http://www.riversidehealth.org/
Contact: Ms. Jacqueline McMahon, Nursing Instructor and Disability Coordinator. Phone: 914-964-4282. E-mail: jmcm753625@aol.com.

The program or unit includes 1 full-time staff member. Academic advisers, counselors, diagnostic specialists, and regular education teachers are provided collaboratively through on-campus or off-campus services.

Subject-area Tutoring Tutoring is offered in small groups for some subjects. Tutoring is provided collaboratively through on-campus or off-campus services via computer-based instruction, graduate assistants/students, LD specialists, and professional tutors.

Basic Skills Remediation Remediation is offered one-on-one for computer skills, learning strategies, math, reading, spelling, spoken language, study skills, time management, visual processing, and written language. Remediation is provided collaboratively through on-campus or off-campus services via computer-based instruction, professional tutors, and regular education teachers.

Application For admittance to the program or unit, students are required to provide a psychoeducational report (3 years old or less) and provide documentation of high school services. It is recommended that students provide documentation of more recent services if necessary. Upon application, materials documenting need for services should be sent to both admissions and the LD program or unit. Upon acceptance, documentation of need for services should be sent only to the LD program or unit. *Application deadline (institutional):* Continuous. *Application deadline (LD program):* Rolling/continuous for fall and rolling/continuous for spring.

Written Policies Written policies regarding general/basic LD accommodations and substitutions and waivers of admissions requirements are outlined in the school's catalog/handbook. Written policies regarding general/basic LD accommodations and substitutions and waivers of admissions requirements are available through the program or unit directly.

College of Alameda
Programs and Services for Students with Disabilities

555 Atlantic Avenue
Alameda, CA 94501-2109
http://www.peralta.cc.ca.us/
Contact: Ms. Helene M. Maxwell, Coordinator of Programs and Services for Students with Disabilities. Phone: 510-748-2326. Fax: 510-748-2339. E-mail: hmaxwell3@earthlink.net.

Programs and Services for Students with Disabilities Approximately 150 registered undergraduate students were served during 2002-03. The program or unit includes 1 full-time and 4 part-time staff members. Academic advisers, coaches, counselors, diagnostic specialists, LD specialists, professional tutors, remediation/learning specialists, skill tutors, and strategy tutors are provided through the program or unit. Academic advisers, counselors, regular education teachers, skill tutors, and trained peer tutors are provided collaboratively through on-campus or off-campus services.

Orientation The program or unit offers a mandatory orientation for new students individually by special arrangement.

Unique Aids and Services Aids, services, or accommodations include career counseling, digital textbooks, faculty training, and priority registration.

Subject-area Tutoring Tutoring is offered one-on-one and in small groups for some subjects. Tutoring is provided through the program or unit via LD specialists and professional tutors. Tutoring is also provided collaboratively through on-campus or off-campus services via computer-based instruction and trained peer tutors.

Diagnostic Testing Testing is provided through the program or unit for auditory processing, learning strategies, learning styles, math, motor skills, reading, spelling, spoken language, visual processing, and written language. Testing for math, reading, and written language is provided collaboratively through on-campus or off-campus services.

Basic Skills Remediation Remediation is offered in small groups for computer skills, learning strategies, math, reading, study skills, time management, and written language. Remediation is provided through the program or unit via LD specialists and professional tutors. Remediation is also provided collaboratively through on-campus or off-campus services via computer-based instruction, regular education teachers, and other.

Enrichment Enrichment programs are available through the program or unit for college survival skills, learning strategies, math, practical computer skills, self-advocacy, study skills, test taking, time management, vocabulary development, and written composition skills. Programs for career planning, college survival skills, health and nutrition, math, oral communication skills, practical computer skills, reading, stress management, and written composition skills are provided collaboratively through on-campus or off-campus services. Credit is offered for career planning, college survival skills, math, oral communication skills, practical computer skills, reading, study skills, test taking, time management, vocabulary development, and written composition skills.

Fees *LD Program or Service* fee is $11. *Diagnostic Testing* fee is $11.

Application For admittance to the program or unit, students are required to apply to the program directly. It is recommended that students provide a psychoeducational report (3 years old or less), provide documentation of high school services, and provide other documentation of disability. Upon application, materials documenting need for services should be sent only to the LD program or unit. Upon acceptance, documentation of need for services should be sent only to the LD program or unit. *Application deadline (institutional):* Continuous. *Application deadline (LD program):* Rolling/continuous for fall and rolling/continuous for spring.

Written Policies Written policies regarding course substitutions, general/basic LD accommodations, grade forgiveness, reduced course loads, substitutions and waivers of admissions requirements, and substitutions and waivers of graduation requirements are outlined in the school's catalog/handbook. Written policies regarding course substitutions, general/basic LD accommodations, grade forgiveness, reduced course loads, substitutions and waivers of admissions requirements, and substitutions and waivers of graduation requirements are available through the program or unit directly.

College of DuPage

425 Fawell Boulevard
Glen Ellyn, IL 60137-6599
http://www.cod.edu/

Contact: Ms. Katie Ricketts, Coordinator of Special Student Services. Phone: 630-942-2306. Fax: 630-942-2071. E-mail: ricketts@cdnet.cod.edu.

The program or unit includes 1 full-time and 2 part-time staff members. Academic advisers are provided through the program or unit. Academic advisers, counselors, LD specialists, professional tutors, regular education teachers, remediation/learning specialists, skill tutors, trained peer tutors, and other are provided collaboratively through on-campus or off-campus services.

Orientation The program or unit offers an optional 2-hour orientation for new students before registration and during summer prior to enrollment.

Unique Aids and Services Aids, services, or accommodations include career counseling and digital textbooks.

Subject-area Tutoring Tutoring is offered one-on-one and in small groups for most subjects. Tutoring is provided collaboratively through on-campus or off-campus services via graduate assistants/students, LD specialists, professional tutors, and trained peer tutors.

Basic Skills Remediation Remediation is offered one-on-one for learning strategies, math, reading, spelling, study skills, time management, and written language. Remediation is provided collaboratively through on-campus or off-campus services via graduate assistants/students, LD specialists, regular education teachers, special education teachers, and trained peer tutors.

Enrichment Programs for career planning, college survival skills, health and nutrition, learning strategies, math, oral communication skills, practical computer skills, reading, self-advocacy, stress management, study skills, test taking, time management, vocabulary development, and written composition skills are provided collaboratively through on-campus or off-campus services. Credit is offered for health and nutrition, math, oral communication skills, and reading.

Student Organization Psi Sigma Chi consists of 8 members.

Application For admittance to the program or unit, students are required to provide a psychoeducational report (3 years old or less). It is recommended that students provide documentation of high school services. Upon application, materials documenting need for services should be sent only to the LD program or unit. Upon acceptance, documentation of need for services should be sent only to the LD program or unit. *Application deadline (institutional):* Continuous. *Application deadline (LD program):* Rolling/continuous for fall and rolling/continuous for spring.

Written Policies Written policies regarding general/basic LD accommodations and grade forgiveness are available on the program Web site. Written policies regarding general/basic LD accommodations and grade forgiveness are outlined in the school's catalog/handbook. Written policy regarding general/basic LD accommodations is available through the program or unit directly.

College of Lake County

19351 West Washington Street
Grayslake, IL 60030-1198
http://www.clcillinois.edu/

Contact: Ms. Amy Chapin, Learning Disability Specialist. Phone: 847-543-2454. Fax: 847-543-2428. E-mail: lac825@clcillinois.edu. Head of LD Program: Ms. Elizabeth Marie Link, Director of Office for Students with Disabilities. Phone: 847-543-2473. Fax: 847-543-2428. E-mail: bllink@clcillinois.edu.

Approximately 600 registered undergraduate students were served during 2002–03. The program or unit includes 2 full-time and 10 part-time staff members. Academic advisers, coaches, counselors, LD specialists, professional tutors, remediation/learning specialists, special education teachers, and trained peer tutors are provided collaboratively through on-campus or off-campus services.

Unique Aids and Services Aids, services, or accommodations include faculty training and priority registration.

Subject-area Tutoring Tutoring is offered one-on-one for most subjects. Tutoring is provided collaboratively through on-campus or off-campus services via computer-based instruction, LD specialists, professional tutors, and trained peer tutors.

College of Lake County (continued)

Basic Skills Remediation Remediation is offered one-on-one and in small groups for auditory processing, computer skills, handwriting, learning strategies, math, motor skills, reading, social skills, spelling, study skills, time management, visual processing, and written language. Remediation is provided collaboratively through on-campus or off-campus services via regular education teachers.

Application For admittance to the program or unit, students are required to provide a psychoeducational report. It is recommended that students provide documentation of high school services. Upon application, materials documenting need for services should be sent only to the LD program or unit. Upon acceptance, documentation of need for services should be sent only to the LD program or unit. *Application deadline (institutional):* Continuous. *Application deadline (LD program):* Rolling/continuous for fall and rolling/continuous for spring.

Written Policies Written policy regarding grade forgiveness is outlined in the school's catalog/handbook. Written policy regarding course substitutions is available through the program or unit directly.

College of St. Catherine-Minneapolis
Learning Center

601 25th Avenue South
Minneapolis, MN 55454-1494
http://stkate.edu/learningcenter.nsf

Contact: Melissa Engstrom McClellan, Supportive Services Coordinator. Phone: 651-690-8160. Fax: 651-690-7849. Head of LD Program: Ms. Susan Mae Pauly, Director of the Learning Center. Phone: 651-690-7833. Fax: 651-690-7849. E-mail: smpauly@stkate.edu.

Learning Center Approximately 40 registered undergraduate students were served during 2002-03. The program or unit includes 1 full-time staff member. LD specialists are provided through the program or unit. Academic advisers, counselors, professional tutors, remediation/learning specialists, and trained peer tutors are provided collaboratively through on-campus or off-campus services.

Unique Aids and Services Aids, services, or accommodations include career counseling, digital textbooks, and personal coach.

Subject-area Tutoring Tutoring is offered one-on-one for most subjects. Tutoring is provided collaboratively through on-campus or off-campus services via professional tutors and trained peer tutors.

Basic Skills Remediation Remediation is offered one-on-one and in class-size groups for computer skills, learning strategies, math, reading, study skills, time management, and written language. Remediation is provided collaboratively through on-campus or off-campus services via professional tutors and regular education teachers.

Enrichment Enrichment programs are available through the program or unit for self-advocacy. Programs for career planning, health and nutrition, learning strategies, math, medication management, practical computer skills, reading, stress management, study skills, test taking, time management, and written composition skills are provided collaboratively through on-campus or off-campus services. Credit is offered for learning strategies, math, practical computer skills, reading, study skills, and written composition skills.

Application For admittance to the program or unit, students are required to provide a psychoeducational report (5 years old or less) and provide diagnostic material and associated recommendations from a professional . Upon acceptance, documentation of need for services should be sent only to the LD program or unit. *Application deadline (institutional):* Continuous. *Application deadline (LD program):* Rolling/continuous for fall and rolling/continuous for spring.

Written Policies Written policy regarding general/basic LD accommodations is available on the program Web site. Written policy regarding general/basic LD accommodations is available through the program or unit directly.

College of the Canyons

26455 Rockwell Canyon Road
Santa Clarita, CA 91355-1899
http://www.coc.cc.ca.us/

Contact: Dr. Christi Franklin, LD Specialist. Phone: 661-362-3341. Fax: 661-254-5716. E-mail: christi.franklin@canyons.edu.

Approximately 150 registered undergraduate students were served during 2002-03. The program or unit includes 5 full-time staff members. Academic advisers, counselors, LD specialists, professional tutors, and skill tutors are provided through the program or unit. Academic advisers, counselors, professional tutors, and skill tutors are provided collaboratively through on-campus or off-campus services.

Orientation The program or unit offers a mandatory 1-hour orientation for new students before registration, before classes begin, during summer prior to enrollment, during registration, after classes begin, and individually by special arrangement.

Summer Program To help prepare for the demands of college, there is an optional summer program prior to entering the school. Degree credit will be earned.

Unique Aids and Services Aids, services, or accommodations include career counseling, faculty training, and priority registration.

Subject-area Tutoring Tutoring is offered in small groups for some subjects. Tutoring is provided through the program or unit via computer-based instruction, professional tutors, and trained peer tutors.

Diagnostic Testing Testing is provided through the program or unit for auditory processing, intelligence, learning strategies, learning styles, math, reading, spelling, visual processing, and written language.

Enrichment Enrichment programs are available through the program or unit for college survival skills. Programs for career planning and college survival skills are provided collaboratively through on-campus or off-campus services. Credit is offered for career planning and college survival skills.

Fees *Diagnostic Testing* fee is $6.

Application For admittance to the program or unit, students are required to apply to the program directly. It is recommended that students provide a psychoeducational report (3 years old or less), provide documentation of high school services, and provide assessment results. Upon application, materials documenting need for services should be sent only to the LD program or unit. Upon acceptance, documentation of need for services should be sent only to the LD program or unit. *Application deadline (institutional):* 8/22. *Application deadline (LD program):* Rolling/continuous for fall and rolling/continuous for spring.

Written Policies Written policy regarding general/basic LD accommodations is available on the program Web site. Written policy regarding general/basic LD accommodations is outlined in the school's catalog/handbook. Written policy regarding general/basic LD accommodations is available through the program or unit directly.

College of the Desert

43-500 Monterey Avenue
Palm Desert, CA 92260-9305
http://desert.cc.ca.us/

Contact: Mr. Paul Magg, Alternative Media Specialist and Counselor. Phone: 760-773-2534. Fax: 760-776-2598. E-mail: pmagg@dccd.cc.ca.us. Head of LD Program: Mr. Michael James O'Neill Jr., Coordinator and Learning Disability Specialist. Phone: 760-773-2534. Fax: 760-776-0198. E-mail: moneill@dccd.cc.ca.us.

Approximately 287 registered undergraduate students were served during 2002-03. The program or unit includes 1 full-time and 2 part-time staff members. Counselors, diagnostic specialists, LD specialists, remediation/learning specialists, and trained peer tutors are provided through the program or unit.

Orientation The program or unit offers individually by special arrangement.

Unique Aids and Services Aids, services, or accommodations include digital textbooks and priority registration.

Subject-area Tutoring Tutoring is offered one-on-one for all subjects. Tutoring is provided collaboratively through on-campus or off-campus services via computer-based instruction and other.

Diagnostic Testing Testing is provided through the program or unit for auditory processing, intelligence, learning strategies, learning styles, math, reading, spelling, spoken language, visual processing, and written language.

Basic Skills Remediation Remediation is offered in class-size groups for computer skills, learning strategies, math, reading, spelling, study skills, time management, visual processing, and written language. Remediation is provided through the program or unit via computer-based instruction, LD specialists, and special education teachers. Remediation is also provided collaboratively through on-campus or off-campus services via computer-based instruction.

Enrichment Enrichment programs are available through the program or unit for career planning, learning strategies, math, practical computer skills, reading, self-advocacy, study skills, test taking, time management, vocabulary development, and written composition skills. Programs for career planning, college survival skills, health and nutrition, learning strategies, math, oral communication skills, practical computer skills, reading, self-advocacy, study skills, test taking, time management, vocabulary development, and written composition skills are provided collaboratively through on-campus or off-campus services.

Application For admittance to the program or unit, students are required to apply to the program directly. It is recommended that students provide a psychoeducational report (3 years old or less) and provide documentation of high school services. Upon applica-

tion, materials documenting need for services should be sent only to the LD program or unit. Upon acceptance, documentation of need for services should be sent only to the LD program or unit. *Application deadline (institutional):* Continuous. *Application deadline (LD program):* Rolling/continuous for spring.

Written Policies Written policies regarding course substitutions, general/basic LD accommodations, and substitutions and waivers of graduation requirements are available through the program or unit directly.

College of the Sequoias
Disability Resource Center

915 South Mooney Boulevard
Visalia, CA 93277-2234
http://www.cos.edu/
view_page.asp?nodeid=1298&parentid=1279&moduleid=5

Contact: Ms. Kathleen Conway, Learning Specialist. Phone: 559-730-3805. Fax: 559-730-3803. E-mail: kathc@cos.edu.

Disability Resource Center Approximately 260 registered undergraduate students were served during 2002-03. The program or unit includes 6 full-time and 11 part-time staff members. Academic advisers, counselors, diagnostic specialists, graduate assistants/students, LD specialists, remediation/learning specialists, strategy tutors, and trained peer tutors are provided through the program or unit. Academic advisers, coaches, counselors, regular education teachers, remediation/learning specialists, and trained peer tutors are provided collaboratively through on-campus or off-campus services.

Unique Aids and Services Aids, services, or accommodations include career counseling and priority registration.

Subject-area Tutoring Tutoring is offered one-on-one and in small groups for most subjects. Tutoring is provided through the program or unit via computer-based instruction, graduate assistants/students, and trained peer tutors. Tutoring is also provided collaboratively through on-campus or off-campus services via computer-based instruction, graduate assistants/students, and trained peer tutors.

Diagnostic Testing Testing is provided through the program or unit for auditory processing, handwriting, intelligence, learning strategies, learning styles, math, motor skills, reading, spelling, spoken language, visual processing, and written language.

Basic Skills Remediation Remediation is offered one-on-one for learning strategies, math, reading, spelling, study skills, and written language. Remediation is provided through the program or unit via computer-based instruction, LD specialists, and trained peer tutors.

Enrichment Enrichment programs are available through the program or unit for college survival skills, learning strategies, study skills, test taking, time management, and vocabulary development. Programs for career planning, college survival skills, learning strategies, study skills, test taking, time management, and vocabulary development are provided collaboratively through on-campus or off-campus services.

Application It is recommended that students provide a psychoeducational report (3 years old or less) and provide documentation of high school services. Upon application, materials documenting need for services should be sent only to the LD program or unit. Upon

College of the Sequoias (continued)

acceptance, documentation of need for services should be sent only to the LD program or unit. *Application deadline (institutional):* 8/15. *Application deadline (LD program):* Rolling/continuous for fall and rolling/continuous for spring.

Written Policies Written policy regarding general/basic LD accommodations is available on the program Web site. Written policy regarding general/basic LD accommodations is outlined in the school's catalog/handbook. Written policy regarding general/basic LD accommodations is available through the program or unit directly.

College of the Siskiyous

800 College Avenue

Weed, CA 96094-2899

http://www.siskiyous.edu/

Contact: Marlys Ann Cordoba, Learning Disabilities Specialist. Phone: 530-938-5884. Fax: 530-938-5228. E-mail: cordoba@siskiyous.edu.

Approximately 150 registered undergraduate students were served during 2002-03. The program or unit includes 2 full-time staff members. Academic advisers, coaches, counselors, diagnostic specialists, and LD specialists are provided through the program or unit. Academic advisers, coaches, counselors, and diagnostic specialists are provided collaboratively through on-campus or off-campus services.

Subject-area Tutoring Tutoring is offered one-on-one, in small groups, and in class-size groups for most subjects. Tutoring is provided through the program or unit via computer-based instruction, LD specialists, and trained peer tutors. Tutoring is also provided collaboratively through on-campus or off-campus services via computer-based instruction, LD specialists, and trained peer tutors.

Diagnostic Testing Testing is provided through the program or unit for auditory processing, intelligence, math, reading, spelling, spoken language, visual processing, and written language. Testing for auditory processing, intelligence, math, reading, spelling, spoken language, visual processing, and written language is provided collaboratively through on-campus or off-campus services.

Basic Skills Remediation Remediation is offered one-on-one, in small groups, and in class-size groups for auditory processing, computer skills, learning strategies, math, reading, spelling, study skills, time management, visual processing, and written language. Remediation is provided through the program or unit via computer-based instruction, LD specialists, and trained peer tutors. Remediation is also provided collaboratively through on-campus or off-campus services via computer-based instruction, LD specialists, and trained peer tutors.

Enrichment Enrichment programs are available through the program or unit for reading and self-advocacy. Programs for career planning, college survival skills, health and nutrition, learning strategies, math, oral communication skills, practical computer skills, reading, stress management, study skills, test taking, time management, vocabulary development, and written composition skills are provided collaboratively through on-campus or off-campus services. Credit is offered for career planning, college survival skills, health and nutrition, learning strategies, math, oral communication skills, practical computer skills, reading, stress management, study skills, test taking, time management, vocabulary development, and written composition skills.

Student Organization Disabled Students Alliance consists of 20 members.

Application For admittance to the program or unit, students are required to provide a psychoeducational report (3 years old or less) and provide results of cognitive and achievement tests. Upon application, materials documenting need for services should be sent only to the LD program or unit. Upon acceptance, documentation of need for services should be sent only to the LD program or unit. *Application deadline (institutional):* Continuous. *Application deadline (LD program):* Rolling/continuous for fall and rolling/continuous for spring.

Written Policies Written policies regarding course substitutions, general/basic LD accommodations, grade forgiveness, reduced course loads, substitutions and waivers of admissions requirements, and substitutions and waivers of graduation requirements are available on the program Web site. Written policy regarding general/basic LD accommodations is outlined in the school's catalog/handbook. Written policies regarding course substitutions, general/basic LD accommodations, grade forgiveness, reduced course loads, substitutions and waivers of admissions requirements, and substitutions and waivers of graduation requirements are available through the program or unit directly.

Colorado Mountain College, Alpine Campus
Special Populations Program

1330 Bob Adams Drive

Steamboat Springs, CO 80487

http://www.coloradomtn.edu/services/disabilitysvcs/spalpine.html

Contact: Ms. Debra Farmer, Coordinator of Special Populations Program. Phone: 970-870-4450. Fax: 970-870-0485. E-mail: dfarmer@coloradomtn.edu.

Special Populations Program Approximately 100 registered undergraduate students were served during 2002-03. The program or unit includes 1 full-time staff member. LD specialists are provided through the program or unit. Academic advisers, counselors, professional tutors, regular education teachers, remediation/learning specialists, skill tutors, strategy tutors, and trained peer tutors are provided collaboratively through on-campus or off-campus services.

Summer Program To help prepare for the demands of college, there is an optional 4-week summer program prior to entering the school.

Unique Aids and Services Aids, services, or accommodations include career counseling.

Subject-area Tutoring Tutoring is offered one-on-one and in small groups for most subjects. Tutoring is provided through the program or unit via computer-based instruction and LD specialists. Tutoring is also provided collaboratively through on-campus or off-campus services via computer-based instruction, professional tutors, and trained peer tutors.

Basic Skills Remediation Remediation is offered one-on-one, in small groups, and in class-size groups for computer skills, learning strategies, math, reading, spelling, study skills, time management, and written language. Remediation is provided collaboratively through on-campus or off-campus services via computer-based instruction, professional tutors, and regular education teachers.

Enrichment Enrichment programs are available through the program or unit for learning strategies, self-advocacy, study skills, test taking, and time management. Programs for career planning, college survival skills, health and nutrition, learning strategies, math, practical computer skills, reading, stress management, study skills, test taking, time management, vocabulary development, and written composition skills are provided collaboratively through on-campus or off-campus services. Credit is offered for career planning, college survival skills, health and nutrition, learning strategies, math, practical computer skills, reading, stress management, study skills, test taking, time management, and written composition skills.

Fees *Summer Program* fee is $1200 to $2800.

Application For admittance to the program or unit, students are required to apply to the program directly and provide a psychoeducational report (3 years old or less). Upon application, materials documenting need for services should be sent only to the LD program or unit. Upon acceptance, documentation of need for services should be sent only to the LD program or unit. *Application deadline (institutional):* Continuous. *Application deadline (LD program):* Rolling/continuous for fall and rolling/continuous for spring.

Written Policies Written policy regarding general/basic LD accommodations is available on the program Web site. Written policies regarding course substitutions, general/basic LD accommodations, grade forgiveness, reduced course loads, and substitutions and waivers of graduation requirements are outlined in the school's catalog/handbook. Written policies regarding course substitutions, general/basic LD accommodations, and substitutions and waivers of graduation requirements are available through the program or unit directly.

Columbia State Community College

PO Box 1315

Columbia, TN 38402-1315

http://www.coscc.cc.tn.us/

Contact: Dr. Paula J. Petty-Ward. Phone: 931-540-2572.

Approximately 38 registered undergraduate students were served during 2002-03. The program or unit includes 2 full-time staff members. Counselors and LD specialists are provided through the program or unit. Academic advisers, counselors, LD specialists, professional tutors, regular education teachers, and trained peer tutors are provided collaboratively through on-campus or off-campus services.

Orientation The program or unit offers an optional 4-hour orientation for new students before classes begin and after classes begin.

Unique Aids and Services Aids, services, or accommodations include advocates, career counseling, peer counseling support.

Subject-area Tutoring Tutoring is offered one-on-one and in small groups for some subjects. Tutoring is provided through the program or unit via computer-based instruction and LD specialists. Tutoring is also provided collaboratively through on-campus or off-campus services via professional tutors and trained peer tutors.

Basic Skills Remediation Remediation is offered in class-size groups for learning strategies, math, reading, spelling, study skills, time management, and written language. Remediation is provided collaboratively through on-campus or off-campus services via computer-based instruction, regular education teachers, and trained peer tutors.

Enrichment Enrichment programs are available through the program or unit for self-advocacy, stress management, test taking, and time management. Programs for career planning, college survival skills, health and nutrition, learning strategies, math, practical computer skills, reading, study skills, and written composition skills are provided collaboratively through on-campus or off-campus services. Credit is offered for learning strategies, practical computer skills, reading, study skills, and written composition skills.

Application For admittance to the program or unit, students are required to provide a psychoeducational report and provide documentation of high school services. It is recommended that students apply to the program directly and provide documentation of current level of functioning. Upon application, materials documenting need for services should be sent to both admissions and the LD program or unit. Upon acceptance, documentation of need for services should be sent only to the LD program or unit. *Application deadline (institutional):* Continuous. *Application deadline (LD program):* Rolling/continuous for fall and rolling/continuous for spring.

Written Policies Written policy regarding general/basic LD accommodations is available through the program or unit directly.

Columbus State Community College

Box 1609

Columbus, OH 43216-1609

http://www.cscc.edu/

Contact: Mr. Ron Lofton, LD Specialist. Phone: 614-287-5396. Fax: 614-287-6054. E-mail: rlofton@cscc.edu. Head of LD Program: Mr. Wayne Cocchi, Director. Phone: 614-287-2629. Fax: 614-287-6054. E-mail: wcocchi@cscc.edu.

Approximately 225 registered undergraduate students were served during 2002-03. The program or unit includes 2 full-time staff members and 1 part-time staff member. Counselors, LD specialists, and remediation/learning specialists are provided through the program or unit. Academic advisers, regular education teachers, remediation/learning specialists, and trained peer tutors are provided collaboratively through on-campus or off-campus services.

Unique Aids and Services Aids, services, or accommodations include textbooks on tape, note-taking, assistive computer software, extra time on exams, reader, scribe.

Subject-area Tutoring Tutoring is offered one-on-one for some subjects. Tutoring is provided through the program or unit via LD specialists. Tutoring is also provided collaboratively through on-campus or off-campus services via trained peer tutors.

Basic Skills Remediation Remediation is offered one-on-one for computer skills, learning strategies, math, reading, social skills, study skills, time management, and written language. Remediation is provided through the program or unit via LD specialists and professional tutors. Remediation is also provided collaboratively through on-campus or off-campus services via trained peer tutors.

Columbus State Community College (continued)

Enrichment Enrichment programs are available through the program or unit for oral communication skills, self-advocacy, time management, and written composition skills. Programs for career planning, college survival skills, math, oral communication skills, practical computer skills, and reading are provided collaboratively through on-campus or off-campus services. Credit is offered for college survival skills.

Application For admittance to the program or unit, students are required to provide a psychoeducational report (5 years old or less) and provide multifactored evaluation (assessment of disability conducted by the secondary school psychologist). It is recommended that students provide documentation of high school services. Upon application, materials documenting need for services should be sent only to the LD program or unit. Upon acceptance, documentation of need for services should be sent only to the LD program or unit. *Application deadline (institutional):* Continuous. *Application deadline (LD program):* Rolling/continuous for fall and rolling/continuous for spring.

Written Policies Written policy regarding general/basic LD accommodations is available on the program Web site. Written policies regarding general/basic LD accommodations and reduced course loads are available through the program or unit directly.

Commonwealth Technical Institute

727 Goucher Street
Johnstown, PA 15905-3092
http://www.hgac.org/

Contact: Phone: 814-255-8200. Head of LD Program: Mr. William R. Cover, Education Director. Phone: 814-255-8321. Fax: 814-255-5709. E-mail: wcover@state.pa.us.

Approximately 350 registered undergraduate students were served during 2002-03.

Community College of Aurora

16000 East Centre Tech Parkway
Aurora, CO 80011-9036
http://www.ccaurora.edu/

Contact: Ms. Reniece A. Jones, Accessibility Services Office Coordinator. Phone: 303-361-7395. Fax: 303-340-7543. E-mail: reniece.jones@ccaurora.edu.

Approximately 40 registered undergraduate students were served during 2002-03. The program or unit includes 1 full-time staff member. Academic advisers, graduate assistants/students, professional tutors, regular education teachers, remediation/learning specialists, skill tutors, and strategy tutors are provided collaboratively through on-campus or off-campus services.

Orientation The program or unit offers an optional orientation for new students individually by special arrangement.

Unique Aids and Services Aids, services, or accommodations include advocates, career counseling, digital textbooks, faculty training, and personal coach.

Subject-area Tutoring Tutoring is offered one-on-one and in small groups for some subjects. Tutoring is provided through the program or unit via LD specialists. Tutoring is also provided collaboratively through on-campus or off-campus services via computer-based instruction, graduate assistants/students, professional tutors, and trained peer tutors.

Diagnostic Testing Testing for math, reading, and written language is provided collaboratively through on-campus or off-campus services.

Basic Skills Remediation Remediation is offered one-on-one and in small groups for computer skills, handwriting, learning strategies, math, reading, spelling, study skills, time management, and written language. Remediation is provided through the program or unit via LD specialists. Remediation is also provided collaboratively through on-campus or off-campus services via computer-based instruction, graduate assistants/students, professional tutors, regular education teachers, and trained peer tutors.

Enrichment Enrichment programs are available through the program or unit for self-advocacy, test taking, and other. Programs for career planning, college survival skills, health and nutrition, learning strategies, math, oral communication skills, practical computer skills, reading, stress management, study skills, time management, vocabulary development, and written composition skills are provided collaboratively through on-campus or off-campus services. Credit is offered for college survival skills, health and nutrition, learning strategies, math, oral communication skills, practical computer skills, reading, stress management, study skills, time management, vocabulary development, and written composition skills.

Fees *LD Program or Service* fee is $23 to $57 (fee varies according to academic program).

Application For admittance to the program or unit, students are required to apply to the program directly and provide a psychoeducational report. It is recommended that students provide documentation of high school services and provide documentation of other disabilities. Upon application, materials documenting need for services should be sent only to the LD program or unit. Upon acceptance, documentation of need for services should be sent only to the LD program or unit. *Application deadline (institutional):* Continuous. *Application deadline (LD program):* Rolling/continuous for fall and rolling/continuous for spring.

Written Policies Written policy regarding general/basic LD accommodations is available on the program Web site. Written policies regarding general/basic LD accommodations and grade forgiveness are outlined in the school's catalog/handbook. Written policy regarding general/basic LD accommodations is available through the program or unit directly.

The Community College of Baltimore County-Catonsville Campus
Student Support Services

800 South Rolling Road
Baltimore, MD 21228-5381

http://www.ccbc.cc.md.us/

Contact: Jill Hodge, Counselor and Coordinator of Support Services. Phone: 410-455-4718. E-mail: jhodge@ccbcmd.edu.

Student Support Services Approximately 150 registered undergraduate students were served during 2002-03. The program or unit includes 1 full-time and 3 part-time staff members. Academic advisers, counselors, diagnostic specialists, LD specialists, regular education teachers, remediation/learning specialists, skill tutors, trained peer tutors, and other are provided through the program or unit.

Orientation The program or unit offers an optional 2-hour orientation for new students before classes begin.

Unique Aids and Services Aids, services, or accommodations include career counseling, digital textbooks, and support groups.

Subject-area Tutoring Tutoring is offered one-on-one for all subjects. Tutoring is provided collaboratively through on-campus or off-campus services via graduate assistants/students, LD specialists, and trained peer tutors.

Diagnostic Testing Testing for learning strategies, learning styles, personality, reading, study skills, and written language is provided collaboratively through on-campus or off-campus services.

Basic Skills Remediation Remediation is offered in class-size groups for auditory processing, computer skills, learning strategies, math, reading, study skills, time management, visual processing, and written language. Remediation is provided collaboratively through on-campus or off-campus services via LD specialists and regular education teachers.

Student Organization Students with Disabilities Organization consists of 30 members.

Application For admittance to the program or unit, students are required to provide a psychoeducational report (5 years old or less). It is recommended that students provide documentation of high school services. Upon application, materials documenting need for services should be sent only to the LD program or unit. Upon acceptance, documentation of need for services should be sent only to the LD program or unit. *Application deadline (institutional):* Continuous. *Application deadline (LD program):* Rolling/continuous for fall and rolling/continuous for spring.

Written Policies Written policy regarding general/basic LD accommodations is available on the program Web site. Written policies regarding course substitutions and general/basic LD accommodations are available through the program or unit directly.

Supportive Services Office The program or unit includes 1 full-time and 4 part-time staff members. Skill tutors, strategy tutors, and trained peer tutors are provided through the program or unit. Academic advisers, counselors, graduate assistants/students, professional tutors, regular education teachers, and remediation/learning specialists are provided collaboratively through on-campus or off-campus services.

Orientation The program or unit offers an optional orientation for new students individually by special arrangement.

Unique Aids and Services Aids, services, or accommodations include career counseling, personal coach, testing accommodations.

Subject-area Tutoring Tutoring is offered one-on-one and in small groups for most subjects. Tutoring is provided through the program or unit via graduate assistants/students and trained peer tutors. Tutoring is also provided collaboratively through on-campus or off-campus services via computer-based instruction, graduate assistants/students, professional tutors, and trained peer tutors.

Diagnostic Testing Testing is provided through the program or unit for learning styles and study skills.

Basic Skills Remediation Remediation is offered in class-size groups for math, reading, and written language. Remediation is provided collaboratively through on-campus or off-campus services via regular education teachers.

Enrichment Enrichment programs are available through the program or unit for college survival skills, learning strategies, self-advocacy, stress management, study skills, test taking, and time management. Programs for career planning, college survival skills, math, practical computer skills, reading, vocabulary development, and written composition skills are provided collaboratively through on-campus or off-campus services.

Student Organization TRI-C's .

Application For admittance to the program or unit, students are required to apply to the program directly and provide a psychoeducational report (3 years old or less). Upon application, materials documenting need for services should be sent only to the LD program or unit. Upon acceptance, documentation of need for services should be sent only to the LD program or unit. *Application deadline (institutional):* Continuous. *Application deadline (LD program):* 8/11 for fall. 12/8 for spring.

Written Policies Written policies regarding course substitutions, general/basic LD accommodations, and grade forgiveness are outlined in the school's catalog/handbook. Written policy regarding general/basic LD accommodations is available through the program or unit directly.

Community College of Beaver County
Supportive Services Office

One Campus Drive
Monaca, PA 15061-2588
http://www.ccbc.cc.pa.us/

Contact: Cheryl Herrington, Special Populations Coordinator. Phone: 724-775-8561 Ext. 161. Fax: 724-728-7599. E-mail: cheryl.herrington@ccbc.edu. Head of LD Program: Mrs. Cheryl Herrington, Special Populations Coordinator. Phone: 724-775-8561 Ext. 161. Fax: 724-728-7599. E-mail: cheryl.herrington@ccbc.edu.

Community College of Southern Nevada
Disability Resource Center

3200 East Cheyenne Avenue
North Las Vegas, NV 89030-4296
http://www.ccsn.nevada.edu/drc

Contact: Ms. Traci McGee, Disability Specialist. Phone: 702-651-4045. Fax: 702-651-4179. E-mail: traci_mcgee@ccsn.nevada.edu.

Disability Resource Center Approximately 400 registered undergraduate students were served during 2002-03. Academic advisers,

Community College of Southern Nevada (continued)

coaches, counselors, diagnostic specialists, graduate assistants/ students, LD specialists, professional tutors, regular education teachers, remediation/learning specialists, skill tutors, special education teachers, strategy tutors, teacher trainees, trained peer tutors, and other are provided collaboratively through on-campus or off-campus services.

Unique Aids and Services Aids, services, or accommodations include advocates, career counseling, support groups, note-takers, books on tape, extended testing.

Subject-area Tutoring Tutoring is offered one-on-one for most subjects. Tutoring is provided collaboratively through on-campus or off-campus services via professional tutors and trained peer tutors.

Enrichment Programs for career planning, college survival skills, health and nutrition, learning strategies, math, medication management, oral communication skills, practical computer skills, reading, self-advocacy, stress management, study skills, test taking, time management, vocabulary development, written composition skills, and other are provided collaboratively through on-campus or off-campus services.

Application For admittance to the program or unit, students are required to provide a psychoeducational report (3 years old or less). Upon application, materials documenting need for services should be sent only to the LD program or unit. Upon acceptance, documentation of need for services should be sent only to the LD program or unit. *Application deadline (institutional):* Continuous. *Application deadline (LD program):* Rolling/continuous for fall and rolling/continuous for spring.

Written Policies Written policies regarding general/basic LD accommodations and substitutions and waivers of admissions requirements are available on the program Web site. Written policies regarding course substitutions, general/basic LD accommodations, substitutions and waivers of admissions requirements, and substitutions and waivers of graduation requirements are outlined in the school's catalog/handbook. Written policies regarding course substitutions, general/basic LD accommodations, reduced course loads, substitutions and waivers of admissions requirements, and substitutions and waivers of graduation requirements are available through the program or unit directly.

Community College of Vermont

PO Box 120
Waterbury, VT 05676-0120
http://www.ccv.edu/
Contact: Phone: 802-241-3535.

Academic advisers, regular education teachers, skill tutors, strategy tutors, and trained peer tutors are provided collaboratively through on-campus or off-campus services.

Subject-area Tutoring Tutoring is offered one-on-one and in small groups for some subjects. Tutoring is provided collaboratively through on-campus or off-campus services via professional tutors, trained peer tutors, and other.

Basic Skills Remediation Remediation is offered in class-size groups for learning strategies, reading, study skills, and written language. Remediation is provided collaboratively through on-campus or off-campus services via regular education teachers.

Application For admittance to the program or unit, students are required to provide documentation of diagnosis and recommendations. Upon acceptance, documentation of need for services should be sent to both admissions and the LD program or unit. *Application deadline (institutional):* Continuous. *Application deadline (LD program):* Rolling/continuous for fall and rolling/continuous for spring.

Written Policies Written policy regarding general/basic LD accommodations is available on the program Web site. Written policies regarding course substitutions, general/basic LD accommodations, grade forgiveness, and reduced course loads are outlined in the school's catalog/handbook.

Consolidated School of Business

2124 Ambassador Circle
Lancaster, PA 17603
http://www.csb.edu/
Contact: Ms. Millie G. Liberatore, Admissions Director. Phone: 717-394-6211. Fax: 717-394-6213. E-mail: mliberatore@csb.edu.

Services are provided collaboratively through on-campus or off-campus services.

Fees *LD Program or Service* fee varies according to disability.

Application Upon application, materials documenting need for services should be sent only to admissions with institutional application materials. *Application deadline (institutional):* Continuous.

Consolidated School of Business

1605 Clugston Road
York, PA 17404
http://www.csb.edu/
Contact: Ms. Millie G. Liberatore, Admissions Director. Phone: 717-764-9550. Fax: 717-764-9469. E-mail: admissions@csb.edu.

Fees *LD Program or Service* fee varies according to disability.

Application Upon application, materials documenting need for services should be sent only to admissions with institutional application materials. *Application deadline (institutional):* Continuous.

Contra Costa College
Disabled Students Programs and Services

2600 Mission Bell Drive
San Pablo, CA 94806-3195
http://www.contracosta.cc.ca.us/dsps/index.html

Contact: Peggy Fleming, Learning Disability Specialist. Phone: 510-235-7800 Ext. 7200. Fax: 510-234-1544. E-mail: pfleming@contracosta.edu.

Disabled Students Programs and Services Approximately 275 registered undergraduate students were served during 2002-03. The program or unit includes 2 full-time staff members. Academic advisers, LD specialists, and remediation/learning specialists are provided through the program or unit. Academic advisers, counselors, professional tutors, regular education teachers, and skill tutors are provided collaboratively through on-campus or off-campus services.

Orientation The program or unit offers an optional 3-hour orientation for new students during summer prior to enrollment.

Unique Aids and Services Aids, services, or accommodations include advocates, career counseling, digital textbooks, faculty training, and priority registration.

Subject-area Tutoring Tutoring is offered in small groups for most subjects. Tutoring is provided through the program or unit via computer-based instruction and LD specialists. Tutoring is also provided collaboratively through on-campus or off-campus services via computer-based instruction and professional tutors.

Diagnostic Testing Testing is provided through the program or unit for auditory processing, learning strategies, learning styles, math, reading, spelling, visual processing, and written language. Testing for learning styles is provided collaboratively through on-campus or off-campus services.

Basic Skills Remediation Remediation is offered in class-size groups for learning strategies, math, reading, and spelling. Remediation is provided through the program or unit via computer-based instruction and LD specialists. Remediation is also provided collaboratively through on-campus or off-campus services via computer-based instruction, professional tutors, regular education teachers, and trained peer tutors.

Enrichment Enrichment programs are available through the program or unit for learning strategies, math, reading, study skills, vocabulary development, and written composition skills. Programs for career planning, college survival skills, health and nutrition, math, oral communication skills, practical computer skills, reading, study skills, time management, vocabulary development, and written composition skills are provided collaboratively through on-campus or off-campus services. Credit is offered for career planning, college survival skills, health and nutrition, learning strategies, math, oral communication skills, practical computer skills, reading, study skills, time management, vocabulary development, and written composition skills.

Application It is recommended that students provide a psychoeducational report (3 years old or less). Upon application, materials documenting need for services should be sent only to the LD program or unit. Upon acceptance, documentation of need for services should be sent only to the LD program or unit. *Application deadline (institutional):* Continuous. *Application deadline (LD program):* Rolling/continuous for fall and rolling/continuous for spring.

Written Policies Written policy regarding general/basic LD accommodations is available on the program Web site. Written policies regarding general/basic LD accommodations and substitutions and waivers of graduation requirements are outlined in the school's catalog/handbook. Written policy regarding general/basic LD accommodations is available through the program or unit directly.

Copper Mountain College
Disabled Student Program and Services

6162 Rotary Way

Joshua Tree, CA 92252

http://www.cmccd.cc.ca.us/

Contact: Ms. Carolyn Beaver, LD Specialist. Phone: 760-366-3791. Fax: 760-366-1299. E-mail: cbeaver@cmccd.edu.

Disabled Student Program and Services Approximately 45 registered undergraduate students were served during 2002-03. The program or unit includes 1 part-time staff member. Diagnostic specialists, remediation/learning specialists, and other are provided through the program or unit. Academic advisers, counselors, professional tutors, regular education teachers, and skill tutors are provided collaboratively through on-campus or off-campus services.

Orientation The program or unit offers an optional 5-week orientation for new students during summer prior to enrollment.

Summer Program To help prepare for the demands of college, there is an optional 5-week summer program prior to entering the school.

Unique Aids and Services Aids, services, or accommodations include advocates, career counseling, digital textbooks, faculty training, priority registration, adaptive computer lab.

Subject-area Tutoring Tutoring is offered one-on-one and in small groups for most subjects. Tutoring is provided through the program or unit via computer-based instruction and LD specialists. Tutoring is also provided collaboratively through on-campus or off-campus services via computer-based instruction and trained peer tutors.

Diagnostic Testing Testing is provided through the program or unit for auditory processing, handwriting, intelligence, math, neuropsychological, personality, spelling, spoken language, visual processing, written language, and other services.

Basic Skills Remediation Remediation is offered in class-size groups for computer skills, learning strategies, math, reading, study skills, time management, and written language. Remediation is provided through the program or unit via computer-based instruction. Remediation is also provided collaboratively through on-campus or off-campus services via regular education teachers and trained peer tutors.

Enrichment Enrichment programs are available through the program or unit for career planning, college survival skills, practical computer skills, reading, and self-advocacy. Programs for career planning, college survival skills, health and nutrition, learning strategies, math, practical computer skills, reading, stress management, study skills, test taking, time management, vocabulary development, and written composition skills are provided collaboratively through on-campus or off-campus services.

Fees *Summer Program* fee is $0 to $11. *Orientation* fee is $0 to $11.

Application For admittance to the program or unit, students are required to apply to the program directly, provide a psychoeducational report (5 years old or less), and provide documentation of high school services. Upon application, materials documenting need for services should be sent only to the LD program or unit. Upon acceptance, documentation of need for services should be sent only to the LD program or unit. *Application deadline (LD program):* Rolling/continuous for fall and rolling/continuous for spring.

Copper Mountain College (continued)

Written Policies Written policies regarding general/basic LD accommodations and reduced course loads are available on the program Web site. Written policy regarding general/basic LD accommodations is outlined in the school's catalog/handbook. Written policies regarding general/basic LD accommodations, grade forgiveness, and reduced course loads are available through the program or unit directly.

Corning Community College

One Academic Drive
Corning, NY 14830-3297
http://www.corning-cc.edu/
Contact: Phone: 607-962-9011. Fax: 607-962-9456.

The program or unit includes 1 full-time and 1 part-time staff member. Academic advisers, counselors, diagnostic specialists, and LD specialists are provided through the program or unit. Academic advisers, counselors, professional tutors, remediation/learning specialists, and trained peer tutors are provided collaboratively through on-campus or off-campus services.

Summer Program To help prepare for the demands of college, there is an optional 2-week summer program prior to entering the school. Degree credit will be earned.

Unique Aids and Services Aids, services, or accommodations include career counseling, digital textbooks, and faculty training.

Subject-area Tutoring Tutoring is offered one-on-one and in small groups for most subjects. Tutoring is provided collaboratively through on-campus or off-campus services via computer-based instruction, graduate assistants/students, professional tutors, and trained peer tutors.

Diagnostic Testing Testing is provided through the program or unit for auditory processing, handwriting, intelligence, learning strategies, learning styles, math, motor skills, reading, spelling, spoken language, study skills, visual processing, and written language.

Basic Skills Remediation Remediation is offered in class-size groups for computer skills, learning strategies, math, reading, study skills, time management, and written language. Remediation is provided collaboratively through on-campus or off-campus services via computer-based instruction, professional tutors, and regular education teachers.

Enrichment Enrichment programs are available through the program or unit for learning strategies, self-advocacy, study skills, and test taking. Programs for career planning, college survival skills, health and nutrition, learning strategies, math, oral communication skills, practical computer skills, reading, stress management, study skills, test taking, time management, and written composition skills are provided collaboratively through on-campus or off-campus services. Credit is offered for career planning, college survival skills, health and nutrition, learning strategies, math, oral communication skills, practical computer skills, reading, stress management, study skills, test taking, time management, and written composition skills.

Application For admittance to the program or unit, students are required to apply to the program directly and provide a psychoeducational report. Upon application, materials documenting need for services should be sent only to the LD program or unit. Upon

acceptance, documentation of need for services should be sent only to the LD program or unit. *Application deadline (institutional):* Continuous. *Application deadline (LD program):* Rolling/continuous for fall and rolling/continuous for spring.

Written Policies Written policy regarding general/basic LD accommodations is available on the program Web site. Written policy regarding general/basic LD accommodations is outlined in the school's catalog/handbook. Written policy regarding general/basic LD accommodations is available through the program or unit directly.

Cottey College
Student Disabilities Services

1000 West Austin
Nevada, MO 64772
http://www.cottey.edu/
Contact: Ms. Mary W. McNerney, Coordinator of Student Disability Services. Phone: 417-667-6333 Ext. 2131. E-mail: mcnerney@cottey.edu.

Student Disabilities Services Approximately 15 registered undergraduate students were served during 2002-03.

Unique Aids and Services Aids, services, or accommodations include career counseling and priority registration.

Subject-area Tutoring Tutoring is offered one-on-one for some subjects. Tutoring is provided collaboratively through on-campus or off-campus services via computer-based instruction and other.

Diagnostic Testing Testing is provided through the program or unit for learning strategies, learning styles, and study skills. Testing for auditory processing, intelligence, neuropsychological, personality, and visual processing is provided collaboratively through on-campus or off-campus services.

Enrichment Programs for career planning, college survival skills, health and nutrition, learning strategies, math, reading, stress management, study skills, test taking, time management, and written composition skills are provided collaboratively through on-campus or off-campus services. Credit is offered for learning strategies and study skills.

Application For admittance to the program or unit, students are required to apply to the program directly, provide a psychoeducational report (3 years old or less), and provide appropriate documentation from the professional making the diagnosis. It is recommended that students provide documentation of high school services. Upon acceptance, documentation of need for services should be sent only to the LD program or unit. *Application deadline (institutional):* Continuous. *Application deadline (LD program):* Rolling/continuous for fall and rolling/continuous for spring.

Written Policies Written policies regarding course substitutions, grade forgiveness, reduced course loads, and substitutions and waivers of graduation requirements are outlined in the school's catalog/handbook. Written policy regarding general/basic LD accommodations is available through the program or unit directly.

County College of Morris
Horizons

214 Center Grove Road
Randolph, NJ 07869-2086

http://www.ccm.edu/horizons/

Contact: Dr. David C. Nast, Director. Phone: 973-328-5274. Fax: 973-328-5286. E-mail: dnast@ccm.edu.

Horizons Approximately 500 registered undergraduate students were served during 2002-03. The program or unit includes 5 full-time and 15 part-time staff members. Academic advisers, counselors, LD specialists, professional tutors, remediation/learning specialists, and strategy tutors are provided through the program or unit. Academic advisers, counselors, professional tutors, and trained peer tutors are provided collaboratively through on-campus or off-campus services.

Orientation The program or unit offers an optional 2-hour orientation for new students before classes begin and individually by special arrangement.

Summer Program To help prepare for the demands of college, there is an optional 4-week summer program prior to entering the school. Degree credit will be earned.

Unique Aids and Services Aids, services, or accommodations include advocates, faculty training, and support groups.

Subject-area Tutoring Tutoring is offered one-on-one and in small groups for most subjects. Tutoring is provided collaboratively through on-campus or off-campus services via professional tutors and trained peer tutors.

Basic Skills Remediation Remediation is offered in class-size groups for learning strategies, math, reading, spoken language, study skills, time management, visual processing, and written language. Remediation is provided through the program or unit via special education teachers. Remediation is also provided collaboratively through on-campus or off-campus services via regular education teachers.

Enrichment Enrichment programs are available through the program or unit for college survival skills, learning strategies, oral communication skills, reading, self-advocacy, stress management, study skills, test taking, time management, and written composition skills. Programs for career planning, math, and written composition skills are provided collaboratively through on-campus or off-campus services. Credit is offered for career planning, college survival skills, learning strategies, oral communication skills, reading, self-advocacy, stress management, study skills, test taking, time management, and written composition skills.

Student Organization Horizons Student Support Group consists of 10 members.

Fees *Summer Program* fee is $500.

Application For admittance to the program or unit, students are required to apply to the program directly, provide a psychoeducational report (3 years old or less), and provide documentation of high school services. Upon application, materials documenting need for services should be sent only to the LD program or unit. *Application deadline (LD program):* 4/15 for fall. 11/15 for spring.

Written Policies Written policy regarding general/basic LD accommodations is available on the program Web site. Written policies regarding course substitutions, general/basic LD accommodations, grade forgiveness, and reduced course loads are available through the program or unit directly.

Craven Community College
Academic Skills Center

800 College Court
New Bern, NC 28562-4984

http://cravencc.edu

Contact: Director of the Academic Skills Center. Phone: 252-638-7294. Fax: 252-638-4232.

Academic Skills Center Approximately 37 registered undergraduate students were served during 2002-03. The program or unit includes 1 full-time and 33 part-time staff members. Counselors, diagnostic specialists, professional tutors, remediation/learning specialists, and trained peer tutors are provided collaboratively through on-campus or off-campus services.

Unique Aids and Services Aids, services, or accommodations include support groups.

Subject-area Tutoring Tutoring is offered one-on-one and in small groups for most subjects. Tutoring is provided collaboratively through on-campus or off-campus services via computer-based instruction, graduate assistants/students, LD specialists, professional tutors, trained peer tutors, and other.

Diagnostic Testing Testing is provided through the program or unit for learning strategies, learning styles, math, personality, study skills, and written language. Testing for auditory processing, handwriting, intelligence, math, motor skills, neuropsychological, reading, social skills, spelling, spoken language, and visual processing is provided collaboratively through on-campus or off-campus services.

Basic Skills Remediation Remediation is offered one-on-one for auditory processing, computer skills, learning strategies, math, reading, study skills, time management, and written language. Remediation is provided collaboratively through on-campus or off-campus services via computer-based instruction, graduate assistants/students, professional tutors, regular education teachers, and trained peer tutors.

Enrichment Enrichment programs are available through the program or unit for learning strategies, math, practical computer skills, reading, self-advocacy, study skills, test taking, time management, and written composition skills. Programs for career planning, college survival skills, health and nutrition, learning strategies, math, practical computer skills, reading, self-advocacy, study skills, test taking, time management, vocabulary development, and written composition skills are provided collaboratively through on-campus or off-campus services. Credit is offered for college survival skills, health and nutrition, learning strategies, math, practical computer skills, reading, study skills, test taking, time management, vocabulary development, and written composition skills.

Application For admittance to the program or unit, students are required to provide a psychoeducational report (3 years old or less). It is recommended that students provide documentation of high school services. Upon application, materials documenting need for services should be sent only to the LD program or unit. Upon acceptance, documentation of need for services should be sent only to the LD program or unit. *Application deadline (institutional):* Continuous. *Application deadline (LD program):* Rolling/continuous for fall and rolling/continuous for spring.

Written Policies Written policy regarding substitutions and waivers of admissions requirements is available on the program Web site. Written policies regarding general/basic LD accommodations and substitutions and waivers of admissions requirements are out-

Craven Community College (continued)
lined in the school's catalog/handbook. Written policies regarding general/basic LD accommodations and substitutions and waivers of admissions requirements are available through the program or unit directly.

Cuesta College
Disabled Student Programs and Services (DSPS)

PO Box 8106
San Luis Obispo, CA 93403-8106
http://academic.cuesta.edu/access/

Contact: Disabled Student Program and Services Department. Phone: 805-546-3148. Fax: 805-546-3930. E-mail: dspsinfo@cuesta.edu. Head of LD Program: Ms. Linda L. Long, Director of Academic Support and Disabled Student Programs and Services. Phone: 805-546-3148. Fax: 805-546-3930. E-mail: dspsinfo@cuesta.edu.

Disabled Student Programs and Services (DSPS) Approximately 300 registered undergraduate students were served during 2002-03. The program or unit includes 21 full-time and 2 part-time staff members. Academic advisers, counselors, diagnostic specialists, LD specialists, professional tutors, regular education teachers, remediation/learning specialists, skill tutors, special education teachers, and strategy tutors are provided through the program or unit. Coaches, counselors, professional tutors, regular education teachers, skill tutors, strategy tutors, and trained peer tutors are provided collaboratively through on-campus or off-campus services.
Orientation The program or unit offers an optional 2-day orientation for new students with specific English and math assessment/orientation/registration advising workshop in April.
Unique Aids and Services Aids, services, or accommodations include alternative testing, note-taking assistance, taped text, and specialized tutoring.
Subject-area Tutoring Tutoring is offered one-on-one and in small groups for most subjects. Tutoring is provided through the program or unit via professional tutors. Tutoring is also provided collaboratively through on-campus or off-campus services via trained peer tutors.
Diagnostic Testing Testing is provided through the program or unit. Testing is provided collaboratively through on-campus or off-campus services.
Basic Skills Remediation Remediation is offered in class-size groups for computer skills, learning strategies, math, reading, spelling, study skills, time management, written language, and test and performance anxiety. Remediation is provided through the program or unit via regular education teachers and special education teachers. Remediation is also provided collaboratively through on-campus or off-campus services via regular education teachers and special education teachers.
Enrichment Enrichment programs are available through the program or unit for college survival skills, math, practical computer skills, reading, vocabulary development, and written composition skills. Programs for career planning, college survival skills, health and nutrition, learning strategies, math, oral communication skills, practical computer skills, reading, stress management, study skills,

test taking, time management, and written composition skills are provided collaboratively through on-campus or off-campus services. Credit is offered for career planning, college survival skills, health and nutrition, learning strategies, math, oral communication skills, practical computer skills, reading, stress management, study skills, test taking, time management, vocabulary development, and written composition skills.
Application For admittance to the program or unit, students are required to apply to the program directly, provide a psychoeducational report (3 years old or less), and provide documentation of high school services. Upon application, materials documenting need for services should be sent only to the LD program or unit. Upon acceptance, documentation of need for services should be sent to both admissions and the LD program or unit. *Application deadline (institutional):* Continuous. *Application deadline (LD program):* Rolling/continuous for fall and rolling/continuous for spring.
Written Policies Written policies regarding course substitutions, general/basic LD accommodations, and substitutions and waivers of graduation requirements are available on the program Web site. Written policies regarding course substitutions, general/basic LD accommodations, and substitutions and waivers of graduation requirements are available through the program or unit directly.

Cumberland County College
Project Assist

PO Box 1500, College Drive
Vineland, NJ 08362-1500
http://www.cccnj.net/

Contact: Debra A. Emery, Assistant Director of Project Assist. Phone: 856-691-8600 Ext. 282. Fax: 856-690-0059. E-mail: daemery@cccnj.edu.

Project Assist Approximately 86 registered undergraduate students were served during 2002-03. The program or unit includes 1 full-time and 1 part-time staff member. Academic advisers and counselors are provided through the program or unit. Academic advisers, counselors, diagnostic specialists, LD specialists, professional tutors, and skill tutors are provided collaboratively through on-campus or off-campus services.
Orientation The program or unit offers a mandatory 5 to 12-hour orientation for new students during summer prior to enrollment and individually by special arrangement.
Summer Program To help prepare for the demands of college, there is an optional 1-week summer program prior to entering the school.
Unique Aids and Services Aids, services, or accommodations include advocates, career counseling, faculty training, personal coach, and support groups.
Subject-area Tutoring Tutoring is offered one-on-one and in small groups for most subjects. Tutoring is provided through the program or unit via professional tutors and trained peer tutors. Tutoring is also provided collaboratively through on-campus or off-campus services via computer-based instruction, LD specialists, and trained peer tutors.
Diagnostic Testing Testing is provided through the program or unit for auditory processing, handwriting, intelligence, learning strategies, learning styles, motor skills, study skills, and visual processing. Testing for auditory processing, handwriting, intelligence, learning

strategies, learning styles, math, motor skills, neuropsychological, personality, reading, social skills, spelling, spoken language, study skills, and visual processing is provided collaboratively through on-campus or off-campus services.

Basic Skills Remediation Remediation is offered one-on-one and in small groups for auditory processing, computer skills, learning strategies, math, reading, social skills, spoken language, study skills, time management, visual processing, and written language. Remediation is provided through the program or unit via professional tutors, regular education teachers, special education teachers, and trained peer tutors. Remediation is also provided collaboratively through on-campus or off-campus services via computer-based instruction, LD specialists, teacher trainees, and trained peer tutors.

Enrichment Enrichment programs are available through the program or unit for career planning, college survival skills, learning strategies, practical computer skills, self-advocacy, stress management, study skills, test taking, and time management. Programs for career planning, college survival skills, health and nutrition, math, medication management, oral communication skills, practical computer skills, reading, self-advocacy, stress management, study skills, test taking, and time management are provided collaboratively through on-campus or off-campus services. Credit is offered for learning strategies.

Student Organization There is a student organization consisting of 15 members.

Fees *Diagnostic Testing* fee is $150.

Application For admittance to the program or unit, students are required to apply to the program directly and provide documentation of high school services. It is recommended that students provide a psychoeducational report. Upon application, materials documenting need for services should be sent only to the LD program or unit. *Application deadline (institutional):* Continuous. *Application deadline (LD program):* Rolling/continuous for fall and rolling/continuous for spring.

Written Policies Written policy regarding general/basic LD accommodations is available on the program Web site. Written policies regarding general/basic LD accommodations, reduced course loads, and substitutions and waivers of graduation requirements are outlined in the school's catalog/handbook. Written policies regarding course substitutions, general/basic LD accommodations, reduced course loads, substitutions and waivers of admissions requirements, and substitutions and waivers of graduation requirements are available through the program or unit directly.

Cuyahoga Community College

700 Carnegie Avenue
Cleveland, OH 44115-2878
http://www.tri-c.edu/

Contact: Mrs. Maryann Syarto-Sender, ACCESS Director. Phone: 216-987-2034. Fax: 216-987-2423. E-mail: maryann.syarto@tri-c.edu. Head of LD Program: Ms. Maryann Syarto-Sender, ACCESS Director. Phone: 216-987-2034. Fax: 216-987-2423. E-mail: maryann.syarto@tri-c.edu.

Approximately 367 registered undergraduate students were served during 2002-03. The program or unit includes 8 full-time and 12

part-time staff members. Academic advisers, counselors, diagnostic specialists, LD specialists, professional tutors, regular education teachers, remediation/learning specialists, skill tutors, special education teachers, strategy tutors, trained peer tutors, and other are provided through the program or unit. Academic advisers, counselors, diagnostic specialists, professional tutors, regular education teachers, remediation/learning specialists, skill tutors, and strategy tutors are provided collaboratively through on-campus or off-campus services.

Orientation The program or unit offers an optional 1-week orientation for new students before registration, before classes begin, and during summer prior to enrollment.

Summer Program To help prepare for the demands of college, there is an optional 4-week summer program prior to entering the school. Degree credit will be earned.

Unique Aids and Services Aids, services, or accommodations include advocates, career counseling, digital textbooks, faculty training, parent workshops, personal coach, priority registration, support groups, and weekly meetings with faculty.

Subject-area Tutoring Tutoring is offered one-on-one for most subjects. Tutoring is provided through the program or unit via computer-based instruction, LD specialists, professional tutors, and trained peer tutors. Tutoring is also provided collaboratively through on-campus or off-campus services via computer-based instruction and professional tutors.

Diagnostic Testing Testing is provided through the program or unit for auditory processing, handwriting, intelligence, learning strategies, learning styles, math, motor skills, neuropsychological, personality, reading, social skills, spelling, spoken language, study skills, visual processing, written language, and other services.

Basic Skills Remediation Remediation is offered one-on-one, in small groups, and in class-size groups for auditory processing, computer skills, handwriting, learning strategies, math, motor skills, reading, social skills, spelling, spoken language, study skills, time management, visual processing, and written language. Remediation is provided through the program or unit via computer-based instruction, LD specialists, professional tutors, regular education teachers, special education teachers, and trained peer tutors. Remediation is also provided collaboratively through on-campus or off-campus services via computer-based instruction, professional tutors, and regular education teachers.

Enrichment Enrichment programs are available through the program or unit for career planning, college survival skills, learning strategies, math, oral communication skills, practical computer skills, reading, self-advocacy, stress management, study skills, test taking, time management, vocabulary development, and written composition skills. Programs for career planning, college survival skills, health and nutrition, learning strategies, math, medication management, oral communication skills, practical computer skills, reading, self-advocacy, stress management, study skills, test taking, time management, vocabulary development, and written composition skills are provided collaboratively through on-campus or off-campus services. Credit is offered for career planning, college survival skills, health and nutrition, math, practical computer skills, reading, vocabulary development, and written composition skills.

Student Organization ACCESS Group consists of 35 members.

Fees *Diagnostic Testing* fee is $150 to $250.

Application For admittance to the program or unit, students are required to apply to the program directly, provide a psychoeducational report (3 years old or less), and provide documentation of high school services. Upon application, materials documenting need for services should be sent only to the LD program or unit. Upon

Cuyahoga Community College (continued)
acceptance, documentation of need for services should be sent only to the LD program or unit. *Application deadline (institutional):* Continuous. *Application deadline (LD program):* Rolling/continuous for fall and rolling/continuous for spring.
Written Policies Written policy regarding general/basic LD accommodations is available on the program Web site. Written policies regarding general/basic LD accommodations and grade forgiveness are outlined in the school's catalog/handbook. Written policies regarding course substitutions, general/basic LD accommodations, reduced course loads, substitutions and waivers of admissions requirements, and substitutions and waivers of graduation requirements are available through the program or unit directly.

Dabney S. Lancaster Community College

100 Dabney Drive, PO Box 1000
Clifton Forge, VA 24422
http://www.dl.vccs.edu/
Contact: Elizabeth Davis, Project Director, Student Support Services Program. Phone: 540-863-2860. Fax: 540-863-2915. E-mail: ldavis@dl.vccs.edu.

Approximately 20 registered undergraduate students were served during 2002-03.
Unique Aids and Services Aids, services, or accommodations include advocates.
Subject-area Tutoring Tutoring is offered one-on-one and in small groups for most subjects. Tutoring is provided collaboratively through on-campus or off-campus services via professional tutors and trained peer tutors.
Basic Skills Remediation Remediation is offered in class-size groups for math, reading, and written language. Remediation is provided collaboratively through on-campus or off-campus services via regular education teachers.
Enrichment Programs for career planning, college survival skills, learning strategies, self-advocacy, stress management, study skills, test taking, and time management are provided collaboratively through on-campus or off-campus services.
Application *Application deadline (institutional):* Continuous. *Application deadline (LD program):* Rolling/continuous for fall and rolling/continuous for spring.
Written Policies Written policy regarding general/basic LD accommodations is available on the program Web site. Written policy regarding general/basic LD accommodations is outlined in the school's catalog/handbook.

Dakota County Technical College
Academic Support Center/Disability Services

1300 East 145th Street
Rosemount, MN 55068

http://www.dctc.mnscu.edu/
Contact: Anne K. Swanberg, Disability Services Adviser. Phone: 651-423-8469. Fax: 651-423-8775. E-mail: anne.swanberg@dctc.mnscu.edu.

Academic Support Center/Disability Services Approximately 100 registered undergraduate students were served during 2002-03. The program or unit includes 1 full-time and 4 part-time staff members. Academic advisers, LD specialists, professional tutors, and other are provided through the program or unit. Academic advisers, counselors, professional tutors, regular education teachers, remediation/learning specialists, trained peer tutors, and other are provided collaboratively through on-campus or off-campus services.
Unique Aids and Services Aids, services, or accommodations include advocates, individualized services according to student's needs.
Subject-area Tutoring Tutoring is offered one-on-one and in small groups for most subjects. Tutoring is provided through the program or unit via professional tutors and trained peer tutors. Tutoring is also provided collaboratively through on-campus or off-campus services via computer-based instruction.
Basic Skills Remediation Remediation is offered one-on-one, in small groups, and in class-size groups for computer skills, learning strategies, math, reading, spelling, spoken language, study skills, time management, and written language. Remediation is provided through the program or unit via professional tutors. Remediation is also provided collaboratively through on-campus or off-campus services via regular education teachers, trained peer tutors, and other.
Enrichment Programs for career planning, college survival skills, learning strategies, math, study skills, test taking, vocabulary development, and written composition skills are provided collaboratively through on-campus or off-campus services. Credit is offered for college survival skills, math, and written composition skills.
Application For admittance to the program or unit, students are required to provide documentation of high school services and provide team assessment report or other psychoeducational testing. It is recommended that students provide a psychoeducational report (3 years old or less). Upon application, materials documenting need for services should be sent only to the LD program or unit. Upon acceptance, documentation of need for services should be sent only to the LD program or unit. *Application deadline (LD program):* Rolling/continuous for fall and rolling/continuous for spring.
Written Policies Written policy regarding general/basic LD accommodations is outlined in the school's catalog/handbook.

Darton College
Disability Services

2400 Gillionville Road
Albany, GA 31707-3098
http://www.darton.edu/students/Stu_Aff/disabilityservices.htm
Contact: Ms. Tanya Anderson, Coordinator of Disability Services. Phone: 229-430-6865. Fax: 229-420-1100. E-mail: andersot@darton.edu.

Disability Services Approximately 45 registered undergraduate students were served during 2002-03. The program or unit includes 1 full-time staff member.

Subject-area Tutoring Tutoring is offered one-on-one and in small groups for some subjects. Tutoring is provided collaboratively through on-campus or off-campus services via trained peer tutors.
Diagnostic Testing Testing for auditory processing, handwriting, intelligence, math, motor skills, personality, reading, social skills, spelling, spoken language, visual processing, and written language is provided collaboratively through on-campus or off-campus services.
Basic Skills Remediation Remediation is offered in class-size groups for math, reading, and written language. Remediation is provided collaboratively through on-campus or off-campus services via regular education teachers.
Fees *Diagnostic Testing* fee is $400.
Application For admittance to the program or unit, students are required to provide a psychoeducational report (3 years old or less). It is recommended that students provide documentation of high school services. Upon application, materials documenting need for services should be sent only to the LD program or unit. Upon acceptance, documentation of need for services should be sent only to the LD program or unit. *Application deadline (institutional):* 7/20. *Application deadline (LD program):* Rolling/continuous for fall and rolling/continuous for spring.
Written Policies Written policies regarding course substitutions, general/basic LD accommodations, reduced course loads, substitutions and waivers of admissions requirements, and substitutions and waivers of graduation requirements are available on the program Web site. Written policies regarding course substitutions, general/basic LD accommodations, substitutions and waivers of admissions requirements, and substitutions and waivers of graduation requirements are available through the program or unit directly.

Davidson County Community College
JobLink Career Center, Vocational Rehabilitation

PO Box 1287
Lexington, NC 27293-1287
http://www.davidson.cc.nc.us/
Contact: Phone: 336-249-8186. Fax: 336-249-0379.

JobLink Career Center, Vocational Rehabilitation Approximately 100 registered undergraduate students were served during 2002-03. The program or unit includes 1 full-time staff member. Academic advisers, counselors, trained peer tutors, and other are provided collaboratively through on-campus or off-campus services.
Unique Aids and Services Aids, services, or accommodations include special testing arrangements, tape recorders.
Subject-area Tutoring Tutoring is offered one-on-one for most subjects. Tutoring is provided collaboratively through on-campus or off-campus services via trained peer tutors.
Basic Skills Remediation Remediation is offered in small groups for learning strategies, study skills, and time management. Remediation is provided collaboratively through on-campus or off-campus services via trained peer tutors and other.
Enrichment Programs for career planning, college survival skills, learning strategies, reading, stress management, study skills, test taking, and time management are provided collaboratively through on-campus or off-campus services.

Application For admittance to the program or unit, students are required to provide a psychoeducational report. It is recommended that students provide documentation of high school services. Upon acceptance, documentation of need for services should be sent only to the LD program or unit. *Application deadline (institutional):* Continuous. *Application deadline (LD program):* Rolling/continuous for fall and rolling/continuous for spring.
Written Policies Written policy regarding general/basic LD accommodations is outlined in the school's catalog/handbook. Written policies regarding course substitutions and substitutions and waivers of graduation requirements are available through the program or unit directly.

Dawson Community College
Student Support Services

Box 421
Glendive, MT 59330-0421
http://www.dawson.edu/
Contact: Mr. Kent Dion, Director of Student Support Services. Phone: 406-377-9416. Fax: 406-377-8132. E-mail: kent_d@dawson.edu.

Student Support Services Approximately 12 registered undergraduate students were served during 2002-03. The program or unit includes 5 full-time and 2 part-time staff members. Academic advisers, counselors, diagnostic specialists, professional tutors, remediation/learning specialists, skill tutors, strategy tutors, and trained peer tutors are provided through the program or unit. Academic advisers, coaches, counselors, and regular education teachers are provided collaboratively through on-campus or off-campus services.
Unique Aids and Services Aids, services, or accommodations include career counseling.
Subject-area Tutoring Tutoring is offered one-on-one and in small groups for most subjects. Tutoring is provided through the program or unit via computer-based instruction, professional tutors, and trained peer tutors.
Diagnostic Testing Testing is provided through the program or unit for learning styles, math, reading, and written language.
Basic Skills Remediation Remediation is offered one-on-one and in small groups for computer skills, learning strategies, math, reading, study skills, and written language. Remediation is provided through the program or unit via computer-based instruction and professional tutors.
Enrichment Enrichment programs are available through the program or unit for career planning, college survival skills, math, reading, study skills, and written composition skills.
Application For admittance to the program or unit, students are required to apply to the program directly. It is recommended that students provide a psychoeducational report (3 years old or less) and provide documentation of high school services. Upon application, materials documenting need for services should be sent to both admissions and the LD program or unit. Upon acceptance, documentation of need for services should be sent only to the LD program or unit. *Application deadline (institutional):* Continuous. *Application deadline (LD program):* Rolling/continuous for fall and rolling/continuous for spring.

Dawson Community College (continued)

Written Policies Written policies regarding course substitutions, general/basic LD accommodations, substitutions and waivers of admissions requirements, and substitutions and waivers of graduation requirements are outlined in the school's catalog/handbook. Written policy regarding general/basic LD accommodations is available through the program or unit directly.

Daytona Beach Community College

PO Box 2811

Daytona Beach, FL 32120-2811

http://www.dbcc.cc.fl.us/

Contact: Ms. Sue Ayres, Student Disability Specialist. Phone: 386-255-8131 Ext. 3892. Fax: 386-947-3152. E-mail: ayress@dbcc.edu. Head of LD Program: Mr. Idris Muhammad, Director. Phone: 386-255-8131 Ext. 3807. Fax: 386-947-3152.

Approximately 200 registered undergraduate students were served during 2002-03. The program or unit includes 7 full-time staff members. Academic advisers, counselors, regular education teachers, skill tutors, strategy tutors, and trained peer tutors are provided collaboratively through on-campus or off-campus services.
Orientation The program or unit offers a mandatory 1-hour orientation for new students after classes begin and individually by special arrangement.
Unique Aids and Services Aids, services, or accommodations include priority registration and support groups.
Subject-area Tutoring Tutoring is offered one-on-one and in small groups for some subjects. Tutoring is provided collaboratively through on-campus or off-campus services via computer-based instruction and trained peer tutors.
Enrichment Programs for career planning, college survival skills, health and nutrition, learning strategies, math, practical computer skills, reading, stress management, study skills, test taking, and written composition skills are provided collaboratively through on-campus or off-campus services.
Student Organization SNAPS Club consists of 15 members.
Application For admittance to the program or unit, students are required to provide a psychoeducational report (3 years old or less). Upon application, materials documenting need for services should be sent only to the LD program or unit. Upon acceptance, documentation of need for services should be sent only to the LD program or unit. *Application deadline (institutional):* Continuous. *Application deadline (LD program):* Rolling/continuous for fall and rolling/continuous for spring.
Written Policies Written policies regarding general/basic LD accommodations, substitutions and waivers of admissions requirements, and substitutions and waivers of graduation requirements are available on the program Web site. Written policy regarding general/basic LD accommodations is outlined in the school's catalog/handbook. Written policies regarding course substitutions, general/basic LD accommodations, substitutions and waivers of admissions requirements, and substitutions and waivers of graduation requirements are available through the program or unit directly.

DeKalb Technical College
Special Services Office

495 North Indian Creek Drive

Clarkston, GA 30021-2397

http://www.dekalbtech.org

Contact: Ms. Lisa M. Peters, Special Service Coordinator. Phone: 404-297-9522 Ext. 1155. Fax: 404-294-3424. E-mail: petersl@dekalbtech.org.

Special Services Office Approximately 16 registered undergraduate students were served during 2002-03. The program or unit includes 1 full-time staff member. Academic advisers are provided through the program or unit. Academic advisers and remediation/learning specialists are provided collaboratively through on-campus or off-campus services.
Unique Aids and Services Aids, services, or accommodations include career counseling, faculty training, and priority registration.
Subject-area Tutoring Tutoring is offered in small groups for some subjects. Tutoring is provided collaboratively through on-campus or off-campus services via computer-based instruction and other.
Basic Skills Remediation Remediation is offered in class-size groups for math, reading, and written language. Remediation is provided collaboratively through on-campus or off-campus services via computer-based instruction and regular education teachers.
Enrichment Programs for career planning, learning strategies, math, oral communication skills, practical computer skills, reading, stress management, study skills, test taking, time management, vocabulary development, and written composition skills are provided collaboratively through on-campus or off-campus services. Credit is offered for learning strategies, math, oral communication skills, practical computer skills, reading, stress management, study skills, test taking, vocabulary development, and written composition skills.
Application For admittance to the program or unit, students are required to apply to the program directly and provide a psychoeducational report. It is recommended that students provide documentation of high school services. Upon application, materials documenting need for services should be sent only to the LD program or unit. Upon acceptance, documentation of need for services should be sent only to the LD program or unit. *Application deadline (institutional):* Continuous. *Application deadline (LD program):* Rolling/continuous for fall and rolling/continuous for spring.
Written Policies Written policy regarding general/basic LD accommodations is outlined in the school's catalog/handbook.

Delaware County Community College
Office of Special Needs Services

901 South Media Line Road

Media, PA 19063-1094

http://www.dccc.edu/studentservices/accom_dis/index.php

Contact: Ms. Ann S. Binder, Director of Special Needs Services. Phone: 610-325-2748. Fax: 610-355-7162. E-mail: abinder@dccc.edu.

Office of Special Needs Services Approximately 300 registered undergraduate students were served during 2002-03. The program or unit includes 1 full-time and 2 part-time staff members. Academic advisers, coaches, and counselors are provided through the program or unit. Academic advisers, counselors, diagnostic specialists, professional tutors, regular education teachers, skill tutors, strategy tutors, and trained peer tutors are provided collaboratively through on-campus or off-campus services.

Orientation The program or unit offers an optional 1-hour orientation for new students individually by special arrangement.

Unique Aids and Services Aids, services, or accommodations include career counseling and priority registration.

Subject-area Tutoring Tutoring is offered one-on-one and in small groups for most subjects. Tutoring is provided collaboratively through on-campus or off-campus services via computer-based instruction, graduate assistants/students, professional tutors, and trained peer tutors.

Basic Skills Remediation Remediation is offered in class-size groups for computer skills, learning strategies, math, reading, spelling, study skills, time management, and written language. Remediation is provided collaboratively through on-campus or off-campus services via computer-based instruction, professional tutors, and regular education teachers.

Enrichment Programs for career planning, college survival skills, health and nutrition, learning strategies, math, medication management, oral communication skills, practical computer skills, reading, self-advocacy, stress management, study skills, test taking, time management, vocabulary development, and written composition skills are provided collaboratively through on-campus or off-campus services. Credit is offered for career planning, math, oral communication skills, practical computer skills, reading, vocabulary development, and written composition skills.

Application For admittance to the program or unit, students are required to provide a psychoeducational report, provide documentation of high school services, and provide a comprehensive evaluation report. Upon application, materials documenting need for services should be sent only to the LD program or unit. Upon acceptance, documentation of need for services should be sent only to the LD program or unit. *Application deadline (institutional):* Continuous. *Application deadline (LD program):* Rolling/continuous for fall and rolling/continuous for spring.

Written Policies Written policy regarding general/basic LD accommodations is available on the program Web site. Written policy regarding general/basic LD accommodations is outlined in the school's catalog/handbook.

The program or unit includes 4 full-time staff members and 1 part-time staff member. Counselors and trained peer tutors are provided through the program or unit. Academic advisers, coaches, and remediation/learning specialists are provided collaboratively through on-campus or off-campus services.

Orientation The program or unit offers an optional 1 to 2-hour orientation for new students individually by special arrangement.

Unique Aids and Services Aids, services, or accommodations include advocates, career counseling, faculty training, personal coach, and priority registration.

Subject-area Tutoring Tutoring is offered one-on-one and in small groups for most subjects. Tutoring is provided through the program or unit via trained peer tutors. Tutoring is also provided collaboratively through on-campus or off-campus services via computer-based instruction and trained peer tutors.

Basic Skills Remediation Remediation is offered in class-size groups for computer skills, learning strategies, social skills, study skills, and time management. Remediation is provided through the program or unit via trained peer tutors. Remediation is also provided collaboratively through on-campus or off-campus services via computer-based instruction, regular education teachers, and trained peer tutors.

Enrichment Enrichment programs are available through the program or unit for career planning, college survival skills, learning strategies, self-advocacy, stress management, study skills, test taking, and time management. Programs for career planning, college survival skills, health and nutrition, learning strategies, math, medication management, oral communication skills, practical computer skills, reading, vocabulary development, and written composition skills are provided collaboratively through on-campus or off-campus services. Credit is offered for college survival skills, math, oral communication skills, reading, and written composition skills.

Application For admittance to the program or unit, students are required to provide documentation of high school services and provide disability documentation by a licensed professional. Upon application, materials documenting need for services should be sent only to the LD program or unit. Upon acceptance, documentation of need for services should be sent only to the LD program or unit. *Application deadline (institutional):* Continuous. *Application deadline (LD program):* Rolling/continuous for fall and rolling/continuous for spring.

Written Policies Written policy regarding general/basic LD accommodations is available on the program Web site. Written policy regarding general/basic LD accommodations is outlined in the school's catalog/handbook. Written policy regarding general/basic LD accommodations is available through the program or unit directly.

Delaware Technical & Community College, Jack F. Owens Campus

PO Box 610
Georgetown, DE 19947
http://www.dtcc.edu/

Contact: Mrs. Heather Statler, Student Enrichment Coordinator. Phone: 302-855-1681. Fax: 302-858-5469. E-mail: hstatler@college.dtcc.edu.

Delaware Technical & Community College, Terry Campus
Student Support Services and Designated Disability Coordinator

100 Campus Drive
Dover, DE 19904-1383
http://www.dtcc.edu/terry/

Delaware Technical & Community College, Terry Campus (continued)

Contact: Ms. Nancy Rockey, Counselor. Phone: 302-857-1000. Fax: 302-857-1094.

Student Support Services and Designated Disability Coordinator Approximately 40 registered undergraduate students were served during 2002-03. Counselors, professional tutors, regular education teachers, skill tutors, and other are provided collaboratively through on-campus or off-campus services.

Summer Program To help prepare for the demands of college, there is summer program prior to entering the school.

Subject-area Tutoring Tutoring is offered one-on-one and in small groups for all subjects. Tutoring is provided collaboratively through on-campus or off-campus services via computer-based instruction and trained peer tutors.

Basic Skills Remediation Remediation is offered one-on-one and in small groups for computer skills, learning strategies, math, reading, study skills, time management, and written language. Remediation is provided collaboratively through on-campus or off-campus services via computer-based instruction, professional tutors, regular education teachers, and trained peer tutors.

Application For admittance to the program or unit, students are required to provide a psychoeducational report (3 years old or less). It is recommended that students provide documentation of high school services. Upon application, materials documenting need for services should be sent only to admissions with institutional application materials. Upon acceptance, documentation of need for services should be sent only to admissions. *Application deadline (institutional):* Continuous. *Application deadline (LD program):* Rolling/continuous for fall.

Written Policies Written policy regarding general/basic LD accommodations is available on the program Web site. Written policy regarding general/basic LD accommodations is outlined in the school's catalog/handbook.

Diagnostic Testing Testing is provided through the program or unit for math, reading, spelling, and written language.

Basic Skills Remediation Remediation is offered in class-size groups for math, reading, social skills, study skills, time management, and written language. Remediation is provided through the program or unit.

Enrichment Programs for career planning, college survival skills, learning strategies, stress management, study skills, test taking, time management, and other are provided collaboratively through on-campus or off-campus services. Credit is offered for career planning, college survival skills, learning strategies, stress management, study skills, test taking, time management, and other.

Application For admittance to the program or unit, students are required to provide a psychoeducational report (3 years old or less). It is recommended that students provide documentation of high school services and provide medical documentation. Upon application, materials documenting need for services should be sent only to the LD program or unit. Upon acceptance, documentation of need for services should be sent only to the LD program or unit. *Application deadline (institutional):* Continuous. *Application deadline (LD program):* Rolling/continuous for fall and rolling/continuous for spring.

Written Policies Written policy regarding general/basic LD accommodations is available on the program Web site. Written policies regarding course substitutions, general/basic LD accommodations, grade forgiveness, reduced course loads, substitutions and waivers of admissions requirements, and substitutions and waivers of graduation requirements are outlined in the school's catalog/handbook. Written policies regarding course substitutions, general/basic LD accommodations, grade forgiveness, reduced course loads, substitutions and waivers of admissions requirements, and substitutions and waivers of graduation requirements are available through the program or unit directly.

Delgado Community College
Office of Disability Services

501 City Park Avenue
New Orleans, LA 70119-4399
http://www.dcc.edu/

Contact: Ms. Tina M. Simpson, Special Needs Coordinator for Westbank Campus. Phone: 504-361-6450. Fax: 504-362-6257. E-mail: tsimps@dcc.edu.

Office of Disability Services Approximately 45 registered undergraduate students were served during 2002-03. The program or unit includes 1 full-time staff member. Academic advisers, coaches, counselors, LD specialists, and skill tutors are provided through the program or unit. Academic advisers, coaches, counselors, LD specialists, professional tutors, and skill tutors are provided collaboratively through on-campus or off-campus services.

Unique Aids and Services Aids, services, or accommodations include career counseling and faculty training.

Subject-area Tutoring Tutoring is offered in small groups for most subjects. Tutoring is provided through the program or unit via computer-based instruction and trained peer tutors.

Delta College
Disability Support Services

1961 Delta Road
University Center, MI 48710
http://www.delta.edu/disabilityservices

Contact: Ms. Prudence R. Coonan, Director. Phone: 989-686-9322. Fax: 989-667-2228. E-mail: pcoonan@alpha.delta.edu.

Disability Support Services Approximately 300 registered undergraduate students were served during 2002-03. The program or unit includes 1 full-time and 3 part-time staff members. Academic advisers, counselors, professional tutors, and trained peer tutors are provided collaboratively through on-campus or off-campus services.

Orientation The program or unit offers an optional 1-hour orientation for new students individually by special arrangement.

Unique Aids and Services Aids, services, or accommodations include digital textbooks, alternate testing arrangements.

Subject-area Tutoring Tutoring is offered in small groups for most subjects. Tutoring is provided collaboratively through on-campus or off-campus services via computer-based instruction, professional tutors, and trained peer tutors.

Basic Skills Remediation Remediation is offered in class-size groups for developmental education classes. Remediation is provided collaboratively through on-campus or off-campus services via regular education teachers.

Enrichment Programs for career planning, learning strategies, study skills, test taking, and time management are provided collaboratively through on-campus or off-campus services. Credit is offered for career planning and learning strategies.

Application For admittance to the program or unit, students are required to provide a psychoeducational report (3 years old or less) and provide documentation of high school services. It is recommended that students provide results of other current testing and reports, if applicable. Upon application, materials documenting need for services should be sent only to the LD program or unit. *Application deadline (institutional):* Continuous. *Application deadline (LD program):* Rolling/continuous for fall and rolling/continuous for spring.

Written Policies Written policy regarding general/basic LD accommodations is available on the program Web site. Written policies regarding course substitutions, general/basic LD accommodations, reduced course loads, substitutions and waivers of admissions requirements, and substitutions and waivers of graduation requirements are available through the program or unit directly.

Des Moines Area Community College
Student Support Services, Special Needs Office

2006 South Ankeny Boulevard

Ankeny, IA 50021-8995

http://www.dmacc.edu/student_services/disabilities.htm

Contact: Ms. Pamela J. Parker, Coordinator of Special Needs. Phone: 515-964-6857. Fax: 515-965-7150. E-mail: pjparker@dmacc.edu. Head of LD Program: Ms. Sharon G. Bittner, Supervisor of Student Support Services. Phone: 515-964-6857. Fax: 515-965-7150. E-mail: sgbittner@dmacc.edu.

Student Support Services, Special Needs Office Approximately 22 registered undergraduate students were served during 2002-03. The program or unit includes 2 full-time staff members. Graduate assistants/students are provided through the program or unit. Academic advisers, counselors, diagnostic specialists, professional tutors, regular education teachers, remediation/learning specialists, and trained peer tutors are provided collaboratively through on-campus or off-campus services.

Unique Aids and Services Aids, services, or accommodations include career counseling, digital textbooks, testing accommodations.

Subject-area Tutoring Tutoring is offered one-on-one and in small groups for most subjects. Tutoring is provided collaboratively through on-campus or off-campus services via trained peer tutors.

Diagnostic Testing Testing for reading is provided collaboratively through on-campus or off-campus services.

Basic Skills Remediation Remediation is offered in class-size groups for math, reading, and written language. Remediation is provided collaboratively through on-campus or off-campus services via regular education teachers.

Application For admittance to the program or unit, students are required to apply to the program directly. It is recommended that students provide a psychoeducational report and provide documentation of high school services. Upon acceptance, documentation of need for services should be sent only to the LD program or unit. *Application deadline (institutional):* Continuous. *Application deadline (LD program):* Rolling/continuous for fall and rolling/continuous for spring.

Written Policies Written policies regarding course substitutions, general/basic LD accommodations, grade forgiveness, substitutions and waivers of admissions requirements, and substitutions and waivers of graduation requirements are available on the program Web site. Written policies regarding course substitutions, general/basic LD accommodations, grade forgiveness, substitutions and waivers of admissions requirements, and substitutions and waivers of graduation requirements are outlined in the school's catalog/handbook. Written policies regarding course substitutions, general/basic LD accommodations, substitutions and waivers of admissions requirements, and substitutions and waivers of graduation requirements are available through the program or unit directly.

Dixie State College of Utah
Disability Resource Center

225 South 700 East

St. George, UT 84770-3876

http://www.dixie.edu/drc

Contact: Sherri Dial, Disability Resource Center. Phone: 435-652-7516. E-mail: sdial@dixie.edu.

Disability Resource Center Approximately 150 registered undergraduate students were served during 2002-03. The program or unit includes 1 full-time and 1 part-time staff member. Academic advisers and counselors are provided through the program or unit. Academic advisers, coaches, counselors, and professional tutors are provided collaboratively through on-campus or off-campus services.

Unique Aids and Services Aids, services, or accommodations include advocates, career counseling, faculty training, priority registration, books on tape, note-takers, readers, scribes, tape recorders, Dragon Naturally Speaking.

Subject-area Tutoring Tutoring is offered in class-size groups for most subjects. Tutoring is provided collaboratively through on-campus or off-campus services via trained peer tutors.

Basic Skills Remediation Remediation is offered in class-size groups for computer skills, learning strategies, math, reading, spelling, study skills, and written language. Remediation is provided collaboratively through on-campus or off-campus services via regular education teachers and trained peer tutors.

Enrichment Programs for career planning, college survival skills, health and nutrition, learning strategies, math, oral communication skills, practical computer skills, reading, stress management, study skills, test taking, time management, vocabulary development, and written composition skills are provided collaboratively through on-campus or off-campus services. Credit is offered for college survival skills, health and nutrition, math, oral communication skills, practical computer skills, reading, stress management, study skills, vocabulary development, and written composition skills.

Dixie State College of Utah (continued)

Application For admittance to the program or unit, students are required to apply to the program directly. It is recommended that students provide a psychoeducational report (3 years old or less) and provide documentation of high school services. Upon application, materials documenting need for services should be sent only to the LD program or unit. Upon acceptance, documentation of need for services should be sent to both admissions and the LD program or unit. *Application deadline (institutional):* Continuous. *Application deadline (LD program):* Rolling/continuous for fall and rolling/continuous for spring.

Written Policies Written policy regarding general/basic LD accommodations is available on the program Web site. Written policy regarding general/basic LD accommodations is available through the program or unit directly.

Draughons Junior College

2424 Airway Drive

Bowling Green, KY 42103

http://www.draughons.org/

Contact: Mr. Mickey H. Finn Jr., Student Services Coordinator. Phone: 270-843-6750. Fax: 270-843-6976. E-mail: mfinn@draughons.org.

The program or unit includes 1 full-time staff member. Academic advisers are provided through the program or unit.

Unique Aids and Services Aids, services, or accommodations include career counseling.

Application Upon application, materials documenting need for services should be sent only to admissions with institutional application materials. Upon acceptance, documentation of need for services should be sent to both admissions and the LD program or unit. *Application deadline (LD program):* Rolling/continuous for fall and rolling/continuous for spring.

Written Policies Written policy regarding general/basic LD accommodations is outlined in the school's catalog/handbook.

Durham Technical Community College
Disability Services

1637 Lawson Street

Durham, NC 27703-5023

http://www.durhamtech.edu/

Contact: Paula J. Rubio, Counselor, Disability Services. Phone: 919-686-3741. Fax: 919-686-3742. E-mail: rubiop@gwmail.dtcc.cc.nc.us. Head of LD Program: D. Thomas Jaynes, Associate Dean of Counseling and Student Development. Phone: 919-686-3652. Fax: 919-686-3742. E-mail: jaynest@gwmail.dtcc.cc.nc.us.

Disability Services Approximately 120 registered undergraduate students were served during 2002-03. The program or unit includes 1 full-time staff member. Coaches, counselors, LD specialists, skill tutors, and strategy tutors are provided through the program or unit.

Academic advisers, diagnostic specialists, professional tutors, regular education teachers, remediation/learning specialists, skill tutors, strategy tutors, and trained peer tutors are provided collaboratively through on-campus or off-campus services.

Unique Aids and Services Aids, services, or accommodations include career counseling and priority registration.

Subject-area Tutoring Tutoring is offered one-on-one and in small groups for some subjects. Tutoring is provided collaboratively through on-campus or off-campus services via computer-based instruction, professional tutors, and trained peer tutors.

Basic Skills Remediation Remediation is offered in class-size groups for math, reading, and written language. Remediation is provided collaboratively through on-campus or off-campus services via regular education teachers.

Enrichment Enrichment programs are available through the program or unit for learning strategies, stress management, study skills, test taking, and time management. Programs for career planning, health and nutrition, learning strategies, math, oral communication skills, practical computer skills, reading, study skills, test taking, time management, vocabulary development, and written composition skills are provided collaboratively through on-campus or off-campus services. Credit is offered for health and nutrition, learning strategies, math, oral communication skills, practical computer skills, reading, study skills, vocabulary development, and written composition skills.

Application For admittance to the program or unit, students are required to provide a psychoeducational report (5 years old or less). Upon application, materials documenting need for services should be sent only to the LD program or unit. Upon acceptance, documentation of need for services should be sent only to the LD program or unit. *Application deadline (institutional):* 8/4.

Written Policies Written policy regarding general/basic LD accommodations is available on the program Web site. Written policy regarding general/basic LD accommodations is available through the program or unit directly.

Dyersburg State Community College
Office of Student Disability Services

1510 Lake Road

Dyersburg, TN 38024

http://www.dscc.edu/

Contact: Ms. Pam B. Dahl, Coordinator. Phone: 731-286-3242. Fax: 731-286-3354. E-mail: dahl@dscc.edu.

Office of Student Disability Services Approximately 11 registered undergraduate students were served during 2002-03. The program or unit includes 1 full-time staff member. Counselors are provided through the program or unit. Counselors are provided collaboratively through on-campus or off-campus services.

Unique Aids and Services Aids, services, or accommodations include career counseling and priority registration.

Subject-area Tutoring Tutoring is offered one-on-one and in small groups for most subjects. Tutoring is provided collaboratively through on-campus or off-campus services via trained peer tutors.

Basic Skills Remediation Remediation is offered in class-size groups for math, reading, study skills, and written language. Remediation is provided collaboratively through on-campus or off-campus services via regular education teachers.

Application For admittance to the program or unit, students are required to provide a psychoeducational report. It is recommended that students provide documentation of high school services. Upon application, materials documenting need for services should be sent only to the LD program or unit. Upon acceptance, documentation of need for services should be sent only to the LD program or unit. *Application deadline (institutional):* Continuous. *Application deadline (LD program):* Rolling/continuous for fall and rolling/continuous for spring.

Written Policies Written policies regarding course substitutions, general/basic LD accommodations, grade forgiveness, reduced course loads, substitutions and waivers of admissions requirements, and substitutions and waivers of graduation requirements are available through the program or unit directly.

East Arkansas Community College

1700 Newcastle Road
Forrest City, AR 72335-2204
http://www.eacc.cc.ar.us/
Contact: Melvin Tinsley, Counselor and Administrator of Evening Services. Phone: 870-633-4480 Ext. 304. Fax: 870-633-3840. E-mail: mtinsley@eacc.edu.

The program or unit includes 7 full-time staff members. Academic advisers, counselors, regular education teachers, remediation/learning specialists, and trained peer tutors are provided through the program or unit. Regular education teachers are provided collaboratively through on-campus or off-campus services.

Unique Aids and Services Aids, services, or accommodations include career counseling and support groups.

Subject-area Tutoring Tutoring is offered one-on-one and in small groups for most subjects. Tutoring is provided collaboratively through on-campus or off-campus services via computer-based instruction and trained peer tutors.

Basic Skills Remediation Remediation is offered one-on-one and in small groups for computer skills, math, reading, study skills, time management, and written language. Remediation is provided collaboratively through on-campus or off-campus services via computer-based instruction, regular education teachers, and trained peer tutors.

Enrichment Programs for career planning, college survival skills, math, oral communication skills, reading, stress management, study skills, test taking, time management, vocabulary development, and written composition skills are provided collaboratively through on-campus or off-campus services. Credit is offered for career planning, college survival skills, math, oral communication skills, and reading.

Application It is recommended that students provide a psychoeducational report (2 years old or less) and provide documentation of high school services. Upon application, materials documenting need for services should be sent only to the LD program or unit. *Application deadline (institutional):* Continuous. *Application deadline (LD program):* Rolling/continuous for fall and rolling/continuous for spring.

Written Policies Written policy regarding general/basic LD accommodations is outlined in the school's catalog/handbook.

East Central College
Access Services

1964 Prairie Dell Road
PO Box 529
Union, MO 63084-0529
http://www.eastcentral.edu/
Contact: Ms. Wendy J. Pecka, Counselor. Phone: 636-583-5195. Fax: 636-583-1011.

Access Services Approximately 40 registered undergraduate students were served during 2002-03.

Unique Aids and Services Aids, services, or accommodations include career counseling.

Subject-area Tutoring Tutoring is offered one-on-one and in small groups for most subjects. Tutoring is provided collaboratively through on-campus or off-campus services via trained peer tutors.

Basic Skills Remediation Remediation is offered in class-size groups for math, reading, spelling, and study skills. Remediation is provided collaboratively through on-campus or off-campus services via computer-based instruction and regular education teachers.

Enrichment Programs for career planning, college survival skills, and stress management are provided collaboratively through on-campus or off-campus services. Credit is offered for college survival skills.

Application For admittance to the program or unit, students are required to provide a psychoeducational report. It is recommended that students provide documentation of high school services. Upon application, materials documenting need for services should be sent only to the LD program or unit. *Application deadline (institutional):* Continuous. *Application deadline (LD program):* Rolling/continuous for fall and rolling/continuous for spring.

Eastern Idaho Technical College
Disabled Student Services Office

1600 South 25th East
Idaho Falls, ID 83404-5788
http://www.eitc.edu/
Contact: Ms. Irene Jones, Disabled Student Services Officer. Phone: 208-524-3000 Ext. 3376. Fax: 208-524-3007. E-mail: ijones@eitc.edu.

Disabled Student Services Office Approximately 15 registered undergraduate students were served during 2002-03. The program or unit includes 1 part-time staff member. Services are provided through the program or unit. Academic advisers, counselors, regular education teachers, remediation/learning specialists, skill tutors, and other are provided collaboratively through on-campus or off-campus services.

Eastern Idaho Technical College (continued)

Unique Aids and Services Aids, services, or accommodations include advocates, career counseling, digital textbooks, and faculty training.

Subject-area Tutoring Tutoring is offered one-on-one and in small groups for some subjects. Tutoring is provided collaboratively through on-campus or off-campus services via computer-based instruction and other.

Diagnostic Testing Testing for math, reading, spelling, and written language is provided collaboratively through on-campus or off-campus services.

Basic Skills Remediation Remediation is offered one-on-one and in class-size groups for computer skills, math, reading, spelling, study skills, and written language. Remediation is provided collaboratively through on-campus or off-campus services via computer-based instruction, regular education teachers, and other.

Enrichment Programs for career planning, college survival skills, learning strategies, math, oral communication skills, practical computer skills, reading, self-advocacy, stress management, study skills, test taking, time management, and written composition skills are provided collaboratively through on-campus or off-campus services. Credit is offered for college survival skills, learning strategies, math, oral communication skills, practical computer skills, stress management, study skills, test taking, time management, and written composition skills.

Application For admittance to the program or unit, students are required to provide a psychoeducational report. It is recommended that students provide documentation of high school services. Upon acceptance, documentation of need for services should be sent only to the LD program or unit. *Application deadline (institutional):* 8/19. *Application deadline (LD program):* Rolling/continuous for fall and rolling/continuous for spring.

Written Policies Written policies regarding general/basic LD accommodations and substitutions and waivers of admissions requirements are outlined in the school's catalog/handbook. Written policy regarding general/basic LD accommodations is available through the program or unit directly.

Eastern Maine Community College
Disability Services

354 Hogan Road
Bangor, ME 04401-4206
http://www.emtc.org/
Contact: Linda Clutterbuck, Coordinator of Disabilities Services. Phone: 207-974-4658. Fax: 207-974-4888. E-mail: lclutterbuck@emtc.org.

Disability Services Approximately 60 registered undergraduate students were served during 2002-03. The program or unit includes 1 full-time staff member. Counselors, professional tutors, and trained peer tutors are provided collaboratively through on-campus or off-campus services.

Subject-area Tutoring Tutoring is offered one-on-one and in small groups for most subjects. Tutoring is provided through the program or unit via professional tutors and trained peer tutors. Tutoring is also provided collaboratively through on-campus or off-campus services via professional tutors and trained peer tutors.

Basic Skills Remediation Remediation is offered in class-size groups for math, reading, study skills, and written language. Remediation is provided collaboratively through on-campus or off-campus services via regular education teachers.

Application For admittance to the program or unit, students are required to provide a psychoeducational report (3 years old or less). It is recommended that students provide documentation of high school services. Upon acceptance, documentation of need for services should be sent only to the LD program or unit. *Application deadline (institutional):* Continuous. *Application deadline (LD program):* Rolling/continuous for fall and rolling/continuous for spring.

Written Policies Written policy regarding general/basic LD accommodations is outlined in the school's catalog/handbook. Written policy regarding general/basic LD accommodations is available through the program or unit directly.

Edison Community College
Program for Students with Disabilities

PO Box 60210
Fort Myers, FL 33906-6210
http://www.edison.edu/
Contact: Phone: 239-489-9300. Fax: 239-489-9399.

Program for Students with Disabilities Approximately 350 registered undergraduate students were served during 2002-03. The program or unit includes 3 full-time staff members and 1 part-time staff member. Services are provided through the program or unit. Academic advisers, counselors, regular education teachers, remediation/learning specialists, skill tutors, strategy tutors, trained peer tutors, and other are provided collaboratively through on-campus or off-campus services.

Subject-area Tutoring Tutoring is offered one-on-one, in small groups, and in class-size groups for most subjects. Tutoring is provided collaboratively through on-campus or off-campus services via computer-based instruction, trained peer tutors, and other.

Basic Skills Remediation Remediation is offered in class-size groups for computer skills, learning strategies, math, spelling, study skills, time management, and written language. Remediation is provided collaboratively through on-campus or off-campus services via computer-based instruction, regular education teachers, special education teachers, and other.

Application For admittance to the program or unit, students are required to apply to the program directly and provide a psychoeducational report (3 years old or less). It is recommended that students provide documentation of high school services. Upon acceptance, documentation of need for services should be sent only to the LD program or unit. *Application deadline (institutional):* 8/18.

Written Policies Written policies regarding course substitutions, general/basic LD accommodations, grade forgiveness, reduced course loads, substitutions and waivers of admissions requirements, and substitutions and waivers of graduation requirements are available on the program Web site. Written policies regarding course substitutions, general/basic LD accommodations, grade forgiveness, reduced course loads, substitutions and waivers of admissions requirements, and substitutions and waivers of graduation requirements are outlined in the school's catalog/handbook.

Edison State Community College

1973 Edison Drive

Piqua, OH 45356-9253

http://www.edisonohio.edu/

Contact: Dick Bollenbacher, Coordinator for Students With Special Needs. Phone: 937-778-8600 Ext. 360. Fax: 937-778-4692. E-mail: bollenbacher@edisonohio.edu.

Approximately 75 registered undergraduate students were served during 2002-03. The program or unit includes 4 part-time staff members. Counselors are provided through the program or unit. Counselors, skill tutors, and trained peer tutors are provided collaboratively through on-campus or off-campus services.

Unique Aids and Services Aids, services, or accommodations include career counseling and personal coach.

Subject-area Tutoring Tutoring is offered one-on-one for some subjects. Tutoring is provided collaboratively through on-campus or off-campus services via computer-based instruction, professional tutors, and trained peer tutors.

Diagnostic Testing Testing for learning strategies, learning styles, math, reading, spelling, and study skills is provided collaboratively through on-campus or off-campus services.

Basic Skills Remediation Remediation is offered in class-size groups for computer skills, learning strategies, math, reading, spelling, study skills, time management, and written language. Remediation is provided collaboratively through on-campus or off-campus services via computer-based instruction, trained peer tutors, and other.

Enrichment Programs for career planning, college survival skills, learning strategies, math, practical computer skills, reading, stress management, study skills, test taking, time management, and written composition skills are provided collaboratively through on-campus or off-campus services.

Application For admittance to the program or unit, students are required to apply to the program directly and provide documentation of high school services. Upon application, materials documenting need for services should be sent only to the LD program or unit. Upon acceptance, documentation of need for services should be sent only to the LD program or unit. *Application deadline (institutional):* Continuous. *Application deadline (LD program):* Rolling/continuous for fall and rolling/continuous for spring.

Written Policies Written policy regarding general/basic LD accommodations is available on the program Web site. Written policy regarding general/basic LD accommodations is outlined in the school's catalog/handbook. Written policy regarding general/basic LD accommodations is available through the program or unit directly.

Edmonds Community College

20000 68th Avenue West

Lynnwood, WA 98036-5999

http://www.edcc.edu/

Contact: Dee Olson, Director of Services for Students with Disabilities. Phone: 425-640-1318. Fax: 425-640-1622. E-mail: dolson@edcc.edu.

Approximately 160 registered undergraduate students were served during 2002-03. The program or unit includes 3 full-time and 3 part-time staff members. Academic advisers, counselors, LD specialists, professional tutors, regular education teachers, remediation/learning specialists, and trained peer tutors are provided collaboratively through on-campus or off-campus services.

Unique Aids and Services Aids, services, or accommodations include advocates, career counseling, and priority registration.

Subject-area Tutoring Tutoring is offered one-on-one for all subjects. Tutoring is provided through the program or unit via LD specialists, professional tutors, and trained peer tutors. Tutoring is also provided collaboratively through on-campus or off-campus services via computer-based instruction and trained peer tutors.

Basic Skills Remediation Remediation is offered one-on-one, in small groups, and in class-size groups for computer skills, learning strategies, math, reading, spelling, study skills, time management, and written language. Remediation is provided through the program or unit via professional tutors and trained peer tutors. Remediation is also provided collaboratively through on-campus or off-campus services via regular education teachers.

Enrichment Enrichment programs are available through the program or unit for self-advocacy. Programs for career planning, college survival skills, health and nutrition, learning strategies, math, practical computer skills, reading, stress management, study skills, test taking, time management, vocabulary development, and written composition skills are provided collaboratively through on-campus or off-campus services. Credit is offered for career planning, college survival skills, health and nutrition, learning strategies, math, practical computer skills, reading, stress management, study skills, test taking, time management, vocabulary development, and written composition skills.

Application For admittance to the program or unit, students are required to apply to the program directly and provide a psychoeducational report (5 years old or less). Upon application, materials documenting need for services should be sent only to the LD program or unit. Upon acceptance, documentation of need for services should be sent only to the LD program or unit. *Application deadline (institutional):* Continuous. *Application deadline (LD program):* Rolling/continuous for fall and rolling/continuous for spring.

Written Policies Written policy regarding general/basic LD accommodations is available on the program Web site. Written policies regarding course substitutions and substitutions and waivers of admissions requirements are outlined in the school's catalog/handbook. Written policies regarding course substitutions, general/basic LD accommodations, substitutions and waivers of admissions requirements, and substitutions and waivers of graduation requirements are available through the program or unit directly.

El Camino College
Special Resource Center, Learning Disabilities Program

16007 Crenshaw Boulevard

Torrance, CA 90506-0001

El Camino College (continued)
http://www.elcamino.edu

Contact: William Hoanzl, Learning Disabilities Program.
Phone: 310-660-3296. Fax: 310-660-3922. E-mail:
srchelp@elcamino.edu.

Special Resource Center, Learning Disabilities Program
Approximately 463 registered undergraduate students were served
during 2002-03. The program or unit includes 2 full-time staff
members and 1 part-time staff member. Diagnostic specialists, LD
specialists, regular education teachers, remediation/learning specialists, skill tutors, and strategy tutors are provided through the program or unit. Academic advisers, coaches, counselors, diagnostic
specialists, graduate assistants/students, professional tutors, remediation/
learning specialists, skill tutors, and strategy tutors are provided
collaboratively through on-campus or off-campus services.

Orientation The program or unit offers a mandatory 2-hour orientation for new students before registration, before classes begin,
during registration, after classes begin, and individually by special
arrangement.

Summer Program To help prepare for the demands of college,
there is an optional summer program prior to entering the school.

Unique Aids and Services Aids, services, or accommodations
include priority registration.

Diagnostic Testing Testing is provided through the program or
unit for auditory processing, intelligence, learning strategies, learning styles, math, motor skills, neuropsychological, reading, social
skills, spelling, study skills, visual processing, and written language.

Basic Skills Remediation Remediation is offered in class-size
groups for auditory processing, computer skills, learning strategies,
math, motor skills, reading, spelling, study skills, time management,
visual processing, and written language. Remediation is provided
through the program or unit via computer-based instruction, LD
specialists, and special education teachers. Remediation is also
provided collaboratively through on-campus or off-campus services
via graduate assistants/students, professional tutors, regular education teachers, teacher trainees, and trained peer tutors.

Application For admittance to the program or unit, students are
required to apply to the program directly and provide documentation of high school services. It is recommended that students provide a psychoeducational report (3 years old or less). Upon
application, materials documenting need for services should be sent
only to the LD program or unit. Upon acceptance, documentation of
need for services should be sent only to the LD program or unit.
Application deadline (institutional): Continuous. *Application deadline (LD program):* Rolling/continuous for fall and rolling/continuous
for spring.

Written Policies Written policy regarding reduced course loads is
available on the program Web site. Written policy regarding reduced
course loads is outlined in the school's catalog/handbook. Written
policies regarding course substitutions, general/basic LD accommodations, grade forgiveness, substitutions and waivers of admissions
requirements, and substitutions and waivers of graduation requirements are available through the program or unit directly.

Elizabethtown Community College
Office of Disability Services

600 College Street Road
Elizabethtown, KY 42701-3081
http://www.elizabethtowncc.com

Contact: Shawna Pelasky Jones, Disability Service
Coordinator. Phone: 270-769-2371 Ext. 4263. E-mail:
shawna.jones@kctcs.edu.

Office of Disability Services Approximately 30 registered undergraduate students were served during 2002-03. The program or unit
includes 1 full-time and 1 part-time staff member. Academic advisers and counselors are provided through the program or unit. Academic advisers, counselors, diagnostic specialists, graduate assistants/
students, LD specialists, professional tutors, regular education
teachers, remediation/learning specialists, skill tutors, special education teachers, strategy tutors, teacher trainees, and trained peer
tutors are provided collaboratively through on-campus or off-
campus services.

Orientation The program or unit offers an optional approximately
1 to 2-hour orientation for new students individually by special
arrangement.

Unique Aids and Services Aids, services, or accommodations
include advocates, career counseling, and priority registration.

Subject-area Tutoring Tutoring is offered for most subjects.
Tutoring is provided collaboratively through on-campus or off-
campus services via computer-based instruction, LD specialists,
professional tutors, and trained peer tutors.

Diagnostic Testing Testing is provided through the program or
unit for learning strategies, learning styles, personality, and study
skills. Testing for auditory processing, intelligence, learning strategies, learning styles, math, motor skills, neuropsychological, reading, social skills, spelling, spoken language, visual processing, and
written language is provided collaboratively through on-campus or
off-campus services.

Basic Skills Remediation Remediation is offered in class-size
groups for math, reading, spelling, study skills, time management,
and written language. Remediation is provided through the program
or unit via regular education teachers.

Enrichment Programs for career planning, college survival skills,
health and nutrition, math, oral communication skills, practical
computer skills, reading, self-advocacy, stress management, study
skills, test taking, time management, vocabulary development, and
written composition skills are provided collaboratively through
on-campus or off-campus services. Credit is offered for college
survival skills, health and nutrition, math, oral communication skills,
practical computer skills, reading, study skills, vocabulary development, and written composition skills.

Application For admittance to the program or unit, students are
required to apply to the program directly and provide a psychoeducational report (3 years old or less). It is recommended that students
provide documentation of high school services. Upon application,
materials documenting need for services should be sent only to the
LD program or unit. *Application deadline (institutional):* Continuous.
Application deadline (LD program): Rolling/continuous for fall and
rolling/continuous for spring.

Written Policies Written policy regarding general/basic LD accommodations is available on the program Web site. Written policies regarding general/basic LD accommodations and grade forgiveness are outlined in the school's catalog/handbook. Written policies regarding course substitutions, general/basic LD accommodations, and reduced course loads are available through the program or unit directly.

Ellsworth Community College

1100 College Avenue
Iowa Falls, IA 50126-1199
http://www.iavalley.cc.ia.us/ece/
Contact: Dr. Laura D. Browne, Associate Dean for Developmental Services. Phone: 641-648-4611 Ext. 459. Fax: 641-648-3128. E-mail: ldbrowne@iavalley.cc.ia.us.

Approximately 25 registered undergraduate students were served during 2002-03. The program or unit includes 1 full-time and 1 part-time staff member. Academic advisers, counselors, regular education teachers, remediation/learning specialists, and trained peer tutors are provided collaboratively through on-campus or off-campus services.

Orientation The program or unit offers an optional 4-hour orientation for new students individually by special arrangement.

Unique Aids and Services Aids, services, or accommodations include digital textbooks, personal coach, and weekly meetings with faculty.

Subject-area Tutoring Tutoring is offered one-on-one and in small groups for most subjects. Tutoring is provided collaboratively through on-campus or off-campus services via computer-based instruction and trained peer tutors.

Basic Skills Remediation Remediation is offered one-on-one, in small groups, and in class-size groups for computer skills, learning strategies, math, reading, spelling, study skills, and time management. Remediation is provided collaboratively through on-campus or off-campus services via regular education teachers and trained peer tutors.

Application For admittance to the program or unit, students are required to apply to the program directly, provide a psychoeducational report (3 years old or less), and provide documentation of disability. It is recommended that students provide documentation of high school services. Upon application, materials documenting need for services should be sent only to the LD program or unit. Upon acceptance, documentation of need for services should be sent only to the LD program or unit. *Application deadline (institutional):* Continuous. *Application deadline (LD program):* Rolling/continuous for fall and rolling/continuous for spring.

Written Policies Written policy regarding general/basic LD accommodations is outlined in the school's catalog/handbook.

Estrella Mountain Community College
Disability Resources and Services

3000 North Dysart Road
Avondale, AZ 85323-1000

http://www.emc.maricopa.edu/
Contact: Phone: 623-935-8000.

Disability Resources and Services Approximately 50 registered undergraduate students were served during 2002-03. The program or unit includes 1 full-time staff member. Academic advisers, counselors, professional tutors, remediation/learning specialists, and skill tutors are provided through the program or unit. Academic advisers, counselors, professional tutors, regular education teachers, remediation/learning specialists, skill tutors, and strategy tutors are provided collaboratively through on-campus or off-campus services.

Orientation The program or unit offers an optional 1-hour orientation for new students before registration, during registration, and individually by special arrangement.

Unique Aids and Services Aids, services, or accommodations include career counseling and priority registration.

Subject-area Tutoring Tutoring is offered one-on-one and in small groups for most subjects. Tutoring is provided through the program or unit via professional tutors. Tutoring is also provided collaboratively through on-campus or off-campus services via computer-based instruction and professional tutors.

Basic Skills Remediation Remediation is offered one-on-one and in small groups for handwriting, reading, and study skills. Remediation is provided through the program or unit via LD specialists and trained peer tutors. Remediation is also provided collaboratively through on-campus or off-campus services via regular education teachers.

Enrichment Enrichment programs are available through the program or unit for career planning, college survival skills, learning strategies, reading, self-advocacy, study skills, test taking, time management, vocabulary development, and written composition skills. Programs for career planning, college survival skills, health and nutrition, learning strategies, math, practical computer skills, reading, study skills, test taking, time management, vocabulary development, and written composition skills are provided collaboratively through on-campus or off-campus services. Credit is offered for career planning, college survival skills, learning strategies, math, practical computer skills, reading, and study skills.

Application For admittance to the program or unit, students are required to apply to the program directly and provide a psychoeducational report (3 years old or less). Upon application, materials documenting need for services should be sent only to the LD program or unit. Upon acceptance, documentation of need for services should be sent only to the LD program or unit. *Application deadline (LD program):* Rolling/continuous for fall and rolling/continuous for spring.

Written Policies Written policies regarding course substitutions, general/basic LD accommodations, and substitutions and waivers of admissions requirements are available on the program Web site. Written policies regarding course substitutions and substitutions and waivers of admissions requirements are outlined in the school's catalog/handbook. Written policies regarding course substitutions, general/basic LD accommodations, and substitutions and waivers of admissions requirements are available through the program or unit directly.

Eugenio Maria de Hostos Community College of the City University of New York
Services for Students with Disabilities

500 Grand Concourse

Bronx, NY 10451

http://www.hostos.cuny.edu/

Contact: Prof. Michael R. Stimola, Director of Services for Students with Disabilities. Phone: 718-518-4454. Fax: 718-518-4433. E-mail: mstimola@hostos.cuny.edu.

Services for Students with Disabilities Approximately 20 registered undergraduate students were served during 2002-03. The program or unit includes 4 part-time staff members. Academic advisers, counselors, skill tutors, strategy tutors, trained peer tutors, and other are provided through the program or unit. Academic advisers, counselors, diagnostic specialists, regular education teachers, and skill tutors are provided collaboratively through on-campus or off-campus services.

Orientation The program or unit offers an optional 1-day orientation for new students individually by special arrangement.

Unique Aids and Services Aids, services, or accommodations include advocates, career counseling, faculty training, priority registration, support groups, assistive technology services and training.

Subject-area Tutoring Tutoring is offered one-on-one and in small groups for some subjects. Tutoring is provided through the program or unit via computer-based instruction, trained peer tutors, and other. Tutoring is also provided collaboratively through on-campus or off-campus services via computer-based instruction, trained peer tutors, and other.

Diagnostic Testing Testing is provided through the program or unit for learning strategies, learning styles, and study skills. Testing for auditory processing, intelligence, math, motor skills, neuropsychological, reading, social skills, spelling, spoken language, visual processing, written language, and other services is provided collaboratively through on-campus or off-campus services.

Basic Skills Remediation Remediation is offered one-on-one, in small groups, and in class-size groups for computer skills, learning strategies, math, reading, spelling, study skills, time management, and written language. Remediation is provided through the program or unit. Remediation is also provided collaboratively through on-campus or off-campus services via regular education teachers and trained peer tutors.

Enrichment Enrichment programs are available through the program or unit for career planning, college survival skills, learning strategies, math, medication management, practical computer skills, self-advocacy, stress management, study skills, test taking, time management, written composition skills, and other. Programs for career planning, college survival skills, learning strategies, math, practical computer skills, reading, stress management, study skills, test taking, time management, vocabulary development, and written composition skills are provided collaboratively through on-campus or off-campus services.

Fees *Diagnostic Testing* fee is $0 to $1200.

Application For admittance to the program or unit, students are required to provide a psychoeducational report (3 years old or less). It is recommended that students provide documentation of high school services. Upon application, materials documenting need for services should be sent only to the LD program or unit. Upon acceptance, documentation of need for services should be sent only to the LD program or unit. *Application deadline (institutional):* Continuous. *Application deadline (LD program):* Rolling/continuous for fall and rolling/continuous for spring.

Written Policies Written policies regarding general/basic LD accommodations and reduced course loads are available through the program or unit directly.

Feather River Community College District

570 Golden Eagle Avenue

Quincy, CA 95971-9124

http://www.frc.edu/

Contact: Terrie Rose-Boehme, Disabled Student Programs and Services Coordinator. Phone: 530-283-0202 Ext. 247. Fax: 530-283-3757. E-mail: trose-boehme@frc.edu.

The program or unit includes 1 full-time staff member. Academic advisers, counselors, diagnostic specialists, professional tutors, regular education teachers, remediation/learning specialists, skill tutors, trained peer tutors, and other are provided collaboratively through on-campus or off-campus services.

Unique Aids and Services Aids, services, or accommodations include advocates, career counseling, digital textbooks, priority registration, and weekly meetings with faculty.

Subject-area Tutoring Tutoring is offered one-on-one and in small groups for some subjects. Tutoring is provided collaboratively through on-campus or off-campus services via computer-based instruction, graduate assistants/students, professional tutors, and trained peer tutors.

Basic Skills Remediation Remediation is offered one-on-one and in small groups for learning strategies, math, reading, spelling, study skills, time management, and written language. Remediation is provided collaboratively through on-campus or off-campus services via computer-based instruction, graduate assistants/students, professional tutors, and regular education teachers.

Enrichment Programs for career planning, college survival skills, learning strategies, math, oral communication skills, practical computer skills, reading, study skills, test taking, time management, vocabulary development, and written composition skills are provided collaboratively through on-campus or off-campus services.

Application It is recommended that students apply to the program directly, provide a psychoeducational report, and provide documentation of high school services. Upon acceptance, documentation of need for services should be sent only to the LD program or unit. *Application deadline (institutional):* Continuous. *Application deadline (LD program):* Rolling/continuous for fall and rolling/continuous for spring.

Written Policies Written policies regarding course substitutions, substitutions and waivers of admissions requirements, and substitutions and waivers of graduation requirements are outlined in the school's catalog/handbook. Written policies regarding general/basic LD accommodations, grade forgiveness, and reduced course loads are available through the program or unit directly.

Flathead Valley Community College
Learning Resource Center

777 Grandview Drive

Kalispell, MT 59901-2622

http://www.fvcc.edu/

Contact: Phone: 406-756-3822. Fax: 406-756-3815.

Learning Resource Center Approximately 50 registered undergraduate students were served during 2002-03. The program or unit includes 1 full-time staff member. Academic advisers, counselors, diagnostic specialists, LD specialists, and remediation/learning specialists are provided through the program or unit.

Unique Aids and Services Aids, services, or accommodations include advocates, career counseling, and priority registration.

Subject-area Tutoring Tutoring is offered one-on-one and in small groups for most subjects. Tutoring is provided collaboratively through on-campus or off-campus services via computer-based instruction, professional tutors, and trained peer tutors.

Diagnostic Testing Testing is provided through the program or unit for intelligence, learning strategies, learning styles, reading, and study skills. Testing for learning strategies, learning styles, math, personality, reading, spelling, spoken language, study skills, and written language is provided collaboratively through on-campus or off-campus services.

Basic Skills Remediation Remediation is offered in small groups for learning strategies, math, reading, spelling, study skills, and written language. Remediation is provided collaboratively through on-campus or off-campus services via regular education teachers and special education teachers.

Enrichment Enrichment programs are available through the program or unit for self-advocacy. Programs for career planning, college survival skills, health and nutrition, learning strategies, math, oral communication skills, practical computer skills, reading, stress management, study skills, test taking, time management, vocabulary development, and written composition skills are provided collaboratively through on-campus or off-campus services. Credit is offered for career planning, college survival skills, health and nutrition, learning strategies, math, oral communication skills, reading, stress management, study skills, test taking, time management, vocabulary development, and written composition skills.

Fees *Diagnostic Testing* fee is $10.

Application For admittance to the program or unit, students are required to provide a psychoeducational report (3 years old or less). It is recommended that students provide documentation of high school services. Upon application, materials documenting need for services should be sent only to the LD program or unit. Upon acceptance, documentation of need for services should be sent only to the LD program or unit. *Application deadline (institutional):* Continuous. *Application deadline (LD program):* Rolling/continuous for fall and rolling/continuous for spring.

Written Policies Written policy regarding general/basic LD accommodations is outlined in the school's catalog/handbook. Written policies regarding course substitutions and substitutions and waivers of graduation requirements are available through the program or unit directly.

Florida Community College at Jacksonville

501 West State Street

Jacksonville, FL 32202-4030

http://www.fccj.org/

Contact: Mrs. Marilyn Cecilia Sumner, Director of Services for Students With Disabilities. Phone: 904-632-5007. Fax: 904-633-8110. E-mail: mcsumner@fccj.org.

Approximately 413 registered undergraduate students were served during 2002-03. The program or unit includes 5 full-time and 4 part-time staff members. Academic advisers, skill tutors, strategy tutors, trained peer tutors, and other are provided through the program or unit. Academic advisers, counselors, diagnostic specialists, professional tutors, regular education teachers, and remediation/learning specialists are provided collaboratively through on-campus or off-campus services.

Orientation The program or unit offers a mandatory 1-hour orientation for new students before classes begin, after classes begin, and individually by special arrangement.

Unique Aids and Services Aids, services, or accommodations include career counseling, digital textbooks, faculty training, priority registration.

Subject-area Tutoring Tutoring is offered one-on-one and in small groups for all subjects. Tutoring is provided collaboratively through on-campus or off-campus services via computer-based instruction.

Diagnostic Testing Testing for math, reading, spelling, written language, and other services is provided collaboratively through on-campus or off-campus services.

Basic Skills Remediation Remediation is offered one-on-one and in small groups for math, reading, spelling, and written language. Remediation is provided through the program or unit via professional tutors and trained peer tutors. Remediation is also provided collaboratively through on-campus or off-campus services via computer-based instruction and special education teachers.

Enrichment Enrichment programs are available through the program or unit for career planning, self-advocacy, test taking, and time management. Program for career planning is provided collaboratively through on-campus or off-campus services.

Fees *Diagnostic Testing* fee is $15.

Application For admittance to the program or unit, students are required to apply to the program directly, provide a psychoeducational report, and provide other documentation. It is recommended that students provide documentation of high school services. Upon application, materials documenting need for services should be sent only to the LD program or unit. *Application deadline (institutional):* Continuous. *Application deadline (LD program):* Rolling/continuous for fall and rolling/continuous for spring.

Written Policies Written policies regarding course substitutions, general/basic LD accommodations, reduced course loads, and substitutions and waivers of graduation requirements are available on the program Web site. Written policies regarding course substitutions, general/basic LD accommodations, reduced course loads, and substitutions and waivers of graduation requirements are outlined in the school's catalog/handbook. Written policy regarding general/basic LD accommodations is available through the program or unit directly.

Floyd College
Access Center—Serving Students with Disabilities

3175 Cedartown Highway, SE
PO Box 1864
Rome, GA 30162-1864
http://www.floyd.edu/accesscenter
Contact: Phone: 706-802-5000. Fax: 706-295-6610.

Access Center—Serving Students with Disabilities Approximately 25 registered undergraduate students were served during 2002-03. The program or unit includes 3 full-time staff members. Academic advisers are provided collaboratively through on-campus or off-campus services.

Unique Aids and Services Aids, services, or accommodations include priority registration.

Subject-area Tutoring Tutoring is offered in small groups for some subjects. Tutoring is provided collaboratively through on-campus or off-campus services via computer-based instruction and professional tutors.

Basic Skills Remediation Remediation is offered in class-size groups for math, reading, and written language. Remediation is provided collaboratively through on-campus or off-campus services via regular education teachers.

Enrichment Programs for career planning, college survival skills, learning strategies, self-advocacy, stress management, study skills, test taking, and time management are provided collaboratively through on-campus or off-campus services.

Application For admittance to the program or unit, students are required to apply to the program directly, provide a psychoeducational report, and provide documentation that meets Georgia Board of Regents criteria. It is recommended that students provide documentation of high school services. Upon acceptance, documentation of need for services should be sent only to the LD program or unit. *Application deadline (institutional):* Continuous. *Application deadline (LD program):* Rolling/continuous for fall and rolling/continuous for spring.

Written Policies Written policy regarding general/basic LD accommodations is available through the program or unit directly.

Frederick Community College

7932 Opossumtown Pike
Frederick, MD 21702-2097
http://www.fcc.cc.md.us/
Contact: Dr. Rosemary Watson, Learning Specialist. Phone: 301-846-2409. Fax: 301-624-2787. E-mail: rwatson@frederick.edu.

The program or unit includes 1 full-time and 1 part-time staff member. LD specialists are provided through the program or unit. Academic advisers, coaches, counselors, LD specialists, professional tutors, and trained peer tutors are provided collaboratively through on-campus or off-campus services.

Unique Aids and Services Aids, services, or accommodations include career counseling and weekly meetings with faculty.

Subject-area Tutoring Tutoring is offered one-on-one and in small groups for all subjects. Tutoring is provided collaboratively through on-campus or off-campus services via trained peer tutors.

Diagnostic Testing Testing is provided through the program or unit for learning strategies, math, reading, spelling, study skills, and written language. Testing for auditory processing, handwriting, intelligence, learning styles, motor skills, neuropsychological, personality, social skills, spoken language, and visual processing is provided collaboratively through on-campus or off-campus services.

Basic Skills Remediation Remediation is offered one-on-one for learning strategies, reading, study skills, and time management. Remediation is provided through the program or unit via LD specialists.

Enrichment Programs for career planning, learning strategies, stress management, study skills, test taking, and time management are provided collaboratively through on-campus or off-campus services. Credit is offered for career planning and learning strategies.

Application For admittance to the program or unit, students are required to apply to the program directly, provide a psychoeducational report (3 years old or less), and provide documentation of high school services. Upon application, materials documenting need for services should be sent only to the LD program or unit. Upon acceptance, documentation of need for services should be sent only to the LD program or unit. *Application deadline (institutional):* 9/1. *Application deadline (LD program):* Rolling/continuous for fall and rolling/continuous for spring.

Written Policies Written policy regarding general/basic LD accommodations is outlined in the school's catalog/handbook.

Front Range Community College
Special Services

3645 West 112th Avenue
Westminster, CO 80031-2105
http://frcc.cc.co.us/
Contact: Jo Anna Bennett, Director of Special Services. Phone: 303-404-5302. Fax: 303-438-9524. E-mail: joanna.bennett@frontrange.edu.

Special Services Approximately 130 registered undergraduate students were served during 2002-03. The program or unit includes 2 full-time staff members. Professional tutors, skill tutors, strategy tutors, and trained peer tutors are provided through the program or unit. Academic advisers, coaches, counselors, regular education teachers, and remediation/learning specialists are provided collaboratively through on-campus or off-campus services.

Orientation The program or unit offers an optional 1 to 2-hour orientation for new students individually by special arrangement.

Unique Aids and Services Aids, services, or accommodations include advocates.

Subject-area Tutoring Tutoring is offered one-on-one and in small groups for most subjects. Tutoring is provided through the program or unit via professional tutors and trained peer tutors. Tutoring is also provided collaboratively through on-campus or off-campus services via computer-based instruction.

Diagnostic Testing Testing for math, personality, reading, and written language is provided collaboratively through on-campus or off-campus services.

Basic Skills Remediation Remediation is offered one-on-one, in small groups, and in class-size groups for computer skills, learning strategies, math, reading, spelling, study skills, time management, and written language. Remediation is provided through the program or unit via professional tutors and trained peer tutors. Remediation is also provided collaboratively through on-campus or off-campus services via computer-based instruction and regular education teachers.

Enrichment Programs for career planning, college survival skills, learning strategies, math, reading, study skills, test taking, time management, vocabulary development, and written composition skills are provided collaboratively through on-campus or off-campus services. Credit is offered for college survival skills, learning strategies, math, reading, study skills, time management, vocabulary development, and written composition skills.

Application For admittance to the program or unit, students are required to provide a psychoeducational report (3 years old or less) and provide a diagnosis from a qualified professional including testing results. It is recommended that students provide documentation of high school services. Upon application, materials documenting need for services should be sent only to the LD program or unit. Upon acceptance, documentation of need for services should be sent only to the LD program or unit. *Application deadline (institutional):* Continuous. *Application deadline (LD program):* Rolling/continuous for fall and rolling/continuous for spring.

Written Policies Written policy regarding general/basic LD accommodations is available on the program Web site. Written policy regarding general/basic LD accommodations is outlined in the school's catalog/handbook. Written policy regarding general/basic LD accommodations is available through the program or unit directly.

Fulton-Montgomery Community College
The Learning Center

2805 State Highway 67
Johnstown, NY 12095-3790
http://www.fmcc.ws/learning_center.htm
Contact: Mrs. Ellie Fosmire, Learning Disabilities Specialist. Phone: 518-762-4651 Ext. 5502. Fax: 518-762-3834. E-mail: efosmire@fmcc.suny.edu.

The Learning Center Approximately 80 registered undergraduate students were served during 2002-03. The program or unit includes 3 full-time and 2 part-time staff members. Counselors, graduate assistants/students, LD specialists, professional tutors, regular education teachers, and trained peer tutors are provided through the program or unit.

Orientation The program or unit offers an optional 1 or 2 half-day orientation for new students before classes begin.

Unique Aids and Services Aids, services, or accommodations include faculty training.

Subject-area Tutoring Tutoring is offered one-on-one and in small groups for most subjects. Tutoring is provided through the program or unit via professional tutors and trained peer tutors.

Diagnostic Testing Testing is provided through the program or unit for learning strategies and learning styles.

Basic Skills Remediation Remediation is offered one-on-one and in small groups for learning strategies, math, study skills, time management, and written language. Remediation is provided through the program or unit via computer-based instruction, LD specialists, professional tutors, and trained peer tutors.

Enrichment Enrichment programs are available through the program or unit for stress management, study skills, test taking, time management, vocabulary development, and written composition skills. Programs for career planning, college survival skills, stress management, study skills, test taking, time management, vocabulary development, and written composition skills are provided collaboratively through on-campus or off-campus services. Credit is offered for career planning and college survival skills.

Application For admittance to the program or unit, students are required to provide a psychoeducational report (3 years old or less) and provide documentation of high school services. Upon application, materials documenting need for services should be sent only to the LD program or unit. Upon acceptance, documentation of need for services should be sent only to the LD program or unit. *Application deadline (institutional):* 9/10. *Application deadline (LD program):* Rolling/continuous for fall and rolling/continuous for spring.

Written Policies Written policy regarding general/basic LD accommodations is available on the program Web site. Written policies regarding general/basic LD accommodations and grade forgiveness are outlined in the school's catalog/handbook. Written policies regarding general/basic LD accommodations and reduced course loads are available through the program or unit directly.

Gaston College
The Counseling Center

201 Highway 321 South
Dallas, NC 28034-1499
http://www.gaston.edu
Contact: Amy A. Davis, Special Needs Counselor. Phone: 704-922-6224. Fax: 704-922-6233. E-mail: davis.amy@gaston.cc.nc.us.

The Counseling Center Approximately 15 registered undergraduate students were served during 2002-03. The program or unit includes 4 full-time staff members. Academic advisers, counselors, regular education teachers, and remediation/learning specialists are provided through the program or unit. Academic advisers, counselors, regular education teachers, and remediation/learning specialists are provided collaboratively through on-campus or off-campus services.

Unique Aids and Services Aids, services, or accommodations include career counseling.

Subject-area Tutoring Tutoring is offered one-on-one for most subjects. Tutoring is provided through the program or unit via LD specialists. Tutoring is also provided collaboratively through on-campus or off-campus services via computer-based instruction, graduate assistants/students, LD specialists, and other.

Gaston College (continued)

Diagnostic Testing Testing is provided through the program or unit for learning styles, math, personality, reading, social skills, written language, and other services. Testing for learning styles, math, personality, reading, social skills, written language, and other services is provided collaboratively through on-campus or off-campus services.

Basic Skills Remediation Remediation is offered one-on-one, in small groups, and in class-size groups for computer skills, learning strategies, math, reading, spoken language, study skills, time management, and written language. Remediation is provided collaboratively through on-campus or off-campus services via computer-based instruction, graduate assistants/students, regular education teachers, and other.

Enrichment Enrichment programs are available through the program or unit for career planning, college survival skills, learning strategies, self-advocacy, stress management, study skills, test taking, time management, written composition skills, and other. Programs for college survival skills, health and nutrition, learning strategies, math, oral communication skills, practical computer skills, reading, study skills, and written composition skills are provided collaboratively through on-campus or off-campus services. Credit is offered for college survival skills, health and nutrition, math, oral communication skills, practical computer skills, reading, study skills, and written composition skills.

Application For admittance to the program or unit, students are required to provide a psychoeducational report (3 years old or less). Upon application, materials documenting need for services should be sent only to the LD program or unit. Upon acceptance, documentation of need for services should be sent only to the LD program or unit. *Application deadline (institutional):* Continuous. *Application deadline (LD program):* Rolling/continuous for fall and rolling/continuous for spring.

Written Policies Written policies regarding general/basic LD accommodations and grade forgiveness are available on the program Web site. Written policies regarding general/basic LD accommodations and grade forgiveness are outlined in the school's catalog/handbook. Written policy regarding general/basic LD accommodations is available through the program or unit directly.

Gateway Community and Technical College

1025 Amsterdam Road
Covington, KY 41011
http://www.gateway.kctcs.edu/

Contact: Ms. Colleen Nan Kane, Disability Survey Coordinator. Phone: 859-442-4120. Fax: 859-441-4252. E-mail: colleen.kane@kctcs.edu.

Approximately 45 registered undergraduate students were served during 2002-03. The program or unit includes 2 full-time staff members. LD specialists, regular education teachers, strategy tutors, and other are provided collaboratively through on-campus or off-campus services.

Unique Aids and Services Aids, services, or accommodations include advocates, priority registration, texts in alternative format, note-takers, extended time on written evaluation.

Subject-area Tutoring Tutoring is offered one-on-one and in small groups for most subjects. Tutoring is provided collaboratively through on-campus or off-campus services via other.

Basic Skills Remediation Remediation is offered in small groups and in class-size groups for learning strategies, math, reading, study skills, time management, and written language. Remediation is provided collaboratively through on-campus or off-campus services via computer-based instruction, LD specialists, and other.

Enrichment Programs for career planning, learning strategies, study skills, test taking, and time management are provided collaboratively through on-campus or off-campus services.

Application For admittance to the program or unit, students are required to provide a psychoeducational report (5 years old or less). It is recommended that students provide documentation of high school services. Upon application, materials documenting need for services should be sent only to the LD program or unit. Upon acceptance, documentation of need for services should be sent only to the LD program or unit. *Application deadline (LD program):* Rolling/continuous for fall and rolling/continuous for spring.

Written Policies Written policies regarding general/basic LD accommodations and grade forgiveness are outlined in the school's catalog/handbook. Written policies regarding course substitutions, general/basic LD accommodations, and reduced course loads are available through the program or unit directly.

Glendale Community College
Center for Students with Disabilities, Instructional Assistance Center

1500 North Verdugo Road
Glendale, CA 91208-2894
http://www.glendale.edu/

Contact: Ellen Oppenberg, Program Coordinator. Phone: 818-240-1000 Ext. 5529. Fax: 818-551-5283. E-mail: elleno@glendale.edu.

Center for Students with Disabilities, Instructional Assistance Center Approximately 300 registered undergraduate students were served during 2002-03. The program or unit includes 5 full-time and 2 part-time staff members. Academic advisers, counselors, diagnostic specialists, LD specialists, professional tutors, remediation/learning specialists, skill tutors, and strategy tutors are provided through the program or unit. Academic advisers, coaches, counselors, professional tutors, regular education teachers, skill tutors, and strategy tutors are provided collaboratively through on-campus or off-campus services.

Orientation The program or unit offers an optional 16-week orientation for new students after classes begin.

Unique Aids and Services Aids, services, or accommodations include career counseling, digital textbooks, faculty training, priority registration, and support groups.

Subject-area Tutoring Tutoring is offered one-on-one for most subjects. Tutoring is provided through the program or unit via LD specialists and professional tutors. Tutoring is also provided collaboratively through on-campus or off-campus services via computer-based instruction, graduate assistants/students, and trained peer tutors.

Diagnostic Testing Testing is provided through the program or unit for auditory processing, intelligence, math, neuropsychological, reading, spelling, spoken language, visual processing, written language, and other services.

Basic Skills Remediation Remediation is offered one-on-one for math, reading, spelling, and written language. Remediation is provided collaboratively through on-campus or off-campus services via computer-based instruction.

Enrichment Enrichment programs are available through the program or unit for college survival skills, learning strategies, study skills, test taking, and time management. Programs for career planning, college survival skills, math, oral communication skills, practical computer skills, reading, vocabulary development, and written composition skills are provided collaboratively through on-campus or off-campus services. Credit is offered for career planning, college survival skills, learning strategies, math, oral communication skills, practical computer skills, reading, study skills, test taking, time management, vocabulary development, and written composition skills.

Student Organization Delta Sigma Omicron consists of 10 members.

Fees *Diagnostic Testing* fee is $11.

Application It is recommended that students provide a psychoeducational report and provide documentation of high school services. Upon application, materials documenting need for services should be sent only to the LD program or unit. *Application deadline (institutional):* 7/1. *Application deadline (LD program):* Rolling/continuous for fall and rolling/continuous for spring.

Written Policies Written policy regarding general/basic LD accommodations is available on the program Web site. Written policy regarding general/basic LD accommodations is outlined in the school's catalog/handbook. Written policies regarding course substitutions, general/basic LD accommodations, reduced course loads, and substitutions and waivers of graduation requirements are available through the program or unit directly.

Globe College

7166 North 10th Street

Oakdale, MN 55128

http://www.globecollege.com/

Contact: Ms. Diana Stanslaski, Director of Education. Phone: 651-714-7301. Fax: 651-730-5151. E-mail: dstanslaski@globecollege.com.

Approximately 20 registered undergraduate students were served during 2002-03. Academic advisers, graduate assistants/students, regular education teachers, and trained peer tutors are provided collaboratively through on-campus or off-campus services.

Subject-area Tutoring Tutoring is offered one-on-one, in small groups, and in class-size groups. Tutoring is provided collaboratively through on-campus or off-campus services via graduate assistants/students, trained peer tutors, and other.

Enrichment Program for math is provided collaboratively through on-campus or off-campus services.

Written Policies Written policy regarding general/basic LD accommodations is outlined in the school's catalog/handbook.

Gloucester County College

1400 Tanyard Road

Sewell, NJ 08080

http://www.gccnj.edu/

Contact: Mr. Dennis Cook, Director. Phone: 856-415-2281. E-mail: dcook@gccnj.edu.

Approximately 265 registered undergraduate students were served during 2002-03. The program or unit includes 3 full-time staff members and 1 part-time staff member. Counselors and trained peer tutors are provided through the program or unit. Academic advisers, counselors, professional tutors, and trained peer tutors are provided collaboratively through on-campus or off-campus services.

Orientation The program or unit offers an optional orientation for new students before registration, before classes begin, during summer prior to enrollment, and group information sessions are given throughout the year.

Subject-area Tutoring Tutoring is offered in small groups for most subjects. Tutoring is provided through the program or unit via trained peer tutors. Tutoring is also provided collaboratively through on-campus or off-campus services via graduate assistants/students, professional tutors, and trained peer tutors.

Basic Skills Remediation Remediation is offered in class-size groups for learning strategies, math, reading, study skills, and written language. Remediation is provided through the program or unit via trained peer tutors. Remediation is also provided collaboratively through on-campus or off-campus services via professional tutors, regular education teachers, and trained peer tutors.

Application For admittance to the program or unit, students are required to apply to the program directly, provide documentation of high school services, and provide documentation of any additional disability. Upon application, materials documenting need for services should be sent only to the LD program or unit. Upon acceptance, documentation of need for services should be sent only to the LD program or unit. *Application deadline (institutional):* Continuous. *Application deadline (LD program):* Rolling/continuous for fall and rolling/continuous for spring.

Written Policies Written policy regarding general/basic LD accommodations is available on the program Web site. Written policy regarding general/basic LD accommodations is outlined in the school's catalog/handbook. Written policy regarding general/basic LD accommodations is available through the program or unit directly.

Gogebic Community College

E-4946 Jackson Road

Ironwood, MI 49938

http://www.gogebic.cc.mi.us/

Contact: Ms. Amanda J. Delich, Director of Student Support Services. Phone: 906-932-4231 Ext. 272. Fax: 906-932-2339. E-mail: amandad@admin.gogebic.cc.mi.us.

Approximately 60 registered undergraduate students were served during 2002-03. The program or unit includes 1 full-time staff

Gogebic Community College (continued)

member. Academic advisers and LD specialists are provided through the program or unit. Counselors and skill tutors are provided collaboratively through on-campus or off-campus services.

Unique Aids and Services Aids, services, or accommodations include advocates, career counseling, digital textbooks, and faculty training.

Subject-area Tutoring Tutoring is offered one-on-one and in small groups for most subjects. Tutoring is provided collaboratively through on-campus or off-campus services via computer-based instruction, graduate assistants/students, professional tutors, and trained peer tutors.

Basic Skills Remediation Remediation is offered one-on-one, in small groups, and in class-size groups for computer skills, learning strategies, math, reading, spelling, study skills, time management, visual processing, and written language. Remediation is provided collaboratively through on-campus or off-campus services via computer-based instruction, professional tutors, regular education teachers, and trained peer tutors.

Enrichment Enrichment programs are available through the program or unit for learning strategies, math, self-advocacy, stress management, study skills, test taking, time management, vocabulary development, and written composition skills. Programs for career planning, college survival skills, health and nutrition, learning strategies, math, oral communication skills, practical computer skills, reading, stress management, study skills, vocabulary development, and written composition skills are provided collaboratively through on-campus or off-campus services. Credit is offered for college survival skills, math, oral communication skills, practical computer skills, reading, stress management, study skills, test taking, time management, vocabulary development, and written composition skills.

Application For admittance to the program or unit, students are required to apply to the program directly, provide a psychoeducational report (3 years old or less), provide documentation of high school services, and provide diagnostics from evaluation. Upon application, materials documenting need for services should be sent only to the LD program or unit. Upon acceptance, documentation of need for services should be sent only to the LD program or unit. *Application deadline (institutional):* Continuous. *Application deadline (LD program):* Rolling/continuous for fall and rolling/continuous for spring.

Written Policies Written policy regarding general/basic LD accommodations is available through the program or unit directly.

Gordon College
Counseling Services

419 College Drive
Barnesville, GA 30204-1762
http://www.gdn.peachnet.edu/

Contact: Kristina Miller, Director of Counseling. Phone: 770-358-5326. Fax: 770-358-5037. E-mail: kristinam@gdn.edu.

Counseling Services The program or unit includes 1 full-time staff member. Academic advisers, counselors, skill tutors, and trained peer tutors are provided collaboratively through on-campus or off-campus services.

Unique Aids and Services Aids, services, or accommodations include career counseling.

Subject-area Tutoring Tutoring is offered one-on-one for some subjects. Tutoring is provided collaboratively through on-campus or off-campus services via trained peer tutors.

Basic Skills Remediation Remediation is offered in class-size groups for math, reading, and written language. Remediation is provided collaboratively through on-campus or off-campus services via regular education teachers.

Enrichment Programs for career planning, college survival skills, stress management, study skills, test taking, and time management are provided collaboratively through on-campus or off-campus services.

Application For admittance to the program or unit, students are required to apply to the program directly and provide a psychoeducational report (3 years old or less). It is recommended that students provide documentation of high school services. Upon acceptance, documentation of need for services should be sent only to the LD program or unit. *Application deadline (institutional):* Continuous. *Application deadline (LD program):* Rolling/continuous for fall and rolling/continuous for spring.

Written Policies Written policy regarding general/basic LD accommodations is available on the program Web site. Written policy regarding general/basic LD accommodations is outlined in the school's catalog/handbook. Written policies regarding course substitutions, grade forgiveness, reduced course loads, substitutions and waivers of admissions requirements, and substitutions and waivers of graduation requirements are available through the program or unit directly.

Grand Rapids Community College
Disability Support Services

143 Bostwick Avenue, NE
Grand Rapids, MI 49503-3201
http://www.grcc.edu/ShowPage.cfm?PageID=20&C=9

Contact: Anne Sherman, Director of Disability Support Services. Phone: 616-234-4140. E-mail: asherman@grcc.edu.

Disability Support Services Approximately 278 registered undergraduate students were served during 2002-03. The program or unit includes 6 full-time staff members and 1 part-time staff member. Academic advisers and counselors are provided through the program or unit. Professional tutors, regular education teachers, remediation/learning specialists, skill tutors, and trained peer tutors are provided collaboratively through on-campus or off-campus services.

Orientation The program or unit offers an optional orientation for new students before registration, before classes begin, during registration, after classes begin, and individually by special arrangement.

Unique Aids and Services Aids, services, or accommodations include career counseling and priority registration.

Subject-area Tutoring Tutoring is offered one-on-one, in small groups, and in class-size groups. Tutoring is provided collaboratively through on-campus or off-campus services via computer-based instruction, professional tutors, and trained peer tutors.

Diagnostic Testing Testing for auditory processing, handwriting, intelligence, learning strategies, learning styles, math, neuropsychological, personality, reading, social skills, spelling, spoken language, study skills, visual processing, and written language is provided collaboratively through on-campus or off-campus services.

Basic Skills Remediation Remediation is offered one-on-one and in class-size groups for computer skills, math, reading, study skills, and time management. Remediation is provided collaboratively through on-campus or off-campus services via professional tutors, regular education teachers, and trained peer tutors.

Enrichment Enrichment programs are available through the program or unit for career planning. Programs for career planning, college survival skills, learning strategies, practical computer skills, reading, stress management, study skills, test taking, time management, and written composition skills are provided collaboratively through on-campus or off-campus services. Credit is offered for college survival skills, learning strategies, practical computer skills, reading, stress management, study skills, test taking, time management, and written composition skills.

Fees *Diagnostic Testing* fee is $500 to $800.

Application For admittance to the program or unit, students are required to apply to the program directly and provide a psychoeducational report (5 years old or less). It is recommended that students provide documentation of high school services. Upon application, materials documenting need for services should be sent only to the LD program or unit. Upon acceptance, documentation of need for services should be sent only to the LD program or unit. *Application deadline (institutional):* 8/30. *Application deadline (LD program):* Rolling/continuous for fall and rolling/continuous for spring.

Written Policies Written policy regarding general/basic LD accommodations is outlined in the school's catalog/handbook. Written policies regarding general/basic LD accommodations and reduced course loads are available through the program or unit directly.

Grays Harbor College

1620 Edward P Smith Drive
Aberdeen, WA 98520-7599
http://www.ghc.ctc.edu/
Contact: Mr. John Rajcich, Coordinator of Disability Support Services. Phone: 360-538-4068. Fax: 360-538-4293.

Approximately 75 registered undergraduate students were served during 2002-03. Academic advisers and counselors are provided collaboratively through on-campus or off-campus services.

Unique Aids and Services Aids, services, or accommodations include advocates, digital textbooks, and priority registration.

Subject-area Tutoring Tutoring is offered in class-size groups for most subjects. Tutoring is provided collaboratively through on-campus or off-campus services via other.

Application For admittance to the program or unit, students are required to apply to the program directly, provide a psychoeducational report (3 years old or less), and provide other documentation. It is recommended that students provide documentation of high school services. Upon application, materials documenting need for services should be sent only to the LD program or unit. Upon acceptance, documentation of need for services should be sent only to the LD program or unit. *Application deadline (institutional):* Continuous. *Application deadline (LD program):* Rolling/continuous for fall and rolling/continuous for spring.

Written Policies Written policies regarding course substitutions, general/basic LD accommodations, reduced course loads, substitutions and waivers of admissions requirements, and substitutions and waivers of graduation requirements are available through the program or unit directly.

Greenfield Community College

1 College Drive
Greenfield, MA 01301-9739
http://www.gcc.mass.edu/
Contact: Ms. Dawn K. Stevenson, Director of Disability Services. Phone: 413-775-1812. Fax: 413-775-1434. E-mail: stevens@gcc.mass.edu.

The program or unit includes 1 full-time and 1 part-time staff member. Professional tutors, regular education teachers, remediation/learning specialists, and other are provided through the program or unit. Academic advisers, counselors, diagnostic specialists, LD specialists, skill tutors, special education teachers, strategy tutors, and trained peer tutors are provided collaboratively through on-campus or off-campus services.

Orientation The program or unit offers an optional orientation for new students individually by special arrangement.

Unique Aids and Services Aids, services, or accommodations include advocates, career counseling, faculty training, parent workshops, priority registration, consultation with an occupational therapist, adaptive technology aids.

Subject-area Tutoring Tutoring is offered one-on-one and in small groups for most subjects. Tutoring is provided collaboratively through on-campus or off-campus services via computer-based instruction, professional tutors, trained peer tutors, and other.

Basic Skills Remediation Remediation is offered in class-size groups for computer skills, learning strategies, math, motor skills, reading, spelling, study skills, time management, visual processing, and others. Remediation is provided through the program or unit via LD specialists. Remediation is also provided collaboratively through on-campus or off-campus services via regular education teachers and trained peer tutors.

Enrichment Enrichment programs are available through the program or unit for self-advocacy and time management. Programs for career planning, college survival skills, health and nutrition, learning strategies, math, oral communication skills, practical computer skills, reading, stress management, study skills, test taking, and written composition skills are provided collaboratively through on-campus or off-campus services. Credit is offered for career planning, college survival skills, health and nutrition, learning strategies, math, oral communication skills, practical computer skills, reading, stress management, study skills, test taking, and written composition skills.

Application For admittance to the program or unit, students are required to apply to the program directly and provide a psychoeducational report. It is recommended that students provide documentation of high school services and provide other testing/evaluation results as appropriate (e.g. SLP or OT evaluation). Upon application, materials documenting need for services should be sent only to the LD program or unit. Upon acceptance, documentation of need

Greenfield Community College (continued)

for services should be sent only to the LD program or unit. *Application deadline (institutional):* Continuous. *Application deadline (LD program):* Rolling/continuous for fall and rolling/continuous for spring.

Written Policies Written policies regarding course substitutions, general/basic LD accommodations, grade forgiveness, reduced course loads, substitutions and waivers of admissions requirements, and substitutions and waivers of graduation requirements are available on the program Web site. Written policies regarding course substitutions, general/basic LD accommodations, grade forgiveness, reduced course loads, substitutions and waivers of admissions requirements, and substitutions and waivers of graduation requirements are outlined in the school's catalog/handbook. Written policies regarding course substitutions, general/basic LD accommodations, grade forgiveness, reduced course loads, substitutions and waivers of admissions requirements, and substitutions and waivers of graduation requirements are available through the program or unit directly.

Green River Community College

12401 Southeast 320th Street
Auburn, WA 98092-3699
http://www.greenriver.edu/
Contact: Ms. Joanne H. Martin, DSS Coordinator. Phone: 253-833-9111 Ext. 2631. Fax: 253-288-3471. E-mail: jmartin@greenriver.edu.

Approximately 180 registered undergraduate students were served during 2002-03. The program or unit includes 1 full-time and 1 part-time staff member. Academic advisers, counselors, and trained peer tutors are provided collaboratively through on-campus or off-campus services.

Unique Aids and Services Aids, services, or accommodations include extended test times (1.5 times).

Basic Skills Remediation Remediation is offered in class-size groups for math, reading, study skills, and written language. Remediation is provided collaboratively through on-campus or off-campus services via computer-based instruction and regular education teachers.

Enrichment Programs for career planning, college survival skills, health and nutrition, learning strategies, math, oral communication skills, reading, study skills, vocabulary development, and written composition skills are provided collaboratively through on-campus or off-campus services. Credit is offered for college survival skills, health and nutrition, learning strategies, oral communication skills, reading, study skills, vocabulary development, and written composition skills.

Application For admittance to the program or unit, students are required to apply to the program directly and provide a psychoeducational report (3 years old or less). It is recommended that students provide documentation of high school services. Upon application, materials documenting need for services should be sent only to the LD program or unit. Upon acceptance, documentation of need for services should be sent only to the LD program or unit. *Application deadline (institutional):* Continuous. *Application deadline (LD program):* Rolling/continuous for fall and rolling/continuous for spring.

Written Policies Written policy regarding general/basic LD accommodations is available on the program Web site. Written policies regarding course substitutions, substitutions and waivers of admissions requirements, and substitutions and waivers of graduation requirements are outlined in the school's catalog/handbook. Written policy regarding general/basic LD accommodations is available through the program or unit directly.

Grossmont College
Disabled Students Programs and Services

8800 Grossmont College Drive
El Cajon, CA 92020-1799
http://www.grossmont.edu
Contact: Phone: 619-644-7000. Fax: 619-644-7922.

Disabled Students Programs and Services Approximately 350 registered undergraduate students were served during 2002-03. The program or unit includes 2 full-time staff members. LD specialists and strategy tutors are provided through the program or unit. LD specialists and strategy tutors are provided collaboratively through on-campus or off-campus services.

Orientation The program or unit offers an optional 1-hour orientation for new students before registration, before classes begin, during registration, after classes begin, individually by special arrangement, and twice weekly (students are asked to attend only one).

Unique Aids and Services Aids, services, or accommodations include career counseling, digital textbooks, and priority registration.

Diagnostic Testing Testing is provided through the program or unit for auditory processing, handwriting, intelligence, math, motor skills, reading, spelling, visual processing, and written language. Testing for learning strategies, learning styles, and study skills is provided collaboratively through on-campus or off-campus services.

Basic Skills Remediation Remediation is offered in small groups for computer skills, learning strategies, math, study skills, time management, and written language. Remediation is provided through the program or unit via computer-based instruction, LD specialists, and trained peer tutors.

Enrichment Enrichment programs are available through the program or unit for learning strategies, math, oral communication skills, practical computer skills, study skills, test taking, time management, and written composition skills. Programs for career planning, college survival skills, health and nutrition, learning strategies, math, stress management, study skills, time management, and written composition skills are provided collaboratively through on-campus or off-campus services. Credit is offered for career planning, college survival skills, learning strategies, math, study skills, test taking, time management, and written composition skills.

Fees *Diagnostic Testing* fee is $0 to $550.

Application For admittance to the program or unit, students are required to apply to the program directly, provide a psychoeducational report (3 years old or less), and provide documentation of high school services. Upon application, materials documenting need for services should be sent only to the LD program or unit. Upon acceptance, documentation of need for services should be sent only to the LD program or unit. *Application deadline (institutional):* 8/12. *Application deadline (LD program):* Rolling/continuous for fall and rolling/continuous for spring.

Written Policies Written policies regarding course substitutions, general/basic LD accommodations, and substitutions and waivers of admissions requirements are available through the program or unit directly.

Gulf Coast Community College
Services for Students with Disabilities

5230 West Highway 98
Panama City, FL 32401-1058
http://www.gulfcoast.edu

Contact: Mrs. Linda B. Van Dalen, Coordinator of Services for Students with Disabilities. Phone: 850-872-3834. Fax: 850-873-3523. E-mail: lvandalen@gulfcoast.edu.

Services for Students with Disabilities Approximately 130 registered undergraduate students were served during 2002-03. The program or unit includes 4 full-time and 3 part-time staff members. Academic advisers, counselors, LD specialists, professional tutors, regular education teachers, remediation/learning specialists, skill tutors, strategy tutors, and trained peer tutors are provided through the program or unit.

Unique Aids and Services Aids, services, or accommodations include career counseling and priority registration.

Subject-area Tutoring Tutoring is offered one-on-one and in small groups for most subjects. Tutoring is provided through the program or unit via graduate assistants/students, LD specialists, professional tutors, and trained peer tutors.

Basic Skills Remediation Remediation is offered one-on-one, in small groups, and in class-size groups for computer skills, math, reading, study skills, time management, and written language. Remediation is provided through the program or unit via graduate assistants/students, LD specialists, professional tutors, and trained peer tutors.

Enrichment Enrichment programs are available through the program or unit for career planning, college survival skills, learning strategies, math, practical computer skills, reading, self-advocacy, stress management, study skills, test taking, vocabulary development, and written composition skills. Programs for career planning, college survival skills, math, practical computer skills, reading, stress management, study skills, test taking, time management, vocabulary development, and written composition skills are provided collaboratively through on-campus or off-campus services.

Application For admittance to the program or unit, students are required to provide a psychoeducational report (3 years old or less). It is recommended that students provide documentation of high school services. Upon application, materials documenting need for services should be sent only to the LD program or unit. Upon acceptance, documentation of need for services should be sent only to the LD program or unit. *Application deadline (institutional):* Continuous. *Application deadline (LD program):* Rolling/continuous for fall and rolling/continuous for spring.

Written Policies Written policy regarding general/basic LD accommodations is available on the program Web site. Written policies regarding course substitutions, general/basic LD accommodations, reduced course loads, and substitutions and waivers of graduation requirements are outlined in the school's catalog/handbook. Written

policies regarding course substitutions, general/basic LD accommodations, and substitutions and waivers of graduation requirements are available through the program or unit directly.

Gwinnett Technical College

PO Box 1505
Lawrenceville, GA 30046-1505
http://www.gwinnett-tech.org/

Contact: Ms. Michelle J. McIntire, Director of Admissions. Phone: 770-962-7580. Fax: 770-685-1267. E-mail: mmcintire@gwinnett.tec.ga.us.

Approximately 15 registered undergraduate students were served during 2002-03. The program or unit includes 1 full-time staff member. Academic advisers and remediation/learning specialists are provided collaboratively through on-campus or off-campus services.

Subject-area Tutoring Tutoring is offered in small groups for some subjects. Tutoring is provided collaboratively through on-campus or off-campus services via computer-based instruction, trained peer tutors, and other.

Diagnostic Testing Testing for math, reading, and written language is provided collaboratively through on-campus or off-campus services.

Basic Skills Remediation Remediation is offered in class-size groups for math, reading, study skills, and written language. Remediation is provided collaboratively through on-campus or off-campus services via regular education teachers.

Enrichment Programs for career planning, learning strategies, math, reading, stress management, study skills, test taking, time management, and written composition skills are provided collaboratively through on-campus or off-campus services.

Application For admittance to the program or unit, students are required to apply to the program directly and provide a psychoeducational report (3 years old or less). It is recommended that students provide documentation of high school services. Upon acceptance, documentation of need for services should be sent only to the LD program or unit. *Application deadline (institutional):* 8/1. *Application deadline (LD program):* Rolling/continuous for fall and rolling/continuous for spring.

Written Policies Written policy regarding general/basic LD accommodations is available on the program Web site. Written policy regarding general/basic LD accommodations is outlined in the school's catalog/handbook. Written policy regarding general/basic LD accommodations is available through the program or unit directly.

Hagerstown Community College

11400 Robinwood Drive
Hagerstown, MD 21742-6590
http://www.hagerstowncc.edu/

Contact: Mrs. Jaime L. Bachtell, Academic and Special Student Services. Phone: 301-790-2800 Ext. 273. Fax: 301-791-9165. E-mail: bachtellj@hagerstowncc.edu.

Hagerstown Community College (continued)

Approximately 47 registered undergraduate students were served during 2002-03. The program or unit includes 1 full-time and 2 part-time staff members. Academic advisers, graduate assistants/students, LD specialists, remediation/learning specialists, strategy tutors, and other are provided through the program or unit. Academic advisers, coaches, counselors, diagnostic specialists, graduate assistants/students, professional tutors, regular education teachers, remediation/learning specialists, skill tutors, special education teachers, strategy tutors, teacher trainees, trained peer tutors, and other are provided collaboratively through on-campus or off-campus services.

Subject-area Tutoring Tutoring is offered for most subjects. Tutoring is provided through the program or unit via LD specialists. Tutoring is also provided collaboratively through on-campus or off-campus services via computer-based instruction, professional tutors, and trained peer tutors.

Basic Skills Remediation Remediation is offered one-on-one, in small groups, and in class-size groups for auditory processing, computer skills, learning strategies, math, reading, spelling, spoken language, study skills, time management, visual processing, and written language. Remediation is provided through the program or unit via LD specialists. Remediation is also provided collaboratively through on-campus or off-campus services via LD specialists, professional tutors, regular education teachers, special education teachers, and trained peer tutors.

Enrichment Enrichment programs are available through the program or unit for career planning, stress management, study skills, test taking, and time management. Programs for career planning, college survival skills, health and nutrition, learning strategies, math, medication management, oral communication skills, practical computer skills, reading, self-advocacy, stress management, study skills, test taking, time management, vocabulary development, and written composition skills are provided collaboratively through on-campus or off-campus services. Credit is offered for career planning, college survival skills, health and nutrition, learning strategies, math, oral communication skills, practical computer skills, reading, study skills, vocabulary development, and written composition skills.

Application For admittance to the program or unit, students are required to apply to the program directly and provide a psychoeducational report (3 years old or less). It is recommended that students provide documentation of high school services and provide other documentation. Upon application, materials documenting need for services should be sent only to the LD program or unit. Upon acceptance, documentation of need for services should be sent only to the LD program or unit. *Application deadline (institutional):* Continuous. *Application deadline (LD program):* Rolling/continuous for fall and rolling/continuous for spring.

Written Policies Written policies regarding general/basic LD accommodations and reduced course loads are available through the program or unit directly.

Harford Community College

401 Thomas Run Road
Bel Air, MD 21015-1698
http://www.harford.edu/

Contact: Patricia A. Burton, Counselor. Phone: 410-836-4452. Fax: 410-836-4200. E-mail: pburton@harford.edu. Head of LD Program: Dr. Ann Topping, Assistant Vice President for Learning Support Services. Phone: 410-836-4186. Fax: 410-836-4200. E-mail: atopping@harford.edu.

Approximately 200 registered undergraduate students were served during 2002-03. The program or unit includes 3 full-time staff members. Academic advisers and counselors are provided through the program or unit. Professional tutors, skill tutors, strategy tutors, and trained peer tutors are provided collaboratively through on-campus or off-campus services.

Orientation The program or unit offers a mandatory 1.5 hour orientation for new students individually by special arrangement.

Unique Aids and Services Aids, services, or accommodations include career counseling.

Subject-area Tutoring Tutoring is offered one-on-one and in small groups for all subjects. Tutoring is provided collaboratively through on-campus or off-campus services via computer-based instruction, graduate assistants/students, professional tutors, and trained peer tutors.

Diagnostic Testing Testing is provided through the program or unit for learning strategies, learning styles, math, personality, reading, spelling, study skills, and written language. Testing for auditory processing, intelligence, learning strategies, learning styles, math, motor skills, neuropsychological, personality, reading, social skills, spelling, visual processing, and written language is provided collaboratively through on-campus or off-campus services.

Basic Skills Remediation Remediation is offered one-on-one, in small groups, and in class-size groups for computer skills, learning strategies, math, reading, spelling, study skills, time management, and written language. Remediation is provided collaboratively through on-campus or off-campus services via computer-based instruction, professional tutors, regular education teachers, and trained peer tutors.

Enrichment Enrichment programs are available through the program or unit for career planning, learning strategies, self-advocacy, stress management, test taking, and time management. Programs for career planning, college survival skills, health and nutrition, learning strategies, math, oral communication skills, practical computer skills, reading, stress management, study skills, test taking, time management, vocabulary development, and written composition skills are provided collaboratively through on-campus or off-campus services. Credit is offered for career planning, college survival skills, health and nutrition, learning strategies, math, oral communication skills, practical computer skills, reading, study skills, test taking, time management, vocabulary development, and written composition skills.

Fees *Diagnostic Testing* fee is applicable.

Application For admittance to the program or unit, students are required to provide a psychoeducational report (3 years old or less). It is recommended that students provide documentation of high school services. Upon acceptance, documentation of need for services should be sent only to the LD program or unit. *Application deadline (institutional):* Continuous. *Application deadline (LD program):* Rolling/continuous for fall.

Written Policies Written policy regarding general/basic LD accommodations is available on the program Web site. Written policy regarding general/basic LD accommodations is outlined in the

school's catalog/handbook. Written policies regarding course substitutions, general/basic LD accommodations, and reduced course loads are available through the program or unit directly.

Hawaii Community College

200 West Kawili Street
Hilo, HI 96720-4091
http://www.hawcc.hawaii.edu/
Contact: Karen Kane, Counselor and Coordinator. Phone: 808-933-0702. Fax: 808-974-7692. E-mail: kkane@hawaii.edu.

Approximately 60 registered undergraduate students were served during 2002-03. The program or unit includes 1 full-time and 12 part-time staff members. Academic advisers, counselors, graduate assistants/students, skill tutors, strategy tutors, and trained peer tutors are provided through the program or unit. Academic advisers are provided collaboratively through on-campus or off-campus services.
Unique Aids and Services Aids, services, or accommodations include support groups, mid-term monitoring of academic progress (MAP).
Subject-area Tutoring Tutoring is offered one-on-one and in small groups for some subjects. Tutoring is provided through the program or unit via trained peer tutors.
Enrichment Enrichment programs are available through the program or unit for career planning, college survival skills, learning strategies, practical computer skills, reading, self-advocacy, stress management, study skills, test taking, time management, and other. Programs for career planning, college survival skills, learning strategies, math, oral communication skills, practical computer skills, reading, study skills, vocabulary development, and written composition skills are provided collaboratively through on-campus or off-campus services. Credit is offered for math, oral communication skills, practical computer skills, reading, study skills, vocabulary development, and written composition skills.
Student Organization Kokua Ohana consists of 20 members.
Application For admittance to the program or unit, students are required to apply to the program directly and provide documentation of high school services. It is recommended that students provide a psychoeducational report and provide other documentation. Upon application, materials documenting need for services should be sent only to the LD program or unit. Upon acceptance, documentation of need for services should be sent only to the LD program or unit. *Application deadline (institutional):* 8/1. *Application deadline (LD program):* Rolling/continuous for fall and rolling/continuous for spring.
Written Policies Written policy regarding general/basic LD accommodations is available through the program or unit directly.

Hawkeye Community College

PO Box 8015
Waterloo, IA 50704-8015

http://www.hawkeyecollege.edu/
Contact: Phone: 319-296-2320. Fax: 319-296-2874.

The program or unit includes 1 part-time staff member. Counselors are provided through the program or unit. Academic advisers, professional tutors, remediation/learning specialists, and trained peer tutors are provided collaboratively through on-campus or off-campus services.
Subject-area Tutoring Tutoring is offered one-on-one for some subjects. Tutoring is provided collaboratively through on-campus or off-campus services via computer-based instruction, professional tutors, and trained peer tutors.
Basic Skills Remediation Remediation is offered in class-size groups for learning strategies, math, reading, spelling, study skills, time management, and written language. Remediation is provided collaboratively through on-campus or off-campus services via regular education teachers.
Enrichment Programs for career planning, college survival skills, learning strategies, math, practical computer skills, reading, stress management, study skills, test taking, time management, and written composition skills are provided collaboratively through on-campus or off-campus services. Credit is offered for career planning.
Application For admittance to the program or unit, students are required to apply to the program directly and provide a psychoeducational report (3 years old or less). It is recommended that students provide documentation of high school services. Upon application, materials documenting need for services should be sent only to the LD program or unit. Upon acceptance, documentation of need for services should be sent only to the LD program or unit. *Application deadline (institutional):* Continuous. *Application deadline (LD program):* Rolling/continuous for fall and rolling/continuous for spring.
Written Policies Written policies regarding course substitutions and substitutions and waivers of graduation requirements are outlined in the school's catalog/handbook. Written policies regarding course substitutions, general/basic LD accommodations, and substitutions and waivers of graduation requirements are available through the program or unit directly.

Herkimer County Community College
Office of Special Services

Reservoir Road
Herkimer, NY 13350
http://webserv.hccc.suny.edu/Learning_Center/
Contact: Ms. Leslie Cornish, Special Services Coordinator. Phone: 315-866-0300 Ext. 331. Fax: 315-866-6957. E-mail: cornishld@hccc.suny.edu.

Office of Special Services Approximately 160 registered undergraduate students were served during 2002-03. The program or unit includes 1 full-time and 3 part-time staff members. LD specialists are provided through the program or unit. Academic advisers, coaches, counselors, professional tutors, regular education teachers, remediation/learning specialists, skill tutors, strategy tutors, and trained peer tutors are provided collaboratively through on-campus or off-campus services.

Herkimer County Community College (continued)

Unique Aids and Services Aids, services, or accommodations include career counseling and faculty training.

Subject-area Tutoring Tutoring is offered one-on-one, in small groups, and in class-size groups. Tutoring is provided through the program or unit via LD specialists. Tutoring is also provided collaboratively through on-campus or off-campus services via computer-based instruction, professional tutors, and trained peer tutors.

Basic Skills Remediation Remediation is offered one-on-one, in small groups, and in class-size groups for learning strategies, math, reading, spelling, study skills, time management, and written language. Remediation is provided through the program or unit via LD specialists. Remediation is also provided collaboratively through on-campus or off-campus services via computer-based instruction, professional tutors, regular education teachers, and trained peer tutors.

Enrichment Enrichment programs are available through the program or unit for college survival skills, learning strategies, self-advocacy, stress management, study skills, test taking, and time management. Programs for career planning, college survival skills, learning strategies, math, medication management, oral communication skills, practical computer skills, reading, self-advocacy, stress management, study skills, test taking, time management, vocabulary development, and written composition skills are provided collaboratively through on-campus or off-campus services.

Application For admittance to the program or unit, students are required to provide a psychoeducational report (2 years old or less) and provide documentation of high school services. Upon acceptance, documentation of need for services should be sent only to the LD program or unit. *Application deadline (institutional):* 8/20.

Written Policies Written policy regarding general/basic LD accommodations is available on the program Web site. Written policies regarding course substitutions and general/basic LD accommodations are outlined in the school's catalog/handbook.

Herzing College
Life Management Office

5218 East Terrace Drive
Madison, WI 53718
http://www.herzing.edu/
Contact: Mrs. Shannon Marie Livingston, Director of Life Management. Phone: 608-663-0817. Fax: 608-249-8593. E-mail: shannon@msn.herzing.edu.

Life Management Office Approximately 5 registered undergraduate students were served during 2002-03. Counselors are provided through the program or unit. Counselors, regular education teachers, and trained peer tutors are provided collaboratively through on-campus or off-campus services.

Unique Aids and Services Aids, services, or accommodations include advocates, faculty training, resource referral, tutoring, accommodations for testing.

Subject-area Tutoring Tutoring is offered one-on-one, in small groups, and in class-size groups for most subjects. Tutoring is provided through the program or unit via LD specialists. Tutoring is also provided collaboratively through on-campus or off-campus services via computer-based instruction, LD specialists, trained peer tutors, and other.

Basic Skills Remediation Remediation is offered one-on-one and in class-size groups for computer skills, learning strategies, math, study skills, and time management. Remediation is provided through the program or unit via LD specialists. Remediation is also provided collaboratively through on-campus or off-campus services via computer-based instruction, LD specialists, and trained peer tutors.

Enrichment Enrichment programs are available through the program or unit for health and nutrition, learning strategies, stress management, study skills, test taking, and time management. Programs for career planning, college survival skills, math, oral communication skills, practical computer skills, and written composition skills are provided collaboratively through on-campus or off-campus services. Credit is offered for career planning, college survival skills, oral communication skills, practical computer skills, and written composition skills.

Application For admittance to the program or unit, students are required to provide a psychoeducational report (3 years old or less). It is recommended that students provide documentation of high school services. Upon application, materials documenting need for services should be sent to both admissions and the LD program or unit. Upon acceptance, documentation of need for services should be sent only to the LD program or unit. *Application deadline (institutional):* 10/10. *Application deadline (LD program):* Rolling/continuous for fall and rolling/continuous for spring.

Written Policies Written policy regarding general/basic LD accommodations is available through the program or unit directly.

Hesston College
ACCESS Program (Academic Center for College Excellence and Student Success)

Box 3000
Hesston, KS 67062-2093
http://www.hesston.edu/
Contact: Mrs. Deb Roth, Director of ACCESS Program. Phone: 620-327-8239. Fax: 620-327-8800. E-mail: debr@hesston.edu.

ACCESS Program (Academic Center for College Excellence and Student Success) Approximately 15 registered undergraduate students were served during 2002-03. The program or unit includes 1 full-time staff member. Remediation/learning specialists are provided through the program or unit. Academic advisers, counselors, regular education teachers, remediation/learning specialists, and trained peer tutors are provided collaboratively through on-campus or off-campus services.

Subject-area Tutoring Tutoring is offered one-on-one and in small groups for all subjects. Tutoring is provided collaboratively through on-campus or off-campus services via trained peer tutors.

Basic Skills Remediation Remediation is offered one-on-one, in small groups, and in class-size groups for computer skills, learning strategies, math, spelling, study skills, time management, and written language. Remediation is provided collaboratively through on-campus or off-campus services via regular education teachers, special education teachers, and trained peer tutors.

Enrichment Programs for career planning, college survival skills, learning strategies, math, study skills, test taking, time management, and written composition skills are provided collaboratively through on-campus or off-campus services. Credit is offered for career planning, college survival skills, learning strategies, math, study skills, test taking, time management, and written composition skills.

Application It is recommended that students provide a psychoeducational report (2 years old or less) and provide documentation of high school services. Upon acceptance, documentation of need for services should be sent to both admissions and the LD program or unit. *Application deadline (institutional):* Continuous. *Application deadline (LD program):* Rolling/continuous for fall and rolling/continuous for spring.

Written Policies Written policy regarding general/basic LD accommodations is outlined in the school's catalog/handbook.

Highland Community College
Services for Students with Disabilities

2998 West Pearl City Road

Freeport, IL 61032-9341

http://www.highland.cc.il.us/

Contact: Ms. Dawn H. Zuehlke, ADA Coordinator and Coordinator of Needs Assessment. Phone: 815-235-6121 Ext. 3583. Fax: 815-599-3646. E-mail: dawn.zuehlke@highland.edu.

Services for Students with Disabilities Approximately 40 registered undergraduate students were served during 2002-03. The program or unit includes 1 part-time staff member. Academic advisers, counselors, LD specialists, special education teachers, and strategy tutors are provided through the program or unit. Academic advisers, coaches, diagnostic specialists, regular education teachers, skill tutors, strategy tutors, and trained peer tutors are provided collaboratively through on-campus or off-campus services.

Unique Aids and Services Aids, services, or accommodations include advocates, career counseling, digital textbooks, faculty training, optional instructor notices, testing accommodations, word-prediction and screen-reading software.

Subject-area Tutoring Tutoring is offered one-on-one and in small groups for most subjects. Tutoring is provided collaboratively through on-campus or off-campus services via trained peer tutors.

Basic Skills Remediation Remediation is offered one-on-one, in small groups, and in class-size groups for reading and written language. Remediation is provided collaboratively through on-campus or off-campus services via regular education teachers and trained peer tutors.

Enrichment Programs for career planning, college survival skills, learning strategies, math, oral communication skills, practical computer skills, reading, stress management, study skills, test taking, time management, and written composition skills are provided collaboratively through on-campus or off-campus services. Credit is offered for college survival skills, math, and oral communication skills.

Application For admittance to the program or unit, students are required to provide a psychoeducational report (3 years old or less) and provide an interview (student approved support people may also attend) . It is recommended that students provide documentation of high school services. Upon application, materials document-

ing need for services should be sent only to the LD program or unit. Upon acceptance, documentation of need for services should be sent only to the LD program or unit. *Application deadline (institutional):* Continuous. *Application deadline (LD program):* Rolling/continuous for fall and rolling/continuous for spring.

Written Policies Written policy regarding general/basic LD accommodations is available through the program or unit directly.

Highline Community College
Access Services

PO Box 98000

Des Moines, WA 98198-9800

http://www.highline.edu/stuserv/access/

Contact: Ms. Carol L. Jones, Director of Access Services. Phone: 206-878-3710 Ext. 3551. Fax: 206-870-3772. E-mail: cjones@highline.edu.

Access Services Approximately 75 registered undergraduate students were served during 2002-03. The program or unit includes 1 full-time and 2 part-time staff members. Academic advisers, counselors, regular education teachers, remediation/learning specialists, trained peer tutors, and other are provided collaboratively through on-campus or off-campus services.

Unique Aids and Services Aids, services, or accommodations include advocates, career counseling, faculty training, priority registration, additional test time, note-taker, use of tape recorder, assistive technology, reader, books on tape.

Subject-area Tutoring Tutoring is offered in small groups for most subjects. Tutoring is provided collaboratively through on-campus or off-campus services via trained peer tutors.

Basic Skills Remediation Remediation is offered in class-size groups for computer skills, math, reading, study skills, and written language. Remediation is provided collaboratively through on-campus or off-campus services via regular education teachers.

Enrichment Programs for career planning, college survival skills, health and nutrition, learning strategies, math, practical computer skills, reading, stress management, study skills, test taking, time management, and written composition skills are provided collaboratively through on-campus or off-campus services. Credit is offered for career planning, college survival skills, health and nutrition, learning strategies, math, practical computer skills, reading, study skills, and written composition skills.

Application For admittance to the program or unit, students are required to apply to the program directly and provide a psychoeducational report. Upon application, materials documenting need for services should be sent only to the LD program or unit. Upon acceptance, documentation of need for services should be sent only to the LD program or unit. *Application deadline (institutional):* Continuous. *Application deadline (LD program):* Rolling/continuous for fall and rolling/continuous for spring.

Written Policies Written policy regarding general/basic LD accommodations is available on the program Web site. Written policies regarding course substitutions, general/basic LD accommodations, and substitutions and waivers of graduation requirements are available through the program or unit directly.

Hill College of the Hill Junior College District
Student Support Services

PO Box 619
Hillsboro, TX 76645-0619
http://www.hill-college.cc.tx.us/
Contact: Phone: 254-582-2555.

Student Support Services The program or unit includes 4 full-time staff members. Counselors and remediation/learning specialists are provided collaboratively through on-campus or off-campus services.

Unique Aids and Services Aids, services, or accommodations include advocates, career counseling, digital textbooks, and weekly meetings with faculty.

Subject-area Tutoring Tutoring is offered one-on-one and in small groups for most subjects. Tutoring is provided collaboratively through on-campus or off-campus services via trained peer tutors.

Basic Skills Remediation Remediation is offered in class-size groups for math, reading, and spelling. Remediation is provided collaboratively through on-campus or off-campus services via computer-based instruction and regular education teachers.

Enrichment Programs for career planning, college survival skills, learning strategies, math, reading, stress management, study skills, test taking, time management, and written composition skills are provided collaboratively through on-campus or off-campus services. Credit is offered for career planning, college survival skills, learning strategies, math, reading, stress management, study skills, test taking, time management, and written composition skills.

Application For admittance to the program or unit, students are required to provide a psychoeducational report (5 years old or less). It is recommended that students provide documentation of high school services. Upon application, materials documenting need for services should be sent only to the LD program or unit. Upon acceptance, documentation of need for services should be sent only to the LD program or unit. *Application deadline (institutional):* Continuous. *Application deadline (LD program):* Rolling/continuous for fall and rolling/continuous for spring.

Written Policies Written policies regarding course substitutions, general/basic LD accommodations, grade forgiveness, reduced course loads, substitutions and waivers of admissions requirements, and substitutions and waivers of graduation requirements are outlined in the school's catalog/handbook.

Hillsborough Community College
Disability Services

PO Box 31127
Tampa, FL 33631-3127
http://www.hccfl.edu/student/services/disabled.html
Contact: Ms. Kelly Irene Oliver, Learning Disability Specialist. Phone: 813-253-7514. Fax: 813-253-7336. E-mail: koliver@hccfl.edu. Head of LD Program: Ms. Denise Giarrusso, Coordinator of Office of Services for Students with Disabilities. Phone: 813-253-7914. Fax: 813-253-7910. E-mail: dgiarrusso@hccfl.edu.

Disability Services Approximately 800 registered undergraduate students were served during 2002-03. The program or unit includes 3 full-time and 65 part-time staff members. LD specialists, professional tutors, remediation/learning specialists, skill tutors, strategy tutors, trained peer tutors, and other are provided through the program or unit. Academic advisers and counselors are provided collaboratively through on-campus or off-campus services.

Unique Aids and Services Aids, services, or accommodations include advocates.

Subject-area Tutoring Tutoring is offered one-on-one for most subjects. Tutoring is provided through the program or unit via LD specialists, professional tutors, and trained peer tutors. Tutoring is also provided collaboratively through on-campus or off-campus services via professional tutors and trained peer tutors.

Basic Skills Remediation Remediation is offered one-on-one for auditory processing, computer skills, learning strategies, math, reading, social skills, spelling, spoken language, study skills, time management, visual processing, and written language. Remediation is provided through the program or unit via LD specialists, professional tutors, and trained peer tutors. Remediation is also provided collaboratively through on-campus or off-campus services via professional tutors and trained peer tutors.

Enrichment Enrichment programs are available through the program or unit for learning strategies, math, oral communication skills, practical computer skills, reading, self-advocacy, stress management, study skills, test taking, time management, vocabulary development, and written composition skills. Programs for career planning, college survival skills, health and nutrition, math, oral communication skills, practical computer skills, reading, self-advocacy, stress management, study skills, test taking, time management, vocabulary development, and written composition skills are provided collaboratively through on-campus or off-campus services. Credit is offered for career planning, college survival skills, health and nutrition, math, oral communication skills, practical computer skills, reading, stress management, study skills, test taking, time management, vocabulary development, and written composition skills.

Application For admittance to the program or unit, students are required to apply to the program directly and provide a psychoeducational report. It is recommended that students provide documentation of high school services. Upon application, materials documenting need for services should be sent only to the LD program or unit. Upon acceptance, documentation of need for services should be sent only to the LD program or unit. *Application deadline (institutional):* Continuous. *Application deadline (LD program):* Rolling/continuous for fall and rolling/continuous for spring.

Written Policies Written policies regarding course substitutions, general/basic LD accommodations, and substitutions and waivers of admissions requirements are available on the program Web site. Written policies regarding course substitutions, general/basic LD accommodations, and substitutions and waivers of admissions requirements are outlined in the school's catalog/handbook.

Hinds Community College
Disability Support Services

PO Box 1100
Raymond, MS 39154-1100
http://www.hindscc.edu

Contact: Ms. Carol Kelley, Coordinator of Disability Support Services. Phone: 601-857-3310. Fax: 601-857-3482. E-mail: ckelley@hindscc.edu.

Disability Support Services The program or unit includes 10 full-time and 8 part-time staff members. Professional tutors and trained peer tutors are provided through the program or unit. Academic advisers, coaches, counselors, and diagnostic specialists are provided collaboratively through on-campus or off-campus services.

Subject-area Tutoring Tutoring is offered one-on-one for all subjects. Tutoring is provided through the program or unit via professional tutors and trained peer tutors. Tutoring is also provided collaboratively through on-campus or off-campus services via computer-based instruction.

Application For admittance to the program or unit, students are required to apply to the program directly and provide a psychoeducational report. Upon application, materials documenting need for services should be sent only to the LD program or unit. Upon acceptance, documentation of need for services should be sent only to the LD program or unit. *Application deadline (institutional):* Continuous. *Application deadline (LD program):* Rolling/continuous for fall and rolling/continuous for spring.

Written Policies Written policies regarding course substitutions, general/basic LD accommodations, and reduced course loads are available on the program Web site. Written policy regarding general/basic LD accommodations is outlined in the school's catalog/handbook. Written policies regarding course substitutions, general/basic LD accommodations, and reduced course loads are available through the program or unit directly.

Hocking College
Access Center, Office of Disability Services

3301 Hocking Parkway
Nelsonville, OH 45764-9588
http://www.hocking.edu/

Contact: Ms. Kim Forbes Powell, Education Coordinator for Students with Disabilities. Phone: 740-753-3591 Ext. 2230. Fax: 740-753-4097. E-mail: forbes_k@hocking.edu.

Access Center, Office of Disability Services Approximately 250 registered undergraduate students were served during 2002-03. The program or unit includes 2 full-time and 2 part-time staff members. LD specialists, professional tutors, and special education teachers are provided through the program or unit. Academic advisers, counselors, remediation/learning specialists, skill tutors, and strategy tutors are provided collaboratively through on-campus or off-campus services.

Unique Aids and Services Aids, services, or accommodations include priority registration.

Subject-area Tutoring Tutoring is offered one-on-one and in small groups for most subjects. Tutoring is provided through the program or unit via computer-based instruction, LD specialists, and professional tutors. Tutoring is also provided collaboratively through on-campus or off-campus services via computer-based instruction and trained peer tutors.

Diagnostic Testing Testing for math, reading, and written language is provided collaboratively through on-campus or off-campus services.

Basic Skills Remediation Remediation is offered one-on-one, in small groups, and in class-size groups for computer skills, learning strategies, math, reading, social skills, spelling, study skills, time management, and written language. Remediation is provided collaboratively through on-campus or off-campus services via computer-based instruction and regular education teachers.

Enrichment Programs for career planning, learning strategies, math, oral communication skills, practical computer skills, reading, stress management, study skills, test taking, time management, vocabulary development, and written composition skills are provided collaboratively through on-campus or off-campus services. Credit is offered for learning strategies, math, oral communication skills, practical computer skills, reading, stress management, study skills, test taking, time management, vocabulary development, and written composition skills.

Application For admittance to the program or unit, students are required to provide documentation of high school services and provide documentation from BVR, MD, psychiatrist/psychologist, audiologist, ophthalmologist/optometrist. It is recommended that students provide a psychoeducational report. Upon application, materials documenting need for services should be sent only to the LD program or unit. Upon acceptance, documentation of need for services should be sent only to the LD program or unit. *Application deadline (institutional):* Continuous. *Application deadline (LD program):* Rolling/continuous for fall and rolling/continuous for spring.

Written Policies Written policy regarding general/basic LD accommodations is available on the program Web site. Written policy regarding general/basic LD accommodations is outlined in the school's catalog/handbook. Written policy regarding general/basic LD accommodations is available through the program or unit directly.

Housatonic Community College

900 Lafayette Boulevard
Bridgeport, CT 06604-4704
http://www.hctc.commnet.edu/

Contact: Phone: 203-332-5000.

The program or unit includes 1 full-time staff member. Academic advisers, counselors, diagnostic specialists, professional tutors, regular education teachers, trained peer tutors, and other are provided collaboratively through on-campus or off-campus services.

Orientation The program or unit offers an optional 1-evening orientation for new students before registration.

Unique Aids and Services Aids, services, or accommodations include faculty training, parent workshops, priority registration, personal counseling as it relates to school success.

Housatonic Community College (continued)

Subject-area Tutoring Tutoring is offered one-on-one and in small groups for most subjects. Tutoring is provided through the program or unit via LD specialists. Tutoring is also provided collaboratively through on-campus or off-campus services via computer-based instruction, graduate assistants/students, professional tutors, trained peer tutors, and other.

Basic Skills Remediation Remediation is offered one-on-one and in small groups for math, reading, study skills, and written language. Remediation is provided collaboratively through on-campus or off-campus services via computer-based instruction, graduate assistants/students, professional tutors, regular education teachers, and trained peer tutors.

Enrichment Programs for college survival skills, health and nutrition, learning strategies, math, practical computer skills, reading, stress management, study skills, test taking, time management, and written composition skills are provided collaboratively through on-campus or off-campus services. Credit is offered for college survival skills, health and nutrition, learning strategies, math, practical computer skills, reading, study skills, test taking, time management, and written composition skills.

Student Organization Total Access Club consists of 10 members.

Application For admittance to the program or unit, students are required to apply to the program directly, provide a psychoeducational report (3 years old or less), provide documentation of high school services, and provide results of testing done outside of high school. Upon acceptance, documentation of need for services should be sent only to the LD program or unit. *Application deadline (institutional):* Continuous. *Application deadline (LD program):* Rolling/continuous for fall and rolling/continuous for spring.

Written Policies Written policy regarding general/basic LD accommodations is available on the program Web site. Written policy regarding general/basic LD accommodations is available through the program or unit directly.

Howard Community College
Disabled Student Services

10901 Little Patuxent Parkway

Columbia, MD 21044-3197

http://www.howardcc.edu/

Contact: Ms. Kathy McSweeney, Disability Support Services Counselor. Phone: 410-772-4606. Fax: 410-772-4499. E-mail: kmcsweeney@howardcc.edu.

Disabled Student Services Academic advisers and LD specialists are provided through the program or unit. Coaches, counselors, professional tutors, regular education teachers, remediation/learning specialists, skill tutors, strategy tutors, and trained peer tutors are provided collaboratively through on-campus or off-campus services.

Orientation The program or unit offers an optional half-day orientation for new students before classes begin and during registration.

Summer Program To help prepare for the demands of college, there is an optional 6-week summer program prior to entering the school.

Unique Aids and Services Aids, services, or accommodations include faculty training, assistive and adaptive technology training.

Subject-area Tutoring Tutoring is offered one-on-one and in small groups for most subjects. Tutoring is provided through the program or unit via LD specialists. Tutoring is also provided collaboratively through on-campus or off-campus services via computer-based instruction, graduate assistants/students, professional tutors, trained peer tutors, and other.

Basic Skills Remediation Remediation is offered one-on-one and in small groups for computer skills, learning strategies, math, reading, study skills, time management, and written language. Remediation is provided through the program or unit via LD specialists. Remediation is also provided collaboratively through on-campus or off-campus services via computer-based instruction, graduate assistants/students, professional tutors, regular education teachers, and trained peer tutors.

Enrichment Programs for career planning, college survival skills, health and nutrition, learning strategies, math, oral communication skills, practical computer skills, reading, self-advocacy, stress management, study skills, test taking, time management, vocabulary development, and written composition skills are provided collaboratively through on-campus or off-campus services. Credit is offered for career planning, college survival skills, health and nutrition, learning strategies, math, oral communication skills, practical computer skills, reading, study skills, vocabulary development, and written composition skills.

Application For admittance to the program or unit, students are required to provide a psychoeducational report. It is recommended that students apply to the program directly and provide documentation of high school services. Upon acceptance, documentation of need for services should be sent only to the LD program or unit. *Application deadline (institutional):* Continuous. *Application deadline (LD program):* Rolling/continuous for fall and rolling/continuous for spring.

Written Policies Written policies regarding course substitutions, general/basic LD accommodations, reduced course loads, substitutions and waivers of admissions requirements, and substitutions and waivers of graduation requirements are available on the program Web site. Written policy regarding general/basic LD accommodations is outlined in the school's catalog/handbook. Written policies regarding course substitutions, reduced course loads, substitutions and waivers of admissions requirements, and substitutions and waivers of graduation requirements are available through the program or unit directly.

Illinois Valley Community College
Special Populations Office

815 North Orlando Smith Avenue

Oglesby, IL 61348-9692

http://www.ivcc.edu/

Contact: Tina Hardy, Special Populations Coordinator. Phone: 815-224-0284. Fax: 815-224-3033. E-mail: tina_hardy@ivcc.edu.

Special Populations Office Approximately 85 registered undergraduate students were served during 2002-03. The program or unit includes 2 part-time staff members. Diagnostic specialists, LD specialists, remediation/learning specialists, and special education teachers are provided through the program or unit. Academic advisers, counselors, diagnostic specialists, graduate assistants/students, LD specialists, regular education teachers, remediation/learning specialists, special education teachers, and trained peer tutors are provided collaboratively through on-campus or off-campus services.

Orientation The program or unit offers a mandatory 2-hour orientation for new students before registration and individually by special arrangement.

Unique Aids and Services Aids, services, or accommodations include priority registration and weekly meetings with faculty.

Subject-area Tutoring Tutoring is offered one-on-one for some subjects. Tutoring is provided through the program or unit via LD specialists. Tutoring is also provided collaboratively through on-campus or off-campus services via computer-based instruction, graduate assistants/students, and trained peer tutors.

Diagnostic Testing Testing is provided through the program or unit for auditory processing, handwriting, intelligence, learning strategies, learning styles, math, neuropsychological, reading, spelling, spoken language, study skills, visual processing, and written language. Testing for auditory processing, intelligence, math, neuropsychological, personality, reading, social skills, spelling, spoken language, visual processing, and written language is provided collaboratively through on-campus or off-campus services.

Basic Skills Remediation Remediation is offered in small groups and in class-size groups for learning strategies, math, reading, spelling, study skills, time management, and written language. Remediation is provided through the program or unit via special education teachers. Remediation is also provided collaboratively through on-campus or off-campus services via regular education teachers.

Enrichment Enrichment programs are available through the program or unit for learning strategies, study skills, test taking, and time management.

Application For admittance to the program or unit, students are required to apply to the program directly, provide a psychoeducational report, and provide documentation of high school services. Upon application, materials documenting need for services should be sent only to the LD program or unit. Upon acceptance, documentation of need for services should be sent only to the LD program or unit. *Application deadline (institutional):* Continuous. *Application deadline (LD program):* Rolling/continuous for fall.

Written Policies Written policy regarding general/basic LD accommodations is available through the program or unit directly.

Imperial Valley College
Disabled Student Programs and Services

PO Box 158, 380 East Aten Road
Imperial, CA 92251-0158
http://www.imperial.edu

Contact: Ms. Raquel Garcia, Instructional Specialist. Phone: 760-355-6312. Fax: 760-355-6132. E-mail: raquel.garcia@imperial.edu. Head of LD Program: Mr. Ted Ceasar, Director. Phone: 760-355-6312. Fax: 760-355-6132. E-mail: ted.ceasar@imperial.edu.

Disabled Student Programs and Services Approximately 200 registered undergraduate students were served during 2002-03. The program or unit includes 6 full-time and 4 part-time staff members. Academic advisers, counselors, diagnostic specialists, LD special-

ists, professional tutors, regular education teachers, remediation/learning specialists, skill tutors, strategy tutors, and trained peer tutors are provided through the program or unit. Academic advisers, counselors, professional tutors, and regular education teachers are provided collaboratively through on-campus or off-campus services.

Unique Aids and Services Aids, services, or accommodations include digital textbooks, faculty training, and priority registration.

Subject-area Tutoring Tutoring is offered one-on-one and in small groups for all subjects. Tutoring is provided through the program or unit via trained peer tutors. Tutoring is also provided collaboratively through on-campus or off-campus services via trained peer tutors.

Diagnostic Testing Testing is provided through the program or unit for auditory processing, intelligence, learning strategies, learning styles, math, reading, spelling, spoken language, visual processing, and written language.

Enrichment Enrichment programs are available through the program or unit for health and nutrition, learning strategies, medication management, practical computer skills, study skills, and test taking. Programs for career planning, college survival skills, math, reading, and study skills are provided collaboratively through on-campus or off-campus services. Credit is offered for college survival skills, math, practical computer skills, and reading.

Application For admittance to the program or unit, students are required to provide a psychoeducational report (3 years old or less). It is recommended that students provide documentation of high school services. Upon application, materials documenting need for services should be sent only to the LD program or unit. Upon acceptance, documentation of need for services should be sent to both admissions and the LD program or unit. *Application deadline (institutional):* Continuous. *Application deadline (LD program):* Rolling/continuous for fall and rolling/continuous for spring.

Written Policies Written policies regarding course substitutions, general/basic LD accommodations, grade forgiveness, reduced course loads, substitutions and waivers of admissions requirements, and substitutions and waivers of graduation requirements are available through the program or unit directly.

Indian River Community College
Student Disability Services

3209 Virginia Avenue
Fort Pierce, FL 34981-5596
http://www.ircc.cc.fl.us/support/stservices/disabil.html

Contact: Ms. Rhoda J. Brant, Counselor. Phone: 772-462-4328. Fax: 772-462-4699. E-mail: rbrant@ircc.edu.

Student Disability Services Approximately 130 registered undergraduate students were served during 2002-03. The program or unit includes 2 full-time staff members and 1 part-time staff member. Academic advisers and counselors are provided through the program or unit. Academic advisers, counselors, diagnostic specialists, professional tutors, regular education teachers, trained peer tutors, and other are provided collaboratively through on-campus or off-campus services.

Unique Aids and Services Aids, services, or accommodations include career counseling.

Indian River Community College (continued)

Subject-area Tutoring Tutoring is offered in small groups for some subjects. Tutoring is provided collaboratively through on-campus or off-campus services via computer-based instruction, professional tutors, and trained peer tutors.

Diagnostic Testing Testing for learning strategies, learning styles, math, motor skills, personality, reading, spelling, study skills, and written language is provided collaboratively through on-campus or off-campus services.

Basic Skills Remediation Remediation is offered in small groups for math, reading, spelling, and written language. Remediation is provided collaboratively through on-campus or off-campus services via computer-based instruction, professional tutors, regular education teachers, and trained peer tutors.

Enrichment Programs for career planning, college survival skills, health and nutrition, learning strategies, math, oral communication skills, practical computer skills, reading, self-advocacy, stress management, study skills, test taking, time management, vocabulary development, written composition skills, and other are provided collaboratively through on-campus or off-campus services. Credit is offered for career planning, college survival skills, health and nutrition, learning strategies, math, oral communication skills, practical computer skills, reading, self-advocacy, stress management, study skills, test taking, time management, vocabulary development, written composition skills, and other.

Application For admittance to the program or unit, students are required to apply to the program directly, provide a psychoeducational report, and provide documentation of high school services. Upon application, materials documenting need for services should be sent only to the LD program or unit. Upon acceptance, documentation of need for services should be sent only to the LD program or unit. *Application deadline (institutional):* Continuous. *Application deadline (LD program):* Rolling/continuous for fall and rolling/continuous for spring.

Written Policies Written policies regarding course substitutions, general/basic LD accommodations, reduced course loads, substitutions and waivers of admissions requirements, and substitutions and waivers of graduation requirements are available on the program Web site. Written policies regarding course substitutions, general/basic LD accommodations, reduced course loads, substitutions and waivers of admissions requirements, and substitutions and waivers of graduation requirements are outlined in the school's catalog/handbook. Written policies regarding course substitutions, general/basic LD accommodations, reduced course loads, substitutions and waivers of admissions requirements, and substitutions and waivers of graduation requirements are available through the program or unit directly.

Inver Hills Community College
Disability Services Office

2500 East 80th Street
Inver Grove Heights, MN 55076-3224
http://www.inverhills.edu/dss/
Contact: Phone: 651-450-8500. Fax: 651-450-8679.

Disability Services Office The program or unit includes 1 full-time and 1 part-time staff member. Trained peer tutors are provided through the program or unit. Academic advisers, counselors, professional tutors, and regular education teachers are provided collaboratively through on-campus or off-campus services.

Application For admittance to the program or unit, students are required to apply to the program directly and provide a psychoeducational report (3 years old or less). Upon application, materials documenting need for services should be sent only to the LD program or unit. *Application deadline (institutional):* Continuous. *Application deadline (LD program):* Rolling/continuous for fall and rolling/continuous for spring.

Written Policies Written policy regarding general/basic LD accommodations is available on the program Web site. Written policy regarding general/basic LD accommodations is outlined in the school's catalog/handbook. Written policy regarding general/basic LD accommodations is available through the program or unit directly.

Iowa Central Community College

330 Avenue M
Fort Dodge, IA 50501-5798
http://www.iccc.cc.ia.us/
Contact: Mrs. Heather Lundberg, Special Populations Coordinator. Phone: 515-576-0099 Ext. 2245. E-mail: lundberg@triton.iccc.cc.ia.us.

Approximately 70 registered undergraduate students were served during 2002-03. The program or unit includes 1 full-time staff member. Academic advisers, coaches, counselors, professional tutors, and regular education teachers are provided collaboratively through on-campus or off-campus services.

Unique Aids and Services Aids, services, or accommodations include advocates and priority registration.

Subject-area Tutoring Tutoring is offered one-on-one for most subjects. Tutoring is provided through the program or unit via graduate assistants/students and professional tutors. Tutoring is also provided collaboratively through on-campus or off-campus services via graduate assistants/students and professional tutors.

Basic Skills Remediation Remediation is available for computer skills, math, reading, spelling, study skills, time management, and written language. Remediation is provided through the program or unit via graduate assistants/students and professional tutors. Remediation is also provided collaboratively through on-campus or off-campus services via graduate assistants/students and professional tutors.

Enrichment Enrichment programs are available through the program or unit for career planning, college survival skills, learning strategies, math, oral communication skills, practical computer skills, reading, self-advocacy, study skills, test taking, time management, and written composition skills. Programs for career planning, college survival skills, learning strategies, math, oral communication skills, practical computer skills, reading, study skills, test taking, time management, and written composition skills are provided collaboratively through on-campus or off-campus services. Credit is offered for college survival skills, math, oral communication skills, practical computer skills, reading, study skills, and written composition skills.

Application For admittance to the program or unit, students are required to provide documentation of high school services. It is recommended that students provide a psychoeducational report. Upon application, materials documenting need for services should be sent to both admissions and the LD program or unit. Upon acceptance, documentation of need for services should be sent only to the LD program or unit. *Application deadline (institutional):* Continuous. *Application deadline (LD program):* Rolling/continuous for fall and rolling/continuous for spring.

Written Policies Written policy regarding general/basic LD accommodations is available on the program Web site. Written policy regarding general/basic LD accommodations is outlined in the school's catalog/handbook. Written policy regarding general/basic LD accommodations is available through the program or unit directly.

Iowa Western Community College

2700 College Road, Box 4-C
Council Bluffs, IA 51502
http://www.iwcc.edu/
Contact: Phone: 712-325-3200. Fax: 712-325-3720.

Approximately 60 registered undergraduate students were served during 2002-03. The program or unit includes 1 full-time staff member. Academic advisers and counselors are provided through the program or unit. Academic advisers, counselors, and remediation/learning specialists are provided collaboratively through on-campus or off-campus services.

Subject-area Tutoring Tutoring is offered one-on-one and in small groups for some subjects. Tutoring is provided collaboratively through on-campus or off-campus services via computer-based instruction, professional tutors, and trained peer tutors.

Basic Skills Remediation Remediation is offered in class-size groups for math, reading, and written language. Remediation is provided collaboratively through on-campus or off-campus services via regular education teachers.

Enrichment Programs for career planning, college survival skills, stress management, study skills, and test taking are provided collaboratively through on-campus or off-campus services. Credit is offered for college survival skills.

Application For admittance to the program or unit, students are required to apply to the program directly and provide a psychoeducational report (5 years old or less). It is recommended that students provide documentation of high school services. Upon application, materials documenting need for services should be sent only to the LD program or unit. Upon acceptance, documentation of need for services should be sent only to the LD program or unit. *Application deadline (institutional):* Continuous. *Application deadline (LD program):* Rolling/continuous for fall and rolling/continuous for spring.

Isothermal Community College
Disability Services

PO Box 804
Spindale, NC 28160-0804

http://www.isothermal.edu/
Contact: Phone: 828-286-3636. Fax: 828-286-8109.

Disability Services The program or unit includes 1 full-time staff member. Services are provided through the program or unit.

Basic Skills Remediation Remediation is offered in class-size groups for math, reading, and written language. Remediation is provided collaboratively through on-campus or off-campus services via regular education teachers.

Application For admittance to the program or unit, students are required to provide a psychoeducational report (3 years old or less). It is recommended that students provide documentation of high school services. Upon acceptance, documentation of need for services should be sent only to the LD program or unit. *Application deadline (institutional):* Continuous. *Application deadline (LD program):* Rolling/continuous for fall and rolling/continuous for spring.

Written Policies Written policies regarding course substitutions, general/basic LD accommodations, and grade forgiveness are outlined in the school's catalog/handbook.

Itasca Community College
Office for Students with Disabilities

1851 Highway 169 East
Grand Rapids, MN 55744

http://www.itascacc.net/studentservices/disability.asp

Contact: Mrs. Ann Marie Vidovic, Director of Disability Services. Phone: 218-327-4167. Fax: 218-327-4299. E-mail: avidovic@it.cc.mn.us.

Office for Students with Disabilities Approximately 40 registered undergraduate students were served during 2002-03. The program or unit includes 1 full-time staff member. Academic advisers, coaches, counselors, LD specialists, professional tutors, skill tutors, and strategy tutors are provided collaboratively through on-campus or off-campus services.

Orientation The program or unit offers an optional 1 to 3-hour orientation for new students before registration, before classes begin, during summer prior to enrollment, during registration, after classes begin, and individually by special arrangement.

Summer Program To help prepare for the demands of college, there is an optional summer program prior to entering the school.

Unique Aids and Services Aids, services, or accommodations include advocates, career counseling, and priority registration.

Subject-area Tutoring Tutoring is offered one-on-one, in small groups, and in class-size groups for most subjects. Tutoring is provided collaboratively through on-campus or off-campus services via computer-based instruction, graduate assistants/students, LD specialists, professional tutors, and trained peer tutors.

Diagnostic Testing Testing for learning strategies, learning styles, math, reading, study skills, and written language is provided collaboratively through on-campus or off-campus services.

Basic Skills Remediation Remediation is offered one-on-one, in small groups, and in class-size groups for auditory processing, computer skills, learning strategies, math, reading, social skills, spelling, spoken language, study skills, time management, and writ-

Itasca Community College (continued)

ten language. Remediation is provided collaboratively through on-campus or off-campus services via computer-based instruction, graduate assistants/students, LD specialists, professional tutors, and trained peer tutors.

Enrichment Programs for career planning, college survival skills, health and nutrition, learning strategies, math, oral communication skills, practical computer skills, reading, self-advocacy, stress management, study skills, test taking, time management, and written composition skills are provided collaboratively through on-campus or off-campus services. Credit is offered for career planning, college survival skills, health and nutrition, learning strategies, math, oral communication skills, practical computer skills, reading, self-advocacy, stress management, study skills, test taking, time management, and written composition skills.

Application For admittance to the program or unit, students are required to provide a psychoeducational report (3 years old or less). It is recommended that students provide documentation of high school services. Upon application, materials documenting need for services should be sent only to the LD program or unit. *Application deadline (institutional):* Continuous. *Application deadline (LD program):* Rolling/continuous for fall and rolling/continuous for spring.

Written Policies Written policies regarding course substitutions, general/basic LD accommodations, reduced course loads, substitutions and waivers of admissions requirements, and substitutions and waivers of graduation requirements are available on the program Web site. Written policies regarding course substitutions, general/basic LD accommodations, reduced course loads, substitutions and waivers of admissions requirements, and substitutions and waivers of graduation requirements are outlined in the school's catalog/handbook. Written policies regarding general/basic LD accommodations and reduced course loads are available through the program or unit directly.

Ivy Tech State College-Central Indiana
Disability Support Services

1 West 26th Street, PO Box 1763
Indianapolis, IN 46206-1763
http://www.ivytech.edu/

Contact: Mrs. Jan Bennett, ACCESS Counselor and Intake Counselor for DSS. Phone: 317-921-4981. Fax: 317-921-4927. E-mail: jbennett@ivytech.edu.

Disability Support Services Approximately 100 registered undergraduate students were served during 2002-03. The program or unit includes 2 full-time and 2 part-time staff members. Professional tutors and special education teachers are provided through the program or unit. Academic advisers are provided collaboratively through on-campus or off-campus services.

Subject-area Tutoring Tutoring is offered one-on-one and in small groups for some subjects. Tutoring is provided through the program or unit via LD specialists and professional tutors.

Basic Skills Remediation Remediation is offered one-on-one and in small groups for math, reading, study skills, and written language. Remediation is provided through the program or unit via LD specialists and professional tutors.

Student Organization ICARE consists of 20 members.

Application For admittance to the program or unit, students are required to apply to the program directly and provide a psychoeducational report. It is recommended that students provide documentation of high school services. Upon application, materials documenting need for services should be sent only to the LD program or unit. *Application deadline (institutional):* Continuous.

Ivy Tech State College-Columbus

4475 Central Avenue
Columbus, IN 47203-1868
http://www.ivytech.edu/

Contact: Phone: 812-372-9925. Fax: 812-372-0311.

The program or unit includes 1 full-time staff member. Counselors and skill tutors are provided collaboratively through on-campus or off-campus services.

Unique Aids and Services Aids, services, or accommodations include digital textbooks, extended test time, tests read, note-taker/tape recorder, books on tape, separate environment.

Subject-area Tutoring Tutoring is offered one-on-one for some subjects. Tutoring is provided collaboratively through on-campus or off-campus services via professional tutors.

Basic Skills Remediation Remediation is offered one-on-one for math, spelling, study skills, and written language. Remediation is provided collaboratively through on-campus or off-campus services via professional tutors and regular education teachers.

Enrichment Programs for career planning, college survival skills, math, reading, study skills, test taking, time management, vocabulary development, and written composition skills are provided collaboratively through on-campus or off-campus services.

Application For admittance to the program or unit, students are required to provide a psychoeducational report. It is recommended that students apply to the program directly and provide documentation of high school services. Upon application, materials documenting need for services should be sent only to the LD program or unit. *Application deadline (institutional):* Continuous. *Application deadline (LD program):* Rolling/continuous for fall and rolling/continuous for spring.

Written Policies Written policy regarding general/basic LD accommodations is outlined in the school's catalog/handbook. Written policies regarding course substitutions, general/basic LD accommodations, grade forgiveness, reduced course loads, substitutions and waivers of admissions requirements, and substitutions and waivers of graduation requirements are available through the program or unit directly.

Ivy Tech State College-Eastcentral

4301 South Cowan Road, PO Box 3100
Muncie, IN 47302-9448
http://www.ivytech.edu/

Contact: Ms. Alison Hindman, Assistant Director of Student Support and Development. Phone: 765-289-2291 Ext. 388. Fax: 765-282-2414. E-mail: ahindman@ivytech.edu.

The program or unit includes 1 full-time staff member. Academic advisers, coaches, counselors, diagnostic specialists, remediation/learning specialists, skill tutors, and other are provided collaboratively through on-campus or off-campus services.

Orientation The program or unit offers before registration, before classes begin, and individually by special arrangement.

Subject-area Tutoring Tutoring is offered one-on-one and in small groups for some subjects. Tutoring is provided collaboratively through on-campus or off-campus services via computer-based instruction, trained peer tutors, and other.

Basic Skills Remediation Remediation is offered in class-size groups for learning strategies, math, reading, spelling, study skills, time management, and written language. Remediation is provided collaboratively through on-campus or off-campus services via computer-based instruction, regular education teachers, trained peer tutors, and other.

Enrichment Programs for career planning, learning strategies, math, study skills, time management, and written composition skills are provided collaboratively through on-campus or off-campus services.

Application It is recommended that students provide documentation of high school services. Upon application, materials documenting need for services should be sent only to the LD program or unit. *Application deadline (institutional):* Continuous. *Application deadline (LD program):* Rolling/continuous for fall and rolling/continuous for spring.

Written Policies Written policy regarding general/basic LD accommodations is outlined in the school's catalog/handbook. Written policy regarding general/basic LD accommodations is available through the program or unit directly.

Ivy Tech State College-Kokomo
Disability Support Services (DSS)

1815 East Morgan St, PO Box 1373
Kokomo, IN 46903-1373
http://www.ivytech.edu/

Contact: Ms. Cheryl Locke, Assistant Director of Student Support and Development. Phone: 765-459-0561 Ext. 349. Fax: 765-454-5111. E-mail: clocke@ivytech.edu.

Disability Support Services (DSS) Approximately 50 registered undergraduate students were served during 2002-03. The program or unit includes 3 full-time staff members and 1 part-time staff member. LD specialists, professional tutors, and strategy tutors are provided through the program or unit. Academic advisers, diagnostic specialists, regular education teachers, and skill tutors are provided collaboratively through on-campus or off-campus services.

Unique Aids and Services Aids, services, or accommodations include advocates and career counseling.

Subject-area Tutoring Tutoring is offered one-on-one and in small groups for some subjects. Tutoring is provided collaboratively through on-campus or off-campus services via computer-based instruction, LD specialists, professional tutors, and trained peer tutors.

Basic Skills Remediation Remediation is offered in class-size groups for math, reading, and written language. Remediation is provided collaboratively through on-campus or off-campus services via computer-based instruction and regular education teachers.

Enrichment Enrichment programs are available through the program or unit for self-advocacy, study skills, test taking, and time management. Programs for career planning, college survival skills, health and nutrition, learning strategies, math, medication management, oral communication skills, practical computer skills, reading, self-advocacy, stress management, study skills, test taking, time management, vocabulary development, and written composition skills are provided collaboratively through on-campus or off-campus services. Credit is offered for math.

Application For admittance to the program or unit, students are required to apply to the program directly and provide a psychoeducational report (5 years old or less). It is recommended that students provide documentation of high school services and provide exit case conference report. Upon application, materials documenting need for services should be sent only to the LD program or unit. Upon acceptance, documentation of need for services should be sent only to the LD program or unit. *Application deadline (institutional):* Continuous. *Application deadline (LD program):* Rolling/continuous for fall and rolling/continuous for spring.

Written Policies Written policies regarding general/basic LD accommodations and grade forgiveness are available on the program Web site. Written policies regarding general/basic LD accommodations, grade forgiveness, and substitutions and waivers of graduation requirements are outlined in the school's catalog/handbook. Written policy regarding general/basic LD accommodations is available through the program or unit directly.

Ivy Tech State College-Lafayette

3101 South Creasy Lane
Lafayette, IN 47905-5266
http://www.ivytech.edu/

Contact: Mr. Tony L. Criswell, Disability Services Adviser. Phone: 765-772-9245. Fax: 765-772-9214. E-mail: tcriswel@ivytech.edu.

The program or unit includes 1 full-time and 1 part-time staff member. Academic advisers are provided through the program or unit. Regular education teachers and remediation/learning specialists are provided collaboratively through on-campus or off-campus services.

Orientation The program or unit offers an optional orientation for new students individually by special arrangement.

Summer Program To help prepare for the demands of college, there is an optional 11-week summer program prior to entering the school.

Unique Aids and Services Aids, services, or accommodations include career counseling and priority registration.

Subject-area Tutoring Tutoring is offered one-on-one and in small groups for most subjects. Tutoring is provided collaboratively through on-campus or off-campus services via computer-based instruction, graduate assistants/students, LD specialists, professional tutors, and trained peer tutors.

Ivy Tech State College-Lafayette (continued)

Basic Skills Remediation Remediation is offered in small groups and in class-size groups for computer skills, learning strategies, math, reading, spelling, study skills, time management, and written language. Remediation is provided through the program or unit via computer-based instruction, LD specialists, and professional tutors. Remediation is also provided collaboratively through on-campus or off-campus services via computer-based instruction.

Enrichment Programs for career planning, college survival skills, learning strategies, stress management, study skills, test taking, and time management are provided collaboratively through on-campus or off-campus services. Credit is offered for career planning, college survival skills, learning strategies, stress management, study skills, test taking, and time management.

Fees *Summer Program* fee is $221.

Application For admittance to the program or unit, students are required to apply to the program directly and provide a psychoeducational report (3 years old or less). It is recommended that students provide documentation of high school services. Upon application, materials documenting need for services should be sent only to the LD program or unit. Upon acceptance, documentation of need for services should be sent only to the LD program or unit. *Application deadline (institutional):* Continuous. *Application deadline (LD program):* 7/20 for fall. 12/10 for spring.

Written Policies Written policies regarding general/basic LD accommodations and substitutions and waivers of admissions requirements are outlined in the school's catalog/handbook. Written policies regarding course substitutions, general/basic LD accommodations, reduced course loads, substitutions and waivers of admissions requirements, and substitutions and waivers of graduation requirements are available through the program or unit directly.

Ivy Tech State College-North Central

220 Dean Johnson Boulevard

South Bend, IN 46601

http://www.ivytech.edu/

Contact: Phone: 574-289-7001. Fax: 574-236-7181.

The program or unit includes 1 full-time and 1 part-time staff member. Counselors, LD specialists, and professional tutors are provided through the program or unit.

Subject-area Tutoring Tutoring is offered one-on-one for most subjects. Tutoring is provided through the program or unit via computer-based instruction, LD specialists, professional tutors, and trained peer tutors. Tutoring is also provided collaboratively through on-campus or off-campus services via computer-based instruction, professional tutors, and trained peer tutors.

Basic Skills Remediation Remediation is offered in class-size groups for learning strategies, math, reading, spelling, and study skills. Remediation is provided collaboratively through on-campus or off-campus services via regular education teachers.

Enrichment Programs for college survival skills, learning strategies, math, reading, study skills, and written composition skills are provided collaboratively through on-campus or off-campus services. Credit is offered for college survival skills, learning strategies, math, reading, study skills, and written composition skills.

Application For admittance to the program or unit, students are required to provide a psychoeducational report (3 years old or less) and provide documentation of high school services. Upon application, materials documenting need for services should be sent only to the LD program or unit. Upon acceptance, documentation of need for services should be sent only to the LD program or unit. *Application deadline (institutional):* Continuous. *Application deadline (LD program):* Rolling/continuous for fall and rolling/continuous for spring.

Written Policies Written policies regarding course substitutions, general/basic LD accommodations, substitutions and waivers of admissions requirements, and substitutions and waivers of graduation requirements are outlined in the school's catalog/handbook. Written policy regarding general/basic LD accommodations is available through the program or unit directly.

Ivy Tech State College-Southcentral

8204 Highway 311

Sellersburg, IN 47172-1829

http://www.ivytech.edu/

Contact: Denise Shaw, Assistant Director of Support and Disability Services. Phone: 812-246-3301 Ext. 4197. Fax: 812-246-9905. E-mail: dshaw@ivytech.edu.

Approximately 50 registered undergraduate students were served during 2002-03. The program or unit includes 1 full-time staff member. Counselors are provided collaboratively through on-campus or off-campus services.

Summer Program To help prepare for the demands of college, there is an optional 8-week summer program prior to entering the school. Degree credit will be earned.

Unique Aids and Services Aids, services, or accommodations include career counseling and priority registration.

Subject-area Tutoring Tutoring is offered one-on-one for most subjects. Tutoring is provided collaboratively through on-campus or off-campus services via graduate assistants/students, professional tutors, and trained peer tutors.

Basic Skills Remediation Remediation is offered in class-size groups for computer skills, learning strategies, math, reading, spelling, study skills, time management, and written language. Remediation is provided collaboratively through on-campus or off-campus services via computer-based instruction and regular education teachers.

Enrichment Programs for career planning, college survival skills, learning strategies, math, oral communication skills, practical computer skills, reading, stress management, study skills, test taking, time management, and written composition skills are provided collaboratively through on-campus or off-campus services. Credit is offered for college survival skills, learning strategies, math, oral communication skills, practical computer skills, reading, study skills, test taking, time management, and written composition skills.

Student Organization Campus Association to Raise Education (CARE) consists of 15 members.

Fees *Summer Program* fee is $221.

Application For admittance to the program or unit, students are required to provide a psychoeducational report. It is recommended that students provide documentation of high school services. Upon application, materials documenting need for services should be sent only to the LD program or unit. Upon acceptance, documentation of need for services should be sent only to the LD program or unit. *Application deadline (institutional):* Continuous.

Written Policies Written policy regarding general/basic LD accommodations is available on the program Web site. Written policy regarding general/basic LD accommodations is outlined in the school's catalog/handbook. Written policies regarding course substitutions, general/basic LD accommodations, grade forgiveness, reduced course loads, substitutions and waivers of admissions requirements, and substitutions and waivers of graduation requirements are available through the program or unit directly.

Ivy Tech State College-Southeast
Disability Support Services

590 Ivy Tech Drive, PO Box 209

Madison, IN 47250-1883

http://www.ivytech.edu/

Contact: Mr. Don Heiderman, Executive Dean. Phone: 812-265-2580 Ext. 4114. Fax: 812-265-4028. E-mail: dheiderm@ivytech.edu.

Disability Support Services Approximately 75 registered undergraduate students were served during 2002-03. The program or unit includes 2 part-time staff members. Counselors are provided through the program or unit.

Subject-area Tutoring Tutoring is offered one-on-one for most subjects. Tutoring is provided collaboratively through on-campus or off-campus services via trained peer tutors.

Diagnostic Testing Testing for math, reading, and written language is provided collaboratively through on-campus or off-campus services.

Basic Skills Remediation Remediation is offered in class-size groups for math, reading, spelling, study skills, time management, and written language. Remediation is provided collaboratively through on-campus or off-campus services via regular education teachers.

Enrichment Programs for math, practical computer skills, reading, study skills, test taking, time management, vocabulary development, and written composition skills are provided collaboratively through on-campus or off-campus services. Credit is offered for math, practical computer skills, reading, study skills, test taking, time management, vocabulary development, and written composition skills.

Application For admittance to the program or unit, students are required to provide documentation of high school services. It is recommended that students apply to the program directly. Upon application, materials documenting need for services should be sent only to admissions with institutional application materials. Upon acceptance, documentation of need for services should be sent only to the LD program or unit. *Application deadline (institutional):* Continuous. *Application deadline (LD program):* 5/20 for fall. 9/20 for spring.

Written Policies Written policy regarding general/basic LD accommodations is outlined in the school's catalog/handbook.

Ivy Tech State College-Southwest

3501 First Avenue

Evansville, IN 47710-3398

http://www.ivytech.edu/

Contact: Ms. Peg K. Ehlen, Professor Skills Advancement and Coordinator of Disability Services. Phone: 812-429-1386. Fax: 812-429-1423. E-mail: pehlen@ivytech.edu.

Approximately 40 registered undergraduate students were served during 2002-03. The program or unit includes 1 full-time and 1 part-time staff member. LD specialists are provided through the program or unit. LD specialists are provided collaboratively through on-campus or off-campus services.

Orientation The program or unit offers a mandatory 30-minute to 1-hour orientation for new students before registration, before classes begin, during summer prior to enrollment, during registration, after classes begin, and individually by special arrangement.

Unique Aids and Services Aids, services, or accommodations include advocates, career counseling, digital textbooks, and faculty training.

Subject-area Tutoring Tutoring is offered one-on-one and in small groups for most subjects. Tutoring is provided through the program or unit via LD specialists. Tutoring is also provided collaboratively through on-campus or off-campus services via computer-based instruction, graduate assistants/students, professional tutors, and trained peer tutors.

Basic Skills Remediation Remediation is offered in small groups and in class-size groups for learning strategies, math, reading, spelling, study skills, time management, and written language. Remediation is provided collaboratively through on-campus or off-campus services via computer-based instruction, regular education teachers, and trained peer tutors.

Enrichment Enrichment programs are available through the program or unit for self-advocacy. Programs for career planning, college survival skills, health and nutrition, learning strategies, math, oral communication skills, practical computer skills, reading, self-advocacy, stress management, study skills, test taking, time management, and written composition skills are provided collaboratively through on-campus or off-campus services. Credit is offered for college survival skills, learning strategies, math, oral communication skills, practical computer skills, reading, study skills, test taking, time management, and written composition skills.

Application For admittance to the program or unit, students are required to provide a psychoeducational report (3 years old or less) and provide at least a month's notice for some services. It is recommended that students provide documentation of high school services. Upon application, materials documenting need for services should be sent only to the LD program or unit. Upon acceptance, documentation of need for services should be sent only to the LD program or unit. *Application deadline (institutional):* Continuous. *Application deadline (LD program):* Rolling/continuous for fall and rolling/continuous for spring.

Ivy Tech State College-Southwest (continued)

Written Policies Written policy regarding general/basic LD accommodations is available on the program Web site. Written policy regarding general/basic LD accommodations is outlined in the school's catalog/handbook. Written policies regarding course substitutions and general/basic LD accommodations are available through the program or unit directly.

Ivy Tech State College-Whitewater

2325 Chester Boulevard
Richmond, IN 47374-1220
http://www.ivytech.edu/
Contact: Mrs. Desiree Polk-Bland, Director of Student Support and Development. Phone: 765-966-2656 Ext. 334. Fax: 765-962-8741. E-mail: dpolk@ivytech.edu.

Approximately 100 registered undergraduate students were served during 2002-03. The program or unit includes 3 full-time staff members.
Unique Aids and Services Aids, services, or accommodations include advocates, career counseling, and faculty training.
Subject-area Tutoring Tutoring is offered one-on-one and in small groups for most subjects. Tutoring is provided collaboratively through on-campus or off-campus services via professional tutors.
Basic Skills Remediation Remediation is offered in class-size groups for computer skills, learning strategies, math, reading, study skills, and written language. Remediation is provided collaboratively through on-campus or off-campus services via regular education teachers.
Enrichment Programs for career planning, college survival skills, learning strategies, math, reading, stress management, study skills, test taking, time management, and written composition skills are provided collaboratively through on-campus or off-campus services.
Application For admittance to the program or unit, students are required to provide a psychoeducational report (3 years old or less) and provide a written request for accommodations every semester. It is recommended that students provide documentation of high school services. Upon acceptance, documentation of need for services should be sent only to the LD program or unit. *Application deadline (institutional):* Continuous. *Application deadline (LD program):* Rolling/continuous for fall and rolling/continuous for spring.
Written Policies Written policy regarding general/basic LD accommodations is available on the program Web site. Written policy regarding general/basic LD accommodations is outlined in the school's catalog/handbook. Written policy regarding general/basic LD accommodations is available through the program or unit directly.

Jefferson Community College
Jefferson Community College Scanlon Learning Skills Center

1220 Coffeen Street
Watertown, NY 13601

http://www.sunyjefferson.edu/

Contact: Sheree A. Trainham, Learning Skills Disability Specialist. Phone: 315-786-2200 Ext. 2335. E-mail: strainham@sunyjefferson.edu.

Jefferson Community College Scanlon Learning Skills Center Approximately 86 registered undergraduate students were served during 2002-03. The program or unit includes 1 full-time staff member. Counselors, diagnostic specialists, LD specialists, professional tutors, remediation/learning specialists, and trained peer tutors are provided through the program or unit. Academic advisers, counselors, diagnostic specialists, professional tutors, regular education teachers, and remediation/learning specialists are provided collaboratively through on-campus or off-campus services.
Orientation The program or unit offers before registration and individually by special arrangement.
Unique Aids and Services Aids, services, or accommodations include advocates, career counseling, faculty training, parent workshops, and weekly meetings with faculty.
Subject-area Tutoring Tutoring is offered one-on-one and in small groups for all subjects. Tutoring is provided through the program or unit via computer-based instruction, LD specialists, professional tutors, and trained peer tutors. Tutoring is also provided collaboratively through on-campus or off-campus services via computer-based instruction, professional tutors, and trained peer tutors.
Diagnostic Testing Testing for auditory processing, handwriting, intelligence, learning strategies, learning styles, math, reading, spelling, visual processing, and written language is provided collaboratively through on-campus or off-campus services.
Basic Skills Remediation Remediation is offered one-on-one, in small groups, and in class-size groups. Remediation is provided through the program or unit via LD specialists. Remediation is also provided collaboratively through on-campus or off-campus services via computer-based instruction, professional tutors, regular education teachers, and trained peer tutors.
Enrichment Enrichment programs are available through the program or unit for self-advocacy, stress management, study skills, test taking, and time management. Programs for career planning, college survival skills, health and nutrition, learning strategies, math, oral communication skills, practical computer skills, reading, stress management, study skills, test taking, time management, vocabulary development, and written composition skills are provided collaboratively through on-campus or off-campus services. Credit is offered for college survival skills, health and nutrition, learning strategies, math, oral communication skills, practical computer skills, reading, vocabulary development, and written composition skills.
Fees *Diagnostic Testing* fee is $0 to $300.
Application For admittance to the program or unit, students are required to provide a psychoeducational report (3 years old or less). It is recommended that students provide documentation of high school services. Upon application, materials documenting need for services should be sent only to the LD program or unit. Upon acceptance, documentation of need for services should be sent only to the LD program or unit. *Application deadline (institutional):* 9/6. *Application deadline (LD program):* Rolling/continuous for fall.
Written Policies Written policies regarding course substitutions, general/basic LD accommodations, reduced course loads, and substitutions and waivers of graduation requirements are outlined in the school's catalog/handbook.

Jefferson Community College

Access*Ability Resource Center (ARC)

109 East Broadway
Louisville, KY 40202-2005
http://www.jctc.kctcs.edu/
Contact: Ms. Terri F. Martin, Disability Resource Coordinator. Phone: 502-213-2449. Fax: 502-213-2479. E-mail: terrif.martin@kctcs.edu.

Access*Ability Resource Center (ARC) Approximately 250 registered undergraduate students were served during 2002-03. The program or unit includes 2 full-time staff members and 1 part-time staff member. Academic advisers, counselors, graduate assistants/ students, regular education teachers, skill tutors, and strategy tutors are provided collaboratively through on-campus or off-campus services.

Unique Aids and Services Aids, services, or accommodations include career counseling, digital textbooks, and priority registration.

Subject-area Tutoring Tutoring is offered one-on-one and in small groups. Tutoring is provided collaboratively through on-campus or off-campus services via computer-based instruction, graduate assistants/students, and trained peer tutors.

Basic Skills Remediation Remediation is offered one-on-one, in small groups, and in class-size groups for computer skills, reading, spelling, study skills, time management, and written language. Remediation is provided collaboratively through on-campus or off-campus services via computer-based instruction, graduate assistants/ students, professional tutors, regular education teachers, and trained peer tutors.

Enrichment Programs for career planning, college survival skills, health and nutrition, learning strategies, math, oral communication skills, practical computer skills, reading, stress management, study skills, test taking, time management, vocabulary development, and written composition skills are provided collaboratively through on-campus or off-campus services. Credit is offered for career planning, college survival skills, health and nutrition, math, oral communication skills, practical computer skills, reading, vocabulary development, and written composition skills.

Student Organization Disability Awareness Organization consists of 15 members.

Application For admittance to the program or unit, students are required to provide a psychoeducational report (3 years old or less). Upon application, materials documenting need for services should be sent only to the LD program or unit. Upon acceptance, documentation of need for services should be sent only to the LD program or unit. *Application deadline (institutional):* Continuous. *Application deadline (LD program):* Rolling/continuous for fall and rolling/continuous for spring.

Written Policies Written policy regarding general/basic LD accommodations is available on the program Web site. Written policies regarding course substitutions, general/basic LD accommodations, grade forgiveness, substitutions and waivers of admissions requirements, and substitutions and waivers of graduation requirements are outlined in the school's catalog/handbook. Written policies regarding course substitutions, general/basic LD accommodations, reduced course loads, substitutions and waivers of admissions requirements, and substitutions and waivers of graduation requirements are available through the program or unit directly.

Jefferson State Community College

2601 Carson Road
Birmingham, AL 35215-3098
http://www.jscc.cc.al.us/
Contact: Martha Smith, Director of ADA Office. Phone: 205-856-7731 Ext. 205. Fax: 205-856-7993. E-mail: marthas@jeffstateonline.com.

The program or unit includes 2 full-time staff members. Academic advisers, counselors, diagnostic specialists, LD specialists, skill tutors, and trained peer tutors are provided collaboratively through on-campus or off-campus services.

Orientation The program or unit offers a mandatory 1 to 2-hour orientation for new students individually by special arrangement.

Unique Aids and Services Aids, services, or accommodations include advocates, digital textbooks, and priority registration.

Subject-area Tutoring Tutoring is offered one-on-one and in small groups for some subjects. Tutoring is provided collaboratively through on-campus or off-campus services via computer-based instruction, professional tutors, and trained peer tutors.

Diagnostic Testing Testing for learning strategies, learning styles, math, and study skills is provided collaboratively through on-campus or off-campus services.

Enrichment Programs for career planning, college survival skills, learning strategies, oral communication skills, stress management, study skills, test taking, and time management are provided collaboratively through on-campus or off-campus services. Credit is offered for college survival skills.

Application For admittance to the program or unit, students are required to apply to the program directly and provide a psychoeducational report (3 years old or less). Upon application, materials documenting need for services should be sent only to the LD program or unit. Upon acceptance, documentation of need for services should be sent only to the LD program or unit. *Application deadline (institutional):* Continuous. *Application deadline (LD program):* Rolling/continuous for fall and rolling/continuous for spring.

Written Policies Written policies regarding course substitutions, general/basic LD accommodations, grade forgiveness, reduced course loads, substitutions and waivers of admissions requirements, and substitutions and waivers of graduation requirements are available on the program Web site. Written policies regarding course substitutions, general/basic LD accommodations, grade forgiveness, reduced course loads, substitutions and waivers of admissions requirements, and substitutions and waivers of graduation requirements are outlined in the school's catalog/handbook. Written policy regarding general/basic LD accommodations is available through the program or unit directly.

Johnson College

3427 North Main Avenue
Scranton, PA 18508-1495
http://www.johnson.edu/

Johnson College (continued)
Contact: Ms. Linda A. Learn, Assistant Director of Student Support Services. Phone: 570-342-6404 Ext. 131. Fax: 570-348-2181. E-mail: llearn@johnsoncollege.com.

The program or unit includes 3 full-time and 10 part-time staff members. Academic advisers, counselors, LD specialists, professional tutors, regular education teachers, remediation/learning specialists, and trained peer tutors are provided through the program or unit. Academic advisers and diagnostic specialists are provided collaboratively through on-campus or off-campus services.
Orientation The program or unit offers before classes begin and during summer prior to enrollment.
Summer Program To help prepare for the demands of college, there is a mandatory 6-week summer program prior to entering the school. Degree credit will be earned.
Unique Aids and Services Aids, services, or accommodations include career counseling, faculty training, mentoring, counseling.
Subject-area Tutoring Tutoring is offered one-on-one and in small groups for all subjects. Tutoring is provided through the program or unit via computer-based instruction, professional tutors, and trained peer tutors.
Diagnostic Testing Testing for neuropsychological is provided collaboratively through on-campus or off-campus services.
Basic Skills Remediation Remediation is offered one-on-one, in small groups, and in class-size groups for computer skills, learning strategies, math, reading, study skills, time management, and written language. Remediation is provided through the program or unit via professional tutors and trained peer tutors.
Enrichment Programs for career planning, college survival skills, learning strategies, math, practical computer skills, reading, self-advocacy, stress management, study skills, test taking, time management, and written composition skills are provided collaboratively through on-campus or off-campus services.
Application For admittance to the program or unit, students are required to provide documentation of high school services. It is recommended that students apply to the program directly and provide a psychoeducational report. Upon acceptance, documentation of need for services should be sent only to the LD program or unit. *Application deadline (institutional):* Continuous. *Application deadline (LD program):* Rolling/continuous for fall and rolling/continuous for spring.
Written Policies Written policies regarding general/basic LD accommodations and substitutions and waivers of admissions requirements are outlined in the school's catalog/handbook. Written policies regarding course substitutions, grade forgiveness, reduced course loads, substitutions and waivers of admissions requirements, and substitutions and waivers of graduation requirements are available through the program or unit directly.

Johnson County Community College
Access Services for Students with Disabilities

12345 College Boulevard
Overland Park, KS 66210-1299
http://www.johnco.cc.ks.us/
Contact: Phone: 913-469-8500.

Access Services for Students with Disabilities Approximately 180 registered undergraduate students were served during 2002-03. The program or unit includes 2 full-time and 7 part-time staff members. Academic advisers, coaches, counselors, professional tutors, regular education teachers, remediation/learning specialists, skill tutors, strategy tutors, and trained peer tutors are provided collaboratively through on-campus or off-campus services.
Unique Aids and Services Aids, services, or accommodations include faculty training, priority registration, support groups, weekly meetings with faculty, note-takers, tutors, books on tape, testing accommodations .
Subject-area Tutoring Tutoring is offered one-on-one and in small groups for most subjects. Tutoring is provided collaboratively through on-campus or off-campus services via LD specialists, professional tutors, and trained peer tutors.
Basic Skills Remediation Remediation is offered in class-size groups for learning strategies, math, reading, spelling, study skills, time management, and written language. Remediation is provided collaboratively through on-campus or off-campus services via professional tutors and regular education teachers.
Enrichment Programs for career planning, health and nutrition, learning strategies, math, oral communication skills, practical computer skills, reading, self-advocacy, study skills, test taking, time management, vocabulary development, and written composition skills are provided collaboratively through on-campus or off-campus services. Credit is offered for career planning, health and nutrition, learning strategies, math, oral communication skills, practical computer skills, reading, study skills, test taking, time management, vocabulary development, and written composition skills.
Application *Application deadline (institutional):* Continuous.
Written Policies Written policy regarding general/basic LD accommodations is available on the program Web site. Written policy regarding general/basic LD accommodations is outlined in the school's catalog/handbook.

Johnston Community College
Disabilities Services

PO Box 2350
Smithfield, NC 27577-2350
http://www.johnston.cc.nc.us/
Contact: Phone: 919-934-3051. Fax: 919-934-2150.

Disabilities Services Approximately 20 registered undergraduate students were served during 2002-03. Academic advisers, counselors, professional tutors, and regular education teachers are provided collaboratively through on-campus or off-campus services.
Unique Aids and Services Aids, services, or accommodations include career counseling.
Subject-area Tutoring Tutoring is offered one-on-one, in small groups, and in class-size groups for most subjects. Tutoring is provided collaboratively through on-campus or off-campus services via professional tutors and trained peer tutors.
Basic Skills Remediation Remediation is offered in class-size groups for math, reading, study skills, time management, and written language. Remediation is provided collaboratively through on-campus or off-campus services via regular education teachers.

Application For admittance to the program or unit, students are required to provide documentation of high school services. Upon application, materials documenting need for services should be sent only to the LD program or unit. *Application deadline (institutional):* Continuous. *Application deadline (LD program):* Rolling/continuous for fall and rolling/continuous for spring.

Written Policies Written policy regarding general/basic LD accommodations is outlined in the school's catalog/handbook. Written policies regarding general/basic LD accommodations and substitutions and waivers of admissions requirements are available through the program or unit directly.

John Wood Community College
Disability Services

1301 South 48th Street

Quincy, IL 62305-8736

http://www.jwcc.edu/

Contact: Ms. Rose-Marie Akers, Coordinator of Disability Services. Phone: 217-641-4352. Fax: 217-221-0778. E-mail: akers@jwcc.edu.

Disability Services Approximately 20 registered undergraduate students were served during 2002-03. The program or unit includes 1 full-time and 1 part-time staff member. Academic advisers, coaches, professional tutors, remediation/learning specialists, skill tutors, and trained peer tutors are provided collaboratively through on-campus or off-campus services.

Subject-area Tutoring Tutoring is offered one-on-one and in small groups for most subjects. Tutoring is provided collaboratively through on-campus or off-campus services via computer-based instruction, professional tutors, and trained peer tutors.

Basic Skills Remediation Remediation is available for math, reading, and written language. Remediation is provided collaboratively through on-campus or off-campus services via regular education teachers.

Application For admittance to the program or unit, students are required to apply to the program directly and provide a psychoeducational report. It is recommended that students provide documentation of high school services. Upon application, materials documenting need for services should be sent only to the LD program or unit. Upon acceptance, documentation of need for services should be sent only to the LD program or unit. *Application deadline (institutional):* Continuous. *Application deadline (LD program):* Rolling/continuous for fall and rolling/continuous for spring.

Written Policies Written policy regarding general/basic LD accommodations is available on the program Web site. Written policies regarding course substitutions, general/basic LD accommodations, and reduced course loads are available through the program or unit directly.

J. Sargeant Reynolds Community College
Office of Student Accommodations

PO Box 85622

Richmond, VA 23285-5622

http://www.reynolds.edu

Contact: Mrs. Debby G. Wilkerson, Student Support Specialist. Phone: 804-371-3289. Fax: 804-371-3527. E-mail: dwilkerson@reynolds.edu. Head of LD Program: Mrs. Deborah G. Wilkerson, Student Support Services Specialist. Phone: 804-371-3289. Fax: 804-371-3527. E-mail: dwilkerson@jsr.vccs.edu.

Office of Student Accommodations Approximately 175 registered undergraduate students were served during 2002-03. The program or unit includes 3 full-time staff members and 1 part-time staff member. Counselors and other are provided through the program or unit. Academic advisers, regular education teachers, remediation/learning specialists, skill tutors, and trained peer tutors are provided collaboratively through on-campus or off-campus services.

Unique Aids and Services Aids, services, or accommodations include career counseling, digital textbooks, adaptive computer software.

Subject-area Tutoring Tutoring is offered one-on-one and in small groups for most subjects. Tutoring is provided collaboratively through on-campus or off-campus services via computer-based instruction, trained peer tutors, and other.

Basic Skills Remediation Remediation is offered in class-size groups for math, reading, written language, and developmental courses. Remediation is provided collaboratively through on-campus or off-campus services via regular education teachers.

Enrichment Programs for career planning, learning strategies, study skills, test taking, and time management are provided collaboratively through on-campus or off-campus services.

Application For admittance to the program or unit, students are required to apply to the program directly and provide Diagnostic testing by licensed professional in LD. It is recommended that students provide a psychoeducational report and provide documentation of high school services. Upon application, materials documenting need for services should be sent only to the LD program or unit. Upon acceptance, documentation of need for services should be sent only to the LD program or unit. *Application deadline (institutional):* Continuous. *Application deadline (LD program):* Rolling/continuous for fall and rolling/continuous for spring.

Written Policies Written policies regarding course substitutions and general/basic LD accommodations are available on the program Web site. Written policies regarding course substitutions and general/basic LD accommodations are outlined in the school's catalog/handbook. Written policies regarding general/basic LD accommodations and reduced course loads are available through the program or unit directly.

Kansas City Kansas Community College

7250 State Avenue

Kansas City Kansas Community College (continued)
Kansas City, KS 66112-3003

http://www.kckcc.edu/arc

Contact: Phone: 913-334-1100. Fax: 913-696-9646.

Approximately 20 registered undergraduate students were served during 2002-03. The program or unit includes 6 full-time staff members and 1 part-time staff member. LD specialists are provided through the program or unit. Academic advisers, coaches, counselors, professional tutors, and regular education teachers are provided collaboratively through on-campus or off-campus services.

Subject-area Tutoring Tutoring is offered one-on-one and in small groups for all subjects. Tutoring is provided collaboratively through on-campus or off-campus services via professional tutors and trained peer tutors.

Diagnostic Testing Testing is provided through the program or unit for learning styles. Testing for auditory processing, intelligence, neuropsychological, reading, visual processing, and written language is provided collaboratively through on-campus or off-campus services.

Basic Skills Remediation Remediation is offered in class-size groups for math, reading, and written language. Remediation is provided collaboratively through on-campus or off-campus services via computer-based instruction and regular education teachers.

Fees *Diagnostic Testing* fee is $150 to $400.

Application For admittance to the program or unit, students are required to provide a psychoeducational report (3 years old or less) and provide documentation of high school services. It is recommended that students apply to the program directly. Upon application, materials documenting need for services should be sent only to the LD program or unit. Upon acceptance, documentation of need for services should be sent only to the LD program or unit. *Application deadline (institutional):* Continuous. *Application deadline (LD program):* Rolling/continuous for fall and rolling/continuous for spring.

Written Policies Written policy regarding general/basic LD accommodations is available on the program Web site. Written policies regarding grade forgiveness and substitutions and waivers of admissions requirements are outlined in the school's catalog/handbook. Written policy regarding general/basic LD accommodations is available through the program or unit directly.

Kapiolani Community College

4303 Diamond Head Road

Honolulu, HI 96816-4421

http://www.kcc.hawaii.edu/

Contact: Phone: 808-734-9111.

The program or unit includes 4 full-time staff members. Counselors are provided collaboratively through on-campus or off-campus services.

Orientation The program or unit offers an optional orientation for new students individually by special arrangement.

Unique Aids and Services Aids, services, or accommodations include career counseling, digital textbooks, and priority registration.

Subject-area Tutoring Tutoring is offered in small groups for some subjects. Tutoring is provided collaboratively through on-campus or off-campus services via other.

Application It is recommended that students provide a psychoeducational report and provide documentation of high school services. *Application deadline (institutional):* 7/1. *Application deadline (LD program):* Rolling/continuous for fall and rolling/continuous for spring.

Written Policies Written policies regarding general/basic LD accommodations and substitutions and waivers of admissions requirements are available through the program or unit directly.

Kellogg Community College
Support Services Department—Disability Services

450 North Avenue

Battle Creek, MI 49017-3397

http://www.kellogg.edu

Contact: Ms. Holly McKee, Director of Support Services. Phone: 269-965-3931 Ext. 2629. Fax: 269-965-8850. E-mail: mckeeh@kellogg.edu.

Support Services Department—Disability Services Approximately 100 registered undergraduate students were served during 2002-03. The program or unit includes 3 full-time and 5 part-time staff members. Academic advisers, LD specialists, professional tutors, skill tutors, strategy tutors, and trained peer tutors are provided through the program or unit. Academic advisers, coaches, LD specialists, professional tutors, regular education teachers, remediation/learning specialists, skill tutors, and strategy tutors are provided collaboratively through on-campus or off-campus services.

Orientation The program or unit offers an optional 20 to 30-minute orientation for new students before registration, before classes begin, during summer prior to enrollment, during registration, after classes begin, and individually by special arrangement.

Unique Aids and Services Aids, services, or accommodations include advocates and faculty training.

Subject-area Tutoring Tutoring is offered one-on-one, in small groups, and in class-size groups for most subjects. Tutoring is provided collaboratively through on-campus or off-campus services via computer-based instruction, LD specialists, professional tutors, trained peer tutors, and other.

Diagnostic Testing Testing for learning styles, math, reading, study skills, and written language is provided collaboratively through on-campus or off-campus services.

Basic Skills Remediation Remediation is offered in small groups and in class-size groups for math, study skills, and written language. Remediation is provided collaboratively through on-campus or off-campus services via computer-based instruction, regular education teachers, and other.

Enrichment Programs for career planning, college survival skills, health and nutrition, learning strategies, math, oral communication skills, practical computer skills, reading, self-advocacy, study skills, test taking, vocabulary development, written composition skills, and other are provided collaboratively through on-campus or off-campus services.

Application For admittance to the program or unit, students are required to apply to the program directly, provide a psychoeducational report (3 years old or less), and provide documentation of high school services. Upon application, materials documenting need for services should be sent only to the LD program or unit. Upon acceptance, documentation of need for services should be sent only to the LD program or unit. *Application deadline (institutional):* 8/30. *Application deadline (LD program):* Rolling/continuous for fall and rolling/continuous for spring.

Written Policies Written policy regarding general/basic LD accommodations is available on the program Web site. Written policy regarding general/basic LD accommodations is outlined in the school's catalog/handbook. Written policy regarding general/basic LD accommodations is available through the program or unit directly.

Kilgore College
Step Up To Educational Prosperity

1100 Broadway Boulevard

Kilgore, TX 75662-3299

http://www.kilgore.cc.tx.us/

Contact: Mrs. Pam Gatton, Special Population Counselor. Phone: 903-983-8682 Ext. 682. Fax: 903-983-8214 Ext. 214. E-mail: gattonp@kilgore.cc.tx.us.

Step Up To Educational Prosperity Approximately 75 registered undergraduate students were served during 2002-03. The program or unit includes 1 full-time staff member. Academic advisers, coaches, counselors, regular education teachers, strategy tutors, and trained peer tutors are provided collaboratively through on-campus or off-campus services.

Unique Aids and Services Aids, services, or accommodations include advocates, career counseling, and priority registration.

Subject-area Tutoring Tutoring is offered one-on-one and in small groups for most subjects. Tutoring is provided collaboratively through on-campus or off-campus services via computer-based instruction, professional tutors, and trained peer tutors.

Basic Skills Remediation Remediation is offered in class-size groups for learning strategies, math, reading, spelling, study skills, time management, and written language. Remediation is provided collaboratively through on-campus or off-campus services via computer-based instruction, regular education teachers, and trained peer tutors.

Enrichment Programs for career planning, college survival skills, learning strategies, math, reading, study skills, test taking, time management, vocabulary development, and written composition skills are provided collaboratively through on-campus or off-campus services.

Application For admittance to the program or unit, students are required to apply to the program directly and provide a psychoeducational report. It is recommended that students provide documentation of high school services. Upon acceptance, documentation of need for services should be sent only to the LD program or unit. *Application deadline (institutional):* Continuous. *Application deadline (LD program):* Rolling/continuous for fall and rolling/continuous for spring.

Written Policies Written policies regarding course substitutions, general/basic LD accommodations, grade forgiveness, reduced course loads, substitutions and waivers of admissions requirements, and substitutions and waivers of graduation requirements are available through the program or unit directly.

Kingsborough Community College of the City University of New York
Special Services Program

2001 Oriental Blvd, Manhattan Beach

Brooklyn, NY 11235

http://www.kbcc.cuny.edu/

Contact: Dr. A. Colarossi, Director of Special Services Program. Phone: 718-368-5175. Fax: 718-368-4782. E-mail: acolarossi@kbcc.cuny.edu.

Special Services Program Approximately 500 registered undergraduate students were served during 2002-03. The program or unit includes 4 full-time and 10 part-time staff members. Academic advisers, counselors, diagnostic specialists, graduate assistants/students, LD specialists, professional tutors, remediation/learning specialists, skill tutors, and strategy tutors are provided through the program or unit.

Orientation The program or unit offers a mandatory 4 to 5-hour orientation for new students before registration and before classes begin.

Subject-area Tutoring Tutoring is offered one-on-one and in small groups for most subjects. Tutoring is provided through the program or unit via graduate assistants/students, LD specialists, and professional tutors. Tutoring is also provided collaboratively through on-campus or off-campus services via computer-based instruction.

Basic Skills Remediation Remediation is offered one-on-one and in small groups for computer skills, learning strategies, math, reading, social skills, study skills, time management, and written language.

Enrichment Enrichment programs are available through the program or unit for career planning, college survival skills, learning strategies, practical computer skills, self-advocacy, stress management, and study skills. Programs for health and nutrition, math, oral communication skills, practical computer skills, and reading are provided collaboratively through on-campus or off-campus services. Credit is offered for career planning, college survival skills, learning strategies, practical computer skills, and study skills.

Application For admittance to the program or unit, students are required to provide a psychoeducational report and provide psychological evaluation and educational evaluation. It is recommended that students provide documentation of high school services. Upon acceptance, documentation of need for services should be sent only to the LD program or unit. *Application deadline (institutional):* Continuous. *Application deadline (LD program):* Rolling/continuous for fall and rolling/continuous for spring.

Written Policies Written policy regarding course substitutions is available through the program or unit directly.

Labette Community College

200 South 14th Street
Parsons, KS 67357-4299
http://www.labette.edu/
Contact: Phone: 620-421-6700.

The program or unit includes 1 part-time staff member. Academic advisers, counselors, professional tutors, regular education teachers, skill tutors, and other are provided collaboratively through on-campus or off-campus services.
Orientation The program or unit offers an optional 8-week orientation for new students.
Subject-area Tutoring Tutoring is offered one-on-one, in small groups, and in class-size groups for all subjects. Tutoring is provided collaboratively through on-campus or off-campus services via computer-based instruction, professional tutors, and trained peer tutors.
Basic Skills Remediation Remediation is offered one-on-one, in small groups, and in class-size groups for computer skills, handwriting, learning strategies, math, reading, spelling, spoken language, study skills, and time management. Remediation is provided collaboratively through on-campus or off-campus services via computer-based instruction, professional tutors, and trained peer tutors.
Enrichment Programs for career planning, college survival skills, health and nutrition, learning strategies, math, practical computer skills, self-advocacy, stress management, study skills, test taking, and time management are provided collaboratively through on-campus or off-campus services.
Application For admittance to the program or unit, students are required to apply to the program directly and provide a psychoeducational report. Upon application, materials documenting need for services should be sent only to the LD program or unit. Upon acceptance, documentation of need for services should be sent only to the LD program or unit. *Application deadline (institutional):* Continuous. *Application deadline (LD program):* Rolling/continuous for fall and rolling/continuous for spring.
Written Policies Written policies regarding course substitutions, general/basic LD accommodations, grade forgiveness, reduced course loads, substitutions and waivers of admissions requirements, and substitutions and waivers of graduation requirements are outlined in the school's catalog/handbook. Written policies regarding course substitutions, general/basic LD accommodations, substitutions and waivers of admissions requirements, and substitutions and waivers of graduation requirements are available through the program or unit directly.

Laboure College

2120 Dorchester Avenue
Boston, MA 02124-5698
http://www.labourecollege.org/
Contact: Stephanie McCormick, Director of Admissions. Phone: 617-296-8300 Ext. 4015. Fax: 617-296-7947. E-mail: stephanie_mccormick@laboure.edu.

Academic advisers, skill tutors, and other are provided collaboratively through on-campus or off-campus services.

Subject-area Tutoring Tutoring is offered one-on-one and in small groups for most subjects. Tutoring is provided collaboratively through on-campus or off-campus services via computer-based instruction and trained peer tutors.
Basic Skills Remediation Remediation is offered one-on-one for learning strategies, math, reading, study skills, and written language. Remediation is provided collaboratively through on-campus or off-campus services via computer-based instruction.
Application For admittance to the program or unit, students are required to provide documentation of high school services. It is recommended that students provide results of any outside testing that has been done to determine LD . Upon application, materials documenting need for services should be sent only to admissions with institutional application materials. Upon acceptance, documentation of need for services should be sent only to admissions. *Application deadline (institutional):* Continuous.

Lake Tahoe Community College
Disability Resource Center

One College Drive
South Lake Tahoe, CA 96150-4524
http://www.ltcc.cc.ca.us/student_services/disability/
Contact: Dr. Beth Marinelli-Laster, Learning Specialist. Phone: 530-541-4660 Ext. 291. Fax: 530-542-7104. E-mail: marinelli-laster@ltcc.edu. Head of LD Program: Bob Albrecht, Disability Resource Center Director. Phone: 530-541-4660 Ext. 384. Fax: 530-542-7104. E-mail: albrecht@ltcc.cc.ca.us.

Disability Resource Center Approximately 200 registered undergraduate students were served during 2002-03. The program or unit includes 5 full-time and 12 part-time staff members. Academic advisers, counselors, diagnostic specialists, LD specialists, professional tutors, remediation/learning specialists, skill tutors, special education teachers, strategy tutors, and trained peer tutors are provided through the program or unit. Academic advisers, counselors, professional tutors, and regular education teachers are provided collaboratively through on-campus or off-campus services.
Orientation The program or unit offers an optional 1-hour orientation for new students during registration and individually by special arrangement.
Summer Program To help prepare for the demands of college, there is an optional summer program prior to entering the school. Degree credit will be earned.
Unique Aids and Services Aids, services, or accommodations include career counseling, priority registration, and support groups.
Subject-area Tutoring Tutoring is offered in small groups for most subjects. Tutoring is provided through the program or unit via computer-based instruction, LD specialists, professional tutors, and trained peer tutors.
Diagnostic Testing Testing is provided through the program or unit for auditory processing, intelligence, learning strategies, learning styles, math, reading, spelling, visual processing, and written language.

Basic Skills Remediation Remediation is offered in class-size groups for computer skills, learning strategies, math, reading, spelling, study skills, time management, and written language. Remediation is provided through the program or unit via computer-based instruction, LD specialists, professional tutors, special education teachers, and trained peer tutors.

Enrichment Enrichment programs are available through the program or unit for career planning, learning strategies, math, practical computer skills, reading, study skills, test taking, time management, vocabulary development, and written composition skills. Programs for career planning, college survival skills, math, practical computer skills, reading, stress management, and written composition skills are provided collaboratively through on-campus or off-campus services. Credit is offered for career planning, college survival skills, math, practical computer skills, reading, study skills, vocabulary development, and written composition skills.

Fees *Diagnostic Testing* fee is $7.

Application For admittance to the program or unit, students are required to apply to the program directly. It is recommended that students provide a psychoeducational report (5 years old or less), provide documentation of high school services, and provide documentation/verification of disability. Upon application, materials documenting need for services should be sent only to the LD program or unit. Upon acceptance, documentation of need for services should be sent only to the LD program or unit. *Application deadline (institutional):* Continuous. *Application deadline (LD program):* Rolling/continuous for fall and rolling/continuous for spring.

Written Policies Written policies regarding course substitutions, general/basic LD accommodations, grade forgiveness, and reduced course loads are available through the program or unit directly.

Diagnostic Testing Testing for learning strategies, learning styles, and personality is provided collaboratively through on-campus or off-campus services.

Basic Skills Remediation Remediation is offered one-on-one, in small groups, and in class-size groups for computer skills, learning strategies, math, reading, spelling, study skills, time management, and written language. Remediation is provided collaboratively through on-campus or off-campus services via computer-based instruction, graduate assistants/students, professional tutors, regular education teachers, and trained peer tutors.

Enrichment Programs for career planning, college survival skills, health and nutrition, learning strategies, math, oral communication skills, practical computer skills, reading, stress management, study skills, test taking, time management, vocabulary development, and written composition skills are provided collaboratively through on-campus or off-campus services. Credit is offered for college survival skills, health and nutrition, learning strategies, math, oral communication skills, practical computer skills, reading, study skills, test taking, time management, vocabulary development, and written composition skills.

Application For admittance to the program or unit, students are required to apply to the program directly and provide a psychoeducational report (2 years old or less). It is recommended that students provide documentation of high school services. Upon application, materials documenting need for services should be sent only to the LD program or unit. Upon acceptance, documentation of need for services should be sent only to the LD program or unit. *Application deadline (institutional):* 9/16. *Application deadline (LD program):* Rolling/continuous for fall and rolling/continuous for spring.

Written Policies Written policy regarding general/basic LD accommodations is available on the program Web site. Written policy regarding general/basic LD accommodations is outlined in the school's catalog/handbook.

Lamar Community College

2401 South Main Street

Lamar, CO 81052-3999

http://www.lamarcc.edu/

Contact: Mr. Thomas R. Alderman, Affirmative Action Officer. Phone: 719-336-6646. Fax: 719-336-2248. E-mail: tom.alderman@lcc.cccoes.edu.

Approximately 5 registered undergraduate students were served during 2002-03. The program or unit includes 1 part-time staff member. Academic advisers and counselors are provided through the program or unit. Academic advisers, counselors, professional tutors, regular education teachers, skill tutors, and trained peer tutors are provided collaboratively through on-campus or off-campus services.

Summer Program To help prepare for the demands of college, there is an optional 10-week summer program prior to entering the school. Degree credit will be earned.

Unique Aids and Services Aids, services, or accommodations include advocates and career counseling.

Subject-area Tutoring Tutoring is offered one-on-one, in small groups, and in class-size groups for all subjects. Tutoring is provided collaboratively through on-campus or off-campus services via computer-based instruction, graduate assistants/students, professional tutors, and trained peer tutors.

Lamar State College-Orange

410 Front Street

Orange, TX 77630-5899

http://www.lsco.edu/

Contact: Frances Ahearn, Director of Advising, Counseling and Testing. Phone: 409-882-3387. Fax: 409-882-3049. E-mail: frances.ahearn@lsco.edu.

Approximately 30 registered undergraduate students were served during 2002-03.

Unique Aids and Services Aids, services, or accommodations include career counseling, faculty training, priority registration, representatives from institution at graduate ARD meetings.

Enrichment Enrichment programs are available through the program or unit for career planning, college survival skills, health and nutrition, learning strategies, oral communication skills, self-advocacy, stress management, study skills, test taking, time management, and other. Programs for career planning, college survival skills, health and nutrition, learning strategies, math, oral communication skills, practical computer skills, reading, self-advocacy, stress management, study skills, test taking, time management, written composition skills, and other are provided collaboratively through on-campus or off-campus services. Credit is offered for health and nutrition, math, oral communication skills, practical computer skills, reading, written composition skills, and other.

Lamar State College-Orange (continued)

Application For admittance to the program or unit, students are required to apply to the program directly and provide a psychoeducational report (3 years old or less). Upon application, materials documenting need for services should be sent only to the LD program or unit. Upon acceptance, documentation of need for services should be sent only to the LD program or unit. *Application deadline (institutional):* Continuous. *Application deadline (LD program):* Rolling/continuous for fall and rolling/continuous for spring.

Written Policies Written policy regarding general/basic LD accommodations is available on the program Web site. Written policy regarding general/basic LD accommodations is outlined in the school's catalog/handbook. Written policy regarding general/basic LD accommodations is available through the program or unit directly.

Laramie County Community College
Disability Resource Center

1400 East College Drive
Cheyenne, WY 82007-3299
http://www.lccc.cc.wy.us/success/drc.htm

Contact: Ms. Lisa Dignan, Coordinator of Disability Resource Center. Phone: 307-778-1359. Fax: 307-778-1262. E-mail: ldignan@lccc.cc.wy.us.

Disability Resource Center Approximately 150 registered undergraduate students were served during 2002-03. The program or unit includes 1 full-time staff member. Academic advisers and LD specialists are provided through the program or unit. Academic advisers, counselors, professional tutors, regular education teachers, skill tutors, trained peer tutors, and other are provided collaboratively through on-campus or off-campus services.

Unique Aids and Services Aids, services, or accommodations include career counseling, digital textbooks, and faculty training.

Subject-area Tutoring Tutoring is offered one-on-one and in small groups for most subjects. Tutoring is provided collaboratively through on-campus or off-campus services via professional tutors and trained peer tutors.

Basic Skills Remediation Remediation is offered in class-size groups for math, reading, spelling, and written language. Remediation is provided collaboratively through on-campus or off-campus services via computer-based instruction and regular education teachers.

Enrichment Programs for career planning, college survival skills, learning strategies, math, oral communication skills, practical computer skills, reading, self-advocacy, stress management, study skills, test taking, time management, written composition skills, and other are provided collaboratively through on-campus or off-campus services. Credit is offered for learning strategies, math, oral communication skills, practical computer skills, reading, stress management, study skills, written composition skills, and other.

Application For admittance to the program or unit, students are required to apply to the program directly and provide a psychoeducational report. It is recommended that students provide documentation of high school services. Upon application, materials documenting need for services should be sent only to the LD program or

unit. Upon acceptance, documentation of need for services should be sent only to the LD program or unit. *Application deadline (institutional):* Continuous. *Application deadline (LD program):* Rolling/continuous for fall and rolling/continuous for spring.

Written Policies Written policies regarding course substitutions, general/basic LD accommodations, reduced course loads, and substitutions and waivers of graduation requirements are outlined in the school's catalog/handbook. Written policies regarding course substitutions, general/basic LD accommodations, reduced course loads, and substitutions and waivers of graduation requirements are available through the program or unit directly.

Lassen Community College District
Disabled Students Programs and Services

Highway 139
PO Box 3000
Susanville, CA 96130
http://www.lassen.cc.ca.us/

Contact: Ms. Cindy Howe, Learning Disabilities Specialist. Phone: 530-251-8867. Fax: 530-257-6181 Ext. 8914.

Disabled Students Programs and Services Approximately 147 registered undergraduate students were served during 2002-03. The program or unit includes 3 full-time staff members and 1 part-time staff member. Diagnostic specialists, LD specialists, professional tutors, remediation/learning specialists, skill tutors, special education teachers, and strategy tutors are provided through the program or unit. Academic advisers, coaches, counselors, professional tutors, regular education teachers, and trained peer tutors are provided collaboratively through on-campus or off-campus services.

Orientation The program or unit offers an optional 1-hour orientation for new students individually by special arrangement.

Unique Aids and Services Aids, services, or accommodations include career counseling.

Subject-area Tutoring Tutoring is offered one-on-one and in small groups for some subjects. Tutoring is provided through the program or unit via computer-based instruction, LD specialists, professional tutors, and trained peer tutors. Tutoring is also provided collaboratively through on-campus or off-campus services via computer-based instruction and trained peer tutors.

Diagnostic Testing Testing is provided through the program or unit for auditory processing, intelligence, learning strategies, learning styles, math, reading, spelling, visual processing, and written language. Testing for learning styles, math, reading, and written language is provided collaboratively through on-campus or off-campus services.

Basic Skills Remediation Remediation is offered in class-size groups for computer skills, learning strategies, math, reading, spelling, study skills, time management, and written language. Remediation is provided through the program or unit via computer-based instruction, LD specialists, professional tutors, special education teachers, and trained peer tutors. Remediation is also provided collaboratively through on-campus or off-campus services via computer-based instruction, regular education teachers, and trained peer tutors.

Enrichment Enrichment programs are available through the program or unit for learning strategies, math, practical computer skills, reading, study skills, test taking, vocabulary development, and written composition skills. Programs for career planning, college survival skills, health and nutrition, learning strategies, math, oral communication skills, practical computer skills, reading, stress management, study skills, test taking, time management, and written composition skills are provided collaboratively through on-campus or off-campus services. Credit is offered for career planning, college survival skills, health and nutrition, learning strategies, math, oral communication skills, practical computer skills, reading, stress management, study skills, test taking, time management, vocabulary development, and written composition skills.

Fees *Diagnostic Testing* fee is $30.

Application For admittance to the program or unit, students are required to apply to the program directly and provide a psychoeducational report (3 years old or less). It is recommended that students provide documentation of high school services and provide school psychologist's report. Upon application, materials documenting need for services should be sent only to the LD program or unit. Upon acceptance, documentation of need for services should be sent only to the LD program or unit. *Application deadline (institutional):* Continuous. *Application deadline (LD program):* Rolling/continuous for fall and rolling/continuous for spring.

Written Policies Written policy regarding grade forgiveness is outlined in the school's catalog/handbook. Written policies regarding general/basic LD accommodations and reduced course loads are available through the program or unit directly.

Lee College
Office of Disability Services

PO Box 818
Baytown, TX 77522-0818
http://www.lee.edu/counseling/#dis
Contact: Dr. Rosemary A. Coffman, Counselor for Students with Disabilities. Phone: 281-425-6384. Fax: 832-556-4004. E-mail: rcoffman@lee.edu.

Office of Disability Services Approximately 47 registered undergraduate students were served during 2002-03. The program or unit includes 2 full-time and 10 part-time staff members. Counselors, skill tutors, and other are provided collaboratively through on-campus or off-campus services.

Unique Aids and Services Aids, services, or accommodations include career counseling, faculty training, and priority registration.

Subject-area Tutoring Tutoring is offered one-on-one and in small groups for most subjects. Tutoring is provided collaboratively through on-campus or off-campus services via computer-based instruction and trained peer tutors.

Basic Skills Remediation Remediation is offered in class-size groups for math, reading, study skills, and written language. Remediation is provided collaboratively through on-campus or off-campus services via computer-based instruction and regular education teachers.

Enrichment Programs for career planning, college survival skills, learning strategies, math, practical computer skills, reading, study skills, test taking, time management, and written composition skills are provided collaboratively through on-campus or off-campus services.

Application For admittance to the program or unit, students are required to provide a psychoeducational report. It is recommended that students provide documentation of high school services. Upon application, materials documenting need for services should be sent only to the LD program or unit. *Application deadline (institutional):* Continuous. *Application deadline (LD program):* Rolling/continuous for fall and rolling/continuous for spring.

Written Policies Written policy regarding general/basic LD accommodations is available on the program Web site. Written policy regarding general/basic LD accommodations is outlined in the school's catalog/handbook.

Leeward Community College
Kako'o 'Ike—Disabilities Services for Students

96-045 Ala Ike
Pearl City, HI 96782-3393
http://www.lcc.hawaii.edu/
Contact: Ms. Tamara A.M. Watson-Wade, KI Coordinator and Disabilities Services Specialist. Phone: 808-455-0421. Fax: 808-455-0421. E-mail: tamaraww@hawaii.edu.

Kako'o 'Ike—Disabilities Services for Students Approximately 65 registered undergraduate students were served during 2002-03. The program or unit includes 1 full-time staff member. Services are provided through the program or unit. Academic advisers, counselors, diagnostic specialists, LD specialists, professional tutors, regular education teachers, remediation/learning specialists, skill tutors, strategy tutors, trained peer tutors, and other are provided collaboratively through on-campus or off-campus services.

Orientation The program or unit offers an optional orientation for new students individually by special arrangement.

Summer Program To help prepare for the demands of college, there is an optional 14-week (summer semester) summer program prior to entering the school.

Unique Aids and Services Aids, services, or accommodations include priority registration, tutors, audiotexts, in-class and testing accommodations, adaptive software, furniture and equipment.

Subject-area Tutoring Tutoring is offered one-on-one and in small groups for most subjects. Tutoring is provided through the program or unit via computer-based instruction and trained peer tutors. Tutoring is also provided collaboratively through on-campus or off-campus services via computer-based instruction, graduate assistants/students, and trained peer tutors.

Basic Skills Remediation Remediation is offered one-on-one, in small groups, and in class-size groups for handwriting, math, reading, spelling, spoken language, and written language. Remediation is provided through the program or unit via trained peer tutors and other. Remediation is also provided collaboratively through on-campus or off-campus services via trained peer tutors and other.

Enrichment Enrichment programs are available through the program or unit for college survival skills, learning strategies, math, oral communication skills, practical computer skills, self-advocacy, stress management, study skills, test taking, and time management. Programs for career planning, college survival skills, health and nutrition, learning strategies, math, oral communication skills, prac-

Leeward Community College (continued)

tical computer skills, reading, self-advocacy, stress management, study skills, test taking, time management, vocabulary development, and written composition skills are provided collaboratively through on-campus or off-campus services. Credit is offered for career planning, college survival skills, health and nutrition, math, oral communication skills, practical computer skills, reading, self-advocacy, stress management, study skills, test taking, time management, and written composition skills.

Student Organization Friends of Kako'o 'Ike consists of 150 members.

Application For admittance to the program or unit, students are required to apply to the program directly. It is recommended that students provide a psychoeducational report (3 years old or less), provide documentation of high school services, and provide ability and achievement scores. Upon application, materials documenting need for services should be sent only to the LD program or unit. Upon acceptance, documentation of need for services should be sent to both admissions and the LD program or unit. *Application deadline (institutional):* 8/15. *Application deadline (LD program):* Rolling/continuous for fall and rolling/continuous for spring.

Written Policies Written policies regarding course substitutions, general/basic LD accommodations, grade forgiveness, reduced course loads, substitutions and waivers of admissions requirements, and substitutions and waivers of graduation requirements are outlined in the school's catalog/handbook. Written policies regarding course substitutions, general/basic LD accommodations, grade forgiveness, reduced course loads, substitutions and waivers of admissions requirements, and substitutions and waivers of graduation requirements are available through the program or unit directly.

Lehigh Carbon Community College

4525 Education Park Drive

Schnecksville, PA 18078-2598

http://www.lccc.edu/

Contact: Ms. Joann Mackesy, Director of Educational Support Services. Phone: 610-799-1156. E-mail: jmackesy@lccc.edu.

The program or unit includes 1 full-time staff member. Remediation/learning specialists are provided through the program or unit. Academic advisers, counselors, professional tutors, remediation/learning specialists, and trained peer tutors are provided collaboratively through on-campus or off-campus services.

Unique Aids and Services Aids, services, or accommodations include career counseling.

Subject-area Tutoring Tutoring is offered one-on-one and in small groups for most subjects. Tutoring is provided collaboratively through on-campus or off-campus services via computer-based instruction, professional tutors, and trained peer tutors.

Basic Skills Remediation Remediation is offered in small groups and in class-size groups for computer skills, learning strategies, math, reading, spelling, study skills, time management, and written language. Remediation is provided collaboratively through on-campus or off-campus services via computer-based instruction, professional tutors, regular education teachers, and trained peer tutors.

Enrichment Programs for career planning, college survival skills, learning strategies, stress management, study skills, test taking, time management, and written composition skills are provided collaboratively through on-campus or off-campus services.

Application It is recommended that students apply to the program directly, provide a psychoeducational report, and provide documentation of high school services. Upon application, materials documenting need for services should be sent only to the LD program or unit. Upon acceptance, documentation of need for services should be sent only to the LD program or unit. *Application deadline (institutional):* Continuous. *Application deadline (LD program):* Rolling/continuous for fall and rolling/continuous for spring.

Written Policies Written policies regarding general/basic LD accommodations and substitutions and waivers of graduation requirements are available on the program Web site. Written policies regarding general/basic LD accommodations and substitutions and waivers of graduation requirements are outlined in the school's catalog/handbook. Written policy regarding general/basic LD accommodations is available through the program or unit directly.

Lincoln Land Community College
Special Needs Office

5250 Shepherd Road

PO Box 19256

Springfield, IL 62794-9256

http://www.llcc.cc.il.us/

Contact: Ms. Linda D. Chriswell, Special Needs Professional. Phone: 217-786-2828. Fax: 217-786-2251. E-mail: linda.chriswell@llcc.edu.

Special Needs Office Approximately 204 registered undergraduate students were served during 2002-03. The program or unit includes 2 full-time staff members. Academic advisers, counselors, diagnostic specialists, professional tutors, skill tutors, strategy tutors, and trained peer tutors are provided through the program or unit. Academic advisers, counselors, professional tutors, regular education teachers, remediation/learning specialists, skill tutors, strategy tutors, and trained peer tutors are provided collaboratively through on-campus or off-campus services.

Orientation The program or unit offers an optional 3 to 4-hour orientation for new students before registration, before classes begin, during summer prior to enrollment, and individually by special arrangement.

Unique Aids and Services Aids, services, or accommodations include career counseling, faculty training, and priority registration.

Subject-area Tutoring Tutoring is offered one-on-one and in small groups for all subjects. Tutoring is provided through the program or unit via computer-based instruction, professional tutors, and trained peer tutors. Tutoring is also provided collaboratively through on-campus or off-campus services via computer-based instruction, professional tutors, and trained peer tutors.

Diagnostic Testing Testing is provided through the program or unit for math, reading, spelling, and written language. Testing for learning strategies, learning styles, math, and study skills is provided collaboratively through on-campus or off-campus services.

Basic Skills Remediation Remediation is offered one-on-one and in class-size groups for computer skills, learning strategies, math, reading, spelling, study skills, time management, and written language. Remediation is provided through the program or unit via computer-based instruction, professional tutors, and trained peer tutors. Remediation is also provided collaboratively through on-campus or off-campus services via professional tutors, regular education teachers, and trained peer tutors.

Enrichment Enrichment programs are available through the program or unit for career planning, learning strategies, self-advocacy, stress management, and study skills. Programs for career planning, college survival skills, learning strategies, math, practical computer skills, reading, stress management, study skills, test taking, time management, vocabulary development, and written composition skills are provided collaboratively through on-campus or off-campus services. Credit is offered for college survival skills, learning strategies, math, reading, study skills, test taking, time management, vocabulary development, and written composition skills.

Application For admittance to the program or unit, students are required to apply to the program directly and provide a psychoeducational report (3 years old or less). It is recommended that students provide documentation of high school services. Upon application, materials documenting need for services should be sent only to the LD program or unit. Upon acceptance, documentation of need for services should be sent to both admissions and the LD program or unit. *Application deadline (institutional):* Continuous. *Application deadline (LD program):* Rolling/continuous for fall and rolling/continuous for spring.

Written Policies Written policies regarding course substitutions, general/basic LD accommodations, grade forgiveness, and substitutions and waivers of admissions requirements are outlined in the school's catalog/handbook. Written policies regarding general/basic LD accommodations and substitutions and waivers of admissions requirements are available through the program or unit directly.

Linn-Benton Community College

6500 Southwest Pacific Boulevard

Albany, OR 97321

http://www.linnbenton.edu/

Contact: C. E. Allison PhD, Coordinator Disability Services. Phone: 541-917-4690. Fax: 541-917-4808. E-mail: adero.allison@linnbenton.edu.

The program or unit includes 3 full-time and 3 part-time staff members. Academic advisers, skill tutors, and strategy tutors are provided through the program or unit. Academic advisers, counselors, professional tutors, regular education teachers, and trained peer tutors are provided collaboratively through on-campus or off-campus services.

Orientation The program or unit offers a mandatory orientation for new students during registration, after classes begin, and individually by special arrangement.

Unique Aids and Services Aids, services, or accommodations include career counseling, time management, study strategies, organization skills through Disability Services staff advocates.

Subject-area Tutoring Tutoring is offered one-on-one, in small groups, and in class-size groups for some subjects. Tutoring is provided collaboratively through on-campus or off-campus services via professional tutors and trained peer tutors.

Diagnostic Testing Testing for learning styles, math, reading, spelling, and written language is provided collaboratively through on-campus or off-campus services.

Basic Skills Remediation Remediation is offered one-on-one, in small groups, and in class-size groups for learning strategies, math, reading, spelling, study skills, time management, and written language. Remediation is provided through the program or unit via professional tutors and regular education teachers. Remediation is also provided collaboratively through on-campus or off-campus services via computer-based instruction, professional tutors, and regular education teachers.

Enrichment Enrichment programs are available through the program or unit for college survival skills, learning strategies, math, self-advocacy, stress management, study skills, test taking, time management, vocabulary development, and written composition skills. Programs for career planning, college survival skills, health and nutrition, learning strategies, math, oral communication skills, practical computer skills, reading, self-advocacy, stress management, study skills, test taking, time management, vocabulary development, and written composition skills are provided collaboratively through on-campus or off-campus services. Credit is offered for career planning, college survival skills, health and nutrition, learning strategies, math, oral communication skills, practical computer skills, reading, stress management, study skills, test taking, time management, vocabulary development, and written composition skills.

Fees *Diagnostic Testing* fee is $2.

Application It is recommended that students apply to the program directly, provide documentation of high school services, and provide re-certifying documentation within 3 years for high school students. Upon application, materials documenting need for services should be sent only to the LD program or unit. Upon acceptance, documentation of need for services should be sent only to the LD program or unit. *Application deadline (institutional):* Continuous. *Application deadline (LD program):* Rolling/continuous for fall and rolling/continuous for spring.

Written Policies Written policies regarding course substitutions, general/basic LD accommodations, grade forgiveness, and substitutions and waivers of graduation requirements are available on the program Web site. Written policies regarding course substitutions, general/basic LD accommodations, grade forgiveness, and substitutions and waivers of graduation requirements are outlined in the school's catalog/handbook. Written policy regarding general/basic LD accommodations is available through the program or unit directly.

Los Angeles Trade-Technical College
Disabled Student Programs and Services (DSP&S)

400 West Washington Boulevard

Los Angeles, CA 90015-4108

http://www.lattc.edu/

Los Angeles Trade-Technical College (continued)

Contact: Dr. Susan Gamble, Learning Disability Specialist. Phone: 213-763-3773. Fax: 213-763-5391. E-mail: gamblesr@lattc.edu.

Disabled Student Programs and Services (DSP&S) Approximately 135 registered undergraduate students were served during 2002-03. The program or unit includes 1 full-time and 3 part-time staff members. Academic advisers, counselors, LD specialists, special education teachers, and trained peer tutors are provided through the program or unit. Regular education teachers and skill tutors are provided collaboratively through on-campus or off-campus services.

Orientation The program or unit offers an optional orientation for new students before registration, during summer prior to enrollment, during registration, and individually by special arrangement.

Unique Aids and Services Aids, services, or accommodations include career counseling and priority registration.

Subject-area Tutoring Tutoring is offered one-on-one for some subjects. Tutoring is provided through the program or unit via trained peer tutors. Tutoring is also provided collaboratively through on-campus or off-campus services via computer-based instruction.

Diagnostic Testing Testing is provided through the program or unit for auditory processing, handwriting, intelligence, math, motor skills, reading, spelling, visual processing, and written language. Testing for learning styles is provided collaboratively through on-campus or off-campus services.

Basic Skills Remediation Remediation is offered in class-size groups for computer skills, math, reading, spelling, study skills, and written language. Remediation is provided through the program or unit via LD specialists. Remediation is also provided collaboratively through on-campus or off-campus services via computer-based instruction.

Enrichment Enrichment programs are available through the program or unit for learning strategies, math, study skills, and vocabulary development. Programs for career planning, college survival skills, health and nutrition, math, practical computer skills, reading, stress management, study skills, test taking, time management, vocabulary development, and written composition skills are provided collaboratively through on-campus or off-campus services. Credit is offered for college survival skills, health and nutrition, learning strategies, math, practical computer skills, reading, study skills, and vocabulary development.

Fees *Diagnostic Testing* fee is $11.

Application For admittance to the program or unit, students are required to apply to the program directly. It is recommended that students provide a psychoeducational report and provide documentation of high school services. Upon application, materials documenting need for services should be sent only to the LD program or unit. *Application deadline (institutional):* 8/28. *Application deadline (LD program):* Rolling/continuous for fall and rolling/continuous for spring.

Written Policies Written policies regarding general/basic LD accommodations and substitutions and waivers of graduation requirements are available through the program or unit directly.

Louisiana State University at Eunice

PO Box 1129

Eunice, LA 70535-1129

http://www.lsue.edu/

Contact: Mrs. Angela M. Soileau, Student Support Services Coordinator. Phone: 337-550-1254. Fax: 337-550-1268. E-mail: asoileau@lsue.edu.

Approximately 40 registered undergraduate students were served during 2002-03. The program or unit includes 1 full-time staff member. Counselors, LD specialists, professional tutors, and trained peer tutors are provided through the program or unit. Academic advisers, coaches, diagnostic specialists, regular education teachers, and remediation/learning specialists are provided collaboratively through on-campus or off-campus services.

Summer Program To help prepare for the demands of college, there is an optional summer program prior to entering the school. Degree credit will be earned.

Unique Aids and Services Aids, services, or accommodations include career counseling.

Subject-area Tutoring Tutoring is offered one-on-one for most subjects. Tutoring is provided through the program or unit via computer-based instruction and trained peer tutors.

Basic Skills Remediation Remediation is offered one-on-one for computer skills, learning strategies, math, reading, social skills, spelling, spoken language, study skills, time management, and written language. Remediation is provided through the program or unit via computer-based instruction, LD specialists, and trained peer tutors.

Enrichment Enrichment programs are available through the program or unit for career planning, college survival skills, learning strategies, math, practical computer skills, self-advocacy, stress management, study skills, test taking, time management, vocabulary development, and written composition skills. Programs for career planning, college survival skills, health and nutrition, reading, study skills, test taking, time management, vocabulary development, and written composition skills are provided collaboratively through on-campus or off-campus services. Credit is offered for college survival skills, health and nutrition, reading, study skills, test taking, time management, vocabulary development, and written composition skills.

Fees *Summer Program* fee is $60.

Application For admittance to the program or unit, students are required to apply to the program directly and provide documentation of disability and recommendations for accommodations from provider. It is recommended that students provide a psychoeducational report (2 years old or less) and provide documentation of high school services. Upon application, materials documenting need for services should be sent only to the LD program or unit. Upon acceptance, documentation of need for services should be sent only to the LD program or unit. *Application deadline (institutional):* 8/7. *Application deadline (LD program):* Rolling/continuous for fall and rolling/continuous for spring.

Written Policies Written policies regarding course substitutions, general/basic LD accommodations, grade forgiveness, reduced course loads, substitutions and waivers of admissions requirements, and substitutions and waivers of graduation requirements are outlined in the school's catalog/handbook.

Macomb Community College
Special Services

14500 East Twelve Mile Road

Warren, MI 48088-3896

http://www.macomb.edu/

Contact: Ms. Dina Aiuto, Counselor. Phone: 586-445-7420. Fax: 586-445-7223. E-mail: aiutod@macomb.edu. Head of LD Program: Mr. Robert Penkala, Director of Counseling and Career Services at South Campus. Phone: 586-445-7636. Fax: 586-445-7223. E-mail: penkalar@macomb.edu.

Special Services Approximately 600 registered undergraduate students were served during 2002-03. The program or unit includes 6 full-time and 4 part-time staff members. Counselors are provided through the program or unit. Academic advisers, coaches, counselors, diagnostic specialists, graduate assistants/students, LD specialists, professional tutors, regular education teachers, special education teachers, and trained peer tutors are provided collaboratively through on-campus or off-campus services.

Orientation The program or unit offers a mandatory 3-hour orientation for new students before registration, before classes begin, during summer prior to enrollment, during registration, after classes begin, and individually by special arrangement.

Unique Aids and Services Aids, services, or accommodations include advocates, career counseling, personal coach, priority registration, and support groups.

Subject-area Tutoring Tutoring is offered one-on-one, in small groups, and in class-size groups for some subjects. Tutoring is provided collaboratively through on-campus or off-campus services via trained peer tutors.

Enrichment Programs for career planning, college survival skills, health and nutrition, learning strategies, math, practical computer skills, reading, stress management, study skills, test taking, and written composition skills are provided collaboratively through on-campus or off-campus services. Credit is offered for career planning, college survival skills, health and nutrition, learning strategies, math, practical computer skills, reading, and written composition skills.

Application For admittance to the program or unit, students are required to apply to the program directly, provide a psychoeducational report (2 years old or less), provide documentation of high school services, and provide medical documentation or documentation for mental illness. Upon application, materials documenting need for services should be sent only to the LD program or unit. Upon acceptance, documentation of need for services should be sent only to the LD program or unit. *Application deadline (institutional):* Continuous. *Application deadline (LD program):* Rolling/continuous for fall and rolling/continuous for spring.

Written Policies Written policy regarding general/basic LD accommodations is available on the program Web site. Written policy regarding general/basic LD accommodations is outlined in the school's catalog/handbook. Written policies regarding course substitutions, general/basic LD accommodations, reduced course loads, substitutions and waivers of admissions requirements, and substitutions and waivers of graduation requirements are available through the program or unit directly.

Marion Technical College
Office of Students with Disabilities

1467 Mount Vernon Avenue

Marion, OH 43302-5694

http://www.mtc.edu

Contact: Mr. Mike S. Stuckey, Director of the Student Resource Center. Phone: 740-389-4636 Ext. 271. Fax: 740-389-6136. E-mail: stuckeym@mtc.edu.

Office of Students with Disabilities Approximately 200 registered undergraduate students were served during 2002-03. The program or unit includes 2 full-time staff members and 1 part-time staff member. Academic advisers, coaches, counselors, LD specialists, professional tutors, remediation/learning specialists, skill tutors, strategy tutors, and trained peer tutors are provided through the program or unit. Regular education teachers and special education teachers are provided collaboratively through on-campus or off-campus services.

Unique Aids and Services Aids, services, or accommodations include advocates, career counseling, digital textbooks, faculty training, personal coach, and priority registration.

Subject-area Tutoring Tutoring is offered one-on-one and in small groups for most subjects. Tutoring is provided through the program or unit via LD specialists, professional tutors, and trained peer tutors. Tutoring is also provided collaboratively through on-campus or off-campus services via computer-based instruction.

Basic Skills Remediation Remediation is offered in small groups for computer skills, learning strategies, math, reading, study skills, written language, and science. Remediation is provided collaboratively through on-campus or off-campus services via regular education teachers.

Application For admittance to the program or unit, students are required to apply to the program directly, provide a psychoeducational report (5 years old or less), provide documentation of high school services, and provide a complete psych evaluation if applicable. Upon application, materials documenting need for services should be sent only to the LD program or unit. Upon acceptance, documentation of need for services should be sent only to the LD program or unit. *Application deadline (institutional):* Continuous. *Application deadline (LD program):* Rolling/continuous for fall and rolling/continuous for spring.

Written Policies Written policy regarding general/basic LD accommodations is outlined in the school's catalog/handbook.

Marshalltown Community College
Success Center

3700 South Center Street

Marshalltown, IA 50158-4760

http://www.marshalltowncommunitycollege.com/

Contact: Dr. Laura D. Browne, Associate Dean for Developmental Services. Phone: 641-752-4643 Ext. 237. Fax: 641-754-1442. E-mail: ldbrowne@iavalley.cc.ia.us.

Marshalltown Community College (continued)

Success Center Approximately 25 registered undergraduate students were served during 2002-03. The program or unit includes 2 full-time staff members. Academic advisers, coaches, skill tutors, and trained peer tutors are provided through the program or unit. Academic advisers and counselors are provided collaboratively through on-campus or off-campus services.

Unique Aids and Services Aids, services, or accommodations include advocates and weekly meetings with faculty.

Subject-area Tutoring Tutoring is offered one-on-one and in small groups for most subjects. Tutoring is provided through the program or unit via computer-based instruction and trained peer tutors.

Basic Skills Remediation Remediation is offered one-on-one, in small groups, and in class-size groups for computer skills, learning strategies, math, reading, spelling, study skills, time management, and written language. Remediation is provided through the program or unit via regular education teachers and special education teachers.

Enrichment Enrichment programs are available through the program or unit for career planning, health and nutrition, learning strategies, math, practical computer skills, reading, self-advocacy, stress management, study skills, test taking, time management, vocabulary development, and written composition skills. Programs for career planning, health and nutrition, learning strategies, math, practical computer skills, reading, self-advocacy, stress management, study skills, test taking, time management, vocabulary development, and written composition skills are provided collaboratively through on-campus or off-campus services. Credit is offered for health and nutrition, learning strategies, math, practical computer skills, and reading.

Application For admittance to the program or unit, students are required to provide a psychoeducational report (3 years old or less) and provide documentation of high school services. Upon application, materials documenting need for services should be sent only to the LD program or unit. Upon acceptance, documentation of need for services should be sent only to the LD program or unit. *Application deadline (institutional):* Continuous. *Application deadline (LD program):* Rolling/continuous for fall and rolling/continuous for spring.

Written Policies Written policies regarding course substitutions, general/basic LD accommodations, reduced course loads, substitutions and waivers of admissions requirements, and substitutions and waivers of graduation requirements are available on the program Web site. Written policies regarding course substitutions, general/basic LD accommodations, reduced course loads, substitutions and waivers of admissions requirements, and substitutions and waivers of graduation requirements are outlined in the school's catalog/handbook.

Marymount College, Palos Verdes, California
Disability Resources

30800 Palos Verdes Drive East
Rancho Palos Verdes, CA 90275-6299
http://www.marymountpv.edu/

Contact: Ms. Ruth Proctor, Coordinator of Disability Resources. Phone: 310-377-5501 Ext. 367. Fax: 310-377-6223. E-mail: rproctor@marymountpv.edu.

Disability Resources Approximately 70 registered undergraduate students were served during 2002-03. The program or unit includes 1 full-time staff member. Academic advisers, coaches, LD specialists, and strategy tutors are provided through the program or unit. Academic advisers, counselors, regular education teachers, skill tutors, and trained peer tutors are provided collaboratively through on-campus or off-campus services.

Orientation The program or unit offers an optional 1-hour orientation for new students before classes begin.

Unique Aids and Services Aids, services, or accommodations include advocates, faculty training, personal coach, and priority registration.

Subject-area Tutoring Tutoring is offered one-on-one for most subjects. Tutoring is provided through the program or unit via LD specialists. Tutoring is also provided collaboratively through on-campus or off-campus services via trained peer tutors and other.

Basic Skills Remediation Remediation is offered one-on-one for learning strategies, math, reading, study skills, and time management. Remediation is provided through the program or unit via special education teachers. Remediation is also provided collaboratively through on-campus or off-campus services via regular education teachers and trained peer tutors.

Enrichment Enrichment programs are available through the program or unit for learning strategies, reading, self-advocacy, study skills, test taking, and time management. Programs for health and nutrition, learning strategies, math, reading, stress management, study skills, test taking, time management, and written composition skills are provided collaboratively through on-campus or off-campus services. Credit is offered for health and nutrition, reading, and written composition skills.

Application For admittance to the program or unit, students are required to provide a psychoeducational report (3 years old or less). It is recommended that students apply to the program directly and provide documentation of high school services. Upon application, materials documenting need for services should be sent only to the LD program or unit. Upon acceptance, documentation of need for services should be sent only to the LD program or unit. *Application deadline (institutional):* 7/1. *Application deadline (LD program):* Rolling/continuous for fall and rolling/continuous for spring.

Written Policies Written policy regarding general/basic LD accommodations is available through the program or unit directly.

Massasoit Community College

1 Massasoit Boulevard
Brockton, MA 02302-3996
http://www.massasoit.mass.edu/
Contact: Phone: 508-588-9100. Fax: 508-427-1220.

The program or unit includes 2 full-time and 2 part-time staff members. Academic advisers and counselors are provided through the program or unit. Academic advisers, counselors, LD specialists, professional tutors, regular education teachers, and trained peer tutors are provided collaboratively through on-campus or off-campus services.

Summer Program To help prepare for the demands of college, there is an optional half-day summer program prior to entering the school.

Unique Aids and Services Aids, services, or accommodations include career counseling.

Subject-area Tutoring Tutoring is offered one-on-one and in small groups for most subjects. Tutoring is provided collaboratively through on-campus or off-campus services via computer-based instruction, LD specialists, professional tutors, and trained peer tutors.

Basic Skills Remediation Remediation is offered one-on-one for computer skills, learning strategies, math, reading, study skills, time management, written language, and others. Remediation is provided collaboratively through on-campus or off-campus services via LD specialists, professional tutors, regular education teachers, and trained peer tutors.

Application For admittance to the program or unit, students are required to provide a psychoeducational report (3 years old or less). It is recommended that students provide documentation of high school services. Upon application, materials documenting need for services should be sent only to the LD program or unit. Upon acceptance, documentation of need for services should be sent only to the LD program or unit. *Application deadline (institutional):* Continuous. *Application deadline (LD program):* Rolling/continuous for fall.

Written Policies Written policy regarding general/basic LD accommodations is outlined in the school's catalog/handbook. Written policies regarding course substitutions, general/basic LD accommodations, reduced course loads, substitutions and waivers of admissions requirements, and substitutions and waivers of graduation requirements are available through the program or unit directly.

Maui Community College

310 Kaahumanu Avenue
Kahului, HI 96732
http://mauicc.hawaii.edu
Contact: Ms. Lisa Correa, Special Needs Coordinator.
Phone: 808-984-3496 Ext. 3496. Fax: 808-242-9618. E-mail: lisacorr@hawaii.edu.

Approximately 25 registered undergraduate students were served during 2002-03. The program or unit includes 1 part-time staff member. Academic advisers, counselors, and remediation/learning specialists are provided collaboratively through on-campus or off-campus services.

Unique Aids and Services Aids, services, or accommodations include advocates and career counseling.

Subject-area Tutoring Tutoring is offered one-on-one for some subjects. Tutoring is provided collaboratively through on-campus or off-campus services via professional tutors and trained peer tutors.

Diagnostic Testing Testing for auditory processing, learning strategies, learning styles, math, neuropsychological, personality, reading, social skills, spelling, spoken language, visual processing, and other services is provided collaboratively through on-campus or off-campus services.

Basic Skills Remediation Remediation is offered one-on-one for computer skills, learning strategies, math, reading, spelling, study skills, time management, and written language. Remediation is provided collaboratively through on-campus or off-campus services via professional tutors and trained peer tutors.

Enrichment Programs for career planning, learning strategies, math, oral communication skills, practical computer skills, reading, stress management, study skills, test taking, time management, vocabulary development, and written composition skills are provided collaboratively through on-campus or off-campus services. Credit is offered for career planning, learning strategies, math, oral communication skills, practical computer skills, reading, study skills, test taking, time management, vocabulary development, and written composition skills.

Fees *Diagnostic Testing* fee is $150 to $600.

Application For admittance to the program or unit, students are required to provide a psychoeducational report. It is recommended that students provide documentation of high school services. Upon application, materials documenting need for services should be sent only to the LD program or unit. Upon acceptance, documentation of need for services should be sent only to the LD program or unit. *Application deadline (institutional):* Continuous. *Application deadline (LD program):* Rolling/continuous for fall and rolling/continuous for spring.

Written Policies Written policy regarding general/basic LD accommodations is outlined in the school's catalog/handbook.

Mayland Community College
SOAR Program

PO Box 547
Spruce Pine, NC 28777-0547
http://www.mayland.cc.nc.us/
Contact: Nancy Godwin, Director of the SOAR Program.
Phone: 828-765-7351 Ext. 232. E-mail: ngodwin@mayland.edu.

SOAR Program Approximately 15 registered undergraduate students were served during 2002-03. The program or unit includes 4 full-time and 2 part-time staff members. Academic advisers, counselors, LD specialists, professional tutors, regular education teachers, remediation/learning specialists, skill tutors, strategy tutors, and trained peer tutors are provided through the program or unit. Academic advisers, counselors, professional tutors, regular education teachers, remediation/learning specialists, skill tutors, strategy tutors, and trained peer tutors are provided collaboratively through on-campus or off-campus services.

Orientation The program or unit offers a mandatory 1-hour orientation for new students individually by special arrangement.

Unique Aids and Services Aids, services, or accommodations include advocates, career counseling, digital textbooks, and faculty training.

Subject-area Tutoring Tutoring is offered one-on-one and in small groups. Tutoring is provided through the program or unit via computer-based instruction, LD specialists, professional tutors, and trained peer tutors. Tutoring is also provided collaboratively through on-campus or off-campus services via trained peer tutors.

Basic Skills Remediation Remediation is offered one-on-one and in small groups for computer skills, learning strategies, math, reading, study skills, time management, and written language. Reme-

Mayland Community College (continued)

diation is provided through the program or unit via computer-based instruction, LD specialists, and trained peer tutors. Remediation is also provided collaboratively through on-campus or off-campus services via trained peer tutors.

Enrichment Enrichment programs are available through the program or unit for learning strategies, math, oral communication skills, practical computer skills, reading, self-advocacy, stress management, study skills, test taking, time management, and written composition skills. Programs for career planning, health and nutrition, math, reading, study skills, test taking, time management, vocabulary development, and written composition skills are provided collaboratively through on-campus or off-campus services. Credit is offered for math, oral communication skills, practical computer skills, reading, stress management, study skills, test taking, time management, vocabulary development, and written composition skills.

Application For admittance to the program or unit, students are required to apply to the program directly, provide a psychoeducational report (3 years old or less), and provide documentation of high school services. *Application deadline (institutional):* Continuous. *Application deadline (LD program):* Rolling/continuous for fall and rolling/continuous for spring.

Written Policies Written policy regarding general/basic LD accommodations is available through the program or unit directly.

Mercer County Community College

1200 Old Trenton Road, PO Box B
Trenton, NJ 08690-1004
http://www.mccc.edu/
Contact: Arlene Stinson, Director of Academic Support Services. Phone: 609-586-4800 Ext. 3525. E-mail: stinsona@mccc.edu.

Approximately 350 registered undergraduate students were served during 2002-03. The program or unit includes 2 full-time and 2 part-time staff members. Academic advisers, counselors, LD specialists, and professional tutors are provided through the program or unit. Academic advisers, counselors, LD specialists, and professional tutors are provided collaboratively through on-campus or off-campus services.

Orientation The program or unit offers an optional orientation for new students during registration and after classes begin.

Unique Aids and Services Aids, services, or accommodations include advocates and career counseling.

Subject-area Tutoring Tutoring is offered one-on-one, in small groups, and in class-size groups for all subjects. Tutoring is provided collaboratively through on-campus or off-campus services via professional tutors and trained peer tutors.

Basic Skills Remediation Remediation is offered in class-size groups for math, reading, and written language. Remediation is provided collaboratively through on-campus or off-campus services via LD specialists and professional tutors.

Enrichment Programs for career planning, college survival skills, learning strategies, math, self-advocacy, stress management, study skills, test taking, and time management are provided collaboratively through on-campus or off-campus services. Credit is offered for math.

Application For admittance to the program or unit, students are required to apply to the program directly, provide a psychoeducational report (3 years old or less), and provide documentation of high school services. Upon application, materials documenting need for services should be sent only to the LD program or unit. *Application deadline (institutional):* Continuous. *Application deadline (LD program):* Rolling/continuous for fall.

Written Policies Written policy regarding general/basic LD accommodations is available on the program Web site. Written policies regarding course substitutions, general/basic LD accommodations, substitutions and waivers of admissions requirements, and substitutions and waivers of graduation requirements are outlined in the school's catalog/handbook. Written policy regarding general/basic LD accommodations is available through the program or unit directly.

Metropolitan Community College
Special Support Services

PO Box 3777
Omaha, NE 68103-0777
http://www.mccneb.edu/
Contact: Mr. James Grotrian, Executive Dean of Campus and Student Services. Phone: 800-228-9553. Fax: 402-457-2788. E-mail: jgrotrian@metropo.mccneb.edu.

Special Support Services Approximately 150 registered undergraduate students were served during 2002-03. The program or unit includes 4 full-time and 15 part-time staff members. Academic advisers, counselors, professional tutors, regular education teachers, remediation/learning specialists, skill tutors, trained peer tutors, and other are provided collaboratively through on-campus or off-campus services.

Orientation The program or unit offers an optional orientation for new students before registration, during registration, and individually by special arrangement.

Unique Aids and Services Aids, services, or accommodations include advocates, career counseling, digital textbooks, faculty training, meetings with faculty as needed.

Subject-area Tutoring Tutoring is offered one-on-one and in small groups for most subjects. Tutoring is provided collaboratively through on-campus or off-campus services via computer-based instruction, professional tutors, trained peer tutors, and other.

Basic Skills Remediation Remediation is offered one-on-one, in small groups, and in class-size groups for computer skills, math, reading, study skills, and written language. Remediation is provided collaboratively through on-campus or off-campus services via computer-based instruction, professional tutors, regular education teachers, trained peer tutors, and other.

Enrichment Programs for career planning, college survival skills, learning strategies, math, oral communication skills, practical computer skills, reading, self-advocacy, stress management, study skills, test taking, time management, vocabulary development, written composition skills, and other are provided collaboratively through on-campus or off-campus services.

Application For admittance to the program or unit, students are required to provide a psychoeducational report. It is recommended that students provide documentation of high school services and provide other documentation. Upon application, materials documenting need for services should be sent only to the LD program or unit. Upon acceptance, documentation of need for services should be sent only to the LD program or unit. *Application deadline (institutional):* Continuous. *Application deadline (LD program):* Rolling/continuous for fall and rolling/continuous for spring.

Written Policies Written policy regarding general/basic LD accommodations is available on the program Web site. Written policy regarding general/basic LD accommodations is outlined in the school's catalog/handbook. Written policy regarding general/basic LD accommodations is available through the program or unit directly.

Middlesex Community College

100 Training Hill Road

Middletown, CT 06457-4889

http://www.mxcc.commnet.edu/

Contact: Mrs. Diane von Hardenberg, Learning Specialist. Phone: 860-343-5879. Fax: 860-343-5735. E-mail: dvonhardenberg@mxcc.commnet.edu.

Approximately 125 registered undergraduate students were served during 2002-03.

Unique Aids and Services Aids, services, or accommodations include advocates, career counseling, faculty training, priority registration, and support groups.

Subject-area Tutoring Tutoring is offered one-on-one and in small groups for most subjects. Tutoring is provided through the program or unit via LD specialists. Tutoring is also provided collaboratively through on-campus or off-campus services via computer-based instruction and trained peer tutors.

Basic Skills Remediation Remediation is offered one-on-one for learning strategies, social skills, spoken language, study skills, time management, and written language. Remediation is provided through the program or unit via LD specialists.

Enrichment Enrichment programs are available through the program or unit for learning strategies, self-advocacy, stress management, study skills, test taking, and time management. Programs for career planning, math, reading, and written composition skills are provided collaboratively through on-campus or off-campus services.

Application For admittance to the program or unit, students are required to provide a psychoeducational report. It is recommended that students provide documentation of high school services. Upon application, materials documenting need for services should be sent only to the LD program or unit. Upon acceptance, documentation of need for services should be sent only to the LD program or unit. *Application deadline (institutional):* Continuous.

Written Policies Written policy regarding general/basic LD accommodations is outlined in the school's catalog/handbook. Written policy regarding general/basic LD accommodations is available through the program or unit directly.

Middlesex Community College
Disability Support Services

Springs Road

Bedford, MA 01730-1655

http://www.middlesex.cc.ma.us/student_Serv/disability_support/www.middlesex.cc.ma.us/student_Serv/disability_support/

Contact: Pamela B. Flaherty, Assistant Dean of Student Development. Phone: 781-280-3631. E-mail: flahertyp@middlesex.cc.ma.us.

Disability Support Services Approximately 550 registered undergraduate students were served during 2002-03. The program or unit includes 2 full-time and 3 part-time staff members. Academic advisers, counselors, LD specialists, professional tutors, remediation/learning specialists, skill tutors, and strategy tutors are provided through the program or unit. Academic advisers, counselors, diagnostic specialists, professional tutors, regular education teachers, remediation/learning specialists, skill tutors, and strategy tutors are provided collaboratively through on-campus or off-campus services.

Summer Program To help prepare for the demands of college, there is an optional 1-week summer program prior to entering the school.

Unique Aids and Services Aids, services, or accommodations include advocates, career counseling, digital textbooks, faculty training, and weekly meetings with faculty.

Subject-area Tutoring Tutoring is offered one-on-one, in small groups, and in class-size groups for most subjects. Tutoring is provided through the program or unit via LD specialists. Tutoring is also provided collaboratively through on-campus or off-campus services via computer-based instruction, professional tutors, and trained peer tutors.

Basic Skills Remediation Remediation is offered in class-size groups for auditory processing, computer skills, learning strategies, math, motor skills, reading, social skills, spelling, spoken language, study skills, time management, visual processing, and written language. Remediation is provided through the program or unit via LD specialists. Remediation is also provided collaboratively through on-campus or off-campus services via computer-based instruction, LD specialists, professional tutors, regular education teachers, and other.

Enrichment Enrichment programs are available through the program or unit for career planning, college survival skills, learning strategies, oral communication skills, reading, self-advocacy, stress management, study skills, test taking, time management, vocabulary development, written composition skills, and other. Programs for career planning, college survival skills, health and nutrition, learning strategies, math, medication management, oral communication skills, practical computer skills, reading, self-advocacy, stress management, study skills, test taking, time management, vocabulary development, written composition skills, and other are provided collaboratively through on-campus or off-campus services.

Application For admittance to the program or unit, students are required to apply to the program directly and provide a psychoeducational report (3 years old or less). It is recommended that students provide documentation of high school services. Upon application,

Middlesex Community College (continued)

materials documenting need for services should be sent only to the LD program or unit. *Application deadline (institutional):* Continuous. *Application deadline (LD program):* Rolling/continuous for fall.
Written Policies Written policies regarding general/basic LD accommodations and reduced course loads are available through the program or unit directly.

Midland College

3600 North Garfield
Midland, TX 79705-6399
http://www.midland.edu/
Contact: Mr. Dale Edward Williams, Director of Career Center/Counselor. Phone: 915-685-4695. Fax: 915-685-4774. E-mail: dewilliams@midland.edu.

Approximately 30 registered undergraduate students were served during 2002-03. The program or unit includes 2 full-time staff members. Academic advisers, counselors, and skill tutors are provided through the program or unit.
Unique Aids and Services Aids, services, or accommodations include career counseling, priority registration, and weekly meetings with faculty.
Subject-area Tutoring Tutoring is offered one-on-one for all subjects. Tutoring is provided through the program or unit via graduate assistants/students.
Basic Skills Remediation Remediation is offered in class-size groups for math, reading, spelling, study skills, and time management. Remediation is provided collaboratively through on-campus or off-campus services via regular education teachers.
Enrichment Enrichment programs are available through the program or unit for career planning, college survival skills, math, reading, and study skills.
Application For admittance to the program or unit, students are required to provide a psychoeducational report (5 years old or less). Upon application, materials documenting need for services should be sent only to the LD program or unit. Upon acceptance, documentation of need for services should be sent only to the LD program or unit. *Application deadline (institutional):* Continuous. *Application deadline (LD program):* Rolling/continuous for fall and rolling/continuous for spring.
Written Policies Written policies regarding course substitutions, general/basic LD accommodations, grade forgiveness, reduced course loads, substitutions and waivers of admissions requirements, and substitutions and waivers of graduation requirements are available through the program or unit directly.

Midlands Technical College

PO Box 2408
Columbia, SC 29202-2408
http://www.midlandstech.com/
Contact: Ms. Karen Pettus, Director of Counseling Services. Phone: 803-822-3508. E-mail: pettusk@midlandstech.com.

Approximately 87 registered undergraduate students were served during 2002-03. The program or unit includes 7 full-time staff members and 1 part-time staff member. Counselors are provided through the program or unit. Academic advisers, diagnostic specialists, regular education teachers, remediation/learning specialists, skill tutors, strategy tutors, and trained peer tutors are provided collaboratively through on-campus or off-campus services.
Unique Aids and Services Aids, services, or accommodations include career counseling and parent workshops.
Subject-area Tutoring Tutoring is offered one-on-one, in small groups, and in class-size groups for some subjects. Tutoring is provided collaboratively through on-campus or off-campus services via computer-based instruction and trained peer tutors.
Basic Skills Remediation Remediation is offered in class-size groups for learning strategies, math, reading, study skills, time management, and written language. Remediation is provided collaboratively through on-campus or off-campus services via regular education teachers.
Enrichment Enrichment programs are available through the program or unit for career planning. Programs for career planning, college survival skills, learning strategies, math, practical computer skills, reading, study skills, test taking, time management, and written composition skills are provided collaboratively through on-campus or off-campus services. Credit is offered for college survival skills, learning strategies, math, practical computer skills, reading, study skills, test taking, time management, and written composition skills.
Application For admittance to the program or unit, students are required to apply to the program directly and provide a psychoeducational report (3 years old or less). Upon application, materials documenting need for services should be sent only to the LD program or unit. Upon acceptance, documentation of need for services should be sent only to the LD program or unit. *Application deadline (institutional):* 7/20. *Application deadline (LD program):* Rolling/continuous for fall and rolling/continuous for spring.
Written Policies Written policies regarding general/basic LD accommodations, reduced course loads, and substitutions and waivers of graduation requirements are available on the program Web site. Written policy regarding substitutions and waivers of graduation requirements is outlined in the school's catalog/handbook. Written policies regarding general/basic LD accommodations and reduced course loads are available through the program or unit directly.

Mid Michigan Community College

1375 South Clare Avenue
Harrison, MI 48625-9447
http://www.midmich.cc.mi.us/
Contact: Ms. Susan M. Cobb, Special Populations Coordinator/Counselor. Phone: 989-386-6636. Fax: 989-386-2411. E-mail: scobb@midmich.edu.

Approximately 40 registered undergraduate students were served during 2002-03. The program or unit includes 1 full-time staff member. Counselors are provided through the program or unit. Academic advisers, remediation/learning specialists, skill tutors, and trained peer tutors are provided collaboratively through on-campus or off-campus services.

Orientation The program or unit offers an optional orientation for new students individually by special arrangement.

Unique Aids and Services Aids, services, or accommodations include advocates and career counseling.

Subject-area Tutoring Tutoring is offered one-on-one and in small groups for most subjects. Tutoring is provided collaboratively through on-campus or off-campus services via computer-based instruction and trained peer tutors.

Diagnostic Testing Testing for auditory processing, learning strategies, learning styles, math, personality, and reading is provided collaboratively through on-campus or off-campus services.

Basic Skills Remediation Remediation is offered in small groups for math, reading, study skills, time management, and written language. Remediation is provided collaboratively through on-campus or off-campus services via computer-based instruction, regular education teachers, and trained peer tutors.

Enrichment Programs for career planning, learning strategies, math, oral communication skills, practical computer skills, reading, stress management, study skills, test taking, time management, and written composition skills are provided collaboratively through on-campus or off-campus services. Credit is offered for math, oral communication skills, practical computer skills, reading, stress management, and written composition skills.

Application For admittance to the program or unit, students are required to apply to the program directly. It is recommended that students provide documentation of high school services. Upon application, materials documenting need for services should be sent only to admissions with institutional application materials. Upon acceptance, documentation of need for services should be sent only to the LD program or unit. *Application deadline (institutional):* Continuous. *Application deadline (LD program):* 6/1 for fall. 11/1 for spring.

Written Policies Written policy regarding general/basic LD accommodations is available on the program Web site. Written policy regarding general/basic LD accommodations is outlined in the school's catalog/handbook.

Mid-South Community College

2000 West Broadway

West Memphis, AR 72301

http://www.midsouthcc.edu/

Contact: Dr. Nancy M. Vandett, Vice President for Learning Support and Student Disability Services Coordinator. Phone: 870-733-6779. Fax: 870-733-6719. E-mail: nvandett@midsouthcc.edu.

Approximately 20 registered undergraduate students were served during 2002-03. Academic advisers, counselors, remediation/learning specialists, and skill tutors are provided collaboratively through on-campus or off-campus services.

Unique Aids and Services Aids, services, or accommodations include faculty training.

Subject-area Tutoring Tutoring is offered in small groups for most subjects. Tutoring is provided collaboratively through on-campus or off-campus services via computer-based instruction and trained peer tutors.

Diagnostic Testing Testing for learning strategies, learning styles, reading, and study skills is provided collaboratively through on-campus or off-campus services.

Basic Skills Remediation Remediation is offered in class-size groups for math, reading, and written language. Remediation is provided collaboratively through on-campus or off-campus services via computer-based instruction and regular education teachers.

Enrichment Programs for career planning, college survival skills, learning strategies, math, oral communication skills, practical computer skills, reading, self-advocacy, stress management, study skills, test taking, time management, and written composition skills are provided collaboratively through on-campus or off-campus services. Credit is offered for college survival skills, learning strategies, math, oral communication skills, practical computer skills, reading, study skills, and written composition skills.

Fees *Diagnostic Testing* fee is $5.

Application For admittance to the program or unit, students are required to provide a psychoeducational report (5 years old or less). It is recommended that students provide documentation of high school services. Upon acceptance, documentation of need for services should be sent only to the LD program or unit. *Application deadline (institutional):* Continuous. *Application deadline (LD program):* 8/15 for fall. 1/5 for spring.

Written Policies Written policies regarding course substitutions, general/basic LD accommodations, grade forgiveness, and substitutions and waivers of graduation requirements are available on the program Web site. Written policies regarding course substitutions, general/basic LD accommodations, grade forgiveness, and substitutions and waivers of graduation requirements are outlined in the school's catalog/handbook. Written policies regarding general/basic LD accommodations and substitutions and waivers of graduation requirements are available through the program or unit directly.

Mid-State Technical College
Disability Services

500 32nd Street North

Wisconsin Rapids, WI 54494-5599

http://www.mstc.edu/

Contact: Ms. Patti J. Lloyd, Disability Services Coordinator. Phone: 715-422-5452. Fax: 715-422-5440. E-mail: patti.lloyd@mstc.edu.

Disability Services Approximately 180 registered undergraduate students were served during 2002-03. The program or unit includes 3 full-time staff members. Services are provided through the program or unit. Academic advisers, counselors, regular education teachers, skill tutors, and other are provided collaboratively through on-campus or off-campus services.

Summer Program To help prepare for the demands of college, there is an optional 1-day summer program prior to entering the school.

Unique Aids and Services Aids, services, or accommodations include advocates, career counseling, digital textbooks, and faculty training.

Subject-area Tutoring Tutoring is offered one-on-one, in small groups, and in class-size groups for most subjects. Tutoring is provided collaboratively through on-campus or off-campus services via professional tutors and trained peer tutors.

Mid-State Technical College (continued)

Basic Skills Remediation Remediation is offered one-on-one, in small groups, and in class-size groups for learning strategies, math, reading, spelling, study skills, time management, and written language. Remediation is provided collaboratively through on-campus or off-campus services via computer-based instruction, regular education teachers, and trained peer tutors.

Enrichment Programs for career planning, college survival skills, learning strategies, math, practical computer skills, reading, self-advocacy, stress management, study skills, test taking, time management, and written composition skills are provided collaboratively through on-campus or off-campus services. Credit is offered for college survival skills, math, practical computer skills, reading, study skills, and written composition skills.

Application For admittance to the program or unit, students are required to apply to the program directly, provide a psychoeducational report (5 years old or less), and provide documentation of high school services. Upon application, materials documenting need for services should be sent only to the LD program or unit. Upon acceptance, documentation of need for services should be sent only to the LD program or unit. *Application deadline (institutional):* Continuous. *Application deadline (LD program):* Rolling/continuous for fall and rolling/continuous for spring.

Written Policies Written policy regarding general/basic LD accommodations is available on the program Web site. Written policy regarding general/basic LD accommodations is outlined in the school's catalog/handbook.

Mineral Area College
ACCESS Office

PO Box 1000
Park Hills, MO 63601-1000
http://www.mineralarea.edu/
Contact: Phone: 573-431-4593.

ACCESS Office Approximately 25 registered undergraduate students were served during 2002-03. The program or unit includes 1 full-time staff member.

Unique Aids and Services Aids, services, or accommodations include career counseling, texts on tape, out-of-class testing, readers or writers for tests.

Subject-area Tutoring Tutoring is offered one-on-one and in small groups for some subjects. Tutoring is provided collaboratively through on-campus or off-campus services via professional tutors, trained peer tutors, and other.

Basic Skills Remediation Remediation is offered one-on-one for math and written language. Remediation is provided collaboratively through on-campus or off-campus services via professional tutors.

Enrichment Enrichment programs are available through the program or unit for learning strategies, self-advocacy, stress management, study skills, test taking, time management, and other. Programs for career planning, college survival skills, health and nutrition, math, medication management, oral communication skills, practical computer skills, reading, vocabulary development, and written composition skills are provided collaboratively through on-campus or off-campus services. Credit is offered for career planning, college survival skills, oral communication skills, and practical computer skills.

Application For admittance to the program or unit, students are required to apply to the program directly and provide a psychoeducational report (5 years old or less). It is recommended that students provide documentation of high school services. Upon application, materials documenting need for services should be sent only to the LD program or unit. Upon acceptance, documentation of need for services should be sent only to the LD program or unit. *Application deadline (institutional):* Continuous.

Written Policies Written policies regarding general/basic LD accommodations and substitutions and waivers of graduation requirements are outlined in the school's catalog/handbook. Written policy regarding general/basic LD accommodations is available through the program or unit directly.

Minnesota State College-Southeast Technical
Learning Resource Center

1250 Homer Road, PO Box 409
Winona, MN 55987
http://www.southeastmn.edu/

Contact: Mrs. Alice Zimmer, Director of Learning Resources. Phone: 507-453-2723. Fax: 507-453-2715. E-mail: azimmer@southeastmn.edu.

Learning Resource Center Approximately 50 registered undergraduate students were served during 2002-03. The program or unit includes 1 full-time staff member. LD specialists, professional tutors, and remediation/learning specialists are provided through the program or unit. Academic advisers, counselors, diagnostic specialists, regular education teachers, skill tutors, and trained peer tutors are provided collaboratively through on-campus or off-campus services.

Orientation The program or unit offers an optional orientation for new students before registration, before classes begin, during summer prior to enrollment, and individually by special arrangement.

Unique Aids and Services Aids, services, or accommodations include advocates, career counseling, priority registration, and weekly meetings with faculty.

Subject-area Tutoring Tutoring is offered one-on-one and in small groups for all subjects. Tutoring is provided through the program or unit via LD specialists, professional tutors, and trained peer tutors. Tutoring is also provided collaboratively through on-campus or off-campus services via trained peer tutors.

Basic Skills Remediation Remediation is offered one-on-one and in small groups for computer skills, learning strategies, math, reading, spelling, spoken language, and written language. Remediation is provided through the program or unit via LD specialists, professional tutors, and trained peer tutors. Remediation is also provided collaboratively through on-campus or off-campus services via regular education teachers.

Enrichment Enrichment programs are available through the program or unit for math, oral communication skills, practical computer skills, reading, vocabulary development, and written composition skills. Programs for career planning, college survival skills, learning strategies, self-advocacy, stress management, study skills, test taking, and time management are provided collaboratively through on-campus or off-campus services.

Application For admittance to the program or unit, students are required to provide a psychoeducational report (2 years old or less). It is recommended that students apply to the program directly, provide documentation of high school services, and provide physiological evaluations. Upon application, materials documenting need for services should be sent only to admissions with institutional application materials. Upon acceptance, documentation of need for services should be sent only to admissions. *Application deadline (institutional):* Continuous. *Application deadline (LD program):* Rolling/continuous for fall and rolling/continuous for spring.

Written Policies Written policies regarding course substitutions, general/basic LD accommodations, and substitutions and waivers of admissions requirements are available on the program Web site. Written policies regarding course substitutions, general/basic LD accommodations, and substitutions and waivers of admissions requirements are outlined in the school's catalog/handbook.

MiraCosta College

One Barnard Drive

Oceanside, CA 92056-3899

http://www.miracosta.edu/

Contact: Ms. Nancy Klump Schaefer, Learning Disabilities Specialist. Phone: 760-795-6658. Fax: 760-795-6604. E-mail: nschaefer@miracosta.edu. Head of LD Program: Ms. Loretta Bohl, DSPS Coordinator. Phone: 760-795-6658. Fax: 760-795-6604. E-mail: lbohl@miracosta.edu.

Approximately 225 registered undergraduate students were served during 2002-03. The program or unit includes 5 full-time and 2 part-time staff members. Academic advisers, counselors, diagnostic specialists, LD specialists, remediation/learning specialists, and special education teachers are provided through the program or unit. Academic advisers, counselors, professional tutors, and regular education teachers are provided collaboratively through on-campus or off-campus services.

Orientation The program or unit offers an optional orientation for new students individually by special arrangement.

Unique Aids and Services Aids, services, or accommodations include career counseling, priority registration, and support groups.

Subject-area Tutoring Tutoring is offered one-on-one and in small groups for most subjects. Tutoring is provided collaboratively through on-campus or off-campus services via trained peer tutors.

Diagnostic Testing Testing is provided through the program or unit for auditory processing, intelligence, learning strategies, learning styles, math, reading, spelling, study skills, visual processing, and written language.

Basic Skills Remediation Remediation is offered in class-size groups for learning strategies, math, reading, study skills, time management, and written language. Remediation is provided through the program or unit via LD specialists and special education teachers. Remediation is also provided collaboratively through on-campus or off-campus services via computer-based instruction and regular education teachers.

Enrichment Programs for career planning, college survival skills, health and nutrition, learning strategies, math, oral communication skills, reading, study skills, and written composition skills are provided collaboratively through on-campus or off-campus services.

Credit is offered for career planning, college survival skills, health and nutrition, learning strategies, math, oral communication skills, reading, study skills, and written composition skills.

Fees *LD Program or Service* fee is $11 (fee varies according to course level and degree level). *Diagnostic Testing* fee is $6.

Application For admittance to the program or unit, students are required to apply to the program directly, provide a psychoeducational report (3 years old or less), and provide documentation of high school services. Upon application, materials documenting need for services should be sent only to the LD program or unit. Upon acceptance, documentation of need for services should be sent only to the LD program or unit. *Application deadline (institutional):* Continuous. *Application deadline (LD program):* Rolling/continuous for fall and rolling/continuous for spring.

Written Policies Written policies regarding course substitutions, general/basic LD accommodations, reduced course loads, and substitutions and waivers of graduation requirements are available on the program Web site. Written policies regarding course substitutions, general/basic LD accommodations, and substitutions and waivers of graduation requirements are outlined in the school's catalog/handbook. Written policies regarding course substitutions, general/basic LD accommodations, and substitutions and waivers of graduation requirements are available through the program or unit directly.

Montana State University-Great Falls College of Technology
Disability Services

2100 16th Avenue, South

Great Falls, MT 59405

http://www.msugf.edu/sservices/

Contact: Jill M. Davis, Disability Services Coordinator. Phone: 406-771-4311. Fax: 406-771-4317. E-mail: jdavis@msugf.edu.

Disability Services Approximately 30 registered undergraduate students were served during 2002-03. The program or unit includes 1 full-time and 2 part-time staff members. Counselors, diagnostic specialists, LD specialists, and strategy tutors are provided through the program or unit. Academic advisers, counselors, professional tutors, regular education teachers, remediation/learning specialists, and skill tutors are provided collaboratively through on-campus or off-campus services.

Subject-area Tutoring Tutoring is offered one-on-one for most subjects. Tutoring is provided through the program or unit via LD specialists and trained peer tutors. Tutoring is also provided collaboratively through on-campus or off-campus services via computer-based instruction and trained peer tutors.

Enrichment Enrichment programs are available through the program or unit for career planning, college survival skills, learning strategies, practical computer skills, self-advocacy, stress management, study skills, test taking, and time management. Programs for career planning, college survival skills, practical computer skills, study skills, test taking, time management, and written composition skills are provided collaboratively through on-campus or off-campus services.

Montana State University-Great Falls College of Technology (continued)

Application For admittance to the program or unit, students are required to apply to the program directly and provide a psychoeducational report (3 years old or less). It is recommended that students provide documentation of high school services. Upon application, materials documenting need for services should be sent only to the LD program or unit. Upon acceptance, documentation of need for services should be sent only to the LD program or unit. *Application deadline (institutional):* Continuous. *Application deadline (LD program):* Rolling/continuous for fall and rolling/continuous for spring.

Written Policies Written policy regarding general/basic LD accommodations is available through the program or unit directly.

Montgomery College
Special Services Office

3200 College Park Drive

Conroe, TX 77384

http://wwwmc.nhmccd.edu/

Contact: Special Services Office. Phone: 936-273-7239. Fax: 936-273-7234.

Special Services Office Approximately 155 registered undergraduate students were served during 2002-03. Academic advisers, counselors, professional tutors, regular education teachers, and remediation/learning specialists are provided collaboratively through on-campus or off-campus services.

Unique Aids and Services Aids, services, or accommodations include career counseling and faculty training.

Subject-area Tutoring Tutoring is offered in small groups for most subjects. Tutoring is provided collaboratively through on-campus or off-campus services via computer-based instruction and professional tutors.

Basic Skills Remediation Remediation is offered in small groups and in class-size groups for learning strategies, math, reading, spelling, study skills, time management, and written language. Remediation is provided collaboratively through on-campus or off-campus services via computer-based instruction, professional tutors, and regular education teachers.

Enrichment Programs for career planning, college survival skills, health and nutrition, learning strategies, math, oral communication skills, practical computer skills, reading, self-advocacy, stress management, study skills, test taking, time management, vocabulary development, and written composition skills are provided collaboratively through on-campus or off-campus services. Credit is offered for health and nutrition, math, oral communication skills, practical computer skills, reading, and written composition skills.

Application For admittance to the program or unit, students are required to provide a psychoeducational report (3 years old or less). It is recommended that students provide documentation of high school services. Upon application, materials documenting need for services should be sent only to the LD program or unit. Upon acceptance, documentation of need for services should be sent only to the LD program or unit. *Application deadline (institutional):* Continuous. *Application deadline (LD program):* Rolling/continuous for fall and rolling/continuous for spring.

Written Policies Written policies regarding course substitutions and general/basic LD accommodations are available on the program Web site. Written policies regarding course substitutions and general/basic LD accommodations are outlined in the school's catalog/handbook. Written policy regarding general/basic LD accommodations is available through the program or unit directly.

Moorpark College
ACCESS (Accessibility Coordination Center and Educational Support Services)

7075 Campus Road

Moorpark, CA 93021-1695

http://www.moorparkcollege.edu/access/

Contact: Ms. Melanie Masters, LD Specialist. Phone: 805-378-1461. Fax: 805-378-1598. E-mail: mmasters@vcccd.net.

ACCESS (Accessibility Coordination Center and Educational Support Services) Approximately 330 registered undergraduate students were served during 2002-03. The program or unit includes 12 full-time and 3 part-time staff members. Academic advisers, counselors, diagnostic specialists, graduate assistants/students, LD specialists, remediation/learning specialists, and special education teachers are provided through the program or unit. Academic advisers, counselors, diagnostic specialists, graduate assistants/students, LD specialists, professional tutors, regular education teachers, remediation/learning specialists, skill tutors, special education teachers, and trained peer tutors are provided collaboratively through on-campus or off-campus services.

Orientation The program or unit offers a mandatory 1 to 2-hour orientation for new students before registration, before classes begin, during summer prior to enrollment, and individually by special arrangement.

Summer Program To help prepare for the demands of college, there is an optional 4-week summer program prior to entering the school.

Unique Aids and Services Aids, services, or accommodations include advocates, career counseling, digital textbooks, faculty training, priority registration, support groups, and weekly meetings with faculty.

Subject-area Tutoring Tutoring is offered in small groups for most subjects. Tutoring is provided through the program or unit via computer-based instruction and LD specialists. Tutoring is also provided collaboratively through on-campus or off-campus services via computer-based instruction, graduate assistants/students, and trained peer tutors.

Diagnostic Testing Testing is provided through the program or unit for auditory processing, intelligence, learning strategies, learning styles, math, motor skills, neuropsychological, reading, spelling, spoken language, study skills, visual processing, and written language. Testing for spoken language, study skills, and written language is provided collaboratively through on-campus or off-campus services.

Basic Skills Remediation Remediation is offered in small groups and in class-size groups for auditory processing, computer skills, learning strategies, math, reading, social skills, spoken language, study skills, time management, visual processing, and written language. Remediation is provided through the program or unit via computer-based instruction, LD specialists, and special education teachers. Remediation is also provided collaboratively through on-campus or off-campus services via computer-based instruction, regular education teachers, and trained peer tutors.

Enrichment Enrichment programs are available through the program or unit for career planning, college survival skills, health and nutrition, learning strategies, math, practical computer skills, reading, self-advocacy, stress management, study skills, test taking, time management, vocabulary development, and written composition skills. Programs for career planning, college survival skills, health and nutrition, learning strategies, math, practical computer skills, reading, stress management, study skills, test taking, time management, vocabulary development, and written composition skills are provided collaboratively through on-campus or off-campus services. Credit is offered for career planning, college survival skills, health and nutrition, learning strategies, math, practical computer skills, reading, stress management, study skills, test taking, time management, vocabulary development, and written composition skills.

Fees *Diagnostic Testing* fee is $6.

Application For admittance to the program or unit, students are required to apply to the program directly. It is recommended that students provide a psychoeducational report (3 years old or less) and provide documentation of high school services. Upon application, materials documenting need for services should be sent only to the LD program or unit. Upon acceptance, documentation of need for services should be sent only to the LD program or unit. *Application deadline (institutional):* Continuous. *Application deadline (LD program):* Rolling/continuous for fall and rolling/continuous for spring.

Written Policies Written policies regarding course substitutions, general/basic LD accommodations, reduced course loads, and substitutions and waivers of graduation requirements are available on the program Web site. Written policies regarding course substitutions, general/basic LD accommodations, reduced course loads, and substitutions and waivers of graduation requirements are outlined in the school's catalog/handbook. Written policy regarding general/basic LD accommodations is available through the program or unit directly.

Moraine Valley Community College

10900 South 88th Avenue
Palos Hills, IL 60465-0937
http://www.morainevalley.edu/
Contact: Mrs. Debbie Sievers, Director. Phone: 708-974-5711. Fax: 708-974-1184. E-mail: sievers@morainevalley.edu.

Approximately 225 registered undergraduate students were served during 2002-03. The program or unit includes 2 full-time and 4 part-time staff members. Academic advisers, counselors, diagnostic specialists, and LD specialists are provided through the program or unit. Academic advisers, counselors, professional tutors, regular education teachers, remediation/learning specialists, and trained peer tutors are provided collaboratively through on-campus or off-campus services.

Orientation The program or unit offers an optional 3-hour orientation for new students before registration, before classes begin, during summer prior to enrollment, and during registration.

Unique Aids and Services Aids, services, or accommodations include advocates, career counseling, priority registration, and support groups.

Subject-area Tutoring Tutoring is offered in small groups for some subjects. Tutoring is provided collaboratively through on-campus or off-campus services via computer-based instruction, professional tutors, and trained peer tutors.

Diagnostic Testing Testing is provided through the program or unit for auditory processing, handwriting, intelligence, learning strategies, learning styles, math, reading, visual processing, and written language.

Basic Skills Remediation Remediation is offered in class-size groups for math, reading, study skills, time management, and written language. Remediation is provided collaboratively through on-campus or off-campus services via regular education teachers.

Enrichment Programs for career planning, college survival skills, health and nutrition, learning strategies, math, practical computer skills, reading, stress management, study skills, test taking, time management, and written composition skills are provided collaboratively through on-campus or off-campus services. Credit is offered for career planning, college survival skills, health and nutrition, math, practical computer skills, reading, and study skills.

Student Organization Friendly, Informative Students of Success (FISOS) consists of 12 members.

Fees *Diagnostic Testing* fee is $100.

Application For admittance to the program or unit, students are required to apply to the program directly, provide a psychoeducational report (3 years old or less), provide documentation of high school services, and provide medical documentation for additional disabilities. Upon application, materials documenting need for services should be sent only to the LD program or unit. Upon acceptance, documentation of need for services should be sent only to the LD program or unit. *Application deadline (institutional):* Continuous. *Application deadline (LD program):* 5/1 for fall. 10/1 for spring.

Written Policies Written policy regarding general/basic LD accommodations is available on the program Web site. Written policy regarding general/basic LD accommodations is outlined in the school's catalog/handbook. Written policy regarding general/basic LD accommodations is available through the program or unit directly.

Morton College

3801 South Central Avenue
Cicero, IL 60804-4398
http://www.morton.cc.il.us/
Contact: Mr. George Russo, Special Populations Coordinator. Phone: 708-656-8000 Ext. 383. Fax: 708-656-3924. E-mail: russog@morton.cc.il.us. Head of LD Program: Ms. Sue Martin, Director of Counseling and Testing. Phone: 708-656-8000 Ext. 151. E-mail: martins@morton.cc.il.us.

Approximately 70 registered undergraduate students were served during 2002-03. The program or unit includes 4 full-time and 4

Morton College (continued)

part-time staff members. Academic advisers, counselors, diagnostic specialists, professional tutors, regular education teachers, strategy tutors, and trained peer tutors are provided collaboratively through on-campus or off-campus services.

Subject-area Tutoring Tutoring is offered one-on-one and in small groups for some subjects. Tutoring is provided collaboratively through on-campus or off-campus services via computer-based instruction and professional tutors.

Basic Skills Remediation Remediation is offered one-on-one and in small groups for computer skills, learning strategies, math, reading, spoken language, and written language. Remediation is provided collaboratively through on-campus or off-campus services via computer-based instruction and professional tutors.

Enrichment Programs for career planning, college survival skills, math, reading, and written composition skills are provided collaboratively through on-campus or off-campus services.

Application For admittance to the program or unit, students are required to provide a psychoeducational report (3 years old or less) and provide documentation of high school services. Upon application, materials documenting need for services should be sent only to the LD program or unit. Upon acceptance, documentation of need for services should be sent only to the LD program or unit. *Application deadline (institutional):* Continuous. *Application deadline (LD program):* Rolling/continuous for fall and rolling/continuous for spring.

Written Policies Written policy regarding general/basic LD accommodations is available on the program Web site. Written policies regarding general/basic LD accommodations, grade forgiveness, and substitutions and waivers of admissions requirements are outlined in the school's catalog/handbook. Written policies regarding course substitutions, general/basic LD accommodations, grade forgiveness, reduced course loads, and substitutions and waivers of graduation requirements are available through the program or unit directly.

Mt. San Antonio College
Disabled Student Programs and Services (DSP&S)

1100 North Grand Avenue

Walnut, CA 91789-1399

http://DSPS.mtsac.edu

Contact: Dr. James Andrews, Counselor/Psychologist. Phone: 909-594-5611 Ext. 5641. Fax: 909-468-3943. E-mail: jandrews@mtsac.edu. Head of LD Program: Mrs. Grace Hanson, Director of DSP&S. Phone: 909-594-5611 Ext. 4290. Fax: 909-468-3943. E-mail: ghanson@mtsac.edu.

Disabled Student Programs and Services (DSP&S) Approximately 600 registered undergraduate students were served during 2002-03. The program or unit includes 12 full-time and 12 part-time staff members. Academic advisers, counselors, diagnostic specialists, LD specialists, remediation/learning specialists, and special education teachers are provided through the program or unit. Academic advisers, coaches, counselors, graduate assistants/students,

professional tutors, regular education teachers, remediation/learning specialists, skill tutors, special education teachers, strategy tutors, teacher trainees, and trained peer tutors are provided collaboratively through on-campus or off-campus services.

Orientation The program or unit offers a mandatory 1½-hour orientation for new students before registration.

Unique Aids and Services Aids, services, or accommodations include career counseling, digital textbooks, faculty training, and priority registration.

Subject-area Tutoring Tutoring is offered for some subjects. Tutoring is provided collaboratively through on-campus or off-campus services via computer-based instruction, professional tutors, and trained peer tutors.

Diagnostic Testing Testing is provided through the program or unit for auditory processing, intelligence, learning styles, math, reading, and visual processing. Testing for spoken language is provided collaboratively through on-campus or off-campus services.

Basic Skills Remediation Remediation is offered in class-size groups for auditory processing, computer skills, learning strategies, math, reading, spelling, spoken language, study skills, time management, and written language. Remediation is provided through the program or unit via LD specialists. Remediation is also provided collaboratively through on-campus or off-campus services via computer-based instruction, LD specialists, professional tutors, regular education teachers, and trained peer tutors.

Enrichment Enrichment programs are available through the program or unit for career planning, college survival skills, learning strategies, math, oral communication skills, reading, stress management, study skills, test taking, time management, vocabulary development, and written composition skills. Programs for career planning, college survival skills, health and nutrition, learning strategies, math, oral communication skills, practical computer skills, reading, stress management, study skills, test taking, time management, vocabulary development, and written composition skills are provided collaboratively through on-campus or off-campus services. Credit is offered for career planning, college survival skills, health and nutrition, learning strategies, math, oral communication skills, practical computer skills, reading, stress management, study skills, test taking, time management, vocabulary development, and written composition skills.

Student Organization Strength in Diversity Club consists of 30 members.

Application For admittance to the program or unit, students are required to apply to the program directly and provide a psychoeducational report (3 years old or less). Upon application, materials documenting need for services should be sent only to the LD program or unit. *Application deadline (institutional):* 8/16.

Written Policies Written policies regarding course substitutions, general/basic LD accommodations, grade forgiveness, and substitutions and waivers of graduation requirements are outlined in the school's catalog/handbook. Written policies regarding course substitutions, general/basic LD accommodations, and substitutions and waivers of graduation requirements are available through the program or unit directly.

Mount Wachusett Community College
Visions Program (TRIO)

444 Green Street

Gardner, MA 01440-1000

http://www.mwcc.mass.edu/

Contact: Joyce Kulig, Learning Disabilities Specialist. Phone: 978-630-9185. E-mail: j_kulig@mwcc.edu.

Visions Program (TRIO) Approximately 200 registered undergraduate students were served during 2002-03. The program or unit includes 1 full-time and 2 part-time staff members. Academic advisers, counselors, LD specialists, professional tutors, remediation/learning specialists, skill tutors, and strategy tutors are provided through the program or unit. Academic advisers, counselors, professional tutors, remediation/learning specialists, skill tutors, strategy tutors, trained peer tutors, and other are provided collaboratively through on-campus or off-campus services.

Orientation The program or unit offers upon request.

Unique Aids and Services Aids, services, or accommodations include career counseling, digital textbooks, faculty training, priority registration, and support groups.

Subject-area Tutoring Tutoring is offered one-on-one, in small groups, and in class-size groups for all subjects. Tutoring is provided through the program or unit via LD specialists and professional tutors. Tutoring is also provided collaboratively through on-campus or off-campus services via computer-based instruction, professional tutors, trained peer tutors, and other.

Basic Skills Remediation Remediation is offered one-on-one and in small groups for auditory processing, computer skills, learning strategies, math, reading, social skills, study skills, time management, visual processing, and written language. Remediation is provided through the program or unit via LD specialists and professional tutors. Remediation is also provided collaboratively through on-campus or off-campus services via computer-based instruction, professional tutors, trained peer tutors, and other.

Enrichment Enrichment programs are available through the program or unit for college survival skills, learning strategies, math, oral communication skills, practical computer skills, reading, self-advocacy, stress management, study skills, test taking, time management, vocabulary development, and written composition skills. Programs for career planning, college survival skills, health and nutrition, learning strategies, math, medication management, oral communication skills, practical computer skills, reading, self-advocacy, stress management, study skills, test taking, time management, vocabulary development, and written composition skills are provided collaboratively through on-campus or off-campus services. Credit is offered for math, reading, self-advocacy, study skills, test taking, time management, vocabulary development, and written composition skills.

Application For admittance to the program or unit, students are required to apply to the program directly and provide a psychoeducational report (3 years old or less). It is recommended that students provide documentation of high school services. Upon acceptance, documentation of need for services should be sent only to the LD program or unit. *Application deadline (institutional):* Continuous. *Application deadline (LD program):* Rolling/continuous for fall and rolling/continuous for spring.

Written Policies Written policies regarding course substitutions, general/basic LD accommodations, and substitutions and waivers of graduation requirements are available through the program or unit directly.

Muscatine Community College

152 Colorado Street

Muscatine, IA 52761-5396

http://www.eicc.edu/

Contact: Kathryn Trosen, Disability Support Provider. Phone: 563-288-6013. Fax: 563-288-6104. E-mail: ktrosen@eicc.edu.

The program or unit includes 1 full-time staff member. LD specialists are provided through the program or unit.

Unique Aids and Services Aids, services, or accommodations include advocates, career counseling, faculty training, and priority registration.

Subject-area Tutoring Tutoring is offered one-on-one for most subjects. Tutoring is provided through the program or unit via LD specialists. Tutoring is also provided collaboratively through on-campus or off-campus services via trained peer tutors.

Basic Skills Remediation Remediation is offered in class-size groups for learning strategies, math, reading, study skills, time management, and grammar/writing. Remediation is provided collaboratively through on-campus or off-campus services via regular education teachers.

Enrichment Programs for career planning, college survival skills, health and nutrition, learning strategies, practical computer skills, reading, study skills, test taking, and time management are provided collaboratively through on-campus or off-campus services. Credit is offered for career planning, college survival skills, health and nutrition, learning strategies, practical computer skills, reading, study skills, test taking, and time management.

Application For admittance to the program or unit, students are required to apply to the program directly and provide a psychoeducational report. It is recommended that students provide documentation of high school services. Upon acceptance, documentation of need for services should be sent only to the LD program or unit. *Application deadline (institutional):* Continuous. *Application deadline (LD program):* Rolling/continuous for fall.

Written Policies Written policies regarding course substitutions, general/basic LD accommodations, reduced course loads, substitutions and waivers of admissions requirements, and substitutions and waivers of graduation requirements are available through the program or unit directly.

Muskegon Community College
Special Service Programs Office

221 South Quarterline Road

Muskegon, MI 49442-1493

Muskegon Community College (continued)
http://www.muskegon.cc.mi.us/
Contact: Mrs. Janice Walker Alexander, Coordinator and Counselor. Phone: 231-777-0309. Fax: 231-777-0209. E-mail: alexandj@muskegoncc.edu.

Special Service Programs Office Approximately 100 registered undergraduate students were served during 2002-03. The program or unit includes 1 full-time and 1 part-time staff member. Counselors are provided through the program or unit. Academic advisers, counselors, regular education teachers, and trained peer tutors are provided collaboratively through on-campus or off-campus services.

Unique Aids and Services Aids, services, or accommodations include career counseling, digital textbooks, and faculty training.

Subject-area Tutoring Tutoring is offered one-on-one and in small groups for most subjects. Tutoring is provided collaboratively through on-campus or off-campus services via trained peer tutors.

Diagnostic Testing Testing for math, reading, and written language is provided collaboratively through on-campus or off-campus services.

Basic Skills Remediation Remediation is offered one-on-one, in small groups, and in class-size groups for math and reading. Remediation is provided collaboratively through on-campus or off-campus services via regular education teachers, teacher trainees, and trained peer tutors.

Enrichment Programs for career planning, college survival skills, health and nutrition, math, oral communication skills, practical computer skills, reading, study skills, test taking, and written composition skills are provided collaboratively through on-campus or off-campus services. Credit is offered for college survival skills, health and nutrition, math, oral communication skills, practical computer skills, reading, and written composition skills.

Application For admittance to the program or unit, students are required to apply to the program directly and provide a psychoeducational report (5 years old or less). It is recommended that students provide documentation of high school services. Upon application, materials documenting need for services should be sent only to the LD program or unit. Upon acceptance, documentation of need for services should be sent only to the LD program or unit. *Application deadline (institutional):* Continuous. *Application deadline (LD program):* Rolling/continuous for fall and rolling/continuous for spring.

Written Policies Written policy regarding general/basic LD accommodations is available on the program Web site. Written policy regarding general/basic LD accommodations is outlined in the school's catalog/handbook. Written policy regarding general/basic LD accommodations is available through the program or unit directly.

Nassau Community College
Center for Students with Disabilities

1 Education Drive
Garden City, NY 11530-6793
http://www.ncc.edu
Contact: Prof. Janis Schimsky, Director of the Center for Students with Disabilities. Phone: 516-572-7241. Fax: 516-572-9874. E-mail: schimsj@ncc.edu.

Center for Students with Disabilities The program or unit includes 7 full-time and 2 part-time staff members. Academic advisers, counselors, LD specialists, professional tutors, remediation/learning specialists, skill tutors, special education teachers, strategy tutors, trained peer tutors, and other are provided through the program or unit. Professional tutors, regular education teachers, and remediation/learning specialists are provided collaboratively through on-campus or off-campus services.

Orientation The program or unit offers an optional 1-day orientation for new students during summer prior to enrollment.

Unique Aids and Services Aids, services, or accommodations include advocates, career counseling, faculty training, parent workshops, priority registration, and support groups.

Subject-area Tutoring Tutoring is offered one-on-one and in small groups for some subjects. Tutoring is provided through the program or unit via computer-based instruction, LD specialists, professional tutors, trained peer tutors, and other. Tutoring is also provided collaboratively through on-campus or off-campus services via computer-based instruction.

Basic Skills Remediation Remediation is offered one-on-one and in small groups for computer skills, learning strategies, math, reading, social skills, study skills, time management, and written language. Remediation is provided through the program or unit via computer-based instruction, LD specialists, professional tutors, special education teachers, and trained peer tutors. Remediation is also provided collaboratively through on-campus or off-campus services via computer-based instruction and trained peer tutors.

Enrichment Enrichment programs are available through the program or unit for career planning, college survival skills, learning strategies, math, practical computer skills, reading, self-advocacy, study skills, test taking, time management, vocabulary development, and written composition skills. Programs for career planning, college survival skills, health and nutrition, learning strategies, math, practical computer skills, reading, stress management, study skills, test taking, time management, vocabulary development, and written composition skills are provided collaboratively through on-campus or off-campus services. Credit is offered for career planning, college survival skills, health and nutrition, practical computer skills, reading, vocabulary development, and written composition skills.

Student Organization Access Club consists of 45 members.

Application For admittance to the program or unit, students are required to provide a psychoeducational report (3 years old or less) and provide documentation of high school services. Upon acceptance, documentation of need for services should be sent only to the LD program or unit. *Application deadline (institutional):* 8/1. *Application deadline (LD program):* Rolling/continuous for fall and rolling/continuous for spring.

Written Policies Written policy regarding general/basic LD accommodations is available through the program or unit directly.

New England Culinary Institute

250 Main Street
Montpelier, VT 05602-9720
http://www.neci.edu/

Contact: Mr. Matt Trybus, Learning Services Coordinator. Phone: 802-225-3327. Fax: 802-223-8029. E-mail: mattt@neci.edu.

Approximately 15 registered undergraduate students were served during 2002-03. The program or unit includes 2 full-time staff members. LD specialists, professional tutors, skill tutors, strategy tutors, and trained peer tutors are provided through the program or unit. Teacher trainees and trained peer tutors are provided collaboratively through on-campus or off-campus services.

Unique Aids and Services Aids, services, or accommodations include career counseling and faculty training.

Subject-area Tutoring Tutoring is offered one-on-one and in small groups for all subjects. Tutoring is provided through the program or unit via computer-based instruction, LD specialists, professional tutors, and trained peer tutors. Tutoring is also provided collaboratively through on-campus or off-campus services via trained peer tutors.

Basic Skills Remediation Remediation is offered one-on-one for computer skills, learning strategies, math, reading, social skills, spelling, spoken language, study skills, time management, written language, and cooking skills and techniques. Remediation is provided through the program or unit via LD specialists, professional tutors, and trained peer tutors. Remediation is also provided collaboratively through on-campus or off-campus services via trained peer tutors.

Enrichment Programs for career planning, health and nutrition, oral communication skills, practical computer skills, study skills, and written composition skills are provided collaboratively through on-campus or off-campus services. Credit is offered for career planning, health and nutrition, oral communication skills, practical computer skills, and written composition skills.

Application It is recommended that students provide a psychoeducational report (4 years old or less), provide documentation of high school services, and provide other documentation. Upon application, materials documenting need for services should be sent to both admissions and the LD program or unit. Upon acceptance, documentation of need for services should be sent to both admissions and the LD program or unit. *Application deadline (institutional):* Continuous. *Application deadline (LD program):* Rolling/continuous for fall.

Written Policies Written policy regarding general/basic LD accommodations is outlined in the school's catalog/handbook.

New Hampshire Community Technical College, Nashua/Claremont

505 Amherst Street

Nashua, NH 03063-1026

http://www.ncctc.edu/

Contact: Mary Oswald, Disability Coordinator. Phone: 603-882-6923 Ext. 1451. Fax: 603-882-8690. E-mail: moswald@nhctc.edu. Head of LD Program: Mary G. Oswald, Disability Coordinator. Phone: 603-882-6923 Ext. 1451. Fax: 603-882-8690. E-mail: moswald@nhctc.edu.

Approximately 30 registered undergraduate students were served during 2002-03. The program or unit includes 1 full-time staff member. Academic advisers and LD specialists are provided through the program or unit.

Subject-area Tutoring Tutoring is offered one-on-one and in small groups for some subjects. Tutoring is provided through the program or unit via computer-based instruction, professional tutors, and trained peer tutors.

Application For admittance to the program or unit, students are required to apply to the program directly and provide a psychoeducational report (3 years old or less). It is recommended that students provide documentation of high school services. Upon application, materials documenting need for services should be sent only to the LD program or unit. Upon acceptance, documentation of need for services should be sent only to the LD program or unit. *Application deadline (institutional):* Continuous. *Application deadline (LD program):* Rolling/continuous for fall and rolling/continuous for spring.

Written Policies Written policy regarding general/basic LD accommodations is available through the program or unit directly.

New Mexico State University-Alamogordo

2400 North Scenic Drive

Alamogordo, NM 88311-0477

http://alamo.nmsu.edu/

Contact: Phone: 505-439-3600.

The program or unit includes 1 full-time staff member. Academic advisers and counselors are provided through the program or unit. Academic advisers, professional tutors, regular education teachers, remediation/learning specialists, and skill tutors are provided collaboratively through on-campus or off-campus services.

Unique Aids and Services Aids, services, or accommodations include career counseling.

Subject-area Tutoring Tutoring is offered one-on-one and in small groups for most subjects. Tutoring is provided collaboratively through on-campus or off-campus services via computer-based instruction, graduate assistants/students, professional tutors, and trained peer tutors.

Diagnostic Testing Testing for auditory processing, intelligence, math, motor skills, neuropsychological, personality, reading, spelling, and written language is provided collaboratively through on-campus or off-campus services.

Basic Skills Remediation Remediation is offered one-on-one, in small groups, and in class-size groups for computer skills, learning strategies, math, reading, spelling, study skills, time management, and written language. Remediation is provided collaboratively through on-campus or off-campus services via computer-based instruction, professional tutors, regular education teachers, and trained peer tutors.

Enrichment Programs for career planning, math, study skills, test taking, time management, and written composition skills are provided collaboratively through on-campus or off-campus services.

Fees *Diagnostic Testing* fee is applicable.

Application For admittance to the program or unit, students are required to apply to the program directly. It is recommended that students provide a psychoeducational report and provide documen-

New Mexico State University-Alamogordo (continued)

tation of high school services. Upon application, materials documenting need for services should be sent only to the LD program or unit. Upon acceptance, documentation of need for services should be sent only to the LD program or unit. *Application deadline (institutional):* Continuous. *Application deadline (LD program):* Rolling/continuous for fall and rolling/continuous for spring.

Written Policies Written policy regarding general/basic LD accommodations is available on the program Web site. Written policy regarding general/basic LD accommodations is outlined in the school's catalog/handbook. Written policy regarding general/basic LD accommodations is available through the program or unit directly.

New Mexico State University-Carlsbad

1500 University Drive

Carlsbad, NM 88220-3509

http://cavern.nmsu.edu/

Contact: Kay Rankin-Williams, Coordinator of Special Needs Services. Phone: 505-234-9321. Fax: 505-885-4951. E-mail: kwilliams@cavern.nmsu.edu.

Approximately 10 registered undergraduate students were served during 2002-03. The program or unit includes 1 full-time staff member. Academic advisers are provided through the program or unit. Academic advisers, counselors, diagnostic specialists, regular education teachers, remediation/learning specialists, skill tutors, and trained peer tutors are provided collaboratively through on-campus or off-campus services.

Unique Aids and Services Aids, services, or accommodations include career counseling, faculty training, weekly meetings with faculty, books on tape, extended time and quiet testing, note-takers, priority book buy, and others.

Subject-area Tutoring Tutoring is offered one-on-one and in small groups for most subjects. Tutoring is provided collaboratively through on-campus or off-campus services via computer-based instruction and trained peer tutors.

Diagnostic Testing Testing for auditory processing, intelligence, learning strategies, learning styles, math, motor skills, neuropsychological, personality, reading, spelling, study skills, visual processing, and written language is provided collaboratively through on-campus or off-campus services.

Basic Skills Remediation Remediation is offered one-on-one and in small groups for computer skills, learning strategies, math, reading, spelling, study skills, time management, and written language. Remediation is provided through the program or unit via computer-based instruction and trained peer tutors. Remediation is also provided collaboratively through on-campus or off-campus services via computer-based instruction, regular education teachers, trained peer tutors, and other.

Enrichment Enrichment programs are available through the program or unit for self-advocacy, stress management, study skills, test taking, time management, vocabulary development, and written composition skills. Programs for career planning, college survival skills, health and nutrition, learning strategies, math, oral communication skills, practical computer skills, reading, self-advocacy, stress management, study skills, test taking, time management,

vocabulary development, written composition skills, and other are provided collaboratively through on-campus or off-campus services. Credit is offered for career planning, college survival skills, health and nutrition, learning strategies, math, oral communication skills, practical computer skills, reading, stress management, study skills, test taking, time management, vocabulary development, and written composition skills.

Application For admittance to the program or unit, students are required to provide a psychoeducational report (3 years old or less). It is recommended that students provide documentation of high school services. Upon application, materials documenting need for services should be sent only to the LD program or unit. Upon acceptance, documentation of need for services should be sent only to the LD program or unit. *Application deadline (institutional):* Continuous. *Application deadline (LD program):* Rolling/continuous for fall and rolling/continuous for spring.

Written Policies Written policy regarding general/basic LD accommodations is available on the program Web site. Written policy regarding general/basic LD accommodations is outlined in the school's catalog/handbook. Written policy regarding general/basic LD accommodations is available through the program or unit directly.

Northampton County Area Community College
Disability Services

3835 Green Pond Road

Bethlehem, PA 18020-7599

http://www.northampton.edu/

Contact: Laraine A. Demshock, Coordinator of Disability Services. Phone: 610-861-5342. Fax: 610-861-5075. E-mail: ldemshock@northampton.edu.

Disability Services Approximately 350 registered undergraduate students were served during 2002-03. The program or unit includes 4 full-time and 2 part-time staff members. LD specialists are provided through the program or unit. Academic advisers, counselors, and professional tutors are provided collaboratively through on-campus or off-campus services.

Orientation The program or unit offers an optional 3-hour orientation for new students during summer prior to enrollment and during registration.

Unique Aids and Services Aids, services, or accommodations include career counseling and priority registration.

Subject-area Tutoring Tutoring is offered one-on-one and in small groups for all subjects. Tutoring is provided collaboratively through on-campus or off-campus services via LD specialists, professional tutors, and trained peer tutors.

Basic Skills Remediation Remediation is offered one-on-one, in small groups, and in class-size groups for learning strategies, reading, study skills, time management, and written language. Remediation is provided through the program or unit via LD specialists. Remediation is also provided collaboratively through on-campus or off-campus services.

Application For admittance to the program or unit, students are required to provide a psychoeducational report (3 years old or less). It is recommended that students provide documentation of high school services. Upon application, materials documenting need for services should be sent only to the LD program or unit. Upon acceptance, documentation of need for services should be sent only to the LD program or unit. *Application deadline (institutional):* Continuous. *Application deadline (LD program):* Rolling/continuous for fall and rolling/continuous for spring.

Written Policies Written policy regarding general/basic LD accommodations is available on the program Web site. Written policies regarding course substitutions and substitutions and waivers of graduation requirements are outlined in the school's catalog/handbook. Written policies regarding course substitutions, general/basic LD accommodations, and substitutions and waivers of graduation requirements are available through the program or unit directly.

North Central Michigan College

1515 Howard Street
Petoskey, MI 49770-8717
http://www.ncmc.cc.mi.us/
Contact: Mr. Scott L. Hickman, Director. Phone: 231-348-6817. Fax: 231-348-6818. E-mail: scotth@ncmc.cc.mi.us.

The program or unit includes 1 full-time and 1 part-time staff member. Counselors and professional tutors are provided through the program or unit. Academic advisers and diagnostic specialists are provided collaboratively through on-campus or off-campus services.

Unique Aids and Services Aids, services, or accommodations include advocates and career counseling.

Subject-area Tutoring Tutoring is offered one-on-one and in small groups for all subjects. Tutoring is provided collaboratively through on-campus or off-campus services via computer-based instruction, graduate assistants/students, professional tutors, and trained peer tutors.

Basic Skills Remediation Remediation is offered one-on-one for computer skills, math, reading, study skills, time management, and written language. Remediation is provided collaboratively through on-campus or off-campus services via computer-based instruction.

Application It is recommended that students provide a psychoeducational report (3 years old or less) and provide documentation of high school services. Upon acceptance, documentation of need for services should be sent only to the LD program or unit. *Application deadline (institutional):* Continuous. *Application deadline (LD program):* Rolling/continuous for fall and rolling/continuous for spring.

Written Policies Written policies regarding general/basic LD accommodations and reduced course loads are available through the program or unit directly.

North Central State College

2441 Kenwood Circle, PO Box 698
Mansfield, OH 44901-0698
http://www.ncstatecollege.edu/

Contact: Mrs. Sandra Luckie, Coordinator of Specialized Supportive Services. Phone: 419-755-4727. Fax: 419-755-4750. E-mail: sluckie@ncstatecollege.edu.

Approximately 100 registered undergraduate students were served during 2002-03. The program or unit includes 1 full-time and 1 part-time staff member. Academic advisers, trained peer tutors, and other are provided collaboratively through on-campus or off-campus services.

Subject-area Tutoring Tutoring is offered one-on-one, in small groups, and in class-size groups for some subjects. Tutoring is provided collaboratively through on-campus or off-campus services via trained peer tutors and other.

Basic Skills Remediation Remediation is offered in class-size groups for computer skills, learning strategies, reading, study skills, time management, and written language. Remediation is provided collaboratively through on-campus or off-campus services.

Application For admittance to the program or unit, students are required to provide a psychoeducational report (3 years old or less). It is recommended that students provide documentation of high school services and provide multi-factored team report. Upon application, materials documenting need for services should be sent only to the LD program or unit. Upon acceptance, documentation of need for services should be sent only to the LD program or unit. *Application deadline (institutional):* Continuous. *Application deadline (LD program):* Rolling/continuous for fall and rolling/continuous for spring.

Written Policies Written policy regarding general/basic LD accommodations is available on the program Web site. Written policy regarding general/basic LD accommodations is outlined in the school's catalog/handbook. Written policy regarding general/basic LD accommodations is available through the program or unit directly.

North Country Community College

Student Affairs—Learning Assistance Center

20 Winona Avenue, PO Box 89
Saranac Lake, NY 12983-0089
http://www.nccc.edu/

Contact: Dr. Al Iantorno, Dean of Student Affairs. Phone: 518-891-2915 Ext. 204. Fax: 518-891-0898. E-mail: aiantorno@nccc.edu.

Student Affairs—Learning Assistance Center Approximately 100 registered undergraduate students were served during 2002-03. The program or unit includes 5 full-time staff members. Academic advisers, counselors, diagnostic specialists, LD specialists, professional tutors, regular education teachers, remediation/learning specialists, skill tutors, strategy tutors, and trained peer tutors are provided through the program or unit.

Orientation The program or unit offers an optional 1-day orientation for new students before classes begin, during summer prior to enrollment, during registration, and individually by special arrangement.

Unique Aids and Services Aids, services, or accommodations include career counseling, digital textbooks, faculty training, support groups, and weekly meetings with faculty.

North Country Community College (continued)

Subject-area Tutoring Tutoring is offered one-on-one and in small groups for all subjects. Tutoring is provided through the program or unit via computer-based instruction, LD specialists, professional tutors, and trained peer tutors.

Diagnostic Testing Testing is provided through the program or unit for learning strategies, learning styles, math, reading, spelling, study skills, and written language. Testing for auditory processing, handwriting, intelligence, motor skills, neuropsychological, personality, social skills, spoken language, and visual processing is provided collaboratively through on-campus or off-campus services.

Basic Skills Remediation Remediation is offered in small groups and in class-size groups for computer skills, math, reading, spelling, study skills, and written language. Remediation is provided through the program or unit via computer-based instruction, LD specialists, professional tutors, regular education teachers, and trained peer tutors.

Enrichment Enrichment programs are available through the program or unit for career planning, college survival skills, health and nutrition, learning strategies, math, oral communication skills, practical computer skills, reading, self-advocacy, stress management, study skills, test taking, time management, and written composition skills. Credit is offered for career planning, college survival skills, health and nutrition, learning strategies, math, oral communication skills, practical computer skills, reading, study skills, and written composition skills.

Fees *Diagnostic Testing* fee is applicable.

Application For admittance to the program or unit, students are required to provide a psychoeducational report (1 year old or less) and provide documentation of high school services. Upon application, materials documenting need for services should be sent only to admissions with institutional application materials. Upon acceptance, documentation of need for services should be sent only to the LD program or unit. *Application deadline (institutional):* Continuous. *Application deadline (LD program):* Rolling/continuous for fall.

Written Policies Written policy regarding general/basic LD accommodations is outlined in the school's catalog/handbook. Written policy regarding general/basic LD accommodations is available through the program or unit directly.

North Dakota State College of Science
Disability Support Services

800 North Sixth Street

Wahpeton, ND 58076

http://www.ndscs.nodak.edu/student/asc.dss.html

Contact: Ms. Joy Eichhorn, Disability Services Coordinator. Phone: 701-671-2623. Fax: 701-671-2440. E-mail: joy.eichhorn@ndscs.nodak.edu. Head of LD Program: Ms. Bunnie R. Johnson, Academic Services Center Director. Phone: 701-671-2335. Fax: 701-671-2440. E-mail: bunnie.johnson@ndscs.nodak.edu.

Disability Support Services Approximately 85 registered undergraduate students were served during 2002-03. The program or unit includes 1 full-time staff member. Academic advisers, counselors, regular education teachers, remediation/learning specialists, and trained peer tutors are provided collaboratively through on-campus or off-campus services.

Summer Program To help prepare for the demands of college, there is an optional 4 to 8-week summer program prior to entering the school.

Subject-area Tutoring Tutoring is offered in small groups for most subjects. Tutoring is provided collaboratively through on-campus or off-campus services via computer-based instruction, trained peer tutors, and other.

Basic Skills Remediation Remediation is offered in class-size groups for computer skills, learning strategies, math, reading, spelling, study skills, time management, and written language. Remediation is provided collaboratively through on-campus or off-campus services via computer-based instruction and regular education teachers.

Enrichment Programs for learning strategies, math, practical computer skills, reading, study skills, test taking, time management, vocabulary development, and written composition skills are provided collaboratively through on-campus or off-campus services. Credit is offered for learning strategies, math, practical computer skills, reading, study skills, test taking, time management, vocabulary development, and written composition skills.

Application For admittance to the program or unit, students are required to apply to the program directly, provide a psychoeducational report, and provide documentation of high school services. Upon application, materials documenting need for services should be sent only to the LD program or unit. Upon acceptance, documentation of need for services should be sent only to the LD program or unit. *Application deadline (institutional):* Continuous. *Application deadline (LD program):* Rolling/continuous for fall and rolling/continuous for spring.

Written Policies Written policies regarding course substitutions, general/basic LD accommodations, reduced course loads, and substitutions and waivers of graduation requirements are available through the program or unit directly.

Northeast Wisconsin Technical College

2740 W Mason Street, PO Box 19042

Green Bay, WI 54307-9042

http://www.nwtc.edu/

Contact: Mary Van Haute, Special Needs Counselor. Phone: 920-498-5498. E-mail: maryvanhaute@nwtc.edu.

The program or unit includes 5 full-time staff members and 1 part-time staff member. Academic advisers and counselors are provided through the program or unit. Academic advisers, counselors, regular education teachers, remediation/learning specialists, and trained peer tutors are provided collaboratively through on-campus or off-campus services.

Summer Program To help prepare for the demands of college, there is an optional 3 half-day summer program prior to entering the school.

Unique Aids and Services Aids, services, or accommodations include career counseling.

Subject-area Tutoring Tutoring is offered one-on-one and in small groups for all subjects. Tutoring is provided through the program or unit via graduate assistants/students. Tutoring is also provided collaboratively through on-campus or off-campus services via graduate assistants/students.

Basic Skills Remediation Remediation is offered in class-size groups for math, reading, and written language. Remediation is provided collaboratively through on-campus or off-campus services via computer-based instruction and regular education teachers.

Enrichment Enrichment programs are available through the program or unit for self-advocacy, stress management, study skills, test taking, and time management. Programs for career planning, college survival skills, learning strategies, math, oral communication skills, reading, study skills, test taking, and time management are provided collaboratively through on-campus or off-campus services.

Application For admittance to the program or unit, students are required to provide a psychoeducational report (10 years old or less) and provide documentation of high school services. Upon application, materials documenting need for services should be sent only to admissions with institutional application materials. Upon acceptance, documentation of need for services should be sent only to the LD program or unit. *Application deadline (institutional):* Continuous. *Application deadline (LD program):* Rolling/continuous for fall and rolling/continuous for spring.

Written Policies Written policy regarding general/basic LD accommodations is available on the program Web site. Written policy regarding general/basic LD accommodations is available through the program or unit directly.

Northern Marianas College

Box 501250

Saipan, MP 96950-1250

http://www.nmcnet.edu/

Contact: Daisy Villagomez-Bier, Director Disability Support Services, Counseling Programs and Services. Phone: 670-234-5498 Ext. 1341. Fax: 670-234-0759. E-mail: daisyv@nmcnet.edu.

Approximately 9 registered undergraduate students were served during 2002-03. The program or unit includes 1 full-time staff member. Academic advisers, counselors, skill tutors, strategy tutors, and trained peer tutors are provided through the program or unit. Academic advisers, counselors, diagnostic specialists, LD specialists, regular education teachers, remediation/learning specialists, skill tutors, special education teachers, strategy tutors, and trained peer tutors are provided collaboratively through on-campus or off-campus services.

Unique Aids and Services Aids, services, or accommodations include advocates, career counseling, faculty training, and priority registration.

Subject-area Tutoring Tutoring is offered one-on-one for most subjects. Tutoring is provided through the program or unit via trained peer tutors. Tutoring is also provided collaboratively through on-campus or off-campus services via computer-based instruction and trained peer tutors.

Basic Skills Remediation Remediation is offered one-on-one for reading, study skills, time management, and written language. Remediation is provided through the program or unit via trained peer tutors. Remediation is also provided collaboratively through on-campus or off-campus services via trained peer tutors.

Enrichment Enrichment programs are available through the program or unit for career planning, college survival skills, learning strategies, self-advocacy, stress management, study skills, test taking, and time management. Programs for career planning, college survival skills, health and nutrition, learning strategies, math, medication management, oral communication skills, practical computer skills, reading, self-advocacy, stress management, study skills, test taking, time management, vocabulary development, and written composition skills are provided collaboratively through on-campus or off-campus services. Credit is offered for college survival skills, health and nutrition, learning strategies, math, oral communication skills, practical computer skills, reading, study skills, test taking, time management, vocabulary development, and written composition skills.

Application For admittance to the program or unit, students are required to apply to the program directly and provide a psychoeducational report (3 years old or less). It is recommended that students provide documentation of high school services. Upon application, materials documenting need for services should be sent only to the LD program or unit. Upon acceptance, documentation of need for services should be sent only to the LD program or unit. *Application deadline (institutional):* Continuous. *Application deadline (LD program):* Rolling/continuous for fall and rolling/continuous for spring.

Written Policies Written policy regarding general/basic LD accommodations is outlined in the school's catalog/handbook. Written policy regarding general/basic LD accommodations is available through the program or unit directly.

Northern Oklahoma College

1220 East Grand Avenue, PO Box 310

Tonkawa, OK 74653-0310

http://www.north-ok.edu/

Contact: Fachaitte Kinslow, Counselor. Phone: 580-628-6652. Fax: 580-628-6209. Head of LD Program: Sue Ann Rodgers, Director of Counseling. Phone: 580-628-6651. Fax: 580-628-6209. E-mail: srodgers@north-ok.edu.

Approximately 91 registered undergraduate students were served during 2002-03. Counselors, professional tutors, regular education teachers, remediation/learning specialists, and trained peer tutors are provided collaboratively through on-campus or off-campus services.

Unique Aids and Services Aids, services, or accommodations include career counseling and weekly meetings with faculty.

Subject-area Tutoring Tutoring is offered one-on-one and in small groups. Tutoring is provided through the program or unit via professional tutors. Tutoring is also provided collaboratively through on-campus or off-campus services via trained peer tutors.

Diagnostic Testing Testing for learning strategies and reading is provided collaboratively through on-campus or off-campus services.

Basic Skills Remediation Remediation is offered one-on-one for reading, study skills, and time management. Remediation is provided collaboratively through on-campus or off-campus services via computer-based instruction.

Northern Oklahoma College (continued)

Enrichment Programs for career planning, college survival skills, learning strategies, math, reading, stress management, study skills, test taking, time management, and written composition skills are provided collaboratively through on-campus or off-campus services.

Application For admittance to the program or unit, students are required to provide a psychoeducational report and provide documentation of high school services. *Application deadline (institutional):* Continuous. *Application deadline (LD program):* Rolling/continuous for fall and rolling/continuous for spring.

Written Policies Written policy regarding general/basic LD accommodations is outlined in the school's catalog/handbook. Written policy regarding general/basic LD accommodations is available through the program or unit directly.

Northern Virginia Community College

4001 Wakefield Chapel Road
Annandale, VA 22003-3796
http://www.nv.cc.va.us/

Contact: Ms. Carol Sweetser, Counselor, Disability Services. Phone: 703-323-3018. Fax: 703-323-3229. E-mail: csweetser@nvcc.edu.

Approximately 800 registered undergraduate students were served during 2002-03. The program or unit includes 3 full-time staff members. Counselors and LD specialists are provided through the program or unit. Diagnostic specialists and professional tutors are provided collaboratively through on-campus or off-campus services.

Orientation The program or unit offers a mandatory 8-week orientation for new students as a semester course.

Summer Program To help prepare for the demands of college, there is an optional 3-day summer program prior to entering the school.

Unique Aids and Services Aids, services, or accommodations include advocates, career counseling, faculty training, and priority registration.

Subject-area Tutoring Tutoring is offered one-on-one for most subjects. Tutoring is provided collaboratively through on-campus or off-campus services via trained peer tutors.

Basic Skills Remediation Remediation is offered in class-size groups for computer skills, learning strategies, math, reading, spelling, study skills, time management, and written language. Remediation is provided collaboratively through on-campus or off-campus services via computer-based instruction and regular education teachers.

Enrichment Enrichment programs are available through the program or unit for career planning, college survival skills, learning strategies, self-advocacy, stress management, study skills, test taking, and time management. Programs for career planning, college survival skills, health and nutrition, learning strategies, math, practical computer skills, reading, study skills, test taking, time management, vocabulary development, and written composition skills are provided collaboratively through on-campus or off-campus services. Credit is offered for career planning, college survival skills, health and nutrition, learning strategies, math, practical computer skills, reading, study skills, test taking, time management, vocabulary development, and written composition skills.

Fees *Orientation* fee is $5654.

Application For admittance to the program or unit, students are required to provide a psychoeducational report (3 years old or less), provide documentation of high school services, and provide documentation from MD. Upon application, materials documenting need for services should be sent only to the LD program or unit. Upon acceptance, documentation of need for services should be sent only to the LD program or unit. *Application deadline (institutional):* Continuous. *Application deadline (LD program):* Rolling/continuous for fall and rolling/continuous for spring.

Written Policies Written policy regarding general/basic LD accommodations is available on the program Web site. Written policy regarding general/basic LD accommodations is outlined in the school's catalog/handbook. Written policy regarding general/basic LD accommodations is available through the program or unit directly.

North Harris College
Disability Services Office

2700 W. W. Thorne Drive
Houston, TX 77073-3499
http://www.nhmccd.edu

Contact: Ms. Beth Case, Counselor, Disability Services. Phone: 281-681-5481 Ext. 5471. Fax: 281-618-7107. E-mail: beth.case@nhmccd.edu. Head of LD Program: Ms. Sandi Patton, Coordinator of Disability Services. Phone: 281-618-5481 Ext. 5401. Fax: 281-618-7107. E-mail: sandi.patton@nhmccd.edu.

Disability Services Office Approximately 800 registered undergraduate students were served during 2002-03. The program or unit includes 3 full-time and 2 part-time staff members. Counselors and LD specialists are provided through the program or unit. Academic advisers, counselors, diagnostic specialists, graduate assistants/students, LD specialists, professional tutors, regular education teachers, remediation/learning specialists, skill tutors, and trained peer tutors are provided collaboratively through on-campus or off-campus services.

Unique Aids and Services Aids, services, or accommodations include career counseling.

Subject-area Tutoring Tutoring is offered one-on-one and in small groups for some subjects. Tutoring is provided collaboratively through on-campus or off-campus services via computer-based instruction, graduate assistants/students, professional tutors, and trained peer tutors.

Basic Skills Remediation Remediation is offered one-on-one and in small groups for math, reading, and written language. Remediation is provided collaboratively through on-campus or off-campus services via computer-based instruction and regular education teachers.

Application For admittance to the program or unit, students are required to apply to the program directly, provide a psychoeducational report (5 years old or less), and provide documentation of high school services. Upon application, materials documenting need for services should be sent only to the LD program or unit. Upon acceptance, documentation of need for services should be sent only to the LD program or unit. *Application deadline (institutional):* Continuous. *Application deadline (LD program):* Rolling/continuous for fall and rolling/continuous for spring.

Written Policies Written policy regarding general/basic LD accommodations is outlined in the school's catalog/handbook.

North Iowa Area Community College

500 College Drive
Mason City, IA 50401-7299
http://www.niacc.edu/
Contact: Phone: 641-423-1264. Fax: 641-423-1711.

The program or unit includes 1 part-time staff member. Academic advisers, counselors, remediation/learning specialists, and trained peer tutors are provided collaboratively through on-campus or off-campus services.

Unique Aids and Services Aids, services, or accommodations include priority registration.

Subject-area Tutoring Tutoring is offered one-on-one and in small groups for most subjects. Tutoring is provided collaboratively through on-campus or off-campus services via professional tutors and trained peer tutors.

Basic Skills Remediation Remediation is offered in class-size groups for math, reading, spelling, and written language. Remediation is provided collaboratively through on-campus or off-campus services via regular education teachers.

Enrichment Programs for career planning, college survival skills, learning strategies, practical computer skills, study skills, time management, and written composition skills are provided collaboratively through on-campus or off-campus services. Credit is offered for career planning, college survival skills, learning strategies, and study skills.

Application For admittance to the program or unit, students are required to provide documentation of high school services. It is recommended that students provide psychologist report or other medical documentation. Upon application, materials documenting need for services should be sent only to the LD program or unit. Upon acceptance, documentation of need for services should be sent only to the LD program or unit. *Application deadline (institutional):* Continuous. *Application deadline (LD program):* Rolling/continuous for fall and rolling/continuous for spring.

Written Policies Written policy regarding general/basic LD accommodations is available on the program Web site. Written policy regarding general/basic LD accommodations is outlined in the school's catalog/handbook. Written policies regarding course substitutions, general/basic LD accommodations, and substitutions and waivers of graduation requirements are available through the program or unit directly.

Northland Community and Technical College
The Learning Center

1101 Highway One East
Thief River Falls, MN 56701
http://www.northlandcollege.edu

Contact: Mr. Dean L. Dalen, Director of the Learning Center. Phone: 218-681-0835. Fax: 218-681-0811. E-mail: dean.dalen@northlandcollege.edu.

The Learning Center Approximately 30 registered undergraduate students were served during 2002-03. The program or unit includes 5 full-time staff members. Professional tutors, remediation/learning specialists, skill tutors, and trained peer tutors are provided through the program or unit.

Orientation The program or unit offers an optional orientation for new students individually by special arrangement.

Subject-area Tutoring Tutoring is offered one-on-one and in small groups for most subjects. Tutoring is provided through the program or unit via computer-based instruction, graduate assistants/students, professional tutors, and trained peer tutors. Tutoring is also provided collaboratively through on-campus or off-campus services via computer-based instruction and graduate assistants/students.

Basic Skills Remediation Remediation is offered one-on-one, in small groups, and in class-size groups for computer skills, learning strategies, math, reading, spelling, spoken language, study skills, time management, and written language. Remediation is provided through the program or unit via computer-based instruction, graduate assistants/students, professional tutors, and trained peer tutors. Remediation is also provided collaboratively through on-campus or off-campus services via computer-based instruction, graduate assistants/students, regular education teachers, and trained peer tutors.

Enrichment Enrichment programs are available through the program or unit for college survival skills, learning strategies, math, oral communication skills, practical computer skills, reading, self-advocacy, study skills, test taking, time management, vocabulary development, and written composition skills. Programs for career planning and health and nutrition are provided collaboratively through on-campus or off-campus services. Credit is offered for college survival skills, learning strategies, math, oral communication skills, practical computer skills, reading, study skills, vocabulary development, and written composition skills.

Application It is recommended that students provide a psychoeducational report (5 years old or less) and provide documentation of high school services. Upon application, materials documenting need for services should be sent only to the LD program or unit. Upon acceptance, documentation of need for services should be sent only to the LD program or unit. *Application deadline (institutional):* 9/2. *Application deadline (LD program):* Rolling/continuous for fall.

Written Policies Written policies regarding course substitutions, general/basic LD accommodations, reduced course loads, and substitutions and waivers of graduation requirements are available on the program Web site. Written policies regarding course substitutions, general/basic LD accommodations, reduced course loads, and substitutions and waivers of graduation requirements are outlined in the school's catalog/handbook. Written policy regarding reduced course loads is available through the program or unit directly.

North Shore Community College

1 Ferncroft Road
Danvers, MA 01923-4093
http://www.nscc.cc.ma.us/

North Shore Community College (continued)
Contact: Phone: 978-762-4000. Fax: 978-762-4021.

Approximately 125 registered undergraduate students were served during 2002-03. The program or unit includes 5 part-time staff members. Academic advisers, counselors, LD specialists, professional tutors, remediation/learning specialists, and trained peer tutors are provided collaboratively through on-campus or off-campus services.
Subject-area Tutoring Tutoring is offered in small groups for some subjects. Tutoring is provided collaboratively through on-campus or off-campus services via computer-based instruction, professional tutors, and trained peer tutors.
Diagnostic Testing Testing is provided through the program or unit for learning strategies, learning styles, math, reading, and study skills. Testing for auditory processing, intelligence, learning strategies, learning styles, math, reading, study skills, and visual processing is provided collaboratively through on-campus or off-campus services.
Basic Skills Remediation Remediation is offered in class-size groups for learning strategies, math, reading, study skills, and time management. Remediation is provided collaboratively through on-campus or off-campus services via computer-based instruction, professional tutors, and regular education teachers.
Enrichment Programs for career planning, college survival skills, learning strategies, math, reading, stress management, study skills, test taking, time management, and written composition skills are provided collaboratively through on-campus or off-campus services. Credit is offered for career planning, college survival skills, learning strategies, math, reading, stress management, study skills, test taking, time management, and written composition skills.
Fees *Diagnostic Testing* fee is applicable.
Application For admittance to the program or unit, students are required to provide a psychoeducational report (3 years old or less), provide documentation of high school services, and provide documentation of intellectual ability, information processing, and academic achievement. Upon application, materials documenting need for services should be sent only to the LD program or unit. *Application deadline (institutional):* Continuous. *Application deadline (LD program):* Rolling/continuous for fall.
Written Policies Written policy regarding general/basic LD accommodations is available on the program Web site. Written policies regarding course substitutions, reduced course loads, substitutions and waivers of admissions requirements, and substitutions and waivers of graduation requirements are outlined in the school's catalog/handbook. Written policies regarding course substitutions, general/basic LD accommodations, reduced course loads, and substitutions and waivers of graduation requirements are available through the program or unit directly.

Northwest College

231 West 6th Street
Powell, WY 82435-1898
http://www.northwestcollege.edu/
Contact: Phone: 307-754-6000. Fax: 307-754-6700.

The program or unit includes 3 full-time staff members. Academic advisers, LD specialists, remediation/learning specialists, skill tutors, strategy tutors, teacher trainees, and trained peer tutors are provided

through the program or unit. Academic advisers, counselors, diagnostic specialists, regular education teachers, remediation/learning specialists, skill tutors, strategy tutors, and trained peer tutors are provided collaboratively through on-campus or off-campus services.
Orientation The program or unit offers an optional 2-hour orientation for new students individually by special arrangement.
Unique Aids and Services Aids, services, or accommodations include advocates, career counseling, digital textbooks, faculty training, personal coach, priority registration, and support groups.
Subject-area Tutoring Tutoring is offered one-on-one and in small groups for all subjects. Tutoring is provided through the program or unit via LD specialists. Tutoring is also provided collaboratively through on-campus or off-campus services via professional tutors and trained peer tutors.
Diagnostic Testing Testing is provided through the program or unit for learning strategies, learning styles, math, personality, reading, and study skills. Testing for intelligence, learning strategies, learning styles, math, personality, social skills, and study skills is provided collaboratively through on-campus or off-campus services.
Basic Skills Remediation Remediation is offered in class-size groups for math, reading, study skills, time management, and written language. Remediation is provided collaboratively through on-campus or off-campus services via regular education teachers.
Enrichment Enrichment programs are available through the program or unit for reading, self-advocacy, and study skills. Programs for career planning, college survival skills, health and nutrition, learning strategies, math, oral communication skills, practical computer skills, reading, stress management, study skills, test taking, time management, and written composition skills are provided collaboratively through on-campus or off-campus services. Credit is offered for health and nutrition, math, oral communication skills, practical computer skills, reading, and written composition skills.
Student Organization There is a student organization consisting of 10 members.
Application For admittance to the program or unit, students are required to apply to the program directly and provide a psychoeducational report (5 years old or less). It is recommended that students provide documentation of high school services and provide medical information from physician if applicable. Upon application, materials documenting need for services should be sent only to the LD program or unit. Upon acceptance, documentation of need for services should be sent only to the LD program or unit. *Application deadline (institutional):* 8/15. *Application deadline (LD program):* Rolling/continuous for fall and rolling/continuous for spring.
Written Policies Written policy regarding general/basic LD accommodations is available on the program Web site. Written policies regarding general/basic LD accommodations, grade forgiveness, and reduced course loads are outlined in the school's catalog/handbook. Written policies regarding course substitutions, general/basic LD accommodations, substitutions and waivers of admissions requirements, and substitutions and waivers of graduation requirements are available through the program or unit directly.

Northwest State Community College
Accessibility Services

22-600 State Route 34
Archbold, OH 43502-9542

http://www.nscc.cc.oh.us/StudentServices/
SuccessCenter.asp

Contact: Ms. Lana Evans, Success Center Director. Phone: 419-267-5511 Ext. 225. Fax: 419-267-3688. E-mail: levans@nscc.cc.oh.us.

Accessibility Services Approximately 45 registered undergraduate students were served during 2002-03. The program or unit includes 1 full-time and 1 part-time staff member. Academic advisers and regular education teachers are provided collaboratively through on-campus or off-campus services.

Subject-area Tutoring Tutoring is offered one-on-one, in small groups, and in class-size groups for some subjects. Tutoring is provided through the program or unit via computer-based instruction, professional tutors, and trained peer tutors. Tutoring is also provided collaboratively through on-campus or off-campus services via computer-based instruction, professional tutors, and trained peer tutors.

Enrichment Programs for career planning, college survival skills, learning strategies, math, reading, stress management, study skills, test taking, time management, vocabulary development, and written composition skills are provided collaboratively through on-campus or off-campus services. Credit is offered for college survival skills, learning strategies, math, reading, stress management, study skills, test taking, time management, vocabulary development, and written composition skills.

Application For admittance to the program or unit, students are required to apply to the program directly. It is recommended that students provide a psychoeducational report (3 years old or less). Upon application, materials documenting need for services should be sent only to the LD program or unit. Upon acceptance, documentation of need for services should be sent only to the LD program or unit. *Application deadline (institutional):* Continuous. *Application deadline (LD program):* Rolling/continuous for fall and rolling/continuous for spring.

Written Policies Written policies regarding general/basic LD accommodations and grade forgiveness are outlined in the school's catalog/handbook. Written policy regarding general/basic LD accommodations is available through the program or unit directly.

Oakton Community College

1600 East Golf Road
Des Plaines, IL 60016-1268
http://www.oakton.edu/

Contact: Linda McCann, Special Needs Coordinator. Phone: 847-635-1759. E-mail: lindamc@oakton.edu.

The program or unit includes 11 part-time staff members. Academic advisers, counselors, diagnostic specialists, LD specialists, professional tutors, remediation/learning specialists, skill tutors, and strategy tutors are provided through the program or unit. Academic advisers, counselors, and regular education teachers are provided collaboratively through on-campus or off-campus services.

Orientation The program or unit offers an optional 2-day orientation for new students before classes begin.

Summer Program To help prepare for the demands of college, there is an optional 7-week summer program prior to entering the school. Degree credit will be earned.

Unique Aids and Services Aids, services, or accommodations include career counseling and faculty training.

Subject-area Tutoring Tutoring is offered one-on-one and in small groups for most subjects. Tutoring is provided through the program or unit via LD specialists and professional tutors. Tutoring is also provided collaboratively through on-campus or off-campus services via computer-based instruction, graduate assistants/students, professional tutors, and trained peer tutors.

Diagnostic Testing Testing is provided through the program or unit for auditory processing, learning strategies, learning styles, math, motor skills, neuropsychological, reading, spelling, study skills, visual processing, and written language. Testing for learning strategies, learning styles, personality, reading, study skills, and written language is provided collaboratively through on-campus or off-campus services.

Basic Skills Remediation Remediation is offered one-on-one for computer skills, learning strategies, math, reading, spelling, study skills, time management, and written language. Remediation is provided through the program or unit via LD specialists, professional tutors, regular education teachers, and special education teachers. Remediation is also provided collaboratively through on-campus or off-campus services via computer-based instruction, professional tutors, regular education teachers, and trained peer tutors.

Enrichment Enrichment programs are available through the program or unit for career planning, learning strategies, and stress management. Programs for college survival skills, math, reading, stress management, study skills, test taking, time management, vocabulary development, and written composition skills are provided collaboratively through on-campus or off-campus services. Credit is offered for college survival skills, vocabulary development, and written composition skills.

Fees *Summer Program* fee is $160. *Diagnostic Testing* fee is $0 to $150.

Application It is recommended that students provide a psychoeducational report (5 years old or less) and provide documentation of high school services. Upon application, materials documenting need for services should be sent only to the LD program or unit. Upon acceptance, documentation of need for services should be sent only to the LD program or unit. *Application deadline (institutional):* Continuous. *Application deadline (LD program):* Rolling/continuous for fall and rolling/continuous for spring.

Written Policies Written policy regarding general/basic LD accommodations is available on the program Web site. Written policies regarding general/basic LD accommodations and grade forgiveness are outlined in the school's catalog/handbook. Written policies regarding course substitutions, general/basic LD accommodations, and reduced course loads are available through the program or unit directly.

Ocean County College

College Drive, PO Box 2001
Toms River, NJ 08754-2001
http://www.ocean.edu/

Contact: Mrs. Geraldine E. Parrish, Project Specialist. Phone: 732-255-0400 Ext. 2359. Fax: 732-255-0458. E-mail: gparrish@ocean.edu.

Ocean County College (continued)

The program or unit includes 4 full-time and 3 part-time staff members. Academic advisers, counselors, diagnostic specialists, LD specialists, professional tutors, regular education teachers, remediation/learning specialists, skill tutors, and strategy tutors are provided through the program or unit. Counselors, professional tutors, regular education teachers, remediation/learning specialists, skill tutors, and strategy tutors are provided collaboratively through on-campus or off-campus services.

Orientation The program or unit offers an optional half-day orientation for new students before classes begin.

Unique Aids and Services Aids, services, or accommodations include career counseling, faculty training, parent workshops, priority registration, and support groups.

Subject-area Tutoring Tutoring is offered one-on-one for most subjects. Tutoring is provided through the program or unit via professional tutors.

Diagnostic Testing Testing is provided through the program or unit for auditory processing, intelligence, learning strategies, learning styles, math, reading, spelling, spoken language, study skills, visual processing, written language, and other services.

Basic Skills Remediation Remediation is offered one-on-one and in class-size groups for auditory processing, computer skills, learning strategies, math, reading, spoken language, study skills, time management, visual processing, and written language. Remediation is provided through the program or unit via computer-based instruction, LD specialists, professional tutors, and regular education teachers. Remediation is also provided collaboratively through on-campus or off-campus services via computer-based instruction, LD specialists, professional tutors, and regular education teachers.

Enrichment Enrichment programs are available through the program or unit for career planning, college survival skills, health and nutrition, learning strategies, math, oral communication skills, practical computer skills, reading, self-advocacy, stress management, study skills, test taking, time management, and written composition skills. Programs for career planning, college survival skills, health and nutrition, learning strategies, math, oral communication skills, practical computer skills, reading, self-advocacy, stress management, study skills, test taking, time management, and written composition skills are provided collaboratively through on-campus or off-campus services.

Fees *Diagnostic Testing fee is $575.*

Application For admittance to the program or unit, students are required to provide a psychoeducational report (3 years old or less), provide documentation of high school services, and provide medical documentation if no IEP is available. Upon application, materials documenting need for services should be sent only to the LD program or unit. Upon acceptance, documentation of need for services should be sent only to the LD program or unit. *Application deadline (institutional):* Continuous. *Application deadline (LD program):* Rolling/continuous for fall.

Written Policies Written policy regarding general/basic LD accommodations is available on the program Web site. Written policy regarding general/basic LD accommodations is outlined in the school's catalog/handbook. Written policy regarding general/basic LD accommodations is available through the program or unit directly.

Odessa College
Student Development Center

201 West University Avenue
Odessa, TX 79764-7127
http://www.odessa.edu/dept/counseling/students.htm

Contact: Ms. Martha Kunkel, Counselor, Special Populations. Phone: 432-335-6346. Fax: 432-335-6860. E-mail: mkunkel@odessa.edu. Head of LD Program: Dr. Sherrie Lang, Director of Title V and Student Development. Phone: 432-335-6433. Fax: 432-335-6860. E-mail: slang@odessa.edu.

Student Development Center Approximately 50 registered undergraduate students were served during 2002-03. The program or unit includes 1 full-time staff member. Academic advisers, counselors, regular education teachers, trained peer tutors, and other are provided collaboratively through on-campus or off-campus services.

Unique Aids and Services Aids, services, or accommodations include career counseling, priority registration, copies of notes and handouts, books on tape as available, tutoring and study management.

Subject-area Tutoring Tutoring is offered one-on-one, in small groups, and in class-size groups for most subjects. Tutoring is provided collaboratively through on-campus or off-campus services via computer-based instruction, trained peer tutors, and other.

Basic Skills Remediation Remediation is offered in class-size groups for math, reading, and written language. Remediation is provided collaboratively through on-campus or off-campus services via computer-based instruction, professional tutors, regular education teachers, and trained peer tutors.

Enrichment Programs for career planning, college survival skills, learning strategies, math, reading, study skills, test taking, and time management are provided collaboratively through on-campus or off-campus services.

Application For admittance to the program or unit, students are required to apply to the program directly and provide a psychoeducational report (3 years old or less). Upon acceptance, documentation of need for services should be sent only to the LD program or unit. *Application deadline (institutional):* Continuous. *Application deadline (LD program):* Rolling/continuous for fall and rolling/continuous for spring.

Written Policies Written policy regarding general/basic LD accommodations is available on the program Web site. Written policy regarding general/basic LD accommodations is outlined in the school's catalog/handbook. Written policy regarding general/basic LD accommodations is available through the program or unit directly.

Okaloosa-Walton Community College

100 College Boulevard
Niceville, FL 32578-1295
http://www.owcc.edu/

Contact: Ms. Jody Swenson, Coordinator of Services to Students with Special Needs. Phone: 850-729-6079. Fax: 850-729-5323. E-mail: swensonj@owcc.net.

Approximately 50 registered undergraduate students were served during 2002-03. Counselors are provided collaboratively through on-campus or off-campus services.

Unique Aids and Services Aids, services, or accommodations include career counseling and priority registration.

Subject-area Tutoring Tutoring is offered for some subjects. Tutoring is provided collaboratively through on-campus or off-campus services via computer-based instruction and trained peer tutors.

Basic Skills Remediation Remediation is offered in class-size groups for math, reading, study skills, and written language. Remediation is provided collaboratively through on-campus or off-campus services via computer-based instruction and regular education teachers.

Application It is recommended that students apply to the program directly, provide a psychoeducational report, and provide documentation of high school services. Upon application, materials documenting need for services should be sent only to the LD program or unit. Upon acceptance, documentation of need for services should be sent only to the LD program or unit. *Application deadline (institutional):* Continuous. *Application deadline (LD program):* Rolling/continuous for fall and rolling/continuous for spring.

Written Policies Written policy regarding general/basic LD accommodations is available on the program Web site. Written policy regarding general/basic LD accommodations is outlined in the school's catalog/handbook. Written policies regarding course substitutions, general/basic LD accommodations, and substitutions and waivers of graduation requirements are available through the program or unit directly.

Oklahoma State University, Oklahoma City
Disability Support Services

900 North Portland
Oklahoma City, OK 73107-6120
http://osuokc.edu/disabled
Contact: Mrs. Shelly Bell, Adviser to Students with Disabilities. Phone: 405-945-3385. Fax: 405-945-3329. E-mail: shelldc@osuokc.edu.

Disability Support Services Approximately 15 registered undergraduate students were served during 2002-03. The program or unit includes 1 full-time staff member. Academic advisers, counselors, professional tutors, regular education teachers, skill tutors, and strategy tutors are provided collaboratively through on-campus or off-campus services.

Summer Program To help prepare for the demands of college, there is an optional 6-week summer program prior to entering the school. Degree credit will be earned.

Subject-area Tutoring Tutoring is offered one-on-one and in small groups for some subjects. Tutoring is provided collaboratively through on-campus or off-campus services via computer-based instruction and professional tutors.

Basic Skills Remediation Remediation is offered in small groups for computer skills, learning strategies, math, reading, study skills, and time management. Remediation is provided collaboratively through on-campus or off-campus services via professional tutors and regular education teachers.

Enrichment Programs for college survival skills, health and nutrition, learning strategies, math, practical computer skills, reading, stress management, study skills, test taking, time management, and written composition skills are provided collaboratively through on-campus or off-campus services. Credit is offered for college survival skills, health and nutrition, learning strategies, math, practical computer skills, reading, stress management, study skills, test taking, time management, and written composition skills.

Fees *Summer Program* fee is $65.

Application For admittance to the program or unit, students are required to provide a psychoeducational report (3 years old or less). It is recommended that students provide documentation of high school services. Upon acceptance, documentation of need for services should be sent only to the LD program or unit. *Application deadline (institutional):* Continuous. *Application deadline (LD program):* Rolling/continuous for fall and rolling/continuous for spring.

Written Policies Written policy regarding general/basic LD accommodations is available on the program Web site. Written policy regarding general/basic LD accommodations is available through the program or unit directly.

Ozarks Technical Community College

PO Box 5958
Springfield, MO 65801
http://www.otc.cc.mo.us/
Contact: Phone: 417-895-7000. Fax: 417-895-7161.

Approximately 342 registered undergraduate students were served during 2002-03. The program or unit includes 5 full-time and 2 part-time staff members. Remediation/learning specialists and other are provided collaboratively through on-campus or off-campus services.

Unique Aids and Services Aids, services, or accommodations include advocates and career counseling.

Subject-area Tutoring Tutoring is offered one-on-one, in small groups, and in class-size groups for some subjects. Tutoring is provided collaboratively through on-campus or off-campus services via trained peer tutors.

Basic Skills Remediation Remediation is offered in class-size groups for learning strategies, math, reading, and written language. Remediation is provided collaboratively through on-campus or off-campus services via computer-based instruction and trained peer tutors.

Application For admittance to the program or unit, students are required to provide documentation of high school services. It is recommended that students provide a psychoeducational report. Upon application, materials documenting need for services should be sent only to the LD program or unit. Upon acceptance, documentation of need for services should be sent only to the LD program or unit. *Application deadline (LD program):* Rolling/continuous for fall and rolling/continuous for spring.

Written Policies Written policies regarding general/basic LD accommodations and substitutions and waivers of admissions requirements are available on the program Web site. Written policies regarding general/basic LD accommodations and substitutions and waivers of admissions requirements are outlined in the school's catalog/handbook.

Panola College
Disability Support Services

1109 West Panola Street
Carthage, TX 75633-2397
http://www.panola.edu/student_services
Contact: Ms. Teresa Washington, Vocational Counselor.
Phone: 903-693-1123. Fax: 903-693-5588. E-mail:
twashington@panola.edu.

Disability Support Services Approximately 6 registered under-graduate students were served during 2002-03. The program or unit includes 1 full-time staff member. Counselors are provided through the program or unit.

Unique Aids and Services Aids, services, or accommodations include career counseling.

Subject-area Tutoring Tutoring is offered one-on-one for most subjects. Tutoring is provided collaboratively through on-campus or off-campus services via computer-based instruction and trained peer tutors.

Diagnostic Testing Testing is provided through the program or unit for learning styles, personality, and study skills.

Basic Skills Remediation Remediation is offered in class-size groups for math, reading, and written language. Remediation is provided collaboratively through on-campus or off-campus services via computer-based instruction, special education teachers, and trained peer tutors.

Enrichment Programs for career planning, college survival skills, health and nutrition, learning strategies, stress management, study skills, test taking, and time management are provided collaboratively through on-campus or off-campus services.

Application For admittance to the program or unit, students are required to apply to the program directly. It is recommended that students provide a psychoeducational report (5 years old or less) and provide documentation of high school services. Upon applica-tion, materials documenting need for services should be sent only to the LD program or unit. Upon acceptance, documentation of need for services should be sent only to the LD program or unit. *Appli-cation deadline (institutional):* Continuous. *Application deadline (LD program):* Rolling/continuous for fall and rolling/continuous for spring.

Written Policies Written policy regarding general/basic LD accom-modations is available on the program Web site. Written policy regarding general/basic LD accommodations is outlined in the school's catalog/handbook. Written policy regarding general/basic LD accommodations is available through the program or unit directly.

Paradise Valley Community College

18401 North 32nd Street
Phoenix, AZ 85032-1200
http://www.pvc.maricopa.edu/
Contact: Ms. Donna G. Young, Manager, Disability Resource Center. Phone: 602-787-7174. Fax: 602-787-7230. E-mail: donna.young@pvmail.maricopa.edu.

Approximately 102 registered undergraduate students were served during 2002-03. The program or unit includes 1 full-time staff member. Academic advisers and counselors are provided collabora-tively through on-campus or off-campus services.

Unique Aids and Services Aids, services, or accommodations include career counseling, digital textbooks, faculty training, and support groups.

Subject-area Tutoring Tutoring is offered in small groups for all subjects. Tutoring is provided collaboratively through on-campus or off-campus services via computer-based instruction and trained peer tutors.

Basic Skills Remediation Remediation is offered in class-size groups for learning strategies, reading, study skills, time manage-ment, and written language. Remediation is provided collaboratively through on-campus or off-campus services via computer-based instruction, regular education teachers, and other.

Enrichment Programs for career planning, college survival skills, health and nutrition, learning strategies, math, reading, stress man-agement, study skills, test taking, time management, and written composition skills are provided collaboratively through on-campus or off-campus services. Credit is offered for career planning, col-lege survival skills, learning strategies, stress management, study skills, test taking, time management, and written composition skills.

Application For admittance to the program or unit, students are required to provide a psychoeducational report (3 years old or less). Upon application, materials documenting need for services should be sent only to the LD program or unit. Upon acceptance, docu-mentation of need for services should be sent only to the LD program or unit. *Application deadline (institutional):* Continuous. *Application deadline (LD program):* Rolling/continuous for fall and rolling/continuous for spring.

Written Policies Written policies regarding course substitutions, general/basic LD accommodations, grade forgiveness, reduced course loads, substitutions and waivers of admissions requirements, and substitutions and waivers of graduation requirements are available on the program Web site. Written policies regarding grade forgive-ness, reduced course loads, substitutions and waivers of admissions requirements, and substitutions and waivers of graduation require-ments are outlined in the school's catalog/handbook. Written poli-cies regarding general/basic LD accommodations, reduced course loads, substitutions and waivers of admissions requirements, and substitutions and waivers of graduation requirements are available through the program or unit directly.

Paris Junior College
Student Development

2400 Clarksville Street
Paris, TX 75460-6298
http://www.paris.cc.tx.us/
Contact: Ms. Barbara O. Thomas, Director of Student Development. Phone: 903-782-0426. Fax: 903-782-0796. E-mail: bthomas@paris.cc.tx.ux.

Student Development Approximately 25 registered undergradu-ate students were served during 2002-03. The program or unit includes 2 part-time staff members. Trained peer tutors are provided through the program or unit.

Unique Aids and Services Aids, services, or accommodations include career counseling and faculty training.
Subject-area Tutoring Tutoring is offered one-on-one and in small groups for most subjects. Tutoring is provided through the program or unit via trained peer tutors. Tutoring is also provided collaboratively through on-campus or off-campus services via computer-based instruction.
Basic Skills Remediation Remediation is offered in class-size groups for learning strategies, math, reading, study skills, and written language. Remediation is provided collaboratively through on-campus or off-campus services via computer-based instruction and regular education teachers.
Enrichment Programs for career planning, learning strategies, math, study skills, and written composition skills are provided collaboratively through on-campus or off-campus services.
Application For admittance to the program or unit, students are required to apply to the program directly and provide a psychoeducational report. It is recommended that students provide documentation of high school services. Upon application, materials documenting need for services should be sent only to the LD program or unit. Upon acceptance, documentation of need for services should be sent only to the LD program or unit. *Application deadline (institutional):* Continuous. *Application deadline (LD program):* Rolling/continuous for fall and rolling/continuous for spring.
Written Policies Written policies regarding general/basic LD accommodations and substitutions and waivers of admissions requirements are available on the program Web site. Written policies regarding general/basic LD accommodations and substitutions and waivers of admissions requirements are outlined in the school's catalog/handbook. Written policies regarding course substitutions, general/basic LD accommodations, reduced course loads, and substitutions and waivers of graduation requirements are available through the program or unit directly.

Pasco-Hernando Community College
Office of Disabilities Services

10230 Ridge Road
New Port Richey, FL 34654-5199
http://www.phcc.edu/contact/studentserv.htm
Contact: Mr. Reinhardt Thiessen III, Coordinator of Disabilities Services. Phone: 727-816-3236. Fax: 727-816-3712. E-mail: thiessr@phcc.edu.

Office of Disabilities Services Approximately 600 registered undergraduate students were served during 2002-03. The program or unit includes 2 full-time staff members. Academic advisers, strategy tutors, and trained peer tutors are provided through the program or unit. Academic advisers, coaches, strategy tutors, and trained peer tutors are provided collaboratively through on-campus or off-campus services.
Unique Aids and Services Aids, services, or accommodations include priority registration.
Subject-area Tutoring Tutoring is offered one-on-one and in small groups for some subjects. Tutoring is provided through the program or unit via trained peer tutors and other. Tutoring is also provided collaboratively through on-campus or off-campus services via computer-based instruction and trained peer tutors.

Basic Skills Remediation Remediation is offered one-on-one and in small groups for computer skills, math, reading, and written language. Remediation is provided through the program or unit via trained peer tutors and other. Remediation is also provided collaboratively through on-campus or off-campus services via computer-based instruction and trained peer tutors.
Enrichment Programs for career planning, college survival skills, math, reading, vocabulary development, and written composition skills are provided collaboratively through on-campus or off-campus services. Credit is offered for college survival skills, math, reading, vocabulary development, and written composition skills.
Student Organization People Accepting Challenges Together (PACT) and Courage And Strength Together (CAST) consists of 35 members.
Application For admittance to the program or unit, students are required to apply to the program directly and provide a psychoeducational report (3 years old or less). It is recommended that students provide documentation of high school services and provide documentation meeting AHEAD standards. Upon application, materials documenting need for services should be sent only to the LD program or unit. Upon acceptance, documentation of need for services should be sent only to the LD program or unit. *Application deadline (institutional):* Continuous. *Application deadline (LD program):* Rolling/continuous for fall and rolling/continuous for spring.
Written Policies Written policies regarding course substitutions, substitutions and waivers of admissions requirements, and substitutions and waivers of graduation requirements are available on the program Web site. Written policies regarding course substitutions, substitutions and waivers of admissions requirements, and substitutions and waivers of graduation requirements are outlined in the school's catalog/handbook. Written policy regarding general/basic LD accommodations is available through the program or unit directly.

Patrick Henry Community College
Student Support Services

PO Box 5311
Martinsville, VA 24115-5311
http://www.ph.vccs.edu
Contact: Lisa B. Via, Learning Disabilities Specialist. Phone: 276-656-0223. Fax: 276-656-0327. E-mail: lvia@ph.vccs.edu. Head of LD Program: Scott D. Guebert, Director of Student Support Services. Phone: 276-656-0257. Fax: 276-656-0327. E-mail: sguebert@ph.vccs.edu.

Student Support Services Approximately 102 registered undergraduate students were served during 2002-03. The program or unit includes 5 full-time and 11 part-time staff members. Counselors, graduate assistants/students, LD specialists, professional tutors, and trained peer tutors are provided through the program or unit. Counselors, diagnostic specialists, graduate assistants/students, professional tutors, remediation/learning specialists, and trained peer tutors are provided collaboratively through on-campus or off-campus services.
Orientation The program or unit offers an optional 1-day orientation for new students before classes begin and during registration.

Patrick Henry Community College (continued)

Unique Aids and Services Aids, services, or accommodations include career counseling, faculty training, priority registration, support groups, adaptive testing, extended time, assistive technology, recorded textbooks, readers/scribes.

Subject-area Tutoring Tutoring is offered one-on-one and in small groups for most subjects. Tutoring is provided through the program or unit via computer-based instruction, graduate assistants/students, LD specialists, professional tutors, and trained peer tutors.

Diagnostic Testing Testing is provided through the program or unit for learning styles, reading, and study skills. Testing for intelligence and other services is provided collaboratively through on-campus or off-campus services.

Basic Skills Remediation Remediation is offered one-on-one and in small groups for computer skills, learning strategies, math, reading, social skills, spelling, study skills, time management, and written language. Remediation is provided through the program or unit via graduate assistants/students, LD specialists, professional tutors, and trained peer tutors. Remediation is also provided collaboratively through on-campus or off-campus services via computer-based instruction.

Enrichment Enrichment programs are available through the program or unit for learning strategies, math, oral communication skills, practical computer skills, study skills, test taking, and time management. Programs for college survival skills, learning strategies, math, oral communication skills, practical computer skills, stress management, study skills, test taking, and time management are provided collaboratively through on-campus or off-campus services. Credit is offered for college survival skills.

Student Organization Academic Success Group (ASG) consists of 20 members.

Application It is recommended that students apply to the program directly, provide a psychoeducational report, provide documentation of high school services, and provide documentation from vocational rehabilitation, mental health, or other community service providers. Upon application, materials documenting need for services should be sent only to the LD program or unit. Upon acceptance, documentation of need for services should be sent only to the LD program or unit. *Application deadline (institutional):* Continuous. *Application deadline (LD program):* Rolling/continuous for fall and rolling/continuous for spring.

Written Policies Written policy regarding general/basic LD accommodations is available through the program or unit directly.

The Pennsylvania State University Delaware County Campus of the Commonwealth College

25 Yearsley Mill Road

Media, PA 19063-5596

http://www.de.psu.edu/

Contact: Ms. Sharon Manco, Disability Contact Liaison. Phone: 610-892-1461. Fax: 610-892-1357. E-mail: de-learningcenter@psu.edu.

Approximately 40 registered undergraduate students were served during 2002-03. The program or unit includes 2 full-time and 17 part-time staff members. Coaches, counselors, diagnostic specialists, graduate assistants/students, LD specialists, professional tutors, regular education teachers, remediation/learning specialists, skill tutors, strategy tutors, and trained peer tutors are provided through the program or unit. Academic advisers, regular education teachers, and skill tutors are provided collaboratively through on-campus or off-campus services.

Summer Program To help prepare for the demands of college, there is an optional 30-day summer program prior to entering the school.

Unique Aids and Services Aids, services, or accommodations include career counseling and faculty training.

Subject-area Tutoring Tutoring is offered one-on-one and in small groups for most subjects. Tutoring is provided through the program or unit via graduate assistants/students, LD specialists, professional tutors, and trained peer tutors. Tutoring is also provided collaboratively through on-campus or off-campus services via trained peer tutors.

Basic Skills Remediation Remediation is offered one-on-one, in small groups, and in class-size groups for learning strategies, math, reading, spelling, spoken language, study skills, time management, and written language. Remediation is provided through the program or unit via graduate assistants/students, LD specialists, professional tutors, regular education teachers, special education teachers, and trained peer tutors. Remediation is also provided collaboratively through on-campus or off-campus services via graduate assistants/students.

Enrichment Enrichment programs are available through the program or unit for college survival skills, learning strategies, math, oral communication skills, practical computer skills, reading, stress management, study skills, test taking, time management, vocabulary development, and written composition skills. Programs for career planning, college survival skills, health and nutrition, learning strategies, math, oral communication skills, stress management, study skills, test taking, time management, and written composition skills are provided collaboratively through on-campus or off-campus services. Credit is offered for career planning, college survival skills, health and nutrition, learning strategies, math, oral communication skills, and reading.

Application For admittance to the program or unit, students are required to provide a psychoeducational report (3 years old or less). It is recommended that students provide documentation of high school services. Upon acceptance, documentation of need for services should be sent only to the LD program or unit. *Application deadline (institutional):* Continuous. *Application deadline (LD program):* Rolling/continuous for fall and rolling/continuous for spring.

Written Policies Written policy regarding general/basic LD accommodations is available on the program Web site. Written policies regarding course substitutions, general/basic LD accommodations, reduced course loads, and substitutions and waivers of admissions requirements are outlined in the school's catalog/handbook. Written policies regarding course substitutions, general/basic LD accommodations, reduced course loads, and substitutions and waivers of admissions requirements are available through the program or unit directly.

The Pennsylvania State University Hazleton Campus of the Commonwealth College
Disability Services

Hazleton, PA 18202-1291

http://www.hn.psu.edu/tlrc/disable.htm

Contact: Mrs. Jacqueline Walters, Coordinator of Disability Services. Phone: 570-450-3005. Fax: 570-450-3182. E-mail: jxw2@psu.edu.

Disability Services Approximately 18 registered undergraduate students were served during 2002-03. The program or unit includes 1 full-time staff member. Academic advisers are provided through the program or unit. Academic advisers, counselors, professional tutors, and other are provided collaboratively through on-campus or off-campus services.

Unique Aids and Services Aids, services, or accommodations include career counseling, faculty training, and priority registration.

Subject-area Tutoring Tutoring is offered one-on-one and in small groups for all subjects. Tutoring is provided collaboratively through on-campus or off-campus services via professional tutors and trained peer tutors.

Basic Skills Remediation Remediation is offered in class-size groups for math and written language. Remediation is provided collaboratively through on-campus or off-campus services via regular education teachers.

Enrichment Enrichment programs are available through the program or unit for career planning and self-advocacy. Programs for career planning, college survival skills, stress management, study skills, test taking, time management, and written composition skills are provided collaboratively through on-campus or off-campus services. Credit is offered for college survival skills.

Application For admittance to the program or unit, students are required to provide a psychoeducational report (3 years old or less). Upon acceptance, documentation of need for services should be sent only to the LD program or unit. *Application deadline (institutional):* Continuous.

Written Policies Written policies regarding course substitutions, general/basic LD accommodations, grade forgiveness, reduced course loads, substitutions and waivers of admissions requirements, and substitutions and waivers of graduation requirements are available on the program Web site. Written policies regarding course substitutions, general/basic LD accommodations, grade forgiveness, reduced course loads, substitutions and waivers of admissions requirements, and substitutions and waivers of graduation requirements are outlined in the school's catalog/handbook. Written policies regarding course substitutions, general/basic LD accommodations, grade forgiveness, reduced course loads, substitutions and waivers of admissions requirements, and substitutions and waivers of graduation requirements are available through the program or unit directly.

The Pennsylvania State University McKeesport Campus of the Commonwealth College

4000 University Drive
McKeesport, PA 15132-7698

http://www.mk.psu.edu/

Contact: Dr. Patrick Boyle, Director of Student Affairs. Phone: 412-675-9160. Fax: 412-675-9036. E-mail: jpb12@psu.edu.

Approximately 10 registered undergraduate students were served during 2002-03. Academic advisers, professional tutors, regular education teachers, remediation/learning specialists, skill tutors, strategy tutors, and trained peer tutors are provided collaboratively through on-campus or off-campus services.

Application For admittance to the program or unit, students are required to provide a psychoeducational report (3 years old or less). Upon acceptance, documentation of need for services should be sent only to the LD program or unit. *Application deadline (institutional):* Continuous. *Application deadline (LD program):* Rolling/continuous for fall and rolling/continuous for spring.

Written Policies Written policy regarding general/basic LD accommodations is available on the program Web site. Written policy regarding general/basic LD accommodations is available through the program or unit directly.

The Pennsylvania State University Mont Alto Campus of the Commonwealth College
The Learning Center

Campus Drive
Mont Alto, PA 17237-9703

http://www.ma.psu.edu/~malc

Contact: Nanette M. Hatzes, Learning Center Coordinator. Phone: 717-749-6045. E-mail: nmh2@psu.edu.

The Learning Center Approximately 35 registered undergraduate students were served during 2002-03. The program or unit includes 30 full-time and 2 part-time staff members. LD specialists, professional tutors, skill tutors, strategy tutors, and trained peer tutors are provided through the program or unit.

Unique Aids and Services Aids, services, or accommodations include career counseling, digital textbooks, faculty training, and priority registration.

Subject-area Tutoring Tutoring is offered one-on-one, in small groups, and in class-size groups for most subjects. Tutoring is provided through the program or unit via computer-based instruction, LD specialists, professional tutors, and trained peer tutors.

The Pennsylvania State University Mont Alto Campus of the Commonwealth College (continued)

Enrichment Enrichment programs are available through the program or unit for college survival skills and self-advocacy. Programs for career planning, learning strategies, math, oral communication skills, practical computer skills, reading, stress management, study skills, test taking, time management, vocabulary development, and written composition skills are provided collaboratively through on-campus or off-campus services. Credit is offered for career planning.

Application For admittance to the program or unit, students are required to provide a psychoeducational report (3 years old or less). It is recommended that students provide documentation of high school services. Upon acceptance, documentation of need for services should be sent only to the LD program or unit. *Application deadline (institutional):* Continuous. *Application deadline (LD program):* Rolling/continuous for fall and rolling/continuous for spring.

Written Policies Written policies regarding course substitutions, general/basic LD accommodations, reduced course loads, substitutions and waivers of admissions requirements, and substitutions and waivers of graduation requirements are available on the program Web site. Written policies regarding course substitutions, general/basic LD accommodations, reduced course loads, substitutions and waivers of admissions requirements, and substitutions and waivers of graduation requirements are outlined in the school's catalog/handbook. Written policies regarding course substitutions, general/basic LD accommodations, reduced course loads, substitutions and waivers of admissions requirements, and substitutions and waivers of graduation requirements are available through the program or unit directly.

The Pennsylvania State University Shenango Campus of the Commonwealth College
Disability Services

147 Shenango Avenue
Sharon, PA 16146-1537
http://www.shenango.psu.edu/
Contact: Kathryn Watson, Director of Student affairs.
Phone: 724-983-2835. Fax: 724-983-2820. E-mail: kew1@psu.edu.

Disability Services Approximately 35 registered undergraduate students were served during 2002-03. Professional tutors, remediation/learning specialists, and skill tutors are provided collaboratively through on-campus or off-campus services.

Summer Program To help prepare for the demands of college, there is an optional 3-week summer program prior to entering the school.

Unique Aids and Services Aids, services, or accommodations include advocates, career counseling, and faculty training.

Subject-area Tutoring Tutoring is offered one-on-one and in small groups for all subjects. Tutoring is provided through the program or unit via professional tutors and trained peer tutors. Tutoring is also provided collaboratively through on-campus or off-campus services via professional tutors and trained peer tutors.

Basic Skills Remediation Remediation is offered one-on-one and in class-size groups for computer skills, learning strategies, math, study skills, time management, and written language. Remediation is provided through the program or unit via professional tutors and regular education teachers. Remediation is also provided collaboratively through on-campus or off-campus services via professional tutors and regular education teachers.

Student Organization On Campus and Community Advocacy Club consists of 10 members.

Application For admittance to the program or unit, students are required to provide a psychoeducational report (5 years old or less). Upon acceptance, documentation of need for services should be sent only to the LD program or unit. *Application deadline (institutional):* Continuous. *Application deadline (LD program):* Rolling/continuous for fall and rolling/continuous for spring.

Written Policies Written policies regarding course substitutions, general/basic LD accommodations, grade forgiveness, reduced course loads, substitutions and waivers of admissions requirements, and substitutions and waivers of graduation requirements are available on the program Web site. Written policies regarding course substitutions and substitutions and waivers of admissions requirements are outlined in the school's catalog/handbook. Written policies regarding general/basic LD accommodations, grade forgiveness, reduced course loads, and substitutions and waivers of graduation requirements are available through the program or unit directly.

Phoenix College
Disability Support Services, Special Services

1202 West Thomas Road
Phoenix, AZ 85013-4234
http://www.pc.maricopa.edu/departments/SpecialServices/DSS/index.html
Contact: Mr. Gene W. Heppard, Coordinator, Disability Support Services. Phone: 602-285-7477. Fax: 602-285-7663. E-mail: gene.heppard@pcmail.maricopa.edu. Head of LD Program: Ms. Mitra Mehraban, Director of Special Services. Phone: 602-285-7476. Fax: 602-285-7663. E-mail: mitra.mehraban@pcmail.maricopa.edu.

Disability Support Services, Special Services Approximately 150 registered undergraduate students were served during 2002-03. The program or unit includes 4 full-time and 3 part-time staff members. Academic advisers, counselors, diagnostic specialists, LD specialists, and strategy tutors are provided through the program or unit. Coaches, graduate assistants/students, professional tutors, regular education teachers, remediation/learning specialists, skill tutors, special education teachers, teacher trainees, and trained peer tutors are provided collaboratively through on-campus or off-campus services.

Orientation The program or unit offers an optional approximately 2-hour orientation for new students before classes begin and individually by special arrangement.

Unique Aids and Services Aids, services, or accommodations include career counseling and digital textbooks.

Subject-area Tutoring Tutoring is offered one-on-one and in small groups for most subjects. Tutoring is provided collaboratively through on-campus or off-campus services via computer-based instruction, graduate assistants/students, professional tutors, and trained peer tutors.

Enrichment Enrichment programs are available through the program or unit for career planning. Programs for career planning, college survival skills, health and nutrition, learning strategies, oral communication skills, practical computer skills, reading, self-advocacy, stress management, study skills, test taking, time management, vocabulary development, and written composition skills are provided collaboratively through on-campus or off-campus services. Credit is offered for college survival skills, health and nutrition, learning strategies, oral communication skills, practical computer skills, reading, self-advocacy, stress management, study skills, test taking, time management, vocabulary development, and written composition skills.

Application For admittance to the program or unit, students are required to provide a psychoeducational report (3 years old or less). It is recommended that students provide documentation of high school services. Upon application, materials documenting need for services should be sent only to the LD program or unit. Upon acceptance, documentation of need for services should be sent only to the LD program or unit. *Application deadline (institutional):* Continuous. *Application deadline (LD program):* Rolling/continuous for fall and rolling/continuous for spring.

Written Policies Written policies regarding general/basic LD accommodations, reduced course loads, and substitutions and waivers of admissions requirements are available on the program Web site. Written policies regarding course substitutions, grade forgiveness, and substitutions and waivers of graduation requirements are outlined in the school's catalog/handbook. Written policies regarding general/basic LD accommodations, reduced course loads, and substitutions and waivers of admissions requirements are available through the program or unit directly.

Piedmont Community College
Students with Special Needs

PO Box 1197
Roxboro, NC 27573-1197
http://www.piedmont.cc.nc.us

Contact: Counseling Center. Phone: 336-599-1181 Ext. 272. Fax: 336-598-9283.

Students with Special Needs Approximately 30 registered undergraduate students were served during 2002-03. The program or unit includes 1 full-time staff member. Counselors, trained peer tutors, and other are provided collaboratively through on-campus or off-campus services.

Subject-area Tutoring Tutoring is offered one-on-one and in small groups for some subjects. Tutoring is provided collaboratively through on-campus or off-campus services via trained peer tutors and other.

Basic Skills Remediation Remediation is offered in small groups for math, reading, and written language. Remediation is provided collaboratively through on-campus or off-campus services.

Enrichment Programs for career planning, college survival skills, health and nutrition, learning strategies, practical computer skills, reading, stress management, study skills, test taking, time management, and other are provided collaboratively through on-campus or off-campus services.

Application For admittance to the program or unit, students are required to provide a psychoeducational report. It is recommended that students provide documentation of high school services. Upon application, materials documenting need for services should be sent to both admissions and the LD program or unit. Upon acceptance, documentation of need for services should be sent to both admissions and the LD program or unit. *Application deadline (institutional):* Continuous. *Application deadline (LD program):* Rolling/continuous for fall and rolling/continuous for spring.

Written Policies Written policy regarding general/basic LD accommodations is available through the program or unit directly.

Piedmont Technical College
Student Disability Services

PO Box 1467
Greenwood, SC 29648-1467
http://ptc.edu/SSC/Disability-Services/

Contact: Ms. Alice Hodges, Disability Services Coordinator. Phone: 864-941-8378 Ext. 8378. Fax: 864-941-8709. E-mail: hodges.a@ptc.edu.

Student Disability Services Approximately 102 registered undergraduate students were served during 2002-03. The program or unit includes 1 full-time staff member. Academic advisers, counselors, LD specialists, professional tutors, remediation/learning specialists, skill tutors, strategy tutors, trained peer tutors, and other are provided through the program or unit. Academic advisers, counselors, diagnostic specialists, LD specialists, professional tutors, regular education teachers, remediation/learning specialists, skill tutors, strategy tutors, trained peer tutors, and other are provided collaboratively through on-campus or off-campus services.

Unique Aids and Services Aids, services, or accommodations include advocates, career counseling, and faculty training.

Subject-area Tutoring Tutoring is offered one-on-one for most subjects. Tutoring is provided through the program or unit via LD specialists and trained peer tutors. Tutoring is also provided collaboratively through on-campus or off-campus services via LD specialists and trained peer tutors.

Basic Skills Remediation Remediation is offered one-on-one for learning strategies, math, reading, social skills, spelling, study skills, time management, and written language. Remediation is provided through the program or unit via trained peer tutors. Remediation is also provided collaboratively through on-campus or off-campus services via trained peer tutors.

Enrichment Enrichment programs are available through the program or unit for career planning, college survival skills, learning strategies, math, oral communication skills, practical computer skills, reading, self-advocacy, stress management, study skills, test taking, time management, and written composition skills. Programs for career planning, college survival skills, learning strategies, math, oral communication skills, practical computer skills, reading, self-advocacy, stress management, study skills, test taking, time management, vocabulary development, and written composition skills

Piedmont Technical College (continued)

are provided collaboratively through on-campus or off-campus services. Credit is offered for college survival skills, oral communication skills, practical computer skills, reading, vocabulary development, and written composition skills.

Application For admittance to the program or unit, students are required to apply to the program directly. It is recommended that students provide a psychoeducational report (3 years old or less) and provide documentation of high school services. Upon application, materials documenting need for services should be sent only to the LD program or unit. Upon acceptance, documentation of need for services should be sent only to the LD program or unit. *Application deadline (institutional):* Continuous. *Application deadline (LD program):* Rolling/continuous for fall and rolling/continuous for spring.

Written Policies Written policy regarding general/basic LD accommodations is available on the program Web site. Written policies regarding course substitutions, general/basic LD accommodations, grade forgiveness, reduced course loads, substitutions and waivers of admissions requirements, and substitutions and waivers of graduation requirements are outlined in the school's catalog/handbook.

Pikes Peak Community College
Office of Accommodative Services and Instructional Support (OASIS)

5675 South Academy Boulevard
Colorado Springs, CO 80906-5498
http://www.ppcc.edu/
Contact: Mrs. Sandra L. Johannsen, Disability Specialist. Phone: 719-540-7124. Fax: 719-540-7090. E-mail: sandra.johannsen@ppcc.edu.

Office of Accommodative Services and Instructional Support (OASIS) Approximately 143 registered undergraduate students were served during 2002-03. The program or unit includes 2 full-time staff members. LD specialists, skill tutors, and other are provided collaboratively through on-campus or off-campus services.
Orientation The program or unit offers an optional 2½ to 3-hour orientation for new students before classes begin.
Summer Program To help prepare for the demands of college, there is an optional 2½ to 3-hour summer program prior to entering the school.
Unique Aids and Services Aids, services, or accommodations include career counseling, digital textbooks, faculty training, and personal coach.
Subject-area Tutoring Tutoring is offered one-on-one, in small groups, and in class-size groups for most subjects. Tutoring is provided through the program or unit via computer-based instruction, professional tutors, and trained peer tutors.
Basic Skills Remediation Remediation is offered in class-size groups for computer skills, learning strategies, math, reading, study skills, time management, and written language. Remediation is provided collaboratively through on-campus or off-campus services via computer-based instruction, regular education teachers, and trained peer tutors.

Enrichment Programs for career planning, college survival skills, learning strategies, math, oral communication skills, practical computer skills, self-advocacy, stress management, study skills, test taking, time management, vocabulary development, and written composition skills are provided collaboratively through on-campus or off-campus services.
Student Organization Disabled Students Club consists of 5 members.
Application For admittance to the program or unit, students are required to apply to the program directly and provide a psychoeducational report (5 years old or less). It is recommended that students provide documentation of high school services. Upon application, materials documenting need for services should be sent only to the LD program or unit. Upon acceptance, documentation of need for services should be sent only to the LD program or unit. *Application deadline (institutional):* Continuous. *Application deadline (LD program):* Rolling/continuous for fall and rolling/continuous for spring.
Written Policies Written policy regarding general/basic LD accommodations is available on the program Web site. Written policy regarding general/basic LD accommodations is outlined in the school's catalog/handbook. Written policy regarding general/basic LD accommodations is available through the program or unit directly.

Pima Community College
Disabled Student Resources (DSR)

4905 East Broadway
Tucson, AZ 85709-1010
http://www.pima.edu/
Contact: Ms. Jane Irey, Disability Specialist. Phone: 520-206-6688. Fax: 520-206-3139. E-mail: jane.irey@pima.edu. Head of LD Program: Mr. Eric Morrison, DSR 504 Coordinator. Phone: 520-206-6688. Fax: 520-206-3139. E-mail: eric.morrison@pima.edu.

Disabled Student Resources (DSR) Approximately 300 registered undergraduate students were served during 2002-03. The program or unit includes 7 full-time staff members. Academic advisers, counselors, LD specialists, regular education teachers, and trained peer tutors are provided collaboratively through on-campus or off-campus services.
Unique Aids and Services Aids, services, or accommodations include career counseling, priority registration, assistive technology (Kurzweil 3000), text help, Dragon Naturally Speaking.
Subject-area Tutoring Tutoring is offered one-on-one and in small groups for some subjects. Tutoring is provided collaboratively through on-campus or off-campus services via trained peer tutors.
Basic Skills Remediation Remediation is offered one-on-one, in small groups, and in class-size groups for math, reading, spelling, study skills, time management, and written language. Remediation is provided collaboratively through on-campus or off-campus services via regular education teachers and trained peer tutors.
Enrichment Programs for career planning, math, reading, stress management, study skills, test taking, time management, vocabulary development, and written composition skills are provided collaboratively through on-campus or off-campus services. Credit is offered for career planning, math, reading, stress management, study skills, test taking, time management, vocabulary development, and written composition skills.

Application For admittance to the program or unit, students are required to provide a psychoeducational report and provide documentation of high school services. Upon application, materials documenting need for services should be sent only to the LD program or unit. Upon acceptance, documentation of need for services should be sent only to the LD program or unit. *Application deadline (institutional):* Continuous. *Application deadline (LD program):* Rolling/continuous for fall and rolling/continuous for spring.

Written Policies Written policies regarding course substitutions and general/basic LD accommodations are available on the program Web site. Written policies regarding course substitutions and general/basic LD accommodations are available through the program or unit directly.

Pine Technical College

900 4th Street SE

Pine City, MN 55063

http://www.ptc.tec.mn.us/

Contact: Mrs. Gloria Jean Baker, Director of Disability Services. Phone: 320-629-5174. Fax: 320-629-5101. E-mail: bakerg@ptc.tec.mn.us.

Approximately 40 registered undergraduate students were served during 2002-03. The program or unit includes 1 full-time and 2 part-time staff members. LD specialists, professional tutors, skill tutors, strategy tutors, and trained peer tutors are provided through the program or unit. Academic advisers, counselors, diagnostic specialists, graduate assistants/students, regular education teachers, remediation/learning specialists, and special education teachers are provided collaboratively through on-campus or off-campus services.

Unique Aids and Services Aids, services, or accommodations include career counseling and support groups.

Subject-area Tutoring Tutoring is offered one-on-one and in small groups for most subjects. Tutoring is provided through the program or unit via computer-based instruction, LD specialists, professional tutors, and trained peer tutors. Tutoring is also provided collaboratively through on-campus or off-campus services via computer-based instruction.

Diagnostic Testing Testing is provided through the program or unit for learning strategies, learning styles, math, reading, study skills, and written language. Testing for auditory processing, handwriting, intelligence, motor skills, neuropsychological, personality, social skills, spelling, spoken language, and visual processing is provided collaboratively through on-campus or off-campus services.

Basic Skills Remediation Remediation is offered one-on-one and in small groups for learning strategies, math, reading, study skills, time management, and written language. Remediation is provided through the program or unit via computer-based instruction, LD specialists, professional tutors, regular education teachers, and trained peer tutors. Remediation is also provided collaboratively through on-campus or off-campus services via computer-based instruction and special education teachers.

Enrichment Enrichment programs are available through the program or unit for career planning, learning strategies, math, self-advocacy, stress management, study skills, test taking, and time management. Programs for career planning, college survival skills, learning strategies, math, practical computer skills, reading, stress management, study skills, test taking, time management, vocabulary development, and written composition skills are provided collaboratively through on-campus or off-campus services.

Application For admittance to the program or unit, students are required to provide other health disability documentation . It is recommended that students provide a psychoeducational report (3 years old or less) and provide documentation of high school services. Upon application, materials documenting need for services should be sent only to the LD program or unit. Upon acceptance, documentation of need for services should be sent only to the LD program or unit. *Application deadline (institutional):* Continuous. *Application deadline (LD program):* Rolling/continuous for fall and rolling/continuous for spring.

Written Policies Written policy regarding general/basic LD accommodations is available through the program or unit directly.

Polk Community College

999 Avenue H, NE

Winter Haven, FL 33881-4299

http://www.polk.edu/

Contact: Mr. Sylvester Little, Coordinator of Academic Advising. Phone: 863-297-1000 Ext. 5227. Fax: 863-297-1060. E-mail: slittle@polk.edu. Head of LD Program: Mr. Jonathan Morrell DD, Dean of Student Services. Phone: 863-297-1010 Ext. 5344. Fax: 863-297-1060. E-mail: jmorrell@polk.edu.

Approximately 75 registered undergraduate students were served during 2002-03. The program or unit includes 4 part-time staff members. Academic advisers are provided through the program or unit. Professional tutors and trained peer tutors are provided collaboratively through on-campus or off-campus services.

Orientation The program or unit offers an optional orientation for new students before registration, before classes begin, and individually by special arrangement.

Unique Aids and Services Aids, services, or accommodations include career counseling and priority registration.

Subject-area Tutoring Tutoring is offered one-on-one for most subjects. Tutoring is provided collaboratively through on-campus or off-campus services via professional tutors and trained peer tutors.

Basic Skills Remediation Remediation is offered in class-size groups for math, reading, and written language. Remediation is provided collaboratively through on-campus or off-campus services via regular education teachers.

Enrichment Enrichment programs are available through the program or unit for career planning. Programs for college survival skills, learning strategies, math, reading, study skills, test taking, time management, and written composition skills are provided collaboratively through on-campus or off-campus services.

Application For admittance to the program or unit, students are required to apply to the program directly and provide a psychoeducational report (10 years old or less). It is recommended that students provide documentation of high school services. Upon application, materials documenting need for services should be sent only to the LD program or unit. Upon acceptance, documentation of need for services should be sent only to the LD program or unit. *Application deadline (institutional):* Continuous. *Application deadline (LD program):* Rolling/continuous for fall and rolling/continuous for spring.

Polk Community College (continued)

Written Policies Written policies regarding grade forgiveness and substitutions and waivers of graduation requirements are outlined in the school's catalog/handbook. Written policies regarding course substitutions, general/basic LD accommodations, grade forgiveness, substitutions and waivers of admissions requirements, and substitutions and waivers of graduation requirements are available through the program or unit directly.

Prince George's Community College

301 Largo Road
Largo, MD 20774-2199
http://www.pgcc.edu/
Contact: Ms. Daria Price, Learning Specialist. Phone: 301-322-0198. Fax: 301-808-0418. E-mail: pricedl@pgcc.edu. Head of LD Program: Mr. Thomas Oliver Mays, Manager of Disability Support Services. Phone: 301-322-0838. Fax: 301-386-7542. E-mail: maysto@pgcc.edu.

Approximately 250 registered undergraduate students were served during 2002-03. The program or unit includes 2 full-time staff members and 1 part-time staff member. Academic advisers, counselors, LD specialists, professional tutors, and trained peer tutors are provided collaboratively through on-campus or off-campus services.

Unique Aids and Services Aids, services, or accommodations include career counseling, priority registration, a retention services program.

Subject-area Tutoring Tutoring is offered one-on-one and in small groups for most subjects. Tutoring is provided collaboratively through on-campus or off-campus services via computer-based instruction, graduate assistants/students, LD specialists, professional tutors, and trained peer tutors.

Diagnostic Testing Testing is provided through the program or unit for learning strategies, learning styles, and study skills. Testing for auditory processing, handwriting, intelligence, math, motor skills, neuropsychological, personality, reading, social skills, spelling, spoken language, visual processing, and written language is provided collaboratively through on-campus or off-campus services.

Basic Skills Remediation Remediation is offered in class-size groups for computer skills, learning strategies, math, reading, social skills, study skills, time management, and written language. Remediation is provided collaboratively through on-campus or off-campus services via computer-based instruction, LD specialists, professional tutors, regular education teachers, and trained peer tutors.

Enrichment Enrichment programs are available through the program or unit for self-advocacy, stress management, study skills, test taking, and time management. Programs for career planning, college survival skills, learning strategies, math, oral communication skills, practical computer skills, reading, self-advocacy, stress management, study skills, test taking, time management, vocabulary development, and written composition skills are provided collaboratively through on-campus or off-campus services. Credit is offered for career planning, college survival skills, math, oral communication skills, practical computer skills, reading, study skills, vocabulary development, and written composition skills.

Fees *Diagnostic Testing* fee is $400 to $2000.

Application For admittance to the program or unit, students are required to apply to the program directly and provide a psychoeducational report (3 years old or less). Upon application, materials documenting need for services should be sent only to the LD program or unit. Upon acceptance, documentation of need for services should be sent only to the LD program or unit. *Application deadline (institutional):* Continuous. *Application deadline (LD program):* Rolling/continuous for fall and rolling/continuous for spring.

Written Policies Written policy regarding general/basic LD accommodations is available on the program Web site. Written policies regarding general/basic LD accommodations and grade forgiveness are outlined in the school's catalog/handbook. Written policy regarding general/basic LD accommodations is available through the program or unit directly.

Pueblo Community College
Disability Resources

900 West Orman Avenue
Pueblo, CO 81004-1499
http://www.pueblocc.edu/
Contact: Mrs. Nancy E. Hunt, Adaptive Services Adviser. Phone: 719-549-3044. Fax: 719-549-3467. E-mail: nancy.hunt@pueblocc.edu.

Disability Resources Academic advisers, counselors, professional tutors, regular education teachers, trained peer tutors, and other are provided collaboratively through on-campus or off-campus services.

Subject-area Tutoring Tutoring is offered one-on-one and in small groups for all subjects. Tutoring is provided collaboratively through on-campus or off-campus services via computer-based instruction, professional tutors, and trained peer tutors.

Basic Skills Remediation Remediation is offered one-on-one, in small groups, and in class-size groups for computer skills, learning strategies, math, reading, study skills, time management, and written language. Remediation is provided collaboratively through on-campus or off-campus services via computer-based instruction, professional tutors, regular education teachers, and trained peer tutors.

Application Upon acceptance, documentation of need for services should be sent to both admissions and the LD program or unit. *Application deadline (institutional):* Continuous. *Application deadline (LD program):* Rolling/continuous for fall and rolling/continuous for spring.

Written Policies Written policy regarding general/basic LD accommodations is available on the program Web site. Written policy regarding general/basic LD accommodations is available through the program or unit directly.

Pulaski Technical College
Counseling Services

3000 West Scenic Drive
North Little Rock, AR 72118

http://www2.pulaskitech.edu/

Contact: Ms. Beth Trafford, Counselor. Phone: 501-812-2220. Fax: 501-812-2316. E-mail: btrafford@pulaskitech.edu.

Counseling Services Approximately 100 registered undergraduate students were served during 2002-03. The program or unit includes 1 part-time staff member. Counselors are provided through the program or unit. Academic advisers, counselors, and skill tutors are provided collaboratively through on-campus or off-campus services.

Unique Aids and Services Aids, services, or accommodations include priority registration.

Subject-area Tutoring Tutoring is offered one-on-one for some subjects. Tutoring is provided collaboratively through on-campus or off-campus services via computer-based instruction and trained peer tutors.

Basic Skills Remediation Remediation is offered in class-size groups for learning strategies, math, reading, and written language. Remediation is provided collaboratively through on-campus or off-campus services via computer-based instruction and regular education teachers.

Application For admittance to the program or unit, students are required to provide a psychoeducational report (5 years old or less). It is recommended that students provide documentation of high school services. Upon application, materials documenting need for services should be sent only to the LD program or unit. Upon acceptance, documentation of need for services should be sent only to the LD program or unit. *Application deadline (institutional):* Continuous. *Application deadline (LD program):* Rolling/continuous for fall and rolling/continuous for spring.

Written Policies Written policies regarding course substitutions, general/basic LD accommodations, substitutions and waivers of admissions requirements, and substitutions and waivers of graduation requirements are available through the program or unit directly.

Quinebaug Valley Community College

742 Upper Maple Street

Danielson, CT 06239-1440

http://www.qvcc.commnet.edu/

Contact: Mr. Chris Scarborough, Learning Specialist. Phone: 860-774-1130 Ext. 403. Fax: 860-774-7768. E-mail: cscarborough@qvcc.commnet.edu.

Approximately 50 registered undergraduate students were served during 2002-03. The program or unit includes 1 full-time staff member. LD specialists are provided through the program or unit.

Unique Aids and Services Aids, services, or accommodations include advocates, career counseling, digital textbooks, faculty training, and personal coach.

Subject-area Tutoring Tutoring is offered one-on-one and in small groups for most subjects. Tutoring is provided collaboratively through on-campus or off-campus services via computer-based instruction, graduate assistants/students, LD specialists, and trained peer tutors.

Basic Skills Remediation Remediation is offered in small groups and in class-size groups for learning strategies, math, reading, study skills, time management, and written language. Remediation is provided collaboratively through on-campus or off-campus services via regular education teachers.

Application It is recommended that students provide a psychoeducational report (5 years old or less) and provide documentation of high school services. Upon acceptance, documentation of need for services should be sent only to the LD program or unit. *Application deadline (institutional):* 9/1. *Application deadline (LD program):* Rolling/continuous for fall and rolling/continuous for spring.

Written Policies Written policies regarding course substitutions, general/basic LD accommodations, reduced course loads, substitutions and waivers of admissions requirements, and substitutions and waivers of graduation requirements are available on the program Web site.

Ranken Technical College
Student Achievement Center

4431 Finney Avenue

St. Louis, MO 63113

http://www.ranken.edu/

Contact: Ms. Andra L. Dorlac, Director of Student Achievement Center. Phone: 314-286-3687. Fax: 314-371-0241. E-mail: aldorlac@ranken.edu.

Student Achievement Center Approximately 24 registered undergraduate students were served during 2002-03. The program or unit includes 1 full-time and 7 part-time staff members. Professional tutors, remediation/learning specialists, and trained peer tutors are provided through the program or unit. Academic advisers, counselors, professional tutors, regular education teachers, and trained peer tutors are provided collaboratively through on-campus or off-campus services.

Subject-area Tutoring Tutoring is offered one-on-one and in small groups for most subjects. Tutoring is provided through the program or unit via computer-based instruction, professional tutors, and trained peer tutors. Tutoring is also provided collaboratively through on-campus or off-campus services via computer-based instruction, professional tutors, and trained peer tutors.

Basic Skills Remediation Remediation is offered one-on-one and in class-size groups for computer skills, learning strategies, math, reading, study skills, time management, and written language. Remediation is provided through the program or unit via computer-based instruction, professional tutors, and trained peer tutors. Remediation is also provided collaboratively through on-campus or off-campus services via professional tutors, regular education teachers, and trained peer tutors.

Enrichment Enrichment programs are available through the program or unit for college survival skills, learning strategies, math, reading, study skills, test taking, time management, and written composition skills. Programs for career planning, practical computer skills, stress management, and written composition skills are provided collaboratively through on-campus or off-campus services.

Application For admittance to the program or unit, students are required to provide a psychoeducational report (3 years old or less). Upon application, materials documenting need for services should be sent only to the LD program or unit. Upon acceptance, docu-

Ranken Technical College (continued)

mentation of need for services should be sent only to the LD program or unit. *Application deadline (institutional):* Continuous. *Application deadline (LD program):* Rolling/continuous for fall and rolling/continuous for spring.

Written Policies Written policy regarding general/basic LD accommodations is outlined in the school's catalog/handbook.

Reading Area Community College
Center for Counseling and Academic Development

PO Box 1706
Reading, PA 19603-1706
http://racc.edu
Contact: Ms. Tomma Lee Furst, Tutor Coordinator and Learning Specialist. Phone: 610-372-4721 Ext. 5069. Fax: 610-607-6257. E-mail: tfurst@racc.edu. Head of LD Program: Ms. Stephanie Giddens, Special Populations Coordinator. Phone: 610-372-4721 Ext. 5070. Fax: 610-607-6257. E-mail: sgiddens@racc.edu.

Center for Counseling and Academic Development Approximately 75 registered undergraduate students were served during 2002-03. The program or unit includes 2 full-time staff members and 1 part-time staff member. Academic advisers, counselors, professional tutors, remediation/learning specialists, and trained peer tutors are provided through the program or unit.
Unique Aids and Services Aids, services, or accommodations include career counseling.
Subject-area Tutoring Tutoring is offered one-on-one and in small groups for most subjects. Tutoring is provided collaboratively through on-campus or off-campus services via professional tutors and trained peer tutors.
Application For admittance to the program or unit, students are required to provide a psychoeducational report (3 years old or less). It is recommended that students provide documentation of high school services and provide ER report. Upon application, materials documenting need for services should be sent only to the LD program or unit. Upon acceptance, documentation of need for services should be sent only to the LD program or unit. *Application deadline (institutional):* Continuous. *Application deadline (LD program):* Rolling/continuous for fall and rolling/continuous for spring.
Written Policies Written policy regarding general/basic LD accommodations is available on the program Web site. Written policies regarding course substitutions, general/basic LD accommodations, and substitutions and waivers of admissions requirements are outlined in the school's catalog/handbook.

Red Rocks Community College
Office of Special Services

13300 West 6th Avenue
Lakewood, CO 80228-1255

http://www.rrcc.edu/
Contact: Ms. Donna Smith, Coordinator of Special Services. Phone: 303-914-6733. Fax: 303-914-6721. E-mail: donna.smith@rrcc.edu.

Office of Special Services Approximately 250 registered undergraduate students were served during 2002-03. The program or unit includes 3 full-time and 3 part-time staff members. Academic advisers, counselors, LD specialists, and professional tutors are provided through the program or unit. Academic advisers, professional tutors, regular education teachers, and trained peer tutors are provided collaboratively through on-campus or off-campus services.
Unique Aids and Services Aids, services, or accommodations include advocates, career counseling, digital textbooks, and faculty training.
Subject-area Tutoring Tutoring is offered one-on-one and in small groups for most subjects. Tutoring is provided through the program or unit via professional tutors. Tutoring is also provided collaboratively through on-campus or off-campus services via computer-based instruction, professional tutors, and trained peer tutors.
Basic Skills Remediation Remediation is offered one-on-one and in class-size groups for learning strategies, math, reading, spelling, study skills, written language, and vocabulary. Remediation is provided through the program or unit via professional tutors. Remediation is also provided collaboratively through on-campus or off-campus services via professional tutors and regular education teachers.
Enrichment Enrichment programs are available through the program or unit for math, practical computer skills, reading, self-advocacy, and written composition skills. Programs for career planning, college survival skills, health and nutrition, learning strategies, math, oral communication skills, practical computer skills, reading, stress management, study skills, test taking, time management, vocabulary development, and written composition skills are provided collaboratively through on-campus or off-campus services. Credit is offered for career planning, college survival skills, health and nutrition, learning strategies, math, oral communication skills, practical computer skills, reading, study skills, vocabulary development, and written composition skills.
Application For admittance to the program or unit, students are required to apply to the program directly, provide a psychoeducational report (3 years old or less), and provide documentation of high school services. Upon application, materials documenting need for services should be sent only to the LD program or unit. Upon acceptance, documentation of need for services should be sent only to the LD program or unit. *Application deadline (institutional):* Continuous. *Application deadline (LD program):* Rolling/continuous for fall and rolling/continuous for spring.
Written Policies Written policy regarding general/basic LD accommodations is available through the program or unit directly.

Reedley College
Disabled Students Programs and Services (DSP&S)

995 North Reed Avenue
Reedley, CA 93654-2099
http://www.reedleycollege.edu60

Contact: Mrs. Linda Reither, Learning Disability Specialist. Phone: 559-638-0332 Ext. 3183. Fax: 559-638-0382. E-mail: linda.reither@reedleycollege.edu. Head of LD Program: Dr. Janice M. Emerzian, District Director Disabled Students Programs and Services. Phone: 559-442-8237. Fax: 559-485-7304. E-mail: janice.emerzian@scccd.com.

Disabled Students Programs and Services (DSP&S) Approximately 60 registered undergraduate students were served during 2002-03. The program or unit includes 3 full-time staff members. Academic advisers, counselors, diagnostic specialists, LD specialists, remediation/learning specialists, and strategy tutors are provided through the program or unit. Academic advisers, coaches, counselors, regular education teachers, skill tutors, strategy tutors, and trained peer tutors are provided collaboratively through on-campus or off-campus services.

Orientation The program or unit offers an optional orientation for new students individually by special arrangement.

Summer Program To help prepare for the demands of college, there is an optional 2-day summer program prior to entering the school.

Unique Aids and Services Aids, services, or accommodations include career counseling, digital textbooks, faculty training, priority registration, and support groups.

Subject-area Tutoring Tutoring is offered one-on-one, in small groups, and in class-size groups for most subjects. Tutoring is provided through the program or unit via LD specialists. Tutoring is also provided collaboratively through on-campus or off-campus services via trained peer tutors.

Diagnostic Testing Testing is provided through the program or unit for auditory processing, intelligence, learning strategies, learning styles, math, reading, spelling, spoken language, study skills, visual processing, and written language. Testing for study skills is provided collaboratively through on-campus or off-campus services.

Basic Skills Remediation Remediation is offered one-on-one, in small groups, and in class-size groups for auditory processing, computer skills, learning strategies, math, reading, social skills, spelling, spoken language, study skills, time management, visual processing, and written language. Remediation is provided through the program or unit via LD specialists. Remediation is also provided collaboratively through on-campus or off-campus services via computer-based instruction, regular education teachers, and trained peer tutors.

Enrichment Enrichment programs are available through the program or unit for college survival skills, learning strategies, oral communication skills, practical computer skills, study skills, test taking, time management, and vocabulary development. Programs for career planning, college survival skills, health and nutrition, learning strategies, math, oral communication skills, practical computer skills, reading, study skills, test taking, time management, and written composition skills are provided collaboratively through on-campus or off-campus services. Credit is offered for college survival skills, health and nutrition, learning strategies, math, oral communication skills, practical computer skills, reading, study skills, test taking, time management, vocabulary development, and written composition skills.

Student Organization Students with Disabilities Club consists of 30 members.

Fees *Summer Program* fee is $30.

Application For admittance to the program or unit, students are required to provide a meeting with DSP&S counselor, who will refer the student to the LD specialist. It is recommended that students provide a psychoeducational report (3 years old or less) and provide documentation of high school services. Upon application, materials documenting need for services should be sent only to the LD program or unit. Upon acceptance, documentation of need for services should be sent only to the LD program or unit. *Application deadline (institutional):* Continuous. *Application deadline (LD program):* Rolling/continuous for fall and rolling/continuous for spring.

Written Policies Written policies regarding course substitutions, general/basic LD accommodations, grade forgiveness, reduced course loads, substitutions and waivers of admissions requirements, and substitutions and waivers of graduation requirements are outlined in the school's catalog/handbook. Written policies regarding general/basic LD accommodations, substitutions and waivers of admissions requirements, and substitutions and waivers of graduation requirements are available through the program or unit directly.

Remington College-Jacksonville Campus

7011 A.C. Skinner Parkway
Jacksonville, FL 32256
http://www.remingtoncollege.edu/
Contact: Phone: 904-296-3435. Fax: 904-296-9097.

Academic advisers, coaches, counselors, diagnostic specialists, graduate assistants/students, LD specialists, professional tutors, regular education teachers, remediation/learning specialists, skill tutors, special education teachers, strategy tutors, teacher trainees, trained peer tutors, and other are provided collaboratively through on-campus or off-campus services.

Subject-area Tutoring Tutoring is offered one-on-one for all subjects. Tutoring is provided through the program or unit via other.

Application Upon application, materials documenting need for services should be sent only to admissions with institutional application materials. Upon acceptance, documentation of need for services should be sent only to admissions. *Application deadline (LD program):* Rolling/continuous for fall and rolling/continuous for spring.

Written Policies Written policies regarding general/basic LD accommodations and substitutions and waivers of admissions requirements are outlined in the school's catalog/handbook.

Richard Bland College of The College of William and Mary

11301 Johnson Road
Petersburg, VA 23805-7100
http://www.rbc.edu/
Contact: Phone: 804-862-6100. Fax: 804-862-6189.

Richard Bland College of The College of William and Mary (continued)

The program or unit includes 1 full-time staff member. LD specialists are provided through the program or unit. Academic advisers, counselors, professional tutors, and trained peer tutors are provided collaboratively through on-campus or off-campus services.

Summer Program To help prepare for the demands of college, there is an optional 6-week summer program prior to entering the school. Degree credit will be earned.

Unique Aids and Services Aids, services, or accommodations include advocates, career counseling, and personal coach.

Subject-area Tutoring Tutoring is offered one-on-one, in small groups, and in class-size groups for all subjects. Tutoring is provided collaboratively through on-campus or off-campus services via computer-based instruction, trained peer tutors, and other.

Basic Skills Remediation Remediation is offered one-on-one, in small groups, and in class-size groups for auditory processing, computer skills, learning strategies, math, spoken language, study skills, time management, visual processing, and written language. Remediation is provided collaboratively through on-campus or off-campus services via computer-based instruction, regular education teachers, trained peer tutors, and other.

Enrichment Enrichment programs are available through the program or unit for self-advocacy and stress management. Programs for career planning, college survival skills, health and nutrition, learning strategies, math, oral communication skills, practical computer skills, self-advocacy, stress management, study skills, test taking, time management, and written composition skills are provided collaboratively through on-campus or off-campus services. Credit is offered for college survival skills, health and nutrition, learning strategies, math, oral communication skills, practical computer skills, stress management, study skills, test taking, time management, and written composition skills.

Fees *LD Program or Service* fee is $921 (fee varies according to academic program). *Summer Program* fee is $921.

Application For admittance to the program or unit, students are required to provide a psychoeducational report (3 years old or less) and provide documentation of high school services. Upon acceptance, documentation of need for services should be sent only to the LD program or unit. *Application deadline (institutional):* 8/15. *Application deadline (LD program):* Rolling/continuous for fall.

Written Policies Written policies regarding course substitutions, general/basic LD accommodations, grade forgiveness, reduced course loads, substitutions and waivers of admissions requirements, and substitutions and waivers of graduation requirements are outlined in the school's catalog/handbook. Written policies regarding general/basic LD accommodations and substitutions and waivers of admissions requirements are available through the program or unit directly.

Richland College

12800 Abrams Road
Dallas, TX 75243-2199
http://www.rlc.dcccd.edu/
Contact: Phone: 972-238-6106. Fax: 972-238-6957.

The program or unit includes 3 full-time staff members and 1 part-time staff member. Academic advisers, counselors, skill tutors, and trained peer tutors are provided collaboratively through on-campus or off-campus services.

Unique Aids and Services Aids, services, or accommodations include career counseling, digital textbooks, and priority registration.

Subject-area Tutoring Tutoring is offered one-on-one, in small groups, and in class-size groups for most subjects. Tutoring is provided collaboratively through on-campus or off-campus services via professional tutors and trained peer tutors.

Basic Skills Remediation Remediation is offered one-on-one for computer skills, learning strategies, math, reading, spelling, study skills, time management, and written language. Remediation is provided collaboratively through on-campus or off-campus services via professional tutors and trained peer tutors.

Enrichment Programs for career planning, college survival skills, health and nutrition, learning strategies, math, reading, stress management, test taking, time management, vocabulary development, and written composition skills are provided collaboratively through on-campus or off-campus services. Credit is offered for career planning.

Application It is recommended that students provide a psychoeducational report (3 years old or less). Upon acceptance, documentation of need for services should be sent only to the LD program or unit. *Application deadline (institutional):* Continuous.

Written Policies Written policy regarding general/basic LD accommodations is available on the program Web site. Written policy regarding general/basic LD accommodations is outlined in the school's catalog/handbook. Written policy regarding general/basic LD accommodations is available through the program or unit directly.

Richland Community College

One College Park
Decatur, IL 62521-8513
http://www.richland.edu/
Contact: Phone: 217-875-7200. Fax: 217-875-6991.

The program or unit includes 1 full-time and 1 part-time staff member. Diagnostic specialists, LD specialists, remediation/learning specialists, skill tutors, special education teachers, and strategy tutors are provided through the program or unit. Academic advisers, counselors, graduate assistants/students, professional tutors, regular education teachers, and trained peer tutors are provided collaboratively through on-campus or off-campus services.

Orientation The program or unit offers an optional 2-hour orientation for new students before classes begin.

Summer Program To help prepare for the demands of college, there is an optional 2-week summer program prior to entering the school. Degree credit will be earned.

Unique Aids and Services Aids, services, or accommodations include support groups.

Subject-area Tutoring Tutoring is offered one-on-one and in small groups for all subjects. Tutoring is provided through the program or unit via computer-based instruction, graduate assistants/students, LD specialists, professional tutors, and trained peer tutors. Tutoring is also provided collaboratively through on-campus or off-campus services via graduate assistants/students, professional tutors, and trained peer tutors.

Diagnostic Testing Testing is provided through the program or unit for auditory processing, learning strategies, learning styles, math, reading, social skills, spelling, study skills, visual processing, and written language.

Basic Skills Remediation Remediation is offered one-on-one and in class-size groups for auditory processing, computer skills, learning strategies, math, reading, social skills, spelling, study skills, time management, visual processing, and written language. Remediation is provided through the program or unit via computer-based instruction, LD specialists, professional tutors, special education teachers, and trained peer tutors. Remediation is also provided collaboratively through on-campus or off-campus services via computer-based instruction, professional tutors, regular education teachers, and trained peer tutors.

Enrichment Enrichment programs are available through the program or unit for college survival skills, health and nutrition, learning strategies, math, practical computer skills, reading, stress management, study skills, test taking, time management, vocabulary development, and written composition skills. Programs for career planning, learning strategies, math, practical computer skills, reading, stress management, study skills, test taking, time management, vocabulary development, and written composition skills are provided collaboratively through on-campus or off-campus services. Credit is offered for career planning.

Student Organization Students Unlimited consists of 10 members.

Fees *Summer Program* fee is $54.

Application For admittance to the program or unit, students are required to apply to the program directly, provide a psychoeducational report, and provide documentation of high school services. Upon application, materials documenting need for services should be sent only to the LD program or unit. Upon acceptance, documentation of need for services should be sent only to the LD program or unit. *Application deadline (institutional):* Continuous. *Application deadline (LD program):* 8/26 for fall. 1/23 for spring.

Written Policies Written policy regarding general/basic LD accommodations is available on the program Web site. Written policy regarding general/basic LD accommodations is outlined in the school's catalog/handbook. Written policies regarding course substitutions, general/basic LD accommodations, and reduced course loads are available through the program or unit directly.

Riverland Community College
Student Success Center

1900 8th Avenue, NW

Austin, MN 55912

http://www.riverland.cc.mn.us/

Contact: Mindi Federman Askelson, Director of Student Success Services. Phone: 507-433-0569. E-mail: maskelso@river.cc.mn.us.

Student Success Center Approximately 15 registered undergraduate students were served during 2002-03. The program or unit includes 3 full-time and 2 part-time staff members. Professional tutors and trained peer tutors are provided through the program or unit. Academic advisers and counselors are provided collaboratively through on-campus or off-campus services.

Orientation The program or unit offers a mandatory 1-hour orientation for new students individually by special arrangement.

Unique Aids and Services Aids, services, or accommodations include advocates, digital textbooks, priority registration, extended testing, private room.

Subject-area Tutoring Tutoring is offered one-on-one, in small groups, and in class-size groups for most subjects. Tutoring is provided through the program or unit via professional tutors and trained peer tutors. Tutoring is also provided collaboratively through on-campus or off-campus services via computer-based instruction.

Basic Skills Remediation Remediation is offered in class-size groups for reading and written language. Remediation is provided collaboratively through on-campus or off-campus services via regular education teachers.

Application For admittance to the program or unit, students are required to apply to the program directly and provide a psychoeducational report (3 years old or less). It is recommended that students provide documentation of high school services. Upon application, materials documenting need for services should be sent only to the LD program or unit. Upon acceptance, documentation of need for services should be sent only to the LD program or unit. *Application deadline (institutional):* Continuous. *Application deadline (LD program):* Rolling/continuous for fall and rolling/continuous for spring.

Written Policies Written policy regarding general/basic LD accommodations is available through the program or unit directly.

Roane State Community College
Counseling and Career Services

276 Patton Lane

Harriman, TN 37748-5011

http://www.rscc.cc.tn.us/

Contact: Mr. Jeff A. Snell, Counselor. Phone: 865-481-2003 Ext. 2274. Fax: 865-481-2009. E-mail: snell_ja@roanestate.edu.

Counseling and Career Services Approximately 50 registered undergraduate students were served during 2002-03. The program or unit includes 4 full-time staff members. Counselors are provided through the program or unit. Academic advisers, professional tutors, and regular education teachers are provided collaboratively through on-campus or off-campus services.

Unique Aids and Services Aids, services, or accommodations include advocates, career counseling, digital textbooks, faculty training, weekly meetings with faculty, interpreters.

Subject-area Tutoring Tutoring is offered one-on-one for some subjects. Tutoring is provided through the program or unit via LD specialists. Tutoring is also provided collaboratively through on-campus or off-campus services via computer-based instruction, graduate assistants/students, and trained peer tutors.

Diagnostic Testing Testing is provided through the program or unit for learning strategies, math, personality, reading, and written language.

Basic Skills Remediation Remediation is offered one-on-one, in small groups, and in class-size groups for learning strategies, math, reading, study skills, and written language. Remediation is provided

Roane State Community College (continued)

through the program or unit via LD specialists. Remediation is also provided collaboratively through on-campus or off-campus services via computer-based instruction, regular education teachers, and trained peer tutors.

Enrichment Enrichment programs are available through the program or unit for career planning, college survival skills, health and nutrition, learning strategies, math, oral communication skills, practical computer skills, reading, stress management, study skills, test taking, time management, written composition skills, and other. Programs for college survival skills, health and nutrition, learning strategies, math, oral communication skills, practical computer skills, reading, study skills, written composition skills, and other are provided collaboratively through on-campus or off-campus services. Credit is offered for college survival skills, health and nutrition, learning strategies, math, oral communication skills, practical computer skills, reading, study skills, and written composition skills.

Fees *Diagnostic Testing* fee is $20.

Application For admittance to the program or unit, students are required to provide proof of disability. It is recommended that students provide a psychoeducational report (3 years old or less) and provide documentation of high school services. Upon application, materials documenting need for services should be sent only to the LD program or unit. Upon acceptance, documentation of need for services should be sent only to the LD program or unit. *Application deadline (institutional):* Continuous. *Application deadline (LD program):* Rolling/continuous for fall and rolling/continuous for spring.

Written Policies Written policies regarding general/basic LD accommodations and grade forgiveness are outlined in the school's catalog/handbook.

Rockingham Community College

PO Box 38

Wentworth, NC 27375-0038

http://www.rcc.cc.nc.us/

Contact: Ms. LaVonne Waugh James, Counselor. Phone: 336-342-4261 Ext. 2243. Fax: 336-342-1809. E-mail: jamesl@rockinghamcc.edu. Head of LD Program: Mr. Terry Kent, Counselor. Phone: 336-342-4261 Ext. 2127. Fax: 336-342-1809. E-mail: kentt@rockinghamcc.edu.

The program or unit includes 2 part-time staff members. Academic advisers, coaches, counselors, and trained peer tutors are provided collaboratively through on-campus or off-campus services.

Application *Application deadline (institutional):* Continuous.

Rock Valley College

3301 North Mulford Road

Rockford, IL 61114-5699

http://www.rockvalleycollege.edu/

Contact: Phone: 815-921-7821. Fax: 815-654-5568.

The program or unit includes 10 full-time and 53 part-time staff members. Academic advisers, counselors, diagnostic specialists, professional tutors, remediation/learning specialists, trained peer tutors, and other are provided collaboratively through on-campus or off-campus services.

Unique Aids and Services Aids, services, or accommodations include career counseling and priority registration.

Subject-area Tutoring Tutoring is offered in small groups for most subjects. Tutoring is provided collaboratively through on-campus or off-campus services via computer-based instruction, professional tutors, and trained peer tutors.

Diagnostic Testing Testing for auditory processing, handwriting, intelligence, learning strategies, learning styles, math, motor skills, neuropsychological, personality, reading, social skills, spelling, spoken language, study skills, visual processing, written language, and other services is provided collaboratively through on-campus or off-campus services.

Enrichment Programs for career planning, health and nutrition, learning strategies, math, oral communication skills, practical computer skills, reading, stress management, study skills, time management, vocabulary development, and written composition skills are provided collaboratively through on-campus or off-campus services. Credit is offered for career planning, health and nutrition, math, oral communication skills, practical computer skills, reading, and written composition skills.

Fees *Diagnostic Testing* fee is $350.

Application For admittance to the program or unit, students are required to provide a psychoeducational report (3 years old or less), provide documentation of high school services, and provide medical, psychological reports when appropriate. Upon application, materials documenting need for services should be sent only to the LD program or unit. Upon acceptance, documentation of need for services should be sent only to the LD program or unit. *Application deadline (institutional):* 8/24. *Application deadline (LD program):* Rolling/continuous for fall and rolling/continuous for spring.

Written Policies Written policies regarding course substitutions, general/basic LD accommodations, and reduced course loads are available through the program or unit directly.

Rose State College
Disability Services and Resources

6420 Southeast 15th Street

Midwest City, OK 73110-2799

http://www.rose.edu/cstudent/stuserv/disable.htm

Contact: Ms. Janet Griffith, Counselor. Phone: 405-733-7407. Fax: 405-733-7549. E-mail: jgriffith@rose.edu.

Disability Services and Resources Approximately 50 registered undergraduate students were served during 2002-03. The program or unit includes 1 full-time staff member. Academic advisers, counselors, and strategy tutors are provided through the program or unit. Academic advisers, counselors, professional tutors, and trained peer tutors are provided collaboratively through on-campus or off-campus services.

Unique Aids and Services Aids, services, or accommodations include career counseling.

Subject-area Tutoring Tutoring is offered one-on-one and in small groups for some subjects. Tutoring is provided collaboratively through on-campus or off-campus services via computer-based instruction, professional tutors, and trained peer tutors.

Basic Skills Remediation Remediation is offered one-on-one, in small groups, and in class-size groups for math, reading, and written language. Remediation is provided collaboratively through on-campus or off-campus services via computer-based instruction, professional tutors, and trained peer tutors.

Enrichment Enrichment programs are available through the program or unit for career planning, college survival skills, and self-advocacy. Programs for career planning, college survival skills, learning strategies, math, reading, study skills, test taking, time management, and written composition skills are provided collaboratively through on-campus or off-campus services.

Student Organization Abled Disabled Association consists of 4 members.

Application For admittance to the program or unit, students are required to apply to the program directly and provide documentation relating to disability and impact on classroom activities. Upon application, materials documenting need for services should be sent only to the LD program or unit. Upon acceptance, documentation of need for services should be sent only to the LD program or unit. *Application deadline (institutional):* Continuous. *Application deadline (LD program):* Rolling/continuous for fall and rolling/continuous for spring.

Written Policies Written policies regarding general/basic LD accommodations and grade forgiveness are outlined in the school's catalog/handbook.

Roxbury Community College
Counselor for Students with Disabilities

1234 Columbus Avenue
Roxbury Crossing, MA 02120-3400
http://www.rcc.mass.edu

Contact: Ms. Linda B. O'Connor, Counselor for Students with Disabilities. Phone: 617-427-0060 Ext. 5006. Fax: 617-541-5371. E-mail: loconn@rcc.mass.edu.

Counselor for Students with Disabilities Approximately 20 registered undergraduate students were served during 2002-03. The program or unit includes 1 part-time staff member. Academic advisers, skill tutors, and trained peer tutors are provided through the program or unit.

Unique Aids and Services Aids, services, or accommodations include career counseling, digital textbooks, and priority registration.

Subject-area Tutoring Tutoring is offered one-on-one, in small groups, and in class-size groups for most subjects. Tutoring is provided through the program or unit via LD specialists. Tutoring is also provided collaboratively through on-campus or off-campus services via computer-based instruction, professional tutors, and trained peer tutors.

Diagnostic Testing Testing for learning styles, math, reading, and spelling is provided collaboratively through on-campus or off-campus services.

Basic Skills Remediation Remediation is offered in class-size groups for computer skills, learning strategies, math, reading, spelling, study skills, time management, and written language. Remediation is provided collaboratively through on-campus or off-campus services via computer-based instruction, professional tutors, regular education teachers, and trained peer tutors.

Enrichment Programs for career planning, college survival skills, health and nutrition, learning strategies, math, practical computer skills, reading, self-advocacy, study skills, test taking, time management, vocabulary development, and written composition skills are provided collaboratively through on-campus or off-campus services. Credit is offered for career planning, college survival skills, practical computer skills, reading, and written composition skills.

Application For admittance to the program or unit, students are required to provide a psychoeducational report (3 years old or less). It is recommended that students provide documentation of high school services. Upon application, materials documenting need for services should be sent only to the LD program or unit. Upon acceptance, documentation of need for services should be sent only to the LD program or unit. *Application deadline (institutional):* Continuous. *Application deadline (LD program):* Rolling/continuous for fall and rolling/continuous for spring.

Written Policies Written policies regarding general/basic LD accommodations and reduced course loads are available through the program or unit directly.

Saddleback College
Special Services

28000 Marguerite Parkway
Mission Viejo, CA 92692-3635
http://www.saddleback.edu/serv/couns/dsps

Contact: Ms. Diane Crary, Learning Disabilities Specialist. Phone: 949-582-4291. E-mail: dcrary@saddleback.edu. Head of LD Program: Mr. Randy Anderson, Director of Special Services. Phone: 949-582-4750. Fax: 949-347-1526. E-mail: randerson@saddleback.edu.

Special Services Approximately 475 registered undergraduate students were served during 2002-03. The program or unit includes 2 full-time and 5 part-time staff members. Diagnostic specialists, LD specialists, remediation/learning specialists, and teacher trainees are provided through the program or unit. Academic advisers, coaches, counselors, professional tutors, regular education teachers, skill tutors, strategy tutors, and trained peer tutors are provided collaboratively through on-campus or off-campus services.

Orientation The program or unit offers an optional orientation for new students before classes begin and during summer prior to enrollment.

Unique Aids and Services Aids, services, or accommodations include career counseling, digital textbooks, faculty training, priority registration, and support groups.

Subject-area Tutoring Tutoring is offered one-on-one and in small groups for some subjects. Tutoring is provided through the program or unit via computer-based instruction and professional tutors. Tutoring is also provided collaboratively through on-campus or off-campus services via trained peer tutors.

Saddleback College (continued)

Diagnostic Testing Testing is provided through the program or unit for auditory processing, intelligence, learning strategies, spelling, spoken language, and written language. Testing for auditory processing, handwriting, learning styles, math, reading, and study skills is provided collaboratively through on-campus or off-campus services.

Basic Skills Remediation Remediation is offered in class-size groups for auditory processing, computer skills, handwriting, learning strategies, math, reading, spelling, spoken language, study skills, time management, and written language. Remediation is provided through the program or unit via computer-based instruction, LD specialists, and trained peer tutors. Remediation is also provided collaboratively through on-campus or off-campus services via computer-based instruction and LD specialists.

Enrichment Enrichment programs are available through the program or unit for learning strategies, math, oral communication skills, practical computer skills, reading, self-advocacy, time management, vocabulary development, and written composition skills. Programs for career planning, college survival skills, learning strategies, practical computer skills, reading, stress management, study skills, test taking, time management, vocabulary development, and written composition skills are provided collaboratively through on-campus or off-campus services. Credit is offered for college survival skills, learning strategies, math, oral communication skills, practical computer skills, reading, self-advocacy, study skills, test taking, vocabulary development, and written composition skills.

Application For admittance to the program or unit, students are required to apply to the program directly. It is recommended that students provide a psychoeducational report (5 years old or less) and provide documentation of high school services. Upon application, materials documenting need for services should be sent only to the LD program or unit. Upon acceptance, documentation of need for services should be sent only to the LD program or unit. *Application deadline (institutional):* Continuous. *Application deadline (LD program):* Rolling/continuous for fall and rolling/continuous for spring.

Written Policies Written policies regarding course substitutions and general/basic LD accommodations are available on the program Web site. Written policies regarding grade forgiveness and reduced course loads are outlined in the school's catalog/handbook. Written policies regarding course substitutions and general/basic LD accommodations are available through the program or unit directly.

St. Clair County Community College

323 Erie Street, PO Box 5015
Port Huron, MI 48061-5015
http://www.sc4.edu/
Contact: Phone: 810-984-3881. Fax: 810-984-4730.

The program or unit includes 5 full-time and 63 part-time staff members. Academic advisers, counselors, professional tutors, and trained peer tutors are provided collaboratively through on-campus or off-campus services.

Unique Aids and Services Aids, services, or accommodations include career counseling.

Subject-area Tutoring Tutoring is offered one-on-one and in small groups for all subjects. Tutoring is provided collaboratively through on-campus or off-campus services via computer-based instruction, professional tutors, and trained peer tutors.

Basic Skills Remediation Remediation is offered one-on-one and in small groups for math, reading, study skills, time management, and written language. Remediation is provided collaboratively through on-campus or off-campus services via computer-based instruction, professional tutors, and trained peer tutors.

Enrichment Programs for career planning, college survival skills, learning strategies, math, reading, stress management, study skills, test taking, time management, and written composition skills are provided collaboratively through on-campus or off-campus services. Credit is offered for career planning, college survival skills, learning strategies, math, reading, stress management, study skills, test taking, time management, and written composition skills.

Application It is recommended that students provide a psychoeducational report and provide documentation of high school services. Upon application, materials documenting need for services should be sent only to the LD program or unit. Upon acceptance, documentation of need for services should be sent only to the LD program or unit. *Application deadline (institutional):* Continuous. *Application deadline (LD program):* Rolling/continuous for fall and rolling/continuous for spring.

Written Policies Written policy regarding general/basic LD accommodations is outlined in the school's catalog/handbook. Written policy regarding general/basic LD accommodations is available through the program or unit directly.

St. Johns River Community College

Services for Students with Disabilities Office

5001 Saint Johns Avenue
Palatka, FL 32177-3897
http://www.sjrcc.cc.fl.us
Contact: Counselor for Students with Disabilities Office. Phone: 386-312-4137. Fax: 386-312-4292. E-mail: bevans_s@firn.edu.

Services for Students with Disabilities Office The program or unit includes 5 full-time staff members. Academic advisers and counselors are provided through the program or unit. Academic advisers, counselors, graduate assistants/students, regular education teachers, and remediation/learning specialists are provided collaboratively through on-campus or off-campus services.

Unique Aids and Services Aids, services, or accommodations include digital textbooks, priority registration, note-takers, readers, testing accommodations.

Subject-area Tutoring Tutoring is offered one-on-one and in small groups for some subjects. Tutoring is provided collaboratively through on-campus or off-campus services via computer-based instruction and trained peer tutors.

Basic Skills Remediation Remediation is offered in class-size groups for math, reading, and written language. Remediation is provided collaboratively through on-campus or off-campus services via computer-based instruction, regular education teachers, and special education teachers.

Enrichment Programs for career planning, college survival skills, health and nutrition, learning strategies, math, oral communication skills, practical computer skills, reading, self-advocacy, stress management, study skills, test taking, time management, vocabulary development, and written composition skills are provided collaboratively through on-campus or off-campus services. Credit is offered for career planning, college survival skills, health and nutrition, learning strategies, math, oral communication skills, practical computer skills, reading, stress management, study skills, test taking, time management, vocabulary development, and written composition skills.

Application For admittance to the program or unit, students are required to apply to the program directly and provide a psychoeducational report (3 years old or less). It is recommended that students provide documentation of high school services. Upon application, materials documenting need for services should be sent only to the LD program or unit. Upon acceptance, documentation of need for services should be sent only to the LD program or unit. *Application deadline (institutional):* Continuous. *Application deadline (LD program):* Rolling/continuous for fall and rolling/continuous for spring.

Written Policies Written policies regarding course substitutions, substitutions and waivers of admissions requirements, and substitutions and waivers of graduation requirements are outlined in the school's catalog/handbook. Written policies regarding course substitutions, general/basic LD accommodations, substitutions and waivers of admissions requirements, and substitutions and waivers of graduation requirements are available through the program or unit directly.

St. Louis Community College at Florissant Valley
Access Office, Services for Students with Disabilities

3400 Pershall Road
St. Louis, MO 63135-1499
http://www.stlcc.cc.mo.us/access/
Contact: Ms. Suelaine M. Matthews, Manager. Phone: 314-595-4549. Fax: 314-595-2376. E-mail: smatthews@stlcc.edu. Head of LD Program: Ms. Mary S. Wagner, Access Office Specialist. Phone: 314-595-2188. Fax: 314-595-2376. E-mail: mwagner@stlcc.edu.

Access Office, Services for Students with Disabilities
Approximately 80 registered undergraduate students were served during 2002-03. The program or unit includes 2 full-time and 2 part-time staff members. Academic advisers, counselors, and LD specialists are provided through the program or unit. Academic advisers, coaches, counselors, regular education teachers, remediation/learning specialists, skill tutors, strategy tutors, and trained peer tutors are provided collaboratively through on-campus or off-campus services.

Orientation The program or unit offers an optional 1-day orientation for new students before classes begin.

Unique Aids and Services Aids, services, or accommodations include career counseling, digital textbooks, and faculty training.

Subject-area Tutoring Tutoring is offered one-on-one and in small groups for all subjects. Tutoring is provided collaboratively through on-campus or off-campus services via trained peer tutors.

Basic Skills Remediation Remediation is offered one-on-one, in small groups, and in class-size groups for computer skills, math, reading, study skills, time management, and written language. Remediation is provided collaboratively through on-campus or off-campus services via computer-based instruction, regular education teachers, and trained peer tutors.

Enrichment Enrichment programs are available through the program or unit for career planning, college survival skills, self-advocacy, stress management, study skills, test taking, and time management. Programs for career planning, college survival skills, health and nutrition, learning strategies, math, oral communication skills, practical computer skills, reading, stress management, study skills, test taking, time management, vocabulary development, and written composition skills are provided collaboratively through on-campus or off-campus services.

Application For admittance to the program or unit, students are required to provide a psychoeducational report (5 years old or less). It is recommended that students provide documentation of high school services. Upon application, materials documenting need for services should be sent only to the LD program or unit. Upon acceptance, documentation of need for services should be sent only to the LD program or unit. *Application deadline (institutional):* 8/19. *Application deadline (LD program):* Rolling/continuous for fall and rolling/continuous for spring.

Written Policies Written policies regarding general/basic LD accommodations and reduced course loads are available on the program Web site. Written policies regarding course substitutions, grade forgiveness, and substitutions and waivers of graduation requirements are outlined in the school's catalog/handbook. Written policies regarding general/basic LD accommodations and reduced course loads are available through the program or unit directly.

St. Louis Community College at Forest Park

5600 Oakland Avenue
St. Louis, MO 63110-1316
http://www.stlcc.edu/
Contact: Phone: 314-644-9100.

The program or unit includes 2 full-time and 11 part-time staff members. Counselors, LD specialists, and other are provided collaboratively through on-campus or off-campus services.

Orientation The program or unit offers an optional 3-hour orientation for new students before classes begin and once a year in August.

Unique Aids and Services Aids, services, or accommodations include career counseling and digital textbooks.

Subject-area Tutoring Tutoring is offered one-on-one, in small groups, and in class-size groups for some subjects. Tutoring is provided collaboratively through on-campus or off-campus services via computer-based instruction and trained peer tutors.

Basic Skills Remediation Remediation is offered in class-size groups for computer skills, math, reading, study skills, time management, and written language. Remediation is provided collaboratively through on-campus or off-campus services via computer-based instruction, regular education teachers, and trained peer tutors.

St. Louis Community College at Forest Park (continued)

Enrichment Programs for career planning, math, practical computer skills, reading, stress management, study skills, test taking, time management, and written composition skills are provided collaboratively through on-campus or off-campus services.

Application For admittance to the program or unit, students are required to provide a psychoeducational report (5 years old or less). It is recommended that students provide documentation of high school services. Upon application, materials documenting need for services should be sent only to the LD program or unit. Upon acceptance, documentation of need for services should be sent only to the LD program or unit. *Application deadline (institutional):* 8/22. *Application deadline (LD program):* Rolling/continuous for fall and rolling/continuous for spring.

Written Policies Written policies regarding course substitutions, general/basic LD accommodations, reduced course loads, and substitutions and waivers of graduation requirements are available on the program Web site. Written policies regarding course substitutions, general/basic LD accommodations, reduced course loads, and substitutions and waivers of graduation requirements are available through the program or unit directly.

St. Louis Community College at Meramec

11333 Big Bend Boulevard
Kirkwood, MO 63122-5720

http://www.stlcc..edu/

Contact: ACCESS Office. Phone: 314-984-7673. Fax: 314-984-7123. E-mail: dkoenig@stlcc.edu.

Approximately 350 registered undergraduate students were served during 2002-03. The program or unit includes 6 full-time staff members and 1 part-time staff member. Academic advisers, coaches, counselors, diagnostic specialists, and LD specialists are provided through the program or unit. Academic advisers, counselors, professional tutors, regular education teachers, skill tutors, strategy tutors, and trained peer tutors are provided collaboratively through on-campus or off-campus services.

Orientation The program or unit offers a mandatory 3-hour orientation for new students before registration, before classes begin, during summer prior to enrollment, during registration, after classes begin, individually by special arrangement, and available to a large group of students with disabilities prior to fall .

Unique Aids and Services Aids, services, or accommodations include advocates, career counseling, digital textbooks, faculty training, advising.

Subject-area Tutoring Tutoring is offered one-on-one, in small groups, and in class-size groups for all subjects. Tutoring is provided collaboratively through on-campus or off-campus services via computer-based instruction, graduate assistants/students, professional tutors, trained peer tutors, and other.

Diagnostic Testing Testing is provided through the program or unit for personality. Testing for learning styles and personality is provided collaboratively through on-campus or off-campus services.

Basic Skills Remediation Remediation is offered one-on-one, in small groups, and in class-size groups for computer skills, learning strategies, math, reading, study skills, time management, and writ-

ten language. Remediation is provided collaboratively through on-campus or off-campus services via computer-based instruction, professional tutors, regular education teachers, trained peer tutors, and other.

Enrichment Programs for career planning, health and nutrition, learning strategies, math, oral communication skills, practical computer skills, reading, stress management, study skills, test taking, time management, vocabulary development, and written composition skills are provided collaboratively through on-campus or off-campus services. Credit is offered for career planning, health and nutrition, learning strategies, math, oral communication skills, reading, stress management, study skills, test taking, time management, vocabulary development, and written composition skills.

Application For admittance to the program or unit, students are required to apply to the program directly, provide a psychoeducational report (5 years old or less), and provide adult testing (5 years old or less) or adult testing with continued college services provided. It is recommended that students provide documentation of high school services. Upon application, materials documenting need for services should be sent only to the LD program or unit. Upon acceptance, documentation of need for services should be sent only to the LD program or unit. *Application deadline (institutional):* Continuous. *Application deadline (LD program):* Rolling/continuous for fall and rolling/continuous for spring.

Written Policies Written policy regarding general/basic LD accommodations is available on the program Web site. Written policy regarding general/basic LD accommodations is outlined in the school's catalog/handbook. Written policies regarding general/basic LD accommodations and reduced course loads are available through the program or unit directly.

Salish Kootenai College

PO Box 117
Pablo, MT 59855-0117

http://www.skc.edu/

Contact: Phone: 406-675-4800. Fax: 406-675-4801. Head of LD Program: Mr. John Domitrovich, Instructor. Phone: 406-275-4889. E-mail: john_domitrovich@skc.edu.

Subject-area Tutoring Tutoring is offered one-on-one and in small groups for most subjects. Tutoring is provided collaboratively through on-campus or off-campus services via trained peer tutors.

Basic Skills Remediation Remediation is offered one-on-one, in small groups, and in class-size groups for learning strategies, math, reading, study skills, and time management. Remediation is provided collaboratively through on-campus or off-campus services via regular education teachers.

Application Upon application, materials documenting need for services should be sent only to the LD program or unit. Upon acceptance, documentation of need for services should be sent only to the LD program or unit. *Application deadline (institutional):* Continuous.

Written Policies Written policy regarding general/basic LD accommodations is outlined in the school's catalog/handbook. Written policy regarding general/basic LD accommodations is available through the program or unit directly.

San Diego Mesa College
Disabled Students Programs and Services

7250 Mesa College Drive

San Diego, CA 92111-4998

http://www.sdmesa.sdccd.net

Contact: Prof. Jill Jansen, LD Specialist and Counselor. Phone: 619-388-2780. Fax: 619-388-2460. E-mail: jjansen@sdccd.net. Head of LD Program: Prof. Gail Conrad, Coordinator of Disabled Students Programs and Services. Phone: 619-388-2780. Fax: 619-388-2460. E-mail: gconrad@sdccd.net.

Disabled Students Programs and Services Approximately 250 registered undergraduate students were served during 2002-03. The program or unit includes 2 full-time staff members. Academic advisers, counselors, diagnostic specialists, LD specialists, and remediation/learning specialists are provided through the program or unit. Academic advisers, counselors, diagnostic specialists, professional tutors, skill tutors, and strategy tutors are provided collaboratively through on-campus or off-campus services.

Orientation The program or unit offers a mandatory online orientation for new students at any time after application is received at Disabled Students Programs and Services Office.

Unique Aids and Services Aids, services, or accommodations include career counseling, digital textbooks, priority registration, accommodations based on disability verification.

Subject-area Tutoring Tutoring is offered in small groups for most subjects. Tutoring is provided through the program or unit via computer-based instruction. Tutoring is also provided collaboratively through on-campus or off-campus services via computer-based instruction, LD specialists, and professional tutors.

Diagnostic Testing Testing is provided through the program or unit for auditory processing, intelligence, learning styles, math, reading, spelling, visual processing, and written language.

Basic Skills Remediation Remediation is offered in small groups for auditory processing, computer skills, learning strategies, math, reading, spelling, study skills, time management, visual processing, and written language. Remediation is provided through the program or unit via computer-based instruction and LD specialists. Remediation is also provided collaboratively through on-campus or off-campus services via trained peer tutors.

Enrichment Enrichment programs are available through the program or unit for learning strategies, math, practical computer skills, reading, self-advocacy, stress management, study skills, and written composition skills. Programs for career planning, college survival skills, health and nutrition, learning strategies, math, oral communication skills, practical computer skills, reading, study skills, test taking, time management, and written composition skills are provided collaboratively through on-campus or off-campus services. Credit is offered for career planning, college survival skills, health and nutrition, learning strategies, math, oral communication skills, practical computer skills, reading, study skills, test taking, time management, and written composition skills.

Fees *Diagnostic Testing* fee is $6 to $14.

Application For admittance to the program or unit, students are required to apply to the program directly. It is recommended that students provide a psychoeducational report (3 years old or less) and provide documentation of high school services. Upon application, materials documenting need for services should be sent only to the LD program or unit. Upon acceptance, documentation of need for services should be sent only to the LD program or unit. *Application deadline (LD program):* Rolling/continuous for fall and rolling/continuous for spring.

Written Policies Written policy regarding general/basic LD accommodations is available on the program Web site. Written policies regarding general/basic LD accommodations and grade forgiveness are outlined in the school's catalog/handbook. Written policy regarding general/basic LD accommodations is available through the program or unit directly.

San Diego Miramar College

10440 Black Mountain Road

San Diego, CA 92126-2999

http://www.miramar.sdccd.cc.ca.us/

Contact: Ms. Sandra J. Smith, Educational Psychologist and Counselor. Phone: 619-388-7312. Fax: 619-388-7917. E-mail: ssmith@sdccd.net.

Approximately 185 registered undergraduate students were served during 2002-03. The program or unit includes 1 full-time and 2 part-time staff members. Academic advisers, diagnostic specialists, LD specialists, remediation/learning specialists, and strategy tutors are provided through the program or unit. Coaches, counselors, professional tutors, regular education teachers, skill tutors, and trained peer tutors are provided collaboratively through on-campus or off-campus services.

Orientation The program or unit offers an optional 1-hour orientation for new students before registration, before classes begin, during summer prior to enrollment, during registration, after classes begin, and individually by special arrangement.

Unique Aids and Services Aids, services, or accommodations include career counseling, digital textbooks, faculty training, and priority registration.

Subject-area Tutoring Tutoring is offered one-on-one and in small groups for most subjects. Tutoring is provided through the program or unit via computer-based instruction. Tutoring is also provided collaboratively through on-campus or off-campus services via graduate assistants/students and trained peer tutors.

Diagnostic Testing Testing is provided through the program or unit for auditory processing, intelligence, learning strategies, learning styles, math, motor skills, neuropsychological, reading, social skills, spelling, spoken language, visual processing, and written language. Testing for study skills is provided collaboratively through on-campus or off-campus services.

Basic Skills Remediation Remediation is offered one-on-one and in small groups for auditory processing, computer skills, handwriting, learning strategies, math, motor skills, reading, spelling, spoken language, study skills, time management, visual processing, and written language. Remediation is provided through the program or unit via computer-based instruction. Remediation is also provided collaboratively through on-campus or off-campus services via computer-based instruction and trained peer tutors.

Enrichment Enrichment programs are available through the program or unit for college survival skills, learning strategies, math, oral communication skills, practical computer skills, reading, self-advocacy, stress management, study skills, test taking, time management, vocabulary development, and written composition skills.

San Diego Miramar College (continued)

Programs for career planning, health and nutrition, learning strategies, and medication management are provided collaboratively through on-campus or off-campus services. Credit is offered for career planning, college survival skills, health and nutrition, math, oral communication skills, practical computer skills, reading, self-advocacy, stress management, study skills, test taking, time management, vocabulary development, and written composition skills.

Application It is recommended that students apply to the program directly, provide a psychoeducational report (5 years old or less), and provide documentation of high school services. Upon application, materials documenting need for services should be sent only to the LD program or unit. Upon acceptance, documentation of need for services should be sent to both admissions and the LD program or unit. *Application deadline (institutional):* 9/4. *Application deadline (LD program):* Rolling/continuous for fall and rolling/continuous for spring.

Written Policies Written policies regarding general/basic LD accommodations and grade forgiveness are outlined in the school's catalog/handbook. Written policies regarding course substitutions, substitutions and waivers of admissions requirements, and substitutions and waivers of graduation requirements are available through the program or unit directly.

San Jacinto College South Campus

13735 Beamer Road
Houston, TX 77089-6099
http://www.sjcd.edu/
Contact: Ms. Connie Ginn, Special Populations Coordinator. Phone: 281-922-3453. Fax: 281-929-4626. E-mail: connie.ginn@sjcd.edu.

The program or unit includes 1 full-time and 1 part-time staff member. Academic advisers, coaches, counselors, professional tutors, remediation/learning specialists, skill tutors, trained peer tutors, and other are provided through the program or unit.

Orientation The program or unit offers an optional orientation for new students individually by special arrangement.

Summer Program To help prepare for the demands of college, there is an optional summer program prior to entering the school.

Subject-area Tutoring Tutoring is offered one-on-one, in small groups, and in class-size groups for all subjects. Tutoring is provided through the program or unit via computer-based instruction, graduate assistants/students, professional tutors, and trained peer tutors. Tutoring is also provided collaboratively through on-campus or off-campus services via computer-based instruction, graduate assistants/students, professional tutors, and trained peer tutors.

Basic Skills Remediation Remediation is offered in class-size groups for learning strategies, math, study skills, and time management. Remediation is provided through the program or unit via computer-based instruction and professional tutors. Remediation is also provided collaboratively through on-campus or off-campus services via computer-based instruction, professional tutors, and other.

Enrichment Enrichment programs are available through the program or unit for career planning, learning strategies, study skills, test taking, time management, and vocabulary development. Pro-

grams for career planning, college survival skills, learning strategies, math, reading, study skills, test taking, time management, vocabulary development, and written composition skills are provided collaboratively through on-campus or off-campus services. Credit is offered for math and reading.

Application For admittance to the program or unit, students are required to apply to the program directly, provide a psychoeducational report (3 years old or less), and provide documentation of disability. It is recommended that students provide documentation of high school services. Upon application, materials documenting need for services should be sent only to the LD program or unit. *Application deadline (institutional):* Continuous. *Application deadline (LD program):* Rolling/continuous for fall and rolling/continuous for spring.

Written Policies Written policy regarding substitutions and waivers of graduation requirements is outlined in the school's catalog/handbook. Written policies regarding general/basic LD accommodations and substitutions and waivers of graduation requirements are available through the program or unit directly.

Santa Barbara City College
DSPS

721 Cliff Drive
Santa Barbara, CA 93109-2394
http://www.sbcc.edu
Contact: Phone: 805-965-0581. Fax: 805-963-SBCC Ext. 2220.

DSPS Approximately 410 registered undergraduate students were served during 2002-03. The program or unit includes 8 full-time and 50 part-time staff members. Coaches, counselors, diagnostic specialists, LD specialists, professional tutors, strategy tutors, and trained peer tutors are provided through the program or unit. Academic advisers, regular education teachers, and skill tutors are provided collaboratively through on-campus or off-campus services.

Summer Program To help prepare for the demands of college, there is an optional 6-week summer program prior to entering the school.

Unique Aids and Services Aids, services, or accommodations include career counseling, digital textbooks, faculty training, priority registration, support groups, weekly meetings with faculty, testing accommodations, assistive technology, alternate media, adaptive equipment, auxiliary aids.

Subject-area Tutoring Tutoring is offered one-on-one, in small groups, and in class-size groups for most subjects. Tutoring is provided through the program or unit via computer-based instruction, LD specialists, professional tutors, and trained peer tutors. Tutoring is also provided collaboratively through on-campus or off-campus services via computer-based instruction, professional tutors, and trained peer tutors.

Diagnostic Testing Testing is provided through the program or unit for auditory processing, handwriting, intelligence, learning strategies, learning styles, math, motor skills, reading, social skills, spelling, spoken language, study skills, visual processing, and written language. Testing for auditory processing, handwriting, intelligence, learning strategies, learning styles, math, motor skills,

neuropsychological, personality, reading, social skills, spelling, spoken language, study skills, visual processing, and written language is provided collaboratively through on-campus or off-campus services.
Basic Skills Remediation Remediation is offered in class-size groups for computer skills, learning strategies, math, reading, spelling, study skills, time management, and written language. Remediation is provided through the program or unit via LD specialists, professional tutors, and trained peer tutors. Remediation is also provided collaboratively through on-campus or off-campus services via computer-based instruction, professional tutors, regular education teachers, and trained peer tutors.
Enrichment Enrichment programs are available through the program or unit for learning strategies, math, practical computer skills, reading, self-advocacy, stress management, study skills, test taking, time management, vocabulary development, and written composition skills. Programs for career planning, college survival skills, health and nutrition, learning strategies, math, medication management, oral communication skills, practical computer skills, reading, stress management, study skills, test taking, time management, vocabulary development, and written composition skills are provided collaboratively through on-campus or off-campus services. Credit is offered for career planning, college survival skills, oral communication skills, practical computer skills, and reading.
Application It is recommended that students provide a psychoeducational report (3 years old or less). Upon application, materials documenting need for services should be sent only to the LD program or unit. *Application deadline (institutional): 8/18. Application deadline (LD program):* Rolling/continuous for fall and rolling/continuous for spring.
Written Policies Written policy regarding general/basic LD accommodations is available on the program Web site. Written policies regarding course substitutions, general/basic LD accommodations, reduced course loads, substitutions and waivers of admissions requirements, and substitutions and waivers of graduation requirements are available through the program or unit directly.

Santa Monica College
Learning Disabilities Program

1900 Pico Boulevard
Santa Monica, CA 90405-1628
http://www.smc.edu/
Contact: George Marcopulos, Professor, Learning Disabilities Specialist. Phone: 310-434-4684. Fax: 310-434-3694. E-mail: marcopulos_george@smc.edu.

Learning Disabilities Program Approximately 400 registered undergraduate students were served during 2002-03. The program or unit includes 3 full-time and 6 part-time staff members. Diagnostic specialists, LD specialists, strategy tutors, and trained peer tutors are provided through the program or unit. Counselors and trained peer tutors are provided collaboratively through on-campus or off-campus services.
Orientation The program or unit offers an optional 1-day orientation for new students before classes begin and during registration.
Summer Program To help prepare for the demands of college, there is an optional 6-week summer program prior to entering the school.

Unique Aids and Services Aids, services, or accommodations include digital textbooks, faculty training, and priority registration.
Subject-area Tutoring Tutoring is offered one-on-one, in small groups, and in class-size groups for some subjects. Tutoring is provided through the program or unit via computer-based instruction, LD specialists, and trained peer tutors. Tutoring is also provided collaboratively through on-campus or off-campus services via trained peer tutors.
Diagnostic Testing Testing is provided through the program or unit for auditory processing, intelligence, learning strategies, learning styles, math, reading, spelling, spoken language, visual processing, and written language.
Basic Skills Remediation Remediation is offered in class-size groups for computer skills, learning strategies, math, reading, study skills, time management, and written language. Remediation is provided through the program or unit via LD specialists. Remediation is also provided collaboratively through on-campus or off-campus services via computer-based instruction and regular education teachers.
Enrichment Enrichment programs are available through the program or unit for college survival skills, learning strategies, practical computer skills, self-advocacy, study skills, test taking, time management, and vocabulary development. Programs for career planning, college survival skills, learning strategies, math, practical computer skills, reading, study skills, test taking, time management, vocabulary development, and written composition skills are provided collaboratively through on-campus or off-campus services. Credit is offered for career planning, college survival skills, learning strategies, math, practical computer skills, reading, study skills, test taking, time management, vocabulary development, and written composition skills.
Application For admittance to the program or unit, students are required to provide a psychoeducational report (3 years old or less) and provide documentation of high school services. It is recommended that students apply to the program directly and provide results of assessment to determine eligibility under California Community College guidelines . Upon acceptance, documentation of need for services should be sent only to the LD program or unit. *Application deadline (institutional): 8/30. Application deadline (LD program):* Rolling/continuous for fall.
Written Policies Written policy regarding general/basic LD accommodations is outlined in the school's catalog/handbook. Written policy regarding substitutions and waivers of graduation requirements is available through the program or unit directly.

Santa Rosa Junior College
Disability Resources Department

1501 Mendocino Avenue
Santa Rosa, CA 95401-4395
http://www.santarosa.edu/disability_resources.html
Contact: Catherine Reisman, Learning Disabilities Specialist. Phone: 707-527-4279. E-mail: creisman@santarosa.edu.

Disability Resources Department Approximately 350 registered undergraduate students were served during 2002-03. The program or unit includes 3 full-time and 2 part-time staff members. Academic advisers, counselors, diagnostic specialists, LD special-

Santa Rosa Junior College (continued)

ists, professional tutors, skill tutors, special education teachers, and strategy tutors are provided through the program or unit. Academic advisers and counselors are provided collaboratively through on-campus or off-campus services.

Orientation The program or unit offers an optional 2 half-day orientation for new students after classes begin.

Unique Aids and Services Aids, services, or accommodations include career counseling, digital textbooks, and priority registration.

Subject-area Tutoring Tutoring is offered one-on-one and in small groups for most subjects. Tutoring is provided through the program or unit via computer-based instruction and professional tutors. Tutoring is also provided collaboratively through on-campus or off-campus services via computer-based instruction, graduate assistants/students, professional tutors, and trained peer tutors.

Diagnostic Testing Testing is provided through the program or unit for auditory processing, intelligence, learning strategies, math, motor skills, reading, spelling, visual processing, written language, and other services.

Basic Skills Remediation Remediation is offered one-on-one, in small groups, and in class-size groups for auditory processing, learning strategies, math, spelling, study skills, and written language. Remediation is provided through the program or unit via computer-based instruction, LD specialists, and professional tutors. Remediation is also provided collaboratively through on-campus or off-campus services via computer-based instruction, LD specialists, professional tutors, and regular education teachers.

Enrichment Enrichment programs are available through the program or unit for career planning, college survival skills, learning strategies, math, self-advocacy, stress management, study skills, time management, and written composition skills. Programs for career planning, college survival skills, health and nutrition, learning strategies, math, medication management, oral communication skills, practical computer skills, reading, stress management, study skills, test taking, time management, vocabulary development, and written composition skills are provided collaboratively through on-campus or off-campus services. Credit is offered for career planning, college survival skills, learning strategies, math, oral communication skills, practical computer skills, reading, self-advocacy, stress management, study skills, test taking, time management, vocabulary development, and written composition skills.

Application For admittance to the program or unit, students are required to provide a psychoeducational report (3 years old or less). It is recommended that students apply to the program directly and provide documentation of high school services. Upon application, materials documenting need for services should be sent only to the LD program or unit. *Application deadline (institutional):* Continuous. *Application deadline (LD program):* Rolling/continuous for fall and rolling/continuous for spring.

Written Policies Written policy regarding general/basic LD accommodations is available on the program Web site. Written policy regarding general/basic LD accommodations is outlined in the school's catalog/handbook. Written policies regarding course substitutions, general/basic LD accommodations, and reduced course loads are available through the program or unit directly.

Schoolcraft College
Learning Assistance Center

18600 Haggerty Road

Livonia, MI 48152-2696

http://www.schoolcraft.edu/lac/

Contact: Mr. Carl R. Monroe, Equal Access Counselor. Phone: 734-462-4436. Fax: 734-462-4542. E-mail: cmonroe@schoolcraft.edu. Head of LD Program: Dr. Deborah Daiek, Associate Dean Academic and Assessment Services. Phone: 734-462-4436. Fax: 734-462-4542. E-mail: ddaiek@schoolcraft.edu.

Learning Assistance Center Approximately 150 registered undergraduate students were served during 2002-03. The program or unit includes 4 full-time and 6 part-time staff members. Academic advisers, coaches, counselors, LD specialists, skill tutors, trained peer tutors, and other are provided through the program or unit. Regular education teachers are provided collaboratively through on-campus or off-campus services.

Orientation The program or unit offers an optional 1-hour orientation for new students individually by special arrangement.

Unique Aids and Services Aids, services, or accommodations include advocates, career counseling, and personal coach.

Subject-area Tutoring Tutoring is offered one-on-one and in small groups for most subjects. Tutoring is provided through the program or unit via trained peer tutors. Tutoring is also provided collaboratively through on-campus or off-campus services via LD specialists and professional tutors.

Diagnostic Testing Testing is provided through the program or unit for study skills. Testing for auditory processing, intelligence, learning strategies, learning styles, neuropsychological, reading, visual processing, and written language is provided collaboratively through on-campus or off-campus services.

Basic Skills Remediation Remediation is offered one-on-one, in small groups, and in class-size groups for learning strategies, math, reading, study skills, time management, and written language. Remediation is provided through the program or unit via regular education teachers and trained peer tutors. Remediation is also provided collaboratively through on-campus or off-campus services via LD specialists and professional tutors.

Enrichment Enrichment programs are available through the program or unit for college survival skills, learning strategies, self-advocacy, study skills, test taking, time management, and written composition skills. Programs for career planning, math, oral communication skills, reading, stress management, test taking, time management, vocabulary development, and written composition skills are provided collaboratively through on-campus or off-campus services. Credit is offered for career planning, college survival skills, learning strategies, oral communication skills, reading, self-advocacy, study skills, time management, and vocabulary development.

Fees *Diagnostic Testing* fee is $150.

Application For admittance to the program or unit, students are required to apply to the program directly. It is recommended that students provide a psychoeducational report (3 years old or less) and provide documentation of high school services. Upon application, materials documenting need for services should be sent only to the LD program or unit. Upon acceptance, documentation of need for services should be sent only to the LD program or unit. *Application deadline (institutional):* Continuous. *Application deadline (LD program):* Rolling/continuous for fall and rolling/continuous for spring.

Written Policies Written policies regarding course substitutions, general/basic LD accommodations, substitutions and waivers of admissions requirements, and substitutions and waivers of graduation requirements are available through the program or unit directly.

Seminole Community College

100 Weldon Boulevard
Sanford, FL 32773-6199
http://www.scc-fl.edu/
Contact: Ms. Dottie Paishon, Coordinator of Disability Support Services. Phone: 407-327-2109. Fax: 407-328-2484. E-mail: paishond@scc-fl.edu.

Approximately 258 registered undergraduate students were served during 2002-03. The program or unit includes 3 full-time staff members and 1 part-time staff member. Diagnostic specialists, LD specialists, remediation/learning specialists, and trained peer tutors are provided through the program or unit. Academic advisers, counselors, skill tutors, and trained peer tutors are provided collaboratively through on-campus or off-campus services.

Unique Aids and Services Aids, services, or accommodations include career counseling and digital textbooks.

Subject-area Tutoring Tutoring is offered one-on-one for most subjects. Tutoring is provided through the program or unit via professional tutors and trained peer tutors. Tutoring is also provided collaboratively through on-campus or off-campus services via trained peer tutors.

Diagnostic Testing Testing is provided through the program or unit for auditory processing, intelligence, math, neuropsychological, reading, spelling, spoken language, visual processing, and written language. Testing for learning styles is provided collaboratively through on-campus or off-campus services.

Basic Skills Remediation Remediation is offered in class-size groups for math, reading, and written language. Remediation is provided collaboratively through on-campus or off-campus services via regular education teachers.

Enrichment Programs for career planning, college survival skills, study skills, test taking, and written composition skills are provided collaboratively through on-campus or off-campus services. Credit is offered for career planning, college survival skills, and written composition skills.

Student Organization disAbled Students Lead (DSL) consists of 25 members.

Application For admittance to the program or unit, students are required to apply to the program directly and provide a psychoeducational report (3 years old or less). It is recommended that students provide documentation of high school services. Upon application, materials documenting need for services should be sent only to the LD program or unit. Upon acceptance, documentation of need for services should be sent only to the LD program or unit. *Application deadline (institutional):* Continuous. *Application deadline (LD program):* Rolling/continuous for fall and rolling/continuous for spring.

Written Policies Written policies regarding course substitutions, general/basic LD accommodations, and substitutions and waivers of graduation requirements are available on the program Web site.

Shasta College
Disability Resource Center (DSPS)— Learning Disabilities

PO Box 496006
Redding, CA 96049-6006
http://www.shastacollege.edu/stuinfo/studentservices.htm#studentdis
Contact: Mr. Kendall Glen Crenshaw, Learning Disability Counselor. Phone: 530-225-3973. Fax: 530-225-4876. E-mail: kcrenshaw@shastacollege.edu. Head of LD Program: Mr. Thomas Morehouse, Director of Disability Resource Center. Phone: 530-225-3973. Fax: 530-225-4876. E-mail: tmorehouse@shastacollege.edu.

Disability Resource Center (DSPS)—Learning Disabilities
Approximately 175 registered undergraduate students were served during 2002-03. The program or unit includes 6 full-time and 7 part-time staff members. Academic advisers, counselors, diagnostic specialists, LD specialists, regular education teachers, remediation/learning specialists, skill tutors, special education teachers, strategy tutors, and trained peer tutors are provided through the program or unit.

Orientation The program or unit offers an optional 3-hour orientation for new students before registration and before classes begin.

Unique Aids and Services Aids, services, or accommodations include digital textbooks, faculty training, priority registration, extra time on tests, note-takers, tutoring.

Subject-area Tutoring Tutoring is offered one-on-one and in small groups for most subjects. Tutoring is provided through the program or unit via trained peer tutors.

Diagnostic Testing Testing is provided through the program or unit for auditory processing, intelligence, math, reading, spelling, visual processing, written language, and other services.

Basic Skills Remediation Remediation is offered in class-size groups for computer skills, handwriting, learning strategies, math, reading, social skills, spelling, study skills, time management, and written language. Remediation is provided through the program or unit via LD specialists and special education teachers.

Enrichment Enrichment programs are available through the program or unit for career planning, college survival skills, learning strategies, math, practical computer skills, reading, self-advocacy, study skills, test taking, and time management. Programs for career planning, college survival skills, health and nutrition, math, study skills, and written composition skills are provided collaboratively through on-campus or off-campus services. Credit is offered for career planning, college survival skills, math, practical computer skills, reading, and written composition skills.

Application It is recommended that students provide a psychoeducational report and provide documentation of high school services. Upon application, materials documenting need for services should be sent only to the LD program or unit. Upon acceptance, documentation of need for services should be sent only to the LD program or unit. *Application deadline (institutional):* Continuous. *Application deadline (LD program):* Rolling/continuous for fall.

Shasta College (continued)

Written Policies Written policy regarding substitutions and waivers of admissions requirements is outlined in the school's catalog/handbook. Written policies regarding course substitutions and substitutions and waivers of graduation requirements are available through the program or unit directly.

Shoreline Community College

16101 Greenwood Avenue North

Seattle, WA 98133-5696

http://www.shore.ctc.edu/

Contact: Kimberley A. Thompson, Coordinator of Services to Students with Disabilities. Phone: 206-546-4545. Fax: 206-533-5109.

The program or unit includes 2 full-time and 2 part-time staff members. Academic advisers, coaches, counselors, regular education teachers, and trained peer tutors are provided collaboratively through on-campus or off-campus services.

Unique Aids and Services Aids, services, or accommodations include advocates, career counseling, and priority registration.

Subject-area Tutoring Tutoring is offered one-on-one for most subjects. Tutoring is provided collaboratively through on-campus or off-campus services via trained peer tutors.

Basic Skills Remediation Remediation is offered in class-size groups for learning strategies, social skills, study skills, and time management. Remediation is provided collaboratively through on-campus or off-campus services via regular education teachers.

Enrichment Programs for career planning, college survival skills, learning strategies, math, reading, stress management, study skills, test taking, time management, vocabulary development, and written composition skills are provided collaboratively through on-campus or off-campus services. Credit is offered for college survival skills, reading, stress management, study skills, vocabulary development, and written composition skills.

Application For admittance to the program or unit, students are required to apply to the program directly and provide summary assessment or psychoeducational report (3 years old or less). It is recommended that students provide documentation of high school services. Upon application, materials documenting need for services should be sent only to the LD program or unit. Upon acceptance, documentation of need for services should be sent only to the LD program or unit. *Application deadline (institutional):* Continuous. *Application deadline (LD program):* Rolling/continuous for fall and rolling/continuous for spring.

Written Policies Written policies regarding general/basic LD accommodations and reduced course loads are available on the program Web site. Written policies regarding course substitutions, general/basic LD accommodations, reduced course loads, and substitutions and waivers of graduation requirements are available through the program or unit directly.

Skagit Valley College
Disability Support Services

2405 College Way

Mount Vernon, WA 98273-5899

http://www.skagit.edu/news.asp_Q_pagenumber_E_355

Contact: Mr. Eric L. Anderson, Counselor/Coordinator of Disability Support Services. Phone: 360-416-7818. Fax: 360-416-7950. E-mail: anderson@skagit.ctc.edu.

Disability Support Services Approximately 175 registered undergraduate students were served during 2002-03. The program or unit includes 2 full-time staff members. Academic advisers and counselors are provided through the program or unit. Regular education teachers, remediation/learning specialists, and trained peer tutors are provided collaboratively through on-campus or off-campus services.

Unique Aids and Services Aids, services, or accommodations include career counseling, digital textbooks, and priority registration.

Subject-area Tutoring Tutoring is offered one-on-one and in small groups for most subjects. Tutoring is provided collaboratively through on-campus or off-campus services via trained peer tutors.

Basic Skills Remediation Remediation is offered in class-size groups for computer skills, learning strategies, math, reading, spelling, study skills, time management, and written language. Remediation is provided collaboratively through on-campus or off-campus services via computer-based instruction and regular education teachers.

Enrichment Programs for career planning, college survival skills, health and nutrition, learning strategies, math, practical computer skills, reading, study skills, test taking, time management, vocabulary development, and written composition skills are provided collaboratively through on-campus or off-campus services. Credit is offered for career planning, college survival skills, health and nutrition, learning strategies, math, practical computer skills, reading, study skills, test taking, time management, vocabulary development, and written composition skills.

Application For admittance to the program or unit, students are required to provide a psychoeducational report (5 years old or less). It is recommended that students provide documentation of high school services. Upon application, materials documenting need for services should be sent only to the LD program or unit. Upon acceptance, documentation of need for services should be sent only to the LD program or unit. *Application deadline (institutional):* Continuous. *Application deadline (LD program):* Rolling/continuous for fall and rolling/continuous for spring.

Written Policies Written policies regarding course substitutions, general/basic LD accommodations, substitutions and waivers of admissions requirements, and substitutions and waivers of graduation requirements are outlined in the school's catalog/handbook.

Southeast Arkansas College
Student Services—Disabled Student Services

1900 Hazel Street

Pine Bluff, AR 71603

http://www.seark.edu/

Contact: Phone: 870-543-5900.

Student Services—Disabled Student Services The program or unit includes 1 full-time staff member. Counselors are provided through the program or unit. Counselors are provided collaboratively through on-campus or off-campus services.

Unique Aids and Services Aids, services, or accommodations include career counseling.

Subject-area Tutoring Tutoring is offered in small groups for some subjects. Tutoring is provided collaboratively through on-campus or off-campus services via professional tutors.

Basic Skills Remediation Remediation is offered in small groups for computer skills, learning strategies, math, reading, and written language. Remediation is provided collaboratively through on-campus or off-campus services via regular education teachers.

Fees *LD Program or Service* fee is $55 (fee varies according to level/tier of service).

Application For admittance to the program or unit, students are required to provide a psychoeducational report (10 years old or less). It is recommended that students provide documentation of high school services. Upon application, materials documenting need for services should be sent to both admissions and the LD program or unit. Upon acceptance, documentation of need for services should be sent to both admissions and the LD program or unit. *Application deadline (institutional):* 8/21. *Application deadline (LD program):* Rolling/continuous for fall.

Written Policies Written policy regarding general/basic LD accommodations is outlined in the school's catalog/handbook.

Southeast Community College

700 College Road

Cumberland, KY 40823-1099

http://www.soucc.kctcs.net/

Contact: Ms. Veria J. Baker, Director of Admissions and Coordinator of Disability Services Cumberland Campus. Phone: 606-589-2145 Ext. 2108. Fax: 606-589-5423. E-mail: cookie.baker@kctcs.edu.

Approximately 4 registered undergraduate students were served during 2002-03. The program or unit includes 1 full-time staff member. Academic advisers, counselors, and remediation/learning specialists are provided through the program or unit. Academic advisers and counselors are provided collaboratively through on-campus or off-campus services.

Unique Aids and Services Aids, services, or accommodations include career counseling.

Subject-area Tutoring Tutoring is offered one-on-one for all subjects. Tutoring is provided through the program or unit via professional tutors and trained peer tutors.

Basic Skills Remediation Remediation is offered one-on-one for computer skills, math, reading, study skills, and written language. Remediation is provided through the program or unit via trained peer tutors. Remediation is also provided collaboratively through on-campus or off-campus services via regular education teachers.

Application It is recommended that students provide documentation of high school services. Upon application, materials documenting need for services should be sent only to the LD program or unit. Upon acceptance, documentation of need for services should be sent only to the LD program or unit. *Application deadline (institutional):* 8/20. *Application deadline (LD program):* 8/19 for fall. 1/16 for spring.

Written Policies Written policy regarding general/basic LD accommodations is available on the program Web site. Written policies regarding course substitutions, general/basic LD accommodations, substitutions and waivers of admissions requirements, and substitutions and waivers of graduation requirements are outlined in the school's catalog/handbook.

Southeast Community College, Milford Campus
Assessment Office

600 State Street

Milford, NE 68405-8498

http://www.southeast.edu/

Contact: Larry Meyer, Dean of Students. Phone: 402-761-8270. Fax: 402-761-8439.

Assessment Office Approximately 50 registered undergraduate students were served during 2002-03. The program or unit includes 1 full-time staff member. Services are provided through the program or unit. Services are provided collaboratively through on-campus or off-campus services.

Summer Program To help prepare for the demands of college, there is an optional 11-week summer program prior to entering the school.

Application For admittance to the program or unit, students are required to provide a psychoeducational report (5 years old or less). It is recommended that students provide documentation of high school services. Upon acceptance, documentation of need for services should be sent only to the LD program or unit. *Application deadline (institutional):* Continuous. *Application deadline (LD program):* Rolling/continuous for fall and rolling/continuous for spring.

Written Policies Written policy regarding general/basic LD accommodations is available on the program Web site. Written policy regarding general/basic LD accommodations is outlined in the school's catalog/handbook. Written policy regarding general/basic LD accommodations is available through the program or unit directly.

Southeastern Community College
Disability Services

PO Box 151

Whiteville, NC 28472-0151

http://www.southeastern.cc.nc.us/

Southeastern Community College (continued)

Contact: Mrs. Sharon W. Jarvis, Counselor. Phone: 910-642-7141 Ext. 263. Fax: 910-642-5658. E-mail: sjarvis@mail.southeast.cc.nc.us.

Disability Services Approximately 20 registered undergraduate students were served during 2002-03. The program or unit includes 1 part-time staff member. Academic advisers, counselors, regular education teachers, and trained peer tutors are provided collaboratively through on-campus or off-campus services.
Unique Aids and Services Aids, services, or accommodations include career counseling and weekly meetings with faculty.
Subject-area Tutoring Tutoring is offered one-on-one, in small groups, and in class-size groups for most subjects. Tutoring is provided collaboratively through on-campus or off-campus services via computer-based instruction and trained peer tutors.
Basic Skills Remediation Remediation is offered one-on-one, in small groups, and in class-size groups for computer skills, learning strategies, math, reading, spelling, study skills, time management, and written language. Remediation is provided collaboratively through on-campus or off-campus services via computer-based instruction, regular education teachers, and trained peer tutors.
Enrichment Programs for career planning, college survival skills, learning strategies, stress management, study skills, test taking, and time management are provided collaboratively through on-campus or off-campus services. Credit is offered for college survival skills, learning strategies, stress management, study skills, test taking, and time management.
Application For admittance to the program or unit, students are required to provide a psychoeducational report (3 years old or less) and provide a list of accommodation requests. It is recommended that students provide documentation of high school services. Upon application, materials documenting need for services should be sent only to admissions with institutional application materials. Upon acceptance, documentation of need for services should be sent only to admissions. *Application deadline (institutional):* Continuous. *Application deadline (LD program):* Rolling/continuous for fall.
Written Policies Written policy regarding general/basic LD accommodations is available on the program Web site. Written policies regarding general/basic LD accommodations and reduced course loads are outlined in the school's catalog/handbook. Written policy regarding general/basic LD accommodations is available through the program or unit directly.

Southern Maine Community College

2 Fort Road
South Portland, ME 04106
http://www.smccme.edu/
Contact: Phone: 207-741-5500. Fax: 207-741-5751.

The program or unit includes 1 full-time and 1 part-time staff member. Academic advisers, counselors, skill tutors, and trained peer tutors are provided collaboratively through on-campus or off-campus services.
Subject-area Tutoring Tutoring is offered one-on-one for most subjects. Tutoring is provided collaboratively through on-campus or off-campus services via computer-based instruction, professional tutors, and trained peer tutors.

Basic Skills Remediation Remediation is offered in class-size groups for math, reading, and written language. Remediation is provided collaboratively through on-campus or off-campus services via regular education teachers.
Application For admittance to the program or unit, students are required to apply to the program directly and provide a psychoeducational report. It is recommended that students provide documentation of high school services. Upon application, materials documenting need for services should be sent only to the LD program or unit. Upon acceptance, documentation of need for services should be sent only to the LD program or unit. *Application deadline (institutional):* Continuous. *Application deadline (LD program):* Rolling/continuous for fall and rolling/continuous for spring.
Written Policies Written policy regarding general/basic LD accommodations is available on the program Web site. Written policy regarding general/basic LD accommodations is outlined in the school's catalog/handbook. Written policies regarding course substitutions, reduced course loads, substitutions and waivers of admissions requirements, and substitutions and waivers of graduation requirements are available through the program or unit directly.

Southern Union State Community College

PO Box 1000, Roberts Street
Wadley, AL 36276
http://www.suscc.cc.al.us/
Contact: Phone: 256-395-2211. Fax: 256-395-2215. Head of LD Program: Mr. Gary L. Branch Jr., Director of Counseling. Phone: 334-745-6437 Ext. 5351. E-mail: gbranch@suscc.edu.

Approximately 150 registered undergraduate students were served during 2002-03. Academic advisers and counselors are provided collaboratively through on-campus or off-campus services.
Unique Aids and Services Aids, services, or accommodations include career counseling, faculty training, and priority registration.
Subject-area Tutoring Tutoring is offered one-on-one and in small groups for all subjects. Tutoring is provided collaboratively through on-campus or off-campus services via computer-based instruction, professional tutors, and trained peer tutors.
Basic Skills Remediation Remediation is offered in small groups for math, reading, spelling, and written language. Remediation is provided collaboratively through on-campus or off-campus services via computer-based instruction, graduate assistants/students, and professional tutors.
Enrichment Programs for career planning, math, reading, and written composition skills are provided collaboratively through on-campus or off-campus services.
Application For admittance to the program or unit, students are required to apply to the program directly and provide a psychoeducational report (3 years old or less). Upon application, materials documenting need for services should be sent only to the LD program or unit. Upon acceptance, documentation of need for services should be sent to both admissions and the LD program or unit. *Application deadline (institutional):* Continuous. *Application deadline (LD program):* Rolling/continuous for fall and rolling/continuous for spring.

Written Policies Written policies regarding general/basic LD accommodations and grade forgiveness are outlined in the school's catalog/handbook. Written policy regarding general/basic LD accommodations is available through the program or unit directly.

South Piedmont Community College
Disability Services

PO Box 126
Polkton, NC 28135-0126
http://www.spcc.edu

Contact: Mrs. Rhonda Williams Treadaway, Acting Director of Counseling and Testing. Phone: 704-272-7635 Ext. 225. Fax: 704-272-8904. E-mail: rtreadaway@spcc.edu. Head of LD Program: Mrs. Elaine Clodfelter, Acting Dean of Student Services. Phone: 704-272-7635 Ext. 218. Fax: 704-272-8904. E-mail: eclodfelter@spcc.edu.

Disability Services Approximately 14 registered undergraduate students were served during 2002-03. The program or unit includes 4 full-time staff members. Academic advisers, counselors, diagnostic specialists, regular education teachers, remediation/learning specialists, and trained peer tutors are provided through the program or unit. Academic advisers, counselors, diagnostic specialists, regular education teachers, remediation/learning specialists, and trained peer tutors are provided collaboratively through on-campus or off-campus services.

Unique Aids and Services Aids, services, or accommodations include career counseling and priority registration.

Subject-area Tutoring Tutoring is offered one-on-one and in small groups for all subjects. Tutoring is provided through the program or unit via trained peer tutors. Tutoring is also provided collaboratively through on-campus or off-campus services via trained peer tutors.

Basic Skills Remediation Remediation is offered one-on-one for computer skills, learning strategies, math, reading, study skills, and time management. Remediation is provided collaboratively through on-campus or off-campus services via computer-based instruction and professional tutors.

Enrichment Enrichment programs are available through the program or unit for career planning, math, reading, study skills, and written composition skills. Programs for career planning, college survival skills, health and nutrition, math, oral communication skills, practical computer skills, reading, and written composition skills are provided collaboratively through on-campus or off-campus services. Credit is offered for college survival skills, health and nutrition, math, oral communication skills, practical computer skills, reading, and written composition skills.

Application For admittance to the program or unit, students are required to provide a psychoeducational report (3 years old or less). It is recommended that students provide documentation of high school services. Upon application, materials documenting need for services should be sent only to the LD program or unit. Upon acceptance, documentation of need for services should be sent only to the LD program or unit. *Application deadline (institutional):* Continuous. *Application deadline (LD program):* Rolling/continuous for fall and rolling/continuous for spring.

Written Policies Written policies regarding course substitutions, general/basic LD accommodations, grade forgiveness, and substitutions and waivers of graduation requirements are outlined in the school's catalog/handbook. Written policies regarding course substitutions, general/basic LD accommodations, and substitutions and waivers of graduation requirements are available through the program or unit directly.

South Seattle Community College
Special Student Services

6000 16th Avenue, SW
Seattle, WA 98106-1499
http://www.sccd.ctc.edu/
Contact: Phone: 206-764-5300.

Special Student Services Approximately 170 registered undergraduate students were served during 2002-03. The program or unit includes 2 full-time and 2 part-time staff members. LD specialists and trained peer tutors are provided through the program or unit.

Unique Aids and Services Aids, services, or accommodations include digital textbooks and priority registration.

Subject-area Tutoring Tutoring is offered one-on-one and in small groups for all subjects. Tutoring is provided through the program or unit via trained peer tutors.

Application For admittance to the program or unit, students are required to provide a psychoeducational report (3 years old or less). It is recommended that students provide documentation of high school services and provide a neuropsychological evaluation. Upon application, materials documenting need for services should be sent only to the LD program or unit. Upon acceptance, documentation of need for services should be sent only to the LD program or unit. *Application deadline (institutional):* Continuous. *Application deadline (LD program):* Rolling/continuous for fall and rolling/continuous for spring.

Written Policies Written policy regarding general/basic LD accommodations is available on the program Web site. Written policy regarding course substitutions is outlined in the school's catalog/handbook.

South Suburban College

15800 South State Street
South Holland, IL 60473-1270
http://www.ssc.cc.il.us/
Contact: Phone: 708-596-2000.

The program or unit includes 1 full-time staff member. Counselors, regular education teachers, remediation/learning specialists, and trained peer tutors are provided collaboratively through on-campus or off-campus services.

Unique Aids and Services Aids, services, or accommodations include career counseling and priority registration.

South Suburban College (continued)

Subject-area Tutoring Tutoring is offered one-on-one, in small groups, and in class-size groups for most subjects. Tutoring is provided collaboratively through on-campus or off-campus services via computer-based instruction and trained peer tutors.

Diagnostic Testing Testing for intelligence, learning styles, math, personality, reading, spoken language, visual processing, and written language is provided collaboratively through on-campus or off-campus services.

Basic Skills Remediation Remediation is offered in class-size groups for math, reading, study skills, and written language. Remediation is provided collaboratively through on-campus or off-campus services via computer-based instruction and regular education teachers.

Enrichment Programs for career planning, college survival skills, health and nutrition, oral communication skills, reading, stress management, study skills, vocabulary development, and written composition skills are provided collaboratively through on-campus or off-campus services. Credit is offered for career planning, college survival skills, health and nutrition, oral communication skills, reading, study skills, vocabulary development, and written composition skills.

Application It is recommended that students provide a psychoeducational report (5 years old or less) and provide documentation of high school services. Upon application, materials documenting need for services should be sent only to the LD program or unit. *Application deadline (institutional):* Continuous. *Application deadline (LD program):* Rolling/continuous for fall and rolling/continuous for spring.

Written Policies Written policy regarding general/basic LD accommodations is available through the program or unit directly.

South University

3810 Main Street

Columbia, SC 29203-6400

http://www.southuniversity.edu/

Contact: Ms. Ute Lowery, Dean of Student Affairs. Phone: 803-799-9082. Fax: 803-799-9038. E-mail: ulowery@southuniversity.edu.

Approximately 4 registered undergraduate students were served during 2002-03. The program or unit includes 1 full-time staff member. Academic advisers and trained peer tutors are provided collaboratively through on-campus or off-campus services.

Subject-area Tutoring Tutoring is offered one-on-one for most subjects. Tutoring is provided collaboratively through on-campus or off-campus services via trained peer tutors.

Application For admittance to the program or unit, students are required to provide a psychoeducational report (5 years old or less). It is recommended that students provide documentation of high school services. Upon application, materials documenting need for services should be sent only to the LD program or unit. Upon acceptance, documentation of need for services should be sent only to the LD program or unit. *Application deadline (institutional):* Continuous.

Written Policies Written policy regarding general/basic LD accommodations is outlined in the school's catalog/handbook.

South University

1760 North Congress Avenue

West Palm Beach, FL 33409

http://www.southuniversity.edu/

Contact: Ms. Deborah Casey, Dean of Student Affairs. Phone: 561-697-9200. Fax: 561-697-9944. E-mail: dpowell@southuniversity.edu.

Approximately 25 registered undergraduate students were served during 2002-03. The program or unit includes 1 full-time staff member. Academic advisers and trained peer tutors are provided collaboratively through on-campus or off-campus services.

Unique Aids and Services Aids, services, or accommodations include career counseling.

Subject-area Tutoring Tutoring is offered one-on-one for most subjects. Tutoring is provided collaboratively through on-campus or off-campus services via trained peer tutors.

Application For admittance to the program or unit, students are required to provide a psychoeducational report (5 years old or less). It is recommended that students provide documentation of high school services. Upon application, materials documenting need for services should be sent only to the LD program or unit. Upon acceptance, documentation of need for services should be sent only to the LD program or unit. *Application deadline (institutional):* Continuous.

Written Policies Written policy regarding general/basic LD accommodations is outlined in the school's catalog/handbook.

Southwestern College
Disability Support Services

900 Otay Lakes Road

Chula Vista, CA 91910-7299

http://www.swc.cc.ca.us/

Contact: Dr. Malia M. Flood, Coordinator. Phone: 619-482-6512. Fax: 619-482-6511. E-mail: mflood@swc.cc.ca.us.

Disability Support Services Approximately 650 registered undergraduate students were served during 2002-03. The program or unit includes 4 full-time staff members. Academic advisers, counselors, diagnostic specialists, LD specialists, remediation/learning specialists, strategy tutors, and trained peer tutors are provided through the program or unit. Academic advisers, coaches, counselors, regular education teachers, skill tutors, and trained peer tutors are provided collaboratively through on-campus or off-campus services.

Orientation The program or unit offers an optional 6-week orientation for new students during a one-unit summer school course.

Unique Aids and Services Aids, services, or accommodations include digital textbooks and priority registration.

Subject-area Tutoring Tutoring is offered one-on-one and in small groups for most subjects. Tutoring is provided through the program or unit via computer-based instruction. Tutoring is also provided collaboratively through on-campus or off-campus services via graduate assistants/students and trained peer tutors.

Diagnostic Testing Testing is provided through the program or unit for auditory processing, intelligence, learning strategies, learning styles, math, reading, spelling, spoken language, visual processing, and written language.

Basic Skills Remediation Remediation is offered in class-size groups for computer skills, learning strategies, math, reading, spelling, spoken language, study skills, and written language. Remediation is provided through the program or unit via computer-based instruction and LD specialists. Remediation is also provided collaboratively through on-campus or off-campus services via regular education teachers.

Enrichment Enrichment programs are available through the program or unit for college survival skills, learning strategies, oral communication skills, and practical computer skills. Programs for career planning, college survival skills, learning strategies, and practical computer skills are provided collaboratively through on-campus or off-campus services. Credit is offered for career planning, college survival skills, oral communication skills, and practical computer skills.

Student Organization ABLE Club consists of 20 members.
Fees *Orientation* fee is $11. *Diagnostic Testing* fee is $11.
Application For admittance to the program or unit, students are required to apply to the program directly and provide a psychoeducational report (3 years old or less). It is recommended that students provide documentation of high school services. Upon application, materials documenting need for services should be sent only to the LD program or unit. Upon acceptance, documentation of need for services should be sent only to the LD program or unit. *Application deadline (institutional):* Continuous. *Application deadline (LD program):* Rolling/continuous for fall and rolling/continuous for spring.

Written Policies Written policy regarding general/basic LD accommodations is outlined in the school's catalog/handbook. Written policies regarding course substitutions, general/basic LD accommodations, reduced course loads, and substitutions and waivers of graduation requirements are available through the program or unit directly.

Southwestern Community College
Student Support Services

447 College Drive
Sylva, NC 28779
http://www.southwest.cc.nc.us/

Contact: Cheryl Contino-Conner, Director Student Support Services. E-mail: cheryl@southwest.cc.nc.us.

Student Support Services Approximately 90 registered undergraduate students were served during 2002-03. The program or unit includes 3 part-time staff members. Counselors and other are provided through the program or unit. Counselors, professional tutors, remediation/learning specialists, skill tutors, trained peer tutors, and other are provided collaboratively through on-campus or off-campus services.

Unique Aids and Services Aids, services, or accommodations include advocates, career counseling, and priority registration.

Subject-area Tutoring Tutoring is offered one-on-one, in small groups, and in class-size groups for all subjects. Tutoring is provided through the program or unit via professional tutors, trained peer tutors, and other. Tutoring is also provided collaboratively through on-campus or off-campus services via professional tutors, trained peer tutors, and other.

Basic Skills Remediation Remediation is offered in class-size groups for computer skills, handwriting, learning strategies, math, reading, social skills, spelling, study skills, time management, and written language. Remediation is provided through the program or unit via computer-based instruction. Remediation is also provided collaboratively through on-campus or off-campus services via computer-based instruction and regular education teachers.

Enrichment Enrichment programs are available through the program or unit for career planning, college survival skills, learning strategies, oral communication skills, stress management, study skills, test taking, and time management. Programs for career planning, college survival skills, learning strategies, study skills, test taking, and time management are provided collaboratively through on-campus or off-campus services. Credit is offered for college survival skills and learning strategies.

Application For admittance to the program or unit, students are required to provide a psychoeducational report and provide medical documentation when appropriate. It is recommended that students provide documentation of high school services. Upon application, materials documenting need for services should be sent only to the LD program or unit. *Application deadline (institutional):* Continuous. *Application deadline (LD program):* Rolling/continuous for fall.

Written Policies Written policy regarding general/basic LD accommodations is available on the program Web site. Written policy regarding general/basic LD accommodations is outlined in the school's catalog/handbook.

Southwestern Michigan College

58900 Cherry Grove Road
Dowagiac, MI 49047-9793
http://www.swmich.edu/

Contact: Mrs. Susan H. Sullivan, Coordinator of Special Populations Services. Phone: 269-687-4801. Fax: 269-684-2281. E-mail: ssullivan@swmich.edu.

The program or unit includes 2 full-time staff members and 1 part-time staff member. Academic advisers, counselors, professional tutors, regular education teachers, strategy tutors, and trained peer tutors are provided through the program or unit. Academic advisers, counselors, professional tutors, regular education teachers, skill tutors, strategy tutors, and trained peer tutors are provided collaboratively through on-campus or off-campus services.

Unique Aids and Services Aids, services, or accommodations include advocates, career counseling, digital textbooks, instructional accommodations, assistive technology.

Subject-area Tutoring Tutoring is offered one-on-one, in small groups, and in class-size groups for most subjects. Tutoring is provided through the program or unit via computer-based instruction. Tutoring is also provided collaboratively through on-campus or off-campus services via computer-based instruction, graduate assistants/students, professional tutors, and trained peer tutors.

Southwestern Michigan College (continued)

Diagnostic Testing Testing is provided through the program or unit for learning strategies, learning styles, and study skills. Testing for learning strategies, learning styles, math, reading, study skills, and written language is provided collaboratively through on-campus or off-campus services.

Basic Skills Remediation Remediation is offered in class-size groups for math, reading, study skills, and written language. Remediation is provided collaboratively through on-campus or off-campus services via computer-based instruction, regular education teachers, and trained peer tutors.

Enrichment Enrichment programs are available through the program or unit for career planning, college survival skills, learning strategies, self-advocacy, stress management, study skills, test taking, and time management. Programs for career planning, college survival skills, learning strategies, math, reading, self-advocacy, stress management, study skills, test taking, time management, and written composition skills are provided collaboratively through on-campus or off-campus services.

Application For admittance to the program or unit, students are required to apply to the program directly and provide medical or professional documentation of disability. It is recommended that students provide a psychoeducational report (3 years old or less) and provide documentation of high school services. Upon application, materials documenting need for services should be sent only to the LD program or unit. Upon acceptance, documentation of need for services should be sent only to the LD program or unit. *Application deadline (institutional):* Continuous. *Application deadline (LD program):* Rolling/continuous for fall and rolling/continuous for spring.

Written Policies Written policy regarding general/basic LD accommodations is available on the program Web site. Written policies regarding course substitutions, general/basic LD accommodations, grade forgiveness, and substitutions and waivers of graduation requirements are outlined in the school's catalog/handbook. Written policy regarding reduced course loads is available through the program or unit directly.

Southwest Georgia Technical College

15689 US 19 North
Thomasville, GA 31792
http://www.swgtc.net/

Contact: Dr. Tammy Pfister, Retention Coordinator. Phone: 229-225-5060 Ext. 2668. Fax: 229-227-2666. E-mail: tpfister@swgtc.net.

Approximately 11 registered undergraduate students were served during 2002-03. The program or unit includes 1 full-time staff member. Counselors, professional tutors, and regular education teachers are provided through the program or unit.

Unique Aids and Services Aids, services, or accommodations include career counseling.

Subject-area Tutoring Tutoring is offered one-on-one and in small groups for some subjects. Tutoring is provided collaboratively through on-campus or off-campus services via computer-based instruction and professional tutors.

Diagnostic Testing Testing is provided through the program or unit for math, reading, and written language.

Basic Skills Remediation Remediation is offered one-on-one, in small groups, and in class-size groups for math, reading, and written language. Remediation is provided collaboratively through on-campus or off-campus services via computer-based instruction.

Application It is recommended that students provide a psychoeducational report and provide documentation of high school services. Upon acceptance, documentation of need for services should be sent only to admissions. *Application deadline (institutional):* 8/1. *Application deadline (LD program):* Rolling/continuous for fall and rolling/continuous for spring.

Written Policies Written policy regarding general/basic LD accommodations is outlined in the school's catalog/handbook.

Southwest Missouri State University-West Plains
Academic Support Center

128 Garfield
West Plains, MO 65775
http://www.wp.smsu.edu

Contact: Phone: 417-255-7255. Head of LD Program: Janice Faye Johnson, Disability Support Coordinator. Phone: 417-255-7943. Fax: 417-255-7944. E-mail: janicejohnson@wp.smsu.edu.

Academic Support Center Approximately 22 registered undergraduate students were served during 2002-03. The program or unit includes 4 full-time and 8 part-time staff members. Diagnostic specialists, LD specialists, professional tutors, skill tutors, strategy tutors, and trained peer tutors are provided through the program or unit. Academic advisers and regular education teachers are provided collaboratively through on-campus or off-campus services.

Subject-area Tutoring Tutoring is offered in small groups for some subjects. Tutoring is provided collaboratively through on-campus or off-campus services via computer-based instruction, trained peer tutors, and other.

Diagnostic Testing Testing for auditory processing, handwriting, intelligence, learning strategies, learning styles, math, motor skills, neuropsychological, personality, reading, social skills, spelling, spoken language, study skills, visual processing, and written language is provided collaboratively through on-campus or off-campus services.

Basic Skills Remediation Remediation is offered one-on-one for auditory processing, reading, study skills, time management, and visual processing. Remediation is provided through the program or unit via computer-based instruction and professional tutors.

Fees *Diagnostic Testing* fee is $0 to $700.

Application For admittance to the program or unit, students are required to apply to the program directly and provide a psychoeducational report (3 years old or less). It is recommended that students provide documentation of high school services and provide documentation from a psychologist. Upon application, materials documenting need for services should be sent only to the LD program or unit. Upon acceptance, documentation of need for services should be sent only to the LD program or unit. *Application deadline (institutional):* Continuous. *Application deadline (LD program):* Rolling/continuous for fall.

Written Policies Written policy regarding general/basic LD accommodations is available on the program Web site. Written policy regarding general/basic LD accommodations is outlined in the school's catalog/handbook.

Southwest Tennessee Community College

PO Box 780
Memphis, TN 38101-0780
http://www.southwest.tn.edu/
Contact: Ms. Maxine Ford, Director. Phone: 901-333-4223. Fax: 901-333-4505. E-mail: mford@southwest.tn.edu.

The program or unit includes 1 full-time staff member. LD specialists are provided through the program or unit. Academic advisers, professional tutors, regular education teachers, and trained peer tutors are provided collaboratively through on-campus or off-campus services.

Summer Program To help prepare for the demands of college, there is a mandatory half-day summer program prior to entering the school.

Unique Aids and Services Aids, services, or accommodations include priority registration, support groups, weekly meetings with faculty, extended time on tests.

Subject-area Tutoring Tutoring is offered one-on-one and in small groups for some subjects. Tutoring is provided collaboratively through on-campus or off-campus services via professional tutors and trained peer tutors.

Diagnostic Testing Testing for personality is provided collaboratively through on-campus or off-campus services.

Basic Skills Remediation Remediation is available for math, reading, and study skills. Remediation is provided collaboratively through on-campus or off-campus services via regular education teachers.

Enrichment Program for career planning is provided collaboratively through on-campus or off-campus services.

Application For admittance to the program or unit, students are required to provide a psychoeducational report. Upon application, materials documenting need for services should be sent only to the LD program or unit. Upon acceptance, documentation of need for services should be sent only to the LD program or unit. *Application deadline (institutional):* 9/1. *Application deadline (LD program):* Rolling/continuous for fall and rolling/continuous for spring.

Written Policies Written policy regarding general/basic LD accommodations is available on the program Web site. Written policies regarding course substitutions, general/basic LD accommodations, substitutions and waivers of admissions requirements, and substitutions and waivers of graduation requirements are outlined in the school's catalog/handbook. Written policies regarding general/basic LD accommodations and reduced course loads are available through the program or unit directly.

Southwest Virginia Community College

PO Box SVCC
Richlands, VA 24641-1101

http://www.sw.edu/
Contact: Mr. G. Michael Rush, Vice President of Student Development Services. Phone: 276-964-7286. E-mail: mike.rush@sw.vccs.edu.

Academic advisers, counselors, diagnostic specialists, regular education teachers, remediation/learning specialists, and skill tutors are provided collaboratively through on-campus or off-campus services.

Unique Aids and Services Aids, services, or accommodations include career counseling, digital textbooks, priority registration, support groups, extended time, oral tests, scribe, private test area.

Subject-area Tutoring Tutoring is offered one-on-one and in small groups for most subjects. Tutoring is provided collaboratively through on-campus or off-campus services via computer-based instruction and trained peer tutors.

Diagnostic Testing Testing for auditory processing, intelligence, learning strategies, learning styles, reading, spelling, study skills, visual processing, and written language is provided collaboratively through on-campus or off-campus services.

Basic Skills Remediation Remediation is offered one-on-one and in small groups for learning strategies, math, reading, study skills, and time management. Remediation is provided collaboratively through on-campus or off-campus services via computer-based instruction, regular education teachers, and trained peer tutors.

Enrichment Programs for career planning, college survival skills, health and nutrition, learning strategies, math, medication management, oral communication skills, practical computer skills, reading, stress management, study skills, test taking, time management, and written composition skills are provided collaboratively through on-campus or off-campus services. Credit is offered for career planning, college survival skills, health and nutrition, math, medication management, oral communication skills, practical computer skills, reading, and study skills.

Student Organization Project ACHIEVE consists of 300 members.

Application For admittance to the program or unit, students are required to provide documentation of high school services. Upon application, materials documenting need for services should be sent only to the LD program or unit. Upon acceptance, documentation of need for services should be sent only to the LD program or unit. *Application deadline (institutional):* Continuous. *Application deadline (LD program):* Rolling/continuous for fall and rolling/continuous for spring.

Written Policies Written policies regarding course substitutions, general/basic LD accommodations, reduced course loads, substitutions and waivers of admissions requirements, and substitutions and waivers of graduation requirements are available on the program Web site. Written policies regarding course substitutions, general/basic LD accommodations, reduced course loads, substitutions and waivers of admissions requirements, and substitutions and waivers of graduation requirements are outlined in the school's catalog/handbook. Written policies regarding course substitutions, general/basic LD accommodations, reduced course loads, substitutions and waivers of admissions requirements, and substitutions and waivers of graduation requirements are available through the program or unit directly.

Southwest Wisconsin Technical College
Support Services Center (SSC)

1800 Bronson Boulevard

Fennimore, WI 53809-9778

http://www.southwest.edu/

Contact: Mr. Alan L. Propst, Support Services Specialist. Phone: 608-822-3262 Ext. 2130. Fax: 608-822-6019. E-mail: apropst@swtc.edu.

Support Services Center (SSC) Approximately 55 registered undergraduate students were served during 2002-03. The program or unit includes 2 full-time and 2 part-time staff members. Academic advisers, coaches, graduate assistants/students, professional tutors, remediation/learning specialists, skill tutors, and trained peer tutors are provided through the program or unit. Counselors and regular education teachers are provided collaboratively through on-campus or off-campus services.

Summer Program To help prepare for the demands of college, there is an optional 4-day summer program prior to entering the school.

Unique Aids and Services Aids, services, or accommodations include advocates, digital textbooks, personal coach, voice input computer training, FM tape recorders, note-takers.

Subject-area Tutoring Tutoring is offered one-on-one and in small groups for most subjects. Tutoring is provided collaboratively through on-campus or off-campus services via other.

Diagnostic Testing Testing for learning styles, math, reading, spelling, study skills, and written language is provided collaboratively through on-campus or off-campus services.

Basic Skills Remediation Remediation is offered one-on-one, in small groups, and in class-size groups for learning strategies, math, reading, spelling, spoken language, study skills, time management, written language, and general science. Remediation is provided collaboratively through on-campus or off-campus services via computer-based instruction, regular education teachers, and special education teachers.

Fees *Summer Program* fee is $0 to $25. *Diagnostic Testing* fee is $10.

Application For admittance to the program or unit, students are required to provide a psychoeducational report, provide documentation of high school services, and provide psychological reports for adults. Upon application, materials documenting need for services should be sent only to the LD program or unit. *Application deadline (institutional):* Continuous. *Application deadline (LD program):* Rolling/continuous for fall and rolling/continuous for spring.

Written Policies Written policies regarding course substitutions, general/basic LD accommodations, substitutions and waivers of admissions requirements, and substitutions and waivers of graduation requirements are available on the program Web site. Written policies regarding course substitutions, general/basic LD accommodations, substitutions and waivers of admissions requirements, and substitutions and waivers of graduation requirements are outlined in the school's catalog/handbook. Written policy regarding reduced course loads is available through the program or unit directly.

Spokane Community College

1810 North Greene Street

Spokane, WA 99217-5399

http://www.scc.spokane.cc.wa.us/

Contact: Mr. Ric Villalobos, Counselor. Phone: 509-533-7169. Fax: 509-533-8877. E-mail: rvillalobos@scc.spokane.edu.

Approximately 125 registered undergraduate students were served during 2002-03. The program or unit includes 1 full-time staff member. Counselors are provided through the program or unit. Trained peer tutors are provided collaboratively through on-campus or off-campus services.

Orientation The program or unit offers an optional orientation for new students individually by special arrangement.

Subject-area Tutoring Tutoring is offered one-on-one for some subjects. Tutoring is provided collaboratively through on-campus or off-campus services via trained peer tutors.

Diagnostic Testing Testing is provided through the program or unit for learning strategies, learning styles, and study skills.

Student Organization Disability Awareness League consists of 15 members.

Application For admittance to the program or unit, students are required to apply to the program directly, provide a psychoeducational report (3 years old or less), and provide results of any testing on which the IEP is based. It is recommended that students provide documentation of high school services. Upon application, materials documenting need for services should be sent only to the LD program or unit. Upon acceptance, documentation of need for services should be sent only to the LD program or unit. *Application deadline (institutional):* Continuous. *Application deadline (LD program):* Rolling/continuous for fall and rolling/continuous for spring.

Written Policies Written policy regarding general/basic LD accommodations is available on the program Web site. Written policies regarding course substitutions, general/basic LD accommodations, grade forgiveness, reduced course loads, substitutions and waivers of admissions requirements, and substitutions and waivers of graduation requirements are available through the program or unit directly.

Spoon River College
Disability Support Services

23235 North County 22

Canton, IL 61520-9801

http://www.spoonrivercollege.com/services/specialneeds.html

Contact: Janet Munson, Student Development Specialist/Disability Support Services. Phone: 309-649-6273. Fax: 309-649-6393. E-mail: jmunson@spoonrivercollege.edu.

Disability Support Services Approximately 25 registered undergraduate students were served during 2002-03. The program or unit includes 1 full-time staff member. Academic advisers are provided through the program or unit. Academic advisers, counselors, regular education teachers, trained peer tutors, and other are provided collaboratively through on-campus or off-campus services.

Unique Aids and Services Aids, services, or accommodations include note-takers, readers.

Subject-area Tutoring Tutoring is offered one-on-one and in small groups for some subjects. Tutoring is provided collaboratively through on-campus or off-campus services via trained peer tutors and other.

Basic Skills Remediation Remediation is offered one-on-one and in class-size groups for math, reading, study skills, time management, and written language. Remediation is provided collaboratively through on-campus or off-campus services via regular education teachers and other.

Application For admittance to the program or unit, students are required to apply to the program directly and provide a psychoeducational report. It is recommended that students provide documentation of high school services. Upon application, materials documenting need for services should be sent only to the LD program or unit. *Application deadline (institutional):* Continuous. *Application deadline (LD program):* Rolling/continuous for fall and rolling/continuous for spring.

Written Policies Written policy regarding general/basic LD accommodations is available on the program Web site. Written policy regarding general/basic LD accommodations is outlined in the school's catalog/handbook. Written policy regarding general/basic LD accommodations is available through the program or unit directly.

Springfield College in Illinois
Learning Center

1500 North Fifth Street
Springfield, IL 62702-2694
http://www.sci.edu/learningcenter.html

Contact: Mr. Kevin David Broeckling, Dean of Student Affairs. Phone: 217-525-1420 Ext. 239. Fax: 217-525-1497. E-mail: broeckling@sci.edu. Head of LD Program: Ms. Eva Mae Moats, Director of the Learning Center. Phone: 217-525-1420 Ext. 229. Fax: 217-525-1497. E-mail: moats@sci.edu.

Learning Center Approximately 4 registered undergraduate students were served during 2002-03. The program or unit includes 1 full-time and 6 part-time staff members. Academic advisers, counselors, LD specialists, professional tutors, remediation/learning specialists, skill tutors, strategy tutors, and trained peer tutors are provided through the program or unit. Academic advisers, coaches, counselors, LD specialists, regular education teachers, and teacher trainees are provided collaboratively through on-campus or off-campus services.

Summer Program To help prepare for the demands of college, there is a mandatory 5-week summer program prior to entering the school. Degree credit will be earned.

Subject-area Tutoring Tutoring is offered one-on-one for most subjects. Tutoring is provided through the program or unit via computer-based instruction, graduate assistants/students, and trained peer tutors. Tutoring is also provided collaboratively through on-campus or off-campus services via professional tutors.

Diagnostic Testing Testing for math, reading, spoken language, study skills, and written language is provided collaboratively through on-campus or off-campus services.

Basic Skills Remediation Remediation is offered one-on-one for learning strategies, reading, social skills, study skills, and written language. Remediation is provided through the program or unit via computer-based instruction, LD specialists, professional tutors, and trained peer tutors. Remediation is also provided collaboratively through on-campus or off-campus services via regular education teachers.

Enrichment Enrichment programs are available through the program or unit for learning strategies, study skills, test taking, and time management. Programs for college survival skills, health and nutrition, math, oral communication skills, practical computer skills, reading, stress management, study skills, test taking, time management, and written composition skills are provided collaboratively through on-campus or off-campus services.

Fees *Summer Program* fee is $0 to $150.

Application For admittance to the program or unit, students are required to provide a psychoeducational report (10 years old or less). It is recommended that students provide documentation of high school services. Upon application, materials documenting need for services should be sent to both admissions and the LD program or unit. Upon acceptance, documentation of need for services should be sent only to the LD program or unit. *Application deadline (institutional):* Continuous. *Application deadline (LD program):* Rolling/continuous for fall and rolling/continuous for spring.

Written Policies Written policies regarding course substitutions, general/basic LD accommodations, grade forgiveness, reduced course loads, substitutions and waivers of admissions requirements, and substitutions and waivers of graduation requirements are available on the program Web site. Written policies regarding course substitutions, general/basic LD accommodations, grade forgiveness, reduced course loads, substitutions and waivers of admissions requirements, and substitutions and waivers of graduation requirements are outlined in the school's catalog/handbook.

Springfield Technical Community College
Office of Disability Services

1 Armory Square, PO Box 9000
Springfield, MA 01102-9000
http://www.stcc.edu/

Contact: Mrs. Jane Kmon. Phone: 413-755-4474. Head of LD Program: Dr. Peter M. Shea, Learning Disabilities Specialist. Phone: 413-755-4474. E-mail: shea@stcc.edu.

Office of Disability Services Approximately 200 registered undergraduate students were served during 2002-03. The program or unit includes 6 full-time staff members. Counselors and LD specialists are provided through the program or unit. Academic advisers, professional tutors, regular education teachers, skill tutors, and strategy tutors are provided collaboratively through on-campus or off-campus services.

Orientation The program or unit offers a mandatory 1-hour orientation for new students individually by special arrangement.

Springfield Technical Community College (continued)

Unique Aids and Services Aids, services, or accommodations include career counseling, digital textbooks, priority registration, and weekly meetings with faculty.

Subject-area Tutoring Tutoring is offered one-on-one for most subjects. Tutoring is provided through the program or unit via computer-based instruction and LD specialists. Tutoring is also provided collaboratively through on-campus or off-campus services via graduate assistants/students, professional tutors, and trained peer tutors.

Basic Skills Remediation Remediation is offered one-on-one and in class-size groups for auditory processing, computer skills, learning strategies, math, reading, study skills, and time management. Remediation is provided through the program or unit via computer-based instruction. Remediation is also provided collaboratively through on-campus or off-campus services via professional tutors, regular education teachers, and trained peer tutors.

Enrichment Enrichment programs are available through the program or unit for self-advocacy. Programs for career planning, college survival skills, learning strategies, math, medication management, oral communication skills, practical computer skills, reading, stress management, study skills, test taking, time management, vocabulary development, and written composition skills are provided collaboratively through on-campus or off-campus services. Credit is offered for college survival skills, practical computer skills, reading, study skills, test taking, time management, vocabulary development, and written composition skills.

Application For admittance to the program or unit, students are required to provide a psychoeducational report (2 years old or less) and provide psychoeducational assessment. It is recommended that students provide documentation of high school services. Upon application, materials documenting need for services should be sent only to the LD program or unit. *Application deadline (institutional):* Continuous. *Application deadline (LD program):* 9/1 for fall. 1/6 for spring.

Written Policies Written policies regarding course substitutions, general/basic LD accommodations, and reduced course loads are available on the program Web site. Written policies regarding course substitutions, general/basic LD accommodations, and reduced course loads are available through the program or unit directly.

Stanly Community College
Disabilities Services Office

141 College Drive
Albemarle, NC 28001-7458
http://www.stanly.cc.nc.us/
Contact: Phone: 704-982-0121. Fax: 704-982-0819.

Disabilities Services Office Approximately 15 registered undergraduate students were served during 2002-03. The program or unit includes 2 full-time staff members and 1 part-time staff member. Academic advisers, counselors, diagnostic specialists, regular education teachers, remediation/learning specialists, and skill tutors are provided collaboratively through on-campus or off-campus services.

Unique Aids and Services Aids, services, or accommodations include extended time.

Subject-area Tutoring Tutoring is offered one-on-one, in small groups, and in class-size groups for most subjects. Tutoring is provided collaboratively through on-campus or off-campus services via computer-based instruction, graduate assistants/students, and trained peer tutors.

Basic Skills Remediation Remediation is offered one-on-one, in small groups, and in class-size groups for computer skills, math, reading, and study skills. Remediation is provided collaboratively through on-campus or off-campus services via computer-based instruction, graduate assistants/students, and trained peer tutors.

Enrichment Programs for career planning, college survival skills, learning strategies, math, oral communication skills, practical computer skills, reading, study skills, test taking, time management, and written composition skills are provided collaboratively through on-campus or off-campus services. Credit is offered for college survival skills, learning strategies, and written composition skills.

Application For admittance to the program or unit, students are required to apply to the program directly and provide a psychoeducational report (3 years old or less). It is recommended that students provide documentation of high school services. *Application deadline (institutional):* Continuous. *Application deadline (LD program):* Rolling/continuous for fall and rolling/continuous for spring.

Written Policies Written policy regarding general/basic LD accommodations is available on the program Web site. Written policy regarding general/basic LD accommodations is outlined in the school's catalog/handbook. Written policy regarding general/basic LD accommodations is available through the program or unit directly.

Stark State College of Technology

6200 Frank Avenue, NW
Canton, OH 44720-7299
http://www.starkstate.edu/
Contact: Phone: 330-494-6170. Fax: 330-497-6313.

The program or unit includes 1 full-time staff member. Academic advisers and counselors are provided through the program or unit. Academic advisers, counselors, graduate assistants/students, professional tutors, regular education teachers, strategy tutors, and trained peer tutors are provided collaboratively through on-campus or off-campus services.

Orientation The program or unit offers an optional 2-hour orientation for new students before classes begin, during summer prior to enrollment, and individually by special arrangement.

Unique Aids and Services Aids, services, or accommodations include career counseling and faculty training.

Subject-area Tutoring Tutoring is offered one-on-one and in small groups for most subjects. Tutoring is provided collaboratively through on-campus or off-campus services via computer-based instruction, professional tutors, and trained peer tutors.

Basic Skills Remediation Remediation is offered one-on-one and in class-size groups for computer skills, learning strategies, math, reading, study skills, time management, and written language. Remediation is provided collaboratively through on-campus or off-campus services via computer-based instruction, graduate assistants/students, professional tutors, regular education teachers, and trained peer tutors.

Application For admittance to the program or unit, students are required to apply to the program directly and provide a psychoeducational report. It is recommended that students provide documentation of high school services. Upon application, materials documenting need for services should be sent only to the LD program or unit. Upon acceptance, documentation of need for services should be sent only to the LD program or unit. *Application deadline (institutional):* Continuous. *Application deadline (LD program):* Rolling/continuous for fall and rolling/continuous for spring.

Written Policies Written policy regarding general/basic LD accommodations is available on the program Web site. Written policy regarding general/basic LD accommodations is outlined in the school's catalog/handbook. Written policy regarding general/basic LD accommodations is available through the program or unit directly.

State Fair Community College
Vocational Special Needs

3201 West 16th Street
Sedalia, MO 65301-2199
http://www.sfcc.cc.mo.us

Contact: Mrs. Diane M. Watkins, Vocational Special Needs Counselor. Phone: 660-530-5800 Ext. 253. Fax: 660-530-5546. E-mail: watkins@sfcc.cc.mo.us.

Vocational Special Needs Approximately 120 registered undergraduate students were served during 2002-03. The program or unit includes 2 full-time staff members. Academic advisers and counselors are provided through the program or unit. Academic advisers, coaches, counselors, diagnostic specialists, LD specialists, professional tutors, regular education teachers, remediation/learning specialists, and skill tutors are provided collaboratively through on-campus or off-campus services.

Unique Aids and Services Aids, services, or accommodations include digital textbooks, faculty training, support groups, TRIO Program.

Subject-area Tutoring Tutoring is offered one-on-one, in small groups, and in class-size groups for most subjects. Tutoring is provided collaboratively through on-campus or off-campus services via computer-based instruction, graduate assistants/students, professional tutors, and trained peer tutors.

Basic Skills Remediation Remediation is offered in class-size groups for math, reading, and written language. Remediation is provided collaboratively through on-campus or off-campus services via computer-based instruction, professional tutors, regular education teachers, and trained peer tutors.

Enrichment Programs for career planning, college survival skills, learning strategies, math, stress management, study skills, test taking, time management, and written composition skills are provided collaboratively through on-campus or off-campus services. Credit is offered for career planning, college survival skills, learning strategies, math, stress management, study skills, test taking, time management, and written composition skills.

Application For admittance to the program or unit, students are required to apply to the program directly, provide a psychoeducational report (3 years old or less), and provide medical documentation for secondary disability. It is recommended that students provide doc-

umentation of high school services. Upon application, materials documenting need for services should be sent only to the LD program or unit. *Application deadline (institutional):* Continuous. *Application deadline (LD program):* Rolling/continuous for fall and rolling/continuous for spring.

Written Policies Written policy regarding general/basic LD accommodations is available on the program Web site. Written policy regarding general/basic LD accommodations is outlined in the school's catalog/handbook. Written policies regarding course substitutions, general/basic LD accommodations, reduced course loads, substitutions and waivers of admissions requirements, and substitutions and waivers of graduation requirements are available through the program or unit directly.

State University of New York College of Technology at Alfred

Alfred, NY 14802
http://www.alfredstate.edu/

Contact: Heather Meacham, Coordinator of Services for Students with Disabilities. Phone: 607-587-4122. Fax: 607-587-3210. E-mail: meachahm@alfredstate.edu.

Approximately 80 registered undergraduate students were served during 2002-03. The program or unit includes 1 full-time and 2 part-time staff members. Services are provided through the program or unit.

Subject-area Tutoring Tutoring is offered one-on-one and in small groups for most subjects. Tutoring is provided through the program or unit via professional tutors and trained peer tutors. Tutoring is also provided collaboratively through on-campus or off-campus services via professional tutors and trained peer tutors.

Diagnostic Testing Testing is provided through the program or unit for learning styles. Testing for learning styles is provided collaboratively through on-campus or off-campus services.

Enrichment Programs for career planning, college survival skills, and learning strategies are provided collaboratively through on-campus or off-campus services.

Application For admittance to the program or unit, students are required to provide a psychoeducational report (3 years old or less) and provide documentation of high school services. Upon application, materials documenting need for services should be sent only to the LD program or unit. Upon acceptance, documentation of need for services should be sent only to the LD program or unit. *Application deadline (institutional):* Continuous. *Application deadline (LD program):* Rolling/continuous for fall and rolling/continuous for spring.

Written Policies Written policies regarding course substitutions, general/basic LD accommodations, grade forgiveness, reduced course loads, substitutions and waivers of admissions requirements, and substitutions and waivers of graduation requirements are available through the program or unit directly.

State University of New York College of Technology at Canton
Office of Accommodative Services

Cornell Drive
Canton, NY 13617
http://www.canton.edu/can/
can_start.taf?page=serve_accomodate
Contact: Phone: 315-386-7392. Fax: 315-379-3877. E-mail: leev@canton.edu.

Office of Accommodative Services Approximately 171 registered undergraduate students were served during 2002-03. The program or unit includes 2 full-time staff members. Academic advisers, counselors, professional tutors, and trained peer tutors are provided collaboratively through on-campus or off-campus services.
Unique Aids and Services Aids, services, or accommodations include advocates, career counseling, digital textbooks, and priority registration.
Subject-area Tutoring Tutoring is offered one-on-one, in small groups, and in class-size groups for all subjects. Tutoring is provided collaboratively through on-campus or off-campus services via professional tutors, trained peer tutors, and other.
Basic Skills Remediation Remediation is offered one-on-one, in small groups, and in class-size groups for computer skills, learning strategies, math, reading, spelling, study skills, time management, and written language. Remediation is provided collaboratively through on-campus or off-campus services via professional tutors, trained peer tutors, and other.
Enrichment Programs for career planning, college survival skills, learning strategies, math, oral communication skills, practical computer skills, reading, self-advocacy, stress management, study skills, test taking, time management, vocabulary development, and written composition skills are provided collaboratively through on-campus or off-campus services.
Application For admittance to the program or unit, students are required to provide a psychoeducational report (3 years old or less). It is recommended that students provide documentation of high school services. Upon acceptance, documentation of need for services should be sent only to the LD program or unit. *Application deadline (institutional):* Continuous. *Application deadline (LD program):* Rolling/continuous for fall.
Written Policies Written policy regarding general/basic LD accommodations is outlined in the school's catalog/handbook. Written policy regarding general/basic LD accommodations is available through the program or unit directly.

Sullivan County Community College
Department of Learning and Student Development Services

112 College Road
Loch Sheldrake, NY 12759
http://www.sullivan.suny.edu/
Contact: Ms. Eileen Howell, Learning Services Assistant. Phone: 845-434-5750 Ext. 4328. Fax: 845-434-4806. E-mail: ehowell@sullivan.suny.edu. Head of LD Program: Ms. Helene Joseph Laurenti, Director, Department of Learning and Student Development Services. Phone: 845-434-5750 Ext. 4229. Fax: 845-434-4806. E-mail: hlaurent@sullivan.suny.edu.

Department of Learning and Student Development Services Approximately 45 registered undergraduate students were served during 2002-03. Academic advisers, counselors, professional tutors, remediation/learning specialists, trained peer tutors, and other are provided collaboratively through on-campus or off-campus services.
Subject-area Tutoring Tutoring is offered one-on-one, in small groups, and in class-size groups for most subjects. Tutoring is provided collaboratively through on-campus or off-campus services via computer-based instruction, professional tutors, and trained peer tutors.
Basic Skills Remediation Remediation is offered one-on-one, in small groups, and in class-size groups for computer skills, learning strategies, reading, spelling, study skills, time management, and written language. Remediation is provided collaboratively through on-campus or off-campus services via computer-based instruction, professional tutors, trained peer tutors, and other.
Enrichment Programs for career planning, college survival skills, health and nutrition, learning strategies, math, practical computer skills, reading, self-advocacy, stress management, study skills, test taking, time management, vocabulary development, and written composition skills are provided collaboratively through on-campus or off-campus services. Credit is offered for college survival skills, health and nutrition, math, reading, vocabulary development, and written composition skills.
Application For admittance to the program or unit, students are required to provide a psychoeducational report (3 years old or less) and provide documentation of high school services. Upon acceptance, documentation of need for services should be sent only to the LD program or unit. *Application deadline (institutional):* Continuous. *Application deadline (LD program):* Rolling/continuous for fall and rolling/continuous for spring.
Written Policies Written policy regarding general/basic LD accommodations is available on the program Web site. Written policy regarding general/basic LD accommodations is outlined in the school's catalog/handbook.

Surry Community College
Special Programs/ADA Office

630 South Main Street
PO Box 304
Dobson, NC 27017
http://www.surry.cc.nc.us/
Contact: Laura Bracken, Special Programs and ADA Coordinator. Phone: 336-386-3264. Fax: 336-386-3690. E-mail: brackenl@surry.cc.nc.us.

Special Programs/ADA Office Approximately 40 registered undergraduate students were served during 2002-03. The program or unit includes 1 full-time staff member. Academic advisers, counselors, professional tutors, remediation/learning specialists, trained peer tutors, and other are provided through the program or unit.

Unique Aids and Services Aids, services, or accommodations include career counseling, priority registration, support services adviser.

Subject-area Tutoring Tutoring is offered one-on-one for all subjects. Tutoring is provided through the program or unit via computer-based instruction, graduate assistants/students, professional tutors, trained peer tutors, and other. Tutoring is also provided collaboratively through on-campus or off-campus services via LD specialists.

Diagnostic Testing Testing is provided through the program or unit for handwriting, learning strategies, learning styles, math, personality, reading, social skills, spelling, study skills, and written language. Testing for intelligence, motor skills, neuropsychological, spoken language, visual processing, and other services is provided collaboratively through on-campus or off-campus services.

Basic Skills Remediation Remediation is offered one-on-one for handwriting, learning strategies, math, reading, social skills, spelling, study skills, time management, written language, and developmental courses. Remediation is provided through the program or unit via computer-based instruction, graduate assistants/students, professional tutors, trained peer tutors, and other. Remediation is also provided collaboratively through on-campus or off-campus services via LD specialists, regular education teachers, special education teachers, and teacher trainees.

Enrichment Enrichment programs are available through the program or unit for self-advocacy. Programs for career planning, college survival skills, health and nutrition, learning strategies, math, oral communication skills, practical computer skills, reading, stress management, study skills, test taking, time management, vocabulary development, and written composition skills are provided collaboratively through on-campus or off-campus services.

Application For admittance to the program or unit, students are required to apply to the program directly, provide a psychoeducational report (3 years old or less), and provide results of medical, psychological or emotional diagnostic tests or other professional evaluations. Upon application, materials documenting need for services should be sent only to the LD program or unit. Upon acceptance, documentation of need for services should be sent only to the LD program or unit. *Application deadline (LD program):* Rolling/continuous for fall and rolling/continuous for spring.

Written Policies Written policy regarding general/basic LD accommodations is available on the program Web site. Written policy regarding general/basic LD accommodations is outlined in the school's catalog/handbook.

Sussex County Community College
Disabilities Assistance Program (DAP)

1 College Hill
Newton, NJ 07860
http://www.sussex.cc.nj.us/

Contact: Dr. Kathleen Okay, Associate Director of the Learning Center. Phone: 973-300-2153. Fax: 973-300-2156. E-mail: kokay@sussex.edu.

Disabilities Assistance Program (DAP) Approximately 75 registered undergraduate students were served during 2002-03. The program or unit includes 1 full-time and 2 part-time staff members. Academic advisers, counselors, and remediation/learning specialists are provided through the program or unit. Academic advisers, counselors, diagnostic specialists, professional tutors, remediation/learning specialists, strategy tutors, and trained peer tutors are provided collaboratively through on-campus or off-campus services.

Orientation The program or unit offers an optional 45-minute to 1-hour orientation for new students individually by special arrangement.

Unique Aids and Services Aids, services, or accommodations include career counseling, digital textbooks, faculty training, and priority registration.

Subject-area Tutoring Tutoring is offered one-on-one and in small groups for most subjects. Tutoring is provided collaboratively through on-campus or off-campus services via computer-based instruction, professional tutors, and trained peer tutors.

Diagnostic Testing Testing for intelligence is provided collaboratively through on-campus or off-campus services.

Basic Skills Remediation Remediation is offered in class-size groups for learning strategies, math, reading, and written language. Remediation is provided collaboratively through on-campus or off-campus services via regular education teachers and special education teachers.

Enrichment Enrichment programs are available through the program or unit for college survival skills, learning strategies, study skills, test taking, and written composition skills. Programs for career planning, college survival skills, learning strategies, math, reading, study skills, test taking, time management, and written composition skills are provided collaboratively through on-campus or off-campus services. Credit is offered for college survival skills, learning strategies, and math.

Fees *Diagnostic Testing* fee is $150.

Application For admittance to the program or unit, students are required to apply to the program directly and provide a psychoeducational report (5 years old or less). It is recommended that students provide documentation of high school services. Upon application, materials documenting need for services should be sent only to the LD program or unit. *Application deadline (institutional):* Continuous. *Application deadline (LD program):* Rolling/continuous for fall and rolling/continuous for spring.

Written Policies Written policy regarding general/basic LD accommodations is available on the program Web site. Written policies regarding course substitutions, general/basic LD accommodations, substitutions and waivers of admissions requirements, and substitutions and waivers of graduation requirements are outlined in the school's catalog/handbook. Written policies regarding course substitutions, general/basic LD accommodations, substitutions and waivers of admissions requirements, and substitutions and waivers of graduation requirements are available through the program or unit directly.

Tallahassee Community College

444 Appleyard Drive
Tallahassee, FL 32304-2895
http://www.tcc.fl.edu/

Tallahassee Community College (continued)

Contact: Mark J. Linehan, Counselor. Phone: 850-201-8430. Fax: 850-201-8433. E-mail: linehanm@tcc.fl.edu.

Approximately 900 registered undergraduate students were served during 2002-03. The program or unit includes 5 full-time and 5 part-time staff members. Academic advisers and counselors are provided through the program or unit. Coaches, graduate assistants/students, and regular education teachers are provided collaboratively through on-campus or off-campus services.

Unique Aids and Services Aids, services, or accommodations include career counseling and priority registration.

Enrichment Programs for career planning, college survival skills, reading, stress management, study skills, and test taking are provided collaboratively through on-campus or off-campus services. Credit is offered for career planning, college survival skills, and reading.

Application For admittance to the program or unit, students are required to provide a psychoeducational report. It is recommended that students provide documentation of high school services. Upon application, materials documenting need for services should be sent only to the LD program or unit. Upon acceptance, documentation of need for services should be sent only to the LD program or unit. *Application deadline (institutional):* 8/1. *Application deadline (LD program):* Rolling/continuous for fall and rolling/continuous for spring.

Written Policies Written policies regarding course substitutions, general/basic LD accommodations, and substitutions and waivers of admissions requirements are available on the program Web site. Written policies regarding course substitutions, general/basic LD accommodations, and substitutions and waivers of admissions requirements are outlined in the school's catalog/handbook. Written policy regarding substitutions and waivers of graduation requirements is available through the program or unit directly.

Tarrant County College District
Disability Support Services

1500 Houston Street
Fort Worth, TX 76102-6599
http://www.tccd.edu/dss

Contact: Coordinator. Phone: 817-515-4554. Fax: 817-515-4895. E-mail: carrie.cummings@tccd.edu. Head of LD Program: Mr. Daniel R. Chacon, Dean of Student Development and Educational Services. Phone: 817-515-4504. Fax: 817-515-4028. E-mail: dan.chacon@tccd.edu.

Disability Support Services Approximately 916 registered undergraduate students were served during 2002-03. The program or unit includes 3 full-time staff members and 1 part-time staff member. Graduate assistants/students, skill tutors, strategy tutors, trained peer tutors, and other are provided through the program or unit. Academic advisers, counselors, professional tutors, regular education teachers, and remediation/learning specialists are provided collaboratively through on-campus or off-campus services.

Unique Aids and Services Aids, services, or accommodations include advocates, digital textbooks, faculty training, and support groups.

Subject-area Tutoring Tutoring is offered one-on-one and in small groups for most subjects. Tutoring is provided through the program or unit via trained peer tutors. Tutoring is also provided collaboratively through on-campus or off-campus services via computer-based instruction and professional tutors.

Basic Skills Remediation Remediation is offered in class-size groups for learning strategies, math, reading, study skills, and written language. Remediation is provided through the program or unit via trained peer tutors. Remediation is also provided collaboratively through on-campus or off-campus services via computer-based instruction, professional tutors, regular education teachers, and other.

Enrichment Enrichment programs are available through the program or unit for self-advocacy. Programs for career planning, college survival skills, health and nutrition, learning strategies, math, oral communication skills, practical computer skills, reading, stress management, study skills, test taking, time management, vocabulary development, and written composition skills are provided collaboratively through on-campus or off-campus services. Credit is offered for health and nutrition, math, oral communication skills, practical computer skills, reading, vocabulary development, and written composition skills.

Student Organization Organization for Human Awareness consists of 20 members.

Application For admittance to the program or unit, students are required to apply to the program directly, provide a psychoeducational report (5 years old or less), and provide a letter from a doctor if disability has a physical component. It is recommended that students provide documentation of high school services. Upon application, materials documenting need for services should be sent only to the LD program or unit. Upon acceptance, documentation of need for services should be sent only to the LD program or unit. *Application deadline (institutional):* Continuous. *Application deadline (LD program):* Rolling/continuous for fall and rolling/continuous for spring.

Written Policies Written policy regarding general/basic LD accommodations is available on the program Web site. Written policy regarding general/basic LD accommodations is outlined in the school's catalog/handbook. Written policy regarding general/basic LD accommodations is available through the program or unit directly.

Texas State Technical College-Waco

3801 Campus Drive
Waco, TX 76705-1695
http://www.tstc.edu/

Contact: Mr. Brent A. Burns, Coordinator. Phone: 254-867-3600. Fax: 254-867-3601. E-mail: brent.burns@tstc.edu.

The program or unit includes 3 full-time staff members. Academic advisers and skill tutors are provided through the program or unit.

Orientation The program or unit offers an optional orientation for new students individually by special arrangement.

Unique Aids and Services Aids, services, or accommodations include advocates, digital textbooks, and priority registration.

Subject-area Tutoring Tutoring is offered one-on-one for some subjects. Tutoring is provided through the program or unit via computer-based instruction and trained peer tutors.

Diagnostic Testing Testing is provided through the program or unit for math, reading, and written language.

Basic Skills Remediation Remediation is offered one-on-one for math, reading, written language, and technical classes. Remediation is provided through the program or unit via computer-based instruction and trained peer tutors.

Enrichment Enrichment programs are available through the program or unit for math, reading, self-advocacy, and written composition skills.

Fees *Diagnostic Testing* fee is $20.

Application For admittance to the program or unit, students are required to apply to the program directly, provide a psychoeducational report, provide documentation of high school services, and provide reports from vocational rehabilitation and/or Commission for the Blind. Upon application, materials documenting need for services should be sent only to the LD program or unit. Upon acceptance, documentation of need for services should be sent only to the LD program or unit. *Application deadline (institutional):* Continuous. *Application deadline (LD program):* Rolling/continuous for fall and rolling/continuous for spring.

Written Policies Written policy regarding general/basic LD accommodations is available on the program Web site. Written policy regarding course substitutions is outlined in the school's catalog/handbook. Written policy regarding general/basic LD accommodations is available through the program or unit directly.

Texas State Technical College-West Texas
Counseling and Testing Department

300 College Drive

Sweetwater, TX 79556-4108

http://www.westtexas.tstc.edu/sweetwater/counseling_testing/

Contact: Donnie Armstrong, Counseling and Testing Coordinator. Phone: 325-235-7414. Fax: 325-235-7443. E-mail: donnie.armstrong@sweetwater.tstc.edu.

Counseling and Testing Department Approximately 50 registered undergraduate students were served during 2002-03. The program or unit includes 3 full-time staff members. Academic advisers, counselors, regular education teachers, and remediation/learning specialists are provided collaboratively through on-campus or off-campus services.

Summer Program To help prepare for the demands of college, there is an optional 1-week summer program prior to entering the school.

Unique Aids and Services Aids, services, or accommodations include advocates, career counseling, and faculty training.

Subject-area Tutoring Tutoring is offered one-on-one, in small groups, and in class-size groups for most subjects. Tutoring is provided through the program or unit via computer-based instruction, professional tutors, and trained peer tutors. Tutoring is also provided collaboratively through on-campus or off-campus services via computer-based instruction, professional tutors, and trained peer tutors.

Basic Skills Remediation Remediation is offered one-on-one, in small groups, and in class-size groups for learning strategies, math, reading, social skills, spelling, study skills, and time management. Remediation is provided through the program or unit via computer-based instruction, regular education teachers, teacher trainees, and trained peer tutors. Remediation is also provided collaboratively through on-campus or off-campus services via computer-based instruction, regular education teachers, teacher trainees, and trained peer tutors.

Enrichment Enrichment programs are available through the program or unit for career planning, college survival skills, health and nutrition, learning strategies, math, oral communication skills, practical computer skills, reading, self-advocacy, stress management, study skills, test taking, and time management. Programs for career planning, college survival skills, health and nutrition, learning strategies, math, oral communication skills, practical computer skills, reading, stress management, study skills, test taking, time management, vocabulary development, and written composition skills are provided collaboratively through on-campus or off-campus services. Credit is offered for career planning, college survival skills, health and nutrition, learning strategies, math, oral communication skills, practical computer skills, reading, stress management, study skills, test taking, time management, vocabulary development, and written composition skills.

Application For admittance to the program or unit, students are required to apply to the program directly. It is recommended that students provide a psychoeducational report (3 years old or less) and provide documentation of high school services. Upon application, materials documenting need for services should be sent only to the LD program or unit. Upon acceptance, documentation of need for services should be sent only to the LD program or unit. *Application deadline (institutional):* Continuous. *Application deadline (LD program):* Rolling/continuous for fall and rolling/continuous for spring.

Written Policies Written policies regarding course substitutions, general/basic LD accommodations, grade forgiveness, reduced course loads, substitutions and waivers of admissions requirements, and substitutions and waivers of graduation requirements are available on the program Web site. Written policies regarding course substitutions, general/basic LD accommodations, grade forgiveness, reduced course loads, substitutions and waivers of admissions requirements, and substitutions and waivers of graduation requirements are outlined in the school's catalog/handbook.

Thaddeus Stevens College of Technology

750 East King Street

Lancaster, PA 17602-3198

http://www.stevenscollege.edu/

Contact: Phone: 717-299-7730. Fax: 717-391-6929.

Approximately 45 registered undergraduate students were served during 2002-03. The program or unit includes 1 full-time staff member. Counselors and professional tutors are provided through the program or unit. Academic advisers, counselors, professional tutors, regular education teachers, trained peer tutors, and other are provided collaboratively through on-campus or off-campus services.

Thaddeus Stevens College of Technology (continued)

Summer Program To help prepare for the demands of college, there is a mandatory 5-week summer program prior to entering the school.

Unique Aids and Services Aids, services, or accommodations include career counseling and faculty training.

Subject-area Tutoring Tutoring is offered one-on-one and in small groups for most subjects. Tutoring is provided through the program or unit via professional tutors and trained peer tutors. Tutoring is also provided collaboratively through on-campus or off-campus services via professional tutors and trained peer tutors.

Diagnostic Testing Testing is provided through the program or unit for auditory processing, handwriting, learning strategies, learning styles, social skills, and study skills. Testing for learning strategies, learning styles, math, reading, social skills, spelling, spoken language, study skills, and written language is provided collaboratively through on-campus or off-campus services.

Basic Skills Remediation Remediation is offered one-on-one and in small groups for computer skills, learning strategies, math, reading, spelling, study skills, and time management. Remediation is provided collaboratively through on-campus or off-campus services via computer-based instruction, professional tutors, regular education teachers, and trained peer tutors.

Enrichment Programs for learning strategies, math, reading, study skills, test taking, time management, and written composition skills are provided collaboratively through on-campus or off-campus services.

Fees *Diagnostic Testing* fee is applicable.

Application For admittance to the program or unit, students are required to provide a psychoeducational report. It is recommended that students provide 504, or physician's letter. Upon application, materials documenting need for services should be sent only to the LD program or unit. Upon acceptance, documentation of need for services should be sent only to the LD program or unit. *Application deadline (institutional):* 6/30. *Application deadline (LD program):* Rolling/continuous for fall and rolling/continuous for spring.

Written Policies Written policy regarding general/basic LD accommodations is available on the program Web site. Written policy regarding general/basic LD accommodations is outlined in the school's catalog/handbook.

Thomas Nelson Community College
Disabled Students Services

PO Box 9407
Hampton, VA 23670-0407
http://www.tncc.vccs.edu/

Contact: Ms. Nancy E. Bailey, Counselor. Phone: 757-825-2833. Fax: 757-825-3697. E-mail: baileyn@tncc.vccs.edu.

Disabled Students Services Approximately 75 registered undergraduate students were served during 2002-03. The program or unit includes 2 full-time staff members and 1 part-time staff member. Academic advisers, counselors, skill tutors, and strategy tutors are provided through the program or unit. Academic advisers, counselors, skill tutors, strategy tutors, and trained peer tutors are provided collaboratively through on-campus or off-campus services.

Subject-area Tutoring Tutoring is offered one-on-one for some subjects. Tutoring is provided through the program or unit via trained peer tutors and other. Tutoring is also provided collaboratively through on-campus or off-campus services via computer-based instruction and trained peer tutors.

Basic Skills Remediation Remediation is offered in class-size groups for learning strategies, math, reading, study skills, time management, and written language. Remediation is provided collaboratively through on-campus or off-campus services via computer-based instruction and regular education teachers.

Application For admittance to the program or unit, students are required to apply to the program directly, provide a psychoeducational report, and provide documentation of high school services. Upon application, materials documenting need for services should be sent only to the LD program or unit. Upon acceptance, documentation of need for services should be sent only to the LD program or unit. *Application deadline (institutional):* Continuous. *Application deadline (LD program):* Rolling/continuous for fall and rolling/continuous for spring.

Written Policies Written policy regarding general/basic LD accommodations is outlined in the school's catalog/handbook. Written policies regarding course substitutions, general/basic LD accommodations, and reduced course loads are available through the program or unit directly.

Three Rivers Community College

7 Mahan Drive
Norwich, CT 06360
http://www.trcc.commnet.edu/

Contact: Chris Scarborough, Learning Specialist. Phone: 860-892-5751. E-mail: cscarborough@qvcc.commnet.edu.

Approximately 80 registered undergraduate students were served during 2002-03. The program or unit includes 1 full-time staff member. LD specialists are provided through the program or unit.

Subject-area Tutoring Tutoring is offered for most subjects. Tutoring is provided collaboratively through on-campus or off-campus services via trained peer tutors.

Basic Skills Remediation Remediation is offered in class-size groups for math, reading, spelling, study skills, time management, and written language. Remediation is provided collaboratively through on-campus or off-campus services via LD specialists, regular education teachers, and trained peer tutors.

Application It is recommended that students provide a psychoeducational report and provide documentation of high school services. Upon application, materials documenting need for services should be sent only to the LD program or unit. Upon acceptance, documentation of need for services should be sent only to the LD program or unit. *Application deadline (institutional):* Continuous. *Application deadline (LD program):* Rolling/continuous for fall.

Written Policies Written policies regarding course substitutions, general/basic LD accommodations, grade forgiveness, reduced course loads, substitutions and waivers of admissions requirements, and substitutions and waivers of graduation requirements are available through the program or unit directly.

Tidewater Community College
Learning Disabilities Services

121 College Place
Norfolk, VA 23510
http://www.tcc.edu/disabilityservices/index.htm
Contact: Sue R. Rice, Coordinator of Learning Disabilities Services. Phone: 757-822-1213. Fax: 757-822-1214. E-mail: srice@tcc.edu.

Learning Disabilities Services Approximately 215 registered undergraduate students were served during 2002-03. The program or unit includes 1 full-time and 4 part-time staff members. Academic advisers, counselors, diagnostic specialists, graduate assistants/students, LD specialists, and regular education teachers are provided through the program or unit. Academic advisers, counselors, professional tutors, regular education teachers, remediation/learning specialists, skill tutors, strategy tutors, and trained peer tutors are provided collaboratively through on-campus or off-campus services.
Unique Aids and Services Aids, services, or accommodations include advocates, career counseling, digital textbooks, faculty training, priority registration, and support groups.
Subject-area Tutoring Tutoring is offered one-on-one, in small groups, and in class-size groups for all subjects. Tutoring is provided collaboratively through on-campus or off-campus services via computer-based instruction, graduate assistants/students, trained peer tutors, and other.
Diagnostic Testing Testing is provided through the program or unit for auditory processing, handwriting, intelligence, learning strategies, learning styles, math, motor skills, neuropsychological, reading, spelling, spoken language, study skills, visual processing, written language, and other services. Testing for learning strategies, learning styles, math, reading, and study skills is provided collaboratively through on-campus or off-campus services.
Basic Skills Remediation Remediation is offered one-on-one, in small groups, and in class-size groups for computer skills, learning strategies, math, motor skills, reading, spelling, study skills, time management, and written language. Remediation is provided collaboratively through on-campus or off-campus services via computer-based instruction, graduate assistants/students, regular education teachers, teacher trainees, trained peer tutors, and other.
Enrichment Enrichment programs are available through the program or unit for college survival skills, health and nutrition, learning strategies, math, medication management, practical computer skills, reading, self-advocacy, stress management, study skills, test taking, time management, vocabulary development, and written composition skills. Programs for career planning, college survival skills, health and nutrition, learning strategies, math, practical computer skills, reading, self-advocacy, stress management, study skills, test taking, and time management are provided collaboratively through on-campus or off-campus services. Credit is offered for college survival skills, health and nutrition, math, practical computer skills, reading, stress management, study skills, test taking, time management, vocabulary development, and written composition skills.
Application For admittance to the program or unit, students are required to provide a psychoeducational report (3 years old or less). Upon application, materials documenting need for services should be sent only to the LD program or unit. Upon acceptance, docu-

mentation of need for services should be sent only to the LD program or unit. *Application deadline (institutional):* Continuous. *Application deadline (LD program):* Rolling/continuous for fall.
Written Policies Written policies regarding course substitutions and general/basic LD accommodations are available on the program Web site. Written policy regarding grade forgiveness is outlined in the school's catalog/handbook. Written policies regarding course substitutions and general/basic LD accommodations are available through the program or unit directly.

Tri-County Technical College

PO Box 587, 7900 Highway 76
Pendleton, SC 29670-0587
http://www.tctc.edu/
Contact: Mrs. Croslena Johnson, Coordinator of Academic and Career Counseling. Phone: 864-646-8361 Ext. 1568. Fax: 864-646-1890. E-mail: cjohnso5@tctc.edu.

Approximately 7 registered undergraduate students were served during 2002-03. The program or unit includes 2 full-time staff members. Counselors are provided through the program or unit. Academic advisers and counselors are provided collaboratively through on-campus or off-campus services.
Subject-area Tutoring Tutoring is offered in small groups for most subjects. Tutoring is provided collaboratively through on-campus or off-campus services via other.
Basic Skills Remediation Remediation is offered one-on-one and in class-size groups for math, reading, and written language. Remediation is provided collaboratively through on-campus or off-campus services.
Enrichment Programs for career planning, college survival skills, oral communication skills, and practical computer skills are provided collaboratively through on-campus or off-campus services. Credit is offered for college survival skills, oral communication skills, and practical computer skills.
Application For admittance to the program or unit, students are required to provide a psychoeducational report (3 years old or less). Upon application, materials documenting need for services should be sent only to the LD program or unit. *Application deadline (institutional):* Continuous. *Application deadline (LD program):* Rolling/continuous for fall and rolling/continuous for spring.
Written Policies Written policy regarding general/basic LD accommodations is available through the program or unit directly.

Trocaire College
Palisano Learning Center

360 Choate Avenue
Buffalo, NY 14220-2094
http://www.trocaire.edu/
Contact: Phone: 716-826-1200. Fax: 716-826-4704.

Palisano Learning Center Approximately 19 registered undergraduate students were served during 2002-03. The program or unit

Trocaire College (continued)

includes 1 full-time and 2 part-time staff members. LD specialists are provided through the program or unit. LD specialists, professional tutors, regular education teachers, remediation/learning specialists, special education teachers, and trained peer tutors are provided collaboratively through on-campus or off-campus services.

Orientation The program or unit offers a mandatory 1-day orientation for new students during summer prior to enrollment and during registration.

Summer Program To help prepare for the demands of college, there is a mandatory summer session summer program prior to entering the school. Degree credit will be earned.

Unique Aids and Services Aids, services, or accommodations include faculty training and support groups.

Subject-area Tutoring Tutoring is offered one-on-one for most subjects. Tutoring is provided through the program or unit via professional tutors. Tutoring is also provided collaboratively through on-campus or off-campus services via computer-based instruction, LD specialists, professional tutors, and trained peer tutors.

Diagnostic Testing Testing is provided through the program or unit for reading. Testing for learning strategies, learning styles, math, reading, and written language is provided collaboratively through on-campus or off-campus services.

Basic Skills Remediation Remediation is offered in small groups for computer skills, handwriting, math, reading, study skills, and time management. Remediation is provided collaboratively through on-campus or off-campus services via computer-based instruction, LD specialists, professional tutors, and trained peer tutors.

Enrichment Programs for career planning, college survival skills, learning strategies, math, practical computer skills, reading, study skills, test taking, time management, vocabulary development, and written composition skills are provided collaboratively through on-campus or off-campus services.

Fees *Summer Program* fee is $350. *Orientation* fee is $350.

Application For admittance to the program or unit, students are required to apply to the program directly, provide a psychoeducational report (2 years old or less), and provide documentation of high school services. Upon application, materials documenting need for services should be sent to both admissions and the LD program or unit. Upon acceptance, documentation of need for services should be sent only to the LD program or unit. *Application deadline (institutional):* Continuous. *Application deadline (LD program):* Rolling/continuous for fall and rolling/continuous for spring.

Written Policies Written policies regarding course substitutions, general/basic LD accommodations, grade forgiveness, reduced course loads, substitutions and waivers of admissions requirements, and substitutions and waivers of graduation requirements are outlined in the school's catalog/handbook. Written policies regarding course substitutions, general/basic LD accommodations, reduced course loads, substitutions and waivers of admissions requirements, and substitutions and waivers of graduation requirements are available through the program or unit directly.

Truckee Meadows Community College

7000 Dandini Boulevard
Reno, NV 89512-3901

http://www.tmcc.edu/

Contact: Ms. Lee Geldmacher, Adviser. Phone: 775-673-7286. Fax: 775-673-7207. E-mail: lgeldmacher@tmcc.edu.

Approximately 300 registered undergraduate students were served during 2002-03. The program or unit includes 2 full-time staff members and 1 part-time staff member. LD specialists, skill tutors, and trained peer tutors are provided through the program or unit. Diagnostic specialists are provided collaboratively through on-campus or off-campus services.

Unique Aids and Services Aids, services, or accommodations include digital textbooks.

Subject-area Tutoring Tutoring is offered one-on-one for all subjects. Tutoring is provided through the program or unit via trained peer tutors.

Diagnostic Testing Testing for auditory processing, intelligence, math, reading, spelling, visual processing, and written language is provided collaboratively through on-campus or off-campus services.

Basic Skills Remediation Remediation is offered one-on-one for computer skills, math, reading, spelling, study skills, time management, and written language. Remediation is provided through the program or unit via professional tutors and trained peer tutors.

Enrichment Enrichment programs are available through the program or unit for math, oral communication skills, practical computer skills, and reading. Programs for career planning, college survival skills, learning strategies, study skills, test taking, time management, vocabulary development, and written composition skills are provided collaboratively through on-campus or off-campus services. Credit is offered for college survival skills, study skills, test taking, time management, vocabulary development, and written composition skills.

Fees *Diagnostic Testing* fee is $150.

Application For admittance to the program or unit, students are required to apply to the program directly, provide a psychoeducational report (3 years old or less), and provide other documentation. It is recommended that students provide documentation of high school services. Upon application, materials documenting need for services should be sent only to the LD program or unit. *Application deadline (institutional):* Continuous.

Written Policies Written policy regarding general/basic LD accommodations is available on the program Web site. Written policy regarding reduced course loads is available through the program or unit directly.

Ulster County Community College
The Learning Center/Student Support Services

Stone Ridge, NY 12484

http://www.sunyulster.edu

Contact: Jean Vizvary, Director of Student Support Services. Phone: 845-687-5057. Fax: 845-687-5083. E-mail: vizvaryj@sunyulster.edu.

The Learning Center/Student Support Services Approximately 100 registered undergraduate students were served during

2002-03. The program or unit includes 2 full-time staff members. Counselors, professional tutors, and trained peer tutors are provided collaboratively through on-campus or off-campus services.

Subject-area Tutoring Tutoring is offered one-on-one and in small groups for some subjects. Tutoring is provided collaboratively through on-campus or off-campus services via professional tutors and trained peer tutors.

Basic Skills Remediation Remediation is offered in class-size groups for learning strategies, math, reading, study skills, and written language. Remediation is provided collaboratively through on-campus or off-campus services via regular education teachers.

Enrichment Programs for career planning, college survival skills, learning strategies, math, reading, stress management, study skills, test taking, time management, and written composition skills are provided collaboratively through on-campus or off-campus services. Credit is offered for college survival skills, math, and written composition skills.

Application For admittance to the program or unit, students are required to apply to the program directly, provide a psychoeducational report, and provide documentation of high school services. Upon application, materials documenting need for services should be sent only to the LD program or unit. Upon acceptance, documentation of need for services should be sent only to the LD program or unit. *Application deadline (institutional):* Continuous. *Application deadline (LD program):* Rolling/continuous for fall and rolling/continuous for spring.

Written Policies Written policy regarding general/basic LD accommodations is available on the program Web site. Written policy regarding general/basic LD accommodations is outlined in the school's catalog/handbook.

Umpqua Community College

PO Box 967
Roseburg, OR 97470-0226
http://www.umpqua.edu/
Contact: Barbara J. Stoner, Coordinator of Disability Services. Phone: 541-677-3215 Ext. 215. Fax: 541-440-4665. E-mail: barb.stoner@umpqua.edu.

Approximately 40 registered undergraduate students were served during 2002-03. The program or unit includes 1 full-time and 1 part-time staff member. Academic advisers, coaches, counselors, LD specialists, regular education teachers, remediation/learning specialists, skill tutors, and trained peer tutors are provided collaboratively through on-campus or off-campus services.

Orientation The program or unit offers an optional orientation for new students before registration, before classes begin, during summer prior to enrollment, and individually by special arrangement.

Unique Aids and Services Aids, services, or accommodations include advocates, career counseling, faculty training, and weekly meetings with faculty.

Subject-area Tutoring Tutoring is offered one-on-one, in small groups, and in class-size groups for most subjects. Tutoring is provided through the program or unit via LD specialists. Tutoring is also provided collaboratively through on-campus or off-campus services via computer-based instruction, graduate assistants/students, and trained peer tutors.

Diagnostic Testing Testing is provided through the program or unit for auditory processing, handwriting, and intelligence. Testing for learning strategies, learning styles, math, personality, reading, social skills, spelling, spoken language, study skills, visual processing, and written language is provided collaboratively through on-campus or off-campus services.

Basic Skills Remediation Remediation is offered one-on-one, in small groups, and in class-size groups for auditory processing, computer skills, handwriting, learning strategies, math, reading, social skills, spelling, spoken language, study skills, time management, and written language. Remediation is provided collaboratively through on-campus or off-campus services via computer-based instruction, LD specialists, regular education teachers, and trained peer tutors.

Enrichment Programs for career planning, college survival skills, health and nutrition, learning strategies, math, oral communication skills, practical computer skills, reading, self-advocacy, stress management, study skills, test taking, time management, vocabulary development, and written composition skills are provided collaboratively through on-campus or off-campus services. Credit is offered for career planning, college survival skills, health and nutrition, learning strategies, math, oral communication skills, practical computer skills, reading, stress management, study skills, test taking, time management, vocabulary development, and written composition skills.

Application It is recommended that students provide a psychoeducational report and provide documentation of high school services. Upon application, materials documenting need for services should be sent only to the LD program or unit. Upon acceptance, documentation of need for services should be sent only to the LD program or unit. *Application deadline (institutional):* Continuous. *Application deadline (LD program):* 9/1 for fall. 3/31 for spring.

Written Policies Written policy regarding general/basic LD accommodations is available through the program or unit directly.

United Tribes Technical College
Disability Support Services

3315 University Drive
Bismarck, ND 58504-7596
http://www.uttc.edu.com
Contact: Carol A. Johnson, Disability Coordinator. Phone: 701-255-3285 Ext. 465. E-mail: caajohns@hotmail.com.

Disability Support Services The program or unit includes 1 full-time staff member. Academic advisers, LD specialists, professional tutors, remediation/learning specialists, and special education teachers are provided through the program or unit. LD specialists, professional tutors, remediation/learning specialists, and special education teachers are provided collaboratively through on-campus or off-campus services.

Unique Aids and Services Aids, services, or accommodations include faculty training.

Subject-area Tutoring Tutoring is offered one-on-one and in small groups for all subjects. Tutoring is provided through the program or unit via LD specialists and professional tutors. Tutoring is also provided collaboratively through on-campus or off-campus services via trained peer tutors.

United Tribes Technical College (continued)

Diagnostic Testing Testing for math, reading, spelling, and written language is provided collaboratively through on-campus or off-campus services.

Basic Skills Remediation Remediation is offered in class-size groups for math, reading, and written language. Remediation is provided collaboratively through on-campus or off-campus services via regular education teachers.

Enrichment Programs for career planning, college survival skills, health and nutrition, learning strategies, math, practical computer skills, stress management, study skills, test taking, time management, vocabulary development, and written composition skills are provided collaboratively through on-campus or off-campus services. Credit is offered for career planning, college survival skills, health and nutrition, learning strategies, math, practical computer skills, stress management, study skills, test taking, time management, vocabulary development, and written composition skills.

Application For admittance to the program or unit, students are required to provide a psychoeducational report (3 years old or less). It is recommended that students provide documentation of high school services. Upon application, materials documenting need for services should be sent to both admissions and the LD program or unit. Upon acceptance, documentation of need for services should be sent to both admissions and the LD program or unit. *Application deadline (institutional):* Continuous. *Application deadline (LD program):* Rolling/continuous for fall and rolling/continuous for spring.

Written Policies Written policy regarding general/basic LD accommodations is outlined in the school's catalog/handbook. Written policy regarding general/basic LD accommodations is available through the program or unit directly.

The University of Akron-Wayne College

1901 Smucker Road
Orrville, OH 44667-9192
http://www.wayne.uakron.edu/

Contact: Dr. Julia R. Beyeler, Director of Learning Support Services. Phone: 330-684-8963 Ext. 8963. Fax: 330-684-8989. E-mail: juliabeyeler@UAkron.edu.

The program or unit includes 1 full-time and 10 part-time staff members. Graduate assistants/students, LD specialists, professional tutors, remediation/learning specialists, skill tutors, strategy tutors, and trained peer tutors are provided through the program or unit. Academic advisers, coaches, counselors, diagnostic specialists, regular education teachers, special education teachers, and teacher trainees are provided collaboratively through on-campus or off-campus services.

Unique Aids and Services Aids, services, or accommodations include career counseling, digital textbooks, and weekly meetings with faculty.

Subject-area Tutoring Tutoring is offered one-on-one for most subjects. Tutoring is provided through the program or unit via professional tutors and trained peer tutors.

Diagnostic Testing Testing is provided through the program or unit for learning strategies, learning styles, math, reading, study skills, and written language. Testing for auditory processing, intel-

ligence, motor skills, neuropsychological, personality, social skills, spelling, spoken language, and visual processing is provided collaboratively through on-campus or off-campus services.

Basic Skills Remediation Remediation is offered in class-size groups for computer skills, learning strategies, math, reading, spelling, spoken language, study skills, time management, and written language. Remediation is provided through the program or unit via regular education teachers.

Enrichment Enrichment programs are available through the program or unit for career planning, college survival skills, learning strategies, math, oral communication skills, practical computer skills, reading, self-advocacy, stress management, study skills, test taking, time management, vocabulary development, and written composition skills.

Application For admittance to the program or unit, students are required to apply to the program directly and provide a psychoeducational report (3 years old or less). It is recommended that students provide documentation of high school services. Upon acceptance, documentation of need for services should be sent only to the LD program or unit. *Application deadline (institutional):* 8/28. *Application deadline (LD program):* Rolling/continuous for fall and rolling/continuous for spring.

Written Policies Written policy regarding general/basic LD accommodations is available on the program Web site. Written policy regarding general/basic LD accommodations is outlined in the school's catalog/handbook. Written policy regarding general/basic LD accommodations is available through the program or unit directly.

University of Alaska Southeast, Ketchikan Campus
Student Services

2600 7th Avenue
Ketchikan, AK 99901-5798
http://www.ketch.alaska.edu/

Contact: Ms. Gail Klein, Student Services Coordinator. Phone: 907-228-4508. Fax: 907-225-3624. E-mail: gail.klein@uas.alaska.edu.

Student Services Approximately 3 registered undergraduate students were served during 2002-03. Academic advisers, LD specialists, professional tutors, and other are provided collaboratively through on-campus or off-campus services.

Unique Aids and Services Aids, services, or accommodations include digital textbooks, additional testing time, extra time for assignments.

Subject-area Tutoring Tutoring is offered one-on-one. Tutoring is provided collaboratively through on-campus or off-campus services via trained peer tutors.

Basic Skills Remediation Remediation is offered one-on-one for learning strategies, math, spelling, study skills, and written language. Remediation is provided collaboratively through on-campus or off-campus services via trained peer tutors.

Application For admittance to the program or unit, students are required to provide documentation of high school services and provide documentation of disability from a professional in the field.

Upon application, materials documenting need for services should be sent only to admissions with institutional application materials. Upon acceptance, documentation of need for services should be sent only to admissions. *Application deadline (institutional):* Continuous. *Application deadline (LD program):* Rolling/continuous for fall and rolling/continuous for spring.

Written Policies Written policies regarding general/basic LD accommodations and substitutions and waivers of admissions requirements are available on the program Web site. Written policies regarding general/basic LD accommodations and substitutions and waivers of admissions requirements are outlined in the school's catalog/handbook.

University of Kentucky, Lexington Community College
Disability Support Services

Cooper Drive
Lexington, KY 40506-0235
http://www.uky.edu/LCC/DSS

Contact: Ms. Veronica Miller, Director. Phone: 859-257-4872 Ext. 4194. Fax: 859-323-7136. E-mail: vimill1@email.uky.edu.

Disability Support Services Approximately 450 registered undergraduate students were served during 2002-03. The program or unit includes 2 full-time and 2 part-time staff members. Academic advisers, counselors, graduate assistants/students, remediation/learning specialists, and trained peer tutors are provided through the program or unit. Academic advisers, counselors, diagnostic specialists, graduate assistants/students, and regular education teachers are provided collaboratively through on-campus or off-campus services.

Subject-area Tutoring Tutoring is offered one-on-one and in small groups for some subjects. Tutoring is provided through the program or unit via trained peer tutors. Tutoring is also provided collaboratively through on-campus or off-campus services via computer-based instruction, professional tutors, and trained peer tutors.

Diagnostic Testing Testing for auditory processing, handwriting, intelligence, learning strategies, learning styles, math, motor skills, neuropsychological, personality, reading, social skills, spelling, spoken language, study skills, visual processing, and written language is provided collaboratively through on-campus or off-campus services.

Basic Skills Remediation Remediation is offered one-on-one and in small groups for learning strategies, math, study skills, time management, and written language. Remediation is provided collaboratively through on-campus or off-campus services via computer-based instruction, regular education teachers, and other.

Enrichment Enrichment programs are available through the program or unit for career planning and self-advocacy. Programs for career planning, college survival skills, health and nutrition, learning strategies, math, medication management, oral communication skills, practical computer skills, reading, stress management, study skills, test taking, time management, vocabulary development, and written composition skills are provided collaboratively through on-campus or off-campus services. Credit is offered for career

planning, college survival skills, learning strategies, oral communication skills, practical computer skills, reading, stress management, study skills, test taking, time management, and written composition skills.

Student Organization The Athena Club.

Fees *Diagnostic Testing* fee is $300.

Application For admittance to the program or unit, students are required to provide a psychoeducational report. It is recommended that students provide documentation of high school services. Upon acceptance, documentation of need for services should be sent only to the LD program or unit. *Application deadline (institutional):* 8/1. *Application deadline (LD program):* Rolling/continuous for fall and rolling/continuous for spring.

Written Policies Written policy regarding general/basic LD accommodations is outlined in the school's catalog/handbook. Written policies regarding course substitutions and substitutions and waivers of graduation requirements are available through the program or unit directly.

University of New Mexico-Valencia Campus

280 La Entrada
Los Lunas, NM 87031-7633

Contact: Dr. Karen O'Kain, Coordinator of The Learning Center and Equal Access Services. Phone: 505-925-8930. E-mail: kokain@unm.edu.

Unique Aids and Services Aids, services, or accommodations include career counseling.

Subject-area Tutoring Tutoring is offered one-on-one and in small groups for most subjects. Tutoring is provided through the program or unit via computer-based instruction, professional tutors, and trained peer tutors.

Diagnostic Testing Testing is provided through the program or unit for learning strategies, learning styles, reading, spelling, and written language. Testing for auditory processing, handwriting, intelligence, learning strategies, learning styles, math, motor skills, neuropsychological, personality, social skills, spoken language, study skills, visual processing, and written language is provided collaboratively through on-campus or off-campus services.

Basic Skills Remediation Remediation is offered one-on-one, in small groups, and in class-size groups for computer skills, learning strategies, math, reading, spelling, study skills, time management, and written language. Remediation is provided through the program or unit via computer-based instruction, professional tutors, and trained peer tutors. Remediation is also provided collaboratively through on-campus or off-campus services via computer-based instruction and regular education teachers.

Enrichment Enrichment programs are available through the program or unit for learning strategies, practical computer skills, study skills, test taking, time management, vocabulary development, and written composition skills. Programs for career planning, college survival skills, health and nutrition, learning strategies, math, practical computer skills, reading, study skills, time management, vocabulary development, and written composition skills are provided collaboratively through on-campus or off-campus services. Credit is offered for math, practical computer skills, and reading.

University of New Mexico-Valencia Campus (continued)

Application For admittance to the program or unit, students are required to apply to the program directly and provide a letter from a diagnostician describing the disability and the accommodations required. It is recommended that students provide a psychoeducational report and provide documentation of high school services. Upon acceptance, documentation of need for services should be sent only to the LD program or unit. *Application deadline (institutional):* Continuous. *Application deadline (LD program):* Rolling/continuous for fall and rolling/continuous for spring.

Written Policies Written policy regarding general/basic LD accommodations is available on the program Web site. Written policies regarding course substitutions, general/basic LD accommodations, and reduced course loads are outlined in the school's catalog/handbook. Written policy regarding general/basic LD accommodations is available through the program or unit directly.

University of South Carolina Lancaster
Office of Disability Services

PO Box 889
Lancaster, SC 29721-0889
http://usclancaster.sc.edu/
Contact: Mrs. Tracey Craig Taylor, Disability Services Coordinator. Phone: 803-313-7066. Fax: 803-313-7116. E-mail: ttaylor@gwm.sc.edu.

Office of Disability Services Approximately 2 registered undergraduate students were served during 2002-03. The program or unit includes 1 part-time staff member. Academic advisers and regular education teachers are provided collaboratively through on-campus or off-campus services.

Subject-area Tutoring Tutoring is offered one-on-one for most subjects. Tutoring is provided collaboratively through on-campus or off-campus services via computer-based instruction, professional tutors, and trained peer tutors.

Application For admittance to the program or unit, students are required to provide a psychoeducational report (3 years old or less) and provide documentation of high school services. Upon application, materials documenting need for services should be sent to both admissions and the LD program or unit. Upon acceptance, documentation of need for services should be sent to both admissions and the LD program or unit. *Application deadline (institutional):* Continuous. *Application deadline (LD program):* Rolling/continuous for fall and rolling/continuous for spring.

Written Policies Written policies regarding course substitutions, general/basic LD accommodations, grade forgiveness, reduced course loads, substitutions and waivers of admissions requirements, and substitutions and waivers of graduation requirements are available on the program Web site.

University of Wisconsin-Marinette

750 West Bay Shore

Marinette, WI 54143-4299
http://www.uwc.edu/mnt
Contact: Ms. Cynthia M. Bailey, Director of Student Services. Phone: 715-735-4302. Fax: 715-735-4304. E-mail: cbailey@uwc.edu.

Approximately 17 registered undergraduate students were served during 2002-03. The program or unit includes 1 full-time staff member. Academic advisers and professional tutors are provided through the program or unit.

Subject-area Tutoring Tutoring is offered one-on-one and in small groups for some subjects. Tutoring is provided collaboratively through on-campus or off-campus services via computer-based instruction and professional tutors.

Basic Skills Remediation Remediation is offered one-on-one and in small groups for computer skills, learning strategies, study skills, and time management. Remediation is provided collaboratively through on-campus or off-campus services via regular education teachers.

Enrichment Programs for career planning, college survival skills, learning strategies, math, stress management, study skills, time management, and written composition skills are provided collaboratively through on-campus or off-campus services.

Application For admittance to the program or unit, students are required to apply to the program directly and provide documentation of high school services. It is recommended that students provide a psychoeducational report (3 years old or less). Upon acceptance, documentation of need for services should be sent only to the LD program or unit. *Application deadline (institutional):* Continuous. *Application deadline (LD program):* Rolling/continuous for fall and rolling/continuous for spring.

Written Policies Written policies regarding general/basic LD accommodations and reduced course loads are available through the program or unit directly.

University of Wisconsin-Rock County
Student Services

2909 Kellogg Avenue
Janesville, WI 53546-5699
http://www.uwc.rock.edu
Contact: Cynthia L. Calvin, Director of Student Services. Phone: 608-758-6523. Fax: 608-758-6564. E-mail: ccalvin@uwc.edu.

Student Services Approximately 25 registered undergraduate students were served during 2002-03. Academic advisers, coaches, counselors, regular education teachers, remediation/learning specialists, skill tutors, and trained peer tutors are provided collaboratively through on-campus or off-campus services.

Orientation The program or unit offers a mandatory 1-hour orientation for new students individually by special arrangement.

Unique Aids and Services Aids, services, or accommodations include TRIO Program.

Subject-area Tutoring Tutoring is offered one-on-one, in small groups, and in class-size groups for some subjects. Tutoring is provided collaboratively through on-campus or off-campus services via computer-based instruction, professional tutors, and trained peer tutors.

Basic Skills Remediation Remediation is offered in class-size groups for math, study skills, time management, and written language. Remediation is provided collaboratively through on-campus or off-campus services via regular education teachers.

Enrichment Enrichment programs are available through the program or unit for self-advocacy and stress management. Programs for career planning, college survival skills, learning strategies, math, oral communication skills, practical computer skills, study skills, test taking, time management, vocabulary development, and written composition skills are provided collaboratively through on-campus or off-campus services. Credit is offered for oral communication skills and written composition skills.

Application For admittance to the program or unit, students are required to provide a psychoeducational report (6 years old or less). It is recommended that students provide documentation of high school services. Upon acceptance, documentation of need for services should be sent only to admissions. *Application deadline (institutional): 7/31. Application deadline (LD program):* Rolling/continuous for fall and rolling/continuous for spring.

Written Policies Written policy regarding general/basic LD accommodations is available on the program Web site. Written policy regarding general/basic LD accommodations is outlined in the school's catalog/handbook.

Valencia Community College
Office for Students with Disabilities

PO Box 3028
Orlando, FL 32802-3028
http://www.valencia.cc.fl.us/
Contact: Phone: 407-299-5000.

Office for Students with Disabilities Approximately 400 registered undergraduate students were served during 2002-03.
Unique Aids and Services Aids, services, or accommodations include career counseling and priority registration.
Subject-area Tutoring Tutoring is offered one-on-one and in small groups for most subjects. Tutoring is provided collaboratively through on-campus or off-campus services via computer-based instruction and trained peer tutors.
Basic Skills Remediation Remediation is offered in class-size groups for math, reading, study skills, and written language. Remediation is provided collaboratively through on-campus or off-campus services via computer-based instruction and regular education teachers.
Enrichment Programs for career planning, health and nutrition, and study skills are provided collaboratively through on-campus or off-campus services. Credit is offered for career planning, health and nutrition, and study skills.
Application For admittance to the program or unit, students are required to apply to the program directly and provide a psychoeducational report (3 years old or less). It is recommended that students provide documentation of high school services. Upon application, materials documenting need for services should be sent only to the LD program or unit. *Application deadline (institutional): 8/5. Application deadline (LD program):* Rolling/continuous for fall and rolling/continuous for spring.

Written Policies Written policy regarding grade forgiveness is outlined in the school's catalog/handbook. Written policies regarding course substitutions, general/basic LD accommodations, substitutions and waivers of admissions requirements, and substitutions and waivers of graduation requirements are available through the program or unit directly.

Victor Valley College
DSPS

18422 Bear Valley Road
Victorville, CA 92392-5849
http://www.vvc.edu/offices/
disabled_student_program_services/index.htm
Contact: Phone: 760-245-4271. Fax: 760-245-9745.

DSPS Approximately 300 registered undergraduate students were served during 2002-03. The program or unit includes 1 full-time and 2 part-time staff members. Counselors, diagnostic specialists, LD specialists, and other are provided through the program or unit. Counselors, diagnostic specialists, professional tutors, regular education teachers, remediation/learning specialists, skill tutors, special education teachers, strategy tutors, and other are provided collaboratively through on-campus or off-campus services.
Orientation The program or unit offers a mandatory 3-hour orientation for new students before registration, before classes begin, during summer prior to enrollment, during registration, after classes begin, and individually by special arrangement.
Unique Aids and Services Aids, services, or accommodations include career counseling, digital textbooks, faculty training, priority registration, support groups, and weekly meetings with faculty.
Subject-area Tutoring Tutoring is offered one-on-one for some subjects. Tutoring is provided through the program or unit via LD specialists and other. Tutoring is also provided collaboratively through on-campus or off-campus services via computer-based instruction, trained peer tutors, and other.
Diagnostic Testing Testing is provided through the program or unit for auditory processing, handwriting, intelligence, learning strategies, learning styles, math, reading, spelling, spoken language, study skills, visual processing, written language, and other services. Testing for learning strategies, neuropsychological, personality, and social skills is provided collaboratively through on-campus or off-campus services.
Basic Skills Remediation Remediation is offered in class-size groups for computer skills, learning strategies, math, reading, spelling, spoken language, study skills, time management, and written language. Remediation is provided through the program or unit via computer-based instruction, LD specialists, regular education teachers, and other. Remediation is also provided collaboratively through on-campus or off-campus services.
Enrichment Enrichment programs are available through the program or unit for career planning, college survival skills, health and nutrition, learning strategies, math, oral communication skills, practical computer skills, reading, self-advocacy, stress management, study skills, test taking, time management, vocabulary development, written composition skills, and other. Programs for career planning, college survival skills, health and nutrition, learning strategies, math, oral communication skills, practical computer skills, reading, self-advocacy, stress management, study skills, test taking,

Victor Valley College (continued)

time management, vocabulary development, written composition skills, and other are provided collaboratively through on-campus or off-campus services. Credit is offered for career planning, college survival skills, health and nutrition, learning strategies, math, oral communication skills, practical computer skills, reading, vocabulary development, and written composition skills.

Application For admittance to the program or unit, students are required to apply to the program directly, provide a psychoeducational report (4 years old or less), provide documentation of high school services, and provide documentation from a clinician. Upon application, materials documenting need for services should be sent only to the LD program or unit. Upon acceptance, documentation of need for services should be sent only to the LD program or unit. *Application deadline (institutional):* Continuous. *Application deadline (LD program):* Rolling/continuous for fall and rolling/continuous for spring.

Written Policies Written policy regarding general/basic LD accommodations is available on the program Web site. Written policies regarding course substitutions, general/basic LD accommodations, reduced course loads, and substitutions and waivers of graduation requirements are available through the program or unit directly.

Virginia Western Community College

PO Box 14007

Roanoke, VA 24038

http://www.vw.vccs.edu

Contact: Dr. Avis C. Quinn, Director/Counselor REACH/ Student Support Services. Phone: 540-857-6489. Fax: 540-857-7918. E-mail: aquinn@vw.vccs.edu.

Approximately 200 registered undergraduate students were served during 2002-03. The program or unit includes 4 full-time and 15 part-time staff members. Academic advisers, counselors, professional tutors, and skill tutors are provided through the program or unit.

Subject-area Tutoring Tutoring is offered one-on-one for most subjects. Tutoring is provided through the program or unit via professional tutors and trained peer tutors.

Enrichment Enrichment programs are available through the program or unit for career planning, learning strategies, self-advocacy, stress management, study skills, test taking, and time management. Programs for college survival skills, health and nutrition, math, oral communication skills, practical computer skills, reading, vocabulary development, and written composition skills are provided collaboratively through on-campus or off-campus services. Credit is offered for college survival skills, health and nutrition, math, oral communication skills, practical computer skills, reading, vocabulary development, and written composition skills.

Application For admittance to the program or unit, students are required to apply to the program directly, provide a psychoeducational report (3 years old or less), provide documentation of high school services, and provide psychological exam from DRS or physician. Upon application, materials documenting need for services should be sent only to admissions with institutional application materials. Upon acceptance, documentation of need for services should be

sent only to the LD program or unit. *Application deadline (institutional):* Continuous. *Application deadline (LD program):* Rolling/continuous for fall and rolling/continuous for spring.

Written Policies Written policy regarding general/basic LD accommodations is available on the program Web site. Written policy regarding general/basic LD accommodations is outlined in the school's catalog/handbook. Written policies regarding general/basic LD accommodations and reduced course loads are available through the program or unit directly.

Warren County Community College
Office of Student Development

475 Route 57 West

Washington, NJ 07882-4343

http://www.warren.edu

Contact: Jan Anthony Mellon, Coordinator of Advisement Services. Phone: 908-835-2300 Ext. 2301. Fax: 908-689-5824. E-mail: mellon@warren.edu.

Office of Student Development Approximately 67 registered undergraduate students were served during 2002-03. The program or unit includes 1 full-time staff member. Academic advisers are provided through the program or unit. Professional tutors and regular education teachers are provided collaboratively through on-campus or off-campus services.

Subject-area Tutoring Tutoring is offered one-on-one and in small groups for all subjects. Tutoring is provided collaboratively through on-campus or off-campus services via professional tutors and trained peer tutors.

Diagnostic Testing Testing for learning strategies, math, reading, study skills, and written language is provided collaboratively through on-campus or off-campus services.

Basic Skills Remediation Remediation is offered in class-size groups for math, reading, and written language. Remediation is provided collaboratively through on-campus or off-campus services via regular education teachers.

Enrichment Programs for career planning, college survival skills, learning strategies, math, oral communication skills, practical computer skills, reading, study skills, time management, and written composition skills are provided collaboratively through on-campus or off-campus services. Credit is offered for career planning, college survival skills, learning strategies, math, oral communication skills, practical computer skills, reading, study skills, time management, and written composition skills.

Fees *Diagnostic Testing* fee is $25.

Application For admittance to the program or unit, students are required to provide a psychoeducational report (3 years old or less) and provide documentation of high school services. Upon application, materials documenting need for services should be sent only to the LD program or unit. Upon acceptance, documentation of need for services should be sent only to the LD program or unit. *Application deadline (institutional):* Continuous. *Application deadline (LD program):* Rolling/continuous for fall.

Written Policies Written policy regarding general/basic LD accommodations is available through the program or unit directly.

Washington State Community College

710 Colegate Drive

Marietta, OH 45750-9225

http://www.wscc.edu/

Contact: Phone: 740-374-8716. Fax: 740-376-0257.

The program or unit includes 1 full-time staff member. LD specialists are provided through the program or unit. Academic advisers, professional tutors, and regular education teachers are provided collaboratively through on-campus or off-campus services.

Subject-area Tutoring Tutoring is offered one-on-one and in small groups for all subjects. Tutoring is provided collaboratively through on-campus or off-campus services via graduate assistants/students, professional tutors, and trained peer tutors.

Application For admittance to the program or unit, students are required to apply to the program directly and provide a psychoeducational report (3 years old or less). It is recommended that students provide documentation of high school services. Upon application, materials documenting need for services should be sent only to the LD program or unit. Upon acceptance, documentation of need for services should be sent only to the LD program or unit. *Application deadline (institutional):* Continuous. *Application deadline (LD program):* Rolling/continuous for fall and rolling/continuous for spring.

Written Policies Written policies regarding course substitutions, general/basic LD accommodations, substitutions and waivers of admissions requirements, and substitutions and waivers of graduation requirements are available on the program Web site. Written policies regarding course substitutions, general/basic LD accommodations, substitutions and waivers of admissions requirements, and substitutions and waivers of graduation requirements are available through the program or unit directly.

Waubonsee Community College
Access Center for Students with Disabilities

Route 47 at Waubonsee Drive

Sugar Grove, IL 60554-9799

http://www.waubonsee.edu/

Contact: Phone: 630-466-7900. Fax: 630-466-4964.

Access Center for Students with Disabilities Approximately 200 registered undergraduate students were served during 2002-03. The program or unit includes 5 full-time and 8 part-time staff members. Academic advisers, counselors, diagnostic specialists, LD specialists, professional tutors, remediation/learning specialists, skill tutors, strategy tutors, and other are provided through the program or unit. Academic advisers, coaches, counselors, professional tutors, regular education teachers, and skill tutors are provided collaboratively through on-campus or off-campus services.

Orientation The program or unit offers an optional orientation for new students before registration, before classes begin, during summer prior to enrollment, during registration, after classes begin, and individually by special arrangement.

Summer Program To help prepare for the demands of college, there is an optional summer program prior to entering the school.

Unique Aids and Services Aids, services, or accommodations include advocates, career counseling, faculty training, and priority registration.

Subject-area Tutoring Tutoring is offered one-on-one and in small groups for most subjects. Tutoring is provided through the program or unit via LD specialists and professional tutors. Tutoring is also provided collaboratively through on-campus or off-campus services via computer-based instruction, professional tutors, and trained peer tutors.

Diagnostic Testing Testing for auditory processing, learning strategies, learning styles, math, reading, visual processing, and written language is provided collaboratively through on-campus or off-campus services.

Basic Skills Remediation Remediation is offered in class-size groups for learning strategies, reading, study skills, and written language. Remediation is provided collaboratively through on-campus or off-campus services via regular education teachers.

Enrichment Programs for career planning, college survival skills, health and nutrition, learning strategies, math, reading, stress management, study skills, test taking, vocabulary development, and written composition skills are provided collaboratively through on-campus or off-campus services.

Fees *Diagnostic Testing* fee is $25.

Application For admittance to the program or unit, students are required to apply to the program directly. It is recommended that students provide a psychoeducational report (3 years old or less) and provide documentation of high school services. Upon application, materials documenting need for services should be sent only to the LD program or unit. Upon acceptance, documentation of need for services should be sent only to the LD program or unit. *Application deadline (institutional):* Continuous. *Application deadline (LD program):* Rolling/continuous for fall and rolling/continuous for spring.

Written Policies Written policy regarding grade forgiveness is outlined in the school's catalog/handbook. Written policy regarding general/basic LD accommodations is available through the program or unit directly.

Waukesha County Technical College
Special Services

800 Main Street

Pewaukee, WI 53072-4601

http://www.wctc.edu

Contact: Deb A. Jilbert, Coordinator of Special Services. Phone: 262-691-5210. Fax: 262-691-5089. E-mail: djilbert@wctc.edu.

Special Services Approximately 200 registered undergraduate students were served during 2002-03. The program or unit includes 4 full-time staff members. Academic advisers, counselors, and LD specialists are provided through the program or unit.

Waukesha County Technical College (continued)

Orientation The program or unit offers an optional orientation for new students individually by special arrangement.

Summer Program To help prepare for the demands of college, there is an optional 1-day summer program prior to entering the school.

Unique Aids and Services Aids, services, or accommodations include career counseling.

Subject-area Tutoring Tutoring is offered in small groups for most subjects. Tutoring is provided through the program or unit via LD specialists.

Basic Skills Remediation Remediation is offered in class-size groups for math, reading, and written language. Remediation is provided collaboratively through on-campus or off-campus services via computer-based instruction and regular education teachers.

Application For admittance to the program or unit, students are required to provide a psychoeducational report, provide documentation of high school services, and provide an assistive technology evaluation (when appropriate). It is recommended that students apply to the program directly. Upon application, materials documenting need for services should be sent only to the LD program or unit. Upon acceptance, documentation of need for services should be sent only to the LD program or unit. *Application deadline (institutional):* Continuous. *Application deadline (LD program):* 7/15 for fall. 11/15 for spring.

Written Policies Written policy regarding course substitutions is outlined in the school's catalog/handbook. Written policies regarding general/basic LD accommodations and reduced course loads are available through the program or unit directly.

Waycross College
Student Life

2001 South Georgia Parkway

Waycross, GA 31503-9248

http://www.waycross.edu/

Contact: Ms. Merry Trammell, Coordinator of Testing, Guidance and Student Development. Phone: 912-285-6012. Fax: 912-285-6158. E-mail: mtrammel@waycross.edu.

Student Life Approximately 12 registered undergraduate students were served during 2002-03. The program or unit includes 1 full-time staff member. Academic advisers are provided through the program or unit. Academic advisers, counselors, diagnostic specialists, and professional tutors are provided collaboratively through on-campus or off-campus services.

Summer Program To help prepare for the demands of college, there is an optional 1-hour summer program prior to entering the school. Degree credit will be earned.

Unique Aids and Services Aids, services, or accommodations include advocates and career counseling.

Subject-area Tutoring Tutoring is offered one-on-one, in small groups, and in class-size groups for all subjects. Tutoring is provided collaboratively through on-campus or off-campus services via trained peer tutors.

Diagnostic Testing Testing for auditory processing, handwriting, intelligence, learning strategies, learning styles, math, motor skills, neuropsychological, personality, reading, social skills, spelling, spoken language, study skills, visual processing, written language, and other services is provided collaboratively through on-campus or off-campus services.

Basic Skills Remediation Remediation is offered in class-size groups for computer skills, learning strategies, math, reading, study skills, time management, and written language. Remediation is provided collaboratively through on-campus or off-campus services via computer-based instruction, regular education teachers, and trained peer tutors.

Enrichment Programs for career planning, college survival skills, health and nutrition, learning strategies, math, oral communication skills, reading, self-advocacy, stress management, study skills, test taking, time management, and written composition skills are provided collaboratively through on-campus or off-campus services.

Fees *Diagnostic Testing* fee is $400.

Application For admittance to the program or unit, students are required to provide a psychoeducational report (2 years old or less). It is recommended that students apply to the program directly and provide documentation of high school services. Upon acceptance, documentation of need for services should be sent only to the LD program or unit. *Application deadline (institutional):* Continuous. *Application deadline (LD program):* Rolling/continuous for fall and rolling/continuous for spring.

Written Policies Written policies regarding course substitutions, general/basic LD accommodations, grade forgiveness, reduced course loads, substitutions and waivers of admissions requirements, and substitutions and waivers of graduation requirements are available on the program Web site. Written policies regarding course substitutions, general/basic LD accommodations, grade forgiveness, reduced course loads, substitutions and waivers of admissions requirements, and substitutions and waivers of graduation requirements are outlined in the school's catalog/handbook. Written policies regarding general/basic LD accommodations and substitutions and waivers of admissions requirements are available through the program or unit directly.

Wayne Community College
Disability Services for Students

PO Box 8002

Goldsboro, NC 27533-8002

http://www.waynecc.edu

Contact: Phone: 919-735-5151. Fax: 919-736-3204.

Disability Services for Students Approximately 40 registered undergraduate students were served during 2002-03. The program or unit includes 1 full-time staff member. Academic advisers and counselors are provided through the program or unit. Academic advisers, remediation/learning specialists, skill tutors, and trained peer tutors are provided collaboratively through on-campus or off-campus services.

Unique Aids and Services Aids, services, or accommodations include digital textbooks, priority registration, meetings with faculty.

Subject-area Tutoring Tutoring is offered one-on-one for most subjects. Tutoring is provided collaboratively through on-campus or off-campus services via computer-based instruction, graduate assistants/students, and trained peer tutors.

Basic Skills Remediation Remediation is offered one-on-one and in class-size groups for computer skills, math, reading, spelling, study skills, and written language. Remediation is provided collaboratively through on-campus or off-campus services via computer-based instruction, graduate assistants/students, and trained peer tutors.

Enrichment Programs for career planning, college survival skills, learning strategies, math, practical computer skills, reading, stress management, study skills, test taking, time management, vocabulary development, and written composition skills are provided collaboratively through on-campus or off-campus services. Credit is offered for college survival skills.

Application For admittance to the program or unit, students are required to apply to the program directly and provide a psychoeducational report (3 years old or less). Upon application, materials documenting need for services should be sent only to the LD program or unit. Upon acceptance, documentation of need for services should be sent only to the LD program or unit. *Application deadline (institutional):* Continuous. *Application deadline (LD program):* Rolling/continuous for fall and rolling/continuous for spring.

Written Policies Written policies regarding course substitutions, general/basic LD accommodations, and substitutions and waivers of graduation requirements are available on the program Web site. Written policies regarding course substitutions, general/basic LD accommodations, and substitutions and waivers of graduation requirements are outlined in the school's catalog/handbook.

Wenatchee Valley College

1300 Fifth Street
Wenatchee, WA 98801-1799
http://www.wvc.ctc.edu/
Contact: Ms. Carla Boyd, Special Populations Coordinator.
Phone: 509-682-6854. E-mail: cboyd@wvc.edu.

The program or unit includes 1 full-time staff member. Academic advisers, coaches, counselors, diagnostic specialists, LD specialists, regular education teachers, remediation/learning specialists, skill tutors, and trained peer tutors are provided collaboratively through on-campus or off-campus services.

Unique Aids and Services Aids, services, or accommodations include priority registration.

Subject-area Tutoring Tutoring is offered in small groups for some subjects. Tutoring is provided collaboratively through on-campus or off-campus services via LD specialists and trained peer tutors.

Basic Skills Remediation Remediation is offered in class-size groups for computer skills, learning strategies, math, reading, spelling, study skills, and written language. Remediation is provided collaboratively through on-campus or off-campus services via regular education teachers.

Application Upon acceptance, documentation of need for services should be sent only to the LD program or unit. *Application deadline (institutional):* Continuous. *Application deadline (LD program):* Rolling/continuous for fall and rolling/continuous for spring.

Written Policies Written policies regarding course substitutions, grade forgiveness, reduced course loads, substitutions and waivers of admissions requirements, and substitutions and waivers of graduation requirements are outlined in the school's catalog/handbook. Written policy regarding general/basic LD accommodations is available through the program or unit directly.

Western Nebraska Community College
Counseling Office

371 College Drive
Sidney, NE 69162
http://www.wncc.net/

Contact: Mr. Norman J. Stephenson, Counseling Director.
Phone: 800-348-4435 Ext. 6090. Fax: 308-635-6055. E-mail: stephens@wncc.net.

Counseling Office Approximately 25 registered undergraduate students were served during 2002-03. The program or unit includes 2 full-time staff members and 1 part-time staff member. Counselors are provided through the program or unit. Academic advisers, counselors, diagnostic specialists, LD specialists, professional tutors, regular education teachers, remediation/learning specialists, skill tutors, special education teachers, and trained peer tutors are provided collaboratively through on-campus or off-campus services.

Unique Aids and Services Aids, services, or accommodations include career counseling, priority registration, and support groups.

Subject-area Tutoring Tutoring is offered one-on-one and in small groups for all subjects. Tutoring is provided through the program or unit via LD specialists. Tutoring is also provided collaboratively through on-campus or off-campus services via computer-based instruction, LD specialists, professional tutors, trained peer tutors, and other.

Basic Skills Remediation Remediation is offered one-on-one and in small groups for math, reading, spelling, study skills, and written language. Remediation is provided through the program or unit via LD specialists. Remediation is also provided collaboratively through on-campus or off-campus services via computer-based instruction, professional tutors, regular education teachers, teacher trainees, and trained peer tutors.

Enrichment Programs for career planning, college survival skills, health and nutrition, learning strategies, math, medication management, oral communication skills, practical computer skills, reading, self-advocacy, stress management, study skills, test taking, time management, vocabulary development, and written composition skills are provided collaboratively through on-campus or off-campus services. Credit is offered for college survival skills, math, oral communication skills, practical computer skills, and vocabulary development.

Application It is recommended that students apply to the program directly, provide a psychoeducational report (3 years old or less), and provide documentation of high school services. Upon application, materials documenting need for services should be sent to both admissions and the LD program or unit. Upon acceptance, documentation of need for services should be sent only to the LD program or unit. *Application deadline (institutional):* Continuous. *Application deadline (LD program):* Rolling/continuous for fall and rolling/continuous for spring.

Written Policies Written policies regarding course substitutions, general/basic LD accommodations, grade forgiveness, reduced course loads, substitutions and waivers of admissions requirements, and substitutions and waivers of graduation requirements are available through the program or unit directly.

Western Texas College
Counseling Center

6200 College Avenue
Snyder, TX 79549-6105
http://wtc.edu
Contact: Phone: 915-573-8511.

Counseling Center Approximately 25 registered undergraduate students were served during 2002-03. The program or unit includes 2 part-time staff members. Academic advisers and counselors are provided collaboratively through on-campus or off-campus services.
Orientation The program or unit offers an optional orientation for new students before classes begin.
Unique Aids and Services Aids, services, or accommodations include career counseling, priority registration, and weekly meetings with faculty.
Subject-area Tutoring Tutoring is offered one-on-one for most subjects. Tutoring is provided collaboratively through on-campus or off-campus services via computer-based instruction and trained peer tutors.
Basic Skills Remediation Remediation is offered one-on-one and in class-size groups for math, reading, and written language. Remediation is provided collaboratively through on-campus or off-campus services via computer-based instruction and regular education teachers.
Application For admittance to the program or unit, students are required to apply to the program directly and provide a psychoeducational report (5 years old or less). It is recommended that students provide documentation of high school services. Upon application, materials documenting need for services should be sent only to the LD program or unit. Upon acceptance, documentation of need for services should be sent only to the LD program or unit. *Application deadline (institutional):* Continuous. *Application deadline (LD program):* Rolling/continuous for fall and rolling/continuous for spring.
Written Policies Written policy regarding general/basic LD accommodations is outlined in the school's catalog/handbook. Written policy regarding general/basic LD accommodations is available through the program or unit directly.

West Hills Community College

300 Cherry Lane
Coalinga, CA 93210-1399
http://www.westhillscollege.com/
Contact: Ms. Joyce K. Smyers, Director and Counselor. Phone: 800-266-1114 Ext. 2337. E-mail: joycesmyers@westhillscollege.com.

Approximately 125 registered undergraduate students were served during 2002-03. The program or unit includes 8 full-time staff members. Coaches, counselors, diagnostic specialists, LD specialists, professional tutors, remediation/learning specialists, skill tutors, and special education teachers are provided through the program or unit. Academic advisers, regular education teachers, strategy tutors, and trained peer tutors are provided collaboratively through on-campus or off-campus services.
Orientation The program or unit offers a mandatory 1-hour orientation for new students individually by special arrangement.
Unique Aids and Services Aids, services, or accommodations include advocates, career counseling, digital textbooks, faculty training, priority registration, and support groups.
Subject-area Tutoring Tutoring is offered one-on-one, in small groups, and in class-size groups for most subjects. Tutoring is provided through the program or unit via computer-based instruction and other. Tutoring is also provided collaboratively through on-campus or off-campus services via computer-based instruction, graduate assistants/students, and trained peer tutors.
Diagnostic Testing Testing is provided through the program or unit for auditory processing, handwriting, intelligence, learning strategies, learning styles, math, reading, spelling, study skills, visual processing, and written language. Testing for learning strategies, learning styles, motor skills, reading, spelling, spoken language, study skills, visual processing, and written language is provided collaboratively through on-campus or off-campus services.
Basic Skills Remediation Remediation is offered in class-size groups for auditory processing, computer skills, handwriting, learning strategies, math, motor skills, reading, spelling, study skills, time management, visual processing, and written language. Remediation is provided through the program or unit via computer-based instruction and special education teachers. Remediation is also provided collaboratively through on-campus or off-campus services via computer-based instruction, graduate assistants/students, regular education teachers, and trained peer tutors.
Enrichment Enrichment programs are available through the program or unit for college survival skills, learning strategies, math, oral communication skills, practical computer skills, reading, self-advocacy, study skills, test taking, time management, vocabulary development, and written composition skills. Programs for career planning, college survival skills, health and nutrition, math, oral communication skills, practical computer skills, reading, study skills, vocabulary development, and written composition skills are provided collaboratively through on-campus or off-campus services. Credit is offered for career planning, college survival skills, health and nutrition, learning strategies, math, oral communication skills, practical computer skills, reading, study skills, vocabulary development, and written composition skills.
Application For admittance to the program or unit, students are required to apply to the program directly and provide a psychoeducational report (1 year old or less). It is recommended that students provide documentation of high school services. Upon application, materials documenting need for services should be sent only to the LD program or unit. *Application deadline (institutional):* Continuous. *Application deadline (LD program):* Rolling/continuous for fall and rolling/continuous for spring.
Written Policies Written policies regarding course substitutions, general/basic LD accommodations, grade forgiveness, substitutions and waivers of admissions requirements, and substitutions and waivers of graduation requirements are available on the program Web site. Written policies regarding general/basic LD accommodations and grade forgiveness are outlined in the school's catalog/handbook. Written policies regarding course substitutions, general/basic LD accommodations, substitutions and waivers of admissions requirements, and substitutions and waivers of graduation requirements are available through the program or unit directly.

West Virginia University at Parkersburg
Disability Services

300 Campus Drive

Parkersburg, WV 26104-8647

http://www.wvup.edu/ada/index.htm

Contact: Catherine A. Mutz, ADA Coordinator and Assistant Professor. Phone: 304-424-8320. Fax: 304-424-8372. E-mail: cathy.mutz@mail.wvu.edu.

Disability Services Approximately 40 registered undergraduate students were served during 2002-03. The program or unit includes 1 full-time and 5 part-time staff members. Counselors and other are provided through the program or unit.

Orientation The program or unit offers an optional orientation for new students individually by special arrangement.

Unique Aids and Services Aids, services, or accommodations include career counseling, faculty training, priority registration, weekly meetings with faculty, testing accommodations, assistive technology and listening, TDD, talking books, reading machines .

Subject-area Tutoring Tutoring is offered one-on-one, in small groups, and in class-size groups for some subjects. Tutoring is provided collaboratively through on-campus or off-campus services via other.

Basic Skills Remediation Remediation is offered one-on-one, in small groups, and in class-size groups for math, reading, study skills, time management, and written language. Remediation is provided collaboratively through on-campus or off-campus services via computer-based instruction and other.

Enrichment Programs for career planning, college survival skills, health and nutrition, learning strategies, math, oral communication skills, practical computer skills, reading, self-advocacy, stress management, study skills, test taking, time management, vocabulary development, written composition skills, and other are provided collaboratively through on-campus or off-campus services. Credit is offered for career planning, reading, and study skills.

Application For admittance to the program or unit, students are required to apply to the program directly and provide a psychoeducational report. Upon acceptance, documentation of need for services should be sent only to the LD program or unit. *Application deadline (LD program):* Rolling/continuous for fall and rolling/continuous for spring.

Written Policies Written policy regarding general/basic LD accommodations is available on the program Web site. Written policy regarding general/basic LD accommodations is outlined in the school's catalog/handbook. Written policy regarding general/basic LD accommodations is available through the program or unit directly.

Whatcom Community College

237 West Kellogg Road

Bellingham, WA 98226-8003

http://www.whatcom.ctc.edu/

Contact: Bill Culwell, Coordinator for Disability Support Services. Phone: 360-676-2170. Fax: 360-676-2171. E-mail: bculwell@whatcom.ctc.edu.

Academic advisers, counselors, professional tutors, regular education teachers, remediation/learning specialists, skill tutors, special education teachers, teacher trainees, and trained peer tutors are provided collaboratively through on-campus or off-campus services.

Orientation The program or unit offers an optional orientation for new students individually by special arrangement.

Unique Aids and Services Aids, services, or accommodations include career counseling and priority registration.

Subject-area Tutoring Tutoring is offered one-on-one and in small groups for some subjects. Tutoring is provided collaboratively through on-campus or off-campus services via computer-based instruction and trained peer tutors.

Basic Skills Remediation Remediation is offered one-on-one, in small groups, and in class-size groups for math, spelling, and study skills. Remediation is provided collaboratively through on-campus or off-campus services via regular education teachers, special education teachers, and trained peer tutors.

Enrichment Programs for career planning, college survival skills, health and nutrition, learning strategies, reading, stress management, study skills, test taking, time management, vocabulary development, and written composition skills are provided collaboratively through on-campus or off-campus services. Credit is offered for career planning, college survival skills, health and nutrition, reading, stress management, study skills, test taking, time management, vocabulary development, and written composition skills.

Application It is recommended that students provide a psychoeducational report (5 years old or less) and provide a professional diagnosis of LD. Upon application, materials documenting need for services should be sent only to the LD program or unit. Upon acceptance, documentation of need for services should be sent only to the LD program or unit. *Application deadline (institutional):* 6/13. *Application deadline (LD program):* Rolling/continuous for fall and rolling/continuous for spring.

Written Policies Written policies regarding substitutions and waivers of admissions requirements and substitutions and waivers of graduation requirements are outlined in the school's catalog/handbook. Written policies regarding course substitutions, general/basic LD accommodations, reduced course loads, and substitutions and waivers of graduation requirements are available through the program or unit directly.

Wilkes Community College
Disability Services

1328 Collegiate Drive, PO Box 120

Wilkesboro, NC 28697

http://www.wilkescc.edu/

Contact: Nancy H. Sizemore, Disability Service Provider. Phone: 336-838-6560 Ext. 6560. Fax: 336-838-6277. E-mail: sizemore@wilkes.cc.nc.us.

Disability Services Approximately 60 registered undergraduate students were served during 2002-03. The program or unit includes 1 full-time and 3 part-time staff members. Counselors and diagnos-

Wilkes Community College (continued)

tic specialists are provided through the program or unit. Counselors, graduate assistants/students, professional tutors, and regular education teachers are provided collaboratively through on-campus or off-campus services.

Unique Aids and Services Aids, services, or accommodations include career counseling, digital textbooks, faculty training, and priority registration.

Subject-area Tutoring Tutoring is offered one-on-one and in small groups for most subjects. Tutoring is provided collaboratively through on-campus or off-campus services via professional tutors and trained peer tutors.

Diagnostic Testing Testing for intelligence, learning strategies, learning styles, math, personality, reading, study skills, and written language is provided collaboratively through on-campus or off-campus services.

Basic Skills Remediation Remediation is offered one-on-one for learning strategies, math, reading, study skills, and written language. Remediation is provided collaboratively through on-campus or off-campus services via regular education teachers.

Enrichment Programs for career planning, college survival skills, learning strategies, stress management, study skills, test taking, and time management are provided collaboratively through on-campus or off-campus services. Credit is offered for college survival skills.

Application For admittance to the program or unit, students are required to provide a psychoeducational report and provide documentation of high school services. Upon application, materials documenting need for services should be sent only to the LD program or unit. *Application deadline (institutional):* Continuous.

Written Policies Written policies regarding course substitutions, general/basic LD accommodations, reduced course loads, and substitutions and waivers of admissions requirements are available through the program or unit directly.

Williston State College
Disabilities Support Services

Box 1326
Williston, ND 58802-1326
http://www.wsc.nodak.edu

Contact: Mrs. Janice Marie Hunter, Director. Phone: 701-774-4594. Fax: 701-774-4275. E-mail: jan.hunter@wsc.nodak.edu.

Disabilities Support Services Approximately 20 registered undergraduate students were served during 2002-03. The program or unit includes 2 full-time staff members. Professional tutors, skill tutors, and trained peer tutors are provided through the program or unit. Professional tutors, skill tutors, and trained peer tutors are provided collaboratively through on-campus or off-campus services.

Unique Aids and Services Aids, services, or accommodations include career counseling.

Basic Skills Remediation Remediation is offered one-on-one and in small groups for learning strategies, math, reading, study skills, and written language. Remediation is provided through the program or unit via computer-based instruction and trained peer tutors. Remediation is also provided collaboratively through on-campus or off-campus services via computer-based instruction and trained peer tutors.

Enrichment Programs for career planning, math, practical computer skills, reading, study skills, and written composition skills are provided collaboratively through on-campus or off-campus services. Credit is offered for career planning, math, practical computer skills, reading, study skills, and written composition skills.

Application For admittance to the program or unit, students are required to apply to the program directly and provide documentation of high school services. It is recommended that students provide a psychoeducational report. Upon application, materials documenting need for services should be sent only to the LD program or unit. Upon acceptance, documentation of need for services should be sent only to the LD program or unit. *Application deadline (institutional):* Continuous. *Application deadline (LD program):* Rolling/continuous for fall and rolling/continuous for spring.

Written Policies Written policy regarding general/basic LD accommodations is outlined in the school's catalog/handbook. Written policy regarding general/basic LD accommodations is available through the program or unit directly.

Windward Community College
Students Toward Academic Achievement and Retention (STAAR)

45-720 Keaahala Road
Kaneohe, HI 96744-3528
http://www.wcc.hawaii.edu

Contact: Ms. Yvette M. Malama, Student Services Specialist. Phone: 808-235-7489. Fax: 808-247-5362. E-mail: malama@hawaii.edu.

Students Toward Academic Achievement and Retention (STAAR) Approximately 10 registered undergraduate students were served during 2002-03. The program or unit includes 2 full-time staff members. Trained peer tutors are provided through the program or unit. Academic advisers, counselors, and regular education teachers are provided collaboratively through on-campus or off-campus services.

Subject-area Tutoring Tutoring is offered one-on-one for some subjects. Tutoring is provided through the program or unit via trained peer tutors.

Basic Skills Remediation Remediation is offered one-on-one for computer skills, math, reading, study skills, and time management. Remediation is provided through the program or unit via trained peer tutors.

Enrichment Programs for learning strategies, math, stress management, study skills, test taking, and time management are provided collaboratively through on-campus or off-campus services. Credit is offered for study skills.

Application It is recommended that students provide a psychoeducational report (3 years old or less). Upon application, materials documenting need for services should be sent only to the LD program or unit. Upon acceptance, documentation of need for services should be sent only to the LD program or unit. *Application deadline (institutional):* Continuous. *Application deadline (LD program):* Rolling/continuous for fall and rolling/continuous for spring.

Written Policies Written policy regarding general/basic LD accommodations is available on the program Web site. Written policies regarding general/basic LD accommodations and substitutions and waivers of admissions requirements are outlined in the school's catalog/handbook. Written policies regarding course substitutions, grade forgiveness, reduced course loads, and substitutions and waivers of graduation requirements are available through the program or unit directly.

Wyoming Technical Institute
Academic Accommodations

4373 North Third Street
Laramie, WY 82072-9519
http://www.wyotech.com/
Contact: Kelley Jean Johnson, ADA/504 Caseworker.
Phone: 307-755-2177. Fax: 307-721-4854. E-mail:
kjohnson@wyotech.com.

Academic Accommodations Approximately 150 registered undergraduate students were served during 2002-03. The program or unit includes 1 full-time staff member. LD specialists are provided through the program or unit. LD specialists, regular education teachers, and trained peer tutors are provided collaboratively through on-campus or off-campus services.

Orientation The program or unit offers an optional ongoing orientation for new students individually by special arrangement.

Unique Aids and Services Aids, services, or accommodations include career counseling and weekly meetings with faculty.

Subject-area Tutoring Tutoring is offered one-on-one for most subjects. Tutoring is provided collaboratively through on-campus or off-campus services via trained peer tutors.

Enrichment Programs for career planning, college survival skills, health and nutrition, learning strategies, stress management, study skills, test taking, and time management are provided collaboratively through on-campus or off-campus services. Credit is offered for career planning, college survival skills, health and nutrition, learning strategies, stress management, study skills, test taking, and time management.

Application For admittance to the program or unit, students are required to provide documentation of high school services. It is recommended that students provide a psychoeducational report (5 years old or less). Upon application, materials documenting need for services should be sent only to admissions with institutional application materials. Upon acceptance, documentation of need for

services should be sent only to the LD program or unit. *Application deadline (institutional):* Continuous. *Application deadline (LD program):* Rolling/continuous for fall and rolling/continuous for spring.

Written Policies Written policies regarding course substitutions, general/basic LD accommodations, grade forgiveness, reduced course loads, substitutions and waivers of admissions requirements, and substitutions and waivers of graduation requirements are outlined in the school's catalog/handbook. Written policies regarding course substitutions, general/basic LD accommodations, grade forgiveness, reduced course loads, and substitutions and waivers of graduation requirements are available through the program or unit directly.

York Technical College
Learning Enhanced Achievement Program (LEAP)

452 South Anderson Road
Rock Hill, SC 29730-3395
http://www.yorktech.com/
Contact: Phone: 803-327-8000. Fax: 803-327-8059.

Learning Enhanced Achievement Program (LEAP) Approximately 55 registered undergraduate students were served during 2002-03. The program or unit includes 2 full-time staff members. Special education teachers are provided through the program or unit.

Unique Aids and Services Aids, services, or accommodations include weekly meetings with faculty.

Subject-area Tutoring Tutoring is offered one-on-one and in small groups for most subjects. Tutoring is provided through the program or unit via trained peer tutors. Tutoring is also provided collaboratively through on-campus or off-campus services via trained peer tutors.

Enrichment Enrichment programs are available through the program or unit for college survival skills, learning strategies, reading, self-advocacy, stress management, study skills, and time management.

Application For admittance to the program or unit, students are required to provide a psychoeducational report (3 years old or less). It is recommended that students provide documentation of high school services. Upon application, materials documenting need for services should be sent only to the LD program or unit. Upon acceptance, documentation of need for services should be sent only to the LD program or unit. *Application deadline (institutional):* Continuous. *Application deadline (LD program):* Rolling/continuous for fall and rolling/continuous for spring.

ALPHABETICAL INDEX OF COLLEGES

The names of colleges with **Structured/Proactive Programs** for students with LD are printed in bold-face type; those with Self-Directed/Decentralized Programs for students with LD are in regular type.

GEOGRAPHIC INDEX OF COLLEGES

The names of colleges with **Structured/Proactive Programs** for students with LD are printed in bold-face type; those with Self-Directed/Decentralized Programs for students with LD are in regular type.

Colleges for Students with Learning Disabilities or ADD

RHODE ISLAND

SOUTH CAROLINA

SOUTH DAKOTA

TENNESSEE

TEXAS

Colleges for Students with Learning Disabilities or ADD

NOTES

NOTES

NOTES

NOTES

NOTES

NOTES